THE
BIBLE
KNOWLEDGE
BACKGROUND
COMMENTARY

ACTS–PHILEMON

THE
BIBLE
KNOWLEDGE
BACKGROUND
COMMENTARY

ACTS–PHILEMON

GENERAL EDITOR

Craig A. Evans

Victor®

The Bible Teacher's Teacher

An Imprint of Cook Communications Ministries
COLORADO SPRINGS, COLORADO • PARIS, ONTARIO
KINGSWAY COMMUNICATIONS, LTD., EASTBOURNE, ENGLAND

Victor®

Victor is an imprint of
Cook Communications Ministries, Colorado Springs, Colorado 80918

Cook Communications, Paris, Ontario
Kingsway Communications, Eastbourne, England

THE BIBLE KNOWLEDGE BACKGROUND COMMENTARY: ACTS–PHILEMON
© 2004 by Cook Communications Ministries

First Printing, 2004

Printed in the United States of America

1 2 3 4 5 6 7 8 9 10 11 12 Printing/Year 14 13 12 11 10 09 08 07 06 05 04

Editor: Craig A. Bubeck
Interior Design: Pat Miller

Library of Congress Cataloging-in-Publication Data

The Bible knowledge background commentary : Acts–Philemon/ Craig A. Evans, general editor.
　　p. cm.

ISBN 0-7814-4006-8

CONTENTS

CONTRIBUTORS

Craig A. Evans, Ph.D., Claremont
        Payzant Distinguished Professor of Biblical Studies
        Acadia Divinity College, Wolfville, Nova Scotia
        General Editor, *Introduction to Volume Two*

Isobel A. H. Combes, Ph.D., Cambridge
        The Vicarage, Parwich
        Ashbourne, England
        Philemon

Daniel M. Gurtner, Ph.D. (cand.), St. Andrews
        St. Mary's College
        University of St. Andrews, Scotland
        Romans, Ephesians, Philippians, Colossians, 1 and 2 Thessalonians

Lee Martin McDonald, Ph.D., Edinburgh
        Principal and Professor of New Testament
        Acadia Divinity College, Wolfville, Nova Scotia
        Acts, 1–2 Corinthians, Galatians

Robert W. Wall, Th.D., Dallas
        Professor of Christian Scriptures
        Chair, Biblical Studies Department
        Seattle Pacific University, Seattle, Washington
        1–2 Timothy, Titus

Abbreviations and Ancient Resources

For a thorough delineation of traditional abbreviations and resources specified in this volume, refer to the first volume of the *Bible Knowledge Background Commentary* series (Matthew–Luke). Additional abbreviations used in this volume are specified below.

ANF   A. Roberts and J. Donaldson (eds.), *The Ante-Nicene Fathers* (10 vols., Edinburgh: T. & T. Clark, 1898; repr. Grand Rapids: Eerdmans, 1989).

ANT   J. K. Elliott, *The Apocryphal New Testament:* A Collection of Apocryphal Christian Literature in an English Translation based on M. R. James (Oxford: Clarendon Press, 1993).

b.   I. Epstein (ed.), *Hebrew-English Edition of the Babylonian Talmud* (30 vols., London: Soncino, 1960; repr. 1990).

Garcia Martinez
Florentino Garcia Martinez. *The Dead Sea Scrolls Translated: The Qumran Texts in English.* Trans. by W. G. E. Watson. 2nd ed. Leiden/New York/Cologne: E. J. Brill/ Grand Rapids: Wm. B. Eerdmans, 1996.

LCL   *Leob Classical Library.* Cambridge, MA/ London England: Harvard University Press.

m.   H. Danby, *The Mishnah:* Translated from the Hebrew with Introduction and Brief Explanatory Notes. Oxford/New York/Toronto: Oxford University Press, 1933.

Macc. (1 and 2), Sir., Bar, etc.
B. M. Metzger, *The Apocrypha of the Old Testament* (Oxford and New York: Oxford University Press, 1977).

NHL   James M. Robinson, ed., *The Nag Hammadi Library in English.* 3rd ed. San Francisco: Harper SanFrancisco, 1990.

NT Apo   W. Schneemelcher, ed., *New Testament Apocrypha* (2 vols., Cambridge: James Clarke; Louisville: Westminster/John Knox Press, 1991–92).

OTP   J. H. Charlesworth (ed.), *The Old Testament Pseudepigrapha* (2 vols., New York: Doubleday, 1983–85).

t.   J. Neusner, *The Tosefta* (6 vols., New York: Ktav, 1977–86).

TOB   Barnstone, Willis, ed., *The Other Bible.* San Francisco: HarperSanFrancisco, 1984.

Vermes   Geza Vermes. *The Complete Dead Sea Scrolls in English.* London/New York: Penguin Books, 1998.

Introduction to Volume Two

Volume two of the *Bible Knowledge Background Commentary* is comprised of the book of Acts and the letters of the Apostle Paul. Even though Acts is the second volume of Luke–Acts, it is appropriate to combine commentary on it with commentary on Paul's letters, for the former clarifies the historical and religious context of the latter, while the latter clarify more fully the theological issues lying behind the narrative of the former.

The book of Acts provides a bridge between Jesus and the Gospels, on the one hand, and the missionary activities of the apostles, on the other. But Acts is especially important for situating the place of Paul, author of about one half of the writings that eventually will make up the New Testament. Linking Paul to the apostles of the Gospels, appointed by Jesus himself, is vital, especially in a church in danger of dividing into two parts: Jewish and Gentile. The author of Acts is careful to show that Paul does indeed have a place among the apostles. Indeed, he not only has a place, but he also emerges as a leader in the mission to Gentiles. The author of Acts accomplishes this, in part, by underscoring the parallels between the major acts of the apostles Peter and Paul (see the "Peter-Paul Parallels" text box).

But the author of Acts also demonstrates the legitimacy of the Pauline mission by a series of careful, logical steps leading from the prominence of Peter and the Jerusalem church, to the conversion, training, call, and apostolic leadership of Paul himself. This demonstration manifests itself in at least seven distinct steps:

1. In Acts 6 seven deacons are chosen. This is significant because they are not part of the original Twelve, and yet two of them (Stephen and Philip) become involved in evangelism. In fact, in Acts 8 Philip takes the gospel to a Gentile. Thus, precedent has been established—before Paul is even converted—that a person who was not among the original apostles could become an evangelist (if not an apostle) and proclaim the good news of the risen Christ.

Peter-Paul Parallels

Peter	Activity	Paul
3:1-10	A lame man is healed	14:8-10
3:11-26	Historical sermon	13:16-41
4:1-22	Brought before religious leaders	22:1-22
5:17-20	Miraculous release from prison	16:19-34
8:9-24	Encounter with a magician	13:4-12
10:1-48	Evangelization of Gentiles	13:44-52
11:1-18	Prominence at a Jerusalem Council	15:1-35

2. In Acts 8 the gospel is preached to Samaritans, which by many were regarded as part-Jewish. The Spirit is poured out upon these new converts as evidence of the reality of their conversion. In the last part of chap. 8 Philip converts the Ethiopian official, thus making it clear that the gospel has now gone to the Gentiles. Again, this important step has been taken without any involvement of Paul.

3. In Acts 9 Paul is converted and begins speaking the gospel boldly, but there is no hint that his Gentile ministry has begun. Paul proclaims the gospel to fellow Jews. (It is important to note that the "Hellenists" of 9:29 are non-Palestinian [Greek-speaking] Jews, not Greeks.)

4. In Acts 10 Peter receives his vision that the gospel may go to the Gentiles. Soon after, Peter takes the gospel to the household of Cornelius, a Roman. They, too, like the Samaritans in Acts 8, have the Spirit poured out upon them, thus validating the legitimacy of their conversion.

5. In Acts 11 the Church holds its first Council, in Jerusalem, in order to decide the validity of Gentile (and Samaritan) conversion. Peter's testimony carries the day: If God has chosen to pour out his Spirit on these people, who are we Jews who believe in Jesus to question it?

6. The beginning of Paul's leadership may be traced to Barnabas, not to Paul himself. In Acts 11:25-26 it was Barnabas who brought Paul to Antioch and got him involved in the ministry there, thus paving the way for his trip to Jerusalem (11:27-30) and his later call to the mission field.

7. In Acts 13 Paul and Barnabas, having returned from Jerusalem, are commissioned by the church of Antioch to undertake the first missionary journey. Up to this point in the narrative of Acts, Paul is referred to by his Hebrew name, Saul, and only by this name (from 7:58 until 13:7, some seventeen times in all). The ministry begins with no intention of going to the Gentiles, but because the Jews reject the gospel, Paul and Barnabas turn to the Gentiles. Even so, every time Paul and Barnabas enter a city, they go to the synagogue to preach the gospel first to the Jews, and only later, usually after rejection, do they evangelize Gentiles.

The way Acts 6–13 is written it is clear that the author wished to portray Paul's Gentile ministry as having both necessity and precedent. Paul is not to be understood as a "maverick" apostle who launched the Gentile mission on his own authority, but as an apostle with Jerusalem links, who took the gospel to the Gentiles with Jerusalem's blessing.

The book of Acts is itself an important part of the background of Paul's various letters. In Acts Paul visits many of the cities to which he will later address his letters. These cities include Corinth (Acts 18:1; 19:1), Thessalonica (17:1, 11, 13), Ephesus (18:19, 21; 19:17, 26, 35; 20:16-17), Philippi (16:12; 20:6), Rome (19:21; 23:11; 28:14, 16), and the region of Galatia (16:6; 18:23).

In his letters Paul also refers to Troas (2 Cor. 2:12; 2 Tim. 4:13), a port city through which he passed (Acts 16:8, 11; 20:5-6). He also mentions Cenchreae, another port city where the apostle made a vow (Acts 18:8; Rom. 16:1). In Greece Paul visits the famous Athens (Acts 17:15-16, 22; 18:1), which he mentions in one of his letters (1 Thess. 3:1). And, of course, Paul travels to and from Jerusalem, the holy city, as a new convert, as a delegate, and as an apostle (Acts 9:26; 15:2, 4; 20:16; 21:17; Rom. 15:19, 25; 1 Cor. 16:3; Gal. 1:17-18; 2:1).

These cities link Acts and Paul's letters. They also attest to Paul's extensive travels, travels accommodated by a network of roads for overland travel and a number of port cities and harbors that support travel by sea. Most of these roads and harbors can be seen today. There have also been excavations at most of the cities that Paul has visited. One can see a large theatre and an impressive two-story library at Ephesus. One can view the harbor of Troas from the cliffs above. The marketplace of

Philippi is in open view, perhaps also the very prison in which Paul was placed. Some of ancient Thessalonica has been uncovered. One may visit the ruins of Corinth, the remnants of the harbor at Cenchreae, and the famous Acropolis of Athens. Travel through Turkey (Asia Minor), Greece, Lebanon, and Israel will bring to life the activities of Paul the letter-writer and traveler.

These sites and many others are described in the commentary on Acts and the commentary on Paul's letters. The commentators not only describe geographical and archaeological features, but they also relate cultural and religious beliefs and conventions and point to many important parallels in literature and inscriptions. Lee McDonald, who wrote the commentary on Acts and on Paul's letters to Corinth and the churches of Galatia, has traveled extensively in Greece, Turkey, and Israel. Robert Wall wrote the commentary on the Pastoral Letters (1–2 Tim. and Titus), Daniel M. Gurtner wrote the commentary on the other letters of Paul, while Isobel Combes, who possesses expertise in the topic of slavery in the Roman Empire, wrote the commentary on Philemon. The editor is grateful to these colleagues for taking on their respective assignments and writing background commentary that readers of this book will find stimulating, clarifying, and enriching.

Paul's Letters, Written on His Journeys and During His Imprisonments

Letter	Number of Letters	Journeys and Imprisonments
GALATIANS	1	After his first missionary journey
1 THESSALONIANS 2 THESSALONIANS	2	On his second missionary journey
1 CORINTHIANS 2 CORINTHIANS ROMANS	3	On his third missionary journey
EPHESIANS PHILPPIANS COLOSSIANS PHILEMON	4	During his first imprisonment
1 TIMOTHY TITUS 2 TIMOTHY	3	Before and during his second imprisonment

Introduction to Acts

Lee Martin McDonald

This is the fifth book of the New Testament, originally written as a companion volume to the Gospel of Luke (Luke 1:1-4; Acts 1:1) by the same author. Considerable debate exists among scholars, however, on the date, origin, provenance, and even the identity of the author of the Book of Acts.

Name. The name "Acts of the Apostles" did not appear on the volume until toward the end of the second century and from then on, the title is regularly employed. The title suggests that the book was about the apostles, but Luke shows little interest in the apostles as a group. His primary focus is rather on the mission activities of Peter and Paul. Although not original to the document, the title is important evidence from the second century of the church's quest for faith to be rooted in apostolicity. The title "Acts" (Greek = *praxeis*) itself reflects an ancient term that denoted special deeds of important personalities, normally those of rulers. A comparable term in the Roman world was *res gestae* that referred to the actions of individuals, for example, the *Res gestae divi Augusti* or "Acts of the divine Augustus." The title appears to have been a special term for a "historical monograph," but while there are some obvious parallels with the literary genre of ancient historiography, the contents of Acts are considerably more than that. The author intends to focus more on Peter and Paul and attributes their ministry activity to the working of the risen Lord or the Holy Spirit (3:12-16; 4:10, 30; 13:2; 15:4, 12; 21:19). The author used sources to tell his story, but his intent included casting the Christian story in a favorable light and edifying the reader(s). The volume is at least a historical monograph, but it can in no sense be considered only from that perspective. The title given to the volume itself was likely added later since its contents are not reflected in the title.

Date. The work could have been written as early as A.D. 65 (if written by Luke, the companion of Paul—cf. Col. 4:14; 2 Tim. 4:11; Phile. 24) and possibly as late as 93–95. Irenaeus (*Adv. Haer.* 1.23.1-5; 3.14.1-2), Clement of Alexandria (*Strom.* 5.12 and 5.82.4), Tertullian (*Adv. Marc.* 5.2), and probably Origen, (Eusebius is citing Origen in *Ecclesiastical History* 6.25.14), claimed that Luke was the author of Acts. Some scholars have placed the writing of the book well into the second century and by an unknown author, but most scholars, while questioning its authorship, date the book ca. 80–85. Was Acts written before Paul's death since the book concludes with Paul in prison in Rome awaiting the opportunity to appeal his case before Caesar? Acts does not tell us what happened to Paul after his imprisonment in Rome as reported in the last decade of the first century by Clement (1 Clem 1.5) and subsequently by Tertullian (*De Praescriptione* 36.3) and Eusebius (*HE* 2.25.5). Is this because Paul, who died sometime around 64–65, was still alive?

Authorship. The traditional argument for Lukan authorship is based on the "we" passages of Acts 16:10-17; 20:5-15; 21:1-18; 27:1–28:16 and also 11:28 in codex Bezae (cf. Irenaeus, *Adv. Haer.* 3.13.3; 3.14.1). In the list of Paul's missionary companions, only Luke and Jesus called Justus appear to be candidates for authorship; all early church tradition supports the former. Whoever wrote the book, the author intended the "we" passages to show that he was a participant in the journeys of Paul and was not simply using the conventional "we." Acts and other ancient historical writings made use of the first person plural in narrations of journeys to indicate participation (cf. esp. Polybius 36.12, but also 12.27.1-6; Lucian, *History* 47; Homer, *Odyssey* 12.402-425). Jerome (ca. 400), who produced the famous Latin version of the Bible, the Vulgate, ascribed two volumes to Luke, the companion of Paul:

> Luke, a doctor of Antioch, was, as his writings show, not ignorant of the Greek language. The follower of the apostle Paul, and his companion in all his journeying, he wrote the gospel, of which the same Paul says, "we have sent with him the brother whose praise is in the Gospel through all the churches" and to the Colossians, "Luke, the beloved doctor, greets you," and to Timothy, "Only Luke is with me." He also published another excellent volume which is entitled "Apostolic Acts:" its story extends as far as the two-year period of Paul's residence in Rome, that is, as far as the fourth year of Nero. From this we learn that the book was composed in that city. . . .
>
> The gospel therefore he wrote as he had heard; but the Acts of the Apostles he composed as he had himself seen. He is buried at Constantinople, to which city his bones, with the remains of the apostle Andrew, were translated in the twentieth year of Constantius [= A.D.

343–44] (*De Viris Illustribus* 7).

Some scholars have questioned these conclusions, noting that were the author a companion of Paul, he would probably have shown more awareness of Paul's epistles and major teachings and would have ascribed the title "apostle" to Paul, who always so referred to himself (Gal. 1:1; 1 Cor. 9:1, passim). Also, they point to the work's tendency to smooth out the differences in the early church (the so-called "catholicizing" tendency, hence "*Tendenz criticism*"), that especially makes Peter and Paul alike in regard to Gentile freedom and in their keeping of the Law (Acts 10-11; 16:3; 18:18; 21:26). This view, often associated with the so-called Tübingen School position was first advocated by F. C. Baur in the 1850s, but is still current in a variety of forms among scholars today who question Luke's authorship of the Gospel and Acts. Nevertheless, while the early Christians did not hesitate to create volumes in the names of apostles, one is hard pressed to understand why they would have attributed the authorship of such an important book to a relatively unimportant nonapostolic name unless there was some merit to the claim.

Aim of the Book. Acts concentrates its narrative around Peter (chaps. 1–12) and Paul (chaps. 13–28). The first part of the book tells the story of the early church in Jerusalem and Palestine/Syria from the resurrection of Christ to the departure of Peter from Jerusalem. Peter serves as the transition and authentication of the Gentile mission of the church, principally carried out by Paul. The career of the latter is structured in three missionary journeys from Antioch and Palestine/Syria to the west and a final journey as a prisoner to Rome. A feature of the contents is the frequent inclusion of speeches that summarize early Christian preaching and teaching (e.g., Acts 2; 3; 7; 13; 17; 20; 22; 26).

While the author produced an "orderly account" (Luke 1:1-4) of the birth and development of the Christian movement for his patron

Theophilus (see commentary below under 1:1), Luke was much more than an unbiased historian interested simply in setting forth the facts. He was also a zealous advocate for the Christian faith. He viewed the early followers of Jesus as models for conduct and wanted to show how the Christian movement, which began as a Jewish sect in Palestine, supplanted that group and grew to have universal appeal to both Jews and Gentiles. The universal appeal of the Christian gospel, the argument that the Christian movement is not a threat to Rome or its interests, and an interest in the growth and development of the Christian movement with propagandist views in mind are all important themes and matters of focus in Acts. What Acts appears to do is to carry on the mission of Jesus through his disciples by the power of the Holy Spirit (1:1). Luke probably had several purposes in mind along with the above, not the least is to show that Christianity was no threat to the Roman Empire. Perhaps he also wanted to prepare them for the impending persecution through Peter and John's example and experience before the Jerusalem authorities (4:5-31 and 5:12-42). Perhaps also he wanted to show that Christianity was the logical successor to Judaism and that salvation from God is only found in the apostolic mission as presented in Acts. (See Fitzmyer 55-69.)

History of Use. Because of the length of Luke-Acts, the books were published in two separate volumes or scrolls of papyrus sheets (or perhaps parchment), making it possible to circulate one without the other. Acts was probably circulating separate from the Gospel of Luke at least by ca. 140, when an edited form of Luke became part of Marcion's "canon" along with ten of Paul's epistles. Acts was probably rejected by Marcion because of its universal focus that affirmed the apostles of Jewish Christianity (Peter and James) as well as the apostleship of Hellenistic church leaders (Stephen, Barnabas, and especially Paul). It is

possible that he was unaware of the document, but that cannot be demonstrated.

Although there are some verbal parallels between Acts and 1 Clement, Barnabas, Polycarp, Didache, and Hermas, this may be evidence only of a common vocabulary in early Christianity. With Justin Martyr in the middle of the second century, however, there are apparent citations from Acts (compare Acts 1:8 with *1 Apol.* 50.12 and Acts 17:23 with *2 Apol.* 10.6). Irenaeus was the first writer to cite Acts in his attacks against Marcion (see *Haer.* 1.23.1-5; 3.14.1-2; 4.15.1 but also 3.1.1; 3.10.1; 3.12.1-5). He uses Acts to argue against the Ebionites who rejected Paul's apostleship (*Adv. Haer.* 3.15.1) and to argue against the Marcionites who only accepted Paul's apostleship (*Adv. Haer* 3.13.1-14.4). Acts is mentioned in the Anti-Marcionite Prologue of Luke (possibly as early as ca. 160–180, but possibly later), which notes that Luke was a Syrian of Antioch, a disciple of the apostles who later followed Paul and who served the Lord as a single man until his death in Boeotia (Bithynia?) at the age of eighty-four. Clement of Alexandria frequently cited Acts in a scripture-like (authoritative) manner (e.g., *Str.* 3.6.49; 7.9.53). Origen made use of several texts in Acts, but was vague about its scriptural status (*Or.* 12.2; 13:6). Tertullian (ca. 200), like Irenaeus, appealed to Acts to refute Marcion (*Marc.* 5.1-2) and added that those who did not accept Acts as Scripture were not of the Holy Spirit (*Praescr.* 22). He is the first to refer to the book by name ("Acts" in *De Bapt.* 7; *De Res. Carnis* 23; *Scorp.* 15; and "Acts of the Apostles" in *De Bapt.* 10; *De Carnis Christi* 15; *De Resur. Carnis* 39; *Praescript.* 1). Until the separation of Luke from Acts and until all four canonical Gospels were grouped together, as in the case of Irenaeus (*Adv. Haer.* 3.11.8-9), there appeared to be no need for a separate title for Acts. As noted above, the title "Acts of the Apostles" was probably attached to the work no later than A.D. 180–200. Acts was permanently separated from the Gospel of

Luke no later than the middle of the second century, and probably sooner, and never appears re-attached to it in the later canonical lists of New Testament books.

In the third century, Hippolytus of Rome showed reliance on Acts for the story of Simon Magus of Samaria *(Haer.* 6.20.1-2); in the fourth, Eusebius used Acts as a model for his own history, claiming that Luke was its author *(HE* 3.4.4-11), and he included it in his undisputed collections of New Testament Scriptures *(Ecclesiastical History* 3.25.1). Acts 7:6 was cited in the account of the *Martyrs of Lyons* (ca. 180–190 —see Eusebius, *Ecclesiastical History* 5.2.5). After Eusebius, Acts was acknowledged as Scripture throughout the church both in the east and the west. By ca. 350, it appeared regularly in all church canons of Scriptures, including Athanasius' *Festal Letter* for 367 and in the *Muratorian Fragment* (ca. 350–375). If this fragment is a second-century document, as many scholars maintain, it would likely be the earliest reference to Acts by name, but the *Muratorian Fragment* probably dates from the late fourth century where its name for Acts has a number of parallels (see Cyril of Jerusalem, *Catech.* 4.36; *Doctrina Addai* [ca. 390–430], Gregory of Nazianzus, *Carm.* 12.13; and Amphilochius, *Iambi ad Seleucum* 296–97).

There was a tendency in the eastern churches in the fourth century to expand the title of Acts. This may have been a response to the collection and circulation of five apocryphal Acts of Paul, Peter, Andrew, Thomas, and John by the Manicheans. These five apocryphal Acts were anonymously written in the late second and early third centuries in Asia Minor and Syria and all were modeled after the New Testament Acts. Unlike Acts, however, they are almost entirely fictional. It may be that their existence led to the adoption of the name that now identifies Acts. In the third and fourth centuries, other apocryphal Acts circulated in some churches, but they had no impact on the church's biblical canon.

Value of the Book. It is all but impossible to establish any chronology of early Christianity without the aid of the book of Acts. This is especially true in regard to Acts 16–19 for the dating of Romans, 1 & 2 Corinthians, and 1 Thessalonians. Acts also offers one of the most important historical dates in the New Testament: namely, the presence of Gallio in Corinth in A.D. 50–51 (see Acts 18:12). The value of Acts for dating the literature and ministry of early Christianity, as well as for understanding the theology and ministry of Paul continues to be matter of dispute among NT scholars. Nevertheless, the historical framework of Acts is essential for positing any historical framework of first-century Christianity. Regardless of the debate over its historical reliability, there is general agreement that Luke-Acts is primarily a theological document with aims and purposes that are significantly more than historical. Many scholars contend, however, that it is also a reliable historical witness to early Christianity.

Place in the NT Canon. In the NT, Acts forms a "bridge" or "hinge" between the two major parts of the NT writings, the gospels and the epistles of Paul. The use of Acts in this role was an important step, since it is difficult to follow the epistles of Paul without the outline provided in the Acts. Likewise, the story of the development of the early church is difficult to trace in Acts without the epistles of Paul to give it clarity. The central structure of the New Testament depends on Acts, which provides the sequel to the Gospels and the background to the Epistles. It may be that the usefulness of Acts as a "hinge" does not *begin* to manifest itself until there is a *new* testament of Scriptures to which one can appeal. This "new testament" *begins* to take shape in the churches at the end of the second century and comes to its more complete form in the fourth century. Origen in the third century still senses the need to clarify the meaning of the terms Old Testament and New Testament (*On first Principles* 4.1.1.

[*Philocalia* 1]), suggesting that they are still new terms. On the other hand, as one looks at the various New Testament canonical lists of the fourth century, Acts did not always provide a hinge or bridge between the gospels and the epistles. In codex Clermont, for instance, Acts comes after Revelation. In the *Mommsen Catalogue* and in Epiphanius, Acts appears after the epistles of Paul. In the *Apostolic Canons*, Acts appears after both the epistles of Paul and the Catholic Epistles including *1 & 2 Clement* and the *Apostolic Constitutions*. In the early fifth-century (A.D. 405) list of Pope Innocent (*Ad Exsuper. Tol.*), Acts follows the epistles of Paul and also the Catholic Epistles. Acts comes between the Epistles of Paul and the Catholic Epistles in Jerome and just before Revelation in Augustine. Its function, therefore, as a bridge in the NT between the gospels and epistles of Paul appears in the fourth century, but is not settled in that position in most of the churches until well beyond that time. The introduction to Acts (1:1-14) suggests that the two volumes, Luke and Acts, were circulating separately probably form the very beginning since, had they been in one volume or scroll, there would have been no need for the duplicate introduction to the second book in the same volume (cf. Luke 1:1-4 and Acts 1:1-2).

Acts as History. Acts does not fit easily into any ancient pattern of historiography, although the author clearly had some acquaintance with the historian's craft and a working knowledge of Greek rhetoric. Acts itself is neither a biography nor a history after the usual ancient patterns, although the author uses both in his own way to underscore the origins and validity of Christianity. There is no question that Luke made use of sources for his work, but he has so completely rewritten them that they are hardly distinguishable. He shares in this practice with many ancient historians, such as Tacitus, Josephus, and even Dionysius of Halicarnassus (*Roman Antiquities* 5; 8) and Lucian (*History* 47), who claim to have neither added nor deleted

anything but who also completely rewrote their sources.

Place of Origin. Irenaeus was the first to say that the book originated in Rome (*Adv haer.* 3.1.1; 3.14.1. So also Eusebius, *Ecclesiastical History* 2.22.6 and later Jerome, *De Viris Illustribus* 7), but it is difficult to establish the origins or validity of this tradition. Rome appears to be as likely a place as any, but various other places of origin have been suggested by scholars over the years such as Antioch of Syria, the birthplace of the Gentile mission.

OUTLINE OF THE BOOK

I. Spread of the Gospel in Jerusalem (1:1–8:3)
II. Prologue and Ascension (1:1–14)
III. Spread of the Gospel to Samaria and the coastal regions (8:4–11:18)
IV. Spread of the Gospel to Gentiles—triumph (11:19–30)
V. Interlude: Persecution of the Church and God's Judgment (12:1–23)
VI. Spread of the Gospel to Gentiles—triumph and conflict (11:19–15:35)
VII. The Second Missionary Journey (Spread of the Gospel to Western Asia and Greece; 15:36–18:22)
VIII. The Third Missionary Journey (Spread of the Gospel from Antioch to Jerusalem; 18:23–21:25)
IX. Spread of the Gospel from Jerusalem to Rome (21:27–28:31)

RESOURCES

Barrett, C. K. *A Critical and Exegetical Commentary on The Acts of the Apostles.* ICC. Eds. J. A. Emerton, C.E.B. Cranfield, G. N. Stanton. Edinburgh: T & T Clark, vol.1 (Acts 1–14), 1994, vol. 2 (Acts 15–28), 1998.

Bauckham, Richard, ed. *The Book of Acts in Its Palestinian Setting,, Vol. 4. The Book of Acts in Its First Century Setting*; B. Winter, series ed., Grand Rapids/Carlisle: Eerdmans/Paternoster, 1995.

Boring, M. Eugene, Klaus Berger, Carsten Colpe, eds. *Hellenistic Commentary to the New Testament*. Nashville: Abingdon, 1995.

Bruce, F. F., *The Acts of the Apostles* (Revised and expanded edition; Grand Rapids: Eerdmans, 1990).

Charlesworth, James H., ed. *The Old Testament Pseudepigrapha* (2 vols.). Garden City, NY: Doubleday, 1983.

Conzelmann, Hans, *Acts of the Apostles*. Hermenia. E. J. Epp and C. R. Matthews, eds. Trans. by J. Limburg, T. Kraabel, and D. Juel. Philadelphia: Fortress Press, 1987. German ed., 1972.

Danby, Herbert, *The Mishnah: Translated from the Hebrew with Introduction and Brief Explanatory Notes*. Oxford/New York/Toronto: Oxford University Press, 1933.

Fitzmyer, J., *The Acts of the Apostles: A New Translation with Introduction and Commentary*. The Anchor Bible. New York/London/Toronto: Doubleday, 1998.

Garcia Martinez, Florentino, *The Dead Sea Scrolls Translated: The Qumran Texts in English*. Second ed. Leiden: E. J. Brill/Grand Rapids: Eerdmans, 1994, 1996.

Haenchen, E., *The Acts of the Apostles: A Commentary*. Trans. R. McL. Wilson. Philadelphia: Fortress Press, 1971/ German edition, 1965.

Hengel, Martin. *Acts and the History of Earliest Christianity*. Trans. by John Bowden. Philadelphia: Fortress Press, 1980 (German ed., *Zur urchristlichen Geschichtsschreibung*. Stuttgart: Calwer Verlag, 1979).

Gill, David and Conrad Gempf, eds. *The Book of Acts in Its Graeco-Roman Setting, Vol. 2. The Book of Acts in Its First Century Setting*, B. Winter, series ed. Grand Rapids/

Carlisle: Eerdmans/Paternoster, 1994.

Horsley, Greg and S. R. Llewelyn, eds. *New Documents Illustrating Early Christianity* (9 vols. presently). Ancient History Documentary Research Centre, Macquarrie University Press/Grand Rapids: Eerdmans, 1981-2002.

Käsemann, Ernst, "Ephesians and Acts," L. E. Keck and J. L. Martyn, eds. *Studies in Luke-Acts* (Nashville: Abingdon, 1966).

Keener, Craig S., *The Bible Background Commentary: New Testament*. Downers Grove: InterVarsity Press, 1993.

Kümmel, W. G., "Lukas in der Anklage der Heutigen Theologie," *ZNW* (1972) 63:149-65.

Parsons, M. C. "Reading Talbert: New Perspectives on Luke and Acts," M. C. Parsons and J. B. Tyson, eds., *Cadbury, Knox, and Talbert: American Contributions to the Study of Acts* (Atlanta: Scholars Press, 1992).

Schneemelcher, Wilhelm, ed. *New Testament Apocrypha*. Revised. 2 vols. Louisville, KY: Westminster/John Knox Press, 1992.

Talbert, Charles H. *Literary Patterns, Theological Themes and the Genre of Luke-Acts* (Missoula, Montana: Scholars Press, 1974).

_____. "Luke-Acts," *The New Testament and its Modern Interpreters*. E. J. Epp and G. W. MacRae, eds.; Atlanta: Scholars Press, 1989, 297-320.

Winter, Bruce and A. D. Clarke, eds. *The Book of Acts in Its Ancient Literary Setting, Vol. 1. The Book of Acts in its First Century Setting*. B. Winter, series ed. Grand Rapids/ Carlisle: Eerdmans/Paternoster, 1993.

Acts

Lee Martin McDonald

I. 1:1-14. PROLOGUE AND ASCENSION

1:1. The first account I composed. This is the second of two volumes, the Gospel of Luke and the Acts of the Apostles, that Luke produced and, as was common in literary works of antiquity, he referred to the first volume in the beginning of the second with a brief review of what had been said in the first volume, "all the things that Jesus began to do and teach up to the day when. . . ." See, for instance, how Philo introduced his second book on Moses: "The former treatise dealt with the birth and nurture of Moses; also with his education and career as a ruler, in which capacity his conduct was not merely blameless but highly praiseworthy; . . . The present treatise is concerned with matters allied and consequent to these" (*Life of Moses* 2.1, LCL). Similarly, an even closer parallel to the introduction of Acts is found in Josephus who begins the volume: "In the first volume of this work, my most esteemed Epaphroditus, I have demonstrated the antiquity of our race . . ." (*Ag. Ap.* 2.1, LCL).

Interestingly, it is not clear when the introduction proper ends and the book begins, but all of 1:1-14 is found in the Gospel of Luke and this whole section is probably intended to be the connection to the first volume. Since Luke was not an eyewitness to the events he reports, it is certain that he made use of sources

(see Gospel of Luke, Introduction), but there are not likely any additional sources used in this section since what is said here is both repetitious and probably common tradition in the early church.

Theophilus. The name Theophilus was a common one in the ancient world, meaning "dear to God" and probably was intended by Luke to address a real person and not employed simply as a generic term for all Christians. The title, "O excellent" (Greek = *o kratiste*) used before the same name in Luke 1:3, is also found in a specific title in reference to Felix (Acts 23:26). It was not unusual in the ancient world for a writer to introduce a patron in the introduction of a volume. See, for example, how Josephus uses the same title (*kratiste*) in the introduction to his *Against Apion*: "In my history of our Antiquities, most excellent Epaphroditus, I have, I think, made sufficiently clear to any who may peruse that work the extreme antiquity of our Jewish race. . . ." (*Ag. Ap.* 1.1, LCL). It is not clear, however, which Theophilus in antiquity is intended, but such dedications in antiquity may have constituted the act of publication and the person to whom the book was dedicated who would give permission, and perhaps pay for, copies of the book to be distributed (Haenchen, 136-7). Theophilus may have been an interested and influential patron who was disposed to

Christianity, or even a person who was a Christian or person familiar with Judaism and the early Christian movement, but that is speculation. It is not clear, however, whether a non-Christian or at least one unacquainted with Judaism in antiquity would have understood the contents of the book.

1:3. The length of the appearances. The differences between the Gospel of Luke and Acts on the length of Jesus' appearances (v. 3) and in the Ascension (vv. 9-11) may be due to theological motives in the text. The "forty" days of the appearances may have other important suggestions about the presence and activity of God since that number is a fairly common holy number in several places in the Bible, e.g., the length of the rains that produced a flood upon the earth, the length of Moses' stay at Mt. Sinai, the wanderings of the children of Israel in the wilderness, Elijah at Mt. Horeb, and Jesus' temptations in the wilderness. The number forty seems to be a special "holy" number in the Bible that is probably not normally to be taken literally. Since the presence and power of God are referred to in the above noted places where the number forty occurs, Luke probably had something like this in mind in Acts 1:3. Perhaps the theological significance of the forty

days for Luke is that they represent a special "holy interval" in sacred history, in which the apostles were being prepared by the coming of the Holy Spirit for their forthcoming task of witness. If that explanation is correct, this may account for the obvious difference in the length of the appearances in Luke 24 where they seem to have taken place all on one day and the departure or ascension took place at the conclusion of that same day. It is possible, however, that the mention of the forty days in Acts 1:3 is simply Luke's attempt, like John's and Paul's, to link the resurrection of Jesus with the coming of the Holy Spirit, but if so, why does Luke stop at "forty days"? Why not "fifty days" to coincide with Pentecost? At any rate, the "forty days" in Acts 1:3 also suggests that there was also a limited time for the resurrection appearances. After a period of time, however long it was, the kind of resurrection appearances experienced by the disciples terminated. This is supported by the Easter tradition in 1 Cor. 15:3-8, in which Paul says that the appearances that the earliest witnesses experienced ceased after a definite period of time, that is, with Paul's Damascus Road experience. The number forty is not repeated in Acts in reference to the length of the appearances (see 10:41 and 13:31).

Miracles by Peter and Paul

Peter

Acts 3:1-11	Healed a man lame from birth
5:15-16	Peter's shadow healed people
5:17	Success caused Jewish jealousy
8:9-24	Dealt with Simon, a sorcerer

Paul

14:8-18	Healed a man lame from birth
19:11-12	Handkerchiefs and aprons from Paul healed people
13:45	Success caused Jewish jealousy
13:6-11	Dealt with Bar-Jesus, a sorcerer
20:9-12	Raised Eutychus to life

1:2, 9-11. The Ascension. Reference to the ascension of Jesus is found elsewhere in the NT only in Luke 24:5, John 20:17-19, and the secondary Mark 16:19. In both Luke and John it appears to be equal to the glorification or exaltation of the risen Lord elsewhere found in such passages as Acts 2:32-33 and 5:30-31, Rom. 8:34, Eph. 1:19-20, Col. 3:1, Phil. 2:9-11, 1 Tim. 3:16, and 1 Peter 3:21-22 where Jesus' resurrection and exaltation appear to be linked. Luke uses the Ascension also to show that there came a time when the appearances of the risen Lord ceased. He only has one other appearance after this (9:3-9; 22:6-11; 26:12-19; and cf. 1 Cor. 9:1; 15:5-8).

The use of an ascension story to proclaim the glory and exaltation of a person was not uncommon in the ancient world. Dio Cassius (A.D. 164–229), for example, in his *Roman History* speaks of events following the death of Caesar Augustus (Octavian) thusly:

> At the time they [these rumors] declared Augustus immortal, assigned to him priests and sacred rites, and made Livia, who was already called Julia and Augusta, his priestess; they also permitted her to employ a lictor when she exercised her sacred office. On her part, she bestowed a million sesterces upon a certain Numerius Atticus, a senator and ex-praetor, because he swore that he had seen Augustus ascending to heaven after the manner of which tradition tells concerning Proculus and Romulus (Bk 56.46, LCL).

The stories about Heracles' ascension to heaven in the sixth century B.C. was transferred to Romulus (Ovid, *Fasti* 2.475-510 and Ovid, *Metamorphoses* 14:805-51). In both cases these men were brought to the gods by an ascension. In the case of Romulus, even his horses and carriage ascended with him. These and similar stories often were accompanied by reports of the absence of the body and bodies of the deceased. See also Livy, *History of Rome* 1.16.2-

8. The Old Testament also has an interesting ascension story that relates how Elijah was taken by God to heaven (2 Kings 2:11-12). It may be that something similar was in view in the brief story of Enoch, (Gen. 5:24; see Heb. 11:5), but it clearly was in the early church. Clement of Rome wrote (ca. A.D. 95), "Let us take Enoch, who was found righteous in obedience, and was translated, and death did not befall him" (*1 Clem* 9.3, LCL). This is clearly found in a pseudepigraphal writing (possibly first cent. B.C. or first cent. A.D.) that probably expresses a widely held view in which Enoch tells of his ascension. Describing two men who came to take him to heaven, he writes: "And the men said to me, 'Be brave, Enoch!' Do not fear! The eternal Lord has sent us to you. And behold, today you will ascend with us to heaven" (*2 Enoch* 1.8, *OT Pseud* 1:109).

1:5. Baptized with the Holy Spirit and fire. See discussion of Luke 3:16-17 in this series. Luke anticipates the promise of the coming of the Spirit and begins his story (chap. 2) with the coming of that power that was promised.

1:8. Passing on the mission of Jesus to his disciples. The "passing of the torch" is common in the Bible as in the case of Moses passing the leadership role to Joshua (Num. 27:18-23; Deut. 34:9) or Elijah passing on the mantle to Elisha (1 Kings 19:16, cf., 2 Kings 2:13-15).

To the remotest part of the earth. Jesus also committed his mission to his successors, the apostles, and the scope of that mission was universal as Luke subsequently shows in Acts, moving the transmission of the Gospel from Jerusalem to Rome, the capital of the empire. This is probably what Luke has in mind since the expression is found elsewhere as a reference to Rome. *Ps. Sol.* 8:1, for instance, describes God as bringing Pompey from "the end of the earth" (that is, Rome) to the land of Israel. This accords well with the conclusion of Acts that has Paul telling the story of God's salvation in Rome, and this is where the book concludes. The mission was to be a witness of Jesus in the entire world, but the means of accomplishing this mission was the power of the Holy Spirit. In this verse, Luke sets the stage for the unfolding of his book beginning with the coming of the Holy Spirit (2:1-4).

1:9. Clouds. Clouds not uncommonly played a role in such ascension stories. Plutarch's *Parallel Lives*, for instance, claims that

> Suddenly there was a great commotion in the air, and a cloud descended upon the earth bringing with it blasts of wind and rain. The throng of common folk were terrified and fled in all directions, but Romulus disappeared, and was never found again either alive or dead. . . . And Proculus, a man of eminence, took oath that he had seen Romulus ascending to heaven in full armor, and had heard his voice commanding that he be called Quirinius (*Life of Numa* 11:2, 3. LCL)

Compare with Plutarch, *Parallel Lives*, "Life of Romulus" 28. See also the coming of a heavenly figure with clouds in Daniel 7:13 and the NT parallels in Mark 13:26; 14:62; and Rev. 1:7. In the transfiguration of Jesus, stories (Matt. 17:1-8; Mark 9:2-8; Luke 9:28-36), which probably prefigure the resurrection of Jesus, the cloud covered the mountain (Mark 9:7; cf. Exod. 24:16), God's voice came from the cloud (Mark 9:7; cf. Exod. 24:16), and a transformed appearance took place (Mark 9:3; cf. Exod. 34:30). In the resurrection of Jesus, after he had appeared to his disciples for forty days, he was taken up in a cloud (Acts 1:9). It is difficult not to draw a parallel with Moses, who also entered the cloud and was with God on the mountain for forty days in Exod. 24:15-18. The clouds probably suggest the presence of God, and in the story of the Ascension, the glory Jesus received in his resurrection. The transfiguration was probably intended by the evangelists to be understood as a foreshadowing of the resurrection which Jesus had predicted in Mark 8:31; 9:1; Luke 9:22, 27; and Matt. 16:21, 28. In an OT ascension story, Elijah was also carried off to heaven by a chariot of fire and a whirlwind (2 Kings 2:11-12).

Ascension stories were fairly common in the first and second centuries A.D., especially in regard to the afterlife of the Roman emperors. In his *Lives of the Caesars*, Suetonius told virtuous stories about the Caesars. In one story, after the death of the Octavian (Caesar Augustus) a person testified to his ascension into heaven. Suetonius reports that following the emperor's death and cremation, "an ex-praetor who took oath that he had seen the form of the Emperor, after he had been reduced to ashes, on its way to heaven" (*Lives, The Deified Augustus* 1.100.4-5, LCL). It is worth noting that after Augustus's (Octavian's) death, reports about his remarkable birth and the various remarkable physical features that attended both his birth and death were noted. Philostratus, *Apollonius of Tyana* 1.4–6, reports that the origins of the first-century itinerant philosopher Apollonius were considered divine, that is, the child bears the image of the divine Proteus, the mother had a remarkable birth, and the child was called a "son of Zeus." In regard to Augustus' birth, Suetonius reports: "According to Julius Marathus, a few months before Augustus was born, a portent was generally observed at Rome, which gave warning that nature was pregnant with a king for the Roman people" (*The Deified Augustus* 94.3, LCL). He reportedly also was able to divine "beforehand the outcome of all his wars" (96.1, LCL). Before he died, he was also aware that this would happen and there were "signs" to point to it.

> His death, too, of which I shall speak next, and his deification after death, were known in advance by unmistakable signs. As he was bringing the lustrum [a sacrifice of purification made every five years] to an end in the

Campus Martius [his eventual place of burial, see 100.4] before a great throng of people, an eagle flew several times about him and then going across to the temple hard by, perched above the first letter of Agrippa's name. On noticing this, Augustus bade his colleague Tiberias recite the vows which it is usual to offer for the next five years; for although he had them prepared and written out on a tablet, he declared that he would not be responsible for vows which he should never pay. At about the same time the first letter of his name was melted from the inscription on one of his statues by a flash of lightning; this was interpreted to mean that he would live only a hundred days from that time, the number indicated by the letter C, and that he would be numbered with the gods, since *aesar* (that is, the part of the name Caesar which was left) is the word for god in the Etruscan tongue (*Augustus* 97.1-3, LCL).

The message of Luke that Jesus had a phenomenal birth (Luke 1:26), that the death of Jesus did not take him unaware (Luke 9:21), that his death was accompanied by signs (Luke 23:44-45), and that Jesus' death was in the plan of God (Acts 2:22-23) are not unfamiliar themes in antiquity. Such stories suggest the above comment that the ascension story was intended by Luke and John to proclaim the exaltation of Jesus in his resurrection. The divine nature of the event Luke is reporting is attested to not only by the apostles, but also by the presence of the interpreting angelic beings in vv. 9-11. For Luke, the ascension of Jesus points to the significance of Jesus and his exaltation. The grave did not have final victory over him.

1:12-14. The Disciples in the Upper Room

1:12. A Sabbath day's journey A sabbath day's journey was about 2,000 cubits (a cubit was 56 cm) or approximately 1,120 meters (= ca. 3,675 feet = 1,224 yards or a little more than half a mile). See *Mekhilta Exod.* 16.29 (59a); *Tg.Ps.-J. Exod.* 16.29; *b. Erubin* 51a; *y. Berakoth* 5.9a 40. The distance allowed at Qumran was about half that amount (*CD* 10.21) unless a person was pasturing a beast and then that distance was extended to 2,000 cubits (*CD* 11.5).

1:13. Time of stay in the upper room. If, as it seems unlikely, the forty days are to be taken literally, then the duration on the meetings in the upper room were about a week to ten days.

The names of the apostles. The listing of the names of the "apostles" (see 1:2) supports the view that this is a second volume and not, as some scholars have suggested, that the two volumes were originally one single volume that was later split into two. The list is the same as in Luke 6:14-16 except that Judas' name has been omitted and the order is slightly different. Compare the list of the apostolic names in Matt. 10:2-4 and Mark 3:16-19. Luke's designation of these disciples of Jesus as apostles (see earlier in Luke 6:14-16) indicates the mission of the Twelve. The term "apostle" (Greek, *apostolos* = "one who is sent") was employed in early Christianity to focus on the mission of Jesus that was passed on to his closest followers. Jesus himself is called an apostle in Heb. 3:1 and the term was not to restricted to the Twelve alone, but also included others such as Paul (Gal. 1:1), Andronicus and Junia (Rom. 16:7), James the Lord's brother (Gal. 1:19), and others besides (1 Cor. 15:7). Paul refers to the appearance he had from the risen Christ to argue for his apostleship (1 Cor. 9:1).

The importance of the Twelve. Because Luke believes that the Twelve were an important group of disciples of Jesus who also were called apostles (Luke 6:13, cf. 22:14, 29-30), he sees the need to replace Judas with another who will, with the rest of the Twelve, lead the reconstituted Israel, the people of God. This is the relationship Luke sees between the Twelve and the twelve tribes of Israel and probably why it is the reconstituted Twelve who are called to proclaim Jesus to the gathered twelve tribes of Israel at the Feast of Pentecost in Jerusalem.

II. 1:15–8:13. THE SPREAD OF THE GOSPEL IN JERUSALEM

1:15-26. The Replacement of Judas Iscariot
1:15. Peter stood up in the midst of the brethren. The word "brethren" (Greek= *adelphoi*) is used for fellow Christians throughout Acts and elsewhere in the New Testament. In Acts, see 1:16; 9:30; 10:23; 11:1, 12, 29; 12:17; 14:2; 15:3, 22, 32–33, 40; 17:6, 10, 14; 18:18, 27; 21:7, 17, 20; 28:14-15; and possibly in 15:7, 13, 23. The term as used here has nothing to do with blood relations, but rather with the close nature of the relationships that Christians experienced as fellow believers and followers of Christ. This kind of kindred relationship is also found at Qumran (1QS 6.22; 1Qsa 1:28; 2.13). Describing how the Essenes shared their wealth with each other and how no one had any need among them, Josephus says that this had the result that "you will nowhere see either abject poverty or inordinate wealth; the individual's possessions join the common stock and all, like brothers, enjoy a single patrimony" (*Wars* 2.122-23, LCL).

1:18-19. The death of Judas Iscariot. The story of Judas' death varies in detail with the one in Matthew 27:3-10, but both have significant parallels with the death of evil people in the ancient world. Our closest example has to do with the death of Herod Agrippa (cf. the later discussion of this in Acts 12:20-23 that also has a parallel in Josephus' *Ant.* 19.8.2). Josephus also relates the painful death of Herod the Great (*J. W.* 1.656-65 and *Ant.* 17. 168-69). *Second Macc.* 9:7-12 reports the terrible death of the ruthless King Antiochus IV Epiphanes. Luke employs the common means of telling of

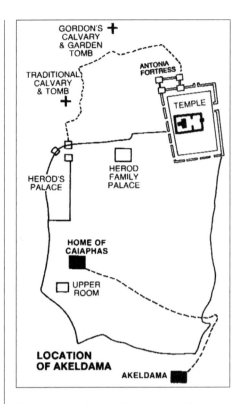

the demise of a wicked person that was intended to describe the just end of an evil person. The early Christians saw Judas as a traitor and the NT reflects his betrayal of Jesus regularly and views him in a negative light (Luke 6:16; 22:3, 47; Mark 3:19; Matt. 10:4; cf. Mark 14:10, 43; Matt. 26:14, 25, 47; John 6:71; 12:4; 13:2; 18:2, 5). Unlike Matthew's account, Luke does not speak of Judas' repentance and so his judgment is final (v. 20). Luke sees Judas' failure as a fulfillment of Scripture and cites Pss. 69:26 and 109:8. In the latter case, he finds justification for replacing Judas with another.

1:21-22. Qualifications for selection. Luke indicates that those who had been with Jesus from the time of his baptism and witnessed his resurrection were qualified to serve with them as one of the Twelve (1:21-22). This suggests that an apostle was one who had known Jesus and that the role would eventually die out in the church. Two names were selected among the gathering in the upper room who were qualified and one was selected.

1:22-26. The casting of lots. The practice of casting lots to determine the will of God has many parallels in the OT and some in the Essene community at Qumran (see 1QS 5.3.). It was also widespread among the Greeks and Romans. In the OT parallels, lots were cast to determine the will of God in dividing up the promised land (Josh. 18:6; 19:51), distributing goods and objects of desire (Nah. 3:10; Ps. 22:18), and even in the selection of residents of post-exilic Jerusalem (Neh. 10:34). They were also used to determine the identity of a guilty party (Josh. 7:10-26; Jonah 1:7; 1 Sam. 14:41-42), and in such matters as who would become king (1 Sam. 10:20) and who would perform sacred duties in the temple (1 Chron. 24:7; 25:8; and 26:13-19). Those who cast the lots believed that God would determine the outcome that was needed in the process (Prov. 16:33). The practice is not condemned in the Bible and is distinguished from magic or soothsaying.

2:1-13. The Coming of the Holy Spirit

Only Luke describes this occasion in the NT. While Paul was aware of the gift of the Spirit having come to the Christians (Gal. 3:1-5), he does not describe the events of Pentecost. This event is the fulfillment of the promise of the risen Christ in Acts 1:8 and what was called "the promise of the Father" in Luke 24:49 and Acts 1:4. This was the occasion when the followers of Jesus received the power that was needed to carry out the mission of Jesus in the world.

2:1. The Day of Pentecost. The setting for the coming of the Holy Spirit is on the Day of Pentecost and in Jerusalem where the Festival of Pentecost was observed. This was one of the three most important festival days in the Jewish calendar, and because of the difficulties with weather in the earlier two, this one was often better attended by Jews living outside of Palestine. Pentecost celebrated the "Feast of Weeks" (Exod. 23:16; 34:22; Lev. 23:15-16; Deut. 16:9-10, 16; 2 Chron. 8:13) or originally the "day of first fruits" of the wheat harvest (Num. 28:26; Exod. 34:22). It was celebrated fifty days after Passover, or on the "morrow after seven weeks" (see also *Jubilees* 15:1; 44:1-4). Pentecost was a time when Jews from all over the Greco-Roman world came for the annual celebration. In time, but it is not clear that it occurred in the first century A.D., the time was eventually set aside in the rabbinic period (probably around A.D. 270) to celebrate the giving of the Law (Exod. 19:1) (see *b. Pesahim* 68b). This may have derived from *Jubilees* 6:15-22 where the Feast of Weeks was interpreted as a renewal of the covenant. The giving of the Law may have been observed first on this occasion by Asa in his renewal or covenant with the Lord (2 Chron. 15:10-12), but that is not clear. Before the time of Jesus, it appears that some Jews were celebrating the Feast of Weeks in the middle of the third month (Siwan) as a renewal of the Sinai covenant, or the giving of the Law (see Jub. 1:1; 6:17-19; 14:20; cf. 22:1-16). The *Manual of Discipline* (1QS 1:8-2:25) records part of the ritual that took place on this day and elsewhere suggests that this was a renewal of the covenant of Sinai (CD 6:19; 8:21; 19:34; 20:12; 1QpHab 2:3).

There may be allusions to the renewal of the Sinai covenant in Luke, but it is not obvious: namely, the reference to the "devout men of every nation" coming to Jerusalem (Fitzmyer 234). See, for example, the parallels between Exod. 19-20 and Acts 2 (all the people together, Exod. 19:8 cf. Acts 2:1; there were sounds, Exod. 19:16 cf. Acts 2:2, 6; which came from heaven, Exod. 20:22, cf. Acts 2:2; the Lord's descent to Sinai comes in fire and likewise in Acts 2:2). Do these parallels suggest that the covenant at Sinai was celebrated at the Pentecost festival? It is instructive that after the beginning of the Christian era, the giving of the Law at Sinai was celebrated by the Jews at the same time as when the Christians celebrated the giving of the Holy Spirit. Whatever was understood at the celebration of Pentecost in the time of Jesus, the Christians adopted and adapted both the Jewish observances of Passover and Pentecost to celebrate the resurrection of Jesus and the giving of the Holy Spirit respectively.

According to the temple Scroll, there were three "pentecost" feasts celebrated by the Jews. These included the Feast of Weeks (third month, fifteenth day, 18:10-13), the Feast of New Wine (fifth month, third day, 19:11-14), and the Feast of New Oil (sixth month, twenty-second day, 21:12-16). Each of these days occurred fifty days apart. Could it be that the feast of New Wine is subtly behind the question in 2:13? What suggests otherwise is that the Feast of New Wine occurred some fifty days later and it would have been too early in the calendar for such an allusion. Some scholars believe that new wine was available earlier, however, and it was celebrated at Qumran (1Qsa 2.17-20; 1QS 6:4-5).

The phenomena that accompanied the coming of the Holy Spirit in Acts suggest the presence and power of God involved in the events.

2:1, 4. All together . . . all of them were filled. The "all" refers to the whole assembly of 120 rather than only to the Twelve (1:15), and the Holy Spirit came upon all of them. This is Luke's theme wherein the Spirit comes upon all who follow Christ (2:17-18, 38; 4:31; 5:32; 10:45; 19:6-7). See the expression "filled with the Holy Spirit" elsewhere in Luke 1:15, 41, 67 and in Acts 4:8, 31; 9:17; 13:9; compare Sirach 48:12 which speaks of Elisha receiving the spirit of Elijah. He was "filled with his spirit." Although there is no definite article before the Holy Spirit in Acts 2:4, there is little doubt that Luke is speaking of the presence and power of the Holy Spirit that enables the followers of Jesus to do the mission to which he had called

them (Acts 1:8). The Spirit empowers the follows of Jesus to proclaim him to the Jews on the Day of Pentecost.

2:2. Wind. Wind and breath are familiar images in the Scriptures employed to depict the presence and often the power of the Holy Spirit or the presence of God (Gen. 2:7; Ezek. 37:9-14; John 3:8). Wind (Greek, *pnoe*) and Spirit (*pneuma*) are related words.

2:3. Tongues of fire. See Exod. 3:2-4; 40:38 and compare Matt. 3:11 and Luke 3:16 at the baptism of Jesus and the promise of the Father. In Exod. 3:2; 14:20, 24; 19:18; 1 Kings 19:11-12, Ps. 104:4, clouds, wind, and fire are sometimes seen together or separately as signs of the presence and power of God. In the book of Exodus, when the Lord descended on Sinai, he did so in fire (19:18). Also interesting because of the parallels with the Acts account of the giving of the Spirit is how Philo describes the giving of the Law. For example, in his *The Decalogue* he writes:

> (33) He [God] at that time wrought a most conspicuous and evidently holy miracle, commanding an invisible sound to be created in the air, more marvelous than all the instruments that ever existed, attuned to perfect harmonies; and that not an inanimate one, nor yet, on the other hand, one that at all resembled any nature composed of soul and body; but rather it was a rational soul filled with clearness and distinctness, which fashioned the air and stretched it out and changed it into a kind of flaming fire, and so sounded forth so loud and articulate a voice like a breath passing through a trumpet, so that those who were at a great distance appeared to hear equally with those who were nearest to it. . . . (44) And moreover, as was natural, he filled the whole place with miraculous signs and works, with

noises of thunder too great for the hearing to support, and with the most radiant brilliancy of flashes of lightning, and with the sound of an invisible trumpet extending to a great distance, and with the march of a cloud, which like a pillar, had its foundation firmly fixed on the earth, but raised the rest of its body even to the height of heaven; and last of all, by the impetuosity of a heavenly fire, which overshadowed everything with a dense smoke.... (46) And a voice sounded forth from out of the midst of the fire which had flowed from heaven, a most marvelous and awful voice, the flame being endowed with articulate speech in a language familiar to the hearers, which expressed its words with such clearness and distinctness that the people seemed rather to be seeing than hearing it ... (48) It is therefore, with great beauty, and also with a proper sense of what is consistent with the dignity of God, that the voice is said to have come forth out of the fire; for the oracles of God are accurately understood and tested like gold by the fire (Philo, *De Decal.* 33, 44, 46, 48, Yonge's transl.).

Interestingly, the so-called Liturgical Text of the Qumran fragment 1Q29 also speaks of three tongues of fire. The condition of this fragment is such that a full understanding of the text is not possible, but the reference to the tongues of fire and the three tongues are discernible. Observe, for instance, Fragments 1-2:

"... the stone. When [...] *by tongues of fire*.... [... until] the priest [...] stops speaking [... who]speaks to you. And the prophet [...] who speaks apostasy [...] YHWH, god of [...]

[... the] right st[one] when the priest leaves [...] *three tongues of fire* [...] And after he shall go up and

remove his shoes [...] YHWH, your God, [...] all Israel [...]with all. Your name [...] the generations of the power of the glorious ones [...] (Trans. By Garcia Martinez, *The Dead Sea Scrolls*, p. 277-78, italics added.)

This phenomenon of fire reflecting a divine presence has several parallels in other ancient literature. An example of this may be seen in Virgil, who describes the words of a prisoner during the Greek-Trojan wars who is called upon to speak and addresses his captors as follows: "You eternal fires of heaven, Godhead inviolable, now bear me witness, and you altars and knives set for unspeakable deeds from which I escaped ...." (*Aeneid* 2.682-4, LCL). See also parallels in Ovid, *Fasti* 6.635, and in Homer, for example, who tells of the radiance with divine fire given to Achilles by the goddess Athena for battle: ". . . Achilles, dear to Zeus, roused him, and round about his mighty shoulders Athene flung her tasseled aegis, and around his head the fair goddess set thick a golden cloud, and forth from the man made blaze a gleaming fire" (*Iliad* 18.214, LCL). Justin, *Trypho* 88, interestingly reports there was a fire in the Jordan River at Jesus' baptism. "And then, when Jesus had gone to the river Jordan, where John was baptizing, and when he stepped into the water, a fire was kindled in the Jordan and when he came out of the water, the Holy Ghost lighted on Him like a dove, [as] the apostles of this very Christ of ours wrote" (ANF Trans., Cf. Acts 1:3 and 2:3). Philo, in his *De Decalogo* (*The Decalogue* 11.44, 46, 48), tells how at the giving of the Law the presence of God was represented in various manifestations, including fire.

And, moreover, as was natural, he filled the whole place with miraculous signs and works, with noises of thunder too great for the hearing to support, and with the most radiant brilliancy of flashes of lightning, and with the sound of an invisible trumpet extending to a great distance, and with the march of a cloud . . . and last of all, by the impetuosity of a heavenly fire, which overshadowed everything around with a dense smoke . . .

And a voice sounded forth from out of the midst of the fire which had flowed from heaven, a most marvelous and awful voice, the flame being endowed with articulate speech in a language familiar to the hearers . . .

It is, therefore, with great beauty, and also with a proper sense of what is consistent with the dignity of God, that the voice is said to have come forth out of the fire; for the oracles of God are accurately understood and tested like gold by the fire . . . (*Decalogue* 11.44, 46, 48; trans. by Yonge, 522).

Sometimes fire is also representative of the consuming judgment of God. (See Isa. 66:15, 18 and also Philo, who writes, "But all those who are stubborn and disobedient are for ever inflamed, and burnt, and consumed by their internal appetites, which, like flame, will destroy all the life of those who possess them" [*The Decalogue* 11.48]).

2:4, 11. Other tongues. Luke intends to say that the followers of Jesus were enabled by the power of the Spirit to speak the languages of those represented in Jerusalem that day. It is not uncommon in the ancient world to find references to all peoples speaking one language and bridging the barriers between people (Alexander the Great, plus see Boring, 486). Part of the success for Alexander's program, apart from his military prowess, had to do with his vision for the peoples he conquered. A good example of this is found in part of a famous speech that Alexander reportedly gave at Opis, a town on the Tigris River near Babylon in 324 B.C. The speech has undoubtedly been embellished to some degree by Eratosthenes, the third director of the library of

Alexandria in the second century B.C., and also by Ptolemy (one of Alexander's famous generals) who heard the speech. Nevertheless, because several parts of the speech have been reported in various contexts with similar ideas and wording it is likely that there is some element of truth in the story. The speech reportedly was given to some 9,000 "dignitaries and notables of all races" and emphasized brotherhood and reconciliation of all persons. The shortest report of this speech comes from the Roman historian Flavius Arrian (ca. A.D. 130), who writes: "And Alexander prayed for all sorts of blessings, and especially for harmony (*homonoian*) and fellowship (*koinonian*) in the empire between Macedonians and Persians" (Arrian, *Anabasis* 7.11.9, LCL). Strabo's version of the story (64 B.C. – ca. A.D. 23) claims that Alexander transcended the old distinctions between Greek and Barbarian and said that the real distinction between people was not a matter of race, but whether they were good or bad (1.4.9). The speech has taken many forms (see also Plutarch, *de Alexandri Fortuna* 1.6), but the themes of brotherhood, the worth of all humanity and the goal of reconciliation are in all of them. This view lies behind the call for linguistic and cultural commonality in Alexander's conquests (see W. W. Tarn, *Alexander the Great.* Cambridge: Cambridge University Press, 1948, 2.434–49, and N. G. L. Hammond, *A History of Greece to 323 B.C.* Oxford: Clarendon Press, 1959, pp. 641–42).

The removal of the language barriers so that everyone could communicate in one Hellenized tongue without cultural barriers was the primary goal of Alexander's conquests, and that was in large part realized throughout the Greco-Roman world in the first century. While there was a common (*koine*) Greek language that was available for communication in the marketplace, this, however, did not mean that various dialects had been replaced or lost. Often the people of various nations could communicate in more than one language. It was important to Luke, however, that the proclamation of Jesus was heard in the mother-tongues of the people gathered in Jerusalem from around the Greco-Roman world. Although Luke does not draw attention to it here, it is not difficult to consider as one of the effects of Pentecost the reversal of the story of the confusion of languages at Babel (Gen. 11:1-9). Philo, the Jewish interpreter of Scripture from Alexandria (roughly in the lifetime of Jesus), for example, shares a tradition that before Babel, all people spoke one language. He passes on the tradition that in the beginning of the human race they all spoke one language but indeed, so did the animals:

> And there is also another story akin to this, related by the deviser of fables, concerning the sameness of language existing among animals: for they say that formerly, all the animals in the world, whether land animals, or aquatic ones, or winged ones, had but one language, and that just as among men Greeks speak the same language as Greeks, and the present race of barbarians speaks the same language as barbarians, exactly in the same manner every animal was able to converse with every other animal with which it might meet, and with which it did anything, or from which it suffered anything , so that they sympathized with one another at their mutual misfortunes, and rejoiced whenever any of them met with any good fortune; (7) for they could impart their pleasures and their annoyances to one another by their sameness of language so that they felt pleasure together and pain together; and this similarity of manners and union of feelings lasted, until being sated with great abundance of good things which they enjoyed, as often happens, they were at last drawn on to a desire of what was unattainable, and even sent an embassy to treat for

immortality, requesting to be released from old age, and to be always endowed with the vigour of youth, saying, that already one animal of their body, and that a reptile, the serpent, had received this gift; for he having put off old age, was allowed again to grow young; and that it was absurd for the more important animals to be left behind by an inferior one, or for their whole body to be distanced by one. (8) However, they suffered the punishment suitable to their audacity, for they immediately were separated in their language, so that from that time forth, they have not been able to understand one another, by reason of the difference in the dialects into which the one common language of them all had been divided (Philo, *De Confusione Linguarum/On the Confusion of Tongues.* 3.6-8, Trans. by Yonge, 234-35).

Similarly, Josephus claims that before the Fall in the Garden of Eden (Gen. 3) all animals spoke a common language as well: "At that epoch all the creatures spoke a common tongue" (*Ant.* 1.41). He probably received this legend from the *Book of Jubilees* (ca. 100 B.C.) which claims: "On that day [the fall of Adam and Eve] the mouth of all the beasts and cattle and birds and whatever walked or moved was stopped from speaking because all of them used to speak with one another with one speech and one language" (*Jub.* 3.28), but he writes that humanity lost the ability to communicate through one speech at the Tower of Babel (*Jub.* 10.22-25). The author/s of the *Testaments of the Twelve Patriarchs*, claim/s that in the coming age people will see the redeemed once again have one language: "And you shall be one people of the Lord, with one language" (*Test. XII Patr, Judah* 25.3).

More than the ability to communicate in languages appears to have been involved in the Acts 2 experience, however. The enabling of the Spirit to speak in *unknown* tongues of the Pauline type (1 Cor. 12-14; Mark 16:17) seems obvious from v. 13. Otherwise, why would the disciples be accused of drunkenness (cf. 1 Cor. 14:23, madness)? Also, why would the local residents of Judea (2:9) be surprised simply to hear the message in their own language (2:12)? This is what they would expect. It is likely that Luke expected both kinds of tongues to be understood since later in Acts the unknown tongues of the Pauline-type accompany the coming of the Holy Spirit (10:45-46; 19:6-7).

Such tongues were not unique to the Christian community in the ancient world. Delphic oracles were known in the ancient world to speak for the god Apollo in a trance and prophets were present who would interpret their meaning. The young woman in Acts 16:16 is said to have a "spirit of divination" which translates the Greek words *pneuma pythona*, (= "a spirit of Python"). Python was the earlier name of Delphi. It is quite possible that the young woman in 16:16 was a Delphic oracle (one who prophesied in the spirit of Apollo at Delphi) who was speaking in tongues. Tongues in the ancient world may also be found in the OT. Scholars disagree on whether this phenomenon was present in the OT times, but some passages suggest that prophecy and tongues may be equated, e.g., 1 Sam. 10:5-13 and 19:18-24. Paul clearly distinguishes prophecy from tongues in 1 Cor. 12:10, 27-30 and 14:5-6, 23-24, but this may not have been the case for Luke since what was attributed to madness and drunkenness in Acts 2:13 was considered a fulfillment of prophecy (Acts 2:17-cf. Joel 2:28-32; 3:1-5).

Other examples of ecstatic speech in the ancient world include Apeleius (born ca. A.D. 125), the so-called Platonic philosopher from Madauros, in his *Metamorphoses* (also known as *The Golden Ass*) in which he describes a certain Greek named Lucius who was transformed into an ass for a year during which time he was passing by a cottage in which several persons were engaged in this experience. He writes:

After passing a number of small cottages in their wandering course, they came to the country house of a rich land-owner. As soon as they reached the entrance-way they frantically flung themselves forward, filling the place with the sound of their discordant shrieks. For a long time they dropped their heads and rotated their necks in writhing motions, swinging their hanging locks in a circle. . . . In the midst of all this one of them started to rave more wildly than the rest, and producing rapid gasps from deep down in his chest, as though he had been filled with the heavenly inspiration of some deity, he simulated a fit of madness—as if, indeed, the gods' presence was not supposed to make men better than themselves, but rather weak or sick. Now we see what sort of reward he earned from divine providence. Shouting like a prophet, he began to attach and accuse himself with a fabricated lie about how he had perpetrated some sin against the laws of holy religion . . . (*Metamorphoses* 8.27-28, LCL).

Likewise, Lucian (A.D. 120–190), the satirist from Samosata on the Euphrates, describes the activities of Alexander, a wandering prophet who came to a village to take advantage of simple people and began to speak strange words in a religious meeting from the high altar in the city's temple. Lucian describes what happened thusly:

The assembly—for almost the whole city, including women, old men, and boys, had come running—marveled, prayed and made obeisance. Uttering a few meaningless words like Hebrew or Phoenician, he dazed the creatures, who did not know what he was saying save only that he everywhere brought in [the gods] Apollo and Asclepius. Then he ran at full speed to the future temple,

Sermons and Speeches in Acts

Speakers			Occasions and/or		
Peter	Paul	Others	Hearers	Cities	References
1. Peter			Selection of successor to Judas	Jerusalem	1:16-22
2. Peter			Signs on the day of Pentecost	Jerusalem	2:14-36
3. Peter			Healing of lame man in the temple	Jerusalem	3:12-26
4. Peter			Before the Sanhedrin, for preaching the resurrection of Christ	Jerusalem	4:8-12
		Gamaliel	Before the Sanhedrin, regarding Peter and others	Jerusalem	5:35-39
		Stephen	Before the Sanhedrin, after Stephen was arrested	Jerusalem	7:2-53
5. Peter			At Cornelius' house, to present the gospel to Gentiles there	Caesarea	10:34-43
6. Peter			Defense to the church about what happened in Caesarea	Jerusalem	11:4-17
	1. Paul		Sabbath sermon to Jews in the synagogue	Antioch of Pisidia	13:16-41
	2. Paul and Barnabas		Crowd who wanted to worship them	Lystra	14:15-17
7. Peter			Church council	Jerusalem	15:7-11
		James	Church council	Jerusalem	15:13-21
	3. Paul		Athenians on Mars' Hill	Athens	17:22-31
		Demetrius	Workman who were disturbed at Paul's preaching	Ephesus	19:25-27
		Town clerk	Riot at Ephesus	Ephesus	19:35-40
	4. Paul		Gathering of Ephesian elders	Miletus	20:18-35
	5. Paul		Mob of people who tried to kill Paul	Jerusalem	22:1-21
	6. Paul		Defense before the Sanhedrin	Jerusalem	23:1-6
	7. Paul		Defense before Felix	Caesarea	24:10-21
	8. Paul		Defense before Festus	Caesarea	25:8, 10-11
	9. Paul		Defense before Herod Agrippa II	Caesarea	26:1-23
	10. Paul		Shipmates in a violent storm	Mediterranean Sea, between Crete and Malta	27:21-26
	11. Paul		Testimony of Jewish leaders	Rome	28:17-20, 25-28

went to the excavation of the previously improvised fountain-head of the oracle, entered the water, and sang hymns in honour of Asclepius and Apollo at the top of his voice, and besought the god, under the blessing of heaven, to come to the city (Lucian, *Alexander the False Prophet* 13, LCLl; see also 22, 49, 51, 53).

He later describes some of the oracles (ecstatic speech) offered by Alexander the prophet and the large sums of money he collected when his interpreters ("expounders") interpreted their meaning. Lucian offers examples of the unintelligible speech that was offered. For example, *"morphen eubargoulis eis skian chnechikrage leipsei phaos"* and *"Sabardalachou malachaattealos en."* There may be a mixture of Sythian and Greek in the former expression, but in both cases the meaning is not clear. Other examples of this are in Herodotus, *History* 8.135; Dio Chrysostom, *Oration* 10.23-24; Plutarch, *De def. or.* 412 A.

Nations gathered. Most scholars agree that Luke is using a list of nations that he has received from other earlier sources. There are many such lists in the ancient world, including in the Bible (Gen. 10:2-31), and while there are some overlaps in a few of these lists, none are exactly like the one Luke presents. Observe that the various lists of nations and their similarities and especially how dated they are: namely, Media was no longer a nation at that time, but had only a few tribes in existence. There are a number of other difficulties with this list, however. For example, why did Luke omit Macedonia and Achaia, significant areas of Paul's later ministry, but also quite significant in the ancient world? There is also some agreement among scholars that Judea (*Ioudaia*) was a late addition to Luke's list since it does not fit geographically in the place it has in the list. Further, it is strange, given the Jerusalem context of the Pentecost event that there is amazement that they (the Jews) were hearing the message in their own tongues when they

were living in their homeland. With the events described occurring in Judea there should have been no amazement that they heard the message in their own tongue. If Judea is omitted, the sequence of the places listed makes more geographical sense. The question is rather when and why Luke added Judea to the list.

2:13. Drunken with new wine. Is this a reference to the Festival of New Wine that occurred fifty days after Pentecost? According to the Temple Scroll discovered at Qumran, there were three festivals celebrated by the Jews, each of which was fifty days apart: the Feast of Weeks (18:10-13, which is the same as Pentecost in Acts 2:1), the Feast of New Wine (19:11-14), and the Feast of New Oil (21:12-16). (For a discussion of these see Fitzmyer 234-35.)

Does this text justify the view that in Acts 2:4, 11 Luke also was describing the Pauline type of *glossalalia* (= speaking in tongues, see 1 Cor. 12)? If the speaking in tongues there is restricted to the communication of the proclamation about Jesus, it is strange that such speaking (vv. 6, 11) did not lead to a response of faith, but only puzzlement and ridicule (vv. 12-13). Peter's explanation of the phenomenon (2:27-36) does lead to a response of belief (2:37-41). Because Luke elsewhere associates the coming of the Holy Spirit with speaking in tongues (10:45-48; 19:2-6), it is quite possible that he intended the tongues in this passage to include more than the phenomenon of dialects or languages.

It was not uncommon in the ancient world to describe those in a state of ecstasy and inspiration as drunken. Philo, for example, claims that the mind, when truly inspired by God to reveal truth, "becomes seized with a sort of sober intoxication like the zealots engaged in the Corybantian festivals, and yields to enthusiasm, becoming filled with another desire, and a more excellent longing, by which it is conducted onwards to the very summit of such things as are perceptible only to the intellect, till it appears to be reaching the great King himself" (Philo, *On the Creation*, 71, Yonge, transl.).

2:14-40. The First Christian Sermon: Content and Structure.

This is the first of several speeches Luke employs in his story of the expansion of the early church's ministry all the way to Rome. Essentially the content is threefold: namely, prophecy, fulfillment, and decision. It could be further described as follows: (1. what Jesus did: miracles; (2. what the Jewish leaders did: crucified him; (3. what God did: raised and exalted him; (4. what the people asked: what must we do; (5. what Peter said they must do: repent and be baptized. Further, there are several parallels in substance with 1 Peter. For example, the term "foreknowledge" occurs only in these two places in the NT (v. 23 and 1 Peter 1:2). Other parallels include the affirmation that Christ is Lord (v. 36; cf. 1 Peter 3:15), Jesus was rejected by his own (v. 23; cf. 1 Peter 2:3, 7), Jesus' ascension/exaltation and place at the right hand of God (v. 33; cf. 1 Peter 3:22), the promise of the Holy Spirit (v. 33; 1 Peter 1:12; 4:14), the glory that follows suffering (v. 36; 1 Peter 1:11; 4:12-14), and the connection between salvation and baptism (v. 38; 1 Peter 3:21). These parallels in thought have led some interpreters to suggest that they reflect the very words of Peter on this occasion and that Peter is behind the writing of 1 Peter. Likewise, since Luke's companion, Silas (or Silvanus), was also Peter's companion at a later time (1 Peter 5:12), that he may be the one behind these parallels.

2:14. Peter standing with the *eleven*. Mattathias (1:26) has now taken Judas' place so the "eleven" plus Peter are complete and ready for mission. For parallels to Peter's call to attention, see Gen. 4:23; Job 32:10-11.

2:15. These men are not drunk. Peter explains that it is too early in the day to be drunk. "It is only the ninth hour," that is, around nine o'clock in the morning. While it was certainly

possible for people to be drunk in the morning, normally this took place at night and was over by the end of the day. Cicero, for example, ridicules those who were drunk and carousing at three o'clock in the morning (Cicero, *Philipp.* 2.41.104).

2:16. This is that. Peter employs a common form of interpreting Scripture in his day, sometimes called *pesher* interpretation, in which he shows how the Scriptures were fulfilled in the present circumstances of the people. See, for instance the 1QHabakkuk Pesher (1QpHab) at Qumran interprets the prophetic book Habakkuk in terms of its own day. After citing part of the text from Habakkuk, the interpreter says, "the interpretation is." For example, citing Hab. 1:17, the interpreter writes: "For this he continually sheathes his sword to kill peoples without pity.... Its interpretation concerns the Kittim (Romans) who will cause many to die by the edge of the sword, youths, adults and old people, women and children; not even children at the breast will they pity" (Col. VI.8-12, Garcia Martinez transl., pp. 199-200).

2:17. In the last days. Peter's quotation is from Joel 3:1-5 (LXX= the Greek Septuagint translation, which Luke would have been citing; or 2:28-32 MT= the Hebrew Masoretic Text translation). The opening words, "in the last days," are not in the LXX translation of Joel's prophecy, but were added by Luke to emphasize the significance of the events he is describing. The Joel text simply says "He believes that what has happened in their midst is the beginning of the great Day of the Lord" (see 1 Thess. 5:1-11) that will not only bring judgment to evildoers, but unleash the blessings of God upon those who call upon him (2:21). Peter's language at Pentecost is eschatological ("in the last days"), that is, related to the future coming of the kingdom of God, when all people will hear the message of God in their own language. The words "in the last days" were added by Luke to clarify to his readers that in the resurrection of Jesus and the giving of the Holy Spirit the end times promised before by God had arrived. He is quoting from the Septuagint (the LXX) or Greek translation which has the words "and it shall be (come to pass) after these things" but Luke wants to tell his readers that in the events that have unfolded, the "last days" of God's plan for a restored humanity have come to them.

2:22. Jesus of *Nazareth* (Greek = "the Nazorean"). Interestingly, Nazareth is not mentioned either in the Old Testament nor in Josephus who served as a general in the region of Galilee in the early stages of the A.D. 66–70 war. The village is also not found in the Mishnah, nor in the Talmud. It was a small and relatively insignificant village in the first century. It may be that the term was used as a reference to Jesus the "Nazarene" as in Luke 4:34; 24:19. See also Acts 3:6; 4:10; 6:14; 22:8; 26:9. The term is used to identify the Christians in 24:5.

The death of Jesus in the will of God. The sermon is apologetic in substance: namely, accounting for the death of Jesus in the will of God, and evidence of this is that God has raised Jesus from the dead and there are witnesses to this. The message of the early Christians was that Jesus was the promised Messiah, but before anyone could accept that, they had to deal with the problem of his death by a scandalous crucifixion (see also Gal. 3:13-14). The early Christians had to overcome the scandal of a crucified Messiah (see 1 Cor. 1:23) before they propagated their faith, and Peter begins this apologetic in his initial sermon. Jesus did many miracles and signs, and even his enemies witnessed this and though he was crucified, it was in the will of God. Evidence of this is that God raised him up (2:22-24). Unlike Paul (1 Cor. 15:3-5; Gal. 1:3-4; 3:13; Rom. 5:6-8; cf. 1 Cor. 2:2), Luke does not say that Jesus died "for our sins." Instead, Luke claims that the death of Jesus was not a surprise but was

according to the plan and will of God (2:23-24). For Luke, God overcame the death of Jesus through the resurrection as was foretold in the Scriptures (Ps. 16:8-11).

2:34-35. The Lord said to my Lord. Luke quotes Ps. 110 (v. 1), a popular psalm in the early church, and argues that since this did not happen to David, that is, David did not ascend, it must refer to the Messiah. The author of Hebrews cites the same psalm to emphasize the superiority of Jesus (Heb. 1:13, cf. Ps. 110:1 and Heb. 7:17 cf. Ps. 110:4). This probably stems from Jesus' use of the text in his teachings (Mark 12:35). Like other early Christian writers, Luke also uses this occasion and the Ps. 110:1 text to affirm that Jesus is confessed as Lord (see also Phil. 2:11; Rom. 10:9-10; 1 Cor. 12:3).

2:26. Lord and Christ. Early Christians included these two titles prominently in their confessions. That these confessions did not first emerge on Hellenistic soil can be shown in 1 Cor. 16:22 in Paul's reference to the Aramaic term, *Marana tha* ("our Lord, come!" or *Maran atha*, "our Lord has come!" See also Rev. 22:20.). as a prayer of the early Christians in the land of Israel. Through the resurrection from the dead and from Scripture, Luke shows that the exaltation of Jesus has been demonstrated.

2:37-41. Response to Peter's Sermon 2:37 Cut to the heart, they said to Peter and to the other apostles. Luke underscores that Peter is only the spokesperson for the twelve apostles who constitute the true church.

2:38. Be baptized. Baptism and repentance were signs of conversion to Judaism from paganism. John the Baptist's practice of baptizing those who were Jews (Mark and parallels) was unusual for the day and was followed by the early followers of Jesus. All persons who repented of their sins were to be baptized whether they were Jews or Gentiles. Baptism is always passive in the NT. No one baptized him/herself. Baptism was administered by someone else.

In the name of Jesus. The baptism "in the name of Jesus" distinguished the kind of baptism the early Christians followed from other Jewish practices: namely, it was a baptism administered in the name of Jesus. These are the typical words used in Acts to identify what kind of baptism was practiced (2:38; 8:16; 10:48; 19:5), and they also indicate the authority of the baptism: namely, that it was done in the authority of Jesus who was confessed as Lord (see Mark 9:38-39 and the authority to cast out demons in the name of Jesus in Acts 16:18). The Trinitarian formula of Matthew 28:19 is a later development in the practice of baptism in early Christianity.

2:38-39. The gift of the Holy Spirit. In Acts, all of those who acknowledge Jesus as Lord receive the Holy Spirit (see 2:17; 8:15; 9:17; 10:47; 19:6). Now the gift of the Spirit appears no longer to be bound to the ecstatic experience observed earlier on the Day of Pentecost. Elsewhere in the NT this gift enables Christians to do a variety of ministries that build up the Christian community and enable them to accomplish their mission (Rom. 12:6-8; 1 Cor. 12:4-11, 28-31; Eph. 4:7-13). It also enables them to practice the fruit or virtues of Christian faith (Gal. 5:22-23).

2:40. He testified with many other arguments. Luke, like other ancient historians, summarizes the content of the rest of Peter's speech. (For nonbiblical examples of this, see Xenophon, *Hellenica* 2.4.42 and Polybius, *Historiae* 21.14.4.) It is highly unlikely that any sermon from the NT is a verbatim account of the whole sermon since in most instances they only take a few moments to read out loud to a congregation. They are rather to be taken as the author's summaries of what took place on that day.

Luke has shown that the Christian commu-

nity is indwelt by the Spirit who also drives and directs that community's life. The Spirit comes to the community of Jesus' followers through the proclaimed message about Jesus Christ and transcends all ethnic boundaries.

2:41-47. A Summary of Life of the Early Church

2:41. About 3,000 souls (persons) received Peter's word and were baptized and added (to the church). This is one of several numerical indicators that Luke employs to indicate the growth and probably the health of the early church (2:41; 4:4; 5:14; 6:1, 7; 9:31; 11:21, 24; 14:1; 19:20). The passage is also one of several summarizing texts. Such summaries were not uncommon in ancient historical narrative. The term souls (*psuchai*) simply refers to persons or individuals. The Greek term *psuche* was a common designation for persons in antiquity (see 7:14; 27:37; Exod. 1:5; Euripides, *Andromache* 611 and *Helena* 52).

2:42. Teaching, fellowship, breaking of bread, prayers.

Teaching. Much has been made of the distinction between teaching (*didache*) and preaching (*kerygma*) in early Christianity, but at this early stage, there is probably very little difference. See, for example, how the term *didache* is used of the disciples' proclamation (5:28; 13:12; 17:19). From the beginning teaching was an important element of the life of the early church: namely, to learn from those who had been with Jesus during his ministry and witnessed his resurrection appearances (1:21-22, cf. 1 Cor. 9:1).

Fellowship (*koinonia*). The practice of fellowship involved more than simply meeting together, though it also meant at least that. It had to do with the sharing of possessions with one another so that no one had any needs (vv. 44-45; 4:32-35; 5:1-11). Many expressed their concern for others by selling their goods and giving the proceeds to the apostles to distribute as people had need (4:32-37), but it was not a requirement (5:4). The concern to care for the needs of others by distributing one's own property and wealth was already known in the OT and in the story of Jesus (1 Kings 19:21; cf. Mark 10:21). The early Christians practiced this sharing in their meetings. While there was no law among the Christians to follow this practice (as it appears to have been in the Essene community), it seemed to the first Christians the appropriate consequence of having the gift of the Spirit: namely, sharing what one had with those who were in need. Josephus shares how the Essenes practiced it (*Jewish War* 2:122-127), and Philo describes similar practices in his *Every Good Man is Free* (77, 79, 84-85). (Compare Plato *Critias* 110 C-D; Ovid's description of the Golden Age in *Metamorphoses* 1.88-111 describes its practice; Plato, *Republic* 420C-422B; 462B-464A; *Laws* 679B-C; 684C-D; 744B-746C; 757A; Aristotle, *Politics* 1261A-1267B; and Iamblichus, *Life of Pythagoras* 20.) The practice of communal fellowship does not appear to have been pursued beyond the early church—at least there is little evidence of it, except that of Christians sharing their wealth to help others, furthering the Christian cause, and alleviating individual need.

Breaking of bread. This was a description not only of a meal together, but probably also a reference to the observance of the Lord's Supper or the early practice of the Eucharist. Acts 20:7 is not clear, but both a common meal and a *eucharistic* celebration is likely. The meal was real and not simply symbolic as it later became in many Christian traditions due to abuse (1 Cor. 11:21-22). Pliny, *Epist.* 10.96 notes that the Christians were known for eating simple meals with no elaborate preparations.

Prayers. While there were probably no prescribed prayers at this time, Christians continued to offer Jewish prayers in the temple (3:1; 10:9). Their practice of praying familiar Jewish prayers in the temple shows that they did not consider themselves a new sect, but rather the true Israelites who had discovered their Messiah. They did not change their practice of prayer as a result of their conversion, but continued their former practice with renewed dedication.

2:43. Awe. Luke uses the term fear (*phobos*) to express the response of the believing community at the remarkable activity of God in their midst, but the sense of the term is also that of awe (see Luke 1:12, 65; 2:9; 8:37; 21:26; Acts 5:5, 11; 9:31; 19:17).

2:43. Wonders and signs. What Jesus was able to do (2:22) is now carried on in the church. What God used to accredit Jesus (wonders and signs) now accredits the community that Jesus left behind (3:1-11; 5:15-16; 9:32-35).

2:44-45. All things in common. . . . see 1QS 1.11f.; 1QS 5.2; Josephus, *War* 2.122; *Ant.* 18.18-22; Philo, *Prob.* 75-87; 1QS 1.11-12 and 6.2-3. This is also expressed in Lucian's *Passing of Peregrinus* 13. Euripides, *Andromache* 376f. Plato taught that "the belongings of friends are held in common" (*Republic* 4.24a; 5.449c). So also Iamblichus, *Vita Pyth.* 20, "They held their property in common" (trans. by Conzelmann, 24). Why the early Christians were willing to pool their resources and share them with others is not clear. They were not unique in seeking to do this, but why is not certain. Perhaps it was because they believed that Jesus would soon return and as a result there was little need for possessions. Barrett says there was no need to "take thought for the marrow" since the Christians did not believe that there would be one (Barrett, 168). There is not much evidence that this practice continued for long, but there were examples of sacrificial sharing to care for the needs of others (Heb. 10:34; Rom. 15:25-29; 2 Cor. 8-9), but it does not appear that the practice of selling all and bringing it to the leaders of the church continued. This principle was widely accepted, but the Christians were known for putting it into effect. By the fourth century, the Christians had the largest social care network in the Roman Empire.

2:47. Day by day the Lord added daily to their number. Since this was what God had planned in the last days (2:21; cf. Joel 2:32–3:5), as Joel had foretold, Luke adds to his first summarizing passage the outcome of the coming of the promise of the Spirit at Pentecost. As we will soon see, it appears that the results of the coming of the Holy Spirit included not only the speaking in tongues and the conversion of some 3,000, but also various healing miracles, the first of which is reported in 3:1-26.

3:1–5:42. Conflict with Religious Authorities

Luke, aware of the many conflicts that faced Christians at a later time, tells how the apostles' example of dealing with conflict can be a model for all believers facing persecution and trial. He shows by their example that opposition must be met with boldness of conviction and confidence in the Lord (4:5-13) as well as obedience to God in the face of opposition (4:20; 5:29). The miracle story (3:1-11) shows how proclaiming the news about Jesus brings change and joy, but also brings the apostles into conflict with the religious authorities.

3:1-11. Miracles in the Name of Jesus

Luke employs this miraculous healing story to enable his readers to see the power of the name of Jesus (2:28), the risen Christ, for all circumstances of life, even for those who have an unfortunate physical condition like the man born lame who was reduced to a beggar's life. He also uses this story as a bridge to two other speeches by Peter.

3:1. The hour of prayer. Peter and John, like faithful Jews living in the area of the temple, made their way to the temple for their daily

prayers. Faithful Jews repeated prayers daily in the synagogue or at home and in their prayers the *Shema* (Hebrew "hear"), the opening word of Deut. 6:4-9 (see also Deut. 11:3-21 and Num. 15:36-41) was recited. The Shema was also accompanied by reciting Benedictions (also known as the *Shemona Esre*), which later numbered eighteen (called the Eighteen Benedictions), and the Ten Commandments. The faithful recited the Shema each morning and afternoon during their prayers. Prayer (*tefillah*) took place in the morning and afternoon (*m. Barakoth* 4.1; 1QS x:11; Josephus, *War* 2.8.5 §§ 128-31). While in some cases prayers took place three times a day (Dan. 6:11; 2 Enoch 51:4). The prayers that Peter and John were attending in the temple were the afternoon prayers offered around 3:00 P.M. (Ferguson, 527).

3:2, 10. The Beautiful Gate. The steps on the west end of the temple gave access to the temple platform. The Levites gathered here to sing the "Psalms of Ascents." At the top of these steps was the Nicanor Gate on the east, made of bronze and known for its extraordinary beauty. The name that Luke gives to the gate is not found outside of Acts, but Josephus claims that besides the nine gates to the temple that were overlaid with silver and gold, there was another gate that was outside the court of the temple ("holy house") that was made of Corinthian brass that surpassed the ones overlaid with gold and silver (Josephus, *War* 5.201). It is described in the Mishnah as follows: "All the gates that were there had been changed [and overlaid] with gold, save only the doors of the Nicanor Gate, for with them a miracle had happened; and some say, because their bronze shone like gold" (*Middoth* 2.3, Danby Trans. p. 592; see *Middoth* 1.4, which only speaks of seven gates and locates Nicanor on the east. See also *b. Yoma* 38a.). These doors may well be the "Beautiful Gate" that Luke refers to here.

3:6. Silver and gold. It may be that the silver and gold that was over the other gates leading to the temple court was the context for Peter's denial of monetary funds, but this was also a common expression in contrasts of virtue in the Hellenistic world. Plutarch, for instance, writes that "money cannot buy peace of mind, greatness of spirit, serenity, confidence, and self-sufficiency. Having wealth is not the same as being superior to it, nor is possessing luxuries the same as feeling no need of them" (*On Love of Wealth*, 1 in his *Moralia* VII, LCL trans.).

In the name of Jesus Christ the Nazorean. Luke focuses on the significance of the name of Jesus throughout this volume underscoring that what was done by the early church was done by the authority and in the power of Jesus. See also 2:21, 38; 3:6, 16; 4:7-10, 12, 17, 18, 30; 5:28, 40; 8:16; 10:48; 19:5 cf. James 2:7. As we will see below, not only is healing offered in the name of Jesus, but so is salvation itself (4:12). Evidently, calling on the name of Jesus meant to invoke faith in him through an appeal to his authority. While Luke elsewhere speaks against the use of magic (chaps. 3, 16, 19), he underscores that what is done on this day is a result of the activity of the exalted Jesus, the Christ and not by the authority or power of Peter and John. It does not seem likely that Luke intended anything other than Nazareth when he called Jesus the Nazorean, but there may be some focus on the religious side of the name (see Luke 1:26; 2:4, 39, 51; 4:16; Acts 10:38 and compare with 2:22; 4:10; 6:14; 22:8; and 26:9).

At its beginning, early Christianity was a Jewish sect that saw itself as following the one true way to God. The early Jewish Christian community did not cease being a Jewish sect until after the Bar Cochba rebellion (A.D. 132–35), and it saw no reason to separate itself from Jewish practices. Many Christians did not consider it necessary to be a bad Jew in order to be a good Christian. As a result, the early Christians continued in their prayers at the temple with other faithful Jews.

3:12-26. Peter Speaks in the Temple This speech was occasioned by the healing of the lame man (3:1-10) and essentially clarifies to all who listen that it was not accomplished either by Peter or John, but by the power of the name of Jesus.

3:11. Solomon's Portico. This is the location not only where Jesus walked with his disciples and taught during the Feast of Dedication (John 10:23), but also where Peter preached in the temple courtyard and other Christians gathered (5:12, compare 2:46). Its location on the Temple Mount is uncertain, but Josephus mentions that it was located on the eastern side of the Temple Mount. He says that it was built where Solomon used to walk (*War* 5.185). He further notes that all of the porticos were magnificent structures, all in double rows of columns of twenty-five-cubit high pillars (a cubit = the distance from the tip of the middle finger to the elbow, that is approximately 17 to 20 inches) made of pure white marble (5.5.2/§§ 190-94). See also m. *Middoth* 1-5 for another elaborate description of the Temple Mount, but one that is inconsistent with that of Josephus who was an eyewitness.

3:12-26. Peter's sermon. The central focus on Peter's proclamation is not on the miracle (v. 16), but rather on the death of Jesus that was in the plan of God (13-15, 18 cf. 2:23) and in his resurrection (15, 22-26) that vindicates their claims about him (his identity). Peter's reference to Jesus as the glorified child or servant (Greek = *pais*) of God (v. 13) is used often of Moses (Josh. 1:7, 13; 9:24; 11:12, 15; 12:6; 14:7; 18:7 and elsewhere) and of the famous servant of the Lord in Isa. 52:13. Matthew uses the term, *pais*, in reference to Jesus (Matt. 12:18), and it is used as a title in Acts 3:26; 4:25, 27, 30 and also in early Christian literature (*Didache* 9:2; 10:2; 1 *Clement* 59:2-4; *Ep. Barn.* 6:1; 9:2; and in the *Martyrdom of Polycarp* 14:1; 20:2). This thought is introduced here and further explained in v. 26. The term "servant" (or child) is an honorific title, possibly from a liturgical setting.

3:19-20. Repent so the times of refreshing may come. Belief that God would restore his kingdom to Israel was common in the first century (1:6), and it was frequently justified by referring to the promise of the prophets (see especially Isa. 40:9-11; Jer. 32:42-44; Ezek. 37:21-28; Hos. 11:9-11; 14:4-7; Amos 9:11-15). The term, "seasons (*kairoi*) of refreshing" is only found here in the New Testament. Peter claims that the fertile soil for the coming of that kingdom was repentance from sin (3:19), that is, everyone turning from their sinful ways (v. 26). See and compare v. 21 in which "times (*chronoi*) of restoration" is used for the same focus: namely, the blessed visitation of God for salvation. The way to receive those blessings from God comes through repentance and turning to God (v. 19).

3:22. Raise up for you a prophet like me. This is a reference to Deut. 18:15-19, and v. 26 shows how it is used to refer to God's raising the servant/child (Greek = *pais*) Jesus from the dead as well as to connect Jesus as a servant to the prophet like Moses who is also worthy of praise.

In the sermon, Peter uses the story of the lame man, who was made to rise by the power of Jesus Christ, to argue that God has raised Jesus from the dead and exalted him (vv. 13-18). The call is for the Jews to repent and be converted (turn to God) and thereby experience the times of refreshing or blessings that God has prepared for them. His scriptural proof (vv. 22-23) comes from Deut. 18:15, 18-19 and Lev. 23:29.

4:1-22. The Apostle's Defense Before the Sanhedrin.

As Peter and John were explaining to the people that Jesus was the cause of the lame man's healing and that it was because God had raised up Jesus that power and authority resided in him not only to heal, but also to bring forgiveness of sins and a right relationship with God (3:15-26), they were arrested (vv. 1-3). Because they continued to proclaim both authority and power in the name of Jesus and also the resurrection of Jesus (one of Luke's central themes), and because many persons came to believe in him, now about 5,000 in number (v. 4), the religious authorities in Jerusalem considered them as a threat and tried to prevent their activities.

4:5-6. And it came about on the next day, that their rulers and elders and scribes were gathered together in Jerusalem; and Annas the high priest was there, and Caiaphas and John and Alexander, and all who were of high-priestly descent. This body constituted the great council of religious leaders of Jerusalem called the Sanhedrin who gathered to bring charges against Peter and John. There were three main groups that made up the Sanhedrin or ruling body of Jerusalem. They were the rulers or chief priests, elders, and the scribes. The former were mostly Sadducees and the latter two groups were mostly Pharisees. The terms "rulers" and "chief priests" are often interchangeable terms (see discussion below at 22:30). The chief priests were more likely to have come from the high priestly families such as the preceding high priest and the current high priest's family from which the high priest was selected. Josephus, for instance writes:

> Upon learning of the death of Festus, Caesar sent Albinus to Judaea as procurator. The king removed Joseph from the high priesthood, and bestowed the succession to this office upon the son of Ananus, who was likewise called Ananus [Annas, see Luke 3:2]. It is said that the elder Ananus was extremely fortunate. For he had five sons, all of whom, after he himself had previously enjoyed the office for a very long period, became high priests of God—a thing that had never happened to any other of our high priests. The younger Ananus, who, as we have said, had been appointed to the

high priesthood, was rash in his temper and unusually daring. He followed the school of the Sadducees, who are indeed more heartless than any of the other Jews, as I have already explained [*Ant.* 13.294], when they sit in judgment. Possessed of such a character, Ananus thought that he had a favourable opportunity because Festus was dead and Albinus was still on the way. And so he convened the judges of the Sanhedrin and brought before them a man named James, the brother of Jesus who was called the Christ, and certain others (*Ant.* 20.197-201, LCL, see also *Ant.* 18.25-35 for the succession of high priests in the first century).

4:6. Annas, Caiaphas, John, Alexander. Annas held the high priestly office in Jerusalem from A.D. 6–15 (cf. Josephus, *Ant.* 18.26-35), and he was followed by his son-in-law Caiaphas (A.D. 18–36, According to Josephus, *Ant.* 20.198 above and John 18:13). Whether Annas was

high priest or Caiaphas at this point, see note on Luke 3:2. Josephus observes that Annas was high priest from A.D. 6–15 and was followed by his son-in-law Caiaphas and also by five sons. The practice of patrimony among high priests was common. He was replaced by John who is possibly the same as Jonathan (support comes from an ancient manuscript, Codex D and some Old Latin manuscripts which read Jonathan instead of John) who may have been the famous rabbi, Rabban (a title of honor meaning "lord") Yohanan ben Zakkai, who was responsible for reconstituting Jewish religious authority after the destruction of the temple in A.D. 70 at Yavneh (Jamnia). According to *m. Avot* 1 and 2.8, he was a student of both Hillel and Shammai (Josephus, *Ant.* 18.95, 123; *m. Shab.* 16.7; 22.3; *m. Shek.* 1.4; *m. Yad.* 4.3, 6, *passim*) who reportedly lived 120 years. If this is incorrect, neither John nor Alexander can presently be identified.

4:11. The stone rejected. The quote from Psalm 118.22 (LXX 117.22) introduces a new theme in

Annas' Family

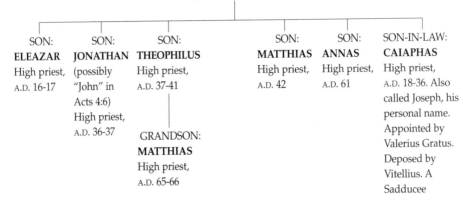

ANNAS
High Priest, A.D. 6-15.
Appointed by
Quirinius, governor of
Syria; deposed by
Valerius Gratus,
procurator of Judea

SON:	SON:	SON:	SON:	SON:	SON-IN-LAW:
ELEAZAR	**JONATHAN**	**THEOPHILUS**	**MATTHIAS**	**ANNAS**	**CAIAPHAS**
High priest, A.D. 16-17	(possibly "John" in Acts 4:6) High priest, A.D. 36-37	High priest, A.D. 37-41	High priest, A.D. 42	High priest, A.D. 61	High priest, A.D. 18-36. Also called Joseph, his personal name. Appointed by Valerius Gratus. Deposed by Vitellius. A Sadducee

GRANDSON:
MATTHIAS
High priest,
A.D. 65-66

Acts that is quite familiar in the NT and may go back to Jesus himself (Matt. 21:42; Mark 12:10; Luke 20:71; see also Rom. 9:33; 1 Peter 2:4, 6-8; Eph. 2:20; and *Ep. Barn.* 6.4). This "stone *testimonia*" refers to the stone (Jesus) that was rejected (v. 10) that has become the most important of all and most prominent of all.

4:12. Salvation [deliverance] in no other. There is a close parallel to this wording in Josephus when he describes how Moses looked to God for deliverance because, "in him, and in no other, is his salvation [deliverance]" (*Ant.* 3.23). "Salvation" (or deliverance) is one of Luke's favorite words (Acts 4:12; 7:25; 13:26, 47; 16:17; 27:34), and the verb form "to save" occurs some thirteen other times in its verbal form (*sodzein*) and referring to the great climactic activity of God at the end of the ages (see also 2:21 that cites the Joel 2:28-32 LXX text = Joel 2:17-21). For Luke, Jesus is always the agent of God's salvation (5:31; 13:23; 16:31).

4:13. Uneducated common men. There is little doubt that the early church began with few educated persons (1 Cor. 1:26-29; compare with the testimony of the early church as in Justin, *Apol.* 1.39.3; Origen, *Cels.* 1.62; Ps.-Clem. *Recog.* 1.62). The remarkable thing to them was how those with so little formal training could speak so boldly. The two terms for unlearned or uneducated (*agrammatos* = to be "unlettered" or without education) and ordinary (*idiotes* from *idios*), were sometimes used in the Greco-Roman world for those not skilled in Greek rhetoric or public speaking (for *agrammatos*). See also Plato, who speaks of the "unlettered and uncultured" (*agrammatous te kai amousous*) in his *Timaeus* 23A, B. Similarly, see Epictetus, *Discourses* 2, 9, 10. For *idiotes*, see Lucian who spoke of "mere illiterate (*idiotai*) serving people" (*Alexander the False Prophet* 30). Paul uses the word *idiotes* in reference to "outsiders" or "unbelievers" who visit the church (1 Cor. 14:16, 23), but also more nar-

rowly in reference to his own lack of proficiency in speech, but not in knowledge (2 Cor. 11:6). In its broader meaning, the term may have the significance of the Hebrew *Am-haaretz* ("people of the land"), or the uninstructed and ordinary people who are ritually unclean (m. *Demai* 2:2-3; 3:4), an unflattering term for ordinary and uninformed people.

4:19-20. The response of Peter and John (see also the similar bold stand in 5:29-32). The words are very similar to those of Socrates who stood before the Athenian judges saying:

And therefore, even if you acquit me now and are not convinced by Anytus, who said that either I ought not to have been brought to trial at all, or since I was brought to trial, I must certainly be put to death, adding that if I were acquitted your sons would all be utterly ruined by practicing what I teach—if you should say to me in reply to this: "Socrates, this time we will not do as Anytus says, but we will let you go, on this condition, however, that you no longer spend your time in this investigation or in philosophy, and if you are caught doing so again you shall die"; if you should let me go on this condition which I have mentioned, I should say to you, "Men of Athens, I respect and love you, but I shall obey the god rather than you, and while I live and am able to continue, I shall never give up philosophy or stop exhorting you and pointing out the truth to any one of you. . . .

Therefore I say to you, men of Athens, either do as Anytus tells you [put him to death], or not, and either acquit me or not, knowing that I shall not change my conduct even if I am to die many times over" (Plato, *Apol.* 29D, 30B, LCL trans.).

This famous story has parallels in the Jewish tradition as well, when people of faith prefer death over compromising the integrity of their faith (see 2 *Macc.* 7:2, "we are ready to die rather than transgress the laws of our ancestors"). When Antiochus Epiphanes tried to force the Jews to violate their eating rituals, Eleazar boldly spoke the following:

> We, Antiochus, who firmly believe that we must lead our lives in accordance with the divine law, consider that no compulsion laid on is is mighty enough to overcome our own willing obedience to the Law (16). . . . I will not violate the solemn oaths of my ancestors to keep the Law, not even if you gouge out my eyes and burn my entrails. . . . Pure shall my fathers welcome me, fearless of your punishments even unto death. Tyrannize as you will over the ungodly, but you will never lord it over my thoughts on the subject of true religion, neither by your words nor through your works"(29). 4 *Macc.* 5:16, 29, 37-38, (H. Anderson, trans. *OT Pseud.* 2:550-51).

Josephus also tells of the courage of Judas and Matthias in pulling down a golden eagle that Herod had erected over the entrance to the temple in Jerusalem. Those who were the doctors of the law reasoned that even if Judas and Matthias would die for this deed, "still to those about to die for the preservation and safeguarding of their father's way of life the virtue acquired by them in death would seem far more advantageous than the pleasure of living" (*Ant.* 17.152). They agreed with this perspective, and when they stood before the king, Josephus reports that they declared, "it is less important to observe your decrees than the laws that Moses wrote as God prompted and taught him, and left behind. And with pleasure we will endure death or whatever punishment you may inflict on us not because of any wrongdoing on our part but because of our devotion to piety" (*Ant.* 17.158-59, LCL). See also the example of Uriah who suffered martyrdom (Jer. 26:20-23).

4:22. More than forty years old. There is some question whether Luke is using this number to make a less obvious statement. The use of the number forty in the Bible and especially in Luke's writings (Luke 4:2; Acts 1:3; 7:23, 30, 36, 42; 13:18, 21; 23:13, 21) suggests more than merely a literal number forty: namely, that God is actively involved in the activity (see comments on 1:3 above). By noting the length of time the infirmity was suffered before a healing took place, Luke is similar to other writers of the New Testament (Mark 5:25; 9:21; John 5:5; 9:1; Luke 8:43; 13:11; Acts 9:33), but also Philostratus in his *Life of Apollonius of Tyana* 3.38.

4:23-31. The Prayer of the Jerusalem Christians.

4:23-30. The prayer. Luke indicates with this story that the early Christians were known to be people of prayer. When Peter and John were released by the Sanhedrin, they joined a group of fellow Christians, probably the other apostles and leaders of the church, but not the whole of the almost 8,000 followers of Jesus in the Jerusalem community. They reported to them probably the prohibition to speak or minister in the name of Jesus (4:18). The words of this prayer are similar to those of Hezekiah in Isa. 37:16-20 and 2 Kings 19:15-19, and they may well have formed the model for Luke. The content is similar except that the Christians do not pray for deliverance here, but for boldness to speak the Word of the Lord (the Gospel). In the prayer, God is recognized as Creator and as the one who controls all human destiny. The reference to David's declarations in the prayer are from Psalm 2:1-2 (see also Ps. 146:6; Exod. 20:11; Neh. 9:6).

4:27. Herod and Pontius Pilate, nations, peoples of Israel. The Herod in view is Herod Antipas who ruled over Galilee from the time of the death of Herod the Great in 4 B.C. until A.D. 39. In Luke 3:1, he is called the "tetrarch [ruler of one fourth of his father's kingdom] of Galilee" and Perea and represents the "kings" of v. 26 while Pontius Pilate (appointed to office A.D. 26–36) represents the "rulers" (v. 26). The passage underscores that all of these were guilty of crucifying Jesus, the anointed of God (v. 26), but that this was in the plan of God. See Exod. 13:3, 14, 16, and Ps. 55:21 which indicate God's complete control of all things and God's ability to harness all things for his purposes.

4:29, 31. Your word, the word of God. Both of these designations are references to the Gospel that the early church proclaimed (see also 6:2, 7; 8:14; 11:1; 12:24; 13:5, 7, 44, 46, 48; 16:32; 17:13; 18:11; 19:10, 20).

4:31. The place trembled. Josephus reports a similar prayer of Moses that recognizes the role of God in creation and in which a sign is requested (*Ant.* 4.40-50). Following Moses' prayer an earthquake occurred. "So spake he [he spoke], weeping withal, when suddenly the earth shook, a tremor moved over its surface as when a wave is tossed by the violence of the wind, and all the people were afraid . . ." (*Ant.* 4.51, LCL). In Acts they request a sign that God had heard their prayer (v. 30). The trembling or quaking is similar to the mountain shaking as a sign of the presence of the Lord in Exod. 19:18. See also Josephus, who speaks of a sign given through the high priest not to attack his enemies until the groves moved without the wind blowing. When that happened, it was a sign that God was involved and the victory belonged to David (*Ant.* 7.76-77). Similarly, Virgil, following a prayer to the god of Thymbra for direction as well as security and protection, concludes by asking a sign: "Grant, father, an omen, and inspire our hearts!" (Aeneid 3.89, LCL). We then see the response:

> Scarcely had I said that, when suddenly it seemed all things trembled, the doors and laurels of the god; the whole hill shook round about and the tripod

moaned as the shrine was thrown open. Prostrate we fall to earth, and a voice comes to our ears: 'Long-suffering sons of Dardanus, the land which bore you first from your parent stock shall welcome you back to her fruitful bosom (3.90-95, LCL).

What began in 2:1-4: namely, the fire, wind, and tongues (languages), is now accompanied with the shaking and boldness of speech (v. 31). These were all signs to Luke of the activity of the Holy Spirit (2:4; 4:31).

4:32–5:11. Second Major Summary and Examples

4:32, 34-35. A sharing community. In Luke's second major summary passage, he repeats the importance of sharing within the community of faith (*koinonia*, 2:42, 44-45). Aristotle once wrote that "among friends everything is common" (*Nicomachean Ethics* 9.8/§1168B) and Luke shows that the friendship within the community of faith is at least this much. He does not say that this kind of sharing was a requirement of the fellowship, and not all gave up all of their possessions to the church. Some Christians continued to own their own homes and those became meeting places for the church (12:12; 16:15, cf. Rom. 16:3-5), but Luke tells how much the church cared for the needs of its community through sacrificial gifts to the church. For parallels to 4:33, see also 2:47 and 5:42. The wording in 34 is similar to the command of Deut. 15:4 and consciously aware of the commands in Deut. 15:10-11. This may be Luke's attempt to show that Scripture was being fulfilled, or at least obeyed, in the apostolic community.

4:33. With great power . . . testimony to the resurrection. Like other sections, Luke repeats one of the consistent themes of Acts: namely, the ability of the apostles to speak of the resurrection of Jesus with power and great grace (*dunamis*).

4:35. At the feet. The laying of funds or property at the feet of the apostles (the Twelve) recognized their authority in the community and also their activity in dispensing the funds to care for the needs of the community (4:37; 5:2; 6:2; see also 7:58 and 22:3). Cicero (*Pro Flacco* 68) and Lucian (*Philopseudes* 20), use a similar expression. There are some parallels also to the Qumran community that called on members of that community to give their possessions to the overseer: "They shall also take steps to incorporate his property, putting it under the authority of the Overseer together with that of general membership, keeping an account of it—but it shall not yet be disbursed along with that of the general membership" (1QS 6:19-20, Garcia Martinez trans., p. 135). The words, "none called anything that he owned his own" (v. 32), is similar in language to Plato's *Critias* 110C-D.

4:36-37. Barnabas. Joseph, a Levite from Cyprus, was named "Barnabas" by the apostles because he was given to encouragement. The name fits his role in the rest of Acts when he introduces the feared Paul to the Jerusalem Christians (see 9:27) and also forgives Mark's weakness and offers him another opportunity for ministry (13:13 and 15:37-38). He is introduced here in Acts, but he returns frequently in conjunction with Paul's ministry (9:27; 11:22, 30; 12:25; 13–14; 15:12, 22, 30, 35) and this relationship ends in 15:36-41 (see also Gal. 2:13), but probably not permanently (1 Cor. 9:6). His name is a difficult issue that cannot currently be resolved on the basis of any investigation of a derivative of "son of encouragement" or "consolation" (Greek = *huios parakleseos*) in Greek, Hebrew, or Aramaic. The Aramaic name probably means "son of Nebo." Nevertheless, he is introduced as a positive example of the practice in vv. 34-35. His significant influence in the church can be seen by the fact that a letter, the *Epistle of Barnabas*, was written in his name in the early second century.

The apostles gave the name. By accepting the name the apostles gave him, Barnabas gave the first indication of his acceptance of their authority over him (see v. 37 below). The practice of renaming a person has a long biblical history (see Gen. 2:19; 17:5; 19:39; 25:26, 36), and it was also followed outside of the biblical tradition, as in the case of the young woman accepting a name from the heavenly man as in *Joseph and Asenath* 15:7 (a Jewish pseudepigraphal book perhaps from Egypt ca. A.D. 115–117). See note on v. 35 above.

Sold a field. According to the Law, Levites were not supposed to own property (Num. 18:20; Deut. 10:9), but that was not always followed. Jeremiah the prophet was also a priest and possessed wealth and was able to purchase property (see Jer. 1:1; 32:7-9). Josephus, the writer and soldier who was also a priest and a Levite, was cheated out of his property by a certain John (*Life* 76).

4:37. Laid . . . at the apostles' feet. This is the first of two examples given of the practice that was common among the Christians in vv. 32, 34-35. The other example (5:1-11) is discussed below. By placing his gift at the feet of the apostles, Barnabas recognized their authority over him and the church. His first recognition of their authority came in his acceptance of their renaming him (v. 36). There is no suggestion that this practice was a requirement within the Christian community (see 5:4) and if it were, there would be no reason to isolate Barnabas as an example of what everyone else was doing.

Ananias and Sapphira (5:1-11). Besides the positive example of Barnabas (4:36-37), Luke also offers a negative example of giving to the church. Perhaps Luke used the example to bring both fear among the Christian community stressing the importance of honesty before the Lord and possibly to remind Christians of an earlier negative example (Achan) in which the people of God suffered through the deceit of one individual (Josh. 7:1-26). The similarities are important: (1) a deceitful holding back of property or valuables; (2) a confrontation with a man of God (Joshua/Peter); (3) the termination of the offender's life by death. The example is reminiscent of Nadab and Abihu in Lev. 10:1-5. In 13:8-11, Paul similarly inflicts punishment on Elymas who opposed his work in at Paphos. The sin was that of deceit against the Holy Spirit: namely, believing that no one within the believing community would know of the deceit. Peter says it was not a deceit against the community, but to lie to or falsify the activity of the Holy Spirit (v. 3), which means that they falsify the actions of the Holy Spirit. The Spirit is so identified with the church that what is done against it or the apostles (see 5:12-13) is also done against the Spirit (9:4). In a somewhat similar text, Gehazi's deceit and greed before his master Elisha caused a curse of leprosy to come upon him (2 Kings 5:20-27).

While some scholars do not believe that the example fits with the model set forth by Jesus of offering forgiveness (Matt. 18:21-22; Luke 17:4), or by Paul (2 Cor. 2:7-10; Phil. 2:1-2; Eph. 4:32; but see 1 Cor. 5:3-5 and in another case 2 Cor. 2:5-7), Luke includes the story to illustrate the importance of honesty in one's dealings with the community of God. The severity of the penalty, however, is not equaled elsewhere in the early church, even in the strict religious community of the Essenes who had their own penalties for those who were dishonest in holding back some of their possessions. In their guidelines it was decided that, "if there be found among them a man who has lied about money and done so knowingly, they shall bar him from the pure meals of the general membership for one year; further, his ration of bread is to be reduced by one-fourth" (1QS 6.24-25, WAC trans., p. 135). There were condemnations (curses) that were spoken at Qumran, but the carrying out of the judgments was the responsibility of God (1QS 2.4-18).

Nothing is known about the identity of either Ananias or Sapphira. Their names were common among the Jews and they were converts to the Christian faith early and perhaps even were among the 120 (1:15), but nothing certain is known about them. It may be assumed that they were financially better off than others and probably were up to that time leading figures in the church.

5:11. Fear. The first example of giving sacrificially to the church (Barnabas) elicited joy and praise, but the second understandably brought fear. While there may be some aspect of reverence in this term (*phobos*), undoubtedly it was more than that as 5:13 suggests. In the Old Testament, fear served as a deterrent to those who would consider similar acts (Deut. 21:21).

The whole church. This is the first time of seventeen (5:11; 8:1, 3; 9:31; 11:22, 26; 12:1, 5; 13:1; 14:23, 27; 15:3, 4, 22; 18:22; 20:17; 20:28) that Luke uses the term *ekklesia* (translated "church") for the whole of the gathered community of faith, who at this point are all residing in Jerusalem. In *I.Berenike* 16, an inscription dated December 3, A.D. 55, the second year of Nero's reign, the Jews in the city erected an inscription in a synagogue to list those who had contributed to the building's repair. Both the building and the members meeting there were called a "synagogue" (*synagoge*). The practice of using the term *synagogue*, not only for a place, but also for the whole community of those who gathered there, is not unlike the later Christian practice of using the term church (*ekklesia*) to refer to both a building and also the Christians who gathered there.

5:12-16. The Third Major Summary. Following the positive and negative examples, remarkable things continued to take place among the Christians not only by Peter and John, but by the rest of the apostles as well. The result was that many more people came to faith, and many nonbelievers heard about the ability of Peter to bring healing, and they carried their sick to him. The stories in this passage illustrate that God has heard the prayer of the Christians in 4:30.

5:12. Solomon's Porch. See previous discussion in 3.11.

5:13-14. No one dared to join them ... more than ever believers were added. These apparently contradictory statements can be resolved by noting that the *"they* were all together in Solomon's Portico" (v. 12) refers to the apostles only and that even believers were fearful of approaching them given what had happened (vv. 1-11). The result of their miraculous activity, however, drew many people into the church ("to the Lord") and it grew considerably (v. 14). It may also be that Luke has brought together two traditions, and the first of these (vv. 12-13) relates to 5:1-11 and the latter in v. 14 to the prayer and activity of 4:30-31 and 5:15-16.

5:15. The shadow of Peter. The reference to healings taking place as a result of Peter's shadow falling on individuals is not unlike Paul's experience in 19:11-12. The superstition behind such healings: namely, that healing was to be found in the individual is set aside by Luke (3:12-13). There is an interesting parallel reported from Epidauros in which the presence of a person with special powers was able to heal those near him (Aelius Aristides, *The Sacred Tales* 2.71; 3.22). The notion of a shadow as a protection is found in many OT texts. The idea was that since the shadow of a person or object protected one from the sun (Job 7:2), so the shadow of God could protect an individual (Judges 9:15; Ps. 17:8; 36:7-8; 57:1-2; 63:7; 91:1; Lam. 4:20; Isa. 9:1-2, cf. Matt. 4:16; see also Hos. 14:7 and Isa. 49:2). The belief that special powers existed in a shadow can also be found in Exod. 40:34-38; Job 15:29-30; Ps. 139:8-12. The idea that the shadow of a human being was an important aspect of one's being was widespread in antiquity, and some persons believed that if a shadow were trampled or urinated

upon, hit or stabbed with a knife, that it could cause considerable harm against the person. One's soul was affected by the shadow. To be touched by the shadow of a criminal could bring harm to the person touched (Cicero, *Tusc.* 3.12, 26; see also Pliny *Natural History* 8.106 and 28.69). The belief that a god could fertilize a woman by his shadow has sometimes been held to be behind Luke 1:35 text where Mary is overshadowed by the Most High and becomes pregnant. It appears obvious that the belief that a shadow could be both a positive or a negative influence lies behind this passage (v. 15).

5:16. They were all cured. This passage brings back to mind what Luke had said earlier about the crowds trying to get close to Jesus for healing and all were cured (Luke 6:17-19). These signs and wonders that were attributed to the apostles by Luke are also mentioned by Paul in his own ministry (2 Cor. 12:12).

5:17-42. The Apostles Before the Council
Luke now returns to the story of Peter and John before the Council or Sanhedrin (4:1-22). Because the apostles did not heed the warning of the council (4:21)—not only Peter and John but also the rest of the apostles—they were arrested and brought before the religious council to account for their refusal to cease proclaiming Jesus. Luke adds that because of the jealousy of the religious leaders, the apostles were arrested and brought to the council. This segment of the passage completes what was started by the miracle of 3:1-10. In some ways it appears as a doublet of 4:1-22 only this time it includes all the apostles and a beating takes place. There are other new elements also that include the beatings, all the apostles (not just Peter and John), and the introduction of Gamaliel into Luke's story.

5:17. Sect of the Sadducees. The Sadducees are referred to as a "sect" (Greek = *hairesis*) or a party, that is, one of the several Judaisms of the first century. Josephus uses this same term (*haireses*) to describe not only the Sadducees, but also the Pharisees (Josephus, *War* 2:166; *Ant.* 13:171, 293-98; 20:199; *Life* 2.10, 12; 38.191; *War* 2.118). Luke also uses the term in reference to the Jewish parties (15:5; 26:5) and of the Christians ("Nazoreans," 24:5, 14; 28:22). At this point there was no negative connotation attached to the word, which eventually became our word "heresy."

5:17, 33. The repeated arrest . . . with jealousy. Luke begins this section with the cause for the re-arrest of Peter and John along with the rest of the disciples. It is obvious that they have violated the earlier admonition not to teach or preach in the name of Jesus (4:17-18, 21, but see 4:31; 5:12-16). Because of the influence they were having on the populous, they were arrested and put in jail awaiting the convening of the council (vv. 17-18). This time they were arrested because of jealousy (or "zeal," Greek = *dzlou*). Jealousy often causes people to consider killing the ones of whom they are jealous, and so does the *Testament of Simeon* 2:7, 11. The term is found in Acts 7:9 of Joseph's brothers' jealousy and then to seek his death. See Philo who shows that their envy and jealousy led to their trying to destroy him (*Joseph* 12). Similarly, in the *Testament of Simeon*, Simeon declares "In the time of my youth I was jealous of Joseph, because my father loved him more than the rest of us. I determined inwardly to destroy him . . ." and again, "I had contemplated an evil deed in the sight of the Lord and of Jacob, my father, on account of Joseph, my brother, because of my envying him" (2:5, 13, Charlesworth, ed. *OT Pseud* 1:783-84). This same jealousy that leads to death is found in the Jews at Thessalonica who tried to destroy Paul (17:5). The relationship between envy, jealousy, and murder is commonplace in the ancient world (*Testament of Gad* 4.5-6; *Testament of Joseph* 1:3; *Testament of Benjamin* 7:1-2). See v. 33 for the continuance of that jealousy and envy that leads to murder.

5:19. An angel of the Lord. Luke frequently refers to angels to facilitate the will and plan of God (1:11, 26; 2:9, 13; 22:43; 24:23; Acts 8:26; 10:3, 7, 22; 11:13; 12:7-15, 23; 27:23). The angel opened the doors and the apostles escaped (v. 19). They returned to the temple to continue their preaching (vv. 20-21). They were then re-arrested and brought to the Sanhedrin for the purpose of deciding what to do with them (vv. 26-27).

5:27-28. The high priest's questions. It is remarkable that the high priest did not ask how the men had escaped from the prison, but only reminded them of his previous warning against teaching in the name of Jesus (4:18) and their failure to follow it. As well, he accused them of blaming Jesus' death on the Sanhedrin. The fact that they had escaped could have cost the guards their lives (12:18-19; 16:27), but nothing is said of this.

5:29-32. Peter's response. Peter's response to the high priest is similar to that in his first appearance before the Sanhedrin (see 4:19 discussion above and the parallel to Socrates). He once again proclaims the resurrection of Jesus and places the blame on the Sanhedrin for putting Jesus to death "on a tree" (v. 30). The curse of crucifixion was already being placed alongside an interpretation of Deut. 21:22-23, and it was not long before the Christians supplied their own theological interpretation of the event (see Gal. 3:13).

Death by crucifixion was practiced long before the first century A.D., and even by the Jews themselves. It was used by the Romans and others, including Jews, as a form of capital punishment from the sixth century B.C. to the fourth century A.D. Josephus reports that the practice was viewed as one of the most horrible manners of death among the Jews and tells that the Hasmonean king, Alexander Janeaus (ruled 103–76 B.C.), used this form of punishment against his Jewish enemies (the Pharisees):

The most powerful among them, however, he shut up and besieged in the city of Bethoma, and after taking the city and getting them into his power, he brought them back to Jerusalem; and there he did a thing that was as cruel as could be: while he feasted with his concubines in a conspicuous place, he ordered some eight hundred of the Jews to be crucified, and slaughtered their children and wives before the eyes of the still living wretches. This was the revenge he took for the injuries he had suffered; but the penalty he exacted was inhuman for all that . . . (*Ant.* 13.380–81 LCL).

Later, the Pharisees under the protection of Queen Alexandra Salome, the successor of Alexander Janeaus, convinced the queen to crucify those who had persuaded Alexander to crucify these 800 men (Josephus, *Ant.* 13.410).

Roman citizens were not generally crucified except in rare cases of very serious crimes such as high treason. Normally this practice was reserved only for slaves and subject peoples. Its practice was banned in A.D. 337 by Constantine out of respect for Jesus Christ. Although it was practiced in the Hellenistic–Hasmonean period (165–63 B.C.), no such practice was used against the Jews by Herod the Great. The Romans, however, did not hesitate to use crucifixion to pacify the people after the invasion of Pompey in 63 B.C. The author of the *Ascension of Moses* (ca. just before A.D. 70 and the fall of the temple) tells of the practice of crucifixion (possibly by Pompey) saying: "there will come into their land a powerful king of the west who will subdue them; and he will take captives, and a part of their temple he will burn with fire. He will crucify some of them around the city" (6:8-9, Charlesworth, *OT Pseud.* trans 1:930). This was a hated form of death among the Jews and the reference in Deut. 21:23 (see also Gal. 3:13) helps explain why a crucified messiah was a stumbling block to the Jews (1 Cor. 1:23). "Hanging on a tree" was already understood as crucifixion well before the time of Jesus and even before the arrival of the Romans in 63 B.C.

5:34. But a certain Pharisee named Gamaliel, a teacher of the Law, respected by all the people, stood up in the Council and gave orders to put the men outside for a short time. The name "Pharisee" (Hebrew = *parush*, "separate") refers to a Jewish sect that came into existence in the late second century B.C. and was dedicated to keeping the law or Torah and also what later became known as the "oral Torah," that is the traditions that later rabbis believed were revealed at Sinai and were preserved in the various prophets of Israel and in its oral traditions such as that found in Mark 7:5-13. Among their distinctive beliefs can be included (1) the belief in the freedom of the will, (2) fate or divine providence, (3) the immortality of the soul of the righteous, (4) the resurrection of the dead, (5) the existence of angels, (6) the notion of the "oral Torah," and (7) their commitment to maintaining their laws of ritual purity. They are often condemned in the New Testament for their emphasis on the letter of the law rather than on its spirit (see Paul's discussion of this in 1 Cor. 3:6, 12-16) and were the strongest opponents of Jesus during his ministry. Josephus speaks well of them, and they are the most prominent sect of Judaism to survive the two wars against Rome (A.D. 66–70 and A.D. 132–35) and form the roots for the emergence of rabbinic Judaism of the second century and following. In a description of their views, he says:

> The Pharisees simplify their standard of living, making no concession to luxury. They follow the guidance of that which their doctrine has selected and transmitted as good, attaching the chief importance to the observance of those commandments which it has seen fit to dictate to them. They show respect and deference to their elders, nor do they rashly presume to contradict their pro-

(Deut. 10:18; 14:29; 16:11, 14; 24:17, 19-21; 26:12-13 and compare James 1:27) was taken to heart both in Jewish and early Christian communities since failure to do so brought forth a curse from God (Deut. 27:19; cf. also Isa. 1:17, 23; 10:2; Jer. 5:28; 7:6; 23:3; Ezek. 22:7; Ps. 93:6; Mal. 3:5). Later in the Mishnah, this admonition continued to serve as an integral part of Jewish piety (*m. Ket.* 4:12; 11:1-6; 12:3-4; *m. Git.* 5:3). Something like soup kitchens were commonplace in ancient Jewish communities (*m. Peah* 5:4; 8:7; *m. Demai* 3:1; *Pirke Aboth* 5:9; *bT Meg.* 27a; *bT Bab. Bat.* 8a-9a; *bT R. H.* 4a-5b).

In the *Testament of Job*, there is a roughly contemporary example of Jewish piety expressed in practical concerns for the unfortunate. It reads:

> And I established on my house thirty tables spread at all hours, for strangers only. I also used to maintain twelve other tables set for the widows. When any stranger approached to ask alms, he was required to be fed at my table before he would receive his need. Neither did I allow anyone to go out of my door with an empty pocket (*Test. Job* 10.1-4, *OT Pseud* 1:843).

6:2. The Twelve. This is the only time that this term is used for the apostles in Acts, though it is hinted at in 1:26 when Matthias' name is added to the "eleven" apostles. After this, Luke uses "apostles" to describe this group, but even that discontinues after 16:4. The reason is not clear.

Ministry. The result of their appointment to the role of "service" or ministry (Greek noun = *diaconia*, vv. 1, 4; verb = *diaconein*, v. 2) was that the mission of the church was advanced (6:7). Whether Luke intended to describe the early stages of the role or office of deacon (Greek = *diaconos*) in the church is doubtful, since he does not use the term here, but the ministry thus described does eventually take on the form of an official office in the church as in the case of Ignatius of Antioch (ca. A.D. 115) who

sees this office as subordinate to the bishop (see his *Eph.* 2.1; *Magn.* 2; 6.1; 13.1; *Did.* 15.1. See also Irenaeus, *Adv. Haer.* 1.26.3; 3.12.10; 4.15). Luke refers to these individuals as the "seven" again in 21:38, which would seem strange if the office of deacon had been specifically intended and he omits any specific reference to it. It is not clear whether the plural term "elders," which is more frequently used in Acts (11:30; 14:23; 15:2, 4, 6, 22, 23; 16:4; 20:17; 21:18), is more what Luke had in mind in the service of ministries indicated in 6:1-6. In both cases, however, the offices "deacon" and "elder" are not clearly distinct in early Christianity. Elsewhere in the New Testament, however, the term "deacon" (*diaconos*) is used for a special office in the church (Rom. 16:1; Phil. 1:1; 1 Tim. 3:8, 12; 4:6). At this point in Acts, only the issue of service or ministry in caring for the needs of the widows is involved, and the seven are appointed to help resolve the problem facing the church. It soon becomes clear, however, that at least two of the seven (Stephen and Philip the Evangelist) will have other functions in the church than simply the distribution of care to the widows.

6:3. Seven. If there is any significance to the number seven in this passage, it is not clear. There is no clear indication why seven were chosen, but the number does, of course, have many parallels in roughly contemporary literature. Josephus, citing Deut. 16.18, indicates that there should be seven persons appointed to bring justice in each city:

> As rulers let each city have seven men long exercised in virtue and in the pursuit of justice; and to each magistracy let there be assigned two subordinate officers of the tribe of Levi. Let those to whom it shall fall to administer justice in the cities be held in all honour, none being permitted to be abusive or insolent in their presence for a respect for human dignitaries will make men

too reverential to be ever contemptuous of God (*Ant.* 4.14-15a, LCL).

This may suggest that there was a Jewish tradition in the first century that called for seven persons to be appointed to carry out important tasks within a community. That seven represents completion is found throughout the book of Revelation e.g., seven churches, seven stars, seven spirits, seven golden lampstands, seven seals, seven vials of wrath, seven trumpets (Rev. 1:4, 11-12, 20; 2:1; 3:1, *passim*).

6:5. Stephen, Philip, Prochorus, Nicanor, Timon, Parmenas, Nicolaus. Outside of Stephen and Philip, nothing is known in the NT about the other five names. While there is a heretical group called the Nicolaitans mentioned in Rev. 2:6, 15, it is Irenaeus in the late second century who first ties them to the Nicolaus of this passage (Irenaeus, *Adv. Haer.* 1.26.3, contrast Clement of Alexandria, *Strom.* 2:20). The only thing that is clear about the group is that they all have Greek names. One, Nicolaus (v. 5), is singled out as a Gentile who is a proselyte from Antioch. This would, by inference, make the others Jews. While much has been made that the people chose seven persons from the group that were being discriminated against, that may not be the case. Many Jews in Palestine in the time of Jesus had Greek names, including three of the twelve apostles (Andrew, Bartholomew, and Philip). Certainly two of the seven were "diaspora" Jews, that is, Jews born on Hellenistic soil and now living in the land of Israel, and that is possible for the rest, but we cannot be certain here.

6:6. Laid hands upon them. The practice of laying on of hands appears to have a number of functions in Scripture, such as the bestowal of a blessing or the transfer of power (see Exod. 29:10, 19; Lev. 1:4, 11; 4:15; 16:21) or the healing of a person (Luke 4:40; 13:13). In Acts it happens in the bestowal of the Spirit (8:17, 19; 19:6) as well as in the ministry of healing (9:12; 17; 28:8). The practice is also used in the ordination of priests as in Num. 8:10. Moses transfers the authority of the Spirit in Num. 27:18, 23 and Deut. 34:9 (cf. 11:25; 1 Tim. 4:14; 2 Tim. 1:6). Here it appears to be used of an ordination to office that suggests the significance Luke attached to this event in the church. Notice also, that while the church selected the Seven, it was the Twelve who commissioned them through the laying on of hands.

6:7. The word grew. The result of the proper caring for those in need in the church was increased spread of the "word of God," that is, the church's witness about Jesus as the Messiah (see 5:42) and the resultant increase of the numbers of those coming to an obedience of faith, including "a great many priests." While some scholars have suggested that these priests were from the Qumran Essene community, there is little to commend that view. That "many priests" are mentioned may not have been so unusual since there is evidence that there were large numbers of priests in the land of Israel in those days, perhaps as many as 20,000. Josephus reports that there were four priestly "tribes" with about 5,000 priests in each, and each tribe or group rotated with the others in their temple responsibilities (Josephus, *Against Apion* 2:108). The Mishnah reflects the large numbers of priests who were involved in the sacrifices and caring for the temple (*m.Yom.* 2:1-7). More importantly, there is evidence of a rift between many of the priests and the ruling high priests in the first century. This rift may also have included how the ruling high priests treated the early Christians that we see in Acts 4 and 5. Josephus tells of the significant opposition of the priests to the practice of the high priests in regard to the collection of funds. The high priests evidently confiscated the funds that were intended for the priests, and this eventually led to the starvation and death of some of the priests (Josephus, *Ant.* 20:181 and compare with *War* 2:409-410).

6:8-15. Stephen accused before the Sanhedrin. The intensity of opposition against the early church moves from harassment to a new level of persecution and opposition in this and the next sections. Stephen was just introduced in the last section as one put into a leadership role of caring for those in need ("serving tables"), but now it is clear that this was not all that the appointment involved. At first glance, 6:1-6 suggests a division of labor within the church: namely, preaching the word (the Twelve) and deeds of charity (the Seven). It seems odd, however, that after their appointment to this office or role in the church, Luke nowhere describes them in that capacity! Both Stephen (6:8–7:53) and Philip the evangelist (8:4-40; 21:8) appear to ignore that role and they become involved in something like the role of the Twelve who were responsible for the "ministry of the word" (6:2). The Twelve were not only evangelists, but also caregivers (4:32-37; 5:2), and they were empowered to do many "signs and wonders" (3:6-10; 4:29-31, 33; cf. 6:8; 8:5-8). The Seven, along with their role as caregivers, were also known for their skills in evangelism and in doing signs and wonders. From several other texts, however, it is clear that the early Christians did not choose preaching over charity, but rather were committed to both ministries (3:1-10; 4:32; 6:1; Rom. 15:25-26; 2 Cor. 9:10-15; passim).

Luke shows how the authority of the Seven derived from the Twelve, and their ministry was in harmony with and complementary to it. The responsibility for charity as well as for witness or preaching originally belonged to the Twelve and was transferred to the Seven. Evidently, the Spirit that resided in the ministry of the Twelve also resided in the Seven who received their recognition and authority from the Twelve. Earlier Luke shows from the example and teaching of Jesus that all who follow him must be willing to serve (*diakonon*) tables (Luke 22:26-27). As the Twelve did charitable deeds and served tables (by implication in 3:6-10; 4:32-3; 6:1-2), so also did the Seven.

Stephen's story (calling/witness/death) in Acts links the ministry of the Word to the church's mission outside of the land of Israel and eventually to the Gentile mission that began in Antioch (8:1, 11:19, 20-27).

6.9. Synagogue of freedmen. For a long time scholars have wondered whether such synagogues existed in the land of Israel in the first century since there is so little conclusive archaeological evidence for them. An inscription dating before A.D. 70 may point to the same synagogue that is mentioned in this passage. It also provides a very practical reason why Paul may have stopped first at synagogues on his missionary journeys: namely, because they offered shelter and food for the traveling Jews. The inscription reads:

Theodotus, son of Vettenus, priest and *archisynagogos* [ruler of the synagogue], son of an *archisynagogos*, grandson of an *archisynagogos*, built this synagogue for the reading of the law and for the teaching of commandments, as well as the hostel, the rooms and the water fittings, as a lodging for those coming from a foreign country, which his fathers established as well as the presbyters and Simonides (*CIJ* = *Corpus Inscriptionum Judaicarum* 1404, trans. by S. Llewelyn, R. A. Kearsley, *New Documents*, 7:89).

The Greek term for "freedmen" (*libertinon*) in 6:9 is a transliterated word from the Latin *libertinus*, a freedman may refer to those Jews who were at one time enslaved but had been manumitted by their Roman masters. Eventually they made their way to the land of Israel and formed a synagogue. In the inscription above, the person Theodotus is called the son of Vettenus (a Latin name); this probably refers to a common practice of slaves taking on the name of their owners. While scholars are divided over whether the synagogue mentioned in the above inscription was the same synagogue that Luke identifies in 6:9, the inscription substantiates that these places of prayer existed for such individuals in the time about which Luke is writing. Philo (first cent. A.D.) refers to Jews who had been freed by their owners, became Roman citizens, and were able to maintain their religious distinctions. Describing the Caesar's approval of the Jews' religious practices he writes:

> How then did he [Caesar] show his approval? He was aware that the great section of Rome on the other side of the Tiber is occupied and inhabited by Jews, most of whom were Roman citizens emancipated. For having been brought as captives to Italy they were liberated by their owners and were not forced to violate any of their native institutions. He knew therefore that they have houses of prayer and meet together in them, particularly on the sacred sabbaths when they receive as a body a training in their ancestral philosophy (*Embassy to Gaius* 155-56a, LCL).

Perhaps, since many Jews had paid the dear price of being taken into slavery because of their religious convictions (see Josephus, *Ant.* 18.1-4; cf. Tacitus, *Annals* 2.85), they were all the more zealous to challenge those whom they believed were attacking their religious beliefs. See, for example, that their charge against Stephen was for alleged words against Moses and God (6:11), speaking against the temple and the law (6:13), and claiming that Jesus would destroy the temple and change the customs believed to have had their origin in Moses (6:14). Notice how these charges are not unlike some of those made earlier against Jesus (Mark 13:1-2; 14:57; Matt. 26:60-61).

6:15. Face of an angel. This expression has several parallels in Judaism and also in early Christianity. As Moses' facial appearance was altered after he had been in the presence of God (Exod. 34:30-35), so also was Jesus' appearance (Luke 9:29, Matt. 17:2; cf. Rev. 1:12-16; and the face of an angel in 10:1). In the second-century story of the martyrdom of Polycarp, it is said that "his face was full of grace so that it not only did not fall with trouble at the things said to him, but that the Pro-Consul, on the other hand, was astounded and sent his herald into the midst of the arena to announce three times: 'Polycarp has confessed that he is a Christian'" (*Mart. Pol.* 12.1, LCL). Likewise, in a second century apocryphal writing, Paul is described as: "a man small of stature, with a bald head and crooked legs, in a good state of body, with eyebrows meeting and nose somewhat crooked, full of friendliness; for now he appeared like a man, and now he had the face of an angel, at times he looked like a man, and at times he had the face of an angel" (*The Acts of Paul and Thecla* 3, NT Apo 2:239). This brief description of Stephen before the Sanhedrin is completed later in 7:55-60.

7:1-53. Stephen's Speech Before the Sanhedrin

In the last section, the case against Stephen was presented and now he is asked to answer these charges (7:1). As he responds, however, he does so in a way that is somewhat foreign to the context, that is, he largely ignores the accusations. More than a few scholars have observed that for a person about to be martyred, this is not the kind of ancient literature one would expect for such an occasion. Rather than respond immediately to the charges, Luke tells of Stephen offering a brief synopsis of the history of Israel beginning with short pieces of history from the lives of Abraham, Joseph, and Moses. He then tells of Israel's falling away from God the first and second times, and finally accuses his accusers of betraying God by failing to keep his law and for killing his

Righteous One. What makes this speech, the longest in Acts, a response to Stephen's accusers? L. T. Johnson (*Acts*, 120) observes that Luke, like several other ancient writers, makes his point by offering a perspective on the history of a people. See, for instance, Herodotus, *Persian Wars* 9:26-27; Thucydides, *Peloponnesian War* 1, 3, 68-70; 2, 6, 35-47. Josephus also told the history of the Jewish people from a biblical perspective to present to them their predicament and how they should respond: namely, by giving in to the Romans (*War* 5:376-419). These examples select a tradition with their slant on it to justify their conclusions. The Qumran sectarians also used the *Book of Jubilees*, the *Genesis Apocryphon*, and the *Damascus Rule* (2:14—6:1; see also 8.9 as that community's accusation against the other inhabitants of Judea) to lay the basis for their claim to be the people of God. Like others before him, Luke weaves the biblical text into a short history to argue who the true people of God are and who are not. In so doing, he offers a summary not unlike other summaries in the Bible (e.g., Josh. 24, Ezek. 20:5-44; Neh. 9:7-27; Pss. 78, 105). Luke selects three well-known biblical personalities to illustrate his point: Abraham (7:2-7), Joseph (7:8-16), and Moses (7:17-41). Moses occupies the largest amount of his speech and, like Jesus, was rejected by the people (35-39). After this, Stephen begins to answer the objections raised against him, at least one of them, viz. whether God lives in buildings made by hands (42-51). Stephen, for Luke, becomes a faithful witness *par excellence* for God both in his speech and in his death.

7:20. Moses' name. Philo continues the tradition found in Exod. 2:10 that Moses' name came from the water. Describing the naming of the child by Pharaoh's daughter, he writes: "since he had been taken up from the water, the princess gave him a name derived from this, and called him Moses, for *Möu* is the Egyptian word for water" (Philo, *Life of Moses*

1.17, LCL trans.). Josephus continues this tradition by noting the two-fold derivation of Moses' name. He explains: "It was indeed from this very incident [the rescue and naming of Moses] that the princess gave him the name recalling his immersion in the river, for the Egyptians call water *mou* and those who are saved *eses*; so they conferred on him this name compounded of both words" (*Ant.* 2.228).

7:36-37. Wonders and signs. According to Deut. 34:10-11, signs and wonders accompany a prophetic ministry. The tradition surrounding Moses' remarkable activity in Egypt and the consequent disbelief was passed along in the *Book of Jubilees*. "And I delivered you [Moses] from his [Pharaoh's] hand and you did the signs and wonders which you were sent to perform in Egypt against Pharaoh, and all his house, and his servants, and his people (48:4, *OT Pseud* 1:39). Philo also tells of Moses' ability to perform signs and wonders, and yet they did not produce faith in the Egyptians except at the end of the tragedies that came their way when they finally had to acknowledge. "'This is the finger of God'; for as for His hand not all the habitable world from end to end could stand against it, or rather not even the whole universe" (*Life of Moses* 1:112, see also 77, 90-112).

7:37. Raise up a prophet like Moses. This is a reference to Deut. 18:15 that is fulfilled in Jesus in 3:22 above.

7:38. He was in the assembly in the wilderness. The term for assembly (Greek = *ekklesia*) is mostly translated "church" in Acts and in the rest of the New Testament. The term used in the Septuagint (LXX) to translate the Hebrew *qahal Yahweh* ("the assembly of the Lord") in Deut. 4:10; 9:10; 18:16; 23:1-2 is also translated "church" in Acts and throughout the New Testament. It appears that the one who stands in the assembly of God's people, Moses in this case, is a picture of the one who will stand in the congregation of God's people, the church: namely, Jesus.

7:38b. "with the angel who spoke to him." Was the Law mediated through an angel or angels? (See v. 53 and cf. Gal. 3:19 and Heb. 2:2.) Josephus tells of "the holiest of our laws from the messengers (Greek = *aggeloi*) sent by God" (*Ant.* 15.136), but there is some question over whether this refers to the prophets or to angelic beings. The Greek is the same for "messengers" as it is for "angels": namely, *aggelon*. In the rabbinic tradition, according to the Midrash *Wayyiqra Rabba*, Rabbi Yohanan claimed that the prophets were the *mal'akim* (Greek = *aggeloi*), and even the high priest was known as a "messenger" or "angel" of God. Since the giving of the Law at Sinai has no mention of a messenger or angelic person giving the law to Moses, what is the source of this tradition? There is scant but debatable evidence in non-Christian sources such as *The Book of Jubilees* 1.27-29; Philo, *On Dreams* 1.141-43, and possibly but unlikely *Testament of Dan* 6.2. While the Hebrew text of Deut. 33:2 does not include angels, the LXX or Greek version does. It is unlikely that this tradition originated in the Christian community, but it is difficult to trace its origins in the extant literature. The intent is easier to determine: namely, that the angels are included to add to the significance of the event of the giving of the Law and heightened level of judgment coming to those who disregard the Law.

7:40-41. "Make gods for us who will lead the way for us." This incident in Israel's history (Exod. 32:1, 23) is singled out among the rabbis as one of the worst acts in Israelite history. Josephus does not include it in his *Jewish Antiquities* (3.98), and Luke minimizes Aaron's role in the act of idol worship.

7:42. Book of the prophets. The quote is from Amos 5:25-27, and the reference in v. 42 is a ref-

erence to the twelve minor prophets which were often seen as one book in antiquity, Amos being but one of the twelve. See Josephus who lists the number of all of the books of the prophets as thirteen and probably incorporates all twelve minor prophets into one book, though he does not name them. He writes: "... the prophets subsequent to Moses wrote the history of events of their own times in thirteen books" (*Against Apion* 1.40, LCL). It is generally agreed that this collection includes the books from Joshua through the historical books and the major prophets plus the Book of the Twelve as they are variously combined in the Hebrew Bible.

7:44-53. Stephen's indictment of Israel's leaders. Opposition to those in leadership in Jerusalem is not unique to Stephen in the first century. Those at Qumran were also known for their pronouncements against the wrong leaders in the land and their predictions of the wrath of God coming upon them. For example, in the Damascus Document found in cave four at Qumran (4Q), we read:

> The princes of Judah are those upon whom the rage will be vented, for they hope to be healed but it will cleave to them (?); all are rebels in so far as they have not left the path of the traitors and have defiled themselves in paths of licentiousness, and with wicked wealth, and avenging themselves, and each one bearing resentment against his brother, and each one hating his fellow, and each one despising his blood relative; they have approached for debauchery and have manipulated with pride for wealth and gain. Each one did what was right in his eyes and each one has chosen the stubbornness of his heart. They did not keep apart from the people and have rebelled with insolence, walking on the path of the wicked, about whom God says: *Deut. 32:23* "Their wine is serpents' venom and the head of cruel

harsh asps" (*The Damascus Document* 8.3-10, Garcia Martinez trans.).

7:48. "The Most High." This reference to God has numerous ancient parallels in several Greek writings, including Pindar, *Nemean Odes* 1.90; 11.2; Aeschylus, *Eumenides* 28. It is also used in the LXX (Gen. 14:18-19, 22; Ps. 46:4) as well as in Philo (*In Flaccum* 7.46 and *Legatio ad Gaium* 36.278).

7:48-50. The Most High does not dwell in buildings made by human hands. There was a longstanding history of persuasion going back into the final stages of the Old Testament that God did not dwell in a temple made by hands. One such text, Isa. 66:1-2, is cited by Stephen in vv. 49-50. While it was true that the religious figures believed that God did dwell among his people in the Tabernacle (tent) in the wilderness and even in the land of Israel/Canaan, this was not necessarily so in regard to the temple built by Solomon (1 Kings 8:27; cf. 2 Chron. 6:18). In the time of Jesus, it was not unusual for Jews to criticize the temple and speak of its inadequacy to be the dwelling place of God. Philo, who argues that it is the soul where God dwells, considers it blasphemy to say that God would dwell in a building of stone and timber. He writes:

> Seeing then that our souls are a region open to His invisible entrance, let us make that place as beautiful as we may, to be a lodging fit for God. Else He will pass silently into some other home, where He judges that the builder's hands have wrought something worthier. . . . What house shall be prepared for God the King of kings, the Lord of all, who in His tender mercy and loving-kindness has deigned to visit created being and come down from the boundaries of heaven to the utmost ends of earth, to show His goodness to our race? Shall it be of stone or timber? Away with

the thought, the very words are blasphemy. For though the whole earth should suddenly turn into gold, though all that wealth should be expended by the builder's skill on porches and porticos, on chambers, vestibules, and shrines, yet there would be no place where His feet could tread. One worthy house there is—the soul that is fitted to receive Him. Justly and rightly then shall we say that in the invisible soul the invisible God has His earthly dwelling-place (*On the Cherub* 98-100, LCL).

Josephus tells the story of God entering Solomon's temple and of Solomon recognizing that his temple cannot contain God.

> "That Thou, O Lord," he [Solomon] said, "hast an eternal dwelling in those things which Thou didst create for Thyself we know—in the heaven and air and earth and sea, through all of which Thou movest and yet art not contained by them. But I have built this temple to Thy name so that from it we may, when sacrificing and seeking good omens, send up our prayers into the air to Thee, and may ever be persuaded that Thou are present and not far removed. For, as Thou seest all things and hearest all things, Thou dost not, even when dwelling here where is Thy rightful place, leave off being very near to all men, but rather art present with everyone who asks for guidance, both by night and by day" (Josephus, *Ant.* 8.107-108, LCL).

Compare also 2 *Macc.* 14:32-36 where the writer speaks of the priests' acknowledgment that God has no need of a temple but has chosen to dwell among his people in that temple, a temple that is being threatened by the Seleucid soldiers with desecration. Interestingly, there are similar parallels in the Hellenistic world as well. In the last quarter of the second century A.D., Clement of Alexandria, citing Zeno of Citium, claims that no building made by hands was worthy of the gods.

Zeno, the founder of the Stoic sect, says in this book of the Republic, "that we ought to make neither temples nor images: for that no work is worthy of the gods." And that he was not afraid to write these very words: "there will be no need to build temples. For a temple is not worth much, and ought not to be regarded as holy. For nothing is worth much and holy, which is the work of builders and mechanics (*Stromata* 5.11.76, ANF trans.).

Luke appears to adopt a view of a temple made with hands that has parallels to that of Strabo (ca. 65 B.C.–A.D. 20), who apparently depends on the tradition of Moses for support. Strabo writes:

For he [Moses] said, and taught, that the Aegyptians were mistaken in representing the Divine being by images of beasts and cattle, as were also the Libyans; and that the Greeks were also wrong in modeling gods in human form; for according to him, God is this one thing alone that encompasses land and sea—the thing which we call heaven, or universe, or the nature of all that exists.

His successors for some time abided by the same course, acting righteously and being truly pious toward God; but afterward, in the first place, superstitious men were appointed to the priesthood, and then tyrannical people; and from superstition arose abstinence from flesh, from which it is their custom to abstain even today, and circumstances and excisions and other observances of the kind. And from the tyrannies arose the bans of rebels . . . (*Geography* 16.35, 37, LCL).

It should be observed that even in the Old Testament, the construction of a temple was not met with unanimous approval (1 Kings 8:2;

cf. 2 Chron. 6:18). Also, subsequent literature in antiquity did not have a unified voice on the temple. There are several ancient texts that point to the dwelling place on God in heaven or a holy mountain or that God's dwelling place will one day be established (see *Book of Jubilees* 1:23-29; 4:26; *1 Enoch* 25:1-7; 53:6; 71:1-17; 90:28-36; *2 Baruch* 4:2-7; *Testament of Benjamin* 9:2-3).

The charge against Stephen (6:9) came from diaspora Jews, that is, those living outside of Palestine who were among the "Hellenists" who spoke Greek but were very dedicated to their religious faith. (See their zeal against Paul and their zeal for the temple in 21:27-29.) In 7:44-50, Stephen responds to the charge of 6:9 by claiming that God does not dwell in a temple made with hands and that they, his accusers, have been guilty of not living in accordance with the traditions of their fathers. Such accusations, in essence the charge of hypocrisy, were common in polemics against both groups and individuals in the ancient world. Seneca (ca. 4 B.C.–A.D. 65) expressed the common belief that deeds must accompany words.

This, however, my dear Lucilius, I ask and beg of you, on your part, that you let wisdom sink into your soul, and test your progress, not by mere speech or writings, but by stoutness of heart and decrease of desire. Prove your words by your deeds.

Far different is the purpose of those who are speech-making and trying to win the approbation of a throng of hearers, far different that of those who allure the ears of young men and idlers by many-sided or fluent argumentation; philosophy teaches us to act, not to speak; it exacts of every man that he should live according to his own standards, that his life should not be out of harmony with his words, and that, further, his inner life should be one hue and not out of harmony with all his activities. This, I say, is the highest duty and the highest proof of wisdom—that deed and word should be in accord, that a man should be equal to himself under all conditions, and always be the same (Epistle 20.1-2, LCL).

For other examples, see Plutarch, *On Stoic Self-Contradiction* 1-2; Lucian of Samosota, *Hermotimus* 79; *Timon* 54-55 and Paul in Rom. 2:17-24 (see L.T. Johnson, *Acts of the Apostles* 134-35).

7:54–8:3. The Martyrdom of Stephen and the Persecution of the Church

As the first martyr of the church, Stephen has a special place in Acts and his speech is the longest that Luke includes. As he finished his speech, Stephen turned the charges against himself toward those who were accusing him of impiety (vv. 51-53) with the result being his martyrdom and expansion of opposition to the early movement of Jesus' followers. It was also the occasion for Luke's introduction of Saul, later to become Paul, into the story of the early church.

There are many parallels in this section to the story of Jesus in the Gospel of Luke and several are quite obvious. For example, the loud cry that Jesus uttered at his death (Luke 23:46) is similar to Stephen's shouting in 7:60. The "Son of Man standing at the right hand of God" (Luke 22:69) is similar to that of Acts 7:56. The cry of Jesus in some manuscripts for the Father to forgive those who have put him on the cross (Luke 23:34) is similar to Stephen's request in Acts 7:60. Both Jesus and Stephen pray that God will receive their spirits (Luke 23:46, cf. Acts 7:59). Again, the heavens opening for Stephen's vision has parallel in the baptism of Jesus (Luke 3:21; cf. Matt. 3:16; John 1:51—though John does not specifically say that Jesus was baptized by John; and Rev.

19:11) and the vision of Peter (Acts 10:11). The pious burying Jesus (Luke 23:50-53) is similar to Stephen's burial (8:2). This is what Fitzmyer calls "imitative historiography" (*Acts,* 390) and underscores one of Luke's aims: namely, to show how those who follow Jesus are enabled by the same Spirit to do the work of God. See, for instance, the role of the Spirit in Jesus' life beginning with his birth (Luke 1:35), his baptism (Luke 3:21-22), his temptation and ministry (Luke 4:1, 14, 18) and how this is seen in the community of those who followed Jesus. See, for instance, Acts 1:8 where the followers of Jesus are promised the Holy Spirit to witness of him. This was true not only for Jesus and the apostles (cf. 2:1-4, 17-18; 3:8-12; 4:31) but also for all who followed him (cf. 6:3, 8, 10; 7:55; 8:5-17, etc.). Luke shows that the same power available to Jesus to be a faithful witness and face hardships is also available to all of those who follow him.

7:54-58. When "they" heard these things … they dragged him out and began to stone him.

There is some question about who is intended as Luke tells of those who stoned Stephen. The reference could be to the Sanhedrin (6:12) or to the witnesses against Stephen (6:13) or both, but if it is to the former, there is a problem. Since, according to John 18:31, the Sanhedrin, or ruling council of Jerusalem, was not allowed to carry out a death sentence, then the execution was inappropriate and illegal. Sentences of death in those days, suggests John, were to be carried out by the Romans. Luke, however, indicates in his Gospel and the Acts that the Sanhedrin and chief priests had the authority to arrest, beat, imprison and kill individuals, and they had a police force capable of inflicting the death penalty (see Luke 9:22; 19:48; Cf. Mark 14:1-2; 55; and Acts 5:33). What limited the actions of the Sanhedrin was apparently their fear of the people (Luke 19:48; 20:6, 19). Luke assumes their vested authority in his account of the arrest of Peter and John by the

Sanhedrin in Acts 5:33-40. In the latter passage, the overriding assumption is that the council did have the authority to punish by death if they chose to do so. According to Luke, they had the authority to arrest, beat, imprison, and even kill the Christians (9:1-2; 22:4-5; and especially 26:9-11). It is likely that what was involved was something of a "lynch law" that erupted when Stephen's words accused the hearers of violating the law of God (7:51-53) rather than answer their charges against him. The ability to inflict capital punishment upon Christians, whether irregular or illegal, stands at the heart of Paul's sense of guilt as a persecutor (1 Cor. 15:9; Gal. 1:13, 23; Phil. 3:6; cf. Acts 22:20). While some scholars have suggested that this event took place during the interim following the departure or recalling of Pilate (ca. A.D. 36–37) to Rome and the arrival of a new prefect to oversee the affairs of Judea when there was little direct supervision of such matters in the land, there is little that is convincing about that proposal and it would date the conversion of Paul far too late. Interestingly, the Mishnah describes a procedure for executions related to blasphemy. After discussing the composition of the Sanhedrin or council of the city (*m. Sanhedrin* 1.6), it discusses various forms of punishment determined by the council. In terms of capital cases, we read in part:

> 6.1. When sentence [of stoning] has been passed they take him forth to stone him. The place of stoning was outside [far away from] the court, as it is written, *Bring forth him that hath cursed without the camp* [Lev. 24:14]... If they [the court] found him innocent, they set him free; otherwise he goes forth to be stoned. A herald goes out before him [calling], "such-a-one, the son of such-a-one, is going for to be stoned for that he committed such or such an offence. Such-a-one and such-a-one are witnesses against him. If any man knoweth aught

> in favour of his acquittal let him come and plead it."

> 2. When he was about ten cubits from the place of stoning they used to say to him, "Make thy confession", for such is the way of them that have been condemned to death to make confession, for every one that makes his confession has a share in the world to come...

> 3. When he was four cubits from the place of stoning they stripped off his clothes. A man is kept covered in front and a woman both in front and behind. So R. Judah. But the Sages say: A man is stoned naked but a woman is not stoned naked.

> . . .

> 6. When the flesh had wasted away they gathered together the bones and buried them in their own place. [After he was put to death] the kinsmen came and greeted the judges and the witnesses as if to say, "We have naught against you in our hearts, for ye have judged the judgment of truth." And they used not to make [open] lamentation but they went mourning, for mourning has place in the heart alone.

> 7.1. The court had power to inflict four kinds of death-penalty: stoning, burning, beheading, and strangling. R. Simeon says: [Their order of gravity is] burning, stoning, strangling, and beheading. This is the ordinance of them that are to be stoned.

> . . .

> 7.4 These are they that are to be stoned: he that has connexion with his mother, his father's wife, his daughter-in-law, a male, or a beast, and the woman that suffers connexion with a beast, and a blasphemer and the idolator, and he that offers any of his seed to Molech, and he that has a familiar spirit and the soothsayer, and he that profanes

the Sabbath, and he that curses his father or his mother, and he that has connexion with a girl that is betrothed, and he that beguiles [others into idolatry], and he that leads [a whole town] astray, and the sorcerer and a stubborn and rebellious son. . . (*m. Sanhedrin* 6.1—7.4, Danby Trans. Italics and all brackets except in 6.1 are his, pp. 389-392).

For some biblical parallels to *m. Sanh.* 7.1 above, see, Lev. 20:2-5, 27; 24:14-16; Num. 15:32-36; Deut. 13:2-6; 17:2-7; 21:18-21; 22:22-23; Josh. 7:25.

7:56. Stephen's vision. Stephen's vision completes the claim that God does not dwell in buildings made with hands, because he is in the heavens. It is not unusual for those facing a martyr's death to receive a vision. A well-known parallel is found in the circumstances surrounding the death of Isaiah, son of Amos, told in the legendary *Ascension* (or *Martyrdom*) *of Isaiah* (perhaps late first cent. A.D.). As he was beginning to be sawed in two he was being derided by his false accuser, Balchira, but instead of responding, "Isaiah was (absorbed) in a vision of the Lord, and though his eyes were open, he saw them [not]" (*Martyrdom of Isaiah* 5.7, C. H. Charles Trans., 162). The early church was not unfamiliar with this pattern as we see in *The Passion of SS. Perpetua and Felicitas* 10-13 and in *The Martyrdom of SS. Carpus, Papylus and Agathonica* 39, 42. The church historian, Eusebius (ca. A.D. 320), refers to Stephen as the "perfect martyr" because he asked God "not to lay this sin to their charge" but prayed for them (*HE* 5.2.5).

Jesus *standing* on the right side. In the gospel of Luke, the Son of Man in his glory is seated (Luke 22:69; cf. Mark 14:62 and Matt. 26:64), so why is he standing here? It could be that the image has legal implications: namely, that of a lawyer interceding on behalf of another or perhaps more likely, the customary way of welcoming individuals by standing and greeting them. Stephen receives a vision of the exalted Christ (see 2:33-36). The title "son of man" is taken over from the common self-designation of Jesus in the Synoptic Gospels.

7:60. He fell asleep (died, Greek = *koimasthai*). The use of this term is a frequent means of describing death in antiquity. Not only is the term commonly used in the New Testament for death (see Matt. 27:52; Acts 7:60, 13:36; 1 Cor. 7:39; 11:30; 15:6, 51; 2 Peter 3:4), it is also used similarly for death in the Greek Old Testament (LXX in Gen. 47:30; Deut. 31:16; Isa. 14:8) and in nonbiblical literature such as Homer's *Iliad* 11.241 ("so there he slept a sleep of bronze" LCL), and in Vergil's *Aenid* (10.745) where the idea is similarly found in the Latin words "stern repose and iron slumber press upon his eyes and their orbs close in everlasting night." See also Sophocles, *Electra* 509 and elsewhere.

7:58, 8:1. Saul/Paul introduced into the story. Luke has introduced the Apostle Paul by his earlier name, Saul, a common name that derives from Israel's first king. The name *Saulos* is the Greek form of the Hebrew name Saul (7:58; 8:1, 3; 9:1, 8, 22, 24; 11:25, 30; 13:1-2, 7). In four places *Saoul* is used (9:4, 17; 22:7; 26:14) when referring to the same person. While interchangeable, the latter is used in Hebraic contexts or solemn address. Saul is the Hebrew name of the Apostle Paul. In 13:9 Luke begins to use the name Paul consistently after that except for the two times in his testimony in 22:7 and 26:14.

There is considerable discussion over Saul/Paul being called a "young man" (Greek = *neanias*) if he was old enough to serve on or for the council and also to give his consent to the death sentence of Stephen (8:1; cf. 26:9-12). It is possible that the term "young man" could refer to anyone from ages 24 to 40, but that is not certain. An obscure and awkward text, Philo, *De Cherubim* 114, leaves that possibility, but it is not clear there. The term *neanias* here is between a youth with a beard (Greek = *protogenios*) and a mature man (Greek = *teleios aner*). Whatever the case, the text in 8:1 does not say that Paul himself (or Saul) actually served on the Sanhedrin nor gave official sanction to the stoning of Stephen. His youth alone, if he was somewhere in his twenties, would not have hindered him from being entrusted with the activities described in Acts 7:58, 8:1a, and 9:1-2.

8:1b-3. The outbreak of persecution. While Luke says that the persecution came to the whole church and all except the apostles were scattered (1b), it is clear that not everyone left Judea or even Jerusalem on a permanent basis. When peace returned to the church, evidently, believers returned to Jerusalem (9:31; 11:2, 22). It seems that most of those who fled for safety were the Jewish Hellenistic Christians.

8:2. Pious men buried Stephen and made loud lamentation over him. Later rabbinic tradition forbids public lamentations over criminals put to death (*m. Sanh.* 6.6), but that does not appear to affect the mourning here. Also, the identity of the pious men is not mentioned by Luke, but it is likely that they were among the pious Jews who were not hostile to the followers of Jesus or they were Christian believers who did not flee. If the law regarding mourning for criminals in the Mishnah was in effect during the time of Stephen's death, the early church, or those who had no cause to fear the authorities, did not follow it.

8:3. Saul was ravaging the church. Although Paul was a young man (7:58), this did not detract from his zeal to persecute the church. The continuation of this story resumes in 11:19. While not explicitly saying so, Saul may well have been behind the plot to kill Stephen. The act of laying the clothes at the feet of Saul (7:58) and his consent (7:60) suggest his active involvement, and this verse confirms his aggressive stance against the followers of Jesus.

III. 8:4–11:18. SPREAD OF THE GOSPEL TO SAMARIA AND THE COASTAL REGIONS

The death of Stephen and the persecution of the church are the foundations of the first major transition in the book of Acts that leads to the mission anticipated in 1:8 from Jerusalem to Judea and Samaria and elsewhere. The activities of the succession of prophetic figures in Acts includes the proclamation of the word of the Lord (or the word about Jesus as Messiah) and the signs that accompanied the proclamation. This succession now continues from the apostles (2:43; 3:1-10; 4:29-33), to Stephen (6:8), now to Philip (8:6-8, 13), and subsequently on to Paul (13:4-12) and all in the power of the Spirit.

In this section we see that the Good News was taken outside of Jerusalem to other places in Judea, Samaria, Damascus, and Antioch, but before that Luke tells how the Gospel or "good news" went from Jerusalem to Samaria (8:4-25) to Gaza and Caesarea (8:26-40), Damascus (9:1), then back to Judea and Galilee (9:31), Lydda and Joppa (9:32–10:23), and then to Caesarea (in 10:23b–11:18).

8:4-40. The spread of the Gospel to Samaria and the Sea Coast. For the first time, the Christian proclamation reaches a non-Jewish population. This is a pivotal transition in the book of Acts, and it was occasioned by the first martyrdom and persecution of the primitive church (8:4).

8:4-25. The Gospel goes to Samaria. The story begins with Philip, one of the seven in Acts 6:5, not 1:13, who does the work of an evangelist taking the message to many of the villages of Samaria (8:5, 25).

8:5. Philip went down to a city of Samaria. Jerusalem was viewed as the holy city in biblical times, and departing from the city always meant going "down" even if geographically Samaria was to the north of Jerusalem. Going to

Jerusalem, conversely, always meant going "up" to Jerusalem. Samaria was both the name of a city in the first century and also of a district or region. The city was rebuilt by Herod the Great and it was renamed *Sebaste* in honor of Caesar Augustus. Philip went to the most important city of the territory at first and subsequently to other villages in the territory (v. 25).

8:9. Simon who had practiced magic in the city. The identity of Simon the magician has an interesting history in the early church. Little is known about him from the first century, but in the second century Simon becomes the founder of gnosticism and the source of all heresy that crept into the church. See, for instance, the report from Justin Martyr, a native of Samaria, in his apology to the emperor who writes:

> There was a Samaritan, Simon, a native of the village called Gitto, who in the reign of Claudius Caesar, and in your royal city of Rome, did mighty acts of magic, by virtue of the art of the devils operating in him. He was considered a god, and as a god was honoured by you with a statue, which statue was erected on the river Tiber, between the two bridges, and bore this inscription, in the language of Rome: "*Simoni Deo Sancto,*" ["To Simon the holy God"]. And almost all the Samaritans, and a few even of other nations, worship him, and acknowledge him as the first god: and a woman Helena, who went about with him at that time, and had formerly been a prostitute, they say is the first idea generated by him (*1 Apology* 26, ANF trans.).

Similar stories are found in the Pseudo-Clementine *Homilies* 2.22.2-3, *The Acts of Peter* 4 in which he reportedly was able to fly or levitate, and even in Eusebius. After describing Simon's fame that came as a result of his magic and noting that he was called *Magos*—a Persian word that came to be used of magicians (*HE* 2.1.10)—Eusebius denies the genui-

ness of his repentance and claims that his heresy continued after him.

> But even he [Simon] was then so overwhelmed by the marvels wrought by Philip by divine power, that he submitted, and feigned faith in Christ even to the point of baptism. It is worthy of wonder that this is still done by those who continue his most unclean heresy to the present day, for following the method of their progenitor they attach themselves to the church like a pestilential and scurfy disease, and ravage to the utmost all whom they are able to inoculate with the deadly and terrible poison hidden in them (*Ecclesiastical History* 2.1.11-12).

Later Christian tradition denies his repentance (8:24) of his attempt at "simony," that is, seeking to purchase spiritual influence. The practice of purchasing religious influence was widespread in antiquity even among the Jews, including the purchase of the high priesthood, but Peter announces that the power of the Spirit was not for sale, but was a gift from God (1:8; 2:38). Simon is mentioned widely in early Christian literature as the founder of the gnostic Christian community, e.g., Irenaeus, *Adversus haereses* 1.23.1-2; Tertullian, *De anima* 34; *Adversus omnes haereses* 1; Clement of Alexandria, *Stromata* 2.52.2; Eusebius 2.13.1-8; Epiphanius, *Panarion* 21.1-4. Luke, however, leaves the impression that Simon's repentance is genuine and says nothing of his subsequent activity.

8:9-11. He did magic. Magic was a common element in Hellenistic religions, but Luke attributes such activity to the demons (13:6-10; 19:13-20).

8:14. When the apostles in Jerusalem had heard ... they sent Peter and John. This section shows the Jerusalem church's role of ratification in the mission of the church. Luke shows the unity of the one church in Acts when the report of the Samaritans' conversion reached the apostles in Jerusalem. The Twelve dispatched Peter and John to confirm the report of the conversion of the Samaritans and also to be involved in the initiation of these new followers of Jesus the Messiah. Luke shows the authority of the Twelve who were still in Jerusalem (8:1) over the church's mission in the act of sending Peter and John.

8:17-19. Peter and John laid their hands on them. The practice of laying on of hands goes back into the Old Testament times (Exod. 29:10; Lev. 1:4, 11; 4:15; 16:21; Num. 27:18-23; Deut. 34:9) and symbolizes the passing on of power or authority from one person to another. Here the practice is also used to bestow the Spirit and with it, the power that accompanied the Spirit (see 19:6). Elsewhere this practice is used for empowering persons for ministry (6:6; 13:3) and for healing (9:12, 17; 28:8).

8:25. Philip's return to Jerusalem. It appears that after the apostles placed hands on the new believers in Samaria, Philip joined Peter and John in visiting several villages of Samaria before returning to Jerusalem. It is likely that his next mission began with his departure from Jerusalem.

8:26-40. Conversion of the Ethiopian.

Philip was called by the "angel of the Lord" to get on the road that leads to Gaza. While on this road, he encountered a high official from Ethiopia who was returning from worshiping in Jerusalem. It is not clear from the passage if the Ethiopian was a Jew or a Gentile who had converted to Judaism. The latter seems unlikely since Luke reserves the time for Gentiles to come to faith in Christ for chap. 10 with the household of Cornelius.

8:27. Was the Ethiopian a diaspora Jew or a Gentile? Does this interrupt or anticipate Luke's story of the Gentile mission in 10:1–11:18? Luke makes a big point that the conversion of Cornelius and his household is the beginning of the Gentile conversions to Christian faith. He inserts this story between Stephen's death and the subsequent scattering of the church and its preaching ministry (8:1-4) and the Antioch story of 11:19, which is the natural consequence of 8:4. Further, according to 11:1, 18, it appears that the conversion of Cornelius and his household was something new in the church: namely, that Gentiles also could find repentance and receive the word of the Lord. It seems unlikely, therefore, that the Ethiopian official was a Gentile, although it may be that he was a Gentile who had converted to Judaism and subsequently became a Christian. There appears to be strong support that he was a Gentile. Eusebius, while telling of the Ethiopian's subsequent preaching, explicitly states that he was a Gentile.

Tradition says that he who was the first of the Gentiles to receive from Philip by revelation the mysteries of the divine word, and was the first-fruits of the faithful throughout the world, was also the first to return to his native land and preach the Gospel of the knowledge of the God of the universe and the sojourn of our Saviour which gives life to men, so that by him was actually fulfilled the prophecy which says, "Ethiopia shall stretch out her hand from God" (*Ecclesiastical History* 2.1.13, LCL).

However, there is a strong tradition that eunuchs were excluded from the assembly in the temple. Along with Deut. 23:1, the Mishnah provides support that such persons were excluded from Jewish worship: namely, "He whose testicles are crushed and whose penis is cut off shall not enter the congregation of the Lord" (*m. Yebamoth* 8.2, Neusner Trans. p. 355). On the other hand, it may be instructive that in each case where there was an advance in the Gospel to the various places mentioned in Acts 1:8, there are representatives from Jerusalem who are present. This takes place in the story of the Samaritans in 8:4-25 and also in the conversion of Cornelius and his household (10:1–11:18). Why would there be no official representation here if the Ethiopian were not a Jew, but in fact a Gentile?

The story of the Ethiopian eunuch was well received in early Christianity and was celebrated for bringing Christianity to Ethiopia. Concerning him, Irenaeus wrote: "This man was also sent into the regions of Ethiopia, to preach what he had himself believed . . ." (*Against Heresies* 3.12.8). Likewise, Eusebius (*Ecclesiastical History* 2.13-14) celebrates the eunuch's subsequent activity of preaching the Gospel in his homeland, a point not made by Luke, but assumed in early Christianity. There is no record, however, of the influence of Christianity in that region until the fourth century.

Conversion to Judaism was not an unusual thing for a Gentile in the first century. Still, Luke does not make any significance of the fact of the Ethiopian's ethnicity, that is, that he was a Gentile. It is likely, therefore, that he was a Jew of the dispersion, that is, a Jew who lived outside of the land of Israel. Conversion to Judaism was not available to those who had become eunuchs by choice. Whether the man was a Jew or Gentile is important only in the sense that if the latter is true, it makes the message of Acts 10:1–11:17 confused in terms of Gentiles coming to faith in Christ: namely, there it is treated as something new. Whatever the case, Barrett is certainly correct that any person filling all of the roles assigned to this individual: namely, an Ethiopian, a eunuch, a member of a ruling class, reading the Bible, and on a pilgrimage to Jerusalem, was certainly a rare find in the ancient world.

8:27. A eunuch from Ethiopia. Ethiopia was the name for the region south of Egypt. In the Old Testament times, it is also known as the land of Cush (Gen. 2:13; cf. 10:6; 1 Chron. 1:8; but see Ezek. 29:10; Zeph. 3:10). The land was ruled by a "candace," that is, a queen. Candace is not a name, but a title like "pharaoh" of the one who ruled the land of Meroe that was located along the Nile River close to the Sudan. While there had also been kings of Ethiopia, well into the fourth century Eusebius speaks of a queen ruling the land. In his description of the conversion of the Ethiopian, he explains: "While the saving preaching was daily progressing and growing [in the early church] some providence brought from the land of the Ethiopians an officer of the queen of that land, for the nation, following ancestral customs, is still ruled by a woman" (*Ecclesiastical History* 2.1.13). Both before and after the New Testament era, the title was used for the queen (see Strabo, *Geography* 17.1.5; Dio Cassius 54.5.4-5).

Homer has an interesting description of the peoples of Ethiopia: "But now Posedion had gone among the far-off Ethiopians—the Ethiopians who dwell divided in two, the farthermost of men, some where Hyperion [a Titan and father through his sister Theia of the Sun, Moon, and Dawn] sets and some where he rises . . ." (*Odyssey* 1.22, LCL) and Herodotus described them as "the tallest and fairest of all men. Their way of choosing kings is different from that of all others, as (it is said) are all their laws; they deem worthy to be their king that townsman whom they judge to be tallest and to have strength proportioned to his stature, handsome of all peoples" (*The Persian Wars* 3.20, LCL). Philostratus describes the people and their location thusly:

"There was then," he said, "a time when the Ethiopians, an Indian race, dwelt in this country, and when Ethiopia as yet was not: but Egypt stretched its border beyond Meroe and the cataracts, and on the one side included in itself the fountains of the Nile, and on the other was bounded by the mouths of the river. Well, at that time of which I speak, the Ethiopians lived here, and were subject to King Ganges, and the land was sufficient for their sustenance, and the gods watched over them ..." (*Life of Apollonius* 3.20, LCL).

Eunuchs were often employed as overseers of a harem or of treasuries in the ancient Near East. In antiquity, eunuchs, that is those who had been castrated, often held significant official positions, but the problem comes when Luke describes the man as having come to Jerusalem to worship (v. 27). According to Deut. 23:1 cf. Lev. 21:17-23, eunuchs were barred from worship. Josephus similarly reports this Jewish tradition thusly:

Shun eunuchs and flee all dealings with those who have deprived themselves of their virility and of those fruits of generation, which God has given to men for the increase of our race; expel them even as infanticides who withal have destroyed the means of procreation. For plainly it is by reason of the effeminacy of their soul that they have changed the sex of their body also. And so with all that would be deemed a monstrosity by the beholders. Ye shall castrate neither man nor beast (*Ant.* 4.290-291, LCL).

Luke does not dwell on the physical condition of the eunuch except to mention that this was his condition. Again, how could such a person be reported as worshiping in Jerusalem? There is another text of Scripture that may have been given priority among the Jews at this time. Isa. 56:3-5 indicates that God will honor faithful eunuchs. This tradition is repeated in the apocryphal (or deutero-canonical) book *The Wisdom of Solomon*.

Blessed also is the eunuch whose hands have done no lawless deed, and who has not devised wicked things against the Lord; for special favor will be shown him for his faithfulness and a place of great delight in the temple of the Lord (*Wisd.* 3:14, NRSV).

Evidently, the earlier views against eunuchs worshiping in the temple were not shared by all Jews.

8:28, 31. He was seated in a chariot. It is not certain what kind of a chariot the Ethiopian was using, but apparently it was large enough for him to be seated in it and also for Philip to join him in it. Josephus, in telling the story of King Ahab (Achab = Ahab) in 1 Kings 20:30b-34, describes Ahab seated in his chariot and a Syrian king, Ben-hadad, was brought to him. Ahab was "seated in a chariot. He [Ben-hadad] then did obeisance to him [Ahab], but Achab gave him his right hand and let him come into the chariot ..." (*Ant.* 8.386-87, LCL).

8:30. Philip heard him reading the prophet Isaiah. It was uncommon in the ancient world to read silently, if not strange. Jews regularly practiced reading aloud in order to aid their memory. Philip would be able to hear if he were near the chariot, what text the official was reading.

8:28, 32-33. Now the passage of Scripture that he was reading. The Ethiopian official was reading a very popular book both in the early church that was frequently cited by Jesus or cited about him, e.g. Matt. 3:3; 4:14-16; 8:17; 12:17; 13:14; 15:7; Mark 1:2; 7:6-7; Luke 3:4; 4:17; John 1:23; 12:38-39, 41; Acts 28:25; Rom. 9:27, 29; 10:16, 20; 15:12. There were also several copies of the scroll of Isaiah found in the Dead Sea Scrolls at Qumran. Isaiah was clearly a popular book in the first centuries B.C. and A.D. The passage that was cited, Isa. 53:7-8, was sometimes cited to speak of Elijah revived (*Sir.* 48:10, cf. Mal. 4:5-6) or possibly the Messiah in 1 Enoch 37-71, especially Isa. 52:13 and 53:11. While the majority of Jewish tradition identifies the suffering servant of Isa. 53 either with one of several righteous individuals (a prophet) or the nation as a whole, it was not common to refer to the passage as reflective of the activity of the Messiah.

Luke, however, identifies Jesus as the suffering servant of Isa. 53 and this was typical in early Christianity.

8:35. Philip opening his mouth and beginning ... proclaimed to him the good news [Gospel]. The expression "opening his mouth beginning" is also found in 10:34 and 18:14, and has a close parallel in Luke 24:45. More importantly, the content of the Gospel in Acts appears to be that Jesus fulfills the Old Testament promises, that God has acted in the death and resurrection of Jesus, and that salvation comes to those who accept this by faith.

[8:37]. This verse is an addition to the original story of Acts. While it occurs in the KJV, it is lacking in the earliest biblical manuscripts and simply was added by a later copier/scribe to clarify what it was that one should believe in order to receive baptism.

8:38-39. Philip and the eunuch went down into the water. Typical of all baptisms where there was no shortage of water, immersion was used in the baptism of the Ethiopian.

8:40. Azotus to Caesarea. This city is the same as the Old Testament Ashdod and is located due west of Jerusalem about four km. from the sea and halfway between Joppa to the north and Gaza to the south. The famous *Via Maris*, a well-known Roman road that passed through this city would have made Philip's journey much easier. A number of towns and villages were on this road, among them were Antipatris (23:31), Lydda (9:32-35), Joppa (9:36-43; 10:5-23), and Jamnia, which was an important center in the survival of Judaism following the destruction of Jerusalem in A.D. 70. Philip's journey stopped at Caesarea where he and his four daughters resided (Acts 21:8-9). It is strange that if he were in Caesarea already as is suggested in Acts, that he plays no part in the evangelization of the household of Cornelius as he

did in Samaria. Caesarea was first settled in the fourth century B.C. and called Strato's Tower, but was rebuilt by Herod the Great 12-10 B.C. along with an important harbor and a well planned aqueduct that brought fresh water in from the north, ruins of which remain today. Josephus' description of the city is instructive:

And when he [Herod the Great] observed that there was a place near the sea, formerly called Strato's Tower, which was very well suited to be the site of a city, he set about making a magnificent plan and put up buildings all over the city, not of ordinary material but of white stone [=marble]. He also adorned it with a very costly palace, with civic halls and—what was greatest of all and required the most labour—with a well-protected harbour, of the size of the Piraeus [the harbor of Athens], with landing-places and secondary anchorages inside. But what was especially notable about this construction was that he got no material suitable for so great a work from the place itself but completed it with materials brought from outside at great expense. Now this city is located in Phoenicia, on the sea-route [the *Via Maris*] to Egypt, between Joppa and Dora (*Ant.* 15.331-333, LCL).

Caesarea was the seat of the Roman prefect Pilate in the time of Jesus and was the home of two Roman legions. It was the most important city in Judea in the time of Jesus and the apostles. Caesarea is where Luke will soon report that the first Gentiles became believers (10:1–11:18), and it is where Paul was imprisoned following his arrest in Jerusalem (Acts 23-33–27:1). In the first century and during the Jewish war with Rome (A.D. 66–70), the Jews massacred a Roman guard and when news of it came to the Romans at Caesarea where some 20,000 Jews resided, the Romans slaughtered all the Jews living there. Josephus describes this event as follows:

The same day and at the same hour, as it were by the hand of Providence, the inhabitants of Caesarea massacred the Jews who resided in their city; within one hour more than twenty thousand were slaughtered, and Caesarea was completely emptied of Jews, for the fugitives were arrested by orders of Florus and conducted in chains, to the dockyards. The news of the disaster at Caesarea infuriated the whole nation. . . (*War* 2.457-58, LCL).

9:1-22. The Conversion and Call of Saul.

One of the most important events in Acts, according to Luke, is the conversion or transformation of Saul/Paul. Unlike any other story in Acts, there are three versions of this story (9:1-22; 22:3-21; 26:9-23; cf. 1 Tim. 1:12-16), and Luke clearly wants to emphasize the importance of this event for the later Gentile mission in Acts (chaps. 13-28) that Paul would pursue. Before that, Luke had to show how the persecutor who later became a missionary was brought into the church. There are some differences between the three stories reported by Luke, but they are negligible compared to the coincidences, and they also find much support in the letters of Paul, especially Gal. 1:15-16 and Phil. 3:6-11. The church's most ferocious persecutor becomes its most zealous ally and spokesman, and Luke wants to tell that story (cf. 8:1-3).

9:2. Saul went to the high priest . . . for letters to the synagogues (cf. 26:10-11).

There is an important ancient parallel from ca. 140 B.C. that shows that Roman authorization was given to the high priest Simon to go after undesirable Jewish citizens who have fled to other countries. The letter in part reads: "Therefore, if any scoundrels have fled to you from their country, hand them over to the high priest Simon, so

that he may punish them according to their law" (*1 Macc.* 15:21, NRSV). The author of *1 Macc.* goes on to say that the consul, Lucius, "wrote the same thing to King Demetrius and to Attalus and Ariarathes and Arsaces, and to all the countries, and . . . [to several other cities around the Greco-Roman world]. They also sent a copy of these things to the high priest Simon" (15:22-24). Josephus knew of such a document, but dates it later than does the author of *1 Macc.* and says that such power was given by the Romans to a subservient king: namely, Herod the Great (37-4 B.C.). He writes:

Herod's formidable influence extended, moreover, beyond his realm to his friends abroad; for no other sovereign had been empowered by Caesar, as he had, to reclaim a fugitive subject even from a state outside his jurisdiction (*War* 1.474, LCL).

There is no independent confirmation that the earlier authority given to Simon the high priest was still in effect during the time of Paul, but the book of Acts assumes that it was.

The Way. This designation for the Christian community is found also in 19:9, 23; 22:4; 24:14, 22. This term is similar and may have much to do with the "two ways" found in ancient Jewish and Christian literature: namely, the way of darkness and the way of light (John 3:19-21; 1 John 1:6-7; 2:8-11). The author of the *Didache* (late first cent. A.D.) begins his collection of teachings of the apostles saying,

There are two Ways, one of Life and one of Death, and there is a great difference between the two Ways. The Way of Life is this: First, thou shalt love the God who made thee, secondly, thy neighbour as thyself; and whatsoever thou wouldst not have done to thyself, do not thou to another (*Did.* 1:1-2, LCL).

Again, he adds: "In the congregation thou shalt not betake thyself to prayer with an evil conscience. This is the way of life. But the Way of Death is this: First of all, it is wicked and full of cursing, murders, adulteries, lusts, fornications, thefts, idolatries, witchcrafts, charms [etc.] . . ." (*Did.* 4:14- 5:1a, LCL). The origin of the use of "the Way" in early Christianity is vague, but it was probably used to distinguish the Christians from other sectarians and perhaps also to emphasize that the Christians believed that they were following the one true way to God and living the way God intended them to live. The term also had a life among the Essenes at Qumran that emphasized observance of the Law of Moses (1QS 9:17-18, 21; CD 1:13; 1QS 4:22; 8:10, 18, 21; 9:5, 9; 11:11). More clearly, at Qumran following the "way" meant following the Law of Moses. Notice, for instance:

> When such men as these come to be in Israel, conforming to these doctrines, they shall separate from the session of perverse men to go to the wilderness, there to prepare the way of truth, as it is written, "In the wilderness prepare the way of the Lord, make straight in the desert a highway for our God" (Isa. 40:3). This means the expounding of the Law, decreed by God through Moses for obedience, that being defined by what has been revealed for each age, and by what the prophets have revealed by His Holy Spirit (1QS 8:12-15, Trans. by Wise, Abegg, Cook, 138).

9:2. Damascus. This city was one of the largest of the Decapolis cities (league of ten cities) of the Galilean region and located on the plain on the eastern side of Mt. Hermon. It is located some 135 miles north of Jerusalem. According to Josephus, there was a large Jewish population there, most of whom died during the A.D. 66–70 war with Rome. "In the end, they [the people of Damascus] fell upon the Jews, cooped up as they were and unarmed, and within one hour slaughtered them all with impunity, to the number of ten thousand five hundred" (*War* 2.561, LCL). Later he claimed that "as you know, there was not a city in Syria

which has not slain its Jewish inhabitants, though more hostile to us than to the Romans. Thus, the people of Damascus, though unable even to invent a plausible pretext, deluged their city with the foulest slaughter, butchering eighteen thousand Jews, with their wives and families" (*War* 7.368, LCL). The latter number includes the women and children and the former probably does not.

Near the time of Paul's visit to Damascus, the city came under the rule of the Nabateans and was governed by King Aretas IV Philopatris (Josephus, *Ant.* 13.387-92 and *War* 1.99-103; cf. Gal. 1:17; 2 Cor. 11:32).

9:3-19a. Saul's conversion. There is considerable debate among scholars over whether what happened to Paul constituted a call or a conversion. While the arguments are considerable for what happened as being a call as opposed to a conversion experience, nevertheless, it is clear that Luke is trying to show how the church's most ardent opponent became its strongest ally and proponent. He does this through an experience that had a radical transformation of Paul's understanding of Jesus and God's activity in him and also a radical change in Paul's behavior. Barrett is correct in concluding that if such a radical set of changes does not constitute a conversion, it is difficult to imagine what would (Barrett 1:442)! This does not, however, negate the call and the Gospel that Paul himself agrees that he received. Paul himself does not separate them (see Gal. 1:12, 15-16, 23; Phil. 3:2-11; 1 Cor. 9:1). For him, these events occurred together. This does not prevent him from receiving confirmation of his call through Ananias or even further instruction in Jerusalem (Gal. 1:18; 2:7-10). It is difficult to imagine that when Paul spent time with the leaders in Jerusalem, who had walked with Jesus, that he did not learn something from them! Indeed, he indicates that he was aware of tradition from Jesus (1 Cor. 7:10-11; 11:23-25; 15:3-8, 11), and he knew that they were in agreement, a difficult matter to determine if there had been no consultation during his visits to Jerusalem.

There is a well-known conversion story in the apocryphal writing, *Joseph and Aseneth* (written sometime between late second cent. B.C. and second cent. A.D. from Palestine), that has a few parallels with Luke's account of Paul's conversion. Aseneth was the Egyptian bride of Joseph, and this apocryphal writing reports the story of her conversion to the Jewish faith. After scorning Joseph, she repented after seven days of fasting (10:17) followed by extensive prayers (12:1-15). Then we read:

> And when Aseneth had ceased making confession to the Lord, behold, the morning star rose out of heaven in the east. And Aseneth saw it and rejoiced and said, "So the Lord God listened to my prayer, because this star rose as a messenger and herald of the great day." And Aseneth kept looking, and behold, close to the morning star, the heaven was torn apart and great and unutterable light appeared. And Aseneth saw (it) and fell on (her) face on the ashes. And a man came to her from heaven and stood by Aseneth's head. And he called her and said, "Aseneth, Aseneth." And she said, "Who is he that calls me, because the door of my chamber is closed, and the tower is high, and how then did he come into my chamber?" And the man called her a second time and said, "Aseneth, Aseneth." And she said, "Behold (here) I (am), Lord. Who are you, tell me." And the man said, "I am the chief of the house of the Lord and commander of the whole host of the Most High. Rise and stand on your feet, and I will tell you what I have to say" (*Jos. & Asen.* 14.1-8, *OT Pseud* 2:224-25).

After changing into her nice clothes from her mourning clothes, she washed her hands and face with "living water" (14:12, 15). There are obvious parallels here to the story of Paul's conversion in terms of the light flashing, the falling on the face, the double calling of the name (see also Exod. 3:4; 1 Sam. 3:4, 10; Luke 8:24; 10:41; 22:31), the asking for identity of the caller, and the subsequent washing (baptism) she is told about her future (15. 2-6). There are also several differences as one might expect. Paul was not involved in fasting and prayer when his vision came, and his encounter was with the risen Christ and not an angelic being.

Perhaps there are better parallels found in the Old Testament (1 Kings 22:19b-22; Isa. 6:1-13; Jer. 1:4-10), but even here there are differences. The call of Ezekiel also has several similar parallels to Paul's conversion story with the presence of light, the falling down on one's face, and a heavenly messenger telling of God's call (Ezek. 1:26–2:3).

9:3. Light from heaven (cf. 22:11; 26:13). Light is a common feature of theophanies (Ps. 27:1; 78:14; Isa. 9:2; 42:16; 60:1, 20; Micah 7:8). Paul understood this event as a revelation from God

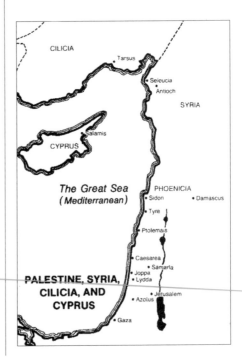

of his Son (Gal. 1:15-16) and that it was on par with the experiences of the other apostles (1 Cor. 9:1; 15:8; cf. 26:19). For hearing without seeing, see Deut. 4:12 and seeing without understanding, Dan. 10:7; but also strangely, Num. 22:22-35. Cf. Isa. 6:9 for a vision that others will not perceive.

9.7. Heard the voice but saw no one. There are differences between this passage and the other accounts 22:9; cf. 26:13.

9:9. Neither ate nor drank. It is not unusual for fasting to be associated with the receiving of a special revelation (Exod. 34:28; Deut. 9:9; Dan. 9:3; 10:2-3).

9:11. A man of Tarsus. This is the first time that Luke mentions the city of Paul's birth (cf. 11:25; 21:39; 22:3). While some have sought to identify it with Tarshish mentioned in Gen. 10:4, there is little to commend it. Tarsus was a highly prosperous city in the fourth century B.C. (Xenophon, *Anabasis* 1.2.23), and Greek coins indicating its Hellenistic influence also date from the fourth century B.C. It had a large community of Jews from the second century B.C. According to 2 *Macc.* 4:30-31, Antiochus the Great offered the city to his concubine, Antiochis, and caused a revolt in Tarsus. It was the home of a famous Stoic teacher of Caesar (Octavian) Augustus by the name of Athenodorus and in the time of Paul was widely known for being a cultural and intellectual center (Strabo, *Geography* 14.5.9-15). Later in Acts 21:39, Paul refers to it as "no mean city" and the place of his citizenship. In his *Discourses*, Dio Chrysostom (late first cent. to early second cent. A.D.) wrote two pieces (the First and Second Tarsic Discourses, also called his 33rd and 34th *Discourses*) to the citizens of Tarsus that were delivered to them in a public gathering upon invitation. He writes of the citizens of Tarsus,

For, men of Tarsus, it has come to pass

that you are foremost among your people, not merely because your city is the greatest of all the cities of Cilicia and a metropolis from the start [probably a reference to their becoming a Roman Province], but also because you beyond all others gained the friendly support of the second Caesar [Augustus]. For the misfortune that befell the city on his account naturally made him well disposed toward you, and eager that the favors received at his hands should appear in your eyes of greater importance than the misfortunes he had occasioned [Loyal to the Caesars, Tarsus opposed Cassius who in 42 B.C. entered the city and levied a contribution of 1500 talents. Cf. Cassius Dio 47.30-31]. Accordingly, everything a man might bestow upon those who were truly friends and allies and had displayed such eagerness in his behalf he has bestowed upon you: land, laws, honour, control of the river and of the sea in your quarter of the world (*Discourse* 34.7-8, LCL).

Following the defeat of Cassius and Brutus at Philippi in 41 B.C., both Augustus and Antony gave special favor to Tarsus, giving to its citizens both independence and exemption from taxation (cf. Appian, *Bellum Civile* 5.7).

9:15. Chosen vessel. Luke uses common biblical language to describe the call of Paul to Christian service (see Gal. 1:15, cf. Isa. 6:9; Jer. 1:5-10; Ezek. 2:3-4; Rom. 9:22-23; 2 Cor. 4.7; 2 Tim. 2:21). Paul uses this unusual designation in Rom. 9:11; 11:5, 7, 28; 1 Thess. 1:4; cf. also Rom. 16:13).

Bear my name before Gentiles. The sense of these words is to be a faithful witness to the risen Christ. A close parallel is found in the later Shepherd of Hermas who writes: "but they [those who are faithful] were never apostates from God, and they *bore the name* gladly, and they gladly received into their houses the servants of God (*Sim.* 8.10.3, LCL, italics added). Likewise, in his next Parable or Similitude he writes: "But you who are *suffering for the name,* ought to glorify God, that God deemed you *worthy to bear this name* and that all your sins should be healed. So then count yourselves blessed; but think that you have done a great deed, *if any of you suffer for God's sake*" (*Sim.* 9.28.5, LCL, italics added).

9:18. Scales from his eyes. Scales, or film, on the eyes was an ancient way of describing blindness (cf. Tobit 2:10; 11:11-13).

9:19b-30. Saul goes from Damascus to Jerusalem. This section is somewhat puzzling since it does not mention Paul's visit to Arabia (Gal. 1:17) nor his three years in Damascus, unless this is found in the "some time had passed" of 9:23. It is not possible to account for all of Paul's activity following his conversion with the available collection of biblical texts. They are all in summary form, including 2 Cor. 11:32, and it may be simply that both Luke's sources and his narrative are summarizing texts that leave open several possibilities. Paul was some ten years in Cilicia that are unaccounted for in Acts. Luke indicates that it was the Jews who wanted to kill Paul, and so he was forced to escape, but Paul attributes the necessity of leaving in haste to the ruler, Aretas (2 Cor. 11:32-33). The book of Acts is silent on Paul's visit to Arabia (probably Nabatea in the Transjordan region south of Damascus and east of Judea), and Paul is silent on what he did while there and how long he stayed. What we can suggest is that since Aretas died in A.D. 39, and since Paul spent some three years in Damascus following his conversion (Gal. 1:17-18), that his conversion took place sometime around or before A.D. 36, the latest possible time. Paul's debate in Jerusalem (v. 29) was with the Hellenists, that is, the Greek-speaking Jews. Their anger against

him prompted fellow Christians to send him to Caesarea and then to Tarsus for safety.

Paul at this point has been integrated into Luke's story. Just prior to the mission to the Gentiles which he does not mention in Damascus, he shows how Paul was transformed from an opponent to an ally of the Christian mission and was, though independent of it, nevertheless fully at one with the church in Jerusalem and the essential Christian message. Paul's letters also agree with this (Gal. 2:1-10; 1 Cor. 15:3-8).

Luke also gives the impression that Paul's visit to Jerusalem after Damascus was quite public: namely, the disciples feared Paul, but Barnabas took him and brought him to the apostles (26-27). And further, "He went in and out among them" (v. 28), but Paul suggests that his visit to Jerusalem after the Damascus ministry was more private (Gal. 1:18-20). It is difficult to bring these two traditions together (public and private visits) and the available sources cannot be harmonized.

While it may be possible, as some scholars contend, that Paul had first a private meeting in Jerusalem with Peter alone and subsequently a more visible ministry, this still does not harmonize with Paul's insistence on the meeting being private: "Behold I do not lie!" (Gal. 1:20, 22). What Paul did during his stay in Cilicia is unknown, and given the fact that Barnabas knew where to find him and also the kind of person Paul was (he immediately began to preach Jesus, 9:20), it may be inferred that Luke simply leaves out a considerable amount of unreported missionary activity. Paul does the same, since he does not indicate what he was doing during that fourteen-year period (Gal. 2:1) following his conversion (or following his first visit to Jerusalem following his conversion).

9:31. Summarizing passage. This is another of Luke's summarizing passages in Acts (see 2:41-47; 4:32-37; 5:12-16; 6:7), letting the reader know that the mission of the church continues to grow and the Holy Spirit is at work in the church.

Galilee. An important observance here is the mission of the church to Galilee. There is ample evidence that churches existed in Galilee, but they are nowhere else mentioned in Acts. This brief notice is all that is known in the New Testament about the mission of the church in Galilee. Galilee is mentioned in 10:37 and 13:31 as the place where Jesus ministered and in 1:11 and 2:7 as the home of Jesus' disciples. The casual mention of Galilee fits in Luke's purpose to show that the Gospel has reached beyond Jerusalem, but there is little evidence that there was a thriving church or churches in Galilee in the first or even second century. Since Matthew, Mark, and John (in chap. 21, the Appendix of John) claim that Jesus made resurrection appearances there, it is likely that some Christian gathering continued there when the appearances ceased, but Galilee does not fit into Luke's scheme for the advancement of the Gospel to the "ends of the earth." Luke clearly subordinates the Galilean appearances to the appearances of Jesus in Jerusalem (Luke 24), but given the other multiple references in Matthew, Mark, and the Johannine Appendix, it is likely that there was some Christian activity there, even if it was not highly significant. Galilee was the starting place of Jesus' ministry and perhaps also for a Gentile ministry in Damascus (so Sean Freyne, *Galilee*, 346-47). Whatever the case, this is Luke's only recognition of Christians existing in the region of Galilee.

9:32-43. Peter's Mission to Lydda and Joppa

As Luke sets the stage for the Gentile mission, Peter is introduced once again as the leader in the mission of the church in its most significant transitions (2:14-41; 8:14-25). These two stories are part of Luke's setting the stage for the most significant activity in the book of Acts and it occupies the next five chapters: namely, the incorporation of Gentiles into the community of those who acknowledge Jesus as Messiah and Lord and possess the Spirit of God. Cornelius' conversion to Christian faith was the first among the Gentiles and was marked as highly significant by Luke (15:7).

Luke does not go into detail about the origin of the churches in these two towns (Lydda and Joppa), but assumes their existence. It could be that they were founded by the scattered Hellenistic Jewish Christians (8:4) or by Philip (8:40) or even perhaps as a result of Peter's proclamation on the Day of Pentecost (2:5-11). Luke is not specific. These two healing stories reflect that Peter was perhaps on a mission to strengthen the churches that had already been founded ("now he went here and there among all the believers" v. 32).

9:32. Lydda. The city of Lydda was located on the Plain of Sharon ten miles southeast of Joppa and was on the main route from both Babylon and Damascus to Egypt. The town is referred to in the OT as Lod (Ezra 2:33; 1 Chron. 8:12; cf. also 1 *Macc.* 11:34). Sometime in the third century it is renamed Diospolis ("City of Zeus") and had a large Christian population residing there. The Roman governor of Syria came here to settle a dispute (Josephus, *Ant.* 6.130), and Pliny the Elder lists it as one of the ten major areas of government in Judea (*Natural History* 5.70). Josephus also speaks of Lydda on several occasions, mostly highlighting the activities of the Roman soldiers who came through here during the 66–70 A.D. war with the Jews (*War* 2.515; 3.54-55; 4.444; see other references in 1 *Macc.* 11:34 and Pliny, *Natural History* 5.70).

9:33. Aeneas. The man who had been lame for eight years has a Greek name, but there is no indication that he was a Gentile. The name itself is known from Homer's *Iliad* 13.541. It was not uncommon in the first century to find Jews with Greek names (Philip, Stephen, etc.).

9:36. Joppa. Joppa was an ancient Philistine city on the Plain of Sharon and on the coast of Palestine. It had its own port and was about thirty miles south of Caesarea. According to Josephus, it was largely a Greek city and was one of two cities that had jurisdiction over the surrounding villages and cities (Josephus, *War* 3.54-56).

A disciple (Greek = *mathetria*). This is the only place in the New Testament where the feminine form of the word is used. Elsewhere, only the masculine form is used.

9:37. Washed her. The washing of a dead person in preparation for burial was widespread in both Greek (see Homer, *Iliad* 18.350; Plato, *Phaedo* 115a; and Virgil, *Aeneid* 6.219) and Jewish communities (*m. Shabb.* 23.5). In the latter source, persons were able to do all that was necessary for a dead person, but some things were not considered necessary.

> They may make ready [on the Sabbath] all that is needful for the dead, and anoint it and wash it, provided that they do not move any member of it. They may draw the mattress away from beneath it and let it lie on sand that it may be the longer preserved; they may bind up the chin, not in order to raise it but that it may not sink lower. . . . They may not close a corpse's eyes on the Sabbath, nor may they do so on a week-day at the moment when the soul is departing; and he that closes the eyes [of the dying man] at the moment when the soul is departing, such a one is a shedder of blood (*m. Shabbath* 23.5).

This story is similar in some respects to the story of Elijah raising the widow's son in 1 Kings 17:19.

9:43. Simon, a tanner. This part of the story is strange since in 10:4 Peter is anxious about keeping the rituals of cleanliness. According to the Jewish tradition, tanners were among the despised of society (in the Mishnah, [*m. Shabbath* 1:2; *Pesharim* 65a; *Kiddushin* 82b; *Megillah* 3:2]). In m. Ketuboth, we find that being married to a tanner was grounds for divorce and also if a wife was married to a tanner, and the brother of the tanner was in the same business, then the wife was under no obligation to marry the brother as was usual in levirate marriages among the Jews.

> And these are they that are compelled to put away their wives: he that is afflicted with boils, or that has a polypus, or that collects [dog's excrements], or that is a coppersmith or a tanner, whether these defects were in them before they married or whether they arose after they married. . . . It once happened in Sidon that a tanner died and had a brother who was a tanner. The sages said: She may say, "thy brother I could endure; but thee I cannot endure" (*m. Ket.* 7:10).

Those who were involved in the tanning business were considered unclean and among the lowest in society. Perhaps Luke is setting up the story of Cornelius to show Peter's willingness to be among those considered "sinners" by the Pharisees.

10:1-48. The Conversion of Cornelius and His Household

As in the case of Paul's conversion, the story of Cornelius is repeated twice (10:1-48; 11:1-18) and referred to again (15:7-9). Without question, Luke finds this conversion story highly significant. Just as the conversion of Paul is necessary for the work among the Gentiles to flourish, so the conversion of Cornelius is a significant turning point in the unfolding plan of redemption (1:8). It is interesting that Luke has carefully designed this story in four parallel scenes: namely, (1) there is a vision of Cornelius that is followed by the vision of Peter (10:1-17); (2) Cornelius' servants arrive at the home where Peter was staying and are welcomed, and then Peter and his companions arrive at Cornelius' house and are welcomed (10:17-29); (3) Cornelius speaks to explain what has happened to him and then Peter speaks to explain his insight into God's impartiality (10:30-43); finally, (4) God's impartiality is confirmed by the giving of the Holy Spirit both in Cornelius' house and back in Jerusalem (10:44-48 and 11:1-18).

That God was involved in the expansion of the mission of the church that was predicted back in 1:8 is clear from the vision and the conclusion that Peter drew from it as well as the confirmation of the Holy Spirit. This passage prepares the reader for understanding the significance of the council meeting of Acts 15. This whole passage flows logically into five parts: namely, Cornelius' vision (10:1-8); Peter's Vision (10:9-16); the welcome for messengers from Cornelius (10:17-23a); Peter's testimony in Cornelius' house (10:23b-48); and Peter's defense at Jerusalem (11:1-18). In this story, Luke makes it clear that it is God who determines the boundaries of the Christian community and that God has his way in all such matters. For Luke, this is confirmed by the visions given to Cornelius and Peter as well as the gift of the Holy Spirit.

10:1. In Caesarea. This city was first settled by a Sidonian king named Strato in the fourth century B.C. It was situated on the seacoast of Israel some 70 miles northwest of Jerusalem. Strato used the town as a center for trade and it became known as Strato's Tower. After a sometimes turbulent history of various conquests, the city was captured by Alexander Jannaeus in 103 B.C., but it declined considerably as an important city, and the city and the harbor lay in ruins by the time of Herod the Great (40–4 B.C.). Herod rebuilt the city between 21 and 9 B.C. and significantly expanded its harbor by using the recently discovered means of drying concrete under water (hydraulic concrete), and he renamed it after Caesar Augustus (Octavian). Following the rebuilding of the city and its harbor, Caesarea (often called Caesarea

Maritima or Caesarea Sebaste/Sabastos) became the capital of Roman Judea during the Roman occupation of that land. It also became one of the most important harbors in the eastern empire because it not only allowed for easy access of the Roman troops into the land of Israel—an important issue for an occupying force—but it also facilitated the spice trade from the east. The harbor provided a major source of income to Herod that also allowed many of his other expensive and extravagant building projects to proceed. Herod built the city to house some 6,000 colonists. It was the most important harbor in the region and became the center for Roman activities in the region in the first century. The city itself was no less important than the famous harbor. It had several temples, paved roads, sewer systems, and water canals throughout, and the materials to build the city were very expensive. Herod imported white stone for many of the construction projects. The chief source of information on this ancient city comes from Flavius Josephus near the end of the first century A.D. He writes:

> The city itself is called Caesarea and is most beautiful both in material and in construction. But below the city the underground passages and sewers cost no less effort than the structures built above them. Of these some led at equal distances from one another to the harbour and the sea, while one diagonal passage connected all of them, so that the rainwater and the refuse of the inhabitants were easily carried off together. And whenever the sea was driven in from offshore, it would flow through the whole city and flush it from below. Herod also built a theatre of stone in the city, and on the south side of the harbour, farther back, an amphitheatre large enough to hold a great crowd of people and conveniently situated for a view of the sea. Now the city was completed in the space of twelve years,

for the king did not slacken in the undertaking and he had sufficient means for the expenses (*Ant.* 15.340-41, LCL).

10:1-2. Cornelius. Luke tells only his *nomen*, that is, the name of his family clan. This was also the name of a famous Roman by the name of P. Cornelius Sulla who freed many slaves who took for themselves the name of their emancipator, but it is not certain that this person was the namesake of the Cornelius of Acts 10. It is instructive, however, of the practice of adopting a name from a benefactor out of gratitude. In the first century A.D., many Romans had three names, often identified as a *praenomen* (a personal name that was more formal than the *cognomen*), a *nomen* (the clan or family name), and a *cognomen* (a nickname that eventually came to be something of a "first" name). Luke only gives the *nomen* of this centurion, Cornelius, and that reflects an older Roman practice that persisted in the late first century B.C. and through the mid-first century A.D. among older and more conservatively minded men in the military.

Cornelius, who was at least a partial Jewish convert, that is, he accepted its teaching without accepting circumcision, was the first Gentile convert to Christianity (see also 11:1-18; 15:6-11). He was also called a devout man who feared God (a "god-fearer," see this term later in 10:22, 35; 13:16, 26), who gave generously to the people, and prayed continually (v. 2). The terms "devout" and "God-fearer" are probably equivalent terms, and most often scholars have argued that both terms have to do with non-Jewish individuals who were sympathetic to Judaism, but who had not yet followed the Law completely or been circumcised. In other words, such individuals so described were on their way to conversion. Recent scholars have pointed to an inscription dating ca. A.D. 200 found in Aphrodisias in modern-day western Turkey that lists a certain man named

Emmonius as a "Godfearer" (Greek = *theosebes*) and also "Antonius, a Godfearer" followed by "Samuel son of Politanus," and finally "Joseph son of Eusebius, a proselyte." Whether this suggests that only Gentiles may become Godfearers is unclear. The inscription seems to distinguish or reserve categories for Jews, Godfearers, and proselytes. These categories in Luke's time may not be entirely separate since the terms apparently could also be used of those who were already proselytes and even of Jews themselves, but Luke uses the terms generally of those who were both attached to and favorable toward the synagogue. That Cornelius was involved in the most esteemed acts of piety (alms giving and prayer, cf. also Jesus' reference to these practices in Matt. 6:1-7) is clear, and Luke indicates that Peter also recognized this in Cornelius (cf. 10:35).

Centurion. As a centurion of the Italian cohort, or a cohort called Italica, Cornelius likely commanded a unit of that cohort of some eighty to one hundred men. Such cohorts were made up of Roman soldiers and were known for their loyalty to Rome. They were often introduced into circumstances where fierce loyalty was a necessity. A cohort consisted of around 500 to 600 men and they were divided into some six units of eighty to a hundred men. Ten cohorts normally equaled the size of an Italian legion (ca. 6,000 men). Reports on the exact numbers of soldiers at Caesarea vary, but Cornelius, as a centurion, was the commander of a unit of the cohort, but probably not all of it. The troops at Caesarea were under the direction of the Roman prefects, as in the case of Pontius Pilate, and helped maintain peace from A.D. 6 until A.D. 40. After a brief reign of the grandson of Herod the Great (Acts 12), the region was once again under Roman rule. Following the death of Herod Agrippa in 44, Josephus indicates that some 2,500 troops were stationed at Caesarea (*Ant.* 19.351-66).

Luke believed that Cornelius was a Gentile since he speaks directly about his conversion as a Gentile in 11:18 and the issue of table fellowship and diet issues (10:9-17, 22, 11:3) would only be important to the Jewish Christians in Jerusalem if Cornelius and his household were Gentiles. Further, the point of Peter's hesitation in his vision to eat unclean food (vv. 9-16) helps explain the immediate story following that vision, in which Cornelius was a Gentile. It also informs the debate among the Jewish Christians in 11:1-18. Further, Jews had difficulty serving in the Roman army because of their ritual purification. Josephus tells how the Romans, upon banishing the Jews from Rome (see Acts 18:2; cf. Josephus, *Ant.* 18.81-84), wanted to enlist 4,000 Jews into their military ranks, but that proved a failure. He explains: "The counsuls drafted four thousand of these Jews for military service and sent them to the island of Sardina; but they penalized a good many of them who refused to serve for fear of breaking the Jewish law" (*Ant.* 18.84). Luke also indicates that Cornelius.

10:22. Summon you to his house. Gentile homes were considered unclean and it was unlawful for a Jew to enter them. According to the Mishnah, "the dwelling-places of Gentiles are unclean" (*m. Oholot* 18:7). Peter's vision prepared him to accept the invitation, but his own inner struggle with the matter can be seen in the story of his vision (10:11-17). It took a vision from God to open Peter to this possibility and the confirmation of the meaning of this vision (10:34) by the servants of Cornelius who told him of the angelic visit to Cornelius.

10:28. It is unlawful for a Jew to associate with a Gentile. The word unlawful is used in 2 *Macc.* 6:5; 7:1; and 3 *Macc.* 5:20. On Jewish and Gentile relations, see Gal. 2:12 and Luke 5:30; 7:33-34; 15:2. Table fellowship symbolized a spiritual unity in the church (2 John 11), but if Gentiles were to be included, how could a faithful Jew who was also a Christian violate the religious traditions widely accepted among the Jews regarding table fellowship? See discussion later on 11:3 and 15:3-29. The church had to deal with the acceptance of Gentiles into its fellowship, but this created problems of violating Jewish laws of ritual purity.

While it was common for Jews to associate with Gentiles, and even to sell to and buy products from Gentiles, both the items purchased and the person having contact with the Gentile needed cleansing from the defilement incurred. According to the apocryphal *Book of Jubilees* (written sometime between 160–140 B.C.), in the story of Abraham blessing Jacob, Jews were forbidden to have contacts with Gentiles.

> And you also, my son, Jacob, remember my words, and keep the commandments of Abraham, your father. Separate yourself from the gentiles, and do not eat with them, and do not perform deeds like theirs, and do not become associates of theirs. Because their deeds are defiled, and all of their ways are contaminated, and despicable, and abominable (*Jub.* 22.16, *OT Pseud* 1:98).

From ancient times, the rabbis, having expanded on the need for keeping the laws of Leviticus 18:3 and 20:3, set about to prohibit Jews from social contacts with Gentiles because of the fear of assimilation and even intermarriage. The injunction against such contacts with the Canaanite nations (Deut. 7:2-4) was eventually extended to all Gentiles. Jews were even prohibited from wearing Gentile costumes and even from imitating their hair dress (*b. Shab.* 67a-b; *b. Sanh.* 52a.). In order to prevent Jews from adopting non-Jewish habits, many laws were set forth that separated Jews from having normal social contacts with Gentiles. There were many biblical traditions that were accepting of Gentiles (Gen. 12:3; Isa. 49:6 and Dan. 1–6 where the foreign kings proclaim the sovereignty of Israel's God), and later the author of *1 Enoch* noted that God's blessings would go to the children of all the world if they adhered to the Torah (10:21; 90:38; 91:14; 100:6; 105:1). On the other hand, the *Book of Jubilees* warns its readers to avoid all contact with Gentiles. The two apocalypses written after the destruction of Jerusalem in A.D. 70 warn that Jews should be antagonistic to the Gentiles and avoid them (*4 Ezra* and *2 Baruch*). The keeping of one's distance from Gentiles became the common practice among Jews of the first century and any involvement in table fellowship was likely to violate that distance and bring back the fear of assimilation of the Jews among the Gentiles.

While Jews had some 613 commandments placed upon them to maintain their ritual holiness, Gentiles only had the so-called seven Noahic commandments (Gen. 9:1-17) that were incumbent upon everyone, Jew or Gentile. According to the Babylonian Talmud, these were listed as follows: "Concerning seven religious requirements were the children of Noah commanded: setting up courts of justice, idolatry, blasphemy [cursing the Name of God], fornication, bloodshed, thievery, and cutting a limb from a living beast" (Neusner, *Talmud, b. Sanhedrin* 56A, Neusnet). Such laws and customs (*ethos*), if maintained within the church, would become a significant barrier to fellowship and acceptance between Jews and Gentiles. The matter of separation was so entrenched in the first century that Luke indicates that it took a special revelation from God to overcome it in the church (10:10-17; 11:3-18; 15:28). See notes in 15:3-29.

10.34. God shows no partiality. Peter concluded this from his vision and from the story that Cornelius had told him.

11:3. You entered the house of uncircumcised men and ate with them. Visiting the house of a Gentile led to ritual uncleanness and was therefore unlawful for observant Jews. See discussion on 10:22, 28 above and 15:3-29 below. With the inclusion of Gentiles into the Christian community, a way was needed to deal with the problem of table fellowship that

emerges here and in Gal. 2:12-14. The matter was settled for the church at a "council" meeting in 15:3-29. See discussion below.

11:1-18. Peter's Defense of His Mission to the Gentiles

Peter's audience in Jerusalem did not object that Cornelius and his household had become Christians and neither did they suggest that Cornelius was not a "godfearer" or a pious man, but rather that Peter had table fellowship with them. This was an issue that is a part of the discussion in Acts 15 and Gal. 2:12 because Gentiles were considered ritually unclean. This section also anticipates the more important question that emerges at the council of Acts 15:1, 5: namely, whether Gentiles must also become Jews before they can be saved from their sins. Thus, in this passage, converts among the Gentiles had not been circumcised and did not keep the laws of Moses, so the controversy arose over the appropriateness of their participation in the Christian community. Peter relates the double vision, one to him and one to Cornelius (vv. 5-14) that God's acceptance of the Gentiles was confirmed by activity of the Holy Spirit (v. 15). This conclusion was revolutionary since Gentiles, who were considered inferior to Jews in every way, could also be accepted like they had been accepted: namely, by faith, but without the necessity of circumcision or a commitment to the laws of Moses. Luke revisits the issue again here, but finally in Acts in 15:3-29.

III. 11:19–30. THE SPREAD OF THE GOSPEL TO GENTILES—TRIUMPH AND CONFLICT

This section has two important parts: the first is the origin of the ministry of the church at Antioch (19-26), and the second is that church's support of the Christians in Jerusalem (27-30). Both sections contain very important information that is central to Luke's purpose of describing the origins, growth, and development of the church.

11:19a. Phoenicia, Cyprus, Antioch. Phoenicia is the name given to the Mediterranean seacoast of the Roman province of Syria. The most important towns or cities in that region included Ptolemais, Acco, Sarepta, Berytus, Tripolis, and Arvad. The name Phoenicia is related to the word "*phoinos*," meaning "redpurple" and is the color of the famous dye from Tyre. The Hebrew term for this dye is related to the name Canaan (see Exod. 16:35 in the LXX and the Heb. text). Cyprus is the large island southwest of Cilicia in Asia Minor or modern Turkey and about sixty miles west of Antioch of Syria. It was the home of Barnabas (4:36) and, according to Philo, there were many Jews on the island. He writes: "And not only are the mainlands full of Jewish colonies but also the most highly esteemed of the islands Euboea, Cyprus, Crete" (Embassy to Gaius §282, LCL).

11:19b-26. The church at Antioch. Antioch, the capital of ancient Seleucid Syria and later capital of the Roman province of Syria, was situated on the edge of a large and fertile plain on the south bank of the Orontes River some fifteen miles from the Mediterranean coast. It was founded ca. 300 B.C. by Seleucus I Nicanor, one of Alexander the Great's generals and the son of Antiochus (after whom he named the city, as was the case with sixteen other cities by that name, also named in honor of Seleucus I's father). Among the well-known Antiochs in the New Testament era is Antioch of Pisidia (Acts 13:14-52). It was originally built at the foot of Mt. Silpius as a convenience city between Seleucus' home in Anatolia and his eastern possessions, but eventually became considerably more important. The king transferred 5,300 residents from Athens and Macedonia to settle the new city. Its closest harbor, Seleucia, was some twelve miles west at the mouth of the Orontes and functioned as the gateway to the city.

Antioch always had a mixed population of Greeks, Macedonians, local Syrians, Jews, and,

after 64 B.C. when it fell to Pompey, also many Romans. It may be that the actual population was just above 100,000, but if the slaves were counted and also the larger geographic area that the city served, then its numbers could well be considerably higher. Antioch had a Jewish population of ca. 25,000 to some 65,000 (Josephus, *JW* 7.43) with the privileges of a political state (a *politeuma*) that included the right to keep the sabbath and other Jewish religious practices and exclusion from obligatory military service (*Ag. Ap.* 2.39; *Ant* 12.119; *JW* 7.43). These privileges may date back to the founding of the city. According to *2 Macc.* 4:33-38, a former Jewish high priest named Onias II lived in the vicinity of Antioch and some of the temple treasures that were stolen from Jerusalem in the days of Antiochus Epiphanes (175-63 B.C.) were taken there. It ranked in importance with Alexandria in Egypt and Seleucia on the Tigris. Nicholas, a "proselyte of Antioch," was one of seven leaders of Hellenists in Jerusalem chosen to do ministries for the church (Acts 6:7).

The story of the church at Antioch actually begins with the story of Stephen's martyrdom and the scattering of the church (Acts 6:8–8:4). Indeed, if the reader read this passage immediately after 8:4, it would be difficult to tell if there was something missing. Luke, however, carefully crafts his story well so that after the scattering of the Hellenistic Christians following Stephen's death, the Gospel is proclaimed to Jews and Gentiles outside of Jerusalem. The proclamation begins with the events of chapter 8 (the Samaritans and the Ethiopian), followed by the conversion of Paul (9:1-30). Paul's Damascus road experience sets up the story of the Gentile mission that begins with Peter and is carried on by Paul and Barnabas (11:19-27 and 13:1–14:28). This scenario sets the stage for the church's recognition of God's will concerning Gentile inclusion in the church (15:1-29). This passage is central to Luke's story of the progress of the Gospel to the city of Rome, and it is clear that he has tied together several pivotal stories to tell of this development. Because there is no evidence that he was an eyewitness, it is obvious that he made use of traditions handed on to him to craft his story. Some scholars have spoken of an "Antiochene" tradition that was used by Luke to tell his story of the growth of the early church: namely, 6:8–8:4; possibly 9:1-30; 11:19-30; and 12:25, 13:1–15:35. While this cannot be proved, the flow of those texts when placed in a connected sequence is suggestive. The connection of Paul and Barnabas with this church also has support in the Pauline literature (Gal. 2:11-14).

11:19. Antioch. Antioch, the capital of ancient Seleucid Syria and later capital of the Roman province of Syria, was situated on the edge of a large and fertile plain on the south bank of the Orontes River some fifteen miles from the Mediterranean coast. Antioch was founded ca. 300 B.C. by Seleucus I Nicanor, one of Alexander the Great's generals and the son of Antiochus, after whom he named the city. Like sixteen other cities by that name, Antioch was named after Seleucus I's father, Antiochus. Among the well-known cities by this name in the New Testament era is Antioch of Pisidia (Acts 13:14-52). It always had a mixed population of Greeks, Macedonians, local Syrians, and Jews; and after 64 B.C. when it fell to Pompey, many Romans also resided there.

After Antioch was annexed by Rome, it became the capital of the province of Syria and was the military headquarters of Rome in the east. The city was allowed to self-govern from the time when Julius Caesar visited the city (47 B.C.) and it even had its own calendar called the Antiochene Era that began on October 1, 49 B.C., the presumed date of the beginning of Julius Caesar's reign. Under Augustus and Tiberias the city was enlarged and, according to Josephus, this expansion was significantly aided by Herod the Great, who built a long, colonnaded street (ca. two and a half miles long)

made of polished marble with a "cloister of the same length," that is, with some 3,200 columns and porticoes on each side of the street with broad walkways. Speaking of Herod's significant contributions to other Roman cities, Josephus writes: "And that broad street in Syrian Antioch—once shunned on account of the mud—was it not he who paved its twenty furlongs with polished marble, and, as a protection from the rain, adorned it with a colonnade of equal length?" (*War* 1.425, LCL). And again: "And for the Antiochenes, who inhabit the greatest city in Syria, which has a street running through it lengthwise, he [Herod] adorned this street with colonnades on either side, and paved the open part of the road with polished stone, thereby contributing greatly to the appearance of the city and to the convenience of its inhabitants" (*Ant.* 16.148, LCL).

Its population varied in size depending on the sources, and ranged from a low of 200,000 residents (Chrysostom, *Pan. Ign.* 4) to 300,000 (Strabo, *Geography* 16.2.5), to a high of 600,000 (Pliny, *HN* 6.122). It may be that the actual population was just above 100,000, but if the slaves were counted and also the larger geographic area that the city served, then its numbers could well have been considerably higher. Josephus, describing Vespasian, the Roman general, activating his troops at Antioch, describes the city as "the capital of Syria, and a city which, for extent and opulence, unquestionably ranks third among the cities of the Roman world" (*War* 3.29, LCL).

Jewish interest in this Gentile city has significant roots well before Herod the Great's contributions to it, and the Jewish community there was of considerable size. Antioch had a large Jewish population of ca. 25,000 to some 65,000 (Josephus, *War* 7.43) with the privileges of a political state (a *politeuma*) that included the right to keep the sabbath and other Jewish religious practices and exclusion from obligatory military service (*Ag. Ap.* 2.39; *Ant.* 12.119; *War* 7.43). These privileges may date back to the founding of the city. According to *2 Macc.* 4:33-38, a former Jewish high priest named Onias II lived in the vicinity of Antioch and some of the temple treasures that were stolen from Jerusalem in the days of Antiochus Epiphanes (175–63 B.C.) were taken there. With such a background, it is not surprising that Jewish Christians made their way to this city to further the Christian mission. It was from this church that the launching of the Gentile mission began with Barnabas and Saul/Paul.

11:24. Full of the Holy Spirit and faith. See the description of Stephen in 6:5, only in reverse.

11:26. Christians. The name is a Latinism (*christianos*) that depends on the Greek *christos* ("anointed one" or "messiah"), a reference to the title that the followers of Jesus gave to him and which became a part of his name within the early church: namely, Jesus the Christ, and eventually Jesus Christ. As the term "called" (Greek = *chrematidzein*) in v. 26 suggests, this term was not so much adopted by the Christian community as one that was given to it by outsiders. It is possible that they also accepted and adopted the term soon afterward, but that is not clear. There are several examples of the non-Christian community referring to the followers of Jesus with this term. There is a more recent parallel in how the Society of Friends (following John 15:14) were often called "Quakers" by outsiders because of their style of worship and they eventually also accepted that designation themselves. In the case of the name "Christian" the grecized Latinism simply refers to those who follow Christ. See also 26:28 below and 1 Peter 4:16. The term is only found in these three passages in the New Testament and it was not until the second century when it became a popular designation for the followers of Jesus widely accepted in the Christian churches. Originally the term may have been a form of mockery or a reference to the Christians as a party or group

such as the Herodians, the Asians, Neronians, and so on. The name is found in Josephus who speaks of the "tribe of the Christians, so called after him [Jesus]" (*Ant.* 18.64), and Pliny (ca. A.D. 100–113) describes his dilemma over what to do with those who call themselves Christians to the Emperor Trajan (*Ep.* 10.96-97). Tacitus (published between A.D. 115–120) tells of how Nero blamed the Christians for the fire that burned Rome and in so doing speaks of the disdain toward the Christians and described them as:

> a class of men, loathed for their vices, whom the crowd styled Christians [Latin = *Christianos*]. Christus, the founder of the name, had undergone the death penalty in the reign of Tiberias, by the procurator, Pontius Pilatus, and the pernicious superstition was checked for a moment, only to break out once more, not merely in Judaea, the home of the disease, but in the capital itself, where all things horrible or shameful in the world collect and find a vogue (*Annals* 15.44, LCL).

Lucian speaks derogatorily of the Christian sect and of their expulsion (Vol. 4, *Alexander the False Prophet* 25, 38) and again of the gullible Christians who accepted as a prophet a charlatan named Proteus Peregrinus who took them for a lot of money (*The Passing of Peregrinus* 11, 12, 16).

There were apparently several Latin ways of spelling the name "Christian." The most common were *christianos, chreistianos,* and *chrestianos.* Suetonius (A.D. 75–140) in his *Lives of the Caesars* (vol. 5) tells how Claudius expelled the Jews from Rome (see later in 18:2) because, as he says, "Since the Jews constantly made disturbances at the instigation of Chrestus, he expelled them from Rome" (*Claudius,* 25.4, LCL). "Chrestus" (in the text, "*Chresto*") is probably an erroneous spelling for Christ and this was occasioned by or led to the various spellings of Christian in the Roman world. While the early Christians probably referred to themselves as disciples (Greek = *mathetai*), believers (Greek = *pisteuontes*), and brethren (Greek = *adelphoi*), it is likely that others would refer to them in less confusing and nonspecific terms such as Christian. Although a sectarian group of Christians at Corinth may have used this term or something like it to refer to themselves (1 Cor. 1:12), it is in the second century when we begin to see the term adopted by the Christians themselves. The first writer to make regular use of the term was Ignatius (*Eph.* 11.2; *Rom.* 3:2; *Magn.* 10.3; *Pol.* 7.3). While the early Christians most likely did not invent this name for themselves, in time they accepted it with honor.

11:27. Prophets came down from Jerusalem to Antioch. Luke uses the word "prophet" or "prophesy" to describe the activity of early Christians (see 2:17-18, but also 13:1; 15:32; 19:6; 21:10; see 21:9 for "prophecy"). According to Paul this is a gift given to the church, e.g. Rom. 12:6; 1 Cor. 12:28-29; and how it is exercised is found in 13:9; 14:1, 3-5, 24, 27, 29-32, 39; and 1 Thess. 5:20 (see also Luke 11:49; Eph. 2:20; 3:5; 4:11). The notion of "false prophets" in the church is also common in the NT (e.g., Matt. 7:15; 24:11, 24; Mark 13:22; 2 Peter 2:11; John 4:1; cf. also Rev. 10:11; 11:10, 18; 16:6; 18:20, 24; 22:9). Many of the wandering prophets in the early church caused problems and the author of the *Didache* (ca. A.D. 80–90) offers several guidelines for receiving such persons in the church, including whether they ask for money for themselves, how long they stay (no longer than three days), and whether they live appropriate lives above reproach (11:1-12). Later, the *Shepherd of Hermas* sets up guidelines on how to discern the false prophet. Among his several ways of discerning the false prophet, he lists the following:

a false prophet, [is one] who is corrupting the understanding of the servants of God. He corrupts the understanding of the double-minded, not of the faithful. Therefore these double-minded men come to him as to a wizard, and ask him concerning the future; and that false prophet, having no power of the Divine Spirit in himself, speaks with them according to their requests, and according to the desires of the their wickedness, and fills their souls, as they themselves wish. For he is empty and makes empty answers to empty men; for whatever question is put he answers according to he emptiness of the man. But he also speaks some true words, for the devil fills him with his spirit, to see if he can break any of the righteous.

. . .

In the first place, that man who seems to have a spirit exalts himself and wishes to have the first place, and he is instantly impudent and shameless and talkative, and lives in great luxury and in many other deceits, and accepts rewards for his prophecy, and if he does not receive them, he does not prophesy . . . You have the life of both the prophets [the true and the false]. Test, then, from his life and deeds, the man who says that he is inspired (*Mandate* 11:1-16, LCL).

11:28. Agabus. Not much is known about this prophet, but Luke mentions him here and again in 21:20. Here he is represented as traveling with other prophets from Jerusalem. In 21:10, he has evidently returned to Judea and made his way to Caesarea.

A severe famine over all the world. There are many references in the ancient world about famines occurring in the first century and especially during the reign of Claudius (A.D. 41–54). Suetonius tells of a time when Claudius came to Rome, and as he was in the Forum a mob shouted insults at him over the scarcity of food and he was pelted with pieces of bread by them. He was barely able to escape back into his palace, and so from that time on Claudius "resorted to every possible means to bring grain to Rome, even in the winter season" (*Life of Claudius* 18, LCL). Tacitus tells a similar story, but adds that following the famine followed many "prodigies" or extraordinary or amazing phenomena such as earthquakes, that:

> a shortage of corn, again, and the famine which resulted, were construed as a supernatural warning. Nor were the complaints always whispered. Claudius sitting in judgment, was surrounded by a wildly clamorous mob, and was driven into the farthest corner of the Forum. . . . It was established that the capital [Rome] had provisions for fifteen days, no more; and the crisis was relieved only by the especial grace of the gods and the mildness of the winter (*Annals* 12:43, LCL).

Josephus also observes "when Claudius being ruler of the Romans and Ishmael our high priest, when our country was in the grip of a famine" that "such dearth prevailed throughout the country" (*Ant.* 3.320-321, LCL). Later he speaks of another famine and says that "it was in the administration of Tiberias Alexander [ca. A.D. 45] that the great famine occurred in Judaea, during which Queen Helena [from Adiabene in northern Mesopotamia] bought grain from Egypt for large sums and distributed it to the needy" (*Ant.* 20.101, LCL). The problem with all available reports of famines is that none of them was universal or empire wide during this time and, if they were, it would seem odd to send funds from Antioch to Jerusalem if they also were faced with the famine. The same could be said of Egypt selling food to Queen Helena if there was a famine there. Since the famine was found in a number of locations from Judaea to Rome, Luke reported through Agabus that it was "over all the world."

This verse also makes an explicit indication that Acts was written after the famine took place.

11:29. Each . . . determined to send. The language here is similar to that in Paul's letters regarding the contribution collected from the churches to bring to Judaea (1 Cor. 16:1-4; 2 Cor. 9:1-15; see also Rom. 15:22-28). There is difficulty, however, in bringing together these two separate traditions about the monies to relieve the suffering of the church in Jerusalem. Only in 24:17 does Luke have Paul bring such funds, but given the number of times that Paul himself mentions the collection in his letters, it is surprising that Luke does not say more in Acts. Is the collection mentioned the same as that discussed in Gal. 2:1-10 and in the Pauline passages noted above? If so, it does not fit neatly with its description toward the end of Paul's missionary journeys in his letters. Finally, the collection that Paul took up for the Christians in Jerusalem (1 Cor. 16:1-4; 2 Cor. 9:1-15; see also Rom. 15:22-28) does not fit easily within the chronological structure of Acts. It is ignored in Paul's last visit to Jerusalem in 21:17-26 and only reported in reflection as Paul defends his Gospel before Felix in 24:17.

Further, the difficulty of trying to harmonize Paul's visit to Jerusalem with Galatians 2:1-10 is well known among scholars. Is it the same as the visit in Acts 15:2-4? If so, why does Paul not mention the decree of the council in Jerusalem (Acts 15:23-29)? Surely this would have strengthened Paul's argument to the Galatians? Because of the silence about the council decision in Acts 15, some scholars believe that the events of Gal. 2:1-10 occurred before the Acts 15 meeting concluding that Paul wrote the letter to the Galatians to the churches in the south of Galatia that Paul and Barnabas established on the first missionary journey (Acts 13-14). Others conclude that the two visits (Gal. 2:1-10 and Acts 15:2-35) are the same and that Paul wrote his letter to the churches of north Galatia. (See the Introduction to Galatians.) It is probably true that the Acts 15 council and its decree regarding Gentiles had not been produced when Paul had his encounters with the Judaizers at Antioch since it would have strengthened his argument in Gal. 2:11-14 had he referred to it.

11:30. Sending it to the elders. This is the first reference to the "elders" in Acts, and Luke gives no clear understanding of who they are nor how they are to be distinguished from the Seven of Acts 6:3-6. Before this text, Luke uses the term only of the elders of Israel, that is, the Jewish leaders. He uses the term *presbuteroi* in 4:5, 8, 23; 6:12; 23:14; 24:1; and 25:15 to refer to authority figures in the Jewish community. In this passage, Luke introduces the term for the first time to refer to those in leadership in the Christian community. It is found again in this sense in 14:23; 15:2, 4, 6, 22-23; 16:4; 20:17; and 21:18. In Acts 15, they, along with the apostles, make important decisions for the church. The term refers to Christian leaders also in 1 Tim. 5:1, 2, 17, 19; Titus 1:5; James 5:14; 1 Peter 5:1, 5; 2 John 1; and 3 John 1. The term is found in the late first century in *1 Clement* 57.1 and in the early second century in Ignatius, *Ephesians* 2.2; 4.1; *Magnesians* 2:1; 3:1; Polycarp, *Philippians* 6.1.

11:30. Barnabas and Saul. Luke initially gives the first reference to Barnabas in this ministry team, but eventually gives it to Saul/Paul. Barnabas is listed first in four passages—11:30; 12:25; 13:1, 2, 7; 14:14; and 15:12, 25, but Paul is mentioned in first place beginning in 13:43, 46, 50; 14:20; and 15:2, 22, 35. It appears that Luke has balanced the number of times each is listed first, but clearly Paul emerges in first place as the mission work is carried out. For a discussion of the name Saul and Paul, see above in 7:58, 8:1 and later in 13:9 where Luke begins to use the name Paul.

V. 12:1-23. INTERLUDE: PERSECUTION OF THE CHURCH AND GOD'S JUDGMENT

12:1-19. Peter's Deliverance
As noted above in 11:19-30, this verse appears

to be part of the supposed Antiochene tradition passages. Indeed, if verse 25 were added to 11:30, and if the reader immediately went to 13:1, then the flow of the book would be much smoother. These passages seem to fit together well, and it seems obvious that Luke is using several sources to piece together his story of the development of the church and its mission. In chapter 12:1-24, Luke inserts an important piece of tradition into his narrative that explains the death of James the apostle, the persecution of the church, and the imprisonment of Peter, and finally the death of Herod Agrippa I, the grandson of Herod the Great, who was born in 10 B.C. and died A.D. 44 on the occasion described in this story.

12.1-5. The Persecution of Christians
12:1. About that time. Presumably this refers to the previous verse, that is, sometime during the famine in the land (11:28) before the death of Herod Agrippa (A.D. 44), and near the time of the Feast of Unleavened Bread (the Passover) (v. 3). Passover was celebrated on the 14th of Nisan and then the Feast of Unleavened Bread for the next seven days after Passover (Exod. 12:6-15; Deut. 16:1-14). In time, Passover became the name for all of the days of celebration (cf. Luke 22:1). This reference, "about that time" however, may simply have been a Lukan expression that is quite general (see 11:30 and 12:25).

Laid violent hands upon ... the church. What led to this state-sponsored persecution is not clear, but perhaps it was because of the increasing numbers of the church that came as a result of its evangelistic ministry. It may be that the ministry of Peter in Lydda (9:92-35) and Joppa (9:36-42), where Peter had a significant ministry that attracted many to faith, was the cause of this persecution. J. Schwartz has raised the possibility that a tradition in Judaism that a Ben Stada at Lod who deceived people may actually be a reference to Peter as a "mesit" (Heb. for "beguiler") who deceived many Jews at Lydda and led them astray, see for instance, the injunction against them in 5:27-28 (Richard Bauckham, Ed., *Acts in Its Palestinian Setting*, 391-414). He argues that the Mishnah speaks against those who would deceive others into idolatry and allows witnesses to entrap such a person and stone him.

'He that beguiles others [to idolatry]'— such is a common man that beguiles another common man. If he said to another, 'There is a god in such a place that eats this, drinks that, does good in this way and does harm in that way' — they may not place witnesses in hiding against any that become liable to the death-penalties enjoined in the law save in this case alone. If he spoke so to one only he may reply, 'I have companions that are so minded'; and if the other was crafty and would not speak before them, witnesses may be placed in hiding behind a wall. Then he says to the other, 'Say [again] what thou didst say to me in private,' and the other speaks to him [as before] and he replies, 'How shall we leave our God that is in heaven and go and worship wood and stone?' If he retracted it shall be well with him, but if he said, 'It is our duty and it is seemly so to do,' they that are behind the wall bring him to the court and stone him (*m. Sanh.* 7:10, Danby trans.).

In the Tosephta (*t. Sanh.* 10.11, Neusner trans.), when this is explained, the name of a person accused of such beguiling is mentioned. A certain Ben Stada was entrapped and arrested in Lydda for his theological crimes and was later executed. After witnesses appeared who had entrapped him, we read: "and they listen to what he says. And so did they to Ben Stada in Lod [Lydda]. They appointed against him two sages [and in consequence of what they heard and saw] they stoned him." Whatever the case in this matter, as the church was growing in size and influence, opposition to it was mounting. With the inclusion of Gentiles in the community of believers, opposition outside the church could have grown just as it did inside the church (11:1-18; 15:1-5).

The Church. Luke uses different terms in Acts to speak of the church, including the "the Way" (Acts 9:2; 19:9, 23; 22:4; 24:14, 22), which may have come from Jesus' reference to himself (John 14:6), but more likely it suggests that the early followers of Jesus thought of themselves as a community of those who had found their way to God or were on the way to God through Jesus Christ. Another term found in Acts is "Christian" (see discussion in 11:26 above).

In this passage, we find Luke's most commonly used designation for the Christians, "assembly" or "gathering" that is translated "church" in the English Bibles. The term is neutral and means "assembly" or "gathering" which is sometimes qualified as the "assembly" or "gathering" of God. Luke uses it frequently throughout his treatise (5:11; 8:1, 3; 9:31; 11:22, 26; 12:1, 5; 13:1; 14:23, 27; 15:3-4, 22; 18:22; 20:17, 28; for the plural, see 15:41; 16:5). The grecized (or transliterated) form of the word is still used in Latin or southern European countries, for example, in French, Italian, Spanish, and Portuguese churches. Sometimes Luke calls the followers of Jesus "believers" or "those believing" (2:44; 4:32; 10:43, 45; 11:21; 18:27; 19:18).

The word "church" is a later term, however, and it begins to appear in Christian communities around the late second and early third centuries, but it did not catch on in all Christian communities. It is a grecized term of the Greek word *kuriakon*, the root word for the English "church" (or Scottish "kirk"), and the German *Kirche* is more widely used in northern European countries. The basic form of the word is *kurios*, or "Lord," the title given to Jesus by the church. The last three letters of *kuriakon* indicate possession in the Greek and therefore the term refers to "those who belong to the Lord." *Kuriakon* is not found in the New Testament, but its derivative, "church," has been used in English and German translations of the New Testament for the Greek term *ecclesia*. On one occasion in the New Testament (James 2:2), the Greek term, *synagoge* (synagogue) is used to refer to the Christian community. Both *synagoge* and *ecclesia* mean much the same thing. Perhaps Christians chose *ecclesia* in order to distinguish themselves from the Jews. It is also possible that the term *kuriakon* came to be used by the church in order to make clearer who its members were: namely, those who belonged to the Lord, although this is uncertain.

12:2. Killed by the sword. The story of James' death is clearly abbreviated and serves only to introduce why Peter was also arrested and imprisoned. A longer version of the story is found in Clement of Alexandria (ca. 170) who preserves in his sixth book (now lost except for some fragments) of his *Hypotyposes* a few more details about the death of James. There we read in the fourth part that after the ascension of the Savior, Peter and James and John "though pre-eminently honoured by the Lord, did not contend for glory, but made James the Just, bishop of Jerusalem" (ANF Trans). Eusebius preserves an additional tradition about the death of James also found in Clement's *Hypotyposes*.

> Concerning this James, Clement adds in the seventh book of the *Hypotyposes* [now lost except in fragmentary form] a story worth mentioning, apparently from the tradition of his predecessors, to the effect that he who brought him to the court was so moved at seeing him testify as to confess that he also was himself a Christian. "So they were both led away together" he says, "and on the way he asked for forgiveness for himself from James. And James looked at him for a moment and said, 'Peace be to you,' and kissed him. So both were beheaded at the same time" (*HE* 2.9.2-3, LCL).

What should be made of this tradition is not clear since it serves the apologetic of the early church, but if James had some leadership role in the church this may account for his earlier death, that is, why he was executed first and not Peter.

Of more interest is the manner of death described here. "By the sword" normally refers to beheading and so Eusebius above takes it. This form of death, according to the Mishnah, was preserved for the worst of criminals. "The ordinance of them that are to be beheaded [is this]: they used to cut off his head with a sword as the government [the Romans] does. R. Judah says: This is shameful for him; but rather, they lay his head on a block and cut it off with an axe. They said to him: There is no death more shameful than this" (*m. Sanh.* 7.3, Danby trans.). Later in the same Tractate, the apostate is also added to this list. "And these are they that are to be beheaded: the murderer and the people of an Apostate City" (*m. Sanh.* 9.1, Danby trans.). This may be an interpretation of the penalty imposed for those who turned others away from the Lord to worship pagan deities (Deut. 13:12-15).

12:3. Pleased the Jews. What Herod Agrippa did on this occasion was well received by "the Jews," probably a reference to the Pharisees with whom Agrippa had a special relationship (Josephus, *Ant.* 19.292-316). More importantly, in Acts from this point forward, "Jews" tends to be those who are hostile to the Gospel, as is the case in Luke.

It is interesting that when James was executed, there was no call to fill his position as we find in 1:15-26 when Judas was replaced. It could be, as Barrett suggests, that the early church distinguished between treachery and martyrdom (*Acts*, 569).

12:7-10. Suddenly an angel of the Lord . . . tapped Peter, chains fell off . . . the iron gate . . . opened. Somewhat like Peter's experience on the rooftop in 10:9-16, in the sense of an angel coming to Peter during his sleep and waking him. The same thing happens here, but this time the angel "tapped" Peter to wake him. This story fits the pattern of several other stories and may be a popular genre of being awakened by a divine or remarkable being used by Luke to describe Peter's escape from prison. For example, Homer tells of the horseman Nestor who came to Odysseus "and woke him, stirring him with a touch of his heel, and roused him, and chid[e] him to his face. . . " (*Iliad* 10.157-59, LCL). Again, Euripides tells of "the fetters from their feet self-sundered fell; Doors, without mortal hand, unbarred themselves" (*Bacchae* 447-48, LCL). In Ovid's writings, he tells of the escape of Tyrrhenian from jail. After being dragged and placed in a dungeon, he says that "while the slaves were getting the cruel instruments of torture ready, the iron, the fire—of their own accord the doors flew open wide; of their own accord, with no one loosing them, the chains fell from the prisoner's arms" (Ovid, *Metamorphoses* 3.695-700, LCL. See also Homer's *Iliad* 24.88).

12:12. Mary, the mother of John whose other name was Mark. Luke tells says nothing more about this woman except that the Christians were gathered in her house and that John "whose other name is Mark" is her son. Is this the same Mary in Mark 15:40? For a discussion of John Mark, see below in 12:25; 13:5, 13; 15:37-39. Marcus was a very common name in the ancient world and there are a number of references to Mark in the New Testament, but they may not all be speaking of the same person. If this is the same John also called Mark as we see in the other references in Acts, Mark or John Mark was a resident of Jerusalem and may also be the cousin of Barnabas (Col. 4:10). This may explain why Barnabas wanted to reinstate him in ministry following his early departure for Barnabas' and Paul's first mission (Acts 13:5, 13; cf. 15:37-39). Mark was evidently reconciled to

Paul and had a significant impact in early Christianity (2 Tim. 4:11, Phile. 24, and 1 Peter 5:13). Eusebius brings these texts together and says that Mark "was Peter's follower" and after Peter's death those who had heard Peter "besought Mark, whose Gospel is extant, seeing that he was Peter's follower, to leave them a written statement of the teaching given them verbally, nor did they cease until they had persuaded him, and so became the cause of the Scripture called the Gospel according to Mark" and that Peter "ratified the scripture for study in the churches" (*Ecclesiastical History* 2.151-2). He also indicates that this same Mark is mentioned in Peter's first epistle that Peter composed in Rome that he referred to metaphorically as Babylon and then Eusebius cites 1 Peter 5:13. He further notes that this same Mark "was the first to be sent to preach in Egypt the Gospel which he had also put into writing, and was the first to establish churches in Alexandria itself" (*Ecclesiastical History* 2.16.1). Eusebius also claims that "in the eighth year after the reign of Nero Annianus was the first after Mark the Evangelist to receive charge of the diocese of Alexandria" (*Ecclesiastical History* 2.24).

12:17. Tell this to James. This is James, the brother of Jesus (Mark 6:3; Matt. 13:55; Acts 1:14; Gal. 1:19, 2:9; 1 Cor. 15:7) and the one to whom the first of the Catholic Epistles is attributed. After Peter left Jerusalem, James took up the leadership role in the church at Jerusalem (15:13-21). Luke introduces him as if everyone knows that James is in a leadership role at this point (see 21:17-18 where James' prominent role is assumed). James' death is mentioned by Josephus who tells of the high priest Ananus, of the school of the Sadducees who "are indeed more heartless than any of the other Jews" who also "convened the judges of the Sanhedrin and brought before them a man named James, the brother of Jesus who was called the Christ, and certain others. He accused them of having transgressed the law and delivered them up to be stoned. Those inhabitants of the city who were strict in observance of the law were offended at this" (*Ant.* 20.199-201, LCL). This same story is retold and expanded in Eusebius (*HE* 2.23.20-24).

12:17b. He left and went to another place. Apart from his place in the council of chapter 15, Peter is not heard of again, but there are other places where he is mentioned in the New Testament (1 Cor. 1:10; 9:5; Gal. 2:11-14). He obviously traveled around to other churches (12:19), and the early church tradition says that he made his way to Rome (1 Peter 5:13; 1 Clement 5.4). Peter's stature in the church is also seen in the number of writings attributed to him in early Christianity. From this point, Luke will shift his focus onto Paul and his missionary activity.

12:19. The guards ... put to death. Common in the ancient world is the responsibility of guards for prisoners (see the *Code of Justinian* 9.4.4).

12:20-23. The Death of Herod Agrippa.
Once again, Luke uses a well-known genre to tell the demise of those who despised God or lived terrible lives. There are many parallels to the kind of death that Agrippa faced in this story, but the most important one is that of Josephus who preserves a similar report: namely, that Agrippa experienced great pain and died very suddenly.

> After the completion of the third year of his reign over the whole of Judaea, Agrippa came to the city of Caesarea, which had previously been called Strato's Tower. Here he celebrated spectacles in honour of Caesar, knowing that these had been instituted as a kind of festival on behalf of Caesar's well-being. For this occasion there were gathered a large number of men who held office or had advanced to some rank in the kingdom. On the second day of the specta-

cles, clad in a garment woven completely of silver so that its texture was indeed wondrous, he entered the theatre at daybreak. There the silver, illumined the touch of the first rays of the sun, was wondrously radiant and by its glitter inspired fear and awe in those who gazed intently upon it. Straightway his flatterers raised their voices from various directions —though hardly for his good—addressing him as a god ... The king did not rebuke them nor did he reject their flattery as impious. But shortly thereafter he looked up and saw an owl perched on a rope over his head. At once, recognizing this as a harbinger of woes just as it had once been of good tidings [see *Ant.* 18.195], he felt a stab of pain in his heart. He was also gripped in his stomach by an ache that he felt everywhere at once and that was intense from the start .... Exhausted after five straight days by the pain in his abdomen, he departed this life in the fifty-fourth year of his life and the seventy years of his reign (*Ant.* 19. 343-50, LCL; cf. also *War* 2.219).

For other examples of someone dying a painful death see 2 *Macc.* 9.5-28 (noted above in 1:18-20 and paralleled in Josephus, *Ant.* 17.169), but also the story of Herod the Great's death in Josephus' writings (*War* 1.656-58; cf. *Ant.* 17.169-170). Finally, Lucian tells the story of the demise of a false prophet by the name of Alexander. "In spite of his prediction in an oracle that he was fated to live a hundred and fifty years and then die by a stroke of lightning, he met a most wretched end before reaching the age of seventy, in a manner that befitted a son of Podaleirus; for his leg became mortified quite to the groin and was infested with maggots. It was then that his baldness was detected when because of the pain he let the doctors foment his head, which they could not have done unless his wig had been removed"

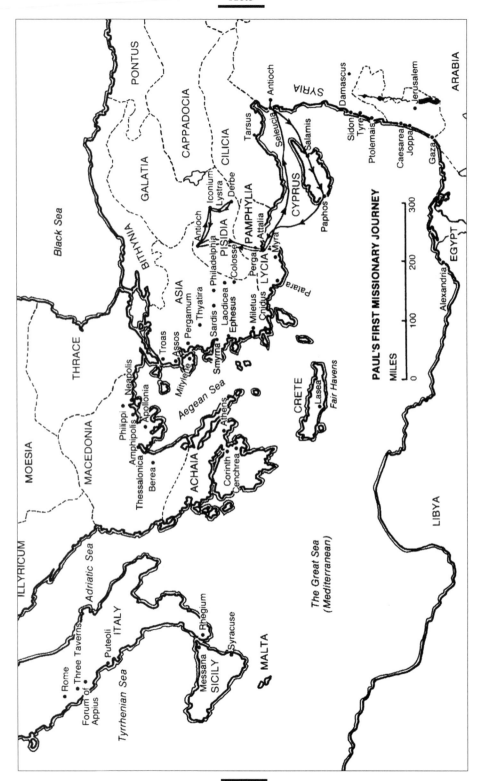

PAUL'S FIRST MISSIONARY JOURNEY

MILES

0   100   200   300

(Lucian, *Alexander the False Prophet* 59, LCL). Besides these examples, see Pausanias, *Description of Greece (Boeotia)* 9.7.2-3, which tells the pitiful end of Thebes Cassander and his sons; and also Herodotus, *History* 4.205.

VI. 12:24–15:35. SPREAD OF THE GOSPEL TO GENTILES—TRIUMPH AND CONFLICT

12:24. The Word of God continued to advance. This is another of Luke's typical summary passages that is inserted here as elsewhere to remind the reader of the purpose of his volume (see 6:7).

12:25. After completing their mission ... Jerusalem. This verse brings the story back to the so-called Antiochene source, which begins with the story of Stephen and persecution or scattering of the Hellenistic Christians in Jerusalem. It also prepares the reader for the first missionary journey of Barnabas and Paul (and with them, John Mark) to Antioch (13:1). There is a problem with the text, however, since it has Barnabas and Saul returning to Jerusalem when, following 11:30, they had not yet left. Their mission was to Jerusalem and upon completing it they would logically have returned to Antioch which is the opening scene in the next passage. There are several textual variants of this passage, but most of them have Barnabas and Saul returning "from" (using the Greek words *ex* or *apo*) Jerusalem instead of "to" (using the Greek *eis*). Most scholars agree that the best textual evidence is the latter which is also the most difficult contextually and geographically to reconcile. Fitzmyer rightly holds that the best solution that also fits the context connects the preposition with the participle (Greek = *plerosantes*) and translates the passage: "And Barnabas and Saul, having completed their mission in Jerusalem, returned ..." Whether this is correct or not, it makes the best sense of the passage.

13:1–14:28. The Missionary Activity of Barnabas and Paul

The beginning and end of this missionary "journey" is Antioch of Syria. While Jerusalem remains the "theological center" of the church for Luke, as Conzelmann calls it, Antioch is the "historical" center of the missionary activity among Gentiles in early Christianity (*Acts* 98).

13:1-3. The Commissioning of Barnabas and Saul/Paul. The geographical context for the launching of this mission is Antioch; the spiritual context is that of prayer, fasting, and worship. Ulitmately, though, Luke stresses here that the context of the mission's beginning is that of the the the Holy Spirit's prompting (13:2, 4).

13:1. Prophets and teachers. While Luke has already introduced a church governed by apostles and whose daily ministries are overseen by the Seven (6:1-7), and later he introduced the activity of the elders in the ministry of the Jerusalem church (11:30), the leadership of the church at Antioch was held by "prophets and teachers." Since the role of the elders plays a significant role in Luke's understanding of the church (11:30; 14:23; 15:2, 6, 22-23; 16:4; 20:17; 21:18; cf. also how the term "elder" [Greek = *presbuteros*] may be interchanged with "bishop" [Greek = *episkopos*] in 20:28), it may seem strange that he does not introduce that view here. This suggests first that all churches were not similarly organized in the first century, but more than that, it also indicates that Luke did not create a different structure in the church than the one he had received from his source(s). Earlier he introduced to his readers the fact that the gift of prophecy would be a part of the community of the faithful in the "last days" (2:17-18) and the traveling prophets were introduced earlier (11:27-28), but now he introduces their role in the leadership of the church and along with them, the role of the teachers. For the first and only time he adds to the prophets the role of the "teachers" (*didaska-*

los). It may be that since this passage begins the primary Lukan focus on Paul, that Paul is the primary source behind much of the material that Luke presents here. It may also be worth noting that Paul emphasizes that in the church there were first apostles, then prophets and teachers (1 Cor. 12:28-29; cf. Rom. 12:7). In Eph. 4:11, prophets and teachers are among the most important gifts given to the church. In terms of the heavy responsibilities of teachers, see James 3:1. The *Didache* (ca. A.D. 80–90) does not clearly distinguish between these roles, and the qualifications for receiving both are apparently the same (chaps. 11, 12, 13). We will see later that as they were sent out by the leaders of the church in Antioch that they were recognized as "apostles" (14:4, 14; cf. notes on 1:13 and 6:2).

Barnabas . . . Saul. The list of those who were prophets and teachers is not divided into those who were prophets and those who were teachers, but the names begin with Barnabas and end with Saul. What was intended by this arrangement is not clear. There is very little that can be said with assurance about any of the individuals in between Barnabas and Saul, but it is worth noting that Manaen (in Hebrew the name is Menahem) was listed as a "member of the court of Herod the ruler [tetrarch, = *tetraarchou*]." This description refers to Manaen's special relationship with Herod Antipas, the king who ruled from Sepphoris in the time of Jesus. There is a tradition told by Josephus that before Herod the Great came to power, he was greeted by a certain Manaemus, an Essene, who predicted that Herod would become the King of the Jews. He reports that

> At the moment Herod paid very little attention to his words, for he was quite lacking in such hopes, but after gradually being advanced to kingship and good fortune, when he was at the height of his power, he sent for Manaemus and questioned him about the length of time he would reign. . . . And from that time on he continued to hold all Essenes in

honour (*Ant.* 15.377-378, LCL).

Scholars have speculated that perhaps Herod the Great adopted this young man as a companion for his son Antipas who later became the Tetrarch of Galilee. This fits with the other term to describe Manaen in 13:1: namely, that he was "brought up" (Greek = *suntrophos*) with Herod the Tetrarch. The word generally refers to a title of honor bestowed on certain youths who were brought up as companions to the princes. The term is used as a child adopted as a playmate for another child in Herodotus, *Persian Wars* 1:99. Lucian tells in his story of Nigrinus what was good about the philosophy and philosophers of Athens and Greece: "the talk began with praise of Greece and of the men of Athens, because Philosophy and Poverty have ever been their foster-brothers [*suntrophoi eisin*], and they do not look with pleasure on any man, be he citizen or stranger, who strives to introduce luxury among them" (*Nigrinus* 12, cf. also 15). An inscription with this term (*suntrophos*) was found on a gravestone with the following tribute:

> In the year 181, month Apellaios, the 12th. Appios, son of Menander and Meltine, honoured their son Apollonios. Charmos, Appion, and Asklepiades his brothers, and Apollonios his brother-in-law together with his wife, his (the deceased Apollonios') mother-in-law, his foster-sister [Greek = *suntrophos*] Tryphosa and her husband Theophilos, the holy association, and his brotherhood honoured him with gold crowns (*SEG* 893; *TAM* 5.1 (1981) 470a. ND 3: 37 with additional samples on 38-39).

Whatever his past, Manaen became a prophet or teacher in the church at Antioch and Luke claims that he was a companion (*suntrophos*) of Herod Antipas.

13:2. Fasting. In Acts, apart from a reference to "the Fast" (a reference to the Day of Atonement, see 27:9), fasting is only found here (v. 2-3) and in 14:23 when Paul and Barnabas appointed elders in the churches. Normally Luke speaks of Christians eating when they gather (e.g., 2:42, 46; 9:19; 10:10). In the Old Testament, fasting is normally accompanied with mourning, as in the loss of a family member (2 Sam. 1:12; 3:35) or in preparation for war (1 Sam. 14:24) and preparation for the Day of Atonement (Lev. 16:29). Fasting was more common in Judaism in the time of Jesus, and following the resurrection of Jesus, it was more common in the church (Matt. 6:16-18).

13:3. Laying on of hands. Along with the fasting and prayers, the prophets and teachers place hands on Barnabas and Saul and sent them away on their mission. This is not the time when Paul becomes an apostle, since he claims that he knew his call from God earlier (Gal. 1:15-17), but rather a time of prayer both of blessing and for power to do the work which these men were sent to accomplish. It is not so much an ordination like what developed in later times, but may well have anticipated it. Since they returned to Antioch and reported what had happened during their mission (14:26-28), it is likely that what took place was something like a commissioning service on the part of the church. It is likely to be more than a simple blessing, but something less than what later became an ordination to ministry. See elsewhere in Acts where the laying on of hands took place (6:6; 8:18; 9:12, 17; 14:23; 19:6; 28:8).

13:4-12. Cyprus. As Barnabas and Paul, accompanied by Mark, set out on their first journey, it is in the power of the Holy Spirit (13:4), and they depart for Cyprus, the homeland of Barnabas (4:36) taking John Mark with them. They departed for Cyprus through Seleucia, the port city 16-20 km. northwest from Antioch on the Orontes River; this was the capital of the province of Syria. The port city was founded in 300 B.C. by Seleucus I Nicanor. In each of the places they stop, beginning with Salamis (v. 5),

they take their witness "to the Jew first" (Rom. 1:16), by going to the synagogue first. Paul went to the synagogues in Antioch of Pisidia (13:14), Iconium (14:1), Philippi (16:13), Thessalonica (17:1-2), Beroea (17:10), Athens (17:17), Corinth (18:4-6), and Ephesus (18:19; 19:8). Josephus indicates that there were many Jewish people living in Cyprus brought there as slaves under Cleopatra's rule. He indicates that in the days of Queen Cleopatra of Egypt, "not only were the Jews in Jerusalem and in the country (of Judaea) in a flourishing condition, but also those who lived in Alexandria and in Egypt and Cyprus" (*Ant.* 13.284, LCL; see also 285-86). Philo also, in his *Embassy to Gaius,* argues that Jerusalem is the mother city of Jews not only in Judaea, but also by the colonies of Jews sent out from their homeland. He claims that "not only are the mainlands full of Jewish colonies but also the most highly esteemed of the islands Euboea, Cyprus, Crete" (*Ant.* 13.282, LCL). Salamis was the first capital of the island during the reign of the Ptolemies, but Paphos replaced it as the provincial capital during the time of Roman rule. There was evidently little or no response to their preaching in Salamis, and so they departed westward to the other side of the island and arrived in Paphos.

At Paphos they met two important individuals: A Jewish false prophet named Bar-Jesus (son of Jesus) (v. 7) also called Elymas (v. 8) who was a magician, and the proconsul of the province named Sergius Paulus, "an intelligent man" who wanted to hear the "word of God" (v. 7). The former tried to hinder the latter from hearing Barnabas and Saul, and as a result, Saul, now identified as Paul (v.9), condemns him for his actions and tells him that he would be smitten with blindness and so it happened (v. 11). The result of this was that Sergius Paulus "believed" because of his amazement over hearing the teaching about the Lord (v. 12). The proconsul was Paul's first recorded convert on his first missionary tour.

13:6, 8. Bar-Jesus/Elymas. It is strange that Luke would employ two different names for the same person. Scholars have long debated this matter. There are several possibilities, but what seems likely is that the name Bar-Jesus was this man's Hebrew name and he was known by that name among his fellow Jews, but the other is an Arabic name and used elsewhere. It is possible that the second name refers to his profession, that is, a magician since there is some similarity, but the passage is still a bit of a puzzle. It is unusual for Luke to use an Arabic name rather than a Greek second name as in the case of Simon Peter, but it may be that the man also had roots in a land where Arabic was spoken such as Philistia. The evidence is not clear, however, and other possibilities may prevail.

13:7. Sergius Paulus. There are three ancient inscriptions that have this name, or a portion of it, and they may refer to the same proconsul mentioned in Acts 13, but certainty cannot be assured. The first inscription identified as *IGR* (*Inscriptiones graecae ad res romanas pertinentes*) III.930, was found on the northern coast of Cyprus at Soloi and refers to a proconsul named Paulus who held office in the tenth year of the emperor, but the *nomen* and *praenomen* are missing. If the emperor refers to Claudius, who began in the year 40, then the date would be A.D. 50, but that is too late for Paul's first journey to Cyprus. The second inscription, identified as *IGR* III. 935, found in northern Cyprus at Kytheria dates sometime in the first century and has been deciphered on line 11 as "Quintus Sergius," but it is difficult to be certain about the identity of this person. More promising is the third Tiber Inscription, identified as *CIL* (or *Corpus inscriptionum latinarum*) 6. 31543. It is a fragment of a boundary stone that was largely intact and was one of several boundary stones used to mark the banks of the Tiber River. The translation of this marker is as follows:

Paullus Fabius Persicus

Gaius Eggius Marullus
Lucius Sergius Paullus
Gaius Obellius Rufus
Lucius Scribonius Libo (?)
custodians of the river banks
and of the bed of the Tiber
in accordance with the authority
of Tiberius Claudius Caesar
Augustus Germanicus
their princeps [Latin perhaps = principis s[en(atus)] = "leader of the senate"]
by placing boundary stones
marked out the bank from the ninth region
to the bridge of Agrippa
(Translation furnished in Nobbs: "Cyprus," *Book of Acts*, 2:285.)

The third line refers all three names of a certain Lucius Sergius Paullus, and this may well be a reference to the same person who was of senatorial rank and in a different role prior to the time of his proconsulship in Cyprus. According to Dio Cassius (57.14.8), Tiberius established a commission of five individuals to check the flooding of the Tiber River. It is possible that Acts 13 refers to the same person. Just as interesting is the report that a person by the same name, L. Sergius Paullus, erected a monument to his father by the same name in Pisidian Antioch (Antioch of Pisidia). His daughter Sergia Paulla was the wife of C. Caristanius Fronto, legate of Lycia and Pamphilia under Domitian near the end of the first century, and their son built a monument to his parents also in Pisidian Antioch. It is perhaps no accident that Paul's next mission stop was in Pisidian Antioch! (Nobbs, "Cyprus" 2:286-87). R. A. Kearsley suggests that Barnabas' and Paul's journey to Pisidian Antioch may have been due to their meeting with Sergius Paullus, the Roman proconsul in Cyprus whose family owned an estate near Antioch (*New Documents*, 7:240-41). It is quite possible that this Paullus provided a letter of recommendation for Barnabas and Paul and their companions, that introduced them to the social network of which Paullus was himself a senior member, though now geographically removed. While nothing here is certain, the parallels are suggestive.

13:9. Saul also known as Paul. Saul (Greek = *Saulos*) was Paul's *supernomen* and Paul (Greek = *Paulos*) was his Roman *cognomen*. While Paul was working primarily around Jews, his *supernomen*, Saul, taken from his namesake (King Saul; see Phil. 3:5) was more appropriate, but when he was among Gentiles, his Roman name was more appropriate. As a Roman citizen, Paul would have had three names. He did not receive this name after he began his ministry, but rather he probably had it from the beginning of his life and used it more in his Gentile relationships. It is the name that Paul uses in all of his letters, but he may have begun the use of this name more regularly during his Gentile mission.

13:13-51. Antioch of Pisidia

13:13. John returned to Jerusalem. John is also known as Mark and the cousin of Barnabas (see notes on 12:12 above and also 12:25; 13:5; 15:37-39). This is the same Mark to whom the Gospel of Mark is attributed. In the fourth century, Eusebius writes about him: "Secondly, that [Gospel] according to Mark, who wrote it in accordance with Peter's instructions whom also Peter acknowledged as his son in the catholic epistle [1 Peter 5:13], speaking in these terms: 'She that is in Babylon, elect together with you, saluteth you; and so doth Mark my son'" (*Ecclesiastical History* 6.25.5, LCL).

13:14. They . . . came to Antioch in Pisidia. Although Paul and Barnabas traveled through Perga and Pamphilia, Luke says nothing about any ministry they may have had there except on their journey back to Antioch of Syria (14:25). It appears that their primary mission was to visit Antioch of Pisidia and perhaps as a

result of letters of introduction from Sergius Paullus or because of his recommendation, since that apparently was his home (see notes on 13:4-12 above). The city of Antioch was located in central Asia Minor northeast of Lake Limnai (modern Lake Egirdir) and close to the modern town of Yalvaç in modern Turkey and had a large Jewish population. In the first century it was in the province of Phrygia and yet was close to the province of Pisidia. It was a Roman city and many of the inscriptions found here were in Latin. In population, it may have been close to the size of Ephesus, and it was known for its remarkable temple of Augustus in a large colonnaded square called Tiberia Platea connected to a triple-arched gate. Barnabas and Paul probably came here sometime between A.D. 46 and 47. They faced considerable Jewish opposition in the city as well as in each of the places where they ministered. It may be that Antioch of Pisidia functioned like something of a paradigm for Luke, forming the typical kind of reception that Paul received in Jewish synagogues and the typical Jewish opposition he faced in most of his synagogue visits. This conclusion is supported by Paul's and Barnabas' revisiting of these churches on their return to Antioch "strengthening" the new believers and encouraging them to continue in their new faith (14:21-22). How successful Paul and Barnabas were in their ministry in this area is not known, but from the Byzantine era (fourth century and following) there was a very large church built on the foundation of the synagogue of Antioch of Pisidia. Whether the church died out and was later revived is not known. It is possible that there was a continual presence of the church in that area from the time of Paul's and Barnabas' missionary visit.

What can be said from Acts is that this is Paul's longest speech, and it parallels in some ways the speeches of Peter in chapter 2 and Stephen in chapter 7 in that Paul recounts a portion of the history of Israel in his witness of

Jesus and emphasizes the fulfillment of the Scriptures in Jesus and the activity of God.

13:15. After reading of the Law. . . . The form of worship in synagogues in antiquity, according to the Mishnah, included the regular recitation of the "Shema" (the term comes from the first word in the Hebrew text of Deut. 6:4-6, "hear"), prayers, readings of the Law and then the Prophets. Such services also included a recitation of the *Shemoneh Esreh*, or the Eighteen Benedictions, which was followed by a sermon. Evidently, for the sermon, Paul and Barnabas were invited to speak.

The officials (rulers) of the synagogue. The Mishnah (*m. Sotah* 7.7-8; see also *m. Yoma* 7.1 for a similar reading) speaks about those who oversee the synagogue and refers to them as the "minister of the synagogue" and the "chief" of the synagogue. In this passage it does seem strange, as some scholars have noted, that the rulers or presidents of the synagogue invited a stranger, Paul, to speak, but the invitation may have come as a result of their knowing Paul's credentials to speak (see Phil. 3:4-6). Philo, describing what takes place on the sabbath day, writes:

So each seventh day there stand wide open in every city thousands of schools [synagogues] of good sense, temperance, courage, justice and the other virtues in which the scholars sit in order quietly with ears alert and with full attention, so much do they thirst for the draught which the teacher's words supply, while one of special experience rises and sets forth what is best and sure to be profitable and will make the whole of life grow to something better (Philo, *The Special Laws* 2.62, LCL).

Evidently, Paul was welcomed as a teacher with special experience.

13:16. Israelites and others who fear God. The term that Luke uses here, "god-fearers" (Greek

= *phoboumenoi*), is most likely a specific reference to Gentile converts in the Jewish community (see notes on 10:1-2 above).

13:19. Seven nations in the land of Canaan. See Deut. 7:1 where these nations are identified as the Hittities, Girgashites, Amorites, Canaanites, Perzzites, Hivites, and the Jebusites (compare also Josh. 14:1–19:51). Josephus states that,

Thus did Joshua divide six of the nations that bore the names of the sons of Canaan and gave their land to the nine and a half tribes for their possession; for Amorites, likewise so called after one of the children of Canaan, had already of yore been taken and apportioned by Moses to the two and a half tribes, as we have previously related (*Ant.* 5.88-89, LCL; cf. also 4.166-72).

13:20. About four hundred and fifty years. The numbers in this verse have posed considerable problems for those trying to reconcile them with other biblical passages (compare 1 Kings 6:1 = 480 years). Josephus himself is inconsistent in the amount of time from the departure from Egypt to the building of the temple (*Ant.* 8.61 = 592 years from departure from Egypt to building of the temple; 10:147-48 = 592 years; 11.112-13 = more than 500 years; 20.230 = 612 years; *Against Apion* 2.19 = 612 years). Can this passage be reconciled by adding the 400 years that the Israelites were in Egypt (Acts 7:6), with the forty years that they were in the desert (Num. 14:33-34), and then add the roughly ten years in the years of conquest as Joshua entered Canaan (Josh. 14)? That would appear to solve the problem in Acts, but not solve the variations in the number of years from other texts. Perhaps the best solution is to take Luke's reference to "about" as merely an approximation of time and not the specifics of it.

13:22. I have found David. This quote comes

from a mixture of Ps. 88:21 (LXX) and 1 Sam. 13:14. Luke cited both passages in messianic terms and this was not unusual in that time. There are parallels in the Qumran literature doing the same, that is, uniting texts about David from the Scriptures in terms of messianic expectation. For instance, in the *Florilegium or Midrash on the Last Days* (4Q174) we read:

> The Lord declares to you that he will build you a House (2 Sam. vii, 11c). I will raise up your seed after you (2 Sam. vii,12). I will establish the throne of his kingdom [for ever] (2 Sam. vii,13). [I will] be his father and he shall be my son (2 Sam. vii, 14). He is the Branch of David who shall arise with the Interpreter of the Law [to rule] in Zion [at the end] of time. As it is written, I will raise up the tent of David that is fallen (Amos ix,11). That is to say, the fallen tent of David is he who shall arise to save Israel (1.10-14, Vermes, Trans., p. 494).

13:30. God raised him from the dead. As we have seen already in Acts 2:24-36; 3:15; 4:10; 10:40, here and elsewhere, this message was at the center of early Christian preaching (see also 1 Cor. 15:3-8, 12-20; Rom. 10:9-10).

13:36. Slept. This is an ancient metaphor for death. See 7:60; 1 Kings 2:10.

13:45. When the Jews saw . . . they were filled with jealousy. This opposition is a response that follows Paul and Barnabas in their subsequent stops in their first missionary journey. Significant opposition regularly grows against them and what takes place here becomes a pattern for their ministry.

13:46. It was necessary. It was an important part of Paul's missionary strategy to go first to the Jews and then to the Gentiles (see 14:1; 16:13; 17:1, 10, 17; 18:4, 19; 19:8). Even though he had received a mission to go to Gentiles, he did not neglect the mission to the Jews and saw them as having priority in his preaching (Rom. 1:16; 2:9-10; 3:1-2).

13:50. Devout women of high standing. Josephus describes the fear of the men of Damascus in carrying out their plan to execute Jews because of the leading women, wives, of the city whose influence was considerable who had converted to Judaism: "they considered that the execution of their plan would present no difficulty whatever; their only fear was of their own wives who, with few exceptions, had all become converts to the Jewish religion, and so their efforts were mainly directed to keeping the secret from them" (*War* 2.560-61, LCL).

It appears that some leading women of the city at Antioch had converted to Judaism as well and exerted considerable influence. For reference to the "leading men" of the Jews, see 25:2 and 28:17.

13:51. Shaking the dust. Luke refers to the word of Jesus when the message of the kingdom is rejected (see Luke 9:4-5; 10:10-11; cf. Mark 6:11 and Matt. 10:14). It appears that those who reject the kingdom of God and the message of salvation are themselves rejected. The practice of shaking the dust from one's feet began when Jews entered the land of Israel from foreign countries and also from outside the temple as they entered the temple courtyard. It was originally a Jewish act of purification from Gentile defilement or other impurities as one entered a place that was holy, but that is clearly not in view here. Paul, as a missionary to Gentiles, would hardly have followed that pattern here. The act clearly has symbolic meaning and could indicate that the missionaries have no further responsibility to the city where this was done. They fulfilled their mission to this city, but, of course, this did not prevent them from returning to strengthen the disciples there (see 14:21-23).

14:1-7. Iconium. Iconium is the modern city of Konya that is located some 85-90 miles southeast of Antioch of Pisidia. It was at times identified with Phrygia (Pliny, *Nat. Hist.* 5.245) and sometimes with Lycaonia (Strabo, 12.568 and Pliny *Nat. Hist.* 5.95), but it was politically tied to Galatia in the first century. It was a Roman colony and was situated at an important crossroads in the region on the Via Sebaste, the main route from Antioch of Pisidia to Iconium.

The city became an important center for Christian witness in the first century. As was their custom, Paul and Barnabas entered the synagogue. It was here that the well-known story emerged in the second century about Paul's ministry at Iconium and his contacts with a young woman named Thecla in which we also have preserved the only description of Paul found in early Christianity. It reads in part as follows:

As Paul went up to Iconium after his flight from Antioch, his traveling companions were Demas and Hermogenes the copper-smith, who were full of hypocrisy and flattered Paul as if they loved him. . . . And a man named Onesiphorus, who had heard that Paul was come to Iconium, went out with his children Simmias and Zeno and his wife Lectra to meet Paul, that he might receive him to his house. For Titus had told him what Paul looked like. For (hitherto) he had not seen him in the flesh, but only in the spirit. And he went along the royal road which leads to Lystra, and stood there waiting for him, and looked at (all) who came, according to Titus' description. And he saw Paul coming, a man small of stature, with a bald head and crooked legs, in a good state of body, with eyebrows meeting and nose somewhat hooked, full of friendliness; for now he appeared like a man, and now he had the face of an angel. (*The Acts of Paul and Thecla* 1-3, *NT Apo* 2:239).

14:5, 14. Apostles. These are the only two passages where Luke calls Paul or Barnabas "apostles." he generally reserves that title for the Twelve. Since Luke had no first-hand knowledge of this part of the first mission journey of Paul and Barnabas, he undoubtedly received this information from other sources and utilized it in his account. He did not change the titles for Paul and Barnabas in the received account and this speaks of his faithfulness to his sources. He seems to underscore the necessary qualification for apostleship to be an eyewitness (see 1:21-22; cf. 13:30-32), and distinguishes what Paul and Barnabas were doing from the apostolic role or function, except in these two connected passages.

14:8-20. Lystra. Ancient Lystra was located some twenty-five miles southwest of Iconium (modern Konya) and probably also on the *Via Sebaste* highway, but if not, no more than a day's journey from it and on the junction of two roads from the Isaurian slopes of the Taurus. Under Augustus, the city was made a colony of Rome in A.D. 26 and named "Colonia Julia Felis Gemina Lustra" (*Corpus inscriptionum latinarum* 3.6786). Unlike sister cities, the common language on coins and inscriptions from the time of Paul and Barnabas (roughly the A.D. 40s) was Latin and not Greek. Even the common term to refer to the citizens of this region was the Latin *populus*. The control of the province of Lycaonia fell to Amyntas, king of Galatia, during Roman rule. Following his death, Augustus made the city and province a part of the Roman province of Galatia. The city has not been excavated, but a significant mound exists where it is believed that the ancient city was situated. The city continued for many centuries and was the seat of a Christian bishop well into the fourth century.

14:11. Saying in Lycaonian. While the major

cities of the Greco-Roman world spoke Greek, many smaller communities continued to use their own local dialects and the more popular languages of Greek and Latin were known mostly by the better educated persons of those communities. That seems to be the case in Lystra. Strabo (12.1) claimed that there were peculiar local dialects in this region. Does the fact that the language they spoke was "Lycaonian" mean that Paul and Barnabas needed an interpreter when they were here? Luke does not say.

14:12. Zeus and Hermes. In this region Zeus was also known as Zeus Ampelites and was portrayed on reliefs as an elderly bearded figure who was sometimes portrayed with a young male assistant. Though the city of Lystra was a Roman colony, the gods have Greek names here, but if in the Latin, they would have been Jupiter (Zeus) and Mercury (Hermes). This may be because Luke was writing in Greek. The identification of Barnabas as Zeus and Paul as Hermes is therefore interesting and may be an indicator of the possible looks and age of Barnabas and Paul as well as the fact that Hermes was the messenger of Zeus and spoke his word and so Paul was the primary spokesperson at this time. The Latin poet Ovid (Publius Ovidius Naso, 43 B.C. to A.D. 17) reported the legend that "Jupiter (Zeus) in the guise of a mortal, and with his father came Atlas' grandson (Hermes or Mercury), he that bears caduceus, his wings laid aside" (Ovid, *Metamorphoses* 8.626, LCL). They (Zeus and Hermes) reportedly visited a thousand homes in the area of Phrygia seeking a place for rest and all of them refused them except for one elderly couple named Philemon and Baucis. As a result, only they escaped the anger and judgment of these gods (see Ovid, *Metamorphoses* 8.6.20–7.24). The fear of such calamities befalling the region again made the whole community more hospitable to strangers.

14:14. They tore their clothes. Jews were trained to tear their clothes as an act of response to blasphemy and words against the holy temple in Jerusalem. See Mark 14:63. It may be in response to death (2 Sam. 3:31; 13:31 but also the Apocrypha has other examples such as *Judith* 14.19; *Ep. Jer.* 30; 2 Macc. 4:38) or as a sign of repentance (Joel 2:12-13; Ezra 9:3-5), but also as a ritual response to blasphemy. According to the Mishnah, after a person has been charged with blaspheming, witnesses are to say expressly what the person has said and then rend their clothes. For example: "'Say expressly what thou heardest' and he says it; and the judges stand up on their feet and rend their garments, and they may not mend them again. And the second witness says, 'I also heard the like' and the third says, 'I also heard the like'" (*M. Sanh.* 7.5, Danby trans.).

14:19. Jews from Antioch and Iconium ... stoned Paul. This appears to be the first fulfillment of the prophecy in 9:16 and Paul may refer to this event in 2 Cor. 11:25. These stories of the trials and persecutions were circulated in the churches and were referred to as common information in 2 Tim. 3:10-11: "Now you have observed my teaching, my conduct, my aim in life, my faith, my patience, my love, my steadfastness, my persecutions and suffering the things that happened to me in Antioch, Iconium, and Lystra." What was prophesied in 9:16 began in Paul's visit to this region. Why Jews would come some 100 miles from Pisidian Antioch to Lystra is not clear, but since Colonia Lystra had put a statue in that city, there may have been a special connection between the cities. It is also worth noting that Luke does not mention a stoning of Barnabas. Since he does not have a tradition about any such incident in Barnabas' life, he did not include it, but he did have one available in 2 Cor. 11:25 if, as seems likely, he was aware of it.

14:20-21a. He went on with Barnabas to Derbe.
Derbe was an ancient city of Lycaonia located along the main road that connected to the leading city of the region, Iconium. Like Lystra, it was in the Roman province of Galatia. This was a Hellenized city that later came under Roman control and was added to Cappadocia ca. A.D. 65. Like Lystra, it came under the control of King Amytas of Galatia, but when he died in 26–25 B.C., it passed over to direct Roman control. In the first century it gained a special title, Claudia Derbe, in honor of the Roman emperor that has been found on coins from that region. The name of a bishop Michael was found on a tombstone there in the fourth century, so it is clear that the mission Paul and Barnabas had started continued for some time. The exact location of the ancient city is uncertain, but there is a small and as yet unexcavated mound called Kerti Huyuk near the village of Sudurya and some fifteen miles northeast of Karaman (ancient Laranda) that is the likely location of this ancient village. This region had no paved roads until around A.D. 80 and so Paul and Barnabas traveled this way on a dirt path. Derbe is about 65 miles southeast of Iconium and about 60 miles east of Lystra on an unpaved pathway. The first paved roads in Galatia came under Roman rule around A.D. 80. There is no mention of any persecution of Paul and Barnabas in this place, unlike the three previous stops. From Acts, we see that Derbe was the home of Gaius who ministered with Paul in Ephesus (Acts 19:29) and is mentioned again in 20:4. There were many converts to the Christian faith at Derbe, but little is known about them or the duration of Paul's and Barnabas' ministry there except that he revisited the town at least once more (16:1) and possibly twice (18:23).

14:21b-28. The return to Antioch of Syria.
After the visit to Derbe, Paul and Barnabas returned to the very cities where they had been forced to flee to strengthen their young disciples.

14:23. After they had appointed elders.
Although there was opposition in three of the four places visited, this did not prevent them from returning to strengthen the churches and establish appropriate leadership within the churches. The term used for this appointment (Greek = *ceirotonein*) can refer both to the act of appointing or even to some form of election as in the case of the *Didache* where the writer(s) call on the readers to "Appoint therefore for yourselves [*ceirotonevsate oun heautois*] bishops and deacons worthy of the Lord" (*Did.* 15.1, LCL). Luke appears to intend that these appointments to leadership roles were made by Paul and Barnabas. The kind of organizational structure introduced here seems similar to that in the Titus 1:5. Whatever the kind of leadership put in place, it is obvious that there were leaders in all of the churches established by Paul (see Gal. 6:6; 1 Thess. 5:12-13; Phil. 1:1).

14:27. God opened a door of faith to the Gentiles. This is one of Luke's major themes and at the end of the first journey to proclaim the word to them, Luke emphasizes that God accomplished this ministry (see also 11:28 and 13:47-48).

15:1-35. The First Church Council: Conflict and Resolution
At the halfway mark of this volume, Luke focuses on a pivotal decision that allows him to complete his story of the Gospel going from Jerusalem to Rome with its universal focus including not only the Jews, but also the Gentiles. A critical decision has to be dealt with once and for all before Luke can complete his story. It appears that this might have been done in 11:18 when the church rejoiced that Gentiles were included, but it is revisited when the question of inclusion into the fellowship of the church was also at stake. How could Jewish Christians continue to be Jews and Gentiles become Christians without becoming Jews? Luke shows how this took place with some

compromise on both sides of the issue.

The success of the early Christian mission to the Gentiles also involved some conflict in the churches. To this point, the majority of Christians were Jews and they continued living as Jews, going to synagogues and in Jerusalem to the temple. They kept the various Jewish rituals and customs as well as its laws of purity and circumcision, observance of holy days, and the like. The question that was posed to them by the influx of Gentiles into the Christian community was whether a Gentile also had to become a Jew in order to be a Christian. In other words, was it important that Gentiles also be circumcised and keep the various Jewish laws of ritual purity related to daily living? This question lies at the heart of the earliest conflict between churches in the first century and is the context for a very significant debate in the early church. Luke describes the nature of this conflict and also the way in which the issue was resolved in Jerusalem by the leaders of the churches. It not only included the way of salvation for Gentiles, but also scope of fellowship in the church: namely, whether Jews and Gentile Christians could also have fellowship with each other. Luke has already introduced this conflict to some extent in 11:18 and resolved that the matter was settled to some extent when Gentiles were admitted into the church. Evidently, the conclusions drawn then were not conclusive for the whole church, and so the matter is revisited here.

The timing of the council meeting in Jerusalem that decided the issue of Gentile freedom from the Law is problematic in that it is difficult to harmonize this decision with Paul's description of a similar event in Galatians 2. Was the meeting that Paul described in that passage the same as the one Luke describes here? Was it a private meeting that was followed by a more open meeting later? If one takes an early dating of the letter to the Galatians: namely, around A.D. 47 or 48,

and if the Jerusalem meeting of Acts 15 was held ca. 48-49, certain difficulties are resolved. For instance, the "private" meeting in Galatians (2:1-2) came before the public one in Acts 15. Many scholars contend that the meeting in Galatians 2:1-10 is the same as the more public meeting listed in Acts 15 and that Luke probably has conveyed the more complete details of the meeting that was mentioned by Paul. The difficulty of bringing these two passages together is well known, and it is made especially difficult because there is no reference to a council decision by the apostles and the elders in the Galatian letter or in any of Paul's letters. Paul does speak about a decision not to impose circumcision on Titus (Gal. 2:3) and that his Gospel to the Gentiles was accepted, but this does not sound like an open meeting among apostles and elders and the church (15:12, 22), but rather a private meeting (Gal. 2:2).

This is important since, if the issue had already been settled when Paul was debating the matter in the Antioch church, and if a decision by the council had already been conveyed to the churches, it would have strengthened Paul's argument considerably with the Galatian Christians. On other occasions he speaks of his unity with the apostles in terms of his Gospel (1 Cor. 15:3-8), and if such a public meeting had taken place earlier, it is strange that Paul did not refer to it. If the "council" had taken place by the time of the conflict in Gal. 2:11-14, why did Paul not refer to it? It is also odd that such an activity as withdrawing from table fellowship with Gentiles in Gal. 2:11-14 could have taken place after the action agreed upon in Acts 15:22-29 had been circulated among the churches. Again, it is difficult to place the events of Gal. 2:1-14 into the chronology of Acts, whether at 9:30; 11:28-30; 15:1-5 or afterward, but it seems that it had not taken place when Paul wrote Galatians. It is more likely that his reference to a meeting with the "pillars" of the church (Gal. 2:1-10) was indeed a private one and only later was it deemed necessary for Paul and Barnabas to return to Jerusalem to argue their case for Gentile freedom from the law and circumcision. This attempt to address the matter more formally in the church came at the request of the Christians in Antioch.

The church "council" of Acts 15 was not a council as such if by that term is meant the type of church councils that emerged near the end of the fourth century. This gathering of the leaders of the church, however, became an important model for church councils in the fourth century and later. The influence of this "council" of church leaders in its position on the inclusion of Gentiles, their freedom from circumcision, and keeping the Mosaic laws, was settled and never revisited in the churches. As such, this meeting became an important model for later churches in dealing with conflict (Fitzmyer 543).

15:2. Paul and Barnabas. Note the sequence of names (cf. also 13:42). Initially it was Barnabas and Saul/Paul (13:2, 7). Paul becomes the spokesperson for the missionary team in 13:9, 13, and thereafter Luke refers to them as Paul and Barnabas (13:42, 46, 50; 14:1, even in 14:11-12; 15:2, 35-36). A return to the original sequence comes in 14:14; 15:12, 25, passages that some scholars believe come from Luke's use of an Antiochene source. See discussion of 14:4, 14 above.

15:3. Phoenicia. See notes on 11:19. **Samaria.** This name refers to that region north of Judea and south of Galilee. This name referred to both the name of a district (1:8) and also the name of a town (see 8:5). The city has ancient roots from OT times and was destroyed, but rebuilt by Herod the Great who renamed the city Sebaste (= "the august" city) after Caesar Augustus. Samaria was visited by Jesus and many believed on him (John 4:4-42) and subsequently by Philip the Evangelist (8:4-25).

15:4. Apostles and Elders. See offices mentioned in 11:30 and 13:1.

15:5. The party of the Pharisees. According to 5:17, 34, there were many Pharisees who became Christians. They apparently were both committed to following Jesus and also to maintaining their religious traditions that included especially the practice of circumcision and the keeping of the laws and customs of Moses. These may be those who visited Antioch and brought division among the Christians there (15:1; see also Gal. 2:11-12). They insisted that Gentile converts must also become Jewish proselytes in order to receive salvation from God.

15:10. Putting God to the test. The idea of putting God to the test comes from the OT (Exod. 15:22-27; 17:2, 7; Num. 14:22; Isa. 7:12; Ps. 77:18, 41, 56; Wisd. 1:2). This likely means approaching God in a spirit of unbelief or mistrust. In the context, Peter says that those who impose regulations that God has not imposed on Gentiles put God to the test. The consequences of such behavior were always undesirable.

Yoke of the Law. Jews saw this "yoke" as a blessing from God that symbolized their duty to God (Exod. 19:5; 34:10). This yoke was not seen by the Jews as a burden, but a blessing. See, for instance, Rabbi Nehunya ben Ha-Kanh who wrote: "He that takes upon himself the yoke of the Law, from him shall be taken the yoke of the kingdom and the yoke of worldly care; but he that throws off the yoke of the Law, upon him shall be laid the yoke of the kingdom and the yoke of worldly care" (m. Aboth 3.5). The yoke of the Law was not seen by him and his contemporaries as a burden to bear. Writing later in the first century, Josephus says after noting how others abandon the yoke of their laws, claims:

From these laws of ours nothing has had power to deflect us, neither fear of our masters, nor envy of the institutions esteemed by other nations. We have trained our courage, not with a view to waging war for self-agrandizement [sic], but in order to preserve our laws . . . Nowadays, indeed, violation of the laws has with most nations become a fine art. Not with us. Robbed though we may be of wealth, of cities, of all good things, our Law at least remains immortal; and there is not a Jew so distant from his country, so much in awe of a cruel despot, but has more fear of the Law than of him. If then our attachment to our laws is due to their excellence, let it be granted that they are excellent (*Against Apion* 2.271-72, 276-77, LCL).

15:13-21. James. See earlier discussion of table fellowship with Gentiles in 10:10-17, 22, 28 and 11:3. The speech does not focus on the preaching nor the missionary appeal that comes from Peter or Barnabas and Paul, but rather focuses on a compromise that will bring a solution to the problem of unity in the church family.

15:14. Symeon. This is the Greek transliterated form of the Hebrew Simeon. As one who was familiar with the Aramaic and Hebrew names for Peter, this would be appropriate. This is a reference to Simon Peter (see 10:5, 18, 32) or simply Peter (15:7). In the rest of the NT, this name is given to Peter only in 2 Peter 1:1.

15:16-21. Amos. James justifies his comments by an appeal to the LXX of Amos 9:11 as a basis for accepting the Gentiles into the church rather than the Hebrew where it is less clear. The Hebrew text reads:

On that day I shall raise up the hut of David that is fallen, and I shall repair its breaches; I shall raise up its ruins and rebuild it as in days of old, that they may possess the remnant of Edom and all the nations that are called by my name—oracle Yahweh who does this.
On the other hand, there is an important

change in the LXX. It reads:

'On that day I shall raise up the tent of David that is fallen and rebuild the ruins of it, and the parts thereof that have been broken down I shall set up, and I shall rebuild it as (in) the days of old, that the rest of humanity my seek (it), even all the nations, upon whom my name has been invoked' says the Lord, who does all these things (trans. by Fitzmyer, 555).

The difference in translation is important and the LXX serves James' purposes better since it shows that God has provided for the Gentiles to become a part of the people of God. Interestingly, the same passage is used in *CD* 7:16 and 4QFlor 1-2, 1 12-13. The Qumran texts do not use Amos 9:11 to include Gentiles into their community nor to show their plan in God's salvation.

15:19-20. See Lev. 18:6-18, 26. The four issues that James believes are essential for the well-being of the church as a whole, and that will help insure unity, are the abstaining from (1) eating food sacrificed to idols (Lev. 17:8 cf. 1 Cor. 8:1-13; 10:19-30), (2) fornication (Lev. 18:6-30), (3) eating what has been strangled, and (4) eating foods made of the blood of animals (Lev. 17:10-14). These codes are similar to the Noahic codes noted earlier, but these are derived from Lev. 17–18 and are in the order found in Leviticus in v. 29. These regulations were to be observed by anyone residing among the Jews in their homeland of Israel.

15:22. It was resolved by the apostles and presbyters and the whole church. It is not clear whether other local churches participated or simply the mother church in Jerusalem, but Luke makes it clear that all who were present agreed with the decision made to bring unity to the church.

Silas. This is the companion of Paul on his

second missionary journey (15:27, 32, 34, 40; 16:19, 25, 29; 17:4, 10, 14-15; 18:5). He is no longer mentioned with Paul after that, but is mentioned in the letters of Paul as Silvanus, perhaps his *supernomen*, in 2 Cor. 1:19; 1 Thess. 1:1; 2 Thess. 1:1 as well as in 1 Peter 5:12 where he is likewise called "Silvanus."

15:23-29. The letter. The form of the letter is typical of ancient Greek letters that have an opening greeting, a body, and a concluding farewell. The "Farewell" at the end of it is a typical conclusion to a Hellenistic letter. Notice, for instance, how Josephus writes a letter to the leaders of the rebellion in Jerusalem following a letter to him from them. He starts his letter thusly: "Josephus to Jonathan and his colleagues, greeting. I am delighted to hear that you have reached Galilee in good health more especially because I shall now be able to hand over to you the charge of affairs here and return home, as I have long wished to do. . . . Do you, therefore, on receipt of this letter, come and visit me. Fare you well" (Josephus, *Life* §226-27, LCL). The "fare you well" [Greek = *errosthe*] is the same word that Luke uses for "farewell" in 15:29. For other parallels, see also *2 Macc.* 11:21, 33; and *3 Macc.* 7:9.

15:23. Syria. This is the first time this province is mentioned in Acts and it will appear again in 15:41; 18:18; 20:3; 21:3. Syria became a Roman province in 64 B.C. and its capital was Antioch on the Orontes. See comments above on Antioch (11:19 above).

15:24. Certain persons . . . from us troubled you. This is a reference to 15:1 and perhaps also to Gal. 2:12.

15:30-35. The Return to Antioch with the Report from the Council.
The council decision in Jerusalem was greeted with favor in Antioch, and Judas and Silas remained for a time to exhort and strengthen the believers there. After a time, they, presumably Judas and Silas, were sent back to Jerusalem, but Paul and Barnabas remained. The awkwardness of Silas' return to Jerusalem in v. 33, but being chosen by Paul to join him on his second missionary journey led to a later addition to the text found in C and D texts. That addition found its way into the Bible as v. 34 in the King James translation of the Bible, but it is not in the earliest manuscripts of this passage. The addition reads: "But it seemed good to Silas to remain there." It may be that in time Silas returned to Antioch or that Paul met him elsewhere (Jerusalem) before beginning his second missionary journey, but there is no clear evidence for this. It is possible that the "they" who returned in v. 33 included others (15:22) besides Judas and Silas who accompanied them to Antioch. In ancient times, it was unusual for individuals to travel alone because of safety's sake. At any rate, Silas is chosen to accompany Paul on his second journey (15:40) and when that occurred, he was obviously back in Antioch. This is, nevertheless, an awkward passage in Luke's story and, as we saw above, there were efforts to smooth it out in the early church, e.g., Codexes C and D.

With the issue settled of Gentile inclusion into the church without the burden of the Law imposed upon them, Luke will now focus his attention on the journeys of Paul to largely Gentile communities in Asia Minor and Greece, and eventually to Rome itself.

Luke has crafted a story that shows how the church faced a very serious dilemma by calling a council, hearing testimony, interpreting sacred texts, declaring its convictions, sending out legations with letters, and establishing peace within its communities of faith. Luke has shown the true identity of the people of God to be based on its messianic faith rather than upon its ethnic origin or ritual practice.

VII. THE SECOND MISSIONARY JOURNEY (15:36–18:22)

15:36–16:5. The Beginning of the Second Missionary Journey

Following the good news of the council decision, Paul and Barnabas remained in Antioch for an undisclosed amount of time before determining to revisit the churches established in their first journey (chaps. 13–14) to check on their well-being and to strengthen them (41).

15:36-41. And there arose such a sharp disagreement that they separated from one another. The launching of the second mission enterprise begins with a dispute between Paul and Barnabas over whether to take John Mark with them on their second missionary journey. Paul took the initiative in this follow-up visit, but as they discussed the trip, Barnabas wanted to take John Mark with them. Paul resisted that suggestion because of Mark's desertion of the team in Pamphylia and his failure to complete the first mission (13:13; 15:38). Whatever the reason for Mark's departure, Paul did not want to take him on another journey. As a result, Barnabas and Paul chose not to go together on the second journey, but Barnabas took Mark and returned to Cyprus (see 4:36 and 13:4) while Paul chose Silas and went through Syria and Cilicia. At this separation, Barnabas, like Peter at the end of the Acts 15 council, is not mentioned again. Like the presence of Silas in Antioch (15:40), Luke did not say specifically how or why Mark returned to Antioch from Jerusalem. Mark's rejection by Paul appears only temporary and he was later considered to be a valuable Christian servant by Paul. Mark may well have returned to him and ministered to him (see Col. 4:10; 2 Tim. 4:11; Phile. 24). In fairness, we should also note that years later, after this split between Paul and Barnabas, Paul continued to see Barnabas as a colleague in Christian ministry (1 Cor. 9:6). Barnabas's inconsistency in Antioch (Gal. 2:13) in regard to table fellowship with Gentiles no doubt put a strain on their relationship, but it does not appear to have been permanent, and Luke shows no awareness of that earlier incident. Whether John Mark also played a role in that heated argument is uncertain. Whatever came of the rift between Paul on the one side and Peter and Barnabas on the other during the incident at Antioch, Paul felt free to return to Antioch at a later time (18:22) and from there began his third missionary journey.

15:41. The churches in Syria and Cilicia (see 15:23). Luke says nothing specifically about the establishing of churches in these areas, but it is possible that they were started by Paul following his departure from Jerusalem (9:30; cf. Gal. 1:21). At the time of Luke's writing, Syria and Cilicia were united as one province.

16:1-5. Timothy Joins Paul and Silas

16:1. And he came also to Derbe. See previous notes on Derbe in 14:20-21a. This is the first town that Paul would have come to given the direction he was traveling stated in 15:41. Either here or in Lystra he came in contact with Timothy.

16:1. Timothy, the son of a Jewish woman who was a believer, but his father was a Greek. Timothy is well known in Acts (here, 17:14-15; 18:5; 19:22; 20:4), but also in the letters of Paul where he is described as a faithful companion in Paul's mission (Rom. 16:21; 1 Cor. 4:17; 16:10; 2 Cor. 1:1, 19; Phil. 1:1; 2:19; Col. 1:1; 1 Thess. 1:1; 3:2, 6; 2 Thess. 1:1; 1 Tim. 1:2, 18; 6:20; 2 Tim. 1:2; Phile. 1; see also Heb. 13:23). In 1 Cor. 4:17, Paul calls him his beloved and faithful son or child. He was born of mixed parentage: namely, a Jewish mother and a Gentile father and Luke assumes that means that he was acknowledged as Jewish, hence the problematic issue of Paul having him circumcised.

Intermarriage for this period between Jews and Gentiles is rare and not well documented. This is one of those rare places where it is men-

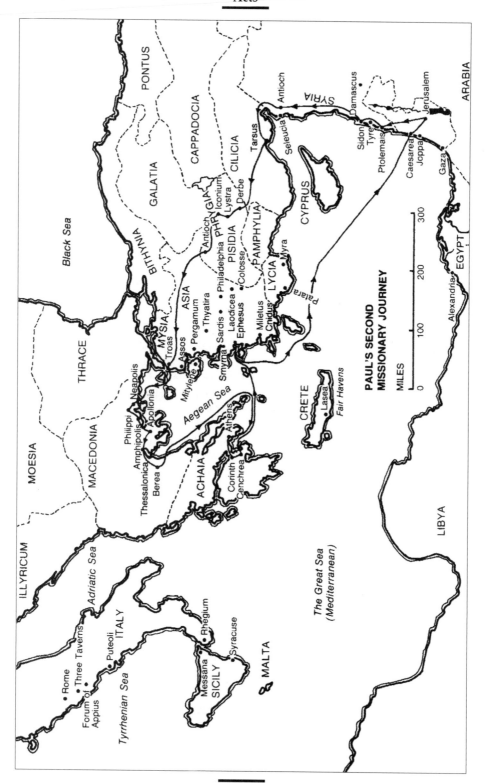

PAUL'S SECOND
MISSIONARY JOURNEY

MILES

0   100   200   300

tioned to justify an act of Paul. Luke fully accepted that with a Jewish mother that Timothy would be viewed as a Jew rather than a Gentile, otherwise, the whole discussion of 15:1-29 would be meaningless if Paul insisted on circumcising a Gentile. This is especially so when Luke indicates that Paul was also going from town to town delivering the decision of the apostles and the elders (16:4). It is unlikely that Luke would have shown the inconsistency of Paul two sentences later! The difficulty with this is that there is no evidence from the first century that indicates that a child born of a Jewish mother and a Gentile father was considered Jewish. There is a rabbinic tradition from the second century that claims this much, but how soon it was acknowledged in the Jewish communities is unknown. In the Mishnah for instance, "But any situation in which a woman has no right to enter into betrothel with this man or with any other man—the offspring is her status" (*Kiddushin* 3.12, Neusner trans.). For an early look at the problem of mixed marriages and Jewish identity, see also Ezra 9:1-10:44; Neh. 13:23-27; Mal. 1:10-16; *Jub.* 30:7-17.

16:3. Had him circumcised. Circumcision was viewed as a sign of the covenant between Abraham and God, and inclusion into the people of God took on the form of this practice. For a biblical history of the practice and the commands regarding it, see Gen. 17:10-14, 23-27; 21:4; 34:15-24; Exod. 12:44, 48; Lev. 12:3; Josh. 5:2-8. It appears to have been a rite related to marriage and also to a covenant with God. Its practice can be dated to the early part of the third millennium B.C. both in Egypt and possibly elsewhere. It came to have special significance for the shedding of blood related to a covenant, but also for the sanctity of the marriage.

Significantly, Ishmael was born to a father (Abraham) who had not yet been circumcised, while in Isaac's case that same father was cir-

cumcised; therefore, Isaac was the child of promise. Those who were of the household of Abraham, (Jews) were therefore circumcised. Timothy, whose Gentile father probably prevented him from being circumcised, was perhaps at this time deceased; and so Paul made a decision to circumcise him since, Luke assumes, his having a Jewish mother made him a Jew. Many commentators argue the inconsistency between Acts and Paul's own letters on the matter of circumcision.

The act of Paul circumcising Timothy seems to fly in the face of another principle stated by Paul: namely, that all believers should stay in the state in which they were called: if uncircumcised, then do not seek to be circumcised (1 Cor. 7:18-19). See also Gal. 2:3 where Paul argues that Titus was not forced to be circumcised and especially Gal. 5:2-3, 6, 11 where Paul seems to be opposed to the idea of circumcision. It may be possible that Paul thought that by circumcising Timothy, it would make his mission in the synagogues more acceptable to the Jews, and in this sense, he would be in keeping with his own missionary principle. On the other hand, in Phil. 3:5 Paul acknowledges with pride that he himself was circumcised, even if he counts it all as rubbish in his pursuit of knowing Christ (Phil. 3:8). He also appears willing to be as one "under the law" to those who are "under the law" in 1 Cor. 9:19-20. If it is true that Paul was more concerned that only Gentiles not be under the Law than Jews, then this would make his observance of Jewish rituals and observances in 18:18 and 21:26, and perhaps in 20:6, more understandable. Paul did not say that it was wrong *for the Jews* to follow the practices of Judaism: namely, circumcision and other Jewish observances. He contended that these traditions, though not wrong, were unable to bring a person into a right relationship with God (Gal. 2:15-21). Luke knows the objections of those who believe that Paul had completely dismissed the practice of the Jewish traditions (21:21), but shows that Paul himself practiced them as a Jew while continuing to insist that Gentiles were not under any such obligations. Paul contended that Gentiles were not under the customs of the Jews and that only faith in Christ and not circumcision would lead to one's salvation, whether for Jews or Gentiles.

What appears to be a significant inconsistency between Paul's letters and Acts, may in fact be a missionary principle, but that would be the case only if Paul saw Timothy as a Jew and not a Gentile. Why Paul did this may not be clear, but Luke seems to imply in v. 3 that everyone knew Timothy's ancestry and therefore Paul circumcised him to make his ministry among the Jews more acceptable by showing that he was not opposed to his Jewish ancestral traditions. If Timothy were not considered Jewish, then the whole passage makes very little sense in light of the Acts 15 council decision.

16:5. Increased in number. This is Luke's usual way of pointing out the continual growth of the church (see 2:41, 47; 4:4; 5:14; 6:7; 8:25, 40; 9:31; 11:24-25; 12:24; 14:21-23).

16:6-10. Paul's Vision

16:6. Phrygian and Galatian region. This is an awkward description of essentially two separate provinces that were probably linked politically from the time of Roman occupation in 25 B.C. See also the equally awkward "Galatian region and Phrygia" in 18:23. As noted above, this region was without paved roads until approximately A.D. 80.

16:7. When they had come to Mysia. The boundaries of the region of Mysia are imprecise in the surviving sources. It was situated in northwest Asia Minor. Strabo indicates the difficulty of locating the region, but it apparently bordered Bithynia and included the well-known cities of Troy, Troas (or Troad), Assos (see Acts 20:13), and Pergamum (see *Geography* 12.4.5-6; 12.8.1), and it was divided into Mysia

Major and Mysia Minor. The former extended to Mt. Olympus, but the latter incorporated the northwest part of Asia Minor. Strabo adds that "Mysia is likewise divided into two parts, I mean Olympene, which is continuous with Bithynia and Phrygia Epictetus, which according to Artemidorus, was colonised by the Mysians who life the far side of Ister, and secondly, the country in the neighbourhood of the Caïcus River and Pergamene [Pergamum]." he later adds that the language of the Mysians is a mixture of the Lydian and Phrygian languages, "for the reason that, although they lived around Mt. Olympus for a time, yet when the Phrygians crossed over from Thrace and slew a ruler of Troy and of the country near it, those people took up their abode there, whereas the Mysians took up their abode above the sources of the Caïcus near Lydia" (*Geography*, 12.8.3, LCL). The region was annexed by the Romans in 133 B.C. and was governed by a procurator.

16:7 They were trying to go into Bithynia. This is a mountainous region of northwestern Asia Minor that was bequeathed to Rome by King Nicomedes in 74 B.C. In the last half of the first century, there were Christian communities founded there (1 Peter 1:1). Around A.D. 111–113, Pliny, the governor of this region and also Pontus, corresponded with the Emperor Trajan about the circumstances of the region and reported to him how he was dealing with those who reported to be Christians (see Pliny, *Letters* 10.96-97). This is one of the earliest non-Christian reports about the presence and activities of the Christians in Bithynia. For whatever reason that Paul was unable to enter this important region, he attributed the change of direction to the "spirit of Jesus" preventing him (16:7). It is not certain what circumstances were involved (illness, opposition, or something else), but Paul attributed it to the will of God. See also 16:6 where the Spirit prevented Paul and his companions from speaking the "word" in Asia. Paul took this inability to enter Bithynia and also his inability to speak in Asia as from God, and so he went instead to Troas (v. 8).

16:8. Passing by Mysia, they came down to Troas. Since Troas was a leading city in Mysia, the narrative here seems awkward. It is probably better to say "passing through Mysia, they arrived in Troas" and that is a possibility that has some support as in 24:7 where similar terminology is used. The second time Paul visits this city will be discussed below in 20:6-12. The ancient coastal town of Troas was situated on the western shores of Asia Minor and located about 10 miles south of the ancient city of Troy. More commonly Troas was known as Alexandrian Troas. Troas (or Troad) was founded at the direction of Alexander the Great and it became a wealthy commercial center as well as the region's main port. It was surrounded on three sides by water and contained a large artificial harbor. It was made a Roman colony by Augustus (*Colonia Augusta Troas*) and was an important port of departure for those sailing to Greece or returning. It was visited twice by Paul on his missionary journeys (here and at 20:5-12) and is the place of his Macedonian vision (16:9). Paul refers to this city in 2 Cor. 2:12-13. In 2 Tim. 4:13, he indicates that he left a cloak, books, and parchments at Troas and requests them. Ottoman Empire architects hauled away most of the stones from building sites in Troas to build up the imperial mosques in Istanbul in the 16th and 17th centuries. Since its treasures were taken for other purposes, the ancient city has never been excavated.

16:9. Come over to Macedonia and help us. As in the case of the call of Paul (9:10) and the way that Peter became open to visit the home of Cornelius (10:9-16, see 11:5), Luke uses a vision to direct Paul on his ministry in Macedonia. In a similar experience, Philostratus tells of a woman appearing to Apollonius of Tyana asking to see him before he left for Rome.

While he was still pondering this project [going to Rome], he had the following dream: It seemed as if a woman both very tall and venerable in years embraced him, and asked him to visit her before he set sail for Italy; and she said that she was the nurse of Zeus, and she wore a wreath that held everything that is on the earth or in the sea. He proceeded to ponder the meaning of the vision, and came to the conclusion that he ought first to sail to Crete, which we regard as the nurse of Zeus, because in that island Zeus was born; although the wreath might perhaps indicate some other island (*Life of Apollonius of Tyana* 4.34, LCL).

Macedonia. This area is the more mountainous region of northern Greece, the boundaries of which are imprecise in antiquity. Under Philip of Macedon (359-336 B.C.), this region became the dominant power in Greece. The region was divided into four districts after Roman control in 168 B.C. and was later established as a Roman province in 148 B.C. Roman colonies were established in Dyrrhachium, Pella, and Philippi.

And when he had seen the vision, immediately we sought to go into Macedonia. This is the place where the well-known "we" passages in Acts begin (see earlier discussion in the introduction). They begin here (16:10-17) and return as Paul makes his way from Troas to Jerusalem (20:5-15; 21:1-18) and then from Caesarea to Rome (27:1-28:16). There is another passage where the first person plural is included at 11:28 in codex Bezae. Whether the presence of the first person plural signifies that the writer is one who accompanied Paul or whether it was a particular literary convention characteristic of ancient historical writing is a matter of significant dispute among biblical scholars. Lucian of Samosata (ca. A.D. 120–190), in his *How to Write History* (16-24) indicates the acceptability of using diaries in writing history and also the acceptability of using the first person in describing history as long as the historical accuracy of the stories are maintained. Luke indicates his awareness and use of such eyewitnesses in the opening passage of his first volume (Luke 1:2). In narratives of sea voyages and other journeys, it was not uncommon for the writer to write in the first person even if the narrator was not involved in the events. For a useful example of this, see Lucian of Samosata, *A True Story* 1.5-42. If the former circumstance is true: namely, that the passages were produced by a companion of Paul, then the question of the identity of that individual arises. The oldest tradition about them is that it was Luke, the beloved physician and companion of Paul (Col. 4:14; 2 Tim. 4:11; Phile. 24). On the other hand, if it was simply a stylistic habit or literary convention of those writing history in antiquity, why are such passages absent from other historical sections of the book? It is more likely that Luke simply carried the "conventional we" from the sources he was using in composing his book (see S. Porter, "The 'We' Passages" in *Acts in Its Greco-Roman Setting*, 2:545-74). For additional discussion, see "Introduction."

16:11-40. Paul's Ministry in Philippi. There are three stories that tell about Paul's ministry in Philippi. They include the story of Lydia's conversion and baptism, Paul's exorcism of the young woman given over to mantic prophecy, and the story of the Philippian jailer's conversion. They are brought together in the final verses of this story (35-40).

16:11: Neapolis. This seaport city was the port used by those at Philippi and was about eight miles west of Neapolis (= New City). At one time, Neapolis served as a naval port for Brutus and Cassius during their battle at Philippi with Antony (Appian, *Civil Wars* 4.13-17; Dio Cassius, *Roman History* 47.42-49). Today, Neapolis is the modern city of Kavala and is the principal port of eastern Macedonia surrounded by the slopes of Mt. Simvolo. It has in its center a Byzantine castle on the acropolis. Paul passed through this port city en route to Philippi on his second missionary journey, but there is no indication that he had a ministry here (Acts 16:11). He left Greece also from this port by ship on his way to Troas at the end of his third missionary journey. While we read that he "sailed from Philippi" (Acts 20:6), the port city of Neapolis was intended since Philippi had no port.

16:12. Philippi. This well-known small city in the ancient world is situated in eastern Macedonia on the famous Roman highway, Via Egnatia, and overlooks an inland plain to the east of Mt. Pangaeus (Pangaion). When work was completed on the famous Via Egnatia highway (145–130 B.C.) it connected Byzantium (later Constantinople) with the Adriatic ports that led to Italy and became Rome's primary route to the East. When the road was finally completed, Philippi became a major stopping place on the way. The original community was founded by immigrants from Thrace and was known for its rich gold mines as well as for its many springs of water that rise in its hills (Strabo *Geography* 7.34). It was surrounded by mountains on three sides and an open plain to the west. The current site was settled ca. 360 B.C. when residents from Thasos annexed the territory and called it Crenides (Greek, *krenai*) because of its springs. It was also known for a brief period as "Datum" or "Daton" (Strabo *Geography* 7.34). Later when its citizens called upon Philip II of Macedonia (the father of Alexander the Great) for help against the Thracians, he came to their aid, but also enlarged their city and renamed it after himself. He built a wall around the city that was later reinforced by the Romans, some of which still remains. Except for the wealth derived from the gold mines, Philippi was relatively unimportant until the Roman conquest of the region in 168–67 B.C. According to Diodorus Siculus (16.3.7, 8.6), Philip II received 1,000 talents a year from the rich mines in the vicinity and treated Philippi as a "free city" within his kingdom. The wealth he got from this region enabled him to enlarge his army and unify his kingdom. Pausanias, who traveled thorough Greece during the reign of Hadrian (A.D. 117–38), called Philippi the "youngest city in Macedonia." The city is mentioned in a number of ancient authors (Dio Cassius, *Hist.*, 47.35-49; Appian, *Civil Wars* 4.102-138; Plutarch, *Brutus* 38-53).

When the work was completed on the famous Via Egnatia highway, that was begun ca. 145 B.C. and completed ca. 130 B.C., the road connected Byzantium (later named Constantinople) with the Adriatic ports that led to Italy. At that time the road became Rome's primary route to the east and finally completed, Philippi became a major stopping place on the way. Besides making it possible to move troops more rapidly throughout the empire, this route was used by Paul on his missionary journey from Neapolis to Philippi, Amphipolis, Apollonia, and Thessalonica (Acts 16:12; 17:1), but he abandoned it when he departed for Beroea (Acts 17:10).

With the emergence of the Second Triumvirate made up of Octavian (later Emperor Augustus), Marcus Antony (Marcus Antonius), and Marcus Aemilius Lepidus in 43 B.C., and following their proscriptions that led to the executions of some 300 senators and 2,000 knights in Rome, they had secured their control of Rome. The only remaining threat to their control over Rome and its vast empire was the Republican army led by Cassius Longinus and Iunius Brutus, the murderers of Julius Caesar. Leaving Lepidus to guard Rome, Octavian and Antony engaged the Republican forces just west of Philippi in two battles and, after defeating them, both Cassius and Brutus committed suicide (Horace, *Odes* 2.7.9-12). Following these battles, Antony settled many veterans from his army in Philippi and enlarged and fortified the city of Philippi. Strabo writes of this expansion:

"In earlier times Philippi was called Crenides, and was only a small settlement, but it was enlarged after the defeat of Brutus and Cassius" (*Geography* 7. frg. 41, LCL). He made it a Roman colony that included Neapolis, Oisyme, and Apollonia, and offered land to many of the triumviral soldiers from Rome who had earlier lost their land in Italy (Strabo, *Geography* 7.41; Pliny the Elder, *Natural History* 4.42; Diodorus, *Hist.* 51, 4.6). Following his victory over Antony at Actium in 31 B.C., Octavian moved more settlers here from Italy. Its colonial status brought with it the significant benefit of equal status with the Italian communities and freedom of its citizens and lands from direct taxation. This was known as the *ius italicum* that conferred the same rights as those granted to Italian cities (Acts 16:12)—the highest privilege possible for a Roman province. This included, as the narrative makes clear below (v. 37), freedom from being put in chains and from flogging. The new settlers, along with the previous residents, constituted the newly reformed colony that became known as *Colonia Augusta Julia Philippensis*. It was common in those days for the Romans to build or reconstitute communities as Roman colonies and then offer property to veteran soldiers and other citizens of Rome.

The official language of Philippi in the first century was Latin, and that is also the language of more than half of the inscriptions found there, but the marketplace language and that of the surrounding community continued to be Greek. Indeed, Paul's letter to the Christians at Philippi and Polycarp's *Letter to the Philippians* in the second century, are both written in Greek. The city was serviced both by the nearby port of Neapolis, modern Kavalla (Acts 16:11) some 10 miles southeast of the city, and by the Via Egnatia. Remains from the Macedonian, Roman, and Byzantine periods including remains of a sanctuary to honor Egyptian gods (Serapis and Isis) have been found on the acropolis at Philippi.

16:13. We went outside the gate to a riverside, where we were supposing that there would be a place of prayer. This designation "a place of prayer" (Greek = *proseuche*) often referred to a synagogue in antiquity. Several Hellenistic inscriptions from Egypt dating from the middle second century to the middle of the first century B.C. used this term, *proseuche*, as a reference to a synagogue. Three of these inscriptions illustrate the point. The first reads, "For King Ptolemy and Queen Kleopatra and their children, Hermias and Philotera, his wife, and their children dedicated this portico for the synagogue [Greek, *proseuche*]" (SGPI 166, ca. 181–145 B.C.). Again, a text from lower Egypt reads "On the orders of the queen and the king: in place of the plaque which was previously situated here concerning the erection of the synagogue [Greek, *proseuches*], the text given below is to be inscribed: 'King Ptolemy Euergetes (has made) the synagogue [*proseuchen*] an asylum. The queen and the king have ordered it'" (AGI 18; OGIS 129; CIJ 1449, ND 4:201). What Paul and his companions visited outside the city of Philippi was likely a synagogue that may simply have been a gathering of Jews and proselytes for prayer. And finally, there is also precedent for this meaning in 3 *Macc.* (early first century B.C.) that concludes with the story of the Jews returning to their land from Egypt under the protection of King Ptolemy Philopator: "They consecrated them with an inscription on a pillar, and having dedicated a place of prayer [*proseuches*] on the site of the banquet, they went away unscathed, free, and filled with joy, and were conducted safely, by ordinance of the king, over land and sea and river, each to his own home" (3 *Macc.* 7:20, OT *Pseud* 2:529).

The location of a "place of prayer" by the riverside may have been both by custom and perhaps also by decree. Josephus reports that a decree from Halicarnassus, on the motion of a Marcus Alexander, a Roman official, stated in part that: "we have also decreed that those Jewish men and women who so wish may observe their Sabbaths and perform their sacred rites in accordance with the Jewish laws, and may build places of prayer [*tas proseuchas*] near the sea, in accordance with their native custom" (*Ant.* 14.258, LCL).

It is not altogether clear why synagogues were built near water, but it is likely that this was done to allow the Jews to ritually wash themselves before their holy service or worship or transcribing their laws. Again, Josephus tells of the practice of washing before the translation of the Law near Ptolemy's palace in Egypt. "And early each day they would go to court, pay their respects to Ptolemy and then go back to the same place and, after washing their hands in the sea and purifying themselves, would betake themselves in this state to the translation of the laws" (*Ant.* 12.106). Whether by decree or custom, the synagogues of Delos, Aegina and Miletus were close to the edge of a shore, and it is possible that the places of prayer were near water to be able to deal adequately by washing with the uncleanness of the Gentiles. In 16:13, Paul and his companions go to the riverside where they supposed there would be a place of prayer. Luke seems to be saying that this was an expected custom in communities that had Jewish populations. It is not clear whether the "place of prayer" was a building or simply a place near the river where Jews and devout Gentile sympathizers met for prayer.

16:14. Lydia of Thyatira. The woman referred to in this passage was named after the region of Lydia and she came from the city of Thyatira, a city that was widely known for its production of purple dye and various pieces of purple cloth (see other mentions of Thyatira in Rev. 1:11; 2:18, 24). Strangely, Lydia is not mentioned in Paul's letter to the Philippians.

The Lord opened her heart to respond. The history behind this statement has a parallel in the opening prayer of 2 *Macc.* where the writer prays: "May he open your heart to his law and his commandments" (2 *Macc.* 1:4, NRSV).

16:15. Come into my house and stay. In similar fashion to Peter in 10:22-23, 48; cf. 11:3), Paul is welcomed to the home of a Gentile.

16:16. A certain slave girl having a spirit of divination. As Paul was on his way to the place of prayer (synagogue, see v. 13), he met and healed a young woman of a "spirit of divination" (literally, a spirit of "*pythona*"). The young woman, a slave of the men who sought to profit from her soothsayings or prophecies, was likely an oracle of Apollo who delivered mantic prophecy. The term used to describe her activity is *mantomene* (or "fortune-telling"), that is, one who acts as a mantic. The name, *Python* was the name of the dragon or snake that guarded the Delphic oracle at the base of Mt. Parnassus. Apollo killed the dragon at Delphi and those who spoke prophecies there were believed to have a spirit of Python (or pythona). Delphi was the most famous city for its practice of mantic prophecy. In time, those who spoke prophecies, or were soothsayers, were believed to have the "spirit of divination" or "*pythones*." Plutarch writes about this practice saying, "Certainly it is foolish and childish in the manner of ventriloquists (who used to be called 'Eurycleis,' but not 'Pythones') enters into the bodies of his prophets and prompts their utterances, employing their mouths and voices as instruments" (*Defect. orac.* 414e). Because the "owners" of the woman (she was a slave) were now robbed of their income from the abilities of the young woman, they took Paul and Silas before the magistrate of the city for compensation and Paul and Silas were thrown in jail.

16:17. The most high God. It is worth noting that this name for God, "most high [Greek, *hupsistos*] God" is used in the gospels by demons to refer to Jesus as the "Son of the most high God" (Mark 5:7l; Luke 8:28).

16:21. Proclaiming customs which it is not lawful for us to accept or to observe, being Romans. There were laws in the empire against converting to nonrecognized religions. According to Cicero, "No one shall have gods to himself, either new gods or alien gods, unless recognized by the state. Privately they shall worship those gods whose worship they have duly received from their ancestors" (*De Leg.* 2.8.19, Conzelmann, 131-32, trans.). In the year A.D. 96, Domitian, the Roman emperor, executed those who abandoned the gods of the Romans and converted to Judaism. Dio Cassius writes of this event:

> ... Domitian slew, along with many others, Flavius Clemens the consul, although he was a cousin and had to wife Flava Domitilla, who was also a relative of the emperor's. The charge brought against them both was that of atheism, a charge on which many others who drifted into Jewish ways were condemned. Some of these were put to death, and the rest were at least deprived of their property (*History*, 67.14.1-2, LCL).

The Christians faced significant opposition from those who believed that any abandonment of their current state-recognized religious practice and beliefs was both antisocial and next to insurrection. Cicero insists from others the loyalty that he himself had for these religious traditions : ". . . I ought to uphold the beliefs about the immortal gods which have come down to us from our ancestors, and the rites and ceremonies and duties of religion. For my part I always shall uphold them . . . and no eloquence . . .shall ever dislodge me from the belief as to the worship of the immortal gods, which I have inherited from our forefathers . . ." (*On the Nature of the Gods* 3.2.5, LCL).

Earlier during the famous trial of Socrates,

he too was accused of introducing strange new deities, and his loyalty to the established deities was doubted. In his defense of Socrates, Xenophon, ca. 430–354 B.C., asked:

"I have often wondered by what arguments those who drew up the indictment against Socrates could persuade the Athenians that his life was forfeit to the state. The indictment against him was to this effect: *Socrates is guilty of rejecting the gods acknowledged by the state and of bringing in strange deities: he is also guilty of corrupting the youth"* (*Memorabilia* 1.1.1, LCL, italics his).

It was dangerous in the ancient world both to deny the credited gods of the state or empire and to introduce new ones. Paul's proclamation of what God had done in Jesus, the Good News, was considered a threat to the stability of society and he was often challenged not only by the Jews, but also by the local authorities.

16:31. Believe in the Lord Jesus, and you shall be saved, you and your household. This is an abbreviated formula that is similar to those in 5:14; 9:42; 11:17, but see also the connection between faith and salvation in 2:38; 14:9; 15:11. The inclusion of the household is not unlike the stories of Cornelius (11:14) and Lydia (16:15).

16:37. They have beaten us in public without trial, men who are Romans, and have thrown us into prison; and now are they sending us away secretly? Paul's apparent indignation at being arrested, beaten, and thrown in prison points to the privileges that Roman citizens had in the first century. Roman citizens received certain protections that were highly prized, among them were the protection against being chained or flogged. Livy writes: "Yet the Porcian law alone seems to have been passed to protect the persons of the citizens, imposing, as it does, a heavy penalty if anyone should scourge or put to death a Roman citizen" (10.9.4, LCL). Similarly, Cicero stated: "By the Julian law on

public violence he is condemned who, endowed with some power, will have killed, or ordered to be killed, should torture, scourge, condemn by law, or order to be incarcerated in the state prison a Roman citizen appealing previously to the people and now to the emperor" (*Rab. post.* 4.12-13, LCL).

Violations of this protection did occur, however, and Josephus cites a well-known example when Gessius Florus, the Roman procurator in Judea (A.D. 64–66), invaded the temple in Jerusalem and had many citizens scourged and crucified. He claims that "Florus ventured that day [in Jerusalem] to do what none had ever done before: namely, to scourge before his tribunal and nail to the cross men of equestrian rank, men, who, if Jews by birth, were at least invested with that Roman dignity" (*War* 2.308, LCL). Despite the inconsistency of the practice, generally speaking, Paul is appealing to what was the widespread practice among the Romans: namely, not to chain or flog Roman citizens. More common was what Cicero argued: "To bind a Roman citizen is a crime, to flog him an abomination, to slay him almost an act of parricide" (*Against Verres* 2.5.66; see also Livy, *Historia* 10.9.4; Cicero, *Pro Rabirio* 4.12-13; Appian, *Civil War* 2.26.98). Paul never mentions his Roman citizenship in his letters, perhaps because in them he was dealing with Christians and not the Roman authorities. When he was with Christians he did not want to demand his rights as an apostle while preaching the Gospel (1 Cor. 9:12-15), but this context is one of dealing with civil authority and he objects to the extreme and unnecessary humiliation that he suffered at Philippi (1 Thess. 2:2).

17:1-9. Ministry in Thessalonica
17:1. Now when they had traveled through Amphipolis and Apollonia. It is not clear why Paul failed to minister at either of these two cities en route to Thessalonica. Perhaps this was because there was no synagogue in either place and his habit was to take the Gospel to

the Jews first (see 16:13, 16 and 17:1b; see also Rom. 1:16). The emphasis on Thessalonica "where there was a synagogue" suggests that neither of the cities he passed through had a Jewish population. The distance between each of the cities mentioned in v. 1 is between 30 to 35 miles apart from the others (Philippi to Amphipolis, Amphipolis to Apollonia, Apollonia to Thessalonica). If the travelers were on horses, the trip could be made in a day from each location to the next. It is difficult to imagine that some stop was not taken at each of the places, but there is no indication that Paul and his companions ministered in them. Amphipolis lies west of Philippi on the Via Egnatia Roman highway on the east bank of the Strymon River and was colonized by the Athenians in 436 B.C. Its original name was *Ennea Hodoi* (Nine Ways or Roads).

Because the Strymon River surrounded the city on three sides, the city was given the name Amphipolis. In the first century Amphipolis was the most important city in the first district of Macedonia. Philip of Macedon (ca. 350 B.C.) captured the region and gave it a favored status so that it became a major stronghold for the Greeks and later a staging place for battles in Roman times. Alexander the Great made the city the chief mint in his domains. Just outside of the modern city today is a majestic stone lion dating from the Hellenistic period that is immediately west of the bridge over the Strymon River. Under the Romans, the city became a "free city" and the capital of the first of four districts of Macedonia. Apollonia, on the other hand, was not as significant a place even though it may have provided shelter on the traveler's journey. The city is named after the Greek god, Apollo. Pliny the Elder (ca. A.D. 23–79) mentions both cities in his description of the boundaries and cities of Macedonia:

Next comes Macedonia, with 150 nations, and famous for two kings [Philip of Macedon and Alexander the Great] and for its former worldwide empire; it was previously called Emathia. It stretches westward to the races of Epirus, at the back of Magnesia and Thessaly, and on this side is exposed to the inroads of the Dardani, but its northern part is protected from the Triballi by Paeonia and Pelagonia. Its towns are . [many towns and districts]. . Heraclea, and the district of Mygdonia lying below, in which at some distance from the sea are Apollonia and Arethusa, and on the coast again Posidium and the bay with the town of Cermorus, the free city of Amphipolis, and the tribe of Bisaltae (*Natural History* 4.33-38, LCL).

17:1b. They came to Thessalonica, where there was a synagogue of the Jews. Thessalonica (modern Thessaloniki or Salonika) became an important city because of its location on the crossroads of important trade routes and its port. The city, since its founding in 315 B.C. by Cassander, one of Alexander's generals, was an important city. It was named after Cassander's wife and continued to prosper long after the Roman conquest of the region. Strabo indicates that in earlier times the place was called Therma, but it was founded, or re-founded, by Cassander, "who named it after his wife, the daughter of Philip the son of Amyntas" (*Geography* 7.Frg. 24, LCL). It was the most important port on the Via Egnatia which also helped its prosperity, and under the Romans the city became the capital of the second district of Macedonia and the seat of the Roman governor in 167 B.C. The city is mentioned elsewhere in Phil. 4:16 and 2 Tim. 4:10.

After leaving Philippi, Paul came to this city and had a brief ministry (17:2) before being driven out of the city by Jewish opposition (vv. 5-10). The response to Paul's message, however, was initially quite positive leading to the establishing of a strong church, but it was also negative due to the opposition that led to an early departure from the city. Because of this early departure, Paul sent Timothy back to the city to check on the well-being of the new congregation (1 Thess. 3:1-7). Timothy brought back good news to Paul, who was in Corinth at the time awaiting word on the welfare of the Christians there (1 Thess. 1:9-10; 3:6-10). Paul responded to this news and wrote to the Thessalonian Christians (1 Thess.) to encourage them in their faith, but also to correct their understanding of the time of the coming of Lord and to encourage them to work quietly and live peacefully among their neighbors. See Introduction to 1 Thessalonians. Later, Aristarchus and Secundus from Thessalonica accompany Paul on his journey back to Jerusalem (20:4).

17.2. Paul went in, as was his custom. Paul's visits to the synagogues were a regular part of his mission strategy. In cities where there was no known synagogue, he appears to have spent little time, e.g., Neapolis, Amphipolis, and Apollonia. Paul's passion for the Gentiles coming to faith in Christ did not reduce his desire for his fellow Jews to do the same. See 13:5, 14; 14:1; 16:13; here; 17:10; 18:4, 19; 19:8; 28:17-28; compare also Rom. 9:3-5; 10:1; 11:1-3. Besides his theological reason for visiting synagogues, it was also common for Jews who were traveling to find shelter and food at such places. In a pre-A.D. 70 inscription found in Jerusalem, we read the following:

> Theotokos, son of Vettenus, priest and *archisynagogos* [ruler of the synagogue], son of an *archisynagogos*, built this synagogue for the reading of the law and for the teaching of commandments, as well as the hostel, the rooms and the water fittings (?), as a lodging for those coming from a foreign country, which his fathers established as well as the presbyters and Simonides (*CIJ* 1404, ND 89).

It was also common to find that discussions were a common feature in synagogues which was also known as a "house of study" (*m. Shab* 16:1).

17:5. But the Jews became jealous. Occasionally, Luke uses the term "Jews" negatively, as he does here and in 12:3; 13:45; 14:2; and 17:13.

With the help of some ruffians in the marketplaces they formed a mob and set the city in an uproar. Plutarch cites a similar example of those who incited others to riot: "Appius saw Scipio rushing into the forum attended by men who were of low birth and had lately been slaves, but who were frequenters of the forum and able to gather a mob and force all issues by means of solicitations and shouting" (*Aem. Paulus* 38, LCL).

17:7. "They are all acting contrary to the decrees of the emperor." See 16:21 above. The term "emperor" translates the more familiar *Kaisaros* ("Caesar") and was the *cognomen* of Gaius Julius Caesar who adopted Octavian, and Octavian became known as Caesar Octavian in 27 B.C. when the Senate of Rome bestowed on him the honorific title *Augustus,* which in the Greek is *Sebastos.* He was thereafter known as Caesar Augustus (Luke 2:1). Those emperors of the Roman Empire who followed Caesar Augustus were regularly referred to as "Caesar." The emperor or Caesar referred to is Claudius (A.D. 41–54). Elsewhere Luke refers to the emperor as "Caesar" in Luke 23:2 and Acts 25:8.

There is another king named Jesus. The Roman emperor was not normally called "king" but occasionally instances of this are found as in recension A of the *Acts of Isodore.* Because of this charge, Christians often had to offer an explanation to show that their king and kingdom was not in competition with Rome (John 18:36).

17:10-15. Beroea

17:10. That very night the believers sent Paul

and Silas off to Beroea. Because of the dangers to Paul, the Christians at Thessalonica took Paul and Silas to Beroea, a town located about fifty miles southwest of Thessalonica on the Astraeus River a few miles south of the Egnatian Way and at the foothills of Mt. Bermius (Strabo, *Geography* 7.frg. 26). Cicero referred to it as a "town off the beaten track" (*In Pisonem* 36.89). Beroea, modern Verria, came under Roman occupation in 168 B.C. and was the first town to surrender to the Romans following the Battle of Pindar. It was in the third of the fourth districts of Macedonia. Pompey made this his winter home in 49–48 B.C. The city was given the title *metropolis* during the reign of Nero, a significant honor that speaks of the importance of this community and also the assembly location of the *koinon* or "council" in the region. It was involved in many military conflicts (Polybius 27.8; 28.8; Livy 44.45; 45.29). Beroea was the center of the imperial cult in the province. Sopater of Beroea (20:4-6) accompanied Paul on his journey from Greece through Macedonia to Troas.

17:11. These Jews were more receptive than those in Thessalonica. "More receptive" comes from the Greek, *eugenesteroi*, and literally means "more well born" or "noble," a title that normally refers to a high social standing. Luke has in mind that the Beroean Jews were more receptive to his message, but it may also refer to their higher social status than those in Thessalonica.

17:14. Silas and Timothy remained behind. This is the first indicator from Luke that Timothy had accompanied Paul on his missionary journey (see also 18:5 and 1 Thess. 3:1-2).

17:15. Now those who conducted Paul brought him as far as Athens. Athens was also the birthplace of democracy. The principles of democratic government of equality and justice by representation was a new phenomenon introduced by Cleisthenes in 507 B.C. and developed by Pericles between 460–30 B.C. An assembly of 500 men (fifty from each of the ten tribes in Athens) met forty times a year on the Pnyx, a western hillside overlooking the Acropolis in Athens. This assembly decided all questions of foreign and domestic policy and Socrates was brought before it in 399 B.C. to defend his philosophy and beliefs. He was condemned to death because the assembly believed that he had corrupted the youth by causing them to be critical of their elders and skeptical of the gods. He was put to death in the state prison in the west end of the *agora* by drinking hemlock. There were occasions when some 5,000 persons would gather and take part in the debates on the Pnyx hill. Similarly, Paul was asked to defend his practice of introducing new deities in Athens (vv. 18-19).

On the north side of the Acropolis is the *agora*, or marketplace, that contains the ruins of the ancient cultural and political center of the city. The *agora* contains one of the best preserved Doric temples of antiquity, the Hephaisteion (begun around 450 B.C. and completed at the end of that century), a beautiful reconstruction of the Stoa of Attalos, the remains of the circular Tholos, the old and new Bouleterion (meeting place of the city council), the Roman Forum, and many other structures. The site was originally a Mycenean cemetery until the end of the seventh century when it was converted into a marketplace or forum in the early sixth century. The reconstructed part of the *agora* is very much like what was present in the first century A.D. when Paul came through here on his second missionary journey.

The Athenian acropolis is one of the most impressive in the world. It has several periods of growth and development, but the primary structures on the hill today (the propylaia, or entry gates, the Parthenon, the Erichtheion, the Odeion of Herodes Atticus and the Theater of Dionysos) were all present when Paul visited Athens. There are remains of ten buildings on the Acropolis dating from the seventh to sixth centuries B.C. The buildings were destroyed by the Persians in 480 B.C. and subsequently rebuilt. The Parthenon was built between 447 and 438, during what is called the Classical period of ancient Greece along with a large statue (39 feet tall) of Athena that was situated on the east side of the temple.

17:16-34. Paul in Athens

17:16. Now while Paul was waiting for them at Athens. Following his brief ministry in Beroea, Paul came to Athens, one of the most cultured cities of antiquity that was known for its academies, art, architecture, philosophy, religious devotion, and idolatry (Acts 17:15-17). Long after Greece's greatness had diminished, Athens continued to have respect and a good reputation in the Greco-Roman world. Long after the Greek empire was over, Cicero (106–43 B.C.) said of Athens that it was a city "where men think humanity, learning, religion, grain, rights, and laws were born, and whence they were spread through all the earth. . . . It has, moreover, such renown that the now shattered and weakened name of Greece is supported by reputation of this city" (*Pro Flacco* 26.62, LCL). In the time of Paul, Athens was essentially a provincial university city and the home of many art treasures. Paul's ship, if he in fact came by ship (vv. 14-15 above may suggest otherwise), would have docked at Pireaus, one of the busiest harbors of Greece in that day. Philostratus, who lived in Athens (ca. A.D. 170), wrote the entrance into Athens of a certain Apollonias, a first-century holy man who was a contemporary of Paul:

> . . . having sailed into the Piraeus at the season of the mysteries, when the Athenians keep the most crowded of Hellenic festivals, he went post haste up from the ship into the city; but as he went forward, he fell in with quite a number of students of philosophy on their way down to Phalerum. Some of

them were stripped and enjoying the heat, for in autumn the sun is hot upon the Athenians; and others were studying books, and some were rehearsing their speeches, and others were disputing (*Life of Apollonius of Tyana* 4.17, LCL).

He was beholding the city full of idols. In his visit to Athens, Pausanias (second cent. A.D.) describes the marketplace (*agora*) thusly:

> In the Athenian marketplace among the objects not generally known is an altar to Mercy, of all divinities the most useful in the life of mortals and in the vicissitudes of fortune, but honoured by the Athenians alone among the Greeks. And they are conspicuous not only for their humanity but also for their devotion to religion. They have an altar to Shamefastness, one to Rumour, and one to Effort. It is quite obvious that those who excel in piety are correspondingly rewarded by good fortune. In the gymnasium not far from the marketplace [*agora*], called Ptolemy's from the founder, are stone Hermae well worth seeing and a likeness in bronze of Ptolemy. Here also is the Juba the Libyan and Chrysippus of Soli (*Description of Greece*, 1.17.1-2, LCL).

Although Paul's ministry in this place was apparently brief, and not too impressive, there were some converts to his message (Acts 17:32-34). Paul saw the numerous idols in the city and used one in particular as a starting place for his message to the leaders of the city (vv. 22-31). As with Socrates and others before him, however, it was dangerous for him to discuss new gods or deny the acceptable ones. Josephus claims that the Athenians considered their city open to everyone, but were nevertheless closed on matters of religion and he describes the fate of those who did not know this or ignored it.

> Apollonius was ignorant of this, and of the inexorable penalty which they [the

Athenians] inflicted on any who uttered a single word about the gods contrary to their laws. On what other ground was Socrates put to death? He never sought to betray his city to the enemy, [and] he robbed no temple. No, because he used to swear strange oaths [e.g., by the dog] and give out (in jest surely, as some say) that he received communications from a spirit, he was therefore condemned to die by drinking hemlock. His accuser brought a further charge against him of corrupting young men, because he stimulated them to hold the constitution and laws of their country in contempt. Such was the punishment of Socrates, a citizen of Athens (*Against Apion* 2.262-64, LCL).

Strabo reports of the Athenians that they were hospitable to "things foreign, so also in their worship of the gods; for they welcomed so many of the foreign rites that they were ridiculed therefore by comic writers" (*Geography* 10.3.18). It appears that the Athenians were hospitable to many new philosophies, but the denial of their accepted deities often carried a penalty. It is interesting that in his proclamation before the Areopagus, Paul did not deny the existence of the "Unknown God" but rather identified him (see v. 28).

17:18. And also some of the Epicurean and Stoic philosophers were conversing with him. The philosophical school of the Epicureans was begun by Epicurus (341–270 B.C.), a moral and natural philosopher who was born in Samos, but came to Athens in 306 and began his school at his home and garden. For the most part, he and has followers lived a modest and austere life and generally avoided the affairs of the city and were often accused of Hedonist practices. In Christian times, the philosophy was rejected and condemned because it taught that the cosmos was the result of an accident, that there was no providential god, and that the criterion of the good life was pleasure. Whether they rejected the existence of God is not clear, but they were accused of this by their practice. Cicero, for instance, accused him of feigning piety to avoid rejection.

Why, but Epicurus (you tell me) actually wrote a treatise on holiness. Epicurus is making fun of us, though he is not so much a humorist as a loose and careless writer. For how can holiness exist if the gods pay no heed to man's affairs? Yet what is the meaning of an animate being [a god] that pays no heed to anything?

It is doubtless truer to say, as the good friend of us all, Posidonius, argued . . . that Epicurus does not really believe in the gods at all, and that he said what he did about the immortal gods only for the sake of deprecating popular odium. Indeed he could not have been so senseless as really to imagine god to be like a feeble human being, but resembling him only in outline and surface, not in solid substance, and possessing all man's limbs but entirely incapable of using them, an emaciated and transparent being, showing no kindness or beneficence to anybody, caring for nothing and doing nothing at all. In the first place, a being of this nature is an absolute impossibility, and Epicurus was of aware of this, and so actually abolishes the gods, although professedly retaining them (*De Natura Deorum* 1.123, LCL).

The Stoics, on the other hand, have their roots in Zeno of Citium (Cyprus) who came to Athens in 313 B.C., and studied Cynicism. He began teaching in the Stoa called the Painted Porch that also served as a public hall. His philosophy took its name from the location of the teaching in Athens, that is, in a stoa, the name given to various types of buildings that generally had a colonnade of Doric style columns and a roof over the space to a rear wall. In the *agora*, they also were places where discussions of political, religious, and philosophical issues took place. Zeno developed a philosophical system consisting of three branches, logic, physics, and theology and ethics. The goal of life, he said was virtue. He argued that a wise person could not be deprived of virtue which is the only true good and therefore such a person is happy (Ferguson, *Backgrounds* 333). Representatives of Stoicism from the Roman times include L. Annaeus Seneca (A.D. 1–65), Musonius Rufus (A.D. 30–101), Epictetus (A.D. 55–135), and Marcus Aurelius (121–180) who became Roman Emperor.

The Stoic understanding of natural theology influenced both Hellenistic Judaism and early Christianity (Rom. 1–2). They viewed life after death, however, as the divine part of humanity returning to the divine whole. It had considerable room for self-respect, but had little concern for love and knew nothing of a loving God. The goal for humanity was self-liberation, and it was an attainable goal. Stoics saw the world as deterministic and argued that the materialistic world of objects interacted according to strict laws, which are called Fate. Human activity, however, is free and morally responsible and expected to live in harmony with nature. For them, virtue was sufficient for happiness and nothing except virtue was good. Emotions were always bad, and even the death of loved ones should not affect the relatives. The true stoic claimed to be indifferent to pain, illness, and death, because happiness cannot depend on the things that are beyond one's control.

17:19. And they took him and brought him to the Areopagus. The Areopagus (Areopagus = *Areon pagos*), also known as Mars Hill, is traditionally understood to be the place where Paul proclaimed his message after being brought to the Council of the Areopagus, the Athenian council of that day. The hill was named after Ares, the Greek god of war, and provided an open space for speakers. Although the hill called Mars Hill, or the Areopagus, is well-attested in antiquity and located on the west side of the Acropolis, this is not necessarily the place where the council met. Often they met in the Royal Stoa in the *agora* (or city marketplace) below the Acropolis on the north side. Paul was led to the council of the Areopagus that dealt with all of the important matters related to the well-being of the city, including its religious and educational matters (see Plutarch, *Vita Cic.* 24). Unlike the earlier assembly of 500 (see above), the Areopagus consisted of aristocrats who were devoted to Rome. Although many of its earlier powers were stripped from it by Rome, the Areopagus council (Greek = *boule*) retained the right to try cases of homicide, wounding of others, arson, and religious matters. It continued existence well into the fourth century when it exercised authority primarily over judicial matters.

17:23. I also found an altar with this inscription, 'TO AN UNKNOWN GOD.' No such altar has been found at Athens, but there are several indications that there were altars erected in honor of unknown gods (plural). The absence of any such find, however, is no evidence that none existed. Apollonius of Tyana, responding to the piety of a young man, said ". . . it is much greater proof of wisdom and sobriety to speak well of all the gods, especially at Athens, where altars are set up in honour even of unknown gods" (Philostratus, *Apollonius of Tyana* 6.3, LCL; similarly, see also Diogenes Laertius, *Lives of Eminent Philosophers* 1:110). In the second century A.D., Pausanius, while describing one of the harbors of the Athenians at Munychia, wrote: "Here there is also a temple of Athena Sciras, and one of Zeus some distance away, and altars of the gods named Unknown, and of heroes, and of the children of Thesus and Phalerus . . ." (*Description of Greece* 1.1.3, LCL). In describing the altars of Olympia,

Pausanius again writes: "An account of the great altar I gave a little way back; it is called the altar of Olympian Zeus. By it is an altar of the Unknown Gods, and after this an altar of Zeus Purifier, one of Victory, and another of Zeus—this time surnamed Underground" (*Description of Greece*, 5.14.8, LCL). Although Paul speaks of an "Unknown God" (singular) there is considerable support for altars erected in antiquity to Unknown Gods (plural). Again, this does not mean that what is reported in this passage is incorrect, but only that presently there is no evidence of such an altar. The independent evidence, however, is enough to suggest that such altars did exist.

7:24. The God who made the world and all things in it. Paul stands in a long line of biblical writers who believed that God was the author of creation (Gen. 1:1; 14:19, 22; Exod. 20:11; Ps. 146:6; Isa. 42:5; see also *Wisd.* 9:9; 11:17; 2 *Macc.* 7:23, 28). The Stoic, Epictetus, ca. 55–130 A.D., of Hierapolis, Phrygia, also concluded that God created the universe.

Therefore, if madness can produce this attitude of mind toward the things which have just been mentioned, and also habit, as with the Galileans [probably Christians], cannot reason and demonstration teach a man that God has made all things in the universe and the whole universe itself, to be free from hindrance, and to contain its end in itself, and the parts of it to serve the needs of the whole (Epictetus, *Discourses* 4.7.6, LCL)?

This is not unlike Pythagoras' view of an ordered world (Plutarch, *De placitis philosophorum* 2.1), or Plato, who spoke of God as maker and father of the universe (*Timaeus* 28C, 76C).

[God] does not dwell in temples made with hands. This is reminiscent of Stephen's speech in 7:48, but see also 1 Kings 8:27; Isa. 57:15. The Jews believed that God did not require anything (2 *Macc.* 14:35; According to 1

Kings 8:22-27, Solomon acknowledges that God cannot be contained in the house that he has built. Josephus, citing this story, shares a widely held Jewish perspective: namely, that "Not by deeds is it possible for men to return thanks to God for the benefits they have received, for the Deity stands in need of nothing and is above any such recompense" (*Ant.* 8.111, LCL). Zeno taught that "one should not build temples of the gods" (Plutarch, *Moralia* 1034B). Lucian, A.D. 120–190, ridicules those who believe that God either dwells in temples or needs their sacrifices at all: "In view of what the dolts do at their sacrifices and their feasts and processions in honour of the gods, what they pray for and vow, and what opinions they hold about the gods, I doubt if anyone is so gloomy and woe-begone that he will not laugh to see the idiocy of their actions" (*On Sacrifices* 1, LCL). Later, he goes on to ridicule the building of temples:

Then too they erect temples, in order that the gods may not be houseless and hearthless, of course; and they fashion images in their likeness, sending for a Praxiteles or a Polycleitus or a Phidias, who have caught sight of a them somewhere and represent Zeus as a bearded man, Apollo as a perennial boy, Hermes with his first moustache, Posidon with sea-blue hair and Athena with green eyes! . . . . Who would not suppose that the gods like to see all this! . . . Actions and beliefs like these on the part of the public seem to me to require, not someone to censure them, but a Heracleitus or a Democritus, the one to laugh at their ignorance, the other to bewail their folly (*On Sacrifices* 11-12, 15. LCL).

17:26. Having determined their appointed times, and the boundaries of their habitation. Paul makes it clear that God is so interested in human beings that he even determines the times and locations of their dwelling. See also

Gen. 11:8; Deut. 32:8; Job 38:4-11; Ps. 74:16-17. Similarly, the author of the *War Scroll* at Qumran asks: "Who is like you, God of Israel, in the heavens or on earth, to do great deeds like your deeds, marvels like your feats?" He then goes on to list the activities of God regarding the earth and all of life within it and observes that God determines "the generations of ..., of the division of tongues, of the separation of peoples, of the dwelling of clans, of the legacy of the nations [. . .] of the sacred seasons, of the cycle of the years and of appointed times for ever. . . ." (1QM 10:8, 14-15, Garcia Martinez trans.).

17:27. He is not far from each one of us. Paul's views on the closeness of God to humanity is shared with other biblical writers (Ps. 145:18; Jer. 23:23), but also with his Stoic contemporary, Seneca (4 B.C.–A.D. 65), who writes:

We do not need to uplift our hands towards heaven, or to beg the keeper of a temple to let us approach his idol's ear, as if in this way our prayers were more likely to be heard. God is near you, he is with you, he is within you. This is what I mean Lucilius: a holy spirit dwells within us, one who marks our good and bad deeds, and is our guardian. As we treat this spirit, so are we treated by it. Indeed, no man can be good without the help of God. Can one rise superior to fortune unless God helps him to rise? He it is that gives noble and upright counsel. In each good man "a god doth dwell, but what god know we not" (*Epistle* 41.1-2, LCL).

Likewise, Dio Chrysostom, ca. 40–120 A.D., argues that what is common to all of humanity is the view that God has a keen interest in humanity.

Now concerning the nature of the gods in general, and especially that of the ruler of the universe, first and foremost an idea regarding him and a conception of him common to the whole human race,

to the Greeks and to the barbarians alike, a conception that is inevitable and innate in every creature endowed with reason, arising in the course of nature without the aid of human teacher and free from the deceit of any expounding priest, has made its way, and it rendered manifest God's kinship with man and furnished many evidences of the truth, which did not suffer the earliest and most ancient men to doze and grow indifferent to them . . . . (Dio Chrysostom, *Twelfth, or Olympic, Discourse* 27-28, LCL. See also Josephus, *Ant.* 8.108 and Philo, *Legum allegoria* 2.2).

17:28. As even some of your own poets have said, 'For we also are His offspring.' Paul cites the words of the Stoic poet Aratus (ca. 315) from *Phaenomena* 5. Paul's understanding of God's close relationship to humanity, however, was first informed by the biblical tradition (Ps. 139:1-16). Luke also shows an awareness of this connection, that is, that human beings are the offspring of God. In his genealogy of Jesus, Luke indicates that Adam was generated by God as those after Adam were generated from him, but God is the origin of humanity (see Luke 3:35-38).

17:29. Being then the offspring of God, we ought not to think that the Divine Nature is like gold or silver or stone. Luke elsewhere shows that God is not an idol and cannot be equated with material items (see 19:26, cf. Deut. 4:28; Isa. 40:18-20; 44:9-10; 46:5-6; Ps. 115:4).

17:32. Now when they heard of the resurrection of the dead, some began to sneer. Although the notion of resurrection became a popular one among the Jews in the intertestamental period (Dan. 12:2), it was rejected by the Greeks. Aeschylus (525–456 B.C.), who lived in Athens, quoted Apollo as having said that "when the dust has soaked up the blood of a man, once he has died, there is no resurrection" (*Eumenides* 647-48, Fitzmyer trans., 612).

17:34. But some men joined him and believed, among whom also were Dionysius the Areopagite. Little else is known of this man except that Eusebius (fourth cent.) passes on a tradition in the church that,

> Dionysius, one of the ancients, the pastor of the diocese of the Corinthians, relates that the first bishop of the church at Athens was that member of the Areopagus, the other Dionysius, whose original conversion after Paul's speech to the Athenians is the Areopagus Luke described in the Acts (*Eccles. Hist.* 3.4.9-10, LCL; see also 4.23.3).

Paul's ministry in Athens, not long by any standards, was nevertheless significant for Luke to show that the Gospel had gone forth to the pagan world and indeed to the heart of the popular philosophical schools of the day and faired well. The evidence that a church was founded at Athens as a result of this ministry comes from Eusebius in the fourth century (noted above), but this display of the Gospel in the marketplace was important preparation for the universal Gospel to make its way not only to the educational center of the Greco-Roman world, but eventually on to the capital of that world, Rome itself.

18:1-17. Paul's Ministry in Corinth.
18:1. After these things he left Athens and went to Corinth.

Corinth. Paul's longest ministry in Greece was at Corinth (Acts 18:1-18) where he wrote his famous letter to the Romans and possibly also letters to the Thessalonians and the Colossians. The many Christian notables in Paul's day who visited Corinth include the Apostle Peter, Timothy, Luke, Silas, Apollos, Prisca (= Prisca) and Aquila, and the Apostle Andrew who was martyred in the city of Patras

west of Corinth. At the end of the first century, Clement of Rome wrote a letter (*1 Clement*) to the church at Corinth to encourage them to respect their leaders, cease their squabbling, and to practice peace, humility, and obedience to their leaders. The most influential bishop in Greece in the second century was Dionysius of Corinth who wrote letters to many churches from there encouraging believers in their Christian faith. He rebuked the Christians at Athens for their tendency toward apostasy.

Because of its location, Corinth was always a strategically important city. Strabo (ca. 64 B.C.–A.D. 25) writes that because of its location and the important high mountain called the Acrocorinth that overshadowed the city, that whoever controlled this mountain and its sister mountain called the Ithome would also control all of the Peloponnesus. He claims that "it is because of their advantageous position that these cities have been objects of contention" (*Geography* 8.4.8, LCL). During the days of Philip V, king of Macedon (ca. 238–179 B.C.), and son of Demetrius II, the Corinthians sided with Philip in his several battles with the Romans (184, 183, and 181 B.C.). They not only took sides against the Romans, but they also threw insults and even human waste at them. Strabo writes:

> The Corinthians, when they were subject to Philip, not only sided with him in his quarrel with the Romans, but individually behaved so contemptuously towards the Romans that certain persons ventured to pour down filth upon the Roman ambassadors when passing by their house. For this and other offenses, however, they soon paid the penalty, for a considerable army was sent thither, and the city itself was razed to the ground by Leucius Mummius (*Geography* 8.6.23, LCL).

When the city was captured by the Roman consul Leucius Mummius in 146 B.C., he severely punished the residents by burning their city and killing most of its residents. The

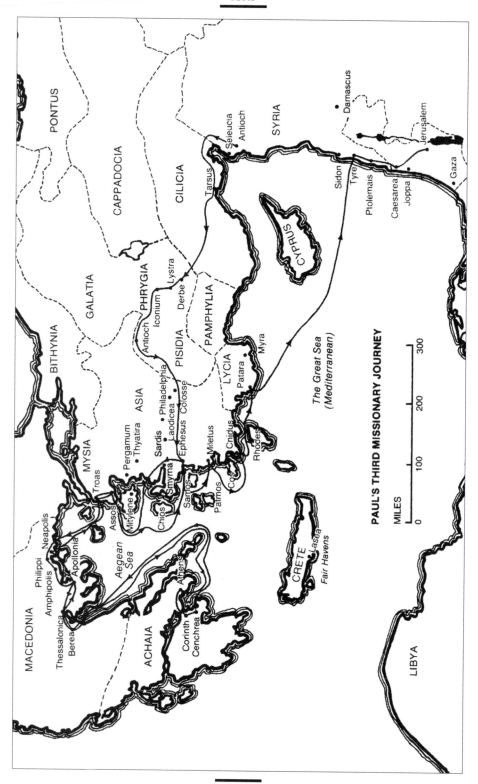

PAUL'S THIRD MISSIONARY JOURNEY

MILES

0   100   200   300

PONTUS

CAPPADOCIA

CILICIA

Tarsus

Seleucia
Antioch

SYRIA

Damascus

Sidon

Tyre

Ptolemais

Caesarea

Joppa

Jerusalem

Gaza

CYPRUS

The Great Sea
(Mediterranean)

GALATIA

PHRYGIA

Lystra

Iconium

Derbe

Antioch

PISIDIA

PAMPHYLIA

LYCIA

Myra

Patara

BITHYNIA

ASIA

Pergamum

Thyatira

Sardis

Philadelphia

Laodicea   Colosse

Ephesus

Miletus   Cnidus

Rhodes

MYSIA

Troas

Assos

Mitylene

Chios

Smyrna

Sardis

Patmos

Cos

Neapolis

Philippi

Amphipolis

Apollonia

Thessalonica

Berea

MACEDONIA

Aegean
Sea

Athens

ACHAIA

Corinth

Cenchrea

CRETE

Lasea

Fair Havens

LIBYA

city was repopulated in 44 B.C. by Julius Caesar and subsequently by Augustus (Octavian) who turned Corinth into a Roman colony. Concerning the rebirth of the city, Strabo writes: "Now after Corinth had remained deserted for a long time [146–44 B.C.], it was restored again, because of its favourable position, by the deified Caesar, who colonised it with people that belonged for the most part to the freedmen class." He continues, after mentioning the significant handcrafts in bronze and earthen vessels produced in the city, that "the city of the Corinthians, then, was always great and wealthy, and it was well-equipped with men skilled both in the affairs of state and in the craftsman's arts" (*Geography* 8.6.23, LCL).

Corinth's strategic location near the isthmus between the Aegean and Ionic Seas (or Corinthian and Saronic Gulfs) insured that it would be rebuilt and once again become a major city. In the first century, it was in many ways an international city at the center of commerce and travel in the first century when Paul was there. Corinth was well known in the ancient world for its springs, baths, classical stonework (especially the widely imitated Corinthian capitals on columns), and its temple of Apollo. It was also the home of an Asklepion, that is, a place of healing named after Asclepius, the god of healing, which was second in importance in Greece only to the Asklepion at Epidauros that lies southwest of Corinth. The city was also known for its low morals and its name was equated with promiscuous activity. To "corinthize" was widely known as the practice of fornication. The decadent community was also known for its worship of Aphrodite and a temple was erected in her honor at the top of the nearby mountain called Acrocorinth (see description below). Later Pausanias (ca. second cent. A.D.) tells a similar but more detailed story of the history of Corinth, noting that "Corinth is no longer inhabited by any of the old Corinthians, but by colonists sent out by the Romans" (*Description*

of Greece 2.1.2). He also offers a lengthy description of the city and also of the Isthmian games nearby, as well as the several attempts from the time of Alexander the Great to dig the Isthmian canal that was later completed in the nineteenth century (see especially his *Description of Greece* 2.1-4). During the first century A.D., the *Diolkos* (Greek, lit. = "haul-across"), a pathway over the isthmus, was built to haul ships overland at the narrowest part of the isthmus to avoid the treacherous voyage around the southern end of the Peloponnese peninsula, especially during winter months. Strabo says that the isthmus "where the ships are hauled overland from one sea to the other, is forty stadia [some six and a half miles], as I have already said" (*Description* 8.2.1; see also 8.6.4, 22, LCL).

The sites at Corinth are impressive, including the Doric temple of Apollo, the Roman baths, the stoa alongside of the main street in the city, or *cardo*. There is also the *bema* ("seat") where Paul stood before Gallio, the proconsul of Achaia who came from Delphi, to answer charges brought against him by the Jews (Acts 18:12-17).

Most of the ruins that survive today come from the Roman period and demonstrate that in the time of Paul, this was a very wealthy community and even more influential at that time than was Athens. In early church history the city also had much more significance than did Athens and was the primary place from which Christian missionaries to the Peloponnese towns and villages were sent.

18.2. Claudius had commanded all the Jews to leave Rome. The expulsion of the Jews from Rome is well attested in antiquity. Josephus, for instance, describes the events leading up to this action as follows:

> About this same time, another outrage threw the Jews into an uproar; and simultaneously certain actions of a scandalous nature occurred in connexion

with the temple of Isis at Rome..... I shall now return to the story, which I promised to tell, of what happened at the same time to the Jews in Rome. There was a certain Jew, a complete scoundrel, who had fled his own country because he was accused of transgressing certain laws and feared punishment on this account. Just at this time he was resident in Rome and played the part of an interpreter of the Mosaic law and its wisdom. He enlisted three confederates not a whit better in character than himself; and when Fulvia, a woman of high rank who had become a Jewish proselyte, began to meet with them regularly, they urged her to send purple and gold to the temple in Jerusalem. They, however, took the gifts and used them for their own personal expenses, for it was this that had been their intention in asking for gifts from the start. Saturnius, the husband of Fulvia, at the instigation of his wife, duly reported this to Tiberius, whose friend he was, whereupon the latter ordered the whole Jewish community to leave Rome. The consuls drafted four thousand of these Jews for military service and sent them to the island of Sardina; but they penalized a good many of them, who refused to serve for fear of breaking the Jewish law. And so because of the wickedness of four men the Jews were banished from the city (Josephus, *Ant.* 18.65, 80–84, LCL).

Dio Cassius preserves another tradition: namely, that earlier the Emperor Tiberius had banished Jews from Rome because they had "flocked to Rome in great numbers and were converting many of the natives to their ways" (Dio Cassius, *Roman History* 57.18.5, LCL). A well-known text from Suetonius (A.D. 75–140) suggests to many biblical interpreters that the cause for the expulsion of the Jews from Rome

had to do with problems between the Jews and Christians in Rome over Jesus the Christ. The text in question states: "Since the Jews constantly made disturbances at the instigation of Chrestus, he [Claudius] expelled them from Rome" (*Lives of the Caesars*, 5.15.4). Some commentators argue that this "Chrestus" is a corruption of a reference to the name Christ, that is, a reference to one of the titles for Jesus. Tacitus (ca. A.D. 55–120) reports that the expulsion was because of conflict or "debate" over Jewish and Egyptian rites. As a result, he claims that,

> A senatorial edict directed that four thousand descendants of enfranchised slaves, tainted with that superstition and suitable in point of age, were to be shipped to Sardina and there employed in suppressing brigandage: "if they succumbed to the pestilential climate, it was a cheap loss." The rest had orders to leave Italy, unless they had renounced their impious ceremonial by a given date (*Annals*, 2.85, LCL).

The Suetonius reference above more closely approximates the time of the expulsion in 18:2 and can be dated with some assurance to A.D. 49. This date best fits the chronology of Acts and also provides an important date for ordering the events of Acts and the missionary activity of Paul. It is also likely that this expulsion had something to do with the conflict among the Jews in Rome over their understanding of Jesus. It is important that Prisca (= Priscilla) and Aquila were Christians prior to their meeting Paul and their activity in sharing their faith may have led to their expulsion from Rome.

18:3. And because he was of the same trade, he stayed with them and they were working; for by trade they were tentmakers. There were many guilds in the Hellenistic world and various associations around such guilds were quite popular. The particular craft shared by Paul, Aquila, and Prisca (= Priscilla) was called by Luke "tentmakers" (Greek, *skenopoioi*), a term also used of those who were leather workers and those who produced overhead shades for theaters. Paul often refers to his practice of working with his hands (1 Cor. 4:12; 9:6; 1 Thess. 2:9; 2 Thess. 3:6-8) and follows a rabbinic tradition of teachers having a responsibility also to work with their hands. In the Mishnah, a Rabban Gamaliel, son of Rabbi Judah the Patriarch, says:

Excellent is study of the Law together with worldly occupation, for toil in them both puts sin out of mind. But all study of the Law without labour comes to naught at the last and brings sin in its train. And let all them that labour with the congregation labour with them for the sake of heaven, for the merit of their fathers supports them and their righteousness endures for ever (*m. Aboth* 2.2, Danby trans.).

Similar attitudes were found among the Greeks and those philosophers who also worked with their hands were praised. The practical Stoic philosopher Epictetus (ca. 54–120 A.D.) admonished all in his guild to combine their scholarly activity with practical work. Showing his disdain for those who refused to work with their hands he concludes that they, "have only to learn the life of healthy men—how the slaves live, the workmen, the genuine philosophers, how Socrates lived—he too with a wife and children—how Diogenes lived, how Cleanthes, who combined going to school and pumping water. If this is what you want, you will have it everywhere, and will live with full confidence" (*Discourses* 3.26.23-24, LCL). He goes on to ask why those in his guild have made themselves so useless that no one would take them in (*Discourses* 3.26.23-24, 26, LCL).

18:6. And when they resisted and blasphemed, he shook out his garments and said to them. See earlier 13:51. The roots of this shaking off the dust is found in 2 Sam. 1:16 and 1 Kings 2:33; and 3:1. See also the instruction of Jesus in Luke 10:11 (see also Matt. 27:25).

"Your blood be upon your own heads! I am clean. From now on I shall go to the Gentiles." Luke has another variation of this in 20:26. This does not mean that Paul no longer went into synagogues or other Jewish places of worship as the rest of Acts shows, but it is his way of showing that he no longer believes that he bears the guilt of responsibility for such preaching.

18:12. But while Gallio was proconsul of Achaia, the Jews with one accord rose up against Paul and brought him before the judgment seat. The visit of Gallio to Corinth (A.D. 51) is one of the few certain dates we have for New Testament events. Gallio, the Roman governor of the region, can be dated with relative certainty. He was the older brother of the contemporary philosopher Seneca (see Seneca, *Ep.*104.1) and his full name was Lucius Junius Gallio Annaeus. He is called by that name by Pliny (A.D. 23–79), who describes and recommends the remedy of Gallio who, after drinking waters that caused illness took a boat ride on the ocean. He writes: "for those attacked by consumption, as I have said, and for Haemoptysis, such as quite recently within our memory was taken by Annaeus Gallio after his consulship" (*Natural History* 31.33, LCL). He is also mentioned in the several fragments of an important inscription found at Delphi. With the most likely restorations to the text in brackets, the inscription is reproduced as follows:

Tiber[ius Claudius C]aes[ar Augus]tus G[ermanicus, Ponttifex Maximus, Holder of the Tribunician Po]wer f[or the twelfth time, Imperator f]or the twenty-sixth time, F[ather of the c]ount[ry, Counsel for the fifth time, and Censor, to the city of the Delphians, greetings.]

For some ti[me past I have been de]vot[ed] to the c[ity of t]he Delph[ians ... and good will from the be]ginning; and I have ever obser[ved th]e worship[ping of the Pythian] Apo[llo ...

But as for the many] current reports and those disco[rds] among the [citi]zens . . . [just as Lucius Ju]nius Gallio, my f[riend] an[d proc]onsul [of Achaia, wrote . . .Therefore I am granting that you] continue to enjoy your for[me]r . . . . (reproduced from *DBSup* 2.358-59).

Gallio's governorship can be determined from the twenty-sixth acclamation of the emperor. According to another inscription, the twenty-fourth acclamation took place in the eleventh year of the tribunate, that is, in the year of the reign of the Emperor Claudius from January 25 to January 24 of the year 51 (*CIL* 3.1977). Another inscription from Carian dates the twenty-sixth acclamation of the emperor in the twelfth tribunate (*B.C.H* 11 ·[1887] 306-7). Another inscription dates the twenty-seventh acclamation of the emperor the year following (*CIL* 6.1256). By means of these and other inscriptions, the Gallio inscription stone has been dated between January 25 and August 1 of the year 51 or 52. The proconsulship of Roman governors lasted one year and, according to Dio Cassius (A.D. 150–235), newly appointed governors left Rome by mid-April. Dio Cassius writes: "He [Claudius] gave notice to the governors chosen by lot, since they were slow even now about leaving the city, that they must begin their journey before the middle of April" (*Roman History* 60.17.3, LCL). Gallio was governor of Achaia sometime between A.D. 51 and 52 (probably July 1, 51 to July 1, 52) and Paul's eighteen months at Corinth (Acts 18:11) overlapped Gallio's term of office. This approximate dating is the most accurate point of reference for the time of Paul's missionary activity. Times are added to or taken from this date to determine other events in the book of Acts and to date Paul's writings.

The Acrocorinth. The imposing mountain called Acrocorinth rises above the ancient city of Corinth and has the remains of fortresses from the Byzantine, Crusader, and Venetian times. In the time of Paul there was a temple on top of the mountain in honor of Aphrodite that reportedly had some 1,000 prostitutes ("courtesans"). Pausanias describes the mountain as follows:

> The Acrocorinthus is a mountain peak above the city, assigned to Helius by Briareos when he acted as adjudicator, and handed over the Corinthians by Helius to Aphrodite. As you go up [to] this Acrocorinthus you see two precincts of Isis, one of Isis surnamed Pelagian (Marine) and the other of Egyptian Isis, and two of Serapis, one of them being of Serapis called "in Canopus." . . .
>
> On the summit of the Acrocorinthus is a temple of Aphrodite. The images are Aphrodite armed, Helius, and Eros with a bow (Pausanias, *Description of Greece* 2.4.6; 2.5.1, LCL).

Only one small part of a pillar base remains of the temple of Aphrodite, but from the top, one has a most impressive view of the famous isthmus and the mountains to the north and south. On a clear day, one can see the acropolis in Athens as well as the waters of the two oceans.

18:18-22. Paul's Return to Antioch via Cenchrea, Ephesus, Caesarea, and Jerusalem. This passage is a summarizing text that Luke uses to draw attention to the end of Paul's second missionary journey and shift focus to his third journey that once again begins in Antioch on the Orontes River in Syria (see 15:40 above).

18:18. In Cenchrea he had his hair cut, for he was keeping a vow. As Paul concluded his mission at Corinth, as well as what is generally called his second missionary journey, he made his way back to Antioch of Syria by way of Ephesus, Caesarea, and Jerusalem. Cenchrea, one of the two harbors of Corinth, was located some six and a half miles east of Corinth on the Saronic Gulf. Lechaeum on the Gulf of Corinth was the other port that led to the west. Cenchrea was also the site of a church (see discussion of Rom. 16:1).

Luke's reference to Paul performing a Jewish ritual vow at Cenchrea is not unlike his earlier act of circumcising Timothy (see discussion above on 16:3 and the later Jewish vow in the temple below in 21:23-26). At Cenchrea Paul cut his hair as a sign of the completion of a Nazirite vow that he had taken. According to the Law, the shaving or cutting of the hair was done at the completion of a vow and an offering was made in the tent (Num. 6:1-21, but especially 5, 13) or later in the temple. See discussion of Paul's understanding of the law in notes on 16:3 above.

The background for understanding such vows in the time of Paul may be seen in *m. Nazir*, the Mishnaic tractate that discusses Nazirite vows in considerable detail. More specifically, 1.4 and 3.2 which discuss the obligations of such vows. Originally, the Nazirite vows were offered as an act of dedication of a person to the service of God for a period of time (see Num. 6:1-21 and Judges 13:5-7). During such vows, the observer accepted prohibitions that were not true of other Jews: namely, an abstinence from wine or other intoxicants, having contact with corpses, and the cutting of one's hair. The observers did not, however, withdraw from community life or abstain from sexual activity. Nazirite vows could be temporary, which was more common, or for a lifetime as in the case of Samson (Judges 13:7) or Samuel (1 Sam. 1:11, 22). In the former case, the cutting of Samson's hair signaled the loss of his remarkable power from God (Judges 16:18-20). In the making of temporary Nazirite vows, the cutting of the hair marked the completion of vows that normally lasted thirty days. According to the Mishnah, the cutting of the hair was an important part of the Nazirite vow. For example, in the case of a man who makes such a vow we read:

> If he said, 'I will be a Nazirite like as the hairs of my head', or 'like as the dust of the earth', or 'like as the sand of the sea',

he becomes a lifelong Nazirite, and he must cut his hair every thirty days. Rabbi says: Such a one does not cut off his hair every thirty days; but who is he that cuts off his hair every thirty days? —he that says, 'I pledge myself to as many Nazirite-vows as the hairs of my head', or 'as the dust of the earth', or 'as the sand of the sea' (*m. Nazir* 1.4, Danby trans.).

If there were two vows made, it was possible that the person would cut his hair after thirty days and again at the end of the period of the vow. The latter came with an offering in the temple (see discussion of 21:23-26 below). According to a later passage,

> If a man vowed two Nazirite vows he should cut off his hair after the first spell on the thirty-first day, and after the second on the sixty-first day. If, after the first spell, he cut off his hair on the thirtieth day, he should cut off his hair after the second spell on the sixtieth day; but if he cut off his hair on the fifty-ninth day, he has fulfilled his obligation.... (*m. Nazir* 3.2, Danby trans.).

What specifically this vow was is not clear, but it may have been related to Paul's vision in 18:9 or to his appearance before Gallio in 18:12. There were many kinds of Nazirite vows in antiquity (see *m. Nazir* 1.1- 2.10). It may be that Paul, like other travelers on the seas, offered prayers to God for safety and took vows prior to entering the dangerous seas from the harbor at Cenchrea. Often these vows were repeated or sacrifices made at the successful completion of a sea voyage. Sea travel in the ancient world was especially dangerous and often took the lives of both crew and passengers. Paul mentions that he himself had been shipwrecked three times (2 Cor. 11:25), and the dangers of sea travel in the ancient world are noted by Luke later in 27:9-44. Juvenal (ca. 100–110 A.D.) describes how sailors who had almost lost their lives on a near-shipwrecked vessel, after reaching harbor, shaved their heads in fulfillment of their vows that they had made prior to their journey. "The skipper, with his crippled ship, makes for the still waters of the inner basin in which any Baian shallop may ride in safety. There the sailors shave their heads and delight, in garrulous ease, to tell the story of their perils" (*Satire* 12.80, LCL). For a discussion of Paul's involvement in other Jewish acts of piety, see Acts 20:6 and 21:21-24 below; and also the discussion of 1 Cor. 11:5-6 on the shaving of heads.

Luke reflects Paul's Jewish piety at a time when the early Christian movement was not completely separate from Judaism. Paul's primary concern over keeping the law had to do with whether Gentiles and not Jews were under its obligations. Paul did not believe that one had to be a bad Jew in order to be a good Christian. Jewish Christians were expected to keep the various religious acts of piety common to their Jewish traditions along with observing their faith in Christ. In both cases, Jews and Gentiles, Paul objected to salvation coming from such observances, but he never forbade the Jews from keeping those traditions and he himself also kept them. Indeed, if he had not, it would have been difficult for him to enter the synagogues and even the temple in Jerusalem (Acts 21:23-26).

18:19. And they came to Ephesus, and he left them there. Now he himself entered the synagogue and reasoned with the Jews. It is not clear why Luke mentions this stop en route to Jerusalem and Antioch, but it may be to show that Paul was involved in the origins of the church there. It is not clear that Paul himself began the church in Ephesus, but whether or not that is true, he left his friends Prisca (= Priscilla) and Aquila there no doubt to participate in the mission in that city. When he returned, there were other believers already present (18:27). His involvement in the establishment of the church there is not clear, but his involvement in its mission in the synagogue and elsewhere is well known to Luke (19:8-40).

Ephesus was one of the great cities of antiquity, probably one of the five largest cities of the Greco-Roman world numbering upwards of 200,000 residents. It is difficult to date the origins of the city with precision, but it may go back to around 900 B.C. It was developed into a major city by the Lydian king, Croesus, in the sixth century B.C. From 560 B.C., the city came under the rule of the Greek Lydian kings and was occupied by Lysimachus, one of the successor generals of Alexander the Great. After he died, the city came under the rule of the Seleucid kings from 290 onward. Ephesus was the leading city of the province of Asia, where Paul had earlier been forbidden to enter (16:6), as well as the residence of the governor of the province. It was also the home of the temple of Artemis (in Latin, Diana) also known as the Artemision. This temple was erected there in the latter part of the eighth century and enlarged in the time of Croesus (550 B.C.) but later destroyed (356 B.C.). Alexander the Great later offered to rebuild the temple, but the people of the city chose to do it themselves. The temple was 361 feet long and 180.5 feet wide, set on a platform that was 420 feet long and 240 feet wide. It was one of the seven wonders of the ancient world and the first building ever built on such a monumental scale. The temple was the pride of the city as Luke correctly shows in the story of 19:34-35. In 133 B.C., Ephesus came under Roman rule.

Paul had a very fruitful ministry at Ephesus and from there many other churches were established in the area, including those at Colossae, Hierapolis, and Laodicea, probably through Paul's fellow workers such as Epaphras (see Col. 1:7; 2:1). Paul wrote his correspondence to the Corinthians from this city (see 1 Cor. 16:8, 19). Paul came here on his second missionary journey and later spent some three years here in ministry (Acts 18:19, 19:1-41). The church at Ephesus was the first of the seven churches of Asia Minor to receive a word from the risen Christ at the end of the first century A.D. (Rev. 2: 1-7).

The view of the city itself is most impressive, especially the ancient (second century A.D.) Library of Celsus, the ruins of the temple of Hadrian (built ca. A.D. 117), and the massive theater that seats some 25,000 persons (see 19:29-31). There was also a beautiful *cardo*, or main street, running through the ancient city and a large stadium that seated some 70,000 persons. The presence of Jews in this city is well attested by Josephus (*Ant.* 14:225-227; 262-264; 16:167-168; 172-173; *Against Apion* 2:38-39). See also the notes on Ephesus below in 19:8 and following.

18:21. But taking leave of them and saying, "I will return to you again if God wills," he set sail from Ephesus. Paul's return to Ephesus in 19:1 is anticipated in 18:20-21 when he is invited to stay longer by the Jews in that city.

If God wills. Luke offers here a common expression of piety not only in the New Testament (1 Cor. 4:19; 16:7; Heb. 6:3; James 4:15), but also in Judaism, as in the case of Josephus' description of the faith of Moses addressing the fear of the Israelites coming out of Egypt. "Be not dismayed at the Egyptians' array, nor because of yonder sea and the mountains behind you offer no means of escape . . . for ye may see these hills leveled to a plain, should God so will, or the land emerge from the deep" (*Ant.* 2.333, LCL; see also *Ant.* 2.347; 7.343). A similar expression was also found in the Greco-Roman world. For example, Epictetus, when asked about when the winds will blow, writes:

> "What wind is blowing?" we ask Boreas. "What have we to do with it? When will Zepherus blow?" When it pleases good sir, or rather when Aeolus pleases [alluding to Homer's *Odyssey* 10.21] for God has not made you steward of the winds, but Aeolus. "What then?" We must make the best of what is under our control, and take the rest as its nature is. "How, then is its nature?"

As God wills (*Discourses*, 1.1.17, LCL; see also, Plato's *Phaedo* 80D and again his *Alcibialdes* I.35 §135d).

18:22. And when he had landed at Caesarea, he went up and greeted the church, and went down to Antioch. As he returns to Antioch, Paul concludes his second missionary journey begun in 15:40. Having once again demonstrated his loyalty and commitment to the church in Jerusalem, Paul returned to the church that welcomed him (11:26-30) and sent him out two times before (13:1-3; 14:26-28; and 15:30-35). The term "having went up" (Greek, *anabas*) is a typical reference to going up to Jerusalem, the holy city (see 8:5; 11:2 above). The opposite term, "he went down" (Greek, *katebe*) follows the same pattern noted earlier. As persons left the city of Jerusalem, they "went down."

VIII. 18:23–21:26. SPREAD OF THE GOSPEL FROM ANTIOCH TO JERUSALEM

The third and last missionary journey of Paul begins at Antioch of Syria once again and concludes with his visit to Jerusalem bringing with him a gift from the churches. While completing a vow in the temple, he was arrested and eventually sent off to Rome (21:27–28:31). The mission journey effectively ends with his report to James and the elders in Jerusalem (21:18-19).

18:23. And having spent some time there, he departed and passed successively through the Galatian region and Phrygia, strengthening all the disciples. The end of Paul's second missionary journey and the beginning of his third was at Antioch. He no doubt reported to the Christians in Antioch about the events related to his second phase of ministry, and he was sent out again to churches that he had established earlier in Galatia and Phrygia. See 16:6 above for a similar journey through this area. There is no reference to the churches he visited en route to Ephesus, and it appears that Luke wants his readers to focus on the significant ministry there rather than on the various churches he had earlier established.

18:24–19:7. Apollos and the disciples of John the Baptist at Ephesus. There are some parallels and differences in these two stories. Both stories happened in Ephesus and there seemed to be something deficient in both. Apollos was not sufficiently informed in the "Way of God" and he knew only the baptism of John. He received additional instruction from Prisca (= Priscilla) and Aquila about "the Way" but was not re-baptized but sent on his way to minister in Achaia, presumably Corinth where Prisca and Aquila had met Paul (18:2). In the latter case, these individuals were called disciples (19:1), who also knew only the baptism of John (19:3), but their understanding was more deficient that that of Apollos since Paul baptized them again but this time in the name of Jesus and placed hands on them so that they might receive the Holy Spirit. The two stories raise a lot of questions, but they do have in common the missionary zeal of those who had been baptized by John.

18:24. Now a certain Jew named Apollos, an Alexandrian by birth, an eloquent man, came to Ephesus. While Apollos is only described here in Acts, it is obvious that his later visit to Achaia in 18:27 (Corinth) was well received and is mentioned by Paul in 1 Cor. 1:12; 3:4-6; 4:6. On the other hand, Paul indicates that Apollos was with him when he wrote to the Christians at Corinth (1 Cor. 16:12). Evidently, Apollos returned since his presence there earlier is assumed (1:12; 3:4-6). Apollos' city of origin, Alexandria, was one of the great learning centers of the ancient world that was begun by Alexander the Great himself and became the capital of Egypt. The city was home of the largest library known in the ancient world as well as a famous museum. It was known for its art, industry, and commerce, but it was also the center for Hellenistic Jewish literature epitomized in the writings of Philo Judaeus. Pharos Island, next to Alexandria, was also the birthplace of the Septuagint, or Greek translation of the Old Testament Scriptures (often called the "LXX"). Later when churches where established there, Alexandria became the home of the first Christian Catechetical School directed first by Pantaenus (ca. 170) in the second century and later by Clement of Alexandria and Origen. Alexandria was one of the five largest cities in the Greco-Roman world of the first century (Rome, Alexandria, Antioch of Syria, Corinth, and Ephesus).

18:25. This man had been instructed in the way of the Lord. The phrase, "in the way of the Lord" has parallels in Isa. 40:3 and Jer. 5:4, but this is more likely a reference to the Christian community and its beliefs about Jesus (see 9:2; 16:17; 18:25-26; 19:9, 23; 22:4; 24:14, 22). Because the Christians adopted for themselves the term "the way" (see note on 9:2), that is probably what Luke intended his readers to understand.

And being fervent in spirit, he was speaking and teaching accurately the things concerning Jesus, being acquainted only with the baptism of John. There is a parallel situation in 19:1-7 where the disciples of John at Ephesus knew only the baptism of John, but in this case Apollos is instructed in the way of the Lord by Prisca (= Priscilla) and Aquila, but not baptized. He evidently had a deficient understanding of the Christian faith that was developed by the teaching of Prisca and Aquila, but he was not in need of the Spirit as the others were in 19:2. The "being fervent in the spirit" (Greek = *dzeon to pneumati*) may have suggested to Luke that Apollos already had the Spirit unlike the disciples of John in 19:1-7. In the latter case, the disciples of John are baptized by Paul, but there is no mention of Apollos being baptized after he gained this additional instruction. It is not clear whether Luke believed that he was already a Christian when he was met by Prisca and

Aquila, but he does not indicate that an act of initiation followed their instruction.

18:27. And when he wanted to go across to Achaia, the brethren encouraged him and wrote to the disciples to welcome him. It was not unusual for Christians to write letters of introduction for others in the ancient world. Paul himself wrote several such introductions (Rom. 16:1-2; 2 Cor. 3:1; Col. 4:10). In a fragmented letter by a patron on behalf of a client from Oxyrhynchos, Egypt in the first century, designated as *CPR 23*, we read a similar letter of recommendation.

> To my master, my really most worthy brother Gerontios, son of Elias, Ktesippos sends greetings. Since Makarios our sailor has loaded a few cabbages at Oxyrhynchos, let your brotherly kindness consider this man worthy to make a sale of them at a good price such as he himself wants to sell them for, and to be unmolested by anyone until he gets the boat ready — it's for me that you're doing this big favor. For God knows that if I had not written to your brotherly kindness and if without a letter he had spoken to you about me you would not have been able to allow him to be interfered with by anyone. And concerning . . .deign to inform me—a very big favour for me you'd be doing. My lord and brother Philip greets you. I greet with pleasure all those who love you. I pray you are very well . . . (verso) to my master, my really most beloved . . . (*ND* 1.65).

19:1-7. Paul having passed through the upper country came to Ephesus, and found some disciples . . . and he said to them, "Did you receive the Holy Spirit when you believed?" And they said to him, "No, we have not even heard whether there is a Holy Spirit." Luke's intention in this passage, as in the previous section on Apollos (18:24-28), is to include everyone into the mainstream of the church, even the so-called "fringe" Christians such as we find here. While Luke normally uses the term "disciple" (Greek, *mathetes*) to refer to those who are Christians (6:2, 7; 9:1, 10, 26, 38; 11:26, 29; 13:52; 14:20, 22, 28; 15:10; 16:1; 18:23, 27; 19:9, 30; 20:1, 30; 21:4, 16), it is not clear if that was his purpose since these "disciples" had not yet received the Holy Spirit. When individuals were baptized, they *usually* have received the Christian proclamation about Jesus and the Spirit has come upon them (2:38; 9:17-18; 10:44-48), but these individuals were unaware that the Holy Spirit was connected to baptism. This situation may not be unlike the situation in Acts 8:12-16 in which persons had believed the proclamation about Jesus and been baptized, but they had not yet received the Holy Spirit. These individuals had received the baptism of John that was a baptism of repentance (Luke 3:3) who also preached that the one coming after him would baptize with the Holy Spirit and fire (Luke 3:16; see also Acts 1:5). Were these "disciples" Christian then in the sense that Luke has shared thus far? Luke suggests that in both cases, Apollos and these "disciples," that there was something missing and that the Christians, in these instances, Prisca, Aquila and subsequently Paul, had to supply what was needed.

19:8–20:1a. Paul's ministry at Ephesus

19:8. And he entered the synagogue and continued speaking out boldly . . . about the kingdom of God. Although Paul felt absolved from the responsibility of preaching to the Jews, he nevertheless continued to enter the synagogues as he had opportunity. One of Luke's important themes is that Paul did not abandon the Jewish ethos or the Jewish people as he proclaimed the Gospel to Gentiles. (See note above on 18:6.) The boldness of speech is a common element in apostolic preaching in Acts (2:29; 4:13, 29, 31; 9:27-28; 13:46; 14:3; 18:26). Paul does not focus much on the kingdom of God in his letters (Rom. 14:17; 1 Cor. 4:20; 6:9-10; 15:24, 50; Gal. 5:21; 1 Thess. 2:12), a term Luke makes synonymous with "the Way" and preaching about the risen Christ Jesus (19:9).

There has been considerable difficulty finding a synagogue in the ruins of Ephesus, but the presence of Jews in that city is well known from antiquity. Josephus, for instance, argues for the right of Alexandrian Jews to refer to themselves as Alexandrians and writes:

All persons invited to join a colony, however different their nationality, take the name of the founders. It is needless to go outside our race for instances. Our Jewish residents in Antioch are called Antiochenes, having been granted rights of citizenship by its founder, Seleucus. Similarly, those at Ephesus and through the rest of Ionia bear the same name as the indigenous citizens, a right which they received from Alexander's successors (*Against Apion* 2.39, LCL).

Further, he also states precisely what the religious rights of the Jews were in Asia and Ephesus in particular. In declaring the rights insured the Jews by Caesar Augustus and Agrippa, he states that Julius Antonius, the son of Mark Antony, also wrote a letter and he sets forth that letter:

To the magistrates, council, and people of Ephesus, greeting. When I was administering justice in Ephesus on the Ides of February, the Jews dwelling in Asia pointed out to me that Caesar Augustus and Agrippa have permitted them to follow their own laws and customs, and to bring the offerings, which each of them makes of his own free will and out of piety toward the Deity, traveling together under escort (to Jerusalem) without being impeded in any way. And they asked that I confirm by my own decision the rights granted by Augustus and Agrippa. I therefore wish you to know that in agreement with the will of

Augustus and Agrippa I permit them to live and act in accordance with their ancestral customs without interference (*Ant.* 16.172-73, LCL).

19:9. Some were . . . speaking evil of the Way before the multitude, he withdrew . . . and took away the disciples, reasoning daily in the school of Tyrannus. Luke uses the common term, *schole*, from which the English word "school" is derived, as a place where Paul and his disciples continued to meet and proclaim Jesus after they were no longer welcome in the synagogue. In this case it was the *schole* or hall of Tyrannus. Earlier the term referred to a group of people who were addressed during their leisure. The notion of *schole* as a place is found in Plutarch, *Moralia.* 42A, but so is the notion of a group of people addressed (*Mor.* 519F). The context (see 19:8 where Paul departs the synagogue to another place) clearly refers to the former: namely, a lecture hall or meeting place. The identity of Tyrannus is unknown even though several inscriptions have been found in Ephesus with that name dating from roughly 54–59 (*I.Eph.* 20B.40) or A.D. 92–93 (*I.Eph.* 1012.4), which may refer to the same person (see also *ND* 1:186, cf. *I.Eph.* IV.1012; 1029.6-7 and *I.Eph.* 1001.5 that speaks of a M. Pacuvius Tyrannus from the time of Tiberias). While Josephus mentions the name of Tyrannus as one of the two bodyguards for Herod (Jucundus and Tyrannus), both esteemed for their size and strength (*Ant.* 16. 314), that is clearly not the person intended in the Acts story.

19:10. And this took place for two years. The two months are added onto the three months that Paul argued in the synagogue (19:8) and should be factored into the total amount of time of three years that Paul spent in this place (20:31). The dates are likely to be between sometime between A.D. 52 and 55. It is probable that the time of the preaching was during the siesta hours in the middle of the day when the hall was not in use.

So that all who lived in Asia heard the word of the Lord, both Jews and Greeks. This does not, of course, suggest that Paul preached in all of the towns in Asia, but rather that his missionary activity was carried on by his disciples, such as Epaphras who evangelized Colossae (Col. 1:7; 2:1).

19:13. But also some of the Jewish exorcists, who went from place to place, attempted to name over those who had the evil spirits the name of the Lord Jesus, saying, "I adjure you by Jesus whom Paul preaches." There are several examples from antiquity that refer to Jewish exorcists. In the "Great Magical Papyri" at Paris, there is an interesting reference to those who practice exorcisms in the name of Jesus. It reads: "I adjure you by Jesus, the God of the Hebrews" (PGM 4.3019-20). In telling of the ability of Solomon to surpass all of his contemporaries, Josephus also shares his experiences with exorcisms.

> And God granted him knowledge of the art used against demons for the benefit and healing of men. He also composed incantations by which illnesses are relieved, and left behind forms of exorcisms with which those possessed by demons drive them out, never to return. And this kind of cure is of very great power among us to this day, for I have seen a certain Eleazar, a countryman of mine, in the presence of Vespasian, his sons, tribunes and a number of other soldiers, free men possessed by demons. (Ant. 8.45-46, LCL).

In the following passage (8.47-47) he describes how the exorcisms were done. The existence of such exorcisms in the name of Jesus is presupposed in Matt. 7:22-23; 12:27; cf. Luke 11:19; Mark 9:38. Origen tells of those who cast out demons in the name of Jesus (C. Celsum 1.6; 6.40).

19:14. And seven sons of one Sceva, a Jewish chief priest, were doing this. While there was no high priest in the first century named Sceva, it is possible that the man was of the household of a chief priest. The name itself is not a Jewish name, but rather a Latin name that was well known in antiquity (Appian, Civil War 2.9.60; Dio Cassius, Roman History 56.16.1; Plutarch, Caesar 16:2). It is also not clear what a high priest from Jerusalem would be doing in Ephesus in the first place or even his sons. Since it is not uncommon for those who practiced such activities to be called priest, or even high priest, that may be what is behind the use of the title here. Juvenal (A.D. 60–140) may offer a parallel to those Jews who practiced exorcisms and other seeming magical activity. He tells of a Jewish woman who was known as a high priestess who told fortunes.

> No sooner has that fellow than a palsied Jewess, leaving her basket and her truss of hay, comes begging to her secret ear; she is an interpreter of the laws of Jerusalem, a high priestess of the tree [from the act of camping under trees], a trusty go-between of highest heaven. She, too, fills her palm, but more sparingly, for a Jew will tell you dreams of any kind you please for the minutest of coins (Satire 6.542-47, LCL, italics added).

The practice of these kinds of activities was not uncommon among the Jews in the first century (see Acts 13:6) and their presence in Ephesus was not unusual.

19:19. And many of those who practiced magic brought their books together and began burning them. The burning of books as a means of preventing the spread of unacceptable ideas has a long history in antiquity. Livy (59 B.C.–A.D. 17) reports that the consuls of Rome, fearing the introduction of new religious practices in Rome, gathered the citizens to warn them of the dangers of practicing the

Bacchic ceremonies and nocturnal rites.

How often in the times of our fathers and grandfathers, have the magistrates been given the task of forbidding the performance of foreign ceremonies, of excluding the dealers in sacrifices and soothsaying from the Forum, the Circus, and the city, of searching out and burning prophetical books, and of abolishing every system of sacrifice except the traditional Roman method? For men of the deepest insight in all matters of divine and human law came to the decision that nothing tended so much to the destruction of religion as a situation where sacrifices were offered not with the traditional ritual but with ceremonies imported from abroad. (*Rome and the Mediterranean, The Consul's Warning* 39.16, Trans. by H. Bettenson).

Likewise, Lucian of Samosata, tells how a certain Alexander gathered up the writings of Epicurus and burned them:

One of Alexander's acts in this connection was most comical. Hitting upon the "Established Beliefs" of Epicurus, which is the finest of his books, as you know, and contains in summary the articles of the man's philosophic creed, he brought it into the middle of the marketplace, burned it on the fagots of fig-wood just as if he were burning the man in person, and threw the ashes into the sea, even adding an oracle also: "Burn with fire, I command you, the creed of a purblind dotard [sic]!" (*Alexander the False Prophet* 47, LCL)

Suetonius also reports that some 2,000 prophetic books were destroyed leaving behind the Sibylline Oracles (*Life of Augustus* 31:1). The writings of Protagoras were also burned in the Athenian marketplace (Diogenes Laertius, *Lives of Eminent Philosophers* 9.52). This practice also was known in Palestine at the beginning of the Exilic period (Jer. 36:20-32)

and later when Antiochus Epiphanes (167 B.C.) committed sacrilege in Jerusalem both by sacrificing in the holy place, but also by burning the sacred books of the people.

Now on the fifteenth day of Chislev, in the one hundred forty-fifth year, they erected a desolating sacrilege on the altar of burnt offering. They also built altars in the surrounding towns of Judah, and offered incense at the doors of the houses and in the streets. The books of the law that they found they tore to pieces and burned with fire. Anyone found possessing the book of the covenant, or anyone who adhered to the law, was condemned to death by decree of the king. They kept using violence against Israel, against those who were found month after month in the towns. On the twenty-fifth day of the month they offered sacrifice on the altar that was on top of the altar of burnt offering (*1 Macc.* 1:54-59, NRSV).

19:22. And having sent into Macedonia two of those who ministered to him, Timothy and Erastus, he himself stayed in Asia for a while. Timothy is well known in the writings of Paul (see Acts 16:1-3; 18:5; Rom. 16:33; 2 Tim. 4:10; 1 Cor. 4:17; 16:10; Phil. 2:19-24) and has been discussed in 16:1-3 above, but Erastus is less known, even if mentioned (see Rom. 16:23; 2 Tim. 4:10). He was known as the *oikonomos* of the city (Rom. 16:23), the probable equivalent of the Latin *aedile*, a term that was found in the Roman colony at Corinth for a magistrate of a city. It is also possible that this term (*oikonomos*) may have been a step below the Roman *aedile*, but in either case, it was a respectable official office in the city. If this title, or its equivalent, belonged to Paul's association with the Erastus mentioned here, then there is evidence that the Christian message appealed also to the socially elite at Corinth. Their presence in the church and the abuse that came to those with more leisure and prestige is what probably also lies behind the conflict over the Lord's Supper in 1 Cor. 11:17-22. There are two ancient inscriptions that mention a person by this name that date from roughly A.D. 54–59 (SIG^3 838/cf. SIG^2 388) and A.D. 128–29 (*I. Eph.* 1487), the earliest of which may refer to the companion of Paul, but the evidence is not compelling. It reads: "Erastus in return for his aedilship laid [this pavement] at his own expense." The Greek term, *oikonomos*, is the same as the Latin *aedile*.

19:23-41. The riots at Ephesus. This story in Acts may have been toned down by Luke or his sources, because the picture of the events in Acts does not seem as threatening for Paul as we see in Paul's own reports of events in Asia (1 Cor. 15:32; 2 Cor. 1:8-11).

19:24. For a certain man named Demetrius, a silversmith, who made silver shrines of Artemis, was bringing no little business to the craftsmen. Although there is another Demetrius mentioned in 3 John 12, this can hardly be the same individual as in Acts 19. An inscription has been found in Ephesus, dating roughly from the time of Claudius in the first century A.D., that mentions the trade of a silversmith (Greek, *argurokopos*). The inscription also mentions that there was an association of such individuals called *neopoioi*. It reads:

> This tomb and the area around it and the subterranean vault belong to M. Antonius Hermeias, silversmith, Neopoios, and Claudia daughter of Erotion, his wife. No one is to be put in this tomb except the aforementioned. If anyone does dare to put in a corpse or excise this text, he shall pay to the silversmiths at Ephesos 1,000 denarii. Responsibility for this tomb rests with the association [or "guild." Greek = *to sunedrion*] of silversmiths [Greek = *argurokopon*], and Erotian dedicated 50,000 denarii. The legacy was provided in the sixth month, on the appointed eighth day (*I.Eph.* VI (1980) 2212; trans. from ND 4.7).

19:27. "And not only is there danger that this trade of ours fall into disrepute, but also that the temple of the great goddess Artemis be regarded as worthless and that she whom all of Asia and the world worship should even be dethroned from her magnificence." Artemis was believed to be the daughter of Zeus and his wife Leto and was given the bow and was known for her bravery.

Although Apollo, her brother, refused to fight against his brother, Posidon, she did not refuse and chided her brother. Homer says that she "railed at him hotly, even the queen of the wild beasts, Artemis of the wild wood, and spake a word of reviling: 'Lo, thou fleest, thou god that workest afar, and to Posidon hast thou utterly yielded the victory, and given him glory for naught?'" (*Iliad* 21.470-73, LCL).

The Romans called Artemis by the name of Diana. During the time of Claudius' marriage to Agrippina in the first century, Roman coins were minted in Ephesus referring to Artemis as Diana Ephesia. Ovid (ca. 43 B.C.–A.D. 17), who refers to Artemis as Diana calls her the "goddess of the wild woods" (3.161). Later, after she caused the death of a man who had seen her nakedness, Ovid says, only then "was the wrath of the quiver-bearing goddess appeased" (*Metamorphoses* 3.251). She was one to be feared.

The protection of the cult of Artemis at Ephesus had a long history well before the time of Paul. Xenophon (ca. 400 B.C.) tells of a certain Thrasyllus who "led his army back to the coast, with the intention of sailing to Ephesus. But when Tissaphernes learned of this plan, he gathered together a large army and sent out horsemen to carry word to everybody to rally at Ephesus for the protection of Artemis" (*Hellenica* 1.2.6, LCL). The worship of Artemis was not simply local, but extended far and wide. Pausanius, describing the cult of Artemis, writes: "Among the people of Calydon, Artemis, who was worshiped by them above all the gods, had the title Laphria, and the Messenians who received Naupactus from the Athenians, being at that time close neighbors of the Aetolians, adopted her from the people of Calydon" (*Description of Greece* 4.31.7. LCL).

The temple of Artemis, called the Artemision, was begun in the eighth century B.C., but later expanded and remodeled in the mid-sixth century B.C. It was burned in 356 B.C. supposedly on the night that Alexander the Great was born, and rebuilt by the "whole of Asia" over a period of some 120 years and exceptional materials and special woods were used in the process, according to Pliny (*Natural History* 16.79.213-15).

While the passage seems like undo hyperbole, this is the very kind of accusation brought against the Christians by their accusers in the second century. In a letter from Pliny the Younger to Trajan the Roman emperor seeking advice on how to deal with the Christians, it is clear that the Christian witness had a significant affect on the religious activity of his community. As a result of his persecutions and punishments of the Christians, crowds were once again returning to the pagan temples.

I think though that it is still possible for it [the Christian faith] to be checked and directed to better ends, for there is no doubt that people have begun to throng the temples which had been almost entirely deserted for a long time; the sacred rites which had been allowed to lapse are being performed again, and flesh of sacrificial victims is on sale everywhere, though up till recently scarcely anyone could be found to buy it. It is easy to infer from this that a great many people could be reformed if they were given an opportunity to repent [of their Christian beliefs] (*Letters* 10.96.9-10, LCL).

The accusation against the Christians that they were trying to destroy the cult of Artemis found some reality not only in the second century, but also in the fourth century. An inscription was found in Ephesus from that period on a marble base that reads: "having destroyed a deceitful image of demonic Artemis, Demeas set up this sign of truth honouring both God the driver-away of idols, and the cross, that victorious, immortal symbol of Christ" (*I.Eph.* IV.13.51 cited in ND 4.256). In the Selçuk Museum near the ancient site of Ephesus, there are two large heads of Augustus and Livia (Livia Drusilla, wife of Octavian or Augustus who became Roman emperor) with a cross on each forehead. At that time, all non-Christian cults became targets by the new majority religion.

19:28. And when they heard this and were filled with rage, they began crying out, saying, "Great is Artemis of the Ephesians!" Such titles for deities are common in the ancient world (Ps. 46:2; 75:1; 94:3; Dan. 9:4; Acts 8:10; Titus 3:4). In the apocryphal Bel and the Dragon, the king who was visiting with Daniel said: "You are great, O Bel, and in you there is no deceit at all!" (*Bel and the Dragon* 18, NRSV).

20:1b-38. Paul's Final Mission to Churches in Greece, Troas, Miletus.

20:6. And we sailed from Philippi after the days of Unleavened Bread, and came to them at Troas within five days; and there we stayed seven days. See 16:8 above for a description of Troas. The celebration of Unleavened Bread was essentially a reference to the Passover feast that was an observance of seven days of rest for Jews (see discussion in Luke 22:1). It may also be that such vows and observances are Luke's way of fixing the chronology of Paul's missionary itinerary by his keeping of another Jewish ritual (see discussions of 16:3 and 18:18 above and 21:15-26 and 27:9 below), an important theme for Luke.

20:7-12. Paul's Final Visit to Troas (See note on 16:8 above.)

20:7. And on the first day of the week, when

we were gathered together to break bread. The first day of the week combined with the breaking of bread together is a reference to a Christian day of worship (see Luke 24:1; 1 Cor. 16:2; Rev. 1:10). In a late first-century Jewish Christian document, we read of the practice of worship that emerged in the Christian church along with admonitions about the attitudes that should be present in such worship. "On the Lord's Day come together, break bread and hold Eucharist, after confessing your transgressions that your offering may be pure; but let none who has a quarrel with his fellow join your meeting until they be reconciled, that your sacrifice be not defiled" (*Didache* 14:1-2, LCL).

20:10. But Paul went down and fell upon him and after embracing him, he said, "Do not be troubled, for his life is in him." The story of this miracle resembles somewhat that of Elisha in 2 Kings 4:33-36. There is also an interesting story of a miracle told by Philostratus about how Apollonius, after coming upon a funeral procession of a young woman who died just prior to her marriage, raised her up.

> A girl had died just in the hour of her marriage, and the bridegroom was following her bier lamenting as was natural his marriage left unfulfilled, and the whole of Rome was mourning with him, for the maiden belonged to a consular family. Apollonius then witnessing their grief, said: "Put down the bier, for I will stay the tears that you are shedding for this maiden." And withal he asked what was her name. The crowd accordingly thought that he was about to deliver such an oration as is commonly delivered as much to grace the funeral as to stir up lamentation; but he did nothing of the kind, but merely touching her and whispering in secret some spell over her, at once woke up the maiden from her seeming death; and

the girl spoke out loud, and returned to her father's house just as Alcestis did when she was brought back to life by Hercules (*Life of Apollonius* 4.45. LCL).

Such accounts of miracles abound in the *Life of Apollonius* story.

20:13-14. But we, going ahead to the ship, set sail for Assos, intending from there to take Paul on board; for thus he had arranged it, intending himself to go by land. And when he met us at Assos, we took him on board and came to Mitylene. It is not certain why Paul came to Assos overland instead of with his companions who arrived there by boat. From a Christian point of view, it is not clear why Paul would have stopped here except for its strategic location and convenient stopping place for those traveling by ship. It may have been that Paul stayed as long as possible with his friends at Troas and traveled overland to meet up with his traveling companions at Assos. Since the ship traveling from Troas to Assos would have had to pass an exposed coast and double Cape Lectum before reaching Assos, there would have been adequate time for Paul to make the journey on foot and meet up with his companions. This was not unusual, of course, because earlier Paul followed his companions after he observed the days of Unleavened Bread in Philippi (20:5-6). The city or village of Assos is mentioned in Acts 20:6, 13-14 as a place from which Paul and his companions boarded a ship around A.D. 55 en route to Mitylene on the island of Lesbos as they were making their way to Jerusalem. For safety's sake, boats stayed close to the land in the ancient world and made frequent stops for rest and shelter.

As in ancient times, the village of Assos today is a small hamlet pressed against sheer cliff walls. The ruins that remain of the ancient city are on a five square city block area on the tip of a hill. The city was founded about 1000 B.C. by the Aeolian Greeks and ruled by the Lydians, Pergamenes, Romans, Byzantines, and finally by the Ottoman Empire from the year 1330. Like Pergamum, the city had a gymnasium, a theater, an agora (marketplace), and carved into the side of the hill, the temple of Athena dating from 530 B.C. The city today is known as Behramkale. Its more modern mosque (Murad Hüdavendigar Mosque), built in the fourteenth century, incorporated materials from an earlier Christian church probably located on the same site. The Greek crosses carved in the lintel over the entrance support this suggestion. Assos was known for its sarcophagi that were made of limestone and shipped throughout the Mediterranean world.

The city carefully cultivated the favor of the Roman emperors and erected buildings in their honor. In a stoa (open porch that is roofed and supported by a colonnade located on a street or city square) near the gymnasium, an inscription was found that read: "The priest of the god Caesar Augustus, himself likewise hereditary king, priest of Zeus Homonoos, and gymnasiarch, Quintus Lollius Philetarios, has dedicated the Stoa to the god Caesar Augustus and the people." When Strabo, Greek historian and philosopher (63 B.C.–A.D. 21), wrote of Assos he said that it was "strong and well-fortified ... [with] a harbor formed by a great mole ... a notable city" (*Geography* 13.1, 57, 66). Aristotle, a student of Plato and teacher of Alexander the Great, lived and taught at Assos prior to going to Macedonia to be tutor to Alexander. During his stay at Assos, he married Pythias, the daughter of the city tyrant, Hermeias, who had invited Aristotle to come to the city. This is where Aristotle began his famous treatise on *Politics*.

20:16. For Paul had decided to sail past Ephesus in order that he might not have to spend time in Asia; for he was hurrying to be in Jerusalem, if possible, on the day of Pentecost. Paul's bypassing Ephesus, where he had been so involved in his ministry, suggests that it was dangerous for him to stop there. This also fits with what Paul indicates

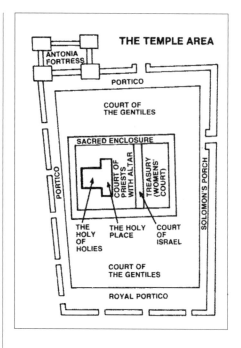

in 1 Cor. 15:32 and 2 Cor. 1:8-11. Had he a choice in the matter, as v. 16 suggests, it is strange that he would have bypassed the community and then asked the elders of the church in Ephesus to join him in Miletus (v. 17). Paul's desire to be in Jerusalem on Pentecost fits with his observance of other Jewish holy days in Acts (see discussion of this occasion in 2:1 and 20:6 above).

20:17-38. Paul's visit with the Ephesian Elders at Miletus. At this point the "we" passages discontinue until 21:1 which suggests that Luke was using a source for the activities and speech that occurred at Miletus. On Ephesus for the Ephesian elders, see discussion at 18:19 above. It was at Miletus that Paul left Trophimus who became ill (2 Tim. 4:20) perhaps on another visit to the city.

Miletus was an important and prosperous harbor city of about 60,000 residents, and at one time, one of the most important in the ancient world, located some thirty miles south of Ephesus on the southwestern coast of

Turkey and near the mouth of the Meander River. The city was founded by the Cretans of the Minoan period and it was occupied and used as an outpost for military actions by the Mycenaeans from Achaia who were located south of Corinth. By the sixth century B.C., Miletus had become the most important and most prosperous city of Asia Minor, but later was surpassed by Ephesus. Pliny describes the city as the capital of Ionia and the "mother of over ninety cities scattered all over the seas." He hastens to add that Miletus must not "be robbed of her claim to Cadmus as her citizen, the author who originated composition in prose" (*Natural History* 5.112, LCL). In the time of Paul, the city could boast of a theater that would seat some 15,000 persons, one of the best preserved ancient Roman theaters in Turkey today. There were also three market areas and four harbors connected to the city. One of the marketplaces near the theater was the largest known in the ancient world. During the first century, there was a temple of Athena, another for Apollo, as well as a stadium and a large gymnasium.

What is more significant for an understanding of Acts is the kind of speech that is present in these verses. It is the only speech in Acts that Paul addresses to Christians, and it can reasonably be called something like a last will and testament. With this speech, Paul concludes his mission. The speech was pastoral in focus and has a familiar sequence in Greco-Roman literature as well as in some of the Old Testament literature. For example, the speech has a recollection of Paul's ministry in Ephesus (vv. 18-19); a statement indicating that he had completed his responsibility to them stated three times which is unusual (vv. 20-21, 26-27, 33-35a) indicating perhaps his addressing special circumstances or problems in the church; a statement of his departure (vv. 22-25); the appointment of successors (vv. 29-30); an exhortation to fidelity (v. 31); and finally, a blessing (vv. 31, 35b). This type of literary form

is essentially followed in several examples of Jewish literature including Gen. 49:1-17 (Jacob's farewell); the whole of Deut. (Moses' farewell); Josh. 23–24 (Joshua's farewell); 1 Samuel 12:1-25 (Samuel's farewell); Tobit 14:3-11 (Tobit's farewell). See also *Jub.* 19:17–21:26; *Jub.* 36:1-16; the *Testaments of the Twelve Patriarchs*; 1 Enoch 91:1-19; 2 Esdras 14:28-36; 2 Baruch 77:1-16; Josephus, *Ant.* 4.309-26 (Moses' farewell). There are also several examples of a similar pattern in Homer's *Iliad* 16.844-53 (Patroclus) and also 22.355-60 (Hector); Sophocles, *Oedipus Colonus* 1518-55 (Oedipus); Herodotus, *History* 3.65 (Cambyses). It may also be that John 14–17 is a similar kind of literature. Paul's speech to the Ephesian elders is presented here in its entirety to illustrate these emphases.

[18] And when they had come to him, he said to them, "You yourselves know, from the first day that I set foot in Asia, [19] how I was with you the whole time, serving the Lord with all humility and with tears and with trials which came upon me through the plots of the Jews; [20] how I did not shrink from declaring to you anything that was profitable, and teaching you publicly and from house to house, [21] solemnly testifying to both Jews and Greeks of repentance toward God and faith in our Lord Jesus Christ. [22] And now, behold, bound in spirit, I am on my way to Jerusalem, not knowing what will happen to me there, [23] except that the Holy Spirit solemnly testifies to me in every city, saying that bonds and afflictions await me. [24] But I do not consider my life of any account as dear to myself, in order that I may finish my course, and the ministry which I received from the Lord Jesus, to testify solemnly of the gospel of the grace of God. [25] And now, behold, I know that all of you, among whom I went about preaching the kingdom, will see my face no more.

26"Therefore I testify to you this day, that I am innocent of the blood of all men. 27For I did not shrink from declaring to you the whole purpose of God. 28Be on guard for yourselves and for all the flock, among which the Holy Spirit has made you overseers, to shepherd the church of God which he purchased with His own blood. 29I know that after my departure savage wolves will come in among you, not sparing the flock;30 and from among your own selves men will arise, speaking perverse things, to draw away the disciples after them. 31Therefore be on the alert, remembering that night and day for a period of three years I did not cease to admonish each one with tears. 32And now I commend you to God and to the word of His grace, which is able to build you up and to give you the inheritance among all those who are sanctified. 33I have coveted no one's silver or gold or clothes. 34You yourselves know that these hands ministered to my own needs and to the men who were with me. 35In everything I showed you that by working hard in this manner you must help the weak and remember the words of the Lord Jesus, that he Himself said, It is more blessed to give than to receive."

36And when he had said these things, he knelt down and prayed with them all. 37And they began to weep aloud and embraced Paul, and repeatedly kissed him, 38grieving especially over the word which he had spoken, that they should see his face no more. And they were accompanying him to the ship.

20:17. And from Miletus he sent to Ephesus and called to him the elders of the church. It appears that the presence of elders in leadership roles in Pauline churches is similar to Luke's account in 14:23, rare and found only in Acts. For a discussion of the elders (Greek = *presbyteroi*), see 11:30 above. Observe that in v. 28 below these elders are also called overseerers (bishops, Greek = *episcopoi*). The difficulty is that except for the Pastorals (1 Tim. 5:1, 2, 17, 19; Titus 1:5) Paul never uses the term "elders" (Greek pl. = *presbyteroi*) in his letters, and only once does he use the term "overseerer" (*episcopos*) in Phil. 1:1. Luke assumes the presbyterial structure of the church from its beginnings (see previous discussion in 11:30 and 14:23 above).

20:20-21. How I did not shrink from declaring to you anything that was profitable, and teaching you publicly and from house to house, solemnly testifying to both Jews and Greeks of repentance toward God and faith in our Lord Jesus Christ. This assertion of Paul's having fulfilled his responsibility and therefore making a declaration of his innocence (see also v. 26) is similar to that in 1 Sam. 12:2-5; 1 Thess. 2:1-12; and 2 Cor. 7:2. There is also a close parallel in the *Testaments of the Twelve Patriarchs* where the writer of The Testament of Simeon indicates that Simeon gathered his children to himself on his deathbed and said: "I was born of Jacob, a second son for my father, and Leah, my mother, called me Simeon because the Lord had heard her prayer. And I became extraordinarily strong; I did not hold back from any exploit, nor did I fear anything. My heart was firm, my courage was high, and my feelings were dispassionate . . . See, I have told you everything, so that I might be exonerated with regard to your sin" (*Testament of Simeon* 2.2-4, *OT Pseud* 1:785-87). Also in the *Testament of Levi* we read: "And now, my children, observe the things which I command you, since what I heard from my ancestors I have told to you. See, I am free of responsibility for your impiety or for any transgression which you may commit until the consummation of the ages . . ." (*Test. Levi* 10:1-2, *OT Pseud* 1:792).

20:27. For I did not shrink from declaring to

you the whole purpose of God. Luke frequently makes use of the term council or will (Greek = *boule*) of God to indicate the plan of God (2:23; 4:28; 5:38; 13:36; 19:1 and here). It is found once in Paul's writings (1 Cor. 4:5) and used here to tell of God's saving purpose for humanity.

20:28-30. Be on guard for yourselves and for all the flock, among which the Holy Spirit has made you overseers, to shepherd the church of God which he purchased with his own blood. I know that after my departure savage wolves will come in among you, not sparing the flock; and from among your own selves men will arise, speaking perverse things, to draw away the disciples after them. On "overseers," see above note in 20:17, but also 11:30 and 14:23. Luke uses the shepherd metaphor here to identify the relationship between leaders and the adherents to the Christian faith and he does so in a text that warns of heresy invading the church following Paul's departure. Apollonius also used this metaphor in reference to protecting his "flock" of followers from others. Philostratus writes:

But certain persons accused him [Apollonius] of avoiding attendance on governors at their visits, and of influencing his hearers rather to live in retirement instead; and one of them uttered the jest that he drove away his sheep as soon as he found any forensic orator approaching. "Yes, by Zeus," said Apollonius, "lest these wolves should fall upon my flock" (*Life of Apollonius* 8.22, LCL).

For parallel warnings of future perverters or twisters of the truth who will do harm to the church, see Mark 13:22; 1 Tim. 4:1-7; 2 Tim. 3:1-4:4; 2 Peter 2:1-3:18. For texts using the sheep attacked by wolves metaphor, see Matt. 7:15. For a different twist on this metaphor, the writer of the *Didache* says: ". . . for in the last days the false prophets and the corrupters shall

be multiplied, and the sheep shall be turned into wolves, and love shall change to hate" (*Did.* 16.3, LCL), but also Ignatius of Antioch (ca. 115–17) who admonishes his hearers: "And follow as sheep where the shepherd is. For there are many specious wolves who lead captive with evil pleasures the runners in God's race, but they will find no place if you are in unity" (*Philadelphians* 2.2-3, LCL. See also 2 Clem 5.2-4 and Justin, *1 Apol.* 1.16.13).

He purchased with His own blood (v. 28). This is the only place where Luke introduces the significance of the death of Jesus or those who have received the Gospel. He normally indicates that the death of Jesus was in the plan of God or emphasizes that the death of Jesus was vindicated through the resurrection (2:23-24, 29-36; 3:13-15; 4:10, 27-29; 10:39-40; 13:28-35). For Luke, the triumph of God comes through his raising of Jesus from the dead. See Paul's writings, however, where the importance of the death of Jesus "for our sins" is quite prominent (Rom. 5:8-9; 8:32; 1 Cor. 15:3-8; Gal. 1:3-4). See also Heb. 9:12.

After my departure savage wolves will come (v. 29). "Departure" is used as a euphemism for death.

20:33. I have coveted no one's silver or gold or clothes. Luke follows a well-known virtuous defense of Paul's conduct by indicating that his actions were not based upon greed. After advising Apollonius to accept a king's generous gift so as not to offend him, after Apollonius had refused the gift, Damis, his companion, reminded him of their own financial needs for travel. Apollonius responds:

a man must fortify himself and understand that a wise man who yields to laziness or anger or passion, or love of drink, or who commits any other action prompted by impulse and inopportune, will probably find his fault condoned; but if he stoops to greed, he will not be pardoned, but render himself odious as a combination of all vices at once. For surely they will not allow that he could be the slave of money, unless he was already the slave of his stomach or fine raiment or of wine or of riotous living ... (Philostratus, *Life of Apollonius* 1.34, LCL).

Dio Chrysostom, who derides the Cynics for their way of obtaining favors from the unsuspecting persons and thereby bringing discredit to philosophers in general, says: "if in the guise of philosophers they do these things with a view to their own profit and reputation, and not to improve you, that indeed is shocking." he goes on to speak of the virtuous persons:

But to find a man who in plain terms and without guile speaks his mind with frankness, and neither for the sake of reputation nor for gain makes false pretensions, but out of good will and concern for his fellow-men stands ready, if need be, to submit to ridicule and to the disorder and the uproar of the mob—to find such a man as that is not easy, but rather the good fortune of a very lucky city, so great is the dearth of noble, independent souls and such the abundance of toadies [those who ate toads that were believed to be poisonous for the purpose of flattery or special gain], mountebanks [itinerant quacks or charlatans], and sophists (*Oration* 32.10-11, LCL).

This view of virtue is also found in Paul's writings (1 Thess. 2:5, cf. Phil. 4:11-18).

20:35. Remember the words of the Lord Jesus, that He Himself said, 'It is more blessed to give than to receive.' See Luke 17:32. The call to remember is a typical example of Hellenistic instruction and is found often in farewell discourses. In his *Demonax*, Lucian of Samosata (A.D. 120–190) calls his readers to remember.

It is now fitting to tell of Demonax for two reasons —that he may be retained in memory by men of culture as far as I can bring it about, and that young

men of good instincts who aspire to philosophy may not have to shape themselves by ancient precedents alone, but may be able to set themselves a pattern from our modern world and to copy that man, the best of all the philosophers whom I know about (*Demonax* 2, LCL).

See other examples in Lucian of Samosata *Nigrinus* 6-7; Plutarch, *Education of Children* 13 [*Moralia* 9F]; *Progress in Virtue* 15 [*Moralia* 85A]. Luke preserves what is commonly known as an *agrapha*, that is, a saying of Jesus that is not found in the canonical gospels. There is a close parallel in thought to this saying found in 1 *Clement* where Clement of Rome praises his readers as follows:

And you were all humble-minded and in no wise arrogant, yielding subjection rather than demanding it, "giving more gladly than receiving," satisfied with the provision of Christ, and paying attention to his words you stored them up carefully in your hearts and kept his sufferings before your eyes (*1 Clem* 2:1, LCL).

This saying is also a well-known Greek aphorism found in various forms in the Greco-Roman world, especially in Thucydides (2.97.4, see also Plutarch, *Moralia* 173d; 181-82; *Moralia* 778c; and *Vita Caes.* 16).

21:1–22:21. Paul in Jerusalem
21:1-16. Paul's Final Journey to Jerusalem. After Paul delivered his closing address to the elders of the church at Ephesus while his ship was docked at Miletus, he began his journey to Jerusalem in order to be there for the Feast of Pentecost (20:16). From this point on, nothing is said about the places where Paul stopped while on his journey to Jerusalem except that he was welcomed by fellow believers in Tyre and stayed seven days with them while the ship was unloading (21:4) and Caesarea where he met with Philip the Evangelist (6:5) and heard from

Agabus (see earlier in 11:28). In this section the "we" passages resume and continue through v. 18. What Luke says about this visit in the warnings of danger to Paul fit with Paul's perception and led him to ask others to pray for him as he made his way to Jerusalem (Rom. 15:30-31).

21:1. We ran a straight course to Cos. This Doric island was situated off the southwest coast of Asia Minor (modern Turkey). It was famous for its shrine of Asclepius, a hero and the healing god who, according to Greek mythology was born in Epidaurus south of Corinth (Pausanias, *Description* 2.26.3-7), but the origin of the cult was at Thessaly in the fourth century B.C. According to Strabo, the actual origin was at Tricca in Thessaly (Strabo, *Geography* 437). These places were therapeutic centers in the ancient world and were accompanied by theaters, gymnasiums, baths, and various dietetic regimens. The founding of the temple at Cos was due largely to the disciples of Hippocrates. These *asclepia* were common throughout the Greco-Roman world, and two were discovered recently in Jerusalem dating probably from the time of Jesus.

Rhodes. This island of about 420 square miles located near the coastland of Caria was settled by the Dorian Greeks. It was a prosperous island from the time of Alexander the Great and well into the time of the Roman Empire. After significant retribution because its citizens did not support Rome, it eventually cooperated with Rome in its campaigns against various rebellious states in the east and was well rewarded by Rome. It became prosperous once again during Roman rule. According to the author of *1 Macc.* 15:23, there evidently were Jews living both in Rhodes and Cos during the occupation of the Seleucids in Palestine.

21:1. The next day to Rhodes and from there to Patara. Patara was a southern coastal city in Lycia with a harbor frequently used by ships with grain coming from Alexandria, Egypt in

the first century. See also 27:5 where Myra is mentioned as a harbor at Lycia. Some manuscripts include Myra to harmonize the location of the harbor in both places.

21:2. And having found a ship crossing over to Phoenicia, we went aboard and set sail. See note on Phoenicia in discussion of 11:19 above.

21:3. And when we had come in sight of Cyprus, leaving it on the left, we kept sailing to Syria and landed at Tyre; for there the ship was to unload its cargo. See notes above on 11:19 and 13:4-12. Tyre was one of the two most important cities in Phoenicia. The other major city was Sidon some twenty miles north of Tyre. Tyre had a rich and lengthy history before the first century dating before the tenth century B.C. and experiencing freedom and independence only occasionally after the conquests of Alexander the Great and later during Rome's rise to power. Strabo's description of the city is telling.

But Tyre is wholly an island, being built up nearly in the same way as Aradus; and it is connected with the mainland by a mole, which was constructed by Alexander when he was besieging it; and it has two harbours, one that can be closed and the other, called "Aegyptian" harbour, open. The houses here, it is said, have many stories, even more than the houses at Rome, and on this account, when an earthquake took place, it lacked but little of utterly wiping out the city. The city was also unfortunate when it was taken by siege by Alexander; but it overcame such misfortunes and restored itself both by means of the seamanship of its people, in which the Phoenicians in general have been superior to all peoples of all times, and by means of their dye-houses for purple . . . The Tyrians were adjudged autonomous, not only by the kings, but also, at small expense to them, by the Romans, when the Romans confirmed the decree of the kings. The number and the size of their colonial cities is an evidence of their power in maritime affairs. Such, then, are the Tyrians.(*Geography* 16.2.23, LCL).

It did not play an important role in New Testament history except that Jesus attracted followers from as far as Tyre (Mark 3:8) and evidently visited there on one occasion (Mark 7:24-31) on a preaching and healing mission before returning to Galilee. Later Jesus indicated if the cities of Tyre and Sidon had received as many miracles or deeds of power as the villages of Chorasin and Bethsaida that they would have repented and also that the cities of Phoenicia would receive better treatment on the day of judgment than those villages in Galilee (Matt. 11:21-22). Nothing else is known of the Christians who lived there, but Luke indicates that Paul and his companions looked up the Christians in the city and stayed with them seven days.

The evident haste of 20:16 is not mentioned here, and there was sufficient time to spend a lengthy time with the "disciples" in Tyre (seven days). The unloading of the ship took place here, and during that time the Christians there warned Paul not to go to Jerusalem. In Paul's speech to the Ephesian elders, he shows that he was aware of the fate that would probably await him in Jerusalem (20:22-23, see also Rom. 15:30-31), but the warnings were not heeded and Paul was willing to experience persecution.

21:7. And when we had finished the voyage from Tyre, we arrived at Ptolemais; and after greeting the brethren, we stayed with them for a day. Little is known about Christians at Ptolemais, but Paul and his friends remained there for a day with "brothers." Ptolemais was another seaport in Phoenicia and built on the ancient site of Acco or Acre (Judges 1:31). That city was destroyed, but rebuilt as a Hellenistic city and named Ptolemais by Ptolemy I who enlarged the city. The city came under Roman rule in 65 B.C. and Claudius settled a colony of Roman veterans there and called it *Colonia Claudia Caesaris Ptolemais*. Pliny noted that the city was located close to the Pacida (or Belus) river and that it was made into "a colony of the Emperor Claudius, formerly called Acce [Acco or Acre] . . ." (*Natural History* 5.17.76, LCL). The Christians are described as the "brothers" (Greek = *tous adelphous*). For further comment on this term, see 1:15 above.

21:8. And on the next day we departed and came to Caesarea; and entering the house of Philip the evangelist, who was one of the seven, we stayed with him. Philip is called for the first time "the evangelist" (this title is found only here and in Eph. 4:11 and 2 Tim. 4:5) and noted as one of the Seven from Acts 6 (see 6:5 above). He has been confused (by Eusebius [*HE* 3.31.3-5; 3.39.9]) with Philip the Apostle (1:13), who lived in Hierapolis (Central Turkey) where a Martyrium was built in his honor and in honor of his four daughters.

21:9. Now this man had four virgin daughters who were prophetesses. The significance of having daughters who prophesied (see 2:17-18 above) is not clear since after they are introduced as those who have the gift of prophecy, that is, the Spirit-given ability to proclaim the Good News, then another individual, Agabus, prophesies (v. 10). It may be that they were introduced to set the tone for the prophecy of Agabus in v. 11. There are parallels in the ancient world of women virgins who were prophetesses. Speaking of the qualifications of the prophetesses at Delphi who uttered prophecies, Plutarch says that the woman brings nothing with her in terms of technical skills or abilities, but rather:

> . . . just as Xenophon believes that a bride should have seen as little and heard as little as possible before she pro-

ceeds to her husband's house, so this girl, inexperienced and uninformed about practically everything, a pure, virgin soul, becomes the associate of the god. Now we cherish the belief that the god, in giving indications to us, makes use of the calls of herons, wrens, and ravens; but we do not insist that these, inasmuch as they are messengers and heralds of the gods, shall express everything rationally and clearly, and yet we insist that the voice and language of the prophetic priestess, like a choral song in the theatre, shall be presented, not without sweetness and embellishment, but also in verse of a grandiloquent and formal style with verbal metaphors and with a flute to accompany its delivery! (*Oracles at Delphi* 22, LCL).

Further, Pausanias tells of an admired Sibyl who was a virgin and prophesied and her prophecies came to pass.

The inhabitants of this Alexandria [in the Troad or Troas] say that Herophile became the attendant of the temple of Apollo Smintheus, and that on the occasion of Hecuba's dream she uttered the prophecy which we know was actually fulfilled. This Sibyl passed the greater part of her life in Samos, but she also visited Clarus in the territory of Colophon, Delos and Delphi. Whenever she visited Delphi, she would stand on this rock and sing her chants. However, death came upon her in the Troad, and her tomb is in the grove of the Sminthian with these elegiac verses inscribed upon the tombstone:—

Here I am, the plain-speaking Sibl of Phoebus,
Hidden beneath this stone tomb.
A maiden [Greek = *parthenos*, "virgin"] once gifted with voice, but now forever voiceless,

By hard fate doomed to this fetter.
But I am buried near the nymphs and this Hermes,
Enjoying in the world below a part of the kingdom I had then (*Description, Phocis, Ozolian Locri* 10.12.5-6, LCL).

Something of this value given to virgins who prophesied is also found in early Christian pseudepigrapha in the well-known story of Paul and Thecla. As the Paul of this story offers his beatitudes, he praises virgins with the words: "Blessed are the bodies of the virgins, for they shall be well pleasing to God, and shall not lose the reward of their purity." Following this we read:

And while Paul was thus speaking in the mist of the assembly in the house of Onesiphorus, a virgin (named) Thecla – her mother was Theocleia – who was betrothed to a man (named) Thamyris, sat at a near-by window and listened night and day to the word of the virgin of life as it was spoken by Paul; and she did not turn away from the window, but pressed on in the faith rejoicing exceedingly. After her baptism, Paul admonishes her to "Go and teach the word of God!" (*Acts of Paul and Thecla* 7, 39. NT Apo. 2:240, 246).

21:10-11. And as we were staying there for some days, a certain prophet named Agabus came down from Judea. And coming to us, he took Paul's belt and bound his own feet and hands, and said, "This is what the Holy Spirit says: 'In this way the Jews at Jerusalem will bind the man who owns this belt and deliver him into the hands of the Gentiles.'" Nothing is known of Agabus except that he appears to have been the same individual who foretold the coming famine in 11:28 (see note there). He exemplifies the actions of the classical prophets who used actions to illustrate their points (Isa. 20:2; Jer. 13:1-13; 16:1-4; 19:1-13; Ezek. 4:1-17;

Hosea 1: 2-11; 3:1-5). Like those at Tyre who warned Paul, Agabus confirms in a prophecy that if Paul went to Jerusalem, his life would be in jeopardy.

This passage recalls Paul's speech to the Ephesian elders that he was **"bound in spirit, I am on my way to Jerusalem not knowing what will happen to me there"** (20:22) and that he did not count his life as dear so that he may finish his course of testifying of the Gospel (20:24). This, of course, fits with his word to the Romans (Rom. 15:31-32).

21:14. And since he would not be persuaded, we fell silent, remarking, "The will of the Lord be done!" This is not a sigh of resignation, but a conclusion of confidence that God's will is going to be done. In a similar passage when Polycarp (ca. 150–60), whose whereabouts were betrayed by a young slave, was about to die, he refused to flee, but accepted the will of God.

> Taking the slave then, police and cavalry went out on Friday at supper-time, with their usual arms, as if they were advancing against a robber. And late in the evening they came up together against him and found him lying in an upper room. And he might have departed to another place, but would not, saying, "the will of God be done." So when he heard that they had arrived he went down and talked with them, while those who were present wondered at his age and courage, and whether there was so much haste for the arrest of an old man of such a kind (*Martyrdom of Polycarp* 7.1-2, LCL).

21:15-18. We got ready and started on our way ... some ... disciples from Caesarea also came with us, taking us to Mnason of Cyprus, with whom we were to lodge ... And when we had come to Jerusalem, the brethren received us ... Paul went in with us to James

... This is the last of the "we" passages while in Jerusalem.

21:16. A disciple of long standing. Perhaps a reference to one of the earliest disciples in Paul and Barnabas's ministry to Cyprus (13:4-ff.) or even one who had been converted early on in the life of the church in Jerusalem (2:9-11, 14, 41).

With whom we were to lodge. The early Christians had a network of hospitality for those traveling to do Christian ministry (see 9:43; 10:6; 16:15, 40; 21:4, 8).

21:17-26. Paul's Welcome, Ritual in the Temple, and Arrest

The distance from Caesarea to Jerusalem was approximately 65 miles and unlikely to be made in one day, even on horseback, in antiquity. Fifteen to thirty miles a day constituted a vigorous full day's journey. This was minimally a two-day journey and frequently overnight stays took place at or near Antipatris (see note below at 23:31). The focus of this passage from this point forward lays the foundation for understanding the rest of the story of Paul's arrest and appeal to Rome in the rest of the book.

21:18 And now the following day Paul went in with us to James, and all the elders were present. Luke clearly intends his readers to understand that James is now the clear leader of the church in Jerusalem. After meeting with some of the "brothers" (see note 1:15 and 21:7 above), they went to see James and all of the elders. James' position in the church at Jerusalem is not described by title, but later Eusebius, after describing the martyrdom of Stephen, says: "At that same time also, James, who was called the brother of the Lord ...[after Peter, James and John did not struggle for glory, the Lord] chose James the Just as bishop [Greek = *episkopon*] of Jerusalem" (*Ecclesiastical History* 2.1.2-3, LCL).

21:19-21. And after he had greeted them, he

began to relate one by one the things which God had done among the Gentiles through his ministry. And when they heard it they began glorifying God. Although Paul tells of his ministry among the Gentiles, nothing is said by Luke about the offering that Paul had collected to bring to Jerusalem (see Rom. 15:15-16, 25-28; 1 Cor. 16:1-4; 2 Cor. 8:1–9:15; Gal. 2:10). While he does refer to it in the defense of Paul before Felix (24:17), it is strange that Luke does not mention this important gift here. Some commentators suggest that Luke's word for "ministry" in v. 19 (Greek = *diakonias*, service or ministry) could well imply the gift that Paul brought, but that is a stretch since the passage says that his ministry was what "God had done among the Gentiles." Also, he does mention a similar gift in 11:29-30 that was brought to the elders in the church, so there should be no reason for not acknowledging it again here. Again, Luke is silent on the matter, however, whether by assuming that everyone would know of the gift for the church, or he did not think it was as important as the issue at hand: namely, Paul's reputation among the Jewish Christians of having abandoned the Law of Moses. If Paul had given the gift, it is not acknowledged by any in the Jerusalem church on this occasion. Paul later mentions the "alms" that he brought to his "nation" in 24:17, but it is both subdued and not given the importance that Paul gave to it in his letters.

21:20. And they said to him, "You see, brother, how many thousands there are among the Jews of those who have believed, and they are all zealous for the Law; and they have been told about you, that you are teaching all the Jews who are among the Gentiles to forsake Moses, telling them not to circumcise their children nor to walk according to the customs." It may be that all of the Hellenizing Christians were chased out of the city earlier following the stoning of Stephen (8:1), but that

is not clear. Luke indicates that all of the Jews who have believed were zealous for the Law. What this suggests is a loyal commitment to keeping the law despite any hardship or fear of loss of life. This notion had important historical roots among the Jews who celebrated the zeal of Phinehas in Num. 25:1-13, who took radical measures in order to purify the nation of Israel in its devotion to God and to prevent the anger of the Lord from falling upon the nation. He was praised by the Lord and given his "covenant of peace" because he was "zealous for his God and made atonement for the Israelites." According to 2 *Macc.* 2:22-54 (see also 2 *Macc.* 4:2), the story of Phinehas was a major part of the inspiration of Mattathias Hasmoneus, the priest of Modein who initiated the Maccabean conflict.

This same commitment motivated those in Palestine during the time of Jesus who were zealous to purify the nation from its corruption brought on by Roman occupation, but it also reflects an eschatological perspective or expectation of the violent overthrow of the Roman armies. Such individuals may have taken radical and even revolutionary measures against Rome, as in the case of Judas the Galilean in A.D. 6 (cf. Acts 5:37; Josephus, *Ant.* 18.4-10). One of Jesus' disciples was called a "zealot" (Luke 6:15; Acts 1:13). Later Luke observes that Paul has been zealous for God and his ancestral traditions (22:3). On the other hand, Paul describes himself as one who was zealous for the traditions of his ancestors (Gal. 1:14; Phil. 3:6) prior to God's revelation to him about the risen Jesus.

Paul had the reputation of abandoning the Law, and this caused significant concern among his fellow Jews who had become followers of Jesus. They had already experienced violence from the leaders in Jerusalem (5:39-41; 7:54–8:1), and they were not inclined to do so again. Paul's message of freedom from the Law was a message to the Gentiles, but not for Jews.

21:21. And they have been told about you, that you are teaching all the Jews who are among the Gentiles to forsake Moses, telling them not to circumcise their children nor to walk according to the customs. Luke's readers have already been made aware of Paul's commitment to the law by his circumcising Timothy (16:3-5) and cutting his hair as a Nazirite vow at Cenchrea (18:18, see notes above). In other words, Luke wants the readers to know that the charges against Paul are false. It is easy, however, to see how Paul's own words could be taken to mean that Jews were no longer under the Law and that he was opposed to circumcision (Gal. 2:16-21; 3:21-25; 5:2, 6 and especially 5:11; Rom. 3:21; *passim*). Luke shows that the keeping of the Law was a custom of the Jews and that Paul carried out these customs, but did not believe that such customs could be imposed on the Gentiles (15:1-5).

The allowance of the Gentiles to be a part of the Christian community without keeping the Law was settled by agreement in Jerusalem earlier (11:1-18; 15:1-22 and 23-29), but this conclusion about the Gentiles did not affect what the Jews were expected to do. Luke wants his readers to understand that Paul has been a faithful Jew, but has not imposed the Jewish customs (6:14; 15:1; 16:21; 26:3; 28:17) on Gentiles. There is nothing in the letters of Paul that tells Jews to abandon the practice of circumcision, but the value of the practice for obtaining the salvation of God is questioned as we see in his letter to the Galatians especially (Gal. 2:16-21; 3:21-25; 5:2, 6; 5:11; but also in Rom. 3:19-21, 31; 4:1-5). The impression Paul gives in his letters is that circumcision, the major issue at hand, is of little value, but still he does not encourage persons to reverse the marks of circumcision by an ancient practice called "epispasm" (1 Cor. 7:18-20). It is clear, however, that the Jewish custom of avoiding Gentiles and refusing to have table fellowship with them (see discussion of 10:9-16, 34-43; 11:1-3 above) was wrong for Paul (Gal. 2:11-14),

and according to Luke, even Peter (11:1-3), even though Peter does not say in his explanation that he had table fellowship with the Gentiles. It is clear that he went into the house of the Gentiles and it is likely that he also ate with them, but Luke does not say that specifically. On the other hand, Peter makes clear that the Gentiles are saved by faith and not by regulations that even the Jews had difficulty keeping (cf. discussion above of 15:6-11).

21:22-23. What, then, is to be done? They will certainly hear that you have come. Therefore do this that we tell you. We have four men who are under a vow. The solution to the problem concerning those who doubt Paul's commitment to the Law, it was thought, was for Paul to join four others who were completing a vow in the temple (see note on 18:18; Num. 6:1-21). For examples of this rhetorical device, see also Rom. 3:31; 4:1; 6:1; 1 Cor. 14:15; 26. The elders of the church have already worked out a plan that will satisfy the believing Jews of Paul's sincerity about keeping the Law and its customs.

21:24. take them and purify yourself along with them, and pay their expenses in order that they may shave their heads; and all will know that there is nothing to the things which they have been told about you, but that you yourself also walk orderly, keeping the Law. See the background and support for this ritual of purification in Num. 8:21; 19:12; 31:19; 1 Chron. 15:12; 2 Chron. 29:16, but these passages do not seem to be related to the Nazirite vow of Num. 6:1-21. Had Paul contaminated himself following the completion of his vow before getting to Jerusalem when he touched a dead person at Troas (20:9-10)? Or did he simply need purification because he had been on Gentile soil? The Mishnah speaks of the kinds of things that might be cause for a ritual cleansing: "These convey uncleanness by contact and carrying, but not by overshadowing: a barleycorn's bulk of bone, earth from a foreign country, [earth from] a grave area, a member from a corpse or a member from a living man that no longer bears its proper flesh, a backbone or a skull in which aught is lacking" (*m. Oholoth* 2.3, Danby trans.).

According to the Mishnah, which indicates that any violation of the purification of this offering of the hair would make the offer of no consequence, describes the kind of uncleanness that requires purification or constitutes a violation of the Nazirite vow.

And great stringency applies to uncleanness than to cutting off the hair, in that uncleanness makes the whole [of the days fulfilled] of none effect, and he is thereby made liable to an offering; whereas cutting off the hair makes only thirty days of none effect and he is not thereby made liable to an offering. What was the rite prescribed for the cutting off of the hair after contracting uncleanness? He was sprinkled on the third and the seventh day, he cut off his hair on the seventh day and brought his offerings on the eighth day; but if he cut off his hair on the eighth day he brought his offerings on the same day. So R. [Rabbi] Akiba. R. Tarfon said to him: How does he differ from the leper [see Lev. 14:10]? he answered: His cleansing is suspended [only] until [the passing of] the days prescribed for him, while the cleansing of the leper is suspended until he cuts off his hair, and he may not bring the offering until he has awaited sunset (*m. Nazir* 6.5-6. Danby trans.).

Luke does not focus much attention on the details of this activity, but the reasoning behind this act of purification was clearly intended to assure those in Jerusalem that Paul was not opposed to the Law.

The actual paying of the expenses for others who are taking a vow was known in ancient times. These expenses were costly and Josephus mentions how Herod Agrippa I paid for such vows for those who were poor. Following the favor of Claudius Caesar in which Agrippa I was given control of the complete kingdom of Israel (A.D. 41–44), Josephus tells how he paid the vows of the poor who had taken vows.

Agrippa naturally, since he was to go back [from Claudius] with improved fortunes, turned quickly homewards. On entering Jerusalem, he offered sacrifices of thanksgiving, omitting none of the ritual enjoined by our law. Accordingly he also arranged for a very considerable number of Nazirites to be shorn (*Ant.* 19.293-94, LCL).

The Mishnah makes provision for others to pay the expenses of those who were taking upon themselves the vows.

[If a man said,] 'I will be a Nazirite and I pledge myself to bring the hair-offering of [another] Nazirite,' and his fellow heard him and said, 'I, too; and I pledge myself to bring the hair-offering of [another]Nazirite,' they are prudent-minded they each bring the hair-offering of the other; but if not, they must bring the hair-offering of other Nazirites. [If a man said,] 'I pledge myself to bring half the hair-offering of a Nazirite,' and his fellow heard him and said, 'I, too, pledge myself to bring half the hair-offering of a Nazirite,' each must bring the whole hair-offering of a Nazirite. So R. Meir. But the Sages say: Each need bring but half of the hair-offering of a Nazirite (*m. Nazir* 2.5-6. Danby trans.).

When the Jews were considering what to do following the desecration of their temple by Antiochus Epiphanes (167 B.C.) and the serious threats to their existence, the author of *1 Macc.* indicates that several people came together at Mizpah to discern the will of God. While there,

They fasted that day, put on sackcloth and sprinkled ashes on their heads, and tore their clothes. And they opened the book of the law to inquire into those matters about which the Gentiles consulted the likenesses of their gods. They also brought the vestments of the priesthood and the first fruits and the tithes, and *they stirred up the Nazirites who had completed their days* and they cried aloud to heaven . . ." (*1 Macc.* 4:47-50a, NRSV, italics supplied).

21:25. But concerning the Gentiles who have believed, we wrote, having decided that they should abstain from meat sacrificed to idols and from blood and from what is strangled and from fornication. Unless this restatement of the agreement of Acts 15:22-29 (see notes on 15:20 and 29 above) was for the sake of Luke's readers to remind them of the decision regarding Gentiles and the keeping of the Law, or for the sake of Paul's companions who may not have been aware of it, it seems that this passage is meant to inform Paul of the decisions made for the Gentile believers already mentioned in 15:29, a decision to which Luke already says that Paul was an eyewitness and participant (15:2-4, 12, 25-26). The latter option would be strange and probably James' reference to it is to remind everyone of the Council's decision and its impact on the Gentiles. It is nevertheless a bit awkward and if the readers only saw this passage, they would naturally conclude that James was informing Paul of previous events. It is important to remember that these conditions of acceptance were intended only for the Gentiles and that Luke did not consider it optional for Jews who became Christians to abrogate the keeping of the Law. For Luke, Paul was a faithful Jew who was also successful in Gentile evangelism. This is an important Lukan theme in Acts.

21:26. Then Paul took the men, and the next day, purifying himself along with them, went into the temple, giving notice of the comple-tion of the days of purification, until the sacrifice was offered for each one of them.** See discussion of the nature of these vows above in 21:20-25. Paul accepted the suggestion by James to prove to the Christian Jews that he was not opposed to the Law and the Jewish sacred traditions and customs. Paul's motive for his involvement in these religious activities is probably spelled out in 1 Cor. 9:19-23 which also fits with the Lukan picture of Paul: namely, as one who advocated Gentile freedom from the Law and the various Jewish religious traditions, but that he himself was an observant Jew.

IX. 21:27–28:31. SPREAD OF THE GOSPEL FROM ROME TO JERUSALEM

21:27–23:11. Paul's Arrest and Defense in Jerusalem

21:27-40. Paul's Arrest in the Temple

21:27. And when the seven days were almost over, the Jews from Asia, upon seeing him in the temple, began to stir up all the multitude and laid hands on him. The number of days involved in this ritual was normally seven days in the first century, but eventually the rabbis in the second century interpreted the tradition as requiring thirty days for its completion. Also, there were various lengths of such vows that also involved the cutting of one's hair.

> A Nazirite-vow that is vowed without a fixed duration is binding for thirty days. If he said, 'I will be a Nazirite for one long spell,' or even 'from now until the end of the world,' he must remain a Nazirite for thirty days. [If he said,] 'I will be a Nazirite for one day more,' or 'I will be a Nazirite and for one hour more,' 'I will be a Nazirite for one spell and a half,' he must remain a Nazirite for two spells. [If he said,] 'I will be a Nazirite for thirty days and one hour,' he must remain a Nazirite for thirty-one

days, since they may not take the vow of a Nazirite by the measure of hours. . . .

[If he said,] 'I will be a Nazirite from here to such-a-place,' they make a reckoning of how many days' journey it is 'from here to such-a-place'; if it is less that thirty days, he becomes a Nazirite for thirty days; otherwise he becomes a Nazirite for as many days as the days of the journey (m. Nazir 1.3, Danby trans.).

The length of the vows and the various circumstances surrounding it during the time of Paul are not clear and it is not always best to use second-century sources for dating purposes. They can be anachronistic. On the other hand, they do give a sense of the importance placed on these vows and their place in Jewish life. There is much about the vows that do not seem to be considered by Luke in his discussion in 18:18 and here, but that may be his assumption of the readers' prior knowledge or that such detail did not fit his purposes. On the Nazirite vow, see above discussion in 21:23-25.

21:28-29. Crying out, "Men of Israel, come to our aid! This is the man who preaches to all men everywhere against our people, and the Law, and this place; and besides he has even brought Greeks into the temple and has defiled this holy place." Paul conceded to the request of James and the elders and began the process that took some seven days. It is likely that Paul's reasons for going through this ritual had more to do with his vision of mission in 1 Cor. 9:19-23. Violent reaction by the Jews to Paul and his ministry is a common occurrence in the book of Acts (9:23; 13:50; 14:2, 5, 19; 17:5-9; 18:12-17; and here). It was also not uncommon for religious pilgrimages to have many skirmishes and so there was a Roman guard posted to keep order. Josephus mentions one set of "skirmishes" that took place at the time of the Feast of Pentecost: "During the daily skirmishes that took place the enemy were waiting for the arrival of the multitude from the coun-

try who were coming for the celebration of Pentecost, as it is called, which is a festival. And when this day came, there were many tens of thousands of armed and unarmed men gathered round the temple" (Ant. 14.337-38, LCL; see also 17.254 and War 2.42-44).

The Jews from Asia who brought these charges of speaking against the Law and profaning the temple were from Ephesus. On these accusations, see how Stephen was dealt with by a religious mob in Jerusalem who were both zealous for their law and their temple (6:11, 13-14, and 7:47-58). The rumor that Stephen was guilty of profaning Moses and the temple provoked the crowds to stone him to death. Those who accused Paul here, mentioned again in 24:19, are enraged by what they thought was true of Paul: namely, that he rejected the Laws of Moses and also that he brought Gentiles into the holy place of the temple area. Luke makes it clear, however, that neither of these charges had merit. In terms of the profaning of the temple by bringing Gentiles into it, an inscription dating to the time before the destruction of the temple in A.D. 70, commonly known as OGIS 598, was placed on one of the walls surrounding the inner courts of the temple and gave a warning to all Gentiles about entering the holy temple area. It reads: "Let no foreigner enter within the screen and enclosure surrounding the sanctuary. Whosoever is taken so doing will be the cause that death overtaketh him" (Trans. supplied by Conzelmann, Acts 183). This wall that kept Gentiles out was sometimes called the "dividing wall," and it was used metaphorically as in reference to all of that religious tradition that divided the Christian community (Eph. 2:14). Josephus describes this second or inner wall surrounding the temple and the warning posted to prevent Gentiles from entering. "Within it and not far distant was a second one [wall] accessible by a few steps and surrounded by a stone balustrade with an inscription prohibiting the entrance of a foreigner

[Greek = *alloethne*] under threat of the penalty of death (*Ant.* 15.417). In another place he adds the following description: "Proceeding across this toward the second court of the temple, one found it surrounded by a stone balustrade, three cubits high and of exquisite workmanship; in this at regular intervals stood slabs giving warning, some in Greek, others in Latin characters, of the law of purification, to wit that no foreigner was permitted to enter the holy place for so the second enclosure of the temple was called" (*Jewish War* 5.193-94, LCL). Philo also speaks of this same wall and the penalty for a Gentile to go beyond it. He writes, "Still more abounding and peculiar is the zeal of them all [Jews] for the temple, and the strongest proof of this is that death without appeal is the sentence against those of other races who penetrate into its inner confines. For the outer are open to everyone wherever they come from." (Philo, *Embassy to Gaius* 212, LCL). During the Jewish war with Rome (A.D. 66–70), Josephus tells of Titus' disappointment with the rebels among the Jews for profaning their own sacred temple, which, had they not done so, he would not have attacked the temple himself. In his criticism of them, Titus was distressed and chided the rebels saying: "Was it not you, he said, most abominable wretches, who placed this balustrade before your sanctuary? Was it not you that ranged along it those slabs, engraved in Greek characters and in our own, proclaiming that none may pass the barrier? And did we not permit you to put to death any who passed it, even were he a Roman?" (*War* 6.124-26, LCL). He then calls on the Jews to abandon the temple as their fortress and to choose another place and he promises that he will preserve the temple (6.126-28).

21:29. For they had previously seen Trophimus the Ephesian in the city with him, and they supposed that Paul had brought him into the temple. While the accusation against Paul bringing a Gentile into the temple area

was false, the one named here was involved in Paul's ministry earlier and accompanied him to Jerusalem (20:4; 2 Tim. 4:20). One of the several inscriptions (*I. Eph.* 1012) places the names of Trophimus, Tyrannius, and Alexander inscribed on the left-front column of the Prytaneum (a building dedicated to the officers or "presidents" of a community). The latter two names, of course, are mentioned in Acts 19:9, 33 (see *ND* 4:186). Whether this was the Trophimus mentioned in 20:4 and here is uncertain. Trophimus is a common name for that community and well attested from inscriptions and other writings in the first century. There were some 297 occurrences of the name in Roman lists of names, making it the twelfth most common name. The name was used both by Gentiles and Jews alike (*ND* 3:91-93). Whether Trophimus was a Jew or a Gentile, this passage suggests that he was the latter and that Paul took him into the temple thereby violating a very important Jewish law. There is no evidence, however, that Paul brought Trophimus into the temple.

21:31-32. And while they were seeking to kill him, a report came up to the commander of the Roman cohort that all Jerusalem was in confusion. And at once he took along some soldiers and centurions, and ran down to them; and when they saw the commander and the soldiers, they stopped beating Paul. The Romans had a fortress beside the temple named the Antonia and from it the Roman soldiers could look into the courtyard of the temple and with steps leading into the courtyard from the Antonia, they could address any riots or disturbances that broke out with quickness. This fortress is described in detail thusly by Josephus:

> It [the fortress] was the work of King Herod [the Great] and a crowning exhibition of the innate grandeur of his genius. For, to begin with, the rock was covered from its base upward with

smooth flagstones, both for ornament and in order that anyone attempting to ascend or descend it might slip off. Next, in front of the actual edifice, there was a wall three cubits [a cubit = the distance from the tip of the elbow to the tip of the middle finger, normally 17 to 20 inches] high; and behind this the tower of Antonia rose majestic to an altitude of forty cubits... The general appearance of the whole was that of a tower with other towers at each of the four corners; three of these turrets were fifty cubits high, while that at the south-east angle rose to seventy cubits, and so commanded a view of the whole area of the temple. At the point where it impinged upon the porticoes of the temple, there were stairs leading down to both of them, by which the guards descended; for a Roman cohort [see 10:1 note above = 500 to 600 men and perhaps as many as 1000] was permanently quartered there, and at the festivals took up positions in arms around the porticoes to watch the people and repress any insurrectionary movement. For if the temple lay as a fortress over the city, Antonia dominated the temple, and the occupants of that post were the guards of all three; the upper town had its own fortress—Herod's palace (*War* 5.238-46, LCL).

The Antonia and its guards were positioned for just such incidents as Luke reports in this story.

21:37. And as Paul was about to be brought into the barracks, he said to the commander, "May I say something to you?" And he said, "Do you know Greek?" A better translation of this question is "Do you know how to speak Greek?" for that is the essence of the question raised by the guard. The question assumes that most Jews with whom he was familiar could not speak both Greek and Hebrew (Aramaic, see below), even if most Jews knew some Greek (sometimes referred to as "secondary bilingualism," as opposed to "primary or productive bilingualism" in which the speaker was fluent in the language. Cf. *ND* 5.24-26). The guard is surprised that Paul is a "productive bilingual," that is, quite fluent in the language. Paul then explains to him that he was a citizen where the primary language was Greek (v. 39). The commander is named Claudius Lysias in 23:2.

21:38. Then you are not the Egyptian who some time ago stirred up a revolt and led the four thousand men of the Assassins out into the wilderness? Prior to this time, an Egyptian had led a revolt against the Romans and escaped. The guard thought Paul might be that person. Josephus describes this Egyptian as follows:

> A still worse blow was dealt at the Jews by the Egyptian false prophet. A charlatan, who had gained for himself the reputation of a prophet, this man appeared in the country, collected a following of about thirty thousand [Luke uses the number 4,000 in 21:38 and is probably the more accurate here, the difference being between the Greek letters *delta* (D) and *lamda* (L) which are easily confused] dupes, and led them by a circuitous route from the desert into Jerusalem and, after overpowering the Roman garrison, to set himself up as tyrant of the people, employing those who poured in with him as his bodyguard. His attack was anticipated by Felix [see Acts 23:24-ff.], who went to meet him with the Roman heavy infantry, the whole population joining him in the defense. The outcome of the ensuing engagement was that the Egyptian escaped with a few of his followers; most of his force were killed or taken prisoners; the remainder dispersed and stealthily

escaped to their several homes. (*War* 2.261-63. LCL).

The word for "of the Assassins" (Greek = *ton sikarion*) is a term that is often associated with the *sicarii*, that is those who carried concealed short knives or daggers and were known as assassins who committed many murders just prior to the Jewish war with Rome. It is not clear that these are the same individuals as the highly feared *sicarii*, since Josephus uses a different term to describe them: namely, the Greek term *lestai*, but it also appears that he equates them, Josephus describes those who assassinated numerous individuals and caused great unrest in the land as follows.

When Festus arrived in Judaea, it happened that Judaea was being devastated by the brigands [Greek = *leston*], for the villages one and all were being set on fire and plundered. The so-called *sicarii* [Greek = *sikarioi*]—these are brigands [Greek = *lestai*]—were particularly numerous at that time. They employed daggers, in size resembling the scimitars [a short oriental sword with a curved single-edged blade, broadening toward the end] of the Persians, but curved and more like the weapons called by the Romans *sciae*, from which these brigands [Greek = *lesteuontes*] took their name because they slew so many in this way. For, as we said previously [*Ant.* 20.164-66], they would mingle at the festivals with the crowd of those who streamed into the city from all directions to worship, and thus easily assassinated any that they pleased. (*Ant.* 20.185-89, LCL).

21:39. But Paul said, "I am a Jew of Tarsus in Cilicia, a citizen of no insignificant city." The well-known significance of this city is elaborated variously and throughout in Dio Chrysostom, *Discourse 33* (= *The First Tarsic Discourse*). See notes above on 9:30 and 11:25. This is an example of the use of *litotes* in Acts. *Litotes* is an ancient rhetorical device of understating something in a negative manner such as "no small amount" or here, "no mean city," in other words, a very important city. Among the many glowing things that Strabo said about Tarsus, he underscores the prominence of people of learning in the city.

The people of Tarsus have devoted themselves so eagerly, not only to philosophy, but also to the whole round of education in general, that they have surpassed Athens, Alexandria, or any other place that can be named where there have been schools and lectures of philosophers. But it is so different from other cities that there the men who are fond of learning are all natives, and foreigners are not inclined to sojourn there; neither do these natives stay there, but they complete their education abroad; and when they have completed it they are pleased to live abroad, and but few go back home (*Geography* 14.5. 13, LCL).

In one ancient inscription Tarsus is described as the "first and greatest and most beautiful metropolis" (*OGIS* 578.7-8).

21:40. And when he had given him permission, Paul, standing on the stairs, motioned to the people with his hand. It is thought by most commentators that it would be highly unusual for the guard, or cohort, to have given Paul permission to speak since they had just dragged him away from an angry crowd, and it was not clear that they had Paul secured from the crowd. It is also strange that the crowd quieted down to listen, even if Paul used the common method in antiquity of quieting the crowd: namely, raising his hand, before he spoke (see also 12:17; 19:33; 26:1). In his famous novel, *The Golden Ass*, Apuleius describes in detail the posture and gestures of one who was about to speak.

And so Thelyphron piled the covers in a heap and propped himself on his elbow, sitting half upright on the couch. He extended his right arm, shaping his fingers to resemble an orator's: having bent his two lowest fingers in, he stretched the others out at long range and poised his thumb to strike, gently rising as he began (*Metamorphoses* 2. 21, LCL).

He spoke to them in the Hebrew dialect, saying. It is quite probable that Paul was actually speaking Aramaic (see 1:19; 6:1; 22:2; 26:14). In several other passages in the New Testament where the text indicates Hebrew is used, the transcriptions into Greek are actually from the Aramaic and not the Hebrew language (John 5:2; 19:13, 17, 20; 20:16; Rev. 9:11; 16:16). Similarly, Josephus calls Hebrew what is Aramaic (*Ant.* 18.228).

22:1-21. Paul's First Defense

This is the first of five defenses that Paul gives in the rest of Acts. In it he gives the second version of his conversion and call experience and the observant reader will find some interesting differences as well as some important similarities. As Luke has been anxious to show through Paul's career, he is an observant Jew and faithful to the traditions of the Jews except that he will not impose them on Gentiles. It is also significant that the two charges against Paul in the previous section: namely, abandoning the Law and bringing a Gentile (Trophimus) into the temple holy area reserved for Jews alone (21:28), are not discussed here, only Paul's faithfulness to his Jewish traditions and his conversion and call. In this story there are several items that are of special interest for background studies.

22:1. Brethren and fathers, hear my defense which I now offer to you. Paul addresses the crowd as "Brethren" or "Brothers" (Greek = *Adelphoi*). See note on this term in 1:15 above. The word used for Paul's defense (Greek =

apologias) is often used as a technical term for a defense. Plato, in his report of the Defense of Socrates (Greek = *Apologia Sokratous*), uses this term to describe Socrates' defense before his accusers. His *Apologia* begins: "How you, men of Athens, have been affected by my accusers, I do not know; but I, for my part, almost forgot my own identity, so persuasively did they talk; and yet there is hardly a word of truth in what they have said" (Plato, *Apology* 1.A, LCL). Later he declares:

Well then, men of Athens, that I am not a wrongdoer according to Meletus's indictment, seems to me not to need much of a defense [Greek = *apologias*], but what has been said is enough. But you may be assured that what I said before is true, that great hatred has arisen against me and in the minds of many persons. And this it is which will cause my condemnation, if it is to cause it, not Meletus or Anytus, but the prejudice and dislike of the many. This has condemned many other good men, and I think will do so; and there is no danger that it will stop with me" (*Apology* 28. A-B, LCL).

In the Apocryphal writing called *The Wisdom of Solomon* (ca. middle to end of first century B.C.), there is a well-known text that focuses on the true defense for a pious Jew. The sage who addressed both kings and judges calls on them to learn true wisdom: namely, "To you then, O monarchs, my words are directed, so that you may learn wisdom and not transgress. For they will be made holy who observe holy things in holiness, and those who have been taught them will find a defense. Therefore set your desire on my words; long for them, and you will be instructed (*Wisd.* 6:9-11. NRSV). Later, Josephus (ca. A.D. 75–79) uses this line of argument when he is defending Moses in his defense against Apion and others who wished to cause the Jews ill-will: "My object is not to compose a panegyric upon [or, laudatory discourse for] our nation; but I consider that, in reply to the numerous false accusations which are brought against us, the fairest defense which we can offer is to be found in the laws which govern our daily life" (*Ag. Apion* 2.247, LCL).

22:3. I am a Jew, born in Tarsus of Cilicia, but brought up in this city, educated under Gamaliel. At the beginning of Paul's defense, Luke employs three well-known Greek biographical terms, born (*gegennemenos*), brought up (*anatethrammenos*), educated (*pepaideumenos*). For example, in one of Socrates' responses to Crito, he says, "Well then, *when you were born and nurtured and educated*, could you say to begin with that you were not our offspring and our slave, you yourself and your ancestors?" (Plato, *Crito* 51E, LCL, italics added). Plato uses words from the same word family as in 22:3. See also Philo's descriptive summary of Moses' early life when he says "The former treatise dealt with the *birth and nurture of Moses; also with his education and career* as a ruler in which capacity his conduct was not merely blameless, but highly praiseworthy" (*On the Life of Moses*. 2.1, LCL, italics added). For a discussion of Gamaliel, see note above at 5:34.

Strictly according to the law of our fathers, being zealous for God, just as you all are today. Paul acknowledges the strictness (Greek = *akribeian*) of his interpretation of the laws and traditions of the Jews. Paul later indicates that he belonged to the "strictest" (*akribestaten*) sect within Judaism, the Pharisees (26:5), and this is the same word Josephus used to describe the Pharisees. "Of the two first-named schools, the Pharisees, who are considered the most accurate [Greek = *akribeias*, "strict"] interpreters of the laws, and hold the position of the leading sect" (*Jewish War* 2.162, LCL). See also 26:5 below. When describing Simon, the son of Gamaliel—probably Gamaliel II, grandson of the Gamaliel mentioned in Acts 5:34 and here—Josephus says that he was "of a noble family, of the sect of the Pharisees, which are supposed to excel others in

the accurate knowledge of the laws of their country" (*Life* 191, LCL). For notes on the Pharisees, see 5:34-35 above and 23:6 below.

22:4. And I persecuted this Way to the death. For Luke's use of "Way" to describe the Christian community, see notes above in 9:2; 19:9, 23. Paul's letters also reflect his persecution of the churches (1 Cor. 15:9; Gal. 1:13; Phil. 3:6).

22:9. And those who were with me beheld the light, to be sure, but did not understand the voice of the One who was speaking to me. In the story of 9:7 (see notes above) the seeing and hearing abilities of Paul's companions are different.

22:17. And it came about when I returned to Jerusalem and was praying in the temple, that I fell into a trance. This is a new introduction into the testimony of Paul from the earlier version in 9:1-18. There Paul's commission appears to come through Ananias by way of a revelation following his Damascus Road experience. Luke apparently is trying to show how Paul's experiences and call are significantly involved in the temple, the place that he has been accused of despising or rejecting (21:28).

22:22-29. The Sequel to Paul's Defense and His Claim to Roman Citizenship
22:24. The commander ordered him to be brought into the barracks, stating that he should be examined by scourging so that he might find out the reason why they were shouting against him that way. The use of torture and flogging to obtain information from prisoners was common among the Romans. In the famous letter of Pliny the younger to Trajan the Roman emperor requesting guidelines on how to deal with those who are found to be Christians, Pliny describes the ways that he has tried to get the Christians to deny their faith and to deal with those who had not.

For the moment this is the line I have taken with all persons brought before me on the charge of being Christians. I have asked them in person if they are Christians, and if they admit it, I repeat the questions a second and third time, with a warning of the punishment awaiting them. If they persist, I order them to be led away for execution; for whatever the nature of their admission, I am convinced that their stubbornness and unshakeable obstinacy ought not to go unpunished . . . .

[After describing his various ways of controlling the spread of the Christian faith, he continues . . .]

This made me decide it was all the more necessary to extract the truth by torture from two slave-women, whom they call deaconesses. I found nothing but a degenerate sort of cult carried to extravagant lengths (*Letters* 96.3-5, 8, LCL).

22:25. And when they stretched him out with thongs. The leather thongs were strips of leather used not only for sandals, but also to make cords for fastening things, especially persons in captivity, and also whips.

Paul said to the centurion who was standing by, "Is it lawful for you to scourge a man who is a Roman and uncondemned?" Paul appeals to a right of Roman citizens to avoid such beatings. Again, Cicero argued: "To bind a Roman citizen is a crime, to flog him an abomination, to slay him almost an act of parricide" (*Against Verres* 2.5.66, LCL). See notes on 16:37 above.

22:28. And the commander answered, "I acquired this citizenship with a large sum of money." It was possible to purchase citizenship in the Roman world, and some were known to have bribed others to receive this important status. Those who received this new status of citizenship were expected to adopt the emperor's name. The tribune, or commander of the military unity in the Antonia Fortress, was named Claudius Lysias (23:26), which would fit with his receiving his citizenship from one of the emperor Claudius's officials or the emperor Claudius himself. In some cases Claudius removed citizenship if the holder was deemed unworthy for various reasons. How this was done is reported in the early third century by Dio Cassius (d. ca. 235) who tells first how one might lose citizenship and then how one could obtain it and the obligations of those who did.

During the investigation of this affair [Lycians who revolted against Roman rule and slew some Romans], which was conducted in the senate, he put a question in Latin to one of the envoys who had originally been a Lycian, but had been made a Roman citizen; and when the man failed to understand what was said, he took away his citizenship, saying that it was not proper for a man to be a Roman who had no knowledge of the Roman's language. A great many other persons unworthy of citizenship were also deprived of it, whereas he granted citizenship to others quite indiscriminately, sometimes to individuals and sometimes to whole groups. For inasmuch as Romans had the advantage over foreigners in practically all respects, many sought the franchise by personal application to the emperor, and many bought it from Messalina and the imperial freedmen. For this reason, though the privilege was at first sold only for large sums. It later became so cheapened by the facility with which it could be obtained that it came to be a common saying, that a man could become a citizen by giving the right person some bits of broken glass. For his course in this matter, therefore, Claudius brought ridicule upon himself; but he was praised for his conduct in another direction. It seems that information was being laid against many of the new citizens, in some instances to the effect that they were not adopting Claudius' name [= not adding Claudius to their original names] and in others that they were not leaving him anything at their death—it being incumbent, they said, upon those who obtained citizenship from him to do both these things (*Roman History* 10. 17. 4-8, LCL).

And Paul said, "But I was actually born a citizen." Paul evidently had the means of proving to the tribune or commander that he was a citizen, otherwise, he could be liable for severe penalties for making such a claim. The wearing of a toga was a common symbol of Roman citizenship, but it is unlikely that Paul was wearing such a garment in the temple area. It is more likely that Paul was carrying a certificate of citizenship. Suetonius tells of Nero conferring Roman citizenship upon some Greek youth following a performance of some war-like dances and "handing each of them certificates of Roman citizenship at the close of his performance" (*Lives of the Caesars*, "Nero" 4.12.1, LCL). Paul may, according to Barrett (*Acts* 2.1048), have been carrying a diploma of citizenship, perhaps a wooden tablet attesting to Paul's birth and citizenship. It is not clear whether he did or did not have such documents, but the penalty for lying about one's citizenship could be serious indeed. Epictetus speaks of the punishment for those who lied about their citizenship:

> Well, but those who falsely claim Roman citizenship are severely punished, and ought those who falsely claim so great and so dignified a calling and title to get off scot-free? Or is that impossible? Whereas the divine and mighty and inescapable law is the law which exacts the greatest penalties from those who are guilty of the greatest offences (*Discourses* 3.24.41, LCL).

22:30–23:11. Paul Before the Sanhedrin

In keeping with Luke's purpose to show that Paul was in harmony with his Jewish traditions and, in terms of the Law, also an observant Jew, it was important that Paul's defense of his loyalty to his Jewish traditions was approved by those who were closest to Paul's theological persuasion, the Pharisees (23:9). More importantly, Luke claims that Paul's testimony before the Sanhedrin was also approved by his Lord (23:11).

22:30. But on the next day, wishing to know for certain why he had been accused by the Jews, he released him and ordered the chief priests and all the Council to assemble, and brought Paul down and set him before them. On "high priest" see note above in 4:5 and on the Sanhedrin or "Council" see notes on 4:5 and 4:6 above.

23:1. And Paul, looking intently at the Council, said, "Brethren, I have lived my life with a perfectly good conscience before God up to this day." See Phil. 1:27. Philo, a Jewish contemporary of Paul, describes the virtues of an exemplary life by illustrating from the life of Moses. He concludes:

> With such instructions he tamed and softened the minds of the citizens of his commonwealth and set them out of the reach of pride and arrogance, evil qualities, grievous and noxious in the highest degree, though embraced as most excellent by the majority of men, particularly when riches and distinctions and high offices bestow their gifts in unstinted superabundance. For arrogance springs up in the insignificant and obscure, as does each of the other passions and diseases and distempers of the soul, though it does not increase to any extent and grows dull as fire does for want of its essential fuel.
>
> . . .

And therefore Moses in his work as Revealer admirably exhorts them to abstain from all sins, but especially from pride. Then he reminds them of the causes which are wont to inflame this passion, unlimited means of satisfying the belly and unstinted superabundance of houses and land and cattle. For men at once lose their self-mastery, and are elated and puffed up, and the one hope of their cure is that they should never lose the remembrance of God (*On the Virtues* 161-162, LCL).

23:2. And the high priest Ananias commanded those standing beside him to strike him on the mouth. The similarities between this passage and John 18:19-24 should not go unnoticed. The Ananias mentioned was son of Nedebaeus who was appointed to this office in the year 47 by Herod of Chalcis. Ananias is well attested in Josephus's writings as a cruel and unpopular man (*Ant.* 20.103, 206-13).

But Ananias had servants who were utter rascals and who, combining operations with the most reckless means, would go to the threshing floors and take by force the tithes of the priests; nor did they refrain from beating those who refused to give. The high priests were guilty of the same practices as his slaves, and no one could stop them. So it happened at that time that those of the priests who in olden days were maintained by the tithes now starved to death (*Ant.* 20.103, LCL; see *Ant.* 20.181 for comment on this).

Observe also Josephus' later comments on this matter: "Ananias, however, kept the upper hand by using his wealth to attract those who were willing to receive bribes" (*Ant.* 20.206-07, 213, LCL).

23:3. Then Paul said to him, "God is going to strike you, you whitewashed wall! And do you

sit to try me according to the Law, and in violation of the Law order me to be struck?"** More than one commentator has asked about the consistency of this passage with what Paul wrote in 1 Cor. 4:12-13: namely, "when reviled, we bless." Luke's point has to do more with the courage of Paul when faced with violence and injustice. He intends to say that Paul is a faithful Jew of the Pharisaic order and that the central issue at stake has to do with the resurrection, more specifically the resurrection of Jesus which is at the heart of Paul's preaching but that is not introduced here. The reference to God's striking Ananias may be Luke's slight allusion to what in fact happened to Ananias: namely, he was killed at the outbreak of the 66–70 war. After the initial success of the rebels, led by a certain Menahem, who took the military strongholds of the city, the remaining Romans fled the city. Josephus reports that, "on the following day the high priest Ananias was caught near the canal in the palace grounds where he was hiding, and, with his brother Exechias, was killed by the brigands" (*War* 2.442, LCL).

23:5. And Paul said, "I was not aware, brethren, that he was high priest; for it is written, 'You shall not speak evil of a ruler of your people.'" While Paul was on his first missionary journey, Ananias came to power (A.D. 47). Paul would not necessarily have known him by face (23:5), having been away from Jerusalem for the many years described in Gal. 1:18-2:1. It is not likely that when Paul returned to Jerusalem (15:2-4) that he would have paid a visit to the high priest. Paul cites Exod. 22:28 in what is apparently an apology for his comments. He did not say that they were wrong, but that it was inappropriate to say them. Luke indicates that the comments were justified and that Paul had the boldness to challenge injustice.

23:6. But perceiving that one part were Sadducees and the other Pharisees, Paul began crying out in the Council, "Brethren, I

am a Pharisee, a son of Pharisees; I am on trial for the hope and resurrection of the dead!" For notes on the Pharisees, see 5:34-35 and 22:4 above. The Sadducees accepted as sacred only the Law of Moses (the Pentateuch), but did not accept the notion of resurrection from the dead. They had their own traditions about the Law, as did the Pharisees who believed in the future hope of resurrection from the dead, but it is difficult to find notions of life after death in the Pentateuch and as a result, the Sadducees rejected it. When the Sadducees questioned Jesus, he challenged their denial of the resurrection by saying that God is the God of Abraham, Isaac, and Jacob (Exod. 3:6) and that he is not the God of the dead, but of the living (see note on Matt. 22:30-32). Josephus explains their views as follows:

The Sadducees hold that the soul perishes along with the body. They own no observance of any sort apart from the laws [= the written Law of Moses]; in fact, they reckon it a virtue to dispute with the teachers of the path of wisdom that they pursue. There are but few men to whom this doctrine has been made known, but these are men of the highest standing. They accomplish practically nothing, however. For whenever they assume some office, though they submit unwillingly and perforce, yet submit they do to the formulas of the Pharisees, since otherwise the masses would not tolerate them. (*Ant.* 18.16-17, LCL).

The first clear passage in the Old Testament on resurrection from the dead comes in Dan. 12:2-3, and there are a few allusions to the possibility earlier (Ps. 49:15; Isa. 26:19; Ezek. 37:2-6; Hos. 6:1-3; 13:14). The Pharisees, who accepted this later literature as sacred, also accepted the notion of life after death through a resurrection from the dead.

23:8. For the Sadducees say that there is no resurrection, nor an angel, nor a spirit; but the

Pharisees acknowledge them all. On the Sadducees' denial of angels and the spirit, there is no additional support in Josephus or elsewhere. Josephus emphasizes the difference between the two schools of thought (Pharisees and Sadducees) and clearly shows his own bias in the matter.

Of the two first-named schools, the Pharisees, who are considered the most accurate [or "strict;" Greek = *akribeias*, see note above (22:3) on this term] interpreters of the laws, and hold the position of the leading sect, attribute everything to Fate and to God; they howl that to act rightly or otherwise rests, indeed, for the most part with men, but that in each action Fate cooperates. Every soul, they maintain, is imperishable, but the soul of the good alone passes into another body, while the souls of the wicked suffer eternal punishment.

The Sadducees, the second of the orders, do away with Fate altogether, and remove God beyond, not merely the commission, but the very sight, of evil. They maintain that man has the free choice of good or evil, and that it rests with each man's will whether he follows the one or the other. As for the persistence of the soul after death, penalties in the underworld, and rewards, they will have none of them (*War* 2.162-65, LCL).

According to Josephus, "The Pharisees are affectionate to each other and cultivate harmonious relations with the community. The Sadducees, on the contrary, are, even among themselves, rather boorish in their behavior, and in their intercourse with their peers are as rude as to aliens. Such is what I have to say on the Jewish philosophical schools" (*War* 2.166, LCL. Similarly, see his *Ant.* 18.14-17).

Luke's readers are already aware of Paul's emphasis on the resurrection of Jesus (see also 1 Cor. 15:12-20). The primary conflict between the

Christians and the Sadducees was whether anyone could rise from the dead. The conflict with the Pharisees was whether Jesus had been raised from the dead. The majority of Jews surviving the destruction of the temple and the Jewish war in Jerusalem (66–70) and also the second rebellion in the second century called the Bar Cochba rebellion (132-53): namely, those of a Pharisaic bent, believed that belief in the resurrection was an essential aspect of their faith. According to the Mishnah there were several kinds of individuals who would not share in the world to come. These include:

All Israelites have a share in the world to come, for it is written, *Thy people also shall be all righteous, they shall inherit the land for ever; the branch of my planting, the work of my hands that I may be glorified* [Isa. 60:21]. And these are they that have no share in the world to come: he that says that there is no resurrection of the dead prescribed in the law, and [he that says] that the Law is not from heaven, and an Epicurean. R. Akiba says: Also he that reads the heretical books [the "external" books], or that utters charms over a wound and says, *I will put none of the diseases upon thee which I have put upon the Egyptians: for I am the Lord that healeth thee* [Exod. 15:26]. Abba Saul says: Also he that pronounces the Name with its proper letters [= the name of God, YHWH or Yahweh] (*m. Sanhedrin* 10.1, Danby trans. Italics are his.).

23:9. And there arose a great uproar; and some of the scribes of the Pharisaic party stood up and began to argue heatedly, saying, "We find nothing wrong with this man; suppose a spirit or an angel has spoken to him?" Luke has succeeded in showing that the Christians have no essential conflict with the Pharisees, the Jewish sect with whom they have the most affinity.

23:10. And as a great dissension was developing, the commander was afraid Paul would be torn to pieces by them and ordered the troops to go down and take him away from them by force, and bring him into the barracks. For protection's sake, Paul is taken back to the barracks (the Antonia Fortress) by orders of Claudius Lysias (see above note on 21:37 and 23:23-25).

23:11. But on the night immediately following, the Lord stood at his side and said, "Take courage; for as you have solemnly witnessed to My cause at Jerusalem, so you must witness at Rome also." Paul's visit to Rome is an important theme in Acts (18:9-10; 22:17-18; 27:23-24), but also Paul himself speaks of his visit to Rome (Rom. 1:11-15; 15:22-29, 32; see also 1 Tim. 2:16-17). Luke underscores in this vision that advances his story not only the Risen Christ's pleasure with Paul's defense, but he also assures him that he will witness of him in Rome. Josephus advances through a vision his own story of a time when he was conflicted inside over whether to depart to be with his family or to stay with the people he was appointed to command.

But wonderful it was what a dream I saw that very night; for when I had betaken myself to my bed, as grieved and disturbed at the news that had been written to me, it seemed to me, that a certain person stood by me, and said, "O, Josephus; leave off to afflict thy soul, and put away all fear; for what now grieves thee will render thee very considerable, and in all respects most happy; for thou shalt get over not only these difficulties, but many others, with great success. However, be not cast down, but remember that thou are to fight with the Romans" (*The Life of Flavius Josephus* 208-209, Whiston trans. See also other dreams in *Ant.* 3.214-18 and *War* 3.350-54).

23:12-22. The Plot to Kill Paul

The source of Luke's information on this matter is probably Paul or the companions of Paul. There are no "we" passages here as one would expect when Paul was imprisoned, but his access to friends and family (23:16) and others who visited him in prison could well receive his report of such events. The kind of imprisonment that Paul experienced in Rome (28:30) allowed him to welcome visitors and that is apparently similar to what he experienced in Roman custody in Jerusalem (see 23:16 below). When Paul makes his journey to Rome, the "we" passages resume (27:1-8, ff. 28:1-16). His rights as a Roman citizen to receive visitors were evidently upheld during his imprisonment in Jerusalem and Caesarea.

23:12. And when it was day, the Jews formed a conspiracy and bound themselves under an oath, saying that they would neither eat nor drink until they had killed Paul. The background for taking such vows lies in the history of Jewish interpretation of such passages as Deut. 13:15; 20:17; Josh. 6:21; Judges 1:17; 21:11; 1 Sam. 15:3. The making of solemn vows is also found in *1 Enoch* (ca. 180 B.C.). The writer indicates that the angels of Gen. 6:1-4 were about to take wives among the "daughters of men" when Semyaz, evidently their leader, expresses concern that if they decide to do this, that he alone would do it and then be found guilty of this sin. The other angels respond: "'Let us all swear an oath and bind everyone among us by a curse not to abandon this suggestion but to do the deed.' And they were altogether two hundred; and they descended into Ardos, which is the summit of Hermon" (*1 Enoch* 6.4-5OT *Pseud* 1:15). Jesus made a resolve or vow not to drink of the vine until he did it anew with his disciples in the kingdom of God (Luke 22:18). The vow in this passage, however, was a most severe kind and involved the abstinence of eating and drinking during the time such a vow is observed. In other words, the failure to

keep such a vow could lead to death. The words of Philo (d. ca. A.D. 40) about the nature of vows are appropriate here. He was aware of the true importance of vows and also of those who used them to accomplish evil purposes.

So then, as I have said, all oaths must be made good so long as they are concerned with matters houourable and profitable for the better conduct of public or private affairs and are subject to the guidance of wisdom and justice and righteousness under which head come also the perfectly lawful vows made in acknowledgement of an abundant measure of blessings either present or expected. But when the oaths have objects of the opposite kind in view, religion forbids us to put them into execution. For there are some who swear at random to commit acts of theft and sacrilege or rape and adultery or assaults and murders or other similar crimes and carry them out without hesitation on the pretext that they must be faithful to their oaths, as though it were not better and more pleasing to God to abstain from wrongdoing than to abstain from breaking their oaths. . . . And everyone who commits a wrong because he has sworn to do so may be assured that the act is not one of faithfulness to a pledge but breaks the oath so worthy of all careful observance with which she sets her seal on what is just and excellent. For he adds guilt to guilt when oaths taken for improper purposes which had better have been left unspoken are followed by actions which violate the law. Let him abstain, then, from wrongful conduct and supplicate God, that he may grant him a share of what His gracious power can give and pardon him for what he has sworn so unadvisedly. For to choose a double measure of ill when he could disburden himself of the half of it is the act of one almost hope-lessly imbecile and insane. But there are some who, either because through excessive moroseness their nature has lost the sense of companionship and fel-low-feeling or because they are con-strained by anger which rules them like a stern mistress, confirm the savagery of their temper with an oath (*Special Laws* 2.12-16, LCL).

The Mishnah taught that there were four kinds of vows that were not binding: namely, "vows of incitement, vows of exaggeration, vows made in error, and vows [that cannot be fulfilled by reason] of constraint" (*m. Nedarim* 3.1, Danby trans.). Luke's readers clearly were led to believe that the vow made to kill Paul was wrong, but he does not complete his story with any indication of what happened to these individuals when they did not complete their vow. He does show how these men collabo-rated with the official Jewish leaders to do harm to Paul (23:14). Further, that those in the Sanhedrin could be involved in such mischief, is acknowledged by Josephus in the story of Ananias (see note on 23:2 above). His known behavior does not set him above the collabora-tion with these assassins.

23:16. But the son of Paul's sister heard of their ambush, and he came and entered the barracks and told Paul. Nothing is known of Paul's family, but his upbringing in Jerusalem suggests a family move to this city and there is nothing that suggests an exaggeration or invention on Luke's part with this story. The nephew's access to Paul is not inconsistent with Paul's treatment under house arrest in Rome (28:30) now with companions traveling with him to Rome. Paul was not considered to be a threat to Rome or the Roman cohort in Jerusalem. How Paul's nephew came by this plot to kill Paul is not told and it is unwise to speculate that he was either a member of that group or that he had friends inside the group

or any of a number of other possibilities. Luke does not believe that this information would further his story, but the disclosure of this plot by the nephew was sufficient and believable to cause the commander of the barracks to act.

23:23. And he called to him two of the centu-rions, and said, "Get two hundred soldiers ready by the third hour of the night to pro-ceed to Caesarea, with seventy horsemen and two hundred spearmen." While the number of soldiers guarding Paul seems excessive: namely, 470 or half of the 1,000-man cohort at the Antonia garrison, these were dangerous times and the tribune or commander of the garrison in Jerusalem wanted to take no chances in getting Paul, a Roman citizen, to Caesarea, especially when his life was being threatened. After their arrival in Antipatris, most of the troops (400 according to v. 32) returned to Jerusalem and only those on horses continued with Paul to Caesarea. It is also pos-sible that the foot soldiers only accompanied the others outside of the city where there was immediate danger to Paul and the soldiers accompanying him. Indeed, a band of some forty assassins could do considerable harm on an even larger number of Roman troops who were trying to navigate the countless narrow pathways en route to Antipatris. Josephus indi-cates the dangers that existed on these same Palestinian roads in those days. When Cestius, the governor of Syria in the fall of the year A.D. 66, began a retreat with his troops from Jerusalem at the outbreak of the war, the Jewish rebels, who were significantly outnum-bered, were able to do savage deeds against his army, the Twelfth Legion, until they could reach Antipatris. He writes:

 . . . all along the route men were contin-ually being struck, torn from the ranks, and dropping on the ground. At length, after numerous casualties, including Priscus, the commander of the sixth legion, Longinus, a tribune, and

Aemilius Jucundus, commander of a troop of horse [cavalry], with difficulty the army reached their former camp at Gabao, having further abandoned the greater part of their baggage (*War* 2.544-45, LCL).

Josephus goes on to tell how the Jewish rebels were able to kill some 5,300 soldiers and 480 cavalry on this retreat to Antipatris, the same route the soldiers were taking Paul (*War* 2.554-55).

23:25-26. And he wrote a letter having this form: "Claudius Lysias, to the most excellent governor Felix, greetings." On the epistolary greeting (Greek = *ho kratistos*, "most excellent", see note in Luke 1:3 and it is also comparable to that used to address the procurator of Judaea and also Vitellius, the governor of Syria. Josephus, reporting correspondence from Emperor Claudius, says of Vitellius, "that excellent man [Greek = *ho kratistos*] for whom I have the greatest esteem" (*Ant.* 20.12, LCL). Whatever his motivation, the Roman commander at Jerusalem felt an obligation to guarantee Paul's safety. In this letter, which is typical of ancient letters in the Greco-Roman world, we see the full name of the commander of the Roman troops in Jerusalem, Claudius Lysias (see above comments at 21:31-33 and 22:28).

Felix's full name was either Antonius Felix (so Tacitus, *Histories* 5.9) or Claudius Felix (so Josephus, *Ant.* 20.137), as the procurator or governor of Palestine (either A.D. 52–60 or A.D. 53–55), has little good said about him either by Josephus or other Roman historians. Tacitus (ca. A.D. 55–120) tells of the problems in Judea and how things were relatively quiet until the death of Tiberias, but when Caligula, his successor, ordered the placing of his statue in the temple in Jerusalem, serious turmoil in the land began again. When Claudius came to the throne after the death of Caligula, Tacitus says that he appointed rulers over Palestine and one such was Antonius Felix, who he claims: "prac-

ticed every kind of cruelty and lust, wielding the power of king with all the instincts of a slave" (*Histories* 5.9, LCL). Josephus is more kind to Felix, but agrees that Claudius "sent Felix, the brother of Pallas, to take charge of matters in Judaea. When he [Claudius] completed the twelfth year of his reign [A.D. 53], granted Agrippa the tetrarchy of Philip together with Batanaea, adding thereto Trachonitis and Lysanias' former tetrarchy of Abila" (*Ant.* 20.137-38, LCL). Suetonius (ca. A.D. 75–140) adds to this that Emperor Claudius was "fond of Felix, giving him the command of cohorts and of troops of horse, as well as the province of Judaea; and he became the husband of three queens [two of which were named Drusilla and the third is unknown]" (*Lives of the Caesars, The Deified Claudius* 5.28, LCL). Josephus tells about Felix's marriages and how he married Drusilla, the sister of Herod Agrippa II, from her husband who was king of Emesa (see above at 24:24). He was later recalled and Festus installed in the same position while Paul was imprisoned (see note below at 25:1). Felix was freed by Claudius's mother, Antonia, and therefore he was called *Antonius* Felix. Tacitus's continued disdain for Felix is reflected in an important passage that also indicates that he had served as procurator of Samaria before going to Caesarea (Paul's comment at 24:10 also lends credence to his appointment). His difficulties and the reason for his recall that took place during Paul's imprisonment at Caesarea is clearly seen in the following:

The like moderation [of his brother Pallas], however, was not shewn [shown] by his brother, surnamed Felix; who for a while past had held the governorship of Judaea, and consideration that with such influences behind him all malefactions would be venial. The Jews, it is true, had given signs of disaffection in the rioting prompted by the demand of Gaius Caesar for an effigy of himself in the temple; and though the news of his murder had made compliance needless, the fear remained that some emperor might issue an identical mandate. In the interval, Felix was fostering crime by misconceived remedies, his worst efforts being emulated by Ventidius Cumanus, his colleague in the other half of the province—which was so divided that the natives of Galilee were subject to Ventidius, Samaria to Felix. The districts had long been at variance, and their animosities were now under the less restraint, as they could despise their regents.

. . . .

At first, the pair rejoiced; then, when the growth of their mischief forced them to interpose the arms of their troops, the troops were beaten, and the province would have been ablaze with war but for the intervention of Quadratus, the governor of Syria. With regard to the Jews who had gone so far as to shed the blood of regular soldiers, there were no protracted doubts as to the infliction of the death penalty: Cumanus and Felix were answerable for more embarrassment, as Claudius, on learning the motives of the revolt [by the Jews], had authorized Quadratus to deal with the case of the procurators themselves (*Annals* 12.54, LCL).

Luke shows the replacing of Felix by Festus (see 24:27 and 25:1 ff.), but he does not go into detail about the cruel activities of the procurator, though the action in 24:26 suggests the unethical practices of the man. What Luke says about Felix is in keeping with the information in Tacitus and also in Josephus noted above.

The letter that Claudius Lysias sends to Felix indicates that Paul is a Roman citizen and that he had to be rescued from the Jews because of their interpretations of their religious traditions and that no Roman offence

was committed. This has some similarities with the story of Paul's arrest in Corinth that also had to do with Jewish religious traditions and likewise was preceded by a vision from the "Lord" (the risen Christ) (see 18:9, 12-15 cf. 23:11, 25-30). In both places, the accusation by the Jews does not impinge on Roman law, and technically Paul could have been freed in Caesarea as he was in Corinth.

23:31. So the soldiers, in accordance with their orders, took Paul and brought him by night to Antipatris. The city and fortress at Antipatris was built by Herod the Great in honor of his father. Josephus describes it as follows:

> After these celebrations and festivals Herod erected another city in the plain of Capharsaba [refers to the Plain of Sharon], as it is called, where he selected a site that was well watered and a region excellent for plants. There was also a river flowing round the city itself, and the grove that surrounded it was most beautiful because of the size of the trees. This city he called Antipatris after his father Antipater (*Ant.* 16.142-43, LCL).

The city was located some thirty-five miles northwest of Jerusalem and some twenty-five miles south and slightly east of Caesarea. The ancient city of Joppa was about ten miles southwest of Antipatris. Many scholars believe that this ancient site has been discovered and excavated near the ancient town of Aphek. Some are still unsure, but the ruins that remain at a probable location exhibit the remains of a fortress that fits with what is known of this city and its likely location.

23:33. And when these had come to Caesarea. For comment on Caesarea, see note at 8:40 above.

23:34. And when he had read it, he asked from what province he was; and when he learned that he was from Cilicia. Paul was from Tarsus of Cilicia, a city governed by the governor of both Syria and Cilicia. The two provinces were separated later under Emperor Vespasian, but were combined in the time of Paul. On Cilicia, see notes on 9:11 above.

23:35. He said, "I will give you a hearing after your accusers arrive also," giving orders for him to be kept in Herod's Praetorium. This was Herod the Great's palace that was subsequently occupied by the procurators of Judaea and also the place where justice was carried out. This is probably the reason Paul is remanded at Caesarea. The palace of Herod, that is, his Praetorium (literally, the term refers to the palace of the governor of a Roman province), has not been found in the recent excavations, but many of the cites mentioned in Josephus's description of this city have. In his lengthy description of the city (*Ant.* 15.331-41), Josephus indicates that Herod the Great adorned the city "with a very costly palace, with civic halls and—what was greatest of all and required the most labour—with a well-protected harbour, of the size of the Piraeus [the harbor that served Athens]" (15.331-32, LCL).

24:1–26:32. Paul's Defense at Caesarea
24:1-23. Paul's Defense before Felix. The following defense is the only debate in Acts and it uses a number of rhetorical devices, including the introductory comments by the advocate for the Jews who have come from Jerusalem.

24:1. And after five days the high priest Ananias came down with some elders, with a certain attorney named Tertullus; and they brought charges to the governor against Paul. "After five days" refers to 23:35, that is, five days after Paul had arrived from Jerusalem. For additional comment on Ananias, see notes on 23:2. The Greek word used for "attorney" is *rhetor* (from which the word *rhetoric* derives) and was a common term for public speakers,

even if it is used with the idea of an advocate or lawyer at a trial. Lucian of Samosata begins his treatise on public speaking with the question: "You ask, my boy, how you can get to be a public speaker [Greek = *rhetor*], and be held to personify the sublime and glorious name of sophist" (*A Professor of Public Speaking* 1, LCL). The term is also frequently used as a legal advocate. For instance, Dio Chrysostom observes that "some laws have not been clearly written, and they are often warped and twisted by the eloquence of the orators [*ton rhetoron*]" (*Seventy-Sixth Discourse* 4, LCL).

24:2-3. And after Paul had been summoned, Tertullus began to accuse him, saying to the governor, "Since we have through you attained much peace, and since by your providence reforms are being carried out for this nation, we acknowledge this in every way and everywhere, most excellent Felix, with all thankfulness." Tertullus's opening remarks of flattery toward Felix are contrary to reality, but customary when addressing one's superior who can act on a request of this nature. As noted above, Felix was commonly viewed as a terrible administrator and responsible for much violence in Palestine (see note on 23:26). It is possible to speak of Felix as a peacemaker in the sense that he directed considerable attention to ridding the land of the "brigands" (Greek = *lestai*) (see note above on 21:38 above). According to Josephus, Felix could be quite cruel (see note above on 23:25), but he also observes that Felix took radical steps to rid the land of the rebels that were causing serious unrest in the land.

> Felix took prisoner Eleazar, the brigand chief, who for twenty years had ravaged the country, with many of his associates, and sent them for trial to Rome. Of the brigands whom he crucified, and of the common people who were convicted of complicity with them and punished by him, the number was incalculable. But

while the country was thus cleared of these pests, a new species of banditti was springing up in Jerusalem, the so-called *sicarii* . . . (*War* 2.252-54, LCL).

Thus, in some sense, he was able to bring peace for a while, but more importantly, this was a customary way of greeting one's superior whether in a court or other matter in which a favor was being requested.

The name Tertullus was a common one and a derivative of Tertius. Pliny later speaks of a person by that name. "I had left Rome for a visit to my native town when news reached me that Cornutus Tertullus had accepted the office of Curator of the Aemilian Road [a road leading to north Italy]" (*Epistles* 5.14.1, LCL).

24:5. For we have found this man a real pest and a fellow who stirs up dissension among all the Jews throughout the world, and a ringleader of the sect of the Nazarenes. Although there is considerable hyperbole introduced with obvious purpose, Paul's identity as "ring leader" is clearly contrary to what the truth of the matter was. Also, the reference to the Christian community as a "sect of the Nazarenes" also has an interesting history. Jesus, for some unknown reason, came to be identified as Jesus the Nazarene and those who followed him were sometimes called Nazoreans. It may be that the term derives not from the village of Nazareth where Jesus grew up, but from the Hebrew *nazir* from which the term Nazarite, as in the Nazirite vows (see notes on 18:18 and 21:24 above) developed. As a sect (Greek = *hairesis*), the Christians were no more or less than other religious groups from the first century within Judaism, such as the Pharisees, Sadducees, or the Essenes, and the term is so used in Josephus as follows: "Now at this time there were three *schools of thought* [Greek = *haireseis*] among the Jews, which held different opinions concerning human affairs" (*Ant.* 13.171, LCL. Italics added).

24:6. And he even tried to desecrate the temple; and then we arrested him. And we wanted to judge him according to our own Law. Among the terrible things the Wicked Priest is accused of doing by the Qumran community in their commentary on Habakkuk 2:17 is that "the /Wicked/Priest performed repulsive acts and defiled the Sanctuary of God" (1QpHab12.7-9, Garcia Martinez trans., p. 202). Profaning the temple was considered an especially evil deed among the Jews and worthy of death (Exod. 31:14; Ps. 73:7; Ezek. 28:18; 2 *Macc.* 8:2).

24:16 "In view of this, I also do my best to maintain always a blameless conscience both before God and before men." Paul's insistence on his striving to maintain a good conscience is a reference to one's moral uprightness. See also 1 Cor. 10:13; Phil. 1:10; 3:13-14.

24:17. Now after several years I came to bring alms to my nation and to present offerings. See above comment on these offerings for the Christians in Jerusalem. See above note on this offering in 21:19-21. It is interesting that Paul does not speak of the offerings for his fellow Christians, but for his country. The latter would be true of those Christians living in Jerusalem who were a part of the church, but Paul did not go into the difference. The offerings Paul presented had to do with James's request (21:26).

24:18-19. But there were certain Jews from Asia who ought to have been present before you, and to make accusation, if they should have anything against me. Paul's argument was that those who have accused a person should be in court to testify against that person. Emperor Claudius held similar views. Suetonius reports that "whenever one party to a suit was absent, he was prone to decide in favour of the one who was present, without considering whether his opponent had failed to appear through his won fault or from a necessary cause" (*The Deified Claudius* 15.2, LCL). Dio

Cassius also reports a similar response by the emperor but as a result of there being so many cases to decide, he wrote: "As the number of lawsuits was now beyond all reckoning and those who expected to lose their cases would no longer put in an appearance, he issued a proclamation announcing that he would decide the cases against them by a given day even in their absence; and he strictly enforced this rule" (*Roman History*, 60.28.6, LCL). Paul's argument was not without merit in that day.

24:22-27. Paul's Imprisonment at Caesarea

24:22. But Felix, having a more exact knowledge about the Way, put them off, saying, "When Lysias the commander comes down, I will decide your case." It was not unusual for those who were leaders in a mixed ethnic and religious community to learn about their subjects. Philo, for instance, tells of a kindly governor named Petronius who studied the views of the Jews living under his rule.

Indeed it appears that he himself had some rudiments of Jewish philosophy and religion acquired either in early lessons in the past through his zeal for culture or after his appointment as governor in the countries where Jews are very numerous in every city, Asia and Syria, or else because his soul was so disposed, being drawn to things worthy of serious effort by a nature which listened to no voice nor dictation nor teaching but its own (*Embassy to Gaius* 245, LCL).

24:23 And he gave orders to the centurion for him to be kept in custody and yet have some freedom, and not to prevent any of his friends from ministering to him. It was not unusual for prisoners who were not thought to be a significant risk or who were not guilty of significant crimes to be treated humanely and allowed regular visitations by friends and family (see 28:30 below). When Agrippa was imprisoned by Tiberias, Antonia, the mother of Claudius, secured for him several privileges including the following:

that the soldiers who were to guard him and that the centurion who would be in charge of them and would also be handcuffed to him should be of humane character, that he should be permitted to bathe every day and receive visits from his freedmen and friends, and that he should have other bodily comforts too. (*Ant.* 18.203, LCL).

24:24. But some days later, Felix arrived with Drusilla, his wife, who was a Jewess, and sent for Paul, and heard him speak about faith in Christ Jesus. Felix married the daughter of Herod Agrippa I through less than honorable means by which he convinced her to leave her present husband (Azizus, king of Emesa, Syria). According to Josephus, Agrippa received a gift from the emperor and gave his sister Drusilla in marriage to the king of Emesa, Syria and the king consented to be circumcised. After that, however, things changed and Josephus reports as follows:

Not long afterwards Drusilla's marriage to Azizus was dissolved under the impact of the following circumstances. At the time when Felix was procurator of Judaea, he beheld her; and, inasmuch as she surpassed all other women in beauty, he conceived a passion for the lady. He sent to her one of his friends, a Cyprian Jew named Atomus, who pretended to be a magician, in an effort to persuade her to leave her husband and to marry Felix. Felix promised to make her supremely happy if she did not disdain him. She, being unhappy and wishing to escape the malice of her sister Berenice—for Drusilla was exceedingly abused by her because of her beauty—was persuaded to transgress the ancestral laws and to marry Felix.

By him she gave birth to a son whom she named Agrippa. How this youth and his wife disappeared at the time of the eruption of Mount Vesuvius in the times of Titus Caesar, I shall describe later (*Ant.* 20.142-44, LCL).

24:25. And as he was discussing righteousness, self-control and the judgment to come, Felix became frightened and said, "Go away for the present, and when I find time, I will summon you." Besides being themes in Paul's letters, Luke may have included these themes because of the immoral conduct of Felix in taking Drusilla as his wife. Paul's comments on the themes of righteousness (see Rom. 3:21-26), self-control (Gal. 5:23), and the judgment of God (Rom. 2:2-3) may have had their desired effect by causing Felix to fear. One should not make too much of the parallel with the example of John the Baptist and his death as a result of judging Herod Antipas on such matters (Matt. 14:1-12; cf. Mark 6:14-16; Luke 9:7-9). Nothing suggests either Felix or Drusilla tried to have Paul executed.

24:26. At the same time too, he was hoping that money would be given him by Paul; therefore he also used to send for him quite often and converse with him. There are two messages here: first that Felix was true to his reputation of trying to extract funds wrongfully by means of a bribe and secondly that for this reason he left Paul in prison rather than free him when there were no grounds for the charges brought against him. Josephus offers a parallel situation and perhaps why Paul remained in prison. He says that Felix's successor, Festus (v. 27), was followed by Lucceius Albinus, who was guilty of terrible crimes against the people.

The administration of Albinus [ca. A.D. 62–64], who followed Festus, was of another order; there was no form of villainy which he omitted to practice. Not only did he, in official capacity, steal and plunder private property and burden the whole nation with extraordinary taxes, but he accepted ransoms from their relatives on behalf of those who had been imprisoned for robbery by the local councils or by former procurators; and the only persons left in gaol [jail or prison] as malefactors were those who failed to pay the price. (*War* 2.272-73, LCL).

24:27. But after two years had passed, Felix was succeeded by Porcius Festus; and wishing to do the Jews a favor, Felix left Paul imprisoned. Little is know about Festus who succeeded Felix who was appointed by Nero and served from A.D. 60–62. He died in office after just two years and was succeeded by Albinus. He was a member of a senatorial clan named Porcii of Tusculum. Josephus says in one place that when Festus became the procurator of Judaea, he "proceed to attack the principal plague of the country: he captured large numbers of the brigands and put not a few to death" (*War* 2.271, LCL). In another he goes into more detail about Festus's most important contribution to the region.

When Festus arrived in Judaea, it happened that Judaea was being devastated by the brigands, for the villages one and all were being set on fire and plundered. These so-called *sicarii*—these are brigands—were particularly numerous at that time. They employed daggers, in size resembling the scimitars of the Persians, but carved more like the weapons called by the Romans *sicae*, from which these brigands took their name because they slew so many in this way (*Ant.* 20.185-86, LCL).

25:1-12. Paul's Appeal Before Festus

25:12. Then when Festus had conferred with his council, he answered, "You have appealed to Caesar, to Caesar you shall go." That a procurator would send a Roman prisoner to

Caesar to deal with matters of justice is not unusual. Felix, his predecessor did so before him. Josephus reports that

> Felix took prisoner Eleazar, the brigand chief, who for twenty years had ravaged the country, with many of his associates, and sent them for trial to Rome. Of the brigands whom he crucified, and of the common people who were convicted of complicity with them and punished by him, the number was incalculable (*War* 2.253, LCL).

Pliny (b. ca. 61, d. ca. 113), while seeking advice from the Emperor on how to deal with Christians in his province, indicated what his practice was with the Christians. Besides torturing and executing those who would not recant of their faith, when he came across Roman citizens who professed the Christian faith, he indicates that he sent them to Rome. "There have been others similarly fanatical who are Roman citizens. I have entered them on the list of persons to be sent to Rome for trial" (*Letters* 10.96.4, LCL). Trajan's response to this was that Pliny had "followed the right course of procedure" (*Letters*, 10.97.1, LCL).

When Quintilius Varus, the governor of Syria, came to Jerusalem to crush a revolt, on advice of council (Achiab, cousin to Herod, cf. Josephus, *War* 1.662), surrendered to Varus and his troops. He "discharged the rank and file and sent the leaders to Caesar for trial" who received pardon from the emperor except those of royal blood who were punished because of their taking arms up against a "sovereign who was of their own family" (War 2.77, LCL). It was not unusual for Roman citizens to be sent to Rome or others with special crimes or of elevated status. For comments on Paul's Roman citizenship see notes on 16:37-38; 22:25-27, 29. Suetonius observes, however, that those who claimed Roman privileges wrongly were punished severely. "He forbade men of foreign birth to use the Roman names so far as those of the clans were concerned. Those who usurped

the privileges of Roman citizenship he [the Emperor Claudius] executed in the Esquiline field" (*The Deified Claudius* 15.3, LCL).

25:13-27. Agrippa's Advice to Festus
25:13. Now when several days had elapsed, King Agrippa and Bernice arrived at Caesarea, and paid their respects to Festus. Agrippa is actually King Agrippa II, son of King Agrippa I (see notes on him in 12:1-4, 20-23), he was educated in Rome and stayed there until his uncle, who ruled Chalcis, had died. Following his uncle's death, Agrippa II was appointed by Emperor Claudius as king over Chalcis and also given control over the temple in Jerusalem with the right of appointing the high priest. He ruled in Palestine from A.D. 48 until ca. A.D. 92 or 93, the longest reigning Herod family member. According to Josephus, "after the death of Herod, sovereign of Chalcis, Claudius presented his kingdom to his nephew Agrippa, son of Agrippa [I]" (*War* 2.§223, LCL). In the year A.D. 52, Nero added to his kingdom also the tetrarchy of his uncle Philip that included both Itureaea and Trachonitis (see Luke 3:1). Later, Nero also added to Agrippa's kingdom parts of Galilee and Perea. "The emperor also bestowed on Agrippa a certain portion of Galilee, giving orders to the cities of Tiberias and Tarichaeae [cities of Galilee] to submit to him. He also gave him Julias, a city of Peraea, and fourteen villages that go with it" (*Ant.* 20.158-59, LCL).

Josephus also mentions that Agrippa was also responsible for new construction of various parts of the temple in Jerusalem and that he "had been appointed by Claudius Caesar to be curator of the temple . . . " and testifies to his ability to appoint the high priest: "He [King Agrippa II] also deprived Jesus son of Gamaliel of the high priesthood and gave it to Matthias the son of Theophilus, under whom the war of the Jews with the Romans began" (*Ant.* 20.222-223, LCL). Josephus also observes that Festus and Agrippa II were apparently in agreement against actions of the Jews regarding the building of a high wall to keep Herod Agrippa from observing the sacrifices in the temple from his palace (*Ant.* 20.189-93).

Bernice was the older sister of Drusilla, wife of Felix (see note on 24:24 above) and like Agrippa, her father was Agrippa I. According to Josephus, when Agrippa I died (see notes on 12:2-23 above), he was survived by his wife Cypros, three daughters (Bernice, Mariamme, and Drusilla), and one son, Agrippa. Bernice married her uncle, Herod, king of Chalcis, (*War* 2.218-220), and when he died she lived with her brother, Agrippa II. This latter action drew scandalous comments from the Jews and Romans alike. Juvenal, or more precisely, Decimus Junias Juvenalis (ca. 60–140), who wrote satires against Roman lifestyle, speaks disrespectfully of Bernice when he describes a gift of a diamond ring given to her by her brother Agrippa II. He says that this diamond was "of great renown, made precious by the finger of Berenice [=Bernice]. It was given as a present long ago by the barbarian Agrippa to his incestuous sister, in that country where kings celebrate festal sabbaths with bare feet [a reference to Bernice]" (*Satire* 6.§155-60, LCL). Dio Cassius also tells of Bernice's relationship with Titus who eventually became the Roman Emperor.

Bernice was at the very height of her power and consequently came to Rome along with her brother Agrippa. The latter was given the rank of praetor, while she dwelt in the palace, cohabiting with Titus. She expected to marry him and was already behaving in every respect as if she were his wife; but when he perceived that the Romans were displeased with the situation, he sent her away. For, in addition to all the other talk that there was, certain sophists of the cynic school managed somehow to slip into the city at this time, too; and first Diogenes, entering the theatre when it was full, denounced the pair in a long, abusive

speech, for which he was flogged; and after him Heras, expecting no harsher punishment, gave vent to many senseless yelpings in true Cynic fashion, and for this was beheaded (*Roman History* 16.15.3-5, LCL).

Suetonius offers an unflattering picture of Titus until it was his time to become emperor, following the death of his father Vespasian, when he apparently changed his way of living. Besides cruelty, he was also suspected of riotous living, since he protracted his revels until the middle of the night with the most prodigal of his friends; likewise of unchastity because of his troops of catamites and eunuchs, and his notorious passion for queen Bernice, to whom it was even said that he promised marriage. He goes on to say that as it came time for him to accept the role of Roman emperor, he sent her from Rome at once, "against her will and against his own. Some of his most beloved paramours, although they were such skilful dancers that they later became stage favourites, he not only ceased to cherish any longer, but even to witness their public performances" (*Lives of Caesars, The Deified Titus* 6.1-2, LCL).

That Paul would shortly stand before Festus, Agrippa, and Bernice to offer his defense (*apologia*), is a fulfillment for Luke of the earlier prediction of his standing before Gentiles, kings, and the people of Israel (9:15).

25:16. "And I answered them that it is not the custom of the Romans to hand over any man before the accused meets his accusers face to face, and has an opportunity to make his defense against the charges." In Emperor Trajan's letter of response to Pliny regarding what to do about those who were accused of being Christians, he rejects accusations by anonymous persons against the Christians and says that "pamphlets circulated anonymously must play no part in any accusation. They create the worst sort of precedent and are quite out of keeping with the spirit of our age" (Pliny, *Letters,* 97.2, LCL). Likewise, Ulpian, the famous Jurist of Roman Law during the reign of the emperor Caracalla (A.D. 212–217), summarizes the rights of accused Roman citizens as follows: "This is the law by which we abide: No one may be condemned without his case being heard" (*Digest* 48.17.1, LCL). On the other hand, it is probable that as a result of the favor that the Jews had from the time of Julius Caesar that they may have tried to use their privilege as an authorized religion in the empire for gaining a special consideration by Festus. Josephus indicates the scope of that favor obtained under Julius Caesar:

I, Julius Caesar, Imperator and Pontifex Maximus, Dictator for the second time, have decided as follows with the advice of the council. [Because of the loyalty of John Hyrcanus in times of peace and war to the Romans] ... it is my wish that Hyrcanus, son of Alexander, and his children shall be ethnarchs of the Jews and shall hold the office of high priest of the Jews for all time in accordance with their national customs, and . .. whatever high-priestly rights or other privileges exist in accordance with their laws, these he and his children shall possess by my command. And if, during this period, any question shall arise concerning the Jews' manner of life, it is my pleasure that the decision shall rest with them. Nor do I approve of troops being given winter-quarters among them or of money being demanded of them (*Ant.* 14.192-95, LCL).

Appian (ca. 98–117) also affirms the civic rights of the accused in a Roman court. "Our law, Senators, requires that the accused shall himself hear the charge preferred against him and shall be judged after he has made his own

defense (*Civil Wars* 3.54.222, Trans. by Conzelmann, *Acts,* 206). Tertullian, himself a lawyer and familiar with Roman law, agrees with this and concludes: "There is freedom to answer cross-question, since in fact it is against the law for men to be condemned, undefended and unheard" (*Apol.* 1.3; 2.2, ANF). Finally, Tacitus observes that because Cingonius and Petronius, generals of Nero, had not received proper defense or had a chance to respond to their accusations before being executed, and observes that "they were killed unheard and undefended, so that men believed them innocent" (*Histories* 1.6, LCL).

25:21. "But when Paul appealed to be held in custody for the Emperor's decision, I ordered him to be kept in custody until I send him to Caesar." Luke's term translated "Emperor" is "Sebaste" (Greek = *sebastou,* Latin = *augustus*). The term that was given to Octavian (Caesar Augustus), the grand-nephew of Julius Caesar. His successors used the title something like that of "his Majesty." In this case, the term refers to Nero Claudius Caesar (A.D. 54–58). Philo speaks of how Octavian received this title justly because of his many remarkable deeds and how it was passed on to his successors.

Again consider him who in all the virtues transcended human nature, who on account of the vastness of his imperial sovereignty as well as nobility of character was the first to bear the name of August [Greek = *sebastos*] or Venerable, a title received not through lineal succession as a portion of its heritage but because he himself became the source of the veneration which was received also by those who followed him. . . . (*Embassy to Gaius* 143, LCL). For discussion of the term Caesar, see note on 17:7.

25:26. "Yet I have nothing definite about him to write to my lord." The use of the term "lord" (Greek = *ho kurios*) for a sitting sovereign was apparently after the time of Tiberius since the use as a reference to the emperor was generally rejected by both Augustus and Tiberias. The reference to an emperor as "lord" was common in Egypt and in other places in the east, but it became more common under Nero. This is the earliest example of the use of the term to speak of the Emperor Claudius. Suetonius claims that Augustus rejected such titles for himself and that

> He always shrank from the title Lord [Latin = *Domini*] as reproachful and insulting. When the words "O just and gracious Lord [*O dominum aequum et bonum*]!" were uttered in a farce at which he was a spectator and all the people sprang to their feet and applauded as if they were said of him, he at once checked their unseemly flattery by look and gesture, and on the following day sharply reproved them in an edict. After that he would not suffer himself to be called Sire even by his children or his grandchildren either in jest or earnest, and he forbade them to use such flattering terms even among themselves. He did not if he could help it leave or enter any city or town except in the evening or at night, to avoid disturbing anyone by the obligations of ceremony (*Lives of the Caesars, The Deified Augustus* 53.1, LCL).

Similarly, Tiberius who, according to Suetonius,

> so loathed flattery that he would not allow any senator to approach his litter, either to pay his respects or on business, and when an ex-consul in apologizing to him attempted to embrace his knees, he drew back in such haste that he fell over backward. In fact, if anyone in conversation or in a set speech spoke of him in too flattering terms, he did not hesitate to interrupt him, to take him to task, and to correct his language on the spot. Being

once called "Lord [Dominus]," he warned the speaker not to address him again in an insulting fashion. When another spoke of his "sacred duties," and still another said that he appeared before the senate "by the emperor's authority," he forced them to change their language, substituting "advice" for "authority" and "laborious" for "sacred."

Tacitus also says of the emperor Tiberias that he rejected the title "Father of his Country" which had been offered to him earlier, but that "he administered a severe reprimand to those who had termed his occupations 'divine,' and himself 'Lord'" [Latin = *dominum*, "lord"] (*Annals* 2.87, LCL). Eventually this hesitation was overcome by the successors of these two emperors and use of the term when referring to Roman emperors became commonplace following the time of Nero. For example, ca. A.D. 150–51, in the registration or notification of the birth of a child, a papyrus document survives that says "We register the son who was born to us, Ischyras, being on year of age in the present fourteenth year of Antoninus Caesar the lord [Greek = *tou kuriou*]" (*Select Papyri: Public Documents*, 309, 8. *Declarations to Officials*, LCL). Luke is apparently aware of this use and is one of the first writers to report its use in reference to Emperor Claudius.

25:27 "For it seems absurd to me in sending a prisoner, not to indicate also the charges against him." Ulpian observed that according to Roman law, "After an appeal has been entered, records must be furnished by the one who made the appeal to the person who is going to conduct the examination concerning the appeal" (*Digest* 49.6.1. Trans. by Conzelmann, *Acts* 207).

26:1- 32. Paul's Defense before Agrippa
Paul's defense (*apologia*) before Agrippa, Bernice, and Festus only begins as a defense and ends as a missionary appeal. This meeting

is not so much a defense, since Paul has already appealed to Rome and the plans are to send him there (see notes on 25:11-12), but rather the opportunity for Festus to find something to say in his accompanying documents as Paul is brought to Rome. Nevertheless, Luke's theme that Paul was a faithful Jew comes out again in this, Paul's final defense, and that his accusers did not have any grounds for accusing him of doing or saying anything against the Law, their traditions, or the temple in Jerusalem.

26:1. And Agrippa said to Paul, "You are permitted to speak for yourself." Then Paul stretched out his hand and proceeded to make his defense. As observed above (21:40), Paul uses the familiar hand gesture of a public speaker.

26:3. Especially because you are an expert in all customs and questions among the Jews; therefore I beg you to listen to me patiently. As at 24:2-3 and 10 when Tertullus and Paul both "curry favor" in their introductory remarks to Felix, so Paul uses what is called the *captatio benevolentiae*, that is "the currying of favor" as he begins his defense. Consider, for example, Pliny's introductory comments to the Emperor Trajan when he was requesting guidance and approval of Pliny's plan to build something for the emperor's honor. Pliny writes: "In consideration of your noble ambition which matches your supreme position, I think I should bring to your notice any projects which are worthy of your immortal name and glory and are likely to combine utility with magnificence." As he concludes the letter he speaks of his enthusiasm for the project and concludes by saying: "This [project], however, only fires me with enthusiasm to see you accomplish what kings could only attempt; you will forgive my ambition for your greater glory" (*Letters* 10.41.1, 5, LCL). Such introductory language was common as a rhetorical device used when addressing a superior individual.

26:5. Since they have known about me for a long time previously, if they are willing to testify, that I lived as a Pharisee according to the strictest sect of our religion. For comments on Paul's life as a Pharisee, see 22:3 above.

26:9. "So then, I thought to myself that I had to do many things hostile to the name of Jesus of Nazareth." Literally, Jesus "the Nazorean." On this see note on 2:22.

26:11. "And as I punished them often in all the synagogues, I tried to force them to blaspheme; and being furiously enraged at them, I kept pursuing them even to foreign cities. Compare 22:3-4 above. Paul's activity against the Christians is even stronger here. An example of how Pliny dealt with Christians when he was sent to Bithynia and Pontus by Trajan, in his correspondence to Trajan describing in effect how he forced the Christians to blaspheme by denying their faith:

> For the moment this is the line I have taken with all persons brought before me on the charge of being Christians. I have asked them in person if they are Christians, and if they admit it, I repeat the question a second and third time, with a warning of punishment awaiting them. If they persist, I order them to be led away for execution . . . " (*Letters* 10.96.3-4, LCL).

> For those who had denied being Christians, Pliny forced them to repeat after him "a formula of invocation to the gods and had made offerings of wine and incense to your statue . . . and furthermore had reviled the name of Christ: none of which things, I understand, any genuine Christian can be induced to do" (*Letters* 10.96.5, LCL). While there is no specific list of things that Paul did to the Christians to cause them to blaspheme and deny their faith, it is clear that he was willing to resort to violent means to accomplish his mission (see 9:1-2, 13-14; 22:4-5). Paul never forgot his actions against

the church (Phil. 3:6; 1 Cor. 15:9).

26:14. "And when we had all fallen to the ground, I heard a voice saying to me in the Hebrew dialect, 'Saul, Saul, why are you persecuting Me? It is hard for you to kick against the goads.'" On the "Hebrew Dialect" see note on 21:40. This appears to be a reference to Aramaic. The reference to "kicking against the goads" is found in Euripides (*Bacc.* 794-95) and was widely used in the ancient world to refer to those who strive against fate, that is, the will of God (see other examples in Julian, *Or.* 8.246 and Aeschylus, *Agam.* 16:24). This notion may also refer to the inner motivation to do the will of God. Philo says that

> Every soul has for its birth-fellow and house-mate a *monitor* whose way is to admit nothing that calls for censure, whose nature is ever to hate evil and love virtue, who is its accuser and its judge in one. If he be once roused as accuser he censures, accuses and puts the soul to shame, and again as judge, he instructs, admonishes and exhorts it to change its ways. And if he has the strength to persuade it, he rejoices and makes peace. But if he cannot, he makes war to the bitter end, never leaving it alone by day or night, but plying it with stabs and deadly wounds until he breaks the thread of its miserable and ill-starred life (*Decalogue* 87, LCL, italics supplied).

He also describes those who have tried to justify their evil deeds but who eventually face up with "Conviction."

> When the true priest, Conviction, enters us, like a pure ray of light, we see in their real value the unholy thoughts that were stored within our soul, and the guilty and blameworthy actions to which we laid our hands in ignorance of our true interests. So conviction, discharging his priest-like task, defiles all

these and bids them all be cleared out and carried away, that he may see the soul's house in its natural bare condition, and heal whatever sicknesses have arisen in it (*Unchangeableness of God* 135, LCL).

See also the pseudepigraphal *Psalms of Solomon* where God uses this kind of a "goad" to bring his children back in line with his will. "Thus my soul was drawn away from the Lord God of Israel, unless the Lord had come to my aid with his everlasting mercy, he jabbed me as a horse is goaded to keep it awake; my savior and protector at all times saved me" (16:3-4, OT Pseud 2:665). Many scholars have taken this passage in Acts to refer to Paul striving against his own conscience, "the goads," but that may not be the focus here. It is also possible that the reference to the "kicking against the goads" can be taken simply as Paul kicking against or going against the will of God that he had not yet perceived. What may suggest this is Paul's own conscience while he was persecuting the church: namely, he saw himself as blameless while he was a persecutor and before he became a Christian (Phil. 3:6). Guilt was not a motive for his conversion, but an intervention by God letting him know that he had been going contrary to the will of God.

26:18. To open their eyes so that they may turn from darkness to light and from the dominion of Satan to God, in order that they may receive forgiveness of sins and an inheritance among those who have been sanctified by faith in Me. See Isa. 42:7, 16. The Christians made frequent use of various metaphors of light and darkness to express their beliefs about their living and relationship with God. This was also common among the Essenes at Qumran who saw themselves as the "sons of light." The War Scroll, for example, begins

> For the Master. The rule of war on the unleashing of the attack of the sons of light against the company of the sons of

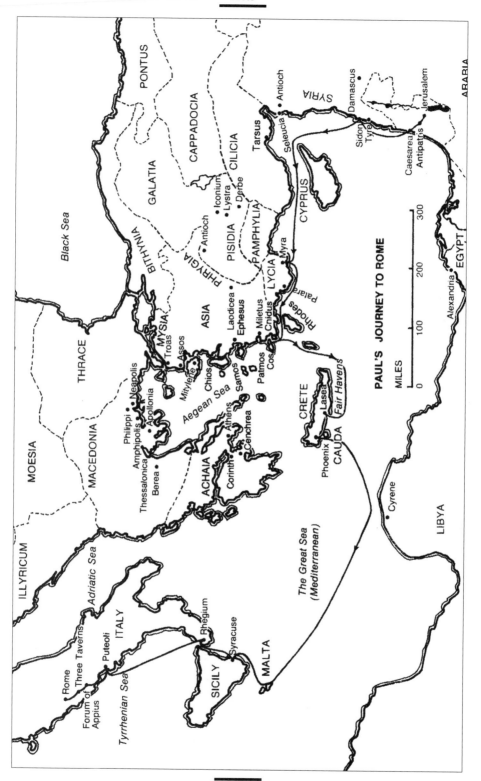

PAUL'S JOURNEY TO ROME

darkness, the army of Belial. . . the sons of Levi, Judah, and Benjamin, the exiles in the desert, shall battle against them in . . . all their bands when the exiled sons of light return from the Desert of the Peoples to camp in the Desert of Jerusalem; and after the battle they shall go up from there (to Jerusalem?) (1QWar Scroll [1 QM, 1Q33] 1.1-3, Trans. Geza Vermes, Complete DSS 163).

Likewise, in a Jewish (and perhaps Christian) pseudepigraphal writing dating from ca. second cent. A.D. and inspired by Gen. 41:45, we read "Lord God of my father Israel, the Most High, the Powerful One of Jacob, who gave life to all (things) and called (them) from the darkness to the light, and from the error to the truth, and from the death to the life" (Joseph and Aseneth 8.10, OT Pseud 2:213). In the New Testament, see also John 3:19-21; 1 John 1:5-7; 2:8-11; Eph. 5:8-14; Col. 1:12-13; 1 Peter 2:9.

26:19. "Consequently, King Agrippa, I did not prove disobedient to the heavenly vision." Paul was obedient to his mission that came from God. In the ancient world, several individuals claimed that what they proclaim or were doing was their mission from God. In his defense, Socrates also claims to have followed the divine will. "As I believe, I have been commanded to do this [teach] by the God through oracles and dreams and in every way in which any man was ever commanded by divine power to do anything whatsoever" (Plato, Apology 33C, LCL). Similarly, as Arrian relates Epictetus's story about Hercules as an example to follow because he obeyed the will of God, he concludes: "It was therefore in obedience to His will that he went about clearing away wickedness and lawlessness" (Epictetus, Discourses 2.16.44, LCL).

26:22. "And so, having obtained help from God, I stand to this day testifying both to small and great, stating nothing but what the Prophets and Moses said was going to take place." This sequence of referring to the Scriptures was unusual. Generally Moses and the Prophets are listed in Luke (see Luke 24:44 and Acts 3:22-23).

26:24-25. And while Paul was saying this in his defense, Festus said in a loud voice, "Paul, you are out of your mind! Your great learning is driving you mad." But Paul said, "I am not out of my mind, most excellent Festus, but I utter words of sober truth." Festus's comment that much "learning is driving you mad [Greek = maine]" has other parallels in antiquity. In the Pap. Oxy. 33.4.9-15 (Acta Appiani) there is a dialogue between the emperor and Appian and it goes as follows: "The emperor: 'Appian, I am accustomed to chasten those who rave and have lost all sense of shame. You speak only so long as I permit you.' Appian: 'By your genius, I am neither mad nor have I lost my sense of shame'" (Trans. by Conzelmann, Acts 212). Lucian of Samosata (ca. A.D. 120–90) speaks disparagingly about a man who collected books, but showed no evidence that he had ever read them. Speaking to the man, he says that everyone "thinks you are still downright daft" (The Ignorant Book Collector 22, LCL). Commenting on the counsel from the wise owl from Aesop's Fables, Dio Chrysostom observed that at first people "considered her foolish, and said she was mad [Greek = mainesthai]; but afterwards through experience they came to admire her and to consider her in very truth exceedingly wise" (Discourse, 12. 8, LCL). See also Sibylline Oracles 1.171-72 and Lucian, Abdicatus 30 for other examples.

26:26. "For the king knows about these matters, and I speak to him also with confidence, since I am persuaded that none of these things escape his notice; for this has not been done in a corner." The expression "in a corner" (Greek = en gonia) is Greek and there are several examples of it in the ancient world. In describing the settling of quarrels that was going on in Rome, Epictetus concludes that "the man who engages in it [settling disputes] will clearly be under obligation not to do it *in a corner* [Greek = *en gonia*]" (*Discourses* 2.12.17, LCL). This proverbial expression is also found in Plato, *Gorgias* 485D, but now in reference to being hidden or secluded. He says of the one who fails to mature in philosophy properly that, "he must cower down and spend the rest of his days whispering *in a corner* [*en gonia*] with three or four lads, and never utter anything free or high spirited" (*Gorgias* 485D, LCL. Italics added).

26:29. And Paul said, "I would to God, that whether in a short or long time, not only you, but also all who hear me this day, might become such as I am, except for these chains." Paul's appearance before Agrippa, Bernice, and Festus in chains appears strange if this were a normal defense, but since Paul has already appealed to Rome, it should not be considered unusual for him to appear before these individuals in chains. There is an edict from Octavian on the matter.

The Emperor Caesar Augustus, *pontifex. maximus*, holding the tribunician power for the seventeenth year declares:

Publius Sextius Scaeva does not merit reproach or censure for ordering Aulus Stlaccius Maximus son of Lucius, Lucius Stlaccius Macedo son of Lucius, and Publius Lacutanius Phileros, freedman of Publius, to be sent on to me from the province of Cyrene under guard because they had said that they had knowledge concerning my security and the commonwealth and wished to declare it. In so doing Sextius performed his duty conscientiously. However, since they have no information that concerns me or the commonwealth but have declared and convinced me that they had misrepresented and lied about this in the province, I have set them free and

am releasing them from custody. But as for Aulus Stlaccius Maximus, whom the envoys of the Cyrenaeans accuse of having removed statues from public places, among them even the one on the base of which the city inscribed my name, I forbid him to depart without my order until I have investigated this matter (*SEG* 9, no. 8.2, trans. *Roman Civilization* 2:38 in Conzelmann, *Acts* 240).

26:30-31. And the king arose and the governor and Bernice, and those who were sitting with them, and when they had drawn aside, they began talking to one another, saying, "This man is not doing anything worthy of death or imprisonment." And Agrippa said to Festus, "This man might have been set free if he had not appealed to Caesar." Once again, Luke concludes that Paul is not guilty of having violated the Law or its traditions or of having profaned the Jewish temple in Jerusalem. He is innocent of the charges leveled against him. How Luke became privy to the conversation between Agrippa and Festus is not known, unless in some way it was shared with Paul by one of them.

27:1–28:10. Paul's Journey to Rome

This portion of Acts has been recognized by all scholars who examine it to be very well versed in sea travel. It includes several important technical nautical names and also considerable familiarity with the geographical landscape of the Mediterranean. There are some commentators who believe that Luke's knowledge of the sea and the nautical routes is too good to be true. In other words, he used another source and placed the Pauline material in the text. There are several places where Luke merges this Pauline tradition into the story (3b, 9-11, 21-26, 31, 33-36, and 43), but Paul is, after all, his chief character. It is unlikely that he would ignore Paul even on the sea voyage to Rome. While some commentators call the passage into question because Paul's role in advising the ship's captain and crew as a prisoner is unlikely, Luke's point is that Paul was an unusual person with courage and spiritual guidance.

If, as the story begins, the centurion, Julius, shows favor to Paul, it would not be unusual for him to listen to Paul's counsel even if he did not take it as in vv. 11-12. It is important to note the return of the "we" passages, a common activity in the journey sections of Paul's mission, but in this passage they appear to be more merged with another source known to Luke. See for instance, how he moves to the third person in 17, which is sandwiched in between two "we" passages. The same is found in 37 where a "we" passage is found in the midst of a third person plural section of the story. The story is in three major parts that include the beginning of the voyage to Rome (1-8), the warning of Paul (9-12), the storm at sea (13-38) with an insert of Paul's counsel in 21-26, and the shipwreck (39-44). There are no exact parallels with this story, but there are many ancient stories about ships at sea and a number of shipwreck stories. Lucian of Samosata tells the story of a man who was thrown overboard during a terrible storm and of his friend who jumped into the sea and saved him from drowning. His story highlights both courage and friendship, but also the dangers at sea. A second tells of a very difficult voyage at sea from Pharos (near Alexandria) en route to Italy during a storm:

> As far as Sicily they had made a fortunate passage, said Simylus; but when they had run through the straits and in due time were sailing in the Adriatic itself, a great tempest fell upon them. Why repeat the many details of his story—huge seas, cyclones, hail, and all the other evils of a storm? But when they were at last abreast of Zacynthos, sailing with the yard bare, and also dragging hawsers [=ropes used for anchoring a ship] in their wake to check the fury of their driving, toward midnight Damon became seasick, as was natural in weather so rough, and began to vomit, leaning outboard. Then, I suppose because the ship was hove down with greater force toward the side over which he was leaning and the high sea contributed a send, he fell overboard head-first; and the poor fellow was not even without his clothes, so as to have been able to swim more easily. So he began at once to call for help, choking and barely able to keep himself above the water. When Euthydicus, who happened to be undressed and in his bunk, heard him, he flung himself into the sea, got to Damon, who was already giving out (all this was visible at a long distance because the moon was shining) and helped him by swimming beside him and bearing him up. The rest of them, he said, wanted to aid the men and deplored their misfortune, but could not do it because the wind that drove them was too strong; however, they did at least something, for they threw them a number of pieces of cork and some spars, on which they might swim if they chanced upon any of them, and finally even the gang plank, which was not small (*Toxaris* 19-20, LCL).

This story illustrates the dangers at sea that we find in the experience of Paul en route to Rome. Other well-known ancient stories of dangerous voyages at sea include Josephus, *Life* 3.13-16; Lucian, *Navigium* 7-10. See notes on 27:16 and 27:14 below. Again, while there are parallels in the sense of dangerous sea voyages that were life threatening, there are no stories exactly like Luke's in circulation, but these and other examples show how realistic such experiences were in the ancient world.

27:1-8. The Journey to Rome Begins
27:1. And when it was decided that we should sail for Italy, they proceeded to deliver Paul and some other prisoners to a centurion of the Augustan cohort named Julius. Nothing is known about the centurion except his name and that he, like other centurions in this work were friendly toward the Christian community (see 10:11-2; 22:25-26).

27:2 And embarking in an Adramyttian ship, which was about to sail to the regions along the coast of Asia, we put out to sea, accompanied by Aristarchus, a Macedonian of Thessalonica. Aristarchus is probably the same as noted in 19:29 above. He was a companion of Paul and is mentioned as a fellow prisoner of Paul (Col. 4:10). It may be possible that he was one of Luke's sources for portions of this story.

27:4. And from there we put out to sea and sailed under the shelter of Cyprus because the winds were contrary. The above noted stories, and especially Lucian's *Navigium* 7, show that strong winds often made sailing very challenging.

27:9-12. Paul's Advice about the Journey
27:9. And when considerable time had passed and the voyage was now dangerous, since even the fast was already over, Paul began to admonish them. The normal sea voyages took place between March 10 to November 11. The closing of the sea often took place in October because it was no longer considered safe to travel by ship. Josephus mentions those who were bringing news of the death of the emperor were "weatherbound for three months at sea" and could not convey the message (*War* 2.203). Because such travel was considered hazardous, Suetonius says that Claudius, in order to insure that adequate grain arrive in Rome during the winter months, "resorted to every possible means to bring grain to Rome, even in the winter season. To the merchants he held out the certainty of profit by assuming the expense of any loss that they might suffer from storms" (*Deified Claudius* 18.2, LCL). Josephus tells the story of Herod the Great making a trip to Rome from Egypt in the dead of winter to seek Antony's help with his enemies. Cleopatra wanted to entrust him with an expedition, but he "eluded the queen's solicitations, and, deterred neither by the perils of mid-winter nor by the disturbances in Italy, set sail for Rome. Nearly shipwrecked off Pamphylia, after throwing overboard the bulk of the cargo, he with difficulty came safe to Rhodesn...." After reaching Rome, he told his story to Antony how "he had left his nearest relatives besieged in a fortress and crossed the sea in the depth of winter to implore his aid." Antony rewarded him in part because of the "heroic qualities of the man in front of him," and "determined then and there to make him king of the Jews" (*War* 1.279-81, LCL). On the other hand, Pliny indicates that the "opening of the seas" took place in early spring.

> Accordingly the spring opens the seas to voyagers; at its beginning the West winds soften the wintry heaven, when the sun occupies the 25th degree of Aquarius; the date of this is Feb. 8. This also practically applies to all the winds whose positions I shall give afterwards, although every leap-year they come a day earlier, but they keep the regular rule in the period that follows (Pliny, *Natural History* 2.47.[§122], LCL).

He then goes on to describe the various winds that arise and when they come as signals of the seasons. This was very important information to those who sailed the seas. He acknowledges at the end of this, however, that "not even the fury of the storms closes the sea; pirates first compelled men by the threat of death to rush into death and venture on the winter seas, but now avarice exercises the same compulsion" (2.47 [125], LCL). Claudius's actions regarding shipping of grain/corn in the winter noted above testify to that!

The fast is that of the Day of Atonement, the tenth day of the seventh month of Tishri (Tishri = roughly October). See Lev. 16:29-31 for the origins of this observance. Philo describes the rationale for this day and how it was observed. While describing the various feast days in the Jewish calendar, he then says:

> The next feast held after the 'Trumpets' is the Fast. Perhaps some of the perversely minded who are not ashamed to censure things excellent will say, "What sort of a feast is this in which there are no gatherings to eat and drink . . . ?" he then offers three reasons for the fast including the need for self-restraint, devotion to prayers and the seeking of remission of sins, and to avoid gluttony since this day occurs after the harvest in October (*Special Laws* 2.193-203).

He noted that on this occasion the "Grand Priest" entered the temple "once a year only on the Fast, as it is called, to offer incense and to pray according to ancestral practice for a full supply of blessings and prosperity and peace for all mankind" (*Embassy to Gaius* 306, LCL). Josephus reports that the siege of the temple in Jerusalem during the war with Rome (66–70) began on the Day of Atonement during the fast (*Ant.* 14.66).

27:13-38. The Storm at Sea

27:14-15. But before very long there rushed down from the land a violent wind, called Euraquilo; and when the ship was caught in it, and could not face the wind, we gave way to it, and let ourselves be driven along. The ship is now out of control and those on board are at the mercy of the winds and waves. Lucian tells of a man who wanted to make a journey to the edge of the sea for the sake of adventure, so he prepared his ship, enlisted fifty men as a crew, and set sail. He reports:

> Well, for a day and a night we sailed before the wind without making much offing, as land was still dimly in sight; but at sunrise on the second day the wind freshened, the sea rose, darkness came on, and before we knew it we could not even get our canvas in. Committing ourselves to the gale and giving up, we drove for seventy-nine days. On the eightieth day, however, the sun came out and suddenly, and at no great distance, we saw a high, wooded island ringed about with sounding surf, which, however, was not rough, as already the worst of the storm was abating.
>
> Putting in and going ashore, we lay on the ground for some time in consequence of our long misery, but finally we rose and told off thirty of our number to stay and guard the ship and twenty to go inland with me and look over the island (*A True Story* 1.6, LCL).

27:17. And after they had hoisted it up, they used supporting cables in undergirding the ship; and fearing that they might run aground on the shallows of Syrtis, they let down the sea anchor, and so let themselves be driven along. They hoisted the lifeboat, or dinghy, that was carried for the safety of the passengers and crew, into the boat, to ensure that it would not damage the ship. Syrtis was located west of Cyrene near modern Libya in North Africa and was notorious for its treacherous shallow waters and quick sands known to all mariners. Dio Chrysostom tells about this place as he reports about mythical beasts in the area who devoured those who were shipwrecked in that location:

> The Syrtis is an arm of the Mediterranean extending far inland, a three days' voyage, they say, for a boat unhindered in its course. But those who have once sailed into it find egress impossible; for shoals, cross-currents, and long sand-bars extending a great distance out make the sea utterly

impassable or troublesome. For the bed of the sea in these parts is not clean, but as the bottom is porous and sandy it lets the sea seep in, there being no solidity to it. This, I presume, explains the existence there of the great sand-bars and dunes, which remind one of the similar condition created inland by the winds, through here, of course, it is due to the surf. The surrounding country is very much the same—a lonely stretch of sandy dunes. However that may be, if shipwrecked mariners came inland or any Libyans were compelled to pass through or lost their way, the beasts would make their appearance and seize them (*Fifth Discourse* 8-11, LCL).

Josephus says that the very mention of the name Syrtes "strikes terror" in people (see *War* 2.381). See also Pliny, *Natural History* 5.4.27).

27:18-19. The next day as we were being violently storm-tossed, they began to jettison the cargo; and on the third day they threw the ship's tackle overboard with their own hands. Juvenal tells of this drastic measure that many have taken to save their lives.

> And now most of the cargo has gone overboard, but even these losses do not ease the vessel; so in his extremity the skipper had to fall back upon cutting away the mast, and so find a way out of his straits—a dire pass indeed when no remedy can be found but one that diminishes the ship! Go trust yourself to a hewn plank, which parts you from death by four finger-breadths of pitch-pine, or seven if it be extra thick! Only remember in the future, besides your net and bread and your bread-basket and your pot-bellied flagon, to take with you axes also for use in a storm (*Satire* 12.52-61, LCL).

27:33-34. And until the day was about to

dawn, Paul was encouraging them all to take some food, saying, "Today is the fourteenth day that you have been constantly watching and going without eating, having taken nothing. Therefore I encourage you to take some food, for this is for your preservation; for not a hair from the head of any of you shall perish."** This is the fourth time Paul is involved in this story and this time everyone listens. The latter part of this statement is similar to a saying in the Old Testament (1 Sam. 14:45 and 2 Sam. 14:11, which is also used in Luke 12:7; 21:17-18).

27:42. And the soldiers' plan was to kill the prisoners, that none of them should swim away and escape. See notes above on 12:19 and 16:27. The escape of a prisoner was a significant danger to those who had responsibility for guarding them.

27:44. And the rest should follow, some on planks, and others on various things from the ship. And thus it happened that they all were brought safely to land. There is another story that speaks of those escaping the treacherous waters of the sea on pieces of a ship that had been broken. After a terrible storm, the ship was wrecked and broken into pieces on some rocks. Most of the passengers died, but others were able to hold onto broken pieces of the ship and eventually get to shore.

> The ship thus broken up, some favouring deity kept whole for us that part of the prow on which Leucippe and I were seated astride, and we floated as the sea carried us. Menelaus and Satyrus, together with some others of the passengers, happened upon the mast, and swam, using it as a support. Close by we saw Clinas swimming with his hands on the yardarm and we heard him cry: "Keep hold of your piece of wood, Clitophon." As he spoke, a wave overwhelmed him from behind. We cried out at the sight, and at the same

time the wave bore down upon us, and we once again saw the spar lifted up on high on the crest of the billow with Clinias upon it. "Have pity," I wailed and cried, "Lord Poseidon, and make a truce with us, the remnants of your shipwreck" (Achilles, *Tatius* 3.1-5, LCL).

28:1-16. Paul's Journey from Malta to Rome

The "we" passages that stopped at the end of Chapter 27 resume again in this section and also conclude here. Once Paul reaches Rome, the "we" is not heard of thereafter. In Acts, when Paul is on a journey, these passages are generally utilized to tell the story of the journey. There are miracles once again attached to Paul's ministry: namely, the incident of the snake and the healings of the people on the island. The journey from Malta after winter continues by ship to Syracuse, a Greek city, then Rhegium, to Puteoli, then over land through the Forum of Appii (some forty-three miles from Rome) and subsequently to Three Taverns (some 33 miles from Rome) and finally Paul and his companions, and presumably the soldiers accompanying him, arrive in Rome. Little is said about the guards accompanying Paul after 27:42 until 28:16 when he arrives in Rome. Paul evidently had significant freedom to move about during that time. It is also unlikely at this time that he was in chains since he is involved gathering wood for the fire in 28:3. Also, it is odd, given a Roman guard escort including a centurion, that Paul had the liberty to stay with fellow believers for seven days in Puteoli (28:13-14). This section emphasizes that Paul was empowered by God to avoid the poisonous venom of snakes (see 28:5 and also Mark 16:18), meet with the most significant person in the community, as was typical throughout his missionary activity and even during his imprisonment, and also to do acts of healings (28:8-9).

28:1. And when they had been brought safely through, then we found out that the island

was called Malta. Malta (Greek = *Melite*, a Semitic word meaning "refuge" suggesting a "safe harbor") is the most likely identity of the place where Paul was shipwrecked, an island south of Sicily. The island is mentioned by Strabo who says that the island (*Melite*) is "five hundred *stadia* from the island Cossurus [now called Pantellaria]" (*Geography* 17.3.16). Elsewhere he identifies it as the home of little dogs called "Melitaean" (*Geography* 6.2.11). It lies roughly sixty miles due south of Sicily and 220 miles north of Tripoli, Libya, and occupies some ninety-five square miles. It is one of five islands that now make up the country of Malta. The island came under Roman control in 218 B.C. when it was captured from the Carthaginians (Livy 21.51) and made a part of the province of Sicily and eventually had its own procurator under Augustus, but they continued to maintain their own Punic/Phoenician culture and language. Even today its dialect is a mixture of Arabic and Italian. They were only granted Roman citizenship under the Emperor Justinian (ca. A.D. 518–65).

28:2. And the natives showed us extraordinary kindness; for because of the rain that had set in and because of the cold, they kindled a fire and received us all. The term translated "natives" is the word *Barbaroi*, a common designation for non-Greek or Latin-speaking people. While it eventually came to be used as a pejorative term, barbarian, meaning rude or uncivilized, that is not the sense here. These *Barbaroi* were friendly and polite to those who were shipwrecked on their shores. See Paul's use of the term in Rom. 1:14; 1 Cor. 14:11; and Col. 3:11. The term is taken from the babble attributed to birds, *bar*, and when reduplicated as in *bar* + *bar*, was used by Greeks to describe unintelligible sounds from those who spoke neither Greek nor Latin. Herodotus preserves something of the sense of the early use of this term in a story about women taken by Phoenicians who spoke a "strange language." he writes:

I suppose that these women were called "doves" by the people of Dodona because they spoke a strange language [Greek = *barbaroi*], and the people thought it like the cries of birds; presently the woman spoke what they could understand, and that is why they say that the dove uttered human speech; as long as she spoke in her foreign language [Greek = *ebarbaridze*], they thought her voice was like the voice of a bird (*The Persian Wars* 2.57, LCL).

28:3. But when Paul had gathered a bundle of sticks and laid them on the fire, a viper came out because of the heat, and fastened on his hand. It is not known what kind of snake existed on Malta in antiquity. There are no snakes on the island today, but the national symbol is a snake: the Coronella Austriaca!

28:4. And when the natives saw the creature hanging from his hand, they began saying to one another, "Undoubtedly this man is a murderer, and though he has been saved from the sea, justice has not allowed him to live." Justice (Greek = *Dike*) is personified as it was in other ancient Greek literature. Hesiod tells the mythological story of Zeus' marriage to Themis "who bare to him Horae (Hours), and Eunomia (Order), Dike (Justice) and blooming Eirene (Peace), who mind the works of mortal men" (*Theogony* 900-903, LCL). Arrian (ca. A.D. 95–175) relates a similar myth relating how Justice operates with Zeus. After telling how Alexander the king had virtuously acknowledged an error, a sophist named Anaxarchus comforted him by reminding him that old philosophers "made Justice sit by the throne of Zeus, because whatever is determined by Zeus is done with Justice, so too the acts of a great king should be held just, first by the king himself and then by the rest of mankind" (*Anabasis of Alexander* 4.9.7, LCL).

28:3-6. But when Paul had gathered a bundle of sticks and laid them on the fire, a viper came out because of the heat, and fastened on his hand. And when the natives saw the creature hanging from his hand, they began saying to one another, "Undoubtedly this man is a murderer, and though he has been saved from the sea, justice has not allowed him to live." However he shook the creature off into the fire and suffered no harm. But they were expecting that he was about to swell up or suddenly fall down dead. But after they had waited a long time and had seen nothing unusual happen to him, they changed their minds and began to say that he was a god. For an understanding of Paul's ability to shake off what was considered to be a poisonous snake by the local residents of the island see Psalm 91:13 where those who put their trust in the Lord will be able to tread even upon the snake or viper and not be hurt. In the New Testament, Jesus gives authority to his disciples and no snake will hurt them. This is also found in the Markan appendix (Mark 16:17-18). In Jewish literature, in the *Mekhilta of Rabbi Ishmael*, dating from the second century A.D., essentially a commentary on Exod. 12:1-23:19, there is a story about a certain man whose fate was concluded with a snakebite.

Judah b. Tabbi came into a ruin and found the slain man writing, with the sword dripping blood from the hand of slayer. Said to him Judah b. Tabbai, "My such-and-so come upon me, if either you or I have killed this man. But what am I going to do? For the Torah has said, 'At the testimony of two witnesses . . . shall a matter be established'" [Deut. 19:15]. But the one who knows and the Master of all intentions is the one who will exact punishment from that man." The man had barely left the place before a snake bit him and he died (3.78.12, cited from *Hellenistic Comm. NT*, p. 332).

In the Talmud, *Berakoth* 33a, it is reported

about the first-century rabbi, Hanina ben Dosa, who was known as a miracle worker, that he stepped over the hole of a snake (or lizard) and the snake bit him and *it* died. It goes as follows:

There was the case concerning a certain place in which a lizard was going around and biting people. They came and told R. Hanina b. Dosa. He said to them, "Show me its hole." They showed him its hole. He put his heel over the mouth of the hole. The lizard came out and bit him and died. He took it on his shoulder and brought it to the school house. He said to them, "See, my sons, it is not the lizard that kills but sin that kills." At that moment they said, "Woe to the man who meets a lizard, and woe to the lizard that meets up with R. Hanina b. Dosa" (cited in *Hellenistic Comm. NT.* Trans. by Neusner, *Talmud*).

There is another interesting story, which turns out differently than this one, about a man who survived a treacherous storm at sea and following a shipwreck was washed up on a beach. Moments later he was bitten by a poisonous snake and died. The relevant part of the text is as follows:

The shipwrecked mariner had escaped the whirlwind and the fury of the deadly sea, and as he was lying on the Libyan sand not far from the beach, deep in his last sleep, naked and exhausted by the unhappy wreck, a baneful viper slew him. Why did he struggle with the waves in vain, escaping then the fate that was his lot on the land (*Greek Anthology*, 7.290, LCL).

28:7. Now in the neighborhood of that place were lands belonging to the leading man of the island, named Publius, who welcomed us and entertained us courteously three days. There is much that is uncertain about this man Publius: namely, whether he was some kind of procurator of the island or a benefactor to the island, but archaeologists may have found his home, a Roman villa, dating from the first cen-

tury at San Pawl Milqi.

28:8. And it came about that the father of Publius was lying in bed afflicted with recurrent fever and dysentery; and Paul went in to see him and after he had prayed, he laid his hands on him and healed him. Laying hands on someone for the sake of healing is not found in the Old Testament, but common in the New Testament (Luke 4:20). At Qumran, a text was found that suggests that Christians were not the only ones to practice this form of healing. When the Pharaoh called upon his wise men to heal him of the plagues that had come up on him from God sending an evil spirit upon him, a certain "HRKNWS" (the meaning of which is unknown), came to Abraham and asked him "to come and pray for the king, and lay my hands upon him so that he would live." And after this the Pharaoh came with the same request: "pray for me and for my household so that this evil spirit will be banished from us. I prayed for [. . .] and laid my hands upon his head, the plague was removed from him; [the evil spirit] was banished [from him] and he lived" (1QapGen. 20:21-22, 28-29, trans., Garcia Martinez, *DSS Translated*, 233-34).

28:11. And at the end of three months we set sail on an Alexandrian ship which had wintered at the island, and which had the Twin Brothers for its figurehead. Alexandrian ships normally were among the first to sail even in inclement weather conditions because of the promise of Claudius to pay for their losses when they bring grain to Rome during the winter months (see note above on Suetonius, *Lives* 28.2). The ship, called "Twin Brothers" (Greek = *Dioskorois*) refers to the twin sons of Zeus, Castor and Pollux, who were believed to protect those at sea. Epictetus refers to this name saying, "Remember God; call upon him to help you and stand by your side, just as voyagers, in a storm, call upon the Dioscuri" (*Discourse* 12.18.29, LCL). They are mentioned variously in other ancient literature such as Lucian of Samosata's, *The Ship*. After describing the journey from Alexandria (Pharos) and making their way to Rome, they encountered a frightening ordeal at sea following a similar path that Luke depicts in Acts, but in the story tells of one of the Dioscuri giving direction to the ship.

The swell is driven by numerous currents and is split on the headland—the rocks are knife-edged, razor-sharp at the sea's edge. So the breakers are terrifying and make a great din, and the wave is often as high as the cliff itself. This is what the captain said they found when it was still night and pitch dark. But the gods were moved by their lamentations, and showed fire from Lycia, so that they knew the place. One of the Dioscuri [Castor and Pollux] put a bright star on the masthead, and guided the ship in a turn to port into the open sea, just as it was driving on to the cliff. Then, having now lost their course, they sailed across the Aegean beating up with the trade winds against them, yesterday, seventy days after leaving Egypt, they anchored in Piraeus, after being driven so far downwind. They should have kept Crete to the starboard, and sailed beyond Malea so as to be in Italy by now (*The Ship or the Wishes* 9, LCL. See also Aelieus Aristides, *Sacred Tales* 4.35-37.).

28:13-14. And from there we sailed around and arrived at Rhegium, and a day later a south wind sprang up, and on the second day we came to Puteoli. There we found some brethren, and were invited to stay with them for seven days; and thus we came to Rome. Rhegium was a Greek colony located in southern Italy in what is commonly called the toe of Italy opposite Messana, Sicily. Strabo (ca. 64–25 B.C.) has much to say about the city including

that it was once heavily fortified and a great city that produced many statesmen. It was generally led by someone from Sicily since it was believed to have been a part of Sicily before its being ripped apart from that island as a result of an earthquake. He also concedes that the name may have come from Rhegium [meaning "Royal"] because many of its citizens had shared in the Roman government and used the Latin language (*Geography* 6.1.6).

Puteoli is a port city on the Bay of Naples and was Italy's most important city during the first century until Claudius had the harbor of Portus built at Ostia (Suetonius, *Deified Claudius* 20.1-3). The city was founded by the Ionians and was finally overcome by the Romans in 194 B.C. and it subsequently became a Roman sea colony. It was about 130 miles overland from Rome. Passengers came ashore at Puteoli and journeyed overland to Rome, but before the harbor built by Claudius at Ostia, so did the grain shipments from Egypt. Strabo comments on the ships coming into and going out of this harbor, both to and from Egypt. "Here the exports from Alexandria also are larger than the imports; and anyone might judge, if he were at either Alexandria or Dicaearchia [= Puteoli] and saw the merchant vessels both at their arrival and at their departure, how much heavier or lighter they sailed thither or there from" (*Geography* 17.1.7, LCL).

This is also where Paul meets "brothers" or Christians from Italy. These are also the first Christians that Paul and his companions have met since leaving Caesarea. There are no reports of the evangelization of the community, but there are reliable reports of Jews living in the area. Speaking of a person who passed himself off to the Jews as Alexander, whom Herod had earlier put to death, this imposter made his way from Crete to Melos and then headed to Rome. "Landing at Dicaearchia [Puteoli], he was loaded with presents by the Jewish colony there and was escorted on his way like a king by the friends of his supposed father" (*War* 2.103-104, LCL). The same story about the false Alexander is told by Josephus in *Ant.* 17.328-38 and also highlighting the Jewish colony at Puteoli. It is not clear why Paul and his companions were encouraged to stay there seven days. Some have suggested that this was to allow word of their arrival to get to Rome ahead of them and to have a delegation meet them as we see in the next verse.

28:15. And the brethren, when they heard about us, came from there as far as the Market of Appius and Three Inns to meet us; and when Paul saw them, he thanked God and took courage. Appius is located forty-three miles southeast of Rome, a fact that is verified by an inscription on a milestone from that era (see CIL 10.6825). The term "Inns" here, literally "taverns" (Latin = *tabernus*) does not refer to a primarily drinking establishment like the British "pub," but rather to an inn where those who travel could stay overnight and be refreshed. The Three Inns is located thirty-three miles southeast of Rome.

28:16. And when we entered Rome, Paul was allowed to stay by himself, with the soldier who was guarding him. The court system in Rome seems to have allowed sufficient time for a trial to take place (two years), and there was evidently a two-year amount of time allowed to appeal a ruling that was considered unjust. In a letter from Trajan to Pliny, after reversing an earlier decision made against one person, he then comments on another saying:

> As for the man who banished for life Julius Bassus, he had two years in which he could have asked for a re-trial if he thought his sentence was unjust, but, as he took no steps to do so, and remained in the province, he must be sent in chains to the officers in command of my imperial guards. It is not sufficient to restore his former sentence when he evaded it by contempt of court

(Pliny, *Letters* 10.57.2, LCL).

28:17-31. Paul and the Jews in Rome. This concluding section of Acts has in many ways furthered Luke's agenda: namely, the outline of the book (1:8) that the followers of Jesus would bear witness of him in Jerusalem, Judea, Samaria, and the ends of the earth. It is also important that Luke shows that the promises that were made to the hero of the book, Paul, would find their fulfillment in his missionary activity, even when that meant that he was in prison and in chains (26:29; 28:20). When Paul finally reached Rome with the Good News, after having testified before Gentiles, kings, and the people of Israel (9:15), the promise of the risen Christ was fulfilled that a witness for him would make it to the ends of earth (1:8). The promise that Paul would bear witness for him in Rome was also fulfilled (23:11). While many modern readers would have wished that Luke had said more about the Christians in Rome, Paul's appeal before Caesar, and his death that was hinted at in 20:22-24 (see comments at the end of this section), it is obvious that Luke nevertheless met the aims that he set forth at the beginning of this volume (1:8) and also demonstrated that the promises made by the risen Lord to Paul were also met (9:15; 18:10; 23:1). What remains is his witness to the Jews in Rome and an acknowledgment that the Gospel that was rejected by them will now go to the Gentiles (28:28). More on this topic will follow after the discussion of this passage.

It has been suggested that the way that Luke concluded Acts indicates that he was closing the door to Jewish evangelism and concluding that only Gentiles will now listen (28:28), but that is not what Luke is saying. In the midst of Paul's Gentile evangelism, he indicates three times in Acts that salvation has come to the Gentiles (13:46; 18:6; and in 28:28), but that after the first two examples, Paul continues to go into the synagogues and preach the Christian message, and there is nothing in this concluding section to suggest otherwise since it is clear that even on this occasion, some Jews were willing to believe the message Paul had given to them (28:24). Indeed, for the next two years Paul received "all" who came to him, and there is no indication in Acts that this was a reference just for Gentiles. While it was certainly becoming clear to Luke that more and more Gentiles were coming into the church and fewer Jews, comparatively speaking, Luke does not disparage of the Jews nor their place in the community of faith. As noted above, one of his constant themes in regard to Paul is his being a faithful Jew who neither spoke against the Law or Moses, the Jewish customs, or the temple. It would be ironic if at the end of his book he rejected all that he had said beforehand. He has frequently made the point, and a big one it has been, that salvation also belonged to the Gentiles, not *only* to the Jews. Furthermore, this action is a fulfillment of the Scriptures.

28:17. And it happened that after three days he called together those who were the leading men of the Jews, and when they had come together, he began saying to them, "Brethren, though I had done nothing against our people, or the customs of our fathers, yet I was delivered prisoner from Jerusalem into the hands of the Romans." Paul's calling of leading men among the Jews to come to him was, of course, not a demand, but an invitation to come as his guest to the home where he was under house arrest. Also, "leading men of the Jews" (Greek = *tous ontas ton Ioudaion protous*, "those who are first among the Jews") may refer to those in the leading roles in the synagogue(s) at Rome. This is the first time in Acts where Paul asked the Jews to come to his home rather than his going to them, but in this circumstance, he is in chains and under house arrest. It would not have been possible otherwise. This verse also presupposes that the Jews who had been expelled by Claudius have now

returned to the city (see note on 18:2). Observe also how Paul addresses these Jewish leaders as "brothers" (Greek = *adelphoi*). Although the early Christians made extensive use of the term to refer to their relationships to one another as a result of their relationship to God through Jesus the Christ, it is likely that the term was first used by the Jews in reference to their fellow countrymen as it is used here. See note on 1:15 above.

28:18-19. "And when they had examined me, they were willing to release me because there was no ground for putting me to death. But when the Jews objected, I was forced to appeal to Caesar; not that I had any accusation against my nation." It is possible that Luke is suggesting that the role of the faithful follower of Jesus will be like that of the master. As Jesus was arrested and considered innocent by the Romans, he was rejected by the Jews (Luke 23:4, 15, 22), so with Paul (Acts 23:29; 25:18, 25; 26:31).

28:20. "For this reason therefore, I requested to see you and to speak with you, for I am wearing this chain for the sake of the hope of Israel." This "hope" may be a reference to the Jewish (Pharisaic) understanding of hope for life through the resurrection (23:6; 24:15).

28:21-22. And they said to him, "We have neither received letters from Judea concerning you, nor have any of the brethren come here and reported or spoken anything bad about you. But we desire to hear from you what your views are; for concerning this sect, it is known to us that it is spoken against everywhere." There is no reason to doubt the veracity of this report, or lack of one, about Paul. What is interesting is the evident lack of understanding and familiarity of the Jews in Rome with the Christians who were also there. The knowledge of them appears to be at a distance rather than first-hand knowledge of them. The Christians are called a "sect" (Greek = *hairesis*) (see 5:17 and 24:5, 14). If there was a rift between Christians and Jews during the time of Claudius, as was suggested in 18:2 above, how could there not be some knowledge of the Christian community living there? It is not clear how to bring the obvious reference to Christians in Rome from Paul's letter to them and also 28:14-15 together with this lack of awareness. Luke is not trying to suggest that Paul started the church at Rome since they are mentioned in 28:14-15. It is also strange that nothing more about the Christians in Rome is said once Paul arrives there. There may be a good reason for this as will be suggested in the discussion following this passage: namely, why Luke does not mention Paul's death or the church in Rome before he concludes his volume.

28:23. And when they had set a day for him, they came to him at his lodging in large numbers; and he was explaining to them by solemnly testifying about the kingdom of God, and trying to persuade them concerning Jesus, from both the Law of Moses and from the Prophets, from morning until evening. Luke uses the term "kingdom of God" as a summary of the Christian Gospel. See above at 1:3; 8:12; 19:8; 20:25. See note above on 1:3. Luke also wants to connect the Christian proclamation as a fulfillment of the Scriptures of the Jews: namely, the Law and the Prophets (26:22-23; cf. Luke 24:44).

28:24. And some were being persuaded by the things spoken, but others would not believe. Again, Luke shows that the Gospel is not completely rejected by the Jews, but rather that some of them believe his words. See note above at the beginning of this section.

28:25-27. And when they did not agree with one another, they began leaving after Paul had spoken one parting word, "The Holy Spirit rightly spoke through Isaiah the prophet to your fathers, saying, 'Go to this people and say, "You will keep on hearing, but will not understand; And you will keep on seeing, but will not perceive; For the heart of this people has become dull, And with their ears they scarcely hear, And they have closed their eyes; Lest they should see with their eyes, And hear with their ears, And understand with their heart and return, And I should heal them."'" The passage that Paul cites is Isa. 6:9-10. It was often used to explain the Jews' failure to respond to the Gospel (Mark 4:12; 8:17-18; Luke 8:10; Matt. 13:14-15; John 12:40; Rom. 11:8). Compare this passage with Rom. 11:30-32 where Paul says that it is because of Jewish disbelief that the Gentiles were brought into the household of faith and because of unbelief mercy could be shown and will be shown again to the Jews. Luke does not say this, but acknowledges what was probably apparent to him at this time: namely, that Gentiles were readily coming into the church and fewer and fewer Jews were responding favorably to the Christian message.

28:28. "Let it be known to you therefore, that this salvation of God has been sent to the Gentiles; they will also listen." This is a possible allusion to Psalm 67:3. See his response to those Jews who reject the Christian Gospel in 13:46 and 18:6.

28:30-31. And he stayed two full years in his own rented quarters, and was welcoming all who came to him, preaching the kingdom of God, and teaching concerning the Lord Jesus Christ with all openness, unhindered. The practice of a prisoner paying his or her own way is not without parallel in antiquity. The length of time that Paul spent waiting to be heard, "two years" is not unusual under Roman law. There are examples of how it was important not to hold a prisoner after that time, but most examples of emperor behavior to the contrary or to support the view of a maximum two-year time constraint in which to bring the accusations against the accused in a court of law are all much later in the history of the empire when the senate adopted guidelines that were to be followed throughout the empire. According to Dio Cassius, Claudius, because of the heavy amount of lawsuits and the jamming of the courts with cases, would dismiss cases after a stated day in which the accusation or defense was to take place. "As the number of lawsuits was now beyond all reckoning and those who expected to lose their cases would no longer put in an appearance, he issued a proclamation announcing that he would decide the cases against them by a given day even in their absence; and he strictly enforced this rule" (*Roman History* 60.28.6, LCL). This, however, was not the practice of every succeeding emperor.

In his letter to the Emperor Trajan, Pliny asked about the actions of a certain Bassus that had been overturned and that the Roman Senate granted that anyone sentenced by him had the right to have a new trial "so long as the appeal was made within two years" (*Letters* 10.54.4, LCL). When Pliny found out that the man had not made such an appeal within the allotted time, he asked Trajan what to do with him. The emperor said "as for the man who was banished for life by Julius Bassus, he had two years in which he could have asked for a re-trial if he thought his sentence was unjust, but as he took no steps to do so, and remained in the province, he must be sent in chains to the officers in command of my imperial guards" (*Letters* 57.2, LCL). Although the two-year "rule" did not become a fixed law of the land for several more centuries (A.D. 529). Theodosius enacted laws in A.D. 385 and 409 stating that any accuser who fails to proceed with his case within a two-year period will be punished! One further example of the references to a two-year allotment of time involved in one coming to trial is from Philo who tells of a certain governor named Lampo who was on

trial for several crimes, including:

> ... impiety to Tiberias Caesar and as the trial had dragged on for two years he had broken down under it. For the ill-will of his judge had concocted post-ponements and delays, as he wished, even if he was acquitted on the charge, to keep hanging over him for as long as possible the fear of uncertain future, and so render his life more painful than death (*Flaccus*, 128-29, LCL).

More importantly, Luke does not suggest anything of the sort about Paul. He was expecting a favorable hearing and Paul awaits trial for two years. Nothing can be inferred from Luke that because Paul was not accused during this time that the charges against him were dropped or that he was imprisoned as a result of a trial. On the other hand, Luke may have concluded here because the death of Paul in Rome was well known to his readers and they were allowed to anticipate his death from Paul's statements in 20:22-24. Luke is anxious to conclude that although Paul was chained in Rome and had been in prison, the Word of God continued. This is not unlike the testimony in 2 Tim. 2:9.

What happened at the end of Paul's two-year imprisonment and why does Luke not say anything about it? How could Luke focus so much attention on Paul and fail to tell the rest of the story? It appears to most readers that this is a strange way to end the book of Acts: namely, with no reference to Paul's appearance before the emperor or a trial, and with no communication with the Christians who were there before him. It also seems odd that with the declared innocence of Paul that Luke so frequently asserts, that he does not show Paul set free or placed in prison. There is also very little said about the Christians in Rome to whom Paul wrote his longest and most carefully crafted letter. There are a number of views about the ending of Acts that have been suggested by commentators including that Luke had intended a third volume to finish the story, but never got to it because of death or some other reason, or that Luke was writing at the time that these events had happened and when he wrote, nothing else had happened to Paul.

It may be that Luke said nothing more because what did, in fact, happen was sad and would not have furthered his message. For example, it appears that no one came to Paul at his "first defense" and all deserted him (2 Tim. 4:16), but this suggests that Paul was released and subsequently re-arrested and suffered the death of a martyr (2 Tim. 4:6-8). In other words, it would not further Luke's cause to say that Paul, his hero throughout most of the book, had been abandoned by the church and even by his closest associates. Is this the reason that there is no reference to the Christians in Rome after Paul arrived there, that is, after 28:15? Certainly the earliest Christian writer from Rome to speak of Paul's death indicates that it was because of the turmoil of envy and jealousy (within the church?) that both Peter and Paul came to their deaths in Rome.

Let us take the noble examples of our own generation. Through jealousy and envy the greatest and most righteous pillars of the church were persecuted and contended unto death. Let us set before our eyes the good apostles: Peter, who because of unrighteous jealousy suffered not one or two but many trials, and having thus given his testimony went to the glorious place which was his due. Through jealousy and strife Paul showed the way to the prize of endurance; seven times he was in bonds, he was exiled, he was stoned, he was a herald both in the East and in the West, he gained the noble fame of his faith, he taught righteousness to all the world, and when he had reached the limits of the West he gave his testimony before the rulers, and thus passed from the world and was taken up into the

Holy place, the greatest example of endurance (1 Clement 4:1-7, LCL).

This testimony suggests that Paul reached the "limits of the West" and this has given rise to much speculation about a first and second imprisonment of Paul. It is often assumed that there was a first release from prison and that Paul made a visit to Spain (Rom. 15: 23-24). During this time he also wrote the letters of 1, 2 Timothy and Titus. Eusebius (ca. A.D. 320) wrote that "Paul's martyrdom was not accomplished during the sojourn in Rome which Luke describes" (Ecclesiastical History 2.22.7, LCL). In a fourth-century fragment that intended to list the writings that were considered among the Christians, the author of what is now called the Muratorian Fragment mentions Paul's trip to Spain thusly: "Moreover, the acts of the apostles were written in one book. For 'most excellent Theophilus' Luke compiled the individual events that took place in his presence—as he plainly shows by omitting the martyrdom of Peter as well as the departure of Paul from the city [of Rome] when he journeyed to Spain" (Muratorian Fragment, lines 34-38). One of the earliest testimonies about Paul's visit to Spain comes from the apocryphal Acts of Peter (ca. A.D. 180–90). It speaks of a time when Paul was in Rome strengthening the believers that the wife (Candida) of a prison officer named Quartus came to faith as a result of Paul's witness and subsequently so did her husband. Quartus then released Paul to go where he chose. After three days of fasting, Paul had a vision and the Lord said to him "'Paul, arise and be a physician to those who are in Spain.' So when he had related to the brethren what God had enjoined, without doubting he prepared to leave the city" (Actus Vercellenses 1.1, trans. NT Apo. 2:287-88). There are a number of references in the early church fathers to Paul's going to Spain, but none of them have much to commend themselves to scholars of the early church.

As noted in the opening comments on this section, however, the last chapter of Acts is well

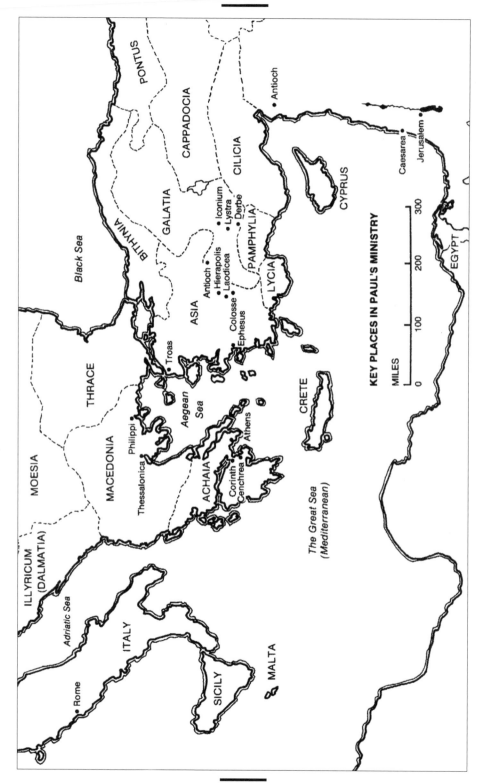

KEY PLACES IN PAUL'S MINISTRY

MILES

0   100   200   300

planned and shows that Paul made a final appeal to the Jews before turning to the Gentiles. Paul's death was acknowledged earlier in the speech at Miletus (20:22-24) and so Luke does not dwell on it here. It may have been too painful for him or, it may not have happened when this volume was completed. For Luke, however, Paul's mission is complete and nothing remains of the story he set out to tell.

Introduction to Romans

Daniel M. Gurtner

The venerable Karl Barth studied Romans with "a joyful sense of discovery" (Barth, 2). Martin Luther (1522) said this letter contained the "purest Gospel." The careful reader of this letter can at times easily forget he is reading a letter and consider himself to be immersed in a theological treatise. Nowhere else has the Apostle Paul drawn so heavily on the Scriptures of his Jewish background to articulate the truths of his Christian faith as in the epistle to the Romans.

Authorship. The authorship of Romans is among the least disputed and, some argue, least disputable issues in New Testament scholarship. The letter claims to have been written by Paul (1:1), and the early church fathers clearly understood it to be the work of that apostle, including Clement of Rome (ca. 95-96; *1 Clem.* 32:2; 35:5), Ignatius (ca. 100-118; *Eph.* 19:3; *Magn.* 6:2; *Trall.* 9:2; *Smyrn.* 1:1), and a number of others. The letter has never been attributed to another, and every extant early list of New Testament books includes it among Paul's letters (Cranfield, 2).

Yet scholars do debate the role played by Tertius in the composition of this letter. Romans 16:22 reads, "I, Tertius, who write this letter, greet you in the Lord." Though it is widely accepted that Paul frequently dictated his letters to an *amanuensis* (see Introduction to the Prison Epistles), some have contended that Tertius fully composed the letter himself under Paul's instructions. Such a view, however, has found little support, and it is generally recognized that either Tertius wrote the letter in longhand as Paul dictated, or that he took it down in shorthand as Paul dictated it and then subsequently wrote it out in longhand (Cranfield, 2).

Another question related to the authorship of Romans concerns its compositional integrity. Rudolf Bultmann claimed to find non-Pauline interpolations in 2:16, 6:17b, 7:25-8:1, and 10:17, but the questions he raises about these texts need not be answered by alternative authorship. A much more difficult and controversial set of questions arises from the text of chapters 15 and 16. First, various manuscript traditions place the doxology of 16:25-27 at different locations from chapters 14 to 16. Second, several reliable Latin Vulgate manuscripts only have 1:1-14:23, followed immediately by 16:24-27. Third, while Tertullian (ca. 166-220) makes use of Romans in his disputes with the heretic Marion (ca. 144), he nowhere cites texts from chapters 15 or 16, which could most strongly support his argument. Finally, Tertullian, Irenaeus (ca. 140-202) and Cyprian (d. 258) seem to know a text of Romans without these two chapters. Scholars have varied widely on how to evaluate this evidence, though their theories could be narrowed to three: First is the unlikely scenario that Paul originally wrote 1:1-14:23 as a general letter for circulation among churches not of his foundation and which he had not visited, and then subsequently adapted it for sending to the church in Rome by the addition of the material which now follows 14:23 (Cranfield, 7). Acts 14:23 does not bring the argument of chap. 14 to a conclusion and is otherwise hardly a suitable conclusion for a letter, particularly one of Paul's. A second theory is that chap. 16 was not part of Paul's original letter to the Romans. This theory argues that Paul wrote 1:1-15:33 to Rome and subsequently sent a revised copy supplemented by chap. 16 to another church, perhaps Ephesus. This argument supposes, among other things, that chapter 16, which contains almost entirely personal greetings, could not have been written by Paul, who had not yet visited that church. He did, however, have a lengthy and personal ministry in Ephesus, where he would have known many people whom he could greet (cf. esp. Acts 20:37). This point, among this view's strongest arguments, fails to recognize Paul's familiarity with people even in churches he had not founded. Moreover, it presupposes that if Paul is writing his addendum (chap. 16) to the Ephesians because he had such an affinity with them, that he had nothing personal to say to them other than a list of individual greetings. The traditional and most sound explanation for the composition of Romans is to presume Paul wrote 1:1-16:23 to the church at Rome. Such is largely the scholarly consensus and is the best way of accounting for all the evidence most convincingly (Cranfield, 11).

Provenance and Date. At the time Romans was written, Paul felt his missionary work in the eastern provinces of the Roman Empire had been completed (15:19, 23). The apostle was either on his way to, or about to set out for, Jerusalem (15:25), a journey which cannot be earlier than that recorded in Acts 20 and 21 (Cranfield, 12). The journey, as recorded in 15:25-28, is in agreement with that of Acts 24:17 in which Luke records Paul saying, "Now after

several years I came to bring alms to my nation and to present offerings." Paul clearly had wanted to visit the Roman church for some time (1:10-13) but was prevented from doing so (1:13; 15:22). Now he hopes to visit them on his way to Spain (15:23, 28) but only after a stop in Jerusalem to deliver the collection for them made by the churches in Macedonia and Achaia to relieve the poor among the Jerusalem saints (15:22-27). It was during Paul's three-month stay in Greece, the province of Achaia, to which Acts 20:2-3 refers, that Romans was written (Cranfield, 12). Specifically, Paul seems to be staying in this province's capital, Corinth, as a number of texts in Romans suggest: Paul commends Phoebe (16:1-2), a servant (*daikonos*) of the church in Cenchrea, which is Corinth's eastern port. Some have suggested that she carried the letter to Rome (Cranfield, 12). Furthermore, the greetings from Gaius in 16:23, in whose house Paul was staying, may be the same man mentioned in 1 Cor. 1:14 as having been baptized by Paul.

This evidence requires a date between late 54 and early 59. An inscription found at Delphi early in this century suggests that Gallio was probably proconsul of Achaia, which typically only served single-year terms, from mid-51 to mid-52. Paul appears before him (Acts 18:22) in what seems to be an early period in Gallio's governorship. After being dismissed by Gallio, Paul remained "many days longer" in Corinth (Acts 18:18), after which he sailed to Syria (Acts 18:18), either in late 51 or early 52. He also spent some time in Ephesus along the way (Acts 18:19-21). He came to Caesarea, went down to Antioch (Acts 18:22), and spent "some time" there (Acts 18:23). While it is possible that the apostle completed all these travels in but a few months, finishing in the summer of 52 (Acts 18:23; 19:1), it seems more probable that his travels ultimately concluded in Ephesus (Acts 19:1) late in 53. With his stay in Ephesus being between two and three years (cf. Acts 19:8, 10; 20:31), his return to Corinth via Macedonia (Acts 20:1-2) was perhaps in late 55 or 56, shortly after which the epistle to the Romans seems to have been written (Cranfield, 14). Thus, it was written during the reign of the Roman emperor Nero (54-68).

Occasion and Purpose: As was indicated in the discussion of Provenance and Date above, Paul has completed his missionary efforts in the east and anticipates going to Spain. Along the way he expects to take the collection from the churches of Macedonia and Achaia to the needy among the church in Jerusalem. He hopes to visit the Roman congregation on his way westward and spend a short time with them, gathering their encouragement and blessing for the ministry that lies ahead. In anticipation of this visit, the apostle writes to the church at Rome to inform them of his plans and to solicit their prayers for the mission.

While this accounts for 1:8-16a and 15:14-33, more needs to be said of the occasion and purpose of the bulk of the letter, 1:16b-15:13. It is not easy to discern whether there was a situation in the Roman church which required such a lengthy treatise on the gospel provided in 1:16b-15:13, or if he simply felt the need to articulate more fully the gospel he mentions in 1:16a. Among the various proposals offered by scholars, many recognize three general purposes of the letter. First, it had a missionary purpose (15:18-24, 28). Paul describes himself as "apostle to the Gentiles" and eager to bring in "the full number of Gentiles" (11:13-15, 25-26), and Rome is the capital of the Gentile world. Moreover, Paul solicits Roman support for his anticipated Spanish mission (Rom. 15:24, 28; cf. 1:16-17). The apostle makes frequent reference to the necessity of his gospel being spread (cf. 15:19, 23).

In addition to a missionary purpose, an apologetic purpose for Romans has also been recognized. Paul seems to have felt a need to defend both himself and his understanding of the gospel (1:16; 3:8; 9:1-2). Perhaps such caveats of defensiveness were to strengthen what he surely saw would become a very influ-

Reigns and Fates of Roman Caesars

Julius Caesar 49–44 B.C.	Murdered by Gaius Cassius and Marcus Brutus.
Mark Antony 44–31 B.C.	Defeated by Octavian; committed suicide.
Augustus 31 B.C.–A.D. 14	Born Octavian; greatest Roman emperor.
Tiberius A.D. 14–37	Pedophile; despised by Roman elite.
Caligula A.D. 37–41	Widely regarded as insane; ordered his statue placed in the Jerusalem temple; murdered by officers of his Praetorian Guard.
Claudius A.D. 41–54	Poisoned by his wife Agrippina so that her son Nero could succeed him.
Nero A.D. 54–68	Forced to commit suicide by the Roman Senate.
Galba A.D. 68–69	Assassinated after a seven-month reign.
Gotho A.D. 69	Committed suicide after reigning 90 days.
Vitellius A.D. 69	Murdered.
Vespasian A.D. 69–79	Having subdued Galilee, hailed emperor.
Titus A.D. 79–81	Finished conquest of Judea and Jerusalem.
Domitian A.D. 81–96	Younger brother of Titus; came to be hated; finally assassinated.

Persecution Policy under Emperor Trajan (A.D. 98-117)

In a famous correspondence from A.D. 112, the Roman legate Pliny the Younger wrote to Emperor Trajan asking what to do about Christians in Bithynia and Pontus. He writes,

"Pliny to the Emperor Trajan: It is my custom to refer all my difficulties to you, Sir, for no one is better able to resolve my doubts and to inform my ignorance. I have never been present at the examination of Christians. Consequently, I do not know the nature or the extent of the punishments usually meted out to them, nor the grounds for starting an investigation and how far it should be pressed. Nor am I at all sure whether any distinction should be made between them on the grounds of age, or if young people and adults should be treated alike; whether a pardon ought to be granted to anyone retracting his beliefs, or if he has once professed Christianity, he shall gain nothing by renouncing it; and whether it is the mere name of Christian which is punishable, even if innocent of crime, or rather the crimes associated with the name.

For the moment this is the line I have taken with all persons brought before me on the charge of being Christians. I have asked them in person if they are Christians, and if they admit it, I repeat the question a second and third time, with a warning of the punishment awaiting them. If they persist, I order them to be led away for execution; for, whatever the nature of their admission, I am convinced that their stubbornness and unshakeable obstinacy ought not go unpunished. There have been others similarly fanatical who are Roman citizens. I have entered them on the list of persons to be sent to Rome for trial.

Now that I have begun to deal with this problem, as so often happens, the charges are becoming more widespread and increasing in variety. An anonymous pamphlet has been circulated which contains the names of a number of accused persons. Among these I considered that I should dismiss any who denied that they were or ever had been Christians when they had repeated after me a formula of invocation to the gods and had made offerings of wine and incense to your statue (which I had ordered to be brought into court for this purpose along with the images of the gods), and furthermore had reviled the name of Christ: none of which things, I understand, any genuine Christian can be induced to do.

Others, whose names were given to me by an informer, first admitted the charge and then denied it; they said that they had ceased to be Christians two or more years previously, and some of them even twenty years ago. They all did reverence to your statue and the images of the gods in the same way as the others, and reviled the name of Christ. They also declared that the sum total of their guilt or error amounted to no more than this: they had met regularly before dawn on a fixed day to chant verses alternately among themselves in honor of Christ as if to a god, and also to bind themselves by oath, not for any criminal purpose, but to abstain from theft, robbery and adultery, to commit no breach of trust and not to deny a deposit when called upon to restore it. After this ceremony it had been their custom to disperse and reassemble later to take

continued on the next page

food of an ordinary, harmless kind; but they had in fact given up this practice since my edict, issued on your instructions, which banned all political societies. This made me decide it was all the more necessary to extract the truth by torture from two slave-women, whom they called deaconesses. I found nothing but a degenerate sort of cult carried to extravagant lengths.

I have therefore postponed any further examination and hasten to consult you. The question seems to me to be worthy of your consideration, especially in view of the number of persons endangered; for a great many individuals of every age and class, both men and women, are being brought to trial, and this is likely to continue. It is not only the towns, but villages and rural districts too which are infected through contact with this wretched cult. I think though that it is still possible for it to be checked and directed to better ends, for there is no doubt that people have begun to throng the temples which had been almost entirely deserted for a long time; the sacred rites which had been allowed to lapse are being performed again, and flesh of sacrificial victims is on sale everywhere, though up till recently scarcely anyone could be found to buy it. It is easy to infer from this that a great many people could be reformed if they were given an opportunity to repent."

Pliny, Epistles 10.96.1-10 LCL

Emperor Trajan replies,

"Trajan to Pliny: You have followed the right course of procedure, my dear Pliny, in your examination of the cases of persons charged with being Christians, for it is impossible to lay down a general rule to a fixed formula. These people must not be hunted out; if they are brought before you and the charge against them is proved, they must be punished, but in the case of anyone who denies that he is a Christian, and makes it clear that he is not by offering prayers to our gods, he is to be pardoned as a result of his repentance however suspect his past conduct may be. But pamphlets circulated anonymously must play no part in any accusation. They create the worst sort of precedent and are quite out of keeping with the spirit of our age."

Pliny, Epistles 10.97.1-2 LCL

ential church or simply a glimpse of an anticipated defense in Jerusalem. Evidence is lacking to draw anything beyond tentative suggestions for the apostle's defensiveness in Romans. Finally, Romans is seen to serve a pastoral purpose. The passage 14:1-15:6 particularly reflects Paul's concern for either real or potential rifts in the Roman congregation. This may reflect some Jew-Gentile tensions (cf. 14:1; 15:7; and "Recipients" below). Paul also seeks to introduce and commend Phoebe to the Roman saints (16:1-2) and offer personal greetings to some in the congregation with whom he had somehow become acquainted (16:3-15).

Recipients. Though known today as the letter "to the Romans," manuscript evidence is not universally in agreement. Several manuscripts, particularly that of Origen (ca. 185-254), omit the phrase "in Rome." However, given the theological significance of this epistle and its importance in the early church, scholars have widely recognized that this phrase occasionally dropped out of a few manuscript traditions to better lend itself to a more universal readership which it could so effectively address. The variant reading should not be seen to be as problematic as that in Ephesians (see Introduction to Ephesians). The epistle was written to the church at Rome.

A more important issue is the history and composition of the congregation to whom Paul wrote. Fortunately, the apostle raises this issue almost from the start. His letter is "to the Jew first and also to the Greek (or Gentile)" (1:16). Simply put, we do not know when, under what conditions, or by whom the church at Rome was founded. Indeed, this epistle is the first historical evidence of the existence of the Roman congregation. Yet much is known of a sizable Jewish community in Rome in the first century, perhaps as large as 40,000-50,000 people. According to Suetonias, "since the Jews constantly made disturbances at the instigation of Crestus, he expelled them from Rome" (*Claudius* 25.4 LCL), with "Crestus" almost universally understood as a reference to Christ. Finally, the number of slave names among those greeted in chap. 16, perhaps more than 14 out of 24, has been understood to suggest that members of the Roman church were descendants of Jewish slaves. These slaves would have been captured during Pompey's subjugation of Palestine and brought to Rome in 62 B.C. (Dunn, xlvi-xlviii). It seems that the church at Rome at least initially started among the Jewish synagogues, perhaps under Peter, who was said to preach the gospel there in the second year of Claudius (ca. A.D. 42; Eusebius, *H.E.* 2.14.6; cf. 2.17.1), and is the apostle traditionally associated with that church and missions particularly to the Jews (Gal. 2:7). This may also explain why this letter is so dominated by the phrase, "to the Jew first and also to the Greek (Gentile)" (Rom. 1:16; cf. 2:9-11; 3:9, 29; 9:24; 10:12). Gentiles were apparently also present in the church (11:13-32; 15:7-12; cf. 1:6, 13; 15:15-16). It is unclear whether there was conflict between them and the Jewish Christians, but if some of the latter were among those expelled from Rome in 49, the church may have lost much of its earliest leadership and depended on the former to rise to leadership.

Contribution. Romans is a virtual treatise on the core of the Christian faith as held by Paul. In it, the apostle illustrates the utter depravity of humanity (1:18-32), including Jews (2:1-3:8), concluding that all are in fact alike under sin and its consequential condemnation (3:9-20). The gospel provides the only answer (3:21-5:21) in which is found faith in Christ (3:21-26). It is offered to Jews and Gentiles (3:27-32), as is illustrated in the case of Abraham alone (4:1-25). This gospel brings peace with God to individual believers (5:1-11) and a new model for obedience (Christ) which all humanity can follow (5:12-21), rather than the failed example of Adam. Yet God's gracious response to sin should not be misunderstood as a license for debauchery (6:1-23), and the Law and human frailty have been manipulated by sin (7:1-25). The Law itself was weakened by sin (8:3), and believers must live in the reality of spiritual sonship (8:1-17) by which they have hope (8:18-30) and assurance (8:31-39). How does Israel fit into this scheme (9:1-5)? They were clearly called by God (9:6-29) but failed to understand their calling and privileges (9:30–10:21). Yet God mysteriously holds a role for them (11:1-36). The Gospel has a wide range of implications for daily living (12:1–15:13). This includes personal living responsibilities (12:1-2) as well as those of a community (12:3-8). Each of these is governed by the overarching principle of love (12:9-21). Paul also applies the gospel's truth to good citizenship (13:1-7), food laws, and holy days (14:1-15:6).

OUTLINE OF THE BOOK

I. Introduction (1:1-17)
II. The Human Condition (Jews and Gentiles) (1:18–3:20)
  A. Humans Are Depraved (1:18-32)

B. Jews Are likewise Depraved (2:1–3:8)

C. All Are Alike Under Sin (3:9-20)

III. The Gospel as the Solution (3:21–5:21)

A. Faith in Christ Is the Key (3:21-26)

B. The Gospel Is Offered to Jew and Gentile (3:27-31)

C. Illustration of Abraham (4:1-25)

D. Implications for Individuals and All Humanity (5:1-21)

IV. The Problems of Sin, the Law, and Death (6:1–8:39)

A. The Problem of Sin (6:1-23)

B. The Problem of the Law (7:1-25)

C. The Problem of Human Frailty and Death (8:1-39)

V. The Problem of Israel (9:1–11:36)

A. Paul's Concern for Israel (9:1-5)

B. God's Call of Israel (9:6-29)

C. Israel's Failure (9:30–10:21)

D. The Mystery of God's Faithfulness (11:1-32)

E. Concluding Hymn of Adoration (11:33-36)

VI. Implications of the Gospel: Christian Conduct (12:1–15:13)

A. Basis for Responsible Living (12:1-2)

B. Live in the Community of Faith (12:3-8)

C. Love in the Christian Community (12:9-21)

D. Practicing Good Citizenship (13:1-7)

E. Love your Neighbor (13:8-10)

F. The End Is Near (13:11-14)

G. Problems Regarding Food Laws and Holy Days (14:1–15:6)

H. Concluding Summary (15:7-13)

VII. Concluding Remarks and Greetings (15:14-16:27)

RESOURCES

Barth, Karl. *The Epistle to the Romans.* Translated by Edwyn C. Hoskyns. Oxford: Oxford University Press, 1933.

Bray, Gerald, ed. *Ancient Christian Commentary on Scripture: Romans.* Chicago/London: Fitzroy Dearborn Publishers, 1998 (=ACCS).

Cranfield, C. E. B. *Romans.* ICC. 2 vols. Edinburgh: T. & T. Clark, 1975.

Dunn, James D. G. *Romans.* WBC 38A-B. 2 vols. Dallas: Word Books, 1988.

Fitzmyer, Joseph A. *Romans.* ABC 33. New York: Doubleday, 1993.

Käsemann, Ernst. *Commentary on Romans.* Grand Rapids: Eerdmans, 1980.

Luther, Martin. *Commentary on the Epistle to the Romans.* Abridged translation by J. Theodore Mueller. Grand Rapids: Zondervan, 1960.

Moo, Douglas J. *The Epistle to the Romans.* NICNT. Grand Rapids: Eerdmans, 1996.

PAUL'S INTRODUCTIONS TO HIS EPISTLES

EPISTLE	PAUL'S TITLES	PAUL'S COMPANIONS	ADDRESSES	ADDRESSES
Romans	Paul, a *servant* of Christ Jesus, called to be an *apostle* and set apart for the gospel	—	To all in Rome who are loved by God and called to be *saints*	Grace and peace to you from God our Father and from the Lord Jesus Christ.
1 Corinthians	Paul, called to be an *apostle* of Christ Jesus *by the will of God*	our brother Sosthenes	To the *church of God* in Corinth, to those *sanctified* ... together with all those everywhere who call on the name of our Lord Jesus Christ	Grace and peace to you from God our Father and the Lord Jesus Christ.
2 Corinthians	Paul an *apostle* of Christ Jesus *by the will of God*	Timothy *our brother*	To the *church* of God in Corinth, together with all the *saints* throughout Achaia	Grace and peace to you from God our Father and the Lord Jesus Christ.
Galatians	Paul an *apostle*—sent not from men nor by man, but by Jesus Christ and God the Father, who raised Him from the dead	and all the *brothers* with me	To the *churches* in Galatia	Grace and peace to you from God our Father and the Lord Jesus Christ.
Ephesians	Paul an *apostle* of Christ Jesus *by the will of God*	—	To all the *saints* in Ephesus, the faithful in Christ Jesus	Grace and peace to you from God our Father and the Lord Jesus Christ.
Philippians	Paul ... *servants* of Christ Jesus	Timothy	To all the *saints* in Christ Jesus at Philippi	Grace and peace to you from God our Father and the Lord Jesus Christ.
Colossians	Paul an *apostle* of Christ Jesus *by the will of God*	Timothy *our brother*	To the *holy* and faithful in Christ at Colosse	Grace and peace to you from God our Father.
1 Thessalonians	Paul	Silas and Timothy	To the *church* of the Thessalonians *in God* the Father and the Lord Jesus Christ	Grace and peace to you.
2 Thessalonians	Paul	Silas and Timothy	To the *church* of the Thessalonians *in God* the Father and the Lord Jesus Christ	Grace and peace to you from God the Father and the Lord Jesus Christ.
1 Timothy	Paul, an *apostle* of Christ Jesus by the command of God our Savior and of Christ Jesus	—	To Timothy, my true son in the faith	Grace, mercy, and peace from God the Father and Christ Jesus our Lord.
2 Timothy	Paul, an *apostle* of Christ Jesus *by the will of God*, according to the promise of life that is in Christ Jesus	—	To Timothy, my dear son	Grace, mercy, and peace from God the Father and Christ Jesus our Lord.
Titus	Paul, a *servant* of God and an *apostle* of Christ Jesus	—	To Titus, my true son in our common faith	Grace and peace from God the Father and Christ Jesus our Savior.
Philemon	Paul, a *prisoner* of Christ Jesus	Timothy *our brother*	To Philemon, our dear friend and fellow worker, to Apphia our sister, to Archippus our fellow soldier, and to the church that meets in your home	Grace to you and *peace* from God our Father and the Lord Jesus Christ.

Romans

Daniel M. Gurtner

I. 1:1-17. INTRODUCTION

1:1. Ancient letters, particularly of an oriental and Jewish model, tended to begin with the names of the sender and the addressees followed by a greeting: "Artaxerxes, king of kings, to Ezra the priest, the scribe of the law of the God of heaven, perfect peace" (Ezra 7:12; cf. Dan. 4:1; 2 Bar. 78:2; Acts 23:26; see comment on Eph. 1:2). **Paul** (*Paulus*) was the Hellenistic-Roman name for his Jewish name "Saul." Jews in Greek-speaking areas took names that closely approximated the sound of their Hebrew and Aramaic names. **A bond-servant** (*doulos*) is a humble but honorable title in the Old Testament and is given to the likes of Abraham (Ps. 105:42), Moses (Ps. 105:26; 2 Kings 18:12; Dan. 9:11), Joshua (Josh. 24:29; Judges 2:8), David (2 Sam. 7:5; Ps. 89:4, 21), and the prophets (Amos 3:7; 1QS 1:3; 1QpHab 2:9; 7:5). Jewish worshipers quite naturally thought of themselves as God's slaves (Neh. 1:6; Pss. 19:11; 27:9; 31:16; 1QH 7:16; 9:10-11; Dunn, 7). Paul's servanthood is **of Christ Jesus. Called as an apostle, set apart for the gospel of God: Called** (*klētos*) is a term frequently used for inviting one to meals (1 Kings 1:41; 3 Macc. 5:14). Here Paul is called to be an **apostle** (*apostolos*), which can also mean a "messenger, delegate, one sent on behalf of" someone. It can be an ambassador or a special envoy (Herodotus, *Histories* 1.21; 5.38; Jos., *Ant.* 17.11.1 §300). **Set apart** (*aphōrismenos*) refers to Paul's

conversion and commissioning on the Damascus road (cf. Gal. 1:15). **Gospel of God.** In the Old Testament, **gospel** (*to euangelion*) appears in Isa. 40:9 as "good news": "Get yourself up on a high mountain, O Zion, bearer of good news, Lift up your voice mightily, O Jerusalem, bearer of good news; Lift it up, do not fear. Say to the cities of Judah, 'Here is your God!'" (cf. *Pss. Sol.* 11:1; 1QH 18:14; 11QMelch 18). In the Greco-Roman world, the term appears as "glad tidings" in a 9 B.C. decree marking the birthday of the emperor Augustus, which proclaims his birth was "the beginning of the world of glad tidings" (*OGIS* 2.458). Rather than looking to the emperor to provide salvation, however, Paul says his gospel is **of God.** That is, God is the source and authority behind the message (Dunn, 10).

1:2. He promised beforehand through His prophets in the holy Scriptures. Though clearly referring to the Old Testament, only here does he call the Scriptures (*graphai*) sacred (*hagiai*), though such was an expression used elsewhere by Jews for their scriptures (Jos., *Ag. Ap.* 2.4 § 45; Philo, *Abr.* 61; *De congr.* 34, 90). Luther said the gospel here provides us an "entrance into the Old Testament." Paul clearly sees the content of his gospel as being continuous with what he studied of the Old Testament as a Pharisee.

1:3. His Son. Jews had a wide variety of beliefs

The "Son of David" and the Glory of Israel

"The Lord speaks to King David through the prophet Nathan about his descendant, and says, 'When your days are complete and you lie down with your fathers, I will raise up your descendant after you, who will come forth from you, and I will establish his kingdom. He shall build a house for My name, and I will establish the throne of his kingdom forever. I will be a father to him and he will be a son to Me; when he commits iniquity, I will correct him with the rod of men and the strokes of the sons of men, but My lovingkindness shall not depart from him, as I took it away from Saul, whom I removed from before you. And your house and your kingdom shall endure before Me forever; your throne shall be established forever.'"

2 Samuel 7:12-16

---

about the Son of God: Some used this phrase as a designation for the king of Israel (2 Sam. 7:14; Pss. 2:7; 89:26-27), Jewish sages (m. Ta'an 3.8), or of Israel as a whole (Exod. 4:22-23; Jer. 31:9; Hos. 11:1; Wisd. 9.7; 18.13; Jub. 1.24-24; Pss. Sol. 17.30; T. Mos. 10.3; Sib. Or. 3.702). **Descendant of David.** Jews long expected a Son of David to rule Israel justly forever (2 Sam. 7:14). This figure was God's Messiah who would bring hope to Israel (Isa. 11:1-15; Jer. 23:5-6; 33:14-16; Ezek. 34:23-31; Pss. Sol. 17.23-51; 4QFlor 1.10-13; 4QpGen. 49; 4QpIsa^a 2:21-28).

1:4. Who was declared the Son of God. Jesus was always the Son of God, but Paul is suggesting that this role is declared at the **resurrection from the dead.** It may reflect a similar declaration of the Old Testament: "I will surely

tell of the decree of the LORD: He said to Me, 'Thou art My Son, Today I have begotten Thee'" (Psalm 2:7).

1:7 In Rome. As was said in the Introduction, this reading is not found in all manuscripts, but is surely original. Rather than being built in a day, Rome was the product of many centuries of development, dating back to its founding by Romulus and Remus in 753 B.C. It developed early as a settlement of shepherds ruled at first by a series of kings, but by around 510 B.C. it had become a republic, under which it was governed by two magistrates called consuls elected each year (Fitzmyer, 25). It controlled all of Italy by 275 B.C., and through a series of wars with Carthage acquired the provinces of Sicily (241 B.C.), Sardinia (238 B.C.), and Spain (206 B.C.) as well. Rome grew to include more Mediterranean provinces such as Macedonia (148 B.C.) and Corinth (146 B.C.), after which it was marred by class struggles and slave wards (135-132 B.C., 103-101 B.C.). Eventually a dictatorship was established (107-100 B.C.), though subsequently deposed (88-79 B.C.). By 60 B.C., Rome came to be governed by the triumvirate of generals, Pompey, Crassus, and Julius Caesar (Fitzmyer, 25), which was subsequently broken up and Julius Caesar assassinated in 44 B.C. Octavian became sole monarch of the Roman world in September, 31 B.C., was conferred the title Augustus (Sebastos, "the Venerable"), and ruled until his death in A.D. 14. During his reign, the Roman life saw great improvements, including a reign of peace (called the Pax Augusta, "the Peace of Augustus"), the army reorganized and made a protector of the people, and the general promotion of arts and letters. His successors, beginning with Tiberius, were soon recognized as gods and worshiped in the Roman Imperial Cult.

Saints. The faithful in the Old Testament were commonly called **saints** (Greek, hagioi literally, "holy ones"). This identification was likewise adopted as the self-designating term

The Roman Imperial Cult

Romans frequently offered divine honors to a living or dead emperor. Though most often deified after their deaths, some emperors recognized or even demanded worship as gods during their own lifetimes.

Tiberius – Refused divine honors for himself and refused to permit a temple to be built in his name. He declared in a speech to the Senate: "I am mortal, and divine honors belong only to Augustus, the real savior of mankind" (Tacitus, *Annals* 4.37-38).

Caligula – Insisted that he was the incarnation of Jupiter, and would dress as other gods and goddesses as well. He had temples erected in his honor in Miletus and Rome (Dio Cassius 59.11.12; 28.1-2). His image was ordered set up in the synagogues of Alexandria. The Jews refused to worship it and complained to Rome (A.D. 39), though they would regard him as "savior and benefactor" (Philo, *Legatio* 75-114; 349-67).

Claudius – Like Tiberius before him, he generally shunned worship of himself as a god, though a temple was built to him following a Roman victory in Britain (Tacitus, *Annals* 14.31).

Nero – Nero had Claudius officially deified, and was himself depicted on coins as "god" and as "Apollo the Lyre Player," wearing the radiate crown of a deified emperor. In 55 the Senate set up a statue of Nero in the temple of Mars Ultor (Tacitus, *Annals* 13.8.1), though in 65 he rejected a proposed temple to "the divine Nero," insisting it was only dead emperors who receive such honors. Yet he was often greeted with titles of deity and ascriptions as a god (Dio Cassius 62.20.5; 63.20.5).

Domitian – Domitian insisted on being recognized as a divine *dues praesens*, an important term for emperor worship. Such was reflected on coins and marble statues. In correspondence he insisted on being addressed as "our lord and god" (Seutonius, *Domitianus* 13).

---

for the Qumran sectarians (1QS 5:13, 18; 8:17, 20, 23; 9:8; 1QM 6:6; 10:10; 16:1; cf. also *1 Enoch* 1:9; 39:1; *Jub.* 31:14). **Grace and peace.** The particular combination of **grace** and **peace** is unusual, but found in some Jewish literature (esp. *2 Bar.* 78:2; cf. *Jub.* 12.29; *1 Enoch* 1:8; 1QS 2:1-4; *2 Bar.* 78:3). Here, however, Paul replaced the standard Hellenistic greeting of "greetings" (*chairein*) with a theological **grace** (*charis*). **Peace** (*eirēnē*) is the Greek equivalent of the Hebrew *shalom*. See comment on Col. 1:2; Eph. 1:2.

1:13. Often I have planned to come to you (and have been prevented thus far). We cannot know for certain Paul's plans to visit the Romans, though that he was detained could suggest he was at work in other churches. If Paul is writing from Corinth (see Introduction), that church could have been a source of his hindrance, as it required a great deal of his time and attention (see Introduction to 1 and 2 Cor.). **Brethren** (*adelphoi*) was commonly used among Christians and other religious groups to designate a fellow member (cf. Exod. 2:11; Deut. 3:18; Tobit 1.3; *2 Macc.* 1:1; 1QS 6:10; 1QM 13:1; 15:4; CD 6:20-7:2). **Some fruit among you.** Bearing fruit is an expression from the Old Testament of growing and multiplying (LXX Gen. 1:22, 28; cf. Gen. 8:17; 9:1, 7; Jer. 3:16; 23:3). Some rabbis used the expression for sin as the fruit of unbelief (*b. Qid.* 40a). Other Jews saw the Law as having power to produce fruit in people (*4 Ezra* 9:31; cf. *4 Ezra* 3:20).

1:14. Both to Greeks and to barbarians. Greeks originally referred only to those of Greek ancestry who spoke the Greek language. After the conquests of Alexander the Great (d. 323 B.C.), however, it was commonly used of anyone who spoke the language and shared in Greek culture and education, regardless of ethnic heritage. **Barbarians** (*barbaroi*) typically referred to one less cultured, including natural enemies. For the Greeks or Romans, a barbarian was anyone not part of their own culture (Josephus, *Ag. Ap.* 2.38 §269).

1:17. For in it the righteousness of God is revealed from faith to faith. This verse echoes the words of Ps. 98:2 which says, "The LORD has made known His salvation; He has revealed His righteousness in the sight of the nations." **Righteousness of God** (*dikaiosynētou theou*). Scholars differ on whether Paul refers here to the righteousness which God gives to believers or God's ability to make things "right." In the Old Testament, from which Paul heavily draws in this verse, the expression of God's **righteousness** was frequently used to depict what caused him to acquit his sinful people (Isa. 46:13; 51:5; 56:1; 61:10; Ps. 40:9-11), where now it is manifest towards people because of what Christ has done (Fitzmyer, 257-58). This is not a moral expression but a legal one, whereby God is not here directing a believer's life but making a judicial decision of innocence (Moo, 70-76, 79-90). **As it is written** is a common way of citing Jewish scriptures in Romans (2:24; 3:10; 4:17; 8:36; etc.), the Old Testament (Dan. 9:13; 2 Kings 14:6), and the Qumran literature (1QS 5:17; 8:14; CD 7:19; 4QFlor 1-2 i 12; 4Q178 3:2). **"But the righteous man shall live by faith."** This is a quotation from Hab. 2:4, which, when cited at Qumran, is understood thus: "The interpretation of it concerns the observers of the law in the house of Judah, whom God shall deliver from the house of judgment because of their striving and their fidelity to the Teacher of Righteousness" (1QpHab 7:5–8:3). This shows evidence of a Palestinian Jewish tradition which understood the prophet's words to promise life for observance of the law *and* fidelity to the person of a Jewish leader. Some scholars see Paul's use of this verse here of Jesus as standing within such a Jewish tradition (Fitzmyer, 264).

Sexuality in the Hellenistic World

Generally speaking, Greek culture was much more tolerant of prostitution, fornication, adultery, and homosexuality than was Judaism. Wealthy men "keep mistresses for pleasure, concubines for daily concubinage, and wives . . . in order to produce children legitimately and to have a trustworthy guardian of our domestic property" (Athenaeus, *Deipnosophistae* 13.573b). Cultic prostitutes were especially common in Asia Minor, such as the temples of Diana or Artemis in Ephesus or that of Aphrodite in Corinth. Extramarital intercourse was generally acceptable among men, but not among their wives. Such affairs were often considered noble, particularly when homosexual relationships were involved (cf. Plato, *Symposium* 178c-180a; Xenophon, *Memorabilia* 2.6.28-39). As men were regarded as superior to women, sexual relations between men were seen as all the more ideal. Zeus himself was attracted to a male, and Emperor Nero's seduction of free-born boys was notorious.

II. THE HUMAN CONDITION
(Jews and Gentiles) (1:18–3:20)

A. 1:18-32. Humans Are Depraved

1:18. For the wrath of God is revealed from heaven against all ungodliness and unrighteousness of men, who suppress the truth in unrighteousness. The wrath of God is primarily thought to be poured out toward the end of time (Isa. 63:3-6; Zeph. 1:15), though it is also seen as a present reality against human sin (Exod. 32:10-12; Num. 11:1; Jer. 21:3-7; *1 Enoch* 84:4; 91:7-9). The present tense of the verb **is revealed** suggests that Paul meant God's wrath as revealed in his own time.

1:19. That which is known about God is evident within them; for God made it evident to them. Paul, here, recognizes a strong Jewish tradition that God cannot be known (Exod. 33:20; Deut. 4:12; *Sir.* 43:31; Philo, *Dreams* 1.11 §§65-66; Josephus, *J.W.* 7.8.7 §346; *Ag. Ap.* 2.16 §167; cf. *Sib. Or.* 3:8-45), except what he chooses to make known (Jer. 40:6; Philo, *Alleg. Interpretation* 3.15 §47; Josephus, *Ant.* 17.2.4 §38; 18.8.7 §294; *Life* 45 §231). Luther said, "These words declare that all earthly gifts must be ascribed to God as their Donor" (27).

1:20. That God had **invisible attributes** was well established in Hellenistic Jewish traditions (Philo, *Moses* 2.12 §65; *Special Laws* 1.3 §20; Josephus, *J.W.* 7.8.7 §346; cf. *2 Bar.* 54:18).

Gregory Nazianzen on Idolatry:

"People like this make it hard to tell which was more contemptible, the worshipers or the worshiped. Perhaps the worshipers by far, since as rational beings and recipients of God's grace, they chose their inferior for patron and better."

Oration on God 28.15 ACCS

Jewish Moral Purity

"Surpassing all men, they [Jewish men] are mindful of holy wedlock, and they do not engage in impious intercourse with male children, as do the Phoenicians, Egyptians, and Romans, spacious Greece and many nations of others, Persians and Galatians and all Asia, transgressing the holy law of immortal God, which they transgressed."

Sibylline Oracles 3:594-600 OTP

1:21. Darkened was a common expression for unbelief. See comment on Eph. 5:8-14.

1:23. Exchanged the glory of the incorruptible God for an image in the form of corruptible man and of birds and four-footed animals and crawling creatures. Paul seems to be particularly dependent on Ps. 106:20, which speaks of the unfaithful Israelites involved in the golden calf incident (Exod. 32:1-34): "Thus they exchanged their glory For the image of an ox that eats grass" (cf. Jer. 2:11; Isa. 44:9-20; *Wisd.* 11:15; 12:24; 15:18-19). The **glory** (*doxa*) **of . . . God** was the radiant external manifestation of his presence in the tabernacle or temple (Exod. 24:17; 40:34-35). In the Old Testament, God's glory (Hebrew, *kabôd*) denoted the weight of esteem or honor that a king or an important person enjoyed (1 Kings 3:13). Yahweh was known as "the king of glory" (Ps. 24:8), and his **glory** filled the earth (Isa. 6:3; Fitzmyer, 283).

1:24. Impurity (*akatharsia*) can refer to a cultic purity, as required both of Old Testament priests and their accompanying sacrifices. Yet, here, it seems to take a plain moral sense (*Wisd.* 2:16; 1 Esdras 1:42) and relates especially to sexual immorality (*1 Enoch* 10:11; *T. Judah* 14:1-15.6; *T. Joseph* 4:6; Dunn, 62).

1:26-27. "Jews" often saw pagans as exchanging their true natural functions for perverted ones (Philo, *Abraham* 135; *Special Laws* 2.50; 3.37; *T. Joseph* 7:8). Homosexual practices were prevalent in the Greco-Roman world (Lucian, *Dailogi meretricum* 5.2; *Amores* 28; Plutarch, *Lycurgus* 18), though roundly condemned among Jews (Lev. 18:22; 20:13; Deut. 23:17; 1 Kings 14:23; 15:12; 22:46; 2 Kings 23:7; cf. *Sib. Or.* 3:594-600).

1:32. They not only do the same, but also give hearty approval to those who practice them. The notion that approval of sin can be worse than one's own sin is attested elsewhere in Jewish thought: "The two-faced are doubly punished because they both practice evil and approve of others who practice it; they imitate the spirits of error and join in the struggle against mankind" (*T. Asher* 6:2 OTP).

B. 2:1–3:8. Jews Are Likewise Depraved 2:1. You is singular in the Greek text, as in 2:17 where he addresses a Jew. Rather than presuming the apostle is singling out a single person in the Roman church, readers are to recognize that Paul is using an ancient literary technique known as *diatribe*. In this style, the author uses a literary device of an imaginary dialogue with a student or opponent. Such a technique is attested in several ancient authors including the New Testament book of James (Moo, 125).

2:2. Paul's appeal to **the judgment of God** was widely used particularly among Jews (cf. Isa. 13:6-16; 34:8; Dan. 7:9-11; Joel 2:1-2; Zeph. 1:14-2:3; Mal. 4:1; *Jub.* 5:10-16; *1 Enoch* 90:20-27) as was the belief that his administration of it would be done **rightly** (cf. 1QS 4:19-20; CD 20:30; *4 Ezra* 7:34; *2 Bar.* 85:9; *m. 'Abot* 3:16).

2:4. Or do you think lightly of the riches of His kindness and forbearance and patience, not knowing that the kindness of God leads you to repentance? There is evidence that some Jews assumed that God's kindness guar-

anteed their exemption from God's judgment: "But thou, our God, art kind and true, patient, and ruling all things in mercy. For even if we sin we are Thine, knowing Thy power; but we will not sin, because we know that we are accounted Thine. For to know Thee is complete righteousness, and to know Thy power is the root of immortality" (*Wisd.* 15:1-3; cf. *T. Abr.* 10:14; *Hel. Syn. Prayer* 11:4).

2:5. Unrepentant heart recalls the hardness of heart in the Old Testament. This is an expression of willful unbelief. It was attributed to Pharaoh (Exod. 4:21; 7:3; 9:12) and at times to Israel (Ps. 94:8; Isa. 6:10; 63:17). It is similarly used in Qumran (1QS 1:6; 2:14; 3:3; 5:4; CD 2:17; 3:5; 8:8). **Day of wrath** is a way of describing God's judgment at the end times particular to the prophet Zephaniah (Zeph. 1:15, 18; 2:2-3; cf. 3:8).

2:6. Who will render to every man according to his deeds. This text is a citation from the Old Testament seeming to combine Ps. 62:12 and Proverbs 24:12. Viewing God as repaying one for his deeds was common enough in Judaism (Job 34:11; Jer. 17:10; Hos. 12:2; *Sir.* 16.12-14; *1 Enoch* 100.7; *Jos. Asen.* 28.3); it was also adopted by the earliest Christians (cf. Matt. 16:27; 2 Cor. 5:10; Col. 3:25; 2 Tim. 4:14; 1 Peter 1:17; Rev. 2:23; Dunn, 85).

2:7. When Paul speaks of **eternal life**, he borrows the Jewish sense of life in the age to come (Dan. 12:2; *2 Macc.* 7:9; *4 Macc.* 15:3; 1QS 4:7; Fitzmyer, 302).

2:8. Wrath and indignation appear in the Old Testament in such pairs in the context of the "day of the Lord" (Isa. 13:9; cf. 30:30; Jer. 7:20; 21:5).

2:9-10. The Greek. See comment on 1:14.

2:11. There is no partiality with God was a common concept in Judaism (Deut. 10:17;

Esteem for the Law in the *Mishnah*

"There are they that have no share in the world to come: he that says that . . . the Law is not from heaven" (*m. Sanhedrin* 10:1).

". . . The rules about what is clean and unclean and the forbidden decrees . . . it is they that are the essentials of the Law" (*m. Hagigah* 1:8).

"He that reads in the Law may not read less than three verses... (he) may leave out verses in the Prophets, but not in the Law" (*m. Megillah* 4:4).

". . . the Law . . . guards (a man) from all evil while he is young, and in old age it grants him a future and a hope" (*m. Kiddushin* 4:14).

"Him (to whom is revealed) the secrets of the Law...is like to a never-failing spring and like to a river that flows ever more mightily; and he becomes modest, long-suffering, and forgiving of insult; and it magnifies him and exalts him above all things" (*m. Aboth* 6:1).

---

2 Chron. 19:7; *Sir.* 35:12-13; *Jub.* 5:16; 21:4; 30:16; 33:16; *Pss. Sol.* 2:18; *2 Bar.* 13:8) and is sometimes used to refer to God's covenant obligations (Deut. 10:18-19; *Jub.* 5:17-18; 33:16-20).

2:12. Law (*nomos*) occurs almost eighty times in Romans. Paul uses the term almost exclusively to refer to the Law of Moses—the commandments given to Israel through Moses, also called *torah*. Those **under the Law** are Jews, while those **apart from the Law** are Gentiles.

2:13 The doers of the Law will be justified. This phrase is similar to Lev. 18:5: "So you shall keep My statutes and My judgments, by which a man may live if he does them; I am the LORD." That life was found in observing the Law was a common sentiment in Judaism (Deut. 4:1, 5-6, 13-14; 30:11-14; *1 Macc.* 2:67; 13:48; Josephus, *Ant.* 20.2.4 §44).

2:14 For when Gentiles who do not have the Law do instinctively the things of the Law, these, not having the Law, are a law to themselves. Though Paul may be referring to Gentile Christians who have the Law written on their hearts (Jer. 31:31-34), it seems more likely that Paul is referring to a widespread Greco-Roman tradition of an "unwritten law." Such was a notion largely articulated by Stoic philosophers

that there was a universal moral standard rooted in all humans. Naturally, Jews such as Philo attached that standard to the Law of Moses: "And right reason is infallible law engraved not by this mortal or that and, therefore, perishable as he, nor on parchment or slabs, and, therefore, soulless as they, but by immortal nature on the immortal mind, never to perish" (*Good Man* 46 LCL; cf. *Special Laws* 1.36-54; *Abraham* 276; Moo, 149-51; cf. *Apoc. Sedr.* 15:4; *2 Bar.* 48:40; *Hel. Syn. Prayer* 11:3; 12:43).

2:15. Work of the Law refers to the works required by the Law (Cranfield, 158; cf. *2 Bar.* 57:2).

2:16. Secrets of men. Jews recognized that God knows the secrets of men's hearts (1 Sam. 16:7; 1 Chron. 28:9; Ps. 139:1-2, 23; Jer. 17:10; cf. *Pss. Sol.* 14:8; 17:25).

2:17. But if you bear the name "Jew," and rely upon the Law, and boast in God. Paul continues to use his *diatribe* (see comment on 2:1) style by criticizing his opponents for not "practicing what they preached" (cf. Epictetus, *Diss.* 2.19-20; 3.7, 17). Precisely what Paul is opposing is well articulated in *2 Baruch* 48:22-24: "In you we have put our trust, because, behold, your Law is with us, and we know that we do not fall as long as we keep your statutes. We shall always be blessed; at least, we did not mingle with the nations. For we are all a people of the Name; we, who received our Law from the One. And that Law that is among us will help us, and that excellent wisdom which is in us will support us" (OTP).

2:19-20. A guide to the blind, a light to those who are in darkness, a corrector of the foolish, a teacher of the immature. These are all descriptions of Israel's role as witnesses of God's power and grace to the world found in the Old Testament and Second Temple Jewish texts. They were **a guide to the blind**. In the Old Testament, God designated Israel to be his "servant" (Isa. 42:6-7) and "to open blind eyes, to bring out prisoners from the dungeon, and those who dwell in darkness from the prison." That Jews continued to see themselves as guides is apparent in later Judaism as well (*Sib. Or.* 3:194-95; *1 Enoch* 105:1; Josephus, *Ag. Ap.* 2.41 §§291-95; Philo, *Abraham* 98). See comment on Matt. 23:16 §182.

They were also **a light to those who are in darkness**. The light which Israel has been given was thought of as the Law (Ps. 119:105; *Wisd.* 18:4; *Sir.* 24:27; *T. Levi* 14:4; 1QSb 4:24). **A corrector of the foolish, a teacher of the immature.** Though no strong Old Testament connection can be made to these descriptions, the Jews at Qumran clearly saw themselves as responsible for giving instruction in their (illuminated) teaching (1QS 3:13; 8:11-12; 9:12-21; 1QH 2:13; 4:27-29; 1QpHab 7:4-5; cf. Prov. 1:22; 16:22; *Wisd.* 10:21; 12:24; 15:14). **Having in the Law the embodiment of knowledge and of the truth.** This may represent the sentiments of Diaspora synagogues (*Sir.* 17:11; 45:5; *Bar.* 3:36; *2 Bar.* 44:14; Dunn, 113).

2:22-23. Here Paul lists three accusations against Jews to demonstrate that even they do not fully obey the Law. **You who say that one should not commit adultery, do you commit adultery?** Cf. Exod. 20:14. **You who abhor idols, do you rob temples?** Though not entirely clear, it seems from Paul's use of "robbing temples" (*hierosyleō*) that he refers to the practice of robbing pagan temples of their idolatrous artifacts to melt them down and profit from their precious medals, a practice specifically forbidden in the Old Testament (Deut. 7:26; Moo, 164-65; cf. Josephus, *Ant.* 4.8.10 §207). Others understand this crime as referring to people taking from sacrifices that rightly belonged to God (cf. Acts 19:37; *T. Levi* 14:5; Fitzmyer, 318). **You who boast in the Law, through your breaking the Law, do you dishonor God?** Such practices may have occurred (cf. *Sir.* 39.8).

2:24. For "the name of God is blasphemed among the Gentiles because of you," just as it is written. This is a quotation from the LXX of Isa. 52:5 and is also similar to Ezek. 36:20. In the context of Isa. 52, the prophet ascribes blasphemy of God's name not to Israel's sin but to her condition of exile, which has led the nations to question God's faithfulness and even his existence. It is perhaps ironic that the responsibility for blaspheming God's name lies at the feet of the Jews (Moo, 166).

2:25. Circumcision for Jews of Paul's time was of paramount importance. Instituted as a sign of God's covenant with Abraham in Genesis 17:9-14, it played a pivotal role as a test of covenant loyalty and mark of Jewish national distinctiveness in the Maccabean period (*1 Macc.* 1:48; 60-61; 2:46; *2 Macc.* 6:10; Dunn, 119). Those without this distinguishing mark were not counted as members of the covenant community of God (Josephus, *Ant.* 13.9.1 §§257-58; 19.7.1 §318; *Jub.* 15:25-34). Its importance as a designating mark of a Jew was even recognized by Gentile writers (Petronius, *Satyricon* 102.14; *Fr.* 37; Tacitus, *Histories* 5.5.2; Juvenal, *Sat.* 14.99).

2:27. And will not he who is physically uncircumcised, if he keeps the Law, will he

not judge you who though having the letter of the Law and circumcision are a transgressor of the Law? Though some Jews in Paul's day, such as Philo of Alexandria, "spiritualized" the commandments of circumcision, they still insisted that the physical rite was essential (*Special Laws* 1.1-11, 304-6; *Abraham* 92).

2:29. Circumcision is that which is of the heart was also a familiar belief among some Jews of Paul's day, and was a metaphor for pious faith which was to accompany physical circumcision (cf. Deut. 10:16; Jer. 4:4; 9:25-26; Ezek. 44:9; 1QpHab 11:13; 1QS 5:5; 1QH 2:18; 18:20; Philo, *Special Laws* 1.305). **Spirit . . . letter. Letter** (*grammata*) was a Greek term used to refer to the Hebrew Scriptures (Josephus, *Ant.* 10.10.4 §210; 13.5.8 §167; 20.12.1 §264) or a single verse of it (Philo, *Migr. Abraham* 15 §85; 25 §139; *De congr.* 12 §58). For Paul, it typically refers to the Decalogue and, as such, is always in contrast to **Spirit** (*pneuma*; Rom. 7:6; 2 Cor. 3:6-7; Fitzmyer, 323).

3:2. Oracles of God here refers to the entire Old Testament (Philo, *Rewards* 1 §1; *Contemplative Life* 3 §25; Josephus, *J.W.* 6.5.4 §§311-13; cf. Num. 24:4, 16; Ps. 106:11). The possession of such oracles had clear advantages, particularly

having the Lord near to the bearers (Deut. 4:7-8; cf. Pss. 147:19-20; 103:7).

3:4. May it never be! The Greek here (*mē genoito*) is a very strong negation, a "negative oath" (Fitzmyer, 327). **Let God be found true, though every man be found a liar.** Jewish writers frequently saw God's truth as the standard by which the teachings and beliefs of others were measured (1QS 11:9-14; cf. Ps. 116:11; *Pss. Sol.* 8.7-8). **As it is written, "That Thou mightest be justified in Thy words, And mightest prevail when Thou art judged."** Paul seems to be quoting his own modified version of the LXX of Ps. 51:4. In this Psalm, the author, probably David, confesses his sin as an offense against God Himself and in so doing acknowledges the just judgments of God. David was a prime example of faithfulness to God yet subject to grievous sin, as this Psalm is traditionally associated with his repentance after being confronted with his sin with Bathsheba (cf. Ps. 89:35; Isa. 55:3; Cranfield, 183). God was frequently seen as establishing his justice through punishing his people in the first-century B.C. book *Psalms of Solomon* (cf. *Pss. Sol.* 2:16-19; 3:3; 4:9, 28; 5:1; 8:27, 29-32, 40; 9:3-4; 10:6; 17:12).

3:5. The righteousness of God, as in 1:17, refers to God's activity in putting sinners into a

---

Let God Be True . . .

". . . I belong to evil humankind, to the assembly of unfaithful flesh; my failings, my iniquities, my sins, {. . .} with the depravities of my heart, belong to the assembly of worms and of those who walk in darkness. For to man (does not belong) his path, nor can a human being steady his step; since the judgment belongs to God, and from his hand is the perfection of the path. By his knowledge everything shall come into being, and all that does exist he establishes with his calculations and nothing is done outside of him. *Blank* As for me, if I stumble, the mercies of God shall be my salvation always . . . he will judge me in the justice of his truth, and in his plentiful goodness always atone for all my sins; in his justice he will cleanse me from the uncleanness of the human being and from the sin of the sons of man, so that I can give God thanks for his justice and The Highest for his majesty."

1QS 11:9-14

right relationship with himself. Specifically, Israel's sin has given God the opportunity of manifesting his righteousness in his judgment: "Now therefore, our God, the great, the mighty, and the awesome God, who dost keep covenant and lovingkindness, Do not let all the hardship seem insignificant before Thee, Which has come upon us, our kings, our princes, our priests, our prophets, our fathers, and on all Thy people, From the days of the kings of Assyria to this day. However, Thou art just in all that has come upon us; For Thou hast dealt faithfully, but we have acted wickedly" (Neh. 9:32-33; Moo, 185).

3:6. For otherwise how will God judge the world? God as judge of the world was a fundamental assumption in Judaism dating back at least to Abraham in Gen. 18:25, where the patriarch pleads for Sodom and Gomorrah to be protected from God's judgment (cf. Deut. 32:4; Job 34:10-12; Isa. 66:16; Joel 3:12; Pss. 94:2; 96:13).

3:8. Slanderously reported (*blasph?moumetha*) is an expression often used of Gentiles who fail to recognize the special favor Israel holds with God (2 Kings 19:4; Ezek. 35:12; 2 *Macc.* 15:24; cf. Josephus, *Ag. Ap.* 1.11 §59; Dunn, 136-37).

C. All Are Alike Under Sin (3:9-20)

3:9. Under sin is an expression denoting Paul's understanding that sin is a force or power within the world, which functions in and upon man to negative effect (cf. *Sir.* 21:2; 27:10; 1QH 1:27; 4:29-30). Its authority is similar to a kingly rule or slave ownership (Rom. 5:21; 6:12-23; 7:14; Dunn, 148).

3:10-18. To support his claim that all are alike under sin (v. 9), Paul quotes a series of Old Testament passages, perhaps six to ten, strung together. Jews at Qumran, for example, sometimes chained together a number of verses as a "proof text" for the point they were trying to

make (cf. 4QTestimonia). Though some Jews would have claimed such verses applied to pagans, the apostle insists that they speak of those "under the law" (v. 19), that is, the Jewish people. The first quotation comes from Eccl. 7:20: **"There is none righteous, not even one"** (cf. Pss. 14:3; 53:4; 1QH 9:14; 1QPs^a 155.8; *b. Sanh.* 101a). The next text (v. 11) is taken from Ps. 14:2: **"There is none who understands, There is none who seeks for God"** and serves as an indictment against not only pagan idolatry but also Jewish self-righteousness (Fitzmyer, 335). Seeking after God is a common Old Testament expression (Exod. 33:7; 2 Chron. 15:12; Ezra 8:22; Pss. 9:10; 24:6; 27:8; Isa. 9:13; Jer. 29:13; Zeph. 1:6), used frequently in the context of seeking guidance from God, intimacy with him, and his deliverance from distress. Verse 12 is taken almost verbatim from Ps. 14:3: **"All have turned aside, together they have become useless; There is none who does good, There is not even one."** In verse 13, Paul first turns to Ps. 5:10, quoted exactly from the LXX: **"Their throat is an open grave, With their tongues they keep deceiving."** This portion of the Psalm depicts the psalmist's ruthless enemies against whom he prays for God's help. The corruption of their throats and tongues depicts the deadly effects of their speech or perhaps the inner corruption which they express (Cranfield, 193). The final text of this verse comes from Ps. 140:3 [LXX: 139:4]: **"The poison of asps is under their lips."** **"Whose mouth is full of cursing and bitterness"** (v. 14) is taken from Ps. 10:7, which depicts the scoffing of God put forth by violent human speech. Verses 15-17 are taken from Isa. 59:7-8, which speaks of the wretched iniquity of God's people. The final text (v. 18) comes from Ps. 36:2b: **"There is no fear of God before their eyes."** Here the psalmist is contrasting the lawbreaker and the upright Jew, who stands in awe of God (cf. Gen. 22:12; Deut. 6:2; Prov. 1:7; Fitzmyer, 336).

3:20. This verse is very similar to Ps. 143:2b.

Some Jews believed that one was unable to stand before God blameless on his own merits (*1 Enoch* 81.5; 1QS 11:9-12; 1QH 9:14-16; *4 Ezra* 7:46). **Works of the Law** probably refers to the things prescribed or required by the Law (4QMMT 3:29; 1QS 5:21; 6:18; Fitzmyer, 338).

III. THE GOSPEL AS THE SOLUTION (3:21–5:21)

A. (3:21-26) Faith in Christ Is the Key

3:21 Law and the Prophets refers to the entire Old Testament corpus (*2 Macc.* 15:9; *4 Macc.* 18:10; Luke 16:16; Acts 13:15; 24:14; 28:23; Matt. 5:17; 7:12; 11:13; 22:40; cf. 1QS 1:3; 8:15-16; CD 5:21-6:1).

3:24. Redemption (*apolytrōsis*) can mean deliverance in a general way (Exod. 21:8) or perhaps the release of a prisoner when the appropriate price is paid (Zeph. 3:1; Dan. 4:34 LXX). The Exodus from Egypt is a primary example of God's **redemption** of Israel from servitude to become his people (Exod. 8:23; Deut. 7:8; 9:26; 13:5; 15:15; 24:18; 1 Chron. 17:21; cf. Ps. 49:7; Job 33:24; Isa. 43:3). **Redemption** is accomplished by God's might (Deut. 7:8; 9:26; Ps. 74:2; 77:15). Israel was to likewise redeem people and property that could not otherwise be freed (Lev. 25:25-26; 47-49). Provisions were made for people to go free from imprisonment by redemption (Exod. 21:29-30). Redemption is seen in Cyrus's decree for the exiles to be restored (Ezra 1:1-11), where the redemption is attributed to God (Isa. 45:1-25; 52:3) in an Exodus-like manner (cf. Isa. 43:1-4, 14). It can also generally refer to a deliverance from imprisonment to Beliar or bondage to evil (*T. Zeb.* 9:8; *T. Joseph* 18:2; cf. Dan. 4:34). The Qumran sectarians saw themselves as ones redeemed by God (1QM 1:12; 9:9; 14:5, 10; 15:1; 17:6). The term was used widely in the ancient world to refer to the process by which prisoners of war or slaves could be bought out of their bondage (Moo, 229; *PTeb*

1.120.41; *PRyl* 2.213.164; Plutarch, *Arat.* 11). Paul says it is accomplished **in Christ Jesus.**

3:25. Displayed publicly may reflect the cultic use of the bread of the presence (Exod. 29:23; 40:23; Lev. 24:8; *2 Macc.* 1:8, 15; Dunn, 170). **Propitiation** (*hilastērion*) is a common word in the LXX of Exodus, Leviticus, and Numbers frequently representing the lid of the Ark of the Covenant, or "mercy seat." Essentially Christ has become the "place" where atonement is accomplished. Clearly Paul was thinking of Jesus' death as a sacrifice of atonement, which is confirmed by the apostle's discussion of Christ's **blood**. Manipulation of blood was a crucial part of the Old Testament sacrificial rituals, particularly that of the Day of Atonement (Lev. 16:1-34). **In the forbearance of God He passed over the sins previously committed. He passed over** (*paresis*) means "postponement of punishment" or "neglect of prosecution," suggesting that sinners in the Old Testament did not receive the punishment for their sins, but it was delayed until Christ.

B. 3:27-31. The Gospel is Offered to Jew and Gentile

3:30. God . . . is one. This is among the most basic of Jewish creeds, found first in Deut. 6:4: "Hear, O Israel! The LORD is our God, the LORD is one!" This is called the *Shema,* from the first Hebrew word of the verse: "Hear!" (cf. Deut. 32:29; Isa. 43:10-12; 44:6; 45:6).

3:31. Do we then nullify the Law through faith? Rabbi Jonathan said, "He that fulfills the Law in poverty shall in the end fulfill it in wealth; and he that neglects the Law in wealth shall in the end neglect it in poverty" (*m. 'Abot* 4.9; cf. *4 Macc.* 5.25, 33).

C. 4:1-25. Illustration of Abraham

4:1-2. Abraham is often appealed to as the father of the Jewish race (Gen. 12:1-24:67; cf. Ps. 105:6; Isa. 41:8; Josephus, *J.W.* 5.9.4 §380). He

---

Jewish Esteem for Abraham

"Abraham was the great father of a multitude of nations, and no one has been found like him in glory; he kept the law of the Most High, and was taken into covenant with him; he established the covenant in his flesh, and when he was tested he was found faithful. Therefore the Lord assured him by an oath that the nations would be blessed through his posterity; that he would multiply him like the dust of the earth, and exalt his posterity like the stars, and cause them to inherit from sea to sea and from the River to the ends of the earth."

Sirach 44:19-21

---

was also regarded for his close relationship with God, and alone was called "the friend of God" (2 Chron. 20:7; Isa. 41:8; *Jub.* 19:9; Philo, *Abraham* 273; *Jos. Asen.* 23:10; Jas. 2:23). The *Prayer of Mannasseh* claims that Abraham did not sin against God (v. 8; *T. Abr.* 10:13), while Sirach says, "no one has been found like him in glory" (44:19). He was also said to be "perfect in all his deeds with the Lord, and well-pleasing in righteousness all the days of his life" (*Jub.* 23:10 OTP), even having obeyed the Law before it was given (*m. Qidd.* 4:14; cf. *2 Bar.* 57:2; CD 3:2; *Jub.* 23:10).

4:3. For what does the Scripture say? "And Abraham believed God, and it was reckoned to him as righteousness." Paul quotes Genesis 15:6 (cf. Gal. 3:6). **Reckoned** (*elogisthō*) is an accounting term figuratively applied to human conduct (Ps. 106:31; *1 Macc.* 2.52; Phlm 19). Some thought that good and bad deeds were being tallied in ledgers (Esther 6:1; Dan. 7:10; *T. Benj.* 11:4; *2 Bar.* 24:1; *Jub.* 30:17; Hermas, *Vision* 1.2.1; Fitzmyer, 373). Later Jews saw Abraham's faith as merit (*4 Ezra* 9:7; 13:23; *b.*

Mekilta 40b). See text box comment on Gal. 3:6.

4:5. Him who justifies the ungoldly. Justifying **the ungodly** or acquitting the wicked was abhorrent to a basic and frequently repeated canon of Jewish justice (Exod. 23:7; Prov. 17:15; 24:24; Isa. 5:23; *Sir.* 42:2; CD 1:19). Those who do so are repeatedly condemned. It seems Paul may see all people as ungodly (3:9-18) and believers are here justified by virtue of Christ's righteousness (3:24).

4:6-8. Here Paul quotes Psalm 32:1-2, attributing it to David, the "man after God's own heart" (1 Sam. 13:14). This is a psalm of personal thanksgiving for healing received, to couple his reference to Gen. 15:6 (v. 3). This is perhaps a mode of Jewish exegesis (which was later called literally "equal decision"), according to which identical words, occurring in two different texts of Scripture, may be used as the basis for a mutual interpretation (Fitzmyer, 376). In this psalm the healing is most readily associated with forgiveness of sins (cf. CD 4:9-10).

4:9. Is this blessing then upon the circumcised, or upon the uncircumcised also? Paul raises this question because there is no mention of circumcision in the psalm just cited (Fitzmyer, 380).

4:10. How then was it reckoned? While he was circumcised, or uncircumcised? Not while circumcised, but while uncircumcised. The circumstances of Gen. 15:6 (vv. 4-8) occur before Abraham's circumcision in Gen. 17:1-27. Rabbis claimed the former preceded the latter by twenty-nine years (Dunn, 211).

4:11. For Jews **circumcision** was a **sign** that one belonged to the covenant (Gen. 17:11; *Jub* 15:26-28). For later Jews it was a **seal** (*Exod. Rab.* 19.5 [on Exod. 12:44]; *Tg. Klet. Cant.* 3:8) of God's ownership.

4:13. Promise (*epangelia*) is a later expression for God's covenant, though that his covenant was based on a promise was a basic element of Israel's faith from the beginning (cf. Exod. 32:13; 1 Chron. 16:14-18; Neh. 9:7-8; Ps. 105:6-11; *Sir.* 44:21; *Wisd.* 12:21; *Pr. Man.* 6; *T. Joseph* 20:1; Dunn, 212). **He would be heir of the world.** From an early time Jews believed inheritance of Canaan was an essential element of their covenant relationship with God. By Paul's day the concept had been broadened out from Canaan to embrace the whole earth (*Sir.* 44:21; *Jub.* 17:3; 22:14; 32:19; 1 *Enoch* 5:7; Philo, *Moses* 1.155; 4 *Ezra* 6:59; Dunn, 213). See comment on Eph. 1:12.

4:14. For if those who are of the Law are heirs, faith is made void and the promise is nullified. Origen said, "Paul says that the promise given to Abraham that he should inherit the world did not come from the law but by faith, which was reckoned to him as righteousness. It doubtless follows that everyone who hopes that God's righteousness will be imputed to him hopes for this by faith and not by the law" (*Commentary on the Epistle to the Romans*, ACCS).

4:17. (As it is written, "A father of many nations have I made you") in the sight of Him whom he believed, even God, who gives life to the dead and calls into being that which does not exist. This quotation is taken from the LXX of Gen. 17:5. **Who gives life to the dead** is a common way of referring to God (Ps. 71:20; Tobit 13:2; *Wisd.* 16:13; *Jos. Asen.* 20.7; *T. Gad* 4:6). While Paul may be referring to the "bringing back to life" of Isaac (Gen. 22:1-14; Heb. 11:19), he may more immediately be referring to the deadness of Abraham's body and Sarah's womb (v. 19). Elsewhere God is described as the **one who gives life** (*zōopoiein*), and it refers to his creative, sustaining, or renewing power (Neh. 9:6; Job 36:6; Eccl. 7:12; *Jos. Asen.* 8:9; John 6:63; 2 Cor. 3:6; Gal. 3:21; Dunn, 217). **Who ... calls into being that which does not exist.** God's work at creation was said to be out of nothing (Latin, *creation ex nihilo*; 2 Macc. 7:28; *Jos. Asen.* 12:2; 2 *Bar.* 21:4; 48:8; 2 *Enoch* 24:2). Similarly, his creation was seen as "calling" things into being (Isa. 41:4; 48:13; *Wisd.* 11:25; Philo, *Special Laws* 4.187; 2 *Bar.* 21:4). A text from *Joseph and Aseneth* clearly describes God in this role: "Lord, God of my father Israel, the Powerful One of Jacob, who gave life to all (things) and called (them) from darkness into light, and from error to truth, and from death to life" (*Jos. Asen.* 8:9 OTP).

4:20. He did not waver in unbelief, but grew strong in faith, giving glory to God. Though originally seen as unbelief, Abraham's laughter at the announcement of Sarah's future pregnancy was later viewed as an expression of great joy (*Jub.* 16:19). Paul also describes it as giving glory to God (cf. 1 Sam. 6:5; 1 Chron. 16:28).

4:21. He was able also to perform. Paul is referring to Gen. 18:14, where God says to Abraham, "Is anything too difficult for the LORD? At the appointed time I will return to you, at this time next year, and Sarah shall have a son." Paul is also drawing from a longstanding tradition that God is able to do all things (Philo, *Dreams* 2.136; *Jos.* 244; *Special Laws* 1.282), and certainly caused this miraculous birth (Philo, *Abraham* 112; *Quest. Gen.* 3.2, 56; Dunn, 221).

4:25. He who was delivered up because of our transgressions, and was raised because of our justification. Here Paul alludes to Isa. 53:4-5, 11-12 and reveals the vicarious character of Christ's suffering in his role as the Servant of the Lord who takes away human sin and achieves justification for human beings (Fitzmyer, 389).

D. 5:1-21. Implications for Individuals and All Humanity

5:1. Having been justified (*dikaiōthentes*) denotes God's acceptance into that relationship and status which Abraham enjoyed as "the friend of God," and which God will acknowledge and vindicate in the final judgment (v. 2; Dunn, 246). **Peace with God** was inextricably related to a covenant relationship with him (Num. 6:22-27; Ps. 55:18-19; Isa. 48:17-22; Jer. 14:19-21; *Sir.* 47:13; *2 Macc.* 1:2-4), and a covenant of peace was particularly associated with the priesthood and zealousness of Phinehas (Num. 25:12; Mal. 2:4-5; *Sir.* 45:24; Dunn, 247). Such peace was thought to be an end-time phenomenon (Isa. 9:6-7; 54:10; Ezek. 34:25-31; 37:26; Mic 5:4; Hag. 2:9; Zech. 8:12; *1 Enoch* 5:7, 9; 10:17; 11:2), suggesting Paul had in mind that Israel's eschatological hope had dawned and is available only **through our Lord Jesus Christ**. On **peace** see comment on 1:7.

5:2. We have obtained our introduction. Introduction (*prosagōgē*) is better translated "access" (cf. Eph. 2:18), and was granted to those permitted an audience with a king (Xenophon, *Cyropaedia* 1.3.8; 7.5.45). The term points to the solemn, though unhindered, approach to a deity (cf. *Odes Sol.* 7:3; 1QS 11:13-15). **Grace in which we stand** is a sphere or dimension marked out and characterized by God's grace (1QH 4:21-22; 7:30-31; Dunn, 248).

5:3. We also exult in our tribulations, knowing that tribulation brings about perseverance. Discipline in Judaism was valued in wisdom traditions for the fruit of character it produces (Prov. 3:11-12; Philo, *Cong.* 31; *Sir.* 2:4-5; *Wisd.* 3:4-7; *Pss. Sol.* 10:1-2; 1QH 9:24-25; *2 Bar.* 52:6), as it is also in Christianity (Jas. 1:2-4; 1 Peter 1:6-7).

5:4. Perseverance, proven character is a common theme in Jewish wisdom literature (Job 23:10; Prov. 8:10; 17:3; *Sir.* 2:5; *Wisd.* 3:6; cf. *Jub.* 19:8; *T. Jos.* 2:7; *4 Macc.* 9:7-8; 17:12).

5:5. Hope does not disappoint. This phrase echoes a recurring theme in the Psalms (22:5; 25:2-3; 31:1; 71:1; 119:31), always related to a

hope based on God and the deliverance He alone can provide. **Holy Spirit who was given to us.** In the Old Testament God's people commonly believed the outpouring of the Holy Spirit would occur as a mark of the new age (Isa. 32:15; 34:16; 44:3; Ezek. 11:19; 36:26-27; 37:4-14; Joel 2:28-32; cf. 1QH 7:6-7).

5:7. For one will hardly die for a righteous man; though perhaps for the good man someone would dare even to die. The possibility of someone being willing to die for another was certainly entertained elsewhere at the time (*T. Ash.* 2:3; Epictetus, *Disc.* 2.7.3; Philostratus, *Vita Apol.* 7.12; Dunn, 256), though it frequently depended on the worthiness of the one for whom such a sacrifice was made.

5:8. But God demonstrates His own love toward us, in that while we were yet sinners, Christ died for us. Pelagius said of this verse, "God becomes the object of love when he conveys how much he loves us. For when someone does something without obligation, one demonstrates love in a special way. And what would be less of an obligation than that a mas-

---

Justification in the Last Day

"He will gather a holy people whom he will lead in righteousness; and he will judge the tribes of the people that have been made holy by the Lord their God. He will not tolerate unrighteousness (even) to pause among them, and any person who knows wickedness shall not live with them. For he shall know them that they are all children of their God. He will distribute them among the land according to their tribes; the alien and the foreigner will no longer live near them. He will judge peoples and nations in the wisdom of his righteousness."

Psalms of Solomon 17.26-29 OTP

ter who is without sin should die for his faithless servants, and that the Creator of the universe should be hanged for the sake of his own creatures? Note that when the apostle says that believers in Christ were once sinners he means that now they are no longer sinners, so that they may recall how they ought to behave" (*Commentary on Romans* ACCS).

5:9. Much more then, having now been justified by His blood. Jews typically believed that one would be justified only in the last day (*Pss. Sol.* 17.26-29). **We shall be saved from the wrath of God through Him.** The righteous in Jewish thought typically looked forward to salvation (*Sir.* 34.13; *Wisd.* 5:2; *1 Enoch* 1:1; 5.6; *T. Naph.* 8:3; 1QpHab 8:1-3).

5:10. For if while we were enemies, we were reconciled to God through the death of His Son, much more, having been reconciled, we shall be saved by His life. Reconciled (*katallassō*) is rarely used in religious texts, perhaps reflecting the less personal conception of the relationship between the gods and men among the Greco-Roman religions. Yet in Judaism, God is thought of in much more personal terms (Josephus, *Ant.* 3.15.2 §315; 6.7.4 §143; 7.7.3 §153, 7.12.1 §295; Philo, *Rewards* 166). Such reconciliation from divine wrath through someone's death is found in later Jewish texts (*2 Macc.* 5:20; 7:33-38; 8:3-5). Mediators who diverted God's wrath included Moses (Ps. 106:23; Josephus, *Ant.* 3.15.2 §315), Aaron (*Wisd.* 18:20-25), and Phinehas (*Sir.* 45:23). The term is used in a later Greek papyrus for the reconciliation sought from a parent estranged from a child (*POxy* 12.1477.6).

5:12. Therefore, just as through one man sin entered into the world, and death through sin, and so death spread to all men, because all sinned. One man. The word for "man" in Hebrew (Gen. 1:26) is "Adam." This may suggest Adam's representative significance for all

humanity (Moo, 319). Jews in particular had a strong notion of "corporate solidarity," that is, people were bound together in various relationships and the deeds of one are representative of the whole. For example, when Achan withheld some of the plunder from the battle of Jericho (Josh. 7:1, 11), his offense was called "Israel's sin" and the cause of God's wrath against the whole community (Josh. 5:1). **Sin entered into the world.** Some Jews believed that "through the devil's envy death entered the world" (*Wisd.* 2:24), or placed the blame on Eve (*Sir.* 25:24). Many believed Adam was responsible for bringing sin into the world. Some rabbis suggest God told Moses "you are to die because of the sin of the first man who brought death into the world" (*Deut. Rab.* 9.8 [on Deut. 31:14]). Others held Adam was not the cause of original sin (*2 Bar.* 54:19), but each person is "his own Adam" (cf. *LAE Apoc.* 14:2).

5:13. Until the Law sin was in the world; but sin is not imputed when there is no law. Paul draws on the idea of heavenly record-keeping of sin already current in Judaism (*Jub.* 30:17-23; *1 Enoch* 104:7; *2 Bar.* 24:1; Dunn, 274).

5:14. Death reigned. Reigned (*basileuō*) means to reign as king (Homer, *Illiad* 2.203; *Odyssea* 2.47; Herodotus, *Histories* 2.173; *POxy* 4.654.8) and denotes the ruler's dominance and lordship. **Adam, who is a type of Him who was to come. Type** (*tupos*) originally meant a mark left by a blow, but came to mean a pattern or example (cf. *PTebt.* 2.342.25; *PLond.* 1122b.3).

5:17. For if by the transgression of the one, death reigned through the one, much more those who receive the abundance of grace and of the gift of righteousness will reign in life through the One, Jesus Christ. The expectation that the faithful would exercise kingly rule in the coming age was a characteristic feature of Jewish hope (Dan. 7:22, 27; *Wisd.* 3:8; 5:15-16; 1QM 12:14-15; Dunn, 282; cf. *LAE Apoc.* 14:2).

IV. 6:1–8:39. THE PROBLEMS OF SIN, THE LAW, AND DEATH

A. 6:1-23. The Problem of Sin

6:3. Or do you not know that all of us who have been baptized into Christ Jesus have been baptized into His death? Though a very difficult text, later rabbis believed that being "washed in the name of" someone signified being bound to that person in whose name one was washed (*b. Yebam.* 45b).

6:4. Walk in newness of life. Walk (*parapateō*) is a metaphorical expression for moral and ethical behavior. In the Old Testament King Hezekiah prayed, "Remember now, O LORD, I beseech Thee, how I have walked before Thee in truth and with a whole heart, and have done what is good in Thy sight" (2 Kings 20:3). Later Jewish laws and traditions called *Halakah* (based on the Hebrew word *hlk*, meaning "to walk") governed daily life (cf. 1 John 2:6; 2 John 6; 3 John 3).

6:5. United with Him. United (*symphyō*) can mean to grow together and was used of the healing of edges of a wound or the broken ends of a bone (Hippocrates, *Aph.* 6.24; *Art* 14; Soranus, 2.57).

6:7. He who has died is freed from sin. Some rabbis believed that only when one is dead is he free from fulfilling the Law (*b. Shab.* 151b; *Sipre Num.* 112 [on Num. 15:31]; cf. *Sir.* 26:29; *T. Sim.* 6:1).

6:9. Death no longer is master over Him. *Mekilta*, on Exod. 20:9, claims R. Jose (ca. 150) said, "The Israelites stood on Mount Sinai (and accepted the Torah) on condition that the angel of death should not exercise lordship over them" (Dunn, 323; cf. *Exod. Rab.* 51.8 [on Exod. 38:21]).

6:10. He lives to God is an expression of devo-tion and obedience. *Fourth Macc.* says, "Only those who with all their heart make piety their first concern are able to conquer the passions of the flesh, believing that to God they do not die, as our patriarchs Abraham, Isaac, and Jacob died not, but live to God" (7:19 OTP).

6:16. Do you not know that when you present yourselves to someone as slaves for obedience, you are slaves of the one whom you obey, either of sin resulting in death, or of obedience resulting in righteousness? Slavery was one of the most well-known institutions in ancient Rome, with between 35 and 40 percent of the population of Rome and the Italian peninsula comprised of slaves. People could sell themselves into slavery for a variety of reasons, including to pay off a debt (Moo, 398-400). See Introduction to Phile.

6:23. For the wages of sin is death, but the free gift of God is eternal life in Christ Jesus our Lord. Wages (*opsōnion*) originally was used of a soldier's subsistence pay or ration of money (1 Esdr. 4:56; *1 Macc.* 3:28; 14:32), but could be used for any type of salary, wage, or allowance (Dunn, 349; cf. *POxy* 3.531; *BGU* 1.69.8; *OGIS* 266.7).

B. 7:1-25. The Problem of the Law

7:1. The Law has jurisdiction. Jurisdiction (*kurieyein*) is the same verb used in 6:9 and 14 of the reign of death and sin.

7:2. Married woman (*hypandros gynē*) literally means "a woman under (her) husband" and is an attested way of referring to a married woman (Polybius, *History* 10.26.3; Artemidorus, 1.78 [74.6]; Num. 5:20; Prov. 6:24; *Sir.* 9:9; 41:23). **If her husband dies, she is released from the law concerning the husband.** Rabbis believed that a woman acquires such freedom either by divorce or by her husband's death (*m. Qidd.* 1.1; *b. Shabb.* 30a).

7:3. So then if, while her husband is living, she is joined to another man, she shall be called an adulteress; but if her husband dies, she is free from the law, so that she is not an adulteress, though she is joined to another man. Because a woman is bound to her husband, any extramarital sexual act of hers was regarded as adultery (Exod. 20:14, 17; 21:22; Lev. 20:10; Num. 30:10-16; Deut. 22:22). Prophets in Judaism frequently used marriage as a description for the relationship between Israel and her covenant God (Isa. 54:5-6; 62:4-5; Jer. 2:2; Ezek. 16:7-8; Hos. 1:2; 2:19; Dunn, 362).

7:5. Flesh (*sarx*) does not simply refer to one's physical existence, but is a metaphor for the sinful tendency that reigns in unregenerate people. Paul likely derives this concept from the Hebrew word in the Old Testament, *basar*, which denotes human beings in their weakness, frailty, and proneness to sin (Gen. 6:3, 12; Ps. 78:39; cf. 1QS 11:7; 1QM 4:3; 1QH 4:29-30; 7:17; 9:16). The Qumran "War Scroll" says, "From God is the hand of battle against all degenerate flesh . . . " (1QM 4:3-4).

7:6. Released. The term is used in ancient papyri to mean "render ineffective" (*POxy* 1.38.17; *PFlor* 2.176.7). **We serve in newness of the Spirit and not in oldness of the letter.** This phrase is thought to recall the prophetic promises of Jeremiah 31:31-34 and Ezekiel 36:26-27.

7:7. What shall we say then? Is the Law sin? May it never be! On the contrary, I would not have come to know sin except through the Law; for I would not have known about coveting if the Law had not said, "You shall not covet." Many Jews believed the Law was present even before Adam and creation itself (*Tg. Yer.* Gen. 3:24; *Pal. Hag.* 2.77c; *Gen. Rab.* 8.2 [on Gen. 1:26]), and the commandment he received not to eat of the fruit (Gen. 2:17) could not be seen as an isolated rule but as an expression of the Torah, and in breaking it Adam could be said to have broken the statutes of God (cf. *4 Ezra* 7.11; *Tg. Neof.* Gen. 2:15; *Gen. Rab.* 16.5 [on Gen. 2:15]; *Gen. Rab.* 16.6 [on Gen. 2:16]; 24.5 [on Job 28:27]; *Deut. Rab.* 2.25 [on Deut. 4:41]; *b. Sanh.* 56b). The quotation is from the tenth commandment in Exod. 20:17 (cf. Deut. 5:21; *4 Macc.* 2.5). The influence of Stoicism led to the belief that desire as such was regarded as something sinful because of its impulsive and non-rational character (cf. *4 Macc.* 1:3, 31-32; 2:1-6; 3:2; Philo, *Allegorical Interpretation* 3.15; *Post.* 26; Dunn, 379). Many Jews held that wrong desire, lust, or covetousness was the root of all sin (Philo, *Opif.* 152; *Decal* 142, 150, 153, 173; *Special Laws* 4.84-85). A Jewish legend

---

The New Covenant in the Old Testament

"'Behold, days are coming,' declares the LORD, 'when I will make a new covenant with the house of Israel and with the house of Judah, not like the covenant which I made with their fathers in the day I took them by the hand to bring them out of the land of Egypt, My covenant which they broke, although I was a husband to them,' declares the LORD. 'But this is the covenant which I will make with the house of Israel after those days,' declares the LORD, 'I will put My law within them, and on their heart I will write it; and I will be their God, and they shall be My people. And they shall not teach again, each man his neighbor and each man his brother, saying, "Know the LORD," for they shall all know Me, from the least of them to the greatest of them,' declares the LORD, 'for I will forgive their iniquity, and their sin I will remember no more.'"

Jeremiah 31:31-34

says that Eve attributed her failure to "lust, the root and beginning of every sin" (*Apoc. Moses* 19:3; cf. *Apoc. Abraham* 24:10).

7:10. This commandment, which was to result in life, proved to result in death for me. Jews widely believed that the Law and its commandments promoted life (Lev. 18:5; Deut. 6:24; Prov. 6:23; *Sir.* 17:1; 45:; *Pss. Sol.* 14:2; *4 Ezra* 14:30; *m. 'Abot* 2:7).

7:11. for sin, taking opportunity through the commandment, deceived me, and through it killed me. *Tg. Ps.-Jonathan* interprets Genesis 2:15 to mean that God put Adam in the Garden to observe the law's commandments (cf. Theophilos of Antioch, *Ad. Autolycum* 2.24; Ambrose, *De Paradiso* 4; Fitzmyer, 468).

7:14. For we know that the Law is spiritual; but I am of flesh, sold into bondage to sin. Bondage (*pepramenos*) resonates with the words from Isa. 50:1: "Thus says the LORD, 'Where is the certificate of divorce, By which I have sent your mother away? Or to whom of My creditors did I sell you? Behold, you were sold for your iniquities, And for your transgressions your mother was sent away.'" 11QPs[a] says, "To death I belonged because of my sins, and my iniquities sold me to Sheol" (cf. 4Q405 1-2 ii:15; Fitzmyer, 474). Bondage (*pepramenos*) was also used as being "sold to do evil" (1 Kings 21:25; 3 Kings 17:17; *1 Macc.* 1:15). The term is used in commercial correspondences for the sale of a product (*PPar* 59.4; *POxy* 14.1672.3; *BGU* 4.1079.16).

7:15. For that which I am doing, I do not understand; for I am not practicing what I would like to do, but I am doing the very thing I hate. Such was not an uncommon complaint among Greek philosophers. Ovid says, "I see the better and approve it, but I follow the words" (*Metamorphoses* 7.20-21; cf. Epictetus, *Diss.* 2.26.4; Dunn, 389). The Qumran sectari-

ans explained the same inner conflict by maintaining that God had put two spirits in human beings to rule until the time of his visitation, a "spirit of truth" and a "spirit of perversity," and they were in conflict (1QS 3:15-4:26; Fitzmyer, 475).

7:17. Sin which indwells me. Indwells (*oikeō*) means simply to live in or inhabit (*PTebt* 1.6.40; *POxy* 8.1101.24; *OGIS* 8.124). Some rabbis believed "the Evil Inclination has sway over" people (*b. Sukkah* 52a).

7:19. For the good that I wish, I do not do; but I practice the very evil that I do not wish. *Fourth Ezra* says, " . . . the first Adam, burdened with an evil heart, transgressed and was overcome, as were also all who were descended from him. Thus the disease became permanent; the law was in the people's heart along with the evil root, but what was good departed, and the evil remained" (3:21-22 OTP).

7:23. I see a different law in the members of my body, waging war against the law of my mind, and making me a prisoner of the law of sin which is in my members. A contrast between God's law and an evil law is found in the *Testament of Naphtali*: "As a person's . . . soul, so also is his thought, whether on the Law of the Lord or the law of Beliar" (2:6 OTP).

7:24. Wretched man that I am! Who will set me free from the body of this death? Wretched (*talaipōros*) can also mean "suffering" or "miserable" (Aeschylus, *Prometheus Vinctus* 233; cf. *PPar* 63.132; *PHamb.* 1.88.10). It is related to a term used several times in the Old Testament to refer to the lot of the wicked in God's judgment (Isa. 47:11; Jer. 6:7). Such wretchedness was also attributed to the patriarch Joseph's wife Aseneth in her brokenness in the presence of her husband (*Jos. Asen.* 6:1-8; cf. 24:14).

C. 8:1-39. The Problem of Human Frailty and Death

8:1. There is therefore now no condemnation for those who are in Christ Jesus. Condemnation (*katakrima*) means the same as "curse" (Gal. 3:10) and is derived from Deut. 27:26: "cursed be the one who fails to fulfill the provisions of this law" (cf. Deut. 28:58-61; Fitzmyer, 461). Such a curse was leveled by the Law itself on those who were subject to it (Fitzmyer, 482). It was used in ancient Greek to refer to the sentence of death being passed upon someone (Herodotus, *Histories* 6.85; 7.146; Xenophon, *Apology* 7; cf. *POxy* 2.298.4; *PTebt* 2.298.65).

8:2. Spirit of life. Jews commonly held that man's breath and life were entirely dependent on the Creator (cf. Gen. 6:17; Ps. 104:29-30; Ezek. 37:5; Tobit 3:6; 2 Macc. 7:23). **Set you free** (*eleutheros*) is an expression frequently used in ancient papyri for the setting free of slaves (*POxy* 3.494.16; *BGU* 2.388.1.16). Paul uses the sense of liberation which the revelation of Christ Jesus brought to him in his understanding of the covenant purpose of God (cf. 2 Cor. 3:17; Dunn, 418).

8:3. For what the Law could not do, weak as it was through the flesh, God did: sending His own Son in the likeness of sinful flesh and as an offering for sin, He condemned sin in the flesh. For sin occurs frequently in the LXX in reference to the sin offering, the sacrifice whereby God dealt with sin on a day-to-day basis and which together with the scapegoat provided the centerpiece of the Day of Atonement (Lev. 16; cf. Lev. 4:24; 5:11; 6:18; Ps. 40:6; Dunn, 439). Hellenistic Greeks similarly had gods who sent messengers or heralds on certain missions (Epictetus, *Diss.* 3.23; Plutarch, *De Alexandri Magni fortuna* 1.6 §329c; cf. Gen. 24:40; Judges 9:23; Isa. 6:8; Ezek. 2:3; *Wisd.* 9:10). Qumran sectarians confessed, "I belong to wicked humanity and to the company of iniquitous flesh" (1QS 11:9; cf. 1QM 4:3; Fitzmyer, 485).

8:4. Requirement. The Greek term here is singular, bringing out the fact that the law's requirements are essentially a unity (Lev. 19:18; Deut. 6:4; Mic 6:8; Cranfield 384). **Fulfilled in us** seems to refer to the final accomplishment of the promises of the new covenant outlined in Jeremiah 31:31-34 (cf. Ezek. 36:26). **Walk.** See comment on 6:4.

8:5. Set their minds on . . . can also mean to "be on someone's side" or "to be of someone's party." Thus Paul uses it to show which "side," that **of the flesh** or that **of the Spirit**, one is on (cf. Herodotus, *Histories* 2.162.6; 7.102.2; Sophocles, *Ajax* 491; Aristophanes, *Pax* 640; Xenophon, *Hell.* 6.3.4; 1 Macc. 10:20; Josephus, *Ant.* 14.15.10 §450).

8:7. Hostile toward God. Hostility in general was thought to be destructive in wisdom traditions (Prov. 10:12), while sin, particularly idolatry, was portrayed as an act of aggression toward God (Ezek. 20:7-49). Rabbis cited the Ezek. 20 text to support their notion that, "The hatred which Israel caused between themselves and their Father who is in Heaven, stirred up against them punishments upon punishments, as R. Samuel b. Nah?man said: For nearly nine hundred years was the hatred between Israel and their Father who is in Heaven in abeyance—from the day on which they went forth from Egypt until it became roused against them in the days of Ezekiel" (*Lev. Rab.* 7.1 [on Lev. 6:1]).

8:11. But if the Spirit of Him who raised Jesus from the dead dwells in you, He who raised Christ Jesus from the dead will also give life to your mortal bodies through His Spirit who indwells you. Some rabbis held that Bezalel, the craftsman who created the tabernacle, merited the Spirit to indwell him for his task by virtue of his relationship to Miriam. Others suggested the Spirit filled Joshua because he was filled with "the spirit of wisdom" (Deut. 34:9). Many believed that the same Spirit that imparted wisdom to these also imparted life (*Exod. Rab.* 48.4 [on Exod. 35:1]).

8:14. Sons of God. Stoics spoke of Zeus as the father of all (cf. Acts 17:28). The expression is used in the Old Testament particularly to denote elect ones (cf. Deut. 14:1).

8:15. Spirit of slavery may recall the usage in the Old Testament (Judges 9:23; 1 Sam. 16:14-16; 1 Kings 22:19-23), where it is used to show that in giving his people the Spirit, God was not working for their downfall (cf. Rom. 11:8; Dunn, 451). It may also be an expression for a force opposed to God, such as the spirit of falsehood, fornication, or jealousy (cf. 1QS 3:18; *T. Reub.* 5:3; *T. Sim.* 2:7; 3:1; 4:7; *T. Levi* 2:3; 9:9; 18:7; *T. Jud.* 13:3; 20:1). **You have received a spirit of adoption as sons.** In rabbinic literature there is no example of the Holy Spirit being brought into connection with the prayer of an Israelite (Dunn, 453). A very rare expression, **adoption as sons** (*huiothesia*) may reflect civic legal adoption. Normally a childless adult would adopt a male child to be his heir. The term is found in a second-century B.C. inscription and first-century B.C. writings of Diodorus Siculus and Nicolaus Damascenus in this respect (cf. *POxy* 3271). 2 Sam. 7:14 suggests the Messiah will be **adopted** as a son, while later Jewish tradition would extend that adoption to sonship to God's people as well (cf. *Jub.* 1:24; *T. Judah* 24:3; 4QFlor 1:11). For Paul, however, the Holy Spirit was the agent of adoption of believers (cf. Gal. 4:4). **Adoption** (*huiothesia*) is a Christian adaptation of the Old Testament idea of God's election of Israel as his chosen people (Fitzmyer, 497). Deut. 4:34 says, "Or has a god tried to go to take for himself a nation from within another nation by trials, by signs and wonders and by war and by a mighty

hand and by an outstretched arm and by great terrors, as the LORD your God did for you in Egypt before your eyes?" Thus, Israel is called God's "firstborn" (Exod. 4:22; cf. Isa. 1:2; Jer. 3:19-22; 31:9; Hos. 11:1). **We cry out** (*krazein*) is used frequently in the LXX to denote urgent prayer, particularly in the Psalms (cf. Pss. 3:4; 4:3; 18:6; 22:2; 34:6; Gal. 4:6). **"Abba! Father!" Abba** is a transliteration of the Aramaic word for "father," *abba*. The term was used by Jesus on the cross (Mark 14:36), and is unattested in the Old Testament. See comment on Mark 14:36 §202.

8:16. The Spirit Himself bears witness with our spirit that we are children of God. Bears witness with (*summartyrei*) is used in ancient papyri in legal contexts where the signature of each attesting witness is accompanied by the words, "I bear witness with and I seal with" (*BGU* 1.86.41; 2.600.6; *PSI* 6.696.5).

8:17. Heirs of God and fellow heirs with Christ. The Israelites were **heirs** of the Promised Land (Exod. 6:8; Num. 26:52ff; 36:1ff; Deut. 18:1-2; Josh. 12:7). Some Jewish writers saw the Law as Israel's inheritance (*Sir.* 24:23; *1 Enoch* 99:14), or even life or eternal life (*Pss. Sol.* 14.7; *1 Enoch* 40:9; cf. *2 Enoch* 50.2; *2 Bar.* 44:13). Israel was itself seen as a "chosen portion" among the nations (Deut. 9:29; 32:8-10; Zech. 2:12 [LXX v. 16]), as were the Qumran sectarians (1QS 2:2; 1QM 1:5; 13:5). In the NT "inheritance" is what was promised (cf. Heb. 11:8), and has been laid up for believers in heaven (1 Peter 1:4; Heb. 9:5; cf. LXX of 1 Sam. 14:41; *Letter to Diognetus* 5:4). According to legend, Joseph forgave his brothers' sins (Gen. 50:15-21) and made them "fellow heirs of all" his possessions (*Jos. Asen.* 24:14 OTP).

The Qumran sectarians believed the elect received a share in the property of angels (1QH 3:22; 6:3; Cf. 1QGenApoc 2:20-21). For Paul it was salvation in the future (Eph. 1:14, 18; 5:5), of which the Holy Spirit is a "down payment" in the present (2 Cor. 1:22; 5:5), and in which Gentiles are "fellow heirs" (Eph. 3:6). Cf. Matt. 21:38; 25:34; Mark 12:7; Luke 12:13; 20:14. See comment on Luke 15:11-32 (§173).

8:18. For I consider that the sufferings of this present time are not worthy to be compared with the glory that is to be revealed to us. Other Jews saw the struggles in the present life as a prelude to the glory in the life to come: "For this world is to them a struggle and an effort with much trouble. And that accordingly which will come, a crown with great glory" (2 *Baruch* 15:8 OTP; cf. Dan. 7:17-27; *Wisd.* 2:1-5.23; 2 *Macc.* 7:1-42; 1 *Enoch* 102:1—104:13; *Jub.* 23:22-31; 1QH 3:28-36; *Sib. Or.* 3:632-56).

8:19. For the anxious longing of the creation waits eagerly for the revealing of the sons of God. In the Old Testament Yahweh made a covenant between himself, Noah, "and every living creature" (Gen. 9:9-10). *Wisdom* 1:14 says, "For he created all things that they might exist, and the generative forces of the world are wholesome, and there is no destructive poison in them; and the dominion of Hades is not on earth." Though made for human beings (*Wisd.* 2:6), creation was cursed because of Adam's sin (Gen. 3:15-17). **Anxious longing** is a term that was used in military contexts to describe Josephus' awaiting a "hail of arrows" from his enemy (Josephus, *J.W.* 3.7.26 §264) or of a military commander awaiting the outcome of a battle (Polybius, *Histories* 16.2.8).

As Paul does here, so the Old Testament occasionally personifies creation, with hills, meadows, and valleys shouting for joy and singing (Ps. 65:12-13), and the earth itself as mourning (Isa. 24:4; Jer. 4:28; 12:4).

8:20. For the creation was subjected to futility, not of its own will, but because of Him who subjected it, in hope. Many Jews believed that creation was drawn into the consequences of Adam's failure (4 *Ezra* 7:11; *b. Sanh.* 108a).

8:21. The creation itself also will be set free from its slavery to corruption into the freedom of the glory of the children of God. Jewish writers held out hope for creation's renewal. A personified renewed creation is depicted in 1 *Enoch* 51:4-5: "In those days, mountains shall dance like rams; and the hills shall leap like kids satiated with milk. And the faces of all the angels in heaven shall glow with joy, because on that day the Elect One has arisen. And the earth shall rejoice; and the righteous ones shall dwell upon her and the elect ones shall walk upon her" (OTP; cf. Isa. 11:6-9; 65:17; 66:22; *Jub.* 1:29; 23:26-29; 1 *Enoch* 91:16-17; Philo, *Praem.* 88-90; *T. Levi* 18:10-11; *Sib. Or.* 3:788-95).

8:22. For we know that the whole creation groans and suffers the pains of childbirth together until now. This metaphor is drawn from several Old Testament texts (Isa. 26:17; 66:8; Jer. 4:31; Hos. 13:13; Mic 4:9), and is a natural expression of severe distress from which a positive and worthy outcome is expected (1QH 3:7-18; 1 *Enoch* 62:4; 4 *Ezra* 10:6-16). (cf. John 16:20b-22; Matt. 24:8). See comment on Mark 13:8 §186.

8:23. First fruits of the Spirit. First fruits was typically associated with the feast of Pentecost, which was the celebration of the first fruits of the annual harvest in the Jewish calendar (Exod. 23:16; 34:22; Deut. 16:9-12; Philo, *Special Laws* 2.179). The association of this feast with the outpouring of the Spirit was already established early in Christian memory (Acts 2:1-47; Dunn, 473).

8:26. And in the same way the Spirit also helps our weakness; for we do not know how to pray as we should, but the Spirit Himself intercedes for us with groanings too deep for words. The Spirit . . . helps. The word for **helps** (*sunantilambanetai*) occurs in the LXX with respect to the seventy elders appointed by

Moses to help decide civil disputes (Exod. 18:22; Num. 11:17). The idea is one of taking part in responsibility or sharing the weight or burden of a task. Though the Greek prefix *sun* typically means "together with," here it functions as an intensive emphasizing the degree of help provided by the Spirit (Cranfield, 425). **The Spirit Himself intercedes.** Such intercession in the Old Testament was ascribed to Abraham (Gen. 18:23-33), Moses (Exod. 8:8), priests (Lev. 16:21-22; Num. 6:23-27), kings (2 Sam. 12:16), prophets (1 Kings 18:22-40), angels (Tobit 12:12; cf. *T. Levi* 3:5), and upright persons in the afterlife (2 *Macc.* 15.12-16; *As. Moses* 11:14-17).

8:27. He who searches the hearts knows what the mind of the Spirit is. Jews typically saw God as one who knows the hearts of individuals (1 Sam. 16:7; 1 Kings 8:39; Pss. 44:21; 139:1-2; Prov. 15:11), while the Spirit is naturally conceived as the searching presence of God (Ps. 139:1-24; *Wisd.* 1:7). **He intercedes for the saints according to the will of God. Intercedes** (*entungchan?*) is sometimes used as a legal term meaning "appeal" in ancient Greek papyri (*PTebt.* 1.58.43; *POxy* 12.1502.3; *BGU* 1.246.12).

8:28. And we know that God causes all things to work together for good to those who love God, to those who are called according to His purpose. Loving God was a pillar of Old Testament faith (Exod. 20:6; Deut. 5:10), which remained essential to Judaism in Paul's day (cf. Deut. 6:5; 7:9; 10:12; Pss. 31:24; 97:10; *Sir.* 1:10; 2:15-16; 47:22). **God causes all things to work together** is seen by some as an expression of God's cooperation in bringing good things to his people (*T. Reub.* 3:6; *T. Issach.* 3:7; *T. Gad* 4:7; Jas. 2:22). **For good.** Sirach says, "From the beginning good things were created for good people, just as evil things for sinners. Basic to all the needs of man's life are water and fire and iron and salt and wheat flour and milk and honey, the blood of the grape, and oil and clothing. All these are for good to the godly, just as

they turn into evils for sinners" (39:25-27). Jews clearly thought of God's purpose as moving history itself as well as through history to its intended end (cf. Ps. 33:11; Prov. 19:21; Jer. 49:20; *Wisd.* 6:4; 1QS 1:8; 2:23; 1QH 4:13; Dunn, 482).

8:29. For whom He foreknew. The Hebrew sense of knowledge among persons involves a relationship experienced and acknowledged (Gen. 18:19; Jer. 1:5; Hos. 13:5; 1QH 9:29-30). **He also predestined to become conformed to the image of His Son.** The **image** here seems to have Adam in mind, a man created in the **image** (*eik?n*) of God (Gen. 1:26-27; cf. *Sir.* 17:3; *Wisd.* 2:23; *T. Naph* 2:5; *Apoc. Mos.* 10:3). For Paul, Christ is the image of God that Adam was intended to be (Dunn, 483).

8:30. Whom He predestined, these He also called; and whom He called, these He also justified; and whom He justified, these He also glorified. Those who are **called** by God were his elect (1QM 3:2; 4:10-11; cf. 1QpHab 10:13).

8:31. What then shall we say to these things? If God is for us, who is against us? Paul seems to be dependent on Ps. 23:4 and 56:9: The former emphasizes the presence of God: "Even though I walk through the valley of the shadow of death, I fear no evil; for Thou art with me; Thy rod and Thy staff, they comfort me," while the latter stresses his protection: "Then my enemies will turn back in the day when I call; This I know, that God is for me."

8:32. He who did not spare His own Son, but delivered Him up for us all, how will He not also with Him freely give us all things? Delivered Him up (*paradidonai*) seems to be an expression of judgment, as Paul uses it elsewhere (1:24, 26, 28) to connote the fate of idolatrous people as a consequence of sin. Christ has vicariously taken the sins of his people (2 Cor. 5:21). Though this reminds one of Abraham's sacrifice of Isaac (Gen. 22), the latter was not understood in a sacrificial sense by early Judaism (cf. *4 Macc.* 7:14; 13:12; 16:20; 18:11; *Jub.* 17:15—18:19; Josephus, *Ant.* 1.13.1-4 §§222-36). It does not seem to have been so understood in Judaism until well after the second century A.D. (cf. *Gen. Rab* 56.8-10 [on Gen. 22:14]).

8:33. Who will bring a charge against God's elect? God is the one who justifies. This may be an allusion to Isa. 50:8-9: "He who vindicates Me is near; Who will contend with Me? Let us stand up to each other; Who has a case against Me? Let him draw near to Me. Behold, the Lord God helps Me; Who is he who condemns Me? Behold, they will all wear out like a garment; The moth will eat them" (cf. 1 Chron. 16:13; Pss. 89:3; 105:6; Isa. 42:1; 45:4; 65:9; *Sir.* 46:1; 47:22; *Wisd.* 3:9; *Jub.* 1:29; *1 Enoch* 5:7-8; CD 4:3-4; 1QM 12:1). **Bring charge** (*enkalesei*) is a legal term for the formal process of laying charges against someone (cf. Prov. 19:5; *Wisd.* 12:12; *Sir.* 46:19; Acts 19:38; 23:28).

8:34. Christ Jesus . . . who is at the right hand of God. The position of Christ **at the right hand of God** is from Ps. 110:1, which is frequently used in the New Testament to denote the high position of Christ (cf. Mark 12:36; Acts 2:34-35; Heb. 1:13). The **right hand** denotes power (Exod. 15:6, 12; Deut. 33:2; Job 40:9; Pss. 17:7; 18:35; *Pss. Sol.* 13:1; Josephus, *J.W.* 1.19.4 §378), and is considered a seat of special honor (1 Kings 2:19; Ps. 45:9; Acts 2:33; 5:31; 7:55-56; Dunn, 503). **Who also intercedes for us.** Intercession was largely attributed to angels in Jewish thought (cf. *1 Enoch* 13.4), or to Adam (*T. Abraham* 11; cf. Job 42:8-10; Isa. 53:12; *T. Benj.* 3:6-8).

8:35. Nakedness was a term naturally associated with human depravity (*T. Zeb.* 7.1; Matt. 25:35-36; 2 Cor. 11:27; Jas. 2:15). Other lists of such tribulations appear in Jewish literature, particularly in eschatological contexts (*Jub.* 23:23; *1 Enoch* 103:8-15; *Pss. Sol.* 15:7; cf. *2 Enoch* 66:6; *Odes. Sol.* 28:5).

Augustine on Assurance

"Paul says he is sure, not merely that he is of the opinion . . . that neither death nor the promise of temporal life nor any of the other things he lists can separate the believer from God's love. No one can separate the believer from God; not someone who threatens death, because he who believes in Christ shall live even if he dies, nor someone who offers earthly life, because Christ gives us eternal life. An angel cannot separate us, because *if an angel comes down from heaven and tells you something other than what you receive, let him be anathema* (Gal. 1:8). Nor can a principality, i.e., an opposing power, because Christ has . . . vanquished them in himself"

Augustine, *On Romans* 58 ACCS

8:36. Just as it is written, "For Thy sake we are being put to death all day long; We were considered as sheep to be slaughtered." Here Paul quotes Ps. 44:23, which was a psalm of community lament, bemoaning the injustice done to faithful Israel by its enemies, recalling its loyalty to Yahweh, and seeking his aid and deliverance. Paul's citation of this text shows that any difficulties suffered by the Roman Christians are typical of those endured by God's people in the past (Fitzmyer, 534). It was used by Jews to refer to the martyrdom during the Maccabean period, who died "for the sake of God's laws" (2 Macc. 7:9, 11; cf. *4 Ezra* 7:89; Dunn, 506), and by rabbis to denote the death of martyrs (*b. Git.* 57b; *Tg. Ps.* 44:23). Such tribulations were seen as necessary precursors to the new age (cf. Rom. 8:18; *1 Enoch* 103:9-15).

8:38-39. Angels (*angeloi*) is a general expression for heavenly beings, though normally conceived of as agents of heaven or intermediaries between heaven and earth (cf. Gal. 1:8; 4:14). It can refer to "good" angels (cf. Rom. 8:26; 2 Cor. 11:14; 2 Thess. 1:7), or hostile angels, typically associated with the beings of Gen. 6:1-4 (*1 Enoch* 6:1-8.4; *Jub.* 5:1; *T. Reub.* 5:6). Evil angels in Jewish apocalyptic thought were said to rule the nations (*Sirach* 17.18; *Jub.* 15.31-32; cf. Deut. 32:8; Dan. 10:13). **Powers** (*dynameis*) is a title for supernatural beings familiar in extra-biblical Greek literature (cf. 2 Kings 17:16; *4 Macc.* 5:13; Philo, *Conf.* 171; Matt. 24:29; Mark 14:62; Acts 8:10; Dunn, 507). See Eph. 3:18.

V. 9:1–11:36. THE PROBLEM OF ISRAEL

A. 9:1-5. Paul's Concern for Israel

9:2. I have great sorrow and unceasing grief in my heart. Sorrow and grief occur together in the Old Testament in Isa. 35:10 and 51:11, where such negative sentiments will "flee away" at the return of the Lord. Such laments were typical in Judaism, however, particularly in reference to the grief associated with the destruction of Jerusalem (cf. Jer. 4:19-22; 14:17; Dan. 9:3; *T. Jud.* 23:1; *2 Bar.* 10:5; 35:1-3).

9:3. For I could wish that I myself were accursed. Accursed (*anathema*) refers to something that is dedicated to God for destruction (Lev. 27:28; Deut. 7:26; 13:17), such as the episode of Achan's sin (Josh. 6:16-18). The term was later used by rabbis to refer to one who was excommunicated from the faith (*m. Sanh.* 2:1).

9:4. Israelites. Israel derives its name from Jacob, whose name was changed to Israel when he wrestled with God (Gen. 32:29). The name was first used to denote the united people of Yahweh (Judges 5:2, 7), but later designated the Northern Kingdom. After the deportation in the Assyrian Captivity (722 B.C.), it was applied to Judah, the Southern Kingdom (Mic. 3:1; Isa. 5:7), in the hope that a restored Israel might be realized. In postexilic

times it became the self-designation of the Jewish people aware of its status as the holy and chosen people of God (cf. Isa. 65:9; *Sir.* 17:18; *Jub.* 33:20; Fitzmyer, 545). **Adoption as sons.** See comment on Rom. 8:15. **The glory** (*doxa*) of Yahweh was seen at the crossing of the Red Sea (Exod. 15:6, 11), in the wilderness (Exod. 16:10; 40:34), and at the temple of Jerusalem (1 Kings 8:11; cf. 11QTemple 29:8). **Covenants** (*diathēkai*) refers to those made with Israel's ancestors: Abraham (Gen. 15:18; 17:2), Isaac (Gen. 26:3-5; Exod. 2:24), Moses (Exod. 24:7-8; *Sir.* 44:12), and David (2 Sam. 23:5). **The temple service** was instituted by Yahweh himself (Exod. 25-31; Josh. 22:27; 1 Chron. 28:13), and was markedly distinct from those of Israel's idolatrous neighbors. **The promises** made to Abraham (Gen. 12:2; 13:14-17; 15:4; 17:4-8; 21:12; 22:16-18), Isaac (Gen. 26:3-5), Jacob (28:13-14), Moses (Deut. 18:18-19), and David (2 Sam. 7:11-16) are still in effect and irrevocable to Paul (Rom. 11:29; Fitzmyer, 547).

B. God's Call of Israel (9:6-29)

9:6. They are not all Israel who are descended from Israel. There was a natural tendency for some Jews to regard descent from the patriarchs as a guarantee of salvation (cf. *m. Sanh.* 10:1; Justin, *Dial.* 140; *b. Qid.* 36a).

9:8. That is, it is not the children of the flesh who are children of God, but the children of the promise are regarded as descendants. Paul is not thinking of the general promise that Abraham would have many descendants (Gen. 15:5), but that the child born of Sarah would be his heir (Gen. 18:10, 14).

9:9. For this is a word of promise. "At this time I will come, and Sarah shall have a son." In this verse Paul combines Gen. 18:10 and 14, showing that God himself takes the initiative in the conception of Isaac.

9:11. God's purpose according to His choice

might stand. Purpose (*prothesis*) conveys a concept found in the Dead Sea Scrolls as "design" (Hebrew *mahahsabâ*): "From the God of knowledge stems all there is and all there shall be. Before they existed he established their entire design. And when they were come into being, at their appointed time, they will execute all their works according to his glorious design, without altering anything" (1QS 3:15-16a).

9:13. "Jacob I loved, but Esau I hated." This quotation is from Mal. 1:2-3, where **Jacob** and **Esau** are used to refer to the nations which they founded. **Loved** and **hated** in Malachi are covenantal terms, and rather than expressing either an emotion or bias, refer to God's covenant relationship with Jacob but not with Esau. **Esau** married Mahalath, the daughter of Ishmael (Gen. 28:9), and became the ancestor of Edom, and of the later Idumaeans (Josephus, *Ant.* 12.8.1 §328). The Idumeans were never really considered Jews, even though John Hyrcanus I defeated them (ca. 108 B.C.), and forced them to be circumcised and observe the Law of Moses. Josephus calls them "half Jews" (*Ant.* 13.9.1 §257; 14.15.2 §403).

9:15. For He says to Moses, "I will have mercy on whom I have mercy, and I will have compassion on whom I have compassion." Here Paul quotes Exod. 33:19, where Yahweh answers Moses after the incident of the golden calf (Exod. 32), when Moses pleaded with the Lord not to punish Israel.

9:16. The man who runs is an expression for human effort, taken from Greco-Roman athletics (Xenophon, *Anabasis* 7.3.45; Herodotus, *Histories* 8.102; cf. 1 Cor. 9:24, 26). **God who has mercy.** That God is merciful is a fixed point in Jewish theology (Isa. 49:10; *Sir.* 50:19; *T. Mos.* 12:7; 1QH 4:32; 6:9; Dunn, 553).

9:17. For the Scripture says to Pharaoh, "For this very purpose I raised you up, to demon- strate My power in you, and that My name might be proclaimed throughout the whole earth."** This text is taken from Exod. 9:16. **I raised you up** means to appoint to a significant role in God's salvation history (cf. Jer. 50:41; Hab. 1:6; Zech. 11:16). **My power** (*dynamis mou*) may refer to God's power as creator or, more probably, as savior. What is to **"be proclaimed throughout the whole earth"** is the Lord's championing and powerful defense of his people in situations where they are under threat from strong adversaries (Pss. 2:7; 59:13; 106:8; 2 *Macc.* 3:34; 1QH 2:24).

9:18. So then He has mercy on whom He desires, and He hardens whom He desires. In the Old Testament the hardening of Pharoah's heart is sometimes attributed to God (Exod. 4:21; 7:3; 9:12; 10:20; 14:8), and sometimes to Pharoah himself (Exod. 7:14; 8:11, 15, 28). The expression used with respect to God is a way of expressing divine reaction to persistent human obstinacy against him, a sealing of a situation arising, not from God, but from the one that

---

God as the Potter

"The word which came to Jeremiah from the Lord saying, Arise and go down to the potter's house, and there I shall announce My words to you. Then I went down to the potter's house, and there he was, making something on the wheel. But the vessel that he was making of clay was spoiled in the hand of the potter; so he remade it into another vessel, as it pleased the potter to make. Then the word of the Lord came to me saying, Can I not, O house of Israel, deal with you as this potter does? declares the Lord. Behold, like the clay in the potter's hand, so are you in My hand, O house of Israel."

Jeremiah 18:1-6

---

rejects his divine intention. It brings out God's utter control of human history (Fitzmyer, 568).

9:20-21. On the contrary, who are you, O man, who answers back to God? The thing molded will not say to the molder, "Why did you make me like this," will it? Again Paul quotes from the Old Testament, this time from Isa. 29:16, which itself may be an allusion to God's creation of man from the dust in Gen. 2:7. God as a potter was a common imagery for his work in creation (Ps. 2:9; Isa. 41:25; Jer. 18:1-6; *T. Naph.* 2:2; 1QS 11:22; 1QH 1:21; 4:29; 11:3). Such **mold**ing (*plassein*) is also used of God's election of Israel (Deut. 32:6; Isa. 43:1, 7; 44:2; Dunn, 557). Few household items were as common to the ancient world as a clay pot. The molding of it was commonly associated with God's work in believers: "As clay in the hand of the potter—for all his ways are as he pleases—so men are in the hand of him who

---

Augustine on the Potter's Vessel

"As long as you are a potter's vessel, you must first be broken by the iron rod of which it was said: *You will rule them with a rod of iron, and you will break them as a potter's vessel* (Ps. 2:9). Then, when the outer man is destroyed and the inner man is renewed, you will be able, rooted and grounded in love, to understand what is the length and breadth and height and depth, to know even the overwhelming knowledge of the love of God (Eph. 3:18). So because from the same lump of clay God has made some vessels for noble use and others for ignoble, it is not for you, whoever you are who still lives according to this lump (that is, who are wise by the standards of earthly sense and the flesh), to dispute what God decreed."

Augustine, *On Romans* 62 ACCS

---

made them, to give them as he decides" (*Sir.* 33:13).

9:22. What if God, although willing to demonstrate His wrath and to make His power known, endured with much patience vessels of wrath prepared for destruction? Vessel of wrath is taken from Jeremiah 50:25 and Isa. 13:5. It refers to one toward which wrath is displayed, a useless pot to be discarded (Fitzmyer, 569). Jews frequently thought such **patience** was afforded by God to the Gentiles to allow them time to become worshipers of Yahweh (2 *Macc.* 6:12-14; cf. *Pss. Sol.* 13:1-5; 4 *Ezra* 7:74; 1QH 15:14-20).

9:25. As He says also in Hosea, "I will call those who were not My people, 'My people,' And her who was not beloved, 'beloved.'" This verse is from Hos. 2:23, which was originally applied to the northern kingdom of Israel. The ten tribes were thrust out into the darkness, but their restoration was foretold by Hosea. Paul applies this verse to be inclusive of Gentiles.

9:26. "And it shall be that in the place where it was said to them, 'you are not My people,' There they shall be called sons of the living God." This is likewise taken from Hos. 2, but verse 1, and is thought by some to refer to an eschatological gathering of the nations at Jerusalem (Isa. 2:2-4; 60:1-22; Mic 4:1-3; Zech. 8:20-23).

9:27-28. And Isaiah cries. See comment on 8:15. **"Though the number of the sons of Israel be as the sand of the sea, it is the remnant that will be saved; for the Lord will execute His word upon the earth, thoroughly and quickly."** The quotation is from Isa. 10:22-23, which speaks of a remnant held during the Assyrian captivity, which Paul applies to Jews called to accept Christ (cf. 1QH 6:7-8; Fitzmyer, 574-75).

9:29. And just as Isaiah foretold, "Except the Lord of Sabaoth had left to us a posterity, We would have become as Sodom, and would have resembled Gomorrah." Again looking to Isa. (1:9), Paul now sees the remnant as what preserves Israel from becoming like the cursed cities destroyed by God (Gen. 19:24-25).

C. 9:30–10:21. Israel's Failure
9:30. Pursue. The Greek term can also mean to hasten or run after, and is an athletic term used of runners on a racecourse (Phil. 3:12; Sir. 11:10; 27:8; Lam. 1:13; OGIS 532.25; PGrenf 2.84.7).

9:33. As it is written, "Behold, I lay in Zion a stone of stumbling and a rock of offense, And he who believes in Him will not be disappointed." This is another mixed quotation, employing both Isa. 28:16 and 8:14. Paul begins with the "stone in Zion" imagery from Isa. 28:16, but turns to a negative portrayal of it as a "stumbling stone" from Isa. 8:14. He thus essentially shows Christ to be a "roadblock" in Israel's pursuit of the law of righteousness (Moo, 628-30). Such **stone** references in the Old Testament were frequently taken messianically (cf. Dan. 2:34). Qumran Jews understood Isa. 28:16 to refer to their own "council of the community" (1QS 8:7; cf. 1QH 6:26-27). The fact that God is the one who lays the **stone of stumbling** shows that for Paul God is behind Israel's fall (Dunn, 584; cf Sib. Or. 8:246).

10:1. Brethren, my heart's desire and my prayer to God for them is for their salvation. Paul stood in a noble tradition of the faithful who prayed for his own people Israel (Exod. 32:11-14; Num. 21:6-9; 1 Sam. 7:8-9; Ps. 99:6; Jer. 42:2-4; Ezek. 11:13; T. Mos. 11:17).

10:2. For I bear them witness that they have a zeal for God, but not in accordance with knowledge. Zeal (zēlos) in the mid-first century was for some a technical term for Jewish nationalism under oppressive Roman occupa-

tion. It hearkens back to Phinehas, whose "zeal for God" caused him to kill an Israelite man and his Midianite mistress, thus rescuing Israel from certain judgment (Num. 26:6-13). He was henceforth viewed as a hero among Israelites (Ps. 106:31; 1 Macc. 2:26; cf. 4 Macc. 18:12; Josephus, Ant. 4.6.12 §152-55; m. Sanh. 9:6; Sifre Num. §131). Zeal for the Law was particularly noble among Jews such as the Pharisees, Zealots, and Qumran sectarians (Josephus, Ant. 12.6.2 §271; Philo, Spec. Laws 1.30; 2.253; Abraham 60; T. Asher 4.5; 1QH 14:14).

10:3. For not knowing about God's righteousness, and seeking to establish their own, they did not subject themselves to the righteousness of God. Establish was a term used of God's establishing his covenants (Gen. 6:18; Exod. 6:4; Lev. 26:9; Deut. 8:18; Jer. 11:5; Sir. 17:12). That Paul writes of people who seek to establish their own ignores the warning of Deut. 9:4-6.

The Warning from God

"Do not say in your heart when the LORD your God has driven them out before you, 'Because of my righteousness the LORD has brought me in to possess this land,' but it is because of the wickedness of these nations that the LORD is dispossessing them before you. It is not for your righteousness or for the uprightness of your heart that you are going to possess their land, but it is because of the wickedness of these nations that the LORD your God is driving them out before you, in order to confirm the oath which the LORD swore to your fathers, to Abraham, Isaac and Jacob. Know, then, it is not because of your righteousness that the LORD your God is giving you this good land to possess, for you are a stubborn people."

Deuteronomy 9:4-6

10:4. For Christ is the end of the law for righteousness to everyone who believes. End (*telos*) means a goal, and is the first word of this sentence in Greek, emphasizing its importance. Paul shows Christ to be both the end and goal of the law, similar to the finish line of a race. Crossing the finish line is the goal and also signifies the end of the race.

10:5. For Moses writes that the man who practices the righteousness which is based on law shall live by that righteousness. Here Paul quotes Lev. 18:5, arguing that, according to Moses, the author of Leviticus, observance of the Torah's prescriptions is the way to life that God promised to his people (Fitzmyer, 589). This is not eternal life, but blessings in the Promised Land (Deut. 30:15, 19). Ezek. 20:13 says, "But the house of Israel rebelled against Me in the wilderness. They did not walk in My statutes, and they rejected My ordinances, by which, if a man observes them, he will live; and My sabbaths they greatly profaned. Then I resolved to pour out My wrath on them in the wilderness, to annihilate them" (cf. *2 Bar.* 67:6).

Romans 10 and the Aramaic Bible

Paul's allusion to Ps. 107:30 ("They rose up to the heavens, they went down to the depths") in his quotation and interpretation of Deut. 30:13 in Rom. 10:6-8 may have been encouraged by the Aramaic version of the Bible. In the Aramaic (i.e., Targum) Deut. 30:13 reads:

> The Law is not in heaven that one
> should say:
> *"Would that we had one like the*
> *prophet Moses*
> *who would ascend to heaven and*
> *fetch it for us*
> and make us hear the commandments
> that we might do them."
> Neither is the Law beyond the Great
> Sea that one may say:
> *"Would that we had one like the*
> *prophet Jonah*
> *who would descend into the depths*
> *of the Great Sea and bring it up for us*
> and make us hear the commandments
> that we might do them."
> (*Tg. Neof.* Deut. 30:12-13)

The italicized portions indicate where the Aramaic text reads differently from the Hebrew, on which modern translations are based. The Aramaic paraphrase speaks of Moses ascending into heaven to fetch the Law and of Jonah descending into the depths to bring up the Law. Paul applies Deut. 30 to the risen Christ in a similar way. For Paul, of course, Christ was the "end of the Law" (Rom. 10:4), so the injunction of Moses in Deuteronomy applies more perfectly to the work of Christ. Remember, too, that early Christians compared Jesus to Moses (as in Matthew and the book of Hebrews) and to Jonah (cf. Matt. 12:39-41; Luke 11:29-32).

10:6-8. But the righteousness based on faith speaks thus, "Do not say in your heart, 'Who will ascend into heaven?'" Paul first quotes part of Deuteronomy 9:4 and of 30:11. He argues that even while Moses had tried to convince the Israelites that the observance of the law did not demand that one scale the heights of heaven, such has indeed been accomplished by Christ (Fitzmyer, 590). **(That is, to bring Christ down)** is an allusion to the incarnation, meaning that a person asked by God to be upright is not being asked by him to bring about the incarnation of Christ (Fitzmyer, 590). **'Who will descend into the abyss?'** alludes to Psalm 107:26, which Paul substitutes for the crossing of the seas in Deuteronomy 30:13 in order to allude to Christ's resurrection (Fitzmyer, 590).

10:9. Jesus as Lord is an early confession. "Jesus is Lord" (Phil. 2:11; 1 Cor. 12:3), along with belief in the resurrection, were key elements of Christian doctrine. Upon their death, emperors were believed to become gods (Suetonius, *Vespasian* 23.4), and were worshiped as **lord** (*kurios*). Indeed, Paul would likely have known of the emperor Caligula (A.D. 37-41), who solicited worship as **lord** (*kurios*), and attempted to place an idol in his image in the Jerusalem temple (Bockmuehl, 143). While Jews often resisted such emperor worship (Josephus, *J.W.* 2.8.1 §118), Gentiles, who were the primary congregants of the Philippian church (see Introduction), would likely have participated (cf. *BGU* 1197.1.15; *POxy* 1.37.5; 2.246; 8.1143.4; *CIG* 4923; *PLond.* 280.6; Tacitus, *Annals* 2.87). Epictetus refers to Caesar as "lord of all," under whom he considered himself a slave (*Disc.* 4.1.11-13).

10:11. For the Scripture says, "Whoever believes in Him will not be disappointed." This is a vindication verse from Isa. 28:16. **Be disappointed** can also translate "put to shame" and refers to a negative judicial verdict, here referring to the final judgment.

10:12. Lord of all is a Jewish formula (1QapGen. 20:13; Josephus, *Ant.* 20.4.22 §90; 11QPs^a 28:17), connoting the sovereignty of Yahweh. **All who call upon Him.** Calling upon God is Jewish language (Deut. 4:7; Pss. 4:1; 14:4; Isa. 55:6; *2 Macc.* 3:22; *Pss. Sol.* 2:36; *T. Jud.* 24:6) frequently used for prayer, but with the character of an appeal to a covenant partner to honor his (covenant) obligations (Dunn, 610-11).

10:13. "Whoever will call upon the name of the Lord will be saved." This time the apostle looks to Joel 3:5, which further speaks of one's being saved and receiving good news. Here, though, Paul sees the Lord as Jesus rather than just Yahweh.

10:14. How then shall they call upon Him in whom they have not believed? And how shall they believe in Him whom they have not heard? And how shall they hear without a preacher? Preaching is a surprisingly rare word in the Old Testament, though when used often refers to the prophets proclaiming a messianic and eschatological message (Isa. 61:1; Joel 2:1; Zeph. 3:14; Zech. 9:9).

10:15. And how shall they preach unless they are sent? Just as it is written, "How beautiful are the feet of those who bring glad tidings of good things!" Paul's quotation here is from Isa. 52:7 (cf. Nah. 2:1), though in a very abbreviated form. This text was understood by some Jews to refer to the Messiah and the age which he inaugurates (11QMelch 15-19; *b. Ber.* 56b).

10:16. However, they did not all heed the glad tidings; for Isaiah says, "Lord, who has believed our report?" From Isa. 53:1, this text originally referred to Israel's rejection of God's offer for mercy (cf. John 12:38).

10:18. But I say, surely they have never heard, have they? Indeed they have; "Their voice has gone out into all the earth, And their words to

the ends of the world." Paul cites Ps. 19:4 to prove that Israel has already heard the good news about Christ. This psalm shows how God is revealed through creation and history.

10:19. But I say, surely Israel did not know, did they? At the first Moses says, "I will make you jealous by that which is not a nation, By a nation without understanding will I anger you." This text is taken from the "Song of Moses" (Deut. 32:21), in which Moses instructs Israel that she will be humiliated by Gentiles (cf. 4Q372 1:12; cf. *3 Bar.* 16:3).

10:20. And Isaiah is very bold and says, "I was found by those who sought Me not, I became manifest to those who did not ask for Me." Here, from Isa. 65:1, the contrast is obvious: Gentiles who do not have the Law come to faith though Jews who do have it do not.

10:21. But as for Israel He says, "All the day long I have stretched out My hands to a disobedient and obstinate people." Now in Isa. 65:2, Paul shows God's divine initiative in reaching out to Israel almost as a man appeals to God (cf. Exod. 9:29; Ezra 9:5; *Sir.* 48:20; 51.19).

D. 11:1-32. The Mystery of God's Faithfulness

11:1. The tribe of Benjamin. Benjamin was a son of Rachel and the only one of Jacob's twelve sons born in the Promised Land (Gen. 35:16-18). From this tribe Israel's first king and the apostle's namesake, Saul, arose. Only the Benjamites remained faithful to Judah and the house of David after the death of Solomon. They went into exile with them and returned with Ezra to resettle the land around Jerusalem.

11:2. God has not rejected His people whom He foreknew. This is taken from both 1 Sam. 12:22 and Ps. 94:14, suggesting Paul's confi-

dence that the scriptural assurance has not been falsified by the present disobedience (10:21) of Israel (Dunn, 636). **Elijah** was the ninth-century B.C. prophet from Tishbe in Gilead and master of Elisha. His loyalty to Yahweh caused him to take the lead in the struggle against the introduction of the worship of Baal into the kingdom of Israel from Tyre under Jezebel. Elijah confronted the prophets of Baal on Mount Carmel to see which would be lord, Baal or Yahweh. In the end, only Yahweh sent fire from heaven to consume the offering as well as the altar on which it was placed (1 Kings 18:1-46). Elijah then slaughtered the prophets of Baal and fled in fear of Jezebel to Beersheba and then Mount Horeb (1 Kings 19:1-8; Fitzmyer, 604).

11:3-4. "Lord, they have killed Thy prophets, they have torn down Thine altars, and I alone am left, and they are seeking my life." Here Paul uses an abridged version of 1 Kings 19:10 to show how Elijah's story illustrates God's plan in the present situation. After his flight from Jezebel, the prophet journeyed forty days and nights to Horeb, took shelter in a cave, and complained bitterly to Yahweh about the infidelity of Israel. Yahweh here announced the impending judgment on his people but the preservation of 7,000 **"who have not bowed the knee to Baal"** (v. 4; 1 Kings 19:18; Fitzmyer, 604). As a result of his faithfulness, Elijah was left alone and the object of scorn.

11:5. In the same way then, there has also come to be at the present time a remnant according to God's gracious choice. The remnant (*leimma*) was an important witness to Yahweh during the crises of the Assyrian and Babylonian tragedies (2 Kings 19:4; Isa. 37:4; Jer. 6:9; 15:9; 23:3; Ezek. 9:8; Ezra 9:8). Qumran sectarians saw themselves as Yahweh's faithful remnant (1QS 8:6).

11:8. "God gave them a spirit of stupor, Eyes to see not and ears to hear not, Down to this very

day." This paraphrase is from Deut. 29:3, where Moses addresses Israel. He tells them that they had witnessed all of the portents sent by God against Pharoah on their behalf, but they had never appreciated their full significance (cf. Isa. 29:10; Fitzmyer, 606).

11:11. To make them jealous. Make . . . jealous refers back to Deut. 32:21 (Rom. 10:19), which refers to God's jealousy for his people or a person's jealousy of another person (1 Kings 14:22; Pss. 37:1; 78:58; 1 Cor. 10:22; *Sir.* 30:3). Apparently Paul thinks the Gentiles' enjoyment of Yahweh's salvation would draw them to faith in Christ as well (cf. *b. Sanh.* 98b).

11:16. And if the first piece of dough be holy, the lump is also. Paul seems to be alluding to the law's requirement of a portion of dough made into cakes (Num. 15:17-21; Philo, *Sac.* 107; *Special Laws* 1.132; Josephus, *Ant.* 4.4.4 §71). Though the metaphor of holiness in dough being spread throughout the batch is not present in Judaism, the holiness of the temple was frequently thought of as extending to Jerusalem and its hills (Neh. 11:1; Isa. 11:9; 48:2; 66:20; Jer. 31:23; Ezek. 20:40; Dunn, 658). **And if the root be holy, the branches are too:** Naturally, branches were known to be dependent on the nourishment obtained from the roots (Job 18:16; Jer. 17:8; Ezek. 31:7; Hos. 9:16; *Sir.* 1:20; 40:15). Paul is drawing on a longstanding tradition that Israel was planted by

---

Israel Was Planted by God

"The Lord's devout shall live by it (the Law) forever; the Lord's paradise, the trees of life, are his devout ones. Their planting is firmly rooted forever; they shall not be uprooted as long as the heavens shall last, for Israel is the portion and inheritance of God."

Psalms of Solomon 14.3-5 OTP

God (Ps. 92:13; Jer. 11:17; *Pss. Sol.* 14:3-4; *1 Enoch* 10:16; *Jub.* 1:16; 7:34; 16:26; *1 Enoch* 10:16). The Jews at Qumran saw themselves as such a planting (1QS 8:4-5; 11:8; CD 1:7). Israel is also depicted as a spreading vine (Ps. 80:8-18; Jer. 2:21; Ezek. 17:1-24; *4 Ezra* 5:23, 28). The Messiah was described as a branch from the root of Jesse (Isa. 11:1, 10; Jer. 23:5; 33:15; Zech. 3:8; 6:12; *T. Jud.* 24:5; cf. 1QH 6:14-17; 8:4-11; Dunn, 659). Sometimes the root of this planting is identified as Abraham (*1 Enoch* 93:5, 8; Philo, *Heres.* 279) or Isaac (*Jub.* 21:24).

11:17. But if some of the branches were broken off, and you, being a wild olive, were grafted in among them and became partaker with them of the rich root of the olive tree. Some scholars consider Paul's urban background to cause him to mishandle this horticultural imagery. Farmers did not graft wild olive shoots into a cultivated olive tree, instead they grafted branches from cultivated trees into wild ones in order to promote their production (Moo, 701-2). Yet Paul seems to simply manipulate the metaphor to make his point. Israel was occasionally likened to an olive tree (Jer. 11:16; Hos. 14:6), probably the most widely cultivated fruit tree in the Mediterranean world (Dunn, 661). Grafting was known to rejuvenate a tree, though *wild* olive trees were notoriously unproductive. Here the root seems to refer to the patriarchs (cf. 11:16), while the natural branches are their descendants, the Jewish people. Wild olive shoots are Gentile Christians, grafted into the olive tree "contrary to nature" (11:24; cf. Theophrastus, *De causis plantarum* 1.6.1-10; *De historia plantarum* 2.1.1-4).

11:20. Do not be conceited, but fear. Jewish wisdom frequently incorporated fear of Yahweh as "the beginning of wisdom" (Prov. 1:7; 3:7; Pss. 2:11; 34:9; 111:10; *Sir.* 1:11-14; 2:7-10).

11:22. Severity of God. Severity (*apotomos*) is used in the *Wisdom of Solomon*, which says, "He

---

The Fear of the Lord

"With him who fears the Lord it will go well at the end; on the day of his death he will be blessed. To fear the Lord is the beginning of wisdom; she is created with the faithful in the womb. She made among men an eternal foundation, and among their descendants she will be trusted. To fear the Lord is wisdom's full measure; she satisfies men with her fruits."

Sirach 1.11-14

---

will come upon you terribly and swiftly, because severe judgment falls on those in high places."

11:25. Mystery (*mysterion*) is a general term often used in reference to the variety of local Greco-Roman "mystery cults" dating from the time of Plato (*Sophist* [*Theaetetus*] 156a; *Gorgias* 497c). These were private groups in the Greco-Roman world into which members were inducted by undergoing secret rituals, which were themselves considered salvific (Plutarch, *How to Study Poetry* 22F; cf. Plutarch, *De Iside et Osiride* 27). Initiates were not permitted to divulge their initiatory rites (Lucius, *Met.* 11.23; Diodorus Siculus, I.27.6), and violation of this and other rules of secrecy were criminal offenses (Plutarch, *Alcibiades* 22.3) and considered a defilement of the god or goddess in view (Plutarch, *Thuc.* 6.60-61; *Life of Alcibiades* 19.1; cf. Ovid, *Amores* 2.601-604). Daily rituals were private affairs, normally involving one's own shrine and regular prayers, but also more public celebrations, including dancing, processionals, and seasonal festivals (Lucian, *Saltatione* 15; *Met.* 11.7-12). Though using the same term, **mystery** for the New Testament entered Christianity from a Jewish background. **Mystery** (*mystērion*) in the OT is a Greek translation of the Aramaic *rz* found in Dan. 2:18-19, 27-30, 47, with reference to some-

thing once hidden and then disclosed. Such "unknown" things were frequently being revealed in Jewish-Christian traditions, such as the meaning of a dream or vision (Dan. 2:19), a description of the end times (Dan. 2:27-29; *2 Bar.* 85:8; 1QpHab 7:1-5; *4 Ezra* 14:5; *1 Enoch* 9:6; 103:2), the divine structure of the universe (*1 Enoch* 71:4; *2 Bar.* 48:2), or an explanation of God's ways in human activity (*1 Enoch* 63:3; 1QM 14:14; 1QH 5:22-25; 9:23). **The fulness of the Gentiles has come in.** Paul may be reflecting a certain Jewish tradition which claimed a fixed number of people would enter the kingdom of God before the end (*4 Ezra* 4.35-37).

11:26. All Israel will be saved. Some Jews thought salvation referred to the restoration of those scattered throughout the Diaspora (Deut. 30:1-5; Neh. 1:9; Jer. 23:3; Ezek. 11:17; Mic 2:12; *Sir.* 36:11; *2 Macc.* 2:18; *Jub.* 1:15; *Pss. Sol.* 17:26-28; 1QSa 1:1-6).

11:27. "And this is My covenant with them, When I take away their sins." Here Paul quotes Isa. 59:21 in which the prophet speaks of teaching one's children and their children about the covenant with Yahweh (cf. Deut. 4:9-10; 6:6-7). It speaks of a renewed, or more effective, covenant (cf. Jer. 31:33; Ezek. 36:27), though here likely refers to the new covenant (Jer. 31:31). The second half of the verse is from Isa. 27:9, changing the original "his sin" (singular) to **their sins** (plural). Jews commonly expected the close connection between a final vindication and the forgiveness of sins (Isa. 4:4; *Jub.* 22:14-15; *Pss. Sol.* 18:5). God taking away sins is a sign of his fulfilling his side of the new pact with Israel (Fitzmyer, 625).

E. 11:33-36. Concluding Hymn of Adoration

11:33. Wisdom (*sophia*) was considered a central attribute of God, contributing to his work in creation, revelation, and redemption of his people (Job 12:13; 38:36-17; Prov. 2:6; *Wisd.* 7:15; 9:2; 10:1; *Sir.* 1:1-10; 15:18; 42:21). **How unsearch-**

able are His judgments and unfathomable His ways! Common in Jewish thought was the notion that God's ways, particularly his judgments, were beyond man's comprehension (Gen. 18:25; Deut. 32:4; Job 40:8; Pss. 10:5; 36:6; 111:7; Isa. 30:18; 40:14; *Wisd.* 17.1; cf. *Hel. Syn. Prayer* 4:30; 1QH 7:31-32; *2 Bar.* 14:8; 20:4).

11:34. For who has known the mind of the Lord, or who became His counselor? This is taken from Isa. 40:13, where the prophet refers to the deliverance of the Jewish people from exile by the Lord and extols his greatness for providing it. It emphasizes that Yahweh is in debt to no one for his plan or his mighty works (cf. *Wisd.* 9:13; Job 15:8; Jer. 23:19; *2 Enoch* 33:4).

11:36. To Him be the glory forever. Amen. This is a Jewish doxology, from the Greek word *doxa,* "glory," commonly found in Jewish praises of Yahweh (*Sir.* 39:14b-16).

VI. 12:1-15:13 IMPLICATIONS OF THE GOSPEL: CHRISTIAN CONDUCT

A. 12:1-2. Basis for Responsible Living
12:1. Urge: A papyrus fragment dating late in the second century contains a letter from a woman entreating a prefect of Egypt to decide

---

Glory to Yahweh

"Scatter the fragrance, and sing a hymn of praise; bless the Lord for all his works; ascribe majesty to his name and give thanks to him with praise, with songs on your lips, and with lyres; and this you shall say in thanksgiving: All things are the works of the Lord, for they are very good, and whatever he commands will be done in his time."

Sirach 39.14b-16

---

a civil dispute (ND 6:144). Another fragment of a letter is written from priests to the Emperor Hadrian (c. A.D. 130?) petitioning him to allow them to excise taxes from certain villagers (*PBerol. Inv.* 16546). "Entreat" was a common word for making an appeal to someone (Aeschylus, *Persae* 380; Euripides, *Phoenissae* 1254; Xenophon, *Anabasis* 3.1.24; Plato, *Republic* 523b). It is used in the NT normally to request ethical behavior consistent with the gospel (1 Thess. 4:1; 10; 1 Cor. 1:10; 4:16; 2 Cor. 6:1; Rom. 12:1). So also here Paul encourages the Romans **to present** (their) **bodies a living and holy sacrifice, acceptable to God.** This phrase is probably contrasting the sacrifices of the Old Testament, which were always killed. **Spiritual service of worship. Spiritual** (*logikōn*) perhaps more properly means "reasonable," in contrast to vague superstitions popular among Roman cults and religions. It connotes sound judgment and a rational decision (cf. Epictetus, *Disc.* 1.16.20-21; Philo, *Special Laws* 1.277).

B. 12:3-8. Live in the Community of Faith
12:4-5. The mention of the church as **one body** may be an allusion to a common Greco-Roman view that the universe was itself a large "body," with each part a member of the cosmic whole (Diogenes Laertes, *Lives of Eminent Philosophers* 7.138, 142-143, 147; Cicero, *de natura deorum* 1.35; 3.9; Seneca, *Naturales Quaestiones* 6.14.1; *Epistulae morales* 95.52; *De Ira* 2.31), a view likewise held by Hellenistic Judaism (cf. Philo, *Noah's Work* 7; *Creation* 82; *Migr. Abraham* 220; *Special Laws* 1:210). Also in Greco-Roman thought the "body" was an image for the state, in which individual "members" have responsibilities for the well-being of the whole (Plato, *Republic* 5:464B; Aristotle, *Politics* 1:1, 2; Cicero, *Phil.* 8:5, 16; *De Off.* 1:25, 85; Seneca, *De Clem.* 1.5.1; Livy, *Histories* 26.16.19; Philo, *Special Laws* 3.131). In some Rabbinic thought people could be seen as parts of Adam's body (*Exod. Rab.* 40.3 [on Exod. 31:2]; cf. Eph. 1:20-23).

12:8. He who exhorts, in his exhortation. Here Paul probably refers to counsel or instruction in ethical conduct (Fitzmyer, 648). **He who gives, with liberality.** This may refer to those who are philanthropists, who share their private wealth (cf. Job 31:17; Prov. 11:26; Luke 3:11; Eph. 4:28; *T. Iss.* 7:5; Hermas, *Vision* 3.9.4).

C. 12:9-21. Love in the Christian Community

12:9. Let love be without hypocrisy. Abhor what is evil; cling to what is good. Cling is a strong term denoting one entering into a close relationship with someone or thing (Ps. 119:31; *T. Iss.* 6:1; *T. Dan* 6:10; *Did* 5:2). Similar moral exhortations are found in Jewish texts roughly contemporary to Paul (1QS 1:4-5; *T. Benj.* 8:1).

12:10. Be devoted to one another in brotherly love. Devoted (*philostorgoi*) also means "loving warmly," and was a common term in ancient wills (*POxy* 3.490.4; 492.6; *PTebt.* 2.408). **Brotherly love** (*philadelphia*) is a love devoted specifically to "brothers," i.e., Christians.

12:11. Fervent in spirit. Fervent (*zeō*) literally means "boil," and may draw from the image of the tumultuous fervor of boiling water.

12:13. Contributing to the needs of the saints, practicing hospitality. Hospitality to a stranger was an aspect of culture in the ancient world whereby one felt a deep sense of obligation to provide for another's needs. Abraham was extolled as a model of hospitality for his entertaining three heavenly visitors in Genesis 18 (Philo, *Abraham* 107-14; Josephus, *Ant.* 1.11.2 §196; *1 Clem.* 10:7).

12:14. Bless those who persecute you; bless and curse not. This seems to echo Jesus' words in Matt. 5:44: "But I say to you, love your enemies, and pray for those who persecute you."

12:15. Rejoice with those who rejoice, and weep with those who weep. Empathy for those in distress was a virtue esteemed in Judaism: "Do not fail those who weep, but mourn with those who mourn" (cf. Job 30:5; Philo, *Jos.* 94; *T. Iss.* 7.5; *T. Zeb.* 6.5; *T. Jos.* 17:7; *b. Ber.* 6b).

12:19. Never take your own revenge, beloved, but leave room for the wrath of God, for it is written, "Vengeance is Mine, I will repay," says the Lord. Retribution was often left in the hands of Israel's leadership (Num. 31:2; Judges 15:7; 1 Sam. 14:24; *Sir.* 46:1; *1 Macc.* 13:6). In the prophetic writings, however, ultimate vengeance is depicted as belonging to Yahweh alone (Jer. 5:9; 23:2; Hos. 4:9; Joel 3:21; Amos 3:2; Nah. 1:2). Individual vengeance was strongly denounced (Lev. 19:18; Prov. 20:22; 24:29; *Sir.* 28:1-7).

12:20. "But if your enemy is hungry, feed him, and if he is thirsty, give him a drink; for in so doing you will heap burning coals upon his head." This is a quotation from Prov. 25:21-22, and the notion of **heaping burning coals upon his head** is just as difficult there as here. **Coals,** along with "fire," are frequently used metaphorically in the Old Testament to refer to God's holy presence and particularly his judgment (2 Sam. 22:9, 13; Ps. 18:8, 12; 140:10; Isa. 5:24). Some scholars argue that this Proverbs text, then, suggests a believer's kindness to his enemies increases the degree of judgment the enemy will receive. But the rather positive context of Paul's use of this text suggests a more positive influence on the unbeliever, leaving other scholars to theorize that the image goes back to an ancient Egyptian practice whereby one carried coals of fire on his head as a sign of repentance; the burning pangs of shame (Moo, 789).

D. 13:1-7. Practicing Good Citizenship

13:1. Let every person be in subjection to the governing authorities. Be in subjection. Being **subject** (*hypotassō*) literally means to "place under" (Plut. *Quaest. Conv.,* IX 2.2 [2.737e]), metaphorically meaning to place under the authority or jurisdiction (Philo, *Creation* 84) even in a political or military context (*OGIS* 2.654.7). A later Jewish legend says that Judah, on his deathbed, said, "And now, children, love Levi so that you may endure. Do not be arrogant toward him or you will be wholly destroyed. To me God has given kingship and to him, the priesthood; and he has subjected (*hypotass?*) the kingship to the priesthood. To me he gave earthly matters and to Levi, heavenly matters. As heaven is superior to the earth, so is God's priesthood superior to the kingdom on earth, unless through sin it falls away from the Lord and is dominated by the earthly kingdom" (*T. Judah* 21:1-4 OTP; cf. Sextus Empiricus, *Against the Mathematicians* 11.102; Plutarch, *Apophthegmata laconica* 66 [II, 213c]; *Letter of Aristeas* 205, 207; Ps. 8:6; *PHaun.* 13.30; etc.). **For there is no authority except from God, and those which exist are established by God.** Josephus likewise held that no one rules apart from God's design (*J.W.* 2.8.8 §140; cf. *Wisd.* 6:1-3).

13:4. It is a minister of God to you for good. Minister (*diakonoi*) is used in the Old Testament for various secular officials (Esth. 1:10; 2:2; 6:3; Jer. 25:9; cf. *Wisd.* 6:4). Yet it is also found in secular texts which likewise see such officials as agents of God: "Rulers are ministers of God for the care and safety of mankind, that they may distribute or hold in safe keeping the blessings and benefits which God gives to man" (Plutarch, *Princip. Inerud.* 5.13.22-14.2). **But if you do what is evil, be afraid; for it does not bear the sword for nothing.** Some scholars see this as referring to the *ius gladii*, the authority of all high officials to inflict a sentence of death (Tacitus, *Histories* 3.68). Or, it may refer to the "sword-bearer" of the Egyptian police officials (Philo, *Special Laws* 2.92-95; 3.159-63). It is difficult to be certain what Paul had in mind beyond the simple notion that governments have the right to enact punishments to those violating their laws.

13:6. For because of this you also pay taxes, for rulers are servants of God, devoting themselves to this very thing. Tax collectors were a constant source of injustice and embitterment in the ancient world (cf. Philo, *Special Laws* 2.92-95; 3.159-63; Josephus, *Ant.* 16.2.4 §45, 16.6.1 §§160-61; Mark 2:15-16). In Rome the subject of taxation was a particularly sensitive issue, as Tacitus (*Annals* 13) says that in A.D. 58 there were persistent complaints against the companies farming indirect taxes and the acquisitiveness of tax collectors (Dunn, 766). Jews, still being allowed their temple tax, would have been particularly sensitive to taxation issues (Cicero, *Flacc.* 28.67; Tacitus, *Histories* 5.5.1).

E. Love your Neighbor (13:8-10)

13:9. The Law is summed up in this saying, "You shall love your neighbor as yourself." That the Law could be summed up in a single command is not new to Paul, nor distinctively Christian. Rabbi Hillel summarized it, "That which you hate do not do it to your fellows; this is the whole law; the rest is commentary; go and learn it" (*b. Shab.* 31a). Rabbi Aqiba claims the same command, "You shall love your neighbor as yourself" (Lev. 19:18) was "the greatest general principle in the Torah" (*Sipra Lev.* §200 [on Lev. 19:15-20]). A third-century rabbi, Simlai, claimed that Amos and Habbakuk had each reduced the law to one principle: "Seek me and live" (Amos 5:4); "The righteous man lives by his faith" (Hab. 2:4) (*b. Mak.* 23b-24a; Dunn, 778-79). The command to **love your neighbor as yourself** is from Lev. 19:18. Some Jews understood the Hebrew for **neighbor** (*ra'*), to refer to only fellow Jews (cf. *Sipra Lev.* §200 [on Lev. 19:15-20]), while others included more people (*T. Zeb.* 5:1; *T. Ash.* 5:7; *T. Naph.* 5:2). See comment on Mark 12:28-34 §179.

13:10. Love does no wrong to a neighbor. This is the negative side of the "golden rule," which was a very ancient Jewish teaching (cf. Ps. 15:3), and a widely held sentiment in Judaism of Paul's day (cf. Zech. 8:17; *Sir.* 10:6; *Ep. Arist.* 168, 207; *Jos. Asen.* 23:12; Tobit 4:15; *b. Shab.* 31b). **Love... is the fulfillment of the law.** *Wisd.* 6:17-19 says, "The beginning of wisdom is the most sincere desire for instruction, and concern for instruction is love of her, and love of her is the keeping of her laws, and giving heed to her laws is assurance of immortality, and immortality brings one near to God."

F. 13:11-14, The End Is Near

13:11. And this do, knowing the time, that it is already the hour for you to awaken from sleep. Sleep was a common euphemism for death (cf. Job 14:12; Isa. 43:17; *Pss. Sol.* 16:1-4; Homer, *Iliad* 11.241; Sophocles, *Electra* 509; see Eph. 5:14). Yet it is also frequently used as a metaphor for insensitivity to the spiritual world (Philo, *Migration* 222; *Dreams* 1.117). **Now salvation is nearer to us than when we believed.** The imminence of the end of time was a common characteristic in Jewish apocalyptic thought (*4 Ezra* 4:33-50; 8:61; 11:44; *2 Bar.* 23:7; 82:2; Dunn, 787).

13:12. The night is almost gone, and the day is at hand. Let us therefore lay aside the deeds of darkness and put on the armor of light. Lay aside... put on is an imagery frequently employed in the ancient world for practicing virtues and getting rid of vices (cf. Demosthenes 8.46; Plutarch, *Coriolanus* 19.4; *Ep. Arist.* 122; Job 29:14; Prov. 31:25; *Wisd.* 5:18; Philo, *Conf.* 31). **Darkness** to **light** is a common expression for conversion (*Jos. Asen.* 8:10; 15:13; Philo, *Virtues* 179; Acts 26:18; Col. 1:12, 13; 1 Peter 2:9; *Odes Sol.* 14:18, 19; cf. Heb. 6:4; 10:32). In the OT light can refer to salvation and life from God (Ps. 27:1; Isa. 9:2; 10:17; 42:6, 16; 41:4; 60:1). At Qumran the "War Scroll" (1QM) depicts a "War of the Sons of Light against the Sons of Darkness" (1QM

1:1-16; 3:6, 9; 13:6; 14:17; cf. 1QS 1:9, 10; 3:13, 19-21, 24, 25). *Testament of Levi* 19:1 says to "choose for yourselves light or darkness, the law of the Lord or the works of Beliar" (OTP; cf. *T. Levi* 14.4; *T. Benj.* 5:3). **Armor** (*t?n panoplian*) **of light** may allude to the armor of God (Eph. 6:11). The term **armor** is a term used for the full equipment, both offensive and defensive, of the heavily armed foot soldier (Polybius 6.23; Thucydides, *Peloponnesian War* 3.114; Judith 14:3; *2 Macc.* 3:25; Luke 11:22). **Of God** (*tou theou*) In the Old Testament the Lord is sometimes portrayed as a warrior (Isa. 42:13; Hab. 3:8, 9; Ps. 35:1-3). In Qumran texts all power and help comes from God (1QM 1:1-19:14; 1QH 3:24-39; 6:28-35).

13:13. Let us behave properly as in the day, not in carousing and drunkenness. Carousing originally referred to the festal processions in honor of Dionysus, and suggests uninhibited revelry to excess (cf. *Wisd.* 14.23; *2 Macc.* 6.4; Gal. 5:21; 1 Peter 4:3). **Drunkenness.** Wine and intoxication were central aspects of the worship of Dionysus. Intense intoxication was the decisive element in being "filled with the spirit" of Dionysus. Drunkenness was widely recognized as a sin in Judaism (Prov. 23:31 LXX; *T. Judah* 11:2; 12:3; 13:6; 14:1-4; 16:1; *T. Iss.* 7:3; Philo, *Plant* 140-7). Cf. Eph. 5:18.

Sensuality is a vice commonly condemned by Jewish and Christian literature and is often associated with sexual sin (Rom. 13:13; 2 Cor. 12:21; Gal. 5:19; *Wisd.* 14:26; *T. Levi* 17:1) or idolatry (*T. Judah* 23:1). It refers to undisciplined behavior often, but not always, sexual in nature (cf. Josephus, *Ant.* 4.6.12 §151; 8.10.2 §252; 8.13.1 §318; 20.5.3 §112).

G. 14:1–15:6. Problems Regarding Food Laws and Holy Days

14:1. Now accept the one who is weak in faith, but not for the purpose of passing judgment on his opinions. Accept (*proslambanomai*) generally means to accept someone into a society, home, or circle of acquaintances. It was used in some ancient papyri as a technical term for enrollment in the army (cf. *PLond* 23.2.21; *POxy* 1.71.2.9).

14:2. One man has faith that he may eat all things, but he who is weak eats vegetables only. The practice of vegetarianism for philosophical or religious reasons is well attested in the ancient world (Diogenes Laertius, 8.38; Philostratus, *Vita Apol.* 1.8). Food laws were very important for Jews (Lev. 11:1-23; Deut. 14:3-21). During the Maccabean period observance of food laws became a test of Jewishness and loyalty to the nation and covenant (*1 Macc.* 1:62-63; *2 Macc.* 5:27; Josephus, *Ant.* 11.8.7 §346).

14:5. One man regards one day above another, another regards every day alike. Let each man be fully convinced in his own mind. In Palestine Sabbath observance was increasingly important (*Jub.* 2:17-33; 50:6-13; CD 10:14-11:18), and the sensitivities over the proper observance of the feast days are indicated by the bitter calendrical disputes of the post-Maccabean period (*Jub.* 6:32-35; *1 Enoch* 74:10-12; 75:2; 82:4-7; 1QS 1:14-15; 1QH 12:8-9; CD 3:14-15; Dunn, 805). Among diaspora Jews Sabbath observance was a mark of ethnic identity and devotion to ancestral custom (Jos., *Ant.* 14.10.20-21 §§241-46; 14.10.23 §258; 14.10.25 §263-64; Philo, *Embassy* 155-58; *Special Laws* 2.59, 70).

14:10. We shall all stand before the judgment seat of God. Stand (*paristēmi*) was a common term in ancient papyri with a technical sense of appearing in court before a judge (*PRyl* 2.94.2; *PAmh* 2.66.40; *POxy* 6.897.10; *PHal* 1.1.218).

14:11. For it is written, "As I live, says the Lord, every knee shall bow to Me, And every tongue shall give praise to God." This is taken from Isa. 45:23, where the prophet claims all who would contest the supreme and final authority of the one God will in the end-time judgment bow and acknowledge that there is no other God than Yahweh, "a righteous God and a Savior" (Isa. 45:23; Dunn, 809).

14:13. Therefore let us not judge one another anymore. Paul may be familiar with Jesus' teaching in Matt. 7:1: "Do not judge lest you be judged." **Determine this—not to put an obstacle or a stumbling block in a brother's way. Obstacle** (*skandalon*) was also used of a trap set for animals (Pollianus, *Greek Anthology* 7.114; 10.156). **Stumbling block** (*proskomma*) can also be an offense, an obstacle, or a bruise from stumbling (Plutarch, *Lives* 2.1048C). Both words were connected with idolatry in Jewish writings (Exod. 23:33; 34:12; Jer. 3:3; 1QS 2:11-12; *Wisd.* 14:11).

14:14. I know and am convinced in the Lord Jesus that nothing is unclean in itself; but to him who thinks anything to be unclean, to him it is unclean. Unclean (*koinos*) is a cultic term referring to ritual impurity (Lev. 11:4-8; Deut. 14:7-10; Judges 13:4; Hos. 9:3). Literally it means "common" and is related to the word used to describe the Greek language of Paul's day: *koine*, means "common" in the sense of being widespread. Jews used the term to designate what is to be avoided by zealous Jews (*1 Macc.* 1:47, 62; Josephus, *Ant.* 12.2.14 §112).

14:18. For he who in this way serves Christ is acceptable to God and approved by men. Approved (*dokimos*) refers to one who is approved by testing (Rom. 16:10; 1 Cor. 11:19; 2 Cor. 10:18; 13:7; 2 Tim. 2:15; Jas. 1:12), but was also used to mean "esteem" or "respect" (Philo, *Creation* 128; *Joseph* 201; Jos. *Ag. Apion* 1.3 §18; *PAmh* 2.89.9; *POxy* 2.265.25).

14:19. Building up of one another. Building up (*oikodomeō*) also means "edification." It is an architectural term used for the construction of a building (*OGIS* 843.104). See comment on Eph. 2:19-22.

14:20. All things are clean has been suggested as a slogan for "the strong" (Dunn, 825). Declaring things **clean** (*katharos*) is the opposite of being unclean (v. 14), and is used of foods approved to eat under the Old Testament dietary laws (cf. Gen. 7:2-3; 8:20; Lev. 4:12; 6:11; 7:19; *Judith* 10:5; *1 Macc.* 1:48; *Pss. Sol.* 8:12; *Let. Aristeas* 166; *T. Levi* 15:1).

14:21. It is good not to eat meat or to drink wine, or to do anything by which your brother stumbles. Some Jews abstained from wine purchased in markets for fear that it was involved in pagan ritual libation rites (cf. Dan. 1:3-16; 10:3; *T. Reub* 1:10; *T. Jud.* 15:4; *Jos. Asen.* 8:5; *m. 'Abod. Zar.* 2:3; 5:2; Dunn, 827).

15:1. It seems there were particularly two groups of people in the Roman church: **We who are strong. Strong** (*dynatos*) also means "capable" and seems to refer to those who, like Paul, are able to understand that in Christ one is freed from the dietary restrictions imposed by the Law. **Those without strength** (*adynaton*), perhaps still deeply attached to Judaism, are probably those who still feel a sense of obligation to the same dietary laws (Moo, 865-66).

15:3. For even Christ did not please Himself; but as it is written, "The reproaches of those who reproached Thee fell upon Me." This quotation is from Ps. 19:9, where the psalmist cries out from personal distress, and for that very reason would hardly commend itself to Jewish thought as messianic in character (Dunn, 838). It shows that Christ willingly accepted his sufferings and bore the reproaches uttered against God by the enemies of God (Fitzmyer, 703).

15:4. For whatever was written in earlier times was written for our instruction, that through perseverance and the encouragement of the Scriptures we might have hope. In *1 Macc.* 12:9 the high priest, Jonathan, writes of the consolation the Jewish people find in their "holy books" in the face of persecution and suffering.

15:6. With one accord you may with one voice. With one accord (*onomthumadon*) probably derives from the political sphere where it refers to the unanimous wishes of an assembled body (cf. Acts 12:20; *Let. Arist.* 178; Philo, *Moses* 1.72; Josephus, *Ant.* 15.8.2 §277).

H. 15:7-13. Concluding Summary
15:9. As it is written, "Therefore I will give praise to Thee among the Gentiles, And I will sing to Thy name." This time Paul quotes from Ps. 18:49 (cf. 2 Sam. 22:50), which does not itself seem to imply Gentiles participating in the praise, though Paul may have this in view. In its original context David praises Yahweh for victory over Gentile nations. Paul puts these words on the lips of Jesus, as for Paul it is Jesus who has conquered the nations and brought them under the blessings of his kingly reign.

15:12. And again Isaiah says, "There shall come the root of Jesse, And He who arises to rule over the Gentiles, In Him shall the Gentiles hope." This quotation is taken from Isa. 11:10. The **root of Jesse** was long known as a title for the Messiah (Isa. 11:1-5; *Sir.* 47:22; cf. Rev. 5:5; 22:16; Jer. 23:5; 4QPat 3-4; 4QFlor 1:11). **Hope.** Some expected the messianic promise to include God's destruction of the Gentiles in vindication of Israel (cf. Pss. 2:8-9; 72:8-9; 110:1; *Pss. Sol.* 17:30). Yet Israel's typical covenant hope has been transformed and Paul articulates it as the outreach of the Gentile mission (Dunn, 850).

VII. CONCLUDING REMARKS AND GREETINGS (15:14–16:27)

15:14. And concerning you, my brethren, I myself also am convinced that you yourselves are full of goodness, filled with all knowl-

edge, and able also to admonish one another. Though to modern readers it may seem Paul indulges in insincere flattery, he may be using an ancient literary device known as *captatio benevolentiae*. By this device the ancient author expressed confidence in his readers to gain adherence for their ideas (Moo, 887-88).

15:16. Minister of Christ Jesus. Minister (*leitourgos*) can also mean "servant" (Josh. 1:1; 2 Sam.·13:18; 1 Kings 10:5), though Paul probably has a more cultic sense of "priest" in mind here (Neh. 10:39; Isa. 61:6; *Sir.* 7:30). Some have suggested that Paul has the Levites in mind here as assistants to "the" priest (Christ; cf. Philo, *Moses* 2.276). **Ministering as a priest the gospel of God.** This is clearly cultic language, and though **ministering as a priest** does not occur in the Old Testament, both Philo and Josephus use the term consistently to connote the priestly offering of sacrifices (Philo, *Allegorical Interpretation* 3.130; *Plant.* 164; *Ebr.* 138; *Conf.* 124; *Migr. Abraham* 67; Josephus, *Ant.* 5.7.10 §263; 6.6.2 §102; 7.13.4 §333; 9.3.2 §43; 14.4.3 §65; 17.6.4 §166), though it is also something the people as a whole could do (Philo, *Moses* 2.229; *Special Laws* 2.145; Josephus, *J.W.* 5.1.3 §§14, 16). **Sanctified by the Holy Spirit. Sanctified** (*hagiazein*) is almost exclusively a biblical word, denoting the act of setting apart, dedicating to God, so as to be his alone, or used solely for his purposes. It was used of sacrifices (Exod. 29:33; 30:29; Lev. 8:15; Num. 18:8-9; 2 Chron. 29:33; Matt. 23:19; Heb. 9:13), priests (Exod. 19:22; 29:1, 21, 44; 30:30; 40:13; Lev. 8:12; 21:8), and the temple (1 Kings 9:3; 2 Chron. 2:4; 7:16; *1 Esdr.* 1:49; *Tobit* 1:4; *Judith* 9:13; *3 Macc.* 2:9; Dunn, 861). The term was also indicative of Israel's election as the people of God (Exod. 19:14; Lev. 11:44; 20:8; 22:32; Deut. 33:3; Ezek. 20:41; 28:25; 37:28; 39:27; *Judith* 6:19; *Sir.* 36:3; *3 Macc.* 6:3).

15:19. Signs and wonders apparently were fixed terms frequently used to recall the mira-

cle of the Exodus (Exod. 7:3; 11:9-10; Deut. 4:34; 7:19; 34:11; Neh. 9:10; Pss. 78:43; 135:9; Jer. 32:20-21; *Wisd.* 10:16; cf. Isa. 8:18; Dan. 4:2-3; 6:27; *Wisd.* 8:8; Philo, *Moses* 1.95; *Special Laws* 2.218; *b. Ber.* 5b; 34b). **From Jerusalem and round about as far as Illyricum I have fully preached the gospel of Christ.** Paul is recounting a geographical portrait of his missionary activity in the eastern Mediterranean world. **Jerusalem** was the starting point of Christianity and at first regarded as the mother church. Christ's death occurred there and was the locus of Paul's meeting with the earlier apostles (Gal. 1:17), where he learned from Peter (Gal. 1:18), and where his gospel met with approval (Gal. 2:2; Fitzmyer, 714). **Illyricum** is in the area of modern Albania, and became an imperial province of the Roman Empire in 11 B.C. It revolted against Rome shortly thereafter and was subdued by Tiberius between A.D. 6 and A.D. 9. Paul probably uses the term to refer to that area north of Macedonia (Strabo, *Geography* 7.7.4; Appian, *Roman History* 10.1.6).

15:24. Whenever I go to Spain—for I hope to see you in passing, and to be helped on my way there by you, when I have first enjoyed your company for a while. Here Paul reveals his plans to visit Spain (see Introduction), which was at that time part of the Roman Empire and known for its gold and silver mines (cf. *1 Macc.* 8:2). Yet it did not come completely under Roman jurisdiction until the time of Augustus. Some have thought Paul was interested in Spain because of an alleged Jewish population there. Others conjecture that the apostle associated that region with the Old Testament "Tarshish," which was considered "the ends of the earth" in which the prophet Isaiah predicted would be the completion of God's eschatological work among the Gentiles (cf. Isa. 66:19; Moo, 900). **Helped** (*propempō*) became a technical term in the earliest church for support of missionary activity, to which

Paul expects the Romans to contribute (Acts 15:3; 20:38; 21:5; 1 Cor. 16:6, 11; 2 Cor. 1:16; Titus 3:13; 3 John 6; *PFlor* 2.206.2).

15:25. I am going to Jerusalem serving the saints. Paul regards his travels to Jerusalem to deliver the collection gathered from churches in Galatia, Achaia, and Macedonia (Gal. 2:10; 1 Cor. 16:1-4; 2 Cor. 8:1-9:15) as an act of service (*diakonia*). Paul was particularly prone to remember those in hardship, particularly the poor (Gal. 2:10). Furthermore, many Jewish people expected the wealth of the nations would flow to Jerusalem at the end of time (Isa. 45:14; 60:5-17; 61:6; Mic 4:13; Tobit 13:11; 1QM 12:13-15; Dunn, 874).

15:26. For Macedonia and Achaia have been pleased to make a contribution for the poor among the saints in Jerusalem. Macedonia had a long, influential, but tumultuous history (cf. Herodotus, *Histories* 5.17-18, 173; 9.45; Polybius, *History* 7.9; 18.22-28; 31.29), including some encounters with Israel during the Babylonian captivity and afterwards (Dan. 2:39; 7:6; 8:5-8; *1 Macc.* 1:1-7; 6:2). In Paul's day, it was a Roman province across which was built a great military road, the Egnatian Way, from the Adriatic Sea to the Aegean. It was made into an imperial province in A.D. 15 (Tacitus, *Annals* 1.76.4; 1.80.1), though divided again into a senatorial province by Claudius in 44 (Dio Cassius, *Historia Romana* 60.24). Within its precincts were located the churches of the Thessalonians and Philippians. **Achaia,** however, was made a separate province under Augustus in 27 B.C. Perhaps Paul had in mind the Philippian church in Macedonia (Phil. 4:15) and the Corinthian church in Achaia (1 Cor. 16:15; 2 Cor. 1:1).

15:28. Therefore, when I have finished this, and have put my seal on this fruit of theirs, I will go on by way of you to Spain. Ancient documents often had a **seal** (*sphagisamenos*) both to simply close them up (Euripides, *Iphigenia Aulidensis* 38; *Frg.* 781.10; cf. *PAmh* 2.41.7), and to authenticate a document. Xenophon records a letter authenticated by "bearing the King's seal" (*Hellenica* 1.4.3; LCL; cf. Jer. 32:11). Such seals were personalized to their owners (Herodotus, *Histories* 1.195, 3.41; cf. Euripides, *Frg* 1063.9; Nicomachus Gerasenus, *Mathematics* 1.23).

16:1. I commend to you our sister Phoebe. Travelers could not depend on public facilities for food and housing, so they depended on letters of commendation written by a mutual friend to find accommodation in a town which they were visiting. It is presumed that as she is listed first and receives Paul's commendation, that she is the bearer of the letter to the Roman church. **Who is a servant of the church which is at Cenchrea. Cenchrea** is a city located about fifty miles east of Corinth, and was the major seaport for that city (cf. Apuleius, *Matamorphoses* 10.35). Scholars conjecture that Phoebe traveled frequently to Corinth on business and became converted through the ministry of the church founded in that city. It is also suggested that her name indicates a pagan background as well as her status as a freed slave (Fitzmyer).

16:2. She herself has also been a helper of many, and of myself as well. The nature of her assistance is unknown, though some have suggested she provided financial assistance or perhaps offered hospitality or assistance in difficulties with secular authorities.

16:3. Greet Prisca and Aquila, my fellow workers in Christ Jesus. Prisca (= Priscilla) and Aquila are regarded by some as two of the most important people in Paul's missionary enterprise (cf. Dunn, 891). Aquila was a Jew from Pontus (Acts 18:2), and one is to perhaps assume Prisca is as well. Both came from Italy to Corinth following the expulsion of the Jews from Rome by the emperor Claudius in A.D. 49 (Acts 18:2). Paul stayed with them during his stay in Corinth, and shared with them in their family trade of tent-making, which probably referred to a leather worker, though not a tanner, as that would have been considered unclean for Jews. Rabbis in Paul's day often had a trade to support themselves in addition to study of the Law (cf. *m. Abot.* 2.2; 4.5). Prisca (= Priscilla) and Aquila traveled with the apostle from Corinth to Ephesus (Acts 18:18-19) and probably established themselves there for some time (1 Cor. 16:19). With Claudius' death in A.D. 54, his decree was relaxed and Prisca and Aquila are apparently once again present in Rome. Scholars often presume they were well-off business people.

16:4. Who for my life risked their own necks. Paul does not specify the incident he has in mind, though they may have played some role to quell the Ephesian riot of the silversmiths (Acts 19:23), or perhaps used their influence to help Paul during his Ephesian imprisonment (1 Cor. 15:32; 2 Cor. 1:8-9).

16:5a. The church that is in their house. This is the earliest reference to churches meeting in individual homes. Having broken away from the temple and synagogue frequented by Jews, Christians naturally turned to homes to meet and worship. Claudius' decree against Jews may likewise have influenced the privacy of such meetings (Dio Cassius, *Historia Romana* 60.6.6), as Christians were initially seen as a sect of Judaism by the Roman government.

16:5b-15. Most of the people listed here are otherwise unknown in Christian history, and it is unclear how Paul, who had not visited the Roman church, had so many acquaintances in it (see Introduction).

16:7. Greet Andronicus and Junias, my kinsmen. Kinsmen probably simply refers to them being fellow Jews, as it does in Rom. 9:3.

16:10. Greet those who are of the household of Aristobulus. Some have suggested, though with uncertainty, that this Aristobulus is the brother of King Herod Agrippa I, ruler of Palestine under Roman jurisdiction from A.D. 41-44 (cf. Acts 12:19-23). Aristobulous was taken with Agrippa to Rome, where he allegedly died in A.D. 48 or 49 (Josephus, *Ant.* 18.8.4 §§273-76; *J.W.* 2.11.6 §221). Yet it is feasible that those remaining of his household were still identified by his name.

16:11. Greet those of the household of Narcissus, who are in the Lord. Narcissus was a well-known freedman who was a secretary under the emperor Claudius and forced to commit suicide after the murder of Claudius (A.D. 54; Tacitus, *Annals* 31.1; Dio Cassius, *Historia Romana* 60.34).

16:13. Greet Rufus, a choice man in the Lord, also his mother and mine. Rufus may be the son of Simon of Cyrene, carrier of Jesus' cross (Mark 15:21). Such is frequently conjectured because of the association of the gospel of Mark with Rome, though Rufus was a very common slave name (Diodorus Siculus 11.60.1; 14.107.1; Josephus, *Ant.* 17.10.3 §266; 17.10.9 §294) and one cannot identify this man with Mark's Rufus with any certainty.

16:14. Greet Asyncritus, Phlegon, Hermes, Patrobas, Hermas and the brethren with them. Hermas was identified by Origen (*Commentary on Romans* 10.31) and Eusebius (*Hist. Eccl.* 3.3.6) as the author of an important Christian writing, *The Shepherd*.

16:16. Greet one another with a holy kiss. Holy kiss. Kisses in the ancient world were used within and outside the family. They communicated love, respect, and reconciliation. Though kissing among the brethren suggests kissing across sexes, kissing of the opposite sex was discouraged in earliest Christianity (*Apostolic Constitutions* 2.57.17). That the **kiss** is called **holy** suggests its religious connotation. Justin Martyr (ca. A.D. 150) spoke of the exchange of kisses during the Eucharistic part of a service (Wanamaker, 208). Pagan religions employed cultic kisses of images to gain supernatural strength (Cicero, *Verr.* 2.4.94; Apul. *Met.* 11.17.3; Dio Cassius, *Historia Romana* 41.9.2; Ovid. *Metam.* 7.631f).

16:20. And the God of peace will soon crush Satan under your feet. Satan (*satanas*) is a Greek transliteration from the Hebrew (*satan*), originally used to denote the accuser within the counsel of God (Job 1:1-2:13; Zech. 3:1-2; cf. 1 Chron. 21:1). **Crush Satan under your feet.** Many Jewish people expected that at the end of time Satan and his minions would be bound and defeated (*Jub.* 5:6; 10:7; 23:29; *1 Enoch* 10:4; 13:1-2; *2 Enoch* 7:1; 1QS 3:18; 4:18-23; 1QM 17:5-6; Rev. 20:20). The wording used by Paul likely reflects that of Gen. 3:15, when God curses the serpent and says, "And I will put enmity between you and the woman, And between your seed and her seed; He shall bruise you on the head, And you shall bruise him on the heel" (cf. Ps. 91:13; *T. Sim.* 6:6; *T. Levi* 18:12; Luke 10:18-19).

16:21. Timothy was a trusted colleague of Paul's who was instrumental in the churches in Thessalonica (3:2, 6), Corinth (1 Cor. 4:17; 16:10), and Philippi (Phil. 2:19). He was a native of a South Galatian city, perhaps Lystra. His mother was a Jew and his father a Greek. He was converted during Paul and Barnabas' first trip to that region, was circumcised, and taken along with Paul as a junior colleague. Timothy accompanied Paul and Silas to Macedonia (Acts 16:1-10; 17:14, 15), and later rejoined Paul in Corinth (Acts 18:5). See comment on Phil. 1:1. **Lucius** was a common name, though some suggest he is Lucius of Cyrene, the prophet and teacher in the church at Antioch (Acts 13:1). He

has even been identified as Luke, as Lucius is a variant way of spelling that name. **Jason** was probably the man who provided shelter for Paul during the apostle's hardships in Thessalonica (Acts 17:5-9). **Sosipater**, also known as Sopater, was from Berea and accompanied Paul when he left Greece toward the end of his third missionary journey (Acts 20:4).

16:22. I, Tertius, who write this letter, greet you in the Lord. Tertius, otherwise unknown in the New Testament, served as Paul's *amanuensis*, or secretary, for the writing of Romans. The employment of an amanuensis was a common practice in antiquity. Cicero frequently dictated letters to his secretary, Tiro, as did other classical writers to theirs. Caesar also seemed to have one (Plutarch, *Vit. Caes.* 17.3), as did many others (Pliny, *Ep.* 3.5; 9.36; Quintilian, *Inst.* 10,3,19). In addition, many papyrus letters preserved from Paul's day were written by secretaries, with a final greeting or closing matter written in the hand of the sender. See Introduction to the Prison Epistles.

16:23. Gaius, host to me and to the whole church, greets you. At least three Christians in the New Testament alone bear the name **Gaius**. There is a Gaius of Derbe (Acts 20:4; cf. 19:29), a Gaius of Corinth (1 Cor. 1:14), and a Gaius who was a leader in a church in Asia Minor (3 John 1). As Paul is writing from Corinth (see Introduction), he probably has the Gaius from that city in mind. **Erastus, the city treasurer greets you.** Erastus was the name of a man Paul sent from Ephesus to Macedonia during his third missionary journey (Acts 19:21-22; cf. 2 Tim. 4:20). An inscription found in Corinth mentioning him as an *aedile* of the city, may be roughly equivalent with Paul's identification of him as **city treasurer** (*oikonomos*), or "director of public works" (Moo, 935).

Introduction to 1 Corinthians

Lee Martin McDonald

I. Context and Background

A. History of Corinth and Its Surroundings.

Paul's final stop in Greece, and his longest, was at the ancient city of Corinth (Acts 18:1-18). While there he wrote his famous letter to the Romans and possibly his letters to the Thessalonians and the Colossians. Corinth is strategically located near the isthmus between the Aegean and Ionic Seas (or Corinthian and Saronic Gulfs). It was well-known for its ancient springs, baths, Classical stonework (especially the widely imitated Corinthian capitals on columns), along with its Temple of Apollo and Asklepion (place of healing and second only to the Asklepion at Epidauros). The city was also known for its low morals (to "corinthize" meant to practice fornication). The decadent community was also known for its worship of Aphrodite, the goddess of love.

Adjacent to the city was the sight of the ancient Isthmian games, (second only to those in Olympia and Athens), as well as the Diolkos, the road built for hauling ships overland to avoid the treacherous voyage around the southern end of the Peloponnese peninsula. Because of its strategic location it was also a wealthy community. Most of what survives in its current ruins comes from the Roman period.

After the city was captured by the Romans in 146 B.C., all of its residents were killed. Corinth was repopulated in 44 B.C. by Julius Caesar and made into a Roman colony. The city remained a significant commercial community until its destruction by an earthquake in 521 A.D. It was largely deserted after the 10th century, even though a small village was built on the eastern side of the ancient city. In early church history the city had much more significance than did Athens and was the primary place from which Christian missions to the Peloponnese towns and villages were launched. The ancient sites at Corinth are impressive, including the Doric temple of Apollo, the Roman baths called Peirene, the *stoa* alongside of the main street, or *maximus cardo*, of the city. Archaeologists have also discovered the ancient Bema ("seat"), or seat of authority in the city, where Paul stood to answer charges brought against him by the Jews before Gallio, the proconsul of Achaia who came from Delphi (Acts 18:12-17).

Many Christian notables in the first-century church visited Corinth, including Paul, Peter, Timothy, Luke, Silas, Apollos, Prisca, and Aquila. Later church history claims that the Apostle Andrew also visited here and was martyred in Patras west of Corinth. At the end of the first century, Clement of Rome wrote a very important letter (*1 Clement*) to the church at Corinth encouraging them to respect their leaders and even to obey them, as well as to cease their quarrellings and practice peace and humility. By far, the most influential bishop in Greece in the second century was the venerable Dionysius of Corinth who wrote many letters to churches encouraging them in their Christian faith. He rebuked the Christians at Athens for their tendency toward apostasy.

Acrocorinth. The imposing acropolis of Acrocorinth rises above the ancient city of Corinth and has the remains of fortresses from the Byzantine, Crusader, and Venetian times. In the time of Paul there was a temple on top in honor of Aphrodite that reportedly had some 1,000 prostitutes ("courtesans"). Only one small part of a pillar base is left of the temple, but from the top, one has the most impressive view of the isthmus and the mountains to the north and south. On a clear day, one can see the acropolis in Athens as well as the waters of the two oceans.

Cenchrea (or Kenchreai). An ancient port on the Saronic Gulf near the ancient Isthmus of Corinth about six miles east of Corinth. The port city is now in ruins, but functioned as the departure city for persons traveling from the Corinthian Gulf on the west to the eastern coast. The city was destroyed along with Corinth in 146 B.C. and rebuilt in 44 B.C. by the decision of Julius Caesar. Marauding Slavs and Avars destroyed it in the 580s. It was never rebuilt after that. According to Acts 18:18, Paul concluded a Jewish vow here prior to setting sail for Syria by way of Ephesus. This was also the home of Phoebe, a deacon (or fellow minister) in the church in this city. Paul recommended her to the Romans as she prepared to travel their way (Rom. 16:1-2). It is also possible that Rom. 16 was written to the Christians at Ephesus and Phoebe was on her way there rather than to Rome.

Because of Corinth's strategic location near the isthmus between the Corinthian and the Aegean Seas, it was always an important location in antiquity both militarily and economically. In the ancient world, one of the most dangerous capes in the Mediterranean Sea for navigation was Cape Malea (now called Cape Matapan) at the southern tip of the Peloponnesus. It was sometimes said of those who went around Cape Malea, "Let him who sails round Malea first make his will." Another

saying was "Let him who sails around Malea forget his home." As a result of the danger incurred by making such a trip around the Peloponnesus, cargo-shipping traffic regularly shortened the journey by going through Corinth. The various cargo ships and passenger ships for that matter were dragged across the "Diolkos" or the pathway over the isthmus that connected the two seas. Today, a canal that was begun by Nero in the first century but was not completed until much later in the early twentieth century, is complete and smaller ships regularly make their way through this Corinthian canal, shortening their journey. In antiquity, larger ships often transferred their cargo to other ships waiting on the other side of the isthmus. Smaller ships, however, were more commonly dragged overland to the other side. Because of the frequent traffic going through, Corinth became a wealthy city. As a result of the popularity of this site, nearby on the eastern side of Corinth was the location of the famous Isthmian games that were second only to those games held at Olympia.

Those Who Lived at Corinth. When the Romans rebuilt the city of Corinth in 44 B.C., the merchants returned along with philosophers, artisans, sailors, freedmen, slaves, and hucksters. There was also a large Jewish population in the city who were prosperous merchants in the area. The name Corinth in time became synonymous with evil and corruption. To "corinthize" meant to live as a drunk and in debauchery. When the ancient Greeks portrayed Corinthians on the stage, they were always drunks. At the top of the hill called Acrocorinth, there was a temple in honor of Aphrodite, the goddess of love, in which there were some 1,000 temple priestesses who were prostitutes who plied their trade at night. Notice what Paul says about those activities among those in the church (1 Cor. 6:9-10). The interpretation of such texts has become very important in the modern culture when Christians are encouraged to be less concerned about those who live together prior to marriage and those who engage in homosexual activity. Corinth was a city that could boast of all of the hopes and promises of a financially prosperous community, but also of all of the evils and vices that were common in such places in both the ancient as well as the modern world. Paul addressed these and other issues that had become problematic to the health of the Corinthian Christians and threatened divisions. He urged the Christians there to come together in peace and love for a more effective witness as believers in the risen Christ.

By all estimates, Corinth was one of the most important cities of ancient Greece because of its strategic location. It was a major trading center and a very wealthy community in the time of Paul and this served, no doubt, as a chief reason for his extended ministry of about a year and a half in this place. When Paul was here, the city was in its second cycle of life as a Roman colony that began in 46 B.C. at the order of Julius Caesar. Following his rejection by the Jews in the city, Paul began a Christian community (2 Cor. 1:1). By the early second century, the city was considered the most beautiful in Greece and was more influential than its older sister city, Athens.

The modern city or town of Corinth is situated on the northeastern shore of the Peloponnesus peninsula and lies about four miles northeast of ancient Corinth.

B. Authorship and Integrity of the Letters to the Christians at Corinth. There are no credible arguments against the traditional position that the Apostle Paul wrote the two letters of the New Testament that are called 1 and 2 Corinthians (see 1 Cor. 1:1; 2 Cor. 1:1). All arguments to the contrary are negligible both historically and in recent times. What is less certain is the integrity of Paul's correspondence to the Christians at Corinth: namely, do the two letters represent more than the two letters? In other words, some scholars contend that 2 Cor. 10–13 may be the "severe letter" that Paul refers to in 2 Cor. 2 and perhaps 2 Cor. 6–7 was the letter referred to in 1 Cor. 5. These are not easy matters

to decide, but there do appear to be breaks in the flow between 2 Cor. 9 and 10 and also between 6:XX and 7:XXX. If these sections were extracted, it is possible that they would form well-constructed letters by themselves. In their current contexts, it appears that the tone of the passages changes as well as the content. Did Paul write these chapters on separate occasions as separate letters? Perhaps, but the arguments are not conclusive. Scholars do make strong cases, however, that all of these letters represent later Christians, or even Paul himself, attempting to bring more than one letter of correspondence into the present two letters.

C. Paul's Ministry in Corinth. The story of Paul's ministry in Corinth is reported in Acts (18:1-17) and indicates that Paul had a productive, if not challenging, ministry here for some eighteen months. After a very dangerous but successful earlier ministry in Macedonia and a rather lackluster ministry in Athens, Paul came to Corinth. Soon after his arrival he met Prisca and Aquila who had recently arrived from Rome following their expulsion by the Roman Emperor Claudius. While in Corinth, the new Roman governor of the area, named Gallio (or more completely), visited Corinth from Delphi. During Paul's visit, he was dragged before Gallio by the Jews who disliked Paul's ministry. Because of the discovery of an inscription at Delphi, scholars have been able to date the visit of Gallio to Corinth and thereby also date Paul's ministry with relative certainty (ca. A.D. 51–52).

The visit of Gallio to Corinth (A.D. 51) is one of the few relatively well-documented dates that we have for New Testament events. The rule of Gallio, the Roman governor of the region, can be dated with some certainty. He was the older brother of the contemporary philosopher Seneca (see Seneca, *Ep*.104.1) and his full name was Lucius Junius Gallio Annaeus. He is called by that name by Pliny (A.D. 23–79), who describes and recommends the remedy of Gallio who, after drinking waters that caused illness by saying, took a boat ride on the ocean. He writes: "for those attacked by consumption, as I have said, and for Haemoptysis, such as quite recently within our memory was taken by Annaeus Gallio after his consulship" (*Natural History* 31.33, LCL). He is also mentioned in the several fragments of an important inscription found at Delphi. With the most likely restorations to the text in brackets, the inscription is reproduced as follows:

Tiber[ius Claudius C]aes[ar Augus]tus G[ermanicius, Ponttifex Maximus, Holder of the Tribunician Po]wer f[or the twelfth time, Imperator f]or the twenty-sixth time, F[ather of the c]ount[ry, Counsel for the fifth time, and Censor, to the city of the Delphians, greetings.]

For some ti[me past I have been de]vot[ed] to the c[ity of t]he Delph[ians . . . and good will from the be]ginning; and I have ever obser[ved th]e worship[ping of the Pythian] Apo[llo . . . But as for the many] recent reports and those disco[rds] among the [citi]zens . . . [just as Lucius Ju]nius Gallio, my f[riend] an[d proc]onsul [of Achaia, wrote . . .Therefore I am granting that you] continue to enjoy your for[me]r . . . . (Reproduced from *DBSup* 2.358-59. Missing letters are in brackets and have been supplied.)

Gallio's governorship is dated from the twenty-sixth acclamation of the emperor. According to another inscription, the twenty-fourth acclamation took place in the eleventh year of the tribunate, that is, in the year of the reign of the Emperor Claudius from January 25 to January 24 of the year 51 (*CIL* 3.1977). Another inscription from Carian dates the twenty-sixth acclamation of the emperor in the twelfth tribunate (*BCH* 11 [1887] 306-7). Another inscription dates the twenty-seventh acclamation of the emperor the year following (*CIL* 6.1256). By means of these and other inscriptions, the Gallio inscription stone has been dated between January 25 and August 1 of the year 51 or 52. The proconsulship of Roman governors lasted one year and, according to Dio Cassius (A.D. 150–235), newly appointed governors left Rome by mid-April. Dio Cassius writes: "he [Claudius] gave notice to the governors chosen by lot, since they were slow even now about leaving the city, that they must begin their journey before the middle of April" (*Roman History* 60.17.3). Gallio was governor of Achaia sometime between A.D. 51 and 52 (probably July 1, 51 to July 1, 52) and Paul's eighteen months at Corinth (Acts 18:11) overlapped Gallio's term of office. The approximate dating here is the most accurate point of reference for the time of Paul's missionary activity. Times are added to or taken from this date to determine other events in the book of Acts and to date Paul's writings.

After a period of some eighteen months of ministry in Corinth, Paul's greatest success there appears to be that the ruler of the synagogue, Crispus, and another fellow Jew named Gaius, became Christians. During his residence in Corinth, Paul enlisted the services of a Christian couple named Pricilla and Aquilla who joined his missionary enterprise that eventually took them to Ephesus where they encountered Apollos who left there and went to Corinth where he was involved in the Corinthian Christian mission in significant ways (cf. Acts 18:xx).

II. The Letters to Corinthian Christians.

The letters are among the earliest writings of the New Testament and receive some of the earliest attestations in the second-century church fathers (Justin, Ignatius, Clement of Rome).

Authorship. There are virtually no credible scholars today who deny Paul's authorship of the Corinthian letters. While there is considerable doubt about the integrity of 2 Cor., that is, whether it was originally produced as it currently exists in its original form or whether it was a collection of two or more of Paul's letters that a later editor put into the letter's current shape and circulated among the churches.

Again, the question is not whether Paul wrote 2 Cor. (see discussion later), but whether it is a composition of several of his writings.

Provenance. It was while Paul was at Ephesus (ca. A.D. 55, see 1 Cor. 16:8) that he learned that things were not going well in the church at Corinth. He received reports of divisions in the church over sexual immorality among its members (1 Cor. 5:9). Paul wrote what was evidently a very strong letter, and it was later followed up with what is now known as 1 Corinthians. The first correspondence dealt with a few of the issues, but now he discusses the problems that some of them had in taking fellow believers to court, family relations when unbelievers are involved, eating meats sacrificed to idols, problems related to the sacred meals in the church, problems related to the gifts of the Spirit, and denials of the resurrection of Jesus, and other matters. It is possible, though not certain, that the letter mentioned in 1 Cor. 5:9 is the same as 2 Cor. 6:14–7:1. If not, it is also possible that this initial letter was lost. Scholars have generally agreed that the Apostle Paul wrote the Corinthian correspondence attributed to him, but they disagree on whether two letters as they now stand are in the form in which they were originally constructed and sent to the church at Corinth. Most of the discussion focuses on the unity of 2 Corinthians. Some scholars suggest that the "painful letter" that Paul says he wrote to the Corinthians in 2 Cor. 2:3-4, is what is found in 2 Cor. 10–13. Since there is a considerable break both in content, continuity, and tone in that section of 2 Cor. (see how 2 Cor. 9 concludes and how 10:1 begins), it is easy to say that even if 2 Cor. was written by Paul, it is not likely that he wrote it at the same time as he wrote chaps. 1–9. There are many ways in which that could be accounted for and so it is not unusual to find a variety of solutions posed. It is not unusual for a person to compose a lengthy letter over several days or even weeks. During that time the tone and content or focus of the letter could change considerably. It could be that new reports were received by Paul in the midst of constructing the letters and that gave rise to the change in tone. What led to the obvious changes in tone within the letters is not clear, but the changes are there and they do not suggest to biblical scholars a change in authorship, but rather a change in the circumstances of the writer or understanding of the writer brought on by the reception of new reports on the church at Corinth or the apostle's own situation. The unity of 1 Corinthians is seldom questioned these days and the unity of 2 Corinthians, though frequently challenged, does not suggest a challenge to its authorship.

It remains possible that 2 Cor. 1–9 was written after the construction of chaps 10–13. Some scholars have suggested that this might well be the letter that Paul refers to in 1 Cor. 5:9-10 or some later correspondence produced after 1 Corinthians, but, again, the authorship is not in question. Much of this is guesswork, but clearly Paul states that he had both written earlier to the Corinthians (1 Cor. 5:9) and that he had also received both written correspondence and personal oral reports from them. The personal reports to which he responded in chaps. 1–6 (except 5:9-13) came from "Chloe's people" (1:11) and from Stephanus and Fortunatus (16:15-18). Paul responded to the written reports point by point in chaps. 7–16 as we can see from his frequent "now concerning" statements introduces another point made in the correspondence (see 1 Cor. 7:1, 25; 8:1, 4; 12:1; 16:1, 12).

III. The Context and Unity of the Letters

It was while Paul was at Ephesus in the year ca. A.D. 55 that he learned that things were not going well in the church at Corinth. He had received by way of correspondence a negative report on the situation in the church that was also leading to schisms in the church. He responded in an initial letter (1 Cor. 5:9), which is now lost, that was perhaps a negative letter, and he followed it up with another letter about the emerging divisions in the church. It is possible that we have that letter in 2 Cor. 6:14–7:1.

Paul's goal was a reconciled church and in 1 Corinthians he addressed the several issues that he was told were dividing the church.

While most scholars have regularly affirmed the internal unity of the letter, more recently several questions have been raised about the internal problems of consistency in the content of the letter and these have led some scholars to question the unity of the letter. For example, how compatible is 4:17-21 with 16:5-11? Does 4:17-21 appear more like the ending of a letter than as a transition to further discussion of issues in a larger letter? Has Timothy already been sent to Corinth (4:17) or is that yet waiting (in 16:10)? In 4:19 Paul says that he will come soon to see them, but in 16:8 he will remain in Ephesus until Pentecost. How soon is "soon"? The section of 4:16-21 with its announcement of travel plans appears more like Paul's conclusions in other letters rather than the ending of a section in the middle of a longer letter. Likewise, does the way that the letter is parted between 1:10–6:21 and 7:1–16:12 suggest the combination of two letters from Paul, one based on a response to oral communication from "Chloe's people" (1:11–6:20) and the second based on a response of Paul to written concerns delivered to him by Stephanus and Fortunatus (7:1–16:12, see 16:15-18)? While these questions cannot be finally decided here, what has been said about the changes of tone in the discussion of 2 Corinthians above could also be said here. It could well be that Paul had about concluded his comments to the Corinthians in 4:17-21 and then fresh news came to him that he considered too important to ignore or postpone and so he added further comment. This is, of course, speculation, but it highlights the difficulty of knowing the context for all such occasional writings in the ancient world. Finally, the apparent differences between the two discussions of the practice of eating meat sacrificed to idols. In 8:1-13 Paul draws the conclusion that there is nothing in and of itself that is wrong with the eating of meat that has been sacrificed to idols (8:4-8),

but he contends that for the sake of those who because of conscience cannot partake of such food that for the sake of unity in the church those who find nothing wrong in the practice should abstain from doing it. He bridges this discussion with a similar one in chap. 10 with a focus in chap. 9 on the need to set aside individual freedoms for a higher goal of strengthening the unity of the church. In chap. 9, he speaks about the rights that he has as an apostle but will not insist on those rights for the sake of Christian unity, and then in chap. 10 he returns to the whole issue of eating foods sacrificed to idols and has a more negative conclusion about the appropriateness of the practice (10:19-21).

Similarly, Paul deals with the matter of spiritual gifts in chap. 12 and then changes direction in chap. 13 to emphasize something more important than these gifts, love. He then returns to the issue of the gifts and specifically focuses on prophecy and tongues in chap. 14. While these are the primary examples that scholars offer for the internal inconsistencies in the volume, they are not sufficient enough to lead most scholars to conclude that 1 Corinthians is a composition of more than one writing produced over a longer period of time with perhaps intervening news reports from Corinth coming to him in Ephesus at different times before the letter was sent back to Corinth.

After the Corinthian Christians' response to Paul's concerns, that included their asking many questions of Paul (see 1 Cor. 7:1), he wrote the letter now called 1 Corinthians that was probably delivered to them by Timothy (1 Cor. 4:14-17). After this, Paul made a second visit to the church (2 Cor. 13:1, 2) and planned on a third (Acts only mentions one trip). His visit apparently did not resolve the conflicts and problems emerged. Consequently, he wrote to them a "severe" letter (2 Cor. 2:4; 7:8), which may be 2 Cor. 10–13. This letter apparently upset a number of people, but it evidently accomplished what Paul wanted to accomplish with it. Paul was so concerned over how the letter was received by the people that he traveled to Macedonia (possibly Philippi) and met with Titus about it (2 Cor. 2:13; 7:5, 13). He was relieved that things were going much better and as a consequence wrote to the Christians at Corinth what is now 2 Cor. 1–9, omitting 6:14–7:1, an irenic piece of correspondence. While this is a possible scenario and explanation for the apparent breaks in the flow of the letters, it is by no means certain and it may be that 2 Corinthians in its totality was written by Paul after the events related in 1 Corinthians, but only that the letter was not written at one time, but with an unspecified break between the time the letter was begun and when it was finished. That could account for the change in tone between chaps. 1–9 and 10–13.

If 2 Cor. 10–13 is the earlier letter that Paul claims he wrote to the Corinthians (1 Cor. 5:9), one can only wonder why the issue he mentions in 5:9-13 is not addressed in 2 Cor. 10–13. It is more likely that Paul wrote an earlier unknown letter to the church at Corinth that predates what we call 1 Corinthians and that we do not possess. It is also possible that 2 Corinthians was written on two separate occasions or that in the midst of writing the letter fresh reports had come to Paul that led to the change in tone and subject matter. It may be that 2 Cor. 10–13 is the painful letter that Paul refers to in 2 Cor. 2:3-4 and that would place it first and make it a separate correspondence from Paul. That would clarify the cause for the change in tone in the second letter from chap. 9 to chap. 10 and help identify the painful letter that Paul mentions in 2 Cor. 2:3-4 and 7:8. Much of this is speculation, however, and cannot be resolved here, so the readers are encouraged to consult with the more important commentaries on the Corinthian letters. See Bibliography.

After a response to an earlier letter (1 Cor. 5:9), which included his addressing many questions passed along to him (see 1 Cor. 7:1, 25; 8:1, etc.), Paul wrote 1 Corinthians and it was probably delivered to them by Timothy (1 Cor. 4:14-

17). After this, he made a second visit to the church (2 Cor. 13:1, 2) and had planned on a third (Acts does not mention this visit). Paul's visit evidently did not accomplish his intended purposes and a number of problems emerged. As a result, he wrote to them a more severe letter (2 Cor. 2:4; 7:8), which, as we suggested above, may be 2 Cor. 10–13, or it may simply be lost. While that letter upset a number of people, it evidently accomplished what Paul wanted to accomplish with it. After this, Paul had become so concerned over how his letter was received by the people that he traveled to Macedonia (possibly Philippi) and met with Titus (2 Cor. 2:13; 7:5, 13). Perhaps from Macedonia he wrote 2 Cor. 1–9, which is a letter of reconciliation.

IV. The Contents of 1 Corinthians.

After his familiar greeting and thanksgiving, Paul responds to the reports he has received about the problems going on in the church at Corinth. He dealt first with the divisions in the church (chaps. 1–4). His introduction to this section (1:10-17) is a summary of the message of the whole letter in that Paul rejects the legitimacy of any divisions among the believers in Corinth whether based on preferences for the leader of the church who baptized them or jealousies over spiritual gifts or other matters. Paul makes it clear that there can be no divisions in the church based on such claims. This is not to say that there were no other kinds of problems among the Christians in Corinth, but that Paul's greatest concern was over the divisions in the church community. Clearly, as we will see later in the letter, there were also moral issues and theological issues that affected the unity and health of that church. Paul's case against the divisions is found in 1:18–4:21 where he argues that there is no basis for boasting, which leads to divisions, in the church.

The second major section of the letter is found in chaps. 5–11 and deals primarily with two specific issues that were dividing the church: namely, sexual immorality and marriage (most of chaps. 5–7) and also the problem of giving individual freedoms priority over unity in the church (8:1–11:1). In 6:1-11, he also argues that Christians should not take each other to public courts because of the adverse effect this will have on their witness in the community (6:1-11), but then returns in 6:12 to the issues related to sexual immorality (*pornea*) that he began in 5:1-13. He then introduces the "body" metaphor in 6:15-17 to argue for the unity of the body, the church. For Paul, unity in the family of Christ is more important than individual freedoms in personal matters. The body metaphor is a familiar theme in Paul and its purpose is consistent: namely, that the body of Christ is a unity and it cannot be divided over individual freedoms. His use of the body metaphor is central to his case for church unity and he returns to it in chap. 12. In chap. 7 Paul takes up the difficult question of marriage and divorce and one's social status (married or single and slave or free). His admonition comes in response to questions the Corinthians had asked him in earlier correspondence (7:1, 25) and deduces from his belief in the soon return of Christ that one's social status in society (married or single, slave, or free) was of less consequence in light of the more important issue of the unity of the family of Christ and its witness in the world. Some individuals in the church were obviously more concerned about their personal freedoms as Christians to participate in various questionable activities than they were about the unity of the church and avoiding conflict. Some of their activities that other Christians found objectionable included issues of promiscuity (6:12-20) and the eating of meat that had been sacrificed to pagan idols (chaps. 8–10), and Paul challenges them to live above reproach.

In the latter case, he tells the Christians at Corinth how to deal with the problem of eating food that had been sacrificed to idols: namely, that there is a higher principle than individual freedom to guide them in such matters (chaps. 8–10). This principle is more important than the

individual rights that anyone had and Paul underscored that personal freedoms are not as important as seeking unity and peace in the fellowship of the church. Unity in the church is found by showing love and consideration for all of the members of the Christian community by not insisting on personal rights (1 Cor. 9:3-20) but rather seeking unity by following the principle of love that does not insist on its own way. Paul returns to this principle in 1 Cor. 13:4-5. He deals with this matter also in his letter to the Romans (Rom. 14). For him, the principle of love brings unity to the Christian community but an insistence on the priority of individual freedoms to pursue pleasure or personal gain destroys that unity.

The third major section of this letter (11:1–14:40) focuses on those issues that divided the church when they came together for worship and service. How should Christians dress when they gather together for worship and how should they participate in their sacred meal? The Christians at Corinth struggled with what the appropriate attire for worship was (whether women should wear a covering or veil in worship or leave their heads uncovered (11:2-16). They were also involved in practices that could divide the church in its most sacred practices: namely, failure to consider the needs and feelings of the poorer members of their congregation when it was time to partake of the Lord's Supper or sacred meal (11:17-34). Paul saw that failure to consider the appropriate attitudes at this sacred meal could adversely affect the unity of the whole family. Rather than eating in their gatherings before everyone, especially the poorer among them, had arrived, Paul urged them to eat at home before coming to the gathering so that they could all participate together in the sacred meal. In dealing with this problem, Paul called upon one of the oldest traditions about the meal that had its origins in Jesus himself.

In this section, Paul also deals with the divisions in the church over the exercise of the gifts of the Spirit (chaps. 12–14). The problems the church faced here were dividing their fellowship and Paul seeks to clarify both the purpose, importance, and use of such gifts in advancing the church's mission. Paul corrected both the jealousies and misunderstandings related to the importance, purpose and function of the gifts of the Spirit for the church. While anxious to maintain that every one had a gift from the Spirit that could build and strengthen the body of Christ, it was unthinkable that those with such gifts would argue over the value of another's gifts or magnify their own within the assembly of believers. Love was the most appropriate attitude in the use of such gifts for Paul (chap. 13), who emphasized the unity of the "body" of Christ (the church) and the necessity for all of the various gifts that God had given to the church (12:14-30). Evidently, there were those who had the gift of speaking in tongues who believed that their particular gift was more important than those who had other gifts. Paul did not devalue the gifts of tongues and prophecy, but he gave clarity on how those gifts were to be exercised in the church. While acknowledging the value of all spiritual gifts in the church, their lasting value was only to be found when they were exercised in love (13:1-13).

In the final section of this letter, Paul dealt with an important doctrinal issue that emerged as a result of a popular understanding of the future of bodily existence in the life to come. Just as those at Athens who heard Paul preach about the resurrection of the dead scoffed at his message (Acts 17:32), there were some who became Christians at Corinth who continued to stumble over the notion of a resurrection from the dead (15:12). The notion of a resurrection of the body from the grave was at odds with the popular Hellenistic thinking held among the Greeks that the body was a prison that enslaved the soul and that the goal of humanity was to be freed from this prison (body) of the soul. When the Christians argued for the Jewish notion of a future bodily existence beyond the grave claiming that the future hope of the believer was in a transformed bodily existence in the presence of God, they were challenging popular Greek notions of life after death. Those persons in the church who were more persuaded by the notions of immortality of the soul and not the body challenged the recent message that Paul preached on Christian views of life after death and the resurrection of the dead.

Paul claimed that belief in the resurrection of Jesus Christ and the Christian believers hope in life beyond the grave were inseparable (1 Cor. 15:12-20; see also Rom. 8:11 and Phil. 3:20-21). In 15:1-57 Paul both clarifies the importance of the resurrection of Jesus for the future of the Christians themselves, but also the nature of the resurrection of the body. Paul reminded the believers of the heart of his message to them about this resurrection itself by first stating the heart of the Gospel which he preached to them: namely, that Jesus Christ died, was buried, was raised, and was seen (15:1-11). On this matter, there was complete agreement among the church's most prominent leaders (Peter and the "twelve" apostles, 500 witnesses, James and the rest of the apostles, and Paul himself). He then argues that if Christ is not raised, then Christian faith itself is futile and vain (15:12-20). This, however, did not clarify to these Hellenistic Christians the nature of the resurrection body so Paul discusses the matter regarding the nature of future existence and the hope of the church. Paul emphasized the importance of the resurrection of Jesus in the hope of the church and that the nature of the Christian's hope was for a transformed bodily existence, like that of Jesus.

V. Conclusion.

Paul concludes his practical and theological arguments as he began his introduction (1:6-9), with the admonition that the church get back to doing the work of the Lord because of what God has in store for his church, and those who labor for God's kingdom will not do so in vain (15:58). The issues that caused disunity in the church are put into their proper perspective and because of the importance of the unity of the Christian community for the sake of its witness for Christ, Paul believed that the Christians should all the more be willing to settle their differences and do the work of the Lord.

In a customary conclusion to a letter, Paul gives final admonitions and greetings. These include his special concern to raise funds for the Christians in Jerusalem who had special financial need (16:1-4), but also his plans to visit them and encouragement to care for others who will be visiting them before Paul arrives (16:5-12). The remainder is both a collection of greetings to individuals and his farewell comments (16:13-24).

OUTLINE OF THE BOOK

I. Introduction (1:1-9)
  A. Salutation. 1:1-3
  B. Thanksgiving. 1:4-9
II. Paul's Response to Oral Reports from Chloe's People (1:10 – 6:20)
  A. Divisions over leadership (1:10 – 4:21)
  B. Divisions over sexual immorality and taking believers to court (5:1–6:20)
    1. Dealing with incest (5:1–13)
    2. Going to court against Christians (6:1-11)
    3. Christians involved with prostitutes (6:12-20)
III. Paul's Response to Written Reports from Stephanus and Fortunatus (7:1–15:58)
  A. Marriage and Social Status (7:1–40)
    1. Advice to those who are married (7:1–16)
    2. Paul's Principle for the single, married, slave or free (7:17–24)
    3. Advice to the virgins (7:25–40)
  B. Food Sacrificed to Idols (8:1–11:1)
    1. The standard to follow in deciding the matter (8:1–13)
    2. Paul's example of giving up rights for a greater unity (9:1–27)
    3. The prohibition of eating foods sacrificed to Idols (10:1–11:1)
  C. Christian Conduct at Christian Gatherings (11:2–14:40)
    1. The appropriate attire for women in worship (11:2–16)
    2. Abuses in eating the sacred meal (11:17–34)
    3. Abuses in exercising the gifts of the Spirit (12:1–14:40)
  D. Misunderstanding Concerning the Resurrection of the Body (15:1–58)
IV. The Closing of the Letter (16:1-24)
  A. Collection for Poor in Jerusalem (16:1–12)
  B. Conclusion of the letter (16:13-24)

RESOURCES

Boring, M. Eugene, Klaus Berger, and Carsten Colpe, eds. *Hellenistic Commentary to the New Testament.* Nashville, TN: Abingdon, 1995.

Bray, Gerald, ed., "1-2 Corinthians," *Ancient Christian Commentary on Scripture.* vol. 7, General Editor, T. C. Oden. Downers Grove, IL: InterVarsity Press, 1999.

F. Collins, Raymond, "First Corinthians," *Sacra Pagina*, vol. 7. D. J. Harrington, S.J., ed., Collegeville, MN: Liturgical Press, 1999.

Conzelmann, Hans, "1 Corinthians." *Hermeneia–A Critical and Historical Commentary on the Bible.* J. W. Leitch (trans.), George W. MacRae (ed.). Philadelphia, PA: Fortress Press, 1975.

Fee, Gordon D., "The Epistle to the Corinthians." *The New International Commentary on the New Testament.* F. F. Bruce, ed. Grand Rapids, MI: Eerdmans, 1987.

Gill, David. W. J., "1 Corinthians," *Zondervan Illustrated Bible Backgrounds Commentary.* Vol. 3, C. E. Arnold, gen. ed., Grand Rapids, MI: Zondervan, 2002.

Goulder, Michael D., "Paul and the Competing Mission in Corinth," *Library of Pauline Studies*, S. E. Porter, ed. Peabody, MA: Hendrickson, 2001.

Horsley, Greg and S. R. Llewelyn, eds. *New Documents Illustrating Early Christianity.* 9 vols. North Ryde, Australia: Macquarrie University/ Grand Rapids, MI/Cambridge, U.K.: Eerdmans, 1981-2002.

Lightfoot, John, "Acts–I Corinthians," *A Commentary on the New Testament from the Talmud and Hebraica*, Vol. 4. Oxford: University Press, 1859; reprint Grand Rapids, MI: Baker Book House, 1979.

Murphy-O'Connor, Jerome, "St. Paul's Corinth: Texts and Archaeology," *Good News Studies 6.* Wilmington, DE: Michael Glazier press, 1983.

Orr, William F. and James Arthur Walthur. "I Corinthians: A New Translation," *The Anchor Bible, Vol. 32.* W. F. Albright and D.N. Freedman, eds., NewYork/London/Toronto/Sydney/ Aukland: Doubleday, 1976.

Robertson, Archibald and Alfred Plummer, "A Critical and Exegetical Commentary on the First Epistle of St. Paul to the Corinthians," 2nd ed., *The International Critical Commentary*, S. R. Driver and C. A. Briggs (eds.). Edinburgh: T & T Clark, 1914.

Sampley, J. Paul, "The First Letter to the Corinthians," *The New Interpreter's Bible*, Vol. X. Leander Keck and William L. Lane, eds., Nashville, TN: Abingdon, 2002.

Thiselton, Anthony C., "The First Epistle to the Corinthians," *The New International Greek Testament Commentary*, I. H. Marshall and D. A. Hagner (eds). Grand Rapids/Cambridge, U.K.: Eerdmans/Carlisle: Paternoster Press, 2002.

1 Corinthians

Lee Martin McDonald

I. 1:1-9. INTRODUCTION

Style. In a typical letter style from the first century, Paul refers to his authorship of the letter, those to whom he is writing, and a typical Christian greeting that invites the blessing of God on those who are the recipients of the letter. (See comment on Rom. 1:1-3 above). It is also Paul's normal practice (see the exception in Gal. 1) to offer a thanksgiving and words of encouragement for his readers. This style of writing in the ancient world was quite common and reflects an important transition for communicating important practical and theological discussion in the early church. The earliest letter that Paul wrote that survives in our Bible is either Galatians or 1 Thessalonians, but 1 Corinthians is one of the best preserved in antiquity and often cited in the church fathers. This is because of its practicality and also the theological discourses that applied to the life of Christians in subsequent generations. The communication of Christian revelation in epistolary (or letter) form became quite common later in the church, but it was innovative at this juncture in the church's development. A typical letter in the first and second century of the Christian era is seen in a son's letter to his mother while he is away on a ship. He writes:

Apollinarius to Taesis, his mother and lady, many greetings. Before all I pray for your health. I myself am well and make supplication for you before the gods of this place. I wish you to know, mother, that I arrived in Rome in good health on the 25th of the month Pachon and was posted to Misenum, though I have not gone to Misenum at the time of writing this letter. I beg you then, mother, look after yourself and do not worry about me; for I have come to a fine place. Please write me a letter about your welfare and that of my brothers and of all your folk. And whenever I find a messenger I will write to you; never will I be slow to write. Many salutations to my brothers and Apollinarius and his children and Karalas and his children. I salute Ptolemaeus and Ptolemais and her children and Heraclous and her children. I salute all who love you, each by name. I pray for your health. (Addressed) Delivered at Karanis to Taesis, from her son Apollinarius of Misenum (*Select Papyri, Private Affairs* #111, From a Recruit in Italy, pp. 303-304, LCL).

This letter has the basic components of ancient correspondence in the first century: namely, the author, the addressee, a typical thanksgiving or prayer, the body of the letter, and a farewell salutation.

1:1. Paul, called as an apostle of Jesus Christ by the will of God, and Sosthenes our brother. Paul frequently uses the term "apostle" (Greek

= *apostolos*) to identify himself to his readers at the beginning of his letters and sometimes within them (see 9:1 below and Gal. 1:11-24; 2 Cor. 12:1-12). While the term literally means "one who is sent," it became a specialized reference by the first-century Christians to those who had seen and represented the risen Lord (see 1 Cor. 9:1; 15:5-8). For Paul it had not yet been restricted to or dominated by references to the "Twelve" apostles. The closest parallel to this term among the Jews in the first and second centuries was the Hebrew term *sheliach* that referred to one who was commissioned as an agent of a congregation with the authority of that congregation so long as the commission was in effect. According to that tradition, the agent (or *sheliach*) was the representative of the congregation and his representation reflected the congregation. According to the Mishnah, "If he that says the *Tefillah* [= Prayer, that is, the prayer of the Eighteen Benedictions] falls into error it is a bad omen for him; and if he was the agent of the congregation [*sheliach*] it is a bad omen for them that appointed him, because a man's agent [*sheliach*] is like to himself" (*m. Berakoth* 5.5, Danby trans.).

For Paul, apostleship was rooted more in the appearance of the risen Christ to him (1 Cor. 9:1; 15:7-9) than in letters of authorization from others in the church. The authorization of his apostleship was not the congregation, but God, as we see in his "by the will of God" (see also Gal. 1:1). His calling as an apostle came from God ("called an apostle"). This is probably what lies behind the notion of apostleship of Andronicus and Junias in Rom. 16:7, but that is not certain. Herodotus used the term apostle as an envoy and this notion is likely behind the church's use of the term. Herodotus (ca. 485 B.C.) writes: "When the Delphic reply was brought to Alyattes, straightway he sent a herald to Miletus, offering to make a truce with Thrasybulus and the Milesians during his building of the temple. So the envoy [Greek = *apostolos*] went to Miletus" (Herodotus, *Persian Wars* 1.21, LCL). Similarly, he writes: "Aristagoras of Miletus . . . bade all to set up governors in each city; and next he went on an embassy [Greek = *apostolos*] in a trireme [= an ancient galley with three banks of oars] to Lacedaemon; for it was needful that he should find some strong ally" (*Persian Wars* 5.38, LCL).

More contemporary with New Testament times is Epictetus (A.D. 54–68) who uses the verb form of *apostolos*: namely, *apostello*, to describe how the "true Cynic" must "know that he has been sent [Greek = *apestaltai*] by Zeus to men" (Epictetus, *Discourses* 3.22.23, LCL). Paul's understanding of the term apostle is more likely a combination of two ideas: namely, that it refers to those who have seen the risen Lord and secondly those who have seen him have been called to proclaim him in missionary activity. More discussion of this topic will be found later in 9:1-3.

Sosthenes. This is a possible reference to the ruler of the synagogue at Corinth in Acts 18:15-27 who became a follower of Jesus ("our brother"). The description of him as a "brother" (Greek = *adelphos*) is similar to other uses of the term to identify those who have become followers of Jesus the Christ (Rom. 16:23; 1 Cor. 16:12; Col. 4:7). He may also have assisted Paul in the writing of 1 Corinthians. For example, see Paul's use of "we" in 1 Cor. 1:18-31 and 2:6-16. The "we" texts may also only refer to a common form of writing in antiquity: namely, using the first person plural. Nevertheless, if the Sosthenes here is the same as in Acts 18:17, then there was at least one Jewish convert under Paul's ministry and two others who worked with him in Corinth, Aquila and Prisca (= Priscilla), mentioned in 1 Cor. 16:19; Acts 18:2-3, 18, 26; and Rom. 16:3.

1:2. To the church of God which is at Corinth. Paul wrote his letter to the Corinthian Christians. The term "church" to describe the followers of Jesus the Christ is quite old and has an interesting history in the early Christian community. The word "church" (Greek = *ekklesia*) is a neutral term that refers simply to a gathering or an assembly of people, perhaps with some political overtones, and it is frequently qualified by "of God" as is the case here. See also 2 Cor. 1:1. While some scholars have argued from the root derivation of the term: namely, *ek-kaleo* (= "call out of") that it referred to the church being called out of the world, that is not the source of the word nor its use in the early church. Likewise, *ekkle˜sia* may have the same idea of the Hebrew *qahal*, which is translated by *ekkle˜sia* in the Septuagint (LXX), but again this will not account for all of the usages found in the New Testament. In meaning it is not unlike the term "synagogue" (Greek, *synago˜ge˜*) that is used almost exclusively of the Jewish community in the New Testament except for James 2:2 where it is used of the gathering of the Christian community. Here we can translate the words literally "to the *assembly* of God" (*te˜ ekkle˜sia tou theou*) and *ekkle˜sia* is one of the most common terms employed by Paul to refer to the community of believers in Jesus the Christ. Often, as here, when Paul uses the term, he qualifies it with the words "of God" (1 Cor. 10:32; 11:16) or something similar such as the churches "of Christ" (Rom. 16:16) or "churches of the saints" (Rom. 14:33). Sometimes the term also stands alone without qualification (1 Cor. 4:17; 11:18). Paul uses the neutral Greek term for a gathering, *ekkle˜sia*, and qualifies it to refer to the whole of the Christian community in a given location: namely, the city of Corinth (e.g., 1 Cor. 1:2; 2 Cor. 1:1). Paul does not qualify it in Gal. 1:2 except by location. He uses this term to refer to the church some thirty times in 1 and 2 Corinthians, more than in all of his other writings combined. While it has been plausibly argued that Jesus himself used this term for an assembly of his followers (see discussion of Matt. 16:18; 18:17), some scholars doubt this.

The word "church" in the English language refers to the Christian gathering and is used in English translations of the Greek New Testament to translate *ekkle˜sia*, however, this is not its actual meaning and it is not found in the New Testament. The term "church" is a later development of the Christians around the end of the second or early third centuries. It did not catch on in all Christian communities, such as the Latin or southern European countries (France, Spain, Portugal, Italy), for example, which continue to prefer to use a transliteration of the New Testament term *ekkle˜sia* ("gathering" or "assembly") to refer to the community of the followers of Christ (Latin *ecclesia*). The Greek word *kuriakon*, however, is the actual root of the word "church" (observe the Scottish "Kirk" and the German *Kirche*), and a form of it is more commonly used in northern European countries (Germany, Netherlands, England, Scotland, and others). The basic form of *kuriakon* comes from the root Greek word *kurios* ("Lord") the title given to Jesus by the Church. The last three letters of *kuriakon* indicate possession and more carefully refers to "those who belong to the Lord." *Kuriakon* is not found in the New Testament, but its derivative, church, has been used in English and German translations of the New Testament for the Greek term *ekkle˜sia*. It is also possible that the term *kuriakon* came to be used by the Church in order to make clear who its members were: namely, those who belonged to the Lord, although this is uncertain.

To those who have been sanctified in Christ Jesus, saints by calling (or "called to be holy"). The origins of this notion of calling the people of God "holy," or separated unto God, go back to Exod. 19:6 where the people of God are to be "a priestly kingdom and a holy nation." It should be noted that the singular form is not used either here or in the letters of Paul, but rather the plural as the whole people of God. The same is true in the New Testament where an individual is *not* called a "saint" (Greek = *hagios*), or a holy person, but rather a community of believers in Christ are called "saints" (Greek = *hagioi*) or "holy people" (Rom. 1:7; 8:27; 12:13; 15:25, 31; 16:2; 6:1, 2; 14:33; 16:1, 15, *passim*). Those who have been made holy in Christ Jesus, says Paul, are "called to be holy." Originally these words were used of those who were the elect of God called to share in the blessings of God (Dan. 7:18, 21, 25, 27). They are also used in the non-canonical writing known as the Psalms of Solomon. For instance, "And he [God] shall gather together a holy people, whom he shall lead in righteousness, and he shall judge the tribes of the people that has been sanctified by the Lord his God" (17:28, Charles, *APOT* 2:649). Also, "And there shall be no unrighteousness in his days in their midst, For all shall be holy and their king the anointed of the Lord," (17:36, Charles, *APOT* 2:650) and finally, "His words (shall be) like the words of the holy ones in the midst of sanctified peoples" (17:49, Charles, *APOT* 2:651). Whether Paul made use of this book at this point or not, the idea is quite similar that the sanctified people of God (= those made holy) are the "saints" or "holy ones" of God. The word parallels are striking in the first and third of these examples. Paul transferred to the followers of Jesus Christ the designation earlier reserved for the people of God (see also 1 Thess. 4:3; 5:23). In the examples from Daniel and the noncanonical *Psalms of Solomon*, the reference is always in the plural and not the singular. In other words, individuals were not called holy or saints, but the corporate people of God. Paul is consistent with this use of the term "holy" or "saint" when he uses it for the followers of Jesus. Paul likewise sees the term as synonymous with the "church (*ekklesia*) of God" (2 Cor. 1:1).

Who in every place call upon the name of our Lord Jesus Christ. The expression of calling upon the name of the Lord has firm roots in the Old Testament (Ps. 99:6; Joel 2:32; see Acts 2:21 and Rom. 10:13). That Jesus is addressed as "our Lord Jesus Christ" is also important. In the New Testament, "Lord" can be translated simply as "sir" (Matt. 8:2; 21:30; 27:63; Mark 7:28; John 4:11, 15, 19, 49; Rev. 7:14) or in the plural, "sirs" (Acts 16:30; 27:10) or it may be a reference to God (Matt. 1:20; 4:7; 11:25; Mark 12:30; Luke 20:42, 44), that is, the one to whom all Christians render their worship, obedience, and loyalty. In this regard, Jesus is also frequently called the Lord in the New Testament (Luke 19:25, 34; John 20:28; Rom. 10:9; 13:14; 1 Cor. 15:31) and especially throughout Paul's writings. For Paul, Jesus was acknowledged as divine through his resurrection from the dead (Rom. 1:3-4) and this title, along with "Christ," is one of the most common titles used of the risen Jesus in the New Testament. It is the latter sense that Paul is using here when he calls Jesus Lord.

In reference to Paul's reference to those who "call on the name of the Lord," the early church's dependence upon the Septuagint (LXX), or Greek translation of the Old Testament, is seen in several passages that focus on the act of acknowledgement of the all sufficiency of God and belief that God can hear and answer those who call on him. This belief is reflected in a common Jewish notion of the importance of calling upon the name of the Lord (see Gen. 4:26; 12:8; Ps. 50:15).

1:3. Grace to you and peace from God our Father and the Lord Jesus Christ. See earlier discussion in Rom. 1:7. This was a common greeting among the early Christians (see Rom. 1:7; 2 Cor. 1:2; Gal. 1:3; Eph. 1:2; Phil. 1:2; Col. 1:2; 1 Thess. 1:1; 2 Thess. 1:2; Titus 1:4; Phile. 3). It is expanded to include mercy in 1 Tim. 1:2 and 2 Tim. 1:2 and 2 John 3, and the grace and peace are multiplied in 1 Peter 1:2 and this is expanded in 2 Peter 1:2 (compare with Daniel 4:1). In the second century, approximately 140–150, Polycarp, the bishop of Smyrna, wrote a letter to the Philippian Christians using a similar introduction. "Polycarp and the Elders with him to the Church of God sojourning in Philippi; mercy and peace from God Almighty and Jesus Christ our Saviour be multiplied to you" (Pol. *Phil.*, Introduction, LCL). Similarly, see also the introduction to 1 Clement that reads: "Grace and peace from God Almighty be multiplied to you through Jesus Christ" (1 Clem, Intro. LCL), which is similar to 1 and 2 Peter, but it also has an earlier parallel in the Jewish pseudepigraphal writing, *2 Baruch.* The beginning of chapter 78 of that work begins:

> These are the words of that epistle which Baruch the son of Neriah sent to the nine and a half tribes, which were across the river Euphrates, in which these things were written. Thus saith Baruch the son of Neriah to the brethren carried into captivity: 'Mercy and peace' (Charles, *APOT* 2:521).

1:4-5. I thank my God always concerning you... in everything you were enriched in Him, in all speech and all knowledge. This is the so-called "Proemium" (Greek = *prooimion*, "prelude"), or thanksgiving, that is typical at the beginning of Paul's letters except in the case of the letter to the Galatians when he was writing both in haste and anger to his recent converts. Here, it is instructive that the Corinthians received the grace from God and did not earn it. This is the basis of his appeal for both humility in the presence of God and one another and not boasting (1:26-31), since all that they have from God came to them by God's grace and was not earned. He gives thanks always to God for what God has done among his readers, the Corinthians. It was Paul's habit to pray regularly for his converts and he began his prayers with thanksgiving for all that God has done for them.

Those who have been made rich because of what God has bestowed upon them is a familiar theme in Paul's thanksgivings for his converts (see below at 3:22; Rom. 2:4; 11:33; Phil. 4:19). Similar forms of thanksgiving are found in Rom. 1:8-13; 1 Cor. 4-9; Phil. 1:3-11; Col. 1:3-14; 1 Thess. 1:2-10; 2 Thess. 1:3-12; Phile. 4-7. In

2 Cor. 1:3-7 (see Eph. 1:3) Paul follows the more Jewish pattern, "Blessed be God" or, more precisely, "Blessed art thou" (*m. Berakoth* 6.3, 8).

1:5-7. Speech, knowledge, spiritual gifts. Paul clarifies for the Corinthians the basis for his regular thanksgiving (1:4) and it is related to the spiritual gifts that God has given to them, especially speech, knowledge, and spiritual gifts (Greek = *logos/gnosis/charismata*), cf. 8:1; 12:8; 13:1-2.

1:8. Who shall also confirm you to the end, blameless in the day of our Lord Jesus Christ. Blameless (Greek = *anegkletous*). This term comes from a judicial context in which those accused of wrongdoing (see Rom. 8:33) have been declared by the judge to be blameless or innocent. Other uses of this word are found in Col. 1:22; 1 Tim. 3:10; Titus 1:6-7. When Paul emphasizes being blameless in a moral or religious sense, he often uses another terms, *amemptos* (Phil. 2:15; 3:6; 1 Thess. 3:13) or *amemptos* (1 Thess. 2:10; 3:13; 5:23).

Day of the Lord. Paul's expression, "Day of the Lord," is a familiar one in the Old Testament (Isa. 13:6, 9; Jer. 25:33; Ezek. 7:10; 13:5; Joel 2:1, 31; 3:14; Amos 5:18-20; Obad. 1:15; Zeph. 1:7, 14; Mal. 4:1) and refers both to God's judgment and to the day of salvation. It plays an important role in Paul's understanding of God's judgments and rewards as well, but for him this is the day of the Lord Jesus Christ or the day of Jesus Christ (2 Cor. 1:14; Phil. 1:6, 10; 2:16; 1 Thess. 5:2). For Paul, the "Lord" is Jesus Christ (Rom. 10:9; 1 Cor. 3:13-15; 5:5).

1:9. God is faithful. The faithfulness of God is a recurrent theme in Jewish beliefs about God. See Deut. 7:9; Isa. 49:7; Ps. 145:13. In roughly contemporary Jewish literature, Philo wrote:

> So then it is best to trust God and not our dim reasonings and insecure conjectures: "Abraham believed God and was held to be righteous" (Gen. xv.6); and

the precedence which Moses takes is testified to by the works he is "faithful in all My house" (Num. xii.7). (*Allegorical Interpretations* 3.228 LCL).

And again,

Now men have recourse to oaths to win belief, when others deem them untrustworthy; but God is trustworthy in his speech as elsewhere, so that His words in certitude and assurance differ not a whit from oaths. And so it is that while with us the oath gives warrant for our sincerity, it is itself guaranteed by God. For the oath does not make God trustworthy; it is God that assures the oath (*Sacrifices of Abel and Cain* 93, LCL).

His Son, Jesus Christ our Lord. This passage contains the longest christological title that Paul uses in any of his letters. We should note here that in the first ten verses of 1 Corinthians, Paul refers to "Christ" ten times! It is clear that he is setting forth the basis for what he is about to say regarding unity in the Christian family: namely, that what God has given to his people in Christ is the basis for their unity in the church.

With this introduction, Paul transitions to the primary reason for writing this letter to the church: namely, the divisions in the church.

II. 1:10–6:20. PAUL'S RESPONSE TO ORAL REPORTS FROM CHLOE'S PEOPLE

Following a usual introduction of a letter to a church, Paul now launches into the concerns that have been shared with him that led to his writing the letter. There are divisions in the church that have been reported to him first by Chloe's people (1:10–6:20) and secondly those reports coming to him by Stephanus and Fortunatus (7:1–16:12). These concerns are dealt with one by one and form the outline of the letter. In the initial section, Paul begins the primary focus of his letter to the Corinthians:

namely, it is a letter of exhortation (Greek = *parakalo*) toward unity. Paul identifies the divisions and also the basis for unity in the Christian community. In the second section, he responds to the specific issues that were dividing the Christian community. Rather than party loyalties, the issues appear to be division over arrogance, boasting, and various personal practices. Some of the problems may have been related to social status as in the case of the wealthier or more leisurely Christians coming to the supper meal before the others arrive and eating better food and more than was left for those who labored longer in their work (1 Cor. 11:17-21). As 1:10–4:21 is pivotal to understanding the context of the Corinthian community that Paul is addressing, so it is also the starting point for the whole letter that focuses on the various causes for divisions in the church. Here Paul is addressing several inappropriate activities among the Corinthian Christians that were reported to him. There is no self-defense here, as we will find later in 2 Corinthians, but rather an at times strongly worded admonition to change their ways.

Many scholars over the years have tried to identify the divisions in the church in terms of party loyalties: namely, those who were loyal to Paul, Apollos, Peter (Cephas) or Christ, but such parties are not mentioned again in the rest of Paul's correspondence to the Corinthians. It is more likely that social distinctions such as the advantages of those with wealth (1 Cor. 11:17-22) and the differences based on spiritual gifts, especially those charismatic gifts such as speaking in tongues and interpreting them, lay behind the divisions in the church (1 Cor. 12:14-26), and these are the areas of conflict that initiate Paul's admonitions toward unity.

A. 1:10–4:21. Divisions over leadership
1:10-17. Divisions in Corinth

1:10. Now I exhort you, brethren, by the name of our Lord Jesus Christ, that you all agree, and

there be no divisions among you. Only here does Paul use the genitive "by" (Greek = *dia*) in reference to the name of Jesus and the idea clearly is that of agency: namely, that by the name of the one who can indeed bring unity, the Lord Jesus Christ, he implores the Corinthian Christians toward that unity in the Christian community and on the basis of the Lord Jesus Christ and as his representative. Normally Paul uses the instrumental dative "in" (Greek = *en*) as in 1 Cor. 5:4 and 6:11. This name is also a part of the baptismal formula (see 1:13-15) employed in the earliest stages of the church's development (see discussion of Acts 2:38; 10:48; 19:3-5), and Paul appeals to the common name in which there ought to be unity among Christians. The title "Christ" is added here and was used regularly by the early Christians as a reference to Jesus, the one who will bring in the salvation of God. The term "messiah" was used earlier by Jews as a reference to a kingly figure who would restore the power of the Davidic kingdom and rule as a righteous king over all the peoples of the earth. This view no doubt stands behind the New Testament use of "Christ." The term, "Christ" or "Messiah" (Hebrew = *mashiah*, "anointed") was used of those who were anointed with oil symbolizing the coming of the Spirit of God upon an individual to perform a sacred office of king or even prophet. The Dead Sea Scrolls have several references to a messianic figure also to a prophet who will recognize the king who comes in the name of the Lord and also to the high priest who will offer sacrifices in the messianic kingdom. In the Rule of the Congregation, for example, this messiah will also join with leaders of the people and priests and bless the first fruits of the bread and of the vine.

This is the assembly of famous men, [those summoned to] the gathering of the community council, when [God] begets the Messiah with them. [The] chief [priest] of all the congregation of Israel shall enter, and all [his brothers, the sons] of Aaron, the priests [summoned] to the assembly, the famous men, and they shall sit befo[re him, each one] according to his dignity. After [the Me]ssiah of Israel shall ent[er] and before him shall sit the chiefs [of the clans of Israel, each] one according to his dignity, according to their p[ositions] in their camps and in their marches. And all the chiefs of the cl[ans of the congre]gation with the wise [men and the learned] shall sit before them, each one according to his dignity. And [when] they gather at the table of community [or to drink] the new wine, and the table of community is prepared [and] the new wine [is mixed] for drinking, [no one should stretch out] his hand to the first-fruit of the bread and of the [new wine] before the priest, for [he is the one who bl]esses the first-fruit of bread and of the new wine [and stretches out] his hand towards bread before them. Afterwards, the Messiah of Israel shall stretch out his hand towards the bread. [And afterwards, shall] bless all the congregation of the community, each [one according to] his dignity. And in accordance with this regulation they shall act at each me[al, when] at least ten m[en are gat]hered. (1Qsa ii.11-22; Trans Garcia Martinez, *The Dead Sea Scrolls Translated* 127-28. The bracketed material [] was supplied by the translator.)

It is not difficult here to see some parallels with the story of Jesus with his disciples at the last supper, but for our interests here, the role of the Messiah at a special banquet is instructive, and those who are gathered together with him (similarly, see 1QS ix.11 2 and 1QM 2.16).

In the early church, Jesus was referred to as a Son of David, and the Christ, or Messiah, in the same context (Matt. 1:1; 17). When Paul refers to Jesus as the Son of David, it is doubtless with his kingship and kingdom in view (Rom. 1:3; see notes). Jesus was also seen as a prophet like unto Moses (Acts 3:20-22) and as a priest who offers intercession on behalf of his people (Heb. 4:14; 8:1-2; 10:11-12). It is remarkable that all three of these roles (prophet, priest, king) are found in the New Testament references to Jesus as Messiah or Christ.

Now I exhort you, brethren. By first calling them brothers (and sisters), Paul lets his readers know that because they are related to God they therefore are his (Paul's) brothers and sisters in the faith, and he appeals to them on the basis of their common family faith ties to agree with one another. We should note that Paul's use of "brethren" (Greek = *adelphoi*) is understood as generic and is not limited to males, even if the term is a masculine plural noun. One commentator has translated the term, "My dear Christian family," (A. Thiselton, *1 Corinthians*, NIGTC) and this is the sense of what Paul has in mind. Throughout the letter, Paul refers to both men and women (1 Cor. 7:1-11; 11:2-16; see also Phil. 4:1-3). Women were regular participants in worship in the churches Paul founded and he addressed members of the churches with their family identity: namely, brothers and sisters. In 1 Corinthians, Paul uses this term, *adelphoi*, some thirty-eight times, which is more than double its use in the rest of his letters combined. Its most poignant use is perhaps found in Phile. 16 when Paul calls upon Philemon to welcome his runaway slave back, not as a slave any longer, but as a brother because he is now a follower of Christ. The schisms in the church provide adequate explanation for Paul's desire to bring peace to the church. The author of *4 Macc.* (perhaps ca. A.D. 60–70) expresses the importance of brotherly love in a manner that is similar to that which Paul presented to the Corinthians. Speaking of the seven martyred brothers he wrote: Their common zeal for beauty and goodness strengthened their goodwill and fellow feeling for one another, and in conjunction with their piety made their brotherly love more ardent" (*4 Macc.* 13:25, *OT Pseud* 2:558).

Plutarch (ca. A.D. 45–120), a younger contemporary of Paul, wrote a treatise on *Brotherly Love* in which he emphasized the importance of treating people as brothers. He bemoans the lack of love in his days saying "brotherly love is as rare in our day as brotherly hatred was among the men of old" (*Moralia 478C*, LCL). He knew that:

If overreaching and factious strife be engendered in them, they corrupt and destroy the animal most shamefully; so through the concord of brothers both family and household are sound and flourish, and friends and intimates, like harmonious choirs, neither do nor say, nor think, anything discordant . . . [but] . . . slander and suspicion entertained against kinsmen ushers in evil and pernicious associations which flow in from outside to fill the vacant room. . . . Indeed it is our very need, which welcomes and seeks friendship and comradeship, that teaches us to honour and cherish and keep our kin, since we are unable and unfitted by Nature to live friendless, unsocial, hermits' lives (*Moralia 479B-C*, LCL).

As a result of the familiar family ties that Christians have because of their faith, the clear implication is that the Corinthian Christians should seek agreement and unity among themselves. The divisions in the church over loyalties to various leaders should be tempered by the above comments and nevertheless understood against the Corinthians' appreciation for those with rhetorical skills. It appears that Paul concedes to Apollos' superior rhetorical skills (1:18–4:21), but continues to call for unity in the body, that is, the family of Christ's followers.

There be no divisions among you, but you be made complete in the same mind and in the same judgment. This is Paul's appeal not to agree on everything, but to allow that on which they agreed to dominate their conversation. Dio Chrysostom (ca. A.D. 40–120), wrote perceptively on the beauty of concord among peoples.

What spectacle of purpose, and what sound is more enchanting than a city of purpose, and what sound is more awe-inspiring than its harmonious voice? What city is wiser in council than that which takes council together? What city is less liable to failure than that which favors the same policies? To whom are blessings sweeter than to those who are of one heart and mind? (*Discourse* 39.3, LCL).

Divisions in the church at Corinth were known long after the death of Paul. Clement of Rome (ca. A.D. 95) addressed the Corinthians about the squabbles among them over their removal from office those leaders who had been appointed over them. Speaking of the causes for divisions in the church at Corinth at the turn of the first century, he writes:

> Our Apostles . . . appointed those who have been already mentioned, and afterwards added the codicil that if they should fall asleep, other approved men should succeed to their ministry. We consider therefore that it is not just to remove from their ministry those who were appointed by them, or later on by other eminent men, with the consent of the whole Church, and have ministered to the flock of Christ without blame, humbly, peaceably, and disinterestedly, and for many years have received a universally favourable testimony. For our sin is not small, if we eject from the episcopate those who have blamelessly and holily offered its sacrifices. Blessed are those Presbyters who finished their course before now, and have obtained a fruitful and perfect release in the ripeness of completed work, for they have now no fear that any shall move them from the place appointed to them. For we see that in spite of their good service, you have removed some from the ministry which they fulfilled blamelessly (*1 Clement* 44.3-6, LCL).

Later he writes:

> Why do we divide and tear asunder the members of Christ, and raise up strife against our own body, and reach such a pitch of madness as to forget that we are members one of another? . . . Your schism has turned aside many, has cast many into discouragement, many to doubt, all of us to grief and your sedition continues (*1 Clement* 46.7, 9, LCL).

He then refers to the schisms mentioned in 1 Cori. 1:10-13 and concludes, "It is a shameful report, beloved, extremely shameful, and unworthy of your training in Christ, that on account of one or two persons the steadfast and ancient church of the Corinthians is being disloyal to the presbyters" (*1 Clement* 47.6, LCL).

The same mind. Paul's concern to bring unity to the church and that they have the same mind (Greek = *aute gnome*) has several parallels in antiquity. This was the goal of Dio Chrysostom's appeal noted above (*Discourses* 39.8) and he uses the same term to call for such unity (*aute gnome*).

1:11. For I have been informed . . . by Chloe's people. It is not altogether clear who Chloe was nor who her people were. Presumably, they were Christians from Corinth who had come to visit Paul. She may have been a wealthy business woman who had slaves or employees working for her in Ephesus. Had these people been Chloe's family, they would have been identified by their father's name even if he had been deceased, therefore, many suggest that Chloe was a business woman of some considerable means. Chloe was probably a Christian who opened her home to the church in Corinth (see Acts 16:15; Rom. 16:10-11; Col. 4:15). Whoever she was, the mentioning of her name gave credence to the report that Paul received and he acted on the information not as gossip, but as fact of what was happening in the church. It is worth noting that the ministry of providing hospitality and a place to meet was something that was generally given to those with financial security in the early church. Wealthy women seemed to play a significant role in the early church and often provided meeting places for worship. See, for instance, Tabitha provided the material needs of the widows in Lydda (Acts 9:36-42), and others provided homes where the church gathered as in the cases of Mary the mother of John Mark (Acts 12:12), Lydia in Philippi (Acts 16:15, 40), and Nymphas in Laodicea (Col. 4:15). What role or roles did other well-known women have in the church, as in the cases of Phoebe in Cenchrea (Rom. 16:1-2), Chloe at Corinth (here), Eudia and Syntyche in Philippi (Phil. 4:2-3), and the wealthy women who converted to Christianity in Thessalonica (Acts 17:4) or Beroea (Acts 17:12)? There are other women mentioned in connection with their husbands and may well have provided hospitality and a meeting place as well, see, for instance, Prisca (= Priscilla) and Aquila (Acts 18:3; 1 Cor. 16:19; Rom. 16:5), Philemon and Apphia at Colossae (Phile. 1-2), and Philologus and Julia in Rome—or Ephesus—(Rom. 16:15). These individuals provided much needed service to the early church and the house-church was at the center of the early church's mission.

There are quarrels among you. The word for "quarrels" or "divisions" is found in a list of vices in the Jewish book of Sirach (ca. 180 B.C.) where we read that: "A hasty quarrel kindles a fire, and hasty dispute sheds blood" (28:11, NRSV). The term is found later and translated "strife" in Sirach 40:5, 9. Paul uses the term again in Rom. 13:13; and 2 Cor. 12:20 where he obviously fears dissension in the church and he even lists "quarrelling" as one of the works of the flesh and sins to avoid in Gal. 5:20.

1:12. "I am of Paul," and "I of Apollos," and "I of Cephas," and "I of Christ." What precisely were these divisions? As noted in the introduction of this section, it is unlikely that the Corinthians actually divided up into three or four units of opposition based on loyalties to three, indeed four, well-known personalities. Paul, however, shows how absurd it was to follow him and he underscored that because everything Christians have comes from Christ, not those who baptized them, that their loyalties and unity should be in him. Paul says that he was not crucified for them nor were they baptized in his name. Christ alone was crucified for them and they were all baptized in the name of Christ (see 1 Cor. 12:12-13). To be baptized in the name of someone meant to be an adherent of that individual. Those who followed Moses through the wilderness and were under the cloud with him were "baptized into Moses" (1 Cor. 10:2).

Apollos. The background for Apollos is found in Acts 18:24-28. He came from Alexandria and became a follower of John the Baptist. He was preaching in Ephesus and was a powerful persuader, but his knowledge was lacking. While he was at Ephesus, he came under the influence of Prisca and Aquila, who taught him more clearly about "the Way" and he became a follower of Jesus Christ. He subsequently went to Corinth and was evidently quite influential in the Corinthian church. Paul did not distance himself from Apollos, but rather let the people know that they were involved in the same work, one who planted and one who watered what was planted (3:1-6; 4:6-7). There is no indication that he and Paul were in any opposition to each other (1 Cor. 16:12).

It is interesting that a recent discovery of a two-handled bowl unearthed at the Asclepion at Corinth, a common place of healing in Greco-Roman cities including Jerusalem in the first century, has the words, "I belong to Apollo." Another bronze dedication found on a sanctuary at Corinth reads: "I belong to Aphrodite," indicating that an individual presented the object in honor of this Greek goddess in her sanctuary at Corinth. (See M. Lang, *Cure and Cult in Ancient Corinth* American Excavations in Old Corinth, Corinth Notes, 3, fig. 2.)

Cephas. The Aramaic name for Peter. Paul regularly uses Peter's Aramaic name Cephas (1:12, 3:22; 9:5; 15:5) rather than the traditional Greek name, but not invariably (Gal. 2:7-8).

Whether he actually came to Corinth is difficult to determine, but his influence was considerable in the early church, and his frequent reference in the Gospel tradition that was circulating in the churches even before the Gospels were written and his tendency toward Jewish Christianity and its commitment to the law may have been an issue that divided the church at Corinth, but if so, it is not obvious from the rest of the letter.

1:13-15. Has Christ been divided? Paul was not crucified for you, was he? Or were you baptized in the name of Paul? I thank God that I baptized none of you except Crispus and Gaius, that no man should say you were baptized in my name. Paul claims that those who have chosen to follow Christ and were baptized in his name are those who have decided to follow him. Because of this, all such loyalties to others and all such divisions based on these loyalties to others are inappropriate. Chrysostom (ca. 347–407), in his *Homilies on the Epistles of Paul to the Corinthians* (3.6), says, "the greatness of baptism does not lie in the baptizer but in the one whose name is invoked in the baptism" and further, that "a person of no singular excellence can baptize." He added that in this passage "Paul downplays his own role in order to show that he was not seeking honor or glory for himself" (NPNF 1, 12:12-13).

Crispus. Crispus was probably a supporter of the Apostle Paul and is likely the same as the ruler or overseer of the synagogue in Corinth (Acts 18:8) who, along with his whole household, became a believer in Christ. Although there were not many in the Corinthian church who were "mighty," Crispus was evidently one of the exceptions. When he became a Christian, his whole household followed him. This suggests both his influence and perhaps also his wealth.

Gaius. Like Crispus, he was baptized by Paul and may well have offered Paul hospitality when he was writing his letter to the Romans from Corinth (Rom. 16:23). That he was host to the entire church in Corinth suggests also that he was a man of wealth. It is possible that the Titius Justus mentioned in Acts 18:7 as the owner of the home where Paul stayed in Corinth is the same as the Gaius mentioned here and that the author of Acts is not giving his full name there and Paul is not giving the full name here. If this is so, it is likely that Gaius' full name, according to Roman order, would be Gaius Titius Justus. It is worth noting that Paul baptized both a Jew (Crispus) and a Gentile (Gaius) in Corinth.

1:16. Now I did baptize also the household of Stephanas. Mentioned only here in the New Testament, Stephanas was a friend to Paul and visited him in Ephesus along with Fortunatus and Achaicus (1 Cor. 16:17). He was a powerful figure in the church at Corinth and both he and his whole household were among Paul's first converts in the province of Achaia where Corinth was situated, and they were actively involved in the ministry of that church (16:15-16).

1:18-31. Christ Crucified, the Wisdom and Power of God
This passage focuses on the distinction between the wisdom of the world and the wisdom of God. Paul says that one does not know God through the former, but only the latter that has its central foundation in the death of Christ on the cross. In this section, Paul briefly abandons his discussion of the divisions among the Corinthians and pursues a corrective in their exaltation of eloquence and wisdom.

1:19. "I will destroy the wisdom of the wise, And the cleverness of the clever I will set aside" (Isa. 29:14). Paul has taken this quote from Isaiah, one of his favorite books that he cites some six times in this letter alone. He cites, however, the Septuagint version (LXX), but changes it by returning to the Hebrew term *satar* meaning "I will set aside" instead of the LXX, "I shall conceal" (Greek = *krupso*). He also changes the third person singular passive to the first person singular active. While scholars do not agree on why Paul made these changes, it is likely that he was citing from memory—it is highly unlikely that he would have had a copy of the Hebrew or Greek Bible with him—and he was using the biblical text in the *pesher* or *midrashic* interpretive fashion common in the first century. Here Paul begins his biblical proof for his argument and in 1:18–3:23, he cites Isa. 29:14 here, Jer. 9:22 in 1:31; Isa. 64:4 in 2:9; Isa. 40:13 in 2:16; Job 5:12-13 in 3:19 and Ps. 94:11 in 3:20.

Paul also focuses on the eschatological nature of God's bringing to nothing the wisdom of the world, "I will set aside." Before him, Hillel (ca. 30 B.C. to A.D. 10), one of the great rabbis of Israel claimed that the cares and possessions of this world one day would end and that only the Law of God and the wisdom that comes from its study would remain. He reportedly taught that:

> . . . the more study of the Law the more life; the more schooling the more wisdom; the more counsel the more understanding; the more righteousness the more peace. If a man has gained a good name he has gained [somewhat] for himself; if he has gained for himself words of the Law he has gained for himself life in the world to come (*m. Aboth* 2.7, Danby Trans.).

1:20. Where is the wise man? Where is the scribe? Where is the debater of this age? Has not God made foolish the wisdom of the world? The reference to the wise man, the scribe, and the debater are interesting social categories. In the social-class-conscious community of Corinth, Paul acknowledges and then discards such categories of distinction for the church. All of the wisdom coming from these three are equal to the wisdom of the world, and Paul says that such wisdom or knowledge will pass away (see also 1 Cor. 13:8-10).

1:21. For since in the wisdom of God the world through its wisdom did not come to know God, God was well-pleased through the foolishness of the message preached to save those who believe. The wisdom of God is contrasted with the wisdom of the world not only in Paul, but long before him Plato argued for a similar conclusion. Reporting the words of Socrates at his trial in Athens, he writes:

> The fact is, men of Athens, that I have acquired this reputation on account of nothing else than a sort of wisdom. What kind of wisdom is this? Just that which is perhaps human wisdom. For perhaps I really am wise in this wisdom; and these men, perhaps, of whom I was just speaking, might be wise in some wisdom greater than human, or I don't know what to say . . .

> And men of Athens, do not interrupt me with noise, even if I seem to you to be boasting; for the word which I speak is not mine, but the speaker to whom I shall refer it is a person of weight. For my wisdom—if it is wisdom at all—and of its nature, I will offer you the god of Delphi as a witness.

> . . .

> Now from this investigation, men of Athens, many enmities have arisen against me, . . . [but] the fact is, gentlemen, it is likely that the god is really wise and by his oracle means this: "Human wisdom is of little or no value." And it appears that he does not really say this of Socrates, but merely uses my name, and makes me an example, as if he were to say: "This one of you, O human beings, is wisest, who, like Socrates, recognizes that he is in truth of no account in respect to wisdom." (Plato, *Apology* 20 DE, 23A, LCL).

Many ancient Jews believed that the wisdom of God was found in the Torah, or Law of God. See for instance, that the writer of the book of Baruch, written sometime between 200 and 60 B.C., speaks of the vain wisdom of the world. Remarkably, he says that those who are perishing do not have wisdom: "God did not choose them, or give them the way to knowledge; so they perished because they had no wisdom, they perished through their folly" (3:27-28, NRSV) and then the writer concludes:

> She [wisdom] is the book of the commandments of God, the law that endures forever. All who hold her [wisdom] fast will live, and those who forsake her will die. Turn, O Jacob, and take her; walk toward the shining of her light. Do not give your glory to another, or your advantages to an alien people. Happy are we, O Israel, for we know that is pleasing to God (*Baruch* 4:1-4, NRSV).

We should note that here as elsewhere in this letter, Paul attributes to Jesus the attributes that in the texts he cites belong to God. See 1:31 (Jer. 9:22-23); 2:16 (Isa. 40:13; 10:9; Ps. 78:18; Num. 21:5-6); 10:22 (Deut. 32:21) and 10:26 (Ps. 24:1). This practice, of course, shows the exaltation of Jesus the Christ in the theology of Paul.

1:22. For indeed Jews ask for signs, and Greeks search for wisdom. The seeking of signs by Jews is demonstrated in the story of Jesus when he tells the Jews that they will not receive a sign (Mark 8:11-12). The Greeks, on the other hand, were known for their interest in learning, or pursuit of wisdom (Greek = *sophia*) and knowledge (Greek = *gnosis*). Herodotus (ca. 485–80 B.C.) tells of this reputation among the Greeks, but also indicates that it may have been produced by the Greeks themselves! He writes:

> I have heard another story told by the Pel[o]ponnesians: namely, that Anacharsis had been sent by the king of Scythia and had been a learner of the ways of Hellas, and after his return told

the king who sent him that all Greeks were zealous for every kind of learning (Greek = *sophien*), save only the Lacedaemonians; but that these were the only Greeks who spoke and listened with discretion. But this is a tale vainly invented by the Greeks themselves ... (*Persian Wars* 4.77, LCL).

1:26. For consider your calling, brethren, that there were not many wise according to the flesh, not many mighty, not many noble. The terms here for "wise" (Greek = *sophos*) and "mighty" (Greek = *dunatos*) are similar to those in the Jeremiah text that Paul cites (1:31) as support for his argument (see Jer. 9:23-24; and compare the boasting of Paul only in the cross of Christ (1:29-31; 2 Cor. 10:17-18; Gal. 6:14).

The word for "noble" (Greek = *eugenes*) literally means "well born" and is likely a reference to the Roman social status that was so highly esteemed. Those who were born free were considered more valuable in society than those who were slaves. The social status issues of the community may well lie behind some of the conflicts in the church, especially as the Christians came together to observe the Lord's Supper (see 11:17-22). The social structure of the Roman Empire consisted essentially of five classes of people. (1) Members of the Roman senatorial families who had such positions because of great wealth. (2) Members of the equestrian class who arrived at their position because of wealth or because of significant contributions of service to the state. (3) Free men and women who were born this way as Roman citizens and who may or may not have been wealthy. (4) Freed men and women, that is, those who had bought their freedom or had had it purchased for them. (5) Slaves, whose range of indenture ran the gamut from immensely dangerous work such as in mines, to trusted positions in a household. Some slaves were allowed to buy their freedom and citizenship, but their wages were often quite low, making it extremely difficult for one person to do.[1] The rights of citizens included the right of appeal, even to the emperor or to his highest court if need be, as well as the right of trial and exemption from some of the local taxes and certain forms of punishment. It was clearly a highly prized possession, and in Acts we can see that Paul's Roman citizenship and consequent rights helped him out of several difficulties and even saved his life (Acts 16:37–39; 22:25–29; 25:9–12).[2]

For years scholars have debated the social structures of the Corinthian church and have generally argued that there were not many wise or powerful or noble people in the church, but there were a few. In contrast, 2 Cor. 8:14 suggests that there may have been more than a few in the church with an abundance of wealth. This may be a bit of hyperbole on Paul's part to encourage the Corinthians to care for the needs of the Christians in Jerusalem. Part of Paul's criticism of the Corinthian Christians stems from their willingness to go to court with one another (1 Cor. 6:1-8). This also suggests that at least some of these Christians were people of means. As noted above, both Chloe and Stephanas were probably people of wealth and influence in the community. Whatever the case, there are hints that there were some persons of means in the church. The extent to which this caused the

divisions in the church is debatable, but seems likely. The Jews in antiquity believed that one was wise who had common sense and a faithfulness to the will of God (see, for example, Prov. 1:7; 5:1-2; 10:23; 13:10; 28:25-26; 11:30). On the other hand, the Hellenists of the first century believed that people who were wise were those who had an understanding of education, philosophy, science, and culture. Those who were "well-born" were generally those who were born free as Roman citizens, or perhaps those who descended from noble families.

The general paucity of well-educated individuals among the Christians was noted in a letter from Pliny the Younger (ca. 61–113), the governor of Bithynia and Pontus serving under the Emperor Trajan. In a letter to Trajan, he asked how he was to treat the Christians in his provinces. He speaks of them with disdain and contempt, calling those who refuse to recant their faith stubborn. He was convinced that those with such "obstinacy ought not to go unpunished" (*Letters* 10.96.4, LCL), and that their faith was "nothing but a degenerate sort of cult carried to extravagant lengths" (*Letters* 10.96.8, LCL), and finally that people in towns, villages, and rural communities were being "infected through contact with this wretched cult" (*Letters* 10.96.9, LCL). Similarly, Lucian of Samosata (ca. 120–180) speaks with contempt at the simplicity and incredulity of the Christians.

---

[1] A recent discussion, with bibliography, of Roman social structure and application to the New Testament, is found in J.N. Kraybill, *Imperial Cult and Commerce in John's Apocalypse* (JSNTSup 132; Sheffield: Sheffield Academic Press, 1996), 57–82. See also A. R. Burn, *The Government of the Roman Empire from Augustus to the Antonines* (London: George Philip, 1952); J. E. Stambaugh and D. L. Balch, *The New Testament in its Social Environment* (LEC; Philadelphia: Westminster, 1986), esp. 138–67. On the social context of the Corinthian letters, see David G. Horrell, *The Social Ethos of the Corinthian Correspondence: Interests and Ideology from 1 Corinthians to 1 Clement*. Studies of the New Testament and its World (Edinburgh: T & T Clark, 1996), 92-198. On slavery in the Roman Empire, see K. R. Bradley, *Slaves and Masters in the Roman Empire: A Study in Social Control* (New York: Oxford University Press, 1987); J.A. Harrill, *The Manumission of Slaves in Early Christianity* (HUT 32; Tübingen: Mohr–Siebeck, 1995).

[2] See B. Rapske, *The Book of Acts in its First Century Setting*. III. *The Book of Acts and Paul in Roman Custody* (Grand Rapids: Eerdmans, 1994), 71–112.

The poor wretches have convinced themselves, first and foremost, that they are going to be immortal and live for all time, in consequence of which they despise death and even willingly give themselves into custody, most of them. Furthermore, their first lawgiver [Jesus] persuaded them that they are all brothers of one another after they have transgressed once for all by denying the Greek gods and by worshiping that crucified sophist himself and living under his laws. Therefore they despise all things indiscriminately and consider them common property, receiving such doctrines traditionally without any definite evidence. So if any charlatan and trickster, able to profit by occasions, comes among them, he quickly acquires sudden wealth by imposing upon simple folk (*On the Death of Peregrinus* 11–14, LCL).

Celsus (ca. A.D. 178–80), a powerful critic of the early Christian movement, showed more understanding of what the Christians believed, taught, and practiced than did many of his contemporaries. He seems to have read a number of Christian writings besides merely listening to the rumors being spread about them and so his arguments against the Christians were taken more seriously than others in the second century. Some fifty years later, Origen in his *Contra Celsum*, responded to Celsus' criticisms. Among them, the criticisms of Christians being irrational and of low social status. Origen responded:

Celsus urges us to "follow reason and a rational guide in accepting doctrines" on the ground that "anyone who believes people without so doing is certain to be deceived." . . . For just as among them scoundrels frequently take advantage of the lack of education of gullible people and lead them wherever they wish, so also," he says, "this happens among the Christians." He says that "some do not even want to give or to receive a reason for what they believe, and use such expressions as 'Do not ask questions; just believe,' and 'Thy faith will save thee'" (Origen, *Contra Celsum* 1.9, ANF).

Origen noted that Celsus further charged that the Christians were largely unprofitable members of society who were weak, women, and slaves. Reflecting Celsus' criticisms of the Christians, he writes:

Their injunctions are like this. "Let no one educated, no one wise, no one sensible draw near. For those abilities are thought by us to be evils. But as for anyone ignorant, anyone stupid, anyone uneducated, anyone who is a child, let him come boldly." By the fact that they themselves admit that these people are worthy of their God, they show that they want and are able to convince only the foolish, dishonorable, and stupid, and only slaves, women, and little children.

Those who summon people to the other mysteries make this preliminary proclamation: "Whoever has pure hands and a wise tongue." And again, others say: "Whoever is pure from all defilement, and whose soul knows nothing of evil, and who has lived well and righteously." Such are the preliminary exhortations of those who promise purification from sins. But let us hear what folk these Christians call. "Whosoever is a sinner," they say, "whosoever is unwise, whosoever is a child, and in a word, whosoever is a wretch, the kingdom of God will receive him."

He asks, "Why on earth this preference for sinners?" (Origen, *Contra Celsum* 3.44, 59, 64, ANF).

It may well be that the majority of the Christians at Corinth were not Roman citizens and were not well educated or of considerable financial means and, as a result, they were despised as a group. Paul's admonition here nevertheless is for those who, for whatever reason—those baptized by a leading apostle, were possessors of special charismatic gifts, or were social superiors—were generally despised for their lack of social status. The value of social superiority, however, was well-known among the Greeks and Romans. Epictetus (ca. 54–120), highlights the importance of social status when describing how one who had moved into a new status ought to act. He indicates that freedom is a high treasure and to be pursued. He writes:

> He is free who lives as he wills, who is subject neither to compulsion, nor hindrance, nor force, whose choices are unhampered, whose desires attain their end, whose aversions do not fall into what they would avoid.... Therefore, there is not a bad man who lives as he wills, and accordingly no bad man is free. (Epict., *Discourses* 4.1.1-4, LCL).

Further, Epictetus, as a Stoic, was familiar with social status in the empire and especially as the Roman social structure was imposed on his fellow Greeks. It was important to be free and not a slave and also to leave behind one's contacts with those of the lower class.

> To this topic [social status] you ought to devote yourself before every other, how: namely, you may avoid ever being so intimately associated with some one of your acquaintances or friends as to descend to the same level with him; otherwise you will ruin yourself. (Epict., *Discourses* 4.2.1, LCL).

It is hard to imagine that the social class orientation of that era had little or no effect upon the Corinthian church, since similar social class differences have continued to affect the church of every generation.

2:1-5. Paul's Arrival in Corinth

Paul underscores that his arrival in Corinth was not in his own strength or remarkable abilities, but rather he came in the power of the Spirit that was manifested in his preaching of the crucified Christ.

2:1. And when I came to you, brethren, I did not come with superiority of speech or of wisdom, proclaiming to you the testimony of God. Paul contrasts the manner that he came to the Corinthians with the well-known eloquent orators that they were used to hearing. Philostratus (ca. 170–205), a sophist from Athens, describes the ancient interest in oratory by telling the story of how Favorinus (ca. 80–150) before him, a pretender to the sophistic mantle, spoke to the people of Rome.

> When he delivered discourses in Rome, the interest in them was universal, so that even those in his audience who did not understand the Greek language shared in the pleasure that he gave; for he fascinated even them by the tones of his voice, by his expressive glance and the rhythm of his speech (Philostratus, *Lives of the Sophists* 492.8, LCL).

He offers an even higher praise for one Gorgias of Leontini in Sicily for his sophistic eloquence and claims that in his delivery of orations in Athens, he set an example to the sophists with his virile and energetic style, his daring and unusual expressions, his inspired impressiveness, and his use of the grand style for great themes; and also with his habit of breaking off his clauses and making sudden transitions, by which devices a speech gains in sweetness and sublimity; and he also clothed his style with poetic words for the sake of ornament and dignity (*Lives of Sophists* 492.9, LCL).

Paul claims that he did not come with such language, but with a simple message delivered in the power of the Spirit.

2:4. And my message and my preaching were ~~not in persuasive words of wisdom, but in~~ **demonstration of the Spirit and of power.** Paul is using two technical terms that were well-known in his day to make his point. **Persuasive** (Greek = *peithos*) words of wisdom and **demon-**

stration (Greek = *apodeixis*) are both found in rhetorical argumentation. For example, Plutarch (ca. 45–120) spoke of the ability of human beings to perceive in contrast to animals.

That "it is day" and that "it is light" assuredly wolves and dogs and birds perceive by their senses; but "if it is day, then it is light," no creature other than man apprehends, for he alone has a concept of antecedent and consequent, of apparent implication and connexion of these things one with the another, and their relations and differences, from which our demonstrations [Greek = *apodeixeis*] derive their most authoritative inception. Since, then, philosophy is concerned with truth, and the illumination of truth is demonstration, and the inception of demonstration [Greek = *apodeixis*] is the hypothetical syllogism, then with good reason the potent element that effects the connexion and produces this was consecrated by wise men to the god who is, above all, a lover of the truth (Plutarch, *Moralia, E At Delphi* 387A, LCL).

2:6-16. Divine Wisdom and Human Wisdom

Paul underscores that true wisdom comes from God and is found not in the wisdom of the world, as observed in 1:21 above, but rather in the secret wisdom of God that comes to us in Jesus Christ through the Spirit of God. While there is a wisdom that is generated through human understanding, the world, that is the natural person, cannot know the wisdom of God except through the discernment and aid of God's Spirit. In this section Paul sets at odds the wisdom of the world and the wisdom of God. He sets up the stage for a later discussion of spiritual gifts and even the resurrection of Jesus from the dead in that God's activity in both are a result of his activity through the Holy Spirit.

2:6. Yet we do speak wisdom among those who are mature. It was common in antiquity to distinguish between those who understood divine mysteries and those who did not by using terms like "mature" (Greek = *teleios*) or children as opposed to adults (see Phil. 3:12-15; cf. 1 Cor. 3:2; Col. 1:28; 4:12; Heb. 5:11–6:1; James 1:4). Philo (ca. A.D. 20–40) also made this distinction in his interpretation of Abraham's migration. Speaking metaphorically while describing wisdom as a land or country, Philo writes:

> In this country there awaiteth thee the nature which is its own pupil, its own teacher, that needs not to be fed on milk as children are fed, that has been stayed by a Divine oracle from going down into Egypt and from meeting with the ensnaring pleasures of the flesh (*Migration of Abraham* 29, LCL).

Elsewhere he claims that there is no need, then, to give injunctions or prohibitions or exhortations to the perfect man [Greek = *teleio*] formed after the (Divine) image, for none of these does the perfect man [*ho teleios*] require. The bad man has need of injunction and prohibition, and the child of exhortation and teaching (*Allegorical Interpretation* 1.94, LCL).

Philo divided persons into three categories: namely, the beginner (Greek = *archomenos*) who has barely started his training, the one who is making gradual progress (Greek = *prokopton*), and the perfect (Greek = *teleios*) person (*Allegorical Interpretation* 3.159). Later, Epictetus (ca. A.D. 64–68) asked his readers, "Make up your mind, therefore, before it is too late, that the fitting thing for you to do is to live as a mature man who is making progress, and let everything which seems to you to be best be for you a law that must not be transgressed" (*Encheiridion* 51.2, LCL). And again, while describing the maturing toward perfection that is essential for every person, he chides his hearers and asks "Are you not willing, at this late date, like children, to be weaned and to partake of more solid food, and not to cry for mammies and nurses—old wives' lamentations?" and he adds, "Man, do something desperate, as the expression goes, now if never before, to achieve peace, freedom, and high-mindedness." (*Discourses* 2.16.40-41,LCL). He later urges the readers to grow up in their understanding and to "advance to perfection [to *teleion*] through the spoken word and such instruction as you receive here" but he fears that some will become satisfied with their immaturity and asks them, "although you have this purpose, because some pretty trick of style, or certain principles, catch your fancy, are you going to stay just where you are and choose to dwell there, forgetful of the things at home and saying 'This is fine'?" (Epictetus, *Discourses*, 2.23.40-41, 43, LCL).

2:7. But we speak God's wisdom in a mystery, the hidden wisdom, which God predestined before the ages to our glory. The reference to the secret wisdom of God as a mystery (Greek = *musterio*) is not unlike the same perspective held by Philo, a contemporary of Paul, who said: "These thoughts, ye initiated, whose ears are purified, receive into your souls as holy mysteries [Greek = *musteria*] indeed and babble not of them to any of the profane." He adds, "I myself was initiated under Moses the God-beloved into his greater mysteries [*musteria*]" (*On the Cherubim* 48-49 LCL). The relationship between wisdom and divine mysteries can also be found in the Jewish tradition. For example, in the Qumran community, we read of the failure of evil persons who do not know God's future mysteries and whose end will be terrible for trying to destroy those mysteries. "And they do not know the future mystery, or understand ancient matters ... And all those who curb the wonderful mysteries will no longer exist. And

all knowledge will pervade the world, and there will never be folly there" (*1QMysteries*/1Q27, 1.3,7, Garcia Martinez trans.). Paul's reference to hidden wisdom is not unlike some Jewish beliefs of his time that there was a special wisdom from God that the world cannot understand. When the author of the apocryphal *4 Ezra* tells the story of God's plan to preserve Israel's sacred writings, he says that there were twenty-four books that all could read, but seventy that were reserved for those who are wise.

So during the forty days ninety-four books were written. And when the forty days were ended, the Most High spoke to me [Ezra], saying "Make public the twenty-four books [perhaps the same as the Old Testament today] that you wrote first and let the worthy and the unworthy read them; but keep the seventy that were written last [perhaps the apocryphal and pseudepigraphal writings], in order to give them to the wise among your people. For in them is the spring of understanding, the fountain of wisdom, and the river of knowledge." And I did so (*4 Ezra* 14:44-48; trans. *OT Pseud*, 1:555).

2:9. But just as it is written, "Things which eye has not seen and ear has not heard, And which have not entered the heart of man, All that God has prepared for those who love Him." There are similarities between this passage and Isa. 64:4, but there are other parallels also in other texts of antiquity, and it is not certain which source Paul was citing in this passage. He introduced the quote with the customary scriptural phrase, "as it is written," and there are some similarities here with Sirach (ca. 180 B.C.), who began his wisdom sayings with the affirmation that "All wisdom is from the Lord, and with him it remains forever" (1:1, NRSV). The author continues, however, that God gives wisdom to all who love him. "It is he who created her [wisdom] and took her measure; he poured her out upon all his works, upon all the living according to his gift; he lavished her upon those who love him" (1:9-10,

NRSV). The church father, "the Ambrosiaster," an unknown commentator of Paul's letters ca. 366–84, concluded that Paul may have been citing the *Apocalypse of Elijah*, but that is difficult to show since the volume is lost. He writes: "These words were expressed somewhat differently by Isaiah [Isa. 64:4], and they are also found in the apocryphal Apocalypse of Elijah. Paul uses them to refer to the incarnation of Christ, which not only goes against human perception but is beyond the understanding of heavenly powers as well" (CSEL 81.26). There is an even a closer parallel in the words of Pseudo-Philo (ca. A.D. 40–70) who, while commenting on the future of those who faithfully follow God, says

And they will be there until I remember the world and visit those inhabiting the earth. And then I will take those and many others better than they are from where eye has not seen nor has ear heard and it has not entered into the heart of man, until the like should come to pass in the world. And the just will not lack the brilliance of the sun or the moon, for the light of those most precious stones will be their light (*Liber Antiquitatum Biblicarum* 26.13, OTP 2.338-39).

Whatever the source, Paul cites it in an authoritative manner to justify the logic of his argument: namely, that there is a wisdom that is known only to God and to those who love God. The relationship between prophecy, knowledge, and wisdom is not as clearly distinguished in antiquity as we find in later generations of Christians. At Qumran, the Jews who produced and collected the literature in the Dead Sea Scrolls, wrote: "My eyes have observed what always is, wisdom that has been hidden from mankind, knowledge and understanding (hidden) from the sons of man, fount of justice and well of strength and spring of glory (hidden) from the assembly of flesh" (1QS [*Rule of the Community*] 11.5-7, Garcia Martinez, trans.).

2:10. For to us God revealed them through the Spirit; for the Spirit searches all things, even the depths of God. The natural rational processes appear to be set aside by the influence of the Spirit of God. Philo speaks of the prophets speaking by the power of God and at the same time, evicting the rational processes.

. . . what the reasoning faculty is in us, the sun is in the world, since both of them are light-bringers, one sending forth to the whole world the light which our senses perceive, the other shedding mental rays upon ourselves through the medium of apprehension. So while the radiance of the mind is still all around us, when it pours as it were a noonday beam into the whole soul, we are self-contained, not possessed. But when it comes to setting, naturally ecstasy and divine possession and madness fall upon us. For when the divine light of God shines, the human light sets; when the divine light sets, the human dawns and rises. This is what regularly befalls the fellowship of the prophets. The mind is evicted at the arrival of the divine Spirit, but when that departs the mind returns to its tenancy. Mortal and immortal may not share the same home (*Who is the Heir* 264-65, LCL).

After Philo, Seneca (fl. ca. 54–65) argued that "reason . . . is nothing else than a portion of the divine spirit set in a human body" (*Epistle* 66.12, LCL).

2:14. But a natural man does not accept the things of the Spirit of God; for they are foolishness to him, and he cannot understand them, because they are spiritually appraised. The argument that "like follows like" is clear in Paul's argument. He argues that the natural person follows the natural things and the spiritual person follows the things that are spiritually discerned. Plutarch likewise assumes this premise when he claims that "the only one of our attributes that is dear to the gods and divine is a virtuous mind, if it be true that it is the nature of like to delight in like" (*Moralia* 11, *How the Young should Study Poetry*, LCL).

The terms "natural" (*psuchikos*) and "spiritually" (*pneumatikos*) discerned are opposite terms and mean essentially that one is driven or motivated by that which is either natural or spiritual.

3:1-17. Warnings Against Partisanship in the Church

Paul chastises the Corinthian Christians because of their divisiveness that evidences the fact that they have not understood the wisdom that comes from God. They are following worldly or "fleshly" ambitions and not spiritual ones, and as a result, Paul must speak to them as he would a child, that is, those who are not spiritually mature. The foundation that Paul has laid through the proclamation of Christ was built upon by others, but he urges the Christians to be cautious about how they build upon it. The foundation of which he speaks is Christ himself and no inappropriate materials such as divisiveness will be able to be placed upon it. He concludes with a warning that anyone who destroys the building of God, the holy temple which is the church, God will destroy.

3:1. And I, brethren, could not speak to you as to spiritual men, but as to men of flesh, as to babes in Christ. Paul returns to the "spiritual" and "carnal" or "fleshly" categories in his discussion of the failures of the Corinthian Christians to urge them to set aside their differences. In the process, he accuses them of immaturity, that is, of being "babes" in Christ. Similar descriptions of immature persons were common in the Greco-Roman world of Paul's era. For instance, Philo draws an allegory from the food that is appropriate both for children and for adults.

But seeing that for babes milk is food, but for grown men wheaten bread, there must also be soul-nourishment, such as

is milk-like suited to the time of childhood, in the shape of the preliminary stages of school-learning, and such as is adapted to grown men in the shape of instructions leading the way through wisdom and temperance and all virtue (*On Husbandry* 9, LCL). See further discussion on Christian maturity in 2:6 above.

3:6. I planted, Apollos watered, but God was causing the growth. The notion of planting and watering or farming produce as metaphors for doing the work of God or judgment are familiar in ancient Judaism (Ruth 4:11; Ps. 28:5; 51:18; 69:35; 147:2; Jer. 1:10; 18:7; 24:6; 31:4, 28; 45:4, Matt. 3:10; Mark 4:1-9; John 15:1-8; Rom. 11:16-23). At Qumran, for instance, the future of faithful Israel is described as a "holy plantation" (1QS [*Rule of the Community*] 8.5). Likewise, the *Damascus Document* speaks of the time of God's visitation with blessing on Israel: "he visited them and caused to sprout from Israel and from Aaron a shoot of the planting, in order to possess his land and to become fat with the good things of his soil" (CD-A 1.7-8, Garcia Martinez trans.).

3:10. According to the grace of God which was given to me, as a wise master builder I laid a foundation, and another is building upon it. Paul turns to a second metaphor to describe his ministry among the Corinthian Christians and how they are to live. This time he uses another familiar example from building. Jesus likewise made use of a builder's foundation to communicate his message about the kingdom of God (Matt. 7:24-27; cf. Heb. 6:1). At Qumran, the people were urged to "lay a foundation of truth for Israel, for the Community of the eternal covenant" (1QS [*Rule of the Community*] 5.5-6). While Paul indicated that he had laid the foundation for their faith, he also made it clear that he was not the foundation (2 Cor. 4:5). That God or Christ is the foundation or foundation stone of faith, see Isa. 28:16; Ps. 118:22; Mark 12:10; Matt. 21:42; Luke 20:17; Acts 4:11; 1 Peter 2:4-8.

3:12. Now if any man builds upon the foundation with gold, silver, precious stones, wood, hay, straw. Philo, an early contemporary of Paul, speaks of similar kinds of things that should not be the focus of those who are mature in their understanding. "Rather as stewards guard the treasure in your own keeping, not where the gold and silver, substances corruptible, are stored, but where lies that most beautiful of all possessions, the knowledge of the Cause and of virtue, and, besides these two, of the fruit which is engendered by them both" (*On the Cherubim* 48, LCL).

3:13-15. Each man's work will become evident; for the day will show it, because it is to be revealed with fire; and the fire itself will test the quality of each man's work. If any man's work which he has built upon it remains, he shall receive a reward. If any man's work is burned up, he shall suffer loss; but he himself shall be saved, yet so as through fire. Once again, Paul uses familiar examples to tell of the importance of living above reproach. The use of fire to destroy and to purify was well-known among the Jews (Prov. 17:3; 27:21; 1 Peter 1:7; Rev. 3:18; cf. Isa. 43:2) and often used metaphorically to teach divine truth. In the *Testament of Abraham* (ca. A.D. 100–125) we read:

> And the fiery and merciless angel, who holds the fire in his hand, this is the archangel Purouel, who has authority over fire, and he tests the work of men through fire. And if the fire burns up the work of anyone, immediately the angel of judgment takes him and carries him away to the place of sinners, a most bitter place of punishment. But if the fire tests the work of anyone and does not touch it, this person is justified and the angel of righteousness takes him and

carries him up to be saved in the lot of the righteous. And thus, most righteous Abraham, all things in all people are tested by fire and balance (*Test. Abr.* 13:11-14, *OT Pseud*1:890).

Likewise in the contemporary writings, the Psalms of Solomon (first century A.D.), we read that "The one [righteous person] who does these things will never be disturbed by evil; the flame of fire and anger against the unrighteous shall not touch him when it goes out from the Lord's presence against sinners to destroy the sinners' every assurance" (*Ps. Sol.* 15:4-5, *OT Pseud* 2:664). The notion of fire as testing is common in the rest of the ancient Greco-Roman world as well. Ovid (43 B.C.–A.D. 17), for instance, writes: "Tis clear that as tawny gold is tested in the flames so loyalty must be proved in times of stress" (*Tristia* 1.5.25, LCL). Paul likely had in mind something like the expression "saved by the skin of one's teeth" (so A. Thiselton, 315).

3:16. Do you not know that you are a temple of God, and that the Spirit of God dwells in you? Paul's question does not imply that he had not taught the Corinthian Christians these things before. This was typical pedagogical style using a pattern found in diatribe that asks questions to remind the readers/listeners of what had already been known to them. While chiding those who place their learning and possessions above harmony, Epictetus writes:

> For if you are acting in harmony, show me that, and I will tell you that you are making progress; but if out of harmony, begone, and do not confine yourself to expounding your books, but go and write some of the same kind yourself? And what will you gain thereby? Do you not know that the whole book costs only five denarii [= a full day's pay]? (*Discourses* 1.4.15-16, LCL).

The very question posed presumes that they know the answer. The people know that

God's Spirit dwells in them. In the days of Paul, this was a belief that was gaining popularity among the non-Christian and non-Jewish communities as well. Seneca, for instance, while rejecting the value of appealing to an idol to draw near to divinity, says: "God is near you, he is with you, he is within you. This is what I mean, Lucilius: a holy spirit indwells within us" (*Epistle* 41.2, LCL, see also the later Porphyry, *Marc.* 19, ca. A.D. 235–305). It was more common to believe among the Jews that God dwelt among them in a temple (2 *Macc.* 14:35; *Wisd.* 3:14, see discussion of Acts 7:48).

3:17. If any man destroys the temple of God, God will destroy him, for the temple of God is holy, and that is what you are. Those who transgress the will of God receive the judgment of God (See Rom. 1:20-22, 24, 26, 28; Jude 22-23).

3:18–4:5. A Summary of the Case

In these verses, Paul summarizes his first major argument in the letter (1:10–3:17) and reminds his readers to avoid the party spirit that destroys the church. In 3:18-23, Paul repeats several important terms that are found earlier: namely, "wisdom," "wise," "boasting," "foolish," "foolishness," and "this age" as opposed to the age to come.

3:18. Let no man deceive himself. If any man among you thinks that he is wise in this age, let him become foolish that he may become wise. Paul returns to this theme below in 8:1-3. Epictetus urges a similar response to his readers. "If you wish to make progress, then be content to appear senseless and foolish in externals, do not make it your wish to give the appearance of knowing anything; and if some people think you to be an important personage, distrust yourself" (*Encheiridion* 13, LCL).

3:21. For all things belong to you. These words comprise a Stoic saying that was applied to a variety of situations (see 6:12, 10:23). Seneca reflects this idea when he speaks of all that comes to the wise man.

> You expressed a wish to know whether a wise man can help a wise man. For we say that the wise man is completely endowed with every good, and has attained perfection; accordingly, the question arises how it is possible for anyone to help a person who possesses the Supreme Good (*Epistles* 109.1, LCL).

In another place, while speaking of those wise persons who have not placed their hope and confidence in material things, Seneca wrote: "And do not suppose that he is content with a little—all things are his, and not in the sense in which they were Alexander's who, although he stood upon the shore of the Indian Ocean, had need of more territory than that he had passed through" (*Benefits* 7.2.5, LCL. See also 7.3.2-3; 7.4.1; 7.8.1; 7.10.6). The phrase is repeated in 3:22.

3:23. And you belong to Christ; and Christ belongs to God. On the matter of Christ's relationship with God, see discussion below at 11:3 and 15:28. Paul repeats that all things belong to Christ in 8:6 and 15:27-28, but also shows that ultimately he is subordinate to the Father in his particular role. Whether this is a veiled reference to the so-called "Christ party" of 1:12 is debatable, but Paul does affirm that a party spirit is inappropriate for those who belong to Christ. Both he and Apollos belong to Christ (3:7, 9) and so do those who follow Christ.

4:1-5. Paul's Application of this Wisdom to Himself

After stating that "all things are yours," Paul shows how this cannot lead to boasting, but rather to faithfulness and gratitude to God.

4:1. Let a man regard us in this manner, as servants of Christ, and stewards of the mysteries of God. Two important terms are used here to describe Paul's and Apollos' roles in the family of Christ. They are servants (*huperetas*) and stewards (*oikonomous*). The former is found only here in Paul's letters and elsewhere it is probably a reference to guards or police or simply a helper (Matt. 5:25; 26:58; Mark 14:54, 65; Luke 1:2; 4:20; John 7:32, 45, 46; 18:3, 12, 18, 22, 36; 19:6; Acts 5:22, 26; 13:5; 26:16). While the term is used variously elsewhere, here it is used in the same sense as in 3:5: namely, as servants (*diakonoi*) or in this place it refers to helpers or fellow workers. Epictetus uses the term in reference to a true Cynic who cares for all persons as sons and daughters and acts like a father to them. "It is as a father he does it, as a brother, and as a servant [*huperetes*] of Zeus, who is Father of us all" (*Discourses* 3.22.82, LCL). The second term, *oikonomous* (= accusative pl.), is translated as steward and has the force of a manager of the house. It is a humble place rather than one of authority. Epictetus uses the term to tell of one who tried to usurp too much authority for himself by calling himself the steward or manager of the house. "For in a well-ordered house, no one comes along and says to himself, 'I ought to be manager [*oikonomon*] of this house'; or if he does, the lord of the mansion, when he turns around and sees the fellow giving orders in a high and mighty fashion, drags him out and gives him a dressing down" (*Discourses* 3.22.3, LCL). The term is also used of a city manager and was used in Corinth to describe the city treasurer. Paul refers to Erastus as a "city manager" or "city treasurer" (*hos oikonomos tes polis*) at Corinth. There is a Latin inscription dating from the mid-first century A.D. that mentions this name on a limestone block found near the municipal theater and reads ". . . Erastus in return for his aedileship laid the [pavement] at his own expense." The aediles originated as subordinate officials who assisted the tribunes in their work including in the administration of public buildings. The Romans employed such people to care for the streets of Rome, public games, and sometimes also they cared for religious temples, the water supply, and the market places. They might be akin today to "middle management." It is possible that Erastus, Paul's friend, is the person named as an *oikonomos* by Paul. It is interesting here that Paul also refers to the "mysteries of God" in conjunction with their service (see discussion of "mystery" above in 2:1, 7).

Paul is self-effacing here and rather than emphasizing his role as an apostle, which he does later (see discussion in 9:1-14 where he does appeal to his office and its rights), he is showing in his actions what he is seeking from the Corinthians. There are some parallels here with Socrates' defense of himself when he is accused by Meletus before the courts in Athens presided over by King Archon. Having been accused of impiety and stirring up the youth of the city, he defends himself by saying that his problem is that others saw him as a wise man, indeed the wisest, and others were jealous of that distinction. Speaking of himself, however, he concludes: "I am conscious that I am not wise either much or little" (Plato, *Apology* 21 B, LCL). He defends himself against the charge, but claims that those who claim to be wise he has not found to be so. In response to such an accusation, he explains:

> For on each occasion those who are present think I am wise in matters in which I confute someone else; but the fact is, gentlemen, it is likely that the god is really wise and by his oracle means this: "Human wisdom is of little or no value." And it appears that he does not really say this of Socrates, but merely uses my name, and makes me an example, as if he were to say: "This one of you, O human beings, is wisest, who, like Socrates, recognizes that he is in truth of no account in respect to wisdom" (*Apology* 23 A-B, LCL).

4:6-21. The Cross as Model for Christian Behavior

Paul offers a catalogue of afflictions that have come to him as a result of faithfulness to the

Gospel. In contrast to his readers, he has no basis for boasting except in the Gospel and no rejoicing over his superior status among them. He appeals to them to follow the way of the cross, but if not, he may come to them with correction rather than love. In the midst of his admonition (4:14), Paul changes his tone from irony and sarcasm to love and appealing to their sense of loyalty to what he was able to bring to them, but then he returns to strong language by the end of this section.

4:6. Now these things, brethren, I have figuratively applied to myself and Apollos for your sakes, that in us you might learn not. The "these things" here is a reference to Paul's argument in 1:10–4:5.

4:7. For who regards you as superior? And what do you have that you did not receive? But if you did receive it, why do you boast as if you had not received it? Socrates reminded his hearers that many teachers were "puffed up" about their teaching and as a result distanced themselves from others.

> You have invented an elixir not of memory, but of reminding; and you offer your pupils the appearance of wisdom, not true wisdom, for they will read many things without instruction and will therefore seem to know many things, when they are for the most part ignorant and hard to get along with, since they are not wise, but only appear wise (Plato, *Phaedrus* 275 A-B, LCL).

4:8. You are already filled, you have already become rich, you have become kings without us; and I would indeed that you had become kings so that we also might reign with you. Paul turns his attention in v. 6 to the Corinthians themselves and now uses irony and sarcasm to bring home his point: namely, no one should boast except in the Lord (see 1:28, 31). His focus on their richness (see 1:5) is couched in irony, but is found in God and not in their gifts or financial wealth. See Eph. 1:7-8; 2:4. Philo spoke of the wealth that belonged to those who acknowledged God as their Master: "But Thou, Master, art my country, my kinsfolk, my great and glorious and inalienable wealth" (*Who Is the Heir?* 27, LCL). In another place he observes that "God loves to give, and so bestows good things upon all, even those who are not perfect (*teleiois*), at the same time encouraging them to a zeal for virtue and a participation in it, by displaying His own overflowing wealth, and how there is abundance even for those who will derive no great benefit from it" (*Allegorical Interpretation* 1.34, LCL). In terms of kingship, Plutarch speaks of how the Stoics saw themselves as kings. "But some think that the Stoics are jesting when they hear that in their sect the wise man is termed not only prudent and just and brave, but also an orator, a poet, a general, a rich man, and a king" (*On Tranquillity of Mind* 472A, LCL).

4:9-13. Catalogue of Paul's Sufferings

There are five times in the Corinthian correspondence when Paul lists his sufferings for his faith (here, 2 Cor. 4:8-9; 6:3-10; 11:23-29; and 12:10).

4:9. For, I think, God has exhibited us apostles last of all, as men condemned to death; because we have become a spectacle to the world, both to angels and to men. Paul appears to be using the well-known Stoic philosopher's struggle to present his case. Sallust (ca. 86–34 B.C.), who served as a governor in Numidia for Rome, tells the pitiable story of his lot to gain the favor of the Roman Senate.

> While I, poor wretch, hurled from my father's throne into this sea of troubles, present a tragedy of human vicissitude, being at a loss what course to take, whether to try to avenge your wrongs when I myself am in need of aid, or to take thought for my throne when the

very question of my life or death hangs upon the help of others. Would that death were an honourable means of escape for one of my estate! Would that, worn out by affliction, I could succumb to oppression without appearing justly contemptible! As it is, life has no charms for me, but death is impossible without shame (Sallust, *War with Jugurtha* 14.23-24, LCL).

Paul tells his story of pain and abuse to say that the way of the cross is not one of pride, boasting, and puffed-up egos, but rather one of humility, grief, and loss. In these circumstances, there can be no boasting or pride that divides the community of Christ. The Cynics wandered about homeless and dependent upon others for food and shelter, and they were despised by the wealthy, many Greek philosophers, but they presented themselves as models to follow. Paul presents himself as a model for others to follow (4:12). The more wealthy individuals in the church would have despised the fact that Paul, the one who brought them to faith in Christ, was an artisan who worked with his hands so as not to be a burden to those he ministered to (cf. Acts 16:19; 18:2-3). When Paul told them that his life was an example to them in this regard, this would have been objectionable to the socially elite of Corinth. As he explains later, this was a part of his strategy in preaching the Gospel (9:16-18). This model was not respected among the ranks of the Corinthians who had economic independence, but Paul sees this as the example that can bring unity and hope to the church.

The Cynics, both before and during Paul's day, would often rebuke their audiences to show that they were independent of them, even though they were looked upon as poor and pitiable by the socially elite of the community. Stoic and Cynic philosophers taught that perseverance in suffering was a mark of their legitimacy. Paul appears to be competing with them on their own terms! Paul, however, acted well within his own Jewish tradition that called upon those who would teach the law also to have a job that required physical labor. According to the Mishnah, "Excellent is the study of the Law together with worldly occupation, for toil in them both puts sin out of mind. But all study of the Law without [worldly] labour comes to naught at the last and brings sin in its train" (*m. Aboth* 2.2, Danby trans).

4:10. We are fools for Christ's sake, but you are prudent in Christ; we are weak, but you are strong; you are distinguished, but we are without honor. Paul later gives a "fool's speech" (11:21–12:20) and appears to snub the social currency of his readers. With his three-fold emphasis on fools, weakness, and being without honor, he claims that the virtues of the Corinthians are inappropriate and need to be revisited. They are wise, strong, and of good reputation, but not Paul and other servants of Christ. Prudence, not foolishness, was one of the most highly valued virtues of the Greeks. Philo identifies the four great virtues as prudence, self-mastery, courage, and justice (*Allegorical Interpretation* 1.63). These virtues have their root in Platonism and were adopted by later Greek philosophers. Philo notes that "Prudence, concerned with things to be done, sets boundaries round them; courage round things to be endured; self-mastery round things to be chosen; justice round things to be awarded" (*Allegorical Interpretation* 1.65). He compares prudence to gold as follows:

> . . . as of all smelted substance the most excellent and most approved is gold, so of the soul too the most approved virtue is prudence . . . prudence is acknowledged to be God's fairest treasure. And in the place where prudence dwells are two corresponding concretes, the man who is prudent, and the man who exercises prudence. These he likens to ruby and emerald (*Allegorical Interpretation* 1.66-67, LCL).

A Jewish perspective on the matter is also interesting and shows that Paul is much closer in his thinking to first-century Jewish tradition than to Greek notions of virtue. Ben Zoma said:

> Who is wise? He that learns from all men, as it is written, *From all my teachers have I got understanding*. Who is mighty? He that subdues his [evil] nature, as it is written, *He that is slow to anger is better than the mighty, and he that ruleth his spirit than he that taketh a city*. Who is rich? He that rejoices in his portion, as it is written, *when thou eatest the labour of thy hands happy shalt thou be, and it shall be well with thee*—in the world to come. Who is honoured? He that honours mankind, as it is written, *For them that honour me I will honour, and they that despise me shall be lightly esteemed* (m. *Aboth* 4.1, Danby trans.).

4:15. For if you were to have countless tutors [*paidagogous*] in Christ, yet you would not have many fathers; for in Christ Jesus I became your father through the gospel. In the Greco-Roman world, slaves were often used to accompany children to school and they were allowed in some cases to discipline the children. They were known as *paidgogoi*. By the first century, they were less often seen as disciplinarians than as teachers and were honored as those having a significant role in a child's development and education (see Gal. 3:24-25; 4:1-3). There could be many teachers or disciplinarians, but Paul's point is that there is only one father. He has "fathered" these Christians and deserves thereby a higher level of respect among them.

4:16. I exhort you therefore, be imitators of me. Xenophon (ca. 430–354 B.C.), using Socrates as an example, says that he "to be sure never professed to teach this; but, by letting his own light shine, he led his disciples to hope that they through imitation of him

would attain to such excellence" (*Memorabilia* 1.2.3, LCL). Seneca (*fl.* A.D. 54–65), contends that the gods are to be imitated. "Would you win over the gods? Then be a good man. Whoever imitates them, is worshiping them sufficiently" (Seneca, *Epistle* 95.50, LCL). Plutarch tells the story of Alexander the Great's desire to follow after Diogenes, but in the end says: "But as things are, forgive me, Diogenes, that I imitate Heracles, and emulate Persus, and follow in the footsteps of Dionysus, the divine author and progenitor of my family . . ." (*Moralia, Fortune of Alexander* 332 A-B). In the Jewish tradition, the imitation of virtue is much stronger. In the apocryphal book, Wisdom of Solomon (ca. late first cent. B.C.), for example, we see: "Better than this is childlessness with virtue, for in the memory of virtue is immortality, because it is known both by God and by mortals. When it is present, people imitate it, and they long for it when it has gone" (*Wisd.* 4:1-2, NRSV). In the story of the torture of the seven brothers by the Greek dynasty, the author of *4 Macc.* relates how the second Jewish brother heroically maintains his faith to the end, even under torturous conditions. As he is about to die, he cries out: "Imitate me, my brothers; do not become deserters in my trial nor forswear our brotherhood in nobility" (*4 Macc.* 9:23, OTP 555).

4:17. For this reason I have sent to you Timothy, who is my beloved and faithful child in the Lord, and he will remind you of my ways which are in Christ, just as I teach everywhere in every church. On Timothy, see Acts 16:1-5 and 2 Tim. 1:5. He was present with Paul in Ephesus and was accompanied by Erastus on his journey to Macedonia (Acts 19:22). According to the Acts account, he arrived at Corinth with Silas shortly after Paul came to Corinth (18:5). He joins Paul in the writing of the second letter to the Corinthians (2 Cor. 1:1) and is at Corinth (or possibly Ephesus) while Paul writes the letter to the

Romans there (Rom. 16:21). He is a trustworthy companion of Paul (2 Tim. 1:2) who sends him to Corinth (here and 16:10) to try to correct the situation as it was emerging. He is later recognized as the first bishop of Ephesus by Eusebius and as the recipient of two pastoral letters, 1 and 2 Timothy (*Ecclesiastical History* 3.4.5). Paul introduces him as his emissary with the appropriate introduction that was common in diplomatic jargon of the day. Timothy's relationship to Paul is expressed and also what his specific responsibility would be (see also Phile. 10, 16).

4:19. But I will come to you soon, if the Lord wills. Frequently Paul indicates that his plans are in the hands of God and that he purposes to come to see them, but only if the Lord wills (Rom. 15:32; 1 Thess. 3:11; Phile. 22). His plans for this visit are stated in 16:5-9.

4:21. Shall I come to you with a rod or with love and a spirit of gentleness? Paul's focus on the use of the rod is like that of a loving parent who uses the "rod" in order to encourage the child to go in the right direction and make proper choices. The roots of this lie in the Old Testament (Prov. 13:24; Ps. 10:13; 23:13-14). In Ps. 89:32-33, the use of the rod and the scourge does not negate the father's love for the one who has transgressed (so also in Heb. 12:5-11). This same perspective is found in the apocryphal Wisdom of Solomon in which God punished the enemies of Israel [the Egyptians] and "tested them [Israel] as a father does in warning" (*Wisd.* 11:10). Likewise the writer of the Psalms of Solomon (ca. first cent. A.D.) claims that God "will admonish the righteous as a beloved son and his discipline is as for a firstborn. For the Lord will spare his devout, and he will wipe away their mistakes with discipline" (*Pss. Sol.* 13:9-10, *OTP* 2:663). The rod is a metaphor here for discipline that draws one's children (in the faith) back to a true reflection of that faith.

B. 5:1–6:20. Divisions over Sexual Immorality and Taking Believers to Court

Having dealt with the general problem of divisions in the church and calling for unity, Paul now focuses on the specific issues that were brought to his attention. The focus of these two chapters is on the nature of the community of God's people, that is, how is it to be holy? Or rather, what does it mean to be holy people? Paul focuses here on the purity of the community.

5:1-13. Dealing with Sexually Immoral People The first of the serious problems facing the church is how to deal with those persons in the church who are guilty of sexually immoral behavior. He has already spoken on this issue before and now reiterates his views on what they are to do. The specific problem had to do with a young man having sexual relations with his mother or stepmother and Paul is responding to reports about it (see also 11:18). This was one of the differences between Jews and Gentiles. The Jews believed that sexual immorality was *the* sin of the Gentiles (see Acts 15:20). What was at issue for Paul was the holiness and witness of the community.

5:1. It is actually reported that there is immorality among you, and immorality of such a kind as does not exist even among the Gentiles, that someone has his father's wife. Sexual activity with someone within one's own family or with the father's wife was strictly forbidden in the Jewish community. This sin was judged worthy of being cut off from the community of faith (Gen. 49:4; Lev. 18:1-18; Deut. 17:7; 22:22, 30; 27:20-23; Ezek. 22:10-11; cf. 1 Cor. 5:13). Ezra banned all Jews from the community of Israel who were involved in illicit sexual relationships (Ezra 7:26; 10:8, 44). According to the Mishnah, a man having sex with his father's wife is to be executed by stoning.

These are they that are to be stoned: He that has connexion [sexual relations] with his mother, his father's wife, his daughter-in-law, a male, or a beast . . ." and again, He that has connexion with his mother is thereby culpable both by virtue of the law of the mother [Lev. 18:7] and of the father's wife [Lev. 18:8]. R. Judah says:

He is culpable by virtue of the law of the mother only. He that has connexion with his father's wife is thereby culpable both by virtue of the law of the father's wife and of another man's wife, whether in his father's lifetime or after his father's death, whether after betrothal [only] or after wedlock (*m. Sanhedrin* 7.4, Danby trans.).

This sin was of the thirty-six transgressions that led to death or extirpation (see *Kerithoth* "Extirpations"). "For thirty-six transgressions is Extirpation prescribed in the Law: if a man has connexion with his mother, his father's wife, his daughter-in-law; [the rest of the thirty-six] . . ." (*m.Kerithoth* 1.1, Danby trans.). Philo reflects contemporary Jewish thought in Paul's day:

What form of unholiness could be more impious than this: that a father's bed, which should be kept untouched as something sacred, should be brought to shame: that no respect should be shown for a mother's ageing years: that the same man should be son and husband to the same woman, and again the same woman wife and mother to the same man: that the children of both should be brothers to their father and grandsons to their mother: that she should be both mother and grandmother of those whom she bore and he both father and half-brother of those whom he begot? (*Special Laws* 3.14, LCL).

Not only in the Jewish community, but also in Roman law, sexual relations and marriage between two persons who became related by marriage or adoption was also ruled out. All forms of incest were strictly forbidden in Roman law as well as in Judaism of the day. According to the *Institutes of Gaius and Rules of Ulpian*, we read: "Neither can I marry her who has aforetime been my mother-in-law or step-mother, or daughter-in-law or step-daughter (*Inst.* 1.63, J. Muirhead, trans.). Sophocles (ca. 497–406 B.C.), one of Athens' greatest Greek poets, wrote disparagingly:

[O] Marriage, marriage, you gave me birth, and after you had some so you brought up the selfsame seed, and displayed fathers who were brothers, children who were fruit of incest, brides who were both wives and mothers to their spouses, and all things that are most atrocious among men (*Oedipus Tyrannus* 1403-1409, LCL).

Cicero later also condemned the practice and said it was so rare that it was also unthinkable. "Oh! To think of the woman's sin, unbelievable, unheard of in all experience save for this single instance!" (Cicero, *Pro Cluentio* 6.15, LCL). Josephus (late first century A.D.) agrees and states clearly:

Adultery he [Moses] prohibited, deeming it blessed that men should be sane-minded concerning wedlock and that it was to the interest alike of the state and the family that children should be legitimate. Again, to have intercourse with one's mother is condemned by the law as grossest of sins; likewise union with a stepmother, an aunt, a sister, or the wife of one's child is viewed with abhorrence as an outrageous crime (*Ant.* 3.274, LCL).

Paul could not think of anything that could undermine the witness of the believing community more than the toleration of such moral failure in its midst. He condemned as sin what the whole civilized Greco-Roman world including the Jewish community also condemned.

5:2. And you have become arrogant, and have not mourned instead, in order that the one

who had done this deed might be removed from your midst. In order to address matters that were worthy of punishment, but that were not prescribed in the Law or found in tradition, the act of excommunication was practiced among the Jews in the time of Jesus. More precise guidelines were drawn up in the post-Talmudic period that began with vilifying a wise man after his death or one who vilifies a member of the Sanhedrin and many other such causes. The length of the period of excommunication varied, but generally until the offense had been addressed and satisfied in the minds of those who imposed the sentence. Moses Maimonides, also known as Rambam (A.D. 1135–1204), listed some twenty-four causes for excommunication. In the *Shulhan Arukh* (or *Orach Chaaim* cap. 359), that listed what became normative practices among the Jews, there was cause for excommunication if a Jew accused a fellow Jew before a heathen tribunal for the purpose of extorting money from the fellow Jew. "Who gives evidence against an Israelite before a heathen tribunal; and by that evidence extorts money from him: they excommunicate him until he pay it back again." That excommunication was in effect until the money was returned. This is not unlike what Paul admonishes his readers in 6:1-7 below.

5:5. I have decided to deliver such a one to Satan for the destruction of his flesh, that his spirit may be saved in the day of the Lord Jesus. Paul says that a person guilty of such an offense must be delivered to Satan, that is, excommunicated from the church. (See also 11:27-30; cf. 1 Tim. 1:20 and Acts 5:1-11). The committal of one's body or flesh to destruction is, of course, death. This may be something akin to Acts 5:1-11, another difficult passage, and by this act, the man's eternal destiny is saved. Although it is clear that some form of excommunication is intended, that is, returning the man to the sphere of Satan, that is the world, but Paul seems to be going beyond that

to something more drastic: namely, the death of an individual (1 Tim. 1:20; Acts 5:1-11). How did Paul intend this? Did he mean that Christians should pray for the death of the individual and that God might save that person's soul? That has certainly been a common interpretation throughout church history and this is also a leading text behind the inquisitions that were so costly in terms of human life in the church of the middle ages. Was there an apostolic authority given over life and death to be used in extreme situations where the witness of the gospel was at stake?

5:6. Your boasting is not good. Do you not know that a little leaven leavens the whole lump of dough? Paul uses a familiar metaphor in the ancient world. Because a little was used in bread and produced a good loaf, too much was detrimental. Hence, too much leaven became a metaphor for too much evil or impurity in one's life. It is prohibited in the preparation of bread for the Jews. As the Jews made their pilgrimage out of Egypt, they were commanded not to put yeast in their bread. The practice among the Jews not only today, but also in Paul's day, reflected the tradition of the Feast of Passover (Exod. 12:15; 13:7) where only unleavened bread would be eaten during the Passover festival called the Feast of Unleavened Bread (Exod. 12:14-20). The yeast later became a symbol of evil. In this case Paul uses it as symbolic of sexual immorality (v. 8) that had to be discarded before the blessing of God would come among the people. Paul has this sense of its use here. See how he uses the metaphor elsewhere (Gal. 5:9). Interestingly, Plutarch asks why it is that the priest of Jupiter was not allowed to touch either flour or yeast (leaven). He responds:

> Yeast is itself also the product of corruption, and produces corruption in the dough with which it is mixed; for the dough becomes flabby and inert, and altogether the process of leavening

seems to be one of putrefaction; at any rate if it goes too far, it completely sours and spoils the flour. (*The Roman Questions* 289. §109, LCL).

5:7b. For Christ our Passover also has been sacrificed. Paul reflects the language and example of Exodus 12:1-27 (cf. Mark 14:12-21; Luke 22:7-23) which tells the story of the Israelites preparing for the Passover meal through the sacrifice of a lamb, the spreading of its blood upon their doorposts, and the removal of the leaven from their homes. See also Exod. 12:43-49. Paul explains the death of Jesus as a sacrifice for the people.

5:9-13. Catalogue of vices. Paul cites three lists of vices in vv. 10-11 and 6:9-10. Such listings of vices were common among the Cynics and Stoics, and Paul makes use of them frequently in his epistles and elsewhere in the New Testament letters (Rom. 1:29-1; 13:13; 2 Cor. 12:20-21; Gal. 5:19-21; cf. Eph. 4:31; 5:3-5; Col. 3:5, 8; 1 Tim. 1:9-10; 6:4-5; 2 Tim. 3:2-5; Titus 1:7; 3:3; 1 Peter 4:15). These vices are often compared and contrasted with a catalogue of virtues as in 2 Cor. 6:6-7a; Gal. 5:22-23; Eph. 4:2-3; 32–5:2; 5:9; Col. 3:12; Phil. 4:8 (see also 1 Tim. 3:2-4, 8-10, 11-12; 4:12; 6:11, 18; 2 Tim. 2:22-25; 3:10; Titus 1:8; 2:2-10; Heb. 7:26). Paul frequently lists avarice along with sexual impurity in his lists of vices. Philo has perhaps the longest list of vices that stem from the pursuit of pleasure. He lists some 146 sinful consequences for those who follow greed or avarice. He introduces this list of consequent behaviors by saying:

> But there are other things which are part and parcel of her, the maladies and plagues which you must needs experience if you choose her gifts, and these she did not tell you, that carried off your feet by windy thoughts of some gain or other you might be caught in her net. Know then, my friend, that if you become a pleasure-lover you will be all these things: [he lists 146 items that are children of seeking after pleasure and concludes] . . . a mass of misery and misfortune without relief (Philo, *The Sacrifices of Abel and Cain*, 31-32, LCL).

The vices in such lists often follow a literary form common in the Hellenistic world but which was also used in Hellenistic Jewish writings. See 1QS 4.9-10 below. See also 1 Peter 2:1; 4:3, 15; Rev. 21:8; 22:15. The early Jewish Christian writing known as the *Didache*, or *Teaching of the Twelve Apostles*, also uses these lists. For instance:

> But the Way of Death is this: first of all, it is wicked and full of cursing, murders, adulteries, lusts, fornications, thefts, idolatries, witchcrafts, charms, robberies, false witness, hypocrisies, a double heart, fraud, pride, malice, stubbornness, covetousness, foul speech, jealousy, impudence, haughtiness, boastfulness. Persecutors of the good, haters of truth, lovers of lies, knowing not the reward of righteousness, not cleaving to the good nor to righteous judgment, spending wakeful nights not for good but for wickedness, from whom meekness and patience is far, lovers of vanity, following after reward, unmerciful to the poor, not working for him who is oppressed with toil, without knowledge of him who made them, murderers of children, corruptors of God's creatures, turning away the needy, oppressing the distressed, advocates of the rich, unjust judges of the poor, altogether sinful; may ye be delivered, my children from all these (*Did.* 1:2-2:7; 5:1-2, LCL).

5:9. I wrote you in my letter not to associate with immoral people. The call to disassociate from the evil ones in their midst has many ancient and contemporary parallels in

Judaism. Paul's justification comes from Scripture in 5:13, a probable reference to the Deut. 17:2-7 passage that calls upon Israel to purge the evil from their midst. This command is found in the Qumran community which also commands adherents not to associate with evildoers.

> May he lift upon you the countenance of his favor for eternal peace. And the Levites shall curse all the men of the lot of Belial [Satan]. They shall begin to speak and shall say: Accursed are you for all your wicked, blameworthy deeds. May he (God) hand you over to dread into the hands of all those carrying out acts of vengeance. Accursed, without mercy, for the darkness of your deeds, and sentenced to the gloom of everlasting fire. May God not be merciful when you entreat him, nor pardon you when you do penance for your faults. May he lift the countenance of his anger to avenge himself on you, and may there be no peace for you in the mouth of those who intercede. And all those who enter the covenant shall say, after those who pronounce blessings and those who pronounce curses: Amen, Amen (1QS 2.4-10, *The Rule of the Community*, Garcia Martinez trans.).

5:10. I did not at all mean with the immoral people of this world, or with the covetous and swindlers, or with idolaters; for then you would have to go out of the world. Paul here brings together those sexually immoral people with other vices and showing the Jewish tendency to view that such activities were more common among the Gentiles. See also 6:9-10.

5:11. I wrote to you not to associate with any so-called brother if he should be an immoral person, or covetous, or an idolater, or a reviler, or a drunkard, or a swindler—not even to eat with such a one. Paul's call to purge relation-ships with evildoers is rooted in the Mosaic law (Deut. 17:7; 19:19; 22:31; 22:22, 24; 24:7). His fear is that the Christians will compromise their witness in the community by allowing such promiscuity and evil in their gathers. The call not to eat with such individuals was quite significant since the gathering for meals was at the heart of their expressions of worship. This is why Paul took offense at Peter's removing himself from table fellowship with Gentiles at Antioch (Gal. 2:11-14). Paul adapts his list of vices to the situation the Corinthians were facing, but it should not be taken for granted that they were guilty of all of the vices he mentions here and in 6:9-10. The context here is sexual immorality and that theme dominates Paul's concern in chaps. 5–7.

6:1-11. Going to the courts with fellow Christians. Because the Roman court system did not allow social inferiors to take their social superiors to court, what takes place here is a reflection of Corinthians of similar social status going before the courts in Corinth. On the other hand, a social superior could bring charges against a social inferior, and this often happened. The jurors were selected from the wealthier social classes and not from among one's peers. The corruption of the courts was well-known in Paul's day and was even addressed by Caesar Augustus in his famous five Cyrene Edicts (7–6 B.C. and 4 B.C.): "There exist certain conspiracies to oppress the Greeks in trials on capital charges . . . I myself have ascertained that some innocent people have in this way been oppressed and carried off to the supreme penalty" (*Rome: The Augustan Age. A Source Book*, C20). Paul finds it highly objectionable that Christians should go to pagan courts with fellow Christians to deal with minor or civil matters (6:2). He admonishes them to judge matters for themselves. Dio Chrysostom (ca A.D. 40–120) refers to the corruption of the legal system in Corinth that involved "lawyers innumerable perverting judgment" (*Eighth Discourse, On Virtue*, 8.9, LCL). Why he discusses Christians before pagan courts here is not clear since the rest of his discussion in this section deals with sexual promiscuity. It could be that the matters taken before the court included such matters of sexual perversion or indiscretion since both are listed in the catalogue of vices in 6:1-10, but that is not clear.

6:1. Dare to go to law before the unrighteous, and not before the saints? Paul may be reflecting here the admonition of Jesus to "turn the other cheek" (see Matt. 5:11, 23-26, 38-42), but also the unjustness of the court system in his day. A contemporary of Paul's, Seneca (Lucius Annaeus Seneca), explaining the unjustness of the court system that favored the wealthy and was unjust to the poor, tells of a rich man taunting a poor man to take him to court, but the poor man asks, "Am I, a poor man, to accuse a rich man?" (*Controversiae* 10.1.2). Like Paul, the Cynic, Epictetus, asks why a Cynic should go before the courts for justice and admonishes those who are flogged to accept it as the Cynic's pattern of life. On the other hand, he describes those who ignore this advice:

> If someone flogs you, go stand in the midst and shout, "O Caesar, what do I have to suffer under your peaceful rule? Let us go before the Proconsul." But what to a Cynic is Caesar, or a Proconsul, or anyone other than He who has sent him into the world and who he serves, that is, Zeus? Does he call upon anyone but Zeus? And is he not persuaded that whatever of these hardships he suffers, it is Zeus that is exercising him? (*Discourses* 3.22.55-56, LCL).

Plutarch speaks of the unjustness and inequality of the court system and this may also have been behind some of Paul's concern. He writes:

> Out of greed and their desire always to

be right, prominent upper-class types avoid local courts and oppress the little people. They appeal to the higher courts, because they don't want to give in to local citizens. The statesman must therefore attempt to keep the trials in the local jurisdiction of the city. But instead of this, people take their cases to orators and advocates in order not to have to give in to one's local fellow citizens (*Precepts of Statecraft* 19, LCL).

6:2. Or do you not know that the saints will judge the world? And if the world is judged by you, are you not competent to constitute the smallest law courts? According to Dan. 7:21-22, the saints of God will judge others. This is similar to what we find in the Apocryphal and Pseudepigraphal literature as well (cf. *Wisd.* 3:7-8; *Jub.* 24:29; *1 Enoch* 1:9; 38:1, 5; 95:3; 96:1; 98:12; 108:12). There was widespread Jewish belief in the time of Paul and earlier that the saints of God would judge the nations. For instance, according to the Qumran community's 1Q Habakkuk Persher, which is a commentary on the book of Habakkuk, we read: "God is not to destroy his people at the hand of nations, but by means of his chosen ones God will judge all the nations; all the evildoers of his people will be pronounced guilty for the reproof of those who have kept his commandments in their hardship" (1QpHab 5:4-6a, Garcia Martinez trans.). Paul declared that the Corinthians are "saints" (1:2), and presupposes their role in future judgment in his shaming of the Corinthians.

6:3. Do you not know that we shall judge angels? Paul appears to draw on the Greek translation (LXX) of Dan. 7:22 which reads: ". . . until the Ancient of days came, and he gave judgment to the saints of the Most High; and the time came on, and the saints possessed the kingdom." The belief in a judgment of God on some of the angels is presupposed in 2 Peter 2:4 and Jude 6, as well as in pre-Christian Jewish literature. Speaking of God's directive to Michael the archangel (see Jude 9), the author of 1 Enoch (ca. 180 B.C.) writes:

> Make known to Semyaza [an angel] and the others who are with him, who fornicated with the women, that they will die together with them in all their defilement. And when they and all their children have battled with each other, and when they have seen the destruction of their beloved ones, bind them for seventy generations underneath the rocks of the ground until the day of their judgment and of their consummation, until the eternal judgment is concluded. In those days they will lead them into the bottom of the fire—and in torment—in the prison (where) they will be locked up forever. And at the time when they will burn and die, those who collaborated with them will be bound together with them from henceforth unto the end of (all) generations (1 Enoch 10:11-14, OT Pseud 1:18).

This view is presupposed in Paul who believed that bringing minor civil issues before a secular court was a scandal in the church and pleads with his hearers to take care of such matters among themselves. Since they will participate in the judgment of angels, surely they can take care of minor or civil issues themselves. Epictetus (ca. A.D. 54–68) encourages his listeners to worthy behavior that will result in participation with the gods in their rule.

> So act [properly] toward children, so toward a wife, so toward office, so toward wealth; and then some day you will be worthy of the banquets of the gods. But if you do not take these things [what is inappropriate to take] even when they are set before you, but despise them, then you will not only share the banquets of the gods, but share also their rule (The Encheiridion of Epictetus 15, LCL).

Similarly, in Sallustius' De deis et mundo (Concerning the Gods and the Universe, ca. A.D. 361–3), he claims that the pious, or religious devotees, will share with the gods the governance of the whole universe (Deor. et mund. 21, LCL).

6:5. I say this to your shame. See also 15:34. This is the first of two times that Paul seeks to shame the Corinthian Christians. Paul was consciously addressing a community that was mindful of the virtue of honor and the disgrace of shame. Paul expects Christians to act in a way that does not compromise their witness before others (10:31-32).

6:6. But brother goes to law with brother, and that before unbelievers? Paul is fearful that Christians will violate a code of conduct considered horrible and unacceptable, even by the unbelievers, to take a brother or other relative to court. Plutarch (A.D. 45–120) also warned against brothers going to court with one another. "For a man who has grown old in lawsuits and quarrels and contentions with his brothers, and then exhorts his children to concord, 'Healer of others, full of sores himself,' weakens the force of his words by his own actions." He goes on to say:

> Therefore it is fitting to cleanse away completely hatred of brothers, which is both an evil sustainer of parents in their old age and a worse nurturer of children in their youth. And it is also a cause of slander and accusations against such brothers; for their fellow-citizens think that, after having been so closely bound together, and their kinship, brothers could not have become deadly enemies unless each were aware of many wicked deeds committed by the other (Moralia, On Brotherly Love 481A,B, LCL).

6:9-10. Or do you not know that the unrighteous shall not inherit the kingdom of God?

Do not be deceived; neither fornicators, nor idolaters, nor adulterers, nor effeminate, nor homosexuals, nor thieves, nor the covetous, nor drunkards, nor revilers, nor swindlers, shall inherit the kingdom of God. This list of vices is simply an expansion of the list found in 5:11 above. Four of those in 5:10 are in 5:11 and this text adds specificity to the list of sexual vices. When Paul asks "do you not know?" he suggests that his readers knew what he was saying and that they had been taught on such matters earlier. His list of vices now includes, for the first time, a judgment against homosexuals (Greek, *arsenokoitai*, literally = "those men who sleep with males"). See later attention given to the issue of homosexuality in 1 Tim. 1:10 (translated "fornicators" by the NRSV). This is followed by "and those effeminate" (Greek = *malakoi*, literally, "the soft ones") and refers to passive partners in homosexual activity. In its broad use in antiquity, the term referred to effeminate males who played the sexual role of females, but the term is broadly translated in antiquity. The practice of homosexuality was condemned in the Greek translation (LXX) of Lev. 18:22 and 20:13 where also the Greek words *arsenos* (Greek for "male") and *koiten* (Greek for "bed") are used in the same sentence, and likely were conflated by the Jews, the likely source of Paul's use of *arsenokoitai*. In 146 B.C. a Roman law, called the *lex Scantinia*, was passed by the Roman tribune Scantinius that limited homosexual behavior and protected Roman citizens from an abuse of its practice. Since Corinth was a Roman colony, this legislation would have applied to Roman citizens there, but not to slaves or those who were not Roman citizens. The Jewish *Sibylline Oracles*, with perhaps a late Christian addition, (ca. late first or second century A.D.), likewise condemns the practice: "Do not practice homosexuality, do not betray information, do not murder" (*Sib. Or.* 2.73, *OT Pseud.* 1:347). Likewise, the third book of Sibylline Oracles (ca. 165 B.C.) reflects an oracle that condemns both practices of homosexuality: namely, adult males with adult males and adult males with boys. "Male will have intercourse with male and they will set up boys in houses of ill-fame and in those days there will be a great affliction among men and it will throw everything into confusion" (*Sib. Or.* 3.185-88, *OT Pseud* 1:366). A later oracle tells of the coming time when there will be no "unlawful love of boys" (*Sib. Or.* 5.430). This coheres with what the Jewish historian, Josephus, a Pharisee (ca. A.D. 37–late first century), wrote on the matter: "What are our marriage laws? The law recognizes no sexual connexions, except the natural union of man and wife, and that only for the procreation of children" (*Against Apion* 2.199, LCL). Similarly, Philo (ca.20 B.C.–A.D. 40) condemned the homosexual practice of the Sodomites because "not only in their mad lust for women did they violate the marriages of their neighbors, but also men mounted males without respect for the sex nature which the active partner shares with the passive," and he adds that 'little by little they accustomed those who were by nature men to submit to play the part of women' and eventually God, out of pity for mankind, destroyed the city and its inhabitants" (*On Abraham* 135, 136, 137-41, LCL). He later adds that the sin of pederasty is one of the gravest sins and effeminate behavior worthy of God's judgment. He contends that those who transform the male nature to the female and practice it as an art are worthy of God's judgment and are "worthy of death by those who obey the law, which ordains that the man-woman who debases the sterling coin of nature should perish unavenged, suffered not to live for a day or even an hour, as a disgrace to himself, his house, his native land and the whole human race" (*The Special Laws* 3.38, LCL).

Paul shares in these familiar and well-established Jewish views on the practice of homosexuality. See discussion in Rom. 1:24-27. His opposition to such practices, however, is also paralleled in Plato who is more opposed to the seduction of the act and the inducing of the young and immature into the practice than he is in its illegality. Nevertheless he argues that such activity as homosexuality and pederasty (sexual activity between men and boys where the boys are generally passive) does not produce virtue among those who practice it.

But when we come to the amorous passions of children of both sexes and of men for women and women for men — passions which have been the cause of countless woes both to individuals and to whole states—how is one to guard against these, or what remedy can one apply so as to find a way of escape in all such cases from a danger such as this? . .. Come then, suppose we grant that this practice is now legalized, and that it is noble and in no way ignoble, how far would it promote virtue? Will it engender in the soul of him who is seduced a courageous character, or the soul of the seducer the quality of temperance? Nobody would ever believe this (Plato, *Laws* 836 A-C, LCL).

He later says that such actions should be illegal and proposes a law banning same-sex relations and pederasty. "So let this law—whether we ought to call it one law or two—be laid down concerning sexual commerce and love affairs in general, as regards right and wrong conduct in our mutual intercourse due to these desires" (*Laws* 841 E, LCL). At a later date, Plutarch (ca. A.D. 45–120), contends that, like Paul in regard to keeping holy days (Rom. 14:5), everyone should be persuaded on matters of sexual activity in themselves. He contends: "Let each be persuaded according to his own convictions" (*Moralia* 12 A, LCL). Sextus Empiricus (ca. A.D. 200) reflects the views in his day about such activity.

... amongst us sodomy is regarded as shameful or rather illegal, but by the Germani, they say, it is not looked on as shameful but as a customary thing. It is said, too, that in Thebes long ago this practice was not held to be shameful,

and they say that Meriones the Cretan was so called by way of indicating the Cretan's custom, and some refer to this the burning love of Achilles for Patroclus. And what wonder, when both the adherents of the Cynic philosophy and followers of Zeno of Citium, Cleanthes and Chrysippus, declare that this practice is indifferent? (*Outlines of Pyrrhonism* 3.199-200, LCL).

Xenophon (ca. 430–354 B.C.) noted the morality of his day:

I think I ought to say something also about intimacy with boys, since this matter also has a bearing on education. In other Greek states, for instance among Boeotians, man and boy live together, like married people; elsewhere, among the Eleians, for example, consent is won by means of favors. Some, on the other hand, entirely forbid suitors to talk with boys. The customs instituted by Lycurgus [a mythological person mentioned in Homer's *Iliad* 6.130-45] were opposed to all of these. If someone, being himself an honest man, admired a boy's soul and tried to make of him an ideal friend without reproach and to associate with him, he approved, and believed in the excellence of this kind of training. But if it was clear that the attraction lay in the boy's outward beauty, he banned the connection as an abomination; and thus he purged the relationship of all impurity, so that in Lacedaemon it resembled parental and brotherly love. I am surprised, however, that people refuse to believe this. For in many states the laws are not opposed to indulgence of these appetites (Xenophon, *The Lacedaemonians* 2.12-14, LCL).

6:12-20. Christians Involved with Prostitutes: Freedom and Sexuality

While Paul acknowledges that Christians are

free in Christ (see also 10:23), there are nevertheless limits to that freedom. Evidently some of the Christians at Corinth were involved with prostitutes, and Paul reminds them that God forbids premarital sexual intercourse or marital sexual intercourse with one who is not his/her spouse. Such comments reflect Paul's understanding of Deut. 22:12-29. Some Greeks of Paul's day argued that sex outside of the bonds of marriage was acceptable as long as it did not control the person. For most Greek males under the age of thirty, sex outside of marriage was available through prostitution and slaves. Fornication was only a problem if it occurred within aristocratic or free families, but not if it occurred with slaves or prostitutes. From the first century B.C., reports were made about Corinth being the home of a thousand prostitutes connected with the temple of Aphrodite that situated on the top of the Acrocorinth, the mountain on the south side of the city of Corinth. In a famous reference from Strabo (65 B.C.–A.D. 25), we read:

The temple of Aphrodite was so rich that it owned more than a thousand temple-slaves, courtesans, whom both men and women had dedicated to the goddess. And therefore it was also on account of these women that the city was crowded with people and grew rich; for instance, the ship-captains freely squandered their money, and hence the proverb, 'Not for every man is the voyage to Corinth' (Strabo, *Geography* 8.6.20, LCL).

While some dispute the reliability of Strabo's report about the 1,000 prostitutes at the temple of Aphrodite, the presence of inappropriate sexual activity in Corinth appears to be well-established.

6:12. All things are lawful for me, but not all things are profitable. For Paul, one is free from sin to serve Christ, but never to live in opposition to the will of God. In the pursuit of freedom to do as one desires, Paul was in keeping with others of his day who saw the pursuit of freedom as a virtuous goal, but even there, his contemporaries also saw the value in putting limits on the extent of that freedom. Epictetus argued that a truly free person also had obligations to morality and virtue. He contends first that all citizens of a community have certain obligations and the completion of these obligations constitutes freedom.

You live in an imperial state; it is your duty to hold office, to judge uprightly, to keep your hands off the property of other people; no woman but your wife ought to look handsome [an object of desire] to you, no boy handsome, no silver plate handsome, no gold plate. . . .

The duties of citizenship, marriage, begetting children, reverence to God, care of parents, in a word, desire, avoidance, choice, refusal, the proper performance of each one of these acts, and that is, in accordance with our nature. And what is our nature? To act as free men, as noble, as self-respecting men (*Discourses* 3.7.21, 27-28, LCL).

Later he entreats those who listen to him to follow purity in sexual habits: "In your sex-life preserve purity, as far as you can, before marriage, and, if you indulge, take only those privileges which are lawful" (*Encheiridion* 33.8, LCL). There are limits to Christian freedom, according to Paul (see 9:1, 12b, 19-23; 10:23-33), because there are also obligations to those who are weaker in their faith (see Rom. 14:5-23). Likewise, Dio Chrysostom (ca. A.D. 40–120), after hearing from a shadow opponent who claims that "whoever has the power to do whatever he wishes is free, and that whoever has not that power is a slave," denies this claim and asks whether "it is permitted to you to do all things, which, while they are not expressly forbidden by the laws, yet are regarded as base and unseemly by mankind? I mean, for example, collecting taxes, or keeping a brothel, or doing other such things?" He concludes the contrary and says "In a word, then, it is not permissible to do mean and unseemly and unprofitable things, but things that are just and profitable and good we must say that it is both proper and permissible to do. . ." He further asks whether one "may do that which is mean and unprofitable without suffering the penalty, whether he be Greek or barbarian . . . ?" (*Discourses, On Slavery and Freedom*, 14.13-14, 16, LCL). He, too, believes that there are limits to human freedom and these limits are governed by human laws and also the virtues of dignity and morality.

6:13-14. Food is for the stomach, and the stomach is for food; but God will do away with both of them. Yet the body is not for immorality, but for the Lord; and the Lord is for the body. Now God has not only raised the Lord, but will also raise us up through His power. Paul is familiar with Hellenistic notions of sexual morality and also of their view of the body. Just as the stomach was for food and food was for the stomach, so it was, as some argued, the body was for sex and sex was for the body and, since the body had no future in the Greek notion of immortality with the gods, many argued that it did not matter what was done sexually in the body. Paul rejects this notion and appeals to the Jewish tradition on human sexuality.

6:16. Or do you not know that the one who joins himself to a harlot is one body with her? For He says, "The two will become one flesh." The reference point for the logic of Paul's argument is in Gen. 2:24, but also Num. 25:3; Jer. 50:5; Hos. 4:17; and Zech. 2:11, that point to God's marriage with his covenant people and that his people are "joined" to God.

6:18. Flee immorality. Every other sin that a man commits is outside the body, but the immoral man sins against his own body. Like the book of Proverbs (5:3; 6:23–7:27) Paul urges his readers to avoid sexual impropriety. There are several parallels here with other Jewish literature roughly just before and contemporary with Paul. In the *Testament of Reuben* (ca. 150 B.C. or later) we see a similar call: "Accordingly, my children, flee from sexual promiscuity" (5:5, *OT Pseud* 1:784). Also, in the Testament of Levi we read: "Be on guard against the spirit of promiscuity, for it is constantly active and through your descendants it is about to defile the sanctuary" (9:9, *OT Pseud* 1:791-92). The parallels to Joseph's fleeing Potiphar's wife in Gen. 39:6b-12) may also be the root of all of these texts: namely, it is always best to flee temptation to promiscuity.

6:19. Or do you not know that your body is a temple of the Holy Spirit who is in you, whom you have from God, and that you are not your own? For a parallel thought, see Rom. 8:11. The idea of deity dwelling in humanity has parallels in both Jewish and Hellenistic literature in the first century A.D. Philo, representing the Jewish parallel, writes:

Be zealous therefore, O soul, to become a house of God, a holy temple, a most beauteous abiding-place; for perchance, perchance the Master of the whole world's household shall be thine too and keep thee under His care as His special house, to preserve thee evermore strongly guarded and unharmed (*On Dreams* 1.149, LCL).

Epictetus, likewise recognizes the presence of the divine living within a person and this affects the way one makes decisions and lives. He says that human beings have the presence of Zeus beside them as a guardian and therefore, "when you close your doors and make darkness within, remember never to say that you are alone, for you are not alone; nay, god is within, and your own genius is within." (*Discourses* 1.14.12-13, LCL). See discussion above in 3:16. What was said there of the community of believers is now transferred to individual believers.

6:20. For you have been bought with a price. It is important to Paul that the Christians at Corinth recognize that they do not belong to themselves, but rather to God who has bought them, and they should therefore lead their lives in a manner that is fitting for those who have the presence of God by his Spirit living within them. In the Hellenistic world, the purchase of a slave was only final after the payment had been made or a large down payment was deposited with the owner. See later discussion in 7:23 where the same notion is presented.

III. 7:1–15:58. PAUL'S RESPONSE TO WRITTEN REPORTS FROM STEPHANUS AND FORTUNATUS

This lengthy portion of 1 Corinthians is in large measure Paul's response to a series questions that came to him in Ephesus from a delegation of persons from Corinth, probably including Stephanus, Fortunatus, and Achaicus (16:15-17). These questions are generally introduced with the familiar, "now concerning" that is found variously throughout the rest of this letter and introduces Paul's discussion of sexual activity and immorality (7:1), the status of the unmarried and the widowed (7:25), freedom to eat food offered to idols (8:1, 4), spiritual gifts (12:1), and the collection for the poor in Jerusalem (16:1, 12). Other subjects are covered in this section that probably also stem from questions asked of Paul, but he discusses them without this simple "now concerning" introduction: namely, head coverings (11:2-16), abuses of the Lord's Supper (11:17-34), matters related to the resurrection of the body (15:1-58). He also suggests that some of their questions to him will be dealt with when he visits them in the near future (11:34b). The use of the "now concerning" was a common feature in ancient writings. The response of an oracle to an inquirer in the first century B.C. begins: "Concerning the things about which you asked. You are well. What you desire night and day will be yours. As for what you want the gods will guide you and your livelihood will be for the better and your life will be distinguished" (*P. Inndob. Salomons* 1, ND).

A. 7:1-40. Marriage and Social Status
1. 7:1-16. Advice to those who are married.
7:1. "It is good for a man not to touch a woman." This statement has traditionally been understood as Paul's reference to his own view of sexual activity, but more recently it has been seen as a quote or slogan of what was in popular currency in Corinth in Paul's day. Marriage was seen as a concession to the frailty of human sexual desires, but more recently the passage is seen as a reflection of views that were circulating in the Christian community in Paul's day. Since Paul only uses the term "touch" (Greek = *haptesthai*) in one other instance (2 Cor. 6:17) and that is in a quotation, it is likely that he is simply citing a popular saying among some at Corinth. Sexual abstinence by devotees of the gods was common among the devotees of the cult of Isis, an Egyptian goddess, who was also widely celebrated and worshiped in Corinth as well as other popular Hellenistic centers such as Pergamum in the first century. There is evidence of worship of Isis at Cenchreae, one of the two port cities of Corinth. There is evidence of the cult of Isis at Corinth and sexual abstinence was a sign of those who were devoted to her. There was a god of the dead named Anubis, whose priests attended the devotees of Isis. Juvenal, the Roman satirist (ca. A.D. 60–140), comments on the priest of Anubis who "obtains pardon for wives who break the law of purity on days that should be kept holy" (*Satire* 6.535-36, LCL). Ovid (ca. 43 B.C.–A.D. 17), likewise, reflects the abstinence from sexual activity by the devotees of Isis when advising women to extract a price for their sexual favors, and comments to them: "Feign headache now, and now let Isis be what affords you pretext. After a time, receive him [the lover], lest he grow used to suffering, and his love grow slack through being oft repulsed"

(Ovid, *The Amores* 1.8.73-76, LCL). The Cynics of Paul's day were more likely to urge sexual abstinence so that the pursuit of their philosophy could go uninterrupted, but this was not Paul's view.

7:2. But because of immoralities, let each man have his own wife, and let each woman have her own husband. Paul is in harmony with Jewish teachings on this matter. In the *Testament of Levi* (ca. 137–107 B.C.) we read: "Be on guard against the spirit of promiscuity, for it is constantly active and through your descendants it is about to defile the sanctuary. Therefore take for yourself a wife while you are still young, a wife who is free of blame or profanation, who is not from the race of alien nations" (*T. Levi* 9:9-10, *OT Pseud.* 1:791-92). Similarly, in the apocryphal book of Tobit (ca. 225–175 B.C.), Tobit calls his son Tobias and says to him: "Beware my son of every kind of fornication. First of all, marry a woman from among the descendants of your ancestors" (*Tob* 4:12, NRSV). See also Prov. 5:19-20 which coincides with Paul's argument here.

7:5. Stop depriving one another, except by agreement for a time that you may devote yourselves to prayer. For Paul, it was expected that men and women would marry (Gen. 1:28), but there were times when it was appropriate with the consent of the spouse to dedicate a time to prayer and during this time it was agreed by both partners to avoid sexual contact. The rabbis followed specific guidelines regarding the length of time for abstinence from sexual activity during prayer or study of the law. Some argued for a two-week period of time and others for one week for the duration of this abstinence. According to the Mishnah,

> If a man vowed to have no intercourse with his wife, the School of Shammai say: [She may consent] for two weeks. And the School of Hillel say: For one week [only]. Disciples [of the Sages]

may continue absent for thirty days against the will [of their wives] while they occupy themselves in the study of the law; and laborers for one week. The duty of marriage enjoined in the Law [Exod. 21:10] is: every day for them that are unoccupied; twice a week for labourers; once a week for ass-drivers; once every thirty days for camel-drivers; and once every six months for sailors. So R. Eliezer (*m. Ketuboth* 5.6, Danby trans.).

Paul is closer in thought to the author of *The Testament of Naphtali* (ca. 137–107 B.C.), however, who writes: There is a time for having intercourse with one's wife, and a time to abstain for the purpose of prayer" (*T. Naph.* 8:8, *OT Pseud* 1:814). Paul contends that abstinence must be mutually agreed to by husband and wife, that it must be for a limited amount of time, and that it should be for the purpose of prayer.

Come together again lest Satan tempt you because of your lack of self-control. See Gal. 5:23; 2 Peter 1:6 where self-control is listed among the Christian virtues. Philo reflects this virtue thusly:

> For when God is gracious He makes all things light and easy, and He does become gracious to those who depart with shame from incontinence to self-restraint and deplore the deeds of their guilty past, abhor the base illusive images which they imprinted on their souls and first earnestly strive to still the storm of the passions, then seek to lead a life of serenity and peace (*On Rewards and Punishments* 116, LCL).

7:7. Yet I wish that all men were even as I myself am. However, each man has his own gift from God, one in this manner, and another in that. Many scholars have inferred that Paul was married since marriage was an important part of his religious training, but there is no evidence that he ever married. According to the Mishnah, "No man may abstain from keeping the law *Be fruitful and multiply*, unless he already has children: according to the School of Shammai, two sons; according to the School of Hillel, a son and a daughter, for it is written, *Male and female created he them*. . . . The duty to be fruitful and multiply falls on the man but not on the woman. R. Johanan B. Baroka says: Of them both it is written, *And God blessed them and God said unto them, Be fruitful and multiply* (*m. Yebamoth* 6.6, Danby trans.).

7:8. But I say to the unmarried and to widows that it is good for them if they remain even as I. Paul now addresses the concerns of those who are unmarried and widowed. While he believes that there are advantages in terms of Christian service for those who are single or widowed to remain single (7:32-35), he knows that not everyone has the ability to remain that way.

7:9. But if they do not have self-control, let them marry; for it is better to marry than to burn. For Paul, it is far better for a person to marry than to burn with passion. In this he is in harmony with longstanding Jewish practices (see discussion in 7:2 above). After hearing Jesus' response to the Pharisees' questions about marriage and divorce, his disciples concluded that it would be better to be single than married (Matt. 19:10). Paul drew similar conclusions based on other considerations: namely, the ability to serve the Lord (7:32-35) with an undivided loyalty and because of an impending crisis (7:26).

7:10-11. But to the married I give instructions, not I, but the Lord, that the wife should not leave her husband (but if she does leave, let her remain unmarried, or else be reconciled to her husband), and that the husband should not send his wife away. Paul finds the topic so important and also potentially divisive in the church that he shares the teaching from Jesus on the matter of divorce. Here and below he separates his views from those of Jesus (see 7:12, 25). See also 9:14, 11:23. Jesus' teaching on divorce is found in Mark 10:2-12, Matt. 19:1-12, and Luke 16:18. The only options for the believing spouse who departs from her husband is either to return to her husband or to remain single. In stating this, Paul is maintaining the tradition from Jesus in Luke 16:18. In the Roman world, on the other hand, divorce was possible for both partners and legal settlements were made regularly. One such settlement was found in a legal contract from Egypt dating from 13 B.C. The document reads:

> To Protarchus from Zois daughter of Heraclides, with her guardian her brother Irenaeus son of Heraclides, and Antipater son of Zenon. Zois and Antipater agree that they have separated from each other, severing the union which they had formed on the basis of an agreement made through the same tribunal in Hathur of the current 17th year of Caesar [Augustus], and Zois acknowledges that she has received from Antipater by hand from his house the material which he received for dowry, clothes to the value of 120 drachmae and a pair of gold earrings. The agreement of marriage shall henceforth be null, and neither Zois nor other person acting for her shall take proceedings against Antipater for restitution of the dowry, nor shall either party take proceedings against the other about cohabitation or any other matter whatsoever up to the present day, and hereafter it shall be lawful both for Zois to marry another man and for Antipater to marry another woman without either of them being answerable. In addition to this agreement being valid, the one who transgresses it shall moreover be liable

both to damages and to the prescribed fine. The 17th year of Caesar, Pharmouthi 2 (6. "Deed of Divorce," *Select Papyri* 1:23-24, LCL).

7:12. But to the rest I say, not the Lord, that if any brother has a wife who is an unbeliever, and she consents to live with him, let him not send her away. Because there were Jews in the church at Corinth (see 1:14; cf Acts 18:8, 17), it is possible that they questioned whether they should live with unbelieving spouses since unbelieving spouses were an abomination to the Lord (2 Chron. 21:6; Ezra 10:2-5, 10-11; Neh. 9:2-3; 10:28-30). Paul does not draw this conclusion, but sees the possibility of the Christian bringing the nonbeliever to faith in Christ (7:16).

2. 7:17-24. Paul's overriding principle: contentment with one's calling.

This is a much misunderstood passage in Paul that has been used variously to support the continuation of slavery and even a failure to recognize women's leadership roles in the church and society. Paul believed that Christ was going to return soon and with impending crisis at hand, all other matters such as singleness or marriage, slavery or freedom—all things had to be seen in light of the most important task of sharing God's Good News as that day of the coming of the Lord was fast approaching. Before that day, there were many hardships also falling on the early Christians and, given the deprivation that some were facing, it seems that singleness was a significant option facing many young Christians and those who had been widowed. While urging that Christians remain in the social condition in which they were called by God, namely—in this case—their married status, Paul appeals to well-known social categories to make his point. Without question the one that has troubled many Christians over the centuries is the call to remain in slavery. In the broader scope of the passage, however, Paul is claiming that there is no social status higher than another

in Christ and, whether married or single, slave or free, Gentile or Jewish, such categories are irrelevant to one's calling of God in Christ. Paul makes the point here and elsewhere (Gal. 3:28) that there are no social distinctions in the salvation that comes to those who are in Christ. This is in the face of those in the ancient world who emphasized such social distinctions. For example, the prayer of Rabbi Judah (second century A.D.), the disciple of Rabbi Aqiba, reportedly prayed: "Blessed are thou . . . who has not made me a heathen . . . who has not made me a woman . . . who has not made me a slave" (*b. Menah.* 43b, cf. *t. Ber.* 7:18; *y. Ber* 9:1, transl. R. F. Collins). For Paul, there is no superior social class in the family of God based on gender, ethnicity, or other arbitrary classes of society.

7:17. Only, as the Lord has assigned to each one, as God has called each, in this manner let him walk. See Rom. 12:3; 2 Cor. 10:13.

7:18. Was any man called already circumcised? Let him not become uncircumcised. In the ancient world, many Jews tried to reverse the visual signs of circumcision by a process known as *"epispasm"* (Greek = *epispastho*), mostly to allow them to attend the baths at gymnasiums and participate in Roman activity without the ridicule that might attend their nakedness in these public places. This operation was most often done during the age of puberty or before so young men could enter into the athletic and gymnastic activities of their Hellenistic counterparts without the stigma of circumcision being a source of ridicule for them. Those who reversed their circumcision by restoring their foreskins usually did so in their youth and it also became a symbol of their abandoning their Jewish covenant. When Antiochus Epiphanes, king of the Seleucid dynasty, came to power, he tried to force the Greek culture and religion upon the Jews (175–165 B.C.). He appointed the puppet king of Israel, Jason, who authorized the Jews "to observe the ordinances of the Gentiles. So they a gymnasium in Jerusalem, according to Gentile custom, and removed the marks of circumcision, and abandoned the holy covenant. They joined with the Gentiles and sold themselves to do evil" (1 Macc. 1:14-15, NRSV). Rejection of one's circumcision was the same as rejecting the covenant that God made with his people. The Maccabean story is likewise told by Josephus (Ant. 12.241). Speaking of the horrible days probably of Antiochus, but saying that these days are ahead for the people of God (the Jews) before the coming of the kingdom of God, the author of the apocryphal book, The Testament of Moses (first century A.D.) claims:

> And there will come upon them [. . .] punishment and wrath such as has never happened to them from the creation till that time when he stirs up against them a king of the kings of the earth who, having supreme authority, will crucify those who confess their circumcision. Even those who deny it, he will torture and hand them over to be led to prison in chains. And their wives will be given to the gods of the nations and their young sons will be cut by physicians to bring forward their foreskins (T. Mos. 8:1-3, OT Pseud 1:930-31).

In the Tosephta, material attributed to first and second century A.D. rabbis, we read:

> One who has his prepuce ["foreskin"] drawn forward has to be circumcised. R. Judah says, "One who has his prepuce drawn forward should not be circumcised, because it is dangerous." They said to him, "Many were circumcised in the time of Ben Koziba, and they had children and did not die, "since it says, circumcising, he shall be circumcised (Gen. 17:13) —even a hundred times. "and it says, My covenant has he destroyed (Gen. 17:14; Any uncircumcised male . . . shall be cut off from his people: he has broken my covenant) —to encompass the one

who has his prepuce drawn forward" (t. Shabbat 15.9, A-E, Neusner Trans.).

Aulius Cornelius Celsus (ca. A.D. 14–37) wrote an encyclopedia on agriculture, medicine, military science, rhetoric, jurisprudence and philosophy. All of what survives in his literary contributions, however, is his eight-volume discussion of medicine. In the seventh of his books on medicine, he describes in considerable detail the ancient practice of epispasm, that is, removing the marks of circumcision, see his On Medicine 7.25.

7:21. Were you called while a slave? Do not worry about it; but if you are able also to become free, rather do that. Paul seems to be reflecting a view held among the Jews that they are not slaves as long as they are obedient to God (see John 8:33). Philo describes the Essenes of Egypt (and probably at Qumran as well) as free people who did not recognize slavery in any form.

> Not a single slave is to be found among them, but all are free, exchanging services with each other, and they denounce the owners of slaves, not merely for their injustice in outraging the law of equality, but also for their impiety in annulling the statute of Nature, who mother-like has born and reared all men alike, and created them genuine brothers, not in mere name, but in reality, though this kinship has been put to confusion by the triumph of malignant covetousness, which has wrought estrangement instead of affinity and enmity instead of friendship (Philo, Every Good Man is Free 79, LCL).

7:22. For he who was called in the Lord while a slave, is the Lord's freedman; likewise he who was called while free, is Christ's slave. Paul is often accused of being indifferent to the plight of slaves, but his overriding concern is the proclamation of the Gospel in light of the coming of the Lord. Some have accused Paul of a Stoic response to the evil of his day, representing something like Epictetus' lack of concern over how one dies since we all die: "what concern is it to you by what road you descend to the House of Hades? They are all equal" (Discourses 2.6.18, LCL). This is not true for Paul, however, his concern is eschatological, that is, on the future and the importance of preaching the Gospel now. Everything else is subordinate to that.

7:23. You were bought with a price; do not become slaves of men. Paul reminds the Corinthians that all Christians are slaves of Christ and that like the purchase of the slave in an open market in their community, Christ paid a price for them. See 6:20 above. Paul understands that true freedom is only found in Christ and slavery is nothing. Epictetus, himself a slave, similarly wrote: "I have considered all of this, no one has authority over me. I have been set free by God, I know His commands, no one has power any longer to make a slave of me, I have the right kind of emancipator, and the right kind of judges" (Discourses, 4.7.16, LCL). Remarkably, there was little interest in the early church to free slaves from their masters. The book of Philemon is, of course, an exception, but even there for different reasons than emancipation.

Slaves in the ancient world could anticipate their freedom after ten to twenty years of service to their master, and many chose to stay slaves when their terms of slavery were over. Slavery in the ancient world must be distinguished from that of slavery in America in the nineteenth century. While it was still slavery, there were many prominent people in the ancient world who were slaves, including teachers, writers, politicians, artisans, philosophers (Epictetus), and others. Some slaves had many financial assets and were better off socially than many who were born free or had purchased their freedom. Epictetus describes

the life of a freedman who was worse off in his freedom than he in his slavery.

It is the slave's prayer that he be set free immediately . . . Then he is emancipated, and forthwith, having no place to which to go and eat, he looks for someone to flatter, for someone at whose house to dine. Next he either earns a living by prostitution, and so endures the most dreadful things, and if he gets a manger at which to eat he has fallen into a slavery much more severe than the first; or even if he grows rich, being a vulgarian he has fallen in love with a chit of a girl, and is miserable, and laments, and yearns for his slavery again. "why, what was wrong with me? Someone else kept me in clothes, and shoes, and supplied me with food, and nursed me when I was sick; I served him in only a few matters" (Discourses 4.1.35-37, LCL).

The process of manumission in Paul's day often included a ritual that took place in a sacred temple, in which, as at the Pythian Apollo temple at Delphi, north of Corinth, a slave would pay the priest the funds to purchase his or her freedom from the owner (slaves could not negotiate the sale on their own) and, once freed, the slave's name was inscribed on the walls of the temple. Several such inscriptions have been found on the walls at Delphi and the following example dating from 200–199 B.C. illustrates what was said:

The Pythian Apollo bought from Sosibus of Amphissa for freedom a female slave, whose name is Nicaea, by race a Roman, at a price of three silver minas and a half-mina. Former seller according to the law was Eumnastus of Amphissa. He received the price. The deed of sale Nicaea has entrusted to Apollo for freedom (Sylloge Inscriptionum Graecarum, second edition, 845).

In this sense, it was believed that the god Apollo actually purchased the freedom of the slave. When Jews were manumitted, it was not unusual for the slaves to go to the synagogue for a similar ritual. For example, an inscription was found at Panticapaeum, in the Crimea, that reads:

In the reign king Tiberius Julius Rhescuporis, friend of Caesar and friend of Rome, the pious; in the year 377 [= A.D. 81], in the month of Penitius, the 20th [or 23rd], I, Chreste, formerly wife of Nicias, son of Sotas, release at the house of prayer my slave Heraclas to be completely free according to my vow. He is not to be retained or disturbed by any heir of mine, but to go wherever he wishes, without let or hindrance according to my vow, except for the house of prayer which is for worship and meeting. Assent is given to this also by my heirs, Pericleides and Heliconias. Joint oversight will be taken also by the synagogue of the Jews (C.I.G. 2114).

From that time, the slave was known as a slave of Apollo. Paul was no doubt aware of this practice and reminded his readers that they were slaves of Christ who purchased them with his own blood. Only rarely did the early Christians seek to purchase the freedom of slaves, and in the early second century Ignatius, Bishop of Antioch, advises Polycarp not to encourage Christians to purchase the freedom of the slaves. He writes:

Do not be haughty to slaves, either men or women; yet do not let them be puffed up, but let them rather endure slavery to the glory of God, that they may obtain a better freedom from God. Let them not desire to be set free at the Church's expense, that they be not found the slaves of lust (Ignatius, *Pol.* 4.3, LCL).

Christians should not equate this lack of interest in the manumission of slaves to indifference, but rather to a different social milieu in the first century than the kind of oppressive slavery that obtained in subsequent centuries. Also, Paul appeals for the stability of the social order here as a means of addressing the issue of marriage. He prefers that those who are

married remain that way and those who are unmarried also to remain that way if they have been so called by God. The appeal to the Corinthian Christians to remain in the condition in which they have found themselves is like the Stoic perspective found in Ovid, who says to Terminus, "thou has not been free to flit: abide in that station in which thou has been placed" (*Fasti* 2.673-74, LCL).

3. 7:25-40. Advice to the Unmarried

Paul now turns his attention to the unmarried and to those widowed. This is a new issue that he is responding to (see his "now concerning" in introduction to C. 7:1 above).

7:25. Now concerning virgins. The most important question involved in interpreting this text has to do with the identity of those he is addressing: namely, who are the "virgins" in the passage? Is it the unmarried male and female? Verse 28 seems to answer that, but Paul holds what is true for one is true for the other. While the term "virgins" (Greek = *parthenoi*) is most commonly used of females only, sometimes it is also used of males (Rev. 14:4). Likewise, in the pseudepigraphal Joseph and Aseneth (ca. 100 B.C. to A.D. 135), we read: "And Joseph [the patriarch of Gen. 37, 39-47, 50] is a man who worships God, and self-controlled, and a virgin like you today, and Joseph is (also) a man powerful in wisdom and experience and the spirit of God is upon him . . ." and later Aseneth's father repeats the same when he tells his daughter, "Greet your brother [Joseph], because he, too, is a virgin like you today and hares every strange woman, as you, too, every strange man" (*JosAs* 4:9; 8:1 *OT Pseud* 2:206-207, 211). It appears that Paul uses the term for both male and female who have not been married. In the context of his discussion of freedom, he tells the Corinthians what is proper and what is best for them. Interestingly, Ignatius of Antioch (ca. A.D. 115) appears to call those who are widowed virgins as well. "I salute the families of my brethren with their wives and children, and the maidens [*parthenous*] who are called widows" (Ign. *Smyrn.* 13:1, LCL). Again, in this passage, Paul seems to refer to both male and female virgins.

I have no command of the Lord, but I give an opinion as one who by the mercy of the Lord is trustworthy. As before (see 7:10-12), Paul distinguishes what he teaches from the direct command of the Lord, but will conclude that he believes that his teaching comes from the prophetic spirit of God (7:40). As Paul makes a claim as a servant of Christ to be trustworthy or faithful (Greek = *pistos*), so Epictetus made the argument that the philosopher is trustworthy. "Next we must learn what the gods are like; for whatever their character is discovered to be, the man [philosopher] who is going to please and obey them must endeavor as best he can to resemble them. If the deity is faithful, he also must be faithful [trustworthy, Greek = *piston*]; if free, he must also be free, . . . in everything he says and does, he must act as an imitator of God" (*Discourses* 2.14.12-13, LCL). Again, he writes: "to be faithful and respectful a man needs judgments of no casual sort," and adds, "Remember, therefore, in general, that confidences require faithfulness and faithful judgments" (*Discourses* 4.13.21, 23, LCL). While what Paul says here is his opinion (Greek, *gnome*), he believes that he is a faithful or trustworthy witness who has the Spirit of God directing him (7:40).

7:26. I think then that this is good in view of the present distress, that it is good for a man to remain as he is. Paul's reference to the "present distress" is paralleled with his comments in 7:29 that reflect his view that the time of the Lord's return and the preceding trials before that time (Rom. 13:11-12; 1 Thess. 1:9-10; cf. Rev. 3:10). His reference to "it is good" here in regard to the unmarried parallels what he has said earlier in 7:1 to the married. He also says that it is good for each person to stay in

the social condition that he or she is in (7:17, 20, 24; cf. Rom. 14:21; Gal. 4:18). The same advice holds true here, but Paul is not adamant about the matter (7:28, 38), but believes that it is good for the unmarried to stay that way, but it is not wrong to be married and have a normal sex life (7:2, 9, 28).

7:27. Are you bound to a wife? Do not seek to be released. Are you released from a wife? Do not seek a wife. What Paul was advocating was in direct opposition to stated custom of his day among the Roman citizens. Tacitus (ca. A.D. 55–120) reported that Caesar Augustus (Octavian), before he died passed a law penalizing those who did not marry "in order to sharpen the penalties of celibacy and to increase the resources of the exchequer [treasurer]. It failed, however, to make marriage and the family popular—childlessness remained vogue" (*Annals*, 3.25, LCL). He had tried to strengthen the laws of Julius Caesar before him called the *lex Iulia de maritundis ordinibus* of 18 B.C. with his own *Lex Papia Poppaea* regulations that he strengthened in A.D. 9, but they were ineffective in promoting marriage and population growth. Dio Cassius reports that the decree of Augustus came as a result of the shrinking Roman population that brought concern to the Emperor Augustus. His plea as he established the law was premised on the need for population growth if the security of Rome was to continue. The following is his impassioned plea for understanding of the law.

Therefore, fellow-citizens—for I believe that I have now persuaded you both to hold fast to the name of citizens and to secure the title of men and fathers as well—I have administered this rebuke to you not for my own pleasure but from necessity, and not as your enemy nor as one who hates you but rather loving you and wishing to obtain many others like you, in order that we may have lawful homes to dwell in and houses full of descendants, so that we may approach the gods together with our wives and our children, and in partnership with one another may risk our all in equal measure and reap in like degree the hopes we cherish in them (Dio Cassius, *Roman History* 46.9, LCL).

Augustus both appealed to the people to marry and have children, offering monetary incentives and eventually strengthening existing laws to do so (Dio Cass., *Roman History* 46.10.1-3). These laws included a shortening of the time of engagement, reducing the three-year period of mourning following the death of a spouse, and setting a limit on the number of divorces one could have (Suetonius, *Lives of the Caesars*, "the Deified Augustus" 2.34.1-2). The laws generally failed because they were hated by the people—especially by the knights of Rome, and were later modified but largely ignored. They do heighten, however, the feelings of the Romans about marriage and having children. In the second century A.D., Pliny, the governor of Bithynia and Pontus, wrote a letter to the emperor on behalf of Suetonius Tranquillus (the Roman Historian ca. A.D. 75–140), asking that he grant Suetonius the privileges that were granted to those with three or more children. The grounds for the appeal is that Suetonius was a scholar, a man of highest integrity and distinction, with considerable literary abilities, but who had no children even though married. Pliny implores the Emperor Trajan: "there are two reasons why he needs the privileges granted to parents of three children: his friends could then effectively express their recognition of his merits, and, as his marriage has not been blessed with children, he can only look to your generosity, at my suggestion, for the benefits which the cruelty of fortune has denied him (*Letters* 10.94, LCL). The emperor granted Pliny's request only reluctantly but declared: "I have conferred on Suetonius Tranquillus the privileges granted to parents of three children, on my usual terms" (*Letters* 10.95, LCL). Precisely what these benefits were is unclear, but it is obvious that what

began with Augusts was continued well into the next century and it offered financial benefits to those getting married and having children. Whether Paul reflects any of these views, whether Jewish or Roman, is doubtful, but his appeal to singleness would have been well received in a Roman colony by the Romans of his day.

7:29. But this I say, brethren, the time has been shortened, so that from now on those who have wives should be as though they had none. This "as though they had none [a wife]" has familiar parallels in *4 Ezra* 16:42, who reflects an impending doom and writes:

O my people; prepare for battle, and in the midst of the calamities be like strangers on the earth. . . . Let him that does business be like one who will not make a profit; and let him that builds a house be like one who will not live in it; let him that sows be like one who will not reap; so also him that prunes the vines, like one who will not gather the grapes; them that marry, like those who will have no children; and them that do not marry like those that are widowed. (*4 Ezra* 16:40-45, *OT Pseud* 1:558).

With the death and resurrection of Christ, the impending "last days" began and will be fulfilled with the coming of Christ that will be preceded with war and crisis (1 Thess. 5:1-11). Because of this, Paul believes that it is better not to marry. Similarly, the author of *4 Ezra* claims that the end of time is near and that they should prepare for it. "Therefore I say to you, O nations that hear and understand, 'Await your shepherd; he will give you everlasting rest, because he who will come at the end of the age is close at hand'" (*4 Ezra* 2:33-34, *OT Pseud* 1:527). And later he says again, "If you are alive, you will see, and if you live long, you will often marvel, because the age is hastening swiftly to its end" (4:26, *OT Pseud* 1:530). Epictetus, when asked whether marriage should be considered by a young man, replied that given:

. . . the order of things at the present,

which is like that of a battlefield, it is a question, perhaps, if the Cynic ought not to be free from distraction, wholly devoted to the service of god, free to go about among men, not tied down by the private duties of men, nor involved in relationships which he cannot violate and still maintain his role as a good and excellent man.... (*Discourses* 3.22.69, LCL).

The Cynics of Paul's day argued that marriage was a distraction for the true philosopher and that it should be avoided. In second-century Christianity, a tradition arose in the famous letter of *Paul and Thecla* that claimed when Paul entered the house of Onesiphorus (see 2 Tim. 1:16; 4:19), he uttered several beatitudes including, "Blessed are they who have wives as if they had them not, for they shall be heirs of God" (*Paul and Thecla* 5, NT Apo 2:239). The Stoics contended that things or possessions such as things or even loved ones who die, ought to be held as temporary and not permanent objects so that one cannot suffer loss. This was accomplished through a love first for the gods. "And what keeps you loving a person as one subject to death, as one who may leave you? Did not Socrates love his won children? But in a free spirit, as one who remembers that it is his first duty to be a friend to the gods" (Epictetus, *Discourses* 3.24.59-60, LCL). Likewise, Epictetus admonishes his readers to remember and keep the law of the God and not to lay claim to what is not ours: namely, persons and things, and to make use of the things that have been given to him and not to yearn for the things that have not been given. He then says, "when something is taken away, to give it up readily and without delay, being grateful for the time in which he had use of it —all this if you do not wish to be crying for your nurse and mammy!" (*Discourses* 2.16.28). He calls upon his readers to do something desperate "to achieve peace, freedom, and high mindedness" and that, he claims will come

when we look toward God and say "I am of one mind with Thee; I am Thine; I crave exemption from nothing that seems good in Thy sight; where thou wilt, lead me; in what raiment Thou wilt, clothe me." The things we must cast off with the help of God include grief, fear, desire, envy, joy at others' ills, greed, effeminacy, and incontinency, bur these can only be cast off by "looking to God alone, being specially devoted to Him only, and consecrated to His commands" (*Discourses* 2.16.42, 45-46, LCL). While Paul's primary motivation is eschatological, it is unclear where he would disagree with Epictetus on how to let go of that which we cannot keep.

7:36. But if any man thinks that he is acting unbecomingly toward his virgin daughter, if she should be of full age, and if it must be so, let him do what he wishes, he does not sin; let her marry. Does this passage refer to a man betrothed to a virgin or a father who has a virgin daughter? In a Jewish document from Alexandria dating from ca. 30 B.C.–A.D. 40, we read some advice given to parents (fathers) about their children: Guard the youthful prime of life of a comely boy, because many rage for intercourse with a man. Guard a virgin in firmly locked rooms, and do not let her be seen before the house until her wedding day" (Pseudo-Phocylides, *Sentences* 213-216, OT Pseud 2:581). Sophocles tells how Oedipus Tyrannus was given a last privilege to see his daughters whom he calls virgins (Greek = *te parthenoin*) and hold them before he is sent away. While it is true that some ancient texts use forms of the term "virgin" (*parthenos*) to refer to a daughter, that is not the case here. The NASB translates this term as a "fiancée" which better fits the context: "If anyone thinks that he is not behaving properly toward his fiancée, if his passions are strong, and so it has to be, let him marry as he wishes; it is no sin" (7:36, NRSV). This is consistent with Paul's earlier comments in 7:7-8, 24, 26-28. He is not focusing his comments on the father of a virgin throughout the passage, but rather upon those who are unmarried, and he is appealing to them to remain in their unmarried state. Paul's teaching here is consistent with his teaching elsewhere on Christian morality (Rom. 13:13; 1 Cor. 14:40; Phil. 4:8; 1 Thess. 4:12).

7:39. A wife is bound as long as her husband lives; but if her husband is dead, she is free to be married to whom she wishes, only in the Lord. Paul was more strict in his views of marriage than were many contemporary Jews who allowed for divorce of a wife on most any grounds of incompatibility. When the divorce came, the wife was free to marry whomever she chose. According to the Mishnah,

'Thou are free to marry any man excepting my father and thy father, my brother and thy brother, a slave or a gentile' . . . the essential formula in the bill of divorce is 'Lo, thou are free to marry any man.' R. Judah says: 'Let this be from me thy writ of divorce and letter of dismissal and deed of liberation, that thou mayest marry whatsoever man thou wilt.' The essential formula in a writ of emancipation is, 'Lo, thou are a freedwoman: lo thou belongest to thyself' (*m. Gittin* 9:2-3, Danby trans.).

Paul's admonition to marry only in the Lord seems to follow standard Jewish views of his day and also reflects Deut. 7:3 and Ezra 9:2 as well as *m. Gittin* 9:2 above.

B. 8:1–11:1. Food Sacrificed to Idols

This section deals primarily with how the Christians in Corinth related to each other in their daily lives and how they observed their religious freedoms they had acquired in Christ. Whether they had the liberty to eat foods sacrificed to idols was a very important matter in the early church and is the central focus of this passage.

8:1. Now concerning things sacrificed to idols, we know that we all have knowledge. Knowledge makes arrogant, but love edifies.

Among the questions asked of Paul from the delegation of persons from Corinth—probably including Stephanus, Fortunatus, and Achaicus (16:15-17) (see introduction to C. above)—is a common issue for the early Christians: namely, whether they should eat meat that had been sacrificed in honor of a pagan deity and served in a pagan temple in the presence of that deity. In the ancient world, many meals of celebration took place in pagan temples to which many Jews and Christians were invited as citizens in that community. Although meat was not a regular part of the average person's diet, it was a part of the food regularly eaten in pagan temples after it had been offered to the pagan deity. If meat were eaten in a house served by a neighbor or friend, Paul encourages the Christians not to ask where it came from, but to eat it if their conscience allowed them to do so (8:10). The key issue that Paul is addressing here is whether Christians may, or should be, involved in eating meals offered to pagan idols in the pagan temples.

In Corinth, some of the wealthy magistrates occasionally invited the whole city to come to a banquet in the temple. In the early- to mid-first century, the first president of the Panhellenic Isthmian games held in the vicinity of Corinth, Lucius Castricius Regulus invited all of the citizens of the Roman colony to a banquet. Three such invitations were discovered in the Oxyrhenchos Papyri dating from the second century A.D. Notice that they include the invitation to dine at a banquet of the "lord"(Serapis).

(a) Nikephorus asks you to dine at a banquet of the lord Serapis in the Birth-House on the 23rd, from the 9th hour.

(b) Herais asks you to dine in the (dining-) room of the Sarapeion [= temple of Asklepios] at a banquet of the Lord Sarapis tomorrow: namely, the 11th, from the 9th hour.

(c) The god calls you to a banquet being held in the Thoereion tomorrow from the 9th hour (*Oxy.* 1.110, ND 1:7).

Plutarch tells about such banquets in honor of the gods held at Corinth during the Isthmian games. "During the Isthmian games, the second time Sospis was president, I avoided the other banquets, at which he entertained a great many foreign visitors at one, and several times entertained all the citizens" (*Quaestionum convivalium libri* vi 723A, LCL). In these temples there was also a statue of a god who was worshiped there. Strabo describes the images of Zeus at a temple near the Olympian games in which there was an image of Zeus "of beaten gold dedicated by Cypselus the tyrant of Corinth," and he goes on to say that the biggest of these was the ivory image of Zeus sitting on a throne. The image (the Greeks did not use the term "statue" to describe these gods erected in their temples), says Strabo,

> . . . was so large that, although the temple was very large, the artist is thought to have missed the proper symmetry, for he showed Zeus seated but almost touching the roof with his head, thus making the impression that if Zeus arose and stood erect he would unroof the temple. (*Geography* 8.3.30, LCL).

Christians eating in such temples would have been exposed to the imagery of a pagan god as well as to the food sacrificed in honor of it. For those Christians who were once among those who served idols (1 Thess. 1:9), it is easy to see their reluctance to return to the place where this imagery was impossible to miss. Eating it at home is another matter that is discussed in 10:1–11:1 below.

At first glance, Paul's conclusion on the matter of eating foods sacrificed to idols seems to be at odds with that taken in 10:1–11:1. Initially he sides with the "strong" who say that they can eat anything and that there is only one God and the pagan gods are not gods at all. On the other hand, he has a more significant concern than whether it is theologically correct to partake of such foods. He is concerned over the unity of the church and what is most appropriate to bring unity to the church as a whole. It appears that Paul is siding with those who are "weak" in their faith and is opposed to those who are "strong" and feel that they can freely eat foods sacrificed to idols. In chap. 10, he takes seriously the arguments from Scripture against such practices and is more in keeping with Jewish practices of his day (Acts 15:29; Rev. 2:14, 20; cf. Num. 22:5, 7; 31:16; Deut. 23:4; Num. 25:1-3). At no point in his argument does Paul refer to the decision of the Acts Council on the matter which welcomes the newly converted Gentiles into the church, but prohibits them from eating foods sacrificed to idols, sexual promiscuity, and eating of blood (Acts 15:19-20, 29; cf. Exod. 34:15-16; Lev. 18:6-23; 17:10-16). There were Jews in the church at Corinth, the number of which cannot be determined, who would naturally be hesitant to participate in eating foods sacrificed to pagan idols, but they are not the ones that Paul has in mind here (8:7). He is speaking about the new Christian who formerly served those idols and now is eating such sacrificed foods in those places of pagan worship. While Paul agrees with the knowledge that these "strong" Christians had (8:4-6), he contends that there is something else that is more important and he seems to side with the "weak" on the matter. He does this, not from theological issues, but rather out of concerns over those for whom Christ died who are not strong.

8:4-5. We know that there is no such thing as an idol in the world, and that there is no God but one. For even if there are so-called gods whether in heaven or on earth, as indeed there are many gods and many lords. Paul concedes the correct theology to those "who have knowledge" (8:1) and repeats with approval their basic point: namely, that there is only one God and the others do not really exist, even though there are demonic powers that do exist. It follows that if such pagan gods do not exist, then there is no power in the idols and the matter of eating food in pagan temples is not a significant problem to those who are free in Christ. Paul nevertheless recognizes that for the unbelievers there are many gods and for those recently converted from those beliefs there is considerable struggle of conscience for them to participate in such activities in honor of these gods.

The most familiar name among the Roman gods, Jupiter was by far the most powerful deity and was lord of heaven's vault of thunderbolts. He became the Roman state deity and was later identified with the Greek god, Zeus. Other gods in the pantheon included Juno (Hera, in Greek mythology), who was the protectress of women, the queen of heaven as well as the wife of Jupiter, and Minerva (Athena), who was known as the goddess of craftsmen. Besides this powerful Roman triad, Mars (Aries) was known as the god of war and of hard labor in the fields, Saturn (Cronus) the god of agriculture, and Vesta (Hestia) the guardian of the fire entrusted to the care of the Vestal Virgins. Also important in the Roman pantheon were Ceres (Demeter), who was the goddess of fertility, Mercury (Hermes), the protector of shopkeepers, and Vulcan (Hephaestos), the god of fire and smiths. Neptune (Poseidon) was recognized as the deity of all waters and seas, Diana (Artemis) became the patron goddess of women and slaves, Fortuna emerged as the mistress of good luck, and later Venus (Aphrodite) was known as the goddess of love. To these more prominent gods, many others were added. Foreign deities were readily accepted by the Romans who were known for wanting to appease the foreign sources of supernatural power. The importance of the gods to the Romans is summarized by Livy, the Roman historian (ca. 59 B.C.–A.D. 17), who concludes: "You will find that those who followed the gods had every success, while those who disregarded them were visited with misfortune" (*History* 5.51.5, LCL).

On the other hand, the Jews and Christians were not the only ones in the ancient world who believed that there was only one God. Plutarch acknowledges the Stoic notion that there is but one God. Plutarch contends that those who advocate many gods "unwittingly erase and dissipate things divine" and claims that "we create in men fearful atheistic opinions which are senseless and inanimate, and are of necessity destroyed by men when they need to use them." He concludes:

It is impossible to conceive of these things as being gods in themselves; for God is not senseless nor inanimate nor subject to human control. As a result of this we have come to regard as gods those who make use of these things and present them to us and provide us with things everlasting and constant. Nor do we think of the gods as different gods among different peoples, nor as barbarian gods and Greek gods, nor as southern and northern gods, but just as the sun and the moon and the heavens and the earth and the sea are common to all, but are called by different names by different peoples, so for that one rationality which keeps all these things in order and the one Providence which watchers over them and the ancillary powers that are set over all, there have arisen different peoples, in accordance with their customs, different honours and appellations (*Isis and Osiris* 66-67, LCL).

8:6. Yet for us there is but one God, the Father, from whom are all things, and we exist for Him; and one Lord, Jesus Christ, by whom are all things, and we exist through Him. Marcus Aurelius (ca 120–180) concludes that "Everything is fitting for me, my universe, which fits thy purpose. Nothing in thy good time is too early or too late for me; everything is fruit for me which thy seasons, nature, bear; from thee, in thee are all things" (*Meditations*

4.23, LCL). Plutarch also made similar claims for Zeus:

> To sum up, then: while every form of creation has, as I say, two causes, the very earliest theological writers and poets chose to heed only the superior one, uttering over all things that come to pass this common generality [taken from the earlier Orphic Fragment 6.10] "Zeus the beginning, Zeus in the midst, and from Zeus comes all being" . . . (*Moralia*, "Obsolescence of Oracles" 436 D, LCL).

8:7. However not all men have this knowledge; but some, being accustomed to the idol until now, eat food as if it were sacrificed to an idol; and their conscience being weak is defiled. Paul speaks as if to the "strong" and shows his concern for the "weak" who have come out of pagan religious practices and are offended by the "strong" entering into the temples and partaking of food sacrificed to the gods the "weak" formerly honored. The crux of his argument in 8:7-13 is that there is something far more significant than freedom to do as one pleases. Paul couches the notion of true Christian freedom here, as in Rom. 14, with the ability to set aside those freedoms for the sake of those who are weak or would stumble over the freedom of those who are "strong," that is, have this "knowledge" that allows them freedom to participate in such ritual activity.

8:12. And thus, by sinning against the brethren and wounding their conscience when it is weak, you sin against Christ. When Paul speaks of the "strong" and "weak" to describe individuals (see 8:7,10, 12, Greek = *asthenes, asthenesin, asthenousan*), he is using familiar language in the Greco-Roman world. Epictetus, for instance, talks about those without education and those who are weak who also puff themselves up with their acquisition of ability and knowledge.

For great is the power of argumentation and persuasive reasoning, and especially if it should enjoy excessive exercise and receive likewise a certain additional ornament from language. The reason is that, in general, every faculty which is acquired by the uneducated and the weak [*asthenesi*] is dangerous for them, as being apt to make them conceited and puffed up over it (*Discourses* 1.8.8-9, LCL).

Elsewhere Plutarch describes the weak as those who are "the unmanly and irrational, the unpracticed and untrained, those who retain from childhood their notions unchanged" (*Moralia*, "Vice Causes Unhappiness" 499D.§4, LCL) and in general he speaks of the weak as those who are prone to false judgments (*Moralia*, "Reply to Colotes" 1122C). Paul uses the term differently here and in chap. 10, but still contrasts them with those who "have knowledge"(the knowledge of 8:4-6), but he argues that those who are consequently "strong" have an obligation to their fellow Christians who might stumble in their faith as a result of unthoughtful actions. He uses his strongest words for those who insist on their freedom and offend the weaker Christians by reminding them they sin against Christ. Sinning against those Christ loves is also sinning against Christ. In Paul's conversion experience, he was reminded that his persecution of the Christians was the same as persecuting Christ himself (see Acts 9:4). He never forgot that important lesson and passes it on here.

8:13. Therefore, if food causes my brother to stumble, I will never eat meat again, that I might not cause my brother to stumble. This is similar to the conclusion on this matter drawn in Rom. 14:13-15, 20-21. Paul returns to this topic again in chap. 10.

D. 9:1–27. Paul's example of giving up rights for a greater unity

The context of this section has to do with freedom, whether to marry or remain single, to eat foods sacrificed to idols, and how to act with freedom as a Christian. Chap. 9 appears to be a digression from the flow of things in Chaps. 8 and 10, but its purpose in the larger whole appears to be in showing his readers the freedom that he has (see 8:1-6), but his unwillingness to use that freedom so that he might achieve a greater cause: namely, the preaching of the Gospel (see parallel with the greater aim of 8:7-13 that emphasizes care for the "weaker" brothers and sisters in Christ). The digressive nature of this chapter, however is noted, but its logic within the context of the argument began in 7:1 is not lost. There are three sections of this chapter that focus on Paul's freedom and rights as an apostle, but failure to demand these rights for the greater purpose of his mission (9:1-14), his defense of his willingness to be all things to all people—again showing the flexibility that is required to achieve a more noble end (9:15-23), and finally his willingness to make sacrifices to achieve his goal of winning the prize (9:24-27). In the latter case, the metaphors of running and boxing are used to show that self-discipline is needed to keep one's eyes on the higher prize. Again, in dealing with those who demand their freedom, Paul indicates that he has the right of freedom as an apostle and servant of Christ, but he does not demand his rights. This is in keeping with the counsel that he gave in 8:7-13, that there was something more important than one's rights: namely, the care for others for whom Christ died. How can he do this? He understands the mission of Christ well enough to know that there is something far more important than personal freedoms. By pursuing a higher calling he can voluntarily set aside his freedoms for the sake of achieving his mission. This is the point he tries to make in the previous argument. A truly free person, like the athlete, can give up all rights to achieve the greater prize in the family of Christ. Certainly one who gives up the rights of a free person to "win the prize" will understand the logic of his argument.

9:1. Am I not free? Am I not an apostle? Have I not seen Jesus our Lord? Are you not my work in the Lord? Using himself as an example to consider, Paul emphasizes that he, like the "strong" in the church, is free and he bases it upon his office of apostleship. For a discussion of this apostleship in the early church, see discussion in 1:1 above. Knowing that about one-third of the population in the Greco-Roman world were slaves, he elsewhere emphasizes what he greatly prized: namely, that he was a Roman citizen and free (see Acts 25:10-12, 21, 25; 26:32) to exercise those rights of all Roman citizens. (See discussion of "free" in 7:21-23 above.) Here, however, his freedom is based on his apostleship rather than his citizenship. Paul knows that those who are free have the right to exercise their freedoms or rights, and here he sets out the rights that he has as one who is free by virtue of his office in the church before stating that he has not made use of such rights so that he might accomplish the greater good, his mission of "saving some" (9:22).

9:5. Do we not have a right to take along a believing wife, even as the rest of the apostles, and the brothers of the Lord, and Cephas? Once again, Paul affirms that he has not married (7:8). Using Peter's nickname, "Cephas," as was his practice (see 1:12; 3:22; 15:5), he refers to a tradition also supported in the Gospels that Peter was married (Matt. 8:14-15; Mark 1:29-31; Luke 4:39-39). Clement of Alexandria (ca. A.D. 170–180), tells the tradition of Peter's wife's death as a martyr before Peter's eyes.

> They say, accordingly, that the blessed Peter, on seeing his wife led to death, rejoiced on account of her call and conveyance home, and called very encour-

agingly and comfortingly, addressing her by name, "Remember thou the Lord." Such was the marriage of the blessed, and their perfect disposition towards those dearest to them (*Stromata* 7.11.47, ANF 2:541).

Later, Eusebius (ca. 320) relates that the Apostles Peter and Philip "begat children, and Philip even gave his daughters to husbands" (*Eccl. Hist.* 3.30.1), who quotes Clement regarding the story of Peter's marriage (3.30.2). Remarkably, Eusebius cites Clement of Alexandria saying that Paul also had a wife and addressed her in a letter (presumably Phil. 4:3) as a yokefellow or wife (*Eccl. Hist.* 3.30.1). Nothing substantiates this tradition, however, and it flies in the face of Paul's own statements.

9:6. Or do only Barnabas and I not have a right to refrain from working? The Jewish teaching of Paul's day called for rabbis, that is, those who taught the Word of God, to have a job that could support them. According to the Mishnah,

> Excellent is study of the Law together with worldly occupation, for toil in them both puts sin out of mind. But all study of the Law without [worldly] labour comes to naught at the last and brings sin in its train. And let all them that labour with the congregation labour with them for the sake of heaven, for the merit of their fathers supports them and their righteousness endures for ever. And as for you, [will God say,] I count you worthy of great reward as though ye [yourselves] had wrought (*m. Aboth* 2.2, Danby trans.).

Likewise, many of Paul's pagan contemporaries also refused to accept gifts for their services and chose instead to work for their living. For example, the Stoic philosopher Cleanthes was a gardener and a miller, the Cynic Dio Chrysostom likewise worked as a gardener and various other jobs. The Cynic philosopher Demetrius of Sunium worked as a porter, and the Stoic philosopher Musonius Rufus had a farm. While many philosophers charged tuition from their students and others begged in the marketplace, some did in fact hold manual labor jobs. The New Testament praises those who work with their hands and condemns those who are idle and do not work. The latter ought not to eat (2 Thess. 3:8-10; cf. Eph. 4:28; 1 Thess. 4:11; Acts 18:3).

9:9. For it is written in the Law of Moses, "You shall not muzzle the ox while he is threshing." God is not concerned about oxen, is He? Citing Deut. 25:4, Paul reflects a Jewish tradition that if God is interested in lesser things (oxen), surely he must be interested in the greater things (human beings). Philo likewise saw that the detail given in Scripture to animal sacrifices in the book of Leviticus, has a higher meaning than merely caring for animals.

> For you will find that all this careful scrutiny of the animal is a symbol representing in a figure the reformation of your own conduct, for the law does not prescribe for unreasoning creatures, but for those that have mind and reason. It is anxious not that the victims should be without flaw but that those who offer them should not suffer from any corroding passion (*On Special Laws* 1.260, LCL).

Paul, like others of his day and later, argues logically for his freedom and then uses the authority of Scripture to bolster his case. Paul is following the widespread tradition of citing three examples to make a point. For instance, Pliny the Younger (ca. A.D. 61–113), in the midst of making a reasoned argument, cited the tradition or rule of his day for schools of rhetoric, citing three examples: "Are two stories enough, or do you want another according to the rule of three?"(*Letters* 2.20.9, LCL, see also Quintilian, *Inst. Orat.* 4.5.3). Likewise, Paul asks whether he has the right to earn a living through his ministry as an apostle, whether he has a right to marry as others do, and whether he and Barnabas have a right to refrain from working (what is normally called today "secular" work) for a living. He then illustrates his point with three examples: those in military service, those who plant a vineyard, and the one who tends a flock (v. 7), and finally appeals to Scripture, his authority (9-10).

9:10. Yes, for our sake it was written, because the plowman ought to plow in hope, and the thresher to thresh in hope of sharing the crops. It is not clear what text Paul is citing, but he treats it as Scripture ("it is written") as in v. 9. This passage is not found in the biblical canon that later emerged as the Bible and it illustrates that lack of precision in such collections of scriptures in Paul's day. Although some scholars have argued that Paul uses here the term "it *was* written" (= *egraphe*, the aorist passive form of *grapho*, = I write") rather that the usual designation "it is written" (*gegraptai*, the perfect passive of *grapho* cf. v. 9) to distinguish Scripture from mere tradition, that will not suffice here since in both cases Paul is using the cited texts as an authoritative guide for Christian behavior in his argument. Paul's text may be an allusion to Sirach 6:19, who writes: "Come to her like one who plows and sows, and wait for her good harvest. For when you cultivate her you will toil but little, and soon you will eat of her produce" (NRSV), but that is not certain. There are slight parallels to this text in the Mishnah and it may be that Paul is appealing to a tradition that was later included by the rabbis in a Mishnah tractate. That text reads:

> These may eat [of the fruits among which they labour] by virtue of what is enjoined in the Law: he that labours on what is still growing after the work is finished, and he that labours on what is already gathered before the work is finished; this applies only to what grows from the soil. (*m. Baba Metzia* 7.2, Danby trans.).

9:12b, 15. If others share the right over you, do we not more? Nevertheless, we did not use this right, but we endure all things, that we may cause no hindrance to the gospel of Christi. . . . 9:15. But I have used none of these things. And I am not writing these things that it may be done so in my case; for it would be better for me to die than have any man make my boast an empty one. Except for his receiving gifts from the church at Philippi, Paul refused to accept gifts for his personal support (Phil. 4:15-18; 1 Thess. 2:9). The purpose was to encourage the Corinthians also to give up their rights for a greater cause.

9:14. So also the Lord directed those who proclaim the gospel to get their living from the gospel. Paul may be referring to the Gospel tradition in which Jesus told his disciples since they "received without payment" they were also to "give without payment" and "take no gold, or silver, or copper in your belts, no bag for your journey, or two tunics, or sandals, or a staff; for laborers deserve their food" (Matt. 10:9-10; cf. Luke 10:7; 1 Tim. 5:18). Once again, Paul underscores his right as an apostle to receive freely from those he ministers to, but he has not made use of that right (9:12b, 15).

9:24-27. In what appears at first glance to be an isolated text in the midst of Paul's argument, this passage demonstrates the presence of athletic metaphors in antiquity. Seneca (ca. 4 B.C.–A.D. 65), teaching his readers how to deal with the pain that people face in life, lifts up the hardships endured by the athletes and then draws peculiarly familiar application.

> What blows do athletes receive on their faces and all over their bodies! Nevertheless, through their desire for fame they endure every torture, and they undergo these things not only because they are fighting but in order to be able to fight. Their training means torture. So let us also win the way to vic-

tory in all our struggles—for the reward is not a garland or a palm or trumpeter who calls for silence at the proclamation of our names, but rather virtue, steadfastness of soul, and a peace that is won for all time, if fortune has once been utterly vanquished in any combat (*Epistle* 78.16, LCL).

9:24. Do you not know that those who run in a race all run, but only one receives the prize? Run in such a way that you may win. Those who ran races were among the most celebrated athletes in the Greek games. Tracks were measured carefully and extended some 630 feet in length. Those who ran various lengths committed to be in training for ten months and were in the vicinity of the track one month before the race occurred. Preparations for running were quite extensive, but only one received a perishable prize. The satirist Lucian from Samosata (A.D. 120–190), in his story about Anacharsis, ridicules the temporal prizes offered for all of the extensive effort and pain that athletes endure.

> [Anacharsis:] So the competitors are all the more ridiculous if they are the flower of the country, as you say, and yet endure so much for nothing, making themselves miserable and defiling their beautiful, great bodies with sand and black eyes to get possession of an apple and an olive-branch when they have won! You see, I like to keep mentioning the prizes, which are so fine! But tell me, do all the contestants get them?
>
> [Solon responds:] Not by any means; only one among them all, the victor. (Lucian, Anacharsis or Athletics, 13, LCL).

Flavius Philostratus (ca. A.D. 170) tells of the mythic and/or aesthetic Apollonius of Tyanna (first century A.D.) addressing those who followed him. He used the games as a metaphor for his disciples and in the process tells of the preparation for the track and field games.

> When the Olympic games are coming on, the people of Elis train the athletes for thirty days in their own country. Likewise, when the Pythian games approach, the natives of Delphi; and when the Isthmian, the Corinthians assemble them and say: 'go now into the arena and prove yourselves men worth of victory.' The Eleans however on their way to Olympia address the athletes thus: 'If ye have laboured so hard as to be entitled to go to Olympia and have banished all sloth and cowardice from your lives, then march boldly on; but as for those who have not so trained themselves, let them depart whithersoever they like' (*Life of Apollonius* 5.43, LCL).

9:26-27. Therefore I run in such a way, as not without aim; I box in such a way, as not beating the air; but I buffet my body and make it my slave, lest possibly, after I have preached to others, I myself should be disqualified. In his only metaphor that speaks of violent physical activity, Paul refers to the untrained and trained boxers. The former are those who beat the air and the latter were those who endured severe hardships in order to be fit for their matches. Virgil (ca. 70 B.C.–A.D. 19), likewise describes the actions of one called Dares, who, after the races were ended and various prizes awarded, challenged all who came to the athletic games to a boxing match. Eventually he is challenged and defeated, but before that Dares is described by Virgil as one who "raises his head high for the fray, displays his broad shoulders, stretches his arms, spars right and left, and lashes the air with blows" (Aeneid 5.375-77, LCL). There were no residents of Corinth, not to mention the Mediterranean world in Paul's day, who were unaware of the Isthmian games and those who ran in them or boxed in them. His metaphors would have been clearly understood by his readers.

At Olympia, those who won the races were given wreaths of olive branches to wear. At Isthmia they were given laurels or wreaths of pine branches. Those who won, however, were often honored with a statue in their honor placed both at the site of the games and also in their hometowns or cities. Those who won these games became instant heroes and were celebrated far and wide around the Mediterranean. Paul uses this metaphor to show what all Christians must go through to win the prize of God's approval in doing what they have been called to do. Self-denial rather than demanding one's rights is the key to achieving the mission of God. Paul uses the "run" metaphor in other contexts as well (Gal. 2:2; 5:7; Phil. 2:16; cf. 2 Tim. 4:8; Heb. 12:1).

The wearing of crowns also took on special religious value as the sign of those who were victors in their divine mission (1 Tim. 4:8; 1 Peter 5:4; James 1:12; Rev. 2:10). In the pseudepigraphal writing, The Testament of Job, the Lord comes to Job promising to him blessing for his faithfulness and obedience and says to him: "And you shall be raised up in the resurrection. For you will be like a sparring athlete, both enduring pains and winning the crown. Then you will know that the Lord is just, true, and strong, giving strength to his elect ones" (*Test. Job*, 4.9-10, *OT Pseud* 1:840).

E. 10:1–11:1. The Prohibition of Eating Foods Sacrificed to Idols

Paul now returns more directly to the theme he introduced in 8:1-3 and having spoken about the importance of exercising one's freedom within the bounds of responsible behavior toward fellow believers (8:7-13; 9:1-18) and even being vigilant in making sure that one maintains self-control and accomplishes God's purposes (9:24-27), he now brings home his point regarding eating sacrificed foods in pagan temples with both Scriptural and rational support. His bottom line is that the Christians who are "strong" and have all knowledge (8:1, 4-6) still need to be reminded of the message of Scripture regarding association with and participation in pagan practices.

10:1-14. An Important Scriptural Lesson (1-13). This passage is in essence a Jewish midrash or interpretation of the Exodus story from the book of Numbers, with a citation from Exod. 32:6, that addresses the extent to which Christians can in good conscience participate in civic activities in a Roman colony that practices religious beliefs that are at variance with those of the Christians. The questions of whether Christians should participate in pagan festivals in pagan temples is once again discussed from a scriptural perspective, and Paul gives a strong word of caution to those who think that they are sufficiently strong in their faith that they are immune from any evil that might come to them as a result of such practices. He argues that the God of the Jews is the same God of the Corinthian Christians and what happened before to the Jews is a lesson from God to them. He mentions five positive things that "all" of the Jews experienced together in their departure from Egypt, using the word "all" in each of them, to illustrate the solidarity that they had (vv. 1-4). Together they experienced the "cloud" (Exod. 13:21-22; cf. Ps. 104:39), the Red Sea (Exod. 14:21-29), baptism into Moses (Exod. 16:35), ate spiritual food (Exod. 16:4-36; Num. 20:11), and drank spiritual drink (Num. 14:29-30). But then he says that God was not pleased with them and most of them were struck down in the wilderness and did not see the promised land (v. 5; cf. Num. 14:16, 30). Paul draws several lessons from this story and admonishes his readers and mentions five things that some of the Israelites were guilty of, and, by implication, so are some of the Corinthians. These included the temptation to become idolaters (v. 7; cf. Exod. 32:6), indulging in sexual immorality (v. 8; cf. Num. 25:1-18), putting Christ to the test (v. 9; cf. Num. 21:5-6), and complaining or grumbling (v. 10; cf. Num. 16:41-49). The Jews' practice of these things prevented most of them from entering God's promised land, and Paul argues that this should be a lesson to some of the Corinthians as well. He makes it clear that special knowledge and having experienced the sacraments of the church are not a refuge from obedience to God. He concludes with a word of hope, however, to those who may have already succumbed to these practices and to those who are tempted to do them (10:13).

10:1. For I do not want you to be unaware, brethren. Paul returns to the address he used in 7:29, "brothers and sisters," and wants to make sure that they are not uninformed ("ignorant") about the important matters of which he has been speaking. This is his usual introduction when he plans to disclose something to his readers (Rom. 1:13; 11:25; 2 Cor. 1:8; 1 Thess. 4:13; 10:1, 11:2; 12:1).

10:1b-2. Our fathers were all under the cloud, and all passed through the sea; and all were baptized into Moses in the cloud and in the sea. Paul makes sure that the Corinthians know that they are the spiritual descendants of the Jews (see Gal. 6:16; Phil. 3:3). In regard to the cloud, see Ps. 105:39. The author of the apocryphal work, The Wisdom of Solomon, refers to God working through Moses by Wisdom to lead the Israelites through the wilderness: "She [Wisdom] gave to holy people the reward of their labors; she guided them along a marvelous way, and became a shelter to them by day and starry flame through the night" (*Wisd.* 10:17, NRSV). Likewise, the writer later says: "The cloud was seen overshadowing the camp, and dry land emerging where water had stood before, an unhindered way out of the Red Sea, and a grassy plain out of the raging waves" (19:7, NRSV).

10:3-4.And all ate the same spiritual food; and all drank the same spiritual drink, for they were drinking from a spiritual rock. Paul is clearly referring to those common things that Christians do together and uses one of his favorite terms, "spiritual" (Greek = *pneumatikos*), which is employed some fifteen times in 1 Cor. alone and many other times in the rest of his letters. What is meant by the term is assumed by Paul and may be his way of speaking typologically or allegorically. In the late first century, the author of the *Didache*, or *The Teaching of the Twelve Apostles*, writes: "Thou, Lord Almighty, didst create all things for thy Name's sake, and didst give food and drink to men for their enjoyment, that they might give thanks to thee, but us hast thou blessed with spiritual [*pneumatiken*] food and drink and eternal light through thy child" (*Did.* 10.3, LCL). The manna that the children of Israel ate was not spiritual food, but real food (Ps. 78:24), but Paul uses it to refer to a heavenly or spiritual food that God's children partake of at the table of the Lord that transcends the physical food that was consumed. Paul's reference to "spiritual" here is his way of drawing out greater implications for his readers than mere daily sustenance suggests.

A spiritual rock which followed them; and the rock was Christ. The story of water coming forth from the rock after Moses hit the rock with his staff in Exod. 17:1-7 has a parallel in Num. 20:2-13 in which Moses was told to command that the rock give forth its water. The rock has an important history among the Jews and Paul may be repeating popular Jewish teachings about it, that is, re-telling an important Jewish midrash. In that tradition, the water, a well, actually follows after the Israelites. It goes as follows:

And so a well which was with the Israelites in the wilderness was a rock, the size of a large round vessel, surging and gurgling upward, as from the mouth of this little flask, rising with them up onto the mountains, and going down with them into the valleys. Wherever the Israelites would encamp, it made camp with them, on a high place, opposite the entry of the Tent of Meeting. The Princes of Israel come and surround it with their staffs, and they sing a song concerning it: *Spring up, O Well! Sing to it; [the well which the princes dug, which the nobles of the people delved with the scepter and with their staves]* (Num. 21:17-18) (*m. Sukkah* 3:11, Neusner trans.).

Similarly, in Pseudo-Philo (ca. first cent. A.D.), the writer tells this story of the Exodus and says of this incident: "Now he led his people out into the wilderness; for forty years *he rained down for them bread from heaven* and brought *quail* to them *from the sea* and brought for a well of water to follow them" (*Ps.-Philo* 10:7, *OT Pseud* 2:317. Itals. theirs), and later in the same book the writer repeats the story:

And he commanded him [Moses] many things *and showed him the tree* of life, from which he cut off and took and *threw into* Marah, and the water of Marah *became sweet*. And it followed them in the wilderness forty years and went up to the mountain with them and went down into the plains (11:15, *OT Pseud* 1:319, Itals. theirs).

Interestingly, Philo (early first cent. A.D.) identified the rock as the wisdom of God!

To return to what I was saying, the soul falls in with a scorpion, which is "scattering," in the wilderness, and the drought of the passions seizes upon it, until God send forth the stream from his strong wisdom and quench with unfailing health the thirst of the soul that had turned from Him. For the flinty rock is the wisdom of God, which He marked off highest and chiefest from His powers, and from which He satisfies the thirsty souls that love God (*Allegorical Interpretation* 2.86, LCL).

Paul's strange reference to the rock that followed them is not at all unique, only that he identified it with Christ. The various Jewish traditions about the rock no doubt gave him opportunity to find a Christian meaning of that tradition. For Paul, the rock that followed them was Christ.

10:7-8. And do not be idolaters, as some of them were; as it is written, "The people sat down to eat and drink, and stood up to play." Nor let us act immorally, as some of them did, and twenty-three thousand fell in one day. The text that Paul cites is Exod. 32:6, but the story of eating and drinking and acting immorally dates back to the time when the Israelites at Peor began to have sexual relations with the daughters of Moab who invited the Israelites to eat the sacrifices to the gods of Moab (Baal) and also to worship them (Num. 25:1-3, 6-9). The author of *Wisdom of Solomon* ties both of these sins together thusly: "for the idea of making idols was the beginning of fornication, and the invention of them was the corruption of life; for they did not exist from the beginning, nor will they last forever" (*Wisd.* 14:12-13, NRSV). The text cited here is Exod. 32:6. Paul draws on this tradition when he combines these two sins (idolatry and sexual immorality). See also Rom. 1:26-31; 1 Thess. 4:5. It should also be noted that there were often prostitutes present at temple festivals such as dinners to satisfy the pleasures of the guests.

10:9-10. Nor let us try the Lord, as some of them did, and were destroyed by the serpents. Nor grumble, as some of them did, and were destroyed by the destroyer. The testing of the Lord is dealt with in Num. 21:5-9 (cf. Deut. 6:16), and there is no distinction made between testing the Lord and grumbling or complaining (Num. 14:2, 27, 36-45; 17:6-12; cf. Exod. 16:2-3; Num. 16:11-35).

10:11. Now these things happened to them as an example, and they were written for our instruction, upon whom the ends of the ages have come. While it is obvious from the allusions and references to what God did to the Jews who failed to obey him, the reasons that these things were written down and passed on among God's people is to remind them of how God expects them to live.

10:12. Therefore let him who thinks he stands take heed lest he fall. The term "fall" is commonly used of those who fall on the battlefield (see 10:8; Num. 14:3), but here it is used of those who are disobedient to God and fall from his favor and blessing. Paul advises those who think that they are strong in their faith to be careful lest they fall. They had too much confidence in their knowledge and not enough awareness of their own vulnerability.

10:14-22. A Warning Against Pride and Over-Confidence

Paul now makes clear what his arguments have been developing. He encourages his readers to consider the experience and downfall of the Israelites, but also to consider their own experience and take heed that they do not follow a similar path that will have similar conclusions. While he continues to agree that the Gentiles do not sacrifice to real gods in Corinth (10:19), nevertheless the demons are involved and great caution is needed. He does not believe that anyone should be partaking of the cup and bread of the Lord and also of the food sacrificed to idols.

10:14. Therefore, my beloved, flee from idolatry. This is the summary of the foregoing argument. Foolish people are those who believe that they are so strong that they could not fall. While there may be nothing physically wrong with the food, Paul says that there is something religiously wrong with eating the food.

10:18. Look at the nation Israel; are not those who eat the sacrifices sharers in the altar? Paul rightly saw what many of his Jewish interpreters of the Law also say: namely, that those who partake of the pagan sacrifices also partake of the altar. They believed that because the food had been sacrificed, it was considered holy and great care was given to its consumption (Lev. 10:12; Num. 17:8-10; Deut. 18:1-5; 12:4-7). While contending for the care of the sacrifices to God, Philo explains that

> The sacrificial meals should not be hoarded, but be free and open to all who have need, for they are now the property not of him by whom but of Him to Whom the victim has been sacrificed, He the benefactor, the bountiful, Who has made the convivial company of those who carry out the sacrifices partners of the altar whose board they share. . . . The final reason is, that the reservation-offering is in fact made in behalf of two: namely, soul and body, to each of which he assigned one day for feasting on the flesh. For it was meet that an equal space of time should be appointed for those elements of our nature which are capable of being preserved, so that on the first day as we eat we obtain a reminder of the soul's preservation, on the morrow of the body's good health (*Special Laws* 1.221-222, LCL).

10:19. What do I mean then? That a thing sacrificed to idols is anything, or that an idol is anything? Paul agreed with his "strong" readers that idols were nothing (8:4), but he does not dismiss the demon presence at such sacrifices and pagan celebrations in the temples.

10:20. No, but I say that the things which the Gentiles sacrifice, they sacrifice to demons, and not to God; and I do not want you to become sharers in demons. While Paul concedes the nonexistence of pagan gods, he does not concede that there is nothing to worry about when being in the company of those who sacrifice to such idols or eat in their presence. He argues that demons are present and that should give cause for hesitation. See Deut. 32:17; Ps. 96:5; 106:37. Paul shares the Old Testament view that worship of pagan gods is a worship of demons. According to the author of the pseudepigraphal book, *Jubilees* (ca. 160–140 B.C.), Moses is told how the people will forsake the Lord when they arrive in the land of promise, "And they will make for themselves high places and grooves and carved idols. And each of them will worship his own (idol) so as to go astray, and they will sacrifice their children to the demons and to every work of the error of their heart" (*Jub.* 1:11, *OT Pseud* 2:53). Finally, the author of 1 Enoch (ca. 105–104 B.C.) wrote about the end of those who worship idols:

> Again I swear to you, you sinners, for sin has been prepared for the day of unceasing blood. (And those) who worship stones, and those who carve images of gold and of silver and of wood and of clay, and those who worship evil spirits and demons, and all kinds of idols not according to knowledge, they shall get no manner of him in them. . . . They shall become wicked and fearful through them, for they wrought all their deeds in falsehood and worshiped stone; so they shall perish instantly. (*1 Enoch* 99:6-9, *OT Pseud* 1:80).

10:21. You cannot drink the cup of the Lord and the cup of demons; you cannot partake of the table of the Lord and the table of demons. It was quite common at pagan festivals in the temple that the cups used by the participants would have the name of the pagan deity inscribed on them. It was therefore impossible not to notice the one in whose honor the dinner was served. Paul makes it clear that those who participate in such activities must make a choice. They cannot partake of the cup of the

Lord and also that of demons. Plato (ca. 427–353 B.C.) earlier wrote that "all sacrifices and ceremonies controlled by divination: namely, all means of communion between gods and men, are only concerned with either the preservation or the cure of Love" (*Symposium* 188 B-C, LCL). Similarly, Publius Aelius Aristides (A.D. 117–181), wrote: "in sacrificing to this one god men severally share genuine communion, both calling him to the altar as their guest and deferring to him as their host . . ." (*Panathenaic Oration* 27, LCL). Paul knows that Christians cannot partake of both the Christian meal and the meals at pagan festivals. It is a serious contradiction of faith to think otherwise. His reference to the "table of the Lord" has an interesting background in the Old Testament where this is a reference to the offerings made to God (Isa. 41:22; 44:16; Mal. 1:7, 12; cf. Isa. 65:11-12).

10:22. Or do we provoke the Lord to jealousy? We are not stronger than He, are we? See Deut. 32:21.

10:23–11:1. The Issue of Freedom and Conscience: A Summary
This final section is where Paul returns to the argument of 8:7-13 and also Rom. 14:13-23. Those who believe that they have the strength and knowledge to partake at such festivals, which Paul clearly does not believe that they do, nevertheless have a higher reason for avoiding such practices: namely, unity of the body of Christ and care for those who are weaker in their faith. Again, the notion of true Christian freedom, according to Paul, is best seen in those who have the ability to set aside their freedom for the sake of others. They are truly free.

10:23. All things are lawful, but not all things are profitable. All things are lawful, but not all things edify. One of the ways that ancient philosophers encouraged their listeners to change cherished perspectives or habits was to show that a change was more beneficial or useful to them than was their old habit or thinking. Once again, Paul agrees with the notion of one's freedom in Christ (6:12; 8:9, 13), but indicates that such freedom is not beneficial if it is exercised without regard to others. Indeed, if exercised without constraint, such freedom will not be beneficial.

10:24. Let no one seek his own good, but that of his neighbor. See Rom. 14:19; 15:2-3; Phil. 2:3-4.

10:25. Eat anything that is sold in the meat market, without asking questions for conscience' sake. There is no evidence that all meat sold in the marketplace had been sacrificed to pagan gods. Plutarch indicates, concerning the Pythagoreans, that "if they tasted flesh, it was most often that of sacrificial animals" (*Moralia*, "*Quaestionum convivalium libri*" 729C, LCL). The "most often" suggests that it was not always the case. The Jewish practice was that a Jew had to determine whether meat bought in the market was slaughtered by a Jew and whether it was related to any pagan cult practice. In the rabbinic tradition care was taken not to consume any meat sacrificed to an idol. "Flesh that is entering in unto an idol is permitted [to eat]. But what comes forth is forbidden, for it is as the sacrifices of the dead" (*m. Abodah Zarah* 2.3, Danby trans. [See Ps. 106:28]). In other words, if a Jew purchases an animal that is designated as one to be used in a pagan sacrifice, it is permitted to eat this animal, but if it has been sacrificed to a pagan deity, it is not.

10:26. For the earth is the Lord's, and all it contains. Paul cites Ps. 24:1 to justify that it is permissible to eat anything. Since everything belongs to God, it is permissible to eat it. The rabbinic tradition that calls for a thanksgiving or benediction for every meal referred to this passage to justify the benediction of thanksgiving to God for each meal.

One must not taste anything until he has [first] recited a benediction [over it], as the Scripture states, *The earth is the Lord's and all that it contains* (Ps. 24:1). One who derives benefit from this world [by eating its produce] without first having recited a benediction has committed sacrilege [viz., it is as if he ate sanctified temple produce, thereby misappropriating God's property], until he has fulfilled all the obligations which permit him [to use the produce; viz., until he has recited the proper benediction]. One should make use of his face, his hands, and his feet only for the honor of his creator, as Scripture states, *the Lord has made everything for its purpose* (Prov. 16:4, read as "Everything that God has made [should be used] for his sake, for his glory") (*T. Berakhot* 4:1, Neusner trans.).

10:27. If one of the unbelievers invites you, and you wish to go, eat anything that is set before you, without asking questions for conscience's sake. It was not unusual for people of antiquity to invite persons either to the temple for a feast following a sacrifice or to invite guests to their home following the sacrifice to consume the meat that was sacrificed. The majority of persons in that day did not have meat very often and when they did, it generally came either as a result of an invitation to a temple banquet (mostly the wealthy came to these) or from an invitation to a home of a friend to eat the remains of what had been sacrificed. Following the athletic games, when many animals were sacrificed in honor of the local deity or deities, the meat that was left over was often sold at a considerable reduction in cost in the open market such as in the large forum in Corinth, and the poorer individuals would normally purchase the meat at considerable savings. It was common, therefore, for the meat that one would serve in a home to be left over from an animal sacrifice in honor of a pagan deity. Xenophon (ca. 430–354 B.C.) reports the story of how Socrates encouraged Criton to get someone for his protection and Criton was able to secure the services of Archedemus for this responsibility. Criton cared for him and gave him many gifts and also invitations to eat at this home following a sacrifice. He writes: "So whenever Criton was storing corn, oil, wine, wool, or other farm produce, he would make a present of a portion to Archedemus, and when he sacrificed, he invited him, and in fact lost no opportunity of showing courtesy" (*Memorabilia* 2.9.4, LCL).

10:28-29. But if anyone should say to you, "This is meat sacrificed to idols," do not eat it, for the sake of the one who informed you, and for conscience's sake; I mean not your own conscience, but the other man's; for why is my freedom judged by another's conscience? It was possible for a Christian who served in a non-Christian home to observe one of the "strong" Christians eating meat that was sacrificed to the local deity and stumble over the "strong" Christian's actions. Paul agrees that there is no judgment over what we eat or drink (in moderation), but he adds the important difference of conscience. If another's conscience is bothered by this action, it is best to refrain, even if Christians are free to partake of it. Paul agrees that if our own conscience does not trouble us, we are free to partake of such food. That is a right of freedom in Christ.

10:30. If I partake with thankfulness, why am I slandered concerning that for which I give thanks? Paul reflects the early Christian practice of giving thanks for food, which no doubt reflects the practice of Jesus (11:23-24; cf. Matt. 26:26-27; Mark 14:22-23; Luke 22:17-19; 24:30; John 6:11) that was also common among the Jews of that day. On this passage, see also Rom. 14:6; 1 Tim. 4:3-5.

10:31. Whether, then, you eat or drink or whatever you do, do all to the glory of God. Strabo (63 B.C.–A.D. 25) describes a group of people in antiquity who abstained from all meats and were held in honor because of their manner of life:

> Poseidonius goes on to say of the Mysians that in accordance with their religion they abstain from eating any living thing, and therefore from their flocks as well; and that they use as food honey and milk and cheese, living a peaceable life, and for this reason are called both "god-fearing" and "capnobatae" [literally = "smoke-eaters," a term that refers to people who live on food of no value] . . . (*Geography* 7.3.3, LCL).

Likewise, Philostratus (ca. A.D. 170), speaking of the diet of Apollonius of Tyana, remarks: "he declined to live upon a flesh diet, on the ground that it was unclean, and also that it made the mind gross; so he partook only of dried fruits and vegetables, for he said that all the fruits of the earth are clean" (*Life of Apollonius of Tyana* 1.8, LCL). Compare Rom. 14:2.

10:32. Give no offense either to Jews or to Greeks or to the church of God. Paul is reflecting a long established model within the Jewish community that sought to live at peace with one's neighbors in the exercise of one's freedom. See Mic. 6:8, but also Matt. 5:9; Rom. 12:18; 14:13-21; 1 Cor. 7:15; Col. 3:15; 1 Thess. 4:12.

11:1. Be imitators of me, just as I also am of Christ. Paul, like the philosophers of his day, did not hesitate to set himself up as an example to follow to the extent that he was a faithful follower of Christ who gave himself for us (11:24). See also Rom. 15:1-3; 1 Cor. 4:16; Phil. 3:17; Eph. 5:1; 1 Thess. 1:6; 2:14.

C. 11:2–14:40. Christian Conduct at Christian Gatherings

This section of 1 Corinthians has received a significant amount of attention due in large measure to current ignorance of the ancient culture and also the historical context of the passage. While much of what we find here will be illumined by a broader historical context, there remain some obscure components in the discussion, but what ties all three topics in this section together is that they all focus on what happens when the Christians gather together for worship and ministry. Without question, one of the most difficult of these topics, women's hairstyle, is complicated because of the clash of cultures not only in the ancient world, but also in the present one, especially in the western societies. How Christians should act when they come together is focused around three major topics: the appropriate hairstyle for women during worship (11:2-16), the abuse of fellow Christians at the table of the Lord during the sacred meal (11:17-34), and the use of the gifts of the Spirit in the life and ministry of the church (12:1-14:40).

1. 11:2-16. The appropriate attire for women in worship. The following passage is one of the most complex in all of Paul's writings, and it is made all the more so because it challenges many modern beliefs about women's roles in society and reflects a more limited ancient middle eastern culture. The complexity of this portion of Scripture stems from the clash of two or more cultural contexts in operation at the same time. It appears that women were coming to worship and prophesying with their heads uncovered. Among the difficulties of this passage are the meanings attached to three words, head (vv. 3, 4, 5, 7, 10), authority (v. 11), and glory (vv. 7, 15). Paul's corrective to a problem appears to be based on the view that women are both subordinate to men and also inferior to them. In the Roman culture, it was appropriate for women to speak with their heads uncov-

ered, but in the Jewish and Greek cultures it was not. Likewise, the length of the hair of the women suggested both their glory and their shame. Paul allows his own Hellenistic Jewish culture to determine how women should dress and yet he offers a possibility for equality between the sexes "in the Lord" (11:11-12). Generally speaking, Paul teaches that men should pray with their heads uncovered and women should pray with their heads covered. Also, he contends that men should have short hair and women long hair. The justification for these cultural guidelines, however, is where most commentators part company and where our sources send mixed signals. From the third century B.C. and later, women were active in the athletic games and increasingly they received financial rewards for their victories. It was not unusual for women to compete in the 200-meter race during the Isthmian games and some even raced war-chariots. Was it such women as these who refused to submit to the social mores that Paul speaks of here? One woman named Hedea won her race at Isthmia in A.D. 43. Paul deals with the matter at hand on the basis of custom, both Jewish and Greek.

11:2. Now I praise you because you remember me in everything, and hold firmly to the traditions, just as I delivered them to you. This passage does not easily fit within the broader context of 1 Corinthians, except in the sense of how Christians should conduct themselves in worship or when they gather together. The passing on of religious traditions among the Jews was believed to have had its origins in God and was received by Moses who passed them along to those who followed him. Paul reflects the practice of handing on "traditions" (Greek = *paradoka*) in 11:23 and 125:2-3, but in this case he is passing on in true Pharisaic style the Christian traditions that had been passed on to him. In the Mishnah, tradition was very important and comprised what came through the prophets from God. "Moses received the

Law from Sinai and committed it to Joshua, and Joshua to the elders, and the elders to the Prophets; and the Prophets committed it to the men of the Great Synagogue" (*m. Aboth* 1:1, Danby trans.). In one of Josephus's distinctions between the Pharisees and the Sadducees, he mentions the observance of traditions.

> For the present I wish merely to explain that the Pharisees had passed on to the people certain regulations handed down by former generations and not recorded in the Laws of Moses, for which reason they are rejected by the Sadducaean group, who hold that only those regulations should be considered valid which were written down (in Scripture), and that those which had been handed down by former generations need not be observed" (*Ant.* 13.297, LCL).

This section is in contrast to the next (see 11:17, 22) in which he indicates twice that he does not commend (or praise) the Corinthians. What Paul is referring to are the "traditions" he had earlier passed on to them regarding women's and men's roles. Because some persons in the church had evidently violated what he had earlier taught was the normative practice for Christians, he revisits the issues once again, but praises his readers for their faithfulness in generally following his teaching on the matter.

There are five primary Christian teachings or traditions in 1 Corinthians that Paul says come from the Lord. These include the prohibition of divorce (7:10), the support of the apostles in their ministry (9:14), the practice of participating at the Lord's Supper (11:23-26), and the custom of women keeping silence in the churches (14:33b-36).

Here the issue has primarily to do with hairstyles. This was not an insignificant issue in the ancient world, and numerous texts address the importance of the matter. The Roman emperors' wives, for example Livia and Octavia, wore their hair in a braided bun on their heads, and wealthy women often wore expensive hairstyles. Poorer women in the community did not have such luxuries. It may be that Paul is addressing only the more wealthy women in the church.

11:3-4. But I want you to understand that Christ is the head of every man, and the man is the head of a woman, and God is the head of Christ. Every man who has something on his head while praying or prophesying, disgraces his head. Paul deals with the issue of who is the head in the family unit and then deals with the issue of covering one's head. Plutarch asks from a Roman perspective questions about Greek habits regarding the covering of their heads:

> Why do they sacrifice to Saturn with the head uncovered? . . . Why do they also sacrifice to the god called "Honor" with the head uncovered? . . . Why do sons cover their heads when they escort their parents to the grave, while daughters go with uncovered heads and hair unbound? Is it because fathers should be honoured as gods by their male offspring, but mourned as dead by their daughters, that custom has assigned to each sex its proper part and has produced a fitting result from both?
>
> Or is it that the unusual is proper in mourning, and it is more usual for women go forth in public with their heads covered and men with their heads uncovered? So in Greece, whenever any misfortune comes, the women cut off their hair and the men let it grow, for it is usual for men to have their hair cut and for women to let it grow (Plutarch, *Moralia,* "The Roman Questions," 266E, F, 267AB, LCL).

In his famous *Metamorphoses,* or *The Golden Ass,* Apuleius (born ca. A.D. 125) tells of those men and women of every rank and age honoring the god Serapis in worship: "They shone with the pure radiance of their linen robes; the women's hair was anointed and wrapped in a transparent covering, while the men's heads were completely shaven and their skulls gleamed brightly—earthly stars of the great religion. (*Met.* 11:10, LCL).

11:5. But every woman who has her head uncovered while praying or prophesying, disgraces her head; for she is one and the same with her whose head is shaved. While Paul seems to favor both men and women prophesying in the church and also praying, the only question for him is not whether they do this, but the way that they are attired when they do. See also Acts 2:17-18.

11:6. For if a woman does not cover her head, let her also have her hair cut off; but if it is disgraceful for a woman to have her hair cut off or her head shaved, let her cover her head. There is evidence that the German tribes of the first century A.D. punished adultery by shaving the head of the woman. Tacitus reports that adulteries were few among these people, but when they were found, "punishment is prompt and is the husband's prerogative: her hair close-cropped, stripped of her clothes, her husband drives her from his house in presence of his relatives and pursues her with a lash through the length of the village" (*Germania* 19, LCL). Jewish women kept their heads covered in public and, for this reason the author of 3 *Macc.* (ca. first century B.C.) indicates that the shame brought upon the Jews in their deportation from Alexandria was made more heinous for them because when they were deported from Egypt,

> the young women who had but recently entered the bridal chamber for the society of married life exchanged their joy for wailing, and, with their perfume-drenched locks covered in dust, they were carried away unveiled and all joined in singing a dirge instead of a

wedding hymn, as if torn asunder by the brutal mangling of the heathen . . . . (*3 Macc.* 4:6, *OT Pseud* 2:522).

For those Jewish women who were caught in adultery, the penalties included the removal of her head covering, a sign of shame. Philo says what happens to the woman after she is brought to the priest. "The priest taking the offering [from the husband] hands it to the woman and removes her kerchief, in order that she may be judged with her head bared and stripped of the symbol of modesty, regularly worn by women who are wholly innocent" (*Special Laws* 3.56, LCL). Josephus tells a similar story with a slightly different judgment on the woman who is suspected by her husband of adultery and brings her to the priests at the temple:

> As for the woman, one of the priests stations her at the gates which face the temple and, after removing the veil from her head, inscribes the name of God upon a skin; he then bids her declare upon oath that she had done her husband no wrong and that if she had violated decency then might her right leg be put out of joint, her belly swell and so might she die" (*Ant.*, 3.270-71, LCL; see also Num. 5:23-28.)

11:7. For a man ought not to have his head covered, since he is the image and glory of God; but the woman is the glory of man. The view that the woman was the glory of her husband has parallels in the Hellenistic Jewish community. The epitaph on a Jewish tomb in Rome reads: "Lucilla, the blessed glory of Sophronius" (Collins, 410). In the Jerusalem Talmud, the Yerushalmi, it is reported that Rabbi Jose, a Galilean, was advised to divorce his wife since "the wife of R. Jose, the Galilean, caused him much annoyance." R. La'azar went up to see him. He said to him: "Rabbi, divorce her for she is not thy glory" (*y. Ketub.* 11:3, Collins trans.).

11:10. Therefore the woman ought to have a symbol of authority on her head, because of the angels. Earlier Paul mentions that the Christians will judge angels (6:3), but why does he mention that women should keep their heads covered because of them? An old tradition is that the angels ("sons of God") were tempted when they saw "the daughters of men" (Gen. 6:1-4), and therefore it is important for women not to be uncovered among them, especially if the angels were present in their acts of worship. In the *Testament of Reuben* (ca. 137–107 B.C.), this story is repeated by way of a warning.

> For women are evil, my children, and by reason of their lacking authority or power over man, they scheme treacherously how they might entice him to themselves by means of their looks.... Indeed the angel of the Lord told me and instructed me that women are more easily overcome by the spirit of promiscuity than are men.... Accordingly, my children, flee from sexual promiscuity, and order your wives and your daughters not to adorn their heads and their appearances so as to deceive men's sound minds. For every woman who schemes in these ways is destined for eternal punishment. For it was thus that they charmed the Watchers, who were before the Flood. As they continued looking at the women, they were filled with desire for them and perpetrated the act in their minds (*Testaments of the Twelve Patriarchs, Testament of Reuben* 5:1-6a, *OT Pseud* 1:784).

The Jews at Qumran also believed that worship took place in the presence of angels and that therefore care should be taken in terms of being ritually pure in the gathering of the assembly for worship so that the angels will not be offended. At Qumran, a fragment was found that forbids any person with a physic or mental defect from entering the congregation (for wor-

ship): "And no one] [stupid or deranged should enter; and any]one feeble-minded or insane, and [those with sightless eyes, the lame or one who stumbles] [or a deaf person, or an underage boy, none of these should enter the congregation, since the holy angels are in its midst]" (4QD^e 10.7b-9, Garcia Martinez).

11:11-12. However, in the Lord, neither is woman independent of man, nor is man independent of woman. For as the woman originates from the man, so also the man has his birth through the woman; and all things originate from God. Paul recognizes the equality of men and women in the presence of God and in Christian service and worship ("in the Lord"). See also discussion of Gal. 3:28.

11:14-15. Does not even nature itself teach you that if a man has long hair, it is a dishonor to him, but if a woman has long hair, it is a glory to her? For her hair is given to her for a covering. Caring for the hair was obviously more important in the ancient world than it is today. In practical terms, Paul seems to follow the maxim: let men look like men and women like women. He follows the guidelines of the Levitical priests who entered the priesthood: namely, "they shall not shave their heads or let their locks grow long; they shall only trim the hair of their heads" (Ezek. 44:20, NSV). This "cropping" of the hair was also common for men in the Greco-Roman world. The standards for such appearance were generally widespread and generally acknowledged. Epictetus seemed to reflect the most popular view that referred to the appearance of men and women in terms of hairstyle. He speaks of Hermes, the messenger god, coming to earth, but leaving "the man a man and the woman a woman." He then tells of Socrates saying to Alcibiades, a handsome young man, do not "dress your locks [of hair] and pluck the hairs out of your legs" but rather "keep the man that you are and were born to be, keep that man clean, a man to be clean as a man, a woman as a woman, a child as a child" (*Discourses* 3.1.39, 42-44. LCL). The question is which culture was Paul conveying to the Christians at Corinth?

In regard to how a man should pray, there is Roman archaeological evidence that shows the Roman Ceasars wearing a headcloth during worship. Plutarch, describing the Roman hair dress in worship explains:

> But if there is anything else to be said, consider whether it be not true that there is only one matter that needs investigation: Why men cover their heads when they worship the gods; and the other follows from this. For they uncover their heads in the presence of men more influential than they: it is not to invest these men with additional honor, but rather to avert from them the jealousy of the gods, that these men may not seem to demand the same honors as the gods, nor to tolerate an attention like that bestowed on the gods, nor to rejoice therein . . .

Or as Castor states when he is trying to bring Roman customs into relation with Pythagoeran doctrines: the Spirit within us entreats and supplicates the gods without, and thus he symbolizes by the covering of the head the covering and concealment of the soul of the body. Why do they sacrifice to Saturn with the head uncovered? (*Moralia*, "The Roman Questions" 266C-E, LCL).

In a Greek inscription from the third century B.C., however, we read in part how women and men were to enter the sanctuary of Despoina: "Nor (let it be permissible to enter) for women with their hair braided, nor for men with their heads covered" (*EG* IV.20/*IG* V,2, 514, *ND* 4:109). The Jewish tradition required that men have their heads covered when they prayed (Exod. 28:36-40; Ezek. 44:18-20). The Greeks, on the other hand required that men pray with their heads uncovered, the practice that was adopted throughout the church and is still present today. In terms of the way the hair is worn, Strabo says: "Speaking generally, the art of caring for the hair consists both in its nurture and in the way it is cut, and both are given special attention by 'girls: and youths' (*Geography* 10.3.8, LCL). In a diatribal fashion, Epictetus describes a youth who wants to look beautiful, but in the process seems to be trying to change his looks to those of a woman. What Epictetus asks this person also indicates what his views are on the matter of hair and what is involved in "being a man" in his culture. He asks:

> Young man, whom do you wish to make beautiful? First learn who you are, and then, in light of that knowledge, adorn yourself. You are a human being; that is, a mortal animal gifted with the ability to use impressions rationally. . . . Your reason is the element of superiority which you posses; adorn and beautify that; but leave your hair to Him who fashioned it as He willed. Come, what other designations apply to you? Are you a man or a woman? A man. Very well then, adorn a man, not a woman. Woman is born smooth and dainty by nature, and if she is very hairy she is a prodigy, and she is exhibited at Rome among the prodigies. But for a man not to be hairy is the same thing, and if he cuts it out and plucks it out of himself what shall we make of him? Where shall we exhibit him and what notice shall we post? "I will show you," we say to the audience, "a man who wishes to be a woman rather than a man." What a dreadful spectacle! . . . Man, what reason have you to complain against your nature? Because it brought you into the world as a man? What then? Ought it to have brought all persons into the world as women? . . . Whom do you wish to please? Frail womankind? Please them as a man.

"Yes, but they liked smooth men." Oh, go hang! And if they liked sexual perverts, would you have become a sexual pervert? (*Discourses* 3.1.24-32, LCL).

In the Jewish literature there was also an acceptable fashion for men and women with respect to their hairstyles. The author of Pseudo-Phocylides (ca. 30 B.C.–A.D. 40) says, "If a child is a boy do not let locks grow on (his) head. Do not braid (his) crown now the cross knots at the top of his head. Long hair is not fit for boys, but for voluptuous women" (*Pseudo-Phocylides* 210-212, *OT Pseud* 2:581). Similarly, Philo describes the behavior and hairstyle of those involved in pederasty (sexual activity of men with boys): "Mark how conspicuously they braid and adorn the hair of their heads, and how they scrub and paint their faces with cosmetics and pigments and the like, and smother themselves with fragrant unguents" (*Special Laws* 3.37, LCL). With regard to hairstyles, Paul appears to argue that the women should wear the Jewish code of dress and the men follow the Greek. The Gnostic Christians of the second century focused on making males and females one as in the case of one of the sayings of Jesus in the Gospel of Thomas: "when you make the male and female one and the same, and so the male not be male nor the female female; and when you fashion eyes in place of an eye, and a hand in place of a hand, and a foot in place of a foot, and a likeness in place of a likeness; then will you enter [the kingdom]" (*Gosp. Thom.* 22, NHL). On the other hand, the writer/collector of these sayings has Jesus conclude these sayings in response to Peter's question about Mary:

Simon Peter said to them, "Let Mary leave us, for women are not worthy of life." Jesus said, "I myself shall lead her in order to make her male, so that she too may become a living spirit resembling you males. For every woman who will make herself male will enter the kingdom of heaven" (*Gosp. Thom.* 114, NHL).

11:16. But if one is inclined to be contentious, we have no other practice, nor have the churches of God. See v. 11 above. After his exposition, Paul says that it is not their custom to be contentious about the matter. This may also be a reference to some balance in what he expects based on his argument in v. 11 above. This is his third time to correct the Corinthians by appealing to the practices of other churches (4:17; 7:17; 11:16). It is interesting that Paul concludes this section without giving a command, but rather refers to what is the practice of other churches. Perhaps he chooses to leave the matter here because what he will discuss in the next passage is of far greater importance to him and potentially of a much greater threat to the stability and unity of the church at Corinth.

2. 11:17–34. Abuses in eating the sacred meal. The circumstance that led to this rebuke from Paul has to do essentially with discrimination at the Lord's table. This is the strongest word that Paul has for the divisive behavior of the Corinthians and he viewed their practice of discrimination at the table of Lord to be one of the worst causes of the divisions among them and, if left unchecked, could destroy the unity of the church and its witness. What was reported to him was opposed to everything that he taught about the inclusiveness of the family of Christ (Gal. 3:28). Where did this behavior originate? There are a number of examples from that region and in the time of Paul that show the widespread nature of discrimination at table fellowships in the wider population and it is likely that some of these practices were simply brought into the church. When public and even private banquets were given, it was not uncommon to reserve special places for the wealthier guests and also to offer to them a better quality of food and wine with their meals. Pliny the Younger (ca. a.d. 61–113) writes of one such example of discrimination.

It would take too long to go into the details . . . of how I happened to be dining with a man—though no particular friend of his—whose elegant economy, as he called it, seemed to me a sort of stingy extravagance. The best dishes were set in front of himself and a select few, and cheap scraps of food before the rest of the company. He had even put the wine into tiny little flasks, divided into three categories, not with the idea of giving his guests the opportunity of choosing, but to make it impossible for them to refuse what they were given. One lot was intended for himself and for us, another for his lesser friends (all his friends were graded) and the third for his and our freedmen. My neighbor at the table noticed this and asked me if I approved. I said I did not. "So what do you do?" he asked. "I serve the same to everyone, for when I invite guests it is for a meal, not to make class distinctions; I have brought them as equals to the same table, so I give them the same treatment in everything." "Even the freedmen?" "Of course, for then they are my fellow-diners, not freedmen." . . . It is this greed which should be put down and "reduced to the ranks" if you would cut down expenses, and you can do this far better by self-restraint than by insults to others (*Letters* 2.6.1-4, LCL).

This portion of Pliny's letter shows his disfavor at the discrimination that was taking place and this is the same kind of thing that Paul condemned at Corinth that Paul also saw as an insult to the "lesser" brothers and sisters in the Christian family. Likewise, Juvenal (ca. A.D. 60–140) speaks with disgust of these kinds of practices and wonders why anyone would leave family to accept an invitation to a dinner where such things were practiced. He speaks at length about the inequity of such discrimination at table fellowship, indeed, the whole of

Satire V is devoted to this subject. He asks:

Is a dinner [hosted by such a person] worth all the insults with which you have to pay for it? Is your hunger so importunate, when it might, with greater dignity, be shivering where you are, and munching dirty scraps of dog's bread? . . .

And what a dinner after all! You are given wine that fresh-clipped wool would refuse to suck up, and which soon converts your revelers into Corybants. . . . The great man himself [the host of the discriminate dinner] drinks wine bottled in the days when Consuls wore long hair; the juice which he holds in his hand was squeezed during the Social Wars [an older and more tasty wine]. . . .

See with what a grumble that you can scarce break in two, or bits of solid dough that have turned mouldy—stuff that will exercise your grinders [teeth] and into which no tooth can gain admittance. For Virro [the host] himself a delicate loaf is reserved, white as snow, and kneaded of the finest flour. [sarcastically] Be sure to keep your hands off it: take not liberties with the bread-basket! . . .

See now that huge lobster being served to my lord, all garnished with asparagus; see how his lordly breast distinguishes the dish, with what a tail he looks down upon the company, borne aloft in the hands of that tall attendant! Before you is placed on a tiny plate a shrimp hemmed in by half an egg—a fit banquet for the dead.

[After lengthy complaints, he concludes]: All we ask of you is that you should dine with us as a fellow citizen [a citizen is as an equal]: do this and remain like so many others nowadays, rich for yourself and poor to your friends. . . . You may perhaps suppose that Virro grudges the expense [of paying for an equal share of the food for the guests]; not a bit of it! His object is to give you pain. For what comedy, what mime, is so amusing as a disappointed belly? His one object, let me tell you, is to compel you to pour out your wrath in tears, and to keep gnashing your squeaking molars. You think yourself a free man, and guest of a grandee; he thinks— and he is not far wrong—that you have been captured by the savoury odours of his kitchen. . . . If you can endure such things, you deserve them! (*Satire* 6.1-170, LCL).

Similar scathing satires are found throughout the ancient world (cf. Martial, *Epigrams* 1.20; 3.49, 60; 4.85; 6.11). On the other hand, addressing these inequities, Plutarch called for equality among all present at such meals ("Table Talk," *Moralia* 613F). Xenophon agrees and tells how Socrates handled the issue of equality at the table.

Whenever some of the members of a dining-club brought more meat than others, Socrates would tell the waiter to either put the small contribution into the common stock or to portion it out equally among the diners. So the high batteners felt obliged not only to take their share of the pool, but to pool their own supplies in return; and so they put their own supplies also into the common stock. And since they thus got no more than those who brought little with them, they gave up spending much on meat (*Memorabilia* 3.14.1, LCL).

What Xenophon refers to, of course, is something like the "potluck" dinner served at churches today, and this is apparently what Paul was calling for, lest the poorer persons among them would get scraps when they gathered together around the Lord's table. As a result of abuse, Paul already had begun to separate the table of the Lord from the regular fellowship meal that took place at the church gatherings. It appears that the wealthier people in the church would gather earlier and eat their food, but took no thought for those who would

come later having worked all day before coming. When the latter showed up, there was not sufficient food remaining and problems arose within the church. The sage words of Sirach (ca. 180 B.C.) are worth recalling here. He first advises his readers about good table manners:

Are you seated at the table of the great?
Do not be greedy at it, and do not say
"How much food there is here!"
Remember that a greedy eye is a bad thing. What has been created more greedy than the eye? Therefore it sheds tears for any reason. Do not reach out your hand for everything you see, and do not crowd your neighbor at the dish. Judge your neighbor's feelings by your own and in every matter be thoughtful. Eat what is set before you like a well brought-up person, and do not chew greedily, or you will give offense. Be the first to stop, as befits good manners, and do not be insatiable or you will give offense. If you are seated among many persons, do not help yourself before they do. How ample a little is for a well-disciplined person! (*Sir.* 31:12-19, NRSV)

He later adds:

If they make you master of the feast, do not exalt yourself; be among them as one of their number. Take care of them first and then sit down; when you have fulfilled all your duties, take your place, so that you may be merry along with them and receive a wreath for your excellent leadership (*Sir.* 32:1-2, NRSV).

Paul believed that appropriate behavior such as this would enhance the community meal in the church and also the unity of the fellowship of believers. When those in the ancient world came together for potluck dinners, they often acted like those Paul condemns in this passage. They brought their food and ate before the others arrived and left them nothing much to eat once they (the poorer ones in the church) arrived.

11:20-21. Therefore when you meet together, it is not to eat the Lord's Supper, for in your eating each one takes his own supper first; and one is hungry and another is drunk. What angered Paul the most in these discriminatory meals is that some believed that they were actually participating in the Lord's Supper by doing these things. Paul told them that when they came together for a meal and there were factions among them, whatever else the meal was, it was not the *Lord's* Supper. Along with a disregard for those who are hungry, there was also excessive behavior at such occasions including drunkenness. Lucian (ca. A.D. 120–190) tells of times when intoxication was so much out of control with arguments and even brawls that banquets had to be cancelled (*The Carousal, or the Lapiths*, 16-20). One ancient papyrus writing lists guidelines to keep civility at such dining clubs. "[it shall not be permissible] for men to enter into one another's pedigrees at the banquet or to chatter or to indict or accuse another or to resign for the course of the year again to bring the drinkings to nought . . ." (*P. Lond.* 2710).

11:22. What! Do you not have houses in which to eat and drink? Paul initiates the separation of the fellowship meal from the "Lord's Supper," the oldest title for what came to be called "communion" and more popularly the "Eucharist" (Greek = *eucharisteo*, "I give thanks"), a term that focuses on the thanksgiving for the sacrificial meal.

11:23. For I received from the Lord that which I also delivered to you. The terms "received" (Greek = *paralambano*, "I receive") and "delivered" (Greek = *paradidomi*, "I give over" or "I hand over" are technical terms from antiquity to speak of the receiving and passing on of tradition. See, for instance, "Moses received the Law from Sinai and committed it to Joshua and Joshua to the elders, and the elders to the Prophets; and the Prophets committed it to

the men of the 'Great Synagogue' [a body of 120 elders accompanying Ezra out of the exile to Babylon back to Jerusalem]" (*m. Aboth* 1:1, Danby trans.). While some of the Jewish traditions were considered by Jesus and the early church to be evasive of the true intent of the law (Mark 7: 5, 9-13), the traditions about Jesus, and even the Jewish traditions, were looked upon by Paul with respect unless they violated what he believed was the intent of the Law or the Gospel itself (1 Cor. 11:2; Gal. 1:14; 2 Thess. 2:15; 3:6). Paul is concerned here with the traditions that were received by him and passed on to the Corinthians about Jesus: namely, what he said and did, and its relevance for the church. Josephus, speaking of the Jewish traditions, writes: "Above all we pride ourselves on the education of our children, and regard as the most essential task in life the observance of our laws and of the pious practices, based thereupon, which we have inherited" (*Against Apion* 1.60, LCL).

11:24. And when He had given thanks, He broke it, and said, "This is My body, which is for you; do this in remembrance of Me." The call to remember reflects the Old Testament call to remember the activity of God (Lev. 24:7; Ps. 37:1; 69:1). See also a later focus on the same call to remember God's activity among the people: "they were troubled for a little while as a warning, and received a symbol of deliverance to remind them of your law's command" (*Wisd.* 16:6, NRSV).

11:25. In the same way He took the cup also, after supper, saying, "This cup is the new covenant in My blood." The Jews believed, and the Christians agreed, that blood had the ability to atone for one's sins (Exod. 24:6-8) and that the new relationship with God that was established through the death (shedding of blood) of Jesus effected this atonement for the Christians (see Mark 14:24; Rom. 3:24 in a quote; Eph. 1:7; Col.

1:20; cf. Heb. 9:15, 20; 1 Peter 1:2, 19; 1 John 1:7; 5:6, 8). The early church agreed: "I have observed that you are established in immovable faith, as if nailed to the cross of the Lord Jesus Christ, both in flesh and spirit, and confirmed in love by the blood of Christ" (Ignatius, *Smyrn.* 1:1, LCL). The blood even began to take on the significance of Jesus Christ himself: "There is a judgment if they do not believe on the blood of Christ" (Ign. *Smyrn.* 6:1, LCL). The reference to the new covenant goes back to Jer. 31:31-34 which is also cited in Heb. 8:8-12. The Bible itself is divided by the titles "Old Covenant" (Testament) and "New Covenant" (Testament). It is also a part of the teaching of Jesus passed on in the early church (Matt. 26:26-28; Mark 14:22-25; Luke 22:15-20). Paul's teaching is firmly rooted in the earliest strands of Christian origins.

11:27. Therefore whoever eats the bread or drinks the cup of the Lord in an unworthy manner, shall be guilty of the body and the blood of the Lord. The logic here is that those who offend against the body of Christ, that is, the community of those who believe in him, have also sinned against the Lord because they have offended his body. Epictetus contends that when a person comes to worship, "a man ought to come also with a sacrifice, and with prayers, and after a preliminary purification, and with his mind predisposed to the idea that he will be approaching holy rites, and holy rites of great antiquity" (*Discourses* 3.21.14, LCL).

11:30. For this reason many among you are weak and sick, and a number sleep. The reference to sleep as a euphemism for death goes back to the times of Homer, but is frequently used in the early church for death. Paul uses the term sleep (Greek = *koimaomai*, "I fall asleep") only of Christians who have died (here; 15:6, 18, 20, 51; 1 Thess. 4:13-15; cf. Matt. 27:52; 28:13; John 11:11-12; 2 Peter 3:4). In terms of judgment from God for inappropriate behavior, Hierocles

the Stoic (second century A.D.) said:

We should certainly not neglect noting that, even though the gods are not the causes of evil, they attach some evils to certain people and surround those who deserve corporal punishment and loss of their property. They do this not because of malice, thinking that man of necessity must live in distress, but for the sake of punishment. . . . the gods sometimes afflict an individual's body or cause him to lose his property in order to punish him and to turn others and make them choose what is better. (*How to Conduct Oneself Toward Gods* 54, Malherbe, *Cynics*, trans.).

Pausanias (second cent. A.D.) tells of the time when Apollo, also known as "Averter of evil" who "by an oracle from Delphi he stayed the pestilence which afflicted the Athenians at the time of the Peloponnesian War" (*Description of Greece, Attica,* 1.3.4, LCL). Evidently the gods were able both to inflict and to relieve affliction. In Jewish tradition, the education of a child or person is not separate from the punishments that come to the child for disobedience (2 Cor. 6:9; 1 Tim. 1:20; Heb. 12:7).

3. 12:1–14:40. Abuses in Exercising the Gifts of the Spirit. In his continuing discussion of appropriate behavior of Christians when they gather together, Paul responds to questions related to spiritual things or gifts that were brought to his attention by reports from Corinth. This can be seen from his "now concerning" (Greek = *peri de*) in 12:1 that introduces a new subject matter (see the others in 7:1, 25; 8:1; 16:1, 12). The larger context of this lengthy section, Paul's longest discussion of any topic in this letter, is the issue of Christians relating to each other as the congregate for their meetings. The dominant issues have been women's apparel, observance of the Lord's Supper, and eating foods sacrificed to idols, and now spiritual matters that center mostly on the gifts of the

Spirit. Paul is most concerned to inform his readers that they are talking about gifts from God and not something that comes to the church as a reflection of God upon an individual's superiority to others. He stresses that all Christians have the Spirit and each one has a spiritual gift that is designed by the Spirit to build up or edify the whole church. He urges that every gift is essential, even the ones that are not in open display, and that their purpose is not to amuse or enhance any individual's position in the church, but rather they are designed to build up the whole church. Given the direction that Paul takes in minimizing in his lists the gift of speaking in tongues and his counsel on how to use them in the fellowship of the church (chapter 14), it is obvious that this had become a problem for the church. Evidently, some were indicating that their possession of this gift indicated a greater share of the Spirit or conversely that those without it seemed to have less of the Spirit. Paul teaches against both conclusions and concludes with the necessity of including the use of all gifts in the church to enable it to accomplish its mission. In a real sense, as others have noted, Paul's focus is not so much on what a gift is as on how to be a "gift" to others in the church.

In the broader context, Paul wants to insure that all persons, whether strong or weak, rich or poor, male or female, are welcomed and valued as an important part of the Christian community. Paul builds his argument for unity on the image of the body (12:14-31) and observes that every part of it was useful, even the parts that are hidden or less obvious. Chapter 12 naturally falls into three categories that are *chaiastic* in structure, that is, Paul begins with a focus on gifts (12:1-11) then introduces the body metaphor to emphasize the necessity for all parts of the body to be connected and function as one whole (12:12-26), and returns again to the issue of spiritual gifts noting that not all have the same gifts (12:27-31). Sandwiched in the middle of this discussion in 12:1–14:40, he has the chap-ter on love (13:1-13), which many have argued was composed separately from the rest of the letter and inserted here, but it fits the context of Paul's argument for unity and harmony in the church very well (e.g., 1:10; 8:11-13; 9:19-22; 10:23-24, 31-32; 11:33-34). In chap. 13, Paul advances that such unity of the Christian gatherings should be based on love and they cannot be based on arrogance, discrimination, or competition, but rather based on love. In fact, the "love chapter" is central to the theme of the whole letter and advances Paul's whole argument for unity. This chapter is often called the *encomium* of the letter: namely, the formal expression of high praise for love. After establishing his foundation for unity in the church, he returns to the specific issue of use of tongues in the church as well as the manner in which prophecy should take place (14:1b-40), and he offers practical guidelines on how to value and utilize these gifts in the church fellowship. Those who could speak with tongues (see 14:1-40) evidently thought that they had more of a "corner on God" than did the others. Paul disagrees with this assessment and calls the church to a better understanding of their value in the church and their use. In regard to the gifts of the Spirit, Paul underscores that the gifts are not for private use or personal gain, but rather they achieve their intended purpose when they are used to build up the members of the church and advance its mission. All members of the body of Christ, the church, have value to the whole church and the gifts distributed to all of its members work best when they are used to build up and not tear down the members of the church.

12:1-3. Paul's Basic Criterion: Speaking by the Spirit.

Paul begins this discussion as a response to questions that had been posed to him. He declares that he will clarify the meaning and function of the gifts of the Spirit or "spiritual things" (Greek = *ton pneumatikon*). Paul presumes, on the basis of the reports, that they do not understand the purpose of spiritual gifts and seeks to inform them of these things. While the church has given evidence of possessing the Spirit of God (3:16), they lack understanding of what that means. In 2:13-16, Paul reminds them that they are spiritual persons. Now he clarifies the meaning of this.

12:2. You know that when you were pagans, you were led astray to the dumb idols, however you were led. This is a reminder of the Corinthian Christians' former days when they were given over to idolatry. It was typical of the Jews to make mocking comments about the worship of idols that cannot speak (1 Kings 18:26-27; Ps. 115:3-8; Hab. 2:18-19). In the Jewish pseudepigraphal writing, Joseph and Aseneth (ca. first cent. B.C. or A.D.), Joseph declares that it is inappropriate for one who serves the living God to "kiss a strange woman who will bless with her mouth dead and dumb idols and eat from their table bread of strangulation and drink from their libation a cup of insidiousness and anoint herself with ointment of destruction (*JosAs* 8:5, OT *Pseud* 2:212). Aseneth confesses her sorrow that God will hate her because she has worshiped "dead and dumb idols, and blessed them, and ate from their sacrifices" (*JosAs* 11:8, *OT Pseud* 2:218). After she confesses to God her sin of worshiping idols (12:5) and recognizes that what she worshiped in ignorance were in fact "dumb and dead idols" (13:11), she received forgiveness (chaps. 14–15).

12:3. Therefore I make known to you, that no one speaking by the Spirit of God says, "Jesus is accursed"; and no one can say, "Jesus is Lord," except by the Holy Spirit. There is little agreement on the significance of "Jesus is accursed" in this text except to say that those who follow Jesus say that "Jesus is Lord." In the latter instance, the acknowledgement of Jesus as Lord is at the heart of the early Christian confessions (Rom. 10:9; Phil. 2:11). Some have postulated that Paul has in mind that the historical Jesus, or the Jesus after the flesh (2 Cor. 5:16), but

this argument presupposes that later Gnostic ideas were present at Corinth during Paul's ministry, but there is no evidence for that. Paul's purpose as he introduces this discussion of spiritual gifts and spiritual people, builds on a foundation he has taught already: namely, that the Holy Spirit is the source of the Christian life when it is lived in obedience to the will of God (see also Rom. 8:15-16, 26; Gal. 3:1-2). A first- or second-century lead tablet contains a curse that. In fact, at the end of the formula of cursing there is a separate line with large letters saying *ANETHEMA* (Greek for "anathema" or "curse") (See *Inscriptiones Graecorum* (*IG*) III.2). In line five of this cure tablet, the word "we curse" is used three times. But who from Corinth would have said such things about Jesus?

There were persecutions of Christians by the end of the first century in Asia Minor, and in the second century many of them were hauled before the Roman courts, and if they denied that they were Christians, they were let go, but if not, they suffered beating and death (see Pliny, *Letters* 10.96-97). None of this was going on in the time of Paul, however, and belonging to the Christian community was not a crime (see Acts 18:14-15). It is possible that the Jews there who rejected Jesus might have said something like this (see Acts 18:5-6, 12-17), and seeing his death on the cross as under the sentence of God's curse (see Deut. 21:23; cf. Gal. 3:13-14), but there is no clear evidence for that view here. Whether there were some at pagan meetings who were inspired by demons and said something like this is not clear. There are no references to such activity and, although some have urged that there were some speaking ecstatically in the Christian gatherings who spoke such slogans, the available evidence does not support that view.

It is likely that the cursing of Jesus is a hypothetical situation or something referring to the Corinthians' pagan past, but it is no longer true. If, in the context, the call is for the Corinthians to recognize that all who acknowledge Jesus as Lord are spiritual persons, then some sense can be made of the passage. As it was true that those who discriminated against one another at the Lord's table were not partaking of the Lord's Supper (11:20), so it is that those who curse Jesus by their deeds are not truly spiritual people and do not reflect the Spirit of Christ. For Paul, the confession of Jesus as Lord is the clearest indication of the Spirit's presence and power and, since this is foundational to one's Christian experience (Rom. 10:9; Phil. 2:11), it is important for all at Corinth to realize that the Christian community is a community of spiritually endowed and enabled persons.

12:4-11. The Variety and Unity of Spiritual Gifts.

This section of Paul's argument underscores that though there are many gifts in the church, they all have one source, the Holy Spirit, and he has given gifts as he chooses and not as a reward for someone's ability or status in the church.

12:4-6. Now there are varieties of gifts, but the same Spirit. And there are varieties of ministries, and the same Lord. And there are varieties of effects, but the same God who works all things in all persons. Paul introduces the discussion of spiritual gifts with three references to their source and empowerment: Spirit, Lord, God (12:4-6). The order of these three varies in Paul's writings (Rom. 8:11; 15:15-16, 30; 2 Cor. 1:21-22; 13:13; Eph. 4:4-6) and elsewhere (Matt. 28:19; 1 Peter 1:2). The Trinitarian tradition was not yet stabilized in terms of sequence (Father, Son, Holy Spirit) in Paul's time. He uses the same word for "varieties" (Greek = *diaipeseis*), but the gifts (*charismaton*), ministries (*diakonion*), and effects (*energematon*) have a different word, but they are not clearly distinguished by their function: namely, to serve for the common good. The gifts are listed in vv. 8-10, but they are not labeled according to these three categories. These categories are likely synonymous and encompass all of the varieties of enablement of the Spirit to build up the church. While *diakonia* is used more frequently of table service (Matt. 25:42-44; Luke 22:26; cf. Also Acts 6:2), and Paul uses it to identify the collection for the church in Jerusalem (2 Cor. 8:4). At this time, it is only beginning to be used generically of office in the church (see discussion of 3:5, 9 above).

12:7. But to each one is given the manifestation of the Spirit for the common good. The reference to the "common good" here comes from the word *sumpheron*, and is similar in meaning to what Paul says elsewhere of the "building up" or "edifying" (Greek = *oikodome*) of the church (see 6:12; 10:23). See also Eph. 4:11-13.

12:8-10. For to one is given the word of wisdom through the Spirit, and to another the word of knowledge according to the same Spirit; to another faith by the same Spirit, and to another gifts of healing by the one Spirit, and to another the effecting of miracles, and to another prophecy, and to another the distinguishing of spirits, to another various kinds of tongues, and to another the interpretation of tongues. The nine gifts in this list are only representative of the variety of gifts. Paul lists others elsewhere and one can see a wider list of gifts in the primary New Testament passages where they are enumerated (vv. 28-31a; Rom. 12:6-8; Eph. 4:11-12; 1 Peter 4:10-11). There is no complete list of the gifts of the Spirit in the New Testament. The only thing that can be said of this list is that tongues and their interpretation appear to be listed in last place precisely because they were promoted beyond their appropriate place among the Corinthians. The distinction between a word of wisdom and that of knowledge are not clearly distinguished here. Interestingly, when speaking of the righteous path that one must follow, those at Qumran listed the following:

These are their paths in the world: to enlighten the heart of man, straighten out in front of him all the paths of justice and truth, establish in his heart respect for the precepts of God; it is a spirit of meekness, of patience, generous compassion, eternal goodness, intelligence, understanding, *potent wisdom which trust in all the deeds of God and depends on his abundant mercy; a spirit of knowledge in all the plans of action*, of enthusiasm for the decrees of justice, holy plans with firm purpose, of generous compassion with all the sons of truth concerning the mysteries of knowledge. These are the counsels of the spirit for the sons of truth in the world. And the visitation of those who walk in it will be fore healing, plentiful peace in a long life, fruitful offspring with all everlasting blessings, eternal enjoyment with endless life, and a crown of glory with majestic raiment in eternal light. (*Rule of the Community*, 1QS 3.4-8, Garcia Martinez trans., *italics* ours).

The miraculous gifts of healing and miracles follow them but prophecy is listed lower here in the list than they are later in vv. 28-30. There they are clearly listed in order of importance to the church. We note here that while Paul does not claim that he has the gifts of healings and miracles, they are certainly represented in his ministry in Acts (Acts 14:8-10; 16:18; 19:11-12; 20:7-20; 28:8-9). It is interesting that Paul mentions the gift of healing in a community where Asklepios, the god of healing, was honored. Corinth had one of the two hundred sanctuaries throughout the Greco-Roman world where healing was commonplace. Every major population in the ancient world had an Askelpion where various healings were practiced, including one in Jerusalem in the time of Jesus! The Asklepieia were places where baths, drama, religious rituals, and dreams were common, and those who found healing would often offer a replica of the part of their body

that was healed. At Corinth, many such parts of the body were found in the ruins of the Asklepion. Again, Paul makes clear that healing could be done in the power of the Holy Spirit to a community that was used to such activity in the power of Asklepios.

At the end of chap. 12, prophecy is listed second in terms of importance in the church behind the role of apostle and, following the pursuit of love, it is the gift of preference in 14:1. Here, however, it is lower in the scale, but again, the order of these gifts in vv. 8-10 is not as important to Paul as their function in the church: namely, to enable the church to care for the "common good," that is, to build up the church. It is possible that such gifts can be misused and merely issue forth in arrogance or being "puffed up" with oneself (8:1).

The tongues that are mentioned here are more than mere languages (*dialects*) as some scholars have insisted, but are seen as a "heavenly language" spoken by angels (13:1). What is referred to is the ancient and modern inarticulate expressions of sound that are commonly found in enthusiastic Christian worship. In the ancient world, this experience was not identified with the Christians only, but was also found among the Jews and also various religious sects such as the Delphic oracles who spoke in tongues, and "prophets" were employed to interpret their divine meaning. In the pseudepigraphal book, *The Testament of Job* (ca. first century B.C. or A.D.), we read that

> when Hemera (a woman's name meaning "Day") arose, she wrapped around her own string just as her father said. And she took on another heart—no longer minded toward earthly things—but she spoke ecstatically in the angelic dialect, sending up a hymn to God in accord with the hymnic style of the angels. And as she spoke ecstatically, she allowed "The spirit" to be inscribed on her garment (48:1-3, *OT Pseud* 1:865-66). Following this, another woman, Kasia,

"had her heart changed so that she no longer regarded worldly things. And her mouth took on the dialect of the archons and she praised God for the creation of the heights" (*Test. Job* 49:1-2, *OT Pseud* 1:866). Similarly, she is followed by Amaltheia who "spoke ecstatically in the dialect of those on high, since her heart also was changed, keeping aloof from worldly things. For she spoke in the dialect of the cherubim, glorifying the Master of virtues" (50:1-2; *OT Pseud* 1:866). It is likely that King Saul was speaking in tongues when it is reported that he prophesied (1 Sam. 10:9-13). For a brief discussion of this phenomenon in the Greco-Roman world, see discussion on Acts 2:3; 10:46; 19:6; cf. also 16:16. Apart from the three references in Acts and those in 1 Cor. 12-14 (12:10, 28, 30; 13:1, 8; 14:5, 6, 18, 21, 22, 23, 39), there are no other references to speaking in tongues in the New Testament. See further discussion in 14:1 ff. below.

By emphasizing that all of these gifts came from the same Spirit, Paul prepares his readers for his next emphasis on the unity of the Church as the one body of Christ (vv. 12-26).

12:11-26. The Church as the Body of Christ

As there has been discrimination in the church both at the Lord's Supper and in terms of the highly prized gifts of the Spirit, Paul emphasizes the importance that all Christians are "of the Spirit" and all have spiritually endowed gifts to be used to build up the church. Clearly some thought that their gifts were not as important as those of others who could either speak in tongues or interpret the tongues or prophesy. This is the thrust of Paul's "because I am not . . . I do not belong" and he incorporates the metaphor of the body to show the unity of the Christian community.

12:12. For even as the body is one and yet has many members, and all the members of the body, though they are many, are one body, so also is Christ. The body metaphor was quite common in antiquity. Josephus, for instance, refers to it to speak of the Jews in their battle against the Romans: "And as in the body when inflammation attacks the principal member all the members catch the infection, so the sedition and disorder in the capital gave the scoundrels in the country free license to plunder" (*Jewish War* 4.406-407, LCL; for further examples cf. also his *War* 1.507; 2.264; 5.277-279). Philo also is familiar with the metaphor and speaking of the role of the high priest to intercede on behalf of all Jews writes:

> so too the whole nation has a kinsman and close relative common to all in the high priest, who as ruler dispenses justice to litigants according to the law, who day by day offers prayers and sacrifices and asks for blessings, as for his brothers and parents and children, that every age and every part of the nation regarded as a single body may be united in one and the same fellowship, making peace and good order their aim (*Special Laws* 3.131, LCL).

Even more like Paul's example in 1 Corinthians, Seneca (4 B.C.–A.D. 65) contends that:

> To injure one's country is a crime; consequently, also to injure a fellow-citizen—for he is a part of the country, and if we reverence the whole, the parts are sacred—consequently to injure any man is a crime, for he is your fellow-citizen in the greater commonwealth. What if the hands should desire to harm the feet, or the eyes the hands? As all the members of the body are in harmony with one another because it is to the advantage of the whole that the individual members be unharmed, so mankind should spare the individual man, because all are born for a life of fellowship, and society can be kept unharmed only by the mutual protection and love of its parts (*On Anger* 2.31.7-8, LCL).

Later he writes: "I can lay down for mankind a rule, in short compass, for our duties in human relationships: all that you behold, that which comprises both god and man, is one—we are the parts of one great body" (*Epistles* 95.51b-52, LCL). Speaking of the relationship of a person to the state, Epictetus also uses the body metaphor.

For I will assert of the foot as such that it is natural for it to be clean, but if you take it as a foot, and not as a thing detached, it will be appropriate for it to step into much and trample on thorns and sometimes to be cut off for the sake of the whole body . . . We ought to hold some such view also about ourselves . . . Do you not know that as the foot, if detached, will no longer be a man? For what is a man? A part of a state; first of that state which is made up of gods and men, and then of that which is said to be very close to the other, the state that is a small copy of the universal state (*Discourses* 2.5.24-27, LCL. See also 2.10.3-6).

Plutarch uses the body metaphor to focus on the need for every member to come to the aid of the others. "in the body itself she [Nature] has contrived to make most of the necessary parts double and brothers and twins: hands, feet, eyes, ears, nostrils; and she has thus taught us that she has divided them in this fashion for mutual preservation and assistance, not for variance and strife" (*On Brotherly Love* 478D, LCL). The Christian community continued this metaphor after Paul as well. Clement of Rome, while writing to the Corinthians near the end of the first century, used this familiar metaphor with the same meaning that Paul attached to it, including Paul's admonitions in 1 Cor. 8:7-13.

The great cannot exist without the small, nor the small without the great; there is a certain mixture among all, and herein lies the advantage. Let us take our body; the head is nothing without the feet, likewise the feet are nothing without the head; and the smallest members of our body are necessary and valuable to the whole body, but all work together and are united in a common subjection to preserve the whole body.

Let, therefore, our whole body be preserved in Christ Jesus, and let each be subject to his neighbor, according to the position granted him. Let the strong care for the weak and let the weak reverence the strong. Let the rich man bestow help on the poor and let the poor give thanks to God, that he gave him one to supply his needs (*1 Clement* 37: 4-6, 38:1-2, LCL).

See also the references to the body in a similar fashion in Eph. 4:1-6 and Col. 1:18-24.

12:15-16. If the foot should say, "Because I am not a hand, I am not a part of the body," it is not for this reason any the less a part of the body. And if the ear should say, "Because I am not an eye, I am not a part of the body," it is not for this reason any the less a part of the body. Philo, a contemporary with Jesus and Paul, asks a similar question with a logical response intended:

And so the other element, the air, must needs be filled with living beings, though indeed they are invisible to us, since even the air itself is not visible to our senses. Yet the fact that our powers of vision are incapable of any perception of the forms of these souls is no reason why we should doubt that there are souls in the air, but they must be apprehended by the mind, that like may be discerned by like (*On the Giants* 9, LCL).

12:19. And if they were all one member, where would the body be? Plato recognized that human beings have different abilities but that all are necessary for the common good. He claims:

"it occurs to me myself that, to begin with, our several natures are not all alike but different. One man is naturally fitted for one task, and another for another" (*The Republic* 370B, LCL).

12:22. On the contrary, it is much truer that the members of the body which seem to be weaker are necessary. Paul may be referring to the "necessary members" euphemistically as in v. 23 below: namely, as the genitals. The term is so used in the Hellenistic word to refer to the male genitals (Artemidorus, *Dream Handbook* 1.45, 79, 80). Perhaps the reference is to those members who are less exposed than others: namely, the ones who serve "behind the scenes" as it were and they are quite valuable to the whole "body."

12:23. And those members of the body, which we deem less honorable, on these we bestow more abundant honor, and our unseemly members come to have more abundant seemliness. The term "unseemly members" (Greek = *ta aschemona*) is generally used of that which is not done in the open, that is, it is a term used of the unmentionable, shameful, or indecent. It is also used in the ancient world euphemistically of the genitals, as is the case here. Dio Chrysostom uses the term to speak of the "indecent harlots who are not ashamed to utter licentious phrases, each from her respective chamber" (*Discourses* 40.29, LCL). In the Septuagint (LXX), the term is used for sexually inappropriate activity, for example in Deut. 24:3 (LXX = 24:1), the term is used in reference to a man wanting to divorce his wife because "he has found some unbecoming thing [*aschemon*] in her." Similarly, in the LXX version of Genesis, "the sons of Jacob came from the plain; and when they heard, the men were deeply pained, and it was very grievous to them, because the man wrought folly [*aschemon*] in Israel" (Gen. 34:7). Josephus uses the term in reference to Herod accusing his sons before the governors of Syria. He offered

"arguments in advocacy of these that were a disgrace [*aschemona*] for a father to use against his sons" (*Ant.* 16.363, LCL).

12:26. And if one member suffers, all the members suffer with it; if one member is honored, all the members rejoice with it. The apostle wants the whole family to show compassion for those who are weak and to rejoice with those who have been blessed. See also Rom. 12:15; 2 Cor. 11:29; Gal. 6:2; 1 Thess. 5:14.

12:27-31a. You are the body of Christ! Paul now returns to the focus on the gifts and prioritizes them in two ways, first by listing them and then by his series of questions. The list of gifts in this collection (v. 28) is different from that in vv. 8-10 above in that only four of them overlap, a further indication that the lists are only illustrative and not exhaustive of all of the gifts of the Spirit. The purpose for prioritizing these gifts will become evident when Paul deals directly with the use of tongues in the church gatherings in 14:1-40. There are essentially two lists in this passage: namely, those that are listed in terms of priority in v. 28 and those that come by way of the seven questions in 29-30. No list here or elsewhere contains all of the gifts, so it is best to conclude that Paul was only illustrative. As he concludes this section, Paul is more concerned to draw attention to what is most important and admonishes his readers to pursue the most important gifts, which was for him, prophecy (14:1), but he contends that the gift of love, which is the fruit of the Spirit, is the best way to pursue (12:31b–13:13).

12:27. Now you are Christ's body, and individually members of it. The reference to the Corinthian Christians being members of the body of Christ is similar to Seneca's reference to the unity of the human race as a "body." "I can lay down for mankind a rule, in short compass, for our duties in human relationships: all that you behold, that which comprises both god and man, is one—we are the parts of one great body" (*Epistles* 95.52, LCL).

12:28. And God has appointed in the church, first apostles, second prophets, third teachers, then miracles, then gifts of healings, helps, administrations, various kinds of tongues. It is strange that in this list neither the terms "bishop"/"overseer" nor deacon (Phil. 1:1) are used in the categories of gifts. In Paul's ministry "deacon" (*diakonos*) is apparently used of recognized church offices (Rom. 16:1). Only later are they explicated in terms of their qualifications (1 Tim. 3). The term "deacon" (*diakonos*) is one of the oldest Christian terms for office in the church, and is used of both Paul and Apollos (1 Cor. 3:5). "Bishop" did not apparently have the same implications of absolute authority and power as it did later in the ministry of Ignatius (c. 115). The term "elder" (*presbuteros*) is mentioned in Acts (11:30; 15:2, 6, 22, 23), but it is not as common in the Pauline churches until later in the first century, where it is mentioned in Titus 1:5 along with "bishop/overseer" (Titus 1:7). This could signify the lack of any influence from Jerusalem in the leadership of the Gentile churches, although this is not certain. Paul, who proudly defended his apostleship on several occasions (Gal. 1:1, 11-18; 1 Cor. 9:1-14; 2 Cor. 12:1-12), nevertheless uses the term "deacon" of himself in 1 Cor. 3:5 and 2 Cor. 6:4, but does not use it here. Instead, here he uses the terms "administrators" (Greek = *kuberneseis*) and "helpers" (Greek = *antilempsis*). Xenophon used the former term to refer to the rule of Cyrus who ruled Asia and Egypt. He indicates that everyone feared him and they wished to "be guided by [*kubernasthai*] his rule" (*Cyrodaedia* 1.1.5, LCL). Paul's use of these terms is strange since the New Testament elsewhere calls all Christians *diakonoi* ("deacons;" cf. John 12:26; Mark 9:35; 10:43). There are close parallels in Paul's use of the term "bishop"

(*episkopos*) in Phil. 1:1. Also, gift of "helper" or "servant" (*antilempsis*) is not unlike the role of the "deacon" or "servant" mentioned elsewhere by Paul. Indeed, both terms here appear to be equivalent to the functions of bishop and deacon elsewhere. Note also, in vv. 29-30, Paul does not ask if all Christians are "administrators" or "helpers," since those offices were elected in the early Church and anyone could hold them, unlike the other functions mentioned in the lists in vv. 8-10, 28-30.

12:29-30. All are not apostles, are they? All are not prophets, are they? All are not teachers, are they? All are not workers of miracles, are they? All do not have gifts of healings, do they? All do not speak with tongues, do they? All do not interpret, do they? Each of these seven sentences is framed with the Greek particles *ou me*, thereby implying that a negative answer to each of the questions is anticipated. In the first case, for instance, "Not all are apostles, are they? No!" is the anticipated response for the way that each of the questions is stated.

12:31a. But earnestly desire the greater gifts. Paul concludes this discussion with a call to pursue not the lesser gifts, but the greater ones (prophecy and teaching).

12:31b–13:13. The Call to a More Excellent Way: Love

Since Paul does not list love as a gift, nor faith and hope (13:13), it seems odd that what follows upon the end of 12:31a is a focus on love rather than prophecy (14:1). Some scholars contend that this passage was inserted into the text after the letter had been completed. Nevertheless, it is possible to bring all of Paul's focus together as he culminates his discussion of how Christians relate to each other when they come together and he finds this an appropriate place to insert what he has been driving at since the beginning of his letter, that Christians should not be divided, but should mutually care for one another. If this passage were not in Paul's letter, one could easily make a logical connection between the end of chap. 12 and the beginning of chap. 14. It appears that Paul wrote this passage in typical encomium style that praises the virtue of something over the value of other highly esteemed qualities. See below in 13:13. The praise of love in the ancient world is not unusual and there are a number of praises of the value of love in ancient writers. While later Christian scholars tried to make distinctions between the various and commonly used words for love—*agape, philia,* and *eros*—ancient writers did not do so and it can be argued that neither do the New Testament writers. For example, Plato (b. ca. 427 B.C.) praises the virtue of love (*eros*), that he also characterizes as a god, not as a sexual pleasure, but rather in a similar fashion as Paul in 1 Cor. 13. Speaking of the gentleness of love, he enters his praise of this virtue as follows:

The same method will serve us to prove the delicacy of Love. Not upon earth goes he, nor on our crowns, which are not very soft; but takes his way and abode in the softest things that exist. The tempers and souls of gods and men are his chosen habitation: not indeed any soul as much as another; when he comes upon one whose temper is hard, away he goes, but if it be soft, he makes his dwelling there . . . Love is in every quarter allowed to excel: unshapeliness and Love are ever at war with one another. Beauty of hue in this god is evinced by his haunting among flowers: for Love will not settle on body or soul or aught else that is flowerless or whose flower has faded away; while he has only to light on a plot of sweet blossoms and scents to settle there and stay. . . .

The strongest plea for this [Love's goodness] is that neither to a god he gives nor from a god receives any injury, nor from men receives it nor to men gives it. For neither is the usage he himself gets a violent usage, since violence takes not hold of Love; nor is there violence in his dealings, since Love winds all men's willing service; and agreements on both sides willingly made are held to be just by "our city's sovereign, the law." Then, over and above his justice, he is richly endowed with temperance. We all agree that temperance is a control of pleasures and desires, while no pleasure is stronger than Love: if they are the weaker, they must be under Love's control, and he is their controller; so that Love, by controlling pleasures and desires, must be eminently temperate . . . If Apollo invented archery and medicine and divination, it was under the guidance of Desire and Love; so that he too may be deemed a disciple of Love, as likewise may the Muses in music, Hephaestus in metal-work, Athene in weaving and Zeus 'in pilotage of gods and men.' Hence also those dealings of the gods were contrived by Love—clearly love of beauty—astir in them, for Love has no concern with ugliness; though aforetime, as I began by saying, there were many strange doings among the gods, as legend tells, because of the dominion of Necessity. But since this god [Love] arose, the loving of beautiful things has brought all kinds of benefits both to gods and to men.

Thus I conceive, Phaedrus, that Love was originally of surpassing beauty and goodness, and is latterly the cause of similar excellences in others (*Symposium* 195D – 197B, LCL).

The division of the chapters and verses in the Bible are a late addition to it that were intended to make reference to various texts more easily and with less time consumed when searching for or referring to various biblical texts. While the work of those who provided this service is greatly appreciated (Stephen Langton [d. 1228] and Robert Estienne [d. 1559], it was not always carefully done, and the chapter division here as well as in 11:1 are such examples; 12:31b clearly belongs in scope with the next chapter. See above on 11:1 and below on 14:1 as well for similar results. The following section of this letter naturally falls into three passages that follow Paul's familiar chiastic style. Verses 1-3 introduce the theme, or encomium, of the greatness of love and in typical fashion three important contrasts at the beginning. He picks out three examples that have special significance to Christian people, especially in Corinth, and says that even here, these are nothing without love. Verses 4-7 focus on the essence of love and what it is and is not, and the final section, vv. 8-14:1a, returns to the contrast between love and other important Christian values. Paul uses the first person to discuss this issue in true rhetorical skill and draws home his point in an ascending fashion in each of the three portions of this section.

12:31b. And I show you a still more excellent way. The figure of "the way" (Greek = *hodos*) has many ancient parallels. There are a number of "ways" that are mentioned in ancient biblical and extra literature, including in both early Christian and Jewish literature. Philo, for instance, speaks of the "royal way" (or "way") to God.

> . . . for since God is the first and sole King of the universe, the road leading to Him, being a King's road, is also naturally called royal. . . . This royal road then, which we have just said to be true and genuine philosophy, is called in the Law the utterance and word of God. For it is written "Thou shalt not swerve aside from the word which I command thee this day to the right hand nor to the left hand" (Deut. 28:14). Thus it is clearly proved that the word of God is

identical with the royal road. He treats the two as synonymous, and bids us decline from neither, but with upright mind tread the track that leads straight on, a central highway (*The Prosperity and Exile of Cain* 101-102, LCL).

Both during and after the time of Paul it was common among both Jews and Christians to speak about "two ways" of life that generally use the light/dark metaphor. The Qumran community, for example, spoke of two ways of life that are contrasted by light and darkness.

> For the wise man, that he may inform and teach all the sons of light about the history of the sons of man, concerning their deeds and their generations, and concerning the visitation of their punishment and the moment of their reward. From the God of knowledge stems all there is and all there shall be. . . . He created man to rule the world and placed within him two spirits so that he would walk with them until the moment of his visitation: they are the spirits of truth and deceit. In the hand of the Prince of Lights is dominion over all the sons of justice; they walk on paths of light. And in the hand of the Angel of Darkness is total dominion over the sons of deceit; they walk on paths of darkness. Due to the Angel of Darkness all the sons of justice will stray, and all their sins, their iniquities, their failings, and their mutinous deeds are under his dominion in compliance with the mysteries of God, until his moment; and all their punishments and their periods of grief are caused by the dominion of his enmity; and all the spirits of their lot cause the sons of light to fall. However, the God of Israel and the angel of his truth assist all the sons of light. He created the spirits of light and darkness and on them established all his deeds [on their p]aths all his

labours. God loved one of them for all . . . (*The Rule of the Community*, 1QS 3.13-26, Garcia Martinez trans).

At the end of the first century, the Christians began circulating a writing known as the Teaching of the Twelve Apostles, abbreviated the *Didache* (Greek = "Teaching"), and it begins with a focus on two ways of life and contrasts them for the first six chapters of the small book. It begins: "there are two Ways, one of Life and one of Death, and there is a great difference between the two Ways" (*Did.* 1:1, LCL). Likewise, the early second-century writing, *The Epistle of Barnabas* also has a section on the two Ways that parallels that of the *Didache*. In the opening section of its discussion of the two Ways, similar contrasts are made:

Now let us pass to another lesson and teaching. There are two ways of teaching and power, one of Light and one of Darkness. And there is a great difference between the two Ways. For over the one are set light-bringing angels of God, but over the other angels of Satan. And the one is Lord from eternity and to eternity, and the other is the ruler of the present time of iniquity (*Ep. Barn.* 18:1-2, LCL. See also 19:1–20:2).

The two Ways here contrast the way of life from a Christian perspective and the way of death that is also the way of darkness that leads to the judgment of God. The roots of this perspective may well have come from an interpretation of the Old Testament (see also Deut. 30:19-20; Ps. 1:1-6; Deut. 30:19; Jer. 21:8), but the view of the two ways also has several parallels in the New Testament, including Matt. 7:13-14 that focuses on two ways with one leading to life and the other to death. For the contrast between light and darkness, see John 3:19-21; cf. Acts 9:2; 18:25; 19:9, 23; 22:4; 24:14, 22; Rom. 3:17; Eph. 4:20-22; Phil. 4;1; Heb. 10:20. Similar to Paul is Ignatius (ca. 115-117), who claims that "love is the way that leads to God" (*Eph.* 9:1).

Epictetus praises the One who points to him the way: "O great good fortune! O the great benefactor who points the way!" (*Discourses* 1.4.29, LCL).

13:1. If I speak with the tongues of men and of angels, but do not have love, I have become a noisy gong or a clanging cymbal. For a discussion of the "tongues of angels" see 12:8-10 above. The Corinthians would have been well aware of the implication of gongs or cymbals since they were well-known for their production of such instruments in their community. The "noisy gong" is more likely translated "sounding brass" that was also quite familiar to the Corinthians. Brass containers were placed in niches around a theater to echo sound. The theater at Corinth may have had these instruments to enhance the sound of the voice in performances. Vitruvius (ca. 30–27 B.C.) described how these brass "gongs" were designed and used in the theaters, not just in Corinth, but elsewhere:

1. Hence in accordance with these enquires, bronze vases are to be made in mathematical ratios corresponding with the size of the theatre. They are to be so made that, when they are touched, they can make a sound from one to another of a fourth, a fifth and so on, to the second octave.

Then compartments are made among the seats of the theater, and the vases are to be placed that they do not touch the wall, and have an empty space around them and above. They are to be placed upside down. On the side looking towards the stage, they are to have wedges put under them not less than half a foot high. Against these cavities openings are to be left in the faces of the lower steps two feet long and half a foot high . . . .

7. Someone will say, perhaps, that many theatres are built every year in Rome without taking any account of these matters. He will be mistaken in this.

. . . But when theatres are built of solids, that is, of rubble walling, stone or marble which cannot resound, the use of bronze vases is to be followed (*On Architecture* 5.5.1, 7, Murphy-O'Connor trans. 75).

It is quite possible that Paul was familiar with these instruments. The theater at Corinth seated some 14,000, and it is easy to understand how some sound enhancement would have been used. Paul was also, no doubt familiar with the reference to clashing cymbals in Ps. 150:5.

13:2. And if I have the gift of prophecy, and know all mysteries and all knowledge; and if I have all faith, so as to remove mountains, but do not have love, I am nothing. Compare here with 8:1-3 and 14:6. The example of the removal of mountains may reflect the teaching of Jesus on faith (Mark 11:23).

13:3 And if I give all my possessions to feed the poor, and if I deliver my body to be burned, but do not have love, it profits me nothing. This is the third instance of Paul's use of comparative hyperbole to highlight the importance of love. Jesus called upon the rich young ruler to give away his wealth and to follow him (Matt. 19:16-30; Mark 10:17-31; Luke 18:18-30). Examples of courage to die for a noble cause are found throughout the ancient world. Courage was an enviable virtue among Greeks and Romans alike. The Jews also picked up on this and celebrated those who would willingly give up their lives before turning against their religious beliefs. In the story of the death of the seven sons in *4 Macc.*, the writer tells the story of the remaining sons who gather to encourage each other toward faithfulness to their beliefs.

They formed a holy choir of piety as they encouraged each other with the words, "Let us die like brothers all, brothers, for the Law's sake. Let us follow the example of the three youths in Assyria, who despised the same trial by ordeal in the furnace [the three in the furnace in Dan. 3]" (*4 Macc.* 13:8-9, *OT Pseud* 2:558).

Likewise, the author of *1 Enoch* (ca. second century B.C.), praises those who stood fast for their faith in the face or torment and persecution.

Those who love God have loved neither gold nor silver, nor all the good things which are in the world, but have given over their bodies to suffering—who from the time of their very being have not longed after earthly food, and who regarded themselves as a (mere) passing breath. And they have observed this matter, the Lord having put them through much testing; then he received their pure spirits so that they should bless his name. And I have recounted in the books all their blessings. He has caused them to be recompensed, for they were all found loving God more than the fire of their eternal souls; and while they were being trodden upon by evil people, experiencing abuse and insult by them, they continued blessing us (*1 En* 108:8-10, *OT Pseud* 1:88-89).

Courage in the face of fire was a highly prized theme in the Greco-Roman world as well. Dio Chrysostom tells of Diogenes' praise of the virtue of an ideal noble man who came to the athletic events in Greece and proclaimed that his real opponents were those of the various hardships of life and his victory was not yielding to them.

He is not afraid of those opponents, nor does he pray to draw another antagonist, but challenges them one after another, grappling with hunger and cold, withstanding thirst, and disclosing no weakness even though he just endure the lash or give his body to be cut or burned. Hunger, exile, loss of reputation, and the like have no terrors for him; nay, he holds them as mere trifles, often as sportive as boys with their dice and their coloured balls (*Discourses* 8.16, LCL).

Lucian (ca. A.D. 120–190), in his satire against Peregrinus, speaks with distrust of those who are willing to offer their bodies to be burned: "but for what reason does this man throw himself bodily into the fire? On yes! To demonstrate his fortitude, like the Brahmans [of India], for Theagenes thought fit to compare him with them, just as if there could not be fools and notoriety-seekers even among the Indians" (*Passing of Peregrinus* 25, LCL). Strabo (ca. 64 B.C.–A.D. 25) tells of the story of a man accompanying an embassy from India to meet with Caesar Augustus who burned himself in a fire in Athens. Strabo explains the reason:

Whereas some commit suicide when they suffer adversity, seeking release from the ills at hand, others do so when their lot is happy, as was the case with that man; for, he adds, although that man had fared as he wished up to that time, he thought it necessary then to depart this life, lest something untoward might happen to him if he tarried here; and that therefore he leaped upon the pyre with a laugh, his naked body anointed, wearing only a loin-cloth; and that the following words were inscribed on his tomb: "Here lies Zarmanochegas, an Indian from Bargosa, who immortalized himself in accordance with the ancestral customs of Indians" (*Geography* 15.1.73, LCL).

Such traditions often reflect the current crises that the people of faith were going through and Paul says that even if he had paid the ultimate sacrifice for his faith, that is insufficient and nothing at all if there is no love. Paul may also be reflecting Jesus' comments at his Last Supper in which he offers his body and blood as a sacrifice for many (Mark 14:22-25; cf. Mark 8:34-36). See also 1 Cor. 11:23-24.

13:4. Love is patient, love is kind, and is not jealous; love does not brag and is not arrogant. Patience has a longstanding approval rating among the Jews. Sirach (ca. mid-second century B.C.), for instance, admonishes his readers to patience in the face of adversity: "Accept whatever befalls you, and in times of humiliation be patient. For gold is tested in the fire, and those found acceptable in the furnace of humiliation" (*Sir.* 2:4, NASV). See also Rom. 2:4; 2 Cor. 6:6; Gal. 5:22. On the latter instance, love is not arrogant, earlier Paul says that knowledge puffs up (8:1), or makes one arrogant, but Christians should rather build up.

13:5. does not act unbecomingly; it does not seek its own, is not provoked, does not take into account a wrong suffered. Love does not act in a way that is rude or unbecoming for a Christian and behaves itself. See 7: 36. Not seeking one's own fulfillment, but that of others is a recurrent theme in Paul. See 10:24; Phil. 2:4.

13:6. does not rejoice in unrighteousness, but rejoices with the truth. See this contrast between lawlessness and righteousness in Romans (1:18, 29; 2:8; 3:5; 6:13; 9:14). For Paul, love is at variance with evil. "Love rejoices" is Paul's way of emphasizing joy in the Christian community (Rom. 12:12; Phil. 2:1-2; 4:4; 1 Thess. 3:9; 5:16). Here the rejoicing is in the truth, not in the lawlessness of individuals or ungodly behavior.

13:7. bears all things, believes all things, hopes all things, endures all things. Two of the characteristics of love that are at the end of Paul's praise of love are listed here (belief/faith and hope) are expressed here as they clarify the meaning of love. In Hellenistic Judaism, both faith and love are listed as important virtues. In *2 Enoch* (ca. first cent. B.C.–second cent. A.D.), for example, there is an appeal to walk in love as one faces the various trials and circumstances of life.

Walk, my children, in long-suffering, in meekness [honesty], in affliction, in distress, in faithfulness, in truth, in hope, in weakness, in derision, in assaults, in temptation, in deprivation, in nakedness, having love for one another until you go out from this age of suffering, so that you may become inheritors of the never-ending age. (*2 Enoch* 66:6, *OT Pseud* 1:194).

Similarly, the author of *Jubilees* (ca. 161–140 B.C.) also extols the value of love and faith in the example of Abraham: "And in everything in which he tested him, he was found faithful. And his soul was not impatient. And he was not slow to act because he was faithful and a lover of the Lord" (*Jub.* 17:9, *OT Pseud* 2:90).

13:8-14:1a. Love Stands Alone. As Paul concludes this section, he has praised the value of love in action in the most ordinary places of life.

13:8. Love never fails; but if there are gifts of prophecy, they will be done away; if there are tongues, they will cease; if there is knowledge, it will be done away. Now he returns to a comparison of love to the prized gifts of the Spirit in Corinth and indicates that they will all pass away but love will endure forever. See discussion in 12:8-10, 28; 13:2. Plutarch (ca. A.D. 45–125) makes a similar plea about the importance of learning over other prized inherited characteristics of birth and valued opportunities in life.

Good birth is a fine thing, but it is an advantage which must be credited to one's ancestors. Wealth is held in esteem, but it is a chattel of fortune. Beauty is highly prized, but short-lived. Health is a valued possession, but inconstant. Strength is much admired, but it falls an easy prey to disease and old age. But learning, of all things in this world, is alone immortal and divine. Two elements of man's nature are supreme over all—mind and reason. The mind exercises control over reason, and reason is the servant of the mind,

unassailable by fortune, impregnable to calumny, uncorrupted by disease, unimpaired by old age. For the mind alone grows young with increase of years, and time, which takes away all things else, but adds wisdom to old age (*Moralia*, "The Education of Children" 8, LCL).

13:9-10. For we know in part, and we prophesy in part; but when the perfect comes, the partial will be done away. The focus here is on the limited nature of the prized gifts that are now in place, but when the kingdom of God comes, there will no longer be a need for them.

13:11 When I was a child, I used to speak as a child, think as a child, reason as a child; when I became a man, I did away with childish things. In the ancient world, as now, a child was used metaphorically of an immature adult. Epictetus writes:

What sort of teacher, then, do you still wait for, that you should put off reforming yourself until he arrives? You are no longer a lad, but already a full-grown man.... Make up your mind, therefore, before it is too late, that the fitting thing for you to do is to live as a mature man who is making progress, and let everything which seems to you to be best be for you a law that must not be transgressed (Epictetus, *Encheiridion* 51.1-2, LCL).

Likewise, Xenophon (430–354 B.C.) uses the metaphor of a boy in contrast to the maturity of an adult as he tells the story of the death of Cyrus: "For when I was a boy, I think I plucked all the fruits that among boys count for the best; when I became a youth, I enjoyed what is accounted best among young men; and when I became a mature man, I had the best that men can have" (Xenophon, *Cyropaedia* 8.7.6, LCL). Philo, in telling the story of the Patriarchs, says that "when Ishmael had apparently lived about twenty years, Moses calls him a child by comparison with Isaac, who is full grown in virtues" (*On Sobriety* 8, LCL).

13:12 For now we see in a mirror dimly, but then face to face; now I know in part, but then I shall know fully just as I also have been fully known. In the ancient world, mirrors were made by a disk of polished metal, generally silver, and attached to a handle. Corinth was famous for producing mirrors. They were not the bright and crisp mirrors that are used today. Plutarch uses the metaphor of a mirror in a way that is similar to Paul's. "in all likelihood, we should welcome those peculiar properties existent in nature which possess the power of perception and have a soul and feeling and character. It is not that we should honour these, but that through these we should honour the Divine since they are the clearer mirrors of the divine by their nature also" (Plutarch, *Moralia, Isis and Osiris* 382B, LCL). In the *Odes of Solomon* (ca. A.D. 100), the writer exclaims: "Behold, the Lord is our mirror. Open (your) eyes and see them in him" (*Ode* 13, *OT Pseud* 2:747). A statue of Aphrodite on the Acrocorinth (mountain near Corinth) depicted her looking at herself in the mirror of a shield. Philo claims that "nothing so much assures its predominance as that through it is best given the revelation of the Father and Maker of all, for in it, as in a mirror, the mind has a vision of God as acting and creating the world and controlling all that is" (*Decalogue* 105, LCL). See also Num. 12:8.

13:13. But now abide faith, hope, love, these three; but the greatest of these is love. The comparison of highly praised characteristics with the selection of one of them as highest has parallel in Plato (see introduction of 12:31b–14:1a above). Another example is found in the latter part of the first century in *4 Ezra*, a pseudepigraphal writing. The author of that comparison makes different choices than Paul,

and places three above the others: "The most High shall be revealed on the seat of judgment, and compassion shall pass away, and patience shall be withdrawn. Only judgment shall remain, truth shall stand, and faithfulness shall grow strong" (*4 Ez* 7:33-34, NRSV). For Paul, the three virtues of faith, hope and love, which are found side-by-side elsewhere in Paul in Rom. 5:1-5; 1 Thess. 1:3; and 5:8—where the order is different—are highly praised, but he chooses love as the most important. All three are in a list of virtues in Rom. 5:1-5 with love at the apex of the list that has come through the power of the Holy Spirit. It is interesting that Paul likewise includes an emphasis on love in the context of speaking about the gifts of the Spirit. See also Rom. 8:24 and 2 Cor. 5:7. Love is the greatest of the commandments in the Synoptic Gospels (Matt. 22:34-40; Mark 12:28-34; Luke 10:25-28; cf. Lev. 19:18). Also, Jesus' commandment to love is found repeatedly elsewhere in the New Testament (John 13:34; 15:17; 1 John 3:18, 23; 4:7-11) and is also an evidence of the presence of the Spirit of God (1 John 4:12).

14:1-40. Prophecy and Tongues. Again, it appears that Paul has inserted the previous chapter into the flow of his argument in order to strengthen his case, but the flow of his argument shows that speaking in tongues was the most highly prized spiritual gift among the Corinthians, and Paul claims that prophecy is a greater gift and should be pursued over tongues. In prioritizing the gifts of the Spirit, the Corinthians maximized to the point of spiritual pride a gift that Paul thought was valuable, but not nearly as much as the gift of prophecy by which the church could be informed of the will of God. The act of speaking in tongues was well-known in the ancient world and it apparently meant rather universally that those with the gift were enabled to speak in the language of God. Likewise, those who interpreted this phenomenon were seen as having the ability to communicate the will of the gods or a god on various important matters. Generally speaking, the Greeks saw little difference between speaking in tongues and prophesying. Paul, however, distinguishes them in this passage. Speaking in tongues was well-known in the ancient Greco-Roman world among the pagans and the best-known place for its practice was at Delphi where the famous Apollo oracles entered into a trance to receive a divine message. The message given by the gods came to the oracles (the women priestesses who spoke in tongues) and was interpreted to the people by the "prophets." Delphi is located roughly sixty miles north of Corinth and was that community that also hosted athletic games. Drama was highly influential throughout the region and indeed the whole of the Mediterranean world. This was the place to discover the will of the gods in political, social, and personal matters. What took place there was highly valued and this no doubt influenced the value attributed to the practice of speaking in tongues in the church at Corinth. For the practice of speaking in tongues, see discussion in Acts 2:4; 16:16 and 1 Cor. 12:8-10 above.

Lucian of Samosata, the second-century satirist (ca. A.D. 120–190) told the story of a false prophet who tricked people with his so-called mantic prophesies. He tells the story of how a whole city came to hear Alexander and "uttering a few meaningless words like Hebrew or Phoenician, he dazzled the creatures, who did not know what he was saying save only that he everywhere brought in Apollo and Asclepius" (*Alexander the False Prophet* 13-14, LCL). At Delphi, prophets were enlisted to interpret the tongues of the priestess or oracle, who received it from the god Apollo, to the inquirers who came seeking the divine will on important matters such as whether one nation should go to war against another and even whether a man should marry a particular woman. Plato spoke of those who both were diviners and also inter-

preters of the gods and what he says reflects well on the practice of speaking in tongues and their interpretation in the ancient world.

> But it belongs to a man when in his right mind to recollect and order both the things spoken in drama or waking vision by the divine and inspired nature, and all the visionary forms that were seen, and by means of reasoning to discern about them all wherein they are significant and for whom they portend evil or good in the future, the past, or the present. But it is not the task of him who has been in a state of frenzy, and still continues therein to judge the apparition and voices seen or uttered by himself; for it was well said of old that to do and to know one's own and oneself belongs only to him who is sound of mind. Wherefore also it is customary to set the tribe of prophets to pass judgment upon these inspired divinations; and they, indeed, themselves are named "diviners" by certain who are wholly ignorant of the truth that they are not diviners but interpreters of the mysterious voice and apparition, for whom the most fitting name would be "prophets of things divined" (*Timaeus* 71E–72B, LCL).

Plutarch describes this activity in some detail:

> However, even if anybody were to grant that no word of prophecy is uttered in our time without being in verse, such a person would be in much more perplexity regarding the oracles of ancient times which gave their responses at one time in verse and at another time without versification. However, neither of these, my young friend, goes counter to reason if only we hold correct and uncontaminated opinions about the god, and do not believe that it was he himself who used to compose the verses in earlier times, while now he suggests the oracles to the prophetic priestess as

if he were prompting an actor in a play to speak his words . . .

I imagine that you are familiar with the saying found in Heracleitus, to the effect that the Lord whose prophetic shrine is at Delphi neither tells nor conceals, but indicates. Add to these words, which are so well said, the thought that the god of this place employs the prophetic priestess for men's ears just as the sun employs the moon for men's eyes. . . . what is called inspiration seems to be a combination of two impulses, the soul being simultaneously impelled through one of these by some external influence, and through the other by its own nature (*Moralia*, "The Oracles at Delphi," 404A-F, LCL).

Finally, Heracleitus writes: "the Sybil [the ecstatic oracle] with raving mouth uttering her unlaughing, unadorned, unincensed words reaches out over a thousand years with her voice, through the (inspiration of the) god" (*Ancilla, Fr.* 92, Conzelmann 234).

This chapter is divided into several arguments from Paul. Verses 1b-12 emphasize the greater gift of prophecy utilizing three analogies. Verses 13–19 argue the value of prophecy over tongues within the gatherings of the whole community for worship. Here Paul argues that the mind is not inactive during worship and communion with God, unlike what Plato and contemporary philosophers taught. In vv. 20-25, Paul deals with the problem of unbelievers coming into the fellowship of the church when the gift of tongues is being practiced: namely, they are confused and consider the Christians to be "mad" or beside themselves. The final section, vv. 26-40 has to do with Paul's view that there should be order in the church when the Christians gather together for worship. It also brings to a close Paul's discussion of the confusion in the church over the issue of spiritual gifts.

14:1. Pursue love, yet desire earnestly spiritual gifts, but especially that you may prophesy. As noted above at the beginning of 11:1 and 12:1, so here. The division of the chapters in these cases are not in their logical place. Since the thought of 14:1a is clearly with 12:31b–13:13, it is better to place it there since it captures the essence of the "Love chapter" in Paul. Likewise, the call to pursue the gifts of the Spirit fits best with 12:31a. The transition from one section to the other is not smooth and shows signs of being inserted into the primary letter that Paul has produced. This is not to say that Paul did not write the previous section, but rather that it was probably prepared by him on another occasion and inserted here for purposes of making clear to the Corinthians that without love, none of his discussion about spiritual gifts had much value. The pursuit of love in the exercise of one's gifts of the Spirit is at the heart of Paul's thinking in this section, but he now goes on to show how to use the gifts for their intended purpose: namely, to build up the body of Christ. For Paul, the prophetic ministry of the church builds up the church much more than does the use of tongues.

The distinction between prophecy and the speaking in tongues was noted above by Plato and Plutarch in the introductory comments for this passage. Now Philo enters his understanding of the differences in prophetic communication, some of which is apparently the practice of tongues, some the interpretation of those tongues, and others the spokesperson for God directly.

Of the divine utterances, some are spoken by God in his own person with His prophet for interpreter, in some the revelation comes through question and answer, and others are spoken by Moses in his own person, when possessed by God and carried away out of himself. The first kind are absolutely and entirely signs of the divine excellencies, graciousness and beneficence, by which He incites all men to noble conduct, and particularly the nation of His worshipers, for whom He opens up the road which leads to happiness. In the second kind we find combination and partnership: the prophet asks questions of God about matters on which he has been seeking knowledge, and God replies and instructs him. The third kind are assigned to the lawgiver himself: God has given to him of His own power of foreknowledge and by this he will reveal future events. Now, the first kind must be left out of the discussion. They are too great to be lauded by human lips; scarcely indeed could heaven and the world and the whole existing universe worthily sing their praises. Besides, they are delivered through an interpreter, and interpretation and prophecy are not the same thing. The second kind I will at once proceed to describe, interweaving with it the third kind, in which the speaker appears under that divine possession in virtue of which he is chiefly and in the strict sense considered a prophet (*The Life of Moses* 2.188-191, LCL).

Paul does not share the view that a person speaking by inspiration is necessarily out of control of one's mind or abilities. In fact, he contends that those speaking in tongues and prophesying can control the exercise of these gifts (vv. 27-28).

14:2. For one who speaks in a tongue does not speak to men, but to God; for no one understands, but in his spirit he speaks mysteries. Paul says here and through v. 5 why the gift of tongues is inferior in the church gatherings to the gift of prophecy. With prophecy one can edify or build up the church and though it appears also possible if the tongues are interpreted (v. 5), Paul clearly prefers the gift that allows for clarity of thought in the church gatherings. Prophecy is the only gift found in all four of Paul's lists of gifts (Rom. 12:6; 1 Cor. 12:10, 28-29).

14:6. But now, brethren, if I come to you speaking in tongues, what shall I profit you, unless I speak to you either by way of revelation or of knowledge or of prophecy or of teaching? These are gifts that emphasize a word from God that brings clarity about his will. Paul contends that this has greater value than the other gifts and enables the church to be built up (see below in 14:31-32).

14:7-8. Yet even lifeless things, either flute or harp, in producing a sound, if they do not produce a distinction in the tones, how will it be known what is played on the flute or on the harp? For if the bugle produces an indistinct sound, who will prepare himself for battle? Paul's point here is that sometimes the use of instruments or the use of music accompanied exercise of mantic prophecy (speaking in tongues) at Hellenistic meetings. Plutarch describes these instruments in his discussion of the tongues experiences at Delphi (*Moralia*, "The Oracles at Delphi" 404F). Strabo, while speaking of the many activities that accompanied the sacred rites and "frenzy" of the prophecies (tongues) says: "and fourthly, music, which includes dancing as well as rhythm and melody, at the artistic beauty brings us in touch with the divine, which is to avoid being perceived by our human senses" (*Geography* 10.3.9, LCL). The New Testament does not put much emphasis on the use of instruments and only a few passages such as this one are to be found. The use of pipes or bugles could both be for celebration (Matt. 11:17; Luke 7:32), but also the bugle or trumpet was used in a battle call to bring the troops together or advance to or withdraw from battle. The harp and the flute were well-known in the Jewish and Christian tradition and were used in promoting religious experience (1 Sam. 10:5; 2 Kings 3:15). When the harp was quiet, this was a sign of judgment (Rev. 18:22; cf. Isa. 24:8; Ezek. 26:13). Paul refers to the trumpet to speak of when the end of the ages will arrive (1 Cor. 15:52; 1 Thess. 4:16), and it figures prominently in the unfolding of the drama of the book of Revelation (Rev. 1:10; 4:1; 8:2, 6,13; 9:14). Paul says very little about musical instruments, perhaps because of the Jewish proscription against their use on the Sabbath and in the synagogue. Since instruments were used in Jewish worship in the Old Testament, e.g., Ps. 150, it is not certain when and for what reason they ceased being used. It became more pronounced following the destruction of Jerusalem in A.D. 70 when the Jews restricted the use of musical instruments and musical rhythm in their gatherings on the Sabbath. In a text from the Mishnah that has been used to argue against their use in Jewish worship, we read:

> Any act that is culpable on the Sabbath, whether by virtue of the rules concerning Sabbath rest or concerning acts of choice or concerning pious duties, is culpable also on a Festival-day. And these [acts are culpable] by virtue of the rules concerning Sabbath rest: none may climb a tree or ride a beast or swim on water or clap the hands or slap the thighs or stamp the feet" (*m. Betzah* [*Yom Tob*] 5.2, Danby trans.)

There is very little in the New Testament that focuses on the use of instruments in worship, but several texts suggest that musical instruments may have been used (Matt. 26:30; Mark 14:26; Acts 16:25; Eph. 5:19; Col. 3:16; Rev. 5:8; 14:2; 15:2), but because instruments were a regular part of pagan worship, Christians often restricted their use in their gatherings.

14:11. If then I do not know the meaning of the language, I shall be to the one who speaks a barbarian, and the one who speaks will be a barbarian to me. The term "barbarian" (Greek = *barbaros*) was a reference to one who did not have facility in the use of the Greek language. As in the case of anyone not familiar with a foreign language in a foreign land, those who could not speak Greek well were often called "barbarians." In a lengthy description of the term, Strabo explains the origin of its use.

> I suppose that the word "barbarian" was at first uttered onomatopoetically

in reference to people who enunciated words only with difficulty and talked harshly and raucously, like our words "*battarizein*" ["stutter"], "*traulizein*" ["lisp"], and "*psellizein*" ["speak falteringly"]; for we are by nature very much inclined to denote sounds by words that sound like them, on account of their homogeneity. Wherefore onomatopoetic words abound in our language . . . Accordingly, when all who pronounced onomatopoetically, it appeared that the pronunciations of all alien races were likewise thick, I mean of those that were not Greek. Those, therefore, they called barbarians in a special sense of the term, at first derisively, meaning that they pronounced words thickly or harshly; and then we misused the word as a general ethnic term, thus making a logical distinction between the Greeks and all other races.

. . .

And there appeared another faulty and barbarian-like pronunciation in our language, whenever any person speaking Greek did not pronounce it correctly, but pronounced the words like barbarians who are only beginning to learn Greek and are unable to speak it accurately, as is also the case with us in speaking their languages.

. . .

So, therefore, we must interpret the terms "speak barbarously" and "barbarously speaking" as applying to those who speak Greek badly (Strabo, *Geography* 14.2.28, LCL).

These foreigners were considered uneducated and uncultured as well and often they were spoken of with disapproval, even within the Jewish community. The author of *2 Macc.* tells of the conquests of Judas Maccabeus and his brothers as they cleansed the temple and fought bravely against the

Seleucid king, Antiochus Epiphanes. He says that they "seized the whole land and pursued the barbarian hordes, and regained possession of the temple" (*2 Macc.* 2:21-22, NRSV).

14:12. So also you, since you are zealous of spiritual gifts, seek to abound for the edification of the church.

14:13-19. The goal of the gifts: to build up! Paul stresses order and coherence when the community of faith gather and he also underscores here the necessity of building up the church over individual experiences that enrich the individual (tongues) but do not build up the family of Christ.

14:13-14. Therefore let one who speaks in a tongue pray that he may interpret. For if I pray in a tongue, my spirit prays, but my mind is unfruitful. The emphasis here is a common one in the Hellenistic world. While there the highest value was given to the spirit, Paul emphasizes the use of the mind (*vous*) in worship.

14:15-16. What is the outcome then? I shall pray with the spirit and I shall pray with the mind also; I shall sing with the spirit and I shall sing with the mind also. Otherwise if you bless in the spirit only, how will the one who fills the place of the ungifted say the "Amen" at your giving of thanks, since he does not know what you are saying? The reference here is to singing within the congregation. Compare with Rom. 15:9 (cf. Ps. 17:50). Paul may have in mind an experience of "singing in the spirit," that is, singing in tongues. This kind of experience is referred to in the pseudepigraphal writing *The Testament of Job* (ca. first century B.C. or A.D.).

> Thus, when the one called Hemera arose, she wrapped around her own string [=herself] just as her father said. And she took on another heart—no longer minded toward earthly things—

but she spoke ecstatically in the angelic dialect, sending up a hymn to God in accord with the hymnic style of the angels. And as she spoke ecstatically, she allowed "The Spirit" to be inscribed on her garment (*Test. Job* 48:1-3, OT *Pseud* 1:865-66).

The reference to the "Amen" (v. 16) reflects the Jewish liturgical forms of worship that Paul passed on to his readers (see also Rom. 1:25 and earlier 1 Chron. 16:36; Neh. 5:13; 8:6; Rev. 1:7; 5:14; 22:20, etc.). In the Jewish community it was the normal response to the benedictions. The Qumran community, for example reflect in their *Rule of the Community* that everyone entering the community shall enter also into a covenant with God to carry out all of God's commands and "when they enter the covenant, the priests and the levites shall bless the God of salvation and all the works of his faithfulness and all those who enter the covenant repeat after them: 'Amen, Amen'" (1QS 1.18-20, Garcia Martinez trans.).

14:20-25. A call to Christian maturity to consider unbelievers. After urging the Corinthians toward clarity and coherence in their communications with one another, he now argues for the credibility of their witness in the community by urging them to consider their conduct when unbelievers attend their meetings. It was obvious that for Paul the church was never separated from unbelievers and that many came to their meetings and Christians often went to meetings and gatherings of the unbelievers (1 Cor. 1:18-25; 5:1; 6:1-11; 7:12-16; chapters 8–10; 10:27; 12:2), so it was important that Christian behavior be above reproach and that there be clarity in the witness that they presented to the unbelieving community.

14:20. Brethren, do not be children in your thinking; yet in evil be babes, but in your thinking be mature. The call to be "babes in evil" is not found elsewhere in the Bible, but its meaning is not in doubt. It is similar to what Paul writes later in urging the Roman Christians to be "wise in what is good and guileless in what is evil" (Rom. 16:19). This is similar to what Philo earlier wrote about the status of Adam and Eve before their disobedience before God.

> "And the two were naked, Adam and his wife, and were not ashamed." . . . The mind that is clothed neither in vice nor in virtue, but absolutely stripped of either, is naked, just as the soul of an infant, is bared and stripped of coverings: for these are the soul's clothes, by which it is sheltered and concealed. Goodness is the garment of the worthy soul, and evil that of the worthless (*Allegorical Interpretation* 2.53, LCL).

14:23. If therefore the whole church should assemble together and all speak in tongues, and ungifted men or unbelievers enter, will they not say that you are mad? It is not clear what Paul means by the "whole church" but it is likely that this is a reference to the gathering of all of the house churches into one location (cf. Rom. 16:23). In contrast to the madness that Paul is opposed to in Christian gatherings, Plato seems to have embraced it when speaking of the "gift" of divination (tongues). "And that God gave unto man's foolishness the gift of divination a sufficient token is this: no man achieves true and inspired divination when in his rational mind, but only when the power of his intelligence is fettered in sleep or when it is distraught by disease or by reason of some divine inspiration" (*Tim.* 71E, LCL). When telling the story of Socrates and Phaedrus, he claims that madness is something to be welcomed since most of what good there is that happens comes through such madness. He cites as an example the priestesses at Delphi and Dodona:

> for if it were a simple fact that insanity

is an evil, the saying would be true; but in reality the greatest of blessings comes to us through madness, when it is sent as a gift of the gods. For the prophetess at Delphi and the priestesses at Dodona when they have been mad have conferred many splendid benefits upon Greece both in private and in public affairs, but few or none when they have been in their right minds; and if we should speak of the Sybil and all the others who by prophetic inspiration have foretold many things to many persons and thereby made them fortunate afterwards, anyone can see that we should speak a long time . . . The ancients, then testify that in proportion as prophecy (*mantike*) is superior to augury, both in name and in fact, in the same proportion madness, which comes from god, is superior to sanity, which is of human origin (*Phaedrus*, 244.A-D, LCL).

This view, which was perhaps made popular by Socrates, contends that the Spirit of God must expel the mind in order to have a vision from God. Philo appears to have agreed with that conclusion.

> Mortal and immortal may not share the same home. And therefore the setting of reason and the darkness which surrounds it produce ecstasy and inspired frenzy. To connect what is coming with what is here written he says "it was said to Abraham" (Gen. 15:3). For indeed the prophet, even when he seems to be speaking, really holds his peace, and his organs of speech, mouth and tongue, are wholly in the employ of Another, to shew forth what He wills (*Who Is the Heir* 265-266, LCL).

The relationship between ecstasy and intoxication was widely known in antiquity and Paul calls for "sobriety" within the Christian fellowship (cf. also Eph. 5:18). Philo was aware of this "inebriation" of the soul who was in a right relationship with God. He tells the story of Samuel and his mother Hannah and tells of God's grace to Hannah. Philo then explains the apparent intoxification of one inspired of God:

> when grace fills the soul, that soul thereby rejoices and smiles and dances, for it is possessed and inspired, so that to many of the unenlightened it may seem to be drunken, crazy and beside itself. . . . For with the God-possessed not only is the soul wont to be stirred and goaded as it were into ecstasy but the body also is flushed and fiery, warmed by the overflowing joy within which passes on the sensation to the outer man and thus many of the foolish are deceived and suppose that the sober are drunk (*On Drunkenness* 146-47, LCL).

14:24-25. But if all prophesy, and an unbeliever or an ungifted man enters, he is convicted by all, he is called to account by all; the secrets of his heart are disclosed; and so he will fall on his face and worship God, declaring that God is certainly among you. This distinction between prophecy and speaking in tongues was unknown in the ancient world, even among Judaism, where the two notions were not distinguished (cf. 1 Sam. 10:10-13). To speak in tongues was believed also to speak prophetically, but that is not the case with Paul. The reference to falling on one's face, or bowing, before God is a common Jewish expression having to do with the act of worship (cf. Isa. 45:14). While conversion is certainly a matter of the heart before God, its manifestation comes in one's worship of God (1 Kings 18:39). In the mystery religions, non-initiates were generally not allowed to come into the meetings, and even if occasionally they were, they were not allowed to speak of what they saw. Speaking of the Eleusinians who danced and sang in praise of the goddess Artemis, in the sanctuary of

Demeter at Eleusis, Pausanias described some of their activities and concludes: "My dream forbade the description of the things within the wall of the sanctuary, and the uninitiated are of course not permitted to learn that which they are prevented from seeing" (*Description of Greece* 1.38.7, LCL).

14:26-40. A Call to Order.
This section completes what was begun in 12:1: namely, Paul's guidance on the purpose and function of the gifts of the Spirit in the church. The summary in 39-40 provides Paul's primary concern over the exercise of such gifts in the church.

14:26. What is the outcome then, brethren? When you assemble, each one has a psalm, has a teaching, has a revelation, has a tongue, has an interpretation. Let all things be done for edification. Observe that it was a customary thing to stand when speaking prophetically (see also v. 30; cf. Luke 4:16-20; Acts 13:16).

14:29. And let two or three prophets speak, and let the others pass judgment. But if a revelation is made to another who is seated, let the first keep silent. Because there was a tendency for prophets in the church to act inappropriately (see Matt. 24:24), guidelines were established to control their excessive behavior. Lucian tells of a prophet in the Christian churches who was leading the uninformed Christians astray. He makes critical remarks about a certain Proteus Peregrinus who tricked the Christians and also gathered to himself many of their possessions and made himself a prophet among them.

> It was then that he learned the wondrous lore of the Christians, by associating with their priests and scribes in Palestine. And—how else could it be?—in a trice he made them all look like children; for he was prophet, cult-leader, head of the synagogue, and everything,

all by himself. He interpreted and explained some of their books and even composed many, and they revered him as a god, made use of him as a lawgiver, and set him down as a protector, next after that other, to be sure, whom they still worship, the man who was crucified in Palestine because he introduced this new cult into the world (*The Passing of Peregrinus* 11, LCL).

He adds that he tricked the Christians into giving him large sums of money and concludes that Christians are gullible and therefore, "if any charlatan and trickster, able to profit by occasions, comes among them [Christians], he quickly acquires sudden wealth by imposing upon simple folk" (*Pass. Peregr.* 13, LCL). The writer(s) of the Didache (end of first century A.D.), set up guidelines for the church to receive and respond to the traveling prophets in the early church. If a traveling prophet came among the Christians, they were to receive him, but if he stayed more than three days or asked for money for himself, he was considered a false prophet. While all prophets spoke what they believed was the will of God, not all spoke an acceptable message. The Didachist writes: "not everyone who speaks in a spirit is a prophet, except he have the behavior of the Lord. From his behavior, then, the false prophet and the true prophet shall be known" (*The Didache* 12.8, LCL).

14:34. Let the women keep silent in the churches; for they are not permitted to speak, but let them subject themselves, just as the Law also says. This is the only place in the New Testament where women are forbidden to speak in Christian gatherings. From a modern western world perspective, this is a troubling passage, and it even appears to be inconsistent with Paul's earlier advice about how women were to prophesy in the church (see 11:5-6, 13), where the only concern was to be properly attired when women pray and prophesy in the church meetings. Some scholars have argued that this passage was later inserted into the writings of Paul by a later Pauline school (Eph. 5:22-24; Col. 18; 1 Tim. 2:11-15; cf. also 1 Peter 3:1-6). The view of women keeping a proper public profile that is subordinate to men, however, is in keeping with the cultural milieu of that day. Sophocles (497–406 B.C.) expressed the contemporary view of women in public places in his day as he tells of Tecmessa's response to an interruptive Ajax: "'Woman, silence makes a woman beautiful.' Hearing this, I ceased, and he sped off alone." (*Ajax* 292-93, LCL). Women were expected to be quiet and covered with a veil over the face in public in the ancient world, but when they were home, most such restrictions were put aside. When the Christians began gathering in homes for worship, it was natural for the women to act in such gatherings like they did in their own homes because this was the only place where the community cultural standards were relaxed. The very location of the church gatherings in private homes was conducive to a relaxing of such rules of behavior for women. Paul, however, appears to be saying that while women could speak prophetically and pray in the assembly, there were certain acts of propriety that should be observed that were in keeping with the cultural standards of the day.

14:35. And if they desire to learn anything, let them ask their own husbands at home; for it is improper for a woman to speak in church. Women learning from their husbands in the home was a long standing practice. There were no schools for women, and it was understood that only the sons of wealthy families would receive an education. In both Jewish and Hellenistic families, the husband was responsible for teaching his wife to carry out her responsibilities, most of which were indoors and most of his were outdoors. Xenophon conveys this practice in his discussion of Socrates meeting up with a certain gentleman named

Ischomachus. The latter married a young woman not yet age fifteen and so Socrates asks: "But in other respects did you train your wife yourself, Ischomachus, so that she should be competent to perform her duties?" "Oh no, Socrates; not until I had first offered sacrifice and prayed that I might really teach, and she learn what was best for us both." "Did not your wife join with you in these same sacrifices and prayers?" "Oh yes, earnestly promising before heaven to behave as she ought to do; and it was easy to see that she would not neglect the lessons I taught her" (*Oeconomicus* 7.5-8, LCL).

14:37-38. If anyone thinks he is a prophet or spiritual, let him recognize that the things which I write to you are the Lord's commandment. But if anyone does not recognize this, he is not recognized. Paul acknowledges the role of the prophet and teacher in the church, but concludes that what he has told them comes from the Lord and should be obeyed. See discussion earlier in 7:6, 10, 12, 25; 11:23 where Paul distinguishes what he says from the Lord (Jesus Christ) and gives what the Lord says more authority in the churches. Here, again, he says that what he is saying comes from the Lord and must be followed in the church.

14:39. Therefore, my brethren, desire earnestly to prophesy, and do not forbid to speak in tongues. This brings to a conclusion the admonition begun in 14:1b and summarizes Paul's argument in 12:1–14:40.

14:40. But let all things be done properly and in an orderly manner. Describing the life of the Essene community, Josephus says that after they have eaten and worked during the day, they return for their evening meal and "no clamour or disturbance ever pollutes their dwelling; they speak in turn, each making way for his neighbor. To persons outside, the silence of those within appears like some awful mystery; it is in fact due to their invariable sobriety and to the limitation of their allotted portions of meat and drink to the demands of nature" (*Jewish War* 2.132-33, LCL). This call for order in community gatherings is also found in the Testament of Naphtali (first century B.C.) which urges: "thus my children you exist in accord with order for a good purpose in fear of God; do nothing in a disorderly manner, arrogantly, or at an inappropriate time" (*Test. Naph.* 2.9, *OT Pseud* 1:811). Like those who worshiped in his earlier Jewish context, Paul likewise urges what is "seemly" and in order in Christian gatherings.

D. 15:1-58. Misunderstanding Concerning the Resurrection of the Body

In Paul's last major theological treatise in this letter, he focuses on a problem that Christians had in expressing the heart of Christian faith in the Hellenistic world. Will there be a life after death and what form will it take? These two questions occupy this whole chapter. Paul does not begin this section as a response to questions that came to him by way of letter or first-hand report from those visiting Corinth (7:1, 25; 8:1; 12:1; 16:1, 12), but rather because of rumors (v. 12; cf. 11:18) that have come his way. Questions about resurrection life were brought to him following his brief ministry at Thessalonika (1 Thess. 4:13-17), but not here. Evidently there were those in Corinth who did not deny the resurrection of Jesus, but they did deny the resurrection of the body and taught rather the immortality of the soul, that is, the body dies and the soul lives on in the presence of the gods. The ones who rejected Paul's teaching on the resurrection from the dead in Athens (Acts 17:32) were similar in belief to those at Corinth who also rejected notions of bodily resurrection. Paul responds to the whole church with an affirmation of the proclamation that had been handed down to him and consequently to them when he established their church, and then he expounds both on the matter of unbelief in the resurrection of the body and also on the nature of that resurrection. The key issue that Paul faces here is stated in 15:12-29, but he has to set the stage for his discussion by setting forth the proclamation that lies at the heart of early Christianity. The whole of the chapter is divided into six sections of unequal length, namely: the foundational proclamation (vv. 1-11), the first and second arguments for the reality of the resurrection of the body (vv. 12-19 and 20-34), the two arguments on the nature of the resurrection body argument (vv. 35-49 and 50-57), and finally a short conclusion calling upon the Corinthian Christians to be steadfast in their belief and in their labor in the Gospel (v. 58). Throughout the passage, Paul refers to Jesus as "Christ" throughout the chapter without additional titles added. For Paul the essential elements of the office were sacrifice and intercession. The former of these is in view in the initial proclamation, but also throughout the chapter.

a. 15:1-11. The Foundational Proclamation. Paul repeats the Gospel proclamation that he had shared with the Corinthians when he established their church. Again, every aspect of this section, and most of what is found in the whole chapter, derives from Jewish apocalyptic teachings: namely, use of and discussion of the terms Christ, sin, Scripture, resurrection, the Twelve, Cephas, and the like. The core of Paul's proclamation is in vv. 3-5 and is united with the witnesses to the risen Christ, that is, he appeared to them in vv. 5b-8. They "received" (Greek = *parelabete*) it and he has "passed" (or "delivered" = *paredoka*) it on to them. The language here is technical and used in the passing on of traditions. After indicating that he was the last person to receive an appearance from the risen Christ, Paul speaks of his unworthiness to have this privilege of seeing the risen Christ because he was a perse-

cutor of the church (Gal. 1:13; Phil. 3:6; cf. 1 Tim. 1:13-16; Acts 8:1-3; 9:1-5; 22:3-5; 26:12-15). He then concludes this foundation by saying that both he and the other apostles preached the same message and they had received it (v. 11). See discussion at 11:23 above.

Every aspect of this passage, especially in vv. 3-8, is steeped in Jewish tradition and Jewish apocalyptic beliefs about life after death. While it is not clear which Scripture texts Paul has in mind in vv. 3-4, Isa. 53:3-5 has been suggested by many scholars. This passage is organized in a well-balanced format to make it easier for memory and teaching in the churches. For example, as shown in the structure below, there are two parts to this proclamation, each in a three/one emphasis balance and each part is introduced by the word "that" (Greek = *hoti*). Often creedal formulations in the New Testament have a "that" (*hoti*) at the beginning (e.g., Rom. 10:9-10). The subsequent appearance stories are also presented in a well-balanced form introduced by a "then" (Greek = *eita/epeita*) plan. Paul's use of "then" has a rhythmic sound to it with the sequence of *eita/epeita* variation. Should any part of this tradition drop out, it would be noticed right away and could be corrected. While the balance throughout this passage is more obvious in the Greek, it is still clear even in English translation.

For I delivered to you as of first importance what I also received,

- that (*hoti*) Christ died—for our sins—according to the Scriptures, and (*kai*)
- that (*hoti*) He was buried, and (*kai*)
- that (*hoti*) He was raised—on the third day—according to the Scriptures, and (*kai*)
- that (*hoti*) He appeared to Cephas then (*eita*) to the Twelve,
- then (*epeita*) He appeared to more than five hundred brethren at one time, most of whom remain until now, but some have fallen asleep;

- then (*eita*) He appeared to James then (*epeita*) to all the apostles; and (*de*) last of all,
- as it were to one untimely born, He appeared to me also (vv. 3-8).

The balance can be seen in the *eita/epeita* as well as in Peter and the Twelve followed by a larger and less balanced group still introduced by the *epeita* and then (*eita*) comes James followed by the rest of the apostles. Paul's name comes next with additional qualifiers like those following the "more than five hundred brethren." It seems clear that Paul added his name to this list since he does not add the *eita* ("then") to the list nor the "and" (*kai*), but rather a different connective for "and" (*de*). The balance is still quite remarkable and would allow those who were teaching this tradition in the church to pass it on relatively unchanged. This reflects the oral stage of development of this tradition and one which Paul himself received, probably from the apostles themselves (Gal. 2:1-10).

15:3. For I delivered to you as of first importance what I also received, that Christ died for our sins according to the Scriptures. The reference to Christ "dying for" our sins would have been well understood in the Greco-Roman world. The dying of a person for a friend or loved one was highly praised among the Greeks and the Romans. Writing about the peculiar power of love, Plato wrote: "Only such as are in love will consent to die for others; not merely men will do it, but women too. Sufficient witness is borne to this statement before the people of Greece by Alcestis, daughter of Pelias, who alone was willing to die for her husband . . ." (*Symposium* 179B, LCL). Similarly, Philostratus tells how much admired the laying down of one's life for another or for a cause when he relates the story of one named Damis, who saw little personal value in his life, but he was willing to die for philosophy, especially that of Apollonius: "I admit that one

ought to die in the cause of philosophy in the sense of dying for one's temples, one's own walls, and one's sepulchers; for there are many famous heroes who have embraced death in order to say and protect such interests as those" (*Life of Apollonius* 7.13, LCL). The Jews considered it a privilege to die for the preservation of the Law and refused to forsake their traditions in order to live. The author of *2 Macc.*, in telling the story of the seven brothers and their mother who all died because they refused to forsake the keeping of the Law, tells of how the first brother died: After being whipped and beaten in order to force the brothers to eat the forbidden swine's flesh, the first brother responds for all of them, "What do you intend to ask and learn from us? For we are ready to die rather than transgress the laws of our ancestors" (*2 Macc.* 7:2, NRSV). This is not unlike what Josephus wrote in his defense of the Jews: "For, although such long ages have now passed, no one has ventured either to add, or to remove, or to alter a syllable; and it is an instinct with every Jew, from the day of his birth, to regard them as the decrees of God, to abide by them, and, if need be, cheerfully to die for them" (*Against Apion* 1.42, LCL).

15:5. And that He appeared to Cephas, then to the twelve. The verb "appeared" (Greek = *ophthe*) is commonly used in antiquity to describe visions or appearances from God. In the Greek translation of the Old Testament (the LXX), the term is used to describe the appearance of God in Gen. 12:7; 26:24; 35:9; 48:3; Exod. 6:3; 1 Kings 3:5; 9:2; 2 Chron. 1:7; 3:1; 7:12, and in a manifestation of the glory of God (Exod. 16:10; Lev. 9:23; Num. 14:10; 16:19; 17:7; 20:6). While the verb does not indicate the nature of such appearances, as some scholars allege, it does indicate that God was involved in revealing himself to his people. In this passage the use of *ophthe* is an indication of the divine presence manifested through Jesus Christ in his resurrection appearances. The reference to the

"Twelve," which in fact was only eleven, indicates how imbedded the number "twelve" was in the Christian community at the time of Paul. It was continued in the gospels (Matt. 28:16-20; Luke 24:36-53; cf. Mark 16:14-18).

Remarkably, Paul does not mention any appearance to the women that is a prominent feature of the gospels (Matt. 28:9-10; Mark 16:1-8; cf. 16:9-11; Luke 24:10-11; John 20:14-18). Perhaps, given the cultural context where women were not to speak, but rather to learn from their husbands (see 14:35 above), Paul chose not to include this part of the early church tradition. It is easier to understand why Paul omitted this tradition than why the gospels included it.

15:6. After that He appeared to more than five hundred brethren at one time, most of whom remain until now, but some have fallen asleep. The reference to "falling asleep" (Greek = *koimaomai*) as a metaphor for death in Paul's writings (7:39; 11:30; 15:6, 18, 20, 51; 1 Thess. 4:13-15) has nonbiblical roots well before the time of Paul. Sophocles (497–406 B.C.) may well have begun the use of this metaphor for death. He describes how a certain Myrtilus, who won a chariot race against King Pelops by bribing his charioteer to loosen the lynchpins of the king's chariot, was executed when he came to collect his reward for winning the race. "O ride Pelops long ago, bringer of many sorrows, how dire was your effect upon this land! For since Myrtilus fell asleep, plunged into the sea, hurled headlong from the golden chariot with cruel torment, never yet has the torment of many troubles departed from this house" (*Electra* 502-515, LCL).

15:7. Then He appeared to James, then to all the apostles. James here is James the Lord's brother (Mark 6:3; Gal. 1:19; 2:9; Acts 15:13; 21:18-25; James 1:1). The New Testament does not tell the story of the actual appearance of Jesus to James, but one apocryphal gospel, known as the Gospel of the Hebrews, comes from the second century and was used by Origen and translated by Jerome. What took place in that appearance is described thusly:

> And when the Lord had given the linen cloth to the servant of the priest, he went to James and appeared to him. For James had sworn that he would not eat bread from that hour in which he had drunk the cup of the Lord until he should see him risen from among them that sleep. And shortly thereafter the Lord said: Bring a table and bread! And immediately it is added: he took the bread, blessed it and brake it and gave it to James the Just and said to him: My brother, eat thy bread, for the Son of man is risen from among them that sleep (*Gosp. Heb. Fr. 7, NT Apo* 1:178).

Another such story is preserved in the gnostic Gospel of Thomas (early to mid-second century A.D.). The author tells of Jesus' disciples asking Jesus who they are to follow when he departs from them. "The disciples said to Jesus: We know that you will depart from us; who is it who will be great over [lead] us? Jesus said to them: Wherever you have come, you will go to James the Just, for whose sake heaven and earth came into being" (*Gosp. Th.*12, *NT Apo* 1:119).

15:10. But by the grace of God I am what I am, and His grace toward me did not prove vain. Frequently in his letters Paul expresses concern that he or his fellow workers not labor in vain (15:2, 10, 14, 58; 2 Cor. 6:1; Gal. 2:2; Phil. 2:16; 1 Thess. 2:1; 3:5). This notion is also found earlier in the Old Testament (Isa. 49:4; 65:23; Ezek. 24:12; cf. Mal. 3:14).

15:12-19. The Problem and First Argument for the Reality of the Resurrection

After setting the grounds for his argument by tracing the core of the Christian proclamation, Paul now goes on to argue his case against those who claim that the dead do not rise. He concludes that if the dead do not rise, then Christ is not alive, and if that is so, then Christian faith is vain. He concludes this passage in chiastic form by asserting that Christ is alive and the implications for Christian faith. Who in the church would have claimed this? It appears that those mentioned in 2:6 and 3:1: namely, those who are "spiritual" who believed that they already had new life within them and there was no need of a resurrected body. A resurrected body would be in conflict with the Greek notions of immortality of the soul and so it was rejected. Paul's affirmation of the resurrection of Christ is affirmed five times in these verses (12, 13, 14, 16, 17), and his argument centers on seven conditional clauses with the logic appearing after each one, that is, what one can conclude if the condition is true or not true (vv. 12, 13, 14, 15, 16, 17, 19). The conditional clause in v. 13 is the basis for the rest of the argument. It may be that Paul's opponents in Corinth were like those mentioned in 2 Tim. 2:18 who claimed that the resurrection had already taken place and that there was no need for any resurrection of the body.

15:12. Now if Christ is preached, that He has been raised from the dead, how do some among you say that there is no resurrection of the dead? This is the issue that Paul is dealing with in this chapter. Some in the Corinthian church were denying that there was a resurrection of the dead. Paul links their assertion with the lynchpin of the Christian faith: namely, the resurrection of Jesus. If there is no resurrection of the dead, then Christ has not been raised (vv. 13-19).

15:19. If we have hoped in Christ in this life only, we are of all men most to be pitied. Paul reflects here Jewish sentiment. If there is no resurrection, then all else is for nothing. The author of the *Apocalypse of Baruch* (ca. A.D.

100–115) concludes: "for if only this life exists which everyone possesses here, nothing could be more bitter than this" (*2 Bar.* 21:13, *OT Pseud* 1:628). Similarly, a pessimistic inscription was often attached to Greek tombs such as "I was not, I was, I am not, I care not"! This was so common that its initials were often inscribed instead of the whole line, for example NFFN-SNC. One variation of this was found on a Roman tomb of the Imperial period: "I did not exist, I was born; I existed, I do not exist; so much for that." An epigram on a tomb from the Imperial period reads: "One, Chrysogonus hight, lies here, of nymphs an adorer, Saying to each passer-by, 'Drink, for thou seest the end'" (Deissmann, *Light* 295).

15:20-34. The Second Argument. Paul explains the connection between the resurrection of Christ and the future of those who believe in him.

15:20. But now Christ has been raised from the dead, the first fruits of those who are asleep. The resurrection of Christ is seen in terms of an agricultural metaphor. The background for this is the Old Testament command to give the first-fruits of the harvest to God (see Exod. 23:16, 19a; Lev. 23:10-14; Num. 18:8-13; Deut. 18:4; 26:2, 10; 2 Chron. 31:5; Neh. 10:37). The history of the use of this term in the Old Testament does not clarify the origin of Paul's use of it as a metaphor here. The form of argumentation that Paul has followed was also followed by Marcus Aurelius Antonius (ca A.D. 120–180), Roman emperor and Stoic philosopher. At first he says what life would be like if there were no gods and then he affirms that there indeed are gods.

> Let thine every deed and word and thought be those of a man who can depart from life this moment. But to go away from among men, if there are gods, is nothing dreadful; for they would not involve thee in evil. But if indeed there

are no gods, or if they do not concern themselves with the affairs of men, what boots it for me to live in a Universe empty of gods or empty of Providence? Nay, but there are gods, and they do concern themselves with human things; and they have put it wholly in man's power not to fall into evils that are truly such (*Meditations* 2.11, LCL).

15:22. For as in Adam all die, so also in Christ all shall be made alive. As in Rom. 5:12-21, Paul sees Adam as the representative of the human race and he died (Gen. 3:19; 5:3-5). Therefore, all who are in Adam die. Christ is the second Adam and those who are in him will all live. Paul presupposes here the fall of Adam and death coming to the whole human race as a result. The author of *4 Ezra* (ca. A.D. 90–100), like Paul, recognizes that sin and its consequence has come to all humankind as a result of the sin of Adam and he asks the obvious question:

O Adam, what have you done? For though it was you who sinned, the fall was not yours alone, but ours also who are your descendants. For what good is it to us, if an eternal age has been promised to us, but we have done deeds that bring death? And what good is it that an everlasting hope has been promised us, but we have miserably failed? (*4 Ezra* 7:118-19, *OT Pseud* 1:541).

Not all ancient Jewish writers had this view, however. Sirach, for instance, argues, "From a woman sin had its beginning, and because of her we all die" (*Sir.* 25:24, NRSV).

15:23. But each in his own order: Christ the first fruits, after that those who are Christ's at His coming. The coming (Greek = *parousia*) of Christ is used here by Paul and in 1 Thessalonians (2:19; 3:13; 4:15; 5:23). Paul claims that God has set in motion a plan and it will unfold first with Christ the first fruits of

those who sleep and then those who belong to Christ, and finally there comes the end (v. 24). This order of things was current in Jewish apocalyptic writings of the first century. The author of the Apocalypse of Baruch states his order in a manner that reflects Paul not only here, but especially in 1 Thess. 4:13-17:

And it will happen after these things when the time of the appearance of the Anointed One has been fulfilled and he returns with glory, that then all who sleep in hope of him will rise. And it will happen at that time that those treasuries will be opened in which the number of the souls of the righteous were kept, and they will go out and the multitudes of the souls will appear together, in one assemblage, of one mind. And the first ones will enjoy themselves and the last ones will not be sad. For they know that the time has come of which it is said that it is the end of times. But the souls of the wicked will the more waste away when they shall see all these things. For they know that their torment has come and that their perditions have arrived (*2 Bar. 30:1-5, OT Pseud* 1:631).

Generally, Judaism does not focus on the resurrection of the unrighteous, but only on the resurrection of the righteous, that is, those who obey the law of God.

15:24. Then comes the end, when He delivers up the kingdom to the God and Father, when He has abolished all rule and all authority and power. The combination of the worldly powers of authorities, powers, and forces is found elsewhere in Paul (Rom. 8:38-39; cf. Col. 1:16; 2:10; Eph. 1:21), but not much should be made of a distinction in meaning here. In the pseudepigraphal writing, *The Testament of Levi*, such powers reside with God alone: "There with him are thrones and authorities; there praises to God are offered eternally" (*Testament of Twelve*

Patriarchs, Test. of Levi 3:8, *OT Pseud* 1:789).

15:25. For He must reign until He has put all His enemies under His feet. See Phil. 2:5-11 for a similar word about the subjection of all things to Christ.

15:26. The last enemy that will be abolished is death. The personification of death is also found in Isa. 25:8 and Rev. 6:9 (cf. Heb. 2:14; 1 Cor. 10:10). The author of the *Apocalypse of Baruch* likewise personifies death in the person of an angel of death. "From now, therefore, everything is in a state of dying. Therefore, reprove the angel of death, and let your glory appear, and let the greatness of your beauty be known, and let the realm of death be sealed so that it may not receive the dead from this time, and let the treasuries of the souls restore those who are enclosed in them (*2 Bar.* 22:22-23, *OT Pseud* 1:628).

15:27. For He has put all things in subjection under His feet. But when He says, "All things are put in subjection," it is evident that He is excepted who put all things in subjection to Him. Paul introduces Ps. 8:6 and Ps. 110:1 into his argumentation. Both are frequently cited psalms in early Christianity and both prefigured the messiah (cf. Heb. 2:6-8). It has been that since the early church identified the son/man in Ps. 8:6 with the "Son of Man"—even Jesus Christ, that perhaps Paul was familiar with that designation for Jesus even though he never directly used it. Both Pss. 8 and 110 were understood in a christological fashion in the early church and Paul is probably drawing upon that tradition.

15:29-34. Paul's Personal Argument. In this well-crafted argument, Paul, in typical rhetorical fashion, asks why the people do something for the dead if the dead are not raised and why he would put his life in danger if there is no resurrection from the dead.

15:29. Otherwise, what will those do who are baptized for the dead? If the dead are not raised at all, why then are they baptized for them? Without question, this passage is one of the most difficult to discern in the whole of Paul's writings. Much of the controversy hinges over how to translate the "for" (Greek = *huper*), which is one of several possibilities for the Greek preposition. Does it mean "over the dead" in the sense that some Christians were baptized at cemeteries to celebrate the life of those who had died and to complete the sense of Paul's reference to being baptized into Christ's death (Rom. 6:3-4)? Whether the word means "above," "for the sake of," "over," "on behalf of," "because of," or "for," or yet something more or less obvious, or whether the baptisms were done on behalf of those who died before being baptized, it is difficult to determine. Some Christians have urged that the passage refers to those who were baptized because the witness of the martyrs, but there is nothing that suggests that there were martyrs in this part of the Roman Empire at this early date (ca. A.D. 51–53). The passage presupposes the *practice* of persons in the church baptizing individuals on behalf of those who have died.

Several early church fathers rejected this practice calling it heretical. For example, Tertullian (ca. 200), rejected the practice outright (*On the Resurrection of the Flesh* 48; *Against Marcion* 5.10) and likewise John Chrysostom (*1 Cor. Hom.* 40) and Epiphanius (*Against Heresies* 6). It is possible that *huper* in v. 29 refers to those who are converted at the deathbed of a loved one who urges them toward faith. As a result, they are baptized (become Christians) "for the sake of" the dead. There is nothing elsewhere in Paul to suggest or that commends that persons could be baptized on behalf of, or in the stead of, another in order to bring that person who had died into the household of faith. For this reason, this latter view best fits with the theology of Paul expressed elsewhere (Rom. 4:5; 5:1; 10:9; Gal. 2:21–3:5; cf. Eph. 2:8-9).

Paul's point is obvious, even if the practice he refers to is not: namely, if there is no resurrection from the dead, then why do they (some of the Christians at Corinth) practice proxy baptisms for the dead or are baptized for the sake of the dead? He argues that there is folly in the practice if the dead do not rise. There is nothing to suggest that Paul agrees or disagrees with the practice, of whatever sort it was, but what that means is not clear in the early church. There are no other parallels to this practice elsewhere in the New Testament, but there are some parallels in Hellenistic literature. Plato tells of sacrifices on behalf of others in the next life:

And they produce a bushel of books of Musaeus and Orpheus, the offspring of the Moon and of the Muses, as they affirm, and these books they use in their ritual, and make not only ordinary men but states believe that there really are remissions of sins and purifications for deeds of injustice, by means of sacrifice and pleasant sport for the living, and that there are also special rites for the defunct, which they call functions, that deliver us from evils in that other world, while terrible things await those who have neglected to sacrifice (*The Republic* 2.364E-365A, LCL).

There were also vicarious activities in the Dionysian orgies on behalf of the uninitiated dead: "And they will carry out the rites, seeking the release of unconsecrated forbears" (Kern. *Orph. Fr.* 245, Conzelmann 275). It is not clear whether Paul approves of the Corinthian practice, but it does further his argument about the resurrection from the dead. There are many and significantly varied interpretations of this passage and none have gained a majority position among commentators.

15:32. If from human motives I fought with wild beasts at Ephesus, what does it profit me? If the dead are not raised, let us eat and drink, for tomorrow we die. Paul's expression is more easily understood within the framework of his argument than is the understanding of his fight with wild beasts at Ephesus. If there is no resurrection from the dead, Paul asks, why would he put his life in jeopardy to preach the Gospel? That is his question and obviously he does not anticipate any controversy over the statement. The question here is whether Paul meant this figuratively or as a statement of fact. In favor of the former, there is a reference to God saving the psalmist from the wild beats (Ps. 35:17) which appears to be used figuratively there, and also Paul earlier used the athletic images of the runner and the boxer to illustrate his point about fervency in his desire to stay focused on his mission (9:24-27 above).

There is a longstanding tradition that Paul was imprisoned at Ephesus and there are in the ancient city today the ruins of a prison where many believe that Paul was imprisoned. Could he have fought with beasts in some gladiator type combat in an arena at Ephesus? It is likely that Paul's style of communication using himself as a part of his defense, similar to such discourses among the Stoics and Cynics of his day, and his other use of competitive images leans toward the former explanation and refers to Paul's many challenges to continue preaching the Gospel. "What advantage is there for me when I risk my life to preach the Gospel, if there is no resurrection from the dead?" he asks (cf. v. 31 above). Likewise, what also supports this conclusion is Paul's use of "humanly speaking" (Greek = *kata anthropon*). In other words, he is qualifying the statement as he makes it. A similar phrase is used figuratively elsewhere, for example, Philo tells a story in which "the ministers of punishment are already as it were standing at the barriers and press forward eager for my blood; every day or rather every hour I die in anticipation and suffer many deaths instead of the final one" (*Flaccus* 175, LCL). Likewise, Ignatius (ca. 115) tells of his trip to Rome to be martyred and uses similar hyperbole: "From Syria to Rome I am fighting with wild beasts, by land and sea, by night and day, bound to ten 'leopards' (that is, a company of soldiers) and they become worse for kind treatment" (*Ep. Rom.* 5.1, LCL). Philo also, in telling the story of some of the difficulties that Moses faced uses figurative language that depicts his struggles with wild beasts: "For some of the overseers were exceedingly harsh and ferocious, in savageness differing nothing from venomous and carnivorous animals, wild beasts in human shape who assumed in outward form the semblance of civilized beings only to beguile and catch their prey, in reality more unyielding than iron or adamant" (*Life of Moses* 1.43, LCL).

15:33. Do not be deceived: "Bad company corrupts good morals." Paul's quote here comes from Menander, an Athenian playwright who wrote various pieces in the fourth century B.C. (d. 292 B.C.). The specific text comes from the comedy, *Thais* (Frag. 187), and was a popular slogan in Paul's day. Even Earlier, Xenophon writes:

> For this cause fathers try to keep their sons, even if they are prudent lads, out of bad company; for the society of honest men is a training in virtue, but the society of the bad is virtue's undoing. As one of the poets says: 'From the good shalt thou learn good things; but if thou minglest with the bad thou shalt lose even what thou hast of wisdom'" (*Memorabilia* 1.2.20, LCL).

Quoting the slogan does not prove that Paul had studied Menander's works, since in Paul's day, after some three hundred and fifty years of circulation, it would be possible for many "one-liners" from the play to make their way into the social discourse throughout the Hellenistic world. That may be the case here. The quote, however, would also have been familiar to Paul's readers and it is possible that some of them saw some of Menander's plays

in the theater at Corinth. Philo from Alexandria (d. A.D. 40) seems to be familiar with the framework and truth of the quote from Menander. He writes:

> but let worthless men, of whose company Cain is a member, living in constant pains and terrors, gather in a most grievous harvest, in the experience or expectation of evils, groaning over the painful case in which they are already, and trembling and shuddering at the fearful things which they expect (cf. Gen. 4.12; *The Worse Attacks the Better* 140, LCL).

15:34. Become sober-minded as you ought, and stop sinning; for some have no knowledge of God. I speak this to your shame. For a parallel in Paul for the use of sobriety in calling upon readers to stay alert and diligent in their behavior, see 1 Thess. 5:6-8.

15:35-49. The Nature of the Resurrection Body

Paul begins a new section or focus on the same general issue of resurrection, but now the emphasis is on what kind of body one will have in the resurrection. He proceeds to speak to a hypothetical figure in common rhetorical fashion. This was not a problem for those who believed in the immortality of the soul, but it was for those Jewish thinkers who espoused the resurrection of the body. What kind of a body would it be? The author of the Apocalypse of Baruch also asks and answers that question:

> But further, I ask you, O Mighty One; and I shall ask grace from him who created all things. In which shape will the living live in your day? Or how will remain their splendor which will be after that? Will they, perhaps, take again this present form, and will they put on the chained members [his hands had been chained in prison] which are in evil and by which evils are accomplished? Or will you per-

haps change these things which have been in the world, as also the world itself?

And he answered and said to me: Listen Baruch, to this word and write down in the memory of your heart all that you shall learn. For the earth will surely give back the dead at that time; it receives them now in order to keep them, not changing anything in their form. But as it has received them so it will give them back. And as I have delivered them to it so it will raise them. For then it will be necessary to show those who live that the dead are living again, and that those who went away have come back. And it will be that when they have recognized each other, those who know each other at this moment, then my judgment will be strong, and those things which have been spoken of before will come.

. . . Also, as for the glory of those who proved to be righteous on account of my law, those who possessed intelligence in their life, and those who planted the root of wisdom in their heart—their splendor will then be glorified by transformations, and the shape of their face will be changed into the light of their beauty so that they may acquire and receive the undying world which is promised to them . . . . (2 Bar. 49:1-3; 50:1-4; 51:3, OT Pseud 1:637-38).

The Pharisees and Christians in the first century taught that life after death involved a bodily existence. Paul agrees with this and describes the nature of that resurrected body that can inherit the kingdom of God (see also v. 50). It cannot be a body of flesh as human beings have in this life, but it is something much more than that. Since the dead do rise, as Paul has argued, the natural question flows, How are they raised? With what body are they raised? The later rabbis also dealt with such questions as these and in similar fashion as Paul with the question and answer style, give

many responses to such questions as the ability of one to be raised if his or her body has been destroyed or lost at sea (b. Ketub. 11a; b. Sanh. 90b; y. Kil. 9.3; y. Ketub. 12.3; Qoh. Rab. 1.4). This section goes into some detail to say that when a believer dies, his or her body is placed in the ground. When it is raised, it is transformed into a new mode of bodily existence (v. 52). Precisely what that new mode of existence is does not become apparent, but what is clear is that the old is incorporated into the new. It is swallowed up and transformed into a new mode of existence. Elsewhere Paul speaks of a bodily transformation (Rom. 8:11, 22-23; Phil. 3:21).

15:35. But someone will say, "How are the dead raised? And with what kind of body do they come?" In the usual rhetorical fashion, Paul has an imaginary figure ask and then he answers the question. Philo (ca. 20 B.C.–A.D. 40) answers this question by saying that the soul and body are united in the afterlife. "Afterward the time came when he had to make his pilgrimage from earth to heaven and leave this mortal life for immortality, summoned thither by the Father, Who resolved his twofold nature of soul and body into a single entity, transforming his whole being into mind, pure as the sunlight" (Life of Moses 2.288, LCL). The unknown writer known by the title Pseudo-Philo (first cent. B.C. or A.D.) understood death as a transformation of one's being. Regarding the death of Moses, he states: "And when Moses heard this, he was filled with understanding and his appearance became glorious; and he died in glory according to the word of the Lord and he buried him as he has promised him" (Pseudo-Philo 19:16, OT Pseud 2:328).

15:36. You fool! That which you sow does not come to life unless it dies. Again, this verbal attack is reflective of the Stoic and Cynic diatribe in Paul's day. Paul uses the familiar example of the seed in the ground that dies and rises to argue his case. See also Ps. 14:1; Luke 12:20.

15:37. And that which you sow, you do not sow the body which is to be, but a bare grain, perhaps of wheat or of something else. The "bare" grain is a strange thing to say about a seed, but not about the body. It has to do with nakedness. This is not unlike Paul's argument in 2 Cor. 5:1-4. The thought that nakedness occurred at death is a Greek one, but not a Jewish notion. The Jews believed that the soul would not be disembodied at death. This lies behind the picture of the souls under the altar in Rev. 6:9-11 who had been killed for their testimony, but are given robes to clothe themselves until the judgment of God comes upon those who killed them. Plato relates the story of Socrates telling of Zeus' dealings with the unjust who were trying to invade undeservingly the Isles of the Blest (a place of reward for those who are virtuous). He equates death with nakedness and says:

> . . . they must be stripped bare of all those things before they are tried; for they must stand their trial dead. Their judge also must be naked, dead, beholding with very soul the very soul of each immediately upon his death, bereft of all his kin and having left behind on earth all that fine array, to the end that the judgment may be just (*Gorgias* 523E, LCL).

15:42-45. So also is the resurrection of the dead. It is sown a perishable body, it is raised an imperishable body; it is sown in dishonor, it is raised in glory; it is sown in weakness, it is raised in power; it is sown a natural body, it is raised a spiritual body. If there is a natural body, there is also a spiritual body. So also it is written, "The first man, Adam, became a living soul." The last Adam became a life-giving spirit. The notion of a natural and a spiritual body as well as the depiction of two

primal human beings, a first Adam and a spiritual Adam, plays an important role in Jewish thought in the first century B.C. and A.D. Adam, the first man, in Qumran beliefs is considerably different than the Adam we encounter in Paul such as he posits here and in Rom. 5:12-20. If there were two Adams, one spiritual and the other natural, a view taught by Philo (see below), then what Paul says here may be more at home in a broader Jewish context. At Qumran, for instance, we read:

> Meanwhile, God will refine, with his truth, all man's deeds, and will purify for himself the configuration of man, ripping out all spirit of deceit from the innermost part of his flesh, and cleansing him with the spirit of holiness from every irreverent deed. He will sprinkle over him the spirit of truth like lustral water (in order to cleanse him) from all the abhorrences of deceit and from the defilement of the unclean spirit. In this way the upright will understand knowledge of the Most High, and wisdom of the sons of heaven will teach those of perfect behaviour. For these are those selected by God for an everlasting covenant and to them shall belong all the glory of Adam (*Rule of the Community,* IQS 4.20-23, Garcia Martinez trans.).

Likewise, we also see at Qumran: "[You protect] the ones who serve you loyally, so that their posterity is before you all the days. You raise an [eternal] name for them, [forgiving them all] sin, eliminating from them all their depravities, giving them as a legacy all the glory of Adam and plentiful days" (*Hymns,* 1QH 4.14-15, Garcia Martinez trans.).

15:46-47. However, the spiritual is not first, but the natural; then the spiritual. The first man is from the earth, earthy; the second man is from heaven. The two men here, Christ and Adam, have some parallels with the two men in Philo's allegory of the Genesis story.

> "And God formed the man by taking clay from the earth, and breathed into his face a breath of life, and the man became a living soul" [Gen. 2.7]. There are two types of men; the one a heavenly man, the other an earthly. The heavenly man, being made after the image of god, is altogether without part or lot in corruptible and terrestrial substance; but the earthly one was compacted out of the matter scattered here and there, which Moses calls "clay." For this reason he says that the heavenly man was not molded, but was stamped with the image of god; while the earthly is a molded work of the Artificer, but not His offspring. We must account the man made out of the earth to be mind mingling with, but not yet blended with, body. But this earthlike mind is in reality also corruptible, were not God to breathe into it a power of real life; when He does so, it does not any more undergo molding, but becomes a soul, not an inefficient and imperfectly formed soul, but one endowed with mind and actually alive; for he says, "man became a living soul" (*Allegorical Interpretation* 1.31-32, LCL).

15:48. As is the earthy, so also are those who are earthy; and as is the heavenly, so also are those who are heavenly. Philo talks about the transformation that will occur in those who are the righteous and concludes: "having given up and left behind all more kind, he [the righteous one] is changed into the divine, so that such men become kin to God and truly divine" (*Questions and Answers on Exodus* 2.29, LCL). Earlier, he distinguishes between the creation of man in the two creation accounts in Gen. 1-2.

After this he [Moses] says that "God formed man by taking clay from the earth, and breathed into his face the breath of life" [Gen.

2:7]. By this also he shows very clearly that there is a vast difference between the man thus formed and the man that came into existence earlier after the image of God: for the man so formed is an object of sense-perception, partaking already of such or such quality, consisting of body and soul, man or woman, by nature mortal; while he that was after the [Divine] image was an idea or type or seal, an object of thought [only], incorporeal, neither male nor female, by nature incorruptible (*Account of the World's Creation* 134, LCL).

15:50-57. Flesh and Spirit and the Kingdom of God.

Following up on the two primal men picture to illustrate the distinction between natural and spiritual, Paul moves a step further by saying that only the spiritual can inherit the kingdom of God.

15:50. Flesh and blood cannot inherit the kingdom of God; nor does the perishable inherit the imperishable. There are several parallels to Paul's reference to "flesh and blood" (cf. also Gal. 1:16; Eph. 6:12), and all emphasize the natural side of humanity. In the early second-century apocryphal or deutero-canonical document, *Sirach* (also known as *Ecclesiasticus*), the writer says, "Like abundant leaves on a spreading tree that sheds some and puts forth others, so are the generations of flesh and blood: one dies and another is born" (*Sir.* 14:18, NRSV). Likewise, he later concludes: "For not everything is within human capability, since human beings are not immortal. What is brighter than the sun? Yet it can be eclipsed. So flesh and blood devise evil. He marshals the host of the height of heaven; but all human beings are dust and ashes" (*Sir.* 17:30-31, NRSV). In the second-century apocryphal gospel, The Gospel of Philip, some similar concerns are raised about the way a person will be raised and also whether "flesh and blood" can inherit the kingdom of God:

Some are afraid lest they rise naked. Because of this they wish to rise in the flesh. And they do not know that those who bear the f[lesh] are [precisely] the naked. Those who are [able] to lay (it) aside [are precisely those who] are not naked. Flesh [and blood cannot] inherit the kingdom [of God]. . . . I blame others, who say that it (the flesh) will not rise. Then both are at fault. You say that the flesh will not rise. But tell me what will rise, that we may honour you (as a teacher). You say: The spirit is in the flesh, and it is also this (spark of) light in the flesh. . . . It is (therefore) necessary to rise in this flesh, since everything is in it (*Gosp. Phil.* 23a-c, *NT Apo* 1:190-91).

15:52. In a moment, in the twinkling of an eye, at the last trumpet; for the trumpet will sound, and the dead will be raised imperishable, and we shall be changed. The trumpet plays a significant role in apocalyptic literature to announce impending battle or doom, but sometimes the intervention of God into human affairs at the end of the age (see 1 Thess. 4:16; Matt. 24:30-31; cf. Mark 13:26-27; Rev. 4:1; 8:6-7, 8, 10, 12-13; 9:1, 13-14; 10:7; 11:15; cf. also Matt. 6:2). In Jewish literature, it is usually a reference to an apocalyptic event. For example, in the late first-century Jewish document *4 Ezra*, the writer tells of the impending doom when

> The books shall be opened before the firmament, and all shall see it together. Infants a year old shall speak with their voices, and women with child shall give birth to premature children at three or four months, and these shall live and dance. Sown places shall suddenly appear unsown, and full storehouses shall suddenly be found to be empty; and the trumpet shall sound aloud, and when all hear it, they shall suddenly be terrified (*4 Ezra* 6:20-23, *OT Pseud* 1:535).

In the ancient Greek culture, just as in more modern times, the trumpet was used to sound a call to battle or even to retreat from battle. Xenophon (430–354 B.C.) tells the story of an army advancing to battle. One named Pigres, who was an interpreter to the generals of the Greeks "gave orders that the troops should advance arms and the phalanx move forward in a body. The generals transmitted these orders to the soldiers, and when the trumpet sounded, they advanced arms and charged" (*Anabasis* 1.2.18, LCL).

15:54-55. But when this perishable will have put on the imperishable, and this mortal will have put on immortality, then will come about the saying that is written, "Death is swallowed up in victory. O death, where is your victory? O death, where is your sting?" Paul cites two biblical passages here to describe the day of hope for the Christian community (Isa. 25:8; Hos. 13:14). He assigns victory in the place of the normal gloom that accompanies death and says that death is not the final word for those who have the "imperishable" faith. Elsewhere he combines sin and death as its consequence (Rom. 5:12-21; 6:23; 7:7-20).

15:57-58. But thanks be to God, who gives us the victory through our Lord Jesus Christ. Therefore, my beloved brethren, be steadfast, immovable, always abounding in the work of the Lord, knowing that your toil is not in vain in the Lord. See also 14:12; 16:10; Rom. 15:13; Phil. 1:9; cf. 2 Cor. 8:7; 9:8.

IV. 16:1-24. THE CLOSING OF THE LETTER

A. 16:1-11. The Collection for the Poor in Jerusalem

Finally Paul discusses a matter that is special to his own heart: the collection for the Christians in Jerusalem. For Paul, who earlier discussed the supreme virtue of love, it was important for that love to manifest itself in caring for those brothers and sisters in the Lord who were facing hunger in Jerusalem (see Gal. 2:10; 2 Cor. 8:1–9:15; Rom. 15:16, 25-28). Titus was put in charge of the collection (2 Cor. 8:6, 16-23), but it clearly was at the heart of Paul's concern. Not only did the offering provide a practical care for those in need, but it also was useful in building bridges between Jewish and Gentile churches. While some Jewish Christians had difficulty in associating with Gentile believers (Gal. 2:11-14), this act of generosity from those who were despised would go a long way in mending and building better relations among the churches.

16:1. Now concerning the collection for the saints, as I directed the churches of Galatia, so do you also. Observe the "now concerning" once again (cf. 7:1, 25; 8:1; 12:1; 16:1, 12). Paul is responding to questions about this special offering to care for the needs of the church in Jerusalem and in his closing comments to the church is putting into practice what he has said about caring and love (13:1-13). Paul has referred to the churches in Galatia as an example to follow in this regard. His designation of the Christians in Jerusalem as "saints" (see also 2 Cor. 8:4; 9:1, 12) shows the respect that he has for those who were a part of the original church. Observe also that Paul calls the Corinthian believers "saints" (1:2).

16:2-3. On the first day of every week let each one of you put aside and save, as he may prosper, that no collections be made when I come. And when I arrive, whomever you may approve, I shall send them with letters to carry your gift to Jerusalem. The "first day of the week" (Sunday) eventually became the day of choice for Christians to gather for worship and instruction (cf. Acts 20:7; Rev. 1:10). Since Christians had to work on the first day of the week, like the rest of their fellow citizens, they probably met in the early morning, late afternoon, or evening of that day. This practice may have begun initially to avoid conflicts with the synagogue since the earliest followers of Jesus

were Jews and were also observant of the Sabbath. The author(s) of the *Didache* (late first century A.D.) admonish the readers: "On the Lord's Day of the Lord, come together, break bread and hold Eucharist, after confessing your transgressions that your offering may be pure" (*Did.* 14:1, LCL). The contributions to the church appear always to have been voluntary and based on the ability to give (see also 2 Cor. 8:4-8). The practice of those who could do so helping the poor among them and also doing this on the first day of the week is reported in Justin Martyr's *First Apology*.

> And the wealthy among us help the needy; and we always keep together; and for all things wherewith we are supplied, we bless the Maker of all through His Son Jesus Christ, and through the Holy Ghost. And on the day called Sunday, all who live in cities or in the country gather together to one place and the memoirs of the apostles or the writings of the prophets are read . . . . (*1 Apol.* 67.1-2, ANF).

In 2 Cor. 8:9, Paul calls for a generous collection for the poor in Jerusalem and reminds his readers that Christ became poor for their sakes and he may also indicate that the church in Jerusalem likewise gave much. Paul seems to be following the admonition in Deut. 15:14 on caring for the poor as one is enabled to do. There was no prescribed amount that the people had to give, but they were to give as generously as they could to care for those in Jerusalem who were facing difficult times due to the famine that came to them. In 2 Cor. 8–9, as well as here, giving was in accordance with what one had rather than any particular amount (2 Cor. 8:12-14).

16:5-9. Paul's Travel Plans
16:5-6. But I shall come to you after I go through Macedonia, for I am going through Macedonia. For another reference to Paul's journey, see Acts 19:21. Here he goes into more

detail of the plans he has for going to Jerusalem and both how he plans to get there and how long he plans to stay with them en route.

16:7. For I do not wish to see you now just in passing; for I hope to remain with you for some time, if the Lord permits. It was common in the ancient world, including the biblical world, to add to one's plans, "If the Lord permits." This is similar to the James admonition to Christians to seek the will of God rather than simply declaring what we will do (James 4:13-15). Similarly, Plato tells of Socrates' correction of Alcibiades in this matter: "[After Socrates makes a request, Alcibiades says:] 'If it be your wish, Socrates.' [Socrates responds:] 'That is not well said, Alcibiades.' [Alcibiades then asks:] 'Well, what should I say?' [Socrates answers:] 'If it be God's will'" (*Alcibiades* 1.135D, LCL).

16:8. But I shall remain in Ephesus until Pentecost. Ephesus was the capital of the province of Asia in western Asia Minor (modern Turkey) and was located on a west coast harbor. It was a large city and also the place of some significant ministry for Paul (Acts 19). Pentecost (see discussion in Acts 2:1) was fifty days after the Passover and often called the Festival of Weeks. The fifty days was originally counted from the beginning of the harvest, but eventually was begun on the day of the Passover, so that it fell on a Sunday. It is clear from this passage that Paul wrote 1 Corinthians from Ephesus. This may have meant that he wanted to stay in Ephesus until the time of Pentecost, but wanted to make his way to celebrate it in Jerusalem (cf. Acts 20:16-17).

16:10-12. Words About Timothy and Apollos

Earlier Paul mentioned both Apollos and Timothy (1:12; 3:5-9; 4:6 and 4:17). What they both have in common here is that Paul hopes to send both to the Corinthian church, but Timothy is going to go, but not Apollos, at that time.

16:10-11. Now if Timothy comes, see that he is with you without cause to be afraid; for he is doing the Lord's work, as I also am. Let no one therefore despise him. But send him on his way in peace, so that he may come to me; for I expect him with the brethren. Christians often provided hospitality for those traveling through their communities and occasionally there was abuse of this by the traveler. As a result, letters of introduction were often given with an encouragement to help the traveler on his or her way. See for instance Paul's encouragement to welcome Phoebe in Rom. 16:1-2; the call to welcome Mark (Col. 4:10). There are other examples of Paul sending fellow workers to share with the churches (Eph. 6:21; Col. 4:7; see also the encouragement to welcome the stranger in 3 John 3-8, but with caution, cf. 2 John 7-11). The admonition to welcome fellow Christians is wellknown in the early church and it enabled fellow Christians to proclaim the Christian message far and wide throughout the empire. The author of the *Didache*, knowing of the tendency for some to abuse the hospitality offers guidelines on welcoming traveling guests.

> Let everyone who "comes in the Name of the Lord" be received; but when you have tested him you shall know him, for you shall have understanding of true and false. If he who comes is a traveler, help him as much as you can, but he shall not remain with you more than two days, or, if need be, three. And if he wishes to settle among you and has a craft, let him work for his bread. But if he has no craft provide for him according to your understanding, so that no man shall live among you in idleness because he is a Christian. But if he will not do so, he is making traffic of Christ; beware of such (*Did*.12:1-5, LCL).

B. 16:13-24. Conclusion of the Letter

As Paul concludes this letter, there are yet a few final admonitions and greetings as is typical of letters in the ancient world.

16:15. Now I urge you, brethren (you know the household of Stephanas, that they were the first fruits of Achaia, and that they have devoted themselves for ministry to the saints). For a discussion of first fruits, see 15:20. The word for "ministry" here is *diakonia* ("service"), and this may be an early indication of the use of the term for someone who has committed himself to the ministry or service of "saints" (see discussion in 1:2 on "saints"): namely, of the early names for those who hold an office in the church (Rom. 16:1). See also the focus on service for the Seven in Acts 6:1-7. Stephanus and his family were baptized by Paul (1:16). Fortunatus and Achaicus in v. 17 below accompany him to Ephesus to see Paul, and apart from having Roman names, which suggests that they were Roman colonists, nothing more is known of them in the New Testament.

16:20. All the brethren greet you. Greet one another with a holy kiss. The call to greet one another with a "holy kiss" is quite common in Paul's letters (Rom. 16:16; 1 Cor. 16:20; 2 Cor. 13:12; 1 Thess. 5:26, but cf. Col. 4:21). It is also encouraged in 1 Peter 5:14. The kiss became a sign of the fellowship of love that Christians belonged to as a result of their relationship with Christ. This became a regular part of Christian worship in many parts of the church later. There is nothing analogous to it in the Greco-Roman world and it probably had its origins in the church. Kissing in public was often ridiculed in Greco-Roman society and often led to accusations of sexual activity. When the woman "whose sins were many" kissed the feet of Jesus, even though it was intended as an act of reverence and devotion (Luke 7:36-50), those with him objected because he had his feet kissed publicly by a woman of low reputation. Oddly, in the *Gospel of Philip* we read that, "The perfect conceive through a kiss and give birth. Because of this we also kiss one another. We receive conception from the grace which we have among us" (*Gosp. Phil.* 31, *NT Apo* 1:192). Later in the same gospel, the Savior [Jesus] gave Mary Magdalene a kiss on the lips and the disciples were offended by it (*Gosp. Phil.* 55a). Epictetus asks: "Were you ever commanded by your sweetheart to do something you didn't wish to do? Did you never cozen your pet slave? Did you never kiss his feet? Yet if someone should compel you to kiss the feet of Caesar, you would regard that as insolence and most extravagant tyranny. What else, then, is slavery?" (*Discourses* 4.1.15-16, LCL). The kiss in the early church, and certainly in Paul, has to do with a greeting. This would normally take place in their gatherings for worship and appear to stress the importance of Christians loving and caring for one another in the highest ideals of the Christian faith. It is a recognition that the barriers between individuals have been destroyed (Gal. 3:28), and that the unity in the family of Christ is complete.

16:21. The greeting is in my own hand — Paul. Paul often used a secretary to write his letters (Rom. 16:22), which may have been the case here as well, but at the conclusion of the letter, Paul offers his own greeting in his own hand. See Gal. 6:11.

16:22. If anyone does not love the Lord, let him be accursed. Maranatha. This is a highly significant verse in that it uses two rather strange words for Paul and probably pre-date him. In other words, they are words that he has introduced here as a part of that tradition that he has received. In the first instance, this is the only time that Paul uses the Greek word *phileo* ("love") instead of the more popular, and in Paul's case, more usual word *agapao* ("love"). Commentators have tried to make a distinction between the two terms in the past, but that does not bear out in their usage in the New Testament writings. They are used synonymously or interchangeably in the Gospels of Matthew and John. What the single use of *phileo* in this passage indicates, instead of the term *agapao* that Paul otherwise uses throughout his letters, is that he probably received this slogan from the church and passed it along here. Observe how he uses the noun form of *agapao* in v. 24 below "my love [*agape*] is with you all in Christ Jesus."

The second important word is *Maranatha*. This is an Aramaic word and, depending on how it is divided (*maran atha* or *marana tha*), means either "Our Lord come!" or "Our Lord has come!" Commentators do not generally agree which it is, but it is probably the former since this best fits with Paul's eschatology. The author of the Didache (late first century A.D.) concludes his admonition about how to offer prayers for the Eucharist with the following: "If any man be holy, let him come! If any man be not, let him repent: *Maran atha*, Amen" (*Did.* 10.6, LCL). In 11:26 above, Paul says that the celebration of the Lord's Supper proclaims his death "until he comes." Likewise, in Rev. 22:20, the concluding prayer "Come Lord Jesus!" is a translation equivalent of the same prayer in 16:22 here. Because of its language: namely, a transliterated Aramaic word, it is nevertheless clear that the word is an important term from Palestine that was popular among Christians and conveyed their confidence in the coming of Christ for them (1 Thess. 2:19; 3:13; 4:13-17; 5:2-11). In the second century, the "kiss of peace" was a part of the Eucharist celebration. Justin Martyr tells of the usual practice following the baptism of one who has come to accept Christian teachings:

> But we, after we have thus washed him who has been convinced and has assented to our teaching, bring him to the place where those who are called brethren are assembled, in order that we may offer hearty prayers in common for ourselves and for the baptized [illuminated] person, and for all others in every place, that we may be counted worthy, now that we have learned the truth, by our works also to be found good citizens and keepers of the commandments, so that we may be saved with an everlasting salvation. Having ended the prayers, we salute one another with a kiss (*1 Apology* 65.1-2, ANF).

Eventually the Western church passed regulations to prevent abuse of the practice.

Introduction to 2 Corinthians

Lee Martin McDonald

Although scholars continue to debate the integrity of the second canonical letter that Paul wrote to the Corinthians, that is, there is considerable question over the unity of the letter, there is nevertheless little serious doubt about the authorship of 2 Corinthians. Paul wrote it, probably from Philippi in Macedonia, though perhaps from Ephesus (2:12-13; 7:5; 8:1-6; 9:2-4). That is the overwhelming consensus of biblical scholarship. It is also generally conceded that this is Paul's most intensely personal letter in which his heart, affections, and emotions are more revealed than in any of his other letters. On the other hand, the occasion for writing the letter, its date, the opponents that Paul addresses in this correspondence, especially in chaps. 10-13 (e.g., were they Judaizers, Hellenistic Jews, early gnostics, who were they?), and the unity of the letter, namely whether it was a composite of two or more letters, are all questions that continue to be debated among scholars. Remarkably, there is little doubt among them about the authorship of the various parts of the letter with the exception of 6:14-7:1. See discussion below.

The immediate context for the writing of this letter is the crises that Paul had faced in Ephesus (1:8) and also his journey to Troas and Macedonia from there (2:12-13; 7:5; 8:1). In the second of the Corinthians letters, Paul seeks to address several important issues including a reaffirmation of his love and care for the Corinthian believers (chaps. 1–7), his desire to collect funds from them to support the Christians in Jerusalem (chaps. 8–9), and his answer to those who were questioning his apostleship and leadership among the Corinthians (chaps. 10–13). The following introduction is intended to offer a pathway through some of the difficult critical questions. For the relationship between this letter and 1 Corinthians, see the introductory discussion of 1 Corinthians above.

I. THE UNITY OF 2 CORINTHIANS

While a few biblical scholars continue to advocate the unity of 2 Corinthians and present arguments for its logical flow, without doubt, the majority of scholars argue that 2 Corinthians is a composite letter. Minimally the last four chapters do not fit with the tone of the first nine chapters. It would not be appropriate for Paul to ask for these Christians at Corinth to give sacrificially in chaps. 8–9, and then speak so harshly in chaps. 10–13. What gives credibility to that argument is that there is a significant change in persons from 1–9 to 10–13. More specifically, there is a decided shift from the inclusive language of "we" in 1–9, to a mostly singular ("I") focus of argumentation in 10–13. In fact, in 10:1, he states emphatically "I myself appeal to you" suggesting that the setting is different than in chaps. 1–9. Paul uses rather freely "we" some 108 times in 2 Corinthians, but it is remarkably infrequent in the most severe part of the last four chapters, especially in Paul's defense in 11:1 to 12:13. Pauline authorship of the letter is not seriously questioned, but whether Paul could have written the two parts in the same general setting, or in the same letter, is. The unity issue of 2 Corinthians revolves around several significant passages that seem to change the tone and smooth flow of the letter. For example, if one were to skip from 6:13 to 7:2, there would be no argument would be more coherent and would not have an unusual interruption in the midst of an otherwise clearly stated argument. Likewise, after the two chapters in which he asks money from the Corinthians to care for the Christians in Jerusalem, the tone changes from that of joy and praise for the Christians at Corinth to one of judgment and conflict. This could be accounted for on the basis of bad news arriving from Corinth while Paul was constructing this letter, so he quickly and angrily added his rebuttal to objections about him. While this is possible, not many commentators are impressed by it. No one questions, however, the change in tone of the letter and the questionable place of an attack on his enemies immediately after he made an appeal to the Corinthians for financial aid for the Christians in Jerusalem. Because the letter is a rather lengthy one, it is not likely that it was all written on the same day or within a short period of time, but that does not completely answer the question of the composite nature of the correspondence. We will look at the sections in question that call for such speculations.

A. 2 Cor. 6:14–7:1.

The first of these problems has to do with this short passage. There are three issues: (1) the abrupt change in tone from 6:13 to 6:14; (2) 6:13 seems to be a suitable introduction to 7:2. When 6:14–7:1 is removed, it improves the flow of the

argument of the letter; and (3) the subject matter and style of this brief passage appear to be inconsistent with the rest of the Corinthian correspondence. For example, 1 Cor. 5:9 says that one is "not to associate with sexually immoral people," but 6:14–7:1 deals with what some have characterized as the relations of believers and unbelievers; and 2 Corinthians (5:18–21) is a letter of reconciliation. It is therefore argued that 2 Cor. 6:14–7:1 seems too exclusive to be from Paul and is more like the community at Qumran.

The first solution to this problem suggested by some is that this small section is a part of the first letter Paul wrote to the Corinthians (see 1 Cor. 5:9) which is now lost and it was inserted here by the ones who edited Paul's letters shortly after his death (or even by Paul himself) so that they could be more easily circulated in the churches. It is possible, according to this view, that Paul's strong language regarding dissociation was misunderstood and interpreted to mean that there should be absolutely no contact whatsoever with unbelievers. Perhaps 1 Cor. 5:10–11 shows Paul clarifying his original statement, hence his correction that believers are not "to associate with sexually immoral people."

Some scholars argue on the contrary that the shift in tone from 6:13 to 6:14 is not as severe as others have suggested, especially if the language is seen in terms of establishing degrees of relationship. For example, in 6:1-13, Paul makes common cause with the Corinthians that, as fellow workers, there is nothing he has done to discredit the ministry. After recounting a number of trials and triumphs, he urges them that, as he has been open to the Corinthians and generous in his affection toward them, they too are to be open and generous in theirs. In 6:14–7:1, however, Paul addresses the relations of Christians and non-Christians, stating that they should not be yoked, using a term for being joined as animals are joined to pull a plow. He supports this by several quotations of the Old Testament (Lev. 26:12; Isa. 52:11; 2 Sam. 7:14; Hos. 1:10), all of which support the idea of God's people being separate from everything incompatible with his holiness. Second, composition over a space of time might well account for the shift in tone, even if gradual. Finally, why would this "first letter" (if it was a part of Paul's first letter to the Corinthians) have been inserted at this place in the fourth letter? The textual tradition of this letter does not help explain its current location, but that could mean that the decisions were made early in the church when copiers were more free in making changes to the letters than at a later time when they were viewed as Scripture and multiple copies were made to aid churches in their ministries. That this section was a fragment of the first letter by Paul to the Corinthians is not widely held today, but some continue to argue that it was an insertion into the normal flow of the letter and was not an original part of it.

Some contend that this passage is not an inauthentic Pauline fragment, but rather comes from Qumran, or some Essene community, and that it was placed here either by Paul or a later editor. The reasons for this include: (1) nine terms are found in this passage that are found nowhere else in Paul ("Unequally yoked" (*heterodzugountes*), "share" (*metoche*), "harmony" (*sumphonesis*), "Beliar," "agreement" (*sungkatathesis*), "walk" (*emperipateo*), "receive" (*eisdechomai*), "almighty" (*pantokrator*), and "defilement" (*molusmos*); (2) the extreme exclusiveness is out of character for Paul who himself associated with unbelievers and preached his Gospel to them; (3) there are similarities of thought in the passage to the Qumran community, such as its dualism and emphasis upon the temple; and finally, (4) the words "flesh" and "spirit" are not used this way elsewhere in Paul's letters. For these reasons, some have concluded that the passage 6:14–7:1 is non-Pauline, and that it may well have come from an earlier or contemporary Jewish community

that reflected typical Jewish separation from Gentiles and also an emphasis upon the temple, such as that found with the Qumran covenanters.

On the other hand, many of the terms found in this "fragment" have cognates in Paul's other letters (e.g. *metocheµ* is not found, but *metechoµ*, the verb for "share," is). Also, 2 Cor. 6:3-10 also has several unique words in it, but this passage is not suspected as being non-Pauline. Likewise, Pauline "outbursts" often have unique words in them (e.g. 1 Cor. 4:7-13 which has six unique words, and 2 Cor. 6:3-10 has four unique words). Also, some commentators argue that the Old Testament quotations in this passage are largely responsible for the exclusive focus of the passage, not the Pauline material. Finally, some scholars argue that this supposed fragment is not at odds with established Pauline thought. In fact, many of the ideas are found not only at Qumran but in other circles as well (e.g. Greek dualism).

A third proposal claims that this passage may have been pre-formed or borrowed in some way by Paul who incorporated it into his account. This view attempts to accommodate the obvious difficulty in harmonizing its contents with what is typical of Paul in his other letters. Likewise, some have seen a difficulty regarding the change of tone, style, and content of the passage, while at the same time retaining the integrity of its Pauline composition. Indeed, if one read from 6:13 and immediately went to 7:2, there would appear to be little difficulty in the transition from one text to the other. If this is so, it may be that 6:14–7:1 was incorporated very early, before the extant texts were copied, but this is difficult to prove without any supporting evidence. On the other hand, while there may be shift in tone or content, the passage can fit its context. If the subject of this section is the nature and degree of Christian relations, this section fits well in its location since 6:1-13 describes Paul and the Corinthians as fellow workers emphasizing their common cause and mutual openness, but for Paul this openness does not imply compromise (6:14–7:1). Rather the passage is predicated upon not taking advantage of each other (7:2–16). If Paul has used a pre-formed or pre-written section, he has incorporated it in a way that made it his own. See further discussion of the notion that 6:14–7:1 is a separate text introduced into Paul's writing at the beginning of the commentary on that section below.

B. 2 Corinthians 10–13.

There are essentially five problems normally associated with 2 Cor. 10–13: (a) chaps. 1–9 are full of praise for the Corinthian believers, but chaps. 10–13 are characterized by condemnation, making it difficult to see how these two portions of the letter fit together in one integral composition. (b) The vocabulary regarding boasting and commendation is used differently in the two major portions of the letter, implying that the letter is not a unity, but is rather a composition of at least two letters. The problem is seen most clearly in how a common word for boasting (kauchaomai) is used positively in chaps. 1–9, but negatively in chaps. 10–13. For example, in 5:12 commendation is made, while in 10:13 Paul says that he will not boast. (c) Scholars have noted a number of passages in chaps. 10–13 that appear to be forward looking, while chaps. 1–9 appear to be looking backwards. Passages to notice in this regard are 10:2 and 8:2 with regard to confidence, 10:6 and 2:9 on obedience, 12:16 and 4:2 concerning trickery, 12:17 and 7:2 on fraud, 13:2 and 1:23 on sparing the Corinthians, and 13:10 and 2:3 with regard to travel. It has been observed on the basis of this evidence that chaps. 1–9 seem to be looking back at a situation that is now resolved, while chaps. 10–13 seem to be looking forward to resolution. (d) To the minds of many scholars, there appears to be a set of contradictions between chaps. 1–9 and 10–13. For example, in 1:24 Paul apparently sees the Corinthians as being "in the faith," while in 13:5 he admonishes them to see if they are "in the faith." Furthermore, in 7:16 he expresses confidence in them, while in 12:20–21 he is afraid of them. These attitudes seem to reflect a different set of circumstances at Corinth. (e) According to some scholars, Paul's reference to wanting to preach "beyond" Corinth (10:16) makes sense as referring to Rome and Spain if chaps. 10–13 were written from Ephesus as the third Corinthian letter, but not from Macedonia as part of the fourth letter, since the trajectory from Macedonia to Corinth would reach across the Mediterranean to Africa.

Many attempts have been made to resolve the apparent conflict between 2 Cor. 1–9 and 10–13, and they can be divided into two possibilities, namely that either the two sections of this letter represent separate documents or they are part of the same document. In regard to the first of these possibilities, it is often argued by scholars that 2 Cor. 10–13 was written and sent separately from chaps. 1–9 and that this portion of 2 Corinthians (10-13) constitutes the "severe" letter that Paul sent to the Corinthian Christians (2:4) soon after his disastrous visit to them. This could make sense of the change in the general tone of the two parts of the letter (chaps. 1–9 and 10–13). In this case, as the argument goes, chaps. 1–9 reflects a later resolution in which Paul now knows that the problems have been resolved and he now has confidence in them. It is quite possible that 1–9 and 10–13 were written separately and 10–13 came shortly after 1–9, but most interpreters to do not give much weight to that argument. Some scholars contend that the shift in tone in these two sections may not be as clear or severe as is sometimes thought. Chaps. 1–9 reflect some uncertainty on the matter of conflict in the church (e.g. 2:6, 17–18; 4:2–5; 5:11–13), even if the tone here is more conciliatory than in 10–13. This suggests that, even if the majority of Christians in the church at Corinth were convinced by Paul's argument, a minority remained that needed to be won over to Paul.

Similarly, chaps. 10–13 do not categorically reflect complete opposition to Paul, but only that some opposition to his authority was present in the church (e.g. 10:2, 7, 11–12; 11:5, 12–13, 18, 20; 12:11, 21; 13:2). Furthermore, the internal references within chaps. 1–9 and chaps. 10–13 may not necessarily be reflecting a relationship only between these two parts of the letter. This suggests that the word that Paul received from Titus regarding the Corinthian situation was that there had been a positive response to Paul, but that it was not complete, especially if a new group of outsiders had recently arrived (see below). It is possible that after the good news that had come to Paul, as reflected in 7:2-16, but between the writing of that part of the letter, along with chaps. 8–9, there was additional news from Corinth that was threatening Paul's ministry there. Consequently, Paul's comments in 2 Cor. 1–13 might well reflect an appreciation for what had been done (chaps. 1–9) with a hoped-for further response (chaps. 10–13). Again, this is a minority view, but whatever the position taken here, all agree that Paul wrote both sections of the letter and with such a great length, that he probably did not pen the whole document at one setting. A change of tone could have emerged at a later setting for writing this letter and he concluded it with his most passionate comments in 10–13.

C. 2 Corinthians 8 and 9.

These two chapters seem to be able to stand on their own as an appeal by Paul to the Corinthian Christians to give generously to the Christians in Jerusalem who were suffering from a famine. At first glance, they appear to be able to stand alone, and some argue that chap. 8 could stand separately from chap. 9 because of the overlap in them. The usual arguments for their independence include: (1) 9:1 has a connective phrase that separates it from chap. 8 and indicates the possibility of a new letter; (2) chaps. 8 and 9 duplicate information regarding the collection, emissaries, etc.; (3) 8:1–5 and

9:1–2 seem to be addressed to different groups, both out of character with the audience in chap. 7; (4) different purposes for those Paul is sending are given in chaps. 8 and 9—comments remarkably lacking from chap. 7; and (5) there are contradictions in details from chap. 8 to chap. 9. For example, introducing the collection in 9:1 appears superfluous since he has already been discussing it (8:1-5).

On the other hand, one need not emphasize the duplication between the two chapters since this may only be a result of Paul's passion for the offering and the relations that he hopes to establish between the Gentiles and the Jews through it. Using Macedonia as a model for the Greeks in 8:1-5 and the Corinthians as a model in 9:2 appears at first glance to be contradictory, but Paul commends the Macedonians to the Corinthians in chap. 8, and he uses the Macedonians as a witness to what the Corinthians should be doing in chap. 9. Likewise, the reference to Paul sending persons to accompany the gift in 9:3-5 is specified in 8:16-24, with the one clarifying the other. There is no need to separate either chaps. 8 or 9 or both from 2 Cor. 1-7, since the connections of chap. 8 with chaps. 1-7 are strong, and some of the information in chap. 9, such as the identity of the "brothers" (9:3, 5), seems to require chap. 8, thus arguing strongly for the unity of the chapters.

The "disunity" of the letter may not be as obvious as was first believed, but regardless of which conclusion one draws, the authorship of the contents of the whole letter is not in question. It is Paul's. The unity question, however, is not an easy one.

II. Occasion and Purpose

If the occasion that prompted Paul's writing the first two letters to the Corinthians (the earliest one noted in 5:9 and 1 Corinthians itself) was the fragmentation of the church, it appears in 2 Cor. 1–9 that the disunity has been largely overcome, and 10–13 suggests that only some of the Corinthians were at odds with Paul and these may have been a new group either from Jerusalem or other traveling Jewish Christian evangelists, perhaps from Jerusalem, who were personally attacking Paul (11:5, 13, 23; 12:11), questioning his apostolic authority in a potentially persuasive way. What was the nature of their attack? Paul vigorously opposes them, and it appears that chaps. 10–13 and perhaps also other correspondence dealt sufficiently with the problem so that Paul could consider the threat as having been dealt with (chaps. 1–9). This reinforces the view that Paul's opponents in Corinth were a minority who were finally rejected by the church at Corinth.

A. Personal Attacks Against Paul.

The nature of the attack against Paul included an accusation of his instability, as evidenced by a change of plans and vacillation (1:15-18), a lack of clarity on his part as to what he meant (1:13-14), a lack of effectiveness (10:10), his being a tyrant (10:8), his abandoning the Corinthians (2:1; 13:2), his gospel not being clear (4:3), and his speech being pitiful (10:11; 11:6), which probably suggests that he was not as well trained in rhetoric as some of them may have been. Concerning his claim to being a representative of Christ, or an apostle, Paul was also apparently denigrated (see also 1 Cor. 9:1-27) because: he had no formal letters of recommendation, as perhaps did other itinerant preachers and teachers (3:1; 4:2); his claims regarding belonging to Christ were apparently seen as unsupported, perhaps because he had not actually seen Christ in the flesh (10:7); he arrived in Corinth without a clear mandate (10:13-14); and he was said to be inferior to the "super apostles." These were probably those who claimed authority from the church at Jerusalem (11:5; 12:11), a position that Paul himself may well have indirectly endorsed because of refusal of support by the Corinthian congregation (11:7-9).

All of this may well have indicated to some that Paul was not even to be considered an apostle (12:12, 14) and that Christ was not speaking through him (13:3). More than this, Paul may well have been accused of having a deleterious effect upon the congregation, because his behavior seemed to be offensive, including praising himself (3:1, 5; 4:5; 5:11-15; 6:3-5; 10:2, 8; 11:16-18; 12:1, 11). It was perhaps said that he was working duplicitously for gain (7:1; 12:17-18) even by using the collection (8:20-21), that he was a coward (1:23; 8:2; 10:1, 10; 11:32-33), and that he ended up harming the Christian community by abandoning the Corinthians (2:1; 13:2) and exploiting the situation for his own benefit (7:2; 12:16).

B. Minority Accusations.

To Paul's mind, at least as reflected in 2 Corinthians, the kinds of attacks made against him seem to have originated with a minority of people connected with the Christian community in Corinth, and quite possibly with Jewish Christians from Jerusalem (Gal. 2:11-14). Paul had to find a suitable tone in the letter and make his perspective clear. For example, he says that they were a minority (2:6; 10:2), who were paid, implying that they, as opposed to Paul, readily accepted financial compensation (2:17; 11:20), something he believed that he was entitled to, even if he did not use it (1 Cor. 9:3-11). They also gained entrance into the church by letters of recommendation and self-commendation (3:1; 10:12, 18) that Paul did not have. They apparently did not hesitate to boast of their own excellence (5:12; 11:12, 18), to emphasize ecstatic experience that Paul counters with his own (5:13; 12:1-6), and overtly to claim both the apostolic office (11:5, 13; 12:11) and superiority to Moses (3:4-11), but without making known their own Jewish heritage (11:22). In response to such claims, Paul says that they in fact were preaching another gospel (11:4), had encroached on others' missionary territory (10:15-16), were immoral (12:21; 13:2), were boastful (10:12-13), and were led by a particular person (2:5; 7:12; 11:4). The result, to Paul's mind at least, was that they were Satan's servants (11:13-15). By contrast, Paul regarded himself as an apostle (1:1), and the proof of this lay in the Corinthians themselves (3:2-3), among whom he had done mighty things (12:12), reflecting his appointment from God (3:5, 6; 4:7).

It may be possible to characterize these false preachers more definitively, since some scholars have characterized them as Judaizers (Gal. 1:6-9), on the basis of their emphasis upon their Jewish heritage (3:4-7; 11:22). It may also be that the opponents are "gnostics" since they focused on ecstatic experiences, and these were some of the later gnostic tendencies, especially in terms of their taking pride in their having "true knowledge," but a fully developed Christian gnosticism is not likely at this early date. The opponents probably were well-educated and articulate individuals. There is merit for this suggestion, especially in light of 1 Corinthians 1:12, 18-31; 2:1-5, but that is not clear. Paul was more conciliatory in 1 Corinthians, but more confrontational in 2 Cor. 10–13 because the situation had deteriorated in the time between the two letters. It is likely that a group of "false preachers" who opposed Paul originated in Palestine, quite possibly as emissaries (whether legitimate or renegade) of the Jerusalem leaders or "super apostles," or they may have been itinerant preachers who claimed to have been with Jesus. This is not to say that the Jerusalem leaders necessarily were directly opposing Paul at Corinth, but one must not dismiss the degree of suspicion that apparently existed between the Jerusalem Jewish Christians and Paul's missionary efforts (see Acts 15:1-5 and 21:20-21). Quite possibly, the term "super apostles" (11:5) may refer to the leaders in Jerusalem, with those in Corinth claiming the authority of the Jerusalem church, whether they actually had it or not.

In terms of the specific identity of these opponents, the following can be gleaned from Paul's correspondence, namely: (1) they are Jewish (11:22) and yet they do not call upon these Christians to keep the Law of Moses as was the case in the situation in Galatia (Gal. 2:21;

3:10-14; 4:8-11; 5:2-6, 18; 6:12-14). (2) They claim to follow Christ (11:23). (3) They claim the title of apostle (11:5, 13; 12:11). (4) They boast constantly (10:12-17; 11:16-12:11). (5) They oppress and take advantage of others (11:20). (6) They take money from the Corinthians (11:7-15, 20; 12:14-15). (7) They display good oratorical skills and criticize Paul for his (11:5-6). The combination of all of these characteristics suggests that these were Hellenistic Jews who were not insisting on the Corinthians' keeping the Law, but rather were seeking an advantage over the Corinthian Christians, and they rejected Paul's ministry, especially his inability to speak as well as they and also his failure to take financial assistance from them as apostles were expected to do. Paul does not attack their theology or doctrine, but rather their conduct in taking advantage of the Corinthian believers and their arrogance as was typical of the sophists. They appear to have proclaimed a Christ who was humble and self-sacrificing, but they themselves were arrogant, rude, self-promoting, and oppressive. His opponents' specific identity may never be fully known, but the above factors are no doubt key factors in their identity.

In response to them, however, Paul asserts his equal standing and authority with any other apostles, including those in Jerusalem. Anyone who says otherwise is a false apostle (2 Cor. 11:5, 12-15).

III. Date

Most commentators agree that this correspondence, at least chaps. 1–9 of it, were written between A.D. 55-57. Chaps. 10–13 probably came slightly later and were eventually either attached to chaps. 1–9 following the death of Paul when his writings began to be collected and circulated in his churches or they were a part of chaps. 1–9 from the beginning with some delay between the time when Paul concluded the first part and then concluded with the final four chapters when word came to him that called for a strong response.

IV. Outline of 2 Corinthians

A. Introduction of Letter (1:1-2)

B. Blessing (1:3-7)

C. Body—Assurances, Instructions, Offerings (1:12–9:15)

1. Formal Body/Opening (1:8-11)

2. Paul's Change of Plans and Special Concerns (1:12–2:13)

   a. Introduction of His Concerns (1:12-14)

   b. Answer Charge of Vacillation (1:15–2:2)

   c. Paul's Tearful Letter (2:3-11)

   d. Paul's Trip to Macedonia (2:12-13)

3. Paul's Apostolic Ministry (2:14–5:21)

   a. Triumphal Progress of Gospel (2:14-17)

   b. Ministry of New Covenant (3:1–4:6)

   c. Ministry/Life Beyond Death (4:7–5:10)

   d. Ministry of Reconciliation (5:11-21)

4. Paul's Appeal for Reconciliation with God (6:1–7:16)

   Parenthesis: Christians and Non-Christians (6:14–7:1)

5. A Collection for Jerusalem Christians (8:1–9:15)

   a. Corinthian Generosity (8:1–9:5)

   b. Generosity Encouraged (9:6–15)

D. Vindication of Paul's Authority (10:1–13:10)

1. Paul's Personal Appeal Regarding His Apostolic Authority (10:1–12:10)

   a. True Apostleship (10:1-18)

   b. A "Fool's Speech" (11:1–12:13)

2. Notice of an Impending Visit (12:14–13:10)

E. Closing (13:11-14)

1. Call to Unity and Summary (13:11)

2. Greetings (13:12-13)

3. Benediction (13:14)

BIBLIOGRAPHY

Barnett, Paul, *The Second Epistle to the Corinthians*. The New International Commentary on the New Testament. N.B. Stonehouse, F. F. Bruce, and Gordon Fee, eds. Grand Rapids, MI/Cambridge, UK: Eerdmans, 1997.

Betz, Hans Dieter, *2 Corinthians 8 and 9: A Commentary on Two Administrative Letters of the Apostle Paul*. Hermenia. G. W. MacRae, ed. Philadelphia: Fortress Press, 1985.

Danker, Frederick W., *II Corinthians*. Augsburg Commentary on the New Testament. Minneapolis, MN: Augsburg Publishing House, 1989.

Furnish, Victor P., *II Corinthians: A New Translation with Introduction and Commentary*. The Anchor Bible. Editors: F. W. Albright and D. N. Freedman, London, New York, Toronto: Doubleday, 1984.

Goulder, Michael D., *Paul and the Competing Mission in Corinth*. Library of Pauline Studies. Peabody, MA: Hendrickson, 2001.

Grant, Robert M., *Paul in the Roman World: The Conflict at Corinth*. Louisville: Westminster/John Knox, 2001.

Hubbard, Moyer V., *2 Corinthians*. Vol. 3. Zondervan Illustrated Bible Background Commentary. C.E. Arnold, gen. ed. Grand Rapids, MI: Zondervan, 2002.

Lambrecht, Jan, *Second Corinthians*. Sacra Pagina, vol. 8. D. J. Harrington, ed. Collegeville, MN: Liturgical Press, 1999.

Martin, Ralph P., *2 Corinthians*. Word Biblical Commentary, vol. 40. D. A. Hubbard and G. W. Barker, Gen. Eds. Waco, TX: Word, 1986.

Murphy-O'Connor, Jerome, *St. Paul's Corinth: Texts and Archaeology*. Good New Studies 6. Wilmington, DE: Michael Glazier, 1983.

Plummer, Alfred, *A Critical and Exegetical Commentary on the Second Epistle of St. Paul to the Corinthians*. The International Critical Commentary, 1915.

Reicke, Bo, *Re-examining Paul's Letters: The History of the Pauline Correspondence*. eds. D. P. Moessner and I. Reicke, Harrisburg, PA: Trinity Press International, 2001.

Sampley, J. Paul, *The Second Letter to the Corinthians*. The New Interpreter's Bible, Vol XI. L. E. Keck, gen. ed. Nashville: Abingdon, 2000 (pp. 3-180).

Thrall, Margaret E., *A Critical and Exegetical Commentary on The Second Epistle to the Corinthians*. 2 Vols. J. A. Emberton, C.E.B. Cranfield, and G. N. Stanton, eds. Edinburgh: T & T Clark, 2000.

2 Corinthians

Lee Martin McDonald

A. 1:1-2. Introduction. The opening of this letter is similar to other Greco-Roman correspondence at this time, including the traditional listing of the writer(s), the addressee(s), and a greeting or blessing. For example, in a letter dating from 260-250 B.C., we see all three parts of the opening and typical conclusion of a letter.

> Dromon to Zenon greeting. I give thanks to all the gods if you are in good health yourself and everything else has been satisfactory. I too am well, and in accordance with what you wrote to me I am taking the utmost care that no one troubles your people. When you are ready to sail up in good health, order one of your people to buy a cotyla [a cup or small container] of Attic honey; for I require it for my eyes by order of the god. Farewell (*Select Papyri, Private Affairs* 1.92. LCL).

In more desperate conditions, the usual formalities of a letter were often abbreviated or omitted, and even reversed. For example from the third century A.D. comes the following:

> To Stephanus from Hephaestion. On receipt of the letter of my son Theon put off everything and come at once to the homestead because of what has happened to me. If you take no heed, as the gods have not spared me, so I will not spare the gods. Goodbye (Select Papyri, Private Affairs 1.138. LCL).

Paul likewise omitted the usual thanksgiving in his Galatian correspondence because the circumstances were desperate (see Gal. 1:6-7).

1:1. Paul, an apostle of Christ Jesus by the will of God, and Timothy our brother, to the church of God which is at Corinth with all the saints who are throughout Achaia. Paul only identifies himself one more time and that is at the beginning of the second major part of his letter. The second time he does not include Timothy as a partner in his discussion. He uses his typical identification, an "apostle of Jesus Christ" but adds "by the will of God" no doubt to underscore his authority and perhaps also to distinguish himself from those who received such recognition at the hands or authority of others (see Gal. 1:1), and to claim that his authority came directly from God. The most commonly cited Pauline texts that discuss his apostleship are Rom. 1:1-6; 1 Cor. 9:1-27; 15:7-11; and Gal. 1:1–2:10. It was important for Paul to defend his leadership and divine calling among those he had been called to serve and against those who called his leadership into question. This defense becomes most intense in 11:1–12:13.

The reference to **Timothy** as a "co-sender" of the letter does not necessarily mean that he helped in its writing, but probably only that he was with Paul when he was writing and that Paul utilized information that he shared about the church in Corinth. He is also listed as a co-sender of other Pauline letters (Phil. 1:1; Col. 1:1; 1 Thess. 1:1; 2 Thess. 1:1; Phile. 1). Only Sosthenes and Silvanus are also mentioned as "co-senders" with Paul in his other letters (1 Cor. 1:1 and 1 Thess. 1:1). Paul's reference to him as our **"brother"** is very important for Paul since this is the term used of those who are fellow believers and who share in the same spiritual blessings from God (see Rom. 14:10, 13, 15, 21; 1 Cor. 5:11; 6:5-6; 7:12-15; 8:11, 13; 1 Thess. 4:6). The plural of this, "brothers" or "brethren" (this is always generic and inclusive of male and female believers) is likewise found throughout Paul's letters (see e.g., 1 Cor. 1:10, 11, 26; 2:1; 2 Cor. 1:8; 8:1, etc.). Most of these references in the plural are found in Romans, 1 and 2 Corinthians, Galatians, Philippians, and 1 Thessalonians. Timothy is referred to as a "brother" elsewhere in 1 Thess. 3:2 and Phile. 1. Timothy came to faith through Paul (1 Cor. 4:17) and Paul used him as a trusted companion in carrying out his mission in a variety of services (1 Cor. 16:10; Rom. 16:21; Phil. 1:1; 2:19; Col. 1:1; 1 Thess. 1:1; 3:2, 6; 2 Thess. 1:1; Phile. 1; 1 Tim. 1:2, 18; 6:20; see also Acts 16:1; 17:14, 15; 18:5; 19:22; 20:4; Heb. 13:23).

To the church of God which is at Corinth with all the saints who are throughout Achaia. For a more complete discussion of "church" (Greek = *ekklesia* = "assembly") in Paul's writings, see 1 Cor. 1:2 above. The term used to translate "church" is ecclesia and essentially refers to an assembly. There is nothing particularly Christian about the word, but it was used by the Christians with the clarification "of God" to identify those who gathered together in the name of Jesus Christ for worship, fellowship, instruction, and mission. While the term may have been selected by some in the Christian community to distinguish it from the more common term among the Jews for their gatherings, "synagogue" (Greek = *sunagoge* = "gathering" or "assembly" and transliterated as "synagogue"), it was probably chosen with more thought behind it

than that. Paul was quite familiar with the Greek translation of the Hebrew Scriptures, the Septuagint (commonly referred to as the "LXX"), and the term *ekklesia* is often used there for the people of God. In Judges 20:2, for instance, we see "all the tribes of Israel stood before the Lord in the assembly (*ekklesia*) of the people of God." Likewise,

Saints. Paul's use of "saints" (Greek = *hagios*) to refer to Christians stems from its use in the LXX to refer to the people of God. It translates the Hebrew *qdsh* and refers to those who have separated themselves from evil ways unto God to do the will of God (see Dan. 7:18, 21, 25, 27). See 1 Cor. 6:11, but also discussion in 1:2.

Achaia. The province of Achaia, named by Homer after Achilles' men and Agamemnon's followers, is mentioned elsewhere in Rom. 15:26; 1 Cor. 16:15; Acts 18:12, 27; 19:21. It is difficult to know precisely what Paul meant by his reference to this region since the boundaries or the limits of the province in the New Testament are imprecise. For Paul, it probably included the Peloponnese to the south of Corinth and the adjoining regions that included Epirus to the northwest of Corinth and perhaps even Thessaly northeast of Macedonia. On two occasions before the Romans conquered this region in 146 B.C., Achaia was generally synonymous with all of Greece and was its head. In the first century, Achaia included Athens and more sixty miles to the north of that city. In antiquity it was also called Ionia before the Achaeans came. Corinth, as the capitol of Achaia, was a thriving metropolis of some 100,000 residents, a large city by ancient standards. What is problematic is that Paul identifies the household of Stephanus from Corinth as the "first-fruits" of Achaia (1 Cor. 16:15), that is, the first to become

Christians, but Luke reports that there were converts in Athens as a result of Paul's ministry there (Acts 17:32-34) and before he came to Corinth. It appears that Paul referred to the province of Achaia as a smaller entity and more restricted to Corinth and both south and west. It is not clear how many other cities heard and received the Gospel in Achaia, but Paul had a favorable response from some who heard his message in Athens (Acts 17:34) and there was a church at Cenchrea (Rom. 16:1; Acts 18:18). Later it is reported that there was a Christian community west of Corinth at Patras (Greek = *Patrai*) on the Corinthian gulf. According to Jerome, Andrew, one of the Twelve Apostles, was martyred in Patras and later his bones were transferred to Constantinople (*De Vir. Il. 7*).

1:2. Grace to you and peace from God our Father and the Lord Jesus Christ. See discussion of "grace and peace" in 1 Cor. 1:3 above. Paul's reference to the "Lord Jesus Christ" as a name and reflecting the titles of Lord and Christ manifestly show his high regard for Jesus and how Jesus is understood in divine terms. The LXX translates the name of God, Yahweh, with the Greek *kurios* ("Lord") more than 6100 times in the Old Testament. While some scholars believe that when this title is used in reference to Jesus in the Gospels, this could be no more than a simple polite reference such as "sir." While it is true that the vocative form of *kurios*, namely *kurie*, is used in this fashion quite frequently (John 12:21), but this form is also used in reference to Yahweh in the Old and New Testaments (John 12:38 cf. Isa. 53:1). Clearly *kurios* has more important christological connotations in Paul but also in the Gospels (see, for example, Matt. 21:9; Mark 1:3; 2:28; 12:36-37; Luke 10:41; John 13:9; 20:28; 21:12; cf. Acts 1:6; 2:36). In fact, it is inconceivable that the

early Christians were unaware of the divine status of the name *kurios*. More than 700 times in the New Testament, Jesus is referred to as "Lord" (*kurios*) and here the Lord Jesus Christ. With the Christians regular use of the Greek translation of the Hebrew Scriptures (the LXX), where this term is the most common one for translating the so-called Hebrew *tetragrammaton*, YHWH (or Yahweh), it cannot be by accident that it is used also in reference to the risen and glorified Jesus the Christ (Rom. 1:3-4; 10:9, etc.). Three examples will demonstrate the point. Paul cites one of the oldest Christian creeds thusly: "If you confess with your mouth that Jesus is Lord and believe in your heart that God has raised him from the dead, you will be saved . . . For everyone who calls upon the name of the Lord will be saved" (Rom. 10:9, 13). He is clearly referring to Jesus what is said of Yahweh, or God, in Joel 2:32 in the LXX that reads: Whoever will call on the name of the Lord [Greek = *kurios*] will be saved." In 1 Thess. 4:16, Paul says "For the Lord [*kurios*, here = Jesus] himself, with a cry of command, with the archangel's call and with the sound of God's trumpet, will descend from heaven, and the dead in Christ shall rise first." Compare this with the LXX of Ps. 46:5: "God is gone up with a shout, the Lord [*kurios*] with a sound of a trumpet." There parallels are clear. What is said of God in the Old Testament is said of Jesus in the New. For Paul, "at the name of Jesus, every knee will bow and every tongue confess that Jesus Christ is Lord [*kurios*]" (Phil. 2:10-11). This is also a clear reference to the LXX of Isa. 45:22-26 that reads in part:

> I am God and there is no other. By myself I swear righteousness shall surely proceed out of my mouth; my words shall not be frustrated; that to me every knee shall bend, and every tongue shall swear by God, saying, Righteousness and glory shall come to him . . . By the Lord [*kurios*] shall they be justified, and in God shall all the seed of the children of Israel be

glorified (S. Bagster, trans.).

For Paul, what is central to all Christian preaching is the recognition of Jesus as Lord. See also the discussion in 1 Cor. 16:22 and Rev. 22:20. Paul uses the words, "Jesus is Lord" in Rom. 10:9, 1 Cor. 12:3, and Phil. 2:11. See also 2 Cor. 4:5 and 8:5 below. It bears repeating that in the first century, the Roman Caesars were also called "lord" and it was a highly significant moment when the Christians claimed that only Jesus was worthy of this title.

B. 1:3-7. Blessing

This is the third part of the typical letter, or epistolary introduction. In all of Paul's letters, except the one to the Galatians (see comment above), after the salutation, Paul gives a thanksgiving or blessing. This blessing/thanksgiving emphasizes the dangers that Paul and his companions face and also their partnership in prayer over his and the Corinthians' circumstances. The benediction or blessing includes Paul's self-praise for the hardships he has endured that benefited the Corinthians. Typically in such benedictions, God is praised as the giver of the blessing and a recipient is congratulated on receipt of the blessing of God and his/her ability to overcome danger or evil. God is praised for accomplishing both. See, for example, the blessing of Moses by Jethro (Exod. 18:10). This blessing is also congratulatory of the Corinthians and ends with asking God to bless them.

1:3. Blessed be the God and Father of our Lord Jesus Christ, the Father of mercies and God of all comfort. Paul's view of God as "Father" (see also Rom. 8:15) is reflective of his Jewish training that saw God as father because he created the nation of Israel (Deut. 32:6; Ps. 103:13; cf. also Deut. 8:5 ("parent") and saw Israel as the "children" of God (Deut. 14:1). Jesus expressed his prayers to God using similar parental language (e.g., Matt. 6:9), and the early church passed on this tradition (Luke 23:34, 46; John 5:36-37; 8:18-19; 17:1, 5, 11, 21, 25, etc.). At Qumran, there are similar references to God as "Father." In the *Hymns* at Qumran, for instance, we read:

> For my mother did not know me, and my father abandoned me to you. Because you are father to all the sons of your truth. In them you rejoice, like one full of gentleness for her child, and like a wet nurse, you clutch to your chest all your creatures (1QH 17.34-35, Garcia Martinez trans.).

It is interesting that in this passage God is also seen as a woman (nurse). This is similar to Paul's reference to himself acting like a nurse who cherishes her children (1 Thess. 2:7). God is also addressed as a father in Sirach (*Ecclesiasticus*, ca. 180 B.C.). In cry for deliverance, Sirach prays: "O Lord, Father and Master of my life, do not abandon me to their designs" (*Sir.* 23:1, NRSV. For similar references to God as father, see also *Testament of Job* 33.3 and *Joseph and Asenath* 12:7-11.). It is well to remember also that Paul's view of the loving father that is modeled on the belief that God as creator of Israel is also "father," was not the typical view of a father among the Romans. While it was permitted for a father to abuse and even kill his children, the Jews called for appropriate care for one's children. The Christians adopted this Jewish notion that was contrary to Roman life. In the late first century, the author(s) of the *Didache* list the prohibitions of those who follow the way of the Lord. These include: "thou shalt not procure abortion, nor commit infanticide" (*Did.* 2.2). See also the call for fathers not to provoke their children to anger in Eph. 6:4.

1:4. Who comforts us in all our affliction so that we may be able to comfort those who are in any affliction with the comfort with which we ourselves are comforted by God. Paul strikes a familiar chord when he conveys that his ability to comfort is based on the fact that he himself has faced distress in his life. In this he has true affinity with those who suffer. Those who tried to console who had not faced the special hurts of those that they were consoling were often mocked. Aeschylus, for instance, argues: "How light for those who feel no pain to give advice to those whose life is weal and woe" (*Prometheus* 263-265, Danker, 33). Sophocles (ca. 497-406 B.C.) similarly wrote: "Chorus: But when people come to grief though no fault of their own, anger is softened, and you should benefit from this. Deianeira: That is the kind of think that a person who has no trouble of his own would say, but not the one to whom the evil belongs" (*The Women of Trachis*, 727-30, LCL). Paul assures his readers that he can understand because he has experienced hardships.

C. 1:8–9:15. Body—Assurances, Instructions, Offerings

Paul now begins the formal part of his letter and addresses the concerns that led him to write to the Corinthians.

1. 1:8-11. Formal Body/Opening

Paul's catalogue of hardships (here, 6:3-6 and 11:23-29) have several parallels in the ancient world. Virtue and adversity were often seen together. Indeed, the best way to demonstrate the blessing of the gods was to show virtue in the adverse circumstances that life brings one's way. In such cases, the adversity one faced served the purposes for which God sent one. The true philosopher did not brag about the office or role that Zeus had given to him, but rather demonstrated that the proof of one's god-blessed training was in one's proper response to adversity. Epictetus writes:

And now, when the crisis calls, will you go off and make an exhibition of your compositions, and give a reading from them, and boast, "See, how I write dialogues"? Do not so, man, but rather boast as follows: "See how in my desire I do not fail to get what I wish. See how in my

aversions I do not fall into things that I would avoid. Bring on death and shall know; bring on hardships, bring on imprisonment, bring on disrepute, bring on condemnation." This is the proper exhibition of a young man come from school. Leave other things to other people; neither let anyone ever hear a word from you about them, nor, if anyone praises you for them, do you tolerate it, but let yourself be accounted a no-body and a know-nothing. (*Discourses* 2.1.34-36, LCL)

In a second-century A.D. brief letter that shows adversity, a young soldier writes to his father:

Apion to Epimachus his father and lord, many greetings. I pray above all that you are healthy and strong, and that things are going well with you, as well as with my brother and my sister and her daughter. I give thanks to the Lord Serapis that he saved me when I was in danger (BGU 423, Berger trans.).

1:8 For we do not want you to be unaware, brethren, of our affliction which came to us in Asia, that we were burdened excessively, beyond our strength, so that we despaired even of life. It is not clear what particular adversity that Paul was facing when the distress he describes happened. It may have been the riot in Ephesus (Acts 19:23-31) or other public opposition to his ministry (1 Cor. 15:29-32), but it clearly took its toll on him and his companions. It may have been his personal illness (1 Cor. 12:7; cf. Gal. 4:13-15).

1:9-10. Indeed, we had the sentence of death within ourselves in order that we should not trust in ourselves, but in God who raises the dead; who delivered us from so great a peril of death, and will deliver us, He on whom we have set our hope. And He will yet deliver us. Paul's hope in the midst of all of his life-threatening experiences has faced death with confidence in God who had and will deliver him. He does not seem to fear death, but dreads the process of death (1:8). Epictetus speaks similarly when he describes what death means to the one who understands it.

> For it is not death or hardship that is a fearful thing, but the fear of hardship or death. That is why we praise the man who said "Not death is dreadful, but a shameful death." Our confidence ought therefore, to be turned toward death, and our caution toward the fear of death; whereas we do just the opposite—in the face of death we turn to flight, but about the formation of a judgment on death we show carelessness, disregard, and unconcern. . . . What is death: A bugbear. Turn it about and learn what it is; see, it does not bite. The paltry body must be separated from the bit of spirit, either now or later, just as it existed apart from it before. Why are you grieved, then, if it be separated now? For if it be not separated now, it will be later. Why? So that the revolution of the universe may be accomplished . . . (*Discourses* 2.1.14-19, LCL).

Paul does not relish in death nor does he look forward to it, but he has confidence that not even death can separate him from the love and presence of God in Christ Jesus (Rom. 8:38-39). Unlike Epictetus, Paul does not see it simply as fate and unavoidable, but rather that if it comes, God does not abandon his children to hopelessness in the midst of it. Epictetus sought for inner strength to be in the cycle of life and plan of the universe, but Paul has a hope of life beyond death. Here he shares his deep-seated pain to let the people know in advance that, as he explains in the next section, his failure to come to them had nothing to do with his fear of them nor his lack of concern for them, but rather the concerns of his present ministry.

2. 1:12–2:13. Paul's change of plans and special concerns. Paul had to make changes in his travels and could not see the Corinthians when he had hoped. As a result, some in Corinth accused him of vacillation, of being unstable, because he was unable to keep his promises. In this section Paul addresses this concern. Counting on the blessing of God and the unity of the Christian community, Paul now responds to the first criticism that was leveled against him by some in Corinth. At the beginning of this brief section, there is a short introduction (1:12-13), and at the end there is an interrupted narrative (2:12-13), but in between, Paul makes two points: first (1:15-22), he seeks to justify changing his travel plans and second, he tells why he cannot come to Corinth immediately as he had planned (1:23–2:11).

1:12. For our proud confidence is this, the testimony of our conscience, that in holiness and godly sincerity, not in fleshly wisdom but in the grace of God, we have conducted ourselves in the world, and especially toward you. Paul defends himself against claims that he had sought personal gain among the Corinthians. It was not uncommon for traveling philosophers and rhetoricians to seek personal gain at the expense of those who would listen to them. The Stoic philosopher and rhetorician, Dio Chrysostom (A.D. 40-120), in his discourse to the people of Alexandria, chides them for not listening to his own good reasons, but acknowledges that many who call themselves philosophers have not acted appropriately toward them.

> And perhaps this situation [not listening] is not of your own making, but you will show whether it is or not if you bear with me today: the fault may lie rather at the door of those who wear the name philosopher. For some among that company do not appear in public at all and prefer not to make the venture, possibly because they despair of being able to improve the masses; others exercise their

voices in what we call lecture-halls, having secured as hearers men who are in league with them and tractable. And as for the Cynics, as they are called, it is true that the city contains no small number of that sect, and that, like any other thing, this too has had its crop—persons whose tenets, to be sure, comprise practically nothing spurious or ignoble, yet who must make a living—still these Cynics, posting themselves at street-corners, in alleyways, and at temple-gates, pass round the hat and play upon the credulity of lads and sailors and crowds of that sort, stringing together rough jokes and much tittle-tattle and that low badinage that smacks of the market-place. Accordingly they achieve no good at all, but rather the worst possible harm, for they accustom thoughtless people to deride philosophers in general, just as one might accustom lads to scorn their teachers, and, when they ought to knock the insolence out of their hearers, these Cynics merely increase it . . .

To be sure, if they themselves are really poets or orators, perhaps there is nothing so shocking in that, but if in the guise of philosophers they do these things with a view to their own profit and reputation, and not to improve you, that indeed is shocking (*Orations* 32.8-10, LCL).

1:14. Just as you also partially did understand us, that we are your reason to be proud as you also are ours, in the day of our Lord Jesus. The "Day of the Lord" was a reference in Paul's day to the time when God would bring judgment against disobedient people and those who persecuted his people (Isa. 2:12-21; Amos 5:18-20; Zech. 14:1-2), but it was also a time of reward from God for his people (Amos 9:11-15; Zech. 14:6-21). Many saw it as a time when God would restore the kingdom to Israel (Acts 1:6). In the New Testament, the hand of Lord and the coming of the Lord Jesus are essentially

identical, and that day is followed by both judgment from God (Rom. 2:5; 1 Cor. 3:13-15; 1 Thess. 1:10; 5:1-7; 2 Thess. 1:5-10; 2:1-3; Rev. 3:10) and reward for faithfulness and obedience (Matt. 16:27; Rom. 8:22-23; 2 Cor. 6:2; Eph. 4:30; Phil. 2:16; 1 Thess. 4:13; 5:8-11; Rev. 3:10. See also Phil. 1:6, 10; 2:16; Rom. 13:12).

1:16. That is, to pass your way into Macedonia, and again from Macedonia to come to you, and by you to be helped on my journey to Judea. It is not certain which city Paul visited when he was planning this trip. It may be that he visited them all and that the place of his meeting of Titus (2:13; cf. 7:5-7) was Philippi where the church on more than one occasion supplied Paul's needs in ministry (Phil. 4:10, 15-16), but which city is not specified. In his travel from Troas, Philippi would have been the first stop if he traveled overland on the Egnatian Highway from Neapolis (see his first journey through this area in Acts 16:11-12). Philippi was the place where he seems to have visited often and received a warm welcome from the Christians there, as well as having stayed there during a religious holiday (the "Days of Unleavened Bread," Acts 20:6), but there is nothing certain here.

1:17-18. Therefore, I was not vacillating when I intended to do this, was I? Or that which I purpose, do I purpose according to the flesh, that with me there should be yes, yes and no, no at the same time? But as God is faithful, our word to you is not yes and no. The accusation against Paul was that he was not speaking clearly and that he freely changed his words to fit whatever situation gave him the greater advantage. Once again, Dio Chrysostom chides those in his day who were not known for speaking plainly, but who said whatever was popular and brought them personal gain. He acknowledges that there are those who have spoken well and appropriately to help the people, himself among them, but laments that many have not.

But here are only a few who have displayed frankness in your presence, and that but sparingly, not in such a way as to fill your ears therewith nor for any length of time; nay, they merely utter a phrase or two, and then, after berating rather than enlightening you, they make a hurried exit, anxious lest before they have finished you may raise an outcry and send them packing, behaving in very truth quite like men who in winter muster up courage for a brief and hurried voyage out to sea. But to find a man who in plain terms and without guile speaks his mind with frankness and neither for the sake of reputation nor for gain makes false pretensions, but out of good will and concern for his fellow-men stands ready, if need be, to submit to ridicule, and to the disorder and the uproar of the mob—to find such a man as that is not easy, but rather the good fortune of a very lucky city, so great is the dearth of noble, independent souls and such the abundance of toadies, mountebanks, and sophists (*Oration* 32.11, LCL).

Another Stoic, Arius Didymus (ca. first cent. B.C. of Alexandria), expressed popular sentiment when he spoke against those who vacillate:

Nor do [the Stoics] assume that a man with good sense changes his mind, for changing one's mind belongs to false assent, on the grounds of erring through haste. Nor does he change his mind in any way, nor alter his opinion, nor is he confused. For all these things are marks of those who waver in their beliefs, which is alien to the person with good sense (*Epitome of Stoic Ethics* 11m, M. Hubbard trans.).

1:21-22. Now He who establishes us with you in Christ and anointed us is God, who also **sealed us and gave us the Spirit in our hearts as a pledge.** Paul draws from his Jewish background for this reference to an anointing. In the Old Testament it referred to the pouring or rubbing of oil normally on the head of a priest, prophet, or king as an act of consecration for their duties. The notion behind it is that the anointing signified the presence and power of God to carry out the mission or activity of the person anointed (1 Sam. 16:12-13; 1 Kings 1:34, 39, 45; 19:15-16; 2 Kings 9:3, 6, 12; Ps. 23:5; 105:15; Zech. 4:14; cf. also Lev. 4:3, 5; 6:20; 7:36; 8:10; 1 Sam. 10:1; 2 Kings 23:30).

The **seal**, of which Paul speaks, is a metaphor describing God's identity placed on those who have trusted him. It appears for Paul to be the "seal" of God in the believer's life (3:18; 4:4-6). For other examples of the metaphorical use of the seal, see also John 6:27; 1 Cor. 9:2; Eph. 1:13; 4:30; Rev. 7:2-4; 9:4). In the ancient world, a seal was a very important part of important communication or shipments made from one part of the Greco-Roman world to another. The seal functioned both as a means of protecting contents, but also of identifying the sender. The sender would generally have a seal made of bronze, stone, or ivory and after melting hot wax or lead on the correspondence or package, would impress the seal on the hot material, thereby leaving the sender's name and perhaps also symbol. Sometimes the symbol would be that of a cherished deity. Several in the ancient world made reference to the seal as a metaphor of something else. Philo, for instance, speaking of God's seal on humanity at creation, writes: "he that was after the (Divine) image was an idea or type or seal" (*On the Creation* 134, LCL). Likewise, he speaks of the heavenly man and the earthly man. The former is one who "was stamped with the image of God; while the earthly is a molded work of Artificer, but not His offspring" (*Allegorical Interpretation* 1:32, LCL). Elsewhere Philo uses the symbol of the seal (divine "impress") to distinguish between those who have the mark of God—the spirit—and those who do not:

> The man of mark, associate of the true monarchy, has imbibed in full measure the inbred spirit of fellowship, and ... For the world has come into being, and assuredly it has done so under the hand of some Cause; and the Word of Him who makes it is Himself the seal, by which each thing that exists has received its shape ... For the living creature that has come into being is imperfect in quality as is shewn by its constant growth as its age advances, but perfect in quality; for the same quality continues, inasmuch as it is the impress of a Divine Word ever continuing and free from every kind of change (*On Flight and Finding*, 11-13, LCL).

Similarly, Philo observes elsewhere: "Moses likened the fashion of the reasonable soul to no created thing, but averred it to be a genuine coinage of that dread Spirit, the Divine and Invisible One, signed and impressed by the seal of God, the stamp of which is the Eternal Word" (*Noah's Work as a Planter* 18, LCL).

The "**pledge**" of which Paul speaks (Greek = *arrabon*) is found also in 5:4-5 below where Paul is speaking of the Holy Spirit as the pledge or guarantor of the blessing of God, life, coming in full measure at the end times. The pledge is an initial payment of what is on the way. In Rom. 8:23, Paul indicates that believers have received the Holy Spirit as a "first-fruits" of what is to come, namely the redemption of the body. For other texts in 2 Corinthians that deal with the focus here, see also 3:3, 18; 4:6, 16; 5:5, 17.

1:23. But I call God as witness to my soul, that to spare you I came no more to Corinth. To call God as a witness was very important in the ancient world and it has been continued in modern society when in a courtroom, a person takes an oath, with a hand lifted up, pledging with a hand on the Bible to tell the truth "so help me God." Invoking the name of God in a pledge meant that one would incur the wrath of God if the truth were not told or a promised deed not carried out (Ruth 1:17; 2 Sam. 3:9). In the Greco-Roman world, similar oaths were also taken. Zeus was the god of oaths and his name was often invoked during pledges of allegiance to a king or ruler. For instance, at the ancient city of Assos on the western coast of Turkey south of the ancient city of Troas, an inscription was discovered that pledged the city's loyalty to the Roman emperor Caligula. It reads: "We swear by Zeus the Savior and the God of Caesar Augustus ...that we are loyally disposed to Gaius Caesar Augustus .... If we observe this oath, may all go well with us; if not, may the opposite befall" (cited in M. Hubbard, 204). In his description of Corinth, Pausanias (ca. second cent. A.D.) tells of the oaths taken at the temple of Palaemon that had a special place underground called the temple "Holy of Holies" and he reported the seriousness with which oaths offered there were taken. He claimed that anyone, "whether Corinthian or stranger, [who] swears falsely here, can by no means escape from his death" (*Description of Greece* 2.2.1, LCL). For other oaths in Paul, see also Rom. 1:9 and Phil. 1:8.

Paul indicates that in order to spare the Corinthians from his anger and the unpleasantness with which he would have come, he chose not to come to them as he had planned, but rather to delay his visit.

1:24. Not that we lord it over your faith, but are workers with you for your joy; for in your faith you are standing firm. Many traveling philosophers in Paul's day were known for "lording it over" their followers, but Paul wanted no part of that. Perhaps this is similar to the criticism waged against Paul by some in Corinth (see 2:17). They often created problems and sowed unrest among the people. In one example, when a Stoic named Helvidius

Priscus, who was a possible candidate for the throne, insulted the Roman Emperor, in A.D. 71 Vespasian, ordered that the payment of teachers of Greek and Latin from the public treasury and ordered all philosophers, except Mucianus [= Musonius Rufus] from Rome.

Inasmuch as many others too, including Demetrius the Cynic, actuated by the Stoic principles, were taking advantage of the name of philosophy to teach publicly many doctrines inappropriate to the times, and in this way were subtly corrupting some of their hearers, Muscianus, prompted rather by anger than by any passion for philosophy, inveighed at length against them and persuaded Vespasian to expel all such persons from the city (Dio Cassius [ca. A.D. 150-235], *Roman History* 65.13, LCL).

Lucian, a second-century A.D. satirist, described the Stoics and other philosophers with biting sarcasm.

> There is a class of men which made its appearance in the world not long ago, lazy, disputatious, vainglorious, quick-tempered, gluttonous, dotish, addle-pated, full of effrontery and to use the language of Homer, 'a useless load to the soil.' Well, these people, dividing themselves into schools and inventing various word-mazes, have called themselves Stoics, Academics, Epicureans, Peripatetics, and other things much more laughable than these. Then, cloaking themselves in the high-sounding name of virtue, elevating their eyebrows, wrinkling up their foreheads and letting their beards grow long, they go about hiding loathsome habits under false garb, very like actors in tragedy; for if you take away from the latter their masks and their gold-embroidered robes, nothing is left but a comical little creature hired for the show at seven drachmas (*Icaromenippus*, or *The Sky-Man* 29, LCL).

Later, after more biting criticism of these groups, he concludes: "that is what these whelps are like, gods. Moreover some of them who call themselves Epicureans are very insolent fellows indeed and attack us immoderately" (*Icarmenippus* 32, LCL).

2:1-4. The letter of tears. Sometime between the writing of 1 Corinthians and this correspondence, Paul wrote a passionate letter expressing his anguish and disappointment with the Corinthian Christians. It may be that this letter was essentially what follows chapter 9, namely chaps. 10–13, but that is not certain. If so, the language of 10–13 is clearly filled with anger and passion and is not in keeping with the gentle style of his appeal for financial aid for the Christians in Jerusalem (chaps. 8–9). In that correspondence (chaps. 10–13), Paul defends his apostleship and ministry among the Corinthians. It is also quite possible that the "tearful letter" is now lost. See discussion of this problem in the Introduction to 2 Corinthians. These verses constitute Paul's reason for writing his current correspondence. He mentions this letter in 2:4, 9; and 7:12. What resulted from the letter was repentance and Paul rejoices over this response both here and in 7:13-15.

2:1. But I determined this for my own sake, that I would not come to you in sorrow again. Evidently, Paul had already had one painful visit to the Corinthians and chose not to have another one. He chose instead to write a strong "tearful" letter to them and he hoped that it would prepare his way for a more productive visit at a later time.

2:5-11. Dealing with an offending person in the church. These verses suggest that someone in the church has insulted Paul and that the Corinthian Christians have taken steps to censure him. Paul urges them to forgive him and reinstate him in the church. This is not likely the situation described in 1 Cor. 5:1-5. It is unlikely that Paul would have dismissed this offense so easily, and it was not one that was directed against Paul himself. The primary grievance the Corinthians had against Paul was his sending to them the "severe letter" instead of coming to them for a long and pleasant visit as he had promised (1 Cor. 16:5-7). Perhaps the man who offended Paul may have been taken up in the church's disappointment over Paul's failure to come to them and perhaps he challenged Paul's authority, but that is not certain. Whatever the offense was, the man became remorseful as a result of the church's actions against him, and so Paul appeals to the Christians to restore the man to their fellowship. Paul refers to this situation once again in 7:12.

2:10-11. But whom you forgive anything, I forgive also; for indeed what I have forgiven, if I have forgiven anything, I did it for your sakes in the presence of Christ, in order that no advantage be taken of us by Satan; for we are not ignorant of his schemes. Paul urges that the spirit of forgiveness be shown to the one who has expressed remorsefulness. Plutarch urged his readers to resist divisiveness and to seek concessions so that "brothers" may have good relations.

> It is therefore of no slight importance to resist the spirit of contentiousness and jealousy among brothers when it first creeps in over trivial matters, practicing the art of making mutual concessions, of learning to take defeat, and of taking pleasure in indulging brothers rather than in winning victories over them. For the men of old gave the name of "Cadmen victory" to no other than that of brothers at Thebes [who died fighting each other], as being the most shameful and the worst of victories (*On Brotherly Love* 488A, LCL).

Satan. Paul's reference to "Satan" (see also 11:14; 12:7) having a victory over them (v. 11) is one of several names he gives to the primary evil force that Christians face. In 6:12, he is named "Beliar" (see discussion below), at other times he is the "god of this age" (4:4), and even "the prince [or "ruler"] of the power of the air" (Eph. 2:2). Satan is the Greek transliteration (*ho Satanas*) of the Hebrew word for "adversary." He is generally represented in Scripture as the Adversary of God and the people of God. This figure is found only three times in the Old Testament (Job 1-2; possibly 1 Chron. 21:1; and Zech. 3:1-2). At this time, he does appear to be the leader of demonic forces that are opposed to God.

In the New Testament, "Satan" appears frequently in the gospels, whether known as "Satan" or the "Devil" (Greek = *diabolos*, "accuser" or "slanderer") (Matt. 4:1, 3; 5; Luke 4:1, 3, 5, 13; John 13:27), "the prince of this world" (John 12:31; 14:30; 16:11), "accuser" (Rev. 12:10), or "prince of demons" (Luke 11:15), or even the "Evil One" (1 John 5:19). According to Luke 10:18, the Devil appears to be one who desired the prerogatives of God. According to Rev. 20:1-10, the Devil will finally be brought to defeat and tormented forever. According to Luke and John, Satan has the ability to enter and possess individuals and did so in the case of Judas (Luke 22:3 and John 13:27; see also Mark 5:12-13; Luke 8:30-32). According to Luke, Jesus tells Peter that Satan has demanded (requested) to "sift all of you like wheat," but Jesus interceded on his behalf (Luke 22:31-32). God may even use Satan to chasten his apostate followers (1 Cor. 5:5; cf. 1 Tim. 1:20). Paul is aware of the Jewish perspective on Satan and knows of the spiritual dimension of conflict in the church.

d. 2:12-13. Paul's trip to Macedonia
2:12-13. Now when I came to Troas for the gospel of Christ and when a door was opened for me in the Lord, I had no rest for my spirit, not finding Titus my brother; but taking my leave of them, I went on to Macedonia.

According to Luke, after the riot at Ephesus started by the silversmiths over the results of the preaching of Paul, Paul left for Macedonia and then returned to Troas for a short season (Acts 20:1-12). There is no mention in Acts of a further journey back to Macedonia or to Achaia to visit the Corinthians, but it may have been that there was another journey shortly after Timothy and Erastus were sent to Macedonia and Achaia (Acts 19:21-22) just before the outbreak of violence in Ephesus. When Titus returned to Macedonia with good news, he met with Paul and related that repentance had taken place on the Corinthians' part. Paul rejoiced and prepared this correspondence.

3. 2:14–5:21. Paul's Apostolic Ministry
a. 2:14–17. The Triumphal Progress of the gospel

2:14-15. But thanks be to God, who always leads us in His triumph in Christ, and manifests through us the sweet aroma of the knowledge of Him in every place. For we are a fragrance of Christ to God among those who are being saved and among those who are perishing. Thanksgiving to God for his goodness is a familiar theme in Paul (Rom. 6:17; 7:25; 1 Cor. 15:57; 2 Cor. 8:16; 9:15). In his rejoicing, Paul conveys his feelings toward this positive turn of events among the Corinthian believers by means of a familiar public event, the marching of a victorious general coming home from battle and leading captives and in the procession. Far from seeing himself as the victor, Paul sees himself being led as a slave of God in God's triumphal victory. Just as a Roman general would lead a train of captives and exhibits the bounty taken in victory, Paul says that God has led him and his fellow believers in a victory procession (Greek = *thriambeuo*, cf. Col. 2:15). Just as God's victory over Paul (1 Cor. 15:8-9) led to God's triumph in spreading the Good News in the Greco-Roman world, so one's surrender to the will of God is God's victory over self and all evil. Paul is grateful to God for leading him as a captive to the will of God and thereby using him through his beatings and imprisonments to bring God's salvation to others. In this sense, Paul is the bond slave of God and so are his fellow believers (Rom. 6:16-19; 7:6; 2 Cor. 4:5; Eph. 6:6).

The Roman triumph was a spectacular event in Rome and other major cities of antiquity. It took the form of a large parade that marched into the city leading to the temple of the chief deity, Jupiter, for enabling the victory, and also honoring the general and soldiers who won the battle. In the processional, which could last for days, the captives and the booty that was taken were displayed in public and often led before the chariot of the conquering hero. Augustus boasted of his victories thusly: "In my triumphs nine kings or children of kings were led before my chariot" (*Acts of Augustus* [*Res Gestae*] 1.4, Danker, trans). Often the defeated generals or kings were marched in public humiliation and executed in public display. Triumphal arches were also built to celebrate such victories such as we see in the famous Arch of Titus that celebrates the captivity of Judea. In that arch, both Jewish slaves and booty from the Jerusalem Temple are displayed. Josephus describes this processional in some detail, indicating how the soldiers were dressed, the royal garments worn by Vespasian and Titus, the activities preceding the procession and finally the procession itself. In regard to the procession, he writes:

> The spoils [in the procession] were bourne in promiscuous heaps; but conspicuous above all stood out those captured in the temple at Jerusalem. These consisted of a golden table [=table of shew-bread, incense cups, and trumpets], many talents in weight, and a lampstand, likewise made of gold, but constructed on a different pattern from those which

we use in ordinary life. Affixed to a pedestal was a central shaft, from which there extended slender branches, arranged in trident-fashion, a wrought lamp being attached to the extremity of each branch; of these there were seven, indicating the honour paid to that number among the Jews. After these, and last of all the spoils, was carried a copy of the Jewish Law. Then followed a large party carrying images of victory, all made of ivory and gold. Behind them drove Vespasian, followed by Titus; while Domitian rode beside them, in magnificent apparel and mounted on a steed that was itself a sight.

The triumphal procession ended at the temple of Jupiter Capitolinus, on reaching which they halted; for it was a time-honored custom to wait there until the execution of the enemy's general was announced. This was Simon, son of Gioras, who had just figured in the pageant among the prisoners, and then with a halter thrown over him and scourged meanwhile by his conductors, had been haled to the spot abutting on the Forum, where Roman law requires that malefactors condemned to death should be executed. After the announcement that Simon was no more and the shouts of universal applause which greeted it, the princes began the sacrifices, which having been duly offered with the customary prayers, they withdrew to the palace .... For the city of Rome kept festival that day for her victory in the campaign against her enemies, for the termination of her civil dissensions, and for her dawning hopes of felicity (*Jewish War* 7.148-157, LCL).

Other cities in the ancient world contained triumphal arches, but the processions were held only in Rome. The notion of being a captive in a triumphal also appears in 1 Cor. 4:9:

"For, I think, God has exhibited us apostles last of all [at the end of the procession], as men condemned to death; because we have become a spectacle to the world, both to angels and to men."

Sweet aroma. Such aromas, or incense, were common in religious processions and civic rituals in antiquity. The notion of such sweet odors was believed by some Jews to be a part of the "Tree of Fragrance." The author of *1 Enoch* (ca. 180 B.C.) tells the story of Michael the archangel coming to Enoch and asking him why he wants to know about the fragrance of the Tree of Life. Michael explains to him that no one can touch the tree until the day of judgment when God will come and take vengeance on the evil ones. Until then no one has the right to eat of the fragrant tree but afterward, it will be given to the righteous and pious.

And the elect will be presented with its fruit for life. He will plant it in the direction of the northeast, upon the holy place—in the direction of the house of the Lord, the Eternal king.

Then they shall be glad and rejoice in gladness, and they shall enter into the holy [place]; its fragrance shall [penetrate] their bones, long life they will live on earth, such as their fathers lived in their days.

At that moment, I blessed the God of Glory, the Eternal King, for he has prepared such things for the righteous people, as he had created (them) and given it to them (*1 Enoch* 25:4-6, *OT Pseud* 1:26).

The author of the *Testament of Abraham* (ca. first-third cent. A.D.) speaks of the meeting of Abraham with Michael the archangel and the writer says: "and behold a sweet odor came to him and a radiance of light. And Abraham turned around and saw Death coming toward him in great glory and youthful beauty ...." (16:7-8, *OT Pseud* 1:892).

In keeping with the imagery of the procession (v. 14, described above), the Roman triumphal procession also included incense bearers. Appian, for instance, while describing the Roman triumphal procession, indicates that after the trumpeters led the wagons with the booty taken in victory over the enemy, then came various animals and even dancers, but just before the victorious general "came a number of incense-bearers" (*Punic Wars* 66, LCL).

This was true in the practice of Jewish temple rituals and also among the Greco-Roman religious world. According to Plutarch, "every temple was open and filled with garlands and incense" (*Lives, Amelius Paulus* 32, LCL). In Old Testament times when the Levitical sacrifices were carried out, the use of incense was a part of providing what was pleasing to God (Lev. 2:2, 12; 6:14). On the other hand, Paul's use of the imagery of the aroma (Greek = *osmen*) and fragrance (Greek = *euodia*) is similar to that in *Sirach*: "Like cassia and camel's thorn I gave forth perfume [*osmen*], and like choice myrrh I spread my fragrance" (*Sir.* 24:15). This is similar to a contrast in *2 Baruch*: "for so far as Zion has been delivered up and Jerusalem laid waste, the idols in the cities of the nations are happy and the flavor of the smoke of the incense of the righteousness of the Law has been extinguished everywhere in the region of Zion; behold the smoke of impiety is there" (2 *Apoc. Bar. 67.6, OT Pseud* 1:644). Closer to the New Testament is the parallel in the Gnostic Gospel of Thomas (ca. A.D. 100-140):

> For the Father is sweet and in his will is what is good. He has taken cognizance of the things that are yours that you might find rest in them. For by the fruits does one take cognizance of the things that are yours because the children of the Father are his fragrance, for they are from the grace of his countenance. For this reason the Father loves his fragrance and manifests it in every place, and if it mixes with matter he gives his fragrance to the light and in his repose he causes it to surpass every form (and) every sound. For it is not the ears that smell and attract the fragrance to itself and is submerged in the fragrance of the Father, so he thus shelters it and takes it to the place where it came from, from the first fragrance which is grown cold . . . . The Fragrances, therefore, that are cold are from division. For this reason faith came; it dissolved the division, and it brought the warm pleroma of love in order that the cold should not come again but there should be unity of perfect thought (*Gosp. Th.* 33-34, NHL 47).

2:15. For we are a fragrance of Christ to God among those who are being saved and among those who are perishing. Contact with that which is holy can lead both to glory and blessing, but also to judgment (2 Sam. 6:3-7). It mattered in antiquity how one handled holy things and there were two consequences for those who encountered the holy. According to the Babylonian Talmud:

> Whosoever occupies himself with the Torah for its own sake his learning becomes an elixir [a powder for the healing of wounds] of life to him, for it is said, "It is a tree of life to them that grasp it; and it is further said, It shall be as health to thy navel; and it is also said, For whoso findeth me findeth life. But, whosoever occupies himself with the Torah not for its own sake, it becomes to him a deadly poison" (*b. Ta'anith* 7a, Soncino trans).

2:16. To the one an aroma from death to death, to the other an aroma from life to life. And who is adequate for these things? With the triumphal procession in view (2:14 above), Paul observes that to the prisoner in a Roman procession, the aroma of the incense would bring a reminder of the death that awaited them at the end of the parade, but to the conquering general and to the crowds along the parade route, this was a sweet aroma.

2:17. For we are not like many, peddling the word of God, but as from sincerity, but as from God, we speak in Christ in the sight of God. See previous discussion in 1:12 above. Not only were non-Christian philosophers guilty of "peddling their wares" to the unsuspecting, even Christian prophets or teachers who wandered from place to place did the same and Paul resists being identified among them. The early church eventually had to warn churches to put restrictions on such individuals who were known for seeking financial favors among the people. The writer(s) of the *Didache*, for instance, admonishes the churches:

> and concerning the apostles and Prophets, act thus according to the ordinance of the Gospel. Let every apostle who comes to you be received as the Lord, but let him not stay more than one day, or if need be a second as well; but if he stay three days, he is a false prophet. And when an apostle goes forth let him accept nothing but bread till he reach his night's lodging; but if he ask for money, he is a false prophet.... But whosoever shall say in a spirit "Give me money, or something else," you shall not listen to him; but if he tell[s] you to give on behalf of others in want, let none judge him (*Did.* 11.3-6, 12. LCL).

Plato (427-347 B.C.), in telling the story of Socrates' interaction with Hippocrates, acknowledges that the sophist "is really a merchant or dealer in provisions on which a soul is nourished" but reminds him that:

> ... we must take care, my good friend, that the sophist, in commending his wares, does not deceive us, as both merchant and dealer do in the case of our bodily food. For among the provisions, you know, in which these men deal, not only are they themselves ignorant what is good or bad for the body, since in selling they commend them all, but the people who buy from them are so too,

unless one happens to be a trainer or a doctor ....

So then, if you are well informed as to what is good or bad among these wares, it will be safe for you to buy doctrines from Protagoras or from anyone else you please: but if not, take care, my dear fellow, that you do not risk your greatest treasure on a toss of the dice. For I tell you there is far more serious risk in the purchase of doctrines than in that of eatables .... But you cannot carry away doctrines in a separate vessel: you are compelled, when you have handed over the price, to take the doctrine in your very soul by learning it, and so to depart either an injured or benefited man (*Protagoras* 313C-314B, LCL).

Philo, Paul's contemporary, in Alexandria advocated the pursuit of the doctrines of Moses rather than the popular sophists, concluding that:

> the wisdom [that one must pursue] must not be that of the systems hatched by the word-catchers and sophists who sell their tenets and arguments like any bit of merchandise in the market, men who for ever pit philosophy against philosophy without a blush ... (*On the Life of Moses* 2.212, LCL).

Likewise, Dio Chrysostom (ca. A.D. 40-120) speaks disparagingly about those who "in the guise of philosophers they do these things with a view to their own profit and reputation, and not to improve you, that indeed is shocking" (*Orations* 32.10, LCL). Equally critical of those who "peddle" their philosophies, is Lucian's satire (ca. A.D. 120-185) about the tendency to sell one's services for personal benefit. He tells the story of Lycinus responding to Hermotimus and says: "I certainly cannot say how in your view philosophy and wine are comparable, except perhaps at this one point that philosophers sell their lessons as wine-merchants—most of them adulterating and cheating and giving false measure" (*Hermotimus, or Concerning the Sects* 59, LCL).

Paul is not seeking his own advantage by promoting his religious beliefs or personal gain, as many others were accused of doing, but rather he was promoting the Gospel to the advance of God's work and the transformation of his hearers.

b. 3:1–4:6. The Ministry of the New Covenant

3:1-2. Are we beginning to commend ourselves again? Or do we need, as some, letters of commendation to you or from you? You are our letter, written in our hearts, known and read by all men. It was common for the Corinthians to see daily monuments all around them that had self-commendations upon them. These were given to the city by individuals who often spoke of their generosity to the city. Wealthy benefactors often had their names inscribed on various structures throughout the city. One of the more modest inscriptions still preserved is that of Erastus, a city treasurer (Rom. 16:23) and fellow believer, who had his name engraved on the pavement. The inscription reads: "Erastus in return for his aedilship laid [this pavement] at his own expense" (M. Hubbard, 209). An "aedilship" ("Aedile," Latin, *aedilis* = "having to do with buildings") is the Roman name given to an office or magistrate elected to a position of responsibility by the people. Such individuals often felt a sense of obligation to do something for the community that elected them. In this case, Erastus, a Roman magistrate (aedile) who oversaw public works and probably the believer who was "city treasurer" in Corinth mentioned by Paul (Rom. 16:23), made a donation to the city and had his name placed on a stone in honor of the gift. One example of a rather self-focused individual who commended himself to his community is found on the statue of a certain Herodes Atticus. He allowed his statue to be erected in his honor and placed his own inscription on it that reads: "Given by great Herodes Atticus, pre-eminent above others, who had attained the peak of every kind of excellence . . .famous among Hellenes and furthermore a son [of Greece] greater than them all, the flower of Achaia" (J. H. Kent, *Corinth* Vol. 8.3, *Inscriptions 1926-1950*).

Paul says, however, that he does not need recommendation letters from others nor does he need to commend himself to the Corinthians. Since he started their church, he says that he is written, not on stone or in ink, but on their hearts. Letters of reference were very important in the ancient world since those who traveled from place to place had very little else to commend them to others who might offer them hospitality. Paul, for instance, gave such a letter of commendation to Phoebe as she made her way to Rome (Rom. 16:1-2), and the letter sent to Philemon on behalf of Onesimus (Phile. 8-21), and observe that Apollos received such a letter in Acts 18:27. The following two such letters of recommendation come from the first century. The first: "I request you to consider as introduced to you Achilles, who is delivering to you this letter of mine, and to assist him actively in whatever he heeds from you, so that he may bear witness to your eagerness" (supplied by Jerome Murphy-O'Connor, 170). The second was found inscribed on a column in the agora (marketplace) of Corinth. It appeared twice on the band above the columns and on the pedestal that contained several Corinthian columns. It read: "Gnaeus Babbius Philinus, aedile and pontifex, had this monument erected at his own expense, and he approved it in his official capacity as duovir" (supplied by Jerome Murphy-O'Connor, 171).

In this passage, Paul emphasizes that the personal conduct that he had among the Corinthian Christians must stand as his letters of commendation. He may have been criticized by some in the church for not carrying such letters from the apostles or others in the church from Jerusalem, but he reminds them that such letters in their case were not necessary since he founded their church and they were witnesses to it.

3:3. Being manifested that you are a letter of Christ, cared for by us, written not with ink, but with the Spirit of the living God, not on tablets of stone, but on tablets of human hearts. When Paul speaks of the stone tablets (Greek = *plaxin lithinais*), he undoubtedly had in mind several Old Testament texts that reflected the Greek translation of the Pentateuch, the Septuagint (LXX), that refers to Moses receiving "two tablets of testimony, tablets of stone [Greek = *plakas lithinas*] written with the finger of God" (Exod. 24:12; 31:18; cf. 34:1; Deut. 9:10-11). The "heart of stone" (Greek = *he kardia he lithine*) probably is contrasted with a "heart of flesh" (Greek = *kardia sarkine*) in Ezek. 11:19 and 36:26. For the similar expression, "tablet of the heart" see also Prov. 3:3a; 7:3 and Jer. 17:1. Thucydides (ca. 460-400 B.C.), in his funeral address for Pericles, wrote of the distinction between matters of the heart and those engraved in stone: "for the whole world is the sepulcher of famous men, and it is not the epitaph upon monuments set up in their own land that alone commemorates them, but also in lands not their own there abides in each breast an unwritten memorial of them, planted in the heart rather than graven on stone" (*History of the Peloponnesian War* 2.43.2, LCL). In the fourth century B.C., Archytas of Tarentum also spoke of lifeless letters:

> I say now that every society consists of ruler and ruled, the third element being the laws. Among these laws, however, there is the living law represented by the king and the lifeless law of the letter. The law is in the first place, for the king faithful to the law abides in it, the ruler who follows it, those who are ruled are free, and the whole society is happy ("On Law and Righteousness," in *Anthologium* 4.1.135, M. Boring, trans.).

At the end of the first century, Clement of Rome also uses this expression, that alludes to Prov. 7:3, when he says of the Corinthian Christians "the commandments and ordinances of the Lord were written on the tables of your heart" (1 Clem. 2.8, LCL). Tacitus reports that Tiberias Caesar wanted nothing more than to be written on the hearts of his subjects rather than given divine honors and having temples erected in his honor. He cries out:

> "I am mortal, that my functions are the functions of men, and that I hold it enough if I fill the foremost place among them—this I call you to witness, and I desire those who shall follow us to bear it in mind.... These are my temples in your breasts, these my fairest and abiding effigies: for those that are reared of stone, should the judgement [sic] of the future turn to hatred, are scorned as sepulchers! And so my prayer to allies and citizens and to heaven itself is this: To Heaven, that to the end of my life it may endow me with a quiet mind, gifted with understanding of law human and divine; and to my fellow men, that whenever I shall depart, their praise and kindly thoughts may still attend my deeds and the memories attached to my name" (Tacitus, *Annals* 4.38, LCL).

It was said after him that: "He had never asked for the baubles of office: he would rather stand sentry and work like the humblest soldier for the security of the emperor. And yet he had reached the supreme goal—he has been counted worthy of an alliance with the Caesar" (*Annals* 4.39, LCL).

3:6. Who also made us adequate as servants of a new covenant, not of the letter, but of the Spirit; for the letter kills, but the Spirit gives life. Once again, Paul refers to a familiar notion in the Old Testament. Only one time in the whole of the Old Testament literature do we find a reference to a "new covenant" (Jeremiah

31:31), and that text is cited in Heb. 8:8-12, the longest citation of an Old Testament text in the New Testament ("testament" = "covenant"). While many Christians are quite familiar with the term "New Testament" that speaks of a collection of 27 books that comprise the second part of the Christian Bible, that is not what Paul has in mind here. The word "testament" and "covenant" both translate the same Greek word, *diatheke*, and mean the same thing. The words "new testament" were not used of the books that make up the second part of the Christian Bible, the New Testament, until late in the second century A.D. At roughly the same time, Irenaeus, Clement of Alexandria, Tertullian, and Origen begin to use the terms "Old Testament" and "New Testament" to refer to the literature that makes up our Christian Bibles. This, however, is foreign to Paul and Jeremiah. God's gift of a new heart and a new spirit to take the place of a heart of stone is found in Ezek. 36:26, and later he claims that God will make an "everlasting covenant" with his people, a move that is not far from Jeremiah's "new covenant." Paul does not speak of a "new covenant" often (here and 1 Cor. 11:25), and the word "covenant" elsewhere only in Rom. 11:27; 2 Cor. 3:14; Gal. 3:17, but the notion is rooted in Jer. 31:31-34 (in the rest of the New Testament, see Matt. 26:28; Mark 14:24; Luke 1:72; 22:20; Acts 3:25; 7:8; Heb. 7:22; 8:6, 7, 8, 9, 10, 13; 9:1, 4, 15, 18, 20; 10:16, 29; 12:24; 13:20; Rev. 11:19). The vast majority of these are in the book of Hebrews, but the notion of a new covenant in the New Testament has its roots in Jesus' words at the Last Supper. The term "covenant" expressed Israel's relationship with God, and in New Testament times, the Qumran community saw itself as a community of this covenant. For instance, When one was joining the Community, the prescription says: "And if the lot results in him joining the foundations of the Community according to the priests and the majority of the men of the covenant, his wealth and his belongings will also be included at the hands of the Inspector of the belongings of the Many" (*Rule of the Community*, 1QS 6.19, Garcia Martinez trans.). Also in this same document, we read: "And thus, all the men who entered the new covenant in the land of Damascus and turned and betrayed and departed from the well of living waters, shall not be counted in the assembly of the people and shall not be inscribed in their [lis]ts, from the day of the session [of him who te<aches> / of the teacher]" (CD 19.33-35, Garcia Martinez, trans.). Again, according to a 1Qhabakkuk Pesher, "[The interpretation of the word concerns] the traitors with the Man of Lies, since they do not [believe in the words of the] Teacher of Righteousness from the mouth of God; (and it concerns) the traito[rs of the] new [covenant] since they did not believe in the covenant of God [and dishonoured] his name" (*Commentary on Habakkuk*, 1QpHab 2.1-3, Garcia Martinez trans.).

Letter kills vs. Spirit gives life. Paul elsewhere speaks of that which "kills" only in Rom. 7:11; 11:3; and 1 Thess. 2:15. See also his word for "letter" (Greek = *gramma*). The Jews early on taught that there was a connection between the spirit (or "breath" which comes from the same Hebrew and Greek words as does "spirit" and means essentially the same thing) and life (Gen. 1:2; 2:7; 6:17). According to the author of *2 Macc.* (ca. 104-63 B.C.), "the Creator of the world, who shaped the beginning of humankind and devised the origin of all things, will in his mercy give life and breath back to you again, since you now forget yourselves for the sake of his laws" (*2 Macc.* 7:23, NRSV). See also the *Wisdom of Solomon* (ca. 50-10 B.C.) who writes: "Their heart is ashes, their hope is cheaper than dirt, and their lives are of less worth than clay, because they failed to know the one who formed them and inspired them with active souls and breathed a living spirit into them" (15:10-11, NRSV). (See also the *Testament of Abraham* 18:11 and Philo, *Creation*

32.) Paul is not contrasting two ways of inter-preting the biblical text. The "spirit gives life" is close to Paul's message in 1 Cor. 15:45; cf. Rom. 4:17; 1 Cor. 15:22, 36. The closest Old Testament parallel is in Ezek. 36:26-28; 37: 5-6, 9. Sophocles (ca. 497-406 B.C.), in the heroic story of Antigone's defiance of inappropriate laws, describes the distinction between the laws that are man-made and those that that have a divine origin (especially Zeus):

> Yes, for it was not Zeus who made this proclamation, nor was it Justice who lives with the gods below that estab-lished such laws among men, nor did I think your proclamations strong enough to have power to overrule, mor-tal as they were, the unwritten and unfailing ordinances of the gods. For these have life, not simply today and yesterday, but for ever [sic], and no one knows how long ago they were revealed. For this I did not intend to pay the penalty among the gods for fear of any man's pride. I knew that I would die, of course I knew, even if you had made no proclamation. But if I die before my time, I account that gain. For does not whoever lives among many troubles, as I do, gain by death? . . . And if you think my actions foolish, that amounts to a charge of folly by a fool! (*Antigone* 450-470, LCL).

3:7-18. The ministry of the New Covenant. In these verses, Paul makes a shocking argument for Jews of the ancient world and even today who believed that the law brought joy and life, rather than death. Paul has rejected the view that salvation comes through the law and claims instead that God has offered life and hope through a new covenant, of which he and all believers are ministers (see 3:6 above). Pursuing the law as a means of securing hope is what called a "ministry of death (condemna-tion)." Indeed, they widely believed that any

who would change the law of God and alter its words were the "cause of wickedness" The author of *1 Enoch* (ca. 180 B.C.) writes: "woe unto you who alter the words of truth and per-vert the eternal law" (*1 Enoch* 99:2, *OT Pseud* 1:79). While reminding his readers of the value of the Law in keeping a "hedge" about the Jewish people by giving them regulations on life, the author of the *Letter of Aristeas* (ca. 150-100 B.C.) defends the Law of Moses saying: "Do not take the contemptible view that Moses enacted this legislation because of an excessive preoccupation with mice and weasels or such-like creatures. The fact is that everything has been solemnly set in order for unblemished investigation and amendment of life for the sake of righteousness" (*Ep. Arist.* 144, *OT Pseud* 2:22). The Jews of Paul's day and later also offered prayers that blessed the "Torah of Life." Sirach, for instance, wrote: "He [God] bestowed knowledge upon them, and allotted top of them the law of life. He established with them an eternal covenant, and revealed to them his decrees" (*Sir.* 17:11, NRSV), and again, "He allowed him [Moses] to hear his voice, and led him into the dark cloud, and gave him the commandments face to face, the law of life and knowledge, so that he might teach Jacob the covenant, and Israel his decrees" (*Sir.* 45:5, NRSV). Around A.D. 90-100, a Jewish writer, chiding the failure of his fellow countrymen, rehearses their history and concludes: "At first our ancestors lived as aliens in Egypt, and they were liberated from there and received the law of life, which they did not keep, which you also have transgressed after them" (*2 Esdr.* 14:30, NRSV). Finally, another Jewish author, ca. A.D. 100, writes about the Law saying: "Your Law is life, and your wisdom is the right way" (*2 Baruch* 38:2, *OT Pseud* 1:633). Paul's words had to come as something of a shock to his Jewish hearers who saw the Law of Moses as words of life and a covenant not of death, but of life. Knowing this helps to understand why the Jews often responded to Paul's message negatively and even violently (Acts 13:45; 14:2, 5, 19; 17:5, 13; 18:12-17; 21:17-21; 27-31). Jewish opposition, given their understanding of the Law and how that differed from Paul's view of its fading nature, led to conflict wherever Paul visited Jewish synagogues.

3:7-9. But if the ministry of death, in letters engraved on stones, came with glory, so that the sons of Israel could not look intently at the face of Moses because of the glory of his face, fading as it was, how shall the ministry of the Spirit fail to be even more with glory? For if the ministry of condemnation has glory, much more does the ministry of righteousness abound in glory. This pronouncement on the fading glory of the Law had to be a considerable surprise to the Jews who did not see the glory of the Law as fading nor did they see it as an instrument of death or condemnation as Paul did (cf. Gal. 3:10-14). Paul uses a familiar rabbinic form of reasoning that goes as follows: "if so with the lesser, how much more so with the greater" (see other examples of the smaller to the greater in Rom. 5:8-10, 15; 11:12, 24; cf. Phil. 2:12; Phile. 16). Philo, for example, argues from the lesser to the greater thusly: "for if the priest's body, which is mortal by nature, must be scrutinized to see that it is not afflicted by any serious misfortune, much more is that scrutiny needed for the immortal soul, which we are told was fashioned after the image of the Self-existent [God]" (*Special Laws* 1.81, LCL). Here Paul tells the story of Moses coming down from the mountain after being with God with a glory on his face, demonstrating a glory that he had received from God, and that was a "fading" splendor that would not last. Moses had the tablets of stone with the law etched on them by God and, because he had been in the presence of God, his face had a glow that the people could not look upon because of its brilliance (Exod. 34:29-35). Philo also related the story of Moses' transfigured appearance when he met with God on the mountain.

Moses came down from the mount so much more beautiful in countenance than when he ascended that those who beheld him were astonished and dumbfounded and were unable to gaze for any length of time because of the brightness that matched the sun in brilliance (*Life of Moses* 2.70, LCL).

Those Corinthians who were familiar with the stories of Homer would be reminded with this story of the time when Athena placed on Achilles her coat of armor and he went off to battle glistening.

When she had thus spoken, swift-footed Iris departed; but Achilles, dear to Zeus, roused him, and round about his mighty shoulders Athene flung her tasseled aegis [shield or protective armor], and around his head the fair goddess set thick a golden cloud, and forth from the man made blaze a gleaming fire . . . even so from the head of Achilles went up the gleam toward heaven (*Iliad* 18.203-206, 213-214, LCL).

While the parallels are clearly not exact, they do have some similarities. In terms of the stone/heart distinction, Dio Chrysostom (ca. A.D. 40-120) draws a similar distinction between laws that are put on tablets and those laws or customs that are placed in the heart:

Therefore it seems to me that we might liken the written law to the power of tyranny, for it is by means of fear and through injunction that each measure is made effective; but custom might rather be likened to the benevolence of kingship, for of their own volition all men follow custom, and without constraint. Again, we know of many laws which have been repealed by those who made them, because they judged them to be bad; but no one could readily point to a custom which had been dissolved . . . . Besides, while laws are preserved on tablets of wood or of stone, each custom is preserved within our hearts. And this sort of preservation is surer and better. Furthermore, the written law is harsh and stern, whereas nothing is more pleasant than custom. Then too, our laws we learn from others, but our customs we all know perfectly (*Orations* 76.2-3, LCL).

3:11. For if that which fades away was with glory, much more that which remains is in glory. Paul returns to his point of 3:7 above and with the same "from the lesser to the greater" kind of argument. The transient nature of the Law for Paul is not found among the Jews. Indeed, they saw the Law as eternal and bringing light, not darkness. In a first-century A.D. writing, roughly about the time of Jesus, a Jewish writer tells of God who "will kindle for him my lamp that will abide in him, and I will show him my covenant that no one has seen. And I will reveal to him my Law [lit. "super excellence" = Law of God] and statutes and judgments, and I will burn an eternal light for him . . ." (*Pseudo-Philo, Liber Antiquitatum Biblicarum* 9.8, *OT Pseud* 2:316). Again, "Shepherds and lamps and fountains came from the Law and when we go away, the law will abide. If you, therefore, look upon the Law and we are intent upon wisdom, then the lamp will not be wanting and the shepherd will not give way and the fountain will not dry up" (*2 Baruch* 77:15-16, *OT Pseud* 1:647). Paul's statement flies in the face of the contemporary Jewish affirmation, "For we who have received the law and sinned will perish, as well as our hearts that received it; the law, however, does not perish but survives in its glory" (*2 Esdr.* 9:36-37, NRSV).

3:12-13. Having therefore such a hope, we use great boldness in our speech, and are not as Moses, who used to put a veil over his face that the sons of Israel might not look intently at the end of what was fading away. The veil for Moses (Exod. 34:29-35) was to protect the people from the radiance that came to his face as a result of his meeting with God, but Paul says that he was "bold" (Greek = *parresia*) in speaking, not hiding behind a veil. The word here for boldness was used also in the political realm to focus on a person's right to speak openly and publicly. Philo expresses a common sentiment of his day: "Let those whose actions serve the common weal use freedom [*parresia*] of speech and walk in daylight through the midst of the marketplace, ready to converse with crowded gatherings . . ." (*Special Laws* 1.321, LCL). The Greeks at Corinth were well aware of those who would not speak with boldness, but were rather evasive in their speech. Dio Chrysostom tells of the difficulty in finding someone who could speak with frankness and boldness and not for personal gain.

> But there are only a few who have displayed frankness in your presence, and that but sparingly, not in such a way as to fill your ears therewith nor for any length of time; nay, they merely utter a phrase or two, and then, after berating rather than enlightening you, they make a hurried exit, anxious lest before they have finished you may raise an outcry and send them packing . . . . But to find a man who in plain terms and without guile speaks his mind with frankness, and neither for the sake of reputation nor for gain makes false pretensions, but out of good will and concern for his fellow-men stands ready, if need be, to submit to ridicule and to disorder and the uproar of the mob— to find such a man as that is not easy, but rather the good fortune of a very lucky city, so great is the dearth of noble, independent souls and such the abundance of toadies [a servile parasite], mountebanks [an itinerant quack or charlatan], and sophists (*Orations* 32.11, LCL).

3:14. But their minds were hardened; for until

this very day at the reading of the old covenant the same veil remains unlifted, because it is removed in Christ. This is the earliest known the use of the term "old covenant" and if so, it is a Pauline term. In Hebrews 8:13, however, the notion of a new covenant surpassing the "old" one and "what is obsolete and passing away will soon disappear" makes the notion a logical one, but refers instead to the "first covenant" in 9:15. This designation is also in keeping with Paul's contrast with the "new covenant" that he mentions in 3:6 above and implies throughout this passage. There is no reference here to the "Old Covenant" or "Old Testament" as a body of sacred literature. This notion is a late second-century development within the church, first used perhaps by Melito of Sardis (ca. 170), (Eusebius, *Ecclesiastical History* 4.26.13-14).

3:18. But we all, with unveiled face beholding as in a mirror the glory of the Lord, are being transformed into the same image from glory to glory, just as from the Lord, the Spirit. A Samaritan *midrash* (interpretation) of Deut. 34:7 tells how Moses' shining appearance could be associated with the image of God that Adam lost in his disobedience in the Garden (Gen. 3). "Nor his natural force abated [Deut. 34:7], for he was vested with the Form which Adam cast off in the Garden of Eden; and his face shone up to the day of his death" (*M. Marqah* 5.4, Furnish 215). The author of *2 Baruch* also tells of going from one degree of glory to a higher one. Those whose works of the Law were deemed worthy "will live in the heights of the world and they will be like the angels and be equal to the stars. And they will be changed into any shape which they wished, from beauty to loveliness, and from light to the splendor of glory" (*2 Apoc. Bar.* 51.10, *OT Pseud* 1:638).

Mirror.

On the notion of **"from the Lord, the Spirit"** (Greek = *kuriou pneumatos*), Paul may have been influenced by *1 Enoch* who says that

"when the secrets of the Righteous One are revealed," then:

the wicked ones will be driven from the presence of the righteous and the elect and from that time, those who possess the earth will neither be rulers nor princes, for they shall not be able to behold the faces of the holy ones, for the light of the Lord of the Spirits has shined upon the face of the holy, the righteous, and the elect. (*1 En.* 38.3-4, *OT Pseud* 1:30)

4:2 but we have renounced the things hidden because of shame, not walking in craftiness or adulterating the word of God, but by the manifestation of truth commending ourselves to every man's conscience in the sight of God. See discussion above on 2:17.

4:4. In whose case the god of this world has blinded the minds of the unbelieving, that they might not see the light of the gospel of the glory of Christ, who is the image of God. See earlier discussion in 2:10-11. The normal reference of Paul is to "the present age" (Rom. 3:26; 8:18; 11:15). That the evil one, Satan (the Devil), should blind individuals to the truth of God is also expressed in *The Testament of Judah* (second cent. B.C.) in which Judah says that "the prince of error blinded me, and I was ignorant—as a human being, as flesh, in my corrupt sins—until I learned of my own weakness after supposing myself to be invincible" (*Test. Judah* 19.4, *OT Pseud* 1:800). In *The Testaments of the Twelve Patriarchs* (first-third centuries A.D.), the "light" that enlightens both Jews and Gentiles comes through the Law. "you [children of Israel] should be the lights of Israel as the sun and the moon. For what will all the nations do if you become darkened with impiety? You will bring a curse on our nation, because you want to destroy the light of the Law which was granted to you for the enlightenment of every man . . ." (*Test. Levi* 14.3-4, *OT Pseud* 1:793). The author of the *Wisdom of Solomon* (ca. 50-10 B.C.) claims that wisdom "is a reflection of eternal light, a spotless mirror of the working of god, and an image of his goodness" (*Wisd.* 7:26, NRSV).

4:5. For we do not preach ourselves but Christ Jesus as Lord, and ourselves as your bondservants for Jesus' sake. This is one of the places where Paul emphasizes an early Christian creed, namely that "Jesus is Lord" (Rom. 10:9; 1 Cor. 12:3; Phil. 2:10-11; cf. also Phil. 3:8). What does it mean to be a faithful servant of the Lord? The famous Stoic teacher Epictetus said that those who would seek would follow his example of wanting the will of God over his own will. He writes: "For I regard god's will as better than my will. I shall attach myself to Him as a servant and follower, my choice is one with His, my desire one with His, in a word, my will is one with His will" (*Discourses* 4.7.20, LCL). Paul insists that his message is not himself, but Christ. Paul's refusal to proclaim himself is similar to Dio Chrysostom's claim:

And the men whom I met, on catching sight of me, would sometimes call me a tramp and sometimes a beggar, though some did call me a philosopher. From this it came about gradually and without any planning or any self-conceit on my part that I acquired this name. Now the great majority of those styled philosophers proclaim themselves such, just as the Olympian heralds proclaim the victors; but in my case, when the other folk applied this name to me, I was not able always and in all instances to have the matter out with them (*Orations* 13.11-12, LCL).

4:6. For God, who said, "Light shall shine out of darkness," is the One who has shone in our hearts to give the light of the knowledge of the glory of God in the face of Christ. This passage probably reflects what took place in Paul's Damascus Road experience that speaks of light and God actively involved in what took place (Acts 9:3-6; 22:6-18). The rest of the passage reflects imagery from Gen. 1:3 and Ps. 27:1, the latter cited by Philo to emphasize that God is the source of truth (light).

God is light, for there is a verse in one of the psalms, 'the Lord is my illumination and my savior' (Ps. 27.1). And he is not only light, but the archtype of every other light, nay prior to and high above every archtype, holding the position of the model of a model (*On Dreams* 1.75, LCL).

The notion of the splendor of God manifested in someone, in this case Jesus Christ (see 3:18 where there is no veil hiding that image as in the case of Moses), is a familiar theme in the Qumran community and may have its roots in Num. 6:24-26, Ps. 31:16 and Ps. 67:1. In the *Rule of the Blessings*, for instance,

You shall be around, serving in the temple of the kingdom, sharing the lot with the angels of the face and the Council of the Community [. . .] for eternal time and for all the perpetual periods. For [all] your judgments [are truth]. They have made you holy among your people, like a luminary [which lights up] the world with knowledge, and shines on the face of the Many [. . .] consecrated for the holy of holies, because [you shall be made holy] for him and give glory to his name and his holy things (1QSb 4.24b-28, Garcia Martinez trans.).

Likewise, the Teacher of Righteousness also speaks of his face being illuminated by God.

I give you thanks, Lord, because you have brightened my face with your covenant and [. . .] I have looked for you. Like perfect dawn you have revealed yourself to me with your light . . . . Through me you have enlightened the face of the Many, you have increased them, even making them uncountable, for you have shown me your wondrous mysteries (1QH 4 [Col.12] 5-6, 27, Garcia Martinez trans.).

This is similar to what is found in the blessing in the *Rule of the Community* in which a part of the blessing is "May he bless you with everything good, and may he protect you from everything bad. May he illuminate your heart with the discernment of life and grace you with eternal knowledge. May he lift upon you the countenance of his favour for eternal peace" (1QS 2.3-4, Garcia Martinez trans.).

c. 4:7–5:10. The Ministry and Life beyond Death.

To some extent this is the second section of Paul's apology or defense. Although the outward appearance did not tell the best of stories for Paul, inwardly, or spiritually, he was more than adequate for the task that was before him. In 4:7-15 Paul pays close attention to the present: namely, how does one who follows Christ deal with the crises that come to those who are serving the Lord? He argues that suffering and preaching come to him in order to care for the Corinthians. In 4:16–5:10, he focuses his attention on what is true for all Christians, hope beyond this life, and he examines the nature of the life that is yet to come for those who are faithful.

4:7. But we have this treasure in earthen vessels, that the surpassing greatness of the power may be of God and not from ourselves. The "vessels," or jars, Paul speaks of here in a metaphorical sense were made of a variety of materials in the ancient world, including bronze, stone, and clay, but the most common material was clay. Jars made of this substance broke easily, but they were also easily replaced. Paul compares the Christians to clay jars, that is, something not that important and also replaceable, but somehow in the plan of God, he made it so these "clay jars" would contain a priceless treasure, the Gospel of Jesus Christ. Seneca (ca. 4 B.C.- A.D. 65) offers a close parallel to Paul's reference to the human body as a fragile vessel:

What is man? A vessel that the slightest shaking, the slightest toss will break. No mighty wind is needed to scatter you abroad; whatever you strike against will be your undoing. What is man? A body weak and fragile, naked, in its natural state of defenseless [sic], dependent upon another's help, and exposed to all the affronts of fortune . . . a fabric of weak and unstable elements, attractive only in its outer features, unable to bear cold, heat, and toil, yet from mere rust and idleness doomed to decay. . . . (*To Marcia on Consolation* 11.3, LCL)

Plutarch offers a parallel in structure to Paul's catalogue of antitheses.

Confined is not impeded, and thrown from a precipice is not subject to force, and stretched on the rack is not tortured, and being mutilated is not injured, and taking a fall in wrestling is unconquerable, and being sold into slavery by his enemies is not taken captive (*Moralia* 1057 D-E, LCL).

4:8-10. We are afflicted in every way, but not crushed; perplexed, but not despairing; persecuted, but not forsaken; struck down, but not destroyed; always carrying about in the body the dying of Jesus, that the life of Jesus also may be manifested in our body. The Stoics and Cynics of Paul's day made use of antithetical formulation, such as we find here, and the Corinthians would have recognized it readily. This is also known as one of Paul's hardship catalogues (see earlier discussion in 1 Cor. 4:6-12). There are five times in the Corinthian correspondence when Paul lists his sufferings for his faith (here, 2 Cor. 4:8-9; 6:3-10; 11:23-29; and 12:10). While there are some similarities to the Stoic stance on the problems that face humanity, there are also differences. Epictetus could say: "Show me a man who though sick is happy, though in danger is happy, though dying is happy, though condemned to exile is happy, though in disrepute is happy. Show him! By the gods, I would fain see a Stoic!" (*Discourses* 2.24.24, LCL). Paul, on the other hand, never suggested that one should rejoice at the problems that life brings, but rather in a God who does not abandon his children in their hour of need (Rom. 8:38-39; Phil. 4:5-7). Paul's view of facing the difficulties of life was rooted in God's faithfulness and in his view of the impending end of the age in which God would reward his children. The Stoic was more self-reliant and even self-deluded about the trials of life that come to all people. Paul's reference to "not forsaken" has strong roots in the Jewish tradition that God determined not to forsake his people (Gen. 28:15; Deut. 31:6, 8; Hos. 11:8-9). It was in this promise that Paul found the strength to overcome the obstacles that came his way.

4:11. For we who live are constantly being delivered over to death for Jesus' sake, that the life of Jesus also may be manifested in our mortal flesh. The continual and very real bodily danger facing Paul was an important factor in his faith in a God who delivers even from death and one's enemies. Since death is a part of one's understanding of the Christian faith itself, namely Christians are also baptized into the death of Christ (Rom. 6:3-11), Paul can speak of the newness of life only after an acknowledgment of the death to the old life that Christians face in their coming to faith in Christ. Plato spoke of the importance of being free from the fear of death and from the pains of the body in order to find true life.

. . . if we are ever to know anything absolutely, we must be free from the body and must behold the actual realities with the eye of the soul alone. And then, as our argument shows, when we are dead we are likely to possess the wisdom which we desire and claim to be enamored of, but not while we live . . . but keep our selves pure from it [the body] until God himself sets us free . . . . true

philosophers practice dying, and death is less terrible to them than to any other men (*Phaedo* 66DE, 67E, LCL)

Seneca also has a similar view of death. He writes:

I remember one day you [Lucilius] were handling the well-known commonplace—that we do not suddenly fall on death, but advance towards it by slight degrees; we die every day. For every day a little of our life is taken from us; even when we are growing, our life is on the wane. We lose our childhood, then our boyhood, and then our youth. Counting even yesterday, all past time is lost time; the very day which we are now spending is shared between ourselves and death. It is not the last drop that empties the water-clock, but all that which previously has flowed out; similarly, the final hour when we cease to exist does not of itself bring death; it merely of itself completes the death-process. We reach death at that moment, but we have been a long time on the way. (*Epistles* 24.19-20, LCL)

4:13. But having the same spirit of faith, according to what is written, "I believed, therefore I spoke," we also believe, therefore also we speak. Paul continues his defense which he defends more fully later in 10:10; 12:19; and 13:3. Here he cites Ps. 116:10 from the Septuagint (LXX).

4:16. Therefore we do not lose heart, but though our outer man is decaying, yet our inner man is being renewed day by day. Paul's "inner man" is similar to the anthropological terms that were popular in his day. Seneca, for example, speaks of the significant hardships that occur to all individuals, but challenges that they can defeat the sage or philosopher. He contends that:

Nothing can subdue him; nothing that

must be endured annoys him. For he does not complain that he has been struck by that which can strike any man. He knows his own strength; he knows that he was born to carry burdens. I do not withdraw the wise man from the category of man, nor do I deny to him the sense of pain as though he were a rock that has no feelings at all. I remember that he is made up of two parts: the one part is irrational—it is this that may be bitten, burned, or hurt; the other part is rational—it is this which holds resolutely to opinions, is courageous, and unconquerable. In the latter is situated man's supreme Good. Before this is completely attained, the mind wavers in uncertainty; only when it is fully achieved is the mind fixed and steady (*Moral Epistles* 71.27, LCL).

Philo is also aware of the "inner man," of which Paul speaks. He identifies it somewhat differently, however.

But who else could the man that is in each of us be save the mind, whose place it is to reap the benefits derived from all that has been sown or planted? But seeing that for babes milk is food, but for grown men wheaten bread, there must also be soul-nourishment, such as is milk—like suited to the time of childhood, in the shape of preliminary stages of school-learning, and such as is adapted to grown men in the shape of instructions leading the way through wisdom and temperance and all virtue (*On Husbandry* 9, LCL).

Paul's distinction between the outer and inner man is similar to that of rabbinic distinction between evil and good, but he has made use of the terms that he has to accommodate his Greek readers in Corinth. Marcus Aurelius (A.D. 120-180), speaks about the possibility of death and considers that which is unseen or within us to be the real core that survives and the outer things that are visible (the body and all its parts) are ultimately useless. He asks:

What end has the man in view? But begin with thyself; cross-examine thyself first. Bear in mind that what pulls the strings is that Hidden Thing within us: that makes our speech, that our life, that, one may say, makes the man. Never in the mental picture of it include the vessel that overlies it nor these organs that are appurtenances thereof. They are like the workman's adze [a tool for cutting the surface of wood], only differing from it in being naturally attached to the body. Since, indeed, severed from the Cause that bids them move and bids them stay, these parts are as useless as is the shuttle of the weaver, the pen of the writer, and the whip of the charioteer (*Meditations* 10.37-38, LCL).

4:18. While we look not at the things which are seen, but at the things which are not seen; for the things which are seen are temporal, but the things which are not seen are eternal. Paul does not say that the temporal things do not exist, as Plato argued, but that they are not as important as those things that are eternal. Seneca, who adopted the Platonic notion that what is seen is not the reality, but the unseen above, namely a dualism that taught that the only true reality is above and that what is seen is temporal and unreal. He claimed that the physical things that we see:

. . . are therefore imaginary, and though they for the moment present a certain external appearance, yet they are in no case permanent or substantial; none the less, we crave them as if they were always to exist, or as if we were always to possess them. We are weak, watery beings standing in the midst of unrealities; therefore let us turn our minds to the things that are everlasting. Let us look up to the ideal outlines of all things, that flit about on high, and to the God who moves among them and plans how he may defend from death that which he could not make imperishable because its substance forbade, and so by reasons may overcome the defects of the body (*Moral Epistles* 58.27, LCL).

This, of course, does not represent the perspective of Paul. He argues that the "eternal" is the most important aspect of life and that he will focus on what cannot be taken away instead of what he can lose. When this takes place, then he can endure the hardships listed in vv. 8-9 and face with confidence the future God has for those who trust in him. Paul is closer to the perspective of the Jewish author of *4 Macc.* (ca. A.D. 38-50), when telling the story of the seven brothers who were on the verge of being tortured because they would not recant their faith, he described them as follows:

But on the very point of being tortured these young men uttered no such words [or recanting their faith] nor even entertained such thoughts. For they despised the emotions and were masters over pain. Accordingly, no sooner had the tyrant finished counseling them to eat unclean food than they all with one voice and as with one soul said: . . . "By our suffering and endurance, we shall obtain the prize of virtue and shall obtain the prize of virtue and shall be with God, on whose account we suffer" (*4 Macc.* 8.27-29; 9.9, *OT Pseud* 2:554).

Seneca is not far from Paul on his willingness to face death with an eye toward the future and to reject the immobilizing fear that sometimes accompanies the pain of life. After praising those who were brave in the face of tragedy and loss, he goes on to reject praise of those who in fear flee danger or death. He then praises those who faced death with bravery and asks:

Should I weep for Hercules because he was burned alive? Or Regulus because

he was pierced by so many nails? Or for Cato because he wounded his own wounds [a reference to his tearing apart the wounds that were not deep enough to kill him!] [Cf. *Epistles* 67.13?] All these by a slight sacrifice of time found out how they might become eternal, and by dying reached immortality (*On Tranquillity* [sic] *of Mind* 16.4, LCL).

Observe also how he saw that what he was going through was a "slight sacrifice of time"! This, of course, sounds similar to Paul's words about the "momentary, light affliction" in 4:17. There were also those in the ancient world who feared dying without having made a sacrifice that would bring them immortality in the minds of those who remained.

5:1-10. Believers' hope in the face of death. Paul now focuses his attention on the nature of life after death for the believer. The "eternal" that Paul has focused on leads him to discuss what takes place as one goes from this life to the next. For Paul, that includes a transformed bodily existence in which the old is not discarded, but is "further clothed upon." Paul is speaking to a community that was familiar with several notions of life beyond death and even no life beyond death. Paul expands his focus from what has happened to him or will happen to him to what will happen to all believers. He claims that believers will have a transformed bodily existence after death (cf. 15:51-53). This hope, Paul argues, leads us to seek to be pleasing to God in our actions (6-10).

5:1. For we know that if the earthly tent which is our house is torn down, we have a building from God, a house not made with hands, eternal in the heavens. Paul reflects on the temporary nature of housing that took place in and around Corinth during the famous Isthmian games every two years. Tents were sent up in many places and the picture of a tent coming down or being torn down was a familiar scene to the Corinthians. Temporary tents were in sharp contrast to the beautiful and substantial buildings at Corinth, the ruins of which still stand after 2,000 years! Paul says that when the "temporary tent" (body) that believers live in is destroyed, they have a "building not made with hands" that is eternal in the heavens." The use of the tent as a reference to the human body precedes Paul and is found in several Jewish texts. For example, the author of the *Wisdom of Solomon* (ca. 50 B.C.), an Alexandrian document, writes: "for a perishable body weighs down the soul, and this earthly tent burdens the thoughtful mind" (*Wisd.* 9:15, NRSV). Likewise, the use of the "building" (Greek = *oikodomen*) to represent the human body is found at Qumran where we find, "The foundations of my building have crumbled, my bones have been disjointed" (1QH 7.4, Garcia Martinez trans.). Additionally, in Acts 7:48 and 17:24, Stephen and Paul respectively claim that God does not dwell in a building "made with hands." It is interesting that Paul says the same thing here about the future body or dwelling place for those who are believers.

5:2-3. For indeed in this house we groan, longing to be clothed with our dwelling from heaven; inasmuch as we, having put it on, shall not be found naked. The notion of the body having a heavenly dwelling or house has several parallels in Jewish literature. In the New Testament, there are several examples of a heavenly dwelling (John 14:2-3; Jude 6; but for the contrary dwelling place of demons, see Rev. 18:2). Paul saw that the body was a burden that needed transformation, but did not see hope in the separation of the soul from the body. That was nakedness and not a thing to be desired, but rather a new body without the same limitations that plagued all who live in the flesh (cf. Rom. 8:22-23). The importance of the separation of the self from the body at death formed the foundation of the majority opinion of Hellenistic belief about life after death. In one unknown writing from ca. 428-348 B.C., the writer speaks of this dissolution of body and soul (self):

> consider this: once the connection [between body and soul] is dissolved and the soul reaches its place in the heavens, then the boy that is left behind—earthly and without reason— is not the real person. For we are souls, immortal living beings, enclosed in a fleshly dungeon [the body]. Nature enclosed us in a tent to our disadvantage.... therefore being released from life is a change from something bad to something good (*Pseudo-Plato, Axiochus* 365E-366A, M.E. Boring trans).

In the *Corpus Hermeticum*, a non-Christian Gnostic document (ca. A.D. 180-200), Hermes Trismegistus speaks to Poimandres (Greek = the shepherd man) and asks him, "How shall I come to Life?" the gnostic views, which are thoroughly Hellenistic, on the value of the body are made clear by Poimandres. He responds:

> First, with the dissolution of your material body, you yield your character to the Daimon. Your image vanishes. The body senses return to their own sources, becoming part of the cosmos, and, combined in new ways, do other work. And anger and desire enter thoughtless Nature. And then man rises into the harmony, the world of the spheres. In the first zone he leaves behind the force to grow and decrease, in the second the machinations of evil, in the third the guile of lust, in the fourth his domineering arrogance, in the sixth his striving for wealth by evil means, and in the seventh zone the malicious lie—all rendered powerless. Then stripped naked by the force of Harmony, he enters the eighth sphere of the fixed star, Ogdoas, and possessing his own energy he remains there with others, singing

hymns to the Father. And the others are happy at his coming. (*Corpus Hermeticum* 1.24-26, Barnstone, trans.)

Later in the same collection of Gnostic writings, we see again the Gnostic/Hellenistic perspective on the body.

. . . The earthly body cannot support so great an immortality, nor can so great a dignity endure defiling contact with a body subject to passion. Mind, therefore, has taken the soul as a shroud, and the soul, which is itself something divine, uses the spirit as a sort of armouring-servant. The Spirit governs the living being.

Then, when the mind has got free of the earthly body, it immediately puts on its own tunic, a tunic of fire, in which it could not stay when in the earthly body (*Corpus Hermeticum* 10.17-18, M.E. Boring, trans.).

Also, the dominance of this view on the nature and value of the human body can be seen well into the fifth century A.D. when a certain Hierocles of Alexandria explains the Pythagorean method of philosophy:

This is the goal of the Pythagorean method, that everyone be empowered to receive the divine goodness, so that when the moment of death comes they may leave behind on earth this mortal body and take off its nature, and that those who have fought the good fight of philosophy will be well-girded for the heavenly way . . . then they will become participants in the divine nature themselves (*Commentary on Pythagoras' "Carmen Aureum"* 26, M.E. Boring, trans.).

(Observe the parallel with "fighting the good fight" in 2 Tim. 4:7). Finally, Epictetus also saw the body as a burden and could hope for a separation from it and concludes,

. . . for since we are upon the earth and trammeled by an earthy body and by earthy associates, how was it possible

that, in respect of them, we should not be hampered by external things? But what says Zeus? "Epictetus, had it been possible I should have made both the paltry body and the small estate of thine free and unhampered [from the body]. But as it is—let it not escape thee—this body is not thine own, but only clay cunningly compounded. Yet since I could not give thee this, we have given thee a certain portion of ourself, this faculty of choice and refusal, of desire and aversion, or, in a word, the faculty which makes use of external impressions . . ." (*Discourses* 1.1.9-12, LCL).

For Epictetus, the body was something that was a burden that dragged him down (*Discourses* 1.1.14-15), but though Paul certainly knew of its limitations, he did not seek a bodiless existence. Interestingly, the notion that humanity emerges clay "cunningly compounded" with the introduction of the "a certain portion of ourself" from the divine is not far from the Genesis picture of the creation of human beings from dust and the breath of God that animates that body formed from the dust (Gen. 2:7; cf. 3:19). We note that the word for "human" in the English language comes from the Latin *"humus"* meaning ground, earth. This word is in harmony with the biblical tradition that humanity was created by God from the earth or ground.

The Greek word for **naked**, *"gumnos,"* is also the root word for gymnasium. The presence of many gymnasiums in the Hellenistic world where both physical exercise, baths, and dissemination of Greek culture took place. They were frequented by those who were both prosperous and often well educated. As a result, they also became a place of education and often functioned as schools. While the Jews were uncomfortable with nudity, the Corinthians were quite familiar with it and it was a normal part of their lives. It was represented on their statuary, paintings on pottery, all athletic games at the nearby Isthmian games, and at the gymnasiums which served as exercise centers. The Romans sometimes utilized the gymnasiums solely for education and the baths as the place both for exercise and bathing. The exercising and public bathing openly displayed nudity and this was abhorrent to the Jews who saw this activity to be characteristic of Gentiles. See also below in 11:27 and Rom. 8:35 where "nakedness" is listed among hardships endured by those in peril. Among the Jews, nakedness was always a thing to be avoided. Their abhorrence of nakedness stems from the sin of Adam and Eve that revealed to them their nakedness (Gen. 3:7) and the subsequent divine provision of garments made of animal skins to cover their nakedness (Gen. 3:21). When the Greeks occupied Palestine during rule of Alexander the Great (333-323 B.C.), Alexander planned a universal empire of all nations through an introduction of Greek culture in the conquered nations. This was carried out through the introduction of the Greek language and the gymnasium, a place of learning and physical exercise that was done in the nude. Likewise, the Greek athletes participated in the athletic events in the nude as well. When the Seleucid dynasty took control of Palestine from the Ptolemies in Egypt (ca. 198 B.C.), who had been largely tolerant of the Jews, the Seleucids, particularly during the reign of the Seleucid king, Antiochus Epiphanes (175-164 B.C.), tried to impose both the Greek culture and Greek religion on the Jews. They introduced the gymnasium into Palestine and both Jews and Greeks participated in the activities related to the gymnasium in the nude. The very word "gymnasium" comes from the Greek word *gymnos* that means "naked."

This angered the Law observant Jews and led to many conclusions about the Gentile invaders. The author of *Jubilees* (ca. second cent. B.C.) claims, on the basis of Gen. 3:21 that "it is commanded in the heavenly tablets to all who will know the judgment of the Law that they should cover their shame and they should not be uncovered as the gentiles are uncovered" (*Jub.* 3:26, 31, *OT Pseud.* 2:60). Similarly, the author of *1 Macc.* (ca. 104-100 B.C.), speaking of the evil brought to the land by Antiochus Epiphanes, says: "So they built a gymnasium in Jerusalem, according to Gentile custom, and removed the marks of circumcision [through a process called "*epispasm*"], and they abandoned the holy covenant. They [some Jews] joined with the Gentiles and sold themselves to do evil" (*1 Macc.* 1:14-15, NRSV). The author of *2 Macc.* (ca. 104-63 B.C.) also speaks with disdain of this behavior when Jason, the high priest, "shifted his compatriots to the Greek way of life" and adopted "an extreme of Hellenization and increase in the adoption of foreign ways because of the surpassing wickedness of Jason" who also led the priests to despise the sanctuary of the temple and the sacrifices to take part in the "unlawful proceedings in the wrestling arena after the signal for the discus-throwing . . . " (*2 Macc.* 4:10-15, NRSV). The Greeks also held their quadrennial games at Tyre on the coast of northern Palestine, in which the athletes likewise performed their competitions naked. They were generally prepared for competition at the gymnasiums where they exercised naked. Nakedness was also a common feature in the public baths in the Greco-Roman world.

What is important here is that Paul speaks metaphorically of nakedness in terms of life after death, namely that there will not be a nakedness, that is a bodiless existence, in the after-life, but rather that there will be an incorporation of the old body in the new ("further clothed upon," v. 4, Greek = *ependusasthai*). Jewish beliefs about the nature of life after death varied considerably between notions of immortality without a body and the resurrection of the body in the first centuries both B.C. and A.D. Paul was clearly of the view that life after death was a bodily existence, albeit a transformed bodily existence—the present decaying body puts on immortality (see also 1 Cor. 15:35-54). This thought was equally repugnant to the Greeks who believed that the body was a prison and that it would be better to be rid of it rather than be inconvenienced by it in the life to come. Plotinus, the Neoplatonist philosopher (ca. 205-270), for example, contended that: "The body is [a] brute beast touched to life. The true man is the other . . . the soul which even in its dwelling here may be kept apart" (*The Animate and the Man* 10, LCL). For the Greeks in the classical period, nudity became the costume of the citizen, and especially so with male nudity. Only the barbarians, non-Greek speaking tribes of people, saw shame in nakedness and so covered up with clothing. Herodotus (ca. 484-430 B.C.) tells of a certain king named Candaules who was so proud of the beauty of his wife that he asked his guard, Gyges, to look upon her nakedness to witness what was his. The guard responded with fear at the prospect:

> What a pestilent command is this that you lay upon me! That I should see her who is my mistress naked! With the stripping off of her tunic a woman is stripped of the hounour due to her. Men had long ago made wise rules for our learning; one of these is, that we, and none other, should see what is our own. As for me, I fully believe that your queen is the fairest of all women; ask not lawless acts of me, I entreat you (Herodotus 1.8, LCL).

Gyges could not escape the king's command and so he watched the queen disrobe, but she saw that he was watching and,

> . . . perceived what her husband had done. But shamed though she was she never cried out nor let it be seen that she had perceived aught, for she had it in mind to punish Candaules; seeing that among the Lydians and most of the foreign peoples it is held great shame that

even a man should be seen naked (Herodotus 1.10, LCL).

While male nudity was common, it was not so with women except in art related to bathing or portraying women about to be raped or killed. Men, on the other hand, would often be shown without clothing in outdoor settings, especially in competitions, but not indoors. In Roman art, nudity was the costume of the male hero, but not so for the female.

To clothe oneself with heavenly garments is a familiar theme in Jewish literature roughly contemporary with the time of Paul (cf. also Ascension of Isa. 7:22; 8:14, 26; 9:2, 9, 17, 24-26; 11:40).

5:4. For indeed while we are in this tent, we groan, being burdened, because we do not want to be unclothed, but to be clothed, in order that what is mortal may be swallowed up by life. The word translated "clothed" in this passage comes from the Greek, *ependuesthai*, "clothed upon" or "further clothed." The idea is that something is put on over the present garment. See also 1 Cor. 15:53-54; cf. also Rom. 8:22-23. What Paul argues here has Jewish parallels elsewhere and claims that the final or future existence of those who are faithful to God will be in a clothed state, that is, with a heavenly body. For example, the author of *1 Enoch* (ca. second cent. B.C.) speaks about the future clothing of those who are faithful to God: "They shall wear the garments of glory. These garments of yours shall become the garments of life from the Lord of the spirits. Neither shall your garments wear out, nor your glory come to an end before the Lord of the Spirits" (*1 En.* 62:16, *OT Pseud* 2:44). In Ezra's vision, he tells of a multitude of those whom God called and blessed, those who were faithful to God and whose number is complete, and "These are they who have put off mortal clothing and have put on the immortal, and have confessed the name of God. Now they are being crowned and receive palms" (2 *Esdras*

2:45, NRSV). In the *Martyrdom and Ascension of Isaiah* (ca. A.D. 100-150), the writer, who shows clear Christian influence, says that Isaiah is promised that he will have a throne, robes and crown in the heavens above (*Asc. Isa.* 7:22-23, OT Pseud 2:168). He goes on to say that "the holy Isaiah is permitted to come up here [heaven], for his robe is here" (9:2). When he ascends, he sees "Enoch and all who (were) with him, stripped of (their) robes of the flesh; and I saw them in their robes of above" (9:9). The others who come to heaven after Isaiah do not receive their robes "until the Lord Christ ascends and they ascend with him. Then indeed they will receive their robes" (9:17-18, similarly 9:24-26). At the end of the writing, the author has Isaiah say to Hezekiah: "as for you, be in the Holy Spirit that you may receive your robes, and the thrones and crowns of glory, which are placed in the seventh heaven" (11:40, *OT Pseud* 2:168-176). The function of the robe is so that there is no nakedness in heaven (cf. Rev. 6:9-11). More importantly, we see a parallel of getting rid of the flesh and receiving a new covering in the *Odes of Solomon* (ca. late first cent. to early second cent. A.D.). The author of that Jewish writing says, "and I was covered with the covering of your spirit, and I removed from myself my garments of skin" (*Odes Sol.* 25:8, *OT Pseud* 2:758). In the Classical period, we also see early on a sense of "nakedness" of the soul that is covered with a body. Plato (ca. 427-347 B.C.), in portraying the dialogue between Socrates and Hermogenes, tells of Socrates' response to questions about the Greek gods and his understanding of death. He explains the fear of coming before a god without the covering of the body, that is, the fear of being "naked."

> I think people have many false notions about the power of this god, and are unduly afraid of him. They are afraid because when we are once dead we remain in his [Hades] realm for ever, and they are also terrified because the

soul goes to him *without the covering* [Greek = *gumne*, a family word associated with *gumnos*] *of the body* (*Cratylus* 403B, LCL, italics ours).

5:5. Now He who prepared us for this very purpose is God, who gave to us the Spirit as a pledge. For a discussion of the role of the Spirit as a pledge to the future, see 1:22 above.

5:8-9. We are of good courage, I say, and prefer rather to be absent from the body and to be at home with the Lord. Therefore also we have as our ambition, whether at home or absent, to be pleasing to Him. Paul does not look forward to being absent from the body during the "intermediate state" of nakedness in the presence of the Lord, but being "home" with the Lord is preferable. On the other hand, wherever he dwells, it is important to be pleasing to the Lord. This passage has to do with the future existence of believers and Paul, like many of his Jewish fellows believes that this will be in bodily form. If there is a wait to be endured until the time of the resurrection, that does not change the "robes" that all will wear in the presence of God and the change that will take place in their bodies. The author of *2 Baruch* (early second cent. A.D.) affirms that there will be changes in the body and that none of the faithful will be disappointed. Baruch asks of the Lord: "In which shape will the living live in your day? Or how will remain their splendor which will be after that? Will they perhaps take this present form . . .?" (*2 Bar.* 49:1-3, *OT Pseud* 1:637). The answer comes to him as follows:

> For the earth will surely give back the dead at that time; it receives them now in order to keep them, not changing anything in their form. But as it has received them so it will give them back. As I have delivered them to it, so it will raise them. For then it will be necessary to show those who live that the dead are

living again, and that those who went away have come back . . . .

. . . their splendor will then be glorified by transformation, and the shape of their face will be changed into the light of their beauty so that they may acquire and receive the undying world which is promised to them.

. . . And they will be changed into any shape which they wished, from beauty to loveliness, and from light to the splendor of glory. For the extents of paradise will be spread out for them, and to them will be shown the beauty of the majesty of the living beings around the throne . . . (*2 Bar.* 50:2; 51:3, *OT Pseud* 1:638).

Paul's view of life after death is similar in that the body is changed, not discarded, but it is also transformed.

5:10. For we must all appear before the judgment seat of Christ, that each one may be recompensed for his deeds in the body, according to what he has done, whether good or bad. Paul uses a term here that was quite familiar to those in Greek cities: namely, the appearing before a "judgment seat" (Greek = *bema*, also "judicial bench"). Corinth had a beautiful "*bema*," the ruins of which are still visible today, and Paul appealed before Gallio there in Acts 18:12-17. Anyone brought before the courts of that day would appear at the *bema*, or judgment seat, to answer for their crimes or to defend themselves. If the *bema* was not in legal session, it was often used by orators who would speak to those who gathered to hear them. Paul says that every believer must give an accountability of himself/herself before Christ (cf. Rom. 14:12). This word, for Paul, was a message of hope for all believers and elsewhere he uses similar language to bring comfort to the faithful (1 Thess. 4:13-17). Plato spoke also of the life after death and also of a judgment that stood between the possibilities of correction under the earth or

blessings in the heavens. Speaking of those who die, he says,

Now in all these states, whoever lives justly obtains a better lot, and whoever lives unjustly, a worse [lot] . . . . when they have finished their first life, receive judgment, and after the judgment some go to the places of correction under the earth and pay their penalty, while others, made light and raised up into a heavenly place by justice, live in a manner worthy of the life they led in human form (*Phaedrus* 249AB, LCL).

d. 5:11–21. The Ministry of Reconciliation

This passage is a summary of Paul's ministry: namely, that it is one of reconciliation of individuals to God. His motives for this ministry are both "fear" (v. 11) and "love" (v. 14). The discussion of Paul's apostleship concludes with this passage and a transition is made to the preparation of the people for the offering that Paul wants to receive from them to care for the Christians in Jerusalem. This passage is connected with the previous discussion by the "therefore" (v. 11) and with what follows in 6:1-13. Paul reintroduces his theme from 2:14 on a ministry of the new covenant, which he left in 4:14-16 to focus on all believers and their future. Building on that, Paul returns to his own ministry that had been called into question by his opponents who claimed that Paul was merely commending himself and that he was somehow inferior in his ministry, and perhaps even that he was beside himself (v. 13). Finally he describes the basis (love for all persons, v. 14) and nature of his ministry (reconciliation, vv.18-21).

5:12. We are not again commending ourselves to you but are giving you an occasion to be proud of us, that you may have an answer for those who take pride in appearance, and not in heart. Philostratus also observes that the sophists were frequently given renown by cities and cities were given renown from having the sophists among them. He tells of one such sophist named Polemo of whom it was said "for just as its marketplace and a splendid array of buildings reflect luster on a city, so does an opulent establishment; for not only does a city give a man renown, but itself acquires it from a man" (Lives of Sophists 532, LCL). Again, Philostratus tells of a certain Favorinus (ca. A.D. 80-150) who came to Rome and,

> When he delivered discourses in Rome, the interest in them was universal, so much so that even those in his audience who did not understand the Greek language shared in the pleasure that he gave; for he fascinated even them by the tones of his voice. By his expressive glance and the rhythm of his speech. They were enchanted by the epilogue of his orations, which they called "The Ode," though I call it mere affection, since it is arbitrarily added at the close of an argument that has been logically proved (Lives of the Sophists 491, LCL).

These sophists were known for their self-commendation and seeking the recognition of all places where they spoke. Evidently, some at Corinth did not care much for those who were eloquent, and especially paying for their trade. Dio Chrysostom (ca. A.D. 40-120) tells of the time when Herodotus paid a visit to Corinth and after speaking "he expected to receive pay from the city. But failing of obtaining even that—for your forebearers did not deem it fitting to traffic in renown—he devised those tales we all know so well, the tales about Salamis and Adeimantus"! (Orations 37.7, LCL). In order to get even, Herodotus told the tales of a battle that was led by the Corinthian commander, Adeimantus, in which he fled with his contingent and was taunted by other Greek forces for his cowardice! Philostratus, while praising Hippodromus, an eloquent but humble sophist, says of the rest of the profession, "for although he had adopted a profes-

sion that is prone to egotism and arrogance, he never resorted to self-praise, but used to check those who praised him to excess" (Lives of Sophists 616, LCL). While Paul was seeking personal glory nor financial benefit from his work among the Corinthians, he wanted them to be proud of him for the significant work he had done among them. While Paul's labor and ability to speak was not at the level of what they had been used to from the visiting philosophers of the day (see 1 Cor. 2:4), Paul had hoped that the church would be pleased with his effort on their behalf.

5:13. For if we are beside ourselves, it is for God; if we are of sound mind, it is for you. Normally to be accused of being beside oneself suggested that a person was drunk, but it was sometimes used of those who were "in the spirit," that is, those in a state of ecstasy. As one who claimed to have "spoken in tongues more than you all" (1 Cor. 14:18), this may be what lies behind this accusation of him being "beside himself." Philo, a contemporary with Paul, speaks of the state of ecstasy that is sometimes confused with drunkenness: "Now when grace fills the soul, that soul thereby rejoices and smiles and dances, for it is possessed and inspired, so that to many of the unenlightened it may seem to be drunken, crazy and beside itself" (On Drunkenness 146, LCL).

5:14. For the love of Christ controls us, having concluded this, that one died for all, therefore all died. The notion that one person could die for all was a familiar one in antiquity. Caiaphas, the high priest who condemned Jesus, was not the first to put forward this perspective (John 11:50-52; 18:14). Earlier Plato (ca. 427-347 B.C.) wrote that "only such as are in love will consent to die for others; not merely men who will do it, but women too" (Symposium 179B, LCL). The notion is also found in Virgil's writings (ca. 70-19 B.C.): "One only shall there be whom, lost in the flood, you will seek in vain; one life shall be given for many . . ." (*Aeneid* 5.813-815, LCL). Dying for the general public was highly praised in antiquity, just as it is today. The Roman Emperor, Otho, for instance, realizing that his army would soon be defeated by Vitellius, offered himself so that his troops might live. As the reality of the impending defeat closed in on him, he said:

> Enough, quite enough, has already happened. I hate civil war, even though I conquer; and I love all Romans, even though they do not side with me. Let Vitellius be victor, since this has pleased the gods; and let the lives of his soldiers also be spared, since this pleases me. Surely it is far better and far more just that one should perish for all than many for one, and that I should refuse on account of one man alone to embroil the Roman people in civil war and cause so great a multitude of human beings to perish . . . . as for me, I shall free myself, that all men may learn from the event that you chose for your emperor one who would not give you up to save himself, but rather himself to save you (Dio Cassius, *Roman History* 63.13.1-3, LCL).

Epictetus (ca. A.D. 50-130) also tells the story of Diogenes and why he was a great man. "Come, was there anybody that Diogenes did not love, a man who was so gentle and kind-hearted that he gladly took upon himself all those troubles and physical hardships for the sake of the common weal?" (*Discourses* 3.24.64, LCL).

5:17. Therefore if any man is in Christ, he is a new creature; the old things passed away; behold, new things have come. Before the time of Paul, a view of a new order coming that would make the former order of creation void was emerging. This usually meant that there was a judgment from God on the previous days and in a dualistic fashion, those who were

faithful to God were blessed in the new order or new creation. The author of *1 Enoch* claims that after the judgment of God has come to sinners and all sin has been removed and an eternal judgment put in place, then "the first heaven shall depart and pass away; a new heaven shall appear; and all the powers of heaven shall shine forever sevenfold" (*1 En.* 91:16, *OT Pseud* 1:73). Similarly, the author of Jubilees tells of the time when the old creation passes away and

> . . . the day of the new creation when the heaven and earth and all of their creatures shall be renewed according to the powers of heaven and according to the whole nature of earth, until the sanctuary of the Lord is created in Jerusalem upon Mount Zion (*Jub.* 1:29, *OT Pseud* 2:54).

For this same notion in the New Testament, see 2 Peter 3:10-13; Rev. 20:11; 21:1-2. Paul, on the other hand, speaks of a new creation beginning in the life of the believer. In the Hellenistic Jewish romance story of *Joseph and Aseneth* (cf. Gen. 41:45), the writer (ca. first cent. B.C.-second cent. A.D.), speaks of Joseph's prayer for Aseneth:

> You, Lord, bless this virgin, and renew her by your spirit, and form her anew by your hidden hand, and make her alive again by your life, and let her eat your bread of life, and drink your cup of blessing, and number her among your people that you have chosen before all (things) came into being, and let her enter your rest which you have prepared for your chosen ones, and live in your eternal life for ever (and) ever (*Jos. Asen.*8.10-11, *OT Pseud* 2:213).

Paul's focus here is on the radical new change that comes to one who has received the message of the cross and been reconciled to God.

5:18. Now all these things are from God, who reconciled us to Himself through Christ, and

gave us the ministry of reconciliation. The terms used here, "reconciled" (Greek = *katallaksantos*) and "reconciliation" (Greek = *katallages*), like the terms Paul uses or "inner man" and "outer man" in 4:16 above, were familiar to the Greek-speaking world of his day and taken from the political sphere that dealt with resolving conflict between two parties. Diplomats, called "ambassadors" (see v. 20 below) were often sent to reconcile differences between cities and states. Reconciliation was an important theme in Paul's ministry (see Rom. 5:11; 11:15; 2 Cor. 5:18-20; cf. also Rom. 5:10; 1 Cor. 7:11; Eph. 2:16; Col. 1:20, 22) and this may have had some roots in Jesus' own call for persons of faith to reconcile (Matt. 5:24). It is a theme also in pre-Pauline literature. For instance, the author of *2 Macc.* writes: "may he [God] hear your prayers and be reconciled to you" (*2 Macc.* 1:5, NRSV), and again, "If our living Lord is angry for a little while, to rebuke and discipline us, he will again be reconciled with his own servants" (7:33, NRSV), and finally, " . . . they [the Jews] made common supplication and implored the merciful Lord to be wholly reconciled with this servants" (8:29, NRSV). With a renewed focus on his ministry of reconciliation, Paul brings to an end the discussion begun in 2:14 on his apostleship. This was characterized by the focus on the new covenant (3:6), the ministry of the Spirit (3:8) and righteousness (3:9).

5:19. Namely, that God was in Christ reconciling the world to Himself, not counting their trespasses against them, and He has committed to us the word of reconciliation. The "word of reconciliation" for Paul was the same as his message of the cross (1 Cor. 1:18; 2:2). It is important that God was not reconciled, but that the world is reconciled to God through the proclamation of the work of Christ. God took the initiative and did not need to be reconciled.

5:20. Therefore, we are ambassadors for Christ, as though God were entreating through us; we beg you on behalf of Christ, be reconciled to God. In Paul's day, the traveling sophists were often chosen to be "ambassadors" (Greek = *presbeuomen*) for the government because of their facility with language and also their eloquence. In the first and second centuries, such positions in government were commonly filled with those of the *literati*, that is, these highly educated and articulate individuals. One named Scopelian in the second century was especially known for his eloquence and was selected by the Emperor Hadrian to lead an embassy to Asia (Minor) to convince the people not to grow vineyards because in their drunkenness, they plotted against the Empire. Scopelian was quite successful in his mission and was highly praised. Philostratus says of him:

> How great a reputation he won in this contest on behalf of the vines is evident from what he said, for the oration is among the most celebrated; and it is evident too from what happened as a result of the oration. For by it he won such presents as are usually given at an imperial court, and also many compliments and expressions of praise, and moreover a brilliant band of youths fell in love with his genius and followed him to Iona. (*Lives of the Sophists* 520, LCL)

4. 6:1–7:16. Paul's Appeal for Reconciliation with God

6:1-10. The Hardships for Paul's Ministry of Reconciliation. 6:1-2 tie together best with what precedes in 5:20-21 where Paul has shared what God has done for his readers in Christ through his own ministry. Now he calls upon them to respond to it positively now and not to reject his message.

6:1. And working together with Him, we also

urge you not to receive the grace of God in vain. Fear of putting forth effort to no avail, or in vain, is a notion that is also found in several Old and New Testament passages (Lev. 26:20; Job 39:16; Isa. 29:8; Jer. 6:29; 28:58; 1 Thess. 3:5; Gal. 2:2; Phil. 2:16). Here, Paul has in view the grand scheme of God's plan of salvation, but behind that he is arguing for the validity of his apostolic office. He has proclaimed God's salvation and urges his readers not to reject either his ministry or the Gospel that he proclaims since they are inextricably bound together. Most of all, Paul fears that the Corinthians may reject the grace of God that he has shared with them.

6:2. For He says, "At the acceptable time I listened to you, And on the day of salvation I helped you"; behold, now is "the acceptable time," behold, now is "the day of salvation." Paul cites a text from the Greek (Septuagint, LXX) translation of Isa. 49:8 to emphasize the importance of responding to God's grace in due time while it is still possible. It may be that Paul is involved in *"pesher"* interpretation of the Isaiah text: namely, allowing it to come to fulfillment in his own day and circumstance. The "behold" and the "now" are not in the LXX form of the text and Paul is picking up on what he has said earlier in vv. 17 and 16 respectively to emphasize the importance of responding now and favorably to the grace of God. The language here is familiar in the Greco-Roman setting of Paul's day. Seneca, for instance, calls upon his readers "Do not miss your opportunity . . . now the day is yours, yours the opportunity" (*Medea* 1017, LCL).

6:3-10. Paul's credentials as a servant of Christ. Recognition of the value of one's services was highly valued in the ancient world and zealously guarded by those who rendered services. Such value attributed to individuals is found on Hellenic inscriptions throughout the Greco-Roman world. Paul was likewise anxious to show that his service for Christ among the people was not compromised due to ques-

tionable behavior. Epictetus, for instance, says that Diogenes continued invaluable service for Zeus even when his circumstances changed.

As became a servant of Zeus, caring for men indeed, but at the same time subject to God. That is why for him alone the whole world, and no special place, was his fatherland; and when he had been taken prisoner he did not hanker for Athens nor his acquaintances and friends there, but he got on good terms with the pirates and tried to reform them. And later, when he was sold into slavery at Corinth he kept on living there just as he had formerly lived at Athens; yes, and if he had gone off to the Perrhaebians he would have acted in quite the same way. That is how freedom is achieved (*Discourses* 3.24.65-66, LCL).

While self-praise is generally considered inappropriate in this generation, it would hardly have been received that way in the first century. Paul did not want to be "cast away" because of his failure to follow conventions that were common and acceptable to those he ministered to (1 Cor. 9:19-23, 27). For the same reason, he likewise sought to make a favorable rhetorical impression as he preached the Gospel showing considerable familiarity with rhetorical conventions of his day, such as we see in vv. 3-10 where conventional lists of hardships and virtues are displayed. Pindar (ca. 518-438 B.C.) concluded his first *Olympian Ode* with the words "may I join victors whenever they win and be foremost in wisdom among Hellenes everywhere" (*Olympian Odes* 1.115b-117, LCL). As he concludes another ode, he says, "Father Zeus, I pray that with the Graces' aid I may celebrate that achievement and surpass many in honoring victory in words, casting my javelin nearest the target of the Muses" (*Nemean Odes* 9.52-55, LCL). Later, while Pindar shared his own praise about his ability to produce songs, he recognized that he may have "pushed the envelope" a bit, and after self-praise, admits the folly of what he did.

But as for me, while I light up that dear city

with my blazing songs, more swiftly than either a high-spirited horse or a winged ship I shall send this announcement everywhere, if with the help of some skill granted by destiny I cultivate the choice garden of the Graces, for it is they who bestow what is delightful. But men become brave and wise as divinity determines: . . . But cast that story away from me, my mouth! For reviling the gods is a hateful skill, and boasting inappropriately sounds a note of madness. Stop babbling of such things now! (Pindar, *Olympian Odes* 9.21-29, 35-40, LCL).

Plutarch (ca. A.D. 45-120), defending such self-praise, argues that:

> . . . self-praise goes unresented if you are defending your good name or answering a charge, as Pericles was when he said: "Yet I, with whom you are angry, yield to none, I believe, in devising needful measures and laying them before you; and I love my country and cannot be bought." For not only is there nothing puffed up, vainglorious, or proud in taking a high tone about oneself at such a moment, but it displays as well a lofty spirit and greatness of character, which by refusing to be humbled humbles and overpowers envy (*On Inoffensive Self-Praise* 540CD, LCL).

What takes place here seems in conflict with what Paul has said about his self-promotion in 3:1; 5:12 and later in 10:18, but this is still in keeping with what was socially customary in his day. The combination of words backed up by deeds was always highly praised in antiquity. Likewise, Paul has stated here that he has backed up with his life what he has said with his mouth.

6:3-5. Giving no cause for offense in anything, in order that the ministry be not discredited, but in everything commending ourselves as servants of God, in much endurance, in afflictions, in hardships, in distresses, in beatings, in imprisonments, in tumults, in labors, in sleeplessness, in hunger. In the ancient world,

the Romans counted as virtues the following: the ability to endure suffering or hardships, justice, fidelity to a trust; steadfastness of purpose; wisdom and deliberation in action, simplicity of living; unflinching performance in the face of difficulties and hazards; reverence for deity and authority figures; and morality seen especially in honoring marital responsibilities. On the other hand, the Greeks honored as virtues the following: uprightness, self-control, endurance, and courage (Danker 89). Because Paul's ability to endure or be consistent with his message has been challenged, he responds to his opponents with a defense based on his own experiences. These experiences are noted in 12:10, but also in 1 Cor. 3:22; 4:11-13; Phil. 4:11-13 and they show how he measures up to what he has said and has "paid the price" through suffering and endurance for the ideals he proclaims. These "hardship catalogues" (see also 4:8-9 and 11:23-33) speak of Paul's fortitude and patience in his mission. They were a normal part of the teachings and writings of the Cynics and Stoics in the first century and typically indicated that the philosophers/writers were not vulnerable to obstacles that came their way. Seneca, in his letter *On Despising Death*, taught that even death was nothing to be feared. While it was not an encouragement to seek death, there was no need to fear it either because: "death is so little to be feared that through its good offices nothing is to be feared. Therefore, when your enemy threatens, listen unconcernedly" (*Epistles* 24.12, LCL). Epictetus calls upon his listeners to reject the fear of death and hardship: "In your school what did you call exile and imprisonment and bonds and death and disrepute?" he responds, "I called them 'things indifferent.'" (*Discourses* 1.30.2-3, LCL). Paul accepted hardship as having some value (1 Cor. 9:24-27), though not something to pursue with bravado. Unlike the Stoic, however, Paul was also willing to confess his weakness (12:10). The hope that the Stoic sought was found within oneself and not in the possession of material things. Epictetus concludes about the material things of life that God has determined that "'If you wish any good thing, get it from yourself.' You say, 'No, but from someone else.' Do not so, but get it from yourself" (Discourses 1.29.3-4, LCL). This is similar to Paul's comments in 4:16 above, in that Paul would agree with Epictetus that joy and lasting happiness is not found in material possessions or the lack thereof, but he contends that the peace one seeks is not found in what is seen (the material), but in the unseen, the eternal, that is, God (4:16-18).

6:6-7a. In purity, in knowledge, in patience, in kindness, in the Holy Spirit, in genuine love, in the word of truth, in the power of God. Paul lists the virtues that are befitting of a true servant of Christ (see another list in Gal. 5:22-23; cf. Eph. 4:32-5:2; 1 Thess. 2:10; 4:9-12).

6:7b. By the weapons of righteousness for the right hand and the left. The weapons that Paul speaks about here are, of course, different from those of the Roman army (cf. Rom. 13:12; Eph. 6:10-18; 1 Thess. 5:8; 1 Tim. 3:3-4). The Roman soldier carried an offensive weapon in his right hand, often one or two medium-length javelins or a short sword, and a shield in his left hand. According to Roman field tactics, the soldier would throw the javelins from a short distance and then advance using the shorter sword to defeat the enemy and the shield to protect himself from the enemy.

6:8-10. By glory and dishonor, by evil report and good report; regarded as deceivers and yet true; as unknown yet well-known, as dying yet behold, we live; as punished yet not put to death, as sorrowful yet always rejoicing, as poor yet making many rich, as having nothing yet possessing all things. Paul reflects many of the core values of the Greco-Roman world, chief among them had to do with honor and shame. The philosophers who were will-

ing to endure shame, or contempt and deprivation, for the sake of their mission were highly praised. Dio Chrysostom, in his discourse on virtue, says that the noble person

> ... holds hardships to be his greatest antagonists, and with them he is ever wont to battle day and night, not to win a sprig of parsley [the laurels placed on victors' heads at the Isthmian and Nemean athletic games] ... but to win happiness and virtue through all the days of his life. ... He is afraid of none of those opponents nor does he pray to draw another antagonist, but challenges them one after another, grappling with hunger and cold, withstanding thirst, and disclosing no weakness even though he must endure the lash or give his body to be cut or burned. Hunger, exile, loss of reputation, and the like have no terrors for him; nay, he holds them as mere trifles, and while in their very grip the perfect man is often sportive as boys with their dice and their colored balls (Orations 8.15-16, LCL).

Paul has endured hardships. He has also been unduly criticized, he believes, and so he offers this defense of his apostleship and ministry among the Corinthians. While he admits that he has sorrows and disappointments (2 Cor. 1:8-9; 7:5; 11:2-29; Gal. 2:11-14; cf. 2 Tim. 1:15; 4:9-16), such displays were considered by the Stoics to be a sign of weakness. Paul does urge contentment in all circumstances of life (Phil. 4:11-13) and realizes that his hope is not in material things (2 Cor. 2:10, see discussion above). In his claim that he has nothing, "but possesses all things," he is similar to Seneca who told of an important Stoic perspective that though all things are taken away, the true things of value always remain. In his Seneca's letter On Facing Hardships, he speaks against those who complain against every ill that comes their way; he advises his student (Lucilius) with the following words:

When everything seems to go hard and up hill, I have trained myself not merely to obey God, but to agree with His decisions. I follow Him because my soul wills it, and not because I must. Nothing will ever happen to me that I shall receive with ill humour or with a wry face. I shall pay up all my taxes willingly. Now all the things which cause us to groan or recoil are part of the tax of life—things, my dear Lucilius, which you should never hope and never seek to escape (*Epistle* 96.2, LCL).

Whatever Paul believed that he possessed, he had others in his day who would agree with his notion that those who are wealthy in possessions have very little. For example, after speaking about the rich who are troubled about their possessions and commit crimes to hold on to their wealth, Crates praises the teaching of Diogenes (founder of the Cynics ca. 412 B.C. – 321 B.C.) in his letter "To Be Wealthy." ". . . as for us, we observe peace since we have been freed from every evil by Diogenes of Sinope, and *although we possess nothing, we have everything*, but you, though you have everything, really have nothing because of your rivalry, jealousy, fear, and conceit" (*Letter of Crates* 7, Malherbe trans., italics ours).

b. 6:11-13. Paul's Appeal for Better Relationships

6:11-13. Our mouth has spoken freely to you, O Corinthians, our heart is opened wide. You are not restrained by us, but you are restrained in your own affections. Now in a like exchange—I speak as to children—open wide to us also. Paul's passion and emotion for the Corinthians is now laid bare. He expresses his heart to his children in the faith and implores them to open themselves to him in like fashion. He is both open to them and honest with them in everything. He has laid bare his heart with these believers. The transition to the next section of verses is not a smooth one and seems interruptive in the flow of things, but will be discussed presently. The phrase, "Our mouth has spoken freely," uses the Greek idiom = *avoigein to soma*, literally, "to open the mouth." This idiomatic expression is found elsewhere in the Greek version (LXX) of Judges 11:35; Job 3:1; and Matt. 5:1. Sirach, similarly, writes: "I opened my mouth and said, Acquire wisdom for yourselves without money" (*Sir.* 51:25, NRSV). Paul then encourages them to "open wide" to him also (v. 13; cf. 7:2). Although he has been wronged (cf. 7:12), he has himself wronged no one and wants their affection as he has an affection for them.

6:14-7:1. Parenthesis: Christians and non-Christians. On this passage, see Introduction to this letter. Most scholars acknowledge that this passage has been inserted into the flow of Paul's argument. It is not an easy fit and the warmth and tone of the preceding verses is lacking here and returns in 7:2. Also, the focus is much more general here, in the sense of setting forth general guidelines for Christian behavior, rather than specific situations that Paul was facing in regard to his readers. Further, the focus in 6:1-3 is on receiving Paul and his apostleship or ministry of reconciliation which resumes in 7:2, but the focus of 6:14–7:1 has to do with avoiding unbelievers which Paul seems to say elsewhere is impossible in this world (1 Cor. 5:9-10). Clearly, that is not the focus of the context. Paul may have been the one to insert this material, which is thoroughly Jewish and has numerous parallels with the literature found at Qumran (see below), but he was not likely its composer because of the significant differences in vocabulary and thought found in it. Its substance is unlike anything else in Paul's other writings or in 2 Corinthians itself. By eliminating this passage and reading from 6:11-13 directly on to 7:2-4, the transition would be smooth without interruption of thought and the rest of the passage fits clearly the stated intention and logical development of Paul. It is not clear that someone after Paul inserted this passage into 2 Corinthians nor can a good reason for doing so be found, but, since Paul elsewhere includes material that he has adopted from traditions handed on to him, as in the case of Phil. 2:5-11, which most scholars believe that Paul did not write, but rather incorporated it into his argument of his letter. There, however, the inserted tradition is more tied to the argument and flow of the appeal Paul was making (see 1:27–2:5 and 2:12-18). It is possible that this was an insertion into Paul's letter that was made by a subsequent editor (or editors) who gathered the letters of Paul together for circulation, as some scholars argue, but there is no evidence for that and one is hard pressed to find a reason for it. The text itself has a series of questions at the beginning (6:14-16a) and proof-texts that fit the style of "writing with Scripture" to advance the admonition (16b-18), followed by a final appeal (7:1). It is not completely clear why this passage is placed here, either by Paul or a later editor (or editors), but the admonition to holy living is certainly in keeping with other Pauline admonitions. Since there is no copy of 2 Corinthians that has survived without this passage in it, any changes or additions must have taken place at a rather early stage. Finally, the older position that advocated that this passage is the lost letter that Paul refers to in 1 Cor. 5:9 is no longer tenable, since this passage does not deal specifically with sexually immoral people, but with unbelievers, and the text in 1 Cor. 5:1-8, 11 specifically deals with discipline within the Christian community itself. For a more lengthy discussion of this passage, and its place in the argument of 2 Corinthians, see the Introduction to this letter above.

6:14. Do not be bound together with unbelievers; for what partnership have righteousness and lawlessness, or what fellowship has light with darkness? The term "bound together with" (Greek = *heterozygein*, "mis-yoked" or "unequally yoked") is unique in the New Testament but has a parallel in the Greek translation (the LXX) of Lev. 19:19. Deut. 22:10 could have been used to argue against the unequal yoking, or mis-yoking, together of good and evil, but there is no reference to it here. There is a remarkable parallel with a fragment from Philo that reads: "It is impossible that love for the world can agree with love for God, just as it is impossible that light and darkness exist together in agreement" (*Sacra Parallel.des. Joh. V. Damascus*, trans M.E. Boring, p. 456). Sirach likewise asks, "How can the clay pot associate with the iron kettle? The pot will strike against it and be smashed" and he later asks, "What does a wolf have in common with a lamb? No more has a sinner with the devout. What peace is there between a hyena and a dog? And what peace between the rich and the poor?" (*Sir.* 13:2, 17-18, NRSV). Likewise, a sentence from Seneca (ca. A.D. 4 B.C. – A.D. 65) who writes: For neither does evil have any agreement with virtue, nor does freedom have any agreement with slavery (*Sentence of Epictetus*, M.E. Boring, trans., p 456). This passage (6:14-15) has often been used as a prohibition against Christians marrying unbelievers and it has roots in Deut. 7:3; Ezra 9:12; and Neh. 13:25. It may have been in mind as it was inserted into the flow of Paul's letter, but that is not as obvious here.

In terms of the passage itself, there are some parallels with the Qumran writings. For example, the inability of righteousness and lawlessness to exist together is found in various Qumran texts, especially in the following: "To you, God of knowledge, belong all the works of justice and the foundation of truth; to the sons of man, the service of sin and the deeds of deception" (*The Hymns*, 1QH 9[=1].26-27, Garcia Martinez, trans.). More specifically, in the opening lines of the *Rule of the Community* we read that the purpose of the community is to seek to do "what is good and just in his presence, as commanded by means of the hand of

Moses and his servants the Prophets; in order to love everything which he selects and to hate everything that he rejects; in order to keep oneself at a distance from evil, and to become attached to all good works . . . " (1QS 1.2-5, Garcia Martinez trans.). Later in the same document, the author states:

> This is the rule for the men of the Community who freely volunteer to convert from all evil and to keep themselves steadfast in all he prescribes in compliance with his will. They should keep apart from men of sin in order to constitute a Community in law and possessions, and acquiesce to the authority of the sons of Zadok . . . those who persevere steadfastly in the covenant (1QS 5.1-3, Garcia Martinez trans.).

This separation from evil and the "works of darkness" is found in the opening lines from the *War Scroll* at Qumran. It states: "The first attack by the sons of light will be launched against the lot of the sons of darkness, against the army of Belial" (1QM 1.1, Garcia Martinez trans.). It is possible that the focus in this passage is on those who associate with the pagans at the pagan temples and a call to disassociate from those who are involved in pagan sacrifices and temple rituals (see 1 Cor. 8:1-12 and 10:14-30), but that is not clear here that Paul has the eating of meats sacrificed to idols in mind nor discontinuing association with those who do.

The use of questions to reinforce instruction is quite common both in Hellenistic and Jewish moral philosophy. Epictetus, for example, frequently asks a series of questions from his imaginary hearers/readers. For example, the following series of questions allows him to provide an obvious answer following the question: "Well, do we fulfill their promise? . . . How did I render that particular passage? . . . Didn't you, just the other day, praise So-and-so contrary to your honest opinion? . . . Don't these very same persons secretly despise you? . . . What else do you suppose the man says to

himself, but . . . ? . . . What work of genius has he displayed?" (*Discourses* 3.23.9-16, LCL). Philo also strings a series of questions together to elicit a learning from his readers: "For which of us stands up to oppose riches? Who prepares himself to wrestle with glory? How many of those who still live in the mazes of empty opinions have come to despise honour and office?" and then proceeds to answer his questions (*On Drunkenness* 57, LCL).

6:15. Or what harmony has Christ with Belial, or what has a believer in common with an unbeliever? The one Paul calls the "god of this world" in 4:4 is now called "Beliar." The name derives from the Hebrew *beliyya 'al* meaning "wickedness," "evil," or "perversion." It is not found in the Hebrew Bible as a designated reference for Satan, but the term is used some 27 times in various compounds speaking of evil or that contrary to the will of God. The rabbis of the second century and following spoke of the corrupt persons who put off the yoke of god and were lawless (*Sanh.* 111b). The term as a designate for Satan is found only here in the New Testament, but is frequently used for Satan in the Pseudepigraphal literature and at Qumran as noted in the previous verse. In the *War Scroll*, those who make war for the Lord, whether priests or Levites or elders of the people, "shall bless the God of Israel and all the deeds of his truth and there they shall dam Belial and the spirits of his lot" and later, "Accursed be Belial in his malicious plan, may he be damned for his wicked rule. Accursed be all the spirits of his lot in his wicked . . . plan" (1QM 13.1-2, 4). This name is also found in the *Testaments of the Twelve Patriarchs*, and in the same form of the word that is found here. For example, "And now, my children, you have heard everything. Choose for yourselves light or darkness, the law of the Lord or the works of Beliar" (*T. of Levi* 19.1, OT Pseud 1:795). Again, "As a person's strength, so also is his work; . . . as is his soul, so also is his thought, whether on the Law of the Lord or on the law of Beliar" (*T. Napthtali* 2.6, *OT Pseud* 1:811). Finally, the same term is used of Satan in the Testament of Joseph: "You shall carry my bones along with you, for when you are taking my bones up there [to the promised land of Israel], the Lord will be with you in the light, while Beliar will be with the Egyptians in the dark" (*T. Jos.* 20.2, *OT Pseud* 1:825). One other variant is found in the Gnostic *Apocryphon of John* that uses the name "Belias" for "Satan." See above discussion of Paul's terms for Satan in 2:11 and 4:4. The term is also found frequently in *The Testaments of the Twelve Patriarchs* (*T. Reub.* 4:7, 11; 6:3; *T. Simeon* 5:3; *T. Levi* 3:3; 18:12; 19:1; *T. Judah* 25:3; *T. Issachar* 6:1; 7:7; *T. Zebulun* 9:8; *T. Dan* 1:7; 4:7; 5:1, 10-11; *T. Naphtali* 2:6; 3:1; *T. Asher* 1:8; 3:2; 6:4; *T. Joseph* 7:4; 20:2; *T. Benjamin* 3:3-4, 8; 6:1, 7; 7:1-2), and elsewhere in the pseudepigraphal literature (*Jub.* 1:20; 15:33; *Sibylline Oracles* 3:63-74; *Martyrdom and Ascension of Isaiah* 1:8-9; 2:4; 3:11, 13; 4:2, 4, 16, 18; 5:1 and elsewhere).

6:16. Or what agreement has the temple of God with idols? For we are the temple of the living God; just as God said, "I will dwell in them and walk among them; And I will be their God, and they shall be My people. The turning from idols to God has parallels in 1 Thess. 1:9 and in the vice lists such as 1 Cor. 5:10-11; 6:9; Gal. 5:20. Paul discusses the practice of Christians going to temples with idols in 1 Cor. 8 and 10, but see also Rom. 2:22 (cf. Rom. 1:22-25). At Qumran, those who entered the covenant of the Community offered both blessings and curses. In terms of the latter,

the priests and the levites shall continue, saying: Cursed be the idols which his heart reveres whoever enters this covenant leaving his guilty obstacle in front of himself to fall over it . . . May God's anger and the wrath of his verdicts consume him for everlasting destruction. May all the curses of this covenant stick

fast to him. May God segregate him for evil, and may he be cut off from the midst of the sons of light because of his straying from following God on account of his idols and his blameworthy obstacle. May he assign his lot with the cursed ones for ever (1QS 2.11-12,15-16, Garcia Martinez trans.).

Another reference that has parallels to 6:16 is found in the Damascus Document (CD), which is similar to the texts at Qumran, where those who despise the ways of God will have no part in the house (temple) of God: "And (proceed) according to this judgment, with all those who despise, among the first as among the last, for they have placed idols in their heart . . . and have walked in the stubbornness of their heart. For them there shall be no part in the house of the law" (CD 20.8-10, Garcia Martinez trans.).

6:17. "Therefore, come out from their midst and be separate," says the Lord. "And do not touch what is unclean; And I will welcome you." This passage cites the LXX of Isa. 52:11b which says: "Depart ye, depart, go out from thence, and touch not the unclean thing; go ye out from the midst of her; separate yourselves, ye that bear the vessels of the Lord" (Bagster trans.). The "says the Lord" is found frequently in the LXX Old Testament such as in Isa. 49:18. The theme of separation from those who are evil is a familiar one at Qumran. For example, in the *Halachic* letter—commonly known as 4QMMT (*Miqsat Ma'aseh ha-Torah* = "Some works of the Law")—the writer says "we have segregated ourselves from the rest of the peop[le and (that) we avoid] mingling in these affairs, and associating with [them] in these things" (4QMMT *Frags.* 7-8, Garcia Martinez trans.).

"**I will receive you**" is possibly a reference to Exod. 20:34 in the LXX (cf. also Zeph. 3:19-20; Zech. 10:8, 10).

6:18. "And I will be a father to you, And you shall be sons and daughters to Me," Says the

Lord Almighty. This is a free translation from the LXX of 2 Sam. 7:14 (= 2 Kings in the LXX) that says in part: "I will be to him a father, and he shall be to me a son" (Bagster trans.). In the New Testament, "Almighty" (Greek = *pantokrator*) is found only here and in the book of Revelation (1:8; 4:8; 11:17; 15:3; 16:7, 14; 19:6, 15; 21:22).

7:1. Therefore, having these promises, beloved, let us cleanse ourselves from all defilement of flesh and spirit, perfecting holiness in the fear of God. This is the only place in the new Testament where believers are called upon to cleanse themselves (Greek = *katharisomen*, "let us cleanse/purify"), though the notion of cleansing or purifying (same Greek term) by God is found in several places (Eph. 5:26; Titus 2:14; 3:5; Heb. 9:14, 22-23; 10:2). On the other hand, the notion of followers of God cleansing themselves does find a parallel at Qumran.

And by the spirit of uprightness and of humility his sin is atoned. And by the compliance of his soul with all the laws of God his flesh is cleansed by being sprinkled with cleansing waters and being made holy with the waters of repentance. May he, then, steady his steps in order to walk with perfection on all the paths of God, conforming to all he has decreed concerning the regular times of his commands and not turn aside. . . (*Rule of Community*, 1QS 3.7-10, Garcia Martinez trans.).

The word for "defilement" (Greek = *molysmos*) is only found here in the New Testament, though there is a cognate to it in 1 Cor. 8:7 (cf. Rev. 3:4; 14:4). In the Apocryphal literature, the term is used in the context of defilement from idols. In *1 Esdras*, for instance, Ezra prays to the Lord citing the prophets who said: "The land that you are entering to take possession of is a land polluted with the pollution of the aliens of the land, and they have filled it with their uncleanness" (*1 Esd.* 8:83, NRSV). This may be a reference to Lev. 18:19-30.

See also *2 Macc.* where the author tells of Judas Maccabeus taking some nine other individuals into the wilderness so that they might not "share in the defilement" of the land that came with the demand for the Jews to worship pagan gods and offer sacrifices to them (*2 Macc.* 5:27). Likewise, the author of the *Letter of Aristeas* claims that "men who hear anything and give physical expression to it by word of mouth, thus embroiling other people in evil, commit no ordinary act of uncleanness, and are themselves completely defiled with the taint of impiety" (*Ep. Arist.* 166, OT Pseud 2:23).

The reference to **"perfecting holiness in the fear of God"** has no clear equivalent in the New Testament, even though the word "holiness" is found in Romans 1:4 (cf. also 1 Thess. 3:13), but again, in the *Rule of the Community*, the notion of perfection by holiness or perfect holiness was found among those at Qumran. "These are the regulations by which the men of perfect holiness shall conduct themselves, each with his fellow" (1QS 8.20, Garcia Martinez trans.). Again, in the *Damascus Document*, we read: "For all those who walk according to these matters in perfect holiness, in accordance with his teaching, God's covenant is a guarantee for them" (CD 7.4-5, Garcia Martinez trans.).

7:2-16 The good report from Titus.

This section both brings to a close the defense of his apostleship begun in 2:14 and continues his word in 1:15–2:13. This passage resumes the appeal that Paul began in 6:11-13, urging the Corinthians to have more affection for him, Paul now summarizes his plea, going back to the beginning of the letter (2:12-13) and ties things together. Earlier he began the letter indicating that he was afflicted or oppressed (Greek = *thlibo*) (1:6) and now he reiterates that but adds that he is afflicted "in every way" (7:5). The focus here is on the comforting news that Titus brought back to Paul while Paul was in Macedonia. Some scholars have argued that at this point, Paul resumes a letter that he left in 2:12-13, but that is not likely because of the change of persons and because Troas was the location of his restlessness there and here it is Macedonia. We are not certain which city Paul has in mind in Macedonia, the place where he wrote this response to Titus's report, but we know that he founded churches in Philippi, Thessalonica, and Beroea (see discussion above in 1:16). Wherever he met Titus is likely also to be the place where he penned this correspondence to the Christians at Corinth. It is difficult not to consider the similarity of Paul's meeting with Titus in Macedonia and his waiting for news from Timothy about the church in Thessalonica (1 Thess. 3:16; cf. 1 Cor. 16:17).

7:2-4. Paul's Appeal Continued and Joy over the Corinthians.

These verses essentially conclude the lengthy section on Paul's apostleship and his ministry begun by Paul in 2:14. Paul also implies the criticisms that have been raised against him: namely, doing something wrong, corrupting the church, and taking advantage of them, perhaps by the offering he is collecting for the Christians in Jerusalem.

Make room for us in your hearts; we wronged no one, we corrupted no one, we took advantage of no one. I do not speak to condemn you; for I have said before that you are in our hearts to die together and to live together. Great is my confidence in you, great is my boasting on your behalf; I am filled with comfort. I am overflowing with joy in all our affliction. These verses essentially conclude the lengthy section on Paul's apostleship and his ministry begun by Paul in 2:14 and essentially conclude with the statement in 7:4. See discussion in 6:11-13 above. Paul has opened his mouth and his heart to the Corinthians and now wants them to do the same to him. While he has been treated badly by one of them, he does not do so himself to them (7:12). In no other passage does Paul speak more passionately about his love for his readers and the great concern he has for them.

He has written a sorrowful letter to them (7:8), but it was to bring them to their senses and to reconcile them to him. As he began in the plural in 6:11-12 above, he resumes that here, "make room for us," calling on his readers to embrace him just as he has them. In the midst of the suffering and affliction that he is facing, he nevertheless finds joy because of the Corinthian believers.

In saying that he will live or die with the Corinthians (v. 3), Paul indicates that he has so invested his life with the Corinthians, that when they suffer, so does he, and when they rejoice, so does he (cf. 11:1-29). Unlike the Stoics who would despise such attachments to people, Paul embraces freely and openly the objects of his affection. The Stoics wanted to maintain self-sufficiency so that when something precious was taken away, they would not stumble or face despair. Epictetus explains:

> This is what you ought to practice from morning till evening. Begin with the most trifling things, the ones most exposed to injury, like a pot, or a cup, and then advance to a tunic, a paltry dog, a mere horse, a bit of land; thence to yourself, your body, and its members, your children, wife, brothers. Look about on every side and cast these things away from you. Purify your judgments, for fear lest something of what is not your own may be fastened to them, or grown together with them, and may give you pain when it is torn loose (*Discourses* 4.1.111-112, LCL).

Paul throws all such self-protection to the wind and openly declares how much his joy is dependent upon the love and acceptance of those he loves. Likewise, his "confidence in you" (the Corinthian believers) is similar to his boldness of speech in 6:11. The opening words of 7:4 are sometimes translated, "I feel I can speak frankly with you." The word for confidence here is *parresia* "boldness." The quality of boldness in one's speech and conduct was greatly admired in the ancient world, as it is today. The ability to employ frank and open speech stating clearly what one means was one of the important virtues admired by many in Paul's day. Philodemus (ca. 110-40 B.C.), for instance, who came to Rome in 75 B.C. and was widely known as a poet and philosopher, wrote: " . . . a wise man will employ frankness [*parresia*] toward his friends. . . . Although many fine things result from friendship, there is nothing so grand as having one to whom one will saw what is in one's heart and who will listen when one speaks" (*On Frank Criticism* 15, 28, M. Hubbard 230). Philo speaks admirably of those who speak plainly and freely. "But the man of worth has such courage [*parresia*] of speech, that he is bold not only to speak and cry aloud, but actually to make an outcry of reproach, wrung from him by real conviction, and expressing true emotion" (*Who Is the Heir* 19, LCL). Later he says that not all bold speech is good, namely that daring speech without wisdom can be dangerous, but rather one should use "good daring [= wise boldness]" because such persons are friends of God. He concludes: "Frankness [*parresia*] of speech is akin to friendship. For to whom should a man speak with frankness but to his friend?" (*Who is the Heir?* 21, LCL).

7:8. For though I caused you sorrow by my letter, I do not regret it; though I did regret it— for I see that that letter caused you sorrow, though only for a while—. The sorrowful letter that Paul wrote has been the subject of many scholarly debates, but many believe that it is the same as the one attached to 2 Corinthians, namely 2 Cor. 10-13. While there is no way to be sure that this is the letter of which Paul speaks, in its present form, chaps. 10-13 do not resemble a letter in typical Pauline style, but the tone of those chapters is markedly different than we find here, and the content of those chapters is in keeping with the "sorrowful" letter that he wrote to the

Corinthians. It is possible that chaps. 10-13 were simply attached to 2 Cor. 1-9 at a later time—a very popular view today, but caution is needed and certainty is not forthcoming. See further discussion of this in the introduction above and in the introduction of those chapters below. In the opening part of the letter, 2:5-10, Paul acknowledges that the church has dealt with the one who offended Paul and he encourages them to restore that one to their fellowship, but revisits that issue in v. 12 that led to such pain for Paul. Paul saw value in the church grieving for a while over the matter and especially dealing with it, but now he wants it put behind them so that their relationship with him will continue to be an encouragement to him. Paul is satisfied that they have done their best to deal with the situation (11b).

7:9-10. I now rejoice, not that you were made sorrowful, but that you were made sorrowful to the point of repentance; for you were made sorrowful according to the will of God, in order that you might not suffer loss in anything through us. For the sorrow that is according to the will of God produces a repentance without regret, leading to salvation; but the sorrow of the world produces death. For Paul, salvation refers to deliverance from the penalty of sin, but also to the receiving for the future that changes one now. It is more than forgiveness of sins, but also involves a transformation of one's present living through the power of the Holy Spirit (2 Cor. 5:17; Gal. 5:22-23; Rom. 8:22, 35-39). Repentance of one's sins or failures is a mark of the beginning of one's salvation. Jesus himself, following the lead of John the Baptist (Mark 1:4; Matt. 3:2; Luke 3:3), preached repentance as the fertile soil for the work of God in one's life (Mark 1:15). For Paul, repentance leads to saving faith (Rom. 2:4). In the story of *Joseph and Aseneth* (first cent. B.C. to second cent. A.D.), the writer praises the act of repentance and personifies it as essential in pleasing God. He says that:

Repentance is in the heavens, an exceedingly beautiful and good daughter of the Most High. And she herself entreats the Most High God for you at all times and for all who repent in the name of the Most High God, because he is (the) father of Repentance. And she herself is guardian of all virgins, and loves you very much, and is beseeching the Most High for you at all times and for all who repent she prepared a place of rest in the heavens. And she will renew all who repent, and wait on them herself for ever (and) ever. And Repentance is exceedingly beautiful, a virgin pure and laughing always, and she is gentle and meek. And, therefore, the Most High Father loves her, and all the angels stand in awe of her (*Jos. Asen.* 15.7-8, *OT Pseud* 2:226-227).

7:15. And his affection abounds all the more toward you, as he remembers the obedience of you all, how you received him with fear and trembling. In antiquity, ambassadors were received with all the protocol that would befit the head of a nation, for the ambassador indeed represented the head of state in all matters of deliberation. The Corinthians' reception of Titus meant that they were also receiving Paul in like manner and because Titus was well-received, this brought considerable joy to Paul. Philo summarized in a negative way the outcome of the poor reception he and others had as ambassadors of the Jews before Gaius: "For whatever ambassadors suffer recoils upon those who sent them" (*Embassy to Gaius* 369, LCL). More positively, Jesus said, "whoever receives me receives the one who sent me" (John 13:20).

7:16. I rejoice that in everything I have confidence in you. Paul reverts to his use of the singular first person here to make his appeal even more personal. He personally has taken the lead in both his criticisms of the church and

now also in the reconciliation with them. His note of joy and confidence in the Corinthian believers, based upon the return of Titus with favorable news about them is a great source of encouragement for Paul and leads him to his next important agenda item that is especially close to his heart: namely, the offering for the Christians in Jerusalem.

5. 8:1–9:15. The collection for Jerusalem Christians. This portion of 2 Corinthians has a number of complicated issues related to it. Among the most frequently debated questions related to these chapters are the following: Did these two chapters, or just chap. 9, exist independently from chaps. 1–7, or 1–8? If so, when was it incorporated into the Corinthian correspondence? How do these chapters fit into the overall framework of the letter? And finally, who was the collection for?

Along with defending his ministry among the Corinthians, Paul also had a goal of gathering a collection from them that would be taken to Jerusalem to care for "the poor" Christians living there. Paul's joy over Titus's report on the Corinthian Christians is the backdrop for something close to his heart: namely, the collection for the Christians in Jerusalem who have faced a severe famine and were in special need. When Paul met with the leaders of the church in Jerusalem to discuss his ministry among the Gentiles, his ministry was accepted and he was asked to "remember the poor" in Jerusalem, which he also agreed to do (Gal. 2:9-10).

Besides the obvious benefit of caring for the poor believers ("saints") in Jerusalem, there were many practical advantages for this offering, not the least of which was better relations between the Jewish Christians and the Gentile Christians, one of the chief sources of conflict between these two groups within the early church (see 8:13-15). Not only was it important to encourage fellow Christians to care for the practical physical needs of their brothers and sisters in the faith, but also to build bridges between them that would encourage the church's divisions over ethnicity to be abolished. The conflict between Jew and Gentile in the church is noted variously in Acts (11:1-18; 15:1-5, 22-32; but also in Paul's letters (Gal. 2:11-14; 3:27-29; cf. Eph. 2:11-21). This offering is mentioned also in Rom. 15:25-27; 1 Cor. 16:1-4; Gal. 2:10 (cf. 1 Cor. 9:11 and Acts 24:17). Paul states clearly what he has in mind with the offering in 8:24 and 9:12-14 below. While there are some parallels in each of the chapters and the redundancy does not appear necessary, it is possible that chap. 8 is focused on the collection itself and chap. 9 more on the reasons for it. What is clear is that Paul spent a considerable amount of time collecting this financial gift for the Christians in Jerusalem. For whom in Jerusalem was this gift being collected? Those who are called "the poor" (Greek = *ptochoi*) in Gal. 2:10, and called "saints (Greek = *hagious*) in 1 Cor. 16:1 and "the poor among the saints" (Rom. 15:25-26, 31), were evidently those Christians who were in destitute circumstances as a result of the famine that came to their region. While it is true that the term "poor" was later used as a designation for Christians, and earlier for the "righteous" at Qumran, Luke never uses this term as a designation for the Christian communities that he described, and it is not so used elsewhere in the New Testament. The author of the *Psalms of Solomon* (ca. first cent. B.C.) seems to equate those who are righteous with the "poor." "Our Lord is just and holy in his judgments forever, and Israel shall praise the Lord's name in joy. And the devout shall give thanks in the assembly of the people, and God will be merciful to the poor to the joy of Israel" (10:5-6, *OT Pseud* 2:661). Later he writes: "I expected the help of Jacob's God and I was saved. For you, O God, are the hope and refuge of the poor" (15:1, *OT Pseud* 2:664; see also 18:2-3). At Qumran, there is something similar: "By the hand of your anointed ones, seers of decrees, you taught us the times of the wars of your hands, . . . by the

hand of the poor, those you saved, with the strength and peace of your wonderful power" (*War Scroll*, 1QM 11.7-9, Garcia Martinez trans.). Again, in the *Commentary on Habakkuk*, we read:

> The interpretation of the word concerns the Wicked Priest, to pay him the reward for what he did to the poor . . . God will sentence him to destruction, . . . exactly as he intended to destroy the poor . . . The violence against the country are the cities of Judah which he plundered of the possessions of the poor (1QpHab 12.2-3, 5-6, 9-10, Garcia Martinez trans.).

On the other hand, the poor as a community of the righteous or faithful is clearly not in the mind of Paul, except that he collected the funds to care for the "saints" who were poor in Jerusalem. The fact that a *monetary* collection was made, strongly suggests that we should conclude that the offering was for those who were enduring financial hardships and needed the aid.

It is not clear that Luke was aware of the gift, or perhaps for some reason, he chose not to mention the collection when Paul came to Jerusalem (Acts 21:17-26). The book of Acts is strangely silent on the matter except in the one passing text in 24:17. On the other hand, if the gift was offered to the leaders of the church when Paul and his companions arrived in Jerusalem, it is not clear that they accepted the gift from the *Gentiles*. It may be that the concern in Jerusalem by the Jewish Christians over Paul's ministry and his understanding of the Law, as well as his ministry to the Gentiles (Acts 21:17-26), led them to reject the gift and Luke may simply have chosen not to mention it. Paul was anxious about the church ("saints") in Jerusalem accepting the gift (Rom. 15:31). The passing reference in 24:17 is only minimal and says little about that which apparently occupied so much of Paul's time, namely the economic relief for Christians in Jerusalem (or Judea).

For our purposes, we will include both chapters in the one letter written by Paul to the Corinthians (2 Cor. 1–9), but add that there was an insertion into (6:14–7:1) and an addition to (chaps. 10–13) the original letter. We will discuss the addition below. For a more comprehensive understanding of the problem, see the Introduction above.

a. 8:1–9:5. Corinthian Generosity

8:3. For I testify that according to their ability, and beyond their ability they gave of their own accord. The Macedonians were not as wealthy as those from Achaia in the first century and Paul indicates that they had given a very generous offering for the poor Christians in Jerusalem. It has been observed that the poor are often more generous than the wealthy, and this is still true today. In the *Testament of Job*, the story is told of Job's generosity that led him to keep some thirty tables spread at all hours so that he could care for strangers who came to him in need. The author, in the name of Job, says that others came to assist Job in this worthy activity.

There were also certain strangers who saw my eagerness, and they too desired to assist in this service. And there were still others, at the time without resources and unable to invest a thing, who came and entreated me, saying, "we beg you, may we also engage in this service." (*Test. Job* 11:1-2, OT Pseud 1:843)

Later, he adds: "On occasion a man cheerful at heart would come to me saying, 'I am not wealthy enough to help the destitute. Yet I wish to serve the poor today at your table'" (*Test. Job* 12:1-2, OT Pseud 1:844). Dio Chrysostom (ca. A.D. 40-120) experienced the generosity of poor people who helped him when he was shipwrecked on the island of Euboea off the coast of Macedonia. Illustrating the generosity of the poor, he tells his personal story:

Now I have not told this long story idly or, as some might perhaps infer, with the desire to spin a yarn, but to present an illustration of the manner of life that I adopted at the beginning and of the life of the poor—an illustration drawn from my own experience for anyone who wishes to consider whether in words and deeds and in social intercourse the poor are at a disadvantage in comparison with the rich on account of their poverty, so far as living a seemly and natural life is concerned, or in every way have the advantage. . . they [the poor] light a fire more promptly than the rich, and guide one on the way without reluctance— indeed, in such matters a sense of self-respect would compel them—and often they share what they have more readily. When you find a rich man, who will give the victim of a shipwreck his wife's or his daughter's purple gown or any article of clothing far cheaper than that: a mantle, for example or a tunic, though he has thousands of them, or even a cloak from one of his slaves (*Orations* 7.82-83, LCL).

8:8. I am not speaking this as a command, but as proving through the earnestness of others the sincerity of your love also. Earlier, it appears that Paul had been a bit more forceful in his asking for the money for the Jerusalem church (1 Cor. 16:1-4). Whatever changed between the writing of 1 Corinthians and this correspondence, it may be that Paul was accused of trying to lord it over the church or make unreasonable demands of them and so he has softened his approach.

8:12. For if the readiness is present, it is acceptable according to what a man has, not according to what he does not have. This is a call to generosity based on what one has received from God. Paul has carefully crafted his words so that no precise amount is stated in advance, but that a generous amount is what is appropriate. What is generous for one, may be small to another. What Paul says is similar to the Jewish tradition current in his generation. According to the Jewish writer of Tobit (probably early second cent. B.C.):

> To all who practice righteousness, give alms from your possessions, and do not let your eye begrudge the gift when you make it. Do not turn your face away from anyone who is poor, and the face of God will not be turned away from you. If you have many possessions, make your gift from them in proportion; if few, do not be afraid to give according to the little you have. So you will be laying up a good reassure for yourself against the day of necessity. For almsgiving delivers from death and keeps you from going into the Darkness. Indeed, almsgiving, for all who practice it, is an excellent offering in the presence of the Most High (*Tobit* 4:6-10, NRSV).

In parallel fashion, Dio Chrysostom said that in the eyes of temperate and good men, "No gift is inadequate which is prompted by affection" (*Orations* 7.93, LCL).

8:13. For this is not for the ease of others and for your affliction, but by way of equality—. The Greeks, who founded democracy, praised equality. Dio Chrysostom, citing the words of Euripides who urged brothers not to over reach each other, wrote:

> At greed, the worst of deities, my son, why graspest thou? Do not; she is Queen of wrong. Houses many and happy cities enters she, Nor leaves till ruined are her votaries. Though are mad for her! —'tis best to venerate Equality, which knitteth friends to friends, Cities to cities, allies to allies. Nature gave men the law of equal rights, and the less, ever marshaled against the greater, ushers in the dawn of hate (Dio Chrysostom, *Orations* 17.9, citing Euripides, *Phoenician Women* 531-40, LCL)

The Romans were not known for any practice of equality and there was no middle class to speak of under Roman rule. They promoted a class-filled society, but to placate those under their rule, they often minted coins that praised the virtue of equality and personified Equality (Latin = *Aequitas*) and placed the name and the image of a woman with a scale in her hand, the symbol of justice and equity. Some coins from the first century depict a woman with the scale in her hand and a cornucopia (the symbol of prosperity) in her hands with the name "Augustan Equality (*Aequitas*)." Roughly contemporary with Paul, Philo says of equality:

> Moses too above all others shews [shows] himself a eulogist of equality; first by always and everywhere lauding justice too whose special property it is, as the name itself seems to shew [show], to divide into two equal parts things material and immaterial; secondly by censuring injustice, the creator of inequality in its most hateful form. Inequality is the mother of the twins, foreign war and civil war, just as its opposite, equality is the mother of peace (*Who is the Heir* 161-162, LCL).

Philo goes on in the same passage to cite Lev. 19:35-36 and Deut. 25:13-16 to justify his comments about Moses' commitment to equality. Also, citing Gen. 1:4-5, he claims that even though the male is stronger physically than the female, God made them both equal (*Who Is the Heir* 163-164).

8:18, 22. And we have sent along with him the brother whose fame in the things of the gospel has spread through all the churches .... And we have sent with them our brother, whom we have often tested and found diligent in many things, but now even more diligent, because of his great confidence in you. Who this unnamed "brother" and the brother who accompanies him and Titus cannot be known with certainty, but it could be Luke, Timothy, Apollos, Sopater, Aristarchus, or

Secundus; the latter three traveled with Paul on his journey to Jerusalem, probably also with the gift collected from the churches (see Acts 20:4). Ordinarily Paul names those he recommends, but not here. Why? It has been suggested that they had earlier been involved in some unpleasant activity in Corinth and so their names are not mentioned here. This also seems unlikely, but it is possible that the names were erased from the letter by the Corinthians themselves. Could it be that this/these individuals might have departed from the faith at a later time as did Demas (2 Tim. 4:10) or someone like Alexander the coppersmith (2 Tim. 4:14)? There is too much that is not known here and it may be better to say that for some unknown reason, Paul chose to omit the names. Paul may have known of some opposition in advance and chose not to state the names.

8:19. And not only this, but he has also been appointed by the churches to travel with us in this gracious work, which is being administered by us for the glory of the Lord Himself, and to show our readiness. The term "appointed" (Greek = *cheirotonetheis*, literally "vote" or "elect") talks about the way the individuals were selected. The Greek root of the word, *cheir* ("hand"), suggests that decisions were made by a show of hands. The same term is used in the *Didache* (late first century A.D.) to "elect therefore bishops and deacons for yourselves worthy of the Lord" (*Did.* 15:1). See also similar statements about selection of leaders for roles in the church in Ignatius, *To the Philadelphians* 10:1 and *To the Smyrneans* 11:2 where the same word is used in the appointment to office. More importantly, Paul's practice of having congregations elect their representatives to deliver money to Jerusalem has a parallel in Philo who tells of the Jews gathering collections for the temple tax in Jerusalem. Philo also uses the same term that Paul uses ("appointed," literally, "elected,"

Greek = *cheirotonountai*) individuals who were trustworthy to carry the funds to Jerusalem. Philo explains:

> And at stated times there are appointed [Greek = *cheirotonountai*] to carry the sacred tribute envoys selected on their merits, from every city those of the highest repute, under whose conduct the hopes of each and all will travel safely. For it is on these first-fruits, as prescribed by the law, that the hopes of the pious rest (*Special Laws* 1.78, LCL).

The parallels with Paul's practice are obvious and the practice of using local representatives to transport gifts (temple tax) to Israel is essentially what Paul did (1 Cor. 16:3-4). Paul wanted representatives from each of the churches that contributed to the gift for the "saints who were poor" in Jerusalem to accompany the gifts to make sure that nothing inappropriate was done with the money collected for this purpose, but his practice was likely one that he adopted from his Jewish kinsmen who collected the temple tax from the diaspora Jews and brought it to Jerusalem.

8:23. As for Titus, he is my partner and fellow worker among you; as for our brethren, they are messengers of the churches, a glory to Christ. The term Paul uses for "messengers" (Greek *apostoloi*, "apostles") is not to be taken in the same sense in which Paul was called to preach the Gospel, but rather those representatives of their churches to accompany the funds to Jerusalem.

9:2. For I know your readiness, of which I boast about you to the Macedonians: namely, that Achaia has been prepared since last year, and your zeal has stirred up most of them. More than one commentator has expressed surprise at this passage (see also 9:3-4) when compared to the above concerns about whether the Corinthians will supply enough in 8:10-11. The two passages seem to be at odds and this has prompted several to suggest that this means that chap. 9 constitutes a different letter written later by Paul at a time when the church at Corinth had already made more serious contributions and committed themselves to the collection (cf. 1 Cor. 16:1-4 for an earlier commitment). Whatever caused them some hesitation toward this collection, perhaps Paul's opponents who may have suggested that it was for himself, the issue seems now to have been settled and only the final amount is in question.

9:4. Lest if any Macedonians come with me and find you unprepared, we (not to speak of you) should be put to shame by this confidence. Paul very astutely pits the Macedonians against the Achaeans in order to encourage each to give as generously as possible. While there were many poor people in the church at Corinth (1 Cor. 1: 26-28), there were also some like Erastus (Acts 19:21-22; Rom. 16:23), who was a city official in Corinth and who donated an expensive pavement to the city (see discussion above in 3:1-2). Likewise, Chloe (1 Cor. 1:11) had servants that she could send to Ephesus to visit Paul, but this was not the general situation. Nevertheless, Paul believes that they have adequate resources to be generous in their giving. Speaking of the wealth associated with Corinth and also the importance of them leading by example rather than following someone else's example, Dio Chrysostom writes:

> But when you followed the lead of persons who—however, I shall say nothing of them by way of retaliation, save only that it would have been more proper for them to follow your lead than for you to follow theirs. For you are now, as the saying goes, both prow and stern of Hellas, having been called prosperous and wealthy and the like by poets and gods from olden days, days when some of the others too had wealth and might; but now since wealth has deserted both

Orchomenos and Delphi, though they may surpass you in exciting pity, none can do so in exciting envy (*Orations* 37.35-36, LCL).

b. 9:6-15. The Principle of Generosity Encouraged

9:7 Let each one do just as he has purposed in his heart; not grudgingly or under compulsion; for God loves a cheerful giver. God's love for a cheerful giver is a common theme in Paul's day, but may also reflect his understanding of Prov. 22:8 in the LXX (Greek translation of the Old Testament) which says in part: "God blesses [Greek = *eulogei*] a cheerful and liberal man." The change between the LXX "blesses" in Proverbs and "loves" in 9:7 (Greek = *agapao*), is probably Paul's design and for the sake of emphasizing more that the cheerful and generous giver experiences love of God which is even greater than his blessing. This is similar to Sirach who encouraged generous giving to the work of the Lord saying: "Be generous when you worship the Lord, and do not stint the first fruits of your hands. With every gift show a cheerful face, and dedicate your tithe with gladness. Give to the Most High as he has given to you, and as generously as you can" (*Sir.* 35:10-12, NRSV). Philo also understands the value of giving liberally as the opportunity arises. He urges those with means to follow the age-old wisdom of generosity.

> For what one of the men of old aptly said is true, that in no other action does man so much resemble God as in showing kindness, and what greater good can there be than that they should imitate God, . . . So then let not the rich man collect great store of gold and silver and hoard it at his house, but bring it out for general use that he may soften the hard lot of the needy with the unction of his cheerfully given liberality (*Special Laws* 4.73-74, LCL).

9:9. As it is written, "He scattered abroad, he gave to the poor, His righteousness abides forever." The passage Paul cites here is from the LXX of Ps. 112:9. He undoubtedly knew the tradition in Judaism that calls upon all faithful followers of the Lord to care for the poor. This is affirmed in the Proverbs where we see that, "those who are generous are blessed, for they share their bread with the poor" (Prov. 22:9, NRSV). Caring for those in need, the poor and the oppressed, was indeed fundamental to Jewish religious teachings and was deeply rooted in the Old Testament (Exod. 22:25; 23:6, 11; Deut. 15:11; 24:14-15; Ps. 12:5; 22:25-26; 41:1; 74:19, 21; 109:16; 112:9; 113:7-8; 132:15; 140:12; Prov. 22:16, 22-23; 28:8, 27; 29:14; 31:9, 20; cf. also 30:14 cf. Luke 6:20). These scriptures form the context for the many sayings about caring for the poor that were present in the time of Paul. Jesus also affirmed the importance of caring for the poor (Matt. 11:5; 19:21; Mark 14:5; Luke 4:18; 7:22; 14:13, 21; 18:22; cf. Luke 19:8; Jas. 2:5-6). This focus on the poor is likewise found in numerous examples in the apocryphal literature. Sirach, for instance, admonishes those who seek wisdom thusly:

My child, do not cheat the poor of their living, and do not keep needy eyes waiting. Do not grieve the hungry, or anger one in need. Do not add to the troubles of the desperate, or delay giving to the needy. Do not reject a suppliant in distress, or turn your face away from the poor. . . .give a hearing to the poor, and return their greeting politely. Rescue the oppressed from the oppressor . . . Be a father to orphans, and be like a husband to their mother; you will then be like a son of the Most High, and he will love you more than does your mother (*Sir.* 4:1-5a, 8-10, NRSV).

D. 10:1–13:10. A Vindication of Paul's Authority

Whatever led to the emotionally charged words in these chapters, Paul is at his most defensive posture in all of his writings here. In 1 Corinthians, his apostleship does not appear to be seriously questioned, despite his defense in 9:1-27, and this does not seem to be a major concern in his defense of his ministry in 2 Corinthians 2:14–7:2. On the other hand, strong opposition to his claims as an apostle stands behind the whole of these four chapters. Whatever was said or reported against him moved him to his most ardent defense in all of his letters that includes biting sarcasm and even satire. He does what he does not want to do, namely boast of his accomplishments and standing among the leaders of his day. While he does not specifically identify his opponents, it seems that they were Jewish Christians, probably of the Judaizing bent, even though Paul does not focus much attention on the Law or its many practices here. Also, it appears from Paul's comments below that they were also schooled in rhetoric and could expect financial assistance in their ministry, unlike what Paul himself accepted, and evidently they were persons who dressed and acted more officially than did Paul. Since they challenged Paul who had no "letters," it is likely that they themselves had such letters from the leadership in Jerusalem. Paul refers to them as "super-apostles" (11:5) and implies that they accused him of being a "false apostle." The opening and closing sections of these four chapters, 10:1-10 and 13:1-10, act as something like bookends to the heart of the matter and the most impassioned words Paul has penned in all of his letters (chaps. 11–12), especially the "fool's speech" (11:1–12:13). There are a number of parallels here with ancient thought and some of those will be highlighted below. Many scholars contend that these chapters were edited and added onto 2 Cor. 1–8 (or chaps. 1–9), and only differ on whether they were written before 2 Cor. 1–8 or came later as circumstances at Corinth changed for the worse. All agree that because of its length, the volume was not written on one occasion and this may account for some of the rather brittle changes in direction or subject matter as the letter progresses, namely between 1:1–2:13 and 2:14–7:4 (with the insertion of 6:14–7:1), the addition of the two chapters on the collection which might have been two separate letters, and these four chapters. There is little question that Paul wrote all of the contents of 2 Corinthians, with the exception of 6:14–7:1, but it is possible that there were considerable time lags between the writing of these sections and the sending of the final document. It is highly unlikely that chaps. 10–13 were written at, or close to, the same time as chaps. 7–9 since the tone in 10–13 is so opposite that of what is found in the former. It is not likely that Paul would have written so angrily and sarcastically to those he was appealing to for financial assistance for Jerusalem. It is possible that chaps. 10–13 were written after chaps. 1–9 with some delay between the two portions of the letter. It is possible that Paul received information from Corinth by way of his colleagues who had recently arrived from there that triggered the strong words of chaps. 10–13. From a look at 2:1-3 (that was probably penned following the writing of chaps. 8–9); 12:21; 13:1, it seems clear that Paul had planned an additional visit to Corinth and his correspondence here is in preparation for that visit. These are all issues that divide biblical scholars, but, again, the content in 10–13 is all Paul's probably written over an extended period of time or written and sent on more than one occasion. See Introduction above for further discussion on the integrity of the letter.

I. 10:1–12:10. Paul's Personal Appeal Regarding His Apostolic Authority

a. 10:1–18. True apostleship. In this section, as throughout the last four chapters of this letter, Paul is responding to quotes that he has received from his opponents and addresses their criticisms with sarcasm and humility as well as wisdom and attack. This is not unlike the words of Dio Chrysostom (ca. A.D. 40-120), who describes how one ought to deal with one's opponents:

But he who in very truth is manly and high-minded would never submit to any such things [inappropriate and selfish activity], nor would he sacrifice his own liberty and his freedom of speech for the sake of any dishonourable payment of either power or riches, nor would he envy those who change their form and apparel for such rewards; on the contrary, he would think such persons to be comparable to those who change from human beings into snakes or other animals, not envying them, nor yet carping at them because of their wantonness, but rather bewailing and pitying them when they, like the boys, with an eye to gifts have their hair cut off, and grey hair at that! [Long hair was the outward and visible sign of the philosopher.] But as for himself, the man of whom I speak will strive to preserve his individuality in seemly fashion and with steadfastness, never deserting his post of duty, but always honouring and promoting virtue and sobriety and trying to lead all men thereto, partly by persuading and exhorting, partly by abusing and reproaching, in the hope that he may thereby rescue somebody from folly and from low desires and intemperance and soft living, taking them aside privately one by one and also admonishing them in groups every time he finds the opportunity, "With gentle words at times at others harsh," until, methinks, he shall have spent his life in caring for human beings, not cattle or horses or camels and houses, sound in words and sound in deeds, a safe traveling companion for any one to have on land or sea and a good omen for men to behold when offering sacrifice, not arousing strife or greed or contentions and jealousies and base desires for gain, but reminding men of sobriety and righteousness and promoting concord, but as for insatiate greed and shamelessness and moral weakness, expelling them as best he can—in short, a person far more sacred than the bearers of a truce or the heralds who in times of war come bringing an armistice.

Therefore he wishes, yes, is eager, in so far as he can, to aid all men; though sometimes he is defeated by other men and other practices and has little or no power at all (*Orations* 77/78.37-39, LCL).

10:1. Now I, Paul, myself urge you by the meekness and gentleness of Christ—I who am meek when face to face with you, but bold toward you when absent! In contrast to the "super-apostles" (11:5, 12-15; 12:11-12), Paul comes to the Corinthians in humility, even if in boldness. The Jewish anticipation of a "meek and lowly" (= humble) Messiah is cited in the New Testament in regard to Jesus, who is Paul's example here (see Matt. 21:5; cf. Zech. 9:9), and found in various Old Testament texts (Ps. 45:4; Isa. 40:11; 42:3; 53:7. See also Matt. 5:5; 11:29 and John 1:29). According to Plutarch (ca. A.D. 45-120), it was concluded that the Athenian's appreciation for Pericles (ca. 495-429 B.C.), their popular leader and general of Athens, was due to him:

... not only because of his reasonableness and gentleness which he maintained in the midst of many responsibilities and great enmities, but also for his loftiness of spirit, seeing that he regarded it as the noblest of all his titles to honour that he had never gratified his envy or his passion in the exercise of his vast power, nor treated any one of his foes as a foe incurable (*Parallel Lives, Pericles* 39.1, LCL).

How can this appearance of humility in Paul at the beginning of his discourse be harmonized with his boldness of speech that follows, especially in his "fool's speech" in

11:1–12:13)? In Jewish literature there is an abundance of examples of the mercy and love of God being combined with justice and boldness of action, for example, Hos. 11:8-9, but also in non-canonical Jewish literature. In the *Psalms of Solomon* (ca. first century B.C.), for example, we read:

For the destruction of the sinner is terrible; but nothing shall harm the righteous, of all these things. For the discipline of the righteous (for things done) in ignorance is not the same as the destruction of the sinners. In secret the righteous are disciplined lest the sinner gloat over the righteous. For he will admonish the righteous as a beloved son and his discipline is as for a firstborn. For the Lord will spare his devout, and he will wipe away their mistakes with discipline. For the life of the righteous (goes on) forever, but sinners shall be taken away to destruction, and no memory of them will ever be found. But the Lord's mercy is upon the devout and mercy is upon those who fear him (*Ps. Sol.* 13:6-12, *OT Pseud* 2:663; see also 8:28-34 and *Wisd. Sol.* 11:20-26).

The hearers of Paul would likewise not be surprised to find both kindness and love in a passage with judgment and correction. For example, Demosthenes addresses the question of when a person should speak boldly in public. He asks: "But under what circumstances ought the politician and orator to be vehement? Of course, when the city is in any way imperiled and when the public is faced by adversaries. Such is the obligation of a noble and patriotic citizen" (*On the Crown* 278, F. Danker, trans.150). The point is that anger over small matters is inappropriate, but passionate language on behalf of others and their welfare is noble.

10:3-4. For though we walk in the flesh, we do not war according to the flesh, for the weapons of our warfare are not of the flesh,

but divinely powerful for the destruction of fortresses. Paul uses warfare language to describe his opposition to the criticisms and behavior of his opponents. This was common among philosophers of his day and was clearly familiar also to Paul. Epictetus (ca. mid-first century A.D. to mid-second century A.D.), describing how to overcome issues of contention uses metaphorical language to make his point:

How, then, is a citadel destroyed? [the citadel represented the tower from which a tyrant operated in a city.] Not by iron, nor by fire, but by judgments. For if we capture the citadel in the city, have we captured the citadel of ever also, have we captured that of pretty wenches also, in a word, the acropolis within us, and we have lording it over each of us every day, sometimes the say tyrants, and sometimes others? But here is where we must begin, and it is from this side that we must seize the acropolis and cast out the tyrants; we must yield up the paltry body, its members, the faculties, property, reputation, offices, honours, children, brothers, friends—count all these things as alien to us. And if the tyrants be thrown out of the spot, why should I any longer gaze the fortifications of the citadel, on my own account, at least? (*Discourses* 4.1.86-87, LCL).

Like Paul, Philo also speaks of toppling evil through warfare within the community of the righteous. He claims that Justice

Razes to the ground the cities which they [evil persons] fortified to menace the unhappy soul, and the tower whose name is explained in the book of Judges. ... For the stronghold which was built through persuasiveness of argument was built solely for the purpose of diverting and deflecting the mind from honouring God. And what greater sin against justice could there be than this? But there stands ready armed for the destruction of this stronghold the robber who despoils injustice and ever breathes slaughter against her, whom the Hebrews call Gideon swore, we read, to the men of Penuel saying, "When I return with peace I will demolish this tower" (Judges 8:9; *The Confusion of Tongues* 128-30, LCL).

10:5-6. We are destroying speculations and every lofty thing raised up against the knowledge of God, and we are taking every thought captive to the obedience of Christ, and we are ready to punish all disobedience, whenever your obedience is complete. Paul's warfare against the evil spreading in the church at Corinth is here declared. There is a likeness in language from his contemporary, Philo from Alexandria, who spoke against those who bring unrest and cause disturbances. He urges his readers to live without contention, "refusing to engage in the way waged by the sophists, with their unceasing practice of quarrelsomeness and disturbance to the adulteration of the truth: for the truth is dear to peace, and peace has no liking for them" (*On Husbandry* 159, LCL). Of such individuals he says elsewhere,

Day after day the swarm of sophists to be found everywhere wears out the ears of any audience they happen to have with disquisitions on minutiae, unraveling phrases that are ambiguous and can bear two meanings and distinguishing among circumstances such as it is well to bear in mind—and they are set on bearing in mind a vast number (*On Husbandry* 136, LCL).

10:7. You are looking at things as they are outwardly. If anyone is confident in himself that he is Christ's, let him consider this again within himself, that just as he is Christ's, so

also are we. This is Paul's way of saying that both the Corinthians who have ridiculed him and he must recognize that they are both followers of Christ, and that that has important implications for their relationships.

10:10. For they say, "His letters are weighty and strong, but his personal presence is unimpressive, and his speech contemptible." Paul deals with a particularly painful criticism of him and is mindful of the standards of appearance and ability that the rhetoricians of his day were expected to meet. His opponents ridiculed him because of his poor rhetorical skills (1 Cor. 1:17, 21; 2:1-4; 3:18-23; 4:9-13; 2 Cor. 2:17; 5:11-13; here; 11:6; 12:19; 13:3), but also because of his appearance. Dio Chrysostom tells of his addressing those in Phrygia who expected him to have greater rhetorical skills than he possessed and acknowledged before he spoke his own inadequacies.

Gentlemen, I have come before you not to display my talents as a speaker nor because I want money from you, or expect your praise. For I know not only that I myself am not sufficiently well equipped to satisfy you by my eloquence, but also that your circumstances are not such as to need my message. Furthermore, the disparity between what you demand of a speaker and my own powers is very great. For it is my nature to talk quite simply and unaffectedly and in a manner in no wise better than that of any ordinary persons; whereas you are devoted to oratory to a degree that is remarkable, I may even say excessive, and you tolerate as speakers only those who are very clever (*Orations* 35.1, LCL).

These expectations are not unlike those that were expected of Paul in Corinth. Paul was compared with those who spoke in public at banquets and civic activities, and Paul did not fare well in comparison. Besides the oratorical skills, there were also demands in physical appearance. Epictetus identifies the normal expectations of those who speak in public in his

day. Besides rhetorical skills, he contends that
. . . such a man needs also a certain kind of body, since if a consumptive comes forward, thin and pale, his testimony no longer carries the same weight. For he must not merely, by exhibiting the qualities of his soul, prove to the laymen that it is possible, without the help of the things which they admire, to be a good and excellent man, but he must also show, by the state of his body, that his plain and simple style of life in the open air does not inure even his body: "Look," he says, "both I and my body are witnesses to the truth of my contention." That was the way of Diogenes, for he used to go about with a radiant complexion, and would attract the attention of the common people by the very appearance of his body. But a cynic who excites pity is regarded as a beggar; everybody turns away from him, everybody takes offence at him (Epictetus, *Discourses* 3.22.86-89, LCL).

In a mid-second century description of Paul, the only one that survives that describes his appearance, we read that Paul was "a man of small stature, with a bald head and crooked legs, in a good state of body, with eyebrows meeting and nose somewhat hooked, full of friendliness; for now he appeared like a man and now he had the face of an angel" (*Acts of Paul and Thecla* 3, NT APO 2:239). If there is some validity to this description, then Paul certainly would not have the appealing stature of many who spoke in public in his day. One's public appearance in Paul's day was important enough that even highly influential persons were often criticized for their public appearance. Cicero, for instance was criticized for his varicose veins.

This is what was accomplished, O Cicero, —or Cicerculus, or Ciceracius, or Ciceriscus, or Greculus [these are diminutive forms of Cicero's name and were intended to express contempt for him], or whatever you delight in being called, —by the uneducated, the naked, the anointed man; and none of it was done by you, so clever, so wise, you who use much more oil than wine [a reference to staying up late at night], who let your clothing drag about your ankles—not, by Jupiter, as the dancers do, who teach you intricacies of reasoning by their poses, but in order to hide the ugliness of your legs (Dio Cassius, *Roman History* 46.18.2, LCL).

Likewise, Pompey was mocked for scratching his head in public (Plutarch, *Moralia* 89e). Some Corinthians were more concerned with the external appearance of the individual rather than what he said or how he lived among them. This focus on the externals ignored what Paul thought was most important, namely the beauty of a Spirit-filled life and humility. The attention paid to external appearances at Corinth was wellknown in the ancient world. In his discussion of personal adornment, Epictetus describes a young student of rhetoric who wanted to play the role of the philosopher and so adorned himself with hair that was "somewhat too elaborately dressed, and whose attire in general was highly embellished" (*Discourses* 3.1.1, LCL). Epictetus chastised him for ignoring the beauty that was the real person (3.1.14-27). Similarly, Martial ridicules a man who was elaborately dressed:

> Since you boast yourself a fellow townsman of Corinthian bronzes with none to gainsay you, Charmenion, why do you call me "brother," born as I am of Iberians and Celts, a countryman of Tagus. Is it that we look alike? You go around looking smart with your hair in curls, mine is stubborn and Spanish. You are smooth with daily depilatory, my shins and cheeks are hairy. Your mouth lisps and your tongue is feeble; only Silia [or Pilia, that is, a lady with a

loud voice] will speak bolder than I (*Epigrams* 2.10.65, LCL).

The call to be the same in word and deed was common in the ancient world and Paul is aware of this familiar expectation. Epictetus described the philosopher as one who was a model both in word and deed. He writes:

> Then, in the place of all the other relaxations, introduce that which comes from the consciousness that you are obedient to God, and that you are playing the part of the good and excellent man, not ostensibly but in reality. For what a fine thing it is to be able to say to oneself, "Now I am actually performing what the rest talk solemnly about in their lectures, and are thought to be uttering paradoxes . . . " (*Discourses* 3.24.110-111, LCL).

10:12. For we are not bold to class or compare ourselves with some of those who commend themselves; but when they measure themselves by themselves, and compare themselves with themselves, they are without understanding. In a satire against those who compare themselves favorably with others, Lucian (mid-second century A.D.) mocks those who boast about their superiority and offers an example of a philosopher who is addressed by one he sees as his inferior.

> . . . he will address you, I say, using very moderate language about himself: "Prithee, dear fellow [the one addressing him], did Pythian Apollo [a god] send you to me, entitling me the best of speakers, just as, when Chaerephon questioned him, he told who was the wisest in that generation? If that is not the case, but you have come of your own accord in the wake of rumour, because you hear everybody speak of my achievements with astonishment, praise, admiration, and self-abasement, you shall very soon learn what a superhuman person you have come to. Do not expect to see something that you can

compare with So-and-so, or So-and-so; no, you will consider the achievement far too prodigious and amazing even for Tityus or Otus or Ephialtes. Indeed, as far as the others are concerned, you will find that I drown them out as effectively as trumpets drown flutes, or cicadas bees, or choirs their leaders (*A Professor of Public Speaking* 13, LCL).

The practice of comparing oneself with others at their expense was common practice among the sophists and is condemned by Plutarch who claimed that they made such comparisons to a fault. "For it is not like friendship, but sophistry to seek for glory in other men's faults" (*How to Tell a Friend from a Flatterer* 71, LCL). Plutarch condemns those who seek praise from others by comparing themselves with others at the other's expense or by ridiculing the efforts of others who instead deserve praise.

> ... when those who hunger for praise cannot find others to praise them, they give the appearance of seeking sustenance and succour for their vainglorious appetite from themselves, a graceless spectacle. But when they do not even seek to be praised simply and in themselves, but try to rival the honour that belongs to others and set against it their own accomplishments and acts in the hope of dimming the glory of another, their conduct is not only frivolous, but envious and spiteful as well. For the proverb makes of him who sets foot in another's chorus a meddler and a fool; among praises of others should be most diligently avoided; indeed we should not even endure such praise from others, but should give place to those on whom hounour is conferred when they deserve it. If we hold them undeserving and of little worth, let us not strip them of their praise by presenting our own, but plainly refute their claim and show their

reputation to be groundless. Here then is something we clearly must avoid (*On Inoffensive Self-Praise* 450A-B, LCL).

Such comparisons at others' expense were commonplace in the ancient world and evidently Paul was so compared with others who argued that they were his superiors. These are the "false apostles" mentioned in 11:13 below.

10:14-15. For we are not overextending ourselves, as if we did not reach to you, for we were the first to come even as far as you in the gospel of Christ; not boasting beyond our measure, that is, in other men's labors, but with the hope that as your faith grows, we shall be, within our sphere, enlarged even more by you. This principle is also stated in Rom. 15:19-23 where Paul underscores that he does not want to build on another person's foundation and that he desired to reach out to those who have never heard the Good News. The term Paul uses to indicate his "own sphere" is the Greek *kanona*, the word used for "canon" or "rule," and sometimes "authority" (see also v. 16 below). While the word is used variously in the ancient world, it generally refers to a standard or guideline that was established or followed. For Paul, his guideline for missionary activity came from the Lord, and that was that he should not build on another person's foundation, but rather reach the unreached for Christ. An example of this use of *kanona (kanon)* comes from Aeschines (ca. 397-322 B.C.) in Athens. He writes:

> Justice is not something vague and undefined, but is bounded by your own laws. In carpentry, when we want to know whether something is straight, we use a ruler (*kanon*) designed for the purpose. So also in the case of indictments for illegal proposals, the guide (*kanon*) for justice is this public posting of the proposal with accompanying statement of the laws that it violates (*Against Ctesiphon* 199-200, Danker trans.).

10:16. So as to preach the gospel even to the regions beyond you, and not to boast in what has been accomplished in the sphere of another. Again, the words "in the sphere" come from the Greek word *kanona* (here = *kanoni*). This is an indication that Paul is planning on extending his mission to places not yet reached, that is, his "sphere" or "rule" as in Rom. 15:19-23.

10:17-18. But he who boasts, let him boast in the Lord. For not he who commends himself is approved, but whom the Lord commends. It was common in the ancient world to attribute one's favorable actions to a god so as not to appear too self-focused. For example, when Achilles defeated Hector in battle, he exclaims to the people, "My friends, leaders and rulers of the Argives, seeing the gods have vouchsafed us to slay this man, that hath wrought much evil beyond all the host of the others . . . " (Homer, *Iliad* 22.378-380, LCL). Demosthenes likewise, rather than acknowledging his own bravery, thanks the good will of a god for restraining the efforts of Philip of Macedon (*On the Crown* 153). Plutarch writes of this practice and praises it to his readers:

> But those who are forced to speak in their own praise are made more endurable by another procedure as well: not to lay claim to everything, but to disburden themselves, as it were, of honour, letting part of it rest with chance, and part with god. For this reason Achilles did well to say "since I by Heaven's will have slain this man," and Timoleon did well to erect an altar at Syracuse to the Goddess of Accidents in commemoration of his acts, and to consecrate his house to the Good Daemon. Best of all is what Python of Aenos did. After killing Cotys he had come to Athens and the speakers were outdoing one another in extolling him to the assembly. Noticing that some persons were jealous and disaffected he

came forward and said: "this, men of Athens, was the doing of some god; I did but lend my arm." Sulla too got rid of envy by always praising his luck, eventually proclaiming himself the Fortunate. For men would rather be bested by luck than by merit, feeling that in the first event another has had an advantage, in the second, that failure lies in themselves and in their own doing. Thus the code of Zaleucus found favour with the Locrians not least, it is said, because he asserted that Athena had constantly appeared to him and had in each case guided and instructed him in his legislation, and that nothing he proposed was of his own invention or devising (*On Inoffensive Self-Praise* 542E-543A, LCL).

b. 11:1–12:13. A "fool's speech." Some commentators have thought that this passage flies in the face of what Paul has just said about comparisons and boastings, and at first glance it does appear to do so. Paul himself calls what he is about to do foolish because he appears to be boasting. At the end of the last chapter he argues that boasting can only be in the Lord, but here he "lapses" into what he acknowledges as foolishness, but because of the criticism leveled against him, he feels obligated to compare himself to those who have criticized him. He uses the Greco-Roman style of adulation to magnify his office before the Corinthian Christians, acknowledging that even he believes that such argumentation is indeed foolish (11:15) and making him out to be a "madman" (11:23). For him to take such a tactic suggests that his opponents had scored considerable victory against Paul in their criticisms. While he boasts against his opponents' accomplishments saying that he has done more (11:22-28), he also insists that his boasting comes from his weakness (11:30, 12:10). He has three major boasts, namely his preaching the Gospel free of charge to the Corinthians (11:7-15), his sufferings that came as a result of his faithful preaching of the Gospel (11:16-33), and his visions and revelations (12:1-10).

11:2. For I am jealous for you with a godly jealousy; for I betrothed you to one husband, that to Christ I might present you as a pure virgin. It was common especially among the Jews for the father of the bride to protect her chastity prior to marriage and to join with the family and friends to escort her to the husband's home following the wedding ceremony (the purpose of those who lit the way in Matt. 25:6-10). This tradition is reported in a tragic story in which the Maccabees attacked a bridegroom when he came out to the procession that was escorting his new bride to him.

After these things it was reported to Jonathan and his brother Simon, "the family of Jambri are celebrating a great wedding, and are conducting the bride, a daughter of one of the great nobles of Canaan, from Nadabath with a large escort." Remembering how their brother John had been killed, they went up and hid under cover of the mountain. They looked out and saw a tumultuous procession with a great amount of baggage, and the bridegroom came out with his friends and his brothers to meet them with tambourines and musicians and many weapons (*1 Macc.* 9:37-39, NRSV).

Paul uses this tradition as a metaphor of his aim as a father wanting to present the church at Corinth as a pure bride to Christ. The image of the people of God betrothed to God is found in various places in the Jewish tradition beginning in the Old Testament (Isa. 50:1-3; 54:5-6; cf. 62:5; Ezek. 16:8; Hos. 2:19-20) and in the New Testament (Eph. 5:22-33; Rev. 21:2). The notion of a pure bride, that is, a virgin, was also an important responsibility of the father and there were signs of proof that were delivered to the elders of Israel. If the woman was pure, that is, the evidence was convincing, judgment was brought to the person who claimed otherwise. If she was not "pure," she was brought to the city gates and stoned to death (Deut. 22:13-21). The rabbis had laws surrounding the responsibility of the bride to provide proof of her purity. The tractate *Ketuboth* (= "Marriage Deeds") in the *Mishnah* has many laws relating to the woman taken in marriage and these are largely to protect her purity and also the purity of the one who is betrothed to her (see also *m. Yebamoth* 6.1-6). Remarkably, the Law commanded (Deut. 22:22-27), and rabbis taught that any man who violated a woman sexually who was betrothed to another was to be stoned to death. Philo tells how important this purity is and the penalties for violating it, but he also indicates that the one who seeks to preserve the bride as pure is a hero. The one who violates her is worthy of great punishment.

Some consider that midway between the corruption of a maiden and adultery stands the crime committed on the eve of marriage, when mutual agreements have affianced the parties beyond all doubt, but before the marriage was celebrated, another man, either by seduction or violence, has intercourse with the bride. But this too, to my thinking, is a form of adultery. For the agreements, being documents containing the names of the man and woman, and the other particulars needed for wedlock, are equivalent to marriage. And therefore the law ordains that both should be stoned to death, if, that is, they set about their misdeeds by mutual agreement with one and the same purpose. For if they were not actuated by the same purpose, they cannot be regarded as fellow-criminals, where there was no such fellowship. Thus we find that difference of situation makes the criminality greater or less. Naturally it is greater if the act is committed in the city and less if it is committed outside the walls and in a solitude. For here there is no one to help the girl, though she says and does everything possible to keep her virginity intact and invulnerable, while in the town there are council-chambers and law-courts, crowds of controllers of districts, markets and wards, and other persons in authority and with them the common people. For assuredly there is in the soul of every man, however undistinguished he may be, a detestation of evil, and if this emotion is roused, no outside influence is then needed to turn its possessor into a champion ready to do battle for anyone who to all appearances has been wronged. As for the man who perpetrated the violation, justice pursues him everywhere, and difference of situation lends him no help to make good his outrageous and lawless conduct. It is not so with the girl. In the one case pity and forgiveness attend her, as I have said, in the other inexorable punishment (*Special Laws* 3.72-76, LCL; see also 1.107).

This same punishment is also emphasized in the Mishnah: "He that has connexion [sexual relations] with a girl that is betrothed" is not culpable unless she is still in her girlhood, and a virgin, and betrothed, and still in her father's house. If two had connexion with her the first is [liable to death] by stoning, but the second [only] by strangling (*m. Sanh.* 7.9, Danby trans.). According to the author of 2 Enoch (late first cent. A.D.),

> The devil is of the lowest places. And he will become a demon, because he fled from heaven. . . . And he became aware of his condemnation and of the sin which he sinned previously. And that is why he thought up the scheme against Adam. In such a form he entered paradise and corrupted Eve. But Adam he did not contact. But on account of (her) nescience I cursed them (*2 Enoch* 31:3-6, *OT Pseud* 1:154).

For Paul, those who were violating the Corinthian Christians whom he was seeking as a "father" to present to Christ "as a bride" were in great danger of divine judgment (for similar notions of Paul wanting to preserve the holiness and sanctity of his converts, see 1 Cor. 5:6-8; 10:1-13; and 2 Cor. 7:1).

11:3. But I am afraid, lest as the serpent deceived Eve by his craftiness, your minds should be led astray from the simplicity and purity of devotion to Christ. The biblical story of Eve's temptation by the serpent in the Garden (Gen. 3:1-7, 13) is often repeated in biblical and extra-biblical literature. In *1 Enoch*, for instance, the identity of the seducer of Eve is identified as a rebellious angel named Gadreel (*1 Enoch* 69:6). That Paul identified the serpent with Satan, given his reference in 11:14 that has parallels in *Apocalypse of Moses* and the *Life of Adam and Eve* (see discussion below in 11:12-15), seems certain. According to the author of *The Wisdom of Solomon* (ca.100-90 B.C.), God created human beings for incorruption, but "through the devil's envy death entered the world, and those who belong to his company experience it" (*Wisd.* 2:24, NRSV). Paul's assumption of the devil's identity with the snake may be dependent upon this text, but that is not clear. For a similar perspective from one of Paul's contemporaries, Philo equates the serpent as the personification of pleasure and it was with pleasure that Eve was tempted (*Allegorical Interpretation* 3.67-68; cf. 3:59).

In *4 Macc.* (first cent. A.D.), the story is told of a Jewish mother whose seven sons were martyred because they refused to obey King Antiochus Epiphanes' order to worship a pagan god. She proclaimed her faithfulness and purity as a virgin because she was not deceived by the "deceiver" (in this case, the reference is to Antiochus).

The mother of the seven sons also addressed these righteous sayings to her children: "I was a chaste maiden and did not leave my father's house; but I kept guard over the rib built into a woman's body. No seducer of the desert nor deceiver in the field corrupted me, nor did the seducing and beguiling serpent defile my maidenly purity. [She then relates the death of her sons by excruciating tortures and concludes] . . . But the sons of Abraham, together with their mother, who won the victor's prize, are gathered together in the choir of their fathers, having received pure and deathless souls from God, to whom be glory forever and ever. Amen" (*4 Macc.* 18:6-8, 23, *OT Pseud* 2:563-64; see also *Wisd. Sol.* 2:24; *Apoc. Mos* 16; *1 En* 69:9).

11:4. For if one comes and preaches another Jesus whom we have not preached, or you receive a different spirit which you have not received, or a different gospel which you have not accepted, you bear this beautifully. It is not clear who Paul's opponents were, but evidently they were preaching a gospel different from the one he preached, and he saw that the acceptance of theirs would jeopardize the Christians at Corinth. The combination of all of the characteristics noted above in the Introduction suggests that Paul's opponents were Hellenistic Jews who were not insisting on the Corinthians' keeping the Law, but rather were seeking an advantage over the Corinthian Christians and they rejected Paul's ministry. They criticized especially his inability to speak as well as they, and they made much of his failure to take financial assistance from them as apostles were expected to do (1 Cor. 9:1-15). Paul does not attack their theology or doctrine, but rather their conduct in taking advantage of the Corinthian believers and their arrogance, as was typical of the sophists. They proclaimed a humble Christ who was self-sacrificing, but they themselves appeared as arrogant, rude, self-promoting, and oppressive.

In remarkable parallel, Paul's fears of others deceiving the Corinthians and their following the deceivers are similar to those of Demosthenes (384-322 B.C.), the greatest of the Athenian orators, who chides his listeners who are tempted to follow others who are led by their own selfish interests. He writes:

> I could indict Aeschines for ten thousand other items, but let it pass. . . . I could point to many other instances in which this fellow was discovered to be

lending aid and comfort to our enemies and at the same time libeling me. But you have no accurate recollection of these matters, nor do you display appropriate wrath. Instead, through some bad habit of yours, you have bestowed much authority on one who plots to trip up and libel one who seeks your best interests, and thereby you trade off your city's welfare for the pleasure and gratification of being entertained by invective. No wonder that it is always easier and safer to hire oneself out in the service of your enemies than to hold public office and loyally serve the state on your behalf. . . .

> I marvel that you did not immediately turn your backs on him when first you saw him. Or is it that some dense darkness hides the truth from you? (*On the Crown* 138, 159, Danker trans.).

11:5-6. For I consider myself not in the least inferior to the most eminent apostles. But even if I am unskilled in speech, yet I am not so in knowledge; in fact, in every way we have made this evident to you in all things. Paul acknowledges that he is not skilled in the art of communication, but he is skilled in the acquisition of knowledge. He identifies his accusers as "eminent [Greek = *huperlian*, "super" or "exceedingly"] apostles." The term *huperlian* is sometimes translated as "super," as in "super apostles." The use of the term here is clearly used in sarcasm and irony. Paul's acknowledgment of his inferior status in regard to the use of rhetoric or oratory is not unlike Dio Chrysostom's appeal to his hearers to whom he acknowledges up front that he is not skilled as others are in oratory.

Now I am almost sure that you believe me when I speak of my own inexperience and lack of knowledge—evidently on account of your knowledge and sagacity—and it seems to me that you not only believe me on this point, but would have believed Socrates also, when he continually and to all men advanced on his own behalf the same defense—that he knew nothing; but that Hippas and Polus and Gorgias, each of whom was more struck with admiration of himself than of anyone else, you would have considered wise and blessed. But notwithstanding, I declare to you that, great as is your number, you have been eager to hear a man who is neither handsome in appearance nor strong, and in age is already past his prime, one who has no disciple, who professes, I may almost say, no art or special knowledge either of the nobler or of the meaner sort, no ability either as a prophet or a sophist, nay, not even a clever writer, or of interest, but who simply—wears his hair long! "But if you think it a better and wiser course" [cited from Homer, *Odyssey* 1.376] I must do this and try to the best of my ability. However, you will not hear words such as you would hear from any other man of the present day, but words much less pretentious and wearisome, in fact just such as you now observe (*Orations* 12.14-16, LCL).

While Paul agrees that he is not skilled in rhetoric, for which he was severely criticized by his opponents, he defends his understanding of the truth against theirs. Similarly, Dio Chrysostom, when comparing himself to those with such skills, claims, "For they are clever persons, mighty sophists, wonder-workers; but I am quite ordinary and prosaic in my utterance, though not ordinary in my theme. For though the words that I speak are not great in themselves, they treat topics of the greatest possible moment" (*Orations* 32.39, LCL).

Defending oneself through comparison and boasting was accepted in Paul's day if it advanced a greater cause than self-promotion. Plutarch, for instance, speaks of a time when it is important to defend oneself through self-promotion.

> Yet in spite of all this there are times when the statesman might venture on self-glorification, as it is called, not for any personal glory or pleasure, but when the occasion and the matter in hand demand that the truth be told about himself, as it might about another—especially when by permitting himself to mention his good accomplishments and character he is enabled to achieve some similar good. For such praise as this yields a handsome return, as a great harvest of yet nobler raise springs up from it as from a seed (*Moralia, On Inoffensive Self-Praise* 539E, LCL).

Paul's weakness in rhetorical skills does not tell the full story, however. He seems quite aware of the written skills of rhetoricians, but his public oratory skills are what is in question. Josephus reflects the suspicion of the Jewish people for those who have mastered the written and oral rhetorical skills that were so highly prized among the Greeks. As he concludes his lengthy treatise on the history of his people, he acknowledges that he has tried to acquire some skills in the writing of Greek, but admits that he has not attained the best of skills in this area. He explains the reasons for this:

> Our people do not favor those persons who have mastered the speech of many nations, or who adorn their style with smoothness of diction, because they consider that not only is such skill common to ordinary freemen but that even slaves who so choose may acquire it. But they give credit for wisdom to those alone who have an exact knowledge of the law and who are capable of interpreting the meaning of the Holy Scriptures. Consequently, though many have laboriously undertaken this training, scarcely two or three have succeeded (*Ant.* 20.264-265, LCL).

See also his defense of using carefully chosen words in writing history, but not to the extent of obscuring the aim or purpose of the writing (*Ant.*

14.1). He elsewhere acknowledges the superior ability of the Greeks in rhetoric, but denies its importance for historical inquiry. "While, then, for eloquence and literary ability we must yield the palm to the Greek historians, we have no reason to do so for veracity in the history of antiquity, least of all where the particular history of each separate foreign nation is concerned" (*Against Apion* 1.27, LCL).

11:7-9. Or did I commit a sin in humbling myself that you might be exalted, because I preached the gospel of God to you without charge? I robbed other churches, taking wages from them to serve you; and when I was present with you and was in need, I was not a burden to anyone; for when the brethren came from Macedonia, they fully supplied my need, and in everything I kept myself from being a burden to you, and will continue to do so. Paul objects to criticism of him because he did not assume the rights of an apostle, namely to be supported by those he ministered to (1 Cor. 9:1-15), but chose instead not to be a financial burden as he preached the Gospel to them. He allowed the church from Philippi to supply his needs after he left there and with the purpose of advancing the mission of Christ (Phil. 4:15-18). This may be in keeping with a widespread missionary rule, namely giving the Gospel without charge to its hearers (see Matt. 10:8; Acts 8:20; Rev. 21:6; 22:17; cf. Isa. 55:1). Also, in the *Didache* (written ca. A.D. 90), those traveling prophets and teachers who ask for money for themselves or stay longer than a few days are called false prophets (*Did.* 11:3-6, 8b-9, 12). In receiving a vision about what is "earthly, and empty, and has no power" the Shepherd of Hermas writes:

In the first place, that man who seems to have a spirit exalts himself and wishes to have the first place, and he is instantly impudent and shameless and

talkative, and lives in great luxury and in many other deceits, and accepts rewards for his prophecy, and if he does not receive them, he does not prophesy (*Shep. Mand.* 11.12, LCL).

According to Xenophon (ca. 430-354 B.C.), Socrates refused to accept financial aid from those he taught. He justified his actions as follows:

You seem, Antiphon, to imagine that happiness consists in luxury and extravagance. But my belief is that to have no wants is divine; to have as few as possible comes next to the divine; and as that which is divine is supreme, so that which approaches nearest to its nature is nearest to the supreme. (*Memorabilia* 1.6.10, LCL)

But Antiphon pushed the matter further and, while agreeing that because of this policy he thought that Socrates was a just man, nevertheless, he believed that he was unwise because of it. "It may well be that you are a just man because you do not cheat people through avarice; but wise you cannot be, since your knowledge is not worth anything" (1.6.12, LCL).

This may well be something like the kind of criticism that Paul was receiving when he took no money from his listeners in Corinth. Socrates' response to Antiphon is worth noting and perhaps something like it lies behind Paul's motivation for preaching: namely, love. Socrates replied:

. . . it is common opinion among us in regard to beauty and wisdom that there is an hounorable and shameful way of bestowing them. For to offer one's beauty for money to all comers is called prostitution; but we think it virtuous to become friendly with a love who is known to be a man of honour. So it is with wisdom. Those who offer it to all comers for money are known as sophists, prostitutors of wisdom, but we think that he who makes a friend of one whom he knows to be gifted by nature, and teaches him all the good he can, fulfills the duty of a citizen and a gentleman. That is my own view, Antiphon. Others have a fancy for a good horse or dog or bird: my fancy, stronger even than theirs, is for good friends (*Memorabilia* 1.6.13-14, LCL).

The opponents of Paul objected to his lowering himself, in their eyes, to do manual labor while he was preaching the Gospel. This was his usual pattern so that the Gospel would be heard at no cost to the listeners (see Acts 18:1-3; 1 Cor. 4:12; 9:3-18; 2 Cor. 12:15; 1 Thess. 2:9). They compared him to professional orators and found him inadequate. When they also saw that professional orators did not do manual labor, Paul was also found lacking. While it was important for the Jewish rabbi to have a manual labor profession, not all Jews saw the value in that for those who would teach. While acknowledging the value of workers and artisans for the good of society and the health of a community, nevertheless, Sirach concludes that their labor could interfere with the higher calling of being a scribe or one who pursues wisdom:

The wisdom of the scribe depends on the opportunity of leisure; only the one who has little business can become wise. How can one become wise who handles the plow and who glories in the shaft of a goad, who drives oxen and is occupied with their work and whose talk is about bulls? He sets his heart on plowing furrows, and he is careful about fodder for the heifers. So too is every artisan and master artisan who labors by night as well as by day.... Without them no city can be inhabited, and wherever they live they will not go hungry. Yet they are not sought out for the council of the people, nor do they attain eminence in the public assembly. They do not sit in the judge's seat, nor do they understand the decisions of the courts; they cannot expound discipline or judgment, and they are not found among the rulers.

But they maintain the fabric of the world, and their concern is for the exercise of their trade. How different the one who devotes himself to the study of the law of the Most High! (*Sir.* 38:24-27, 32-34, NRSV; cf. also 39:1-11 the author goes on to extol the virtues of those who seek after wisdom.)

Lucian of Samosata (ca. A.D. 120-190) agrees in substance with the words of Sirach and contrasts those who pursue "sublime words" and a "dignified appearance" with those who work with their hands. This, he claims came to him in the form of a vision.

On the other hand, if you turn your back upon these men [Demosthenes, Aeschines, and Socrates] so great and noble, upon glorious deeds and sublime works, upon a dignified appearance, upon honour, esteem, praise, precedence, power and offices, upon fame for eloquence and felicitations for wit, then you will put on a filthy tunic, assume a servile appearance, and hold bars and gravers and sledges and chisels in your hands, with your back bent over your work; you will be groundling, with groundling ambitions, altogether humble; you will never lift your head, or conceive a single manly or liberal thought, and although you will plan to make your works well-balanced and well-shapen, you will not show any concern to make yourself well-balanced and sightly; on the contrary, you will make yourself a thing of less value than a block of stone (*The Dream*, or *Lucian's Career* 13, LCL).

On the other hand, Paul appears to have followed a more common Jewish perspective on the value of working with one's hands. In the *Mishnah*, a Rabban Gamaliel, son of Rabbi Judah the Patriarch, says:

Excellent is study of the Law together with worldly occupation, for toil in them both puts sin out of mind. But all study of the Law without labour comes to naught at the last and brings sin in its train. And let all them that labour with the congregation labour with them for the sake of Heaven, for the merit of their fathers supports them and their righteousness endures for ever (*m. Aboth* 2.2, Danby trans.).

Paul insists that he did not want to burden the Corinthians with financial obligations (11:9; 12:14b), and he also sees value in working with one's hands (1 Thess. 4:10b-12; cf. 2 Thess. 3:6-10). Similar attitudes were found among the Greeks, and those philosophers who also worked with their hands were praised. The practical Stoic philosopher Epictetus (ca. A.D. 54-120) admonished all in his guild to combine their scholarly activity with practical work. Showing his disdain for those who refused to work with their hands he concludes that they

> . . . have only to learn the life of healthy men—how the slaves live, the workmen, the genuine philosophers, how Socrates lived—he too with a wife and children—how Diogenes lived, how Cleanthes, who combined going to school and pumping water. If this is what you want, you will have it everywhere, and will live with full confidence (*Discourses* 3.26.23-24, LCL).

He goes on to ask why those in his guild have made themselves so useless that no one would take them in (*Discourses* 3.26.23-24, 26, LCL). Nevertheless, Paul's opponents appear to be of the view portrayed in the Sirach quote above rather than the more popular tradition that emerged in rabbinic Judaism of a later period. There was considerable debate over how the philosopher ought to make a living in the ancient world. In the third century A.D., Diogenes Laertius wrote a compendium on the lives and teachings of philosophers. Concerning a certain Chrysippus, who wrote a volume called *On the Means of Livelihood*, he speaks about how the philosopher should earn a living. Diogenes Laertius quotes him saying:

> and yet what reason is there that he [the philosopher] should provide a living? For if it be to support life, life itself is after all a thing indifferent. If it be for pleasure, pleasure too is a thing indifferent. While if it be for virtue, virtue in itself is sufficient to constitute happiness. The modes of getting a livelihood are also ludicrous, as e.g., maintenance by a king; for he will have to be humored: or by friends; for friendship will then be purchasable for money; or living by wisdom; for so wisdom will become mercenary (Diogenes Laertius, *Lives of Eminent Philosophers* 7.189, LCL).

Lucian cautions those who receive pay from a wealthy patron for their services about losing their independence (*On Salaried Posts* 19-20) and likewise Musonius makes a similar plea (*Frg.* 11). Dio Chrysostom, on the other hand, while speaking about the value of work, also addresses the value of working with one's hands. He concludes that:

> poverty is no hopeless impediment to a life and existence befitting free men who are willing to work with their hands, but leads them on to deeds and actions that are far better and more useful and more in accordance with nature than those to which riches are wont to attract most men (*Orations* 7.103, LCL; see also Musonius Rufus, *What means of Livelihood is Appropriate for a Philosopher? Frg.* 11).

Paul also knew the obligations of benefaction and what the receipt of such gifts might demand of him. Perhaps knowing the context of his hearers well, he chose to preach the Gospel without charge and without inferred obligations to those who gave gifts to him. This does not, of course, imply that he never took gifts from Christians elsewhere to help him pursue his mission (Phil. 4:15).

11:10-11. As the truth of Christ is in me, this boasting of mine will not be stopped in the regions of Achaia. Why? Because I do not love you? God knows I do! Paul's love and passion for the Corinthian Christians is obvious throughout his correspondence with them and none more telling than here. He is so concerned for their welfare and angered at those who try to disturb them that he openly engages in both "foolish speech" and declarations of his love for them. Demosthenes criticized Aeschines because in his delivery of his message he showed no passion or compassion for his listeners.

> I marveled most of all when in the course of speaking about the misfortunes that had befallen the city (of Athens) he did not have the attitude that any upright citizen of goodwill would have manifested: he did not shed a tear; he did not show so much as a flicker of emotion (*On the Crown* 291, Danker trans. 171).

Paul refused aid from the Corinthians because he loved them and also because he saw himself as responsible for them as their father in the faith (see 11:2; 12:14-15).

11:13-15. For such men are false apostles, deceitful workers, disguising themselves as apostles of Christ. And no wonder, for even Satan disguises himself as an angel of light. Therefore it is not surprising if his servants also disguise themselves as servants of righteousness; whose end shall be according to their deeds. Paul's polemical charges against his opponents are similar to those in other Jewish literature when writers believed that their opponents were involved in evil deeds. Paul calls them "false apostles" and may have been the first to use the term, but it has parallels with what Jesus said about those who call on his name whom he never knew (Matt. 7:21-23), and this comes after his reference to "false prophets" who come to those who follow him (7:15-16; cf. 24:11; Mark 13:22; 2 Peter 2:1; 1 John 4:1; Rev. 19:20; 20:10).

An angel of light. Angels sometimes made their appearances in the form of light or radiance (Luke 2:9; 24:4), and in order for Satan to deceive, he too must appear in similar manner. There is a characterization in the ancient world in both Greek and Latin that depicts Satan both as an angel and as an angel of light. The *Life of Adam and Eve* and the Greek text called the *Apocalypse of Moses* (first cent. A.D.), perhaps written by a Jew from Alexandria, both tell the story of the Garden of Eden from Eve's perspective.

> Then Satan was angry and transformed himself into the brightness of angels and went away to the Tigris River to Eve and found her weeping . . . [and he said to the woman:] "The Lord has heard your sighs and accepted your repentance; and all we angels have entreated for you and interceded with the Lord, and he sent me to bring you up from the water and give you food which you had in Paradise, and for which you have been lamenting" (*Adam and Eve* 9.1, OT Pseud 2:260).

And the story continues:

> "And immediately he [Satan] suspended himself from the walls of Paradise about the time when the angels of God went up to worship. Then Satan came in the form of an angel and sang hymns to God as the angels. And I saw him bending over the wall, like an angel" (*Adam and Eve* 17.1-2, OT Pseud 2.277-279).

Whether Paul knew these documents is uncertain, but the tradition that lies behind them is also assumed by Paul.

It is not surprising if his servants also disguise themselves. The comparison of Satan's activities to those of the ones who follow him is often called a *qal wahomer* ("light and heavy"), that is, proceeding in an argument from the lesser to the greater. If deception was true of Satan, it should not be surprising if his followers are the same. The word "disguise" (Greek = *metaschematizomai*) is the operative word for three things in this passage: namely "false apostles" disguising themselves as apostles of

Christ (v. 13), Satan appearing as an angel of light (v. 14), and servants (of Satan) disguised as servants of righteousness. Paul's accusation that his opponents in Corinth are from Satan has some precedence in Jesus' comments to Peter "Get behind me Satan!" (Mark 833; cf. Matt. 16:23).

In this passage Paul is trying to get his readers to have the same views of his opponents as he does and therefore speaks with strong invective to turn his converts from the "false apostles" who have insulted Paul because of his appearance, his inability to speak with trained rhetorical skills, and his unwillingness to take money from them as he has from others. Paul attacks these opponents because of the intense affection he has for the Corinthians (vv. 10-12), but also because of the things they have done in trying to take away his converts and their loyalty to him. After parading his own accomplishments before his hearers in Athens, Demosthenes severely criticized Aeschines by exposing his poor accomplishments on behalf of the city. In cadencelike fashion, as with Paul later in this passage, he writes:

> Caught in the mire, parasites who merit swift destruction, mutilators of their own homelands, men who have squandered our liberty in a toast to Philip and now to Alexander, men who measure happiness by their bellies and by all that is most shameful as they dismantle liberty and the right of Hellenes to control their own destinies—rights that our ancestors knew to be the definitions and standards of all that is most highly prized (*On the Crown* 296, Danker, trans. See also 259-260 and 314-23).

11:16-12:10. Paul's "Foolish" Boastings and Comparisons. While 11:1-15 initiates Paul's boasting and invective against his opponents, here he starts his "foolish boasting" and it continues through 11:29. There are two parts to this "foolishness" and the first begins with vv. 16-20

in which Paul implores his readers to be patient with him as he goes through this act of "madness" and compares himself to others. In 21-22, he shows that he has the same qualifications according to human standards as his opponents, but in 23-29, he points to things that are not true of his enemies but that show that he is superior to them. In the second part Lambrecht has observed that there are some five uneven strophes for boasting in this construction (16-29) and it is useful to list them here.

(1) 23b more often in hard labor
> more often in prison
> countless floggings
> many times in danger of death

(2) 24 Five times I received forty lashes less one
> 25 three times beaten with rods
> once stoned
> three times shipwrecked

(3) 26 Often involved in traveling
> in danger from rivers
> in danger from robbers
> in danger from fellow-countrymen
> in danger from Gentiles
> in danger in the city
> in danger in the wilderness
> in danger at sea
> in danger from false brethren

(4) 27 in hard labor and toil, often without sleep in hunger and thirst, often without foodin cold and nakedness

(5) 28 Apart from other things, daily pressure and concern for churches

> Who is weak, and I am not weak?
> Who is made to fall,
> and I do not have indignation?

The final phase of this boasting is in two parts: Boasting of revelations or visions (12:1-6) and boasting of his weaknesses (12:7-10).

11:16-19. Again I say, let no one think me foolish; but if you do, receive me even as foolish,

that I also may boast a little. That which I am speaking, I am not speaking as the Lord would, but as in foolishness, in this confidence of boasting. Since many boast according to the flesh, I will boast also. For you, being so wise, bear with the foolish gladly. Paul has just condemned his critics for their boasting (10:12-18) and now moves into the awkward position of doing precisely what he has criticized. Like he did in 1 Cor. 7:10, 12, Paul acknowledges here (v. 17) that what he is saying is not from the Lord, but from himself and it is not something that he is pleased to say. Like many of his contemporaries, Paul believed that self-praise was wrong and inappropriate. He knew how common it was among the sophists and for that reason would have found it objectionable to be lumped into the same camp with them, so he treads carefully albeit passionately in this dangerous arena. Plutarch believed that most self-praise was offensive. He concludes that

> . . . we cannot be too cautious, not allowing ourselves to be drawn out by the praise nor to be led on by the questions. The surest precaution and safeguard is to attend closely to the self-praise of others and to remember the distaste and vexation that was felt by all: no other kind of talk is so odious or offensive. For although we can point to no further harm than the mere hearing of the self-praise, yet as though instinctively irked by the performance and uncomfortable we are eager to escape and breathe freely again. Whey even a flatterer, a hanger-on, a man in need, finds it hard in his necessity to stomach and endure a rich man or satrap or king bestowing praises on himself, and calls it the most exorbitant reckoning he ever paid . . . . These are the feelings and language to which we are prompted not only by soldiers and the newly rich with their flaunting and

ostentatious talk, but also by sophists, philosophers, and commanders who are full of their own importance and hold forth on the theme; and if we remember that praise of oneself always involves dispraise from others, that his vainglory has an inglorious end . . . we shall avoid talking about ourselves unless we have in prospect some great advantage to our hearers or to ourselves (*Moralia, On Inoffensive Self-Praise*, 547D-E, LCL).

He does, however, acknowledge that there were occasions when it might be appropriate to boast. "Yet in spite of all this [criticisms against self-praise] there are times when the statesman might venture on self-glorification, as it is called, not for any personal glory or pleasure, but when the occasion and the matter in hand demand that the truth be told about himself . . . " (*On Inoffensive Self-Praise* 539E, LCL). He goes on to say that one should not engage in self-praise to advance one's self nor to destroy others' value, but rather only to "refute their [one's enemies or opponents] claim and show their reputation to be groundless" (540C, LCL).

11:20. For you bear with anyone if he enslaves you, if he devours you, if he takes advantage of you, if he exalts himself, if he hits you in the face. The reference to hitting or slapping, one in the face, has to do with insults: namely, Paul accuses his opponents of insulting the Corinthian Christians. Dio Chrysostom tells of philosophers who were shouting and verbally tearing apart one another at the Poseidon Temple near the location of the Isthmian games and some six miles from Corinth. He speaks of a time "when one could hear crowds of wretched sophists around Poseidon's temple shouting and reviling one another, and their disciples, as they were called, fighting with one another, many writers reading aloud their stupid works, many poets reciting their poems while others applauded them . . . " (*Orations* 8.9, LCL).

11:21-22. To my shame I must say that we have been weak by comparison. But in whatever respect anyone else is bold (I speak in foolishness), I am just as bold myself. Are they Hebrews? So am I. Are they Israelites? So am I. Are they descendants of Abraham? So am I. The "foolish" message properly begins here since Paul now has begun a comparison of himself with his enemies. He claims that he is just as bold as his enemies and that his Jewish pedigree is just as compelling as theirs. His pedigree may have been a factor in their criticisms of Paul, namely that he came from Tarsus rather than Jerusalem. Paul does not, however, take a backseat to their claims and defends that he is as Jewish as they are. His sarcasm that is couched in self-deprecation has parallels in the ancient world. Demosthenes attacks Aeschines as a traitor and then says, "I confess it. I am weak, but all the more loyal than you [Aeschines] to my fellow citizens" (*On the Crown* 320, Danker trans.). In similar language, Dio Chrysostom, while criticizing the sophists, offers self-deprecating comments and says:

> For I do not take disciples, since I know there is nothing I should be able to teach them, seeing that I know nothing myself; but to lie and deceive by my promises, I have not the courage for that. But if I associated myself with a professional sophist, I should help him greatly by gathering a great crowd to him and then allowing him to dispose of the catch as he wished. However, for some reason or other, not one of the sophists is willing to take me on, nor can they bear the sight of me (*Orations* 12.13, LCL).

11:23. Are they servants of Christ? (I speak as if insane) I more so; in far more labors, in far more imprisonments, beaten times without number, often in danger of death. In the introduction to this section above at 11:16, see the five strophes identified. Paul begins a litany of abuses he has suffered because of his mission. See also the discussion of hardship catalogues in 6:3-13 above. Paul's imprisonments were invariably harsh during which time he was kept in unclean and often lice-infested places having chains around his wrists and feet. It was also common for prisoners to receive beatings as well as insults. For a listing of some of these imprisonments, see Eph. 6:20; Phil. 1:7, 3-17; Col. 4:3, 18; 2 Tim. 2:9; Phile. 10, 13.

11:24. Five times I received from the Jews thirty-nine lashes. The maximum number of lashes that a person could receive was forty because more than that was believed to cause death. Often one less than that suggested that the recipient could be brought to the brink of death in a public beating that was also intended to humiliate the person beaten. Seldom could one bear the pain of one such a beating and Paul lists five! According to the Mishnah, a scourging was carried out as follows:

> They bind his two hands to a pillar on either side, and the minister of the synagogue lays hold of his garments—if they are torn they are torn, if they are utterly rent they are utterly rent—so that he bares his chest. A stone is set down behind him on which the minister of the synagogue stands with a strap of calf-hide in his hand doubled and re-doubled, and two [other] straps that rise and fall [are fastened] thereto. The handpiece of the strap is one hand-breadth long and one handbreadth wide; and its end must reach to his navel. He gives him one-third of the stripes in front and two-thirds behind; and he may not strike him when he is standing or when he is sitting, but only when he is bending low, for it is written, "The judge shall cause him to lie down." And he that smites, smites with his one hand with all his might. . . . If he dies under his hand, the scourger is not

culpable. But if he gave him one strip too many and he died, he must escape into exile because of him (*m. Makkoth* ["Stripes"] 3.12-14, Danby trans.).

See Acts 16:22-23, 37-39 for a description of one of these beatings and 18:17 for the story of Sosthenes' beating in public.

11:25. Three times I was beaten with rods, once I was stoned, three times I was shipwrecked, a night and a day I have spent in the deep. The practice of stoning was primarily a Jewish form of punishment (Deut. 13:6-11; Josh. 7:25; *Jub.* 30:7-9; John 8:53-7; 10:31-33; Acts 7:58; 14:19), though occasionally the Romans used it. Sometimes it was the result of mob violence rather than Jewish or Roman civic punishment. While telling of the terrible punishment given to the Jews by Flaccus, the Roman prefect who ruled Alexandria in the first century A.D., Philo tells how Flaccus allowed mobs to hurt and kill the Jews who were:

> laid low and destroyed with manifold forms of maltreatment, put in practice to serve their bitter cruelty by those whom savagery had maddened and transformed into the nature of wild beasts; for any Jews who showed themselves anywhere, they stoned or knocked about with clubs aiming their blows at first against the less vital parts for fear that a speedier death might give a speedier release from the consciousness of their anguish (*Flaccus* 66, LCL).

Paul's catalogue of boastful things that he has gone through, that his opponents cannot match, is similar to other catalogues in antiquity. Caesar Augustus (Octavian) catalogues the achievements of his reign and repeatedly draws attention to the number of his accomplishments:

> Twice have I the lesser triumph . . . . three times the [full] curule triumph;

twenty-one times have I been saluted as "Imperator." . . . Fifty-five times has the Senate decreed a thanksgiving unto the Immortal Gods . . . .nine kings, or children of kings, have been led before my chariot in my triumphs . . . thirteen times had I been consul (*Acts of Augustus* 1.4, M. Hubbard trans. 3:250).

The hardships endured at sea in the ancient world when the boats were essentially at the mercy of the winds were well-known. Seneca (4 B.C. – A.D. 69) tells of the often horrifying voyages at sea and the accompanying ailment of seasickness (*On the Faults of the Spirit*, Ep. 53.1-6). Dio Chrysostom likewise tells of such stories in which those on a ship barely survived or were drowned. He shares one such story of his own experience in which he was crossing by boat from Chios to Euboea and was caught in a storm and had great difficulty getting to shore so the crew eventually crashed the boat on a rough beach (*Orations* 7.2-3). The book of Acts has the story of Paul's harrowing trip to Rome as a prisoner when he endured great danger at sea along with a frightening shipwreck (Acts 27:13-44). Boats in the time of Paul were controlled not by a rudder, but by oars and normally one large sail. Tacking into the wind was not known in those days and so those in the vessels on the sea often faced dangerous situations. Not infrequently those who returned safely to land dedicated objects to the gods who allowed their safe return.

11:26. I have been on frequent journeys, in dangers from rivers, dangers from robbers, dangers from my countrymen, dangers from the Gentiles, dangers in the city, dangers in the wilderness, dangers on the sea, dangers among false brethren. This summary of travels reveals the many dangers that those who traveled in the ancient world often faced. As a result, it was rare that persons made such trips alone. After describing his fear from a dangerous trip overland because of the roughness of the sea, Seneca says to his friend, "For there are certain emotions, my dear Lucillius, which no courage can avoid; nature reminds courage how perishable a thing it is" (*Ep.* 53.4, *On the Trials of Travel*, LCL). Besides the natural elements that one had to endure, there were also the unclean circumstances in which one might have to stay at an inn, where bedbugs were commonplace, and also the dangers of bandits who would lie in wait for unsuspecting travelers (see, for example, Luke 10:30-35). Epictetus tells of the precautions ancient travelers took when they were about to make a journey through dangerous areas.

This is the way also with the more cautious among travelers. A man has heard that the road which he is taking is infested with robbers; he does not venture to set forth alone, but he waits for a company, either that of an ambassador, or of a quaestor, or a proconsul, and when he has attached himself to them he travels along the road in safety. So in this world the wise man acts. Says he to himself, "There are many robber-bands, tyrants, storms, difficulties, losses of what is most dear. Where shall a man flee for refuge? How shall he travel secure against robbery? . . ." (*Discourses* 4.1.91-93, LCL).

11:27. I have been in labor and hardship, through many sleepless nights, in hunger and thirst, often without food, in cold and exposure. As an artisan seeking to earn his keep, there would no doubt be difficult times when work was scarce, especially for a stranger in a community. Working "night and day" so as not to be a burden to those he ministered to (1 Thess. 2:9; 2 Thess. 3:7-10) caused Paul much inconvenience and hardship.

11:28. Apart from such external things, there is the daily pressure upon me of concern for all the churches. One is reminded here of Cicero's endurance of pain and suffering for the sake of others.

For unless I had been persuaded from my earliest youth by the precepts of many, and by many writings, that there was nothing in life of such importance as the glory of an honourable life, but that in the pursuit thereof, one must experience excruciating bodily pains and constant peril of death and exile, I would never have exposed myself in the interest of your safety to such tremendous risks as are involved in the daily attacks of these wicked men (Cicero, *In Behalf of Archia* 6.14, Danker trans. 184).

In like manner, Seneca speaks of the rights of Caesar, but also how he loses those rights in order to care for those he is responsible for.

Caesar can have anything he wishes, but for this very reason many things are denied to him. His wakefulness provides sound sleep for all others; his toil releases all others from their burdens; his labor brings enjoyment to all others; his industry spells time off for all others (*Consolation of Polybius* 7:2, Danker trans. 185).

Dio Chrysostom reminds his readers that a noble man or a pure sophist is one who is not of afraid of his opponents,

. . . challenges them one after another, grappling with hunger and cold, withstanding thirst, and disclosing no weakness even though he must endure the lash or give his body to be cut or burned. Hunger, exile, loss of reputation, and the like have no terrors for him; nay, he holds them as mere trifles, often as sportive as boys with their dice and their coloured balls (*Orations* 8.16, LCL).

11:30-33. If I have to boast, I will boast of what pertains to my weakness. The God and Father of the Lord Jesus, He who is blessed forever, knows that I am not lying. In Damascus the ethnarch under Aretas the king was guarding the city of the Damascenes in order to seize me, and I was let down in a basket through a window in the wall, and so escaped his hands. It is likely that Paul's opponents criticized the way that he had escaped from Damascus (cowardly?) and so he addresses the issue here (see Luke's account of the escape in Acts 9:23-25). The escape, however, was not unlike the way that the spies escaped from Jericho with the help of Rahab (Josh. 2:15-16) or, with the help of his wife Michal, David escaped through a window (1 Sam. 19:11-12). There is also a story in Plutarch's *Aemilius Paulus* (26.269a) that tells how Perseus of Macedonia escaped with his family through a small window and over the city walls. Whatever the cause for sharing this story, it was among the many dangerous activities Paul endured to carry out his mission of proclaiming the Gospel.

Aretas, the Nabatean King Aretas IV, ruled from Petra from 9 B.C. until A.D. 39-40. Herod Antipas married Aretas' daughter but subsequently divorced her to marry Herodias, the wife of Herod Philip and mother of Salome (Mark 6:17-20). John the Baptist was arrested and executed (ca. A.D. 35) because of his rebuke of Herod Antipas over this marriage (Luke 3:19-20; cf. also Josephus, *Ant.* 18.109-126). Because of Herod Antipas' treatment of his daughter, Aretas waged war against Herod Antipas and severely defeated his army. As a result, Antipas appealed to Rome to wage war against Aretas, but before Vitellius could bring war against him, the emperor Tiberias died (A.D. 36) and Vitellius abandoned the military campaign. Aretas probably governed the city through an *Ethnarch* (Greek = "leader" or "ruler of a people"). The title, Ethnarch, while clear in translation, is only found here in the New Testament and its meaning is vague. It is likely that it refers to a ruler of a group of people in a geographical location who was under the overall rule of a foreign power, as in the case of Herod the Great ruling all of the land of Israel, but serving under the authority of Rome. In this case, Aretas was the foreign power and an ethnarch was responsible to him. Aretas' name helps to fix the time of Paul's residence and ministry in Damascus before A.D. 40.

12:1. Boasting is necessary, though it is not profitable; but I will go on to visions and revelations of the Lord. Once again, Paul hedges his comments with a rhetorical device known as *epidiorthosis*, that is, he makes a precautionary statement that prepares his readers for what he assumes will likely be difficult for them to hear. Examples of this are in 3:5; 7:8; 11:21, 30; 12:11, 16; 1 Cor. 7:10; 15:10; Gal. 1:6; 2:20. Demosthenes also makes frequent use of the *epidiorthosis* when he brings criticism against an opponent that he does not want to criticize, but the circumstances demand it: "Inasmuch as the proper and just vote has been pointed out to all, probably I must, despite the fact that I am not fond of invective, speak about him (Aeschines) because of the reviling statements made by him" (*On the Crown* 126, Danker trans.).

12:2. I know a man in Christ who fourteen years ago—whether in the body I do not know, or out of the body I do not know, God knows—such a man was caught up to the third heaven. Philo, like Paul, can speak of visionary or revelatory experiences in which his circumstances were dominated by God. He writes of frequent ("a thousand times") revelatory kinds of experiences that also enabled him to write in a remarkable manner and to experience a "frenzy" in his experience with the divine.

> I feel no shame in recording my own experience, a thing I know from its having happened to me a thousand times. On some occasions, after making up my mind to follow the usual course of writing on philosophical tenents, and knowing definitely the substance of what I was to set down, I have found my understanding incapable of giving birth to a single idea, and have given it up without accomplishing anything, reviling my understanding for its self-conceit, and filled with amazement at the might of Him that IS to Whom is due

the opening and closing of the soul-wombs. On other occasions, I have approached my work empty and suddenly become full, the ideas falling in a shower from above and being sown invisibly, so that under the influence of the Divine possession I have been filled with corybantic frenzy [a Corybant = a priest of Cybele whose worship involved wild dancing and ecstatic experiences] and been unconscious of anything, place, persons, present, myself, words spoken, lines written. For I obtained language, ideas, an enjoyment of light, keenest vision, pellucid distinctiveness of objects, such as might be received through the eyes as the result of clearest showing (*On the Migration of Abraham* 34-35, LCL).

Paul's introduction of a story (vv. 2-6) that involves himself with a third person, "I know a man," is similar to the way that ancient philosophers told stories to illustrate the consequences of inappropriate actions. Epictetus introduces a story in the same manner as did Paul to tell how philosophers ought to act in given circumstances.

If we philosophers had applied ourselves to our own work as zealously as the old men at Rome have applied themselves to the matters on which they have set their hearts, perhaps we too should be accomplishing something. *I know a man* older than myself. . . .

What then? Do I say that man is an animal made for inactivity? . . . For example, to take myself first. . . . (*Discourses* 1.10.1-2, 7-8, LCL. Italics added).

Demosthenes tells why this is a suitable manner of discourse. The reason for using the third person in such a manner, he argues, "I may speak in what will be accepted as the most inoffensive manner" (*On the Crown* 321, Danker trans.188). Likewise, Plutarch explains why it is wise to shift some of the story to another when he contends that

. . . those who are forced to speak in their own praise are made more endurable by another procedure as well: not to lay claim to everything, but to disburden themselves, as it were, of honour, letting part of it rest with chance, and part with God. For this reason Achilles did well to say "since I by Heaven's will have slain this man" (*Moralia, On inoffensive Self-Praise* 542E, LCL).

Third heaven. Being "caught up to the third heaven" was a way of speaking of one's glorification. The reference to the third heaven appears to depend on a first-century document or tradition preceding that document, called the *Apocalypse of Moses*. Speaking of the death of Adam and God's care for him, the writer says,

He [Adam] lay three hours, and so the Lord of all, sitting on his holy throne, stretched out his hands and took Adam and handed him over to the archangel Michael, saying to him, "Take him up into Paradise, to the third heaven, and leave (him) there until that great and fearful day which I am about to establish for the world" (*Apoc. Mos.* 37:5, *OT Pseud* 2:291).

The Romans believed that some individuals had merited by their conduct a divine status that also placed them among the gods and they therefore became imperishable. Romulus, Alexander the Great, Julius Caesar, Caesar Augustus, the philosopher Empedocles, and the physician Aesclepius were all given this status and believed to have become elevated to immortal status at their death. They were watched by "credible eye-witnesses" as they ascended to the heavens (see discussion of this in Acts 1:9-11).

Whether Paul is speaking as a satirist, with tongue in cheek, or actually telling what happened to him, is a matter of debate among scholars, but his reference to the "third heaven" does refer to his going to the ultimate place in heaven. There are many ancient stories about various levels in heaven, for example, whether there were one, three, five, seven, or even 955 levels of heaven. In each of these numbers, the highest was the place reserved for God alone. According to *1 Enoch*, there is one heaven, but according to the *Testament of Levi* 3:1, there are three, so also in *Apocalypse of Moses* 37. *3 Baruch* 11:1-2 mentions five heavens and *2 Enoch* 20:1, *3 Enoch* 17:1, the *Apocalypse of Abraham* 19:5-6, and the *Ascension of Isaiah* 9:6 speak of seven heavens. Remarkably *3 Enoch* 48:1 speaks of 955 heavens! Paul is evidently familiar with the tradition that speaks of three levels of heaven and he tells of his experience of being transferred (translated?) into that place of paradise where God abides.

12:3-4. And I know how such a man—whether in the body or apart from the body I do not know, God knows—was caught up into Paradise, and heard inexpressible words, which a man is not permitted to speak. Paul is not precise in his description, but adds that "God knows" to express the validity of his experience, but also his inability to describe it. Most apocalyptic language of antiquity speaks in coded language so as not to reveal the divine mysteries. This was characteristically true to the mystery religions as well. Those who experience the ultimate divine experience are unable to share it. Lucian (ca. A.D. 160-161) tells the satirical story of a man named Menippus who both ascended into heaven to discover the truth about nature and into Hades (Hell) to discover the truth about the right way to live. As Menippus responds to his friends' questions about how to live, Menippus hesitates to share the divine mystery that he has discovered, but eventually gives in and says that the rich and powerful, including philosophers (!), do not fare well in the life to come! After saying how difficult it will be for the rich, the friend asks, "has any radical legislation been passed in the lower world affecting the upper?" and

Menippus responds: "Yes, by Zeus, a great deal; but it is not right to publish it broadcast and expose their secrets. Someone might indict me for impiety in the court of Rhadamanthus" [in mythology, this Rhadamanthus is the son of Zeus. He did not die but went to heaven where the most blessed mortals live in bliss.] (*Menippus, or Descent into Hades* 2, LCL). Such fear of sharing the details of the divine mysteries was common in the ancient world. In the Mishnah there is a similar warning about sharing the divine things with others.

> The forbidden degrees may not be expounded before three persons, nor the Story of Creation before two, nor the chapter of the Chariot before one alone, unless he is a sage that understands of his own knowledge. Whoever gives his mind to four things it were better for him had he not come into the world—what is above? what is beneath? what was before time? and what will be hereafter? And whoever takes no thought for the honor of his Maker, it were better for him if he had not come into the world (*m. Hagigah* 2.1, Danby trans.).

Paradise is a reference to heaven and is found in only three places in the Bible, including here, Luke 23:43 and Rev. 27 (cf. Gen. 2:9). The word is also used in *2 Esdras* to speak of the heavenly dwelling of God which is also for those who have found favor with God. The author of *2 Esdras* asks what value there is of a paradise for God's faithful if the faithful have lived wickedly. "Or that a paradise shall be revealed, whose fruit remains unspoiled and in which are abundance and healing, but we shall not enter it because we have lived in perverse ways?"(*2 Esdras* 7:52-54/122-124, NRSV). Later, picking up on the image of the Garden of Eden being a paradise of God, he assures his readers of hope for entering paradise:

> You will receive the greatest glory, for many miseries will affect those who inhabit the world in the last times, because they have walked in great pride. But think of your own case, and

inquire concerning the glory of those who are like yourself, because it is for you that paradise is opened, the tree of life is planted, the age to come is prepared, plenty is provided, a city is built, rest is appointed, goodness is established and wisdom perfected before hand (2 *Esdras* 8:49-52, NRSV. See also 4:7; 6:2; 7:36).

12:7-8. And because of the surpassing greatness of the revelations, for this reason, to keep me from exalting myself, there was given me a thorn in the flesh, a messenger of Satan to buffet me—to keep me from exalting myself! Concerning this I entreated the Lord three times that it might depart from me. Paul now moves to his second example that boasts about his weaknesses and not his strengths. The Corinthians were well aware of many healings that had gone on in their community at the Asclepion in their city, but Paul speaks of a lack of healing, a thorn in his flesh that would not go away.

Clearly Paul believed in a Christ who was able to heal, but God did not choose to heal him. What this thorn in the flesh was is not clear, but it is likely that it was a physical ailment having to do with his eyes. Why else would the Galatian Christians have been willing to "pluck out their eyes" for him (Gal. 4:15) and that he should speak of having to write with such large letters (Gal. 6:11)? While there have been many who have argued that this "thorn" was some kind of epilepsy, there is nothing to suggest that this was what Paul experienced. The only physical ailment he alludes to has to do with his eyes, but there is no certainty that this is what he had in mind here, but whatever it was did not make his ministry to the Corinthians or to others any less effective.

Why Paul asked for healing from the Lord (Jesus Christ) *three* times is not clear, but the number was a common one both in Jewish and Greco-Roman traditions (Euripides, *Hippolytus*

46; Horace, *Odes* 3.22.3; *Satires* 2.1.7; *Epistles* 1.1.37). Paul addresses his petition to the Lord, that is, the risen Lord Jesus Christ, and believed that the Lord could heal him of this ailment, but that did not happen, so he accepted it as the Lord's will for him to endure it by God's grace (v. 9).

12:9. And He has said to me, "My grace is sufficient for you, for power is perfected in weakness." Most gladly, therefore, I will rather boast about my weaknesses, that the power of Christ may dwell in me. Like Paul, Epictetus had a physical ailment that left him lame on his feet, probably from beatings in his youth when he was a slave woman's son and a slave himself. After imploring Zeus for healing that did not come, he states that Zeus responded to him:

"Epictetus, had it been possible I should have made both this paltry body and this small estate of thine free and unhampered. But as it is—let it not escape thee—this body is not thine own, but only clay cunningly compounded. Yet since I could not give thee this, we have given thee a certain portion of ourself, this faculty of choice and refusal, of desire and aversion, or, in a word, the faculty which makes use of external impressions; if thou care for this and place all that thou hast therein, thou shalt never be thwarted, never hampered, shalt not groan, shalt not blame, shalt not flatter any man. What then? Are these things small in thy sight?" [Epictetus responds] "Far be it from me!" [Zeus asks] "Art thou, then, content with them?" [Epictetus replies] "I pray the Gods I may be" (*Discourses* 1.1.10-13, LCL).

More similar to Paul in this regard, however, is Philo who says of the burning bush in Exod. 3:2-3 that was not consumed by the fire, that this was a message of hope (from God) for those who suffer:

> . . . we may think of it as a voice pro-claiming to the sufferers: "Do not lose heart; your weakness is your strength, which can prick, and thousands will suffer from its wounds. Those who desire to consume you will be your unwilling saviours instead of your destroyers. Your ills will work you no ill. Nay, just when the enemy is surest of ravaging you, your frame will shine forth most gloriously." Again fire, the element which works destruction, con-victs the cruel-hearted. "Exult not in your own strength" it says (*Moses* 1.69, LCL).

Paul wants the Corinthians to know that his strength is in fact in Christ, and not in his abil-ities or talents. This is remarkably different from most of the Greek philosophers who would not reveal their weaknesses, but only their strengths to others. We should observe that this passage is the only saying of Jesus that Paul mentions in 2 Corinthians.

12:10. Therefore I am well content with weak-nesses, with insults, with distresses, with per-secutions, with difficulties, for Christ's sake; for when I am weak, then I am strong. This concludes Paul's "foolish speech" that began in 11:15, but technically 11:21. As he concludes with a focus on the power or strength that he has in Christ, he has made his case against his foes. In a remarkably similar turn of words, Philo spoke of his strength in weakness thusly: "All this is a description of the nation's condi-tion as it then stood, and we may think of it as a voice proclaiming to the sufferers: "Do not lose heart; your weakness is your strength . . . " (*Moses* 1.69, LCL).

12:11-12. I have become foolish; you your-selves compelled me. Actually I should have been commended by you, for in no respect was I inferior to the most eminent apostles, **even though I am a nobody. The signs of a true apostle were performed among you with all perseverance, by signs and wonders and miracles.** These are transitional verses prepar-ing for Paul's next visit to Corinth. Paul's argu-ment that he is nothing after saying that he is not inferior to the "super-apostles" has a touch of irony to it. He says that "in nothing" (Greek = *ouden*) was he inferior to them, and then con-cludes that he himself is "nothing" (Greek = *ouden*), or a "nobody"! The wordplay is more obvious in the Greek, but it is not difficult to follow even in English. In keeping with a widely recognized custom, Paul has listed important activities that have been for the ben-efit of the Corinthians, something that they themselves should have been able to see and also commend to others rather than wait for Paul to do it. He would rather have spoken as he did to the Romans as he commended his missionary work to them as the work of Christ (Rom. 15:17-21).

The **"signs and wonders and miracles"** mentioned above are referred to frequently in the Bible. The Old Testament often refers to the "signs and wonders" that accompany the activity of God (Deut. 4:34; 6:22; 7:19; 26:8; 29:3; 34:11; Neh. 9:10; Ps. 135:9; Jer. 32:20-21; Dan. 4:2-3; 6:27) and their frequency in the New Testament is also noteworthy (see also John 4:48; Acts 2:43; 4:30; 5:12; 6:8; 7:36; 14:3; 15:12; Rom. 15:19; here; 2 Thess. 2:9; Heb. 2:4). Paul's healings are frequently mentioned in Acts (13:6-12; 14:8-18; 15:12; 16:16-18; 19:11-12; 28:3-6, 7-10), but none of them were done at Corinth. As a miracle worker, Paul has often been compared to the remarkable figure writ-ten about by the Athenian Philostratus (ca. A.D. 170) called Apollonius of Tyana, an itinerant philosopher who traveled in the early part of the first century A.D. performing a variety of miracles. There is considerable debate over whether the man ever existed, but if he did, there are some parallels between his life and Paul's in their ability to do miracles, such as ridding Ephesus of a severe plague (*Life of Apollonius* 4.10-11).

12:13. For in what respect were you treated as inferior to the rest of the churches, except that I myself did not become a burden to you? Forgive me this wrong! Paul's biting irony here is plain. His only mistake among the Corinthian Christians is that he failed to take advantage of them. He begs their forgiveness! He reminds them of what he said in 10:7-10, namely that he was not a burden to them, but that this comes from his love for them, not his rejection of them.

2. 12:14–13:10. Notice of an Impending Visit. Paul now gives notice that he will once again make a visit to the Corinthian Christians. He has been there twice already, the first time being when he founded the church, and then to make a "painful visit" (2 Cor. 2:1), and now he prepares for a third visit after he has sent them this letter.

12:14. Here for this third time I am ready to come to you, and I will not be a burden to you; for I do not seek what is yours, but you; for children are not responsible to save up for their parents, but parents for their children. Philo states what is the common wisdom circulating among the Jews and what Paul mentions here, namely "since, in the natural order of things, sons are the heirs of their fathers and not fathers of their sons, He [God] left unmentioned this deplorable and sinister possibility, to avoid the idea of a father and mother making profit out of their inconsolable sorrow at the untimely death of their children" (*Moses* 2.245, LCL).

12:15. And I will most gladly spend and be expended for your souls. If I love you the more, am I to be loved the less? Paul assumes that his love for the Corinthians will be received and their love for him will be their response. It is difficult to avoid the mention of what many

parents both ancient and modern have felt when their parents, and Paul sees himself as a parent in this case, love their children, but their children do not show their love for them.

12:16. But be that as it may, I did not burden you myself; nevertheless, crafty fellow that I am, I took you in by deceit. Once again, Paul's sarcasm comes through. He finds it ironic that even though he never took advantage of the Corinthians by taking gifts from them, he nonetheless was deceitful toward them. The statement makes no sense and that, of course, is Paul's point here.

12:17. Certainly I have not taken advantage of you through any of those whom I have sent to you, have I? It may be that Paul's efforts to raise money for the Christians in Jerusalem were the background for the accusation that he took advantage of them. Paul's defense takes the form of that of Demosthenes in an address to Aeschines:

> Did I make a contribution? Yes, and I receive praise for that, without being subject to audit for what I donated. Did I hold offices? Yes, and I rendered an accounting for my discharge of the same, but not for donations. Indeed, but was I a corrupt official? Well, if that were the case, whey did you not accuse me when the auditors called me in? (*On the Crown* 117, Danker trans.)

Paul says that neither he nor his envoys that he sent to them took advantage of them. The way that he makes this argument implies that an obvious acknowledgment of the truth of the statement was expected from them (see discussion earlier of Titus in 8:6, 16-22).

12:18. I urged Titus to go, and sent the brother with him. Titus did not take any advantage of you, did he? Did we not conduct ourselves in the same spirit and walk in the same steps? If chaps. 10–13 were written after the collection obtained by Titus in chaps. 8–9, then Paul is making an appeal that as Titus did not take advantage of them, neither did he. He does not worry about someone contradicting him in this matter.

12:19. All this time you have been thinking that we are defending ourselves to you. Actually, it is in the sight of God that we have been speaking in Christ; and all for your upbuilding, beloved. Paul reiterates that everything that he has done up to this point has been for the believers in Corinth and not for himself.

12:20-21. For I am afraid that perhaps when I come I may find you to be not what I wish and may be found by you to be not what you wish; that perhaps there may be strife, jealousy, angry tempers, disputes, slanders, gossip, arrogance, disturbances; I am afraid that when I come again my God may humiliate me before you, and I may mourn over many of those who have sinned in the past and not repented of the impurity, immorality and sensuality which they have practiced. Greeks were fond of lists and often recited them in plays and public oratory. These two lists of vices are among several that appear in Paul's writings and elsewhere in the New Testament (see Rom. 1:29-30; 13:13; 1 Cor. 5:10-11; 6:9-10; Gal. 5:19-21; Eph. 4:31; 5:3-5; Col. 3:5, 8; cf. also 1 Tim. 1:9-10; 6:4-5; 2 Tim. 3:2-4; Titus 3:31. Elsewhere in the New Testament see Mark 7:21-22; 1 Peter 4:3; Rev. 9:21; 21:8; 22:15; cf. also *4 Macc.* 1:26; 2:15). They are also quite common in the Greco-Roman world. There are also lists of virtues in Paul and in the Greco-Roman writers. Paul, for instance, lists virtues (Gal. 5:22-23; cf. Rom. 12:9-13). Philo also had many lists to display to his readers and on one occasion listed what things would be true of those who became lovers of pleasure (*The Sacrifices of Abel and Cain* 32). He listed 150 vices from "unscrupulous to "without relief" and every-

thing imaginable in between that resulted from following pleasure! Diogenes Laertius, offering the views of Zeno, the founder of Stoicism (335-263 B.C.), has a lengthy catalogue of vices and virtues that enable persons to map their way to what pleases the gods (Diogenes Laertius, Zeno 7.110-116). Some of the vices in Paul's list are also found in Wisdom of Solomon who claims that those who err in their knowledge of God and worship idols are known for the following:

> They no longer keep either their lives or their marriages pure, but they either treacherously kill one another, or grieve one another by adultery, and all is a raging riot of blood and murder, theft and deceit, corruption, faithlessness, tumult, perjury, confusion over what is good, forgetfulness of favors, defiling of souls, sexual perversion, disorder in marriages, adultery, and debauchery. For the worship of idols not to be named is the beginning and cause and end of every evil (*Wisd.* 14:24-27, NRSV).

Paul appears to suggest here that if his opponents continue to do and say what they have, the results will be what is listed in vv. 20-21. Anyone who praises such people can fall into their life-style and be guilty of the same. Plutarch offers similar warnings to his readers:

> . . . where mistaken praise injures and corrupts by arousing emulation of evil and inducing the adoption of an unsound policy where important issues are at stake, it is no disservice to counteract it, or rather to divert the hearer's purpose to a better course by pointing out the difference. One would be well content, I think, to see the multitude, when vice is denounced and censured, willing to abstain from it; but if vice should acquire good standing, and if hounour and reputation should be added to its temptations in the way of pleasure or profit, there is no human nature so fortunate or strong as not to

succumb. It is not then with the praise of persons, but with that of acts, when they are vicious, that the statesman must wage war. For this sort of praise perverts; it brings with it the imitation and emulation of what is shameful as if it were noble (On Inoffensive Self-Praise 545D-E, LCL).

Elsewhere, Plutarch appears to state what it is that Paul has been doing in chapters 10–13. He writes: "When blame is mingled with praise, and is expressed with complete frankness, yet devoid of disdain, and induces repentance rather than ire, it appears well-disposed and remedial" (Moralia, Precepts for Governing a State 810c, Danker trans. 208).

13:1-10. Summary and Prospects for the Future. What follows in 13:1-10, in large measure reflects what Paul said at the beginning of this portion of the letter in 10:1-10. These ten verses have much in common with those and a simple comparison suggests that these were intended as both introduction (10:1-10) and summary (13:1-10) of what lies in between. Both of these passages look to the future rather than the failures and problems of the present (chaps. 11–12).

13:1. This is the third time I am coming to you. Every fact is to be confirmed by the testimony of two or three witnesses. Paul reiterates that he will be coming to the Corinthian believers for the third time. He then warns them that they can expect him to follow the biblical mandate (Deut. 19:5; cf. Matt 18:16; 1 Tim. 5:19) of finding witnesses for slanderous comments that have been made about him and that he will apply the same in regard to church discipline.

13:2-3. I have previously said when present the second time, and though now absent I say in advance to those who have sinned in the past and to all the rest as well, that if I come again, I will not spare anyone, since you are seeking for proof of the Christ who speaks in me, and who is not weak toward you, but mighty in you. Paul lets it be known that those who accused him of being bold in letters (10:10) but meek and weak in his presence will find a surprise when he arrives and he will not spare them. Some Corinthians wanted proof that Paul spoke with authority so he once again indicates that it is Christ who speaks through him (2:17; 12:19; 13:3) or God (5:21) and that his conduct is the proof of what he says, even if he does not have the oratorical skills or appearance to impress those who hear him. Dio Chrysostom tells of a Roman named Favorinus (A.D. 80-150), a sophist, who came among the Greeks and spoke so well that the people praised him and erected a statue in his honor, and concluded that it was apparent that he was divinely enabled to do as he had done.

Indeed it seems that he has been equipped by the gods for this express purpose—for the Greeks, so that the natives of that land may have an example before them to show that culture is not whit inferior to birth with respect to renown; for Romans, so that not even those who are wrapped up in their own self-esteem may disregard culture with respect to real esteem; for Celts, so that no one even of the barbarians may despair of attaining the culture of Greece when he looks upon this man (Orations 37.27, LCL).

What Paul might do to the unrepentant member of the congregation at Corinth is not clear, but earlier he spoke of "handing him over to Satan" (1 Cor. 5:5, see discussion of that text above) and this probably also meant some form of excommunication.

13:4. For indeed He was crucified because of weakness, yet He lives because of the power of God. For we also are weak in Him, yet we shall live with Him because of the power of God directed toward you. The proof of God's activity in Christ is shown in the way that he was crucified in weakness, but raised by the power of God. The city of Corinth respected and admired strength, whether in the athletic ability that they witnessed at the Isthmian games or in the variety of statues and art pieces among them with images of the strength and power of athletes and the gods. Even the coins had images of victor's wreaths! A crucified Christ was surely every bit "foolishness to the Greeks," but for Paul and those who received his message, he was the power of God and the wisdom of God (1 Cor. 1:23-24).

13:5. Test yourselves to see if you are in the faith; examine yourselves! Or do you not recognize this about yourselves, that Jesus Christ is in you—unless indeed you fail the test? The call to examine oneself to see if one was following the truth or the right philosophy was quite common in antiquity beginning with Socrates and continuing well past the time of Paul. Epictetus, for example, recounts the example of Socrates:

> For, just as Socrates used to tell us not to live a life unsubjected to examination, so we ought not to accept a sense-impression unsubjected to examination, but should say, "Wait, allow me to see who you are and whence you come" (just as the night-watch say, "Show me your tokens") [Note: tokens were marks of identification for those who traveled at night.] (*Discourses* 3.12.15, LCL).

The goal of such examination was to see if a person continued to be morally fit. Another example of a call for such examination demonstrates this:

> For the gods did not withhold from non-Greeks the ability to know the good. It is possible, through reasoned examination, to test whether we think good thoughts, and to investigate whether our words correspond to our actions, and whether we are like those who live morally (Ps-Anacharsis, *Epistle* 2, M. Hubbard 3:257-58).

13:7. Now we pray to God that you do no wrong; not that we ourselves may appear approved, but that you may do what is right, even though we should appear unapproved. Paul protects himself from the charge of misunderstanding by the use of a rhetorical ploy called the *epidiorthosis* (see 12:1 above).

13:10. For this reason I am writing these things while absent, in order that when present I may not use severity, in accordance with the authority which the Lord gave me, for building up and not for tearing down. Paul hopes to avoid any confrontation when he comes to Corinth and hopes that the Christians there will take care of the problems he has set before them before he arrives. He also concludes his comments that were begun on this matter in 10:10 above. This is similar to Demosthenes who defended himself against the charges of Aeschines that he manipulated the assembly of people with his rhetorical skill. He responds to the charge: "All of you will discover that whatever skill I possess has been exercised, both in public and in private, on your behalf—never against you" (*On the Crown* 277, Danker trans.).

E. 13:11-14. CLOSING

1. 13:11. Call to Unity and Summary.

13:11. Finally, brethren, rejoice, be made complete, be comforted, be like-minded, live in peace; and the God of love and peace shall be with you. The word "brethren" does not in itself show that Paul had in mind the whole congregation at Corinth. *Adelphos*, the Greek word for "brethren" is used in a generic manner here and is inclusive of all of the church at Corinth.

2. 13:12-13. Greetings

13:12. Greet one another with a holy kiss. The call to greet one another with a "holy kiss" is quite common in Paul's letters (Rom. 16:16; 1 Cor. 16:20; 2 Cor. 13:12; 1 Thess. 5:26, but cf. Col. 4:21). It is also encouraged in 1 Peter 5:14. The kiss became a sign of the fellowship of love that Christians belonged to as a result of their relationship with Christ. This became a regular part of Christian worship in many parts of the church later. There is nothing analogous to it in the Greco-Roman world and it probably had its origins in the church. Kissing in public was often ridiculed in Greco-Roman society and often led to accusations of sexual activity. The kiss in the early church, and certainly in Paul, has to do with a greeting. This would normally take place in their gatherings for worship and appear to stress the importance of Christians loving and caring for one another in the highest ideals of the Christian faith. It is a recognition that the barriers between individuals have been destroyed (Gal. 3:28), and that the unity in the family of Christ is complete.

13:13. All the saints greet you. This is a reminder from Paul that the Corinthian Christians do not live in isolation from other believers, but that they are part of a larger family.

3. 13:14. Benediction
13:14. The grace of the Lord Jesus Christ, and the love of God, and the fellowship of the Holy Spirit, be with you all. This benediction has a "Trinitarian" resemblance in its earlier stages and has parallels in Paul's writings (cf. Rom. 15:30; 1 Cor. 12:4-6). While the term "trinity" itself is not mentioned in the New Testament, the data that led the church to adopt the teaching identified by that name in the fourth century is found in its embryonic form in several contexts in the New Testament. For example, the presence of Father, Son, and Holy Spirit are in the baptismal formula in Matthew 28:19-20, in Paul's prayer above, but also to some extent in 1 Corinthians 6:11; 12:4-5; 2 Corinthians 1:21-22; Galatians 3:11-14; 1 Thess. 5:18-19; 1 Peter 1:2. The Father, Son, and Holy Spirit are often identified in relation to one another as at Jesus' baptism when the Father says "This is my beloved Son" as the Spirit descends upon him (Matthew 3:16-17; Luke 3:22; Mark 1:9-10). Notice also Paul's close association of Jesus with the Father in his prayers (1 Cor. 1:3; Gal. 1:3; Phil. 1:2). The Holy Spirit is not only called the Spirit of God, but also the Spirit of Christ (Rom. 8:9). The activity of God in the Old Testament is sometimes attributed to the Holy Spirit in the New Testament (Isa. 6:9-10, cf. Acts 28:25-27). Finally, the Father, Son, and Holy Spirit are often seen in parallel relationships, for example, the Father and Christ (John 14:1; Rom. 1:7; Rev. 5:13) and the Spirit and Christ (1 Cor. 6:11; Rom. 15:30; Heb. 10:29). Some other examples include Jude 20-21 and Rev. 1:4-7. These passages show that the work of all three —Father, Son, and Holy Spirit— were often viewed together in Paul's writings and in the early church, but the fully developed Trinitarian teaching that was stated a the Council of Nicea in A.D. 325, however, took the church centuries more to both recognize and articulate.

It is interesting that the grace that concludes Paul's other letters is normally "with you" (Rom. 16:20b; 1 Cor. 16:23; 1 Thess. 5:28; cf. Col. 4:18; 1 Tim. 6:21; 2 Tim. 4:22) or "with your spirit" (Gal. 6:18; Phil. 4:23; Phile. 25). In Ephesians it is "with all who have an undying love for our Lord Jesus Christ" (6:24); in 2 Thessalonians and Titus it is "with all of you" (2 Thess. 3:18; Titus 3:15).

Introduction to Galatians

Lee Martin McDonald

It is remarkable that there are no other works in the history of the church that have had a greater impact upon the development of the church than Paul's letter to the Galatians. It would be an overstatement to say that were it not for this document the church would be meeting in synagogues today, a statement sometimes made in popular sermons. But the shallowness of that statement does not take away from the enormous impact this relatively small letter has had upon the church's development. Its emphasis upon justification by faith not only had a significant impact upon such reformers as Luther and Wesley, but also on the early church's separation from Judaism and its consequent freedom from the Jewish initiatory, ceremonial, and social aspects of the Law, as in the case of circumcision, sabbath keeping, dietary laws and purity regulations. The separation of the Christians from Judaism came in large part as a result of the work of the Apostle Paul who insisted that Gentiles were not under the obligations of the Law, but came to a right relationship with God directly by faith in Christ. His message is nowhere more clearly stated than in this brief letter. Later, the letter to the Romans expanded what Paul said here, but without changing its substance.

This letter is emotionally charged and presents one of Paul's strongest responses to those who would pervert his gospel of grace through faith in Christ. In it he powerfully attacks a group of persons who were undermining his ministry among the Gentiles by changing the gospel that he proclaimed and calling Paul's apostleship and authority into question in the Galatian churches. He appeals to his converts not to be diverted from the true gospel that he has presented to them, nor to be tempted to accept the yoke of bondage that adherence to the Law would bring to them. This letter is the only correspondence that Paul wrote in which he did not praise his readers, and it is also one of the least polished in terms of his grammatical construction of sentences. It was clearly written in the context of anger and passion for those believers for whom he had labored so hard to bring into the Christian faith.

While Paul may have used a secretary to write all but the final portion of the letter (6:11-18), it is more likely that he penned the whole letter itself. The argumentation is quite heated throughout, and he reserves his strongest attacks for those who have perverted his gospel and are seeking to compel the Gentiles to live under the bondage of the law. The letter has some parallels with 2 Cor. 10–13 in terms of its passionate and critical tone, but more than any other letter, it also reveals Paul's passion for the gospel that he preached and his love for those who received his message.

The following introductory comments will address some of the important issues related to the letter and its structure, and this will be followed by some historical background that will enhance the meaning and historical context of the letter. The difficulty of harmonizing the Book of Acts with Paul's letter to the Galatians is one of the most difficult problems for interpreters of the two books to deal with. We will examine briefly some of the issues that are important in understanding this important letter from Paul.

1. Authorship. There is no question among biblical scholars today that what we have in the letter to the Galatians is a genuine document from the Apostle Paul. Occasionally there have been some challenges to the authenticity of a few passages in the letter, but most scholars see it in its entirety as a genuine Pauline document.

2. Destination. For much of the history of the church, it was believed that this letter was sent to churches that Paul had founded on his second missionary journey in the northern part of the Roman province called Galatia. One of the major debates over the last hundred years regarding Galatians is whether the letter was addressed to the North Galatians, that is, to those living in the ancient ethnic area of Galatia that was settled in Asia Minor (today central Turkey) by the Gauls in the fourth century B.C. from Europe, or whether the letter was addressed to the Christians from churches established in South Galatia by Paul and Barnabas on their first missionary journey (Acts 13:13-25), that is, to those new Christians living in the southern part of the Roman province of Galatia. There are several implications for this discussion. If the destination was North Galatia, the epistle was probably written during or shortly after the end of Paul's second missionary journey. This also suggests that Paul's account of the "private meeting" with the leaders, or "pillars" (Gal. 2:2, 6) of the church in Jerusalem is the same as the rather public meeting often referred to as the "Jerusalem council"

in Acts 15. If the destination was South Galatia, then the letter could have been written as early as the end of Paul's first missionary journey (ca. A.D. 48-49), before the meeting of the Jerusalem Council. This would not preclude it having been written later, however. If the letter was written as early as the end of the first missionary journey, then Gal. 2:1-10 could be Paul's account of the so-called famine visit to Jerusalem of Acts 11:27-30 and 12:25, or a "private meeting" not mentioned in Acts and unknown to Luke.

The history of discussion of this issue is surprisingly recent in the church. The early church, from the second century on, took the view that the letter was written to the churches in North Galatia, or the ethnic view, since the region of Lycaonia had apparently separated from the province of Galatia and united with Cilicia, thus putting several of the churches founded by Paul on his first missionary journey (e.g. Lystra and Derbe) in a separate province from Galatia. By the fourth century, the Roman province of Galatia had been reduced to its original size. The North Galatian theory regarding the destination of the letter, or the "ethnic" view, persisted without challenge in the church until the nineteenth century when Sir William Ramsay, as a result of his first-hand exploration of the region, concluded that the South Galatian destination, or "provincial" view was more plausible. Bible scholars have been divided on the issue of destination ever since. The main arguments for each theory are listed below.

(1) North Galatia Hypothesis. The North Galatia or ethnic/territorial view has been held by a number of important scholars including J. B. Lightfoot, James Moffatt, W. G. Kümmel, H. D. Betz, and S. L. Martyn, among many others (see Bibliography). The main arguments for this position include:

(a) The term "Galatia" (from which we get the Greek = *Galatai, Keltai*, from the "Gauls" or "Celts") refers to those who migrated from Europe into Asia Minor in the fourth century B.C. It referred not to the political province but to the people who had been subdued by the Romans. The use of the term in Gal. 3:1 in a racial sense ("O foolish Galatians"), would seem to support this interpretation.

(b) Acts 16:6 and 18:23 illustrate the geographical sense of the term, since the author also mentions Phrygia, which was another territory in that area. The emphasis is placed on the word "and" in both verses. These are the only places in the Book of Acts where the province is mentioned by name. Elsewhere, the name Galatia outside Gal. 1:2 and "Galatians" in 3:5, is only found in 1 Cor. 16:1; 2 Tim. 4:10 and 1 Peter 1:1. The churches that Paul strengthened in 18:23 are not necessarily in the north and could just as easily be in the southern part of Galatia, namely in Antioch of Pisidia, Iconium, Lystra and Derbe.

(c) In Acts 16:6, Paul "passed through" Phrygia and Galatia because they "had been forbidden" from preaching in Asia Minor. This implies that Paul and his companions went north to the Galatian region, rather than travel on into Asia Minor.

(d) Luke does not refer to Galatia when he mentions Paul going to Lystra and Derbe during the first missionary journey (Acts 14:6, 20, 21), but rather to Lycaonia, a different province, in which these cities were located.

(e) In Gal. 4:13, the use of "former" (Greek = *proteron*) may imply two visits to the region, which, according to this theory, are those recorded in Acts 16:6 and 18:23. This datum could, however, also be used to argue for a later date and a South Galatia destination.

(f) The style and subject matter of Galatians seems to be most compatible with Romans which was apparently written toward the end of Paul's journeys from Corinth (Rom. 15:25-27), and hence the book should be placed in close chronological proximity to this letter. It is difficult to take Galatians, with its focus on the law, as the first letter of Paul that is followed shortly thereafter by the Thessalonian correspondence that does not mention the law. This argument again only supports a later date of composition, not necessarily the North Galatia hypothesis.

(g) The temperament of the Galatian Christians seems to reflect racial stereotypes from a later period that viewed the Galatian people as fickle, superstitious, and unsophisticated (cf. Gal. 3:1).

(h) According to this view, Gal. 1:21 refers to the first missionary journey in Acts 13-14.

(2) South Galatia Hypothesis. The South Galatian, or provincial, theory advanced first by Sir William Ramsay, and subsequently by E. DeWitt Burton, Bruce, Martin, R. N. Longenecker, Ralph Martin, and others, has been growing in popularity among scholars although not all are agreed as to the time of writing. The major arguments for the South Galatian hypothesis are as follows.

(a) The use of the names "Phrygia and Galatia" in Acts 16:6 and 18:23 is adjectival, thus referring to Phrygian-Galatia, the area of the Galatian province that includes the region of Phrygia. Ramsay was not able to provide an exact parallel of this usage, but he found similar kinds of modification that indicated that this pattern was acceptable usage.

(b) The North Galatian view requires an unnatural detour in Acts 16, in which the normal trade routes along the borders of the province of Asia would not have been followed. Paul tended to follow the main roads and centers of communication in Roman provinces (that is from Syria to Cilicia to Iconium and then to Ephesus). The southern side of the Anatolian plateau consisted of low hills with an adequate water supply, and hence was far more important and strategic in terms of population than the north, which was very difficult to get to. It is true that Lystra and Derbe were also "backward" places, by Ramsay's own admission, but at least these cities were in the area that Paul was traveling, rather than requiring a radical detour. Further, Paul left for these areas in a speedy retreat to get away from persecution (Acts 14:5-6).

(c) Paul is not precise in every instance, but he normally uses Roman provincial titles (unlike Luke), especially with reference to areas where churches are located. Hence he uses Achaia or Greece, rather than Hellas, which Luke uses.

(d) Concerning Acts 16:6, the aorist participle translated "forbid" (Greek = *koluthentes*) does not mean that the forbidding took place before Paul and his companions passed through Phrygia and Galatia, but rather that action took place at the same time or after. Hence the verse is best translated, "they passed through Phrygian-Galatia, then they were forbidden to speak the word in Asia [Ephesus?]." In Greek, this is determined by the word order where the participle normally follows the main verb, rather than being determined by the tense of the participle.

(e) Acts mentions only Paul's time in South Galatia, never speaks of a North Galatian ministry.

(f) In Acts 20:4, when the people involved in the collection are mentioned, there are people from South Galatia (Gaius of Derbe, Timothy of Lystra) but nobody from the north. No one from Corinth is mentioned either, but this is a different kind of omission in light of Paul's travel itinerary and the province of Achaia is mentioned in Rom. 15:25-27.

(g) The mention of Barnabas in Gal. 2:1, 9 and 13 is better explained if Paul founded the churches to which he refers on the first missionary journey when Barnabas accompanied him rather than on the second journey after Paul and Barnabas had parted ways (Acts 15:36-41), since this was the only missionary journey on which Barnabas accompanied Paul.

(h) In the light of the subject matter of Galatians, including the debate over the Jewish legalistic responsibilities of Gentiles, it is difficult to believe that Paul would not have mentioned the meeting in Jerusalem in Acts 15, if that meeting had already occurred (some scholars have questioned whether it really did

take place). The Council decision (Acts 15:22-31) would have greatly strengthened Paul's argument in his letter to the Galatians, especially since some "from James" (Gal. 2:12) were perpetrating the problems in the Galatian churches. If the letter were written *before* the Jerusalem Council, it must have been written to the South Galatia churches.

(i) It is possible that the reference to Paul being received by the Galatians as an "angel of God" and even "as Jesus Christ" (Gal. 4:14) by the Galatians coincides with the identification of Paul with Hermes and Barnabas with Zeus by the residents of Lystra (Acts 14:11-18) and references to his "carrying the marks of Jesus (Gal. 6:17) refer to the physical harm that he suffered (Acts 14:19). Although it is an argument from silence, this is the only known place in Paul's ministry where that kind of adulation occurred.

(j) During the first century, the province of Galatia was a large one that included many regions that brought together ethnic groups of all different sorts. One Latin inscription of the Roman period records the full title of a governor of Galatia, illustrating this diversity: he is described as governor "of Galatia, of Pisidia, of Phrygia, of Lycaonia, of Isauria, of Paphlogonia, of Pontus Galaticus, of Pontus Polemoniacus, of Armenia" (#1017 in *Inscriptiones Latinae Selectae*). It is possible that Paul's letter to the churches of Galatia in the south also reflects the multiple locations that were believed to be a part of this province.

While there are important arguments for each of the two positions above, it seems that the evidence for the South Galatian hypothesis has the greatest strength. In terms of the evidence that is at hand, it is more plausible to think that the letter was addressed to the churches at Lystra, Derbe, Iconium and Antioch that we know Paul visited on his first journey and that were located in an area known in Roman times as Galatia, rather than conjecture a different destination far removed from these churches and in a place where there is no evidence that Paul founded churches (the north). It is not clear how else Paul could have addressed the Christians in these four cities collectively except as "Galatians."

3. Date. The date of this letter depends on its destination. If it was sent to churches in the north, it is later and if in the south, it is most likely earlier.

(1) **North Galatia.** There are three possible dates for those who hold to the North Galatian hypothesis. The first is sometime after the first possible visit by Paul to North Galatia (Acts 16:6), sometime during his second missionary journey (e.g., A.D. 50-52). The second possibility is that the letter was sent early in Paul's Ephesian ministry in Acts 19:1-41 (e.g. A.D. 53-55), taking the word "quickly" of Gal. 1:6 quite literally with reference to their abandoning the faith. Paul had visited the churches of Galatia in 16:6 and 18:23, and then gone to Ephesus, where, according to this view, he must have written to them upon hearing of immediate danger. The third possible date, if adopting the North Galatian theory, is that Paul wrote the letter sometime after leaving Ephesus, giving a little bit of time between Paul's visit and his need for writing. Some scholars date the letter after the Corinthian letters, since there is no reference to the problem with Judaizers in the Corinthian correspondence, but before Romans since there is in that correspondence, perhaps being written in Macedonia, due to the theological similarities but less developed thinking (e.g. ca. A.D. 56-57).

(2) **South Galatia**. There are two possible time-frames for composition for those who hold to the South Galatian hypothesis. The latter time of composition correlates with the dates suggested by the North Galatian hypothesis. In this case the "quickly" of Gal. 1:6 is a term indicating the quickness of their turning away from Paul's gospel after others had come in to stir up problems in the church, rather than the length of time from their conversion. The earlier date of composition argues that Paul

wrote to the churches after his first missionary journey but before the Jerusalem council of Acts 15 (e.g. A.D. 49?). In this case, Gal. 4:13 refers to the two visits on the first missionary journey, namely the "first" refers to the first of two or more times that he preached to them.

4. Paul's Visits to Jerusalem in Acts and Galatians. The discussion concerning the date of the composition of Galatians can be further clarified if reference is made to Paul's visits to Jerusalem that are mentioned in Galatians and in Acts. There are two major schemes for understanding the relationship between the Jerusalem visits of Paul according to Galatians and Acts. The following scheme assumes that the Jerusalem council of Acts 15, so far as its essential subject matter, actually happened. There has probably been unnecessary skepticism over whether the council of Acts 15 ever took place. The conclusions reached by the council promoted Gentile Christian freedom from the law, but called upon them to avoid foods sacrificed to idols, the consumption of blood, eating animals that have been strangled, and to abstain from fornication (Acts 15:29). Some scholars have said that Paul took these admonitions lightly in his subsequent ministry, and therefore are grounds for dismissing its historicity, but that is not easily substantiated. Paul clearly discussed two of these four items of restriction (food sacrificed to idols and fornication) in his letters and it is an argument from silence to say that he made light of the others. One reconstruction of the events of Galatians and Acts is represented on the top of the next page.

In this scheme, there are various explanations of Acts 11:27-30, the so-called famine visit. Some argue that the episode in Acts 11 is not historical, and consequently that Paul does not mention it. Others argue that the two accounts in Acts 11 and 15 are duplicates, which the author of Luke-Acts perhaps found in two separate sources, not realizing it was the same story. A third explanation is that the meeting of Acts

Galatians	Acts
1:18-20 Paul sees Cephas and James.	9:26-29 Barnabas takes Paul to the apostles.
1:21 Paul's visit to Syria and Cilicia.	9:30 Paul departs for Tarsus in Cilicia.
2:1-10 Paul and Barnabas, along with Titus, meet James, Peter, and John.	15:2-29 Paul and Barnabas meet with apostles and elders at council.

11, because it appears to be a private meeting in which the apostles are not mentioned, is passed over in Galatians, since the challenge to which Paul is responding in Galatians is in terms of his relationship to the apostles.

A second reconstruction of the events in Galatians and Acts is represented below.

There are some difficulties with this second equation, most notably the apostles and Titus are not mentioned in Acts 11. It seems that Paul receives confirmation of his message to the Gentiles, even though this precedes his first missionary journey, which would have been the first test of his message. Nevertheless, the latter solution is still a more plausible one first, because there is a place for Acts 11 and 15, without resorting to discrediting Luke's account, as some scholars have done. Secondly, the meetings of Acts 11 and Galatians 2:1-10 (see esp. v. 2) both look like private meetings.

Thirdly, Paul appears to be giving a strict chronology, so it would be surprising if he left out an important incident. Besides, this raises the question of when the incident of Galatians 2:11-14, Paul's confrontation with Peter (probably at Antioch), would have occurred. Most likely, the meeting in Galatians 2:11-14 occurred before the events of Acts 15, otherwise the results of that meeting would have been reported in Galatians.

5. Paul's Opponents and the Occasion of the Letter to the Galatians. The occasion of this letter is linked to the specific circumstance(s) in play at the time of writing, including the composition of the churches, the history of their contact with Paul, and may involve other relevant details regarding activities or problems surrounding this contact. What is the reason or reasons for the composition of this particular letter?

Galatians	Acts
1:18-20 Paul sees Cephas and James.	9:26-29 Barnabas takes Paul to the apostles.
1:21 Paul's visit to Syria and Cilicia.	9:30 Paul departs for Tarsus.
2:1-10 Paul and Barnabas, along with Titus, meet James, Peter, and John.	11:27-30, 12:25 Paul and Barnabas bring famine relief. 15:2-29 Paul and Barnabas meet with apostles and elders at council.

a. The circumstances. There were some individuals who had visited the churches that he and Barnabas had founded soon after they had left (1:7; 5:10, 12), possibly coming from James in Jerusalem (2:12), and they were teaching another message to the people that included not only their questioning of Paul's message, but also their questioning of his apostleship (1:1, 9, 10-11). Paul characterized them as troublemakers (1:7; 5:10) or agitators (5:12), and he saw them trying to impose the requirements of Jewish law, especially circumcision (5:3, 11), and the observance of special days (4:10; 2:16; 3:2, 21b; 4:21; 5:4) on his converts. What they were doing, Paul believed, jeopardized his labor and teachings among them.

b. Paul's response. Paul's response to this threat was a vitriolic one, evidencing his passion for the gospel. He characterizes the opponents' teaching as a perversion of the gospel (1:7) that represents a turning from God (1:6, 5:8), a falling from grace (5:4), and a denial of the promise of the Spirit (3:25). He argued that these persons have substituted a false message for the true one (1:8-9). Paul argues that the message that he proclaimed was received directly from Jesus Christ and was later approved by those in Jerusalem (1:12, 1:13–2:10). Paul says that these opponents are in danger of God's judgment (5:10). He concludes that their teaching is contrary to justification by faith (2:21), and all attempts to make the law a means of justification (3:11) undermine the value of Christ's death and the Good News itself (2:21).

c. Identity of the opponents. Who were those that Paul condemned? It is most likely that Paul's opponents were a legalistic and zealous group of Jewish Christians from Jerusalem (perhaps sent by the Jerusalem apostles, see 2:12) who objected to Gentile freedom from the law (see Acts 15:1) and perhaps also to having any contact with Gentiles such as table fellowship (Acts 11:2-3; cf. Gal. 2:11-14). The most commonly used term to identify these persons is "Judaizers," and they penetrated the churches that Paul founded attempting to persuade the Gentile Christians to accept circumcision and adopt the Jewish laws as a necessary part of their belief in Christ. They probably also argued that even Abraham, the father of their faith, was circumcised as his first great act of faith. This argument is probably the context of Paul's argument in 3:6-18 in which he maintains that Abraham was blessed because of his faith and the promise of God was given to him before he was circumcised.

The fact that these "Judaizers" came from outside the Galatian churches is supported by Paul's use of the third person to refer to these groups. Paul normally uses the second person for insiders (cf. 1 Cor. 5:1-2; 2 Cor. 7:2-4; 11:13-15). These legalists, however, may also have some libertine tendencies (see 6:1), perhaps brought about by proto-Gnostic tendencies (4:9-10), in which their lack of regard for the earthly sphere results in libertinism. However, it is more likely that the references to freedom and indulgence (see 5:13, 16, 6:1, 8) can be explained as simply part of the message of the Judaizers, to which Paul responds by saying that though it may seem that they are free to do these things (using an inversion of Paul's own message?), there is a limit to their freedom.

It is likely that this group was dealing with the Zealotic activities in Jerusalem (that eventually led to the revolt in A.D. 66-70) that were pressuring the Jewish Christians there to maintain the laws and traditions more fervently. As a result, in order to erase all suspicion against them coming from fellow Jews, they tried to persuade Gentile Christians to accept circumcision and the various purity laws that accompanied these laws, including Sabbath keeping. There is no clear evidence that these Jewish Christians in Jerusalem were under such pressure, but given the climate in Israel, Jewish Christians might wish to avoid persecution from fellow Jews because of their association with Gentiles. The language of the letter is concerned with the Jewish practices and beliefs, such as observing the works of the law (3:5), including circumcision (5:6; 6:15), Sabbath keeping, and the observance of holy days in the Jewish calendar (4:10). Paul's opponents, however, were not criticized for rejecting Christ. Evidently, they had accepted Jesus as their messiah and were followers of Jesus, even believing that God had raised him from the dead, but they were also zealous for their Jewish traditions and could not distinguish them from the church's teachings of faith.

It is possible also that besides the Judaizers, there were also libertine pneumatics in the church (Gal. 6:1), who were opposite the Jewish legalists, saying that one's lifestyle was not as important as long as one had faith in Christ (Rom. 6:1?). Paul made sure that how one lived was not separated from the gospel he preached. His cataloguing of unacceptable vices for his readers suggests that some in the churches were not living a life of obedience to God through faith in Christ. They may also have attacked Paul's apostleship and the legitimacy of his gospel. This libertine critique may also reflect a criticism of the Judaizers that Paul's converts were living apart from the Law and in an inappropriate manner. On the other hand, since Paul addresses his opponents as one cohesive group, it is not necessary to posit two sets of opponents. It is possible that some of those in the churches in Galatia misunderstood Paul's teaching about freedom in Christ and allowed it to mean that one could live without restraint. This was never Paul's view, however, and he added the importance of living the life of faith in the power of the Spirit showing evidence of the presence of God in one's life (5:16-26). There are a number of matters related to the identity of Paul's opponents as well as the destination of his letter that remain problematic, but again, they will not detract from the basic message of the necessity of the obedience of faith apart from the works of the Law.

6. Paul and the Greco-Roman World. Those who are familiar with the contemporary Greco-Roman writers of Paul's day recognize almost immediately Paul's familiarity with the conventional practices of argument and speech. Where there are some differences, there are often remarkable similarities as the background comments below will show. Whether Paul was specifically familiar with Aristotle's Art of Rhetoric or his Rhetoric to Alexandria, it is clear that he was familiar with many of the principles set forth in them. This does not mean that such principles or communication skills should be considered as ends in themselves, only that as Paul was communicating the Christian message to a largely Hellenistic world, that he was familiar with the normal communication patterns that were current in his day. In places where there is considerable overlap in thought and substance, it is well to remember that Paul was seeking to reach individuals with his gospel who were familiar with a Hellenistic culture. In order to speak so that they could understand, he frequently used conventions of speech that were familiar to them in order to proclaim the unfamiliar to them. While the form and presentation of his gospel was very much at home in this setting, its content derived not from Hellenistic conventions, but from Paul's encounter with the risen Lord on the road to Damascus. Again, while he was familiar with and frequently used the literary conventions that were common among those who spoke and wrote in the Greek langauge, Paul's gospel was new and it was inextricably bound to God's activity in Jesus the Christ who died for our sins and was raised from the dead. As we will see later, Paul's use of the word "gospel" was both familiar and distinct among them. Paul's audiences would have been familiar with the use of the term euangelion ("glad tiding" or "gospel"), but only in the plural ("glad tidings") and not in the singular form. See discussion of this in 1:6 below. Paul is not the only one in the New Testament to use the singular form of a familiar plural noun, but he is probably the first to use it among Gentiles.

Paul's use of such conventions is certainly in keeping with his stated missionary strategy of becoming "all things to all people" that by all means he might win some (1 Cor. 9:22). How else would he become a Jew to the Jews and a Greek to the Greeks? Paul was remarkably qualified to preach a remarkably Jewish message to the Greco-Roman world precisely because of his familiarity with the literary and rhetorical conventions of this day. This is not to say that he was an expert in such matters, nor that he was a trained rhetorician. His critics at Corinth testified against his abilities in this regard and Paul admitted to the same (see Introduction to 1 Cor. and discussion of 1 Cor. 2:1-4; 2 Cor. 10:10; 11:6), but this does not preclude his awareness of the common features of literary and oral communication in the Greco-Roman world. In what follows, we have highlighted, as in Paul's other writings, his familiarity with these literary and rhetorical devices to add clarity not only to Paul's message, but also to its reception in the Gentile Hellenistic communities where he proclaimed it. On the other hand, it is correct to say that the medium of communication was not the message for Paul, but rather the specifics of his gospel.

7. Structure and Outline of Galatians

General Outline of Galatians. The letter to the Galatians is easy to follow in its broad sections. Chapters 1–2 can be summarized as the historical context of the letter that also presents the issues that Paul confronts. This is followed in chaps. 3–4 by the theological foundation of Paul's gospel. The letter concludes with the last two chapters focusing on the practical implications of Paul's gospel of daily living. This broad outline also helps to see Paul's commitment to the unity of theological belief with the ethical response of one's behavior. We will follow this broad outline below and trace the theme of the book in each of these sections.

OUTLINE OF THE BOOK

I. **Introduction to the Letter (1:1-5) (the** *Exordium/Prooemium***)**

II. **Historical Section (1:6-2:21)**
   A. Occasion: The Judaizers and Paul's Demand for "No Other Gospel" (1:6-10)
   B. How Paul Became an Apostle (1:11-24)
      1. Former Life (1:13-14)
      2. God's Call (1:15-20)
      3. Paul's Independence from Jerusalem (1:21-24)
   C. Paul's Message Accepted in Jerusalem (2:1-10)
   D. Paul Rebukes Peter for His Inconsistency (2:11-14)
   E. Conclusion: Jews & Gentiles Alike Are Saved by Faith (2:15-21)

III. **Paul's Gospel Explained (3:1–4:31)**
   A. An Appeal to Experience and Scripture (3:1-18)
      1. The First Argument: Experience of Spirit vs. Flesh (3:1-5)
      2. The Second Argument: Abraham and Faith (3:6-14)
      3. Faith Is Based upon an Earlier Covenant (3:15-18)
   B. The True Purpose of the Mosaic Law (3:19-29)
      1. To Contain Sin (3:19-22)
      2. To Bring Us to Faith (a Custodial Function) (3:23-29)
   C. Bondage under the Law / Freedom in Christ (4:1-31)
      1. Slavery under the Law vs. Adoption (4:1-7)
      2. Reproof of the Galatians' Conduct (4:8-20)
      3. An Allegory of Hagar and Sarah (4:21-31)

IV. **The Application of Paul's Gospel to Life (5:1–6:10)**
   A. The Nature and Implications of Christian Liberty (5:1-26)
      1. The Futility of Justification by

RESOURCES

Moffatt, James, *An Introduction to the Literature of the New Testament.* 3rd ed., Edinburgh: T. & T. Clark, 1918.

Kümmel, W. G., *Introduction to the New Testament.* Trans. H. C. Kee, Nashville: Abingdon, 1975.

Betz, Hans Dieter D., *Galatians: A Commentary on Paul's Letter to the Churches in Galatia.* Hermeneia; Philadelphia: Fortress, 1979.

Burton, Ernest DeWitt, *A Critical and Exegetical Commentary on the Epistle to the Galatians.* ICC; Edinburgh: T. & T. Clark, 1921.

Bruce, F. F., *The Epistle to the Galatians.* NIGTC, Grand Rapids: Eerdmans, 1982.

Dunn, J. D. G., *The Epistle to the Galatians.* Peabody, MA: Hendrickson, 1993.

———. *The Theology of Paul's Letter to the Galatians.* NTT. Cambridge: Cambridge University Press, 1993.

Edwards, Mark J., ed., *Galatians, Ephesians, Philippians.* T. C. Oden, gen. ed., *Ancient Christians Commentary on Scripture, NT,* vol. 8. Downers Grove, IL: InterVarsity Press, 1999.

Ferguson, Everett, *Backgrounds of Early Christianity,* 2nd ed., Grand Rapids: Eerdmans, 1993. [Abbreviated: Backgrounds]

Fitzmyer, Joseph A., "The Letter to the Galatians," in *The New Jerome Biblical Commentary.* R. ,E. Brown, J. A. Fitzmyer, and R. E. Murphy, eds. Englewood Cliffs, NJ: Prentice Hall, 1990.

Fung, Ronald Y. K., *The Epistle to the Galatians.* G. Fee, gen. ed. NICNT. Grand Rapids, MN: Eerdmans, 1988.

Horsley, G. H. R., and S. R. Llewelyn, eds. *New Documents Illustrating Early Christianity.* 9 vols. North Sydney, Australia: Macquarie University Press/Grand Rapids: Eerdmans, 1981-2002. [Abbreviated: ND]

Krentz, Edgar, *Galatians.* Augsburg Commentary on the New Testament. R. A. Harrisville, J. D. Kingsbury, G. A. Krodel, eds. Minneapolis, MN: Augsburg Publishing House, 1985 (pp. 13-117).

Longenecker, R. N., *Galatians.* WBC 41, Dallas: Word Books, 1990.

Lührmann, Dieter, *Galatians.* A Continental Commentary. Trans. by O. C. Dean, Jr. Minneapolis, MN: Fortress Press, 1992.

Martin, Ralph P., and Julie L. Wu, "Galatians," in *Zondervan Illustrated Bible Backgrounds Commentary,* C. E. Arnold, gen. ed. Grand Rapids, MI: Zondervan, 2002, vol. 3: 265-298.

Martyn, J. Louis, *Galatians: A New Translation with Introduction and Commentary.* Anchor Bible 33A, New York: Doubleday, 1997.

Matera, Frank J., *Galatians.* Sacra Pagina, ed., D. J. Harrington, Collegeville, MN: Michael Glazier, 1992.

Ramsay, William M., *A Historical Commentary on St. Paul's Epistle to the Galatians.* New York: G. P. Putnams's Sons, 1900.

Galatians

Lee Martin McDonald

I. 1:1-5. Introduction to the Letter

In the ancient world, the introduction of a letter was known as its *exordium*, also as the *prooemium* or *principium*. It is common for scholars to use these terms to speak of the introduction to ancient letters, including Paul's letters. The introductions to ancient letters generally follow the guidelines set forth by Aristotle's (ca. 384-322 B.C.) *The Art of Rhetoric* and his *Rhetoric to Alexander*. Aristotle indicated that the most essential and special function of the exordium is to make clear what is the end or purpose of the speech; wherefore it should not be employed, if the subject is quite clear or unimportant. All the other forms of exordia in use are only remedies, and are common to all three branches of Rhetoric (*Rhetoric* 3.14.6-7, LCL; see also Cicero, *De inventione rhetorica* 1.15.20-17.25 and Quintilian, *Institutio oratoria* 4.1.1-79).

In the broad sense, rhetoric in the ancient world was simply an attempt through various conventions to use language in such a way that the hearers or readers would be influenced to think or act in a particular way. The same is true today and has always been the case since the beginning of human communication. Paul felt free to use the rhetorical conventions of his day, but when the situation called for something more creative or useful for his purposes, he often abandoned them, as when he spoke in the heat of emotion in this letter and 2 Cor. 10–13. In Paul's writings, literary conventions were not as carefully followed as we find in Hebrews, Luke–Acts, or even the letters of James and 1 Peter. Nevertheless, he had sufficient familiarity with those literary conventions even if he was not specifically trained in their use (2 Cor. 11:6). The letter to the Galatians shows both Paul's heated attack on those he believed were opponents of his gospel and who challenged his apostolic authority, during which his literary style is rather abrupt and in which some sentences or thoughts are not completed. In other instances he followed the more familiar Hellenistic conventions of his day when communicating with his Gentile audiences. He is also very familiar with the Hebrew Scriptures, as well as the various Jewish laws of observance and other traditions, and he often reflects on them in his presentations of the Christian message. On Paul's use of rhetoric, see Introduction, §6 above.

1:1-3. Paul, an apostle (not sent from men, nor through the agency of man, but through Jesus Christ, and God the Father, who raised Him from the dead), and all the brethren who are with me, to the churches of Galatia: Grace to you and peace from God our Father, and the Lord Jesus Christ. In typical Greco-Roman style of writing, Paul announces himself as the sender, along with those who are with him, and then moves to the greeting, "Grace to you and peace" which has specifically Jewish and

Christian connotations. The notions behind these terms as used by the Christians are unknown in the ancient literature. Usually, grace (*charis*) and peace (*eirene*) were personified in mythology as the two daughters of Zeus. Pindar (ca. 518-438 B.C.) writes in poetic fashion referring to these "Graces,"

> O Graces (*charites*), much sung queens and guardians of the ancient Minyai [= ancient inhabitants of Orchomenos, a town near the ancient Mycenean settlement on the Peloponnese], hear my prayer. For with your help all things pleasant and sweet come about for mortals, whether a man be wise, handsome, or illustrious. Yes, not even the gods arrange choruses or feasts with the august Graces [*Chariton*] . . . (*Olympian Odes* 14:1-9, LCL).

Philo (ca. 20 B.C.-A.D. 40), knowing this tradition, incorporates it into his story of the *Migration of Abraham*: "What fair thing, then, could fail when there was present God the Perfecter, with gifts of grace, His virgin daughters, whom the Father that begat them rears up uncorrupted and undefiled?" (*Migration* 31, LCL; For further discussion of these terms in the early church see Rom. 1:7 and 1 Cor. 1:3).

Epictetus (ca. A.D. 54-138) seemed to understand the nature of a divine mission and wrote of the divine empowerment of true Cynics to do it. After encouraging the one who might be discouraged over the hardships that come in life, he adds:

> In the next place, the true Cynic, when he is thus prepared, cannot rest contented with this, but he must know that he has been sent by Zeus [Greek = Dios *apestaltai*, from *apostello*] to men, partly as a messenger, in order to show them that in questions of good and evil they have gone astray, and are seeking the true nature of the good and the evil where it is not, but where it is they never think; and partly, in the words of

Diogenes, when he was taken off to Philip, after the battle of Chaeroncia, as a scout. (*Discourses* 3.23, LCL)

Dio Chrysostom (ca. A.D. 40-120) tells of the poet Hesiod's inspiration by the gods of poetry to enable him to write. He asks, "Is it really for these and similar reasons that Hesiod came to be regarded as a wise man among the Greeks and by no means unworthy of that reputation, as being one who composed and chanted his poems, not by human art, but because he had held converse with the Muses and had become a pupil of those very beings?" (*Orations* 77/78.1, LCL). Likewise, Plato (ca. 427-347 B.C.), telling the story of Socrates, told a learner of the sacred nature of a poet's work and the inspiration that the gods gave to him (Tynnichus) to enable him to do it. He tells of a certain Tynnichus, the Chalcidian,

> . . . who had never composed a single poem in his life that could deserve any mention, and then produced the paean [a hymn in honor of a god, usually Apollo] which is in everyone's mouth, almost the finest song we have, simply—as he says himself— "an invention of the Muses" [= the goddesses upon whom poets depended]. For the god, as it seems to me, intended him to be a sign to us that we should not waver or doubt that these fine poems are not human or the work of men, but divine and the work of gods; and that the poets are merely the interpreters of the gods, according as each is possessed by one of the heavenly powers. To show this, the god of set purpose sang the finest of songs through the meanest of poets . . . (*Ion* 534D-E, LCL).

For a more complete discussion of the style of letters in the ancient world, including the specific Christian contributions to it, see discussion of 1 Cor. 1:1-9. In this introduction, Paul is perhaps also addressing the criticism of him by his opponents, namely that his apostleship was "man-made" and emphasizes the divine agency of his calling. See 1:11-16 below where Paul elaborates on the origins of his call to be a special ambassador of Jesus Christ. On the meaning of "apostle," see the discussion in 1 Corinthians 1:1 (cf. also Rom. 1:1).

1:4-5. Who gave Himself for our sins, that He might deliver us out of this present evil age, according to the will of our God and Father, to whom be the glory forevermore. Amen. Paul reflects a dualistic perspective on the status of the present and the hope of deliverance from its evil in the age to come. Paul believed that the present evil age was under the power of Satan (4:3, 9; cf. 2 Cor. 4:4; Eph. 2:2:1-2). This perspective is also commonly called an apocalyptic theology, or perspective in which God will bring the present evil to an end and establish his own kingdom on the earth, and those who are faithful to God will be blessed forever in that kingdom. Divine deliverance from this evil age and the evil that is yet to come is a common theme in the New Testament (Mark 13:5-30; Matt. 24:3-34; Acts 1:6-7; 1 Thess. 1:1-10; 4:13–5:1-11; cf. 2 Peter 1:4; 3:10-12; Rev. 2:10; 3:10-11). Such views were quite common in the ancient world, especially in Iran, but they are also in the Bible (e.g., Dan., Isa. 24-26; and elsewhere). This conflict is often seen in cosmic terms and frequently has angels or gods at war with one another. This perspective was also present at Qumran, in which the Essenes were looking for a deliverer to help them escape the present evil and to become victors over such evil through the power of a coming king or messiah. In *The Rule of the Community*, for instance, we see this same dualism between good and evil.

In these lies the history of all men; in their (two) divisions all their armies have share by their generations; in their paths they walk; every deed they do falls into their divisions, dependent on what might be the birthright of the man, great or small, for all eternal time. For God has sorted them into equal parts until the last day and has put an everlasting loathing between their divisions . . . Until now the spirits of truth and of injustice feud in the heart of man and they walk in wisdom or in folly. In agreement with man's birthright in justice and in truth, so he abhors injustice; and according to his share in the lot of injustice he acts irreverently in it and so abhors truth. For God has sorted them into equal parts until the appointed end and the new creation. He knows the result of his deeds for all times [everlas]ting and has given them as a legacy to the sons of men so that they know good [and evil], so they decide the lot of every living being in compliance with the spirit there is in him [at the time of] the visitation (*Rule of the Community* [1QS 4.15-17a, 23b-26], Garcia Martinez trans. 7-8. See also 1QS 3:13-4:26 and Heraclitus, *Frg.* 53)

Amen is found several places in Paul's writings (Rom. 1:25; 9:5; 11:36 15:33—probably the original ending of Rom.; 16:27, Gal. 1:5; 6:18; Eph. 3:21; Phil. 4:20; cf. also 1 Tim. 1:17; 6:16; 2 Tim. 4:18), and, as in the OT where the word normally comes at the end of commands, blessings, curses, doxologies, and prayers, Paul has it here at the end of a doxology. It is not easy to translate the word uniformly in its Hebrew context in the Old Testament, but it is more likely to mean in various contexts "stand firm," "be faithful," "truly," "surely," or "so be it." In the New Testament, it is often used to conclude blessings and doxologies (Rom. 1:25; 9:5; 11:36; 15:33; Gal. 1:5; Phil. 4:20). It is sometimes a liturgical response of the church (1 Cor. 14:16; cf. 2 Cor. 1:20). The word is used 73 times in the gospels and elsewhere in the New Testament, with five exceptions (Heb. 13:21; 1 Peter 4:11; 5:11; 2 Peter 3:18; Jude 25). Fourteen uses are found in Paul and nine in Revelation. Early on, the Christians followed the Jewish tradition and adopted the term for the conclusion of all of their prayers, blessings, and doxologies.

II. HISTORICAL SECTION (1:6–2:21)

In this section, Paul gives the context for writing this letter along with the background for presenting his understanding of the gospel that he proclaimed.

A. 1:6-10. Occasion: The Judaizers and Paul's Demand for "No Other Gospel"

What is unusual about this passage is what is missing before it! The reason for these strong words is Paul's anger and dismay over the abandonment by some of his gospel for something that is not a gospel at all (v. 7), that has caused many of his converts to accept both circumcision and the various Jewish laws that were current among the Jews in Palestine in the first century. There is no thanksgiving in the introduction nor the prayer of gratitude for the readers from Paul, but rather a strong word of rebuke because of his disappointment with them. Indeed, this is the only letter of Paul's without a thanksgiving for the readers (see, for example Rom. 1:8-15; 1 Cor. 1:4-9; and elsewhere). While it is usual for writers in the ancient world to offer some gratitude for something about the recipient(s) of a letter, occasionally there is none. Aristotle indicated that there were three reasons for dispensing with the usual patterns of introductory comments in a speech or letter, these include: "(1) when our cause is discreditable, that is, when the subject itself alienates the hearer from us; (2) when the hearer has apparently been won over by the previous speakers of the opposition; (3) or when the hearer has become wearied by listening to the previous speakers" (*Rhetorica ad Herennium* 1.6.1, Betz trans.). Paul's situation falls most in the middle category since his readers have abandoned his message for another.

1:6-7. I am amazed that you are so quickly deserting Him who called you by the grace of Christ, for a different gospel; which is really not another; only there are some who are disturbing you, and want to distort the gospel of Christ. The Galatians' abandonment of Paul's gospel came rather quickly after he had visited

with them. Some scholars who accept that the letter was sent to the churches in North Galatia believe that this quick departure came after Paul's second, or even third, visit to the area (4:13 is taken to imply two visits or more; cf. Acts 16:6; 18:23). More likely, Paul is speaking to the churches he founded on his first missionary journey (Acts 13–14) that had abandoned his gospel shortly after he returned to Antioch of Syria (South Galatian theory, see introduction).

Deserting. The term Paul used for the Galatians' abandonment of their faith, *metatithesthe* is also used in 4:9 for those who wish to return to the weak and beggarly elements, that is, to bondage. The term is often used of those who change their minds, desert their faith, or convert to another religion. Josephus uses the same word for conversion: "When Izates had learned that his mother was very much pleased with the Jewish religion, he was zealous to convert [*metathesthai*] to it himself; and since he considered that he would not be genuinely a Jew unless he was circumcised, he was ready to act accordingly" (*Ant.* 20.38, LCL). Those who strayed from their faith were well-known in the ancient world and not much good was said about them. At Qumran, for instance, God

... has made known to the last generations what he had done for the last generation, the congregation of traitors. These are the ones who stray from the path. This is the time about which it has been written [Hos. 4:16] "Like a stray heifer so has Israel strayed," when the scoffer arose, who scattered the waters of lies over Israel and made them veer off into a wilderness without path, flattening the everlasting heights, diverging from tracks of justice and removing the boundary with which the very first had marked their inheritance, so that the curses of his covenant would adhere to them, to deliver them up to the sword carrying out the vengeance of the covenant (*The Damascus Document*, CD 1.11b-18a, Garcia Martinez trans. 33).

Those who turned from their faith were often called names in the ancient world, as in the case of Dionysius of Heraclea (ca. 330-250 B.C.) who was called a "renagade" for giving up the doctrines of the Stoics. Because of his problems with ophthalmia—a painful inflammation of the eyes, he became an Epicurean. Diogenes Laertius calls him a "Renegade" who "declared that pleasure was the end of action . . . for so violent was his suffering that he could not bring himself to call pain a thing indifferent" (*Lives of Eminent Philosophers* 7.166; see also 5.92; Athenaeus, *Deipnosophistae* 7.281D-E; cf. 10.437E).

Gospel. Paul's familiar choice of terms to speak of the message that he proclaimed about Jesus was already a well-known word in the Greco-Roman world. The Greek noun for gospel is *euangelion*, in its neuter singular noun form, means "good news," or "glad tiding" and its verb form *euangelidzomai*, "I preach / proclaim good news" or "glad tidings." The plural form of the noun was much more familiar to the Greek speaking communities where Paul preached, however, and the connotation was significantly different from the way he used the term. In the Greek translation of the Old Testament (the LXX, or Septuagint), the noun is found in Isa. 52:7 (in the plural form) and the verb form in Joel 3:5. The verb was used in both the second and third parts of Isaiah (40:9; 52:7 [see Rom. 10:15]; and 61:1, which is cited by Jesus in Luke 4:18), and the noun is found in 2 Kings 4:10, 18:22, 25. In these cases the focus of the verb is upon bringing news or a message, and the noun stresses primarily that a message or news was present (the feminine form, *euangelia*, is found in 2 Kings 18: 20, 27; 2 Chron. 7:10.) In the LXX of Ps. 68:12 (= LXX 67:12), the "glad tidings" are linked to the giving of the law.

The term "gospel" gradually began to be the name that was used to designate the "gospels," but that was not so at the beginning.

The canonical gospels were written well before the term "gospel" was applied to them in the second century A.D., but perhaps the first writing to call itself a "gospel" is the writing called the *Gospel of Thomas*, which may be as early as the late first or early second century A.D. The word, however, was not invented by the early Christians but already had a long history of use in the Old Testament and the pagan world prior to the time of Jesus.

As mentioned in the Introduction (§6), *euangelion* was commonly used in reference to the emperors who brought "glad tidings" to the people by their birth and life. It was used in reference to the Roman emperor, Augustus (Octavian). An inscription found at Priene in Asia Minor dating from the year 9 B.C., celebrates the birthday of Augustus (Octavian), whom divine providence has sent as a "savior" to bring wars to an end and peace to the whole world. Part of the Priene inscription reads as follows:

> Everyone may rightly consider this event as the origin of their life and existence. Providence has marvelously raised up and adorned human life by giving us Augustus . . . to make him the benefactor of mankind, our saviour, for us and for those who will come after us. But the birthday of the god [Augustus] was for the world the beginning of the joyful messages [*euangeliwn*, plural] which have gone forth because of him . . . . (*OGIS* 458; for the entire text, see 2.48–60).

The plural form of the word would have been quite familiar to those who heard Paul preach, but the content of his message had no parallel in the Greco-Roman world. The Christian writings that we know by the name gospels were intended by the earliest Christian communities and those that passed them on to others to proclaim that there was "good news" about Jesus Christ within them, rather than about the emperor. Although, as we have mentioned, early Christians were no doubt influenced in their use of the term gospel or "good news" by imperial propaganda, for them the locus of the good news was in the exalted Jesus rather than in the emperor. Paul uses the term similarly when he says in Rom. 1:1-2 that he is set apart for the "good news" ("glad tiding") of God, promised beforehand through his prophets regarding his son. Paul uses the term to designate the specific oral Christian tradition that was shared in the Christian communities about God's activity in the death and resurrection of Jesus (1 Cor. 15:1–5), but also his coming or *parousia* (1 Cor. 15:23–28).

The preaching of the early Church focused on Jesus, his deeds, and the presence of the kingdom of God in his words and deeds. Also, when Mark began his gospel with the words, "The beginning of the gospel [*euangelion*] of Jesus Christ, the Son of God," he was not referring to a book, but rather to the proclamation of the coming of the kingdom of God through the life, ministry, passion, and resurrection of Jesus that was already being proclaimed in the early churches before he began writing his book. His gospel, which was the first written story of Jesus' ministry, passion and resurrection, used the term *euangelion* in the new sense in which the story of Jesus was understood as "good news."

Paul is the first known writer to use this term to identify his proclamation about Jesus, but he may not have been the originator of this use. In the rest of this letter, the noun form is found in 1:7, 11; 2:2, 5, 7, 14. Some three-fourths of the more than sixty occurrences of this word in the New Testament are in Paul's writings (twelve times in the gospels, two times in Acts, one in 1 Peter and 1 in the book of Revelation). We cannot tell from Galatians what Paul's original message to them was, but a look at his other letters gives a good indication (see, for example, 1 Cor. 15:3-5; Rom. 10:9-10; cf. Rom. 5:1-10). The term appears to refer to both the preaching and the content of what was preached in the writings of Paul (Rom. 15:19; 1 Cor. 9:12; 2 Cor. 2:12; 9:13; 10:14; Phil. 1:27; 1 Thess. 3:2.) Whether there was one gospel for the circumcised and another for the uncircumcised (see the possibilities in 2:7 below), is doubtful even if popular among some modern scholars who want to present two ways to heaven. There is no evidence that Paul saw two different gospels, but rather one way, even if Jews who followed Jesus continued practicing the works of the law. He made it clear that both Jews and Gentiles were sinners and under God's judgment, but that God's gift for both was by faith through Jesus Christ (Rom. 3–5). For Paul, "in Christ" there were no distinctions between Jew and Gentile. There is no indication that he preached a different gospel in the synagogues than the one he preached outside the synagogues. Indeed, he began in the synagogues in most of his ministry and there is nothing to suggest that he thought that his gospel was only for Gentiles.

1:8-9. But even though we, or an angel from heaven, should preach to you a gospel contrary to that which we have preached to you, let him be accursed. As we have said before, so I say again now, if any man is preaching to you a gospel contrary to that which you received, let him be accursed. The language of this "double" curse is very much in keeping with typical Jewish curses in Paul's day. For those who followed his gospel, peace and blessing are bestowed, but not to those who preach another gospel. A familiar curse against those disobedient to God's law is found at Qumran. After offering a blessing for those who are obedient to the ways of God, the writer then turns his attention to the disobedient saying:

> And the levites shall curse all the men of the lot of Belial. They shall begin to speak and shall say: "Accursed are you for all your wicked, blameworthy deeds. May he (God) hand you over to dread into the hands of all those carrying out acts of vengeance. Accursed, without mercy, for the darkness of your

deeds, and sentenced to the gloom of everlasting fire. May God not be merciful when you entreat him, nor pardon you when you do penance for your faults. May he lift the countenance of his anger to avenge himself on you, may there be no peace for you in the mouth of those who intercedes." And all those who enter the covenant shall say, after those who pronounce blessings and those who pronounce curses: "Amen, Amen." [blank] And the priests and the levites shall continue, saying: "Cursed by the idols which his heart reveres whoever enters this covenant leaving his guilty obstacle in front of himself to fall over it. When he hears the words of this covenant, he will congratulate himself in his heart, saying: 'I will have peace, in spite of my walking in the stubbornness of my heart.' However, his spirit will be obliterated, the dry with the moist, mercilessly. May God's anger and the wrath of his verdicts consume him for everlasting destruction. May all the curses of this covenant stick fast to him. May God segregate him for evil, and may he be cut off from the midst of all the sons of light because of his straying from following god on account of his idols and his blameworthy obstacle. May he assign his lot with the cursed ones for ever." And all those who enter the covenant shall begin speaking and shall say after them: "Amen, Amen." (*The Rule of the Community*, 1QS 2.4-18, Garcia Martinez trans.).

Toward the end of the first century A.D., Rabban Gamaliel II required the Jews to recite the *Eighteen Benedictions*, also known as the *Shemoneh Esre*, and more recently the *Amidah* (Hebrew = "standing") (see *m. Berakoth* 4.3). Among the *Eighteen Benedictions*, the twelfth is a curse upon the Christians and "apostates" or "heretics." In that benediction, we read:

For apostates let there be no hope, and the dominion of arrogance [Rome] do Thou speedily root out in our days; and let the Nazarenes [Christians] and the heretics perish as in a moment, let them be blotted out of the book of the living and let them not be written with the righteous. Blessed art Thou, O Lord, who humblest the arrogant! (Trans. supplied by E. Ferguson, *Backgrounds* 543-544).

It was not unusual for curses to be pronounced in Paul's day, and he concludes that those who would pervert his gospel were accursed by God. In the famous so-called "Hippocratic Oath" (Hippocrates lived ca. 469-399 B.C.) that has been appealed to for centuries as a standard for physicians' ethics, a covenant was made between "Apollo, the Physician, Aesclepius and Hygeia" that read: "If I fulfill this oath and do not violate it, it may be granted to me to enjoy life and art, being honored with fame among all men for all time to come; if I transgress it and swear falsely, may the opposite of all of this be my lot" (*The Hippocratic Oath*, Ludwig Edelstein, trans. BHM 1, 2-3).

1:10. For am I now seeking the favor of men, or of God? Or am I striving to please men? If I were still trying to please men, I would not be a bond-servant of Christ. Paul uses a familiar Greek word, *peitho*, to speak of his seeking to please men or God. This word was used by Plato to speak of the art of persuasion. When Socrates asks Gorgias what the greatest good is, he replies: "I call it the ability to persuade with speeches either judges in the law courts or statesmen in the council-chamber or the commons in the Assembly or an audience at any other meeting that may be held on public affairs" (*Gorgias* 452E, LCL). Socrates asks him to clarify what he means by the goal of rhetoric being to persuade others and eventually agrees with Gorgias (*Gorgias* 454BC). Later, Plato tells of Socrates trying to distinguish for his pupil, Theaetetus, the difference between persuasion through the art of rhetoric and the art of teaching. He indicated that it was easier to persuade than to teach and also shows that there is greater value in teaching. Perhaps he is already aware of the suspicions people have of the "smooth talker" who persuades, but does not teach (see *Theaetetus* 201A-202C). He concludes that "true opinion accompanied by reason is knowledge" (202C, LCL).

In time, this word was equated with those who use rhetoric to control and even to deceive others for their own ends (Plato, *Sophist* 222C; cf. also *Apology* 17A, 18A). It is not clear how Paul could have been accused of trying to "persuade God," but Plato does use the term *peitho* in this manner. For example, Plato accuses the sophists of being like soothsayers who are masters of spells and enchantments that "constrain [*peithontes*, 'persuade'] the gods to serve their ends" (*Republic* 364C, LCL). When a man asked Antisthenes (ca. 200-180 B.C.) what he should teach his son, Antisthenes responded, "if you want him to live together with the gods, a philosopher; if, however, with men, a rhetorician" (*Gnom.Vatic.* 7, Betz trans. 55). The associations with this word, *peitho*, were not good in Paul's day and to be accused of trying to persuade either men or God was, for Paul, an insult.

Paul refers to himself as a bond-servant of Christ (Rom. 1:1; Phil. 1:1; cf. Titus 1:1) but also of others who are faithful servants of Christ (Rom. 6:16; 1 Cor. 7:22; Col. 4:12). This term appears to be for Paul a description of all who are faithful followers of Christ.

B. 1:11-24. How Paul Became an Apostle

Paul begins a new thought here as he defends his gospel from the charge of being called a "human" proclamation and not valid. He has stated that he is not a "man-pleaser" and his only purpose is to serve Christ. Now he describes more carefully how he came to faith in Jesus as the Messiah and what happened to him afterwards. He is especially anxious to lead up to the point that both he and his gospel were

presented to the leaders in the church and that they accepted both him and his message (2:1-10). This section is most important for understanding what happened to Paul in his call to follow Christ and to preach his gospel.

1:11. For I would have you know, brethren, that the gospel which was preached by me is not according to man. Paul does not state here what his gospel is because he can assume that his readers have already heard it and they received it. Here he claims that his gospel, like his apostleship (1:1) is not of human origin (see this same claim in 3:15; Rom. 3:5; 1 Cor. 3:3; 9:8; 15:32; 1 Peter 4:6), but has a divine origin. Earlier Plato tells of Socrates' defense before the council that was seeking to kill him saying that the words he gave were not merely human, but rather: "the word I speak is not mine, but the speaker to whom I shall refer it is a person of weight. For of my wisdom—if it is wisdom at all—and of its nature, I will offer you the god of Delphi [= Apollo] as a witness" (*Apology* 20E, LCL). In support of his wisdom as the greatest on earth, he appeals to an oracle from Delphi who will testify that a divine message from Apollo confirms that it is Socrates (*Apology* 21A).

1:12 For I neither received it from man, nor was I taught it, but I received it through a revelation of Jesus Christ. Paul is saying that receiving something from God is superior to receiving it from man. Plato agrees with this and claims that the ancients also agreed saying that "as prophecy (*mantike*) is superior to augury [one who determines the will of God by watching birds], both in name and in fact, in the same proportion madness, which comes from god, is superior to sanity, which is of human origin" (*Phaedrus* 244D, LCL).

In terms of the revelation that Paul received, observe that he speaks similarly elsewhere both of this revelation from God and the mystery of God being revealed (see Eph. 1:9,

17; 3:4-6; Col. 1:26; 2:2). There are interesting accounts of the appearance of the risen Christ to Peter accompanied by his commissioning to preach (John 21:15-19). Interestingly, in the apocryphal *Gospel of the Hebrews*, we hear of the appearance of the risen Christ to James.

And when the Lord had given the linen cloth to the servant of the priest, he went to James and appeared to him. For James had sworn that he would not eat bread from that hour in which he had drunk the cup of the Lord until he should see him risen from among them that sleep [see Mark 14:22, 25; 1 Cor. 1:23-25]. And shortly thereafter the Lord said: Bring a table and bread! And immediately it is added: he took the bread, blessed it and brake it and gave it to James the Just and said to him: My brother, eat thy bread, for the Son of man is risen from among them that sleep (Located in Jerome, *De viris illustribus* 2, Trans. by *NT APO* 1:178).

There are other such stories of a revelation from the risen Lord, as in the case of the revelation to James and Peter in the second century Gnostic Apocryphon of James. After giving them commands to follow, the risen Lord departed from them. After this the rest of the disciples called them and asked:

"What did you (pl.) hear from the Master? And what has he said to you? And where did he go?" But we answered them, "He has ascended and has given us a pledge and promised life to us all and revealed to us children (?) who are to come after us, after bidding [us] love them, as we would be [saved] for their sakes."

And when they heard (this), they indeed believed the revelation, but were displeased about those to be born (*Ap. Jas.* 15.30-16.5, NHL 36-37).

In the early church, if a void occurred or if something happened but was not told in the Scriptures, eventually someone filled in the gap with apocryphal stories whether about Jesus' childhood, secret meetings with well-known biblical figures, or such like. Paul tells his own story about a revelation from the risen Lord to him. See discussion of this revelation in v. 15 below.

1:13-14. For you have heard of my former manner of life in Judaism, how I used to persecute the church of God beyond measure, and tried to destroy it; and I was advancing in Judaism beyond many of my contemporaries among my countrymen, being more extremely zealous for my ancestral traditions. Paul begins the story of his revelation from Christ by sharing how his life was before this encounter. Paul does not often discuss his life before his encounter with the risen Lord (see 1 Cor. 15:8-10; 2 Cor. 11:21b-22; Phil. 3:2-6; cf. Acts 21:39–22:5; 26:4-11; 1). The Galatians had already heard of Paul's remarkable story, but he summarizes it here for them to make sure that they can put the story of his revelation from the risen Lord into its appropriate context. Demosthenes (ca. 384-322 B.C.) does something similar at the beginning of a narration: "to remind you of the position of affairs in those days, so that you may consider each transaction with due regard to its occasion" (*On the Crown* 17, LCL).

Paul uses the term "Judaism" (*Ioudaïsmo*), a Jewish-Hellenistic term for the beliefs and life of the Jewish community, to speak of his past. It is found in the New Testament only in these two verses and in 2:14 (*Ioudaïkos / Ioudaïdzein* = "to live like the Jews"), but is the manner of life that he lived prior to his conversion and illustrated in the accounts of his former life noted above. It is used in the first century before Christ by the author of *2 Maccabees*.

The story of Judas Macabeus and his brothers, and the purification of the great temple, and the dedication of the altar, and further the wars against Antiochus Epiphanes and his son Eupator, and the appearances that came from heaven to those who fought bravely for

Judaism . . . " (*2 Macc.* 2:19-21, NRSV; cf. also 8:1; 14:38; *4 Macc.* 4:26).

The term is also found in early Christian literature, as in the case of Ignatius' *Letter to the Philadelphians* (ca. 115-117) when he contrasts Judaism and Christianity: "But if anyone interpret Judaism [*ioudaïsmon*] to you do not listen to him; for it is better to hear Christianity [*christianismon*] from the circumcised than Judaism [*ioudaïsmon*] from the uncircumcised" (*Philad.* 6.1, LCL). The term is also found in his *Letter to the Magnesians* where he cautions those who might be led "astray" by hearing the teachings of Judaism: "Be not led astray by strange doctrines or by old fables which are profitless. For if we are living until now according to Judaism, we confess that we have not received grace" (*Magn.* 8.1, LCL; see also 10:3). In all cases, the term refers to the life and beliefs of the Jewish religion.

Paul's reference to his persecution of the church is found in several places in the New Testament (Acts 8:1-3; 9:1-2, 4-5; 22:4-8; 26:9-15; 1 Cor. 15:9; Phil. 3:6; 1 Tim. 1:13) and no one seriously questions that this was characteristic of his zeal for the law prior to his encounter with the risen Lord. His "zeal" in doing this was characteristic of those who were committed to making sure that Jews were faithful observers of the law. There was an antecedent who was highly praised for his zeal for the law that led him to kill a Jew who made sacrifice at the order of the evil Seleucid kin, Antiochus Ephiphansses (ca. 167 B.C.).

After killing the Jew, he also slew the king's officer who forced the man to make the sacrifice, and then he tore down the altar. After this we read: "thus he burned with zeal for the law, just as Phinehas did against Zimri son of Salu [Num. 25:6-15]. Then Mattathias cried out in the town with a loud voice, saying: "Let every one who is zealous for the law and supports the covenant come out with me!" (*1 Macc.* 2:25-27, NRSV)

This model of zeal for the law was power-ful among the Jews in the first century and even Josephus, in the last part of the first century A.D., tells this same story with pride of the Jews' zeal for the law (*Ant.* 12.268-278). Philo, Paul's contemporary, tells of the zeal of Jews for the law and their willingness to put to death those that they believed were speaking contrary to it. He tells of the many Jews who are willing to carry out such a sentence because of their zeal for the laws:

> For there are thousands who have their eyes upon him [God] full of zeal for the laws, strictest guardians of the ancestral institutions, merciless to those who do anything to subvert them. Otherwise we must suppose that while it is right to seek the death of one who dishonours a father or a mother, more moderation should be shewn when impious men dishonour the name which is more glorious than majesty itself. Yet none is so foolish as to visit the lesser offenses with death and spare those who are guilty of the greater; and the sacrilege involved in reviling or outraging parents is not so great as that committed by perjury against the sacred title of God (*Special Laws* 2.253-254, LCL).

Concern for the ancestral traditions was not only found among the Jews, but also among the Greeks. Speaking of the Spartan culture, Plato praises the education and commitment to it in his day.

> . . . you can tell what I say is true and that the Spartans have the best education in philosophy and argument by this: if you choose to consort with the meanest of Spartans, at first you will find him making a poor show in the conversation; but soon, at some point or other in the short and compressed—a deadly shot that makes his interlocutor seem like a helpless child. Hence this very truth has been observed by certain persons both in our day and in former

times—that the Spartan cult is much more the pursuit of wisdom than of athletics; for they know that a man's ability to utter such remarks is to be ascribed to his perfect education. [He then names several Spartans and says of them:] All these were enthusiasts, lovers and disciples of the Spartan culture; and you can recognize that character in their wisdom by the short memorable sayings that fell from each of them: they assembled together and dedicated these as the first-fruits of their lore to Apollo in his Delphic temple, inscribing there those maxims which are on every tongue— "Know thyself" and "Nothing overmuch" (Plato, *Protagoras* 342D-E, 343AB, LCL).

1:15-17. But when He who had set me apart, even from my mother's womb, and called me through His grace, was pleased to reveal His Son in me, that I might preach Him among the Gentiles, I did not immediately consult with flesh and blood, nor did I go up to Jerusalem to those who were apostles before me; but I went away to Arabia, and returned once more to Damascus. This is one of the most important passages in Paul's letters that tells the story of what happened to Paul that changed his former conduct into an ardent follower and advocate of Jesus Christ. This took place "when it pleased [*eudokesen*] God," a reference to God's decision in the matter of Paul's transformation (see also 1 Cor. 1:21; Col. 1:19). The reference to his being "set apart from his mother's womb" is reflective of Jer. 1:5, but see also Isa. 42:6; 49:1, 5-6. The Jews at Qumran also used similar language to describe God's activity in their lives.

You created breath on the tongue, you know its words, you instituted the fruits of lips before they came to be; you placed a rhythm for words, and a cadence to the puff of breath from the lips; you may the rhythms emerge by their mysteries and the puffs of breaths by their measures to declare your glory and tell your wonders, in all the deeds of your truth and of your just judgments, to praise your name through the mouth of all. And they will know you by their intellect and they will bless you for everlasting centuries (*The Hymns*, 1QH 9.28-31, Garcia Martinez trans. 327).

In me (Greek = *en emoi*; v.16). There is much debate over the correct translation of these words. Translators are divided over whether these words are a simple dative and can be translated "to me," or, whether they reflect a mystical experience for Paul and are therefore translated "in me." The issue is not settled by the immediate context and must be settled with reference to other texts that speak of Paul's encounter with the risen Lord (1 Cor. 9:1; 15:8). Those who argue that Paul had a visionary experience on the Damascus road (Acts 9:3-9; 22:6-16; 26:12-18) prefer the more literal translation, "in me." Those who prefer more substantive appearances, namely bodily appearances, translate these words as "to me."

The word "**immediately**" (*eutheos*, or "at once") often appears elsewhere in "call" narratives in the New Testament, and even where the word is not used, the notion of an immediate response to follow Christ is present (Mark 1:17-18; 11:2-4; Matt. 4:20, 22; 2:13-14; Luke 9:59-62).

Arabia. This is likely a reference to the Nabataean Kingdom in Petra, that was referred to by Paul as the "province of Arabia," and the likely location from which Damascus itself was ruled at the beginning of Paul's ministry by King Aretas (ca. 9 B.C.-A.D. 40). See discussion in 2 Cor. 11:32. While it is often pointed out that the Nabataean Kingdom did not fall under Roman rule until A.D. 170, when it was officially called Arabia, Paul nevertheless still referred to it as Arabia.

Damascus was a large Hellenistic city in the

first century, but it also had a large Jewish community living there. Josephus tells of the community of Jews who lived there during the outbreak of the A.D. 66-70 Jewish rebellion against Rome. Because the Jews had killed many Romans in Jerusalem and during their retreat to Caesarea Maritima, those residents at Damascus in anger wanted to hold the Jews there accountable. According to Josephus,

> ... the people of Damascus, learning of the disaster which had befallen the Romans, were fired with a determination to kill the Jews who resided among them ... In the end, they fell upon the Jews, cooped up as they were and unarmed, and within one hour slaughtered them all with impunity, to the number of ten thousand five hundred. (*Jewish War* 2.559-561, LCL).

1:18. Then three years later I went up to Jerusalem to become acquainted with Cephas, and stayed with him fifteen days. With this passage, we come to several important questions in regard to the chronology of the New Testament period surrounding the ministry of Paul and the life-setting of the early church. Paul makes it clear that his call to follow Jesus came while he was persecuting the church (1:13, 17), and for three years after that he was ministering in and around Damascus and Arabia. He escaped Damascus by being lowered over the wall in a basket when his life was threatened (see 2 Cor. 11:32-33). From there he came to Jerusalem and spent fifteen days with Peter (Cephas) and departed Jerusalem for the more safe regions of Syria and Cilicia for fourteen years (2:1). The difficulty comes in knowing the point when Paul started the fourteen years. Are they to start fourteen years after his conversion/call or fourteen years after he left the two-week visit with Peter? The former is easier to fit into circumstances prior to the Acts 15 council (Acts 15), but it is not easy to merge the chronology

of Acts with the chronology of Paul's letters. If the book of Galatians was written to the churches in South Galatia that Paul and Barnabas founded on their first missionary journey (Acts 13-14), and that journey was soon followed by an open "council" meeting in Jerusalem involving the apostles and elders of the church (Acts 15) —an event that took place no later than A.D. 48-49, then one can arrive at some important probable dates. If one subtracts the fourteen years of 2:1 as well as the three years of 1:18, and the conversion or call of Paul was probably sometime around A.D. 31-32 and no later than 33. If the three years are a part of the fourteen and the starting time of the fourteen is the call of Paul on the Damascus Road, then his conversion is roughly A.D. 34-35.

A problem arises in equating the "private meeting" (Gal. 2:1-10) with the "open council meeting" (Acts 15), but if they are different meetings, the private one surely must have taken place just prior to the open meeting. All of this poses some awkward fitting of the two chronologies together. One important question is whether the confrontation that Paul had with Peter took place before or after the council meeting in Acts 15. One of the problems with our understanding here has to do with the abbreviated stories both in Acts and in Galatians. The recipients probably knew the more complete picture since Paul had shared it with them before. He is only rehearsing some aspects of it here. See discussion in the introduction for more detail here, but the problems appear fewer if the South Galatian destination is adopted rather than the North Galatian.

Cephas. This is the Aramaic name that Jesus gave to Simon Peter or "Simon the son of John" (John 1:42) and it means "rock." The Greek equivalent is "Peter." This is the same as Simon bar Jona (or "son of Jona") (Matt. 16:17; John 1:43; 21:15-17). He was the leading figure in Jesus' inner circle of "Peter, James, and John" and, until the events of Acts 12 when he fled Jerusalem for safety following his escape from prison, he held the leading role in the church in Jerusalem. After that, James emerges as the leader of that church. Paul identifies him by his Aramaic name, Cephas. See 2 Peter 1:1 where the name appears as "Simeon Peter." His death is anticipated in John 21:18-19 and according to later tradition, he died during Nero's persecution of the Christians in Rome. Clement of Rome (ca. A.D. 90) says of his death, "Peter, who because of unrighteous jealousy suffered not one or two but many trials, and having thus given his testimony went to the glorious place which was his due" (1 Clem 5.4, LCL). Paul met and stayed with him for fifteen days when he went to Jerusalem for the first time following his conversion experience.

1:19-20. But I did not see any other of the apostles except James, the Lord's brother. (Now in what I am writing to you, I assure you before God that I am not lying.) The issue that Paul is addressing is not clear, but obviously someone had suggested that he had met with more than Peter and James. Perhaps the context of a later meeting of several individuals, including the apostles and elders of the church (as recounted by Luke, in Acts 15:1-29), is what lies behind this strong assertion ("I am not lying"). There appears to be some accusation that more were at this meeting.

James. The James mentioned here is the brother of Jesus and the likely author of the letter of James. Like Paul, he came to follow Jesus as the Messiah through a resurrection appearance (1 Cor. 15:7) and came to special prominence in the church soon thereafter. His presence in the early church is quite significant and he was able to influence not only the Jerusalem church, but elsewhere as well. The recognition of his authority by both Peter and Barnabas is seen in 2:11-12 below. He is mentioned in a special class of Jesus' brothers in 1 Cor. 9:5, but also appears to have been considered an apostle by Paul (v. 19 and also 1 Cor. 15:7). Against this is the introduction to the letter of James where the author identifies himself only as "a servant of God and of the Lord Jesus Christ." According to Josephus, James was put to death by Ananus, the high priest.

Possessed of such a character, Ananus thought that he had a favorable opportunity because Festus was dead and Albinus was still on the way. And so he convened the judges of the Sanhedrin and brought before them a man named James, the brother of Jesus who was called the Christ, and certain others. He accused them of having transgressed the law and delivered them up to be stoned. Those of the inhabitants of the city who were considered the most fair-minded and who were strict in observance of the law were offended at this (Ant. 20.200-201, LCL).

Although a few scholars have questioned the authenticity of this passage, unlike the one in Ant. 18.63-64, which apparently has Christian interpolations in it, this one is straightforward and does not overly praise James, but only identifies him. It is likely authentic. His attention to faithful keeping of the law also fits with the image of him in Acts, where he is seen as anxious about Paul keeping the law (21:18-21). Why James was chosen for the leading role in Jerusalem when John was there is not known. After Peter's departure from Jerusalem (Acts 12:19), John is no longer mentioned, and given his close association with Jesus and being in the inner circle of Peter, James and John, he would seem an obvious choice. On the other hand, since there was growing unrest in Palestine on the part of the zealots who were insisting on strict keeping of the law, James who was known for his strictness in matters of the law and piety would make some sense in his selection. This is speculation, of course, but there are no documents that present a rationale for passing over John. A Jewish Christian, James was an acknowledged prominent figure in second-century Jewish Christianity long after his death. In the Pseudo-Clementine literature of the second century, there is a *Letter of Clement to James* that addresses James in laudatory terms:

> Clement to James, the lord and bishop of bishops, who governs the holy church of the Hebrews at Jerusalem and those which by the providence of God have been well founded everywhere, together with the presbyters and deacons and all the other brethren (*Epistula Clementis* 1.1, *NT APO* 2:496-97).

There is also a well-known gnostic writing attributed to him that comes from the second century called the *Apocryphon of James* that speaks of a special appearance of Jesus to James and Peter some 550 days after his resurrection. The risen Lord invites both Peter and James to ascend with him into the heavens. After his departure, they:

> . . . sent our heart(s) upwards to heaven. We heard with our ears, and saw with our eyes, the noise of wars and a trumpet blare and a great turmoil. And when we had passed beyond that place, we sent our mind(s) farther upward and saw with our eyes and heard with our ears hymns and angelic benedictions and angelic rejoicing. And heavenly majesties were singing praise, and we too rejoiced (*Apoc. Jas.* 15.7-24, NHL 36).

1:21. Then I went into the regions of Syria and Cilicia. This agrees with Acts 9:30 that tells that Paul went to Tarsus to protect himself from the angry Jews in Jerusalem. Tarsus was the birthplace of Paul and the capital of Cilicia. While no one knows for sure what he was doing there for some ten to fourteen years, given his zeal for proclaiming the gospel, it is likely that he was involved in some sort of Christian ministry in a place which was familiar to him. What took place there is unknown, but when the church at Antioch of Syria began to attract many Gentiles to faith in Christ, Barnabas knew

where to find him to get him involved in the ministry (Acts 11:25-26).

C. 2:1-10. Paul's Message Accepted in Jerusalem.

Paul continues his narrative on the origin of his gospel and its acceptance by the leaders of the church in Jerusalem. Their acceptance not only provided support for the message Paul had proclaimed to the Galatians, but also showed the unity of the church that was so essential to Paul. As he describes his second visit to Jerusalem flowing his conversion/call, he shares with his readers that they recognized that God had called him with the proclamation to the Gentiles. Interestingly, Paul does not say that the leaders, "James, Cephas, and John" also recognized his apostleship (2:7), but he emphasizes the key ingredients of the meeting: that he, Barnabas, and Titus were well received, that Titus, a Gentile, was not compelled to be circumcised, that his mission to the Gentiles was recognized by them, and that he was committed to remembering the poor. His use of the word "then" (*epeita*) in 1:18, 21, and in 2:1 is to be taken in its temporal and chronological meaning.

It was important for Paul to establish for his readers what precisely happened and when it happened. He appears to be establishing the context for his confrontation with Peter (2:11-14) that may well have led to his separation from the church at Antioch in Syria and also the justification for his actions in this regard. It is likely, given the summarizing depiction of the confrontation, that his readers were already aware of this story and perhaps it had been used by the "Judaizers," who were teaching them a false gospel, to justify their own position regarding the keeping of the Law and especially the need to submit to circumcision.

Even a casual reading of this section shows that the sentence structure is not up to the standards that Paul normally uses in writing. In vv. 4-5 and again in vv. 6-9, Paul has committed what have been dubbed "syntactical slips" because he makes sentences without consistent attention to their structure. Indeed, he does not complete the sentences or changes thoughts before completing them. While he is making a statement, something else comes to his mind and he says it (v. 6). These are known as "anacoluthons" and they tend to be present in highly emotional speech. The style, though choppy, does reflect the anguish and emotion that Paul was facing in writing this letter. The change in focus in a sentence comes when Paul mentions individuals who have caused him anguish.

2:1. Then after an interval of fourteen years I went up again to Jerusalem with Barnabas, taking Titus along also. On the importance and meaning of the "fourteen years," see discussion in 1:18, 21 above. Paul, Barnabas, and Titus have come to Jerusalem representing the church at Antioch that was involved in the Gentile mission (Acts 11:19-26; 13:1–14:28). On the use of "I went up . . . to Jerusalem," (or "I went down from Jerusalem") see discussion of Acts 8:5; 11:2; 18:22.

Barnabas. The book of Acts has much to say about this man who was responsible for introducing Paul to the Christians in Jerusalem and involving him in the mission to the Gentiles in Antioch and on their first missionary journey. He was a Levite from Cyprus who sold his farm and gave the proceeds to the church to care for those in need. As a well-respected leader in the church at Jerusalem, he was sent to Antioch to investigate what was happening in the Gentile mission of that church. He became a leading spokesperson in that church as well and as he was convinced of the validity of their ministry to Gentiles, he found Paul and brought him to Antioch and involved him in that work. Barnabas was so trusted by the Antioch Christians that they also sent him and Paul with funds from their church to assist the Christians in Jerusalem during the famine in Jerusalem (cf. Acts 4:36;

9:27; 11:22, 30; 12:25; 13:1, 2, 7, 43, 46, 50; 14:12, 14, 20; 15:2, 12, 22, 25, 35, 36, 37, 39). He also represented the church at Antioch, along with Paul, during this "private" meeting in Jerusalem (Gal. 2:1) but also later at the more inclusive council meeting (Acts 15:2). He and Paul separated over the issue of Mark's failure on their first missionary journey and Paul's unwillingness to take him on their second (Acts 15:36-39; cf. 13:13-14). Outside of Acts and Galatians (2:1, 9, 13), he is only mentioned two times in the rest of the New Testament (1 Cor. 9:6 and Col. 4:10), but there are several references to him in the extra-canonical literature. In Acts, along with Paul, he is called an "apostle" (Acts 14:4, 14), but this is the only place where this is mentioned.

The *Epistle of Barnabas*, a late-first-century to early-second-century anonymous document in the form of a letter, was produced to warn Christians against a Judaistic understanding of the Scriptures (Hebrew Bible) and interprets its message allegorically very much like Philo of Alexandria did. The letter was widely accepted as having come from Barnabas, the companion of Paul, and was often quoted as "scripture" in many churches well into the fourth century A.D. According to Clement of Alexandria (ca. A.D. 170), Barnabas was "one of the seventy" that Jesus sent out to preach (Luke 10:1) and also a "fellow worker of Paul" (*Stromata* 2.20). Later Eusebius (ca. A.D. 320) supports this tradition: " . . . no list of the Seventy is anywhere extant. It is said, however, that one of them was Barnabas, and of him the Acts of the Apostles has also made special mention" (*Ecclesiastical History* 1.12.1, LCL; see also 2.1.4). Clement of Alexander also believed that Barnabas was the author of the letter ascribed to him and cited it in an authoritative manner (*Str.* 2.20). In the *Pseudo-Clementine Recognitions*, perhaps a late-second- or third-century collection of texts that name Clement of Rome as its author, Barnabas is depicted as one who introduced Clement of Rome to the Christian faith and who later introduced him to Peter (*Ps. Clem. Recogn.* 1.7-13). Complete historical trustworthiness of that document is not generally considered tenable, but that there are some reliable traditions present in it is quite possible. Barnabas is described in it as "a Hebrew by name Barnabas, and stated that he belonged to the circle of disciples of that Son of God and had been sent to the end that he might proclaim this message to those who would hear it" (1.7.7, *NT Apo* 2.505-506). Like Paul, he is portrayed as one who "gives no evidence of schooling in grammar, but who communicates to you the divine commands in simple, artless words so that all hearers can follow and understand what is said" (1.9.4, *NT Apo* 2:506-507). Some early Christians believed that he was the author of the Book of Hebrews, but that was not a popular view.

Titus was a Gentile and fellow traveler on Paul's missionary journeys who became a Christian through Paul's ministry (according to Titus 1:4). Paul utilized him in the collection for the poor Christians in the church at Jerusalem (2 Cor. 2:13; 7:6, 13-14; 8:6, 16, 23; 12:18). He is not mentioned in the Book of Acts, but is identified as working in Dalmatia (2 Tim. 4:10) and was earlier (or later?) sent to Crete by Paul to strengthen the church (Titus 1:5-16). As we see in Gal. 2:1-3, he became a test case for Paul's position on Gentile freedom from the law (and circumcision). According to the church father Eusebius (ca. A.D. 320), Titus became bishop of the churches in Crete: "Thus Timothy is related to have been first appointed bishop of the diocese of Ephesus, as was Titus of the churches in Crete" (*Ecclesiastical History* 3.4.5, LCL).

2:2. And it was because of a revelation that I went up; and I submitted to them the gospel which I preach among the Gentiles, but I did so in private to those who were of reputation, for fear that I might be running, or had run, in vain. The primary concern here is the gospel that Paul preached to the Gentiles. There is no record of the content of his preaching to the Jews. Did he say the same thing to them about their obligation to keep the law and circumcision? There is no evidence that survives in either way, but what he concludes about the purpose and value of the law, as well as its limitations (chaps. 3–4), would certainly give rise to the accusation that he had taught that even the Jews could abandon it. This seems to have been Peter's practice too before those from James arrived in Antioch (2:14).

Paul reflects here the ancient practice of seeking a revelation from God (or the gods) before a major decision was made or action taken. As Xenophon (430-354 B.C.) was about to make an important decision that would have important consequences, he conferred with his friend Socrates, the famous teacher of Athens, who told him to journey to Delphi to receive instruction from the god Apollo on the matter of a journey he was to make. "So Xenophon went and asked Apollo to what one of the gods he should sacrifice and pray in order best and most successfully to perform the journey which he had in mind, and after meeting with good fortune, to return home in safety" (*Anabasis* 3.1.6, LCL). Likewise, Plutarch tells of a man who made a journey to offer libations (offerings) as the result of "certain vivid dreams and apparitions"(*On the Sign of Socrates* 579E, LCL). In telling the story of Balaam (Num. 22–24), Philo speaks of a seer who wanted to pose as a "distinguished prophet" and who indicated that he was acting on the basis of divine guidance, but who was wrong.

Enticed by those offers present and prospective, and in deference to the dignity of the ambassadors, he gave way, again dishonestly alleging a divine command. And so on the morrow he made his preparations for the journey, and talked of dreams in which he said he had been beset by visions so clear that they compelled him to stay no longer but follow the envoys. But, as he proceeded there was given to him on the road an unmistakable sign that the purpose which he was so eager to serve was one of evil men (*Moses* 1.268-269, LCL).

The nature of Paul's revelation is not known, but based on what we see in Acts, it may have been a dream (16:9; 18:9; 23:11; 27:23) or an ecstatic trance (22:17), or a sign from the Holy Spirit (16:6; 19:21; 20:22-23) or even a sign given to him by a prophet (11:28; 21:4, 10). This phrase, "according to a revelation" also occurs in Rom. 16:25 and Eph. 3:3. A later scribe, who evidently edited and preserved the story of Polycarp's martyrdom, explains his actions regarding the writing by saying: "And I, again, Pionius, wrote it out from the former writings, after searching for it, because the blessed Polycarp showed it me in a vision, as I will explain in what follows . . . " (*Mart. Pol.* 22:3, LCL).

The task of Paul's delegation to Jerusalem from Antioch was to lay before the leaders the substance of his gospel for their examination, but the delegation chose to do this "in private" (Greek = *kat' idian*). Josephus relates the story of Petronius, the leader of the Romans in Palestine during the 66-70 rebellion, who "held crowded private (*kat' idian*) conferences" with the aristocracy, but public meetings with the people (Jews) who were seeking his favor (*Jewish War* 2.199, LCL).

Those who were of reputation (Greek = *hoi dokountes*). The reference here is to the same persons as are referred to as the "pillars" (see 2:6, 9). The term was a political one and widely used in rhetoric in Paul's day both positively and negatively (sometimes sarcastically) of those in leadership roles (see Xenophon *Cyr.* 7.1.41; Euripides, *Hec* 295; Plutarch, *Superst.* 166B, *Mul. Virt.* 244E, *Quaest. Rom.* 282A, *Quaest Gr.* 296F, and *Isid. et Os.* 363D). Interestingly, Epictetus advised his hearers:

When you are about to meet somebody, in particular when it is one of those men who are held in very high esteem [*dokounton*], propose to yourself the question, "What would Socrates or Zeno have done under these circumstances?"

and then you will not be at a loss to make proper use of the occasion (*Encheiridion* 33.12, LCL).

Run in vain. Paul uses the metaphor of running in vain to characterize what would happen if his gospel were rejected or caused a division in the church. For his other uses of "running" as a metaphor, see Gal. 5:7; Rom. 9:16; 1 Cor. 9:24, 26; Phil. 2:16; cf. 2 Thess. 3:1; Heb. 12:1).

2:3. But not even Titus who was with me, though he was a Greek, was compelled to be circumcised. An obvious question on this matter has to do with the difference between Titus not being compelled to be circumcised, but Paul circumcising Timothy according to Acts 16:1-5. In the latter instance, Timothy was half Jewish on his mother's side and therefore considered Jewish (see discussion of this in Acts 16:1-5), but here Titus is a Gentile. The subject of circumcision is the focus of Paul's discussion and debate in 2:7-9, 12; 5:1-11; 6:12-13, 15; but see also Rom. 2:25-29; 3:1, 20; 4:9-12; 15:8; 1 Cor. 7:19; Phil. 3:3-5. The practice of circumcision came to be equated with the essence of the law and its variety of legal codes in Paul's writings.

2:4. But it was because of the false brethren who had sneaked in to spy out our liberty which we have in Christ Jesus, in order to bring us into bondage. Paul calls those who would challenge his gospel and place the Gentiles under the bondage of the law "false brethren," that is, not brethren at all. For a similar situation of "false apostles" who were not apostles at all, see 2 Cor. 11:26. In the mid-second century A.D., Polycarp likewise admonished his readers in Philippi to "be zealous for good, refraining from offence, and from the false brethren, and from those who bear the name of the Lord in hypocrisy, who deceive empty-minded men" (Pol. *Phil.* 6:3, LCL). The word that Paul uses to describe his opponents "sneaking in" (*pareiserchesthai*), though used in ancient military and political literature (Plutarch, *Moralia* 261B; Diodorus Sic. *Library of History* 12.41.4; Polybius 1.18.3; 2.7.8), is found nowhere else in the New Testament. It is often used, however, of heretics in early Christianity. Similarly, the "spying out" of the liberty of the Gentile Christians is not found elsewhere in the New Testament, but is used in military campaigns and in subversive warfare. Plutarch, while telling of the preparation for battle, says "exiles have slipped into [*pareiselthontas* = same term, but different form of *pareiserchesthai*] the city and are lying concealed" (*On the Sign of Socrates, Moralia* 596A, LCL; see also 964C, 980B; Philo, *Op.* 150; *Ebr.* 157; *Abr* 96; *T. Judah* 16.2).

The author of the *Epistle of Barnabas* admonishes his readers "carefully to inquire concerning our salvation, in order that the evil one may not achieve a deceitful entry into us and hurl us away from our life" (*Ep Barn.* 2.10, LCL). Likewise, the author of the Testament of Judah admonishes his readers to be vigilant in their drinking of wine because if one drinks wine "without restraint and the fear of God departs, the result is drunkenness and shamelessness sneaks in" (*Test. Jud.* 16.2, OT *Pseud* 1.799). Paul indicates that his opponents were able to get into this "private" meeting with James, Cephas and John. Are they the same as those who came from Judea teaching that circumcision was essential to one's salvation (Acts 15:1)?

2:5. But we did not yield in subjection to them for even an hour, so that the truth of the gospel might remain with you. Paul believed that if he caved in to the demands of these individuals, the essence of the gospel would be lost, so he resisted with all his might against them. The phrase "truth of the gospel" occurs only here and in 2:14 below. He is concerned that the switching of loyalties by the Galatians to the "other gospel" has in effect made these Galatians like those he is speaking about in this passage, because they have forsaken the meaning of grace in their proclamation.

2:6. But from those who were of high reputation (what they were makes no difference to me; God shows no partiality)—well, those who were of reputation contributed nothing to me. Paul does not defer to those in leadership in the Jerusalem church because of who they are. He is speaking of James, the acknowledged leader in the church, Cephas (Peter), and John (note the order in 2:9). Had they been opposed to his gospel, he would doubtless have resisted them. As the philosophers of his day and earlier believed, so Paul also believed that respect for a person's position was not conducive to responsible living. Socrates, as he is about to face death, tells those gathered around him to watch how they raise their children, and he adds:

> . . . if they [his friends' children] seem to you to care for money or anything else more than for virtue, and if they think they amount to something when they do not, rebuke them as I have rebuked you because they do not care for what they ought, and think they amount to something when they are worth nothing. If you do this, both I and my sons shall have received just treatment from you (Plato, *Apology* 41E, LCL).

Paul concludes similarly in Gal. 6:3. He understood from the Scriptures that God is impartial and does not put value on those in high positions (Deut. 10:17; 2 Chron. 19:7; Job 24:19). A similar message is found in the New Testament (Acts 10:34; Jas. 2:1), and Paul himself elsewhere acknowledges this same point (Rom. 2:11). Since God's impartiality is central to Paul's gospel to both Jews and Gentiles (Gal. 3:28), this may be the reason he focuses on the point here. This is important for him, even if he states with perhaps a touch of sarcasm that God is impartial. The door is opened for the follow-up word, that so should God's children be!

2:7-8. But on the contrary, seeing that I had been entrusted with the gospel to the uncircumcised, just as Peter had been to the circumcised (for He who effectually worked for Peter in his apostleship to the circumcised effectually worked for me also to the Gentiles). The same God who was active in Peter's apostleship to the Jews is also active in Paul's to the Gentiles. Much has been made about the omission of the word apostleship (Greek = *apostolen*) before Paul's name, but the Greek allows for the one term to cover both. The emphasis here is not on distinguishing the apostleship of Peter from Paul, but rather the recognition of the validity of both. That is the point of the recognition in 2:9. Paul's apostleship is not on the table for discussion in this visit to Jerusalem. (For references to the Jews being called the "circumcision" Gal. 2:12; Rom. 3:30; 4:9, 12; 15:8; Eph. 2:11; Col. 3:11. The "uncircumcised" often serves as a reference to the unbeliever or heathen (Rom. 3:30; 4:9; Eph. 2:11; Col. 3:11). This distinction was also found in the early church. Ignatius (ca. 115-117), for instance, says "if anyone interpret Judaism to you do not listen to him; for it is better to hear Christianity from the circumcised than Judaism from the uncircumcised" (*Philad.*. 6:1, LCL).

2:9. And recognizing the grace that had been given to me, James and Cephas and John, who were reputed to be pillars, gave to me and Barnabas the right hand of fellowship, that we might go to the Gentiles, and they to the circumcised. Again, it is important to observe the transition of authority in the early church. In all of the gospels, when the inner circle of Jesus' closest disciples is referred to, it is always Peter, James, and John. In 1:18, Paul meets only with Peter for fifteen days and not James, the Lord's brother. The circumstances have now changed and if the time frame is that this letter was written just prior to the

Jerusalem council (A.D. 48-49), when James appears as the undisputed head of the church (Acts 15:12, 19; 21:18), then the sequence of names here reflects the transition having taken place by the time of this letter (perhaps as early as A.D. 48-49). It is interesting that by the end of the first century, Clement of Rome says that both Peter and Paul were "pillars" of the church (*1 Clem* 5:2).

John. As the third of the persons named as "pillars," it is strange how little personal information we have about him. John the son of Zebedee and the brother of James (Mark 1:16-20; 3:17; 10:35-45; 14:33 and parallels) is one of the inner circle of Jesus' disciples and is mentioned in all four gospels (he may be the "Beloved disciple" in John 13:23; 19:26; 21:7, 20) at various times in conjunction with Jesus' ministry, but after Easter he seems to have been largely in Peter's shadow in Acts (Acts 3:1-4, 11; 4:1, 6, 13, 19; 8:14, 17, 25; 12:2). He is essentially unknown, even though several writings of the New Testament have historically been attributed to him (the Gospel of John, 1,2,3 John and even the book of Revelation). The language of the last of these books (Revelation) is so different in focus, style, and vocabulary from the others that many have questioned whether the John referred to in Rev. 1:1-2, 4, 9 is the same as the disciple of Jesus who was also one of the twelve apostles. The early church has a number of traditions about him and those traditions do not all agree: namely, where he died and what his subsequent ministry within Asia Minor (Ephesus?) or Jerusalem consisted of. Eusebius mentions him at length indicating that John stayed and died in Ephesus (*Ecclesiastical History* 3.1.1) and reports of his exile on the island of Patmos (3.18.2) and later identifies him as the disciple whom Jesus loved (3.23.1) and tells of his significant ministry in and around Ephesus (3.23.1-18).

Hand of fellowship. The extension of the handshake is intended to formally conclude the meeting on an agreeable note. The hand-shake in ancient times, as in more recent times, was considered a pledge between honorable persons to honor an agreement. Xenophon tells of such an agreement in his day that resulted in the sealing of a peace agreement.

This man was given me at first by my father, to be my subject; then at the bidding, as he himself said, of my brother, this man levied war upon me, holding the citadel of Sardis, and I, by the war I waged against him, made him count it best to cease from warring upon me, and I received and gave the hand-clasp of friendship (*Anabasis* 1.6.6, LCL).

Among the Jews, the hand-clasp was also a symbol of agreement and even of a sacred covenant. In his report on the treachery that led to the death of Onias of Antioch, the author of *2 Maccabees* says:

Therefore Menelaus [high priest of Jerusalem from 172-162 B.C.], taking Andronicus aside, urged him to kill Onias [who exposed the high priest's theft from the temple]. Andronicus came to Onias, and resorting to treach-ery, offered him sworn pledges and gave him his right hand; he persuaded him though still suspicious, to come out from the place of sanctuary; then with no regard for justice, he immediately put him out of the way. (2 *Macc.* 4:34, NRSV)

Josephus tells of the deceit of a certain King Artabanus of Parthia who gave his word for safe passage through his territory, but when the person receiving this assurance was skepti-cal, the king

... swore by his ancestral gods that he would do no evil to them, if they visited him in reliance on his pledge. He offered him his right hand, and that is for all the barbarians of those parts the highest assurance of security in making visits. For no one would ever prove false when he had given his right hand,

nor would anyone hesitate to trust one that he suspected might harm him, once he had received that assurance of safety . . . [the king was asked permission to slay the one who trusted him and the king responded:] "No," said the king, "I cannot grant you permission against this man who puts confidence in my pledge. Moreover, I have given him my right hand and have made a point of winning his trust by swearing by the gods (*Ant.* 18.326, 328, LCL).

2:10. They only asked us to remember the poor—the very thing I also was eager to do. For a discussion of how this was done, see dis-cussion of the collection Paul received from the church in 2 Cor. 8:1-15. This activity, strangely, receives very little attention in Acts (11:29-30; 24:17; cf.. also 1 Cor. 16:1-3). Quite apart from the obvious benefits produced in good rela-tions between Jews and Gentiles by the gesture of collecting funds for the poor in Jerusalem, Paul knows the importance of caring for human need and its way of authenticating the message that he proclaims. The roots of early Christianity are in the preaching of John the Baptist who indicated that true repentance is manifested in caring for those who are in need (Luke 3:11), and this compassion was also emphasized by Jesus as activity fit for those who are faithful to God (Matt. 6:2-3; 25:35-46). The early church practiced this as well (Acts 2:44-45; 4:34-37; 6:1; 11:27-29; Jas. 2:15-16).

D. 2:11-14. Paul Rebukes Peter for His Inconsistency

After telling how the leaders in the church in Jerusalem had acknowledged the validity of Paul's gospel and ministry among the Gentiles, and even given to him and Barnabas the hand of fellowship in Jerusalem, Paul moves the story back to Antioch when he and Peter and Barnabas and others were joined in table fellow-ship with Gentile believers. During that table fellowship, some "from James" came among them and so intimidated Peter and Barnabas that the Jewish Christians removed themselves from the table fellowship with the Gentiles. Peter's action, that was so contagious, that even Barnabas did the same, so infuriated Paul that he lashed out with a strong verbal attack.

2:11. But when Cephas came to Antioch, I opposed him to his face, because he stood condemned. While the confrontation is only summarized here in a few verses, the full impact of what took place apparently had a lasting affect on Paul's relations not only with Barnabas and Peter, but with the whole church at Antioch.

2:12. For prior to the coming of certain men from James, he used to eat with the Gentiles; but when they came, he began to withdraw and hold himself aloof, fearing the party of the circumcision. Who these "men from James" were is not told, but some have speculated that they were the same ones who troubled the Galatian churches. They apparently came as an official delegation from James the brother of Jesus to meet with Peter, and perhaps over the issue of how to deal with the presence of Gentiles in the church at Antioch. Peter's actions, says Paul, came from his fear of those from the "circumcision party" (Greek = *hoi ek peritōmes*, cf. 1:7; 4:17; 5:10). Who were these people? According to Rom. 4:12, they were individuals who were drawn into the church by faith (Rom. 4:16) from the Jewish community that was observant of the Law and its traditions. They were among the Jews who also became followers of Christ by faith. Eusebius (ca. A.D. 320) uses a similar designation, *ek tes peritomes*, to describe those in the church who came to it as Jews. He observes that all Jerusalem bishops, beginning with James to the time of Hadrian, were Jews by birth and he called them "bishops from the circumcision [*ek peritomes episkopoi*]" and identi-

fied the first fifteen of them:

I have not found any written statement of the dates of the bishops in Jerusalem, for tradition says that they were extremely short-lived, but I have gathered from documents this much—that up to the siege of the Jews by Hadrian [the Roman emperor] the successions of bishops were fifteen in number. It is said that they were all Hebrews by origin who had nobly accepted the knowledge of Christ, so that they were counted worthy even of the episcopal ministry by those who had the power to judge such questions. For their whole church at that time consisted of Hebrews who had continued Christian from the apostles down to the siege at the time when the Jews again rebelled from the Romans [the Bar Kochba rebellion in 132-35] and were beaten in a great war. Since the Jewish bishops [*ek peritomes episkopon*] then ceased, it is now necessary to give their names from the beginning. The first, then was James who was called the Lord's brother . . . " (*Ecclesiastical History* 4.5.1-3, LCL).

Jewish hatred for Gentiles was well-known in antiquity and the Jews did not make a secret of it. The author of *Jub.* (ca. 140 B.C.) indicates that this practice of separation from Gentiles goes back to the time of Abraham who, in his blessing of Jacob, said:

And you also, my son, Jacob, remember my words, and keep the commandments of Abraham, your father. Separate yourself from the gentiles, and do not eat with them, and do not perform deeds like theirs. And do not become associates of theirs. Because their deeds are defiled, and all of their ways are contaminated, and despicable, and abominable (*Jub.* 22:16, OT *Pseud* 2:98).

See discussion of Jewish separation

from Gentiles in Acts 10:28.

2:13. And the rest of the Jews joined him in hypocrisy, with the result that even Barnabas was carried away by their hypocrisy. A part of the hypocrisy that Paul accuses Peter of practicing here has to do with the agreement that they had already made, but also it has to do with Peter's living contrary to the message that he himself proclaims. While there does appear to be a tendency in Acts to make Peter like Paul, is this really a synthesizing of two distinct brands of early Christianity that Luke tried to bring together as some scholars have held? There is no reason to suppose that the story of Peter's going to the household of Cornelius in Acts 10, and the subsequent reaction against this by the Christians in Jerusalem because he had violated Jewish custom of table fellowship with Gentiles, is false. Peter also went among the Samaritans (Acts 8) and evidently made his way to Corinth (1 Cor. 1:12). Paul's accusation has to do with Peter's hypocrisy, not his beliefs nor previous practice. He was, after all, sitting at the table of Gentiles before the men came from James.

In a remarkable text Epictetus (ca. early second century A.D.) challenges his readers toward consistency between belief and action. At a time when Christians were considered by many to be Jews, namely before the Bar Kochba rebellion against Rome in A.D. 132-35, Epictetus claims that they (Jews and Christians) are inconsistent in their beliefs and practices and he wants his readers to do better than that!

Why, then, do you call yourself a Stoic, why do you deceive the multitude, why do you act the part of a Jew, when you are a Greek? Do you not see in what sense men are severally called Jew, Syrian, or Egyptian? For example, whenever we see a man halting between two faiths, we are in the habit of saying, "He is not a Jew, he is only acting the part." But when he adopts the attitude of mind of the man who

has been baptized and has made his choice, then he both is a Jew in fact and is also called one. So we also are counterfeit "Baptists," ostensibly Jews, but in reality something else, not in sympathy with our own reason, far from applying the principles which we profess, yet priding ourselves upon them as being men who know them. So, although we are unable even to fulfil [sic] the profession of man, we take on the additional profession of the philosopher—so huge a burden! It is as though a man who was unable to raise ten pounds wanted to lift the stone of Aias [the huge stone with which Aias beat down Aeneas in Homer's *Iliad* 7.264] (*Discourses* 2.9.19-22, LCL).

2:14. But when I saw that they were not straightforward about the truth of the gospel, I said to Cephas in the presence of all, "If you, being a Jew, live like the Gentiles and not like the Jews, how is it that you compel the Gentiles to live like Jews? Paul, after the meeting and agreement in Jerusalem, found Peter's inconsistency with what had already been agreed to intolerable. Peter and Barnabas and other Jews withdraw from table fellowship with the Gentiles and Paul saw a crisis emerging that had to be addressed and he openly criticized Peter's behavior. Paul does not say how Peter responded to him, but those in the early church who were zealous for Peter's integrity and who were angry with Paul, present an apocryphal legend about the meeting called the *Kerygmata Petrou* ("Preaching of Peter"), a so-called dialogue or debate between Paul and Peter in which Peter clearly gets the upper hand in the matter. After Paul speaks of the value of his vision of the risen Christ and the truth revealed to him in it (17.13), Peter first challenges that Paul has a better understanding of the truth than he does (18.1,6) and he even challenges Paul's vision and authority as a teacher.

And if our Jesus appeared to you also and became known in a vision and met you as angry with an enemy, yet he has spoken only through visions and dreams or through external revelations. But can anyone be made competent to teach through a vision? And if your opinion is, "that is possible," why then did our teacher spend a whole year with us who were awake? How can we believe you even if he has appeared to you, and how can he have appeared to you if you desire the opposite of what you have learned? But if you were visited by him for the space of an hour and were instructed by him and thereby have become an apostle, then proclaim his words, expound what he has taught, be a friend to his apostles and do not contend with me, who am his confidant; for you have in hostility *withstood* me, who am a firm rock, the foundation stone of the Church. If you were not an enemy, then you would not slander me and revile my preaching in order that I may not be believed when I proclaim what I have heard in my own person from the Lord, as if I were undoubtedly *condemned* and you were acknowledged. And if you call me condemned, then you accuse God, who revealed Christ to me, and disparage him who called me blessed on account of the revelation. But if you really desire to cooperate with the truth, then learn first from us what we have learned from him, and, as a learner of the truth, become a fellow-worker with us. (*Pseudo-Clementines, Kerygmata Petrou* 19.1-7, *NT APO* 2:536-37).

However reliable this story is, and not many give it much credibility, it does independently substantiate Paul's confrontation of Peter and offers a response from him that is missing in Galatians. Also, in the apocryphal *Epistle of Peter to James* (*Epistula Petri*), dating probably from the second to third century,

reportedly written by Peter to James the Lord's brother, there is the following defense of Peter apparently with the incident at Antioch in view. The bracketed texts are possible allusions to texts in Paul that the writer is opposed to and from Jesus that he uses for support. In the letter, Peter says to James, the brother of Jesus:

For some from among the Gentiles have rejected my lawful preaching and have preferred a lawless and absurd doctrine of the man who is my enemy. And indeed some have attempted, whilst I am still alive, to distort my words by interpretations of many sorts, as if I taught the dissolution of the law [Gal. 2:18] and, although I was of this opinion, did not express it openly [cf. Gal. 2:11-14]. But that may God forbid! For to do such a thing means to act contrary to the law of God which was made known by Moses and was confirmed by our Lord in its everlasting continuance. For he said: The "*heaven and the earth will pass away, but one jot or one tittle shall not pass away from the law*" [Matt. 5:18; 24-25; Gal. 3:19-25]. This he said *that everything might come to pass*. But those persons who, I know not how, allege that they are at home in my thoughts wish to expound the words which they have heard of me better than myself who spoke them. To those whom they instruct they say that this is my opinion, to which indeed I never gave a thought. But if they falsely assert such a thing whilst I am still alive, how much more after my death will those who come later venture to do so? [Acts 10:45; 11:3].

E. 2:15-21. Conclusion: Jews and Gentiles Alike Are Saved by Faith

Paul now moves to explain the rationale or principle that was behind his actions and also to offer support for the gospel he preaches. Paul wants his readers to see that his behavior is consistent with his gospel. He also summarizes the content of his gospel of freedom and faith. Whether these words are a continuation of the challenge he put to Peter is not clear, but they are intended for his readers in the Galatian churches so they can understand his gospel more clearly. He introduces several important contrasting terms here: namely, righteousness and life (or living) law and works versus faith that he will explain as the letter continues. Paul summarizes his gospel in 15-16 and speaks of the consequences of a Law-based gospel in 17-21.

2:15-16. We are Jews by nature, and not sinners from among the Gentiles; nevertheless knowing that a man is not justified by the works of the Law but through faith in Christ Jesus, even we have believed in Christ Jesus, that we may be justified by faith in Christ, and not by the works of the Law; since by the works of the Law shall no flesh be justified. Paul continues that criticism of Peter that he began in v. 14. Paul appears to accept that Jews and Gentiles have a different standing before God because the Jews stand within the covenant, the Torah, because they have received and keep the commands or statutes of the law (see Ps. 119) and the Gentiles do not. It must be understood that Paul's referring to the Gentiles as "sinners" is said in the context of irony and sarcasm. Both Paul and Peter, as well as the "men from James" all stood within the covenant of Israel, but Paul's point that will be made presently is that both they and the Gentiles all came to salvation through Christ in the same way (see 3:1-5 below). The Jewish understanding that because the Gentiles were outside of the covenant with God they were beyond the opportunity for the salvation of God is rejected by Paul (see Rom. 9:20-31; 3:1-3,19-20; 1 Cor. 6:1; 9:21; 12:2; 1 Thess. 1:9-10; 4:5; Phil. 3:6). Those Jews who stood "within the covenant" believed that if they committed sin by transgressing the Law they could find forgiveness through sacrifice and vicarious suffer-

ings available through the Law. How is the sinfulness of the Jews different from that of the Gentiles? The author of 2 Maccabees explains it this way:

> Now I urge those who read this book not to be depressed by such calamities, but to recognize that these punishments [for breaking the Law] were designed not to destroy but to discipline our people. In fact, it is a sign of great kindness not to let the impious alone for long, but to punish them immediately. For in the case of the other nations the Lord waits patiently to punish them until they have reached the full measure of their sins, but he does not deal in this way with us, in order that he may not take vengeance on us afterward when our sins have reached their height. Therefore he never withdraws his mercy from us. Although he disciplines us with calamities, he does not forsake his own people. Let what we have said serve as a reminder; we must go on briefly with the story. (2 Macc. 6:12-17, NRSV)

When the Jews are punished for their sins, it is with corrective measures in view, but not so for the Gentiles. Their punishment is both justly deserved and permanent. They are beyond the mercy of God. In the days of Mattathias Maccabeus, it was said that, "They [Mattathias and his company of Jews] rescued the law out of the hands of the Gentiles and kings, and they never let the sinner gain the upper hand" (1 Macc. 2:48, NRSV). Without the Law, Gentiles had no hope. On the other hand, Paul challenges this view and says that by faith, justification or righteousness also comes to the Gentiles (see also Rom. 3:21-27). Paul seems to assume the correctness of this assumption about the distinction between Jews and Gentiles, but in v. 16 he shows that that distinction no longer exists in Christ.

For Paul, when the Law is no longer the distinguishing feature between Jew and

Gentile, the older categories must fade away. His reference to being saved by the "works of the Law" clearly in context refers to the outward symbols of Jewish ethnic distinctiveness, namely circumcision, dietary laws, and keeping the Sabbath. By withdrawing from table fellowship with the Gentiles, Peter was trying to maintain the traditional boundaries between Jews and Gentiles.

Justified by faith in Christ. The word "justified" (Greek = *dikaiothomen* from *dikaioo*) is the same in Paul as one who has been "made righteous," or "reconciled" to God, or "saved." This state of being made right with God comes only by faith in Christ according to Paul. See how he uses this term elsewhere (Gal. 2:17; 3:8, 11, 24; 5:4; cf. Rom. 2:13; 3:4, 20, 24, 26, 28, 30; 4:2, 5; 5:1, 9; 6:7; 8:30, 33; 1 Cor. 6:11). For Paul, faith in Christ (1:4; 2:20; 3:1, 13; 4:4-6) is the same as being "in Christ" (2:19-21; 3:26-28; 5:5-6, 24; 6:14). Paul does not say that the works of the Law are wrong, only that they will not produce justification or a right relationship with God. For him, that relationship comes only by faith in Christ. That faith (Greek = *pistos*) is essentially one's obedience to God's call that comes through Jesus Christ (Rom. 1:5). Paul does not have two ways of salvation, that is, one for the Jews (by faith and keeping of the law) and one for the Gentiles (by faith alone). The core content of that faith for Paul is in Rom. 10:9-10, namely Jesus is Lord and God has raised him from the dead. It is summarized also in 1 Cor. 15:3-5, namely that Christ died for our sins and was raised from the dead. There are similarities between Paul and the Qumran writers in the sense that forgiveness of sins comes by the mercies of God and not by human effort. There is a recognition in some writings at Qumran of the failure of such human endeavor and of the grace of God who brings salvation.

However, I belong to evil humankind to the assembly of wicked flesh; my failings, my transgressions, my sins, [. . .] with the depravities of my heart, belong to the assembly of worms and of those who walk in darkness. For to man (does not belong) his path, nor to a human being the steadying of his step; since judgment belongs to God, and from his hand is the perfection of the path. By his knowledge everything shall come into being, and all that does exist he establishes with his calculations and nothing is done outside of him. As for me, if I stumble, the mercies of God shall be my salvation always; and if I fall in the sin of the flesh, in the justice of God, which endures eternally, shall my judgment be; if my grief commences, he will free my soul from the pit and make my steps steady on the path; he will draw me near in his mercies, and by kindnesses set in motion my judgment; he will judge me in the justice of his truth and in his plentiful goodness always atone for all my sins; in his justice he will cleanse me from the uncleanness of the human being and from the sin of the sons of man, so that I can extol God for his justice and The Highest for his majesty. (*Rule of the Community*, 1QS 11.9-15, Garcia Martinez trans.)

Paul cites Ps. 143:2 in a modified fashion to strengthen his argument: namely, that since the works of the Law are done by human beings and since by such works shall no flesh shall be justified, everyone must come by faith. Paul adds to the psalm his own interpretation by adding "works of the Law." On the other hand, Paul is no doubt correct in interpreting the psalm since its author affirms that no human being stands before God in his/her own merit. Compare this with Rom. 3:20 which also depends on the same Ps. 143:2. If this is so, then both Jews and Gentiles come the same way, and if so, there can be no discrimination among those (Jews and Gentiles) who enter into a right relationship with God the same way (see also Gal. 3:11, 28; Rom. 3:28; 4:5; 10:5-13).

2:17. But if, while seeking to be justified in Christ, we ourselves have also been found

sinners, is Christ then a minister of sin? May it never be! This part of this section is Paul's response to charges against him by those in the Galatian churches, namely that he has abandoned the Law, God's only solution for dealing with sin, and has failed to observe the Jewish customs of avoiding table fellowship with the Gentiles. Those who abandoned the Law were strongly condemned in Israel, and Paul's abandonment of it as a means toward righteousness must have been an enormous problem for the Jews and the Jewish Christians to overcome. In the *Testament of Levi* (second century B.C.), the words of warning against ignoring the Law echoed the zeal of the Jews of Paul's day for insuring that their fellow countrymen obeyed it. "You will bring down a curse on our nation, because you want to destroy the light of the Law which was granted to you for the enlightenment of every man, teaching commandments which are opposed to God's just ordinances" (*Test. Levi* 14:4, *OT Pseud* 1:793). The same view is held in the Testament of Asher where the Jews are admonished to keep the Law or they will be scattered from their land and punished: "for I know that you will be thoroughly disobedient, that you will be thoroughly irreligious, heeding not God's Law but human commandments, being corrupted by evil" (*Test. Ash.* 7:5, *OT Pseud* 1:818).

2:18. For if I rebuild what I have once destroyed, I prove myself to be a transgressor. If Paul had, like Peter when those from James appeared, re-established the dietary laws about table fellowship with the Gentiles, which he and Peter had both set aside (besides 2:12, see also Acts 10:48; 11:3), then he would justly be called a "transgressor" of what he knew to be true and he would rebuild the walls of a structure that he had once torn down.

2:20. I have been crucified with Christ; and it is no longer I who live, but Christ lives in me; and the life which I now live in the flesh I live by faith in the Son of God, who loved me, and delivered Himself up for me. How is it that Paul was crucified with Christ? What could that mean? He accepts that Jesus died an agonizing death on a cross (3:1), but what could he mean by identifying himself in the death of Jesus? Paul is, of course, speaking figuratively in regard to his crucifixion, and he is also speaking representatively of all Christians, but in a real sense, he has made a decision not to pursue the old life of self justification through the keeping of the Law, which he found impossible to do (Rom. 7:14-23), and he has chosen the life of faith in Christ. All of his desire to make himself right with God through human effort has gone, and he now seeks that goal through the merits of Jesus Christ alone. Compare Rom. 5:1, 15 in which grace and faith are brought together. Paul combines the notion of faith with the grace of God here as well (see v. 21).

Paul believes that the death of Christ is related directly to the Law, but this is not easy to grasp. At Qumran, there was a view that any persons who violated the Law of God were worthy of a crucifixion and an appeal was made to Deut. 21:22-23 as justification. For instance, in the *Temple Scroll*, we read:

> If there were to be a spy against his people who betrays his people to a foreign nation or causes evil against his people, you shall hang him from a tree and he will die. On the evidence of two witnesses and on the evidence of three witnesses shall he be executed and they shall hang him on the tree. If there were a man with a sin punishable by death and he escapes amongst the nations and curses his people/and/the children of Israel, he also shall you hang on the tree and he will die. Their corpses shall not spend the night on the tree; instead you shall bury them that day because they are cursed by God and man, those hanged on a tree; thus you shall not

defile the land which I give you for inheritance (11Q Temple 64.6-12, Garcia Martinez trans. 178; see also 4QpNah, *Frags.* 3 + 4, 1-7).

Paul believed that the Law was enslaving people and Christ broke with the legalistic system that kept people in bondage. Because of this, he was crucified and Paul also identifies with a dying to the Law and what happened to Jesus by the system of the law of slavery. He has put that away so that he might walk in the newness of life with Christ. This view of dying and rising with Christ is similar to Rom. 6:3-6 that speaks of one's participation in the death of Christ. There is a second-century B.C. tradition among the Jewish people that speaks of such a rising with the end-times (eschatological) Son of Man. In part it says,

The righteous and elect ones shall be saved on that day; and from thenceforth they shall never see the faces of the sinners and oppressors. The Lord of the Spirits will abide over the righteous and elect ones shall rise with that Son of Man forever and ever. The righteous and elect ones shall rise from the earth and shall cease being of downcast face (*1 Enoch* 62:13-15, *OT Pseud* 1:44).

2:21. "I do not nullify the grace of God; for if righteousness comes through the Law, then Christ died needlessly." Paul makes it clear that one's standing before God depends not on his or her righteousness through the Law, but through faith in Christ alone.

III. 3:1–4:31. Paul's Gospel Explained

By way of style of ancient deliveries of communication, oral or written, we are entering what the rhetoricians called the *probatio*, that is, the purpose of the letter itself. Up to this point, Paul has delivered an *exordium* (introduction), a *narratio* (the historical narrative or context), and now he gets to his purpose (the *probation*). Cicero claimed that this part of the delivery involved evidence. He said: "confirmation or proof is the part of the oration which by marshalling arguments lends credit, authority, and support to our case" (*De inv.* 1.24.34, Betz trans. 128). Paul now sets forth his strongest arguments, beginning with the experience of the Galatians themselves, and then his argument from Scripture.

A. 3:1-18. An Appeal to Experience and Scripture

1. 3:1-5. The First Argument: Experience of Spirit vs. Flesh.

Paul now moves from the past events that took place at Antioch and addresses the problems currently facing the Galatian Christians themselves. Having argued that they could not find peace with God, or be made right with God, through the Law, but only through faith in Christ, Paul now deals with their situation, and he does so with anger and passion. He begins his appeal by asking the Galatians to look at their own experience. Knowing that they had experienced the presence of God in their lives apart from the Law, he asks them whether they will be advanced in their journey of faith by it. The value of beginning with the experience of the readers is that they are eye-witnesses to what Paul is saying! They are evidence that one does not begin the journey of faith by the works of the Law.

3:1. You foolish Galatians, who has bewitched you, before whose eyes Jesus Christ was publicly portrayed as crucified? The very tone of this passage, that begins with a rebuke (cf. 1:6-7) as well as an insult, assumes that the teachers who have come among the Galatians to "spy out their liberty," have had considerable success in their efforts with the Galatian Christians who are accepting their message: namely, that faith in Christ is accompanied with the keeping of the Law and even accepting circumcision. It was not uncommon in the ancient world to offer rebuke to those who needed correcting. Clement of Rome, for example, encourages the Corinthians as follows: "Let us offend foolish and thoughtless men, who are exalted and boast in the pride of their words, rather than God" (*1 Clem.* 21:5, LCL). Likewise, the author of 2 Clement (ca. 140-150) addresses some of his hearers who had difficulty believing the promises of God, "O foolish men! Compare yourselves to a tree; take a vine . . . " (*2 Clem.* 11.3, LCL) Hermas (ca. 140-150) also begins one of his *Mandates* by saying to an imaginary hearer: "You are foolish, O man" (Shepherd, *Mand.* 9.10.2, LCL) and later addresses him again, "'Hear now', said he, 'foolish man, how grief wears out the Holy Spirit'" (*Mand.* 10.2.1, LCL). For other examples, see also Luke 24:25; cf. Rom. 1:14; 1 Tim. 6:9; Titus 3:3. Paul would no doubt agree with Dio Chrysostom who acknowledged that some people are hard to teach and easy to deceive.

I am almost certain that while all men are hard to teach, they are easy to deceive. They learn with difficulty—if they do learn anything—from the few that know, but they are deceived only too readily by the many who do not know, and not only by others but by themselves as well. For the truth is bitter and unpleasant to the unthinking, while falsehood is sweet and pleasant. They are, I fancy, like men with sore eyes—they find the light painful, while the darkness, which permits them to see nothing, is restful and agreeable. Else how would falsehood often move mightier than the truth, if it did not win its victories through pleasure? (*Orations* 11.1-2, LCL).

In the Galatians' case, there is little pleasure in circumcision, but they have been deceived by the false teachers coming in among them and are willing to submit to circumcision and the other symbolic acts pertaining to the law. Paul is angry and very concerned over the fate of those he had spent so much time and effort

convincing of the truth of his gospel. More than this, he has a great love for the Galatians and that heightens his anxiety over others coming in to steal their devotion to the gospel and affection for Paul (cf. 4:19-20).

Bewitched (Greek = *ebaskanen* from *baskkaino*). This word is only found here in the New Testament, but is found in the Greco-Roman literature and there it refers to someone with an "evil eye" doing some form of magic (Plutarch, *Quaestionum convivalium libri* 680C-683B). Plato used the word to describe those who would use trickery to deceive: "'My friend,' said Socrates, 'do not be boastful, lest some evil eye put to rout the argument that is to come. That, however, is in the hands of God'" (*Phaedo* 95B, LCL). He also indicates how Socrates was accused of deceit and he wondered how that had affected his judges at this trial.

How you, men of Athens, have been affected by my accusers, I do not know; but I, for my part, almost forgot my own identity, so persuasively did they talk; and yet there is hardly a word of truth in what they have said. But I was most amazed by one of the many lies that they told—when they said that you must be on your guard not to be deceived by me, because I was a clever speaker. (*Apol* 17A, LCL; see also *Gorg.* 452E).

Publicly portrayed (Greek = *hois kat' ofthalmous*, "before whose eyes"). Paul's aim when he first came to the Galatians was to tell the story of the agony and suffering of Jesus on their behalf. He did not spare them a vivid picture. The ancient art of delivering in vivid pictures events that the orators were trying to communicate was well-known. They often used vivid stories and event paintings to evoke emotion and response from their hearers. Aristotle explains the phrase thusly:

We have said that smart sayings are derived from propositional metaphor and expressions which set things before the eyes. We must now explain the meaning of "before the eyes," and what must be done to produce this. I mean that things are set before the eyes by words that signify actuality. For instance, to say that a man is "four-square" is a metaphor, for both these are complete, but the phrase does not express actuality, whereas "of one having the prime of his life in full bloom" does . . . (Aristotle, *Rhetoric* 11.1-2, LCL).

And he ends this lesson by saying: "There is something youthful about hyperboles; for they show vehemence. Wherefore those who are in a passion most frequently make use of them" (*Rhetoric* 11.16, LCL).

Portrayed as crucified. This is a summary of Paul's gospel (1 Cor. 1:23; 2:2; cf. 1:13, 17, 18) that Paul abbreviates in this manner. He did not neglect in his gospel that God raised Christ from the dead (1 Cor. 15:3-5; Rom. 10:9-10). The cross was central to Paul's understanding of the grace of God and so it is also central in his preaching (2 Cor. 13:4; Gal. 5:11, 24; 6:12, 14, 17; Eph. 2:16; Phil. 2:8; 3:18; Col. 1:20; 2:14).

3:2. This is the only thing I want to find out from you: did you receive the Spirit by the works of the Law, or by hearing with faith? Paul can ask this question because he already knows that there is only one response they can give. They received the Spirit by faith and not the Law. For Paul, faith is awakened by the gospel that he proclaimed (Rom. 10:16-17). Paul asks whether the Galatians received the Spirit as a result of the works of the Law (circumcision) or when they heard the message that he proclaimed about the crucified Jesus. The question may assume that they were taught by the Judaizing teachers that the Spirit came as a result of the observance of the Law. This notion may date from the time of Ezekiel who tells of God putting a new spirit in the children of Israel so that they can "follow my statutes and keep my ordinances and obey them"(Ezek. 11:19-20, NRSV). In the *Book of*

Jubilees (ca. second century B.C.) the giving of the Spirit and the keeping of the law are inextricably bound together. See, for example, when Moses requests a favor for the Jews from God:

> "Create a pure heart and a holy spirit for them [the Jews]. And do not let them be ensnared by their sin henceforth and forever."

And the Lord said to Moses, "I know their contrariness and their thoughts and their stubbornness. And they will not obey until they acknowledge their sin and the sins of their fathers. But after this they will return to me in all uprighteousness and with all of (their) heart and soul. And I shall cut off the foreskin of their heart and the foreskin of the heart of their descendants. And I shall create for them a holy spirit, and I shall purify them so that they will not turn away from following me from that day and forever. And their souls will cleave to me and to all my commandments. And they will do my commandments" (*Jub.* 1:21-24, *OT Pseud* 1:54).

3:3. Are you so foolish? Having begun by the Spirit, are you now being perfected by the flesh? While it would be easy to assume that Paul is speaking metaphorically, it is more likely that he is literally speaking of the flesh, namely the flesh of the foreskin (the *akrobystia*) that is removed in circumcision. Considering that the teachers who were troubling the Galatians were boasting of their ability to get the Galatians to submit to circumcision, it fits here that in Paul's irony and sarcasm, that he is thinking of the act of circumcision (see 6:12-13). Earlier in Jewish history, the connection between God's covenant and the flesh was considered inseparable. For example, in the *Wisdom of Jesus Son of Sirach* (ca. 180 B.C.), Sirach combines Abraham's actions in circumcision with the establishment of God's covenant.

Abraham was the great father of a multitude of nations, and no one has been found like him in glory. He kept the law of the Most High, and entered into a covenant with him; he certified the covenant in his flesh, and when he was tested he proved faithful. Therefore the Lord assured him with an oath that the nations would be blessed through his offspring; that he would make him as numerous as the dust of the earth, and exalt his offspring like the stars, and give them an inheritance from sea to sea and from the Euphrates to the ends of the earth (*Sir.* 44:19-21, NRSV).

Perfect in the flesh. Paul elsewhere urges his readers to "cleanse ourselves from every defilement of body and of spirit making holiness perfect in the fear of God" (2 Cor. 7:1). The desires of the body can affect one's holiness becoming perfect. James believed that this "perfection" was related to loving one's neighbor (Jas. 2:8) and even more that faith is brought to completion (perfection) by works (2:22). Compare this with Jesus' comments on all of the law being summarized in loving God and one's neighbor (Matt. 22:37-40).

Paul's reference to Abraham and the blessing that came prior to the Law and circumcision (3:6-10) is important for his argument against those who hinge the blessing of God upon keeping the Law and submitting to circumcision. At Qumran, perfection aimed at subduing the impulsive desires of the flesh. In the *Damascus Document*, for instance, we see that perfection was rejecting the desires of the flesh by keeping the Law of God.

And now, my sons, listen to me and I shall open your eyes so that you can see and understand the deeds of God, so that you can choose what he is pleased with and repudiate what he hates, so that you can walk perfectly on all his paths and not follow after the thoughts of a guilty inclination and lascivious eyes. For many wandered off for these matters. . . All flesh which there was in the dry earth decayed and became as if it had never been, for having realized their desires and failing to keep their creator's precepts, until his wrath flared up against them. (*CD* 2.14-20, Garcia Martinez trans. 34)

In the *Rule of the Community* document, we see something similar, only circumcision is used metaphorically:

No-one should walk in the stubbornness of his heart in order to go astray following his heart and his eyes and the musings of his inclination. Instead he should circumcise in the Community the foreskin of his tendency and of his stiff neck in order to lay a foundation of truth for Israel, for the Community of eternal covenant (1QS 5.4-5, Garcia Martinez trans. 8).

The example of Abraham (see 3:6-10 below) was also used by those at Qumran, and probably by those Paul was addressing, to speak of achieving perfect victory over desire and impulse through the keeping of the commands of God. Again, in the *Damascus Document*, we read:

Abraham did not walk in it [evil?], and was counted as a friend for keeping God's precepts and not following the desire of his spirit. And he passed (them) on to Isaac and to Jacob, and they kept (them) and were written up as friends of God and as members of the covenant for ever (*CD* 3.2-4, Garcia Martinez trans. 34).

In the Mishnah, contrary to the argument that Paul will put forth later, it was believed that Abraham attained perfection by keeping the Law and being circumcised.

R. Nehemiah says: Great is circumcision which overrides the laws of leprosy-signs. Rabbi says: Great is circumcision, for despite all the religious duties which Abraham our father fulfilled, he was not called 'perfect' until he was circumcised, as it is written, *Walk before me and be thou perfect* [Gen. 17:1]. After another fashion [it is said], Great is circumcision: but for it the Holy one, blessed is he, had not created his world, as it is written, *Thus saith the*

Lord, but for my covenant day and night, I had not set forth the ordinances of heaven and earth [Jer. 33:25] (*m. Nedarim* 3.11, Danby trans. 268).

According to the Genesis Rabbah, circumcision removed Abraham's only blemish; after that he was perfect. Paul's question is highly relevant to those who were being taught that perfection did, in fact, come through deeds of the flesh, namely circumcision and keeping the other symbolic laws.

3:4. Did you suffer so many things in vain—if indeed it was in vain? This passage hints that the Galatian Christians may have suffered persecution. If so, this is the only passage that says so. It is possible that the term "suffer" (Greek = *epathete* from *pathein*) can also mean nothing more than "experience," but it is not clear. Paul believed that the Galatians were in great danger and that he may have ministered to them in vain (see 4:11, 20; 5:4; 6:8).

3:5. Does He then, who provides you with the Spirit and works miracles among you, do it by the works of the Law, or by hearing with faith? Paul assumes the answer again (3:2) that the working of miracles continues among them, but argues that it is not because of the working or keeping of the Law, but by their faith in Christ. By examining their own experience, they ought to come to the correct answer, according to Paul. Since the gift of the Spirit is God's gift (Phil. 1:19; cf. Rom. 5:5; 8:15; 2 Cor. 1:22; 1 Thess. 4:8). For Paul, the granting of the Spirit and the working of miracles comes not through the Law, but through faith in God. Paul's conclusion here is not unlike that of later Jewish writers who combine the giving of the Holy Spirit with faith. According to a second-century A.D. Jewish writing,

Great is faith before the One who spoke and brought the world into being. For as a reward for the act of faith that the Israelites made in the Lord, the Holy Spirit rested upon them and they sang the song, as it is said, "and they believed in the Lord and in his servant Moses." Then Moses and the people of Israel sang this song [to the Lord, saying, "I will sing to the Lord, for he has triumphed gloriously; the horse and his rider he has thrown into the sea"].

R.[Rabbi] Nehemiah says, "How do you know that whosoever takes upon himself the obligation to carry out a single religious duty in faith is worth that the Holy Spirit should rest upon him?"

For so we find in the case of our ancestors that as a reward for the act of faith that they made, they achieved merit, so that the Holy Spirit rested on them as it is said, "and they believed in the Lord and in his servant Moses."

> . . . So you find that Abraham our father inherited this world and the world to come only as a reward for the faith that he believed, as it is said, "And he believed in the Lord [Gen. 15:6]." (*Mekhilta Beshallah* 7.25-27, trans. by Neusner, *Mekhilta Rabbi Ishmael* in E. Boring, 462).

2. The Second Argument: Abraham and Faith (3:6-14). At the heart of the illustrations that his contemporaries used to justify the "works of the flesh" was the appeal to Scripture and the example of Abraham. Paul therefore appeals to the Scriptures to show that Abraham was made right with God because of his faith and not because of his obedience to the Law or circumcision. The first argument comes from Abraham's example, which continues through v. 18, and involves a scriptural argument as well. Interestingly, unlike in Rom. 4 where Paul begins with Abraham and proceeds to the consequences of his behavior for those who believe, in this passage Paul focuses first on those who are the legitimate heirs of Abraham, those who believe.

3:6. Even so Abraham "believed God, and it was reckoned to him as righteousness." See discussion of 3:1-3 above. Abraham's role among the Jews is unparalleled. He was the father of the nation and the example par excellence of what it meant to be a Jew. As a result, there were countless references to him and to the promises of God to him that constituted the Jews as a people. The author of the *Book of Jubilee* (second cent. B.C.), concludes the story of Abraham's life saying that he "was perfect in all of his actions with the Lord and was pleasing through righteousness all the days of his life" (*Jub* 23:10, *OT Pseud* 1:100). Later he adds, reflecting upon Isaac's desire to journey to Egypt, that God told him, that if he dwells in the land of promise, "I will give to your seed all of this land. And all of the nations of the earth will bless themselves by your seed because

your father obeyed me and observed my restrictions and my commandments and my laws and my ordinances and my covenant" (*Jub* 24.10-11, *OT Pseud* 1:103). The Jews believed that Abraham's faith coincided with his deeds as in the case of his following the command of God to sacrifice his son Isaac (Gen. 22:1-18). Because he obeyed the commands of God, which are a picture of the commands of God found later in the Law of Moses, God blessed him. Sirach (ca. 180 B.C.) concluded the same about him saying "He kept the law of the Most High, and entered into a covenant with him; he certified the covenant in his flesh and when he was tested he proved

---

Paul and Works of the Law at Qumran

Paul tells the Christians of Galatia: "a man is not justified by the works of the Law but through faith in Christ Jesus, even we have believed in Christ Jesus, that we may be justified by faith in Christ, and not by the works of the Law; since by the works of the Law shall no flesh be justified" (Gal. 2:16). To make this argument, the apostle appeals to the example of Abraham, whose story is told in Genesis, one of the books of the Law: "Even so Abraham 'believed God, and it was reckoned to him as righteousness' [Gen. 15:6]" (Gal. 3:6; cf. Romans 4).

Against whom is Paul arguing? Some critics have claimed that Paul has made a straw man out of the Jewish faith of his time, that no one actually believed that justification came from works, instead of faith. But according to a letter from Qumran, in which the interpretation of the Law is discussed, some apparently did. Six fragmentary copies of this letter were found near the Dead Sea. One part of it reads:

"Now, we have written to you 27some of the works of the Law, those which we determined would be beneficial for you and your people, because we have seen [that] 28you possess insight and knowledge of the Law. Understand all these things and beseech Him to set 29your counsel straight and so keep you away from evil thoughts and the counsel of Belial. 30Then you shall rejoice at the end time when you find the essence of our words to be true. 31And it will be reckoned to you as righteousness, in that you have done what is right and good before Him, to your own benefit 32and to that of Israel" (4QMMT C26-32 = 4Q398 frgs. 14–17 ii 2-8).

Whereas Paul drew upon Gen. 15:6, the author of 4QMMT drew upon Ps. 106:30-31: "Then Phinehas stood up and interposed; And so the plague was stayed. And it was reckoned to him for righteousness, To all generations forever." The men of Qumran preferred the example of Phineas the priest, whose works resulted in his being reckoned righteous. In contrast, the Apostle Paul appealed to the example of Abraham, whose faith resulted in his being reckoned righteous.

faithful" (*Sir* 44:20, NRSV). So also, the author of *1 Maccabees* (late second century B.C.), asks, "Was not Abraham found faithful when tested, and it was reckoned to him as righteousness?" (*1 Macc.* 2:52, NRSV).

To argue contrary to this view, Paul would appear to be fighting an uphill battle and a belief firmly entrenched in his day. In the *Mishnah*, in a saying reserved for Gentiles and Jews who opposed the teachings of the rabbis, that is, those who opposed belief in the resurrection and were opposed to chose to be free from restraint, we read: "and these are they that have no share in the world to come: he that says that there is no resurrection of the dead prescribed in the Law, and [he that says] that the Law is not from Heaven, and an Epicurean" (*m. Sanh* 10.1, Danby trans.).

Paul begins his response by citing Gen. 15:6 that says that Abraham (Abram), "believed the Lord; and the Lord reckoned it to him as righteousness." This famous text is frequently cited in Philo's writings. For example, and for different purposes: namely, to dispel confidence in rational thought (Mind) as opposed to faith in God, Philo concludes, "So then it is best to trust God and not our dim reasonings and insecure conjectures: 'Abraham believed God and was held to be righteous' (Gen. 15:6)" (*Allegorical Interpretation* 3.228, LCL). For other examples of this in Philo, see *On change of Names* 177, 181-186, 218; *On the Migration of Abraham* 44; *Who is Heir* 90-95; *On Abraham* 262-274; *On the Unchangeableness of God* 4; *On the Virtues* 216-218; *On Rewards and Punishments* 27-30). Later the Christians also frequently cite this passage, even if for different purposes, (Rom. 4:3, 9, 22, 23; Jas. 2:20-26, esp. 23). The passage also is frequently cited in the noncanonical early Christian literature such as in the Epistle of Barnabas where the author writes: "What then does he say to Abraham, when he alone was faithful, and it was counted to him for righteousness? "Behold I have made thee, Abraham,

the father of the Gentiles who believe in God in uncircumcision" (*Ep. Barn* 13:7, LCL; see also *1 Clem* 10:6; Justin, *Dial* 23.4; 92.3; 119.6).

Paul uses the Greek (LXX) version of the passage to go back to the beginning of Abraham's story to make his point. There were no laws to keep at that time, but Abraham believed God and this act was what precipitated all that followed, not a keeping of the Law. Paul uses chronology, that he comes back to in 3:17, showing historically that faith came before the Law, and therefore he concludes that faith is apart from the Law. For Paul, those who are people of faith are the true children of Abraham.

3:7. Therefore, be sure that it is those who are of faith who are sons of Abraham. Paul here states the conclusion of his thesis, namely that only those persons of faith receive the blessings of Abraham, because he received them not by works of the Law, but rather by faith. Paul argues that the Gentiles come into the household of faith through Abraham and not the Law. Indeed, all who believe are children of Abraham. This forms a part of Paul's concluding argument for the inclusion of the Gentiles apart from the Law in 4:22-31. For those who took refuge in the fact that Abraham was their father and as a result that they were okay with God, both John the Baptist and Jesus offered challenging words (Matt. 3:9; Luke 3:8; 16:24; John 8:33, 39-59). When one of the seven sons was being tortured and eventually martyred by Antiochus Epiphanes, the author of *4 Maccabees* (first century A.D.), says of him, "Even when his bodily frame was all dissevered, the great-souled youth, a true son of Abraham, uttered not a groan" (*4 Macc.* 9:21, *OT Pseud* 2:555). Later, when all of the sons of the woman have been martyred, the same author concludes their story saying, "But the sons of Abraham, together with their mother, who won the victor's prize, are gathered together in the choir of their fathers, having received pure and deathless souls from God, to whom be glory forever and ever. Amen" (18:23, *OT Pseud* 2:564; see also Philo, *On the Virtues* 195-97).

3:8. And the Scripture, foreseeing that God would justify the Gentiles by faith, preached the gospel beforehand to Abraham, saying, "All the nations shall be blessed in you." See Gen. 12:1-3; 15:5-6. For other references to this blessing, see Gen. 18:18; 22:18; 26:4; 28:14; Ps. 71:17 (both Hebrew and LXX). See also *Sir* 44:21 cited above. The phrase "preached the gospel beforehand" is the translation of one Greek word (*proeuangelidzomai*), which is only found here in the New Testament, but is found in Philo who uses it to speak of the anticipation of the blessings of creation. He writes: "*anticipates* the sunrise with the *glad tidings* of its approach" (*On the Creation* 34, LCL, italics ours). He later uses the same term to describe the anticipated ability of the young bird who shakes its wings "giving a welcome promise of ability to fly hereafter" (*On Change of Names* 158, LCL).

3:9. So then those who are of faith are blessed with Abraham, the believer [literally, "faithful Abraham"]. Abraham as the model in whom others of faith are blessed is found in *2 Maccabees* where the writer says by way of a prayer, "May God do good to you, and may he remember his covenant with Abraham and Isaac and Jacob, his faithful servants" (*2 Macc.* 1:2). See also *1 Macc.* 2:52 and Philo, *On the Posterity and Exile of Cain* 173. This same notion appears in early Christian literature as well (*1 Clem* 10:6-7).

3:10. For as many as are of the works of the Law are under a curse; for it is written, "Cursed is everyone who does not abide by all things written in the book of the law, to perform them." The second Scripture proof of Paul's argument from Scripture comes from Deuteronomy 27:26. The citation does not con-

form easily either to the LXX or the Hebrew text, and is likely Paul's own summary of the force of the passage, namely that if one does not keep all of the Law, he or she is cursed by God. Since no one can do that, according to Paul, it follows that those who seek justification or righteousness on the merits of keeping the Law are doomed to failure.

3:11. Now that no one is justified by the Law before God is evident; for, "The righteous man shall live by faith." The third Scripture proof Paul cites comes from Habakkuk 2:4, "the righteous live by faith." At Qumran, in a commentary on this passage, unlike in Paul, it was concluded, "Its interpretation concerns all observing the Law in the House of Judah, whom God will free from punishment on account of their deeds and of their loyalty to the Teacher of Righteousness" (1QpHab 7:17-8:3, Garcia Martinez trans). Again, the interpretation says that one who keeps the Law is made righteous.

3:12. However, the Law is not of faith; on the contrary, "He who practices them shall live by them." Anticipating his opponents' appeal to Lev. 18:5, he cites a fourth scriptural reference here to justify his argument saying that those who want to be justified by the Law, must be prepared to live by the Law, something that he believes no one can in fact do. When Paul cites Lev. 18:5 in Rom. 10:5-6, he appears to be making Moses responsible, for Christ is the end of the Law that brings death, and Moses is the one who advocates the keeping of the Law. The bringing of these two biblical texts together, Hab. 2:4 and Lev. 18:5, appears to be important for understanding Paul's response to the Judaizers. Both texts speak about future life, but for one (Hab. 2:4) it comes through faith and the other (Lev. 18:5) through the Law. Paul argues that those who live by the Law are those who actually keep the Law—all of it, but his argument is based on the assumption that no one can keep all of the Law, and therefore, the text cited is evidence of the judgment or "curse" of God that comes as a result of trying to keep the Law in order to obtain righteousness or justification before God. How can Paul reconcile these two positions? Remarkably, he does not and indeed appears to show that the two are in opposition. For Paul there is a "good side" and a "bad side" to the Law, and later on as well as elsewhere he shows them both (3:19-21; Rom. 3:31; 7:12, 14). He presupposes that the Law has two major emphases: namely, one that is positive and offers promise (Gen. 15:6; Isa. 54:1; Hab. 2:4), but the other Law and a curse (Lev. 18:5). While this may seem surprising that Paul would pit one part of the Scriptures, namely the Law, against another part, namely the promise of God in Christ, this is not unlike what we see in Hebrew 8:6-8, 13, in which God finds fault with the first covenant (the Law) and so sets forth a second opportunity through Christ. One of the biggest obstacles in the early church was to deal with the problem of neglecting what the Law taught, but at the same time claiming the Law and all OT Scriptures as its Bible. Paul is the first to address this issue and it reappears in the second century first through Justin Martyr in his *Dialogue with Trypho*. He argued that the divine ordinances given to Israel, the Law, were added as a result of Israel's hardness of heart and failure. "Then I answered [Trypho the Jew], saying, 'you perceive that God by Moses laid all such ordinances upon you on account of the hardness of your people's hearts, so that, by the large number of them, you might obey God continually in every action, before your eyes and never again begin to act unjustly or impiously'" (*Dial.* 46.6, *ANF*). Later, he adds an invective that reflects both the historical circumstances following the Jewish Bar Kochba rebellion against Rome (132-35) and the Jews' exclusion from Jerusalem. He writes:

> for the circumcision according to the flesh, which is from Abraham, was given for a sign; that you may be sepa-

rated from other nations, and from us; and that you alone may suffer and your land be made desolate and your cities burned with fire, and so that strangers may eat your fruit in your presence, and not one of you may go up to Jerusalem (*Dial.* 16.2, *ECF*. This line of argument continues in *Dial.* 27.2-4.).

This, of course, raises the question never fully answered in antiquity, If the Christians do not follow the Law, how then can it be "Scripture"? How can it be normative for the church? Paul's response is to see both the positive aspects of the Law (it is holy, just and good—Rom. 7:12, and it was added to bring all to a recognition of a need of Christ—3:19-4:7, especially v. 21), but on the other hand, he reveals its inadequacy in bringing one into a right relationship with God.

In the next section (3:15-18), he will make this more clear. Keeping the Law was an essential feature of the Jewish faith in Paul's day and much Jewish interpretation hinges upon it. In the *Mishnah*, the author of *Aboth* (sometimes called *Pirke Aboth*, "Chapters of the Fathers") begins his tractate with the words about the greatness of the Law and the importance of "putting a hedge" around it so that it would be defended.

> Moses received the Law [a reference to the "Oral Law"] from Sinai and committed it to Joshua , and Joshua to the elders [Josh. 24:31], and the elders to the Prophets [Jer. 7:25]; and the Prophets committed it to the men of the Great Synagogue [= 120 elders who came from exile with Ezra]. They said three things: Be deliberate in judgment [sic], raise up many disciples, and make a fence around the Law.

> Simeon the Just [cf. Josephus, *Ant.* 12.43, "On the death of the high priest Onias, he was succeeded by his son Simon, who was surnamed the Just because of his piety toward God and his

benevolence to his countrymen" ca. 200 B.C.; cf. *Sir.* 50:1-24] was of the remnants of the Great Synagogue. He used to say: By three things is the world sustained: by the Law, by the [Temple-] service, and by the deeds of loving-kindness (*m. Aboth* 1.1-2, Danby trans.).

He further contends that the way of the Law is the way of blessings and exclaims, "Great is the Law, for it gives life to them that practice it both in this world and in the world to come, as it is written, for they are life unto those they find them, and health to all their flesh" (*Abot* 7.1, Danby trans.460). In the New Testament, James also represents this notion of doing rather than simply believing (Jas. 2:20-24). The curse of the Law, namely those who do not live by the Law will die, is echoed variously in the Old Testament, but also in the New and in early Jewish literature (Deut. 27:12-13; *Sir* 2:12; 15:16; Matt. 7:13-14; *m. Abot* 2:1 cited earlier; Jas. 2:8-13). Sirach lets his readers know that life is to be found in keeping the commandments of God and death for those who refuse.

If you choose, you can keep the commandments, and to act faithfully is a matter of your own choice. He has placed before you fire and water; stretch out your hand for whichever you choose. Before each person are life and death, and whichever one chooses will be given (*Sir.* 15:15-17, NRSV).

3:13-14. Christ redeemed us from the curse of the Law, having become a curse for us—for it is written, "Cursed is everyone who hangs on a tree"— in order that in Christ Jesus the blessing of Abraham might come to the Gentiles, so that we might receive the promise of the Spirit through faith. This is the key scriptural text that Paul uses to interpret the death of Jesus. While he elsewhere acknowledges that the death of Jesus took place "for our sins" and "in accordance with the scriptures" (1 Cor. 15:3), the death itself as a curse is not explained elsewhere. The word "redeemed"

(Greek = *exegorasen*, from *exagoradzo*, "buy out," "ransom," or "deliver"; from *agoradzo*, "I buy." A similar term, *lutroo*, cf. noun forms, *lutron/lutrosis* or *apolutrosis* = translated "ransom" or "redemption") was used commonly in the ancient world in reference to emancipation or manumission of slaves (see Diodorus Siculus, first cent. B.C., *Library of History* 15.7.1). Paul often uses the terminology metaphorically to speak of the sinner's salvation and freedom from sin, namely that this was "purchased" or "redeemed" by Christ (see 1 Cor. 6:20). If a slave or a benefactor sought to purchase the freedom of the slave, the price paid was often called a "redemption." In an inscription found at Delphi, where slaves often purchased their own freedom, we read the following:

Date [200-199 B.C.]. Apollo [the Greek god] the Pythian bought from Sosibius or Amphissa for freedom a female slave, whose name is Nicaea, by race a Roman, with a price of three minae of silver and a half-mina. Former seller according to law: Eumnastus of Amphissa. The price he had received. The purchase, however, Nicaea had committed unto Apollo for freedom (Trans. by Deissmann, *Light* 323).

While manumission often took place in a temple, such as at Delphi, it sometimes also took place in or with reference to the synagogue when freedom was purchased from Jews. One such report of a Jewish manumission dating from ca. A.D. 81 (= 377 in the Roman calendar) goes as follows:

In the reign of king Tiberias Julius Rhescuporis, friend of Caesar and friend of Rome, the pious; in the year 377, in the month Penitius, the 20th [or 23rd], I Chreste, formerly wife of Nicias, son of Sotas, release at the house of prayer [Greek = *proseuche*] my slave Heraclas to be completely free according to my vow. He is not to be retained or disturbed by any heir of mine, but to go wherever he wishes, without let or hindrance according to my vow, except for the house of prayer which is for worship and meeting. Assent is given to this also by my heirs, Pericleides and Heliconias. Join oversight will be taken also by the synagogue of the Jews. (*CIJ* 683, *CIG* 2114 *bb*, translated by Barrett, *NT Background*, 56).

This inscription does not have any reference to a pagan god, as in the above example. For a discussion of the issue of slavery and its redemption, see discussion and examples in 1 Cor. 7:23. Paul elsewhere sees himself and humanity as slaves of sin (Rom. 7:13-25) in need of the redemption (purchase) of Christ to liberate all persons from bondage to sin (Rom. 8:1-5, 23). The use of the slavery/emancipation theme as a metaphor for what God has done in Christ for those who believe was one that would have resonated well with the citizens in the Greco-Roman world where slavery was a fact of life. For Paul, before Christ, all of humanity, both Jew and Gentile, was enslaved either to the Law or to the rudiments of the world, but now in Christ, both are liberated.

Paul presents his fifth Scripture text here, Deut. 21:23, to demonstrate his point, but his exegesis appears difficult for modern readers to grasp. The Jews in the time of Jesus assumed that this text showed that anyone who was crucified automatically was under the curse of God. In a commentary on the book of Nahum (2:12), the community at Qumran, speaking of the 800 crucifixions by Alexander Janneus (ca. 90 B.C.), concluded that if a man were hanged on a tree (crucified), it proved his condemnation from God.

Its interpretation concerns the Angry Lion [who filled his den with a mass of corpses, carrying our rev]enge against those looking for easy interpretations, who hanged living men [from the tree, committing an atrocity which had not been committed] in Israel since ancient times, for it is horrible for the one hanged alive from the tree (4Q169 [4QpNah]1.6-8, Garcia

Martinez trans, 195).

Similarly, the *Temple Scroll* supplies additional evidence that death on a cross was a curse for the one who was crucified.

If there were to be a spy against his people, who betrays his people to a foreign nation or causes evil against his people, you shall hang him from a tree and he will die. If there were a man with a sin punishable by death and he escapes amongst the nations and curses his people /and/ the children of Israel, he also you shall hang on the tree and he will die. Their corpses shall not spend the night on the tree; instead you shall bury them that day because they are cursed by God and man, those hanged on a tree; thus you shall not defile the land which I give you for inheritance (11Q 64.6-11, Garcia Martinez trans.).

Both of these Jewish texts pre-date the death of Jesus and the view was evidently widespread before the time of Jesus that the very act of crucifixion meant that the one crucified was cursed of God. The connection between Christ's death and the curse from Deut. 21:23, is also found in the second-century apologist, Ariston of Pella (*Altercatio*, cf. the reference in Jerome's commentary on Galatians in *PL* 26.361 and *Writings of the Ante-Nicene Fathers* or *ANF* 8:749) and in Justin's *Dialogue with Trypho* (32.1; 89.2; 90.1; 94.5).

Paul is using acceptable hermeneutics (or methods of interpretation) of his day, but modern readers are often confused or unconvinced by it. Before Gentiles came to faith, they were under a curse because they did not have the Law and were consequently beyond the scope of God's salvation. Because Christ became a curse, having hung on a tree (cross), he has taken their place and redeemed them from the curse they were under. That is the force of Paul's comments, even if the logic of them is difficult to grasp. Paul also speaks of the curse of the Law, namely that if one is going to live by it, he or she must be faithful in every part of it—something impossible to do, hence, a curse. Paul explains this conflict and curse more in Rom. 7:7-25, even though he does not use the word "curse" there. Likewise, because the Law had a curse for those who did not live up to it, Jesus was put to death by his violation of the Law.

It is interesting that in the second-century gnostic text, *The Apocryphon of James*, there is a saying of Jesus that seems to grasp what Paul has said about Jesus becoming a "curse for us." The author of that document, independently of Paul, says, "Do not be proud because of the light that illumines, but be to yourselves as I myself am to you. For your sakes I [Jesus] have placed myself under the curse, that you may be saved" (*Ap. Jas.* 13.21-25). This same idea is found also in another gnostic text, the *Second Apocalypse of James* which, while speaking of Jesus, says, "He shall be judged with the [unrighteous]. He who lived [without] blasphemy died by means of [blasphemy]. He who was cast out they [...]" (trans. supplied by E. Boring, 464). In both cases, there is no apparent dependence on Gal. 3:13, and this gives separate support for what Paul has presented, namely a cursed Christ. What Paul probably has in mind, and it is by no means certain, is that it was those custodians of the Law who condemned Jesus for violating the Law by committing blasphemy; even burying the body before sundown was a requirement of the Law (Mark 14:53-64; cf. Deut. 21:23).

The reference to the "blessing of Abraham" has its roots in Gen. 28:3-4 in which Isaac blesses Jacob and says "May he [God] give to you the blessing of Abraham, to you and to your off-spring with you, so that you may take posses-sion of the land . . . that God gave to Abraham" (NRSV). Paul concludes that this blessing, which is the promise of the Spirit, does not come by the Law, but by faith.

3. Faith Is Based upon an Earlier Covenant (3:15-18). Continuing with his argument from Abraham, the father of all who believe, both Jew and Gentile, Paul makes the argument that since Abraham was justified 430 years prior to the giving of the Law, then it is reasonable to assume that justification is not based on the Law, but on what it was that brought justifica-tion to Abraham, namely faith.

3:15. Brethren, I speak in terms of human relations: even though it is only a man's covenant, yet when it has been ratified, no one sets it aside or adds conditions to it. Unlike in 3:1, 3, Paul has softened the tone of his address to "brethren" (Greek = *adelphoi*). The term is, of course, a generic one for both male and female, and also acknowledges that the ones he is addressing have a special rela-tionship with him through Jesus Christ. Paul softens his tone as he teaches the rationale for his gospel of faith rather than works, and even adds personal comments about how much the Galatians mean to him (4:12-20, 28), but will revert to strong language once again (5:2-12).

Paul now introduces for the first time the word "covenant" (Greek = *diatheke*) in the form of a last will and testament. He also ties the notion of the covenant with God that saves with Abraham and not the Law, something contrary to widespread Jewish understanding in the time of Paul. He states that once a will is made it cannot be changed, but both the Greeks and Romans knew that certain wills or last testaments could be changed, especially during the lifetime of the one who made the will (often referred to as the "usufruct" or tem-porary use and enjoyment of the estate). The Jews also made a distinction between the kinds of covenants that could be changed and those that could not. The Hebrew terms *mattenat bari'* (= a kind of covenant could not be changed) and the *diyathiki* (Hebrew transliteration of the Greek *diatheke*) could be changed or revoked. Paul seems to be making his case on the first of these two kinds of wills or covenants, namely unconditional and conditional. While these distinctions are Jewish and Paul's audience was Hellenistic, it is likely that the arrangements related to the *mattenat bari'* were fairly widespread in Paul's day and would likely have been understood in a Gentile audience. Whatever the situation, Paul's point is clear. Once a promise or covenant has been made, it cannot be changed, revoked or set aside.

3:16. Now the promises were spoken to Abraham and to his seed. He does not say, "And to seeds," as referring to many, but rather to one, "And to your seed," that is, Christ. The promises made to Abraham (Gen. 12:2-3, 7; 13:15-16; 15:4-6; 17:1-11; 22:16-19; 24:7-9) are all based on a covenant and given to Abraham and his "seed," and these were given prior to the giving of the Law. In the LXX (Greek version) of Gen. 17:1-11, the words "covenant" and "seed" are used several times employing the same Greek words that Paul uses here (*diatheke* for "covenant" and *sperma* for "seed"). Although circumcision was a sign or seal of that covenant, the promise (Greek = *epangeliai*) was made prior to circumcision or the giving of the Law. The notion that Abraham had only one seed, but included more than those who were of Jewish descent is based on Gen. 12:2-3 and 21:13, and was carried on among the Jews in the second century B.C. During the Maccabean wars (ca. 167-164 B.C.) Jonathan, the high priest, sent ambassadors to Rome to seek assistance against the Greek alliance that had occupied Israel. He also sent a letter to the Spartans who had not aligned themselves with the Greek Achaean league against Rome and sought to make alliances with them as well as with the Romans. In the letter he called the Spartans "brothers" in the introduction to his letter: "The High priest Jonathan, the senate of the nation, the priests, and the rest of the Jewish people to their brothers the Spartans, greetings" (*1 Macc.* 12:6, NRSV). The response of the Spartans is also quite telling and supports Paul's view of the seed of Abraham being more

than the Jews alone or even those who have submitted to circumcision. In a letter of response, the king of the Spartans replied:

> King Arius of the Spartans, to the high priest Onias, greetings. It has been found in writing concerning the Spartans and the Jews that they are brothers and are of the family of Abraham. And now that we have learned this, please write us concerning your welfare; we on our part write to you that your livestock and your property belong to us, and ours belong to you. We therefore command that our envoys report to you accordingly. (*1 Macc.* 12:20-23, NRSV).

Likewise, the author of *Jubilees* claims that the seed of Abraham includes the nations. In an important and unusual text that has parallels with Exod. 19:6, 1 Peter 2:9, and Rev. 1:6 and 5:10, we read about the seed of Abraham possibly extending to non-Jews.

> And in the sixth year of the fourth month [following the birth and circumcision of Isaac] we went forth to Abraham at the Well of the Oath. And we appeared to him [just as we said to Sarah that we would return to her. And she had conceived a son. And we returned in the seventh month and we found Sarah pregnant before us.] and we blessed him and we announced to him everything which was commanded for him that he would not die until he begot six more sons and he would see (them) before he died. And through Isaac a name and seed would be named for him. And all the seed of his sons would become nations. And they would be counted with the nations. But from the sons of Isaac one would become a holy seed and he would not be counted among the nations because he would become the portion of the Most High and all his seed would fall (by lot) into

that which God will rule so that he might become a people (belonging) to the Lord, a (special) possession from all people, and so that he might become a kingdom of priests and a holy people. And we went our way and we announced to Sarah everything which we had told him. And both of them rejoiced very greatly (*Jub.* 16:15-19, *OT Pseud* 2:88).

3:17. What I am saying is this: the Law, which came four hundred and thirty years later, does not invalidate a covenant previously ratified by God, so as to nullify the promise. Paul argues that if Abraham could receive the blessing of God some 430 years before the giving of the Law, and that blessing (covenant or promise) cannot be set aside, then justification or righteousness does come from faith and not the works of the law (see Rom. 4:13-22). Again, Paul relates the covenant of God with the promise of Abraham and not with the Law. Abraham received the promise of God, that is, the "blessing of Abraham," on the basis of his faith and not by keeping the Law. There was a Jewish tradition that saw this problem and many argued that Abraham must have had a preview of the Law beforehand. Again, Sirach provides an important text on Abraham's blessing tied to his keeping of the law: "He kept the law of the Most High, and entered into a covenant with him; he certified the covenant in his flesh, and when he was tested he proved faithful. Therefore the Lord assured him with an oath that the nations would be blessed through his offspring" (*Sir.* 44:20, NRSV). See discussion in 3:3 above. The more usual Jewish interpretation of how one receives the blessing of God is through the Law. The author of 2 *Maccabees* sums up the typical Jewish understanding: "It is God who has saved all his people, and has returned the inheritance to all, and the kingship and the priesthood and the consecration, as he promised through the law (2 *Macc.* 2:17-18, NRSV).

3:18. For if the inheritance is based on law, it is no longer based on a promise; but God has granted it to Abraham by means of a promise. Paul summarizes his argument for the believer's inheritance (Greek = *kleronomia*) based on the promise or covenant to Abraham only. In this regard, he appears to have stood alone in his time and no doubt this is reflected in those in the church who opposed his ministry, for example Paul's opponents both in Corinth (2 Cor. 10-13) and in Galatia (cf. also 2 Tim. 1:15) and may even have led to his Christian colleagues abandoning him in Rome (2 Tim. 4:10), but the reasons for their departure are not clear.

B. 3:19-29. The True Purpose of the Mosaic Law

1. 3:19-22. To Contain Sin. Paul continues his argument for his gospel of grace and faith, but a logical question comes, if Christians are not under an obligation to keep the law, then what was its purpose in the first place? Paul seeks to answer that in this section. While he acknowledges that the Law is good, he also says that it cannot accomplish the mission of making persons right with God. The reason, of course, is because no one has or can fully keep it (3:10-15). So why the Law?

3:19. Why the Law then? It was added because of transgressions, having been ordained through angels by the agency of a mediator, until the seed should come to whom the promise had been made. Much has been made in antiquity over the usefulness and viability of laws. The comments range from praise to rejection and almost everything in between. Generally speaking, it was believed by the non-Jewish ancient writers that were it not for evil persons, laws would not be needed and that virtuous people did not have need of them. The Jewish perspective, on the other hand, is that nothing would be possible without them. In his essay, *On Law* (or *Minos*), Plato tells about the essence of law and it begins with Socrates asking a companion, "Tell me, what is law?" (313A, LCL). He then proceeds to instruct his companion that whatever is evil and lacks virtue is not lawful, but law has to do with what is good and just, and virtuous (313B-321D) and tells about the various kinds of laws and their importance or their questionable character. In another place, Plato says that laws were created both for the good persons and also for the bad.

> Laws, it would seem, are made partly for the sake of good men, to afford them instruction as to what manner of intercourse will best secure for them friendly association one with another, and partly also for the sake of those who have shunned education, and who, being of a stubborn nature, have had no softening treatment to prevent their taking to all manner of wickedness. It is because of these men that the laws which follow have to be stated (*Laws* 9.880E, LCL).

In his *Seventy-Fifth Discourse on Law*, Dio Chrysostom (A.D. 40-120) praises the Law and says that "those who strictly observe the law have firm hold on safety; while those who transgress it destroy first of all themselves and then their fellows" (*Oration* 75.1, LCL). He continues that "without law, no city can be administered," but more than that, he called law the "king of men and gods" because "law does away with violence, puts down insolence, reproves folly, chastises wickedness, and in private and public relations helps all who are in need, succouring the victims of injustice" (75.2, LCL). When the law is appropriately constructed, he argues, "it exercises its authority without the use of arms and force—on the contrary, law itself does away with force; nay it rules by persuasion and governs willing subjects. For it is because it first persuades men and secures their approval that law comes into being and acquires its own power" (75.4, LCL). In praise of law, he adds that "Law is a protec-

tor of old age, a schoolmaster of youth, of poverty a fellow labourer, a guard of wealth, to peace an ally, to war a foe" and he concludes that "a city cannot be saved if the law has been destroyed, not even when no dire disaster befalls it from without" and "if one expels the law from his life, just as if he had lost his mind, I believe he will be brought into a state of utter madness and confusion" (75.10, LCL). Similarly, Pindar (518-543 B.C.) concludes that "Law, the king of all, of mortals and immortals, guides them as it justifies the utmost violence with a sovereign hand" (*Frg.* 169a, LCL).

Not everyone thought that laws were as essential as did Plato and Dio Chrysostom; Cynics and Stoics often taught that virtue alone was all that was needed by the wise to live peaceably with others and that laws were for the weak. Diogenes claimed that nobility belonged only to those who were virtuous and that virtue was sufficient to insure happiness in life. For him, the wise man was virtuous and "the wise man will be guided in his public acts not by established laws, but by the law of virtue" (Diogenes Laertius, *Lives of Eminent Philosophers* [*Antisthenes*] 6.11, LCL). Later, in response to a question about the advantage that philosophers have over others, he responds: "Should all laws be repealed, we [philosophers] shall go on living as we do now" (2.68, LCL).

Xenophon (ca. 430-354 B.C.), in telling the story of Socrates' interaction with Hippias regarding matters of law and justice, defined the laws of a state as "covenants made by the citizens whereby they have enacted what ought to be done and what ought to be avoided" (*Memorabilia* 4.4.13, LCL). He recognized that those cities that abide by such laws are the strongest and enjoy the most happiness because such laws were just (4.4.16-18). He acknowledged, however, that there are some "unwritten laws," or customs, that are followed by the people that were made "by the gods" for the people and that is why "for among all men the first law is to fear the gods" (4.4.19), and those who transgress the laws ordained by the gods "pay a penalty that a man can in no wise escape" such as dishonoring one's parents or having sexual intercourse with one's children (4.4.20-23).

The Jews believed that the Law was a "hedge" or "fence" that provided protection for them. The author of the *Epistle of Aristeas* (ca. perhaps 170 B.C. and from Alexandria) claims that Moses was endowed by God with universal truths and, "surrounded us with unbroken palisades and iron walls to prevent our mixing with any of the other peoples in any matter, being kept pure in body and soul, preserved from false beliefs, and worshiping the only god omnipotent over all creation" (*Ep. Arist.* 139, *OT Pseud* 2:22). He continues that God gave the Law to protect his people: "So to prevent our being perverted by contact with others or by mixing with bad influences, he hedged us in on all sides with strict observances connected with meat and drink and touch and hearing and sight, after the manner of the Law" (*Ep. Arist.* 142, *OT Pseud* 2:22). Remarkably, the Mishnah reverses this and puts a fence around the Law:

> Moses received the Law from Sinai and committed it to Joshua, and Joshua to the elders, and the elders to the Prophets, and the Prophets committed it to the men of the Great Synagogue. They said three things: Be deliberate in judgement, raise up many disciples, and *make a fence around the Law* (m. *Aboth* 1.1, Danby trans. 446., italics ours).

Philo claims that God established his laws in the desert and away from cities because of the evil in the cities and because that way no one could say that it was derived from the cities but from God and in this way also the Jews could "clear the sin out of their souls" so that they could be nourished in their minds by the Law (*Decalogue* 2, 13-15). He adds that "He who gave abundance of the means of life also bestowed the wherewithal of a good life; for mere life they needed food and drink which they found without making provision; for the good life they needed laws and ordinances which would bring improvement to their souls" (*Decalogue* 17, LCL).

By all accounts, the Jewish literature of Paul's day and before is at odds with Paul's view of the function and value of the Law. For him, Christ is the end of the Law (Rom. 10:4) and after Christ came, there was no continuing purpose for the legalistic system that was intended like a "tutor" (see 3:23-24 below) to bring one to maturity (Christ). How this occurred is answered by Paul himself, namely that it was because of his change of perspective on the identity of Jesus as the true Law of God. Like Paul, Plato saw the law sometimes as a constrainer rather than as a liberator: "I regard you all as kinsmen and intimates and fellow-citizens by nature, not by law: for like is akin to like by nature, whereas law, despot of mankind, often constrains us against nature" (cf. Plato, *Protagoras* 337, LCL). Paul says the Law is good and holy, but with a temporal purpose, not a permanent one.

Mediated through angels. In the opening part of this letter (1:8) Paul involves the possibility of an angel, or even himself, preaching a gospel contrary to the one he had preached to them, would be accursed. The role of angels or mediators in the giving of the law has roots in Deut. 33:2. Those who translated this text into the LXX used the word "angels" as those who attended the giving of the Law (cf. Acts 7:38, 53; Heb. 2:2). Josephus reflects the growth of this perspective when he says "we have learned the noblest of our doctrines and the holiest of our laws from the messengers [Greek = *angelon*, "angels"] sent by God" (*Ant.* 15.136, LCL). As the role of angels grew in antiquity, it was believed that God used angels to accomplish his work among human beings. In the Testament of Dan (late second century B.C.), we read: "Draw near to God and to the angel who intercedes for you, because he is the mediator between God and men for the peace of Israel" (*T. Dan* 6.2, *OT Pseud* 1:810). In *Jubilees* (ca. second century B.C.), God commands an angel to write for Moses: "And he said to the angel of the presence, 'write for Moses from the first creation until my sanctuary is built in their midst forever and ever...'" (*Jub.* 1:27, *OT Pseud* 2:54). According to the writer of the Hymns at Qumran, "You [God] have brought [your truth and your] glory to all the men of your council and in the lot, together with the angels of the face [presence], without there being an mediator between the intelligent and your holy ones" (1QH 6.12-13 [14:12-13], Garcia Martinez trans.). See also Philo, *On Dreams* 1.140-144 and the *Apocalypse of Moses* 1. In the Christian tradition, Michael the archangel is the one who "put the law into the hearts of those who believe" (Hermas, *Sim.* 8.3.3, LCL). In gnostic Christianity, it was the demons who gave the Torah who also were those who created the world (see Epiphanius, *Panarion* 28.1.3). In the second century, the author of the epistle of Barnabas concluded that circumcision itself came from an evil angel who misled the Jews (*Ep. Barn.* 9.4).

"Until the seed should come." This, for Paul, is a reference to Christ and comes from God's promise to Abraham for a seed (Gen. 17:8). See also 3:23, 25 below.

3:20. Now a mediator is not for one party only; whereas God is only one. The mediator that Paul has in mind here is Moses and his mediation has to do with the giving of the Law at Sinai (see, for example, Exod. 19:7, 9, 21; 20:19; 24:3-4, 12; 31:18; 32:16, 19, 30; 34:1; Deut. 4:14; 5:4). If a mediator is used, the result is inferior to the situation where a mediator is not used, as in the case of Christ.

3:21. Is the Law then contrary to the promises of God? May it never be! For if a law had been given which was able to impart life, then righteousness would indeed have been based on law. As elsewhere, Paul cannot bring himself to say that there is something inherently wrong with the Law, only that keeping it, which is not wrong to try, can never bring a person into a right relationship with God. He contends that this was not its purpose, but rather its purpose was to reveal sin and the need of Christ. Paul does say that the promise of God is opposed to the law's curse (4:21-5:1; 5:17-18). The Jews believed the Law produced life. In the Mishnah, according to Rabbi Meir, or the reviser of *m. Aboth* 1-5:

He that occupies himself in the study of the Law for its own sake merits many things, and, still more, he is deserving of the whole world. He is called friend, beloved [of God], lover of God, lover of mankind; and it clothes him with humility and reverence and fits him to become righteous, saintly, upright, and faithful; and it keeps him far from sin and brings him near to virtue, and from him men enjoy counsel and sound knowledge, understanding and might, for it is written, Counsel is mine and sound knowledge, I am understanding, I have might [Prov. 8:14]. And it gives him kingship and dominion and discernment in judgment; to him are revealed the secrets of the Law, and he is made like to a never-failing spring and like to a river that flows ever more mightily; and he becomes modest, long-suffering, and forgiving of insult; and it magnifies him and exalts him above all things (*m. Aboth* 6.1, Danby trans.).

3:23. But before faith came, we were kept in custody under the law, being shut up to the faith which was later to be revealed. "Under the Law" spoke of its authority or rule over those who submitted to it. For this same idea, see Gal. 4:4-7, 21; 5:18; Rom. 6:14-15; 1 Cor. 9:20; cf. also Rom. 3:9; 7:14, and Gal. 3:10. Plato tells of a view of law shared by one Hippaias of Elis who said, "All you men who are present, I believe that you are all relatives, members of the same family, and [fellow] citizens by nature and not by the law. For like is related to like by nature, but the law is a tyrant that compels much that is contrary to nature" (*Protagoras* 26, LCL). Pindar said of the law, "Law, lord of all, mortals and immortals carrieth everything with a high hand, justifying the extreme of violence" (*Frg.* 169, LCL). Other similar views of law were expressed in Paul's day.

3:24. Therefore the Law has become our tutor to lead us to Christ, that we may be justified by faith. Paul uses a familiar metaphor, the tutor (Greek = *paidagogos*), to speak of the role of the Law in bringing one to faith in Christ. In the ancient world, those who had this role were to prepare a child for the adult world and to keep them distracted from the things that would beset their path to maturity. Generally, the tutor accompanied the child to school and admonished him (for the most part, education was for males only) along the way. Xenophon summarizes the relationship thusly: "When a lad ceases to be a child, and begins to be a lad, others release him from his moral tutor [*paidagogos*] and his schoolmaster: he is then no longer under a ruler and is allowed to go his own way" (*Constitution of the Lacedaemonians* 3.1, LCL). He goes on to tell of the extreme measures of one (Lycurgus) in charge of children that were intended to keep the children looking forward and not being distracted by the pleasures of life. They were given a "ceaseless round of work, and contrived a constant round of occupation" and were to be quiet in their behavior, including not being able "to look about them, but to fix their eyes on the ground." The effect, he says, is that "you would expect a stone image to utter a sound sooner than those lads" (3.2-5, LCL). Plato tells a similar story of the role of those who bring children to maturity through education.

They teach and admonish them from earliest childhood till the last day of their lives. As soon as one of them grasps what is said to him, the nurse, the mother, the tutor [*paidagogos*], and the father himself strive hard that the child may excel, and as each act and word occurs they teach and impress upon him that this is just, and that unjust, one thing noble, another base, one holy, another unholy, and that he is to do this, and not do that. If he readily obeys, — so; but if not, they treat him as a bent and twisted piece of wood and straighten him with threats and blows. After this they send them to school and charge the master to take far more pains over their children's good behaviour than over their letters and harp-playing. (*Protagoras* 325C-D, LCL)

As a *paidagogos* with a child who is charged to bring the child to a place of maturity, so the Law, says Paul, has a function and when that function was over, its function or purpose ceases. The maturity comes when faith is exercised and one lives under the guidance of Christ by the power of the Spirit (3:5).

3:25. But now that faith has come, we are no longer under a tutor. Plato has as clear a statement on the authority of a "tutor" (*paidagogos*) over a child as any in the ancient world. The *paidagogos* exercised complete authority over the child until the child came to maturity. During this time, the slave (tutor) has more authority than does a child. After determining that a tutor was a slave, Socrates asks Lysis whether his parents value the slave more than him, a son, and says to him:

"So it seems that they value a slave more highly than you, their son, and entrust him rather than you with their property, and allow him to do what he likes, while preventing you? And now there is one thing more you must tell me. Do they let you control your own self, or will they not trust you in that either?"

"Of course they do not," he replied.

"But some one controls you?"

"Yes," he said, "my tutor [*paidagogos*] here."

"Is he a slave?"

Why, certainly; he belongs to us," he said.

"What a strange thing," I exclaimed; "a free person controlled by a slave!" (*Lysis* 208C, LCL).

The authority of the tutor over the child until the child grows up was wellknown in the ancient world. And, like the tutor, once the child is raised, the tutor is no longer needed. Similarly, for Paul, those who have come to faith in Christ no longer have need of a tutor (see 2:20; 4:7; 5:18; cf. Rom. 6:9, 14, 15; 7:24-25; 10:4; 11:6; 1 Cor. 9:20).

3:26-29. Although following in the same line of thinking, this passage encapsulates Paul's thinking on the role of faith as an equalizer in the presence of God. Both those without the Law and those under it come to the fullness and blessing of God in their lives the same way, and there are no longer any distinctions in the family of God. This passage goes to the heart of Paul's teaching on the Law and on faith.

3:26. For you are all sons of God through faith in Christ Jesus. See Deut. 14:1; 1 Thess. 5:5; cf. Matt. 23:8; John 13:35. Gentiles have through faith attained the position of sons and daughters of God now (Gal. 3:7, 29; cf. John 1:12; 1 John 3:1-2). In the second century, Justin Martyr (ca. A.D. 150-160) tells of this "sonship" through Christ and detects concern on the part of the Jews for saying it:

And in His name shall the Gentiles trust. As therefore from the one man Jacob, who was surnamed Israel, all your nation has been called Jacob and Israel; so we from Christ, who begat us unto God, like Jacob, and Israel, and Judah, and Joseph, and David, are called and are the true sons of god, and

keep the commandments of Christ.

And when I saw that they were perturbed because I said that we are the sons of God, I anticipated their questioning, and said, "Listen, sirs, how the Holy Ghost speaks of this people, saying that they are all sons of the Highest; and how this very Christ will be present in their assembly, rendering judgment to all men" (*Dialogue with Trypho* 123-124, ANF trans 261).

The Jews, on the other hand, understood that this prize was attained only at the Last Judgement and it came from God himself (2 Cor. 6:17-18). Philo, interestingly, speaks of the children or sons of God and that this for the Jews is not yet, but they are children of the Word!

But they who live in the knowledge of the One are rightly called "sons of God," as Moses also acknowledges when he says, "Ye are sons of the Lord God" (Deut. 14:1), and "God who begat thee" (Deut. 32:18), and "Is not He Himself thy father" (Deut. 32:6). Indeed with those whose soul is thus disposed it follows that they hold more beauty to be the only good, and this serves as a counterwork engineered by veteran warriors to fight the cause which makes Pleasure the end and to subvert and overthrow it. But if there be any as yet unfit to be called a Son of God, let him press to take his place under God's First-born, the Word, who holds the eldership among the angels, their ruler as it were. And many names are his, for he is called, "the Beginning," and the Name of God, and His Word, and the Man after His image, and "he that sees," that is Israel. And therefore I was moved to a few pages above to praise the virtues of those who say that "We are all sons of one man" (Gen. 43:11). For if we have not yet become fit to be thought sons of God yet we may be sons of His invisible image, the most holy Word (*The Confusion of Tongues* 145-47, LCL).

3:27. For all of you who were baptized into Christ have clothed yourselves with Christ. See 1 Cor. 12:13. Baptism "in the name of Jesus" or "Christ" distinguished the kind of baptism that early Christians followed from other Jewish practices: namely, it was a baptism administered in the name of Jesus. These are the typical words used in Acts to identify what kind of baptism was practiced (2:38; 8:16; 10:48; 19:5), and they also indicate the authority of the baptism: namely, that it was done in the authority of Jesus who was confessed as Lord (see Mark 9:38-39 and the authority to cast out demons in the name of Jesus in Acts 16:18). The Trinitarian formula of Matt. 28:19 was not regularly used in the early church until the second century and later.

In the ancient world, those who put on the divine clothing had become one with the deity. In the story commonly known as *The Golden Ass* (or *Metamorphoses*), Lucius Apuleius (ca. A.D. 125) tells of his initiation into the Isis mysteries:

When I had taken the customary bath, he began by asking the god's favour and then cleansed me with purificatory sprinkling. He took me back to the temple, with two-thirds of the day now past, and put me right in front of the goddess's feet. Secretly he gave me certain instructions too holy for utterance, and then openly, with all the company as witnesses, he ordered me to restrain my pleasure in food for the next ten days, not to partake of animal food, and to go without wine.

I duly observed these restrictions with reverent continence. . . . Then all the uninitiated were dismissed, I was wrapped in an unused linen robe, and the priest took me by the hand and led me to the innermost part of the sanctuary (Apuleius, *Metamorphoses* 11:23, LCL).

3:28. There is neither Jew nor Greek, there is neither slave nor free man, there is neither male nor female; for you are all one in Christ Jesus. See the divisions between Jews and Gentiles discussed in 2:12-14 above. For a close parallel, see Col. 3:11, but also for other expressions of equality in Rom. 4:9-12, Rom. 7:19; Phil. 3:3; Col. 2:11; Eph. 2:11-22; cf. also John 1:11-12, 3:16. By taking away the distinctions between Jew and Greek on the basis of the Law, Paul has declared all persons alike. See also the discussion on Paul's views of slavery in 1 Cor. 7:1-23.

Paul's call for the equality of all persons in Christ was not new in the ancient world, even if it was not a part of the Jewish context in which he was raised and trained. Aristotle (ca. 384-322 B.C.), for example, said that for "one man to be another man's master is contrary to nature, because it is only convention that makes the one a slave and the other a freeman and there is no difference between them by nature, and that therefore it is unjust, for it is based on force" (*Politics* 1.2.3, LCL). In Philostratus' *Life of Apollonius of Tyanna* (ca. first century A.D.), he reports the correspondence of Apollonius to those who attended worship in the temple of Artemis in Ephesus thusly:

Your temple is thrown open to all who would sacrifice, or offer prayers, or sing hymns, to suppliants, to Hellenes, barbarians, free men, to slaves. Your law is transcendentally divine. I could recognize the tokens of Zeus of Leto, if these were alone (*Epistles of Apollonius* 67, LCL).

Those in the Hellenistic mystery religions formed clubs or associations and argued that all of their members were equal. In an inscription dating to the second century A.D., we read: God invites all human beings to a banquet, and sets the table for all in common and equally, no matter where they come from" (Inscription about Zeus Panamaros, SEG 4 308.8, trans by M. E. Boring 467). Another inscription is found in Philadelphia in Asia Minor (ca. 125-75 B.C.), the place that is mentioned in Rev. 3:7-13 and to which city a letter was written (*To the Philadelphians*) by Ignatius of Antioch (ca. A.D. 115). Because this town overlaps with early Christianity, the following inscription found there is especially informative.

To good fortune! Written for the health and common good and best regards: the prescriptions give to Dionysus in his sleep, who grants free access to this hour for men and women, free and slaves. For altars are built within for Zeus Eumenes and Hestia, his companion, and the other saving gods. For Prosperity and Wealth, Virtue, Health, good fortune, the good Daemon, Remembrance, the Charities, and Nike [victory]. To this one (i.e., Dionysus) Zeus gave prescriptions for the performance of healings, purifications, and mysteries according to the customs of the ancestors, as they are now written.

When they enter this house, men and women, free and slaves, should swear by all the gods that they bear no lies against man or woman, perform no poison or evil curses against others, that they neither participate themselves nor advise others to participate in love potions, abortions, contraception, nor anything else that kills children, and that they are not accomplices in such.

. . .

These prescriptions are set forth by Agdistis, the very holy supervision and Lady of this house. May they make good hearts for men and women, free and slaves, that they will follow what is here prescribed. And in the monthly and yearly sacrifices, the men and women who are confident are to touch this inscription in which the commandments of the gods are written, so that it may become clear who follows these prescriptions and who does not (trans.

supplied by M.E. Boring 468-69).

Early Christianity did not always follow Paul in abstaining from discrimination, and the trouble in the church between Jews and Gentiles (see Acts 11:1-3; 15:1-29; Eph. 2:11-14) also carried on in terms of slaves and free, or rich and poor, as well as male and female relations. In one expression of gnostic Christianity, the *Gospel of Thomas* (ca. A.D. 130-40) reflects a bias against women when the disciples are with Jesus at the conclusion of his ministry with them and they say about Mary Magdalene:

Simon Peter said to them [the disciples and Jesus], "Let Mary leave us, for women are not worthy of life." Jesus said, "I myself shall lead her in order to make her male, so that she too may become a living spirit resembling you males. For every woman who will make herself male will enter the kingdom of heaven." (*Gosp. Thom.* 114, NHL 138)

Similarly, Plutarch says of those in Lycia:

They say that the lawgiver of the Lycians ordered his citizens, whenever they mourned, to clothe themselves first in women's garments and then to mourn, wishing to make it clear that mourning is womanish, and unbecoming and decorous men who lay claim to the education of the free-born. Yes, mourning is verily feminine, and weak, and ignoble, since women are more given to it than men, and barbarians more than Greeks, and inferior men more than better men; and the barbarians themselves, not the most noble, Celts and Galatians, and all who by nature are filled with a more manly spirit, but rather, if such there are, the Egyptians and Syrians and Lydians and all those who are like them (*Moralia, A Letter to Apollonius*, 112-113, LCL).

On the other hand, the author of the *Tripartite Tractate* (ca. late second or early third century) speaks about equality among the sexes.

For when we confessed the kingdom which is in Christ, [we] escaped from the whole multiplicity of forms and from inequality and change. For the end will receive a unitary existence just as the beginning is unitary, where there is no male nor female, nor slave and free, nor circumcision and uncircumcision, neither angel nor man, but Christ is all in all (*Trip. Tract.* 132.18-29, NHL 101).

Philo approvingly reports that among the Essenes (or Theraputae) there are no slaves and he disapproves of inequality:

They [Essenes] do not have slaves to wait upon them as they consider that the ownership of servants is entirely against nature. For nature has borne all men to be free, but the wrongful and covetous acts of some who pursued that source of evil, inequality, have imposed their yoke and invested the stronger with power over the weaker (*Contemplative Life* 70, LCL; see also *Every Good Man is Free* 79; cf. Josephus, *Antiquities* 18.21).

The early church tended to ignore the issue of slavery, or rather, the emancipation of slaves, even though it acknowledged that in the church there was no difference between slave and free (1 Cor. 7:21-13; Eph. 6:5-8; Col. 3:22; 1 Tim. 6:1-2; Titus 2:9-10; Jas. 2:2-7; 1 Peter 2:18; cf. also *1 Clem.* 55:2; Hermas, *Sim.* 1.8).

Gender bias was a part of the ancient world, and Paul's statement on the equality of men and women in Christ must have landed on rocky soil. In the time of Paul, women were lower-class citizens, especially among the Jews, but elsewhere also. When the Jews gathered for prayers and blessings, women, along with children and slaves, were exempt from saying the Shema (*m. Berakoth* 3.3) and from being included in the Common grace (*m. Berakoth* 7.2). Later among the Jews it was taught that a man should begin his prayer thanking God that he is "not a woman, a slave,

or a Gentile" (*b. Berakoth* 13b). Origen likewise preserves common views about the value of women in the ancient world when he shared Celsus's criticism against the early Christians for accepting them.

"Let no one educated, no one wise, no one sensible draw near. For those abilities are thought by us to be evils. But as for anyone ignorant, anyone stupid, anyone uneducated, anyone who is a child, let him come boldly." By the fact that they themselves admit that these people are worthy of their God, they show that they want and are able to convince only the foolish, dishonorable and stupid, and only slaves, women, and little children (Origen, *Contra Celsum* 3.44, 59, 64, ANF).

The differences between men and women were great in antiquity, and women had very few opportunities in life either for education or freedom of choice. In a very telling distinction between men and women preserved in the Mishnah, we read:

How does a man differ from a woman? He may go with hair unbound and with garments rent, but she may not go with hair unbound and with garments rent; he may impose the Nazirite-vow on his son, but she may not impose the Nazirite-vow on her son; a man may bring the Hair-offering for the Nazirite-vow of his father, but a woman may not bring the Hair-offering for the Nazirite-vow of her father; a man may sell his daughter, but a woman may not sell her daughter; a man may give his daughter in betrothal, but a woman may not give her daughter in betrothal; a man is stoned naked, but a woman may not be stoned naked; a man is hanged, but a woman may not be hanged; a man may be sold [to make restitution] for what he has stolen, but a woman cannot be sold [to make restitution] for what she has stolen (*m. Sotah* 38, Danby trans. 297).

For more discussion on this topic, see background material on 1 Cor. 11:2-16.

3:29. And if you belong to Christ, then you are Abraham's offspring, heirs according to promise. On the resumption of the theme began earlier on Abraham's offspring, see discussion in 3:6-9 above. Belonging to Christ is a particular Pauline theme (Rom. 8:9; Gal. 5:24; 1 Cor. 1:12; 3:23; 15:23; 2 Cor. 10:7).

C. 4:1-31. Bondage Under the Law/ Freedom in Christ

Continuing his primary argument of the letter, Paul now offers proof that the Law is inferior to faith. He equates being under the law to being in bondage as those who were minors were no better off than a slave.

1. Slavery under the Law vs. Adoption (4:1-7).

In this section, Paul draws on his previous argument about the role of a child and its rights in Roman society in order to support his case about the superiority of sonship or adoption by faith in Christ over seeking a right relationship with God through the instrumentality of the Law. Paul draws his illustration from the practice in Roman law called the *tutela impuberis* ("guardianship for a minor") and the *tutela testamentaria* ("guardianship established by testament"). In the latter case, the father appoints a guardian for his children who are heirs (Greek = *kleronomoi*) of their father's property when he dies, if the children are minors when the father dies. The child, though the legal heir of the father's estate, is not allowed to take possession of that property while a minor (Greek = *nepios*). The term for the minor is also found in a figurative use in the New Testament (besides here, see 1 Cor. 13:11; but see also Gal. 4:3; Rom. 2:20; 1 Cor. 3:1; 1 Thess. 2:7; Eph. 4:14). The switching of metaphors in this section, namely from a focus on the minor, though a son, being the same as a slave, to an adopted son out of slavery. In the first instance, Paul insists that all who do not have faith in Christ are enslaved under the Law (2:4; 3:23-25; 4:7-9, 24, 25; 5:1). On the other hand, this is contrasted with faith becoming free in Christ (2:4, 4:22-23, 26, 30-31; 5:1, 13).

4:3. So also we, while we were children, were held in bondage under the elemental things of the world. The "elemental things" (Greek = *stoicheia*; see also 4:9) are those cosmic and demonized elements which were hostile to human beings and the ancient religions tried to appease through prayers, sacrifices, astrology, magic, various rituals, and theurgy (referring to divine agency in human affairs as in magic among the Egyptian Platonists). Paul says until Christ came, we were yet in bondage to these elemental spirits or things of the world. In Apuleius's *The Golden Ass*, the goddess Isis is presented as the one who is over all the "elements." She comes saying:

> Behold, Lucius, moved by your prayers I have come, I the mother of the universe, mistress of all the elements [*elementorum omnium domina*], and first offspring of the ages; mightiest of deities, queen of the dead, and foremost of heavenly beings; my one person manifests the aspect of all gods and goddesses (*Metamorphoses* 11.5, LCL).

Later she is praised as the one to whom "The stars obey you, the seasons return at your will, deities rejoice in you, and the elements are your slaves [*serviunt elementa*]" (1.25, LCL).

4:4-5. But when the fullness of the time came, God sent forth His Son, born of a woman, born under the Law, in order that He might redeem those who were under the Law, that we might receive the adoption as sons. This redemption from slavery to the Law is found elsewhere in Paul in Rom. 8:3-4, 14-17, 23; contrast this with Mark 12:1-9 where evil persons tried to steal the inheritance of the legitimate heir. The notion behind the "fullness of time" is found elsewhere in the New Testament (Eph. 1:10; Mark 1:15; 16:14; John 7:8; cf. Heb. 1:2), but also at Qumran where the days are drawing near for the fulfillment of God's visitation on earth. In the *Rule of the Community*, for instance, we see the following:

> For God has sorted them [good and evil people] into equal parts until the last day and has put an everlasting loathing between their divisions. Deeds of deceit are an abhorrence to truth and all the paths of truth are an abhorrence to deceit. There exists a violent conflict in respect of all his decrees since they do not walk together. God, in the mysteries of his knowledge and in the wisdom of his glory, has determined an end to the existence of deceit and on the occasion of his visitation he will obliterate it for ever (1QS 4.16-19, LCL).

Even more specifically is the *Commentary on Habakkuk* (2:3) that argues:

> For the vision has an appointed time, it will have an end and not fail. *Blank* Its interpretation: the final age will be extended and go beyond all that the prophets say, because the mysteries of God are wonderful. Though it might delay, wait for it; it definitely has to come and will not delay. *Blank* Its interpretation concerns the men of truth, those who observe the Law, whose hands will not desert the service of truth, when the final age is extended beyond them, because all the ages of God will come at the right time, as he established for them in the mysteries of his prudence. (1QpHab 7.5-14, Garcia Martinez trans.)

Born of a woman. This part of Paul's comments are difficult to fit into the context of what he is saying and it is likely a pre-Pauline tradition that he has incorporated here to service his argument. It is clearly not a reference to the virgin birth of Jesus that shows up nowhere else in Paul and is restricted in the New Testament to Matthew (1:18-25) and Luke (1:26-35, 41-45; 2:1-20). The phrase here is intended to focus on Jesus' humanity, not his christology. A similar statement is found at Qumran in the *Rule of the Community* that focuses on humanity in the presence of God. "What, indeed, is man, among all your marvelous deeds? As what shall one born of woman be considered in your presence?" (1QS 11.20-21, Garcia Martinez trans.). The phrase here refers to the fact that a human being was born under the Law (see also Job 14:1; Matt. 11:11), but specifically to the purpose of Christ's coming into the world as a human being to redeem those under the Law (cf. Gal. 3:26-28) and from under the "elemental spirits" (Greek = *stoicheia*).

Adoption. The word (Greek = *huiothesia*) was a legal term referring to legal adoption of sons who are not related by birth, but who, in adoption, receive the full rights of natural born sons.

4:6. And because you are sons, God has sent forth the Spirit of His Son into our hearts, crying, "Abba! Father!" The author of Jubilees ties the reception of the Spirit with sonship, only the sonship is based on keeping the commandments of God, but the parallels otherwise are close.

> And I shall create for them a holy spirit, and I shall purify them so that they will not turn away from following me from that day and forever. And their souls will cleave to me and to all my commandments. And they will do my commandments. And I shall be a father to them, and they will be sons to me. And they will all be called "sons of the living God." And every angel and spirit will know and acknowledge that they are my sons and I am their father in uprightness and righteousness. And I shall love them (*Jub.* 1.23-25, *OT Pseud* 2.54).

Abba, Father. See Rom. 8:15. The logic of adding these words to the conclusion of his argument escapes many, but if seen as an outburst of emotion or ecstasy, then it is more understandable. Also, since Paul has spoken of sonship, it is appropriate for "sons" to speak of God as "father." Abba is the Greek transliteration of the Hebrew word for father (*aba*; pl = *aboth*). The term was used in the early church (*1 Clem* 8:3; *Did.* 10:2) and probably stems from Jesus' use of the term (Mark 14:36; Matt. 26:39; Luke 22:42; cf. Matt. 11:25; John 17:1).

4:7. Therefore you are no longer a slave, but a son; and if a son, then an heir through God. At this juncture, Paul switches to the second person singular ("you," sing.) from the second person plural ("you," pl.), perhaps as a rhetorical device that was common in antiquity. Epictetus makes a similar move in his discourse, and one that reflects the maturity of a son:

> You are no longer a lad, but already a full-grown man . . . Make up your own mind, therefore, before it is too late, that the fitting thing for you to do is to live as a mature man who is making progress, and let everything which seems to you to be best be for you a law that must not be transgressed (*Encheiridion* 51.1-2, LCL).

2. 4:8-20. Reproof of the Galatians' Conduct. This whole section is an emotional appeal from Paul that shows both fear that he has lost those whom he loves and anger for those who have led them astray. The logical flow through the passage therefore is understandably not smooth, but is clear on his point, even if how he arrives at it is strange to modern ears: namely, by the use of allegory. This section is in two parts, namely vv. 8-11 and 12-20. In the former of these Paul presents his fourth argument which is based on his readers' former experience when they did not know God and Paul's fear that they will exchange their bondage to the old "elemental" (*stoicheia*) things of this world for a legalistic bondage to the Law. Throughout the section he raises many questions for his readers.

4:8. However at that time, when you did not know God, you were slaves to those which by nature are no gods. Paul raises the issue of the gods that the Galatians formerly served and adds that they were "by nature" not gods at all. This is similar to Plato's reference to those who worship art, which is not by nature a god.

> The first statement, my dear sir, which these people make about the gods is that they exist by art and not by nature—by certain legal conventions which differ from place to place, according as each tribe agreed when forming their laws. They assert, moreover, that there is one class of things beautiful by nature, and another class beautiful by convention; while as to things just, they do not exist at all by nature, but men are constantly in dispute about them and continually altering them, and whatever alteration they make at any time is at that time authoritative, though it owes its existence to art and the laws, and not in any way to nature (*Laws* 10.889E— 889A, LCL).

The author of the *Letter of Aristeas* (ca. 170 B.C.) criticizes the practice of worshiping objects that are not by nature gods. He says that

> . . . the rest of mankind ("except ourselves," as he said) believe that there are many gods, because men themselves are much more powerful than the gods whom they vainly worship; they make images of stone and wood, and declare that they are likenesses of those who have made some beneficial discovery for their living, and whom they worship, even though the insensibility (of the images) is close at hand to appreciate. For if the existence of any god depended on the criterion of invention, it would be absolutely foolish, because in that case the inventors would have taken some of the created things and given an added demonstration of their usefulness without themselves being

their creators. Therefore it is profitless and useless to deify equals. And yet, even today, there are many of greater inventiveness and learning than the men of old, who nevertheless would be the first to worship them. Those who have invented these fabrications and myths are usually ranked to be the wisest of the Greeks (*Ep. Arist.* 134-137, *OT Pesud* 2.21-22).

In a similar fashion, the Jewish author of *Joseph and Aseneth* (ca. first cent. B.C. to first cent. A.D.) claims:

Behold now, all the gods whom I once used to worship in ignorance: I have now recognized that they were dumb and dead idols, and I have caused them to be trampled underfoot by men, and the thieves snatched those that were of silver and gold. And with you I have taken refuge, O Lord my God (*Jos. Asen.* 13.11-12, *OT Pseud* 2:223).

4:9. But now that you have come to know God, or rather to be known by God, how is it that you turn back again to the weak and worthless elemental things, to which you desire to be enslaved all over again? Paul's reference to "knowing God" is found elsewhere in his writings (Rom. 1:21; 1 Cor. 2:6-16; Phil. 3:10; cf. also Hos. 6:6). The notion that human beings are "known by God" is found in the Psalms (Jer. 1:5; Ps. 1:6; 37:18; 44:21; 94"11; Ps. 139) as well as in the New Testament (Gal. 1:15; 1 Cor. 8:2-3; cf. 2 Cor. 4:6; Acts 1:24; 15:8). Philo contrasts one's ability to know with being known: "Even how in this life, we are ruled rather than the rulers, known rather than knowing. The soul knows us, though we know it not; it lays on us commands, which we must fain obey, as a servant obeys his mistress" (*On the Cherubim* 115, LCL). The superstition that appears to lie behind this "turning back" is a source of great pain to Paul. Plutarch speaks of the ignorance and blindness in regard to true religious belief that leads to either atheism or to superstition that causes fear and results in foolish behavior. He seeks to address the failures of both positions.

. . . atheism, which is incorruptible, seems, by disbelief in the Divinity, to lead finally to a kind of utter indifference, and the end which it achieves in not believing in the existence of gods is not to fear them. But on the other hand, superstition, as the very name (dread of deities) indicates, is an emotional idea and an assumption productive of a fear which utterly humbles and crushes a man, for he thinks that there are gods, but that they are the cause of pain and injury. . . . For in the one man ignorance engenders disbelief in the One who can help him, and on the other it bestows the added idea that He causes injury. Whence it follows that atheism is falsified reason, and superstition is an emotion engendered from false reason (*Superstition* 165B-C, LCL).

He concludes his treatment on this subject with the words: "For thus it is that some persons, in trying to escape superstition, rush into a rough and hardened atheism, thus overleaping true religion which lies between" (171F, LCL).

Also interesting is the use of the Greek word *epistrephein* ("turn around"), which is often used in conversions (1 Thess. 1:9; Acts 3:19; 9:35; 11:21; 14:15; 15:19; 26:18, 20), but here it seems to refer to a reverse of that process.

On the "elemental things," see 4:3 above. The things here appear to be the Galatians' turning back to cultic rituals though in this case they are Jewish rather than Hellenistic.

4:10. You observe days and months and seasons and years. The proof of Paul's preceding statement is demonstrated in the Galatians' observance of the Jewish calendar events. Paul appears to abhor the reduction of faith to ritualistic and cultic practices. Justin Martyr (ca. A.D. 140-50), in his *Dialogue with Trypho* (the Jew), asks whether it is possible always for one to observe the Law of Moses ("Mosaic institutions"). Although Trypho agrees that it is not possible to observe them all, he claims that one can do some of them and these include: "To keep the Sabbath, to be circumcised, to observe months, and to be washed if you touch anything prohibited by Moses, or after sexual intercourse" (*Dial.* 46, ANF 217).

4:11. I fear for you, that perhaps I have labored over you in vain. This statement appears to be Paul's passion for the Galatians, not his fear for himself. Should the Galatians revert back to ritual, even of a Jewish sort, he believes that they have misunderstood his gospel or rejected it. This painful concern forms the backdrop to a collection of disjointed comments in 4:8-20 where there is little consistency in thought and sentence structure. While it is true that the following verses are an argument from the heart, they do have parallel in ancient rhetoric: namely, Paul makes use of a list of examples to argue his point that come from the notion of friendship (see Xenophon, *Mem.* 2.4-10; Plato, *Lysis* and *EN* 8-9) utilizing the diatribe, as in Epictetus, *Diss.* 2.22 and Lucian's *Toxaris* and Dio Chrysostom (3.86; 4.42, 34.76; 44.1) and especially Cicero, *Laelius de amicitia* and Seneca, *De beneficiis*. Dio Chrysostom, for example praises friendship as the most valuable of all riches and cites several examples of the benefits of such relationships.

Friendship, moreover, the good king holds to be the fairest and most sacred of his possessions, believing that the lack of means is not so shameful or perilous for a king as the lack of friends, and that he maintains his happy state, not so much by means of revenues and armies and his other sources of strength, as by the loyalty of his friends. For no one, of and by himself, is sufficient for a single one of even his own needs . . . (*Orations* 3.86, LCL)

He continues that "to friendship alone it has been given to be both the most profitable of all and the most pleasurable of all [possessions and experiences]" and "to enjoy them in solitude is the dreariest thing imaginable, and no one could endure it." (3.94, 96, LCL). Elsewhere, upon returning home to his friends, he writes: "you may rest assured that I find all my honours, both those you now propose and any others there may be, contained in your goodwill and friendship, and I need naught else," and continues, "for one word spoken out of goodwill and friendship is worth all the gold and crowns and everything else deemed splendid that men possess; so take my advice and act accordingly" (44.2, LCL).

Sirach also praises friendship and offers a string of examples of what true friendship is, namely those who are with you when things are not going your way and are a "sturdy shelter " and "life-saving medicine" (see *Sirach* 6:5-17). Cicero, in his famous treatise of friends, defines friendship as "nothing more than an accord in all things, human and divine, conjoined with mutual goodwill and affection" (*De amicitia* 20, Betz trans. 222). Aristotle claimed that "friendship is equality of rights and values, especially the equality of those who are alike in virtue" (*EN* 8.8.5, LCL). Lucian's examples of friendship that were demonstrated in the context of hardship and crisis are well-known. In telling about a dialogue between a Scythian (Toxaris) and a Greek (Mnesippus), the former talks about the deeds of friendship being more valuable than mere talk.

It seems to me that you Greeks can indeed say all that is to be said about friendship better than others, but not only fail to practice its works in a manner that befits your words—no, you are content to have praised it and shown what a very good thing it is, but in its times of need you play traitor to your words about it and beat a hasty retreat, somehow or other, out of the press of deeds. And whenever your tragedians put friendships of this kind on the stage and exhibit them to you, you bestow praise and applause, yes even tears upon them, most of you, when they face danger for each other's sake; yet you yourselves dare not come out with any praiseworthy deed for the sake of your friends. On the contrary, if a friend happens to stand in need of anything, those many tragic histories take wing and vanish from your path on the instant, like dreams, and leave you looking like those empty, silent masks which, for all their open mouths, widely agape, do not utter even the slightest sound. We are your opposites; for we have as much the better of you in practicing friendship as we fall short of you in talking about it. (*Toxaris*, or *Friendship*, 9, LCL)

Paul's content and style in discussing the notion of friendship that he has had with the Galatians are not unlike other rhetorical style in these examples.

4:12. I beg of you, brethren, become as I am, for I also have become as you are. You have done me no wrong. Paul, who is a follower of Christ, encourages his readers to be as he is. This is done frequently in his letters (1 Cor. 4:16; 11:1; 1 Thess. 2:14; Phil. 3:17; cf. 1 Cor. 7:7, 8, 40; 10:33). In Phil. 3:17-18, the context is similar to this one in which Paul encourages his readers to follow his example because there are enemies of the cross seeking to destroy them and he has to share this with them with tears. Paul became like his readers, as a Christian who is outside the boundaries of the Law (1 Cor. 9:19-23; cf. Rom. 11:13-16; 1 Cor. 10:33; 2 Cor. 2:14-17; 1 Thess. 2:14-16).

4:13-14. But you know that it was because of a bodily illness that I preached the gospel to you the first time. And that which was a trial to you in my bodily condition you did not despise or loathe, but you received me as an angel of God, as Christ Jesus Himself. What precisely is meant here is difficult to grasp, but Paul praises the people for not rejecting him on account of his physical ailment(s). Because one of the widely accepted characteristics of true friendship is the acceptance of one despite his or her weaknesses or difficulties, Paul reminds the Galatians that they were true friends to him and accepted him when he came to them with his gospel. Precisely what these bodily ailments were is not clear, but scholars have speculated over the years that it was everything from physical wounds incurred in his preaching mission, his unimpressive appearance, or perhaps a physical ailment that he simply endured, such as an eye problem (cf. v. 15; cf. 6:11). Lucian tells how such ailments can test the nature of a friendship. After explaining that no praise was needed when a friend came to the aid of a friend, he explains:

it would be ridiculous if, after having fused ourselves together long ago and united, as far as we could, into a single person, we should continue to think it a great thing if this or that part of us has done something useful in behalf of the whole body; for it was working in its own behalf as part of the whole organism to which the good was being done (*Toxaris* 53, LCL; cf. also Cicero, *Amic.* 67; Plutarch, *Amic. Mult.* 3; Aristotle, *EN* 8.3.8).

4:15. Where then is that sense of blessing you had? For I bear you witness, that if possible, you would have plucked out your eyes and given them to me. It appears to Paul that those who had joyfully received his message were now turning away from him and that led to great pain. The author of the *Epistle of Barnabas* encourages his readers to "love 'as the apple of thine eye' all who speak to thee the word of the Lord" (*Ep. Barn.* 19.9, LCL). Dio Chrysostom tells the value of friends to those who have problems seeing.

If eyes, ears, tongue, and hands are worthy everything to a man that he may be able merely to live, to say nothing of enjoying life, then friends are not less but more useful than these members. With his eyes he may barely see what lies before his feet; but through his friends he may behold even that which is at the ends of the earth (*Orations* 3.1-4-105, LCL).

Later he cites as support of what true friends will share with each other an old proverb that says "Common are the possessions of friends" (110, LCL).

4:16. Have I therefore become your enemy by telling you the truth? Plutarch shares the characteristics of a true friend and this includes being willing to tell the truth to a friend. He said that he had no use for a friend who simply nodded assent to all that he said or did, or even worse tried to imitate it. He claims that he has "no use for a friend that shifts about just as I do and nods assent just as I do (for my shadow better performs that function), but I want one that tells the truth as I do, and decides for himself as I do," and he adds that "the true fried is neither an imitator of everything nor ready to commend everything, but only the best things" (*How to Tell a Flatterer* 53B-C, LCL). He goes on to say that there are those who in the name of friendship imitated the actions and even illnesses of such well-known persons as Plato (his stoop), Aristotle (his lisp), Alexander the Great (his twisted neck), and even Dionysius (his failing eyesight), but these he called flatterers and not true friends (53D-F).

4:17-19. They eagerly seek you, not commendably, but they wish to shut you out, in order that you may seek them. But it is good always to be eagerly sought in a commendable manner, and not only when I am present with you. Paul attacks the flattery that his enemies share with them because the purpose is to take away their (the Galatians') liberty. How can one tell how to identify those who seek not their good, but their harm? Plutarch explains:

In the first place, it is necessary to observe the uniformity and permanence of his tastes, whether he always takes delight in the same things, he directs and ordains his own life according to one pattern, as becomes a free-born man and a lover of congenial friendship and intimacy; for such is the conduct of a friend. But a flatterer, since he has no abiding-place of character to dwell in, and since he leads a life not of his own choosing but another's, moulding and adapting himself to suit another, is not simple, not one, but variable and many in one, and like water that is poured into one receptacle after another, he is constantly on the move from place to place, and changes his shape to fit his receiver (*How to Tell a Flatterer* 52AB, LCL).

Epictetus is similar when he says,

. . . when you see friends, or brothers, who seem to be of one mind, do not instantly make pronouncement about their friendship, not even if they swear to it, nor even if they say that they cannot be separated from one another. The ruling principle of the bad men is not to be trusted; it is insecure, incapable of judgment, a prey now to one external impression and now to another. Where do they put their interest—outside themselves, or in their moral purpose? If outside, call them not friends, any more than you would call them faithful, steadfast, courageous, or free; nay call them not even human beings, if you are wise (*Discourses* 2.22.24-27, LCL).

Paul knows that it is good to be won over to that which is good, but not to that which is harmful. He also knew what Cicero has said earlier: "ask of friends only what is honorable; do for friends only what is honorable and without even waiting to be asked; let zeal be ever present, but hesitation ablest; dare to give true advice with all frankness . . ." (*De amicitia* 44, Betz trans. 232). True friendship does not shift in the changing circumstances of life. As Plutarch wrote, "friendship seeks for a fixed and steadfast character which does not shift about, but continues in one place and in one intimacy. For this reason a steadfast friend is something rare and hard to find" (*On Having Many Friends* 97B, LCL).

4:19. My children, with whom I am again in labor until Christ is formed in you. Paul's use of these two metaphors is rather surprising for any male, namely calling the Galatians his children and combining this with his reference to being in the pain of giving birth over them. He uses similar language elsewhere in his letters (Rom. 8:22; 1 Thess. 2:7; 5:3). Paul undoubtedly obtained the metaphor from the Hebrew Scriptures (cf. Deut. 32:18; Isa. 42:18; 54:1; Job 29). Epictetus offers a parallel that illustrates Paul's meaning in this text. He similarly referred to those who were not children biologically as children in the sense that all human beings were family. Citing Diogenes who founded the Cynic movement, he answers why a Cynic will never marry or have children:

> Many, the Cynic has made all mankind his children; the men among them he has as sons, the women as daughters; in that spirit he approaches them all and cares for them all. Or do you fancy that it is in the spirit of idle impertinence he reviles those he meets? It is as a father he does it, as a brother, and as a servant of Zeus, who is Father of us all (*Discourses* 3.22.81-82, LCL).

Philo speaks of the womb in a metaphorical sense as follows:

> The words "of all that openeth the womb, the males to the Lord," are indeed true to nature. For as nature has given the womb to women as the proper part for generation of living offspring, so she has set in the soul for the generation of things a power by which the understanding conceives and travails and is the mother of many children (*Sacrifices of Abel and Cain* 102, LCL).

Elsewhere he speaks of birth pangs thusly: "The virtues have their conception and their birth pangs, but when I purpose to speak of them let them who corrupt religion into superstition close their ears and depart" (*On the Cherubim*, LCL; cf. also his *Posterity and Exile of Cain* 135; *On the Unchangeableness of God* 14, 137).

On Paul's desire to have Christ formed within his readers, see also (Gal. 1:16; 2:20; 3:5; 4:6; Rom. 8:9-11; 2 Cor. 13:3, 5; Phil. 1:20; so also Eph. 1:18; 3:17; 5:19; Col. 3:15-17; 2 Tim. 2:22).

4:20. But I could wish to be present with you now and to change my tone, for I am perplexed about you. Purporting to be at the "end of his rope," Paul follows a familiar pattern in rhetorical expression. Using similar words Hermas expresses his frustration over a parable shared with him. "I said to him: 'Sir, tell me what this tree is. For I am perplexed about it, that although so many branches have been cut off, the tree is healthy, and nothing seems to have been cut from it; I am perplexed at this'" (Hermas, *Shepherd, Sim.* 8.3.1).

3. An Allegory of Hagar and Sarah (4:21-31). Paul argues his point using the story of two women allegorically. The story of Sarah the wife and Hagar the concubine, two women at odds with each other and both with a child, illustrates Paul's defense of his gospel. Hagar was a slave woman; Sarah was free. Ishmael, her son, was born naturally, that is of the flesh; but Isaac came by way of a promise and divine intervention. Ishmael represents Mt. Sinai, the giving of the Law, and slavery; Isaac represents Mount Zion, freedom, and the promise of God. Ishmael did not gain an inheritance, but Isaac is free and receives the promise of freedom (4:31). In 4:29-30, Paul cites Gen. 21:10 to urge the Galatian Christians to "drive out" the Judaizers who want to take their liberty away. The use of allegory was common in antiquity and adopted by Philo the Jewish theologian from Alexandria (later first cent. B.C. to mid-first cent. A.D.), and early Christians also made extensive use of it in arguing their positions. In the classical sense, allegory was a manner of speech that aimed for meaning not from the literal understanding of words or stories, but rather by their figurative use. It was believed that the "mysteries" of the divine were revealed through this methodology. Paul's argument suggests that the real meaning of the Law is discovered in the use of allegory, not in its literal implementation.

4:24. This is allegorically speaking: for these women are two covenants, one proceeding from Mount Sinai bearing children who are to be slaves; she is Hagar. The term for allegory (Greek = *allegoroumena* from *allegoreo*) focuses on the figurative and spiritualized interpretation of Scripture and its variety of stories. It was first used by the Greeks to interpret Homer's writings when they became sacred literature for the Greeks and provided for them their listing of gods. Some of the actions of the gods in Homer's Iliad and Odyssey were suspicious in nature and not virtuous as what one expected. As a result, allegory was first attached to these writings to show their deeper meaning and to better understand the actions of the gods. Early Christianity also found this methodology convenient in interpreting its faith and religious traditions, that is, getting into its "deeper meaning" that was not apparent in the literal interpretation of their sacred texts. Paul uses this methodology elsewhere as in 1 Cor. 10:4 and it is paralleled in early Christianity, for example, the *Epistle of Barnabas* seeks to clarify the deeper meaning of the sacrifices in Num. 19.

> But what do you think that it typifies, that the commandment has been given to Israel that the men in whom sin is complete offer a heifer and slay it and burn it, and that boys then take the ashes and put them into vessels and bind scarlet wool on sticks (see again the type of the Cross and the scarlet wool) and hyssop, and that the boys all sprinkle the people thus one by one in order that they all be purified from their sins? Observe how plainly he speaks to you. The calf is Jesus; the sinful men offering it are those who brought him to be slain. Then there are no longer men, no longer the glory of sinners. The boys who sprinkle are they who preached to us the forgiveness of sins, and the purification of the heart, to whom he gave the power of the gospel to preach, and there are twelve tribes of Israel. But why are there three boys who sprinkle? As a testimony to Abraham, Isaac, and Jacob, for these are great before God.... And for this reason the things which were thus done are plain to us, but obscure to them, because they did not hear the Lord's voice (*Ep. Barn.* 8.1-7, LCL).

The early church frequently used allegory to clarify the meaning of obscure texts and also to deal with the difficult problem of how the Old Testament could be the Church's sacred Scriptures when the church was not following the Law, a chief component of those Scriptures. The Scriptures appealed to here include Gen. 16:15; 21:2, 9.

4:25. Now this Hagar is Mount Sinai in Arabia, and corresponds to the present Jerusalem, for she is in slavery with her children. Paul comes to the point of his allegory. Just as slavery is against the promise of freedom, so those who promote the Law are children of Hagar, slaves. The Jews did not believe, of course, that Jerusalem represented any form of slavery. Irenaeus (ca. A.D. 170-80) tells of the view of the Ebionite (Jewish) Christians' views of Paul and of the city of Jerusalem. He observes:

> Those who are called Ebionites agree that the world was made by God; but their opinions with respect to the Lord are similar to those of Cerinthus and Carpocrates. They use the gospel according to Matthew only, and repudiate the

Apostle Paul, maintaining that he was an apostate from the law. As to the prophetical writings, they endeavour to expound them in a somewhat singular manner: they practice circumcision, persevere in the observance of those customs which are enjoined by the law, and are so Judaic in their style of life, that they even adore Jerusalem as if it were the house of God (*Against Heresies* 1.26.2, ANF).

4:26. But the Jerusalem above is free; she is our mother. Paul's opponents stressed the importance of Jerusalem and so he pits the present Jerusalem against the Jerusalem which is above. In Paul's day there existed a Jewish notion of a Jerusalem that is "above" and it is the fulfillment of the blessings of God. This view had its roots in Jewish apocalyptic expectations for the rebuilding of the holy city following its destruction by the Babylonians (Isa. 54:10-12; 62:1-7, 12; 65:17-19; 66:10-13; Ezek. 40-48; *Tob.* 13:9-18; 14:7; *Jub* 4:26; 2 *Apoc. Bar.* 4.2-7; 32.2-3; *Sib. Oracles* 5.420). In the apocryphal Book of Tobit, the promise is given to the city,

> O Jerusalem, the Holy city, he afflicted you for the deeds of your hands, but will again have mercy on the children of the righteous. . . . A bright light will shine to all the ends of the earth; many nations will come to you from far away, the inhabitants of the remotest parts of the earth to your holy name, bearing gifts in their hands for the King of heaven. Generation after generation will give joyful praise in you, the name of the chosen city will endure forever (Tobit 12:9, 11, NRSV).

According to the author of *4 Ezra* (ca. A.D. 90-100), the present Jerusalem will be replaced by a heavenly Jerusalem and temple (*4 Ezra* 10:40-54; cf. also *1 Enoch* 90:28-29). The author of 2 Baruch (ca. early second cent. A.D.), having known of the destruction of the city in A.D. 70, spoke of a new city from God.

> And the Lord said to me: This city will be delivered for a time, and the people will be chastened for a time, and the world will not be forgotten. Or do you think that this is the city of which I said: On the palms of my hands I have carved you? It is not this building that is in your midst now; it is that which will be revealed, with me, that was already prepared from the moment that I decided to create Paradise (*2 Bar* 4.1-3, *OT Pseud* 1:622; for similar comments, see *Testament of Dan* 5:12-ff.).

This notion of a new and renewed Jerusalem can also be seen in the New Testament itself (Heb. 12:22; 13:14; Rev. 3:12; 21:2, 9–22:5). Paul, no doubt, adopted this view from within contemporary strands of apocalyptic Judaism. This same notion is also found later in the early church. Hermas (ca. A.D. 140-50), for example, spoke of a heavenly city toward which Christians are on a journey and will one day realize.

> He said to me, "You know that you, as the servants of god, are living in a strange country, for your city is far from this city. If then you know your city [the heavenly Jerusalem], in which you are going to dwell, why do you here prepare lands and costly establishments and buildings and vain dwellings? He therefore, who prepares these things for this city, is not able to return to his own city (*Shepherd. Sim.* 1.1.1-2, LCL).

4:27. For it is written, "Rejoice, barren woman who does not bear; Break forth and shout, you who are not in labor; For more are the children of the desolate than of the one who has a husband." Paul is citing here Isa. 54:1.

4:30. But what does the Scripture say? "Cast out the bondwoman and her son, For the son of the bondwoman shall not be an heir with the son of the free woman." Paul quotes from the LXX (Greek translation) of Gen. 21:10, but the text here is somewhat different from the LXX version. Starting with Sarah's word to

Abraham, the LXX reads: "Cast out this bond-woman and her son, for the son of this bond-woman shall not inherit with my son Isaac."

4:31. So then, brethren, we are not children of a bondwoman, but of the free woman. Paul concludes that the children of Abraham and the children of the freewoman (Sarah), not of the bondwoman. Some commentators have noticed that it appears that Paul differs here from his later view on whether the Jews are included in God's plan of salvation. In Romans it appears that God has a future for the Jews in the plan of redemption (Rom. 11:25-32), but that hope does not manifest itself here. This does not mean that Jews are excluded, however, for Paul no longer sees the Jews as distinct from the Gentiles, but all are included because of their faith in Jesus Christ (3:28).

IV. 5:1–6:10. THE APPLICATION OF PAUL'S GOSPEL TO LIFE

A. 5:1-26. The Nature and Implications of Christian Liberty

As Paul concludes the exposition of his gospel, he prepares to focus on the ethical implications of his message. No doubt many who heard his message of freedom from the Law accused him of trying to please people (1:10; cf. also Rom. 6:1) and so make the Christian faith one of law-lessness and irresponsibility. Paul is aware of these accusations throughout his exposition and also that his opponents have misunderstood the gospel of God's grace in Christ. It is not a gospel of irresponsibility, but rather there are ethical responsibilities for every person who accepts the grace of God in his or her life. Paul's theology, the exposition of his gospel, is never separate from the ethical response of the believer that is mandated for those who are free from the Law and alive in Christ.

1. 5:2-12. The Futility of Justification by

Works. The question of circumcision is mentioned in 5:2, 3, 6, and 11. Paul has visited this issue earlier and has returned to it once again. He will return to it one final time in 6:12-15. Circumcision was the mark of one's willingness to keep the covenant of God and the some 613 attendant laws related to it. He will once again argue that one cannot be selective. If one chooses to keep the Law, one must keep it all or is guilty of failing or breaking it all (see 3:10-14 above). Paul's argument is not much different here than earlier, but he intensifies his point as he repeats it.

5:1. It was for freedom that Christ set us free; therefore keep standing firm and do not be subject again to a yoke of slavery. Paul summarizes the theme of his gospel, namely freedom from the Law that is found in Christ.

5:2-3. Behold I, Paul, say to you that if you receive circumcision, Christ will be of no benefit to you. And I testify again to every man who receives circumcision, that he is under obligation to keep the whole Law. Circumcision, as the mark of the covenant with God, was the visible mark of one's obedience and compliance to the Law. The obligation to keep all of the Law was of critical importance to the rabbis who argued that one could not be selective in what one would obey or observe, but all of it was essential. In a second-century A.D. rabbinic commentary on Numbers, with the biblical text being interpreted in italics, we read the following:

Because he has despised the word of the Lord and has broken His Commandment. "Despised the word of the Lord" refers to a Sadducee; "and has broken His Commandment"—to an Epicurean. Another explanation: *Because he has despised the Word of the Lord* —is he who breaks the covenant of the flesh [i.e. who opposes circumcision]. Hence R[abbi]. El'azar of Modi'im says: "He who profanes the holy things [the sanctuary], and despises the *festivals*, and breaks the covenant of Abraham our father [*circumcision*], even if he has in his hand many other good deeds, is worthy to be thrust out of the world [i.e. the world to come]." If he says: "I accept the whole torah, with the exception of *this* word," of him it is said: "For he despised the word of the Lord." If he says, "The whole torah was spoken by the mouth of Holiness, and this word Moses himself said," he despises the word of the Lord (*Midrash Sifre* on Numbers 112; Neusner, *Sifre*).

In other Jewish literature, Sirach contends that those who think that God will balance their good deeds with the bad and if they have done some good, then things will be okay with God. He writes: "Do not commit a sin twice: not even for one will you go unpunished. Do not say, 'He will consider the great number of my gifts. And when I make an offering to the Most High God, he will accept it'" (*Sir.* 7:8-9, NRSV). Likewise, the author of *4 Maccabees* cautions his readers about ignoring the less significant laws: "Therefore to not suppose that it would be a petty sin if we were to eat defiling food; to transgress the law in matters either small or great is of equal seriousness, for in either case the law is equally despised" (*4 Macc.* 5:19-21, NRSV). In harmony with what we see in *Sirach* and *4 Maccabees*, Josephus says that nothing one does in regard to the Law has merit if circumcision is neglected. When Izates, son of Queen Helena of Adiabene, was about to assume his role as king of Adiabene, he had been convinced to worship the God of the Jews and when it was time for him to return to his land, he wanted to be circumcised. His mother tried to dissuade him because of the danger the move would pose when he returned to a land where there were no Jews and the people worshiped other gods. When the question was raised whether he could worship the God of the Jews without being circumcised, he was told by a Jew that he should carry out the rite of circumcision (*Antiquities* 20.34-40). The king said that he could

> ... worship God even without being circumcised if indeed he had fully decided to be a devoted adherent of Judaism, for it was this that counted more than circumcision.... another Jew, named Eleazar, who came from Galilee and who had a reputation for being extremely strict when it came to the ancestral laws, urged him to carry out the rite. For when he came to him to pay his respects and found him reading the law of Moses, he said: "In your ignorance, O king, you are guilty of the greatest offence against the law and thereby against God. For you ought not merely to read the law but also, and even more, to do what is commanded in it. How long will you continue to be uncircumcised? If you have not yet read the law concerning this matter, read it now, so that you may know what an impiety it is that you commit.." Upon hearing these words, the king postponed the deed no longer. (*Antiquities* 20.41-46, LCL).

5:7. You were running well; who hindered you from obeying the truth? Paul uses the running metaphor elsewhere to describe the Christian life (1 Cor. 9:24-27; Gal. 2:2; Phil. 3:14; cf. 2 Tim. 4:7; Acts 20:34). The picture here is of a runner who is hindered from finishing his race whether by someone who tripped him or some other means of deflecting him from running the race.

5:8. This persuasion did not come from Him who calls you. Paul uses a common word for persuasion (*peismone*) in the Greco-Roman world, but found only here in Paul's writings. It speaks of the persuasiveness of Paul's opponents in Galatia.

5:9. A little leaven leavens the whole lump of dough. Because the Jews were commanded to eat unleavened bread only (Exod. 12:15, 17-20; Deut. 16:3-8), it came to be understood that anything with yeast in it was evil. The word began to be used metaphorically for anything that was evil and it is commonly used in this fashion in the New Testament. Paul says that the Judaizers (the "yeast"), had an evil influence on the Galatians.

5:10. I have confidence in you in the Lord, that you will adopt no other view; but the one who is disturbing you shall bear his judgment, whoever he is. Paul has in mind those who are perverting the gospel (see 1:7-9; 2:11).

5:11. But I, brethren, if I still preach circumcision, why am I still persecuted? Then the stumbling block of the cross has been abolished. Perhaps the criticism that Paul was facing here was one of hypocrisy since it is reported in Acts 16:3 that he circumcised Timothy. The greatest stumbling block or "offense" for early Christianity had to do with the death of the coming Messiah on a cross. Nothing prepared the Jews for this and the Greeks thought it nonsense (1 Cor. 1:22-23; cf. Deut. 21:22-23; Gal. 3:13; on stumbling blocks and offences in religious faith, see Rom. 9:32-33 and compare with Isa. 8:14; Rom. 11:9 and compare with Ps. 69:23; 14:13; 16:17).

5:12. Would that those who are troubling you would even mutilate themselves. The Galatians were well aware of the crude expressions about those who were castrated and became priests of Cybele in that region. Paul's sarcastic comments here may reflect the widespread sentiments against those who underwent "sacral castration" for religious purposes, but he was also mindful that this was contrary to the Mosaic Law (Deut. 23:1). Philo lists those who are to keep their distance from the temple and the Jewish religious activities. Along with those who are effeminate and homosexual, he adds those who have castrated themselves, or it was done to them: "For it expels those whose generative organs are fractured or mutilated, who husband the flower of their youthful bloom, lest it should quickly wither, and restamp the masculine cast into a feminine form" (*Special Laws* 1.325, LCL; cf. also *Allegorical Laws* 3.8). Epictetus ridicules those who have decided on castration as a means of preparing for sacral service.

Such a powerful and invincible thing is the nature of man. For how can a vine be moved to act, not like a vine, but like an olive, or again an olive to act, not like an olive, but like a vine? It is impossible, inconceivable. Neither, then, is it possible for a man absolutely to lose the affections of a man, and those who cut off their bodily organs are unable to cut off the really important thing—their sexual desires. So with Epicurus: he cut off everything that characterizes a man, the head of a household, a citizen, and a friend, but he did not succeed in cutting of the desires of human beings; for that he could not do, any more than the easy-going Academics are able to cast away or blind their own sense perceptions, although they have made every effort to do so (*Discourses* 2.20.18-20, LCL).

Dio Cassius (ca. A.D. 150-235) tells of a certain Elagabalus who offended the people of his region (Syria) because he introduced a strange god and put him before Jupiter, but also because he caused himself to be voted in as a priest and circumcised himself, but "he had planned, indeed, to cut off his genitals altogether, but that desire was prompted solely by his effeminacy; the circumcision which he actually carried out was a part of the priestly requirements of Elagabalus, and he accordingly mutilated many of his companions in like manner" (Dio Cassius, *Roman History* 80.11, LCL; cf. also Lucian's *Eunuch*, which sports fun at the expense of a eunuch; and Philo, *Allegorical Interpretation* 3.8 and *Special Laws* 1.325).

2. Christians Should Not Abuse Their Liberty (5:13-26). Knowing the criticism that those without law are slothful and contrary to the will of God, Paul addresses the concerns of his critics who question the ethical response to a gospel of grace versus one of law. Paul insists on freedom as the best choice, but not lawlessness.

5:13. For you were called to freedom, brethren; only do not turn your freedom into an opportunity for the flesh, but through love serve one another. Because freedom for the Christian comes by the power of the Holy Spirit and brings freedom from the power of sin, the Law, and the "elemental things of the world." It is easy to see that some abuse might find its way among those enjoying their newly found freedom. Moral laxity was never a Christian option and Paul emphasizes that here.

5:14-15. For the whole Law is fulfilled in one word, in the statement, "You shall love your neighbor as yourself." But if you bite and devour one another, take care lest you be consumed by one another. Paul returns here to the issue of the Law, even though he spent all of chaps. 3 and 4 explaining it in terms of and in opposition to his gospel, to emphasize that the Law's obligations are met in the Christian duty of love. He cites here Lev. 19:18 which is one part of the command of Jesus to love both God and neighbor (Matt. 22:37-40 where Jesus cites Deut. 6:5 and combines it with Lev. 19:18; cf. John 13:34-35; 15:12-13; Jas. 2:8; 1 Peter 4:8; 1 John 3:11-23; 2 John 5). There are rabbinic traditions of a later time in which the rabbis also linked the fulfilling of the Law in loving God and one's fellow human beings (*b. Sabb.* 31a). The "neighbor" was generally considered to be one's fellow Jews or, in the case of early Christianity, one's fellow Christians (see Gal. 6:10).

It was debated among the sophists of antiquity whether the abolition of laws would bring chaos to society and reduce human behavior to that of animals. Plutarch challenges that conclusion, however, and using similar words to Paul's in 5:15, claims that:

> ... if someone takes away the laws, but leaves us with the teaching of Parmenides, Socrates, Heracleitus and Plato, we shall be very far from devouring one another and living the life of wild beasts; for we shall fear all that is shameful and shall honor justice for its intrinsic worth, holding that in the gods we have good governors ... (*Moralia*, "Reply to Colotes" 30, LCL).

5:16. But I say, walk by the Spirit, and you will not carry out the desire of the flesh. Paul sets in opposition two approaches to God, one by the Law and the other by faith. In terms of his exposition in 5:16-18 and elsewhere in this letter, there are several contrasts one sees in the two ways of approaching God:

Law	vs.	Faith
Death		Life
Curse		Blessing
Sin		Righteousness
Flesh		Spirit
Slavery/Bondage		Freedom

5:17. For the flesh sets its desire against the Spirit, and the Spirit against the flesh; for these are in opposition to one another, so that you may not do the things that you please. In the *Testament of Judah*, the author writes about the struggles and weaknesses of the "flesh." He concludes of his struggles, "The prince of error blinded me, and I was ignorant—as a human being, as flesh, in my corrupt sins— until I learned of my own weakness after supposing myself to be invincible" (*T. Jud.* 19.4, *OT Pseud* 1:800). In the *Testament of Zebulon*, the writer also speaks about the conflict between flesh and spirit: " ... you will remember the

Lord and repent, and he will turn you around because he is merciful and compassionate; he does not bring a charge at wickedness against the sons of men, since they are flesh and the spirits of deceit lead them astray in all their actions" (9.7, *OT Pseud* 1:807; cf. also the *Testament of Asher* 1.6).

5:19-21. Catalogue of vices and virtues. The following list or catalogue of vices and virtues has many parallels in the New Testament and early Christianity, but they are absent from the Old Testament. The New Testament lists include: Rom. 1:29-31; 12:9-13; 13:13; 1 Cor. 5:10-11; 6:9-10; 2 Cor. 12:20-21; Gal. 5:19-23; Eph. 4:31; 5:3-5; Col. 3:5, 8; 1 Tim. 1:9-10; 2 Tim. 3:2-5; Titus 3:3; Jas. 3:13-18; 1 Peter 2:1; 4:3, 15; cf. Mark 7:22; Matt. 15:19; Rev. 21:8; 22:15. Early Christianity also seems to have made extensive use of these lists and several examples are found in *Didache* 2.1-5.2; *Epistle of Barnabas* 18-20; Polycarp, *Phil.* 2.2; 4.3; Shepherd of Hermas, *Mand.* 5.2.4, 6.2, 8.3; *Sim.* 6, 9.15; *Apocalypse of Peter* 21-34; ps.-Clement, *Hom.* 11.27-28. There are numerous examples of these, however, in the Greco-Roman literature contemporary with and before the time of Paul. It seems clear that Paul, as he did in a variety of rhetorical expressions, made use of a popular means of presenting the Christian virtues as well as enumerating the vices that were contrary to the Christian lifestyle. In the Christian catalogues, there are no vices or virtues that show up exclusively in the Christian lists, but they are widely represented in non-Christian literature. Diogenes Laertius (perhaps early third cent. A.D.) lists the virtues and vices taught by Zeno, the founder of Stoicism (ca. 325-263 B.C.) as follows:

> Amongst the virtues some are primary, some are subordinate to these. The following are the primary: wisdom, courage, justice, temperance. Particular virtues are magnanimity, continence, endurance, presence of mind, good counsel. And wisdom they define as the knowledge of things good and evil and of what is neither good nor evil; courage as knowledge of what we ought to choose, what we ought to beware of, and what is indifferent; justice . . .;
>
> Similarly, of vices some are primary, others subordinate: e.g. folly, cowardice, injustice, profligacy are accounted primary; but incontinence, stupidity, ill advisedness subordinate. Further, they hold that the vices are forms of ignorance of those things whereof the corresponding virtues are the knowledge (*Lives: Zeno* 7.92-94, LCL).

There are parallels to this practice of producing lists also at Qumran that indicates the widespread influence of the Hellenistic catalogues. At Qumran we see in the *Community Rule* the following:

> There are their ways in the world for the enlightenment of the heart of man, and that all paths of true righteousness may be made straight before him, and that the fear of the laws of God may be instilled in his heart: a spirit of humility, patience, abundant charity, unending goodness, understanding, and intelligence; (a spirit of) mighty wisdom which trusts in all the deeds of God and leans on His great loving kindness; a spirit of discernment in every purpose, of zeal for just laws, of holy intent with steadfastness of heart, of great charity towards all the sons of truth, of admirable purity which detests all unclean idols, of humble conduct sprung from an understanding of all things, and of faithful concealment of the mysteries of truth. These are the counsels of the spirit to the sons of truth in this world.
>
> And as for the visitation of all who walk in this spirit, it shall be healing, great peace in a long life, fruitfulness, together with every everlasting blessing and eternal joy in life without end, a

crown of glory and a garment of majesty in unending light.
[Blank]

But the ways of the spirit of falsehood are these: greed and slackness in the search for righteousness, wickedness and lies, haughtiness and pride, falseness and deceit, cruelty and abundant evil, ill-temper and much folly and brazen insolence, abominable deeds (committed) in a spirit of lust, and ways of lewdness in the service of uncleanness, a blaspheming tongue, blindness of eye and dullness of ear, stiffness of neck and heaviness of heart, so that man walks in all the ways of darkness and guile. (1QS 4.2-6, 9-11; Vermes trans.)

By way of example from the second-century gnostic lists, the *Corpus Hermeticum* says:

Mind conceives every mental product: both the good, when mind receives seeds from god, as well as the contrary kind, when the seeds come from some demonic being. [Unless it is illuminated by god,] no part of the cosmos without a demon that steals into the mind to sow the seed of its own energy, and what has been sown the mind conceives—adulteries, murders, assaults on one's father, acts of sacrilege and irreverence, suicides by hanging or falling from a cliff, and all other such works of demons.

Few seeds come from god, but they are potent and beautiful and good—virtue, moderation and reverence. Reverence is knowledge of god, and one who has come to know god, filled with all good things, has thoughts that are divine and not like those of the multitude (*Corp. Herm.* 9.3-4, M. E. Boring 473).

What seems clear from these non-biblical lists is that the ethics of the New Testament were strongly influenced by the Greco-Roman world. This also substantiates a long-standing argument that the essence of Christianity can-not be reduced to its ethics, though among the list of virtues in the list in Galatians love is in first place of importance and this is common throughout the NT (e.g., Matt. 22:37-40; John 15:12-13; 1 John 2:10; 3:11-23; 4:7-21).

5:19. Now the deeds of the flesh are evident, which are: immorality, impurity, sensuality. Paul clarifies the "works/deeds of the flesh" (1 Cor. 3:13; 11:19; 14:25; 2 Cor. 5:10. See also *2 Clem* 16:3; *Ep. Barn.* 8:7; Hermas, *Sim.* 4.3; *Mand..* 11.10; Ignatius, *Eph.* 14.2). Elsewhere they appear to be the outward activities of a human being, but in Galatians, they appear to be those activities carried on not in the power of the Spirit, but of the "flesh" or Law, namely following one's own passions or evil motivations to do what is wrong (6:1).

5:22-23. But the fruit of the Spirit is love, joy, peace, patience, kindness, goodness, faithfulness, gentleness, self-control; against such things there is no law. These nine so-called "virtues" are aspects of one's character that can be appropriated, Paul says, by the power of the Spirit working in the life of one obedient to God and open to the leading of the Spirit. See examples of virtues and vices at the beginning of this section above.

5:24. Now those who belong to Christ Jesus have crucified the flesh with its passions and desires. Using crucifixion as a metaphor for behavior is not unique to Paul, nor indeed unique to the death of Jesus. Compare Rom. 8:13. As one might imagine, with the large numbers of crucifixions under Roman rule, but even among the Jews as well before Roman control of Palestine, the use of painful death could be used in a variety of illustrations for ethical behavior. Plutarch, for example, asks:

Or will you reduce a man from splendid wealth and house and table and lavish living to a threadbare cloak and wallet and begging of his daily bread? These things were the beginning of happiness for Diogenes, of freedom and repute for Crates. But you will nail him to a cross or impale him on a stake? And what does Theodorus care whether he rots above ground or beneath? Among the Scythians such is the manner of happy burial ... (*Moralia*, "Whether Vice Be sufficient to Cause Unhappiness?" 3-4, LCL.)

Philo also uses crucifixion as a metaphor for other purposes. By way of summarizing his argument, he states, "thus the mind stripped of the creations of its art will be found as it were a headless corpse, with severed neck nailed like the crucified to the tree of helpless and poverty-stricken indiscipline" (*On Dreams* 2.213, LCL). He also speaks of one's having died to passions (*Cherubim* 8).

5:26. Let us not become boastful, challenging one another, envying one another. This caution is found throughout Jewish writings (4 *Macc.* 5:10; 8:24; cf. 2:15; 8:19; *Epistle of Aristeas* 8; Philo, *On Dreams* 2.105; Josephus, *War* 6.172.) and in the time of Paul and earlier as well as in early Christian literature. The author(s) of the *Didache*, for example, write: "My child, be not a liar, for lying leads to theft, nor a lover of money, nor *vain-glorious*, for from all these things are thefts engendered" (*Did.* 3.5, LCL; italics ours). Ignatius says to the Philadelphian Christians, "I know that your bishop obtained the ministry, which makes for the common good, neither from himself nor through men, *nor for vain-glory*, but in the love of God the Father and the Lord Jesus Christ" (*Philad.* 1.1, LCL, italics ours; see also *Mart. Pol.* 10.1; Pol., *Phil.* 2.3; 1 *Clem.*35.5). Again, there are numerous examples of calls to avoid challenging and envying one another in both Jewish and Hellenistic literature. In the Mishnah, there is wise rabbinic wisdom on how to avoid conflict with another: "R. Simeon b. Eleazar said: Appease not thy fellow in the hour of his anger, and comfort him not while his dead lies before him, and question him not in the

hour of his vow, and strive not to see him in the hour of his disgrace" (*m. Aboth* 4.18, Danby trans.). Epictetus asks, "Why shall one man envy another? Why shall he admire those who have great possessions, or those who are stationed in places of power, especially if they be both strong and prone to anger?" (*Discourses* 1.9.20, LCL). Later, while speaking of one who has not won a competitive prize but has to watch it go to another, he says: " ... if I am unable to succeed in something myself, I shall not begrudge another the achievement of some noble deed" (1.27.8, LCL; cf. also Josephus, *Ant.* 7.315; 18.369).

B. 6:1-10. The Call to Charity and Zeal in the Faith

Paul concludes the argument of his letter with a collection of opinions, maxims, or judgments that add to his arguments above. There is little in these concluding comments that is specifically Christian, but the admonitions espoused certainly fit within the ethical responses of early Christianity as well as Judaism and many of the philosophic traditions of that day. While Christianity cannot be reduced to a specific set of ethical responses to the gospel, neither can they be eliminated from a Christian understanding of the gospel.

1. Dealing with the Wayward Brother or Sister (1-5). In the practical application of the law of liberty and love, Paul makes it clear that those who do God's will are those who care for brothers or sisters in need of care and guidance. In the only place where he says it in Galatians, Paul makes it clear that a Christian, that is, the "brother or sister" in Christ, is capable of sinning and he urges the Christians there, rather than deal with the matter with zeal in terms of legal codes that are rigid and strictly enforced, to deal gently and caringly with the offender. For Paul, the experience of the gospel that he preached had practical implications for daily living and one's relations to others in the family of Christ. Philo similarly speaks of happiness being found in the exercise of the truth. "What he says is, 'Lo, I have virtue laid up by me as some precious treasure, and this by itself does not make me happy. For happiness consists in the exercise and enjoyment of virtue, not in its mere possession'" (*The Worse Attacks the Better* 60, LCL). He continues saying that, "I have made up my mind that happiness is the exercise of perfect virtue in a perfect life" (60, LCL).

6:1. Brethren, even if a man is caught in any trespass, you who are spiritual, restore such a one in a spirit of gentleness; each one looking to yourself, lest you too be tempted. Paul's reference to those who are "spiritual" continues his focus on the role of the Spirit in the life of believers (see 3:2-5, 14; 4:6, 29; 5:5, 16, 17, 18, 22-25; 6:8, 18). Plutarch also sought to restore the erring person to the community and said that it was the responsibility of the philosopher/educator "to reduce this man's swollen pride and restore him to conformity with his best interests" (*Cato minor* 65.5, Betz trans. 297). Those who lived at Qumran also encouraged relationships that built up one another and says that those who deal with those with failings, "should reproach his fellow in truth, in meekness and in compassionate love for the man" (1QS 5.24, Garcia Martinez trans. 9). In the *Damascus Document* among the Qumran writings, there was a man, called an Inspector, who was responsible to educate the members of the community in the law. The document adds that,

> He shall instruct the Many in the deeds of God, and shall teach them his mighty marvels, and recount to them the eternal events with their solutions. He shall have pity on them like a father on his sons, and will heal all the strays like a shepherd his flock. He will undo all the chains which bind them, so that there will be neither harassed nor oppressed in his congregation (*CD* 13.7-10, Garcia Martinez 43).

Paul's call for every person to do self-examination is similar to 2 Corinthians 13:3-5.

6:2. Bear one another's burdens, and thus fulfill the law of Christ. Paul uses a strange description of what it is that believers should be doing, namely fulfilling the "law of Christ." He surely would not want to focus on the Law at the conclusion of his letter after he has spent so much time speaking against it. There are a few similar references elsewhere in his writings where the word law is attached to that which comes from the Spirit or by faith (1 Cor. 9:21; Rom. 3:27; 8:2; cf. 1 Thess. 4:2). He does not mean that the Jewish Law is a means of salvation, but rather that one fulfills the law in serving Christ. It is also likely that Paul had in mind the new commandments that Christ gave, namely to love one another (John 13:34-35; cf. Matt. 22:37-40).

6:3. For if anyone thinks he is something when he is nothing, he deceives himself. See 1 Cor. 3:18; 8:2; 10:12; 14:37; 2 Cor. 12:11; cf. Jas. 1:26. Epictetus declared that those who thought that they were somebody were fools (*Discourses* 4.8.39). In his *Encheiridion*, he writes: "If you wish to make progress, then be content to appear senseless and foolish in externals, do not make it your wish to give the appearance of knowing anything; and if some people think you to be an important personage, distrust yourself"(*Ench* 13, LCL). Likewise, in the Mishnah, according to Rabbi Hillel, there is the admonition: "Keep not aloof from the congregation and trust not in thyself until the day of they death, and judge not they fellow until thou art come to his place . . . " (*m. Aboth* 2.5, Danby trans 448). It was commonly taught by the philosophers and rabbis that no one should think more highly of him/herself than reality demanded.

6:4. But let each one examine his own work,

and then he will have reason for boasting in regard to himself alone, and not in regard to another. The call to examine oneself dates back to the Delphic oracle, "know thyself." It has often been attributed to Socrates by Plato who wrote in his *Phaedrus*,

And so I dismiss these matters and accepting the customary belief about them, as I was saying just now, I investigate not these things, but myself, to know whether I am a monster more complicated and more furious than Typhon or a gentler and simpler creature, to whom a divine and quiet lot is given by nature." (*Phaed.* 230A, LCL)

It is the assumption of antiquity that when persons truly know themselves, there is no room for arrogance or boasting. The notion of boasting in oneself and not against others is found also in Rom. 4:2; 1 Cor. 5:6; 9:15, 16; 11:28; 2 Cor. 1:14; 5:12; 9:3; Phil. 1:26; 2:16. One is reminded of the words of Jesus in regard to the man who saw the tax collector and said "God, I thank you that I am not like other people: thieves, rogues, adulterers, or even like this tax collector" (Luke 18:12) Elsewhere Jesus tells the story of the older brother in the parable of the Prodigal Son who is resentful of the attention given to his brother and takes pride in the fact that he is not like him, but is filled with envy that the undeserving younger brother was being celebrated by the father (Luke 15:29-32). For Paul's understanding of boasting, see 1 Cor. 3:21; 2 Cor. 11:18; 12:1-10.

6:5. For each one shall bear his own load. See Phil. 4:11-13 where Paul's ability to be self-sufficient is highlighted, even if he is grateful to those who come to his aid (4:15-18). See also Rom. 14:12; 1 Cor. 3:8; cf. 1 Thess. 4:11.

2. 6. Caring for the Teachers
6:6. And let the one who is taught the word share all good things with him who teaches. While this maxim does not appear to fit the context and is isolated from what goes before it

and what follows, it is an important teaching in antiquity that those who are taught should share with those who teach them. In the *Hippocratic Oath*, there is a place for the student to reward and care for his teacher. " . . . to hold him who has taught me this art as equal to my parents and to live my life in partnership with him, and if he is in need of money to give him a share of mine . . ." (Trans. from Bulletin of History of Medicine, Johns Hopkins). That some teachers could sometimes take advantage of their students is also mentioned in antiquity. Diogenes speaks of a teacher whose custom it was "to adopt certain of your men for gratification of his appetite and in order that he might be protected by their goodwill" (Diogenes Laertius, *Lives of Eminent Philosophers* 4.53, LCL). Paul is simply sharing a principle that those who teach and serve should be reimbursed by those who learn and are served (see also 1 Cor. 9:3-12). In a papyrus dating from the third century, the priest from Philosarapis writes to his former teacher Apion and asks him whether he needs anything from home and he promises to supply it (POxy.1664, Betz 305). Paul appears to calling upon his readers to care for their teachers.

3. 7-10. Preparing for Life with God
6:7. Do not be deceived, God is not mocked; for whatever a man sows, this he will also reap. The metaphor of sowing and reaping to illustrate life's activities precedes Paul and has many parallels both in Scripture (Job 4:8; Prov. 22:8; Hos. 8:7; 10:12; Luke 19:21; 2 Cor. 9:6), in the apocryphal literature, and in noncanonical Jewish literature. For example, Sirach urges his readers, "Do not sow in the furrows of injustice, and you will not reap a sevenfold crop" (*Sir.* 7:3, NRSV). Philo speaks of the mischief that works in the spiritual and physical dimensions of life and in their relations to each other "when the mind reaps what is sown by its follies and acts of cowardice and intemperance and injustice" (*Confusion of Tongues* 21:7, LCL) and in the

Greco-Roman world (Plato, while speaking of those who confuse lies and deceit with the truth asks, "what harvest do you suppose his oratory will reap thereafter from the seed he has sown?" (*Phaedrus* 260C, LCL). Paul's use of this metaphor is in keeping with other Jewish wisdom literature and also the Greco-Roman literature as well.

6:8. For the one who sows to his own flesh shall from the flesh reap corruption, but the one who sows to the Spirit shall from the Spirit reap eternal life. Both flesh and spirit are now seen as metaphors for one's direction in life that has both judgmental consequences (flesh) and eternal reward (spirit). For parallels to one who sows, see Mark 4:13-20; Matt. 13:18-23; Luke 8:4-15 and also Hermas, *Sim.* 9.20.1 and the *Odes of Solomon* 11.1, 18-24; 38.16-21.

6:9. And let us not lose heart in doing good, for in due time we shall reap if we do not grow weary. For those who sow to the spirit (6:7-8), the blessings for the future are assured and they are an incentive not to lose heart (see also Mark 8:3; cf. Matt. 15:32; Heb. 12:3-5). The call to watchfulness is echoed later by the Didachist who says at the beginning of a passage in which he exhorts his readers to faithfulness. " 'Watch' over your life: 'let your lamps' be not quenched 'and your loins' be not ungirded, but be 'ready' for ye know not 'the hour in which our Lord cometh'" (*Did.* 16.1, LCL).

6:10. So then, while we have opportunity, let us do good to all men, and especially to those who are of the household of the faith. This verse summarizes the whole of the section (5:1–6:10). The "doing good" is mentioned earlier in the fruit of the Spirit (5:23). In the Mishnah, Rabbi Hillel admonishes his people "Be of the disciples of Aaron, loving peace and pursuing peace, loving mankind and bringing them nigh to the Law" (*m. Aboth* 1.12, Danby trans. 447). For the notion of a "household of faith," see Eph. 2:19 where the focus is on the "household of God."

V. 6:11-18. Paul's Postscript and Conclusion

In this concluding section, Paul adds a postscript that summarizes what he has been saying and also the interpretive tool by which it can be understood. He begins it by stating that he himself is writing it with large letters, unlike what preceded this paragraph. This means, of course, that Paul used a professional secretary, or amanuensis, to write the letter for him. This passage serves as Paul's *peroratio* or his conclusion. In it, he appears to follow the conventional use of the summary to summarize his major points, to arouse anger or hostility against his opponents, and to stimulate sympathy for him and his position. Aristotle said of the conclusion to a speech or writing that seeks to persuade,

> The epilogue is composed of four parts: to dispose the hearer favourably towards oneself and unfavourably towards the adversary; to amplify and depreciate; to excite the emotions of the hearer; to recapitulate. For after you have proved that you are truthful and that the adversary is false, the natural order of things is to praise ourselves, blame him [the opponent], and put the finishing touches. (*Rhetoric* 3.18.19, LCL).

Quintilian says of the epilogue or peroration that "there are two aspects of it: the factual and emotion." He goes on to explain as follows:

> The recapitulation and assemblage of facts, which in Greek is called *anakephalaiosis* [= "going over the headings"], and by some Latin writers "enumeration," both refreshes the memory of the judge, and places the whole Cause before his eyes at once; even if this had not made much impression when the points were made individually, it is cumulatively powerful. The points to be recapitulated here must be treated as briefly as possible and (as the Greek word shows) we

must run quickly through all the "headings," for if we spend too much time, it will become almost a second speech rather than an enumeration." (*The Orator's Education*, 6.1.1-2, LCL).

Cicero says that the conclusion (or "*Conquestio*") "is a passage seeking to arouse the pity of the audience" (*De inv.* 1.55.106, LCL).

A. 11-16. Final Word on Circumcision.

Aristotle not only spoke of the value and structure of the exordium, the introduction, he also gave guidelines on how to prepare the conclusion or epilogue of a speech or writing.

The epilogue is composed of four parts: to dispose the hearer favourably towards oneself and unfavourably towards the adversary; to amplify and depreciate; to excite the emotions of the hearer; to recapitulate. For after you have proved that you are truthful and that the adversary is false, the natural order of things is to praise ourselves, blame him, and put the finishing touches. One of two things should be aimed at, to show that you are either relatively or absolutely good and the adversary either relatively or absolutely bad . . . . In the exordium [introductory] we should state the subject, in order that the question to be decided may not escape notices, but in the epilogue we should give a summary statement of the proofs.

We should begin by saying that we have kept our promise, and then state what we have said and why . . . We may, therefore, either sum up by comparison, or in the natural order of the statements, just as they were made, our own first, and then again, separately, if we so desire, what has been said by our opponent. To the conclusion of the speech the most appropriate style is that which has no connecting particles, in order that it

may be a peroration [the concluding part of a speech], but not an oration: "I have spoken; you have heard; you know the facts; now give your decision" (*Rhetoric* 3.19.1-2, 4-6, LCL).

6:11. See with what large letters I am writing to you with my own hand. It is not clear why Paul mentions writing with "large letters," though the action is in keeping with an eye problem (see above discussion of 4:15; cf. 2 Cor. 12:7). Plutarch says that Porcius Cato Marcus (ca. 234-149 B.C.) wrote his history in "large characters" and does not mention any problems with eyesight. "His History of Rome, as he tells us himself, he wrote out with his own hand in large characters, that his son might have in his own home an aid to acquaintance with his country's ancient traditions" (Plutarch, *Cato maior* 348B, Betz trans. 314). In a letter entitled "Letter from Asclepiades, an Egyptian landowner, to Portis, his tenant," written on an ostracon, or a potsherd, from Thebes, there is a writing that concludes, "Written for him hath Eumelus, the son of Herma . . . , being desired so to do for that he writeth somewhat slowly [a euphemism for writing largely]. In the year Phamenoth 2" (Deissmann, *Light from the Ancient East* 166). Why Paul chose to say these words is not altogether clear, except that for emphasis and to draw attention to his subject, he writes the epilogue to his work in his own hand. The large letters could have been a result of writing with nimble fingers or perhaps the result of poor eyesight. That Paul would conclude a work in his own hand has parallels in his own work (1 Cor. 16:21; Phile. 19; cf. Col. 4:18; 2 Thess. 3:17).

6:12. Those who desire to make a good showing in the flesh try to compel you to be circumcised, simply that they may not be persecuted for the cross of Christ. One of the compelling arguments from Paul's letter and reflective of his opponents' attempts to circumcise the male Christians in Galatia, Paul in summary says that the motivation for these Jewish Christians is to save their own necks. Times were "heating up" in Jerusalem with a growing religious fervor that eventually led up to the war of A.D. 66-70. At this time (A.D. 45-66) zealous Jews were creating pressure for the Jewish Christians to insure that their Gentile converts were also keeping the law and submitting to circumcision. At this point in time, Gentile converts to Christianity were considered converts to Judaism since the church had not yet formally separated from Judaism. It was therefore important for the Jewish Christians to pressure Gentiles who were converting to the Christian faith also to submit to the act of circumcision. Paul suggests that these "Judaizers" were only interested in saving themselves from persecution by insisting that the Galatian Christians submit to circumcision.

6:13. For those who are circumcised do not even keep the Law themselves, but they desire to have you circumcised, that they may boast in your flesh. Epiphanius reported that the Corinthians adhered to the Law, but only partially (*Anaceph.* 28.1.1). Justin, in his *Dialogue with Trypho the Jew*, claims that the Jews were not keeping the Law in its entirety and Trypho acknowledges this (*Dial.* 46-47).

6:15. For neither is circumcision anything, nor uncircumcision, but a new creation. See 5:6 above.

6:16. And those who will walk by this rule, peace and mercy be upon them, and upon the Israel of God. Paul's benediction is unique, especially in terms of the "Israel of God." Some scholars have concluded that this may have come from Israel's Eighteen Benedictions, often called the *Shemoneh Esre*, or the *Amidah* (= "standing," so named because they were said while standing). The history of this collection is obscure, but many assign it in its present con-

dition to Rabban Gamaliel II (ca. A.D. 80). The last of these benedictions (the 18th), says: "Bestow Thy peace upon Israel Thy people and upon thy city and upon Thine inheritance and bless us, all of us together. Blessed art Thou, O Lord, who makest peace!" (E. Ferguson 544). There are some coincidences, but also several differences between this and the benediction of Paul here, but some themes, such as "peace" and Israel thy People" are suggestive. Paul's reference to "peace and mercy" in a benediction is unique in the New Testament. The Israel of God is no doubt in Paul a reference to those who have been made right with God through faith in Jesus Christ. They are, for him, the "true Jews" (Rom. 2:28-29).

B. 17. A Plea for Peace in the Church
6:17. From now on let no one cause trouble for me, for I bear on my body the brand-marks of Jesus. Paul reminds his readers of the price that he has paid to tell his gospel and pleads for peace. The latter would be possible if they returned to his gospel and rejected the legalists who have come to take away their liberties in Christ. While it is true that many ancients would tattoo their bodies to celebrate their faith in their gods, the practice is unknown in early Christianity and it is more likely that the marks of which he speaks came as a result of beatings and various persecutions that he faced in his missionary journeys (cf. 2 Cor. 11:22-29).

C. 18. Paul's Blessing
6:18. The grace of our Lord Jesus Christ be with your spirit, brethren. Amen. For Paul, grace is the term that is the all-encompassing reference to what God has done in Christ to bring hope and salvation. It is therefore not surprising to see him refer to it in his closing of this letter. It is quite possible that those who read or heard this letter in their church(es) were the ones responsible for adding the "Amen" to it.

Introduction to the Prison Epistles

Daniel M. Gurtner

Three of Paul's letters, those to the Ephesians, Philippians, Colossians, and Philemon claim to have been written while the apostle was imprisoned. These have become known as the Prison or Captivity Epistles. As we will see, such imprisonments were very demanding on the imprisoned, yet served to provide significant background to understanding both these letters and Paul's self-understanding of the nature of his own apostleship.

Paul's Imprisonments. That the Apostle Paul was imprisoned numerous times is well attested in Acts, Paul's letters, and the early church. Clement of Rome (ca. 95-96) claims the apostle was "seven times in chains" (*1 Clem.* 5:6). For himself, the apostle simply says he was in chains "far more" times than the false apostles (2 Cor. 11:23).

Paul's first recorded imprisonment is found in Acts 16:23-40. Paul's and Silas' experience in the Philippian jail is understood by scholars to conform to the worst of situations available in an official prison. They had probably nothing to eat or drink since their trial earlier in the day and were probably prevented from the care of friends or family by the jailer (Acts 16:23). Astonishingly, the repentant jailer after his conversion provides the apostles with a meal about midnight (Acts 16:34). His generosity and the time of his serving would have been very unusual and certainly unexpected.

Though no mention of an Ephesian imprisonment is made in Acts, 2 Corinthians 11:23 has been taken to suggest there were additional imprisonments, perhaps alluding to the seven claimed by Clement of Rome (see above). There are also numerous passages alluding to Paul's hardships in Ephesus (1 Cor. 4:9-13; 2 Cor. 4:8-12; 6:4, 5; 11:23-25; cf. 2 Cor. 1:8; Rom. 16:3, 4), which have been taken to suggest the likelihood of imprisonment there. Based on this, some have placed this imprisonment as a direct consequence of the Demetrius riot (Acts 19:23-41) in the late spring of A.D. 57, though most arguing for an imprisonment in Ephesus regard the time period more generally between A.D. 54 and 57, during a very tumultuous time of Paul's life (Acts 19:1–20:38).

Another imprisonment is one at Caesarea (Acts 21:33), where the apostle is left under guard at Herod's palace, in a seemingly more relaxed atmosphere than that of his imprisonment in Jerusalem (Acts 21:37; 23:16), where he was bound in two chains and held in the "barracks" adjoining the temple area. From Caesarea, the apostle was transferred to Rome, where he was kept for two years under house arrest (*custodia libera*) at his own expense (Acts 28:16) and restrained with light chains (*alysis*, Acts 28:20). Paul's imprisonments, as was common in Roman law, were not strictly a punishment for a crime. Instead, prisons were holding places for those either awaiting trial or execution.

Conditions in Prison: Conditions of the

prison were severely lacking. While generally not subject to overcrowding, prisons could at times be uncomfortable during times of war or civil unrest. Imprisonment in Athens was once noted to be unbearably hot with prisoners suffering dehydration: "What a difficult time it was! With the crowd the heat was stifling!" (*Martyrdom of Perpetua and Felicitas* 3:6; cf. 7.4; A.D. 203; Rapske, 196). Prisons were inadequately ventilated (Plutarch, *Phil.* 19.3; Lucian, *Tox.* 29; Cicero, *Ver* 2.5.23, 160). An Athenian prison was also the locus of numerous POWs who worked in the quarry prison of Syracuse. Thucydides describes it:

Crowded as they were in large numbers in a deep and narrow place, at first the sun and the suffocating heat caused them distress, there being no roof; while the nights that followed were, on the contrary, autumnal and cold, so that the sudden change engendered illness. Besides, they were so cramped for space that they had to do everything in the same place; moreover, the dead were heaped together upon one another, some having died from wounds or because of the change in temperature or like causes, so that there was a stench that was intolerable. At the same time they were oppressed by both hunger and thirst . . . (*History of the Peloponnesian War* 7.87.1-2 LCL).

Prisons were notoriously dark (Tertullian, *Ad. Martyres* 2; *Mart. Let. Lyons & Vienne* 27f; *Mart. Perp. & Felic.* 3.5; Cyprian, *Ep.* 15.2; *Mart. Mary. & James* 6.1, 3). Early Christians saw prison as a device of the Devil to erode the life and faith of the Christian (*Mart. Let. Lyons & Vienne* 27f; A.D. 177; Rapske, 201).

Various means of restraint were used for ancient prisoners. Some were fettered by one or both legs (Livy 32.26.18; Tertuallian, *Ad. Maryteras* 2), one or both wrists (Juvenal 16.560), or even chains on every limb (Seneca, *Con.* 1.6.2; Arrian, *Epict. Diss.* 1.29.5; Heliodorus, *Aeth.* 8.9.1). Some prisoners were confined overnight in stocks, while others were secured by a single length of chain which was run through their fetters (Lucian, *Tox.* 33; Rapske, 207). Chains were normally fashioned of iron (Lucian 72; Josephus, *Ant.* 18.6.10 §237; Tacitus, *Ger.* 31) and were at least ten pounds in weight (Livy 32.26.18; cf. *Dig.* 48.19.8.6). Such chains on a sweaty prisoner in a damp cell would inevitably rust, which frequently did further harm to the prisoner (Lucan 72f; cf. Cyprian, *Ep.* 76.2; Seneca, *Con.* 1.6.2). Often, the prisoners' limbs were "burdened with the weight of chains" (*Cod. Theod.* 9.40.22; cf. Ovid, *Conf. Liv.* 273f; Seneca, *Con.* 1.6.2; Philostratus, *VA* 7.36). Finally, the clanging of chains could keep other prisoners from sleep (Seneca, *Ad Lucilium Ep.* 9.9; Juvenal, 6.560f; Tibullus, 2.6.26; *Mart. Mont. & Luc.* 6.2; Lucian, *Tox.* 29).

Provisions for the personal needs of the imprisoned were almost completely neglected by the prison system, and so the prisoner was dependent on outside means of support and provision. While the *Theodosian Code* (409 A.D.) stipulated the provision of food for those who have none, this was a later development and not universally practiced in the Greek, Roman, or Egyptian worlds. Prisoners who had means for their own care, through personal funds or the assistance of friends or family, were typically not restricted in the quality of their existence in prison (Rapske, 210). Yet the majority of prisoners, particularly the poor and young, were dependent upon the prison ration, which could itself jeopardize one's well-being. Athenian POWs in 413 B.C. received about 14 oz. of bread and a half-pint of water to drink daily, about half the amount typically allotted to slaves (Thucydides, *Peloponysian War* 5.16.1; cf. Plato, *Laws* 10.909C; Seneca, *Con.* 9.4). Only at one's last meal before execution does there seem to be any generosity with food provisions for the incarcerated (Athenaeus, *The Deipnosophists* 4.161.A, B). Finally, particularly poor and unassisted long-term prisoners were known to suffer in the disease and filth associated with being left to live in one's own squalor (Lucan 72f; cf. *Mart. Perp. & Felic.* 7.4; Cyprian,

Ep. 15.3; 76.2). Cleaning, grooming, and fresh clothing were the responsibility of the imprisoned, and were otherwise uncared for (cf. esp. Lucian, *Tox.* 30).

The "Prison Epistles": Paul's imprisonment had a profound influence on his self-understanding as an apostle as well as the way he put forth his gospel in the "Prison Epistles." Claiming to be written from prisons, Ephesians, Philippians, Colossians, and Philemon each bear tell-tale signs of the apostle's detainment. Significantly, he always refers to himself not simply as a prisoner, but one "of Christ Jesus" (Phlmn 1, 9; Eph. 3:1), "in the Lord" (Eph. 4:1), or "of the gospel" (Phlmn 13). He also frequently refers to his "chains" (Phil. 1:7, 13, 14, 17; Col. 4:18), yet speaks with an unhindered joy of the inability of his gospel to be so restrained.

Paul occasionally made use of a secretary, or *amanuensis*. *Amanuensis* is a term taken from Latin ("of the hand") and refers to one who writes what another dictates, and is thus a secretary or scribe. Whether due to the restriction of chains or other reasons, Paul employed such people for his letter writing. A certain Tertius claims to be the transcriber for Paul (Rom. 16:22), and the apostle's practice of adding personal greetings (1 Cor. 16:21; 2 Thess. 3:17; Col. 4:18), asseveration (Phile. 19), or a summary statement (Gal. 6:11-18) in his own handwriting seems to imply that the balance of the letter was written by another at Paul's dictation. The distinguishing "sign" or "mark" of the apostle was a sort of signature which, he claims, is affixed to each of his letters (2 Thess. 3:17; cf. 1 Peter 5:12). The employment of an amanuensis was a common practice in antiquity. Cicero, a Classical writer, frequently dictated letters to his secretary, Tiro. Caesar also seemed to have one (Plutarch, *Vit. Caes.* 17.3), as well as many others (Pliny, *Ep.* 3.5; 9.36; Quintilian, *Inst.* 10.3.19). In addition, many papyrus letters preserved from Paul's day were written by a secretary, with a final greeting or closing matter written in the hand of the sender.

RESOURCES

Bahr, G. J., "Paul and Letter Writing in the First Century." *CBQ* 28 (1966): 465-77.

Bahr, G. J., "The Subscriptions in the Pauline Letters." *JBL* 87 (1968): 27-42.

Bruce, F. F., *Paul: Apostle of the Heart Set Free.* Paternoster: Exeter, 1977.

Carson, D. A., Douglas J. Moo, and Leon Morris. *An Introduction to the New Testament.* Grand Rapids: Zondervan, 1992. (=CMM)

Hawthorne, Gerald F., and Ralph P. Martin, eds., *Dictionary of Paul and His Letters.* Downers Grove, Ill: InterVarsity Press, 1993. (=DPL)

Houlden, J. L., *Paul's Letters from Prison.* London: SCM, 1977.

Longenecker, R. N., "Ancient Amanuenses and the Pauline Epistles." Pages 281-97 in *New Dimensions in New Testament Study.* Edited by R. N. Longenecker and M. C. Tenney. Grand Rapids: Zondervan, 1974.

Murphy-O'Connor, Jerome, *Paul: A Critical Life.* Oxford: Clarendon, 1996. St. M's

Rapske, Brian, *Paul in Roman Custody.* Grand Rapids: Eerdmans, 1994.

Introduction to Ephesians

Daniel M. Gurtner

INTRODUCTION

This tenth book of the New Testament contains some of the richest teaching on the church, specific instructions for Christian households, and the most memorable illustrations of "the armor of God" found in the New Testament. Long valued for its general and universal application, Ephesians has been the subject of considerable scholarly debate because of those very traits.

Recipients. Though known today as the epistle to the "Ephesians," textual evidence for that title is less than certain. The phrase "in Ephesus," (*en Ephesē*), is not found in several of the earliest and most reliable Greek manuscripts of the letter (P^{46}, B, 424^C, 1739), as well as the works of Basil (fl. 357-379), Origen (ca. 185-254), and Tertullian (ca. 160-220). Marcion (ca. 144) knew of the epistle, though he called it "the epistle to the Laodiceans," perhaps seeing it as the epistle referred to in Col. 4:16. Yet even the manuscripts which lack "to the Ephesians" in 1:1 retained it as a title, which was included very early in the manuscript traditions (Kümmel, 353). Irenaeus (*Ag. Heresies* 5.2.36) and Clement of Alexandria (*Miscellanies* 4.65) both cite texts from Eph. 5, attributing them to the "Epistle to the Ephesians."

Some phrases, such as, "ever since I heard about your faith in the Lord Jesus" (1:15) and "surely you have heard . . . " (3:2) could be taken to mean the author did not personally know the recipients. Paul's familiarity with the Ephesians, with whom he spent a great deal of time (Acts 19:8, 10; 20:31) and shared a relationship of mutual fondness (Acts 20:17-38), does not seem to be reflected in this letter as explicitly as in others.

If this epistle was indeed sent to the church in Ephesus, it was a fellowship with which Paul was quite familiar. Having arrived in the late summer of A.D. 52, Paul spent about three years evangelizing the region (Bruce, 288), and the intimacy of his relationship to its people is revealed by his tearful departure (Acts 20:37). It is further conjectured that the letter was intended to be widely circulated. Perhaps the letter we have as "Ephesians" is the descendant of the copy intended for that church, or perhaps such a copy, without an address, was present in the Ephesian church for so long that it was assumed to have been sent to it (CMM, 310).

While there is no decisive evidence against the absence of the address, it should be noted that such an absence in first-century epistles is unprecedented (Kümmel, 355). Also, apart from Marcion's curious reference to the epistle as to the "Laodicians," Ephesians is never known to have circulated under any other name. Some have speculated that Paul sent the letter with Tychicus when he sent Colossians, and it was copied and circulated from Ephesus (CMM, 310). Moreover, the letter seems to be sent along with Tychicus (6:21) whom Paul is sending to the readers. What sense would this make if the letter were not, at least initially, sent to a particular church? Regardless of the letter's destination, or whether Paul even knew those to whom he wrote, the letter strongly betrays characteristics of a general nature which indicate that it is more likely intended for a broad readership than a single congregation. There is no reason to doubt that the Ephesians may have been among that broad readership.

Date and Place of Origin. In Eph. 3:1 and 4:1, Paul speaks of imprisonment. He was imprisoned at least three times (in Philippi [Acts 16:23-40], Caesarea [Acts 21:33.], and Rome [Acts 28:16]; See Introduction to the Prison Epistles). It has been argued that the more placid tone and developed ecclesiology (see below) of the epistle suggest the apostle was aging. This requires a later date and thus likely refers to the Roman imprisonment near the end of his life (Best [1998], 44). He died around A.D. 63, so the epistle was likely written between 61-63 in Rome. See Introduction to Colossians.

Authorship. Ephesians has been traditionally attributed to the Apostle Paul, whose name is found in Eph. 1:1, as it is in all other "undisputed" letters of Paul. The letter contains other references to the apostle (3:1), often uses the first person (especially after 3:1), and betrays a style and theology largely typical of Paul. Similar expressions are found in 2 Cor. 10:11; Gal. 5:2; Col. 1:23; 1 Thess. 2:18; Phile. 9. The author is at least somewhat familiar with those to whom he writes (1:15) and expresses his gratitude to God for them (1:16). Traces of such familiarity, characteristic of Paul's writing, are found elsewhere in the epistle (cf. 3:3, 7, 13-14; 4:17; 5:32; 6:19-22) and are consistent with what is thought to be his then current situation of imprisonment (3:1; 4:1).

Apparently referring to it as "Laodiceans," the early Christian heretic Marcion (ca. 140; according to Tertullian, *Ag. Marcion* 5.17) included Ephesians as Pauline and therefore authoritative for him. It was likewise included in the Muratorian Canon (ca. 180, though perhaps much later) as being Pauline, and is clearly attributed to the apostle by Irenaeus (ca. 140-202; 1.8.5; 5.2.3; 8.1; 14.3; 24.4). The influence of Ephesians is seen in some of the earliest Christian writers, including Clement of Rome (ca. 95-96; *1 Clem* 46.6; 64.1), Ignatius (ca. 100-118; perhaps *Ephesians* 9.1; 12.2; 20.1), Polycarp (ca. 120; *Philadelphians* 1.3), Hermas (ca. 100-150; *Mandate* 3.1-4), and perhaps the *Didache* (ca. 70-80; cf. 4.10). The letter itself contains a characteristic Pauline structure, language, and writing style. Throughout the epistle one finds characteristically Pauline theology, though new dimensions of ecclesiology (doctrine of the church; from Greek *ekklēsia*, "church") are added. Such themes as justification by faith, the role of the "flesh" in the unredeemed, the place of grace, the work of Christ in reconciliation, and the role of the Jews and the Law in God's redemptive plan are abundant in Ephesians.

Despite the above evidence, recent scholarship has challenged Pauline authorship on a number of fronts. Theologically, Ephesians is thought, at times, to contradict the undisputed letters of Paul. For example, not only does Ephesians describe the role of the church in the "heavenly realms" (3:10), a concept found nowhere else in Paul, but it claims believers are "built on the foundation of the apostles and prophets" (2:2), whereas Paul sees Christ as the church's foundation (1 Cor. 3:11). It has also been argued that several words and phrases, such as "wantonness" and "in the heavenlies" are not elsewhere attested in the undisputed letters of Paul. The argument from unique language, however, has been overturned by showing that both 2 Corinthians and Philippians contain proportionately more *hapax legomena* ("something said once"; words which appear only once in the NT (Harrison, 20) than does Ephesians.

Some have suggested that because Ephesians is so similar to Colossians, one author would not have written both books. The relation of Ephesians to Colossians is discussed more fully in the "Introduction" to the latter, as is the place of origin of both letters. Because these two books are so similar, readers are strongly encouraged to refer to cross references provided in each where further comments are provided.

Purpose. Why was Ephesians written? The general nature of the book makes its purpose difficult to determine. One does not see, for example, the problems in worship of 1 Corinthians or the return of an envoy in Philippians which could necessitate such a letter. Because of its close affinity to Colossians, scholars have speculated that Ephesians is, in a sense, a rewritten version of Colossians without mention of the specific background of heresy addressed in the latter book. Others have suggested that after the publication of Acts there was renewed interest in Paul. A disciple of Paul, it is argued, wrote Ephesians as a type of "introduction" to the Pauline corpus or perhaps simply to preserve the apostle's writings (Best [1993], 91-92). However, because of the wide range of issues addressed in this letter (see "Contribution of Ephesians" below), it now bears immense value for edification of the modern church.

Contribution of Ephesians. The epistle begins with a strong emphasis on the role of God bringing about salvation, which ultimately returns to him as glory, as he is the originator of salvation (1:5, 11). The sonship of believers is accomplished through Christ and "sealed" with the Holy Spirit (1:5, 7, 13), which is accomplished by a grace that is emphasized throughout the letter. Christian knowledge is an important element to growth in Ephesians. It is attained through "mystery" (*mustērion*), a word denoting not ambiguity but rather one's inability to attain saving knowledge of Christ apart from grace. They are to be "rooted and established in love," as well as to comprehend the magnitude of Christ's love (3:17-19). Only

in 1 Corinthians and 1 John does the word "love" (*agapē*) occur more times than in Ephesians (CMM, 315). Ephesians is most unique for its teaching on the church (*ecclesiology*, "doctrine of the church," from the Greek *ekklēsia* "church"). She is God's "holy temple" or "household" where "God lives by his Spirit" (2:19-22).

A large portion of Ephesians is dedicated to the moral implications of the grace described previously (4:1–6:17). Though there is a diversity of gifts in the church (4:11-16), she remains unified by divine factors which preclude any differences (4:3-6). Believers are exhorted to abandon past lifestyles and take on new ones (4:17-32). No longer living in darkness (5:8), believers are to be "imitators of God" (5:1), living lives characterized by appropriate moral behavior (5:1-21). Such behavior includes household living which reflects the character of Christ (5:22–6:9). It applies to wives and husbands (5:22-33), children and parents (6:1-4), slaves and masters (6:5-9). Paul then provides his readers with the "armor of God" to equip them with the spiritual tools for the unceasing battle with darkness (6:10-20) before his farewell (6:21-24).

OUTLINE OF THE BOOK

A. Unity in Christ (revisited) (4:1-16)
B. Old and New Ways of Life (4:17–5:21)
C. Christian Household (5:22–6:9)
D. Struggle Against Evil (6:10-20)
E. Final Greetings (6:21-24)

BIBLIOGRAPHY

Barth, Markus, *Ephesians* AB. 2 vol.; New York: Doubleday, 1974.

Best, Ernest, *A Critical and Exegetical Commentary on Ephesians.* ICC. Edinburgh: T&T Clark, 1998.

_____. *Ephesians.* New Testament Guides. Sheffield: JSOT Press, 1993.

Bruce, F. F., *Paul: Apostle of the Heart Set Free.* Exeter: Paternoster, 1977.

Carson, D. A., Douglas J. Moo, and Leon Morris, *An Introduction to the New Testament.* Grand Rapids: Zondervan, 1992. (=CMM)

French, D. H., "The Roman Road System of Asia Minor." *Aufsteig und Niedergang der römischen Welt* II.7.2 (1983): 698-29.

Harrison, P. N., *The Problem of the Pastoral Epistles.* London: Oxford University Press, 1921.

Kümmel, Werner Georg, *Introduction to the New Testament.* Rev. edn. Nashville: Abingdon, 1975.

Lincoln, Andrew T., *Ephesians.* Word Biblical Commentary 42. Dallas, Tex.: Word Books, 1990.

Schnackenburg, Rudolf, *The Epistle to the Ephesians.* Trans. by H. Heron. Edinburgh: T&T Clark, 1991.

Ephesians

Daniel M. Gurtner

I. BELIEVERS' SALVATION ACCOMPLISHED IN CHRIST (1:1–3:21)

A. 1:1-2. Salutation

1:1. The faithful in the Old Testament were commonly called **saints** (Greek, *hagioi* literally, "holy ones") as a way of identifying them as the people of God (cf. Exod. 12:16; Lev. 23:2-9; Num. 28:25). See comment on Col. 1:2.

If we accept **at Ephesus** as original (see Introduction), the city was located on the west coast of Asia Minor (modern-day Turkey) on the mouth of the Cayster River, and reckoned, along with Rome, Alexandria, and Syrian Antioch, among the greatest cities of the Roman Empire. Estimates of the city's population begin around 250,000, which is appropriate for its role as capital of the Roman province of Asia Minor. Studies of excavated ancient milestones reveal that mileage to other cities in the province were measured from Ephesus (French, 698-729). Strabo (*Geography* 14.1.24) called Ephesus "the largest emporium in Asia this side of the Taurus" (LCL; cf. also Aelius Aristides, *Orations* 23.24). The city contains a large theater, capable of seating 24,000, in which crowds gathered against Paul for threatening the livelihood of silversmiths who created idols for the Artemis cult (Acts 19:23-41). Worship of Artemis was certainly the most popular of the Ephesian cults and was an important figure of civic pride. To her was ascribed "unsurpassed cosmic power," including the power to raise people from the dead (Arnold, 21-22). Pliny (*Natural History* 36.96) described her temple as being 220 x 425 feet, with 127 columns each 60 feet in height; "a real and remarkable example" of "grandeur as conceived by the Greeks" (LCL). It was even hailed as one of the seven wonders of the world (Antipater of Sidon, *Greek Anthology* 9.58). Worship of Artemis of the Ephesians included obscure mystery rites and the practice of magic (see comment on Eph. 1:9), which gained Ephesus a reputation for magical practices still common in that city well into the Christian era (Clement of Alexandria, *Exhortation* 2.19). There was apparently a small Jewish presence in Ephesus (Acts 19:8; Jos., *Ant.* 12.3.2 §125), which was exempt from military service, permitted to support the Jerusalem Temple, and granted religious freedom (Jos., *Ant.* 14.10.11-12 §§223-27; 14.10.25 §§262-64). Paul's reference to "fighting with wild beasts" (1 Cor. 15:32) in Ephesus has been taken by some to mean that he was imprisoned in that city, which was his base of ministry operations for three years (cf. Acts 19:1-41; 20:13-38).

1:2. It was customary in letter writing to begin with the name of the sender, the recipient, and a greeting; e.g., "Andron to his brother Milon greeting" (*Select Papyri*; Letters, 96.1 [LCL]). The particular combination of **grace** and **peace** is unusual, but found in some Jewish literature (esp. *2 Bar.* 78.2; cf. *Jub.* 12.29; *1 Enoch* 1.8; 1QS 2:1-4). Here, however, Paul replaced the standard Hellenistic greeting of "greetings" (*chairein*) with a theological **grace** (*charis*). **Peace** (*eirēnē*) is the Greek equivalent of the Hebrew *shalom*. See comment on Col. 1:2.

B. Praise to God for His Blessings in Christ (1:3-14)

Verses 3-14 constitute a single sentence in Greek. This is similar in style to Greco-Roman aretalogy, a narrative of the virtues and achievements of the accomplished by the Caesars to promote them in the eyes of citizens. It appears that Paul used a form of promoting Christ that was quite familiar in antiquity. God is praised following the old Jewish tradition of short "blessings."

1:3. Blessed (*eulogētos*) is an LXX word used to translate the Hebrew *barak*; such *berakah* (pl) are often used when someone is responding to God's act of deliverance (Gen. 24:27; Exod. 18:10; 1 Sam. 25:39; Neh. 9:5; *Tobit* 3.11; *Judith* 13.17), though they could be offered for nearly any reason (1 Kings 8:15; 1 Chron. 29:10; 2 Chron. 6:4; *Tobit* 8.5; Dan. 3:26 [LXX]; *1 Macc.* 4.30; 1QApocGen. 20:12; 1QM 18:6).

Heavenly places. Heaven as well as earth is to be shaken and removed in judgment at the end of time (cf. Isa. 51:6; Hag. 2:6; *T. Job* 33.4) when a new heaven and earth will be created (Isa. 65:17; 66:22; *1 Enoch* 91.6). Future salvation was sometimes seen as already present in heaven (*4 Ezra* 7.14, 83; 13.8; *2 Bar.* 21.12; 48.49; 52.7).

1:4. Jews often thought God **chose** them **before the foundation of the world** (Deut. 7:6; 14:2; *Jub.* 18.30; *1 Enoch* 93.2; *2 Esdr.* 3.13; *2 Bar.* 48.19; 1QS 11:7; 1QM 10:9; 1QH 15:13-22; *Jos. Asen.* 8.9; *Midr. Ps.* 74:1; 93:3). Some believed this verse referred to the pre-existence of the church (*2 Clem.* 14.1; Hermas, *Vision* 1.1.6; 2.4.1). Believers are said to be **holy** and **blameless**. See comment on Col. 1:21.

1:5. A very rare expression, **adoption as sons** (*huiothesia*) may reflect civic legal adoption. Normally a childless adult would adopt a male child to be his heir. The term is found in a second-century B.C. inscription and first-century B.C. writings of Diodorus Siculus and Nicolaus Damascenus in this respect (Lincoln, 25; cf. *POxy* 3271). 2 Sam. 7:14 suggests the Messiah will be **adopted** as a **son**, while later Jewish tradition would extend that adoption to sonship to God's people as well (cf. *Jub.* 1.24; *T. Judah* 24.3; 1QFlor 1:11). For Paul, however, the Holy Spirit was the agent of adoption of believers (cf. Gal. 4:4).

1:7. Redemption. See comment on Col. 1:14. Offering **forgiveness of sins** was something God alone could do. See comment on Mark 2:1-13 §65. **Wisdom and insight** in the OT are seen as characteristics of God's extension of grace to his people (Jer. 10:12; 51[LXX 28]:15; Isa. 40:28; Ps. 104:24; Prov. 3:19; 4Q185 frg 1-2 *col* 1:1-15).

1:9. Mystery of His will. Mystery (*mysterion*) is a general term often used in reference to the variety of local Greco-Roman "mystery cults" dating from the time of Plato (*Sophist* [*Theaetetus*] 156a; *Gorgias* 497c). These were private groups in the Greco-Roman world into which members were inducted by undergoing secret rituals, which were themselves considered salvific (Plutarch, *How to Study Poetry* 22F; cf. Plutarch, *De Iside et Osiride* 27). Initiates were not permitted to divulge their initiatory rites (Lucius, *Met.* 11.23; Diodorus Siculus, I.27.6), and violation of this and other rules of secrecy were criminal offenses (Plutarch, *Alcibiades* 22.3) and considered a defilement of the god or goddess in view (Plutarch, *Thuc.* 6.60-61; *Life of Alcibiades* 19.1; cf. Ovid, *Amores* 2.601-604). Daily rituals were private affairs, normally involving one's own shrine and regular prayers, but also more public celebrations, including dancing, processionals, and seasonal festivals (Lucian, *Saltatione* 15; *Met.* 11.7-12). Though using the same term, **mystery** for the New Testament entered Christianity from a Jewish background. See comment on Col. 1:26.

1.10. Administration (*oikonomian*) can refer to household management (Plato, *Apology* 36b, *Republic* 498a; Xenophon, *Oeconomicus* 1.1; Aristotle, *Nic. Ethics* 1141^{b}18), or a process of accomplishing a task (*PMag. Par* 1.161). It also refers to a plan or blueprint used by surveyors for a village (*P. Wiscon.* 55.1; cf. Prov. 3:19). Rabbinic literature says that God consulted the Torah when creating the earth as an architect consults his plans (*Gen. Rab.* 1.1, 7 [on Gen. 1:1]).

For Paul, the **fullness of time** is when God sent his Son (Gal. 4:4). It is an expression used always with respect to a time being under God's sovereign control (cf. LXX Dan. 2:21; 4:37; *Tobit* 14.5; *4 Ezra* 4.38; *2 Bar.* 40.3; 1QpHab 7:2). Paul uses **fullness** (*plērōmatos*) to denote a climax of God's plan in redemptive history.

1:11. The Israelites were allotted an **inheritance** in the Promised Land (Exod. 6:8; Num. 26:52; 36:1; Deut. 18:1-2; Josh. 12:7). See comment on Col. 1:12.

1:13. Documents were often **sealed** both to simply close them up (Euripides, *Iphigenia Aulidensis* 38; *Frg.* 781.10; cf. *PAmh* 2.41.7) and to authenticate a document. Xenophon records a letter authenticated by "bearing the King's seal" (*Hellenica* 1.4.3; LCL; cf. Jer. 32:11). Such seals were personalized to their owners (Herodotus, *Histories* 1.195, 3.41; cf. Euripides, *Frg* 1063.9; Nicomachus Gerasenus, *Mathematics* 1.23).

In Jewish and Christian language a mark on the forehead was a seal, signifying election (Ezek. 9:4) and protection (cf. Rev. 7:2-8), as was circumcision (*Barn.* 9.6; *m. Ber* 7.13; Gen.

17:11). It established and expressed ownership (Gen. 4:15; Exod. 13:9; Lev. 19:28; Deut. 6:8; 14:1; Ezek. 9:4; *Pss. Sol.* 15.6; Rev. 9:4; 13:16-17; Barth, 136). Cattle or slaves could likewise be marked as property. Such marks could also be used to convey authority (Gen. 41:42; Isa. 22:22; Esther 3:10; Matt. 16:19) or to set approval upon someone (John 3:33; Rom. 15:28). The early church saw baptism as a similar seal of ownership (*2 Clem.* 7.6; 8.6; Hermas, *Similitude* 8.2.3; 9.16.3-7; *Acts of Paul and Thecla* 25; *Testament Truth* IX, 3 69:7-11; *Acts of Thomas* 131). See comment at 2 Cor. 1:22.

1:14. Pledge here (*arrabōn*) is a loan-word from Hebrew ('*erabon*, cf. Gen. 38:17-20) and is an expression from law and commerce referring to a securing deposit, pledging full payment at a later time (Menander, *Frg.* 697; Aristotle, *Politics* 1.11). The *Paris Papyri* 58.14 speaks of a woman receiving 1000 drachmas as a **pledge** for the cow she was selling (cf. *PLond* 143.13; *POxy* 2.299.2). The term can also refer to the fore-payment of a service to be rendered (*PGrenf* 2.67.17). The root of the word is retained in modern Greek in reference to a "betrothed bride" and an "engagement ring." See 2 Cor. 1:22; 5:5.

C. 1:15-23. Thanksgiving and Prayer

1:17. God is described as the **Father of glory** in Ps. 29:3 (LXX 28:3; cf. Acts 7:2). **Spirit of wisdom and revelation.** An epitaph dating from the third century A.D. to the goddess Gellia claims that divinely revealed wisdom enabled her love for her husband (*NIP* 4.8, 75-58, ND 3.48). In the Old Testament the Spirit of God was sometimes called the **Spirit of wisdom** (Exod. 28:3; 31:3; 35:31; Isa. 11:2; cf. Deut. 34:9) by virtue of the wisdom it imparted to those called to a particular task. These include Bezalel, the craftsman of the tabernacle and its articles (Exod. 31:3; 35:31), Joshua for his leadership of Israel in succession to Moses (Deut. 34:9), and the Messiah (Isa. 11:2; *1 Enoch* 49.3).

1:18. Old Testament prayers commonly asked for opening one's eyes, particularly to God's Word (Ps. 119:18) or other spiritual realities (2 Kings 6:17). A certain rabbi, Bar Kappara, said, "The soul and the Torah are compared to a lamp. The soul, as is written, *The soul of man is the lamp of the Lord* (Prov. 20:27)" (*Deut. Rab.* 4.4 [on Deut. 11:22]). Cf. Rom. 3:1. This expression was often used metaphorically for faith (Pss. 13:3; Ezra 9:8; *Barn.* 1.12; *Odes Sol.* 11.14; *4 Ezra* 14.22; 1QS 2:3; 4:2). In later Christianity this enlightening was equated with baptism (cf. *Odes Sol.* 15.1-10; *Sib. Or.* 8.247; Justin Martyr, *Apology* 1.61.12; *Dial* 39.2; 122.1; cf. *1 Clem.* 36.2; 59.3). A blessing found at Qumran reads, "May He illuminate your heart with the discernment of life and grace you with eternal knowledge" (1QS 2:3; cf. 1QS 11:3-6).

1:20-23. Resurrection is an important hope for Paul. It may stem from a corporate idea of resurrection in the Old Testament (Hos. 6:1-3) and was an illustration for new life among the faithful (Ezek. 37:1-14). Other Old Testament prophetical and poetical texts affirm the raising of the dead (Pss. 16:10; 49:15; 73:24; Isa. 25:8; 26:19; 53:9, 10; Dan. 12:1-3, 13), which is carried over to Second Temple Judaism. Sadducees did not believe in resurrection (Jos., *Ant.* 18.1.4 §16; Acts 4:1-2; 23:8), though the Pharisees did (Acts 23:6-8; Jos., *Ant.* 18.1.3 §14; *b. Sanh.* 90b; *b. Ketub.* 111b). Some believed only the faithful of Israel would be raised (*1 Enoch* 22.13; 46.6; 51.1-2; *Pss. Sol.* 3.11-16; 13.9-11; 14.4-10; 15.12-15), while others, normally later, believed resurrection would occur for both the righteous and the wicked (*4 Ezra* 4.41-43; 7.32-38; cf. *T. Benj.* 10.6-8; *2 Bar.* 49.2-51.12; 85.13; *1 Enoch* 92.3-5; 103.4; 104.2, 4). See 1 Cor. 15:12-44.

For being **seated at the right hand** (1:20), see comment on Col. 3:10. The locus of that seating was **in the heavenly places**. *Testament of Job* 33.3 says with respect to the Messiah, "My throne is in the upper world, and its splendor and majesty come from the right hand of the Father" (OTP; cf. 1 Cor. 15:25; Rom. 8:34; Col. 3:1; *2 Enoch* 20.1; *T. Levi* 3.8).

Jesus' authority is exercised over every **rule and authority and power and dominion** (v. 21). See comment on Col. 2:10. These terms are also associated with **every name that is named**. Christians in Ephesus especially would recognize this allusion to magical practices of pagan religions (see Introduction). Names of various deities were invoked in magical incantations for curing various illnesses and even demon-possession (*PGM* 61.2; *CI.*52; 7.580-90; cf. Plutarch, *Quaestionum convivialum libri IX* 7.5). Traditionally a list of six names, known as the "Ephesians Letters" (Latin, *Ephesia grammata*), referred to powerful deities able to provide assistance to those who invoked the names. These names were even worn by athletes to aid in their competitions. The six names, *ASKION, KATASKION, LIX, TETRAX, DAMNAMENEUS,* and *AISIA*, were purportedly inscribed on the statue to Artemis at Ephesus, and recited or written for one's welfare.

Paul says God **gave Him** (Christ) **as head**. In Hebrew "to give" (*natan*) can mean to "appoint" or "install" (1 Sam. 8:5-6; Lev. 17:11; Num. 14:4; Isa. 42:6; cf. 1 Cor. 12:18, 28; Acts 20:28) into a political or priestly office (Barth, 157-58). Though **head** often refers to authority (cf. Deut. 28:13; Judges 10:18; 11:11; 2 Sam. 22:44; Isa. 7:8, 9), here it is used in reference to the cosmos. The benefits of Christ being **head** are then bestowed upon the "church," further described as **His body** (1:23). The mention of the church as **His body** may be an allusion to a common Greco-Roman view that the universe was itself a large **body**, with each part a member of the cosmic whole (Diogenes Laertes, *Lives Phil.* 7.138; Cicero, *de natura deorum* 1.35; 3.9; Seneca, *Naturales Quaestiones* 6.14.1; *Epistulae morales* 95.52; *De Ira* 2.31), similarly found in Hellenistic Judaism (cf. Philo, *Noah's Work* 7; *Creation* 82; *Special Laws* 1.210). Also in Greco-Roman thought, the "body" was an image for the state, in which individual "members" have responsibilities to the well-being of the whole (Plato, *Republic* 5.464B; Aristotle, *Politics* 1.1, 2; Cicero, *Phil.* 8.5, 16; *De Off.* 1.25, 85; Seneca, *De Clem.* 1.5.1; Livy, *Histories* 26.16.19; Philo, *Special Laws* 3.131). In some Rabbinic thought, people could be seen as parts of Adam's body (*Exod. Rab.* 40.3 [on Exod. 31:2]).

D. 2:1-10. Old and New Ways of Life

2:1. The OT describes **sins** and **trespasses**, as well as disease, alienation, captivity, and being under the control of one's enemies, as being **dead** (Pss. 13:1-3; 30:3; 31:12; 88:3-6; 143:3; Hos. 13:4; Jonah 2:6; cf. 1QH 3:9; 11:10-14; Lincoln, 92). Those outside of God's covenant community were already seen as **dead** (*m. 'Ed.* 5.2; *y. Ber.* 2.4; *b. Ber.* 18a; *m. Qoh.* 9.5; *Gen. Rab.* 39.7 [on Gen. 11:32]). See comment on Matt. 8:22//Luke 9:60 §62.

2:2. Prince of the power of the air. For Paul there were hostile evil forces in the "heavenly realms" (cf. Eph. 3:10; 6:12). In Jewish thought such spiritual forces were commonly represented in heavenly locations (Job 1:6; Dan. 10:13, 21; 2 Macc. 5.2; 1 Enoch 61.10; 90.21, 24; cf. Philo, *Special Laws* 1.66; *Noah's Work* 14; *Giants* 6, 7; 2 Enoch 3.1). The **air** reaches to the first heaven (*Asc. Isa.* 7.13) and is where evil forces lurk (*Asc. Isa.* 7.9; 9.4; 10.10, 12; 11.23; cf. *T. Benj.* 3.4 [where Satan is called an "airy spirit"]; *Tg. Job* 5.7; *4 Bar.* 9.17).

2:3. The expression **Children of wrath** is, like "sons of disobedience" (v. 2), a Semitism, similar to "son of stripes" (Deut. 25:2), describing one who deserves a flogging, or "son of death" (1 Sam. 26:16; 2 Sam. 12:5; Ps. 102:20), used of someone doomed to die. For killing his brother Abel (Gen. 4:8), Cain is called a "son of wrath" (*Ap. Moses* 3.1-14; cf. Gen. 4:11).

2:5. Grace (*charis*; see comment on 1:2) is related in concept to God's grace given in the Old Testament (*chanan*) to whom he chose

(Exod. 33:19). It is also closely related to a special term for God's overwhelming, abundant love, *hesed*. *Hesed* is a significant way of expressing God's particular covenant-love for his chosen people (Deut. 5:10; 7:9, 12; Ps. 89:28; Isa. 54:8-10). Cf. Hos. 6:6; see comment on Matt. 9:13 §66; 12:7 §88.

2:6. Seated us with Him in the heavenly places: Jewish apocalyptic literature held that the righteous would enter eternal life and exercise dominion from heavenly thrones (Dan. 7:22, 27; *Wisd.* 3.8; 5.15, 16; 1 Enoch 108.12; *Apoc. Elijah* 37.3, 4; *T. Job* 33.3-5; *Asc. Isa.* 9.18; cf. Matt. 19:28; 1 Cor. 6:2; Rev. 3:21; 20:4; 1QH 3:19-22; 11:10-12). See comment on 1:3, 20.

2:10. People are said to be God's **workmanship** (*poiēma*) in Gen. 2:7, with the word sometimes referring to creation as God's "work" (LXX Ps. 91:4; 142:5). Such creative activity did not cease at creation, but continued (Pss. 64:9; 92:4; Isa. 29:16) and continues into the present (Isa. 41:11-21; 45:7; 51:9-11). That the righteous are **created for** a life of **good works** and obedience is likewise found in other Jewish texts. 1QH 4:30-33 reads "...I know that righteousness is not of man, nor of the sons of men perfection of way; to the Most High belong all the works of righteousness, whereas the way of man is not firm unless it be by the Spirit which God has created for him to make perfect a way for the sons of men, that all His works may know the might of His power and the greatness of His mercy to all the sons of his loving-kindness...." (cf. also *m. Abot* 2.8; Jas. 1:18; 1QH 16:5; cf. 4 Ezra 8.52).

E. 2:11-22. Unity in Christ

2:11. "Uncircumcision" is a way of referring to Gentiles, and was previously regarded with contempt by Jews (Josh. 5:9; Judges 15:18; 1 Sam. 14:6; 17:26; Ezek. 28:10). Those who were Jews are called **"Circumcision"** because that was the distinguishing physical mark of their covenant relationship with God (Gen. 17:9-14).

2:12. The **commonwealth** (*politeia*) of Israel refers to the rights, privileges, and responsibilities of belonging to God's covenant community as both a political and religious entity (*2 Macc.* 13.4; *4 Macc.* 17.8). The *Apocalypse of Elijah* 1.13 describes people who ignore God's laws as ones who are "making themselves **strangers to the covenant** of God and robbing themselves of the glorious **promises**" (OTP). Anything in which Gentiles **hope**, apart from God, is mocked (*Sir.* 15.6; cf. *Sib. Or.* 1.167). Yet in the Messiah even they have **hope** (Isa. 11:10; cf. Isa. 42:4; Rom. 15:12; Matt. 12:21).

2:13. Being **far off** is normally an expression for Israelites who have returned from a long journey (Zech. 6:15; Isa. 43:6; 49:12; 60:4-9). The expression is sometimes spiritualized with Gentile nations being described as **far off** (Deut. 28:49; 29:22; 1 Kings 8:41; Isa. 5:26; Jer. 5:15), and Israel being **near** to God (Ps. 148:14). Rabbi Eliezer exhorted Jews to bring sincere converts **near** and not repel them (*Mekilta* on Exod. 18:5; cf. *Num. Rab.* 8.4 [on Josh. 9:20]). One who came **near** was a proselyte into the Qumran sect (1QH 14:14; 1QS 6:16; 8:18; 9:15; cf. *Midr. Esther* 3:9; 1 Kings 8:41; Pss. 145:18; 148:14; Deut. 4:7; Tg. Isa. 48:16; Isa. 57:19; cf. *2 Bar.* 42.3).

Blood (*haima*) was what allowed worshipers to come near to God, and was required for sacrifice on the Day of Atonement (Lev. 16:1-34; Heb. 9:7). Heb. 9:22 claims that "without the shedding of blood, there is no forgiveness of sins." Life itself was said to be in the blood (Lev. 17:14). In the sacrificial system blood was used to clean the altar (Ezek. 43:20), the incense altar (Exod. 30:10), as well as the sanctuary and temple (Lev. 16:15-16; Ezek. 45:18-20). Jesus referred to the wine given at the last supper as the "blood of the covenant" (cf. Zech. 9:11; John 6:54-56; 1 Cor. 11:25; See comment on Matt. 26:28 §199).

2:14. Peace. See comment on Eph. 1:2. Some see an allusion to the *Pax Romana* ("Roman peace"), a time between 27 B.C. and 180 A.D.

when Rome was relatively free from war. Paul describes Christ's work as breaking down **the barrier of the dividing wall**. This is likely a reference to the temple precincts in Jerusalem, the inner court of which was separated from the outer, the so-called Court of Gentiles, by a **dividing wall**. Josephus describes the inner court as "surrounded by a stone balustrade with an inscription prohibiting the entrance of a foreigner under threat of the penalty of death" (*Ant.* 15.11.5 §417 [LCL]; cf. Jos. *J.W.* 5.2 §193-94; *m. Mid.* 2.3; *2 Bar.* 54.5; *3 Bar.* 2.1). The wall, portions of which were first discovered in 1871, stood about four and one-half feet tall and surrounded the nearly three-quarters of a mile perimeter of the inner court.

2:15. Paul describes Christ's death as **abolishing . . . the enmity**. Jews had little regard for Gentiles. See comment on Eph. 2:12. The area which the wall divided (v. 14), similar to the Law in Jewish thought, separated the Gentiles from the Jews and protected the sanctity of the temple and its worshipers from Gentile defilement (*Let. Aris.* 139; *1 Enoch* 93.6; 69.2; *2 Bar.* 54.5; Prov. 28:4 LXX; Philo, *Virtues* 186; *m. Abot* 3:18; cf. Exod. 19:12). Such walls could also be metaphorical for the same concept of separation between Jews and Gentiles (Mic. 7:11; CD 4:12; 8:12, 18). Hatred for Jews likewise ran deep. Tacitus claims, "the Jews are extremely loyal toward one another, and always ready to show compassion, but toward every other people they feel only hate and enmity" (*History* 5.5). Tacitus goes on to list Jewish practices he finds offensive and his, often ignorant and derogatory, understanding of them (*History* 5.1-13).

2:16. Reconcile (*apokatallaxō*): See comment on Col. 1:22.

2:18. Access . . . to the Father in the Old Testament involved a worshiper bringing sacrifices to the Lord (Lev. 1:3; 3:3; 4:14), but was otherwise strictly limited (Lev. 21:23). It was reserved only for the High Priest and that on the Day of Atonement (Lev. 16). Now **both** Jew and Gentile have **access. Access** was granted to those permitted audience with a king (Xenophon, *Cyropaedia* 1.3.8; 7.5.45), and the term points to the solemn, though unhindered, approach to a deity (Lincoln, 149).

2:19-22. Fellow citizens. In Judaism and Christianity the belief in a heavenly city was common (2 *Bar.* 4.2; *Pss. Sol.* 17.30; Philo, *Conf. Tongues* 78; Gal. 4:26; Phil. 3:20; Heb. 11:9; 12:22). An **alien** had only partial legal responsibilities and rights (Lincoln, 149; Barth, 314-15). In the OT Israel was seen as **God's household** (Exod. 16:31; 2 Sam. 1:12; Num. 12:7; Ps. 127.1; 1QS 8:5; CD 3:19; *1 Enoch* 89:29). Members of a household (*oikeioi*) were neither guests nor slaves, but of equal status with one another (Best [1998], 279) and considered members of a family, regardless of blood relations.

"When these things exist in Israel the Community council shall be founded on truth, *blank* to be an everlasting plantation, a holy house for Israel and the foundation of the holy of holies for Aaron, the true witness for the judgment and chosen by the will (of God) to atone for the land and to render the wicked their retribution. *Blank* This (the Community) is the tested rampart, the precious cornerstone that does not *Blank* (It will be) the most holy dwelling for Aaron with eternal knowledge of the covenant of justice and in order to offer a pleasant /aroma/; and it will be a house of perfection and truth in Israel in order to establish {/ . . . /} a covenant in compliance with the everlasting decrees. . . ."

1QS 8:4b-10a

Foundation of the apostles and prophets. The reference here is likely to the Jerusalem temple, the foundation of which still stands. Each stone of this foundation, today known as the "Temple Mount Platform" in Jerusalem, is larger than an average automobile with the largest estimated to weigh 570 tons. **Corner stone** could either be the foundation stone (corner stone) in a building or the top stone of an edifice (capstone). *Testament of Solomon* 22.7-23.3 describes Solomon's temple with its corner stone clearly at the top, which is probably what is in view here (cf. also 1 Peter 2:1; Ps. 118:22; Mark 12:10; Acts 4:11).

Whole building, being fitted together. Again Paul uses architectural language. A building being assembled as a metaphor for a community of people is common in the OT (Gen. 7:1; 1 Sam. 20:16; Ruth 4:11; Num. 12:7; Jer. 31:4; cf. 1QH 6:25-27; 7:8f.). **Being fitted together** reflects the construction process of a building, perhaps the temple. Stones were prepared by cutting and smoothing the surfaces, and holes were made for dowels. The dowels were then fitted into the holes and held by molten lead. **Holy temple.** The meeting place of God is no longer in a building, but his people are his **holy temple**. This is also seen among the Qumran sectarians (1QS 5:5; 9:5, 6; 11:8; 4QFlor 1:6, 7), where being God's holy temple was the basis for founding the community (1QS 8:4b-10a). The earthly temple was seen as a replica of God's heavenly temple abode (*Wisd.* 9.8; *1 Enoch* 90.29; 2 *Bar.* 4.2-6; *T. Dan.* 5.12; *Asc. Isa.* 7.10). The temple was considered a gateway from earth to heaven (*b. Yoma* 54b; *Gen. Rab.* 4.2 [on Gen. 1:6]; *Gen. Rab.* 68.12 [on Gen. 28:12]; *Pirqe R. El.* §32.35; *Num. Rab.* 12.4 [on Num. 7:1]), where heavenly beings lived and worshiped. See comment on Mark 11:15-19 §163.

F. Paul's Call to Minister to Gentiles (3:1-13)

3:6. A **fellow partaker** seems to be used to refer to those who were joint possessors of a house.

For Paul it was not ethnicity, but faith in Christ that made someone a child of Abraham (Gal. 3:7, 26-29).

3:8. Though translated **very least** (*elachisteros*), the word here means "less than the least" or "the very least amount" (Sextus Empiricus, *Ag. Prof.* 3.54 LCL; cf. 9.406). Paul similarly refers to himself as "least of the apostles" (1 Cor. 15:9; cf. 1 Tim. 1:15). That the Latin of Paul's name, *paulus*, means "little" is ironic, but probably coincidental. See comment on Acts 13:9; Col. 1:1.

God's **grace** (see comment on Eph. 2:5). The adjective **unfathomable** (*anexichniston*) is used to describe God's ways in the world (Job 5:9; 9:10; 34:24; Rom. 11:33; cf. *1 Clem.* 20.5), but here is attributed to Christ. That God's ways are beyond human comprehension is common in Jewish thought (Job 42:3; Pss. 131:1; 139:6; *Odes Sol.* 12.6; cf. *Epistle to Diognetus* 9.5). A prayer attributed to Manasseh (cf. 2 Kings 20:21-21:18), but actually dating between the second century B.C. and first A.D., says " . . . unending and immeasurable are your promised mercies" (*Pr. Man.* 6, OTP).

3:12. Access to God in the Old Testament was limited (see comment on Eph. 2:18), though the **boldness** (*parrēsion*) was sometimes an expression used by Jews to describe pious prayer (LXX Job 22:26; 27:9, 10; Philo, *Special Laws* 1.203; Jos., *Ant.* 2.4.4 §52; cf. *Ant.* 5.1.3 §18). **Boldness** here really means frankness, or freedom of speech. *Letter of Aristeas* 125 speaks of a man receiving "frank (*parrēsion*) advice given him by his friends for his benefit" (OTP; cf. *T. Reub.* 4.2; Rom. 5:2; Heb. 3:6; 4:16; 10:35; 1 John 2:28; 3:21; 4:17; 5:14).

3:13. Sages were at times portrayed as suffering in Greco-Roman literature (Plutarch, *Moralia* 361E-362A; 1057D-E; Epictetus, *Discourses* 2.19.12-32; 4.7.13-15; Seneca, *Epistulae morales* 85.26-27), but for Paul suffering was inextricably linked to his ministry (cf. Acts 9:16; Col. 3:4; 2 Cor. 1:6; 4:12).

G. Paul's Prayer for the Ephesians (3:14-21)

3:14. For Jews standing was the common posture of prayer (*m. Ber.* 5.1; *m. Taan* 2.2; Matt. 6:5; Mark 11:25; Luke 18:11; 1 Sam. 1:26; 1 Kings 8:14, 22; Jos., *Ant.* 10.11.6 §255; 12.1.12 §98; *t. Berak* 3.20). Yet kneeling and prostration were also practiced (1 Chron. 29:20 LXX; Isa. 45:23; Ps. 95:6). In repentance, the wicked King Manasseh allegedly prays, "And now behold I am bending the knees of my heart before you; and I am beseeching your kindness. I have sinned, O Lord, I have sinned" (*Pr. Man.* 11-12a, OTP). For God as **Father** see comment on Matt. 5:16 §30.

3:16. Qumran texts portray a leader speaking to his troops to **strengthen** their **spirits** before the final, eschatological battle. 1QM 10:5 says, "Our [of]ficers shall speak to all those in readiness for battle, to those with resolute hearts, to strengthen them with God's power..." (cf. 1QH 7:17; 12:35; 1QM 10:5). See comment on 6:10.

3:18. Breadth and length and height and depth. In Stoic philosophy people were said to possess sufficient knowledge to walk across the height, depth, length, and breadth of the heavens. Magical texts call upon the magic of light "breadth, depth, length, height" to invoke a god to human servitude (Schnackenburg, 151; *PGM* 4.960-85). However, it probably here refers to the dimensions of God's love, as the rest of the verse suggests. It is, then, an expression of the mystery of salvation made manifest in God's love.

3:20. Concern for the personal well-being of worshipers is an attribute missing in Artemis and the other pagan deities of Asia Minor.

3:21. This verse is often used in churches as a "doxology," which comes from the Greek word *doxa*, "glory, praise, honor," because it describes the glory due to God.

II. Ethical Implications of the Believers' Salvation (4:1–6:24)

A. Unity in Christ (revisited) (4:1-16)

4:1. Paul now begins a practical exhortation for behavior (Eph. 4–6) based on the theological truths he has just expounded (Eph. 1–3). This is a common ancient rhetorical device, which now moves to the *exhortatio,* or exhortations phase. **Entreat** (*parakaleō*) was a common word for making an appeal to someone (Aeschylus, *Persae* 380; Euripides, *Phoenissae* 1254; Xenophon, *Anabasis* 3.1.24; Plato, *Republic* 523b). A papyrus fragment dating late in the second century contains a letter from a woman entreating a prefect of Egypt to decide a civil dispute (*ND* 6.144; cf. *P. Berol. Inv.* 16546). **Walk** is a metaphorical expression for moral and ethical behavior. See comment on Col. 1:10.

4:2. **Humility** (*tapeinofros*) literally refers to a "lowliness of mind" and was looked down upon in the Greco-Roman world (Jos., *J.W.* 4.9.2 §494; Epictetus, *Discourses* 1.9.10; 3.24.56; Lincoln, 235). Jews tended to look on it as a positive quality (Pss. 34:18; 51:7; Isa. 66:2) and it was a valued trait at Qumran (1QS 4:2).

4:4-6. **One hope . . . one Lord . . . one faith . . . one baptism . . . one God and Father:** This type of expression is found in Hellenistic Judaism, where we read "there is one law by One, one world and one end for all who exist" (*2 Bar.* 85.14 OTP). Philo speaks of "one sanctuary" because there is only "one God" (*Special Laws* 1.67). Jews of Paul's day were radically monotheistic (*2 Macc.* 7.37; Philo, *Allegorical Interpretation* 2.1; Jos., *Ant.* 5.1.25 §97; 8.13.6 §343; *Ag. Ap.* 2.23 §193; *Sib. Or.* 3.11, 629). Deut. 6:4, called the *Shema* (from the Hebrew *shma* "to hear"), says, "Hear, O Israel! The Lord is our God, the Lord is one!"

4:7. Rabbi Judan ben Rabbi Simeon (ca. A.D. 320) said, "Even the waters which come down from above are given by [God's] **measure**" (*Lev. Rab.* 15.1 [on Lev. 13:2]; cf. Rom. 8:32).

4:8. **When He ascended on high, He led captive a host of captives, And He gave gifts to men.** This text is taken from Ps. 68:18, originally referring to the Lord's triumphal ascent of either Mt. Zion after delivering his people, or possibly Sinai for the giving of the Law. Here it is used of Christ, whose leading of captives may refer to his dominance over heavenly powers (Eph. 1:21-22). Leading **captives** refers to a triumphal procession in which captives taken in war were marched by victors to flaunt their success. See comment on Col. 2:15.

4:9-10. **Lower parts of the earth.** Paul could mean that Christ descended into Hades (1 Peter 3:19; cf. Rom. 10:6, 7), his "descent" from heaven in the incarnation (cf. Phil. 2:6-11; cf. Ps. 139:15), his descent in the person of the Spirit at Pentecost (Acts 2:1-21), or simply an expression for Jesus' death (Ezek. 32:24). It seems most probable that here Paul is referring to the incarnation, as Eph. 4:10 seems to be alluding to the bodily ascension of Christ (cf. *Gk. Apoc. Ezra* 7.3; *Apoc. Elijah* 1.4).

4:11. To the list found in Eph. 2:20, 3:5, Paul adds **evangelists**, **pastors**, and **teachers**. **Evangelists** (*euangelistas*) were probably missionaries who had the particular responsibility of proclaiming the gospel to other lands (*euangelion*; cf. Acts 21:8; 2 Tim. 4:5). **Pastor** (*poimēn*) can also be translated "shepherd," and is a term used of Jesus himself (John 10:11, 14; Heb. 13:20; 1 Peter 2:25). It suggests a leadership characterized by nurture, guidance, and care (cf. Jer. 23:2; Ezek. 34:11; Zech. 11:16; CD 13:7-11). **Teachers** (*didaskalous*) carried responsibilities closely related to those of the pastor, and in the Greek the term is more closely related to the pastor than the apostles to the prophets. Some have considered "pastor-teacher" to be a single office (cf. 1 Cor. 12:28, 29; 14:26; Rom. 12:7). Their role was to preserve, transmit, expound, interpret, and apply the teachings of the apostles and the Old Testament (Lincoln, 251).

4:12. Equipping (*katartismos*) occurs only here in the New Testament. It is used elsewhere in Greek literature to "reconcile" political opponents, "set bones" in surgery (Heliodorus, *Apud Oribasium*, 49.1.1; Soranus, *Gynecology* 1.73), or simply "furnishing" or "preparation" (*PTeb* 33.12; *PRyl* 127.28; *CMRDM* 1.121). This type of equipping may look forward to the spiritual armor of Eph. 6:10-17.

4:14. Communities familiar with Mediterranean seafaring would know what it meant to be **tossed here and there by waves**. Having been shipwrecked at least three times (2 Cor. 11:25), Paul was intimately familiar with the imagery he uses. Isaiah describes the wicked as "like the tossing sea, For it cannot be quiet, And its waters toss up refuse and mud" (Isa. 57:20; cf. Jas. 1:6; Jude 12). Sailing on the Mediterranean was an important means of commercial trade as well as exportation of the Christian faith (Acts 13:13-15; 14:1-2). Its hazards, however, were well-known. The rabbis warned against traveling on it between the Feast of Tabernacles and Hanukkah (*Gen. Rab.* 6.5 [on Gen. 1:17]).

Paul's third metaphor of **the trickery of men** and **craftiness in deceitful scheming** is taken from dice playing. Though not itself sinful, such games were often associated with deception and dishonesty in the ancient world (*m. San.* 3.3; Epictetus, *Discourses.* 2.19.28). These terms are expressions of deceptive manipulation used to lead people astray (Polycarp, *Philadelphians* 7.1; Philo, *Moses* 2.212; 2 Sam. 19:26-27; cf. Ignatius, *Philadelphians* 7.1).

B. Old and New Ways of Life (4:17–5:21)

4:17-18. To **walk as the Gentiles also walk** was considered particularly deplorable to Jews, who considered Gentiles to be "those who are concerned with meat and drink and cloths,

their whole attitude (to life) being concentrated on these concerns." Yet of Jews it is said, "throughout the whole of their lives their main objective is concerned with the sovereignty of God" (*Let. Aris.* 140-141, OTP; cf. *Wisd.* 12.1-15.19). The **Gentiles** (*ethnō*) is a term often used in the Bible to denote "pagans," indicating that they do not know the true God of Israel or behave appropriately for such knowledge.

Being darkened in their understanding: On his deathbed, Reuben is said to describe his deceptiveness as a youth (cf. Gen. 35:22): "And thus every young man is destroyed, darkening his mind from the truth, neither gaining understanding in the Law of God nor heeding the advice of his fathers—just this was the plight in my youth" (*T. Reub.* 3.8-9a). Estrangement from God is thought to lead to **darkened** reasoning (*T. Gad* 6.2; *T. Dan* 2.4; *T. Levi* 14.4; Rom. 11:10; *1 Clem.* 36.2; *2 Clem.* 19.2; 1QS 3:3; 1QM 11:10). The Qumran sectarians saw unfaithful Jews as in darkness (1QM 15:9-11a).

Ignorance (*agnoia*) is the root of the English *agnostic*, literally meaning "not knowing." Jews at times attributed this ignorance to Gentiles. The *Wisdom of Solomon* says, "For all men who were ignorant of God were foolish by nature; and they were unable from the good things that are seen to know him who exists, nor did they recognize the craftsman while paying heed to his works" (*Wisd.* 13.1; cf. Philo, *Decal.* 8; *Special Laws* 1.15; Jos., *Ant.* 10.8.1 §142; *T. Gad.* 5.7; cf. Acts 17:30; 1 Peter 1:14). Biblical authors likewise exhorted fellow Jews not to live like Gentiles (Lev. 20:23; Deut. 18:9).

The condition of **ignorance** is caused by **hardness** (*pōrōsis*) **of their heart**. This is an expression from the OT of willful unbelief. It was attributed to Pharaoh (Exod. 4:21; 7:3; 9:12) and at times Israel (Ps. 94:8; Isa. 6:10; 63:17). It is similarly used in Qumran (1QS 1:6; 2:14; 3:3; 5:4; CD 2:17; 3:5; 8:8). *Testament of Levi* 13.7 says, " . . . nothing can take away the wisdom of the wise man except the blindness of impiety and the obtuseness (*pōrōsis*) of sin" (OTP).

4:19. Sensuality (*aselgeia*) is a vice commonly condemned by Jewish and Christian literature and is often associated with sexual sin (Rom. 13:13; 2 Cor. 12:21; Gal. 5:19; *Wisd.* 14.26; *T. Levi* 17.1) or idolatry (*T. Judah* 23.1). It refers to undisciplined behavior and is often, but not always, sexual in nature (cf. Jos., *Ant.* 4.6.12 §151; 8.10.2 §252; 8.13.1 §318; 20.5.3 §112).

Impurity (*akatharsia*) is a term perhaps borrowed from the ritual impurity of the Old Testament (esp. Lev. 15). If so, it may suggest one's inability to properly participate in corporate worship (cf. 2 Cor. 12:21; Gal. 5:19; Col. 3:5; Prov. 6:16; 1QS 4:9-11). In *3 Maccabees* Simon the High Priest saw being made unclean as a punishment from God (*3 Macc.* 2.17).

With greediness (*pleonexia*) may suggest, with **sensuality**, a sexual desire motivated by greed (CD 8:5; *T. Levi* 14.5; *T. Judah* 18.2; *T. Dan* 5.5-7) or idolatry (*T. Judah* 19.1; Col. 3:5; Eph. 5:3; cf. Matt. 6:24; Luke 16:13). While truly characteristic of many "Gentiles," such vices were by no means universal. Stoics likewise condemned sexual indulgence (Plutarch, *Moralia* 441A; Seneca, *Epistulae morales* 9.3; 75.7; Epictetus, *Discourses* 2.18.15, 19; 3.7.21; 4.1.122) and anger (Best [1998], 424).

4:22-25. Lay aside the old self . . . put on the new self. Here Paul seems to be borrowing the OT metaphor of being clothed with salvation (2 Chron. 6:41) or qualities such as righteousness (Job 29:14; Ps. 132:9). The **old self** should be laid aside like a garment (Acts 7:58; *Martyrdom of Polycarp* 13.2; cf. Philo, *Conf. Tongues* 31; Demosthenes 8.46; Lucian, *Dial. Mort.* 10.8, 9; *Let. Aris.* 122; Plutarch, *Coriolanus* 19.4). The Bible uses similar expressions for putting on and taking off certain types of behavior (Job 29:14; Pss. 93:1; 109:18; Isa. 61:3, 10; 2 Chron. 6:41). The **new self** is described as made **in the likeness of God**. This rings back to God's creation of man in his likeness (Gen. 1:26-27; Ps. 144:17; Deut. 32:4; cf. John 3:3, 7; 1 Peter 1:23).

4:26-27. The phrase **be angry, and yet do not sin** is taken from Ps. 4:4, which in its original context emphasizes the avoidance of sin against the Lord. Jewish and Christian literature viewed anger very negatively. Eccles. 7:9 says, "Do not be eager in your heart to be angry, For anger resides in the bosom of fools" (cf. Jas. 1:19, 20; Matt. 5:22; Gal. 5:20; Col. 3:8; 1 Tim. 2:8; Titus 1:7; Prov. 15:1; 22:24; 29:8; *Sirach* 1.22; 27.30; *T. Dan* 2.1-5.1; Lucian, *Demonax* 51; Dio, *Orat.* 32; Ps-Phocylides 63-64). Early Christians exhorted, "Never give way to anger, for anger leads to murder" (*Didache* 3.2). The rabbis agreed: "Do not flare up, so that you do not sin" (*b. Ber.* 29b; Lincoln, 301).

Do not let the sun go down on your anger. Sunset was thought of as the time limit for many things (cf. Deut. 24:15). The thought here may have been borrowed from the Pythagoreans, of whom Plutarch says, "if ever they were led by anger into recrimination, never let the sun go down before they joined right hands, embraced each other, and were reconciled" (*Moralia* 488c LCL). A similar principle is found in Qumran: "for each to reprove his brother in accordance with the precept, and not to bear resentment from one day to the next" (CD 7:2, 3; cf. CD 9:6; 1QS 5:26-6:1).

Do not give the devil an opportunity. Anger was often associated with **the devil** (*ho diabolos*). *Testament of Dan* 4.7 says, "Anger and falsehood together are a double-edged evil, and work together to perturb the reason. And when the soul is continually perturbed, the Lord withdraws from it and Beliar rules it" (OTP; cf. also *T. Dan* 1.7, 8; 3.6; 5.1; Hermas, *Mandate* 5.1.3; Lincoln, 302-3).

4:28. Naturally, theft was looked down upon in Judaism (Isa. 1:23; Jer. 7:9; Lev. 19:11; Exod. 20:15) and Greco-Roman culture (Epictetus, *Dissertation* 3.8.10; Xenophon, *Anabasis* 7.6.41; Plato, *Republic* I 344b; Heroditus, *Histories*, 1.186.3). Similarly, work was valued in Jewish (Exod. 20:9; Ps. 104:23; Prov. 6:6; 28:19; Eccles.

7:15; *T. Iss.* 5.3; Jos., *Ag. Ap.* 2.41 §291) and Greco-Roman cultures (Epictetus, *Dissertation* 1.16.16; 3.26.27; 8.26.2; Dio, *Orations* 7.112; 123; Best [1998], 452-53). Idle rich people were often condemned (Amos 6:4-6), and even teachers of the Law were expected to support themselves (*m. Abot* 2.2). Paul himself was cautious to support himself and encourage work (1 Thess. 2:6, 9; 3:8; 2 Thess. 3:10). Rabbi Judah (ca. 150 A.D.) said, "He who does not teach his son a craft teaches him to be a robber" (*b. Qidd.* 29a).

4:29. Let no unwholesome word proceed from your mouth. The Greek phrase here is a Semitism also found in *Testament of Isaac* 4.14, 17 which says, "Be careful that an evil word does not come forth from your mouth . . . . See that you do not make sport with your tongue lest an evil word come forth from your mouth" (Lincoln, 305). The Qumran sectarians were quite strict about the use of careless or unwholesome talk, enacting punishments on the offender: "Whoever utters with his mouth futile words, three months [exclusion from sacred fellowship meals]; and for talking in the middle of the words of his fellow, ten days . . ." (1QS 7:9; cf. CD 10:17). Judaism valued gracious and uplifting speech (Prov. 12:25; 15:23; 25:11; cf. Zech. 1:13).

Unwholesome (*sapros*) can be used of rotting figs (Matt. 7:17), crumbling brickwork (Attic inscription *Syll* 587.24 [328 B.C.]), a decaying tree, or withering flower (Demosthenes, *Epistle* 22.70).

4:30. Do not grieve (*lupeite*) **the Holy Spirit of God.** In Isa. 63:10, it was rebellion that would **grieve** the Lord, resulting in his turning against them. The expression was similarly used of Israel's sins of rebellion in the desert (cf. Num. 20:10; Deut. 3:26; Ps. 106:33). Later, (Hermas, *Mandate* 10.2.4; 10.3.2) it indicated a saddening or disappointing of the Spirit by any action contrary to the Spirit's holy nature.

5:1. Being **imitators** refers to copying the con-

duct of another (*4 Macc.* 9.23; 13.9; *Wisd.* 4.2; *T. Benj.* 3.1; 4.1). Sons were to **imitate** their fathers (Isocrates, *Demonicus* 4.11; *1 Macc.* 2.51; Philo, *Abel* 64), subjects their rulers (Xenophon, *Cyropedeia,* VIII 1.21, 24); students their teachers (Dio Chrysostom, *Discourses* 55.4, 5; Seneca, *Epistulae morales* 6.5-6; Philo, *Moses* 1.158), and the good should be imitated (Isocrates, *Nicocles* 22.38; 38.61; Philo, *Special Laws* 4.83; *Ps-Phoc* 77; cf. Jos. *Ant.* 3.6.4 §123; *T. Asher* 4.3; *Let. Aris.* 188; Best [1998], 466).

5:2. Offering (*prosphorn*) **and a sacrifice** (*thusian*) may be borrowed from Ps. 40:6 (LXX 39:6), and are collective terms referring to all kinds of sacrifices, both grain and animal. However, the qualification of being offered **to God as a fragrant aroma** is a common LXX metaphor for a sacrifice which was particularly pleasing to God (Exod. 29:18; Lev. 2:9, 12; Ezek. 20:41; Lincoln, 312; see comment on Phil. 4:18).

5:3. Immorality (*porneia*) is the source of our English word *pornography*. Here in Eph. 5:3-5 primary attention is given to sins of a sexual nature, including "deeds of darkness" (v. 11)

> "I shall not retain Belial within my heart. From my mouth shall not be heard foolishness or wicked deceptions; sophistries or lies shall not be found on my lips. The fruit of holiness will be on my tongue, profanity shall not be found on it. With hymns shall I open my mouth and my tongue will continually recount both the just acts of God and the unfaithfulness of men until their iniquity is complete. I shall remove from my lips worthless words, unclean things and plotting from the knowledge of my heart. . . ."
>
> 1QS 10:21-23

and "things done in secret" (v. 12). While it particularly refers to adultery and intercourse with prostitutes, it can generally be used of any sexual sins, which is apparent by Paul's expression **any impurity**. Such sins were vehemently condemned in Judaism (*Sir.* 23.16-27; *T. Reub.* 1.6; 2.1; 3.3; 4.6; 5.1, 3; 6.1; *T. Sim.* 5.3; *T. Iss.* 7.2; Philo, *Special Laws* 3.51; Lincoln, 321). **Greed** (*pleonexia*) can also be translated "covetousness," and likewise has reference to sexual desires. Reminding one of the tenth Commandment (Exod. 20:17) not to covet one's neighbor's wife, the recognition of such greed with sexual sin was both widely recognized and condemned in Judaism (*T. Levi* 14.5; *T. Judah* 18.2; 1QS 4:9; CD 4:17; Lincoln, 322). Some rabbis presumed a Gentile child was born "for adultery" (*m. AZ* 2.1).

5:4. filthiness and silly talk . . . coarse jesting. The Jews at Qumran observed strict regulations regarding careless speech. One was sentenced to three months of penance for speaking "foolishly" (1QS 7:14-18). An oath from Qumran swears avoidance of such talk (1QS 10:21-23). Aristotle attributed such talk to the excesses of immature youth (*Nic. Ethics* 4.8.1128a.14-15; *Rhetorica.* 2.12.1389b.10-12; Lincoln, 323). Ephesus was particularly known for its facetious orators (Aristotle, *Nic. Ethics* 2.7.13 1108AB; Barth, 562).

5:5. Paul describes an **immoral or impure person or covetous man** as an **idolater**. See comment on Col. 3:5. The patriarch Reuben is said to have warned his children to avoid sexual promiscuity because it "is the pitfall of life, separating man from God and leading on toward idolatry, because it is the deceiver of the mind and the perceptions, and leads youths down to hell before their time" (*T. Reub.* 4.6 OTP; cf. Philo, *Special Laws* 1.23).

5:6. Let no one deceive you with empty words (*kenois logois*): The word **empty** (*kenois*) is used in a second-century papyrus fragment to refer to a camel that has nothing on its back (*OGIS* 629.166), and later of water running to waste (*Kaibel* 646.10). See comment on Col. 2:8. For **sons of disobedience**, see comment on Eph. 2:2.

5:8-14. Darkness to **light** is a common expression for conversion (*Jos. Asen.* 8.10; 15.13; Philo, *Virtues* 179; Acts 26:18; Col. 1:12, 13; 1 Peter 2:9; *Odes Sol.* 14.18, 19; cf. Heb. 6:4; 10:32; Lincoln, 326). In the OT light can refer to salvation and life from God (Ps. 27:1; Isa. 9:2; 10:17; 42:6, 16; 41:4; 60:1; Lincoln, 327). At Qumran, the "War Scroll" (1QM) depicts a "War of the Sons of Light against the Sons of Darkness" (1QM 1:1-16; 3:6; 14:17; cf. 1QS 1:9, 10; 3:13, 19-21, 24, 25; *T. Levi* 14.4; *T. Benj.* 5.3; Lincoln, 327). **Goodness and righteousness and truth** (v. 9): A list of three virtues designating something particularly **pleasing to the Lord** (v. 10) was an ideal in Jewish literature and was attributed to King Hezekiah (2 Chron. 31:20; cf. Mic. 6:8; 1QS 1:5; 8:2; cf. Gal. 5:22). **Expose** (*elegchein*) probably refers to a verbal reproof (*Sir.* 19.13-17). Lev. 19:17 says, "You shall not hate your fellow countryman in your heart; you may surely reprove your neighbor, but shall not incur sin because of him." The need to correct such sinful behavior was also recognized at Qumran (cf. 1QS 5:24, 26; CD 7:2; 9:8; 10:4; especially 20:3-5).

For this reason it says, "**Awake, sleeper, And arise from the dead, And Christ will shine on you**" (v. 14): This seems to be a baptismal hymn with Semitic influence. The first two lines constitute a synthetic parallelism characteristic of Hebrew poetry related to ethical exhortation while the last expresses the promise of Christ's aid (Lincoln, 318). While such awakening language is used both of the mystery religions for conversion (Aristophanes, *Frags.* 340-43; *Orph. Hymn.* 50.50) and is similarly found in the Gnostic writings (cf. the "Hymn of the Pearl" in *Acts of Thomas* 110.43-48), the concept is in fact borrowed from the Old Testament and early Judaism.

Wine and Spirit in the World of Paul

Paul enjoins his readers: "And do not get drunk with wine, for that is debauchery; but be filled with the Spirit" (Eph. 5:18). His injunction reminds us of Prov. 23:31 "Do not get drunk with wine, but converse with righteous men . . ." But the contrast between being drunk with wine and being filled with the Spirit probably reflects pagan religious practice in late antiquity. Some commentators have suggested that Paul may well have had in mind the cult of Dionysius, the god of wine. According to this cult, when one imbibed wine, one actually imbibed the god himself. According to the play *Bacchae*, authored by Euripides, Dionysius

> "discovered the grape-cluster's liquid drink and introduced it to mortals, that which stops wretched me from suffering, when they are filled with the stream of the vine . . . He (Dionysius) is poured as a libation to the gods, a god himself, so it is through him that people have all good things" (lines 279-285).

> "He (Dionysius) is a prophet, too, this deity; since that which is bacchic and that which is manic possesses great mantic powers; for whenever the god enters the body in full measure he makes those who are maddened tell the future" (lines 298-301).

Sleep was a common euphemism for death (cf. Job 14:12; Isa. 43:17; *Pss. Sol.* 16.1-4; Homer, *Iliad* 11.241; Sophocles, *Electra* 509). Having God **shine on you** was an Old Testament way of expressing God's saving or delivering help (cf. Deut. 33:2; Pss. 50:2; 80:1-3, 7, 19; cf. 1QH 4:5, 6, 23; 9:31; CD 20:25, 26; *T. Zeb.* 9.8), and was likewise an attribute of the Messiah (*T. Levi* 18.2-4; *T. Jud.* 24.1).

5:16. The days are evil. Jewish and Christian writers viewed the "last days" in general as evil (*T. Dan* 5.4; *T. Zeb.* 9.5, 6; *Barn.* 4.9; 2 Tim. 3:1; 2 Peter 3:3; Jas. 5:3). Paul's use of the present tense, **the days *are* evil**, may suggest he understands himself to be in "the last days."

5:18. And do not get drunk with wine, for that is dissipation. . . . Wine and intoxication were central aspects of the worship of the god Dionysus, the Greek god of wine and ecstatic experience, typically also associated with vegetation, death, and rebirth. Intense intoxication was the decisive element in being "filled with the spirit" of Dionysus. Drunkenness was widely recognized as a sin in Judaism (Prov. 23:31 LXX; *T. Judah* 11.2; 12.3; 13.6; 14.1-4; 16.1; *T. Iss.* 7.3; Philo, *Plant* 140-7).

Why mention drunkenness here? Paul describes it as **dissipation**, which generally refers to dissolute behavior (Philo, *Special Laws* 4.91; *Contemplative Life* 47; Jos., *J.W.* 4.11.3 §651). Philo says, "wine acts like a drug producing folly" (*Contemplative Life* 74, LCL; cf. *Drunkenness* 11, 95, 125-26, 154). Those looking for spiritual fulfillment sometimes turn to alcohol (cf. Isa. 28:7; Philo, *Contemplative Life* 85, 89; Macrobius *Saturnalia* I 18.1; Hippolytus, *Ref. Heresies* 5.8.6; Best, [1998], 509; cf. also *Num. Rab.* 10.2 [on Num. 6:2-4]; *m. Sanh.* 8.2). **But be filled with the Spirit:** The coming and filling of the Spirit of God was promised in the Old Testament as a definitive element of the messianic age (Isa. 32:15; 44:3; Ezek. 36:25-27; 39:28-29; Joel 2:28-29).

5:21. The term for **subject**ion here is a common one from the ancient world to depict social orders. It involves voluntary yielding to one in leadership, without making judgments on the

"For without divine grace it is impossible either to leave the ranks of mortality, or to stay for ever among the immortal. Now when grace fills the soul, that soul thereby rejoices and smiles and dances, for it is possessed and inspired, so that to many of the unenlightened it may seem to be drunken, crazy and beside itself. Therefore (Hannah) is addressed . . . in these words: 'How long will you make yourself drunk? Put away your wine from you' (1 Sam. 1:14, NAS). For with the God-possessed not only is the soul wont to be stirred and goaded as it were into ecstasy but the body also is flushed and fiery, warmed by the overflowing joy within which passes on the sensation to the outer main. And thus many of the foolish are deceived and suppose that the sober are drunk. Though, indeed, it is true that these sober ones are drunk in a sense, for all good things are united in the strong wine on which they feast, and they receive the loving-cup from perfect virtue; while those others who are drunk with the drunkenness of wine have lived fasting from prudence without ceasing, and no taste of it has come to their famine-stricken lips."

Philo, *On Drunkenness* 146-48 LCL

innate abilities or qualities of either. It is not an expression of servitude nor obedience, but one of subordination as in a military context, or as a church member yields to a leader (1 Peter 3:5) or all Christians are to yield to civil authorities (Rom. 13:1). In the Greco-Roman world, women were generally seen more favorably (Plato, *Laws* 3.680B; Aristotle, *Politics* I 1252B, 1256B) than in Judaism (Best [1998], 532-33). The nature of such submission is quite unique in the ancient world, as the views of Josephus and Philo, and particularly Paul's description of the *husband's* responsibilities illustrate. Plutarch (*Lives: Aemilius Paullus* 5) describes a certain Aemilius Paullus, who upon divorcing his wife is rebuked by his friends. In his defense he likens his former bride to an uncomfortable shoe, which creates discomfort no one can see and is to be discarded. A pagan

"Wives must be in servitude (*douleuein*) to their husbands, a servitude not imposed by violent ill-treatment but promoting obedience in all things."

Philo, *Hypothetica* 7.3 §358 LCL

love charm from the third or fourth century A.D. pledges his relationship to the "gods of the underworld" with his intended bride to be "obedient" to him for the rest of his life (*BIAO* 76.1, 26, ND 1.33-34).

5:22–6:9. Christian Household

5:22. Wives, be subject to your own husbands, as to the Lord. This does not make the husband her lord, but denotes the way in which she serves her **Lord** in this context, by **being sub-ject** to her husband, and relates her action to the Church (Eph. 5:32). Being **subject** literally means to "place under" (Plutarch, *Quaest. Conv.*, 9.2.2 [II.737e]), metaphorically meaning to place under the authority or jurisdiction (Philo, *Creation* 84) even in a political or military context (Ditt. Or., 2.654.7). A later Jewish legend says that Judah, on his death bed, said,

And now, children, love Levi so that you may endure. Do not be arrogant

"The woman, says the Law, is in all things inferior to the man. Let her accordingly be submissive (*hypokuō*), not for her humiliation, but that she may be directed; for the authority has been given by God to man"

Josephus, *Ag. Ap.* 2.24 §201 LCL

toward him or you will be wholly destroyed. To me God has given kingship and to him, the priesthood; and he has subjected the kingship to the priesthood. To me he gave earthly matters and to Levi, heavenly matters. As heaven is superior to the earth, so is God's priesthood superior to the kingdom on earth, unless through sin it falls away from the Lord and is dominated by the earthly kingdom (*T. Judah* 21.1-4 OTP; cf. Sextus Empiricus, *Ag. Mathematicians* 11.102; Plutarch, *Apophthegmata laconica* 66 [II, 213c]; Jos., *J.W.* 2.8.7 §140; *Let. Aris.* 205; Ps. 8:6; *PHaun.* 13.30; etc.).

5:23. Head (*kephalō*) has been variously understood as either "source or origin" or "authority." In the LXX and most Greek literature it can mean either. In Greek thought it can mean "source" or "beginning" (Plato, *Laws* 4.715E; Plutarch, *De defectu oraculorum* 436D; LXX Isa. 9:14-15; *POxy* XVII.2080.48). Apart from its normal, physical sense, it more prominently referred to an authority, which in light of the other relationships here outlined is probably what is in view in 5:23.

5:25. Exhortations for a husband to love his wife are rare in Greek literature (*Ps.-Phocylides* 195-97). Later Jewish tradition said, "Our Rabbis taught: concerning a man who loves his wife as himself, who honors her more than himself, who guides his sons and daughters in right paths . . . , Scripture says, *And thou shalt know that thy tent is in peace* (Job 5:24)" (*b.Yeb.* 62b). Nowhere in Greco-Roman household codes is love (*agapaō*) indicated as a responsibility of the husband. Such a command, as with Christ's self-denying death, is unique to Christianity. Giving **himself up for her** is probably a reference to Christ's willingness to die for his people (John 10:18, though cf. Phil. 2:8). The husband's responsibilities

are greater than the wife's, while both are equally commanded by Paul in the imperatives *subject* and *love.*

5:26-27. Sanctify her . . . washing of water with the word. Sanctification and baptism were commonly associated in Jewish thought (1QS 3:4, 8-10; 1QH 11:10-12). It also alludes to an Old Testament custom of bridal baths, a marital imagery borrowed in Ezekiel 16:8-14, where the Lord is said to enter into a marriage covenant with Jerusalem and says to her, "Then I bathed you with water, washed off your blood from you, and anointed you with oil" (Ezek. 16:9). The **word** (*hrēma*) seems to refer to a profession of faith accompanying baptism, or simply to the general gospel itself (Eph. 6:17; Rom. 10:8, 17; Heb. 6:5; 1 Peter 1:25). Presenting her in **glory** (*endoxos*) may also refer to Ezek. 16, where the Lord says to his bride, "Then your fame went forth among the nations on account of your beauty, for it was perfect because of My splendor which I bestowed on you," declares the Lord God" (Ezek. 16:14).

A **spot** (*spilon*) is a stain, as in stains of blood (Jos., *Ant.* 13.11.3 §314) and always used negatively (cf. Hippocrates *Epistle* 16; Lucianus, *Amores* 15; Libanius *Declamationes* 26.19; 2 Peter 2.13). **Wrinkle** (*hrutida*; cf. Aristophanes, *Rich Man* 1051, Plato, *Symposium* 190e, 191a), with **spot**, is a sign of imperfection not present in the ideal bride (Song 4:7). **Blameless** (*amemos*) is found on a late first or early second-century coffin as one of the ideal virtues of a deceased woman (*ND* 3.40).

5:28. Paul's command to **love** reminds one of the command in Leviticus 19:18 to "love your neighbor as yourself." The bodily unity of husband and wife is found already in Gen. 2:24. Plutarch says that "control ought to be exercised by the man over the woman, not as the owner has control of a piece of property, but, as the soul controls the body, by entering into her feelings and being knit to her through goodwill"

(*Moralia: Advice to Bride and Groom* 142E LCL).

5:29. Nourishes (*thalpein*) **. . . cherishes** (*trephein*). The language here reflects the loving care of a parent for a child (Eph. 6:4; 1 Thess. 2:7; *T. Naph.* 8.5; Hermas, *Vision* 3.9.1; Deut. 22:6), not in a demeaning way but illustrative of the nature of sincere love and tenderness. Both of these words are used in an ancient papyri marriage contract as the obligations of a husband (Best [1998], 550).

5:32. This relationship between **Christ and the church** derives from the Old Testament where the Lord is depicted as a faithful husband to his unfaithful bride Israel (Hos. 1:1-3:5; Jer. 3:8; Isa. 54:1-8; Ezek. 16:1-63, 23:1-48), and is picked up in later Judaism (Philo, *Abraham* 99; *Cherubim* 40; *Dreams* 1.200; *2 Esdr.* 10.25; *Syb. Or.* 3.356; *Odes Sol.* 38.11).

6:1-4. Respect for parents was expected among Jews (*Sir.* 3.1-9; Philo, *Decal.* 120) and Gentiles (Aristotle, *Nic. Eth.* 9.2, 1165a; Plutarch, *Moralia* 479). **Children** obeying **in the Lord** suggests their obedience to parents is grounded in their relationship with Christ; i.e., they obey because they are Christians. In Judaism, parents were just below God in terms of the hierarchy of obedience, and obedience to them is closely associated with that to him (Philo, *Decal.* 119; *Moses* 2.198; *Special Laws* 2.225, 235; Jos., *Ag. Ap.* 2.27 §206; *Sib. Or.* 3.593; *Ps-Phoc* 8; *T. Reub* 3.8; Best [1998], 564). This is a sentiment similarly shared among the Greeks (Cicero, *De officiis* 1.58; Diogenes Laertes, *Lives Phil.* 7.108, 120; Epictetus, *Dissertation* 2.17.31; 3.7.26; ND 1:11; Best [1998], 564).

Honor your father and mother is similar to Deut. 5:16 but more closely follows Exod. 20:12. **That it may be well with you, and that you may live long on the earth** (v. 3): Exod. 20:12 seems to be cited here with a metaphorical sense toward general prosperity.

And, fathers, do not provoke your children to anger; but bring them up in the discipline and instruction of the Lord (v. 4). In Judaism education was conducted most centrally in the home (Deut. 6:7; Prov. 13:24; *Sir.* 30.1-13; Philo, *Hypothetica* 7.14; Jos., *Ag. Ap.* 1.12 §60) where the Torah was primarily taught (Deut. 4:9; 6:7; 11:19; 32:46) and godly wisdom and discipline were espoused (Prov. 19:18; 22:6; 23:13, 14; 29:15; *Sirach* 7.23; cf. Philo, *Embassy to Gaius* 31; *Special Laws* 2.228; *Hypothetica* 7.14). Josephus says of the Jews of his day, "Our ground is good, and we work it to our utmost, but our chief ambition is for the education of our children . . . . We take most pains of all with the

"But the law-giver of the Romans gave virtually full power to the father over his son, whether he thought proper to imprison him, to scourge him, to put him in chains, and keep him at home in the fields, or to put him to death; and this even though the son were already engaged in public life, though he were numbered among the highest magistrates, and though he were celebrated for his zeal for the commonwealth. Indeed, in virtue of this law men of distinction, while delivering speeches from the rostra hostile to the senate and pleasing to the people, and enjoying great popularity on that account, have been dragged down from thence and carried away by their fathers to undergo such punishment as these thought fit; and while they were being led away through the Forum, none present, neither consul, tribune, nor the very populace, which was flattered by them and thought all power inferior to its own, could rescue them."

Dionysius of Halicarnassus, *Rom. Ant.* 2.26.4 LCL

instruction of children, and esteem the observation of the laws, and the piety corresponding with them, the most important affair of our whole life" (*Ag. Ap.* 1.12 §60; cf. 2.18 §178; 2.25 §204; Lincoln, 401). It was recognized in the ancient world that excessive hardness in a father's instruction can produce **anger** rather than appropriate life in relation to **the Lord** (Plutarch, *Moralia* II 8F-8A; *Ps-Phoc* 207-17; Best [1998], 568). Fathers had a great deal of legal authority (*patria potestas*) over their sons. Dionysius of Halicarnassus, from the first century A.D., says that Roman law gave "greater power to the father over his son than to the master over his slaves" (*Rom. Ant.* 2.27.1), though "Greeks regarded the Romans as cruel and harsh" (*Rom. Ant.* 2.27.1). However, Philo also recognized the special status of a parent in relation to his child. He says, "Parents, in my opinion, are to their children what God is to the world, since just as He achieved existence from the non-existent, so they in imitation of His power, as far as they are capable, immortalize the race. And a father and mother deserve honor, not only on this account, but for many other reasons" (*Special Laws* 2.225, 226; cf. *Decal.* 119, 120; Lincoln, 399).

In the Old Testament, disrespect towards one's parents was punishable by death (Lev. 20:9; Deut. 21:18-21), which was still advocated into the first century (Philo, *Special Laws* 2.232; *Hypothetica* 7.2; Jos., *Ag. Ap.* 2.27 §206). However, children were seen as gifts from God, newly or unborn children were particularly protected, and abortion scorned (Philo, *Special Laws* 3.108-19; *Hypothetica* 7.7; Jos., *Ag. Ap.* 2.24 §202; Lincoln, 400). Josephus lists, "honor to parents ... [is] ... second only to honor to God" (*Ag. Ap.* 2.27 §206 LCL). In later Judaism, though the father had the authority, respect was due to both parents (*m. Qidd* 1.7).

6:5-9. For slavery in the ancient world, see "Introduction to Philemon."

D. 6:10-20. Struggle Against Evil

6:10. Finally, be strong in the Lord, and in the strength of His might: This paragraph begins in a manner resembling a speech given to troops before entering battle (1QM 15:1-18; Thucydides, *Peloponnesian War* 2.89; Xenophon, *Cyropaedia* 1.4; Arrian, *Anabasis* 2.83; Lincoln, 433; Best [1998], 586). **His might** is a source of divine strength (Col. 1:11; 1QH 7:6). David was made strong by the Lord (1 Sam. 30:6) as were the faithful (Zech. 10:12). Some Second Temple Jewish texts predicted an end-time war in which the faithful will experience extreme tribulation, but God will ultimately be victorious (*T. Sim.* 5.5; *T. Dan* 5.10, 11; *1 Enoch* 55.3-57.3; *4 Ezra* 13.1-4; 1QH 3:24-39; 6:28-35).

The command to **be strong in the Lord** resembles the call of Joshua to succeed Moses in leading Israel (Josh. 1:6, 7, 9). A similar call to strength in a "spiritual" warfare is found in Qumran: "Be strong and valiant, become men of valor... Do not be afraid . . . do not turn backwards . . . " (1QM 15:7-9).

6:11. The **full armor** referred to the full equipment, both offensive and defensive, of the heavily armed foot soldier (Polybius 6.23; Thucydides, *Peloponnesian War* 3.114; Judith 14.3; 2 Macc. 3.25; Luke 11:22; Lincoln, 442). **Of God** (*tou theou*): In the Old Testament the Lord is sometimes portrayed as a warrior (Isa. 42:13; Hab. 3:8, 9; Ps. 35:1-3). In Qumran texts all power and help comes from God (1QM 1:1-

---

"The Lord will take his zeal as his whole armor, and will arm all creation to repel his enemies; he will put on righteousness as a breastplate, and wear impartial justice as a helmet; he will take holiness as an invincible shield, and sharpen stern wrath for a sword. . . ."

Wisdom 5.17-20a

19:14; 1QH 3:24-39; 6:28-35). **That you may be able to stand firm against the schemes of the devil.** God also empowers his people for his battles (Pss. 18:1-39; 28:7; 59:11-17; 68:35; 89:21; 118:14; Isa. 52:1). More significantly, the Old Testament describes the armor of Yahweh and his Messiah (Isa. 11:4-5; 59:17), which is clearly in view here for Paul and discussed below.

6:12. Struggle is often used of a wrestling match though, as here, can denote any contest or military battle (Euripides, *Heraclidae* 159; Philo, *Abraham* 243; 2 *Macc.* 10.28; 14.18; 15.19). **Flesh and blood** refers to frail humanity in its weakness (*Sir.* 14.18; 17.31; Matt. 16:17; Gal. 1:16; 1 Cor. 15:50; Heb. 2:14; Lincoln, 444). Stoics also said "life is a battle" (Seneca, *Epistulae morales* 96.5; cf. 107.9). Wisdom is a means of defense and protection (Seneca, *De Const. Sap.* 3.4-5), and reason is a weapon (Seneca, *Epistulae morales* 74.19-21; Lincoln, 437-38). In Qumran texts, it was believed that the community will be in an end-time battle against the angel of darkness and his hosts (1QM 13:1-18; 16:11-16; 17:5-9; Lincoln, 444). **Spiritual forces of wickedness:** Such evil spirits were thought to stir up terror even in one's sleep (*T. Sim.* 4.9). Some associated such wickedness with unfaithful priests (*T. Levi* 18.12), but all such wicked spirits will one day

be "trampled underfoot" (*T. Sim.* 6.6 OTP; cf. 1 *Enoch* 15.8-12; *T. Sol.* 8.3; 18.2; *Life of Adam and Eve* 28.2). The *Ascension of Isaiah* contains a prophecy to Manasseh concerning "the eternal judgments, and the torments of Gehenna, and the prince of this world, and his angels, and his authorities, and his powers..." (1.4 OTP). **In the heavenly places:** See comment on Eph. 2:2.

6:13. Therefore, take up the full armor of God. See comment on v. 11. **The evil day.** Judaism strongly affirmed a time of evil at the end of history (Jer. 17:7, 8; Amos 5:18-20; Dan. 12:1; 1 *Enoch* 50.2; 55.3; 63.8; 96.2; 99.4; *Jub.* 23.16-25; *T. Dan* 5.4-6; *T. Levi* 5.5; 2 *Bar.* 48.31; Lincoln, 446; Joel 1:15). At Qumran, there was a strong belief in a final, end-time war between the forces of good (light) and those of evil (darkness; 1QM 1:10-13). See comment on Eph. 5:16.

6:14. Girded your loins with truth. Fastening one's clothing securely around the waist made rapid movement easier and was vital preparation for any vigorous activity. It probably refers to the leather apron worn by Roman soldiers under their armor (Lincoln, 447). The imagery here is taken from LXX Isa. 11:5, where it is said of the Messiah-King, "righteousness will be the belt about His loins, And faithfulness the belt

---

"On this (day), the assembly of the gods and the congregation of men shall confront each other for great destruction. The sons of light and the lot of darkness shall battle together for God's might, between the roar of a huge multitude and the shout of gods and of men, on the day of calamity. It will be a time of suffering fo[r al]l the nation redeemed by God. Of all their suffering, none will be like this, hastening till eternal redemption is fulfilled. And on the day of their ward against the Kittim, [t]he[y] shall go out [to] destruction. In the war, the sons of light will be the strongest during three lots, in order to strike down wickedness; and in three (others), the army of Belial will gird themselves in order to force the lot of [light] to retreat. There will be infantry battalions to melt the heart, but God's might will strengthen the he[art of the sons of light.] And in the seventh lot, God's great hand will subdue [Belial, and al]l the angels of his dominion and all the men of [his lot.]"

1QM 1:10b-15

> "But with righteousness He will judge the poor, And decide with fairness for the afflicted of the earth; And He will strike the earth with the rod of His mouth, And with the breath of His lips He will slay the wicked. Also righteousness will be the belt about His loins, And faithfulness the belt about His waist."
>
> Isaiah 11:4-5
>
> "And He put on righteousness like a breastplate, And a helmet of salvation on His head; And He put on garments of vengeance for clothing, And wrapped Himself with zeal as a mantle."
>
> Isaiah 59:17

about His waist." Here, though, he is girded with **truth**, which Paul seems to associate with righteousness and faithfulness now attributed to believers. The Lord is elsewhere said to be girded with might (Ps. 65:6) and girds the psalmist with strength for battle (Ps. 18:32, 39; Lincoln, 447). The **breastplate of righteousness** is part of Yahweh's armor in Isa. 59:17 and *Wisd.* 5.18, with righteousness now being a quality put on by believers. A **breastplate** (*th?rax*) was a metal piece of armor protecting the chest, heart, and lungs (cf. 2 Cor. 6:7; cf. *T. Levi* 8.2).

6:15. And having shod your feet with the preparation of the gospel of peace. Military sandals or *caliga* (half-boots) were essential for adequate combat (Xenophon, *Anabasis* 4.5.14; cf. Jos., *J.W.* 6.1.8 §85). But footwear is not so much in mind as readiness of one's feet for a task, again taken from the Old Testament. Paul's statements resonate with the words of LXX Isaiah 52:7: "How lovely on the mountains Are the feet of him who brings good news, Who announces peace And brings good news of happiness, Who announces salvation, And says to Zion, 'Your God reigns!'" (cf. Nah. 1:15; Rom. 10:15). **Preparation** (*hetiomasia*) can mean "firm footing" and refers to readiness, preparedness, or preparation for a task (LXX 9:17; *Wisd.* 13.12; *Let. Aris.* 182; Jos., *Ant.* 10.1.2 §9; Lincoln, 448-49).

6:16. Shield of faith. In the Old Testament the shield was an image of God's protection of his people (Gen. 15:1; Pss. 5:22; 18:2, 30, 35; 28:7; 33:20; 35:2; 59:11; 91:4; 115:9-11; 144:1; Lincoln, 449). Roman shields were made of wood and covered with thick leather (Homer, *Illiad* 5.452; Herodotus, *Histories* 7.91; Pliny, *Nat. Hist.* 8.39). **With which you will be able to extinguish all the flaming missiles of the evil one:** Livy (*History* 21.8.10-12) describes a battle where wooden shields were hit by flaming arrows, and when the bearer of the shield lowered it to extinguish the fire, he was unprotected by incoming javelins. Skins like those that covered the Roman shields were soaked with water used to extinguish flaming arrows and protect workman (Thucydides, *Peloponnesian War* 2.75.5). **Flaming missiles.** These arrows, or spears, were tipped with fabric and dipped in pitch before lighting (Jos., *J.W.* 3.10 §173).

6:17. And take the helmet of salvation. In the Old Testament, God is salvation and deliverance for the oppressed (Pss. 18:2, 46-48; 65:6; Isa. 33:2, 6; 45:17; 51:5; Jer. 31:33; Lincoln, 450). Moreover, in Isaiah 59:17 God is a victorious warrior who wears the helmet of salvation, now here Paul has it given to believers for protection (Best [1998], 602). The **sword** (*machaira*) is a short-handled sword and is a crucial weapon in close combat, for which a longer sword would be cumbersome. **Word of God** (*hrēma tou theou*) refers to the gospel. In Judaism God's word had the power to slay (Hos. 6:5; *Wisd.* 18.16; *Odes Sol.* 29.9-11).

6:19. In the Old Testament **opening** one's **mouth** is an expression for proclaiming God's word (Ps. 78:2; Ezek. 3:27; 33:22; Dan. 10:16; Lincoln, 454).

6:20. Speaking boldly was an ideal trait of an orator (Dio Chrysostom, *Orations* 32.11; Epictetus, *Discourses* 3.22.19; Lucian, *Demonax* 3). To be an **ambassador** meant one was responsible for revealing the power, riches, and dignity of the government he represents.

E. 6:21-24. Final Greetings
6:23. Peace. See comment on Eph. 1:2

6:24. The phrase **those who love our Lord Jesus Christ** is a Christian adaptation of a Jewish phrase used to designate the faithful: "those who love God" (Exod. 20:6; Deut. 5:10; 7:9; Dan. 9:4; Neh. 1:5; *Pss. Sol.* 4.25; 6.6; *T. Sim.* 3.6; *1 Enoch* 108.8; cf. Rom. 8:28; 1 Cor. 2:9; 8:3; Jas. 1:12; 2:5). **With a love incorruptible** (*en aftharsia*) literally means "in immortality," perhaps looking to the imperishability and incorruptibility which characterizes the resurrection (*Wisd.* 2.23; 6.18, 19; *4 Macc.* 9.22; 17.12; 1 Cor. 15:42-54; Rom. 2:7; 2 Tim. 1:10; Lincoln, 466-67).

"The Roman panoply consists firstly of a shield (*scutum*), the convex surface of which measures two and a half feet in width and four feet in length, the thickness at the rim being a palm's breadth. It is made of two planks glued together, the outer surface being then covered first with canvas and then with calf-skin. Its upper and lower rims are strengthened by an iron edging which protects it from descending blows and from injury when rested on the ground. It also has an iron boss (*umbo*) fixed to it which turns aside the more formidable blows of stones, pikes, and heavy missiles in general. Besides the shield they also carry a sword, hanging on the right thigh and called a Spanish sword. This is excellent for thrusting, and both of its edges cut effectively, as the blade is very strong and firm.... The common soldiers wear in addition a breastplate of brass a span square, which they place in front of the heart and call the heart-protector (*pectorale*)...."

Polybius *Histories* 6.23.2-8, 14 LCL

Introduction to Philippians

Daniel M. Gurtner

INTRODUCTION

This eleventh book of the New Testament is the most personal of Paul's letters and has been valued for its exuberant teachings on joy, which occurs sixteen times in this short letter. One scholar has summarized the content of this letter as follows: "I rejoice; do you rejoice?" (Bengel; Hawthorne, xlviii).

Authorship. Philippians claims to have been written by Paul (1:1), and there have been no serious attempts to challenge this. Questions remain, however, regarding the origin of the "hymn" in 2:6-11. See the discussion below. The situation in which the author finds himself coincides strongly with what we know of Paul from other sources (see Introduction to the Prison Epistles). Philippians was attributed to the apostle from the earliest days of the Christian church, including Irenaeus (c. 140-202), Clement of Alexandria (c. 150-c. 215), and Tertullian (c. 140), and its influence is found in the writings of Clement of Rome (c. 95-96), Ignatius (c. 100-118), Hermas (c. 100-150), and Justin Martyr (c. 165). It is likewise listed as Pauline in the earliest lists of Church writings, such as the Muratorian Canon (c. 180, though perhaps much later), and that of Marcion (c. 140). Significant challenges to Pauline authorship began with F. C. Baur of the Tübingen School in the 1840s, who claimed that certain non-Pauline, Gnostic elements were found in the hymn, along with apparent contradictions with other "undisputed" Pauline letters. Such criticisms have found very little support among scholars today, who almost unanimously recognize this letter as the work of the Apostle Paul.

More questions remain, however, regarding the unity of this epistle. Some have suggested that Philippians is a compilation of several letters for at least two reasons. First, it is recognized that there is a sharp change of tone and a disjointed train of thought at the beginning of chapt. 3 (O'Brien, 11). Second, the "thank you" (4:10-20) seems to be out of place as an afterthought. Scholars have thus conjectured that the letter is the product of an early editor combining at least two different letters. Support for this theory based on external, textual evidence, however, is nowhere to be found, as the early manuscripts (especially P^{46}) all maintain its unity.

The Church at Philippi. Paul's evangelistic efforts in Philippi occurred on his second missionary journey between AD 49 and 52. While in Troas, Paul had a vision in which he saw a man of Macedonia pleading, "Come over to Macedonia and help us" (Acts 16:9). Confident that God had called them to go, Paul and his companions crossed by sea from Troas to Neapolis and then journeyed about ten miles along the Egnatian Way to Philippi (Acts 16:10-12; O'Brien, 6). Finding no synagogue in Philippi, the apostle met a small gathering of women, God-fearers, and perhaps some Jewesses assembled outside the city by the River Gangites for worship. The first convert, Lydia, was a God-fearing Gentile who was a native of Thyatira in Asia Minor and traded in the purple cloth which made that city famous (Acts 16:14; O'Brien, 6). She extended warm hospitality to the apostle and convinced him and his companions to stay with her (Acts 16:15).

Conflict arose when Paul cast an "evil spirit" from a slave girl, which had previously enabled her to predict the future, while also earning a profit for her masters (Acts 16:16-24). For this Paul and Silas were beaten and imprisoned. An earthquake shook the prison and its prisoners were freed (Acts 16:25-27), to which the overseeing jailer responded, "Sirs, what must I do to be saved?" (Acts 16:30). Upon the jailer's famous conversion, he and his household were baptized (Acts 16:32). Paul subsequently complained to the chief magistrate about their mistreatment as Roman citizens, for which they seemed to receive an apology and were entreated to leave Philippi (Acts 16:39). After visiting the new church at Lydia's home and encouraging them, they did depart (Acts 16:40).

Paul seems to have shared deep, mutual affection with the Philippians (1:7; 4:16), and certainly wrote to that church several times (Polycarp, *Philippians* 3.2). The names of members of this church – Epaphroditus, Euodia, Syntyche, and Clement (2:25; 4:2-3) – suggest the congregation was primarily comprised of Greeks.

Paul's Opponents in Philippians. The apostle seems to have at least two groups of opposition in the Philippian church. Their identity, however, is among the most disputed subjects in modern scholarship on this epistle (O'Brien, 27). The first group is comprised of Christians (called "brothers") who are preaching Christ with the intent of compounding Paul's difficulties (1:14-15). The second group poses a greater threat. Paul calls them "dogs," "evil workers," and "mutilators of the flesh"

(3:2). They are "enemies of the cross of Christ" (3:18), whose "end is destruction" (3:18). They were advocating circumcision and compliance with certain ritual laws (3:19). Paul's harsh words toward them (3:2) seem to reflect his intense frustration with these Jewish opponents who provided unrelenting confrontation in both Jerusalem and Caesarea (Acts 21:37-26:32; cf. 28:19). See comments on the respective texts cited above.

Provenance. As is the case with that to the Colossians, the origin of Paul's letter to the Philippians is difficult to ascertain. That the apostle was imprisoned is difficult to dispute (1:7, 13, 14; cf. 1:20-24, 30; 2:17). However, it is unclear from which of his many imprisonments, perhaps as many as seven according to Clement of Rome (c. 95-96; *1 Clem.* 5.6), Philippians was written (see Introduction to the Prison Epistles). In addition to Rome (AD 60-62), arguments for imprisonments in Ephesus (c. AD 54-55), Caesarea (AD 57-59), and perhaps Corinth have also been proposed.

Whichever city one chooses for the provenance of this letter, several key factors from the text of the epistle itself must be borne in mind: (1) Paul was imprisoned when he wrote (1:7, 13, 17); (2) He faced a trial that could lead either to his death (1:19-20; 2:17) or acquittal (1:25; 2:24); (3) The location of his imprisonment included a *praetorium* (1:13), as well as members of Caesar's household (4:22); (4) Timothy was with him (1:1; 2:19-23); (5) Evangelistic efforts were still effectively conducted around him (1:14-17); (6) Paul planned to visit the Philippians when acquitted (2:24); and (7) Several trips between Philippi and the place of imprisonment were made by various people during the course of Paul's imprisonment. The tradition going back to Marcion (c. 140) arguing for Paul's Roman imprisonment (AD 60-62) is typically favored. Though not without its problems, the antiquity of this view, along with its strong coherence to what we know of Paul's Roman imprisonment from Acts 28, make the apostle's imprisonment in Rome seem slightly favorable, dating the epistle between AD 60 and 62.

Purposes. A careful reading of this epistle can clearly bring forth several reasons why Paul wrote this letter to the saints at Philippi: First, it seems the apostle wanted to update his friends on his current situation (1:12-26; 2:24). The outcome of his impending trial is uncertain (1:18-24), though he hopes to visit them soon (2:23-24). Second, he wrote to warn the Philippians of false teachings (3:2-21; see Paul's Opponents in Philippians below). Third, Paul wrote to inform them regarding their messenger, Epaphroditus. They sent him to care for Paul's needs, but Epaphroditus turned desperately ill. Having recovered and successfully completed his task, the messenger is being sent back to Philippi and where he should receive honor for his service (2:25-30). Fourth, Paul writes to correct division within the Philippian church (1:27; 2:2-4, 16; 4:1-2). Fifth, the apostle exhorts this church to rejoice regardless of adverse circumstances, as he himself is doing (2:18; 3:1; 4:4). Finally, Paul writes to thank the Philippian saints for their gift, presumably of money, which relieved him in his situation (4:10-20).

The "Hymn" (Phil. 2:6-11). Within the text of Phil. 2 Paul has neatly woven what seems to be an ancient hymn of unknown origin. Scholars have debated whether it is Paul's own work or borrowed from another source. Regardless, the apostle has clearly made use of its teaching about Christ for his own purposes in the letter. That this great Christological hymn is used to illustrate the humble life of a Christian has led some scholars to look not to a Gnostic myth or even the Old Testament for its origin. Rather, it has been suggested that what lies behind its juxtaposition of a lofty doctrine of the deity of Christ and the servant humility of his lifestyle is the tradition of Jesus washing his disciples' feet found in John 13:3-17 (Hawthorne, 78-79). The hymn serves as an appeal to accept not only Christ's authority as

Lord, but to be conformed to the humility he maintained through his earthly life (Phil. 3:10). See Comment on Phil. 2:6-11.

Contribution. Philippians is unique in that it reveals the apostle's general satisfaction with the congregation's progress in the faith. Though he does address some false teaching, the thrust of the letter lies elsewhere. In particular, the "hymn" in 2:6-11 perhaps depicts some of the most ancient of Christian creeds while serving to illustrate the need for believers to remain humble. The letter resonates with joy, with the noun "joy" occurring five times and "to rejoice" nine. Only the much longer gospel of Luke has more occurrences of the verb. Also in this letter, Paul recognizes, perhaps more than elsewhere, his readers' "partnership in the gospel" (1:5). Finally, we learn more of Paul's Jewish pedigree as he warns the Philippians against having "confidence in the flesh" (3:4).

OUTLINE OF THE BOOK

I. Salutation, Thanksgiving, and Prayer (1:1-11)
II. News and Instructions (1:12-2:30)
   A. News about Paul (1:12-26)
   B. Instructions for the Church (1:27–2:18)
   C. News about Timothy and Epaphroditus (2:19-30)
III. Warning Against False Teachers (3:1-21)
IV. Final Exhortations (4:1-9)
V. Paul's Thanks for the Philippians' Gift (4:10-20)
VI. Final Greeting (4:21-23)

BIBLIOGRAPHY

Bockmuehl, Marcus, *The Epistle to the Philippians*. Fourth Edition. Black's New Testament Commentaries. London: A & C Black, 1997.

Fee, Gordon D., *Paul's Letter to the Philippians.* NICNT. Grand Rapids: Eerdmans, 1995.

Hawthorne, Gerald F., *Philippians.* WBC. Waco, Tex.: Word Books, 1983.

Martin, Ralph P., *Carmen Christi: Philippians ii. 5-11 in Recent Interpretation and in the Setting of Early Christian Worship.* Rev. ed. Grand Rapids: Eerdmans, 1983.

Martin, Ralph P., *Philippians.* NCB. Greenwood, S.C.: Attic, 1976.

O'Brien, Peter T., *The Epistle to the Philippians.* NIGTC. Grand Rapids: Eerdmans, 1991.

Silva, Moisés, *Philippians,* WEC. Chicago: Moody, 1988.

Witherington III, Ben, *Friendship and Finances in Philippi: The Letter of Paul to the Philippians.* Valley Forge, Penn.: Trinity Press International, 1994.

PHILIPPIANS

Daniel M. Gurtner

I. SALUTATION, THANKSGIVING, AND PRAYER (1:1-11)

1:1. Ancient letters, particularly of an oriental and Jewish model, tended to begin with the name of the sender and the addressees followed by a greeting: "Artaxerxes, king of kings, to Ezra the priest, the scribe of the law of the God of heaven, perfect peace" (Ezra 7:12; cf. Dan. 4:1; 2 *Bar.* 78.2; see comment on Eph. 1:2). **Paul** is the Hellenistic-Roman name used in place of the Jewish "Saul." Jews in Greek-speaking areas took names that closely approximated the sound of their Hebrew and Aramaic names. See comment on Eph. 3:8. **Timothy** is named here probably because he played an important role in the preaching in Macedonia and Achaia (Acts 16:1-18:28; O'Brien, 44). Paul warmly cites Timothy as an example of Christlikeness (2:19-24) and seems to have placed him in charge of the church at Ephesus (2 Tim. 4:21). He was a native of Lystra in Asia Minor (Acts 16:1-2), whose mother (Eunice, 2 Tim. 1:5) was Jewish and father was Greek (Acts 16:1). Timothy was chosen by Paul to accompany him on his second missionary journey apparently because of his good reputation in that area (Acts 16:2-3). He was certainly involved with Paul's conflict in Philippi (see Introduction). Eusebius later describes him as that church's first bishop (*Ecclesiastical History* 3.4). Heb. 13:23 suggests that Timothy was imprisoned, while a tradition from the fourth century claims he was martyred under Domitian

in A.D. 97 (*Acts of Timothy*; Bockmuehl, 49). He is probably not to be thought of as a co-author, as the extensive use of "I" throughout suggests a single author. Instead, Timothy perhaps served as a secretary, or *amanuenses*, writing letters for the chained apostle as he dictated them (see Introduction to the Prison Epistles). **Bond-servants** (*douloi*) is plural and attributed both to Paul and Timothy. In the LXX a **bond-servant** (*doulos*) often designated someone whom God used for a special ministry or through whom he spoke, such as Moses (Neh. 10:29), Joshua (Josh. 24:29), David (Ps. 89:20), and Jonah (2 Kings 14:25; O'Brien, 45; cf. Exod. 14:3; Num. 12:7; Jer. 25:4; Ezek. 38:17; Amos 3:7; Zech. 1:6). The faithful in the Old Testament were commonly called **saints** (Greek, *hagioi* literally, "holy ones"). This identification was likewise adopted as the self-designating term for the Qumran sectarians (1QS 5:13, 18; 8:17, 20, 23; 9:8; 1QM 6:6; 10:10; 16:1; cf. also *1 Enoch* 1.9; 39.1; *Jub.* 31.14). Philippi, as a Roman colony, would have had many slaves and been familiar with the humble imagery it invokes (cf. Introduction to Philemon).

Philippi was located in northeastern Greece and was the first city in Europe in which the gospel was preached. The ancient city received the attention of Philip II of Macedon, father of Alexander the Great, for the gold and silver mines of nearby Pangaeus. He annexed the entire region to his empire in 356 B.C. and formally established the city of Philippi in his own honor. To protect his assets in the region, Philip II strongly fortified the city and provided a garrison of Macedonian troops. It was the site of Mark Antony and Octavian's defeat of Brutus and Cassius, the assassins of Julius Caesar, in 42 B.C. The victors settled a number of their veteran soldiers there and established Philippi as a Roman colony (O'Brien, 4). It soon received the highest possible status for a Roman provincial municipality, the *ius Italicum*, which meant that it was governed by Roman law. Residents obtained rights to purchase, own, and transfer property as well as participate in civil lawsuits. They were considered Roman citizens and even the plan of the city itself was modeled after Rome. Its language was primarily Latin, and Roman dress was the norm. It was also a stopping point for an important military road.

The city was religiously pluralistic and bore Latin counterparts to Greek gods such as Jupiter, Juno, Minerva, and Mars, though the Emperor Cult was probably dominant. Artemis of the Ephesians (see comment on Eph. 1:1) was represented as Bendis and was associated with fertility cults of agricultural communities (O'Brien, 5). The god Isis from Egypt was also worshiped there, as were Serapis and the Phrygian Cybele. The Jewish community was apparently small. The lack of a synagogue in Philippi (Acts 16:13) suggests there were fewer than ten Jewish men in the city, since this was the minimum requirement to establish a synagogue.

Overseers (*episkopois*) referred, classically, to a deity charged with overseeing a country or people (Job 20:29), but also was a title for men responsible for positions of state, such as judges, councilors, treasurers, military strategists, or overseers of religious communities, such as temple officials (Num. 4:16; 30:14; Judges 29:8; O'Brien, 47; cf. Josephus, *Ant.* 10.4.1 §53; *IMAe* 49.43; *PPar* 63.9.47). The Qumran sect had a similar supervisor who was a spiritual father and shepherd of the community who was also responsible for its legal decisions and welfare funds (CD 13:7-9; 1QS 6:12, 20). This clearly

became an office in the early church, with its qualifications described in 1 Tim. 3:2 and Titus 1:7. **Deacons** (*diakonois*) was a term originally used for those in lowly service, particularly waiting tables (Plato, *Politics* 290C; Herodotus, *Histories* 4.71; *PFlor* 121.3), which may inform their function in the early church (cf. 1 Tim. 3:8-12). Clement of Rome (ca. A.D. 96) cited Isa. 60:17 in support of the authority established in these two offices of the church (*1 Clem.* 42.4-5).

1:2. The particular combination of **grace** and **peace** is unusual, but found in some Jewish literature (esp. *2 Bar.* 78.2; cf. *Jub.* 12.29; *1 Enoch* 1.8; 1QS 2:1-4). Here, however, Paul replaced the standard Hellenistic greeting of "greetings" (*chairein*) with a theological **grace** (*charis*). **Peace** (*eirēnē*) is the Greek equivalent of the Hebrew *shalom*. See comment on Col. 1:2.

1:4. Always offering prayer. In the Old Testament there were set times for prayer (Pss. 5:3; 55:7; Ezra 9:5; Dan. 6:10; 1 Chron. 23:30), which continued into later Judaism (*m. Ber.* 4.1; cf. 4.2-5.5). **With joy** (*meta charas*) begins a long string of joy language and attitude throughout the epistle, which cannot be affected by imprisonment or death (1:18; 2:17) but can be affected by the responsiveness of faith and well-being in those for whom Paul cared (2:2, 27-29; 4:1). **Joy** is a confident attitude, not a feeling, that can be commanded (3:1; 4:4; Rom. 12:12; 1 Thess. 5:16) as it is in the Old Testament (Lev. 23:40; Deut. 12:7; Zeph. 3:14; Joel 2:23) where it was particularly associated with the age of redemption (Isa. 12:3; 25:9; 29:19; 35:1-10; 51:3; 55:12). In the "War Scroll," "God's joy" is written on banners of the victorious army (1QM 4:14). It is God who makes people rejoice (4Q509 1:23), and believers are to participate joyously in heavenly worship (4Q403:36). Philo relates joy to the future inheritance of the faithful (*Worse* 120; *Who is the Heir?* 315) from God alone (*Abraham* 220; *Cherubim* 86). Rabbis saw joy in God's commandments (*b. Pes.* 117a; *b. Shab.* 30b; *y. Suk.* 5.1; Bockmuehl, 59).

1:5. Participation (*koinōnia*) is a word denoting intimate fellowship and, though rare, is most prevalent in Philippians. It can refer to marriage as the most intimate relationship between people (*POxy* 1473.33; *3 Macc.* 4.6), generosity (2 Cor. 9:13), or providing unity through a gift or contribution (Rom. 15:26), each denoting participation or sharing of something (Hawthorne, 19). Here, **the gospel. From the first day until now** suggests their acceptance of Paul's message was both early and unwavering.

1:6. Good work (*ergon agathon*) in the Old Testament is God's activity (Gen. 2:2) and is associated with both creation and Israel (Isa. 40:26; 41:20; 43:1; 45:7; 54:16; O'Brien, 64). **Will perfect** (*epitelesei*) means to bring to completion. Some Jews would see God bringing something to completion as an act of his sovereignty: "God brings to completion the affairs of all men and guides (them) with (his) sovereign power" (*Let. Aris.* 195 OTP; cf. Isa. 48:12; 44:6). **Day of Jesus Christ** (vv. 6, 10): The day of "Christ" was understood by the early Christians as the inauguration of the Messianic age, in which the Messiah (Greek *Christos*) would sit on David's throne forever (2 Sam. 7:14), purge God's people of sin, and rule them justly (Isa. 9:7; Jer. 23:5-6). See comment on Col. 1:13; Eph. 1:5.

1:7. Defense and confirmation are legal terms from the Roman courtroom. The former connotes a defense against a legal accusation. The latter refers to a legal guarantee, such as a receipt of sale (*PFay* 92.19) or the fulfillment of a promise (*BGU* 4.1073.13; see comment on Eph. 1:14).

1:8 For God is my witness, how I long for you all with the affection of Christ Jesus. Affection (*splanchnois*) refers to feelings from the inward parts as the seat of emotions. It seems to be a special term in Christian and some later Jewish writings for the particularly compassionate love of God for his people (*T. Zeb.* 8.2; *T. Naph.* 4.5; *T.*

Levi 4.4; Luke 1:78; Jas. 5:11; *Pr. Man.* 7; *Let. Aris.* 211; *1 Clem.* 29.1; Bockmuehl, 65).

1:10. Sincere and blameless. Sincere (*ilikrineis*) also means "pure" or "honest." The word was used by Plato to refer to someone of pure descent, "without barbarian mixture" (*Menexenus* 245d). **Blameless** (*aptoskopoi*) means doing no injustice and was a term largely used of God which Gentiles also should imitate (*Let. Aris.* 210).

1:11. Fruit of righteousness can either mean that righteousness is itself the fruit (Amos 6:12; Heb. 12:11; Jas. 3:18), that the fruit itself is righteous, or that moral fruit is the result of righteousness (Prov. 11:20; 12:12; 13:2; Isa. 3:10). That the fruit **comes through Jesus Christ** suggests that the first is in mind. **To the glory and praise of God.** Such doxologies were common at the end of Jewish prayers (2 Sam. 22:50; Pss. 21:13; 35:28; 41:13; 1QSb 4:25; O'Brien, 82).

II. 1:12–2:30. News and Instructions

A. 1:12-26. News about Paul

1:12. Ancient letters between family and close friends often contained a portion which began "I want you to know . . . " in which the author would explain some details of his personal situation to his loved ones. Significantly, Paul tells the Philippians more of the advancement of the gospel than of his own circumstances.

Epicurus was said to have written to two of his disciples describing how, in the midst of physical suffering, he set his mind on more pleasurable thoughts (Cicero, *On the Ends of Goods and Evils* 2.30.96; *Tusculan Disputations* 3.16.35-3.17.38).

1:13. The whole praetorian guard: Praetorian (*praitōrion*) is a Greek loanword from the Latin *praetorium*, which by the first century referred to an official residence of a governor or prince (cf. Matt. 27:27; Mark 15:16; John 18:28; Acts 23:35), but here seems to refer to a body of men forming the **praetorian guard**, as the NASB translates (O'Brien, 93). Moreover, if the letter was written from Rome (see Introduction), it can denote the emperor's bodyguard or praetorian cohorts stationed in the city, of which there were about 9,000 (O'Brien, 93).

1:14. My imprisonment. See Introduction to the Prison Epistles.

1:15. Envy and strife occur in legal contexts where opponents in a trial attempt to make one another's tasks more difficult (cf. Dio Chrysostom, *Orations* 78.29, 43; Bockmuehl, 77).

1:17. The former proclaim Christ out of selfish ambition. Selfish ambition (*eritheias*) is a rare word, used by Aristotle to describe a greedy grasp for public office by unjust means (*Politics* 5.3). **To cause me distress** (*thlipsin egeirein*) literally means "to raise up affliction," and though it only occurs here in the NT, similar language is found in Jewish wisdom texts (Prov. 10:12; 15:1; 17:11; *Sir.* 33.7), where it is hatred, harsh words, and evil plotting which raise such hardship. **Selfish ambition . . . pure motives:** Rabbis were quite concerned with mixed motives for serving God, which for them primarily involved study and practice of the Scriptures. Such was not to be done out of selfish motives (*m. Abot* 6.1). One rabbi said, "Do not say, I will work in the Torah with the purpose of being called Sage or Rabbi, or to acquire fortune, or even to be rewarded for it in the world to come. But do it for the sake of your love for God, though the glory will come in the end" (*Sifre Deut.* 41 [on Deut. 11:13]; cf. *b. Ned.* 62a; *Midr. Pss.* 1119.46 [on Ps. 119:113]; Bockmuehl, 78).

1:18. What then? Only that in every way, whether in pretense or in truth, Christ is proclaimed; and in this I rejoice, yes, and I will

rejoice. In the Old Testament the preaching of the word of God was thought to overcome all hindrances (Isa. 55:10-11; 1 Kings 2:27; 13:2; 2 Kings 1:17; 22:16; Hawthorne, 38-39).

1:19. For I know that this shall turn out for my deliverance through your prayers and the provision of the Spirit of Jesus Christ. Job, likewise an innocent sufferer, recognized that in his affliction, "This also will be my salvation" (Job 13:15). Rabbi Nahum of Gimzo was famous for suffering personal affliction, yet responding each time with, "This too will turn out for good" (*b. Ber.* 60a; *b. Taan 21a*; cf. Eccles. 8:12; *Sirach* 39.25; *b. Ber.* 60b; Plato, *Republic* 10.12 [613a], *Apology* 41d; Bockmuehl, 83).

> "Terrible is the Lord and very great, and marvelous is his power. When you praise the Lord, exalt him as much as you can; for he will surpass even that. When you exalt him, put forth all your strength, and do not grow weary, for you cannot praise him enough. Who has seen him and can describe him? Or who can extol him as he is? Many things greater than these lie hidden, for we have seen but few of his works. For the Lord has made all things, and to the godly he has granted wisdom."
>
> *Sirach* 43.29-33

1:20. According to my earnest expectation: Earnest expectation refers to a longing in the midst of uncertainty. It is used by Josephus with respect to the outcome of a battle, or even the anticipation of a "hail of arrows" (*War* 4.5.1 §305 LCL; 4.9.2 §497; 5.1.5 §28; 6.2.5 §135; 6.6.2 §326; 7.3.4 §62; *Ant.* 14.15.12 §461; 17.5.1 §86; 17.9.5 §228; 18.8.7 §294; O'Brien, 113). **Put to shame** in the Old Testament, particularly in the Psalms, alluded to abandonment of God (Pss. 6:10; 22:5; 31:1; 53:5). Such is not the lot, however, of those who trust in the Lord (Ps. 24:3; Isa. 49:23). **Now** occurs over sixty times in Paul, normally referring to his recognition of the present as the time of God's appointing for his activity and glory to be manifest in a situation (cf. 1QpHab 7:1-14) or the opportunity to be a faithful witness in the face of danger (Esther 4:14; Dan. 3:17; 2 Macc. 6.24; m. Abot 1.14; Bockmuehl, 86).

Exalted comes from the Old Testament and refers to the exaltation of God or his oppressed people, particularly in contrast to being put to shame. It was similarly used as an expression of worship for God (cf. Pss. 34:3-5; 70:2; 1QH 4:23-24; 5:35; 1QS 4:23; Odes Sol. 29.1; Sir. 43.31).

1:21. For to me, to live is Christ, and to die is gain (kerdos). Some Greeks saw death as a gain in its escape from suffering (Sophocles, Antigone 463-4; Aeschylus, Prometheus Bound 747-51; Europides, Med. 145-47; Plato, Apology 40c-e). For Paul, death does not seem to be deliverance from suffering but to Christ.

1:22. Revered Greeks such as Socrates were said to **choose** (haireomai) death rather than to betray their beliefs (Xenophon, Apology of Socrates 9; Plato, Apology of Socrates 38E; Epictetus, Discourses 1.9.24; Bockmuehl, 91).

1:23. But I am hard-pressed (sunechomai) can refer to being attacked or tormented by pain, grief, or terror (Job 3:24; Luke 8:37). Blessedness after death was often thought to be found in the eschatological resurrection (1 Enoch 70.1; 102.4-105.2; cf. 2 Bar. 3.7; Tobit 3.6). Being **with Christ** (sun Christ?) may be derived from an OT hope of fellowship with God (LXX Pss. 139:14; 20:7; 138:18; cf. Deut. 33:2; Zech. 14:5), which likewise finds expression in an eternal hope in later Judaism (1 Enoch 62.13-14; 105.2).

1:26. Proud confidence (parousia) in Classical Greek referred to the pomp and pageantry that accompanied the arrival of a king or governor

in a city (Hawthorne, 53). **My coming to you again.** If Philippians was written from Rome (see Introduction), then it seems that Paul changed his plans of a proposed trip to Spain. Rom. 15:23-28 did not anticipate further ministry in the East, but this verse, along with Phile. 22, suggests this may have changed (Bockmuehl, 95).

B. 1:27–2:18. Instructions for the Church

1:27. Conduct yourselves (politeuesthe) is a rare word that meant to live as a citizen of a free state (polis). Its relation to the Greek polis is significant in that it conveys a sense of partnership of lifestyle (Aristotle, Politics A 1252a). For Jews, such an ideal society was Jerusalem. Later the concept spilled over to other cities in Israel, ultimately looking to the participation of other nations (Ps. 87:1-7) and the establishment of the worship of the God of Israel in all the earth (Isa. 66:20; Amos 9:11-12; Zech. 14:8-11). However, for later Jews such conduct relates more of the Jewish way of life (2 Macc. 6.1; 11.25; Jos., Life 12 §62-67). Thus, for Paul, it speaks of allegiance to the heavenly commonwealth and, as its citizens, the need to reflect its lifestyle (Heb. 12:22-23; Rev. 21:2-3; O'Brien, 147). Philippi was conscious of its status as a Roman colony. **Worthy of the gospel of Christ. Worthy** (axiōs) is often used by Paul as a term of moral exhortation, similar to "live" or "walk" (see comment on Col. 1:10). **Standing firm** was an attribute of the ideal soldier who did not flinch regardless of threats (Hawthorne, 56). **Striving together** (sunathleō) is language taken from an athletic, and more specifically, gladiatorial arena where competitors were working together in their task. It also refers to friendship (Aristotle, Nic. Ethics 9.8).

1:28. In no way alarmed can also mean "intimidate" and has been used to refer to an uncontrollable stampede of startled horses (O'Brien, 152). Who Paul's **opponents** were is unclear (see Introduction), though a pagan, rather than Jewish (3:2) background seems more plausible.

Destruction (*apōleia*) seems to refer to death and an eschatological judgment (cf. Deut. 28:20; 22:3; 30:18), while **salvation** here may simply refer to victory over their opponents.

1:29-30. In both Jewish and Christian traditions the righteous were thought to suffer but never in vain. There was also a redemptive element to suffering (Ps. 116:15; Isa. 53:1-12; *Wisd.* 2.1-24; *2 Macc.* 6.1-7.42; cf. *Martyrdom of Polycarp* 14.2; Eusebius, *Ecc. Hist.* 5.1.23).

2:1. If therefore there is any encouragement. Encouragement (*paraklesis*) can also mean "consolation" or "comfort." It refers to a hope offered in Christ from the time of one's salvation (O'Brien, 171). **Consolation of love** (*paramuthion agapēn*) refers to the consolation of Christ's love. **Fellowship** (*koinōnia*) **of the Spirit** is a fellowship marked by a common possession of the Holy Spirit. **Affection** (*splanchna*): See comment on 1:8. **Compassion** (*oiktirmoi*) is chiefly an attribute of God in the Old Testament (Pss. 24:6; 50:1; 102:4; 144:9), as well as in a number of Qumran documents (1QS 1:22; 1QH 1:31; 1QM 11:4). It also describes a person who lives according to God's will (1QS 4:3; cf. 2 Chron. 30:9; Ps. 106:46; O'Brien, 175).

2:3-4. Do nothing from selfishness or empty conceit. Empty conceit (*kenodoxia*) is a prideful opinion that one is of the right opinion (*doxa*) when one is actually in error (*kenos*; cf. *Wis.* 14.4; *4 Macc.* 2.15; 8.18; Hawthorne, 69). **Humility of mind** is a derogatory expression in much of Greek literature (Epictetus, *Discourses* 3.24.56), while in the Old Testament its cognates refer to the Lord's acting in history to bring down the proud and arrogant while exalting the lowly (cf. Amos 2:6; Isa. 2:9; Judges 4:23; 2 Sam. 22:28; Pss. 10:17; 31:7; Job 5:11; Prov. 3:34; 15:33; O'Brien, 180-81). **More important than himself**, in the Old Testament, means to surpass or exceed, as Daniel "surpassed" the wise men of Babylon in wisdom and status (Dan. 5:11; cf. Exod. 26:13;

Lev. 25:27; 2 Chron. 5:9).

Moses was a particular model of humility (Num. 12:3), which was a valued quality among Jews, as God saves the low and humble (Ps. 17:28; cf. 112:4-6), hears their prayers (Ps. 101:18), and gives them grace (Isa. 2:22; Ezek. 17:24). Qumran sectarians held a similar view: "And no one shall move down from his rank nor move up from the place of his lot. For all shall be in a Community of truth, of proper meekness, of compassionate love and upright purpose, towards each other, in a holy council, associates of an everlasting society" (1QS 2:23-25; cf. 4:3; 5:3; cf. *m. Abot.* 5.10).

2:5-11. Though the Hymn in this section may have developed prior to Paul's writing of Philippians, the background of it in its entirety is difficult to discern and is best examined on a phrase-by-phrase basis. Some scholars regard it as a pre-Pauline, self-contained, poetic unit perhaps of Hebrew or Aramaic origin for use among early Jewish-Christian communities in worship. Though likely alluding to Isaiah's famous "Servant Songs" (Isa. 42:1-4; 49:1-6; 50:10-11; 52:13-53:12), the hymn is clearly the product of Christian theology interwoven with Pauline exhortatory material (O'Brien, 198). **Have this attitude in yourselves which was also in Christ Jesus:** Rabbis likewise looked to heaven for a model of humility: "R. Joseph (d. ca. A.D. 333) said: "'Man should always learn from the mind of his Creator; for behold, the Holy One, blessed be He, ignored all the mountains and heights and caused His *Shechinah* (glory) to abide upon Mount Sinai, and ignored all the beautiful trees and caused His *Shechinah* to abide in a bush' (Exod. 3:2)" (*b. Sota* 5a).

2:6. He existed in the form: Form (*morphō*) is a relatively rare word in the Bible and generally refers to a visible shape in Jewish writings (Dan. 4:36; 5:6; 7:28; cf. *4 Macc.* 15.4; *Wisd.* 18.1; *Sir.* 9.8; Philo, *Moses* 1.66). Classically, it means the embodiment of a form, implying participation in its character and nature. It is best understood here as a form which truly and fully expresses the being that underlies it (Hawthorne, 83), i.e., **God**. Jesus **did not regard equality with God a thing to be grasped. A thing to be grasped** (*harpagmos*) can mean "seize," "take," or "use to one's advantage" (KJV "robbery"). The idea is that Jesus did not use his status as being in the form of the Father to his own advantage.

2:7 Emptied Himself (*heauton ekenōsen*): **Emptied** (from *kenoun*) can mean "to pour out." Jesus did not empty himself of his deity, or merely *appear* to be a man (Docetism). Rather it is argued that Jesus poured himself out as an expression of self-denial (Hawthorne, 86), similar to the denial of his own advantage shown in v. 6. **Taking the form of a bond-servant, and being made in the likeness of men:** As with **form** in v. 6, Jesus here takes on the attributes of a **bond-servant**. See comment on 1:1. A Jewish work, perhaps dating from the first century, though edited by later Christians, describes the "God of glory" as having "changed himself to be like a man when he was about to come to us so that he might save us [from flesh]" (*Apoc. Elijah* 1.6 OTP; cf. *Odes Sol.* 41.12). It could be taken from Jewish literature that God "comes down" and relates personally to his people in suffering (Exod. 3:7; Lev. 26:11; Isa. 63:9; cf. *b. Sot.* 31a; *b. Taan.* 16a; Bockmuehl, 134; cf. also Isa. 53:5-12). Christ has, in his incarnation, fully identified himself with humans (cf. Heb. 4:15).

2:8. And being found in appearance as a man, He humbled Himself by becoming obedient to the point of Death. This is the ultimate expression of faithfulness and obedience in the suffering righteous, similarly illustrated in the case of Isa. 53:12 (Bockmuehl, 139). **Even death on a cross.** Crucifixion was both so shameful and brutal that it was considered by Cicero to be a shocking and offensive topic unsuitable for polite conversation (Bockmuehl, 139). Jews considered victims of crucifixion to fall under the

curse of Deut. 21:23 (cf. Gal. 3:13) and were appalled by the Hasmonean rulers' introduction of it as a widespread Jewish punishment (Jos., *Ant.* 13.14.2 §380-83; *J.W.* 1.3.6 §97-98; 4QpNah 1.7-8; cf. 11QTemple 64:9-13; Bockmuehl, 139).

2:9-11. Therefore also God highly exalted Him is an expression used of the Servant in Isa. 52:13, and the highest exaltation held by God (cf. Ps. 96:9; Dan. 3:52-90 LXX; *Pr. Jos.* Frag A; cf. *b. Sanh.* 38b).

2:10. At the name of Jesus. Here Jesus' **name** seems to be associated with that of Yahweh, which was itself the greatest name (Ps. 8:1-9; cf. *b. Shab.* 88b; 1QM 9:15; 1Q19 2:4; 4Q544 3:1-2; Josephus, *J.W.* 2.8.7 §142; see comment on Eph. 1:20-23). Jesus thus receives the name and worship of God, which precludes worship of the emperor so popular in the Roman Empire. See comment on 2:11.

Every knee should bow. Normally worship was conducted in the name of the Lord (1 Kings 8:44; Pss. 43:9; 62:5; 104:3). In the Old Testament God promised, "I have sworn by Myself, The word has gone forth from My mouth in righteousness And will not turn back, That to Me every knee will bow, every tongue will swear allegiance" (Isa. 45:23). One would **bow** as a sign of reverence to acknowledge a person of exceptional authority (Gen. 41:43; 2 Kings 1:13), particularly God (1 Kings 8:54; 19:18; 2 Chron. 6:13; Ezra 9:5; Ps. 95:6; Dan. 6:10; cf. *Ascen. Isa.* 10.16). **Those who are in heaven, and on earth, and under the earth:** This is a conventional way for Jews to express the universality of something (cf. Rev. 5:13; Ps. 148:1-14; Bockmuehl, 145), with **under the earth** sometimes used by Greeks to denote the location of gods who must be appeased of their wrath (Strabo, *Geogr.* 6.2.11).

2:11. Jesus Christ is Lord is like the early confession "Jesus is Lord" (Rom. 10:9; 1 Cor. 12:3), which along with belief in the resurrection were key elements of Christian doctrine. Upon their death, emperors were believed to become gods (Seutonius, *Vespasian* 23.4) and were worshiped as **lord** (*kurios*). Indeed, Paul would have likely known of the emperor Caligula (A.D. 37-41), who solicited worship as **lord** (*kurios*), and attempted to place an idol in his image in the Jerusalem temple (Bockmuehl, 143). While Jews often resisted such emperor worship (Josephus, *J.W.* 2.8.1 §118), Gentiles, who were the primary congregants of the Philippian church (see Introduction), would likely have participated (cf. *BGU* 1197.1.15; *POxy* 1.37.5; 2.246; 8.1143.4; *CIG* 4923; *PLond.* 280.6; Tacitus, *Annals* 2.87). Epictetus refers to Caesar as "lord of all," under whom he considered himself a slave (*Disc.* 4.1.11-13). Paul anticipates that all will **confess that Jesus Christ is Lord** (*kurios*).

2:12. Work out (*katergazomai*) is in the present tense, here suggesting the continuous nature of the work: "continue working out" **your salvation.** This is not to be understood in an individual but corporate sense. Both the verb **work out** and the pronoun **your** are plural. **Salvation** (*sōtēria*) for Paul is both present (1 Cor. 1:18; 9:22; 15:2; 2 Cor. 2:15) and future (Rom. 5:9; 10:9). Some suggest that **salvation** here has the sense of general spiritual well-being, ultimately looking toward completion (Hawthorne, 99). **Fear and trembling** is a common biblical phrase describing the response of due reverence in the face of a major challenge, especially in the presence of God and his mighty acts (Exod. 15:16; Bockmuehl, 153; *2 Enoch* 66.2 [J]; cf. *Jos. Asen.* 9.1).

2:13. For it is God who is at work in you. In the Greek, this phrase begins with **God** (*theos*), suggesting that the fear and trembling (v. 12) is caused by God's presence **to will and to work for His good pleasure.**

2:14. Do all things without grumbling (*gongusmos*) **or disputing** (*dialogismos*). Paul is not suggesting that the Philippians were grum-

bling against God as Israel did in the wilderness (Exod. 15-17; Num. 14-17; 1 Cor. 10:10), but that they may have been acting unfriendly toward one another by such actions (cf. 1 Peter 4:9; John 7:12; Hawthorne, 101).

2:15 Christians are **children of God** by virtue of their participation with Christ (Rom. 8:14-17; Gal. 3:26; 4:5-6; see comment on Eph. 1:5). **Above reproach** is an Old Testament reference to ritually pure sacrificial animals, but can also refer to sincere believers such as Job (Job 1:8; 2:3; 11:4; 33:9; cf. Pss. 15:2; 18:23; 37:18; see comment on Col. 1:22). **Crooked and perverse generation** is a variation from Deuteronomy 32:5, where Moses uses such terms to describe Israel's unfaithfulness to God. Where it is cited elsewhere in the New Testament (Matt. 12:39; 17:17; Acts 2:40), it draws a parallel between the present generation and that of Deuteronomy (cf. 1 Cor. 10:1-11; Pss. 78:8; 95:9-11; Num. 32:13; Bockmuehl, 157).

Among whom you appear as lights in the world. Israel was to be "a light to lighten the Gentiles" (Isa. 42:6; 49:6). Such "illumination" was likewise attributed to those who are raised at the last day (Dan. 12:3 LXX; cf. 1QS 1:9; 2:16; 1QM 13:5). In the Old Testament, light is described as emanating from Yahweh himself (Ps. 27:1; Isa. 60:20; Mic. 7:8; O'Brien, 296). Later Jewish tradition held that God "made the race of these men whom he chose for himself shine, so that they should shine upon the whole aeon" (*Apoc. Adam* 7.52 OTP).

2:16. I did not run in vain. Paul's language is filled with athletic imagery, which he uses elsewhere to indicate the strenuous nature of his ministry (1 Cor. 9:24-27; 2 Tim. 4:6-8; cf. Gal. 2:2).

2:17. But even if I am being poured out as a drink offering. In the Old Testament, there were some spiritual or figurative understandings of sacrifices both in the Psalms (50:14; 51:17; 119:108) and the prophets (Amos 5:21-24; Hos.

6:6; Isa. 1:11-17). Later, Jews began to see acts of piety such as prayer, good works, and the study of the Torah as equivalent to sacrifice (*Sirach* 35.1; *Tobit* 4.10; 12.9; Dan. 3:39 LXX; *m. Abot* 1.2). **Being poured out as a drink offering** has been understood by some to be an allusion to death attested in pagan literature (Tacitus, *Annals* 15.64; 16.35). Both pagan and Jewish sacrifices were completed by a libation of wine poured out either on top of the sacrifice or at the foot of the altar in honor to the deity (2 Kings 16:13; Jer. 7:18; Hos. 9:4). Since these offerings were poured out (*Wisd.* 10.15; 2 Tim. 4:6; Ignatius, *Romans* 2.2) in reference to death, this has been seen as a reference to martyrdom (Hawthorne, 105).

C. 2:19-30. News about Timothy and Epaphroditus

2:22. Proven worth refers to the admirable quality of remaining faithful despite hardships. Josephus uses a similar expression to describe Abraham's obedience to offer Isaac as a sacrifice (*Ant.* 1.13.4 §233; cf. Gen. 22.1-19).

2:25. Epaphroditus. We know little more of him than what we read here and in 4:18. His name seems to be related to the cult of the goddess Aphrodite, and he is therefore likely a convert from a genuinely pagan family background (Bockmuehl, 169). His role seemed to be to bring a financial gift from the Philippian church (4:18) and care for Paul during his imprisonment. The Roman prison system made almost no provisions for the basic needs of its prisoners, thus the Philippians' assistance was required to provide even for the apostle's food (see Introduction to the Prison Epistles).

2:26 Distressed suggests an anguish caused by a perceived inability to change a state of affairs (Mark 14:33-36; Matt. 26:37-39; Josephus, *Ant.* 15.7.2 §211).

2:27 Mercy (*eleeō*) in the Old Testament is usually associated with God's deliverance of his people (Exod. 33:19; Pss. 6:3; 50:3), and in the New is a quality that characterizes Jesus' healing ministry (Mark 10:47; Luke 17:13; Bockmuehl, 172).

2:30 Risking his life (*paraboleuomai*) can be used for playing dice when high sums are at stake. It was used in papyri of one who, in the interest of friendship, had exposed himself to dangers as an advocate in legal strife by taking his client's causes, even to emperors (*LAE* 88).

3:1 Finally, my brethren, rejoice in the Lord. Neh. 8:10 says, "The joy of the Lord is your strength" (cf. Ps. 81:1; 1 Chron. 16:27). Abandoning one's joy and stronghold in the Lord's service and seeking it elsewhere will lead to disaster (Deut. 28:47). At Qumran, joyful praise of God was said to hold power over demons (4Q510 1:4-8; cf. *T. Sol.* 1.5-8; 3.5-7; 25.9; Bockmuehl, 181). **To write the same things again is no trouble to me, and it is a safeguard for you.** Safeguard (*asphales*) is a word reminiscent of Jewish Wisdom literature, where the tree of life is a stronghold for those who hold to it (Prov. 3:18; cf. *Wisd.* 7.23). God protects Israel in safety as a father his children (2 *Macc.* 3.22; 3 *Macc.* 7.6; Bockmuehl, 182). Judas Maccabeas provides exhortation to trust in God as a security rather than armor, which leads his men to rejoice (2 *Macc.* 15.7-16).

3:2. Beware . . . beware . . . beware (*blepete*). The present tense is also an imperative, calling for continuous action: "continually beware of." **Dogs** (*kunas*) in the Old Testament are normally associated with indiscriminate behavior, such as eating refuse, dead animals, and corpses (Exod. 22:31; 1 Kings 14:11; 2 Kings 9:10; Jer. 15:3; cf. Prov. 26:11). Israel's unfaithful leaders are seen as lazy but ravenous dogs (Isa. 56:10). Later Judaism particularly associated dogs with an aggressive disregard for any semblance of moral decency or distinction between clean and unclean (Bockmuehl, 186). **Dogs** can refer to

But Maccabeus did not cease to trust with all confidence that he would get help from the Lord. And he exhorted his men not to fear the attack of the Gentiles, but to keep in mind the former times when help had come to them from heaven, and now to look for the victory which the Almighty would give them. Encouraging them from the law and the prophets, and reminding them also of the struggles they had won, he made them the more eager. And when he had aroused their courage, he gave his orders, at the same time pointing out the perfidy of the Gentiles and their violation of oaths. He armed each of them not so much with confidence in shields and spears as with the inspiration of brave words, and he cheered them all by relating a dream, a sort of vision, which was worthy of belief. What he saw was this: Onias, who had been high priest, a noble and good man, of modest bearing and gentle manner, one who spoke fittingly and had been trained from childhood in all that belongs to excellence, was praying with outstretched hands for the whole body of the Jews. Then likewise a man appeared, distinguished by his gray hair and dignity, and of marvelous majesty and authority. And Onias spoke, saying, "This is a man who loves the brethren and prays much for the people and the holy city, Jeremiah, the prophet of God." Jeremiah stretched out his right hand and gave to Judas a golden sword, and as he gave it he addressed him thus: "Take this holy sword, a gift from God, with which you will strike down your adversaries."

2 Maccabees 15:7-16 RSV

pagans who do not know how to distinguish between the holy and profane (Exod. 22:31; *m. Ned.* 4.3; *m. Bek.* 5.6), including the sacred truths of God (4QMMT 61:1-62:10; Matt. 7:6; *Did* 9.5; *Tg. Ps.* 22:17; 1 *Enoch* 90.4).

Evil workers (*kakous ergatas*), in the Old Testament, was an expression repeatedly used for God's enemies (Pss. 5:5; 6:8; 14:4; 28:3; Hos. 6:8; Job 31:3), whereas the faithful were "workers of righteousness" (Ps. 15:2; Isa. 32:17). **False circumcision.** The Greek *katatomēn* "mutilation" is a play on the Greek word *peritomē* "circumcision," possibly echoing a contemporary anti-Semitic slur about the practice (Bockmuehl, 189). While such a practice was commanded by God (Gen. 17:10-24), it was, from the start, clearly an outward mark of an inward reality (Deut. 10:16; 30:6; Jer. 4:4; Ezek. 44:7). Jeremiah claimed that Jews who had uncircumcised hearts were as bad as pagans and equally under God's judgment (Jer. 4:4; 9:25; cf. 1QS 5:5). Paul's choice of "mutilation" (*katatomēn*) is related to a verb describing pagan religious self-mutilation rites (Lev. 21:5; 1 Kings 18:28; Isa. 15:2; Hos. 7:14). "In other words, circumcision that is not of

the heart is no better than ritual pagan laceration" (Bockmuehl, 189).

3:3. We are the true circumcision. Paul is claiming Christians to be the *true* members of a covenant relationship with God, which was originally established with Abraham on the basis of faith (Gen. 15:6, 18), before it was associated with circumcision (Gen. 17:10). In Greek, the **true circumcision** is modified by a series of three verbs connoting what the **true circumcision** does: **worship, glory,** and **put no confidence in the flesh. Worship in the Spirit of God:** This is an expression in the Old Testament often used to denote the worship or service rendered to Yahweh by his chosen people, Israel (Exod. 23:25; Deut. 6:12; 10:12; Josh. 22:27; Hawthorne, 126). **Glory in Christ Jesus:** Rather than "glorying" or "rejoicing" in their own accomplishments, the "true circumcision" **glory in Christ Jesus. Put no confidence in the flesh** means here, as it does in similar Jewish texts, trust in physical humanity often apart from or in contrast to God (cf. Gen. 6:3; Isa. 31:3; 1QH 7:16-26; Bockmuehl, 194).

3:4. Although I myself might have confidence even in the flesh. Paul has his own claims to nationalistic pride: **If anyone else has a mind to put confidence in the flesh, I far more.** Here Paul introduces his pedigree (vv. 5-6).

3:5. Circumcised the eighth day. This was required of all male Jews (Lev. 12:3). **Of the nation of Israel:** Gentiles never referred to Jews as **Israel**; it was an expression by which a Jew identified with the chosen covenant people of God. **Of the tribe of Benjamin: Benjamin** was the son of Rachel and the only one of Jacob's twelve sons born in the Promised Land (Gen. 35:16-18). From this tribe Israel's first king and the apostle's namesake, Saul, arose. Only the Benjamites remained faithful to Judah and the house of David after the death of Solomon. They went into exile with them and returned with Ezra to resettle the land around Jerusalem (Bockmuehl, 196). **A Hebrew of Hebrews.** While most Jews in the first century spoke only Greek and read the Greek translation of the Scriptures, Paul here denotes that he spoke in Hebrew or Aramaic and prayed and read the Scriptures in Hebrew (cf. Acts 6:1, 2; Philo, *Moses* 2.32; Chrysostom, *Homilies on Philippians* 10). Such was likely the language of his instruction under the great rabbi Gamaliel (Acts 22:3; 26:4). **As to the Law, a Pharisee.** Differing sects in Judaism of the first century had different approaches to the Law (Josephus, *Ant.* 18.1.3-6 §12-23; *J.W.* 2.8.2-14 §120-65). Paul's was that of a **Pharisee.** See comment on Matt. 3:7-10 §20.

3:6. As to zeal, a persecutor of the church: Zeal (*zēlos*) in the mid-first century was for some a technical term for Jewish nationalism under oppressive Roman occupation. It harkenhearkens back to Phinehas, whose "zeal for God" caused him to kill an Israelite man and his Midianite mistress, thus rescuing Israel from certain judgment (Num. 26:6-13). He was henceforth viewed as a hero among Israelites (Ps. 106:31; *1 Macc.* 2.26; cf. *4 Macc.* 18.12; Josephus,

Ant. 4.6.12 §152-55; *m. Sanh.* 9.6; *Sifre Num.* 131). Zeal for the Law was particularly noble among Jews such as the Pharisees, Zealots, and Qumran sectarians (Josephus, *Ant.* 12.6.2 §271; Philo, *Spec. Laws* 1.30; 2.253; *Abraham* 60; *T. Asher* 4.5; 1QH 14:14). Prior to his conversion, Paul was **a persecutor of the church**, as he saw Christ as its founder clearly under God's curse (Deut. 21:23; cf. Gal. 3:10-13; 1 Cor. 15:9).

As to the righteousness which is in the Law, found blameless. Here Paul is referring to his personal observance of the requirements of the Torah, which were considered by some as **righteousness**, apparently adopting a Pharisaic assumption that one could indeed keep the Torah's 613 commandments (Bockmuehl, 202).

3:7. But whatever things were gain to me, those things I have counted as loss for the sake of Christ: Gain (*kerdōs*) and **loss** (*zēmian*) are accounting terms, here suggesting the apostle had carefully counted up the separate items of merit for the heavenly audit, expecting all his accounts to be in order (O'Brien, 384; Aristotle, *Nic. Ethics* 5.4, 1132a). He thought he was in the black when in reality he was deeply in the red.

3:8. Knowing Christ Jesus my Lord: Knowing (*gnōseis*) is used in the Old Testament sense where God "knows" his people "in election and grace" (Exod. 33:12; Amos 3:2), and particularly, God's people knowing him "in love and obedience" to his self-revelation (Jer. 31:34; Hos. 6:3; Hawthorne, 138; cf. *Wisd.* 15.3; *Sib. Or.* 3.693; 1QS 1:12; 4:22; 11:16-20). **Rubbish** (*skubala*) can refer to excrement, food gone bad, or refuse. **Gain Christ** is a play on words, returning to accounting language. Whereas previously (v. 7) Paul considered his obedience to the Torah as "gain" (*kerdō*), he now seeks to **gain Christ**.

3:10. Jews often viewed **resurrection** as accomplished by the power of God (Ezek. 37:12; 2 *Macc.* 7.9; 4Q521 ii 2:12).

3:12. Become perfect (*teleioō*) was understood at Qumran to refer to integrity before God and in their careful observance of the Torah (1QS 1:8; 2:2; 4:20; 8:20; cf. Ps. 119:1, 80; Bockmuehl, 221). **I press on** (*diōkō*) is used in the LXX to describe figuratively the zealous pursuit of godly objectives, such as righteousness, peace, and the knowledge of God (Deut. 16:20; Ps. 34:14; Prov. 15:9; Isa. 51:1) and is likewise used here and elsewhere in the New Testament (Rom. 12:3; 14:9; Heb. 12:14; 1 Peter 3:11; O'Brien, 423-24). In Greek papyri, it was used to describe the carrying forth of one's plans (*PFay* 111.20) or even the pursuit of a lion (*PGrenf* 2.84.7).

3:13. Reaching forward to what lies ahead: The metaphor is from a footrace and pictures the body of a racer leaning forward with hands outstretched toward the goal upon which his eyes are fastened.

3:14. I press on toward the goal for the prize of the upward call of God in Christ Jesus: Again Paul borrows language from the athletic arena, where runners would focus on a marker that denoted the end of the race. A **goal** (*skopos*) was used in navigational language as well as a philosophy on life, in which a pilot kept his eyes on the goal in order to navigate (*Let. Aris.* 251).

3:15. Perfect (*teleios*) likely means "mature," and applies to those whose trust is sincerely placed in God and who follow wholeheartedly in his ways (Gen. 6:9; 1 Kings 8:61; 11:4; Bockmuehl, 225).

3:17. Brethren, join in following my example, and observe those who walk according to the pattern you have in us. For **walk**, see comment on Col. 1:10. In Greco-Roman education, imitation of the teacher's example was an important aspect of learning. In Jewish education, disciples were expected to learn the master's teaching as well as to emulate his behavior (Philo, *Virtues* 66; *Congr.* 70; Bockmuehl, 229).

3:18. For many walk, of whom I often told you, and now tell you even weeping, that they are enemies of the cross of Christ. Christians were routinely mocked for worshiping a crucified man. An early Christian apologist provides a hypothetical, though typical, example: "To say that their ceremonies center on a man put to death for his crime and on the fatal wood of the cross is to assign to these abandoned wretches sanctuaries which are appropriate to them and the kind of worship they deserve" (Minucius Felix, *Octavius* 9).

3:19. Whose end is destruction, whose god is their appetite, and whose glory is in their shame, who set their minds on earthly things. People who abandoned a divine cause were said to do so "for the sake of the belly" (3 *Macc.* 7.11). Such **appetites** were condemned in secular literature as well (Cicero, *De natura deorum* 1.40; Seneca, *De vita beata* 9.4; 14.3). In the OT, **shame** was brought about where immorality caused God to turn glory into dishonor (Hos. 4:7 LXX; Bockmuehl, 231). Other Jewish traditions describe people who set "aside the Law of God" as those who "have made their belly their God" (*Apoc. Elijah* 1.13 OTP; cf. *Ps-Phoc.* 69).

3:20. For our citizenship is in heaven. Philo likewise saw God's people as citizens of the heavenly promised land (*Conf. Tongues* 78; *Giants* 61; cf. *Midr. Ps.* 18:3). **Citizenship** (*politeuma*) referred to a colony of foreigners or relocated veterans whose purpose was to secure the conquered country for the conquering country by spreading abroad that country's way of doing things, its customs, its culture, its laws (Hawthorne, 170). Philippi was such a colony, which achieved *ius Italicum* (see comment on 1:1), the highest legal status obtainable by any provincial municipality. Its citizens were Roman citizens with all the rights and privileges afforded to them. It may be that Paul is saying the Philippian church is a colony of the heavenly empire (Martin, 147). Also, the

Philippians are to consider themselves resident aliens in Philippi, with a true **citizenship . . . in heaven** (cf. *Apoc. Elijah* 1.10).

We eagerly wait (*apekdechometha*) refers to a yearning for the coming of Christ (cf. *T. Sol.* 17.4; *Asc. Isa.* 4.13). **Savior** (*sōtēr*) was commonly used of Caesar in the Roman emperor cult (Bockmuehl, 235), though in the Old Testament it could refer to someone God raised up to rescue Israel from its enemies (Judges 3:9, 15). More importantly, it referred to the Lord himself (Judges 2:18; Deut. 32:!5; 1 Chron. 16:35; Isa. 45:15) as the Vindicator of his people (Isa. 35:4). Here Paul exclusively attributes it to **the Lord Jesus Christ.**

3:21. Transform the body of our humble state into conformity with the body of His glory, by the exertion of the power that He has even to subject all things to Himself. Some later Jews believed that obedience to the Torah "will then be glorified by transformations, and the shape of their face will be changed into the light of their beauty so that they may acquire and receive the undying world which is promised to them" (*2 Bar.* 51.3 OTP; cf. *Ascen. Isa.* 4.18).

4:1. Therefore, my beloved brethren whom I long to see, my joy and crown. Crown (*stephanos*) refers to the world of athletic competition where the victor was crowned with a laurel wreath and wore the crown as a festal garland (1 Cor. 9:25; Martin, 151). It is used metaphorically in Proverbs to connote faithful living and service to God (12:4; 16:31; 17:6). **Stand firm** describes the steadfastness of a soldier despite impending threats. See comment on Eph. 6:16.

4:2-3. I urge Euodia and I urge Syntyche to live in harmony in the Lord. These are apparently two influential women in the Philippian church, though their role is not known. They are apparently in disagreement with one another, though again Paul does not specify, though it seems that the conflict is personal in nature. It is presumed that the Philippian readers know the situation, though the modern reader does not. Paul asks the situation to be mediated by his **true comrade** (v. 3). This **true comrade** (*gnēsei suzuge*) literally translates "true yokefellow" (RSV), or "loyal yokefellow" (NIV). This person's identity is unclear, which has led to abundant scholarly speculation. Some Jewish and Greek texts show that **comrade** (*suzuge*) means "wife" (*T. Reub.* 4:1; Bockmuehl, 240), which has led some to speculate this was Paul's wife (Clement of Alexandria). Others have suggested Timothy (cf. 2:20), Epaphroditus (Lightfoot), or even a person named Sygygus (JB). Given the abundant partnership language throughout the epistle, however, it may be best to see this "yokefellow" as the entire church at Philippi (Hawthorne, 180). **Who have shared my struggle: Struggle** (*sunathle?*) is language from the gladiator arena, connoting two competitors who work together. See comment on 1:27. **Clement** may be, as Origen and Eusebius thought, the later bishop of Rome (ca. A.D. 95-96), though this is uncertain.

The **Book of Life** is frequently found in late apocalyptic texts (Rev. 3:5, 20; 15:21, 27) and at Qumran (1QM 12:3) and is drawn from the OT (Exod. 32:32; Pss. 69:28; 139:16), where it figuratively refers to the register of God's covenant people (Martin, 154; cf. *Apoc. Zeph.* 3.8).

4:5. Forbearing spirit (*epieikes*) is a term variously understood as "gentleness" (NIV), "forebearance" (RSV), or "moderation" (KJV). It is used of God as gentle and compassionate (Ps. 86:5; *Let. Aris.* 211; *1 Clem* 29.1; cf. *Wisd.* 12.18) and of a believer who exercises gentleness even under persecution (*Wisd.* 2.19; cf. Jas. 3:17; *1 Clem.* 21.7; 30.8; Bockmuehl, 245). **The Lord is near** may be best understood primarily in a temporal sense, rather than spatial. In the OT God's people were frequently exhorted by the imminent arrival of the "day of the Lord" (Isa. 13:6; Ezek. 30:3; Joel 1:15; 3:14; Ps. 145:18).

4:7. The peace of God. Peace (*eirēnē*) is the Greek equivalent of the Hebrew *shalom*, a very common OT expression found most prominently in the "Aaronic blessing" (Num. 6:22-27; cf. 10:19). It was associated with divine restoration (Jer. 29:11; 33:6) and a characteristic of the Messianic age (Isa. 66:12; Ezek. 34:25; 37:26; Mic. 5:4-5; Hag. 2:9). **Surpasses all comprehension** (cf. Eph. 3:20). **Guard your hearts.** Guard (*phrourōsei*) is sometimes a military term referring to a military garrison established as a "peace keeping" force present in Philippi (O'Brien, 498).

4:8. Finally, brethren, whatever is ... True (*alēthēs*) comprehensively refers to any truth. In the Old Testament and early Christianity such truth was thought to come from God (Ps. 119:142; Prov. 23:23; Justin, *1 Apol.* 46; *2 Apol* 1; Irenaeus, *Ag. Heresies* 3.16.6; 3.18.1). **Honorable** (*semnos*) in its adjective form was a frequent epithet for divinities and related sacred things, such as the temple, Law, and Sabbath (O'Brien, 504). It denotes a dignified, upright lifestyle in contrast with one that is profane (Prov. 8:6; *Sib. Or.* 5.262; Philo, *Sacrifice* 49; *Decalogue* 136; 1 Tim. 3:8; Titus 2:2). **Right** (*dikaios*) in a broad sense is the high standard that God holds (Ps. 11:7; cf. Ps. 36:4; Amos 8:4-6). **Pure** (*hagnos*) is used both to mean ritual purity and personal integrity (Ps. 11:7; Prov. 20:9; cf. 2 Cor. 7:11). **Lovely** (*prosfilēs*) refers to what is aesthetically pleasing (*Sirach* 4.7; 20.13; Josephus, *Ant.* 1.13.4 §258). **Of good repute** is similar to **lovely. Excellence** (*aretē*) is the highest moral quality inherent in a good person (cf. 1 Peter 2:9; 2 Peter 1:3; *Wisd.* 4.1; 5.13; 8.7; *4 Macc.* 1.2; Bockmuehl, 253). **And if anything worthy of praise, let your mind dwell on these things:** Cicero had a similar list of virtues to consider: "all that is lovely, honorable, of good report" (*Tusc. Disp.* 5.23.67 LCL).

4:9. The things you have learned and received and heard and seen in me, practice these things; and the God of peace shall be with you. *Testament of Dan* 5.2 says, "Each of you speak truth clearly to his neighbor, and do not fall into pleasure and troublemaking, but be at peace, holding to the God of peace. Thus no conflict will overwhelm you" (OTP).

4:10. The Philippian church seems to have sent a monetary gift to Paul by Epaphroditus, which would pay for his expenses during imprisonment. See Introduction to the Prison Epistles.

4:18. But I have received everything in full. This expression is used in commercial circles as a technical term for receiving full payment and giving a receipt (*POxy* 1.91.25; *BGU* 2.584.5). **A fragrant aroma, an acceptable sacrifice, well-pleasing to God:** This phrase is borrowed from the Old Testament (Gen. 8:21; Exod. 29:18; Lev. 1:9; Ezek. 20:41). Such spiritualization of sacrifices was present at Qumran, were prayers were seen as such sacrifices (1QS 8:7-9; 9:3-5; Martin, 167; see comment on Eph. 5:2).

4:19. And my God shall supply all your needs according to His riches in glory in Christ Jesus. *Joseph and Aseneth* records a lament for trusting "in the richness of my glory and in my beauty" (21.16 OTP), while *Odes of Solomon* 14.10 describes the Lord as "sufficient for all our needs" (OTP).

4:22. Those of Caesar's household probably refers to anyone in the imperial services, whether soldiers or government officials in the *praetorium*. Government administrators were found in provinces as well as Rome (Martin, 170).

Introduction to Colossians

Daniel M. Gurtner

One of Paul's shortest letters, Colossians has a unique place in the Pauline corpus of New Testament writings. Though he did not found the congregation to which he writes at Colossae, the apostle conveys warm pastoral affection and clear apostolic authority to this young church. Colossians bears some unique and lofty teaching on the divinity of Jesus as well as a memorable and graphic description of forgiveness as nailing the Christian's debts to the cross (2:14).

Recipients. Not only did Paul not found the church at Colossae, it seems he had not met the fledgling church (1:4; 2:1). Instead, the founding of this church is associated with the vigorous missionary and evangelistic efforts of others involved in the apostle's Ephesian ministry (ca. A.D. 52-55; Acts 19:1-41). Luke claims that Paul's preaching in Ephesus was so effective that "all the residents of Asia heard the word of the Lord, both Jews and Greeks" (Acts 19:10). Additionally, Paul had a number of coworkers who planted churches in the province of Asia. Churches in Colossae, Laodicea, and Hieropolis seem to be the fruit of one coworker's efforts, that of Epaphras (Col. 1:7; 4:12, 13). Epaphras was a native of Colossae (Col. 4:12) and "a faithful minister of Christ" who taught the Colossians the truth of the gospel as Paul's representative (Col. 1:7). He may have been converted to Christianity through Paul's ministry in Ephesus (Acts

19:10), and through him Paul learned of their "love in the Spirit" (1:8). Through Epaphras' efforts, the saints in Colossae seem to have been well instructed in the faith (2:6). References to alienation from God (1:21), lack of circumcision (Col. 2:13), godless minds and deeds (1:21), and a relative lack of references to the Old Testament indicate the church which he founded was predominantly of Gentile background (cf. 1:27).

Place of Origin and Date. The origin of Colossians is uncertain. The letter itself states that Paul was in prison (4:3), that Aristarchus, his fellow-prisoner, was with him (4:10), and that the congregation was asked to remember his imprisonment in prayer (4:18). However, it is unclear from which of his many imprisonments, perhaps as many as seven according to Clement of Rome (ca. 95-96; *1 Clem.* 5.6), Colossians was written. There are primarily three options: Rome, Caesarea, or Ephesus.

For some time it was assumed Colossians was of Roman origin, written during Paul's first imprisonment in that city. Mention of Rome is found on some "subscripts" to some manuscripts of the letter (K L [O'Brien, 1]). Eusebius claims that when Paul was brought to Rome, "Aristarchus was with him, and he naturally called him his fellow-prisoner in a passage in the Epistles," presumably a reference to Col. 4:10 (*Ecclesiastical History* 2.22.1 LCL; cf. Acts 27:2). Moreover, the freedom Paul had while imprisoned, which is described by Eusebius, (cf. also Acts 28:30) seems to relate to the presence of Paul's friends and coworkers in Colossians (4:7-17).

Others have considered a Caesarean imprisonment more likely, citing the possibility of Tychicus' accompaniment with Paul to that city (Acts 20:4; 24:23). However, this situation is far from certain, and objections have been raised whether the small town of Caesarea could have been the locus of the avid missionary activity described in Col. 4:3, 4.

Finally, still others have suggested Paul was likely imprisoned in Ephesus for the penning of Colossians. Marcion's prologue to the letter reads: "The apostle already in fetters writes to them from Ephesus" (O'Brien, lii). Though no mention of an Ephesian imprisonment is made in Acts, a number of passages suggest he may have endured such an imprisonment (see Introduction to the Prison Epistles). Moreover, it is argued that the proximity of Ephesus to Colossae, 100 miles, lends itself more readily to the ease of movement described in the epistle.

While it is difficult to decide between these options with much certainty, the Ephesian or Roman imprisonments seem most feasible. As the Roman theory is an attested imprisonment and seems to make best use of the letter's relationship to Philemon, it appears to be the more likely origin. This would suggest a date during his first Roman imprisonment, between A.D. 61 and 63.

Authorship. There is no evidence that Pauline authorship of Colossians was ever challenged until the nineteenth century. Claims to Pauline authorship are clear from the beginning of the letter (1:1) through the two "I, Paul" statements in its body (1:23) and conclusion (4:18). The letter was accepted as Paul's from the earliest accounts of the church, finding a place in Marcion's exclusively Pauline canon (ca. 144) as well as the Muratorian Canon (ca. 180, though perhaps much later). It may have been used as early as Justin (ca. 100-165;

Dialogue with Trypho the Jew 85.2; 138.2) and is clearly accepted as the work of Paul by Irenaeus (*Against Heresies* 3.14.1), Tertullian (fl. ca. 200; *Prescription against Heretics* 7), and Clement of Alexandria (*Miscellanies* 1.1). Objections to Pauline authorship have been based on three factors: linguistic evidence, theological evidence, and the relation of Colossians to the letter to the Ephesians (see below).

Those who argue against Pauline authorship based upon linguistic evidence recognize the number of *hapax legomena*, or rare words found nowhere else in Paul or even the New Testament. Thirty-four words occur only in Colossians and nowhere else in the New Testament, while twenty-eight words occur nowhere else in Paul's letters. Colossians also joins synonyms such as "wisdom and understanding" (1:9) and "teach and admonish" (3:16), which likewise, it is argued, is not characteristic of Paul's writing style. Those who argue against Pauline authorship on theological grounds highlight the letter's lack of characteristic Pauline topics such as justification, law, salvation, and righteousness. Moreover, the letter's depiction of a "cosmic" Christ (1:16-19; 2:9-10), it is argued, is found nowhere else in Paul. However, such concepts are surely present in other Pauline texts (1 Cor. 8:6; Phil. 2:10; Gal. 4:3, 9), with the result that this is insufficient grounds to doubt Pauline authorship. Finally, some scholars insist that the heresy combated in the letter was a second-century form of Gnosticism, which precludes authorship by Paul, who died ca. A.D. 63 (See "The 'Colossian Heresy'" below).

While the above differences between Colossians and the other Pauline letters are genuine, they are best regarded as being called forth by the circumstances at Colossae (O'Brien, xlix). The letter was written by the Apostle Paul. For Timothy's relation to the letter, see comment on 1:1.

Relation to Ephesians and Philemon. The striking similarities between Ephesians and

Colossians have long been recognized, though the nature of their literary relationship is less than clear. It is generally held that the two epistles are best understood as the expressions of one writer more or less repeating some of the same thoughts on two occasions not very far removed from one another (CMM 334). Both Colossians (4:7, 8) and Ephesians (6:21, 22) speak of Tychicus as the bearer of the letters. Tychicus had Onesimus as his companion on the journey to the Lycus valley; the same Onesimus is returning to Philemon (Phile. 12; O'Brien, xlix). Greetings are sent from nearly the same people in the epistles to the Colossians (1:7; 4:12-19) and Philemon (23). It seems likely that Colossians was written first, with Ephesians often expanding the themes and contents therein. Because these two books are so similar, readers are strongly encouraged to refer to cross references provided in each where further comments are provided.

The "Colossian Heresy." Though no explicit mention of a "heresy" is present in the epistle, it is widely recognized that in Colossians Paul is combating some form of false teaching. Its identity is uncertain, and can only be articulated by tracing it through the letter. It was a "philosophy" (2:8) based on an apparently antiquated "tradition" (2:8). It was probably in some way detracting from the person of Christ, not only because of Paul's stress on Christ's preeminence (1:15-19) but also his denouncing the heresy for its attention to other elements, "rather than on Christ" (2:8). Indeed, Paul seems to be quoting catchwords of the heretics: "all the fullness" (2:9), "Don't handle, don't taste, don't even touch!" (2:21), etc. It clearly bears some Jewish characteristics, as seen in his discussion of circumcision (2:11; 3:11), perhaps the warning against human "traditions" (2:8) and regulations of food, feast, and Sabbath laws (2:16). Its worship of angels (2:18) may have developed from Jewish traditions holding angels to be divine mediators (see comment on 2:18). Scholars are widely divided on how to interpret this evidence and, if possible, identify the group responsible for the heresy. Its apparently strict observance of Jewish law and severe asceticism lead J. B. Lightfoot to identify them as Essene Jews of a Gnostic kind. Such is perhaps the best assessment of the scant evidence.

Occasion and Purpose. Why and under what circumstances was Colossians written? Epaphras visited Paul in Rome and told him of the progress of the gospel among the churches at Colossae, Laodicea, and Hierapolis. Though brought an encouraging report about the Colossians (1:8; 2:5), Paul was also informed about the threat of false teaching in the young congregation. Paul's letter seems to be written in response to this theological and practical need. Paul sees a need early on to emphasize the preeminence of Christ (1:15-19) and his redemptive work (1:20-27), which must be clearly and earnestly taught (1:28-29), and which apparently is opposed by the heresy (2:8). Practically, Paul attacks the ascetic practices as man-made traditions (2:8) and urges his readers to live lives governed by theological truths rather than mere human regulations (3:1-4).

Contribution of Colossians. The theme of the supremacy of Christ and his saving work for his people runs through the entire letter. False teachers threatened to impose a barrier between God and the Colossian saints claiming the authority of other powers and practices such as asceticism. Paul combats the heretics by showing that Christ is the "image of the invisible God" and the creator and sustainer of the universe (1:15). Christ is before all (1:17), all the fullness of God dwells in him (1:19), and he is the head of the church (1:18). It is Christ's blood that brought reconciliation between God and the Colossian saints (1:20). God has made known his mystery (*mustērion*, see comment on 1:26-27) to his saints (1:26), to whom Paul has been made a minister (1:25).

Paul describes them as "knit together in love" (2:2), and having God's mystery, which is

Christ (2:2), so that they may not be misled (2:4). He urges them to avoid false teachings (2:8) because they have already been made complete in Christ (2:10). Unique to Colossians is Paul's description of atonement as God having "canceled out the certificate of debt" and "having nailed it to the cross" (2:14). They have, in a sense, participated in Christ's death (2:20) and are therefore urged to no longer live according to "elementary principles of the world."

Because they have been raised with Christ, the Colossians are exhorted to "keep seeking the things above, where Christ is" (3:1). The members of their earthly body are "dead to immorality, impurity, passion, evil desire, and greed, which amount to idolatry" (3:5). They are to demonstrate unity in Christ who "is all, and in all" (3:11), and to do all in his name, with thanksgiving (3:17). This has implications for the Christian household (3:19–4:1), as well as habits of prayer (4:2-4), and general conduct and speech (4:5-6). The letter concludes with a glimpse of some of the administrative affairs of the apostle (4:7-18). Colossians bears valuable exhortations to Christians and churches in danger of succumbing to popular or attractive philosophies of the day.

RESOURCES

Arnold, Clinton, *The Colossian Syncretism.* Grand Rapids: Baker Books, 1996.

Barth, Markus and Helmut Blanke, *Colossians.* Translated by Astrid B. Beck. AB 34B. New York: Doubleday, 1994.

Carson, D. A., Douglas J. Moo, and Leon Morris. *An Introduction to the New Testament.* Grand Rapids: Zondervan, 1992. (=CMM)

Dunn, James D. G., *The Epistles to the Colossians and to Philemon.* NIGTC. Grand Rapids: Eerdmans, 1996.

Lightfoot, J. B., *Saint Paul's Epistles to the Colossians and to Philemon.* Grand Rapids: Zondervan, 1977 (orig. pub. 1879).

Lohse, Eduard, *Colossians and Philemon.* Trans. W. R. Poehlmann and R. J. Karris. Hermeneia. Philadelphia: Fortress Press, 1971.

O'Brien, Peter T., *Colossians.* WBC 44. Waco, Tex.: Word Books, 1982.

Schweizer, Eduard, *The Letter to the Colossians: A Commentary.* Trans. by A. Chester. London: SPCK, 1982.

OUTLINE OF THE BOOK

Colossians

Daniel M. Gurtner

I. 1:1–2:23 THE SUPREMACY OF CHRIST

A. 1:1-2. Salutation

1:1. Paul (*Paulus*) was the Hellenistic-Roman name for his Jewish name "Saul." Jews in Greek-speaking areas took names that closely approximated the sound of their Hebrew and Aramaic names (O'Brien, 2; see comment on Eph. 3:8). **Timothy our brother.** Though Timothy's name appears with Paul's here and elsewhere (2 Cor. 1:1; Phil. 1:1; 1 Thess. 1:1; 2 Thess. 1:1), he perhaps should not be considered a co-author of the epistle but is included with Paul to indicate to the congregation that they both teach and preach one and the same gospel (Lohse, 7). See comment on 4:18.

1:2. The faithful in the Old Testament were commonly called **saints** (Greek, *hagioi* literally, "holy ones"). This identification was likewise adopted as the self-designating term for the Qumran sectarians (1QS 5:13, 18; 8:17, 20, 23; 9:8; 1QM 6:6; 10:10; 16:1; cf. also *1 Enoch* 1.9; 39.1; *Jub.* 31.14). See comment on Eph. 1:1. **Colossae** is an ancient city located about 100 miles east of Ephesus in Phrygia in modern Turkey, the site of which was discovered in 1835. It was situated on the south bank of the Lycus river, a tributary of the Meander, famous for its many curves (this is the source of our English word "meander" meaning "wander," "wind about," O'Brien, xxvi). It lay along an ancient main road from Ephesus and Sardis to the Euphrates and so finds mention in the itineraries of the armies of King Xerxes and Cyrus the Younger who marched along this road (O'Brien, xxvi). In the fifth century B.C., Herodotus called it "a great city in Phrygia" (*History* 7.30.1 LCL), and Xenophon (*Anabasis* 1.2.6; cf. Pliny, *Nat. Hist.* 5.145) described it as populous, large, and prosperous. Its prosperity was perhaps related to its vibrant wool industry. Sheep were grazed along the slopes of the Lycus valley and their wool dyed a dark red color (Strabo, *Geography* 12.8.16), generally known as "Colossian" (Pliny, *Nat. Hist.* 21.51; O'Brien, xxvi). It was also located along an important trade route between the Asian continent and the Aegean coast.

By Paul's time, Colossae seems to have declined in importance and size (Strabo, *Geography* 12.8.13), particularly in comparison with other, more significant cities such as Laodicea, where Christians were likewise found in relation to the Colossian church (Col. 2:1; 4:13, 15, 16). In A.D. 60/61 the Lycus valley was struck by a severe earthquake (Tacitus, *Annals* 14.27; though cf. Eusebius, *Chronicle* 215, who seems to date it to A.D. 64), which were not uncommon in that area (Strabo, *Geography* 12.8.16; Orosius, *Historiae ad paganos* 7.7.12).

Based on the amount of Temple tax taken by the proconsul Flacus in Laodicea in 62 B.C. (Cicero, *Pro Flacco* 28.68), some have proposed a sizable Jewish population in Colossae, perhaps as many as 11,000. Josephus records two thousand Jewish families brought from Babylon and Mesopotamia to settle in Lydia and Phrygia by Antiochus III in the early part of the second century B.C. (*Antiquities* 12.3.4 §147-53), but Colossae was perhaps mostly populated with indigenous Phyrgian and Greek settlers (O'Brien, xxvii).

Peace (*eirēnē*) is the Greek equivalent of the Hebrew *shalom,* a very common OT expression found most prominently in the "Aaronic blessing" (Num. 6:22-27; cf. 10:19). It was associated with divine restoration (Jer. 29:11; 33:6) and a characteristic of the Messianic age (Isa. 66:12; Ezek. 34:25; 37:26; Mic. 5:4-5; Hag. 2:9). "Mercy" (*eleos*) usually appears alongside **peace** (*eirēnē*) in Jewish letters but not **grace** (Dan. 3:98 [4:1]; *2 Bar.* 78.2; Lohse, 5). See comment on Eph. 1:2.

B. 1:3-8. Thanksgiving

1:3. We give thanks to God. Hellenistic prayers often began with a thanksgiving to the gods (*PHibeh* 79; *BGU* 2.423.6-8; *PLond.* 42.1-10; *2 Macc.* 1.10; Lohse, 12).

1:5. Hope laid up for you in heaven. Some Jewish apocalyptic texts describe God's future salvation as presently being reserved for the faithful (*4 Ezra* 7.14; *2 Bar.* 14.12). In the Old Testament, God's Word, spoken and revealed to men, was the **word of truth** (Ps. 119:43), which Paul here equates with **the gospel** (*tou euangelliou*). By designating the **gospel** as **truth,** Paul is contrasting it with the teachings of the Colossian heretics. **Truth** (*alēthia*) was likewise used by the Qumran sectarians (in Hebrew, *'mt*) to identify themselves as "men of truth" (1QpHab 7:10; cf. 1QH 11:11; 14:2) who obey God's truth (1QS 1:11; 5:10) and have a knowledge of truth (1QS 9:17; 1QH 6:12; 9:10; 10:29; 11:7; 1QH 1:9; Lohse, 21). In each case, **truth** represented (their) proper understanding and application of the Law.

1:6. Bearing fruit and increasing is an expression from the Old Testament of growing and multiplying (LXX Gen. 1:22, 28; cf. Gen. 8:17; 9:1, 7; Jer. 3:16; 23:3). Some rabbis used the expression for sin as the fruit of unbelief (*b. Qid.* 40a). Other Jews saw the Law as having power to produce fruit in people (*4 Ezra* 9.31; cf. *4 Ezra* 3.20).

1:7. You learned (*manthanō*) is related to the word "disciple" (*mathēteis*). A disciple is literally a "learner," both intellectually and practically. See comment on Luke 14:25-35; §171. The term suggests Epaphras gave careful, systematic instruction in the gospel (O'Brien, 15). **Epaphras** (*Epaphras*) is a shortened name for Epaphroditus (*Epaphroditos*; *CIG* 1.268.7; 2.1820.1; 1963.1; 2248.4; Ditt. *Syll.* 3.1112.26; 1243.34; Lohse, 22). In Philemon 23, he is called a "fellow-captive" (*sunaichmalōtos*), suggesting he shared in one of Paul's many imprisonments. It is uncertain whether he is the same Epaphroditus of Philippians 2:25; 4:18. His was a very common name. **Fellow bond-servant** (*sundoulos*) is a term found only here and in Colossians 4:7; both of Epaphras. It is not only an expression to further legitimize Epaphras' ministry but to assure the Colossians that he is a servant of Christ who participates in the same work as Paul (cf. 4:12; Lohse, 22). A servant (*doulos,* twice in v. 7) is an honorable title in the Old Testament and is given to the likes of Abraham (Ps. 105:42), Moses (Ps. 105:26; 2 Kings 18:12; Dan. 9:11), Joshua (Josh. 24:29; Judges 2:8), David (2 Sam. 7:5; Ps. 89:4, 21), and the prophets (Amos 3:7; 1QS 1:3; 1QpHab 2:9; 7:5). Epaphras is also described as a faithful **servant** (*diakonos*), which can also mean "minister," from which the English word "deacon" is derived. See Eph. 3:7.

C. 1:9-12. Prayer

1:9. The **knowledge** of which Paul speaks is not that of higher worlds but of God's **will** (*thelēma*; Pss. 103:7; 143:10). In Jewish thought as seen at Qumran, God alone is the source of understanding (1QS 11:17; 3:15) and the revelation of mysteries (1QpHab 11:1; 1QS 5:11; 1QH 4:27). This is particularly applicable to God's Law (1QS 3.1; 8.9) as a revelation of his will (1QS 1:5; 9:13). **Knowledge** (*epignōsis*), **wisdom** (*sofia*), and **understanding** (*sunesis*), in the Old Testament, were endowed by the Spirit upon particular people to carry out a task assigned by God (Exod. 31:3; 35:5, 31; Deut. 34:9; 1 Chron. 22:14; Isa. 11:2). The Qumran sectarians saw the combination of **knowledge, understanding,** and **wisdom** as gifts of God, which he imparted by his Spirit to the faithful members of the community (1QS 4:3, 4; 1QSb 5:23).

Wisdom and understanding were not only valued in Jewish thought (Deut. 1:13; 4:6; 1 Kings 16:18; Isa. 3:3; 19:11; 29:14; Jer. 4:22; Hos. 14:10; Eccles. 9:11; Dan. 1:4; 2:20), but also in Greco-Roman philosophy, though **wisdom** was regarded as subordinate to prudence, in which was found discernment (Aristotle, *Nic. Ethics* 6.11.1141a; 6.11.1143a; Lohse, 26).

1:10. Walk (*parapateō*) is a metaphorical expression for moral and ethical behavior. In the Old Testament, King Hezekiah prayed, "Remember now, O LORD, I beseech Thee, how I have walked before Thee in truth and with a whole heart, and have done what is good in Thy sight" (2 Kings 20:3). Later Jewish laws and traditions, called *Halakah*, (based on the Hebrew word *hlk*, meaning "to walk") governed daily life. At Qumran obedience to the Law was seen as "walking in the way of His (God's) delight" (1QS 5:10). See comment on 1 John 1:6-7 (cf. 1 John 2:6; 2 John 6; 3 John 3). **Worthy** (*axiōs*) literally means the balancing of scales, making things equivalent.

1:11. Strengthened with all power, according to His glorious might, for the attaining of all steadfastness and patience. This type of fortitude does not derive from personal bravery or a strong will but rather from God. The description is taken from Exod. 34:6, where God is described as "slow to anger, and abounding in lovingkindness and truth." Prayer among the Qumran sect was to make a person aware of God's power (1QS 11:4; cf. 1QH 4:31-33), which then enables him in his cosmic struggle against Belial (1QM 1:11:14; 3:5:8; 4:4:12; 6:2:6; Lohse 30).

1:12. Qualified (*hikanōsanti*) is a rare word, used only here and in 2 Corinthians 3:6 in the New Testament. In a second-century B.C. papyrus, we read that a superior **qualified** a subordinate with his authority in his absence (*PTeb* 1.20.8). In the LXX, it is used to denote sufficiency or satisfaction (Num. 16:7; 1 Kings 12:28; Mal. 3:10; cf. also Dionysius Halacarnassensis, *Roman Ant.* 2.74). **Inheritance:** Some Jewish writers saw the Law as Israel's **inheritance** (*Sir.* 24.23; *1 Enoch* 99.14), or even life or eternal life (*Pss. Sol.* 14.7; *1 Enoch* 40.9; cf. *2 Enoch* 50.2; *2 Bar.* 44.13; cf. Dan. 12:13). Israel was itself seen as a "chosen portion" among the nations (Deut. 9:29; 32:8-10; Zech. 2:12 [LXX v. 16]), as were the Qumran sectarians (1QS 2:2; 1QM 1:5; 13:5). In the New Testament, "inheritance" is what was promised (cf. Heb. 11:8) and has been laid up for believers in heaven (1 Peter 1:4; Heb. 9:5; cf. LXX of 1 Sam. 14:41; *Letter to Diognetus* 5.4). According to legend, Joseph forgave his brothers' sins (Gen. 50:15-21) and made them "fellow heirs of all" his possessions (*Jos. Asen.* 24.14 OTP).

The Qumran sectarians believed the elect received a share in the property of angels (1QH 3:22; 6:3; Cf. 1QGenApoc 2:20-21). For Paul it was salvation in the future (Eph. 1:14, 18; 55), and the Holy Spirit is a "down payment" of this in the present (2 Cor. 1:22; 5:5), of which Gentiles are "fellow heirs" (Eph. 3:6). Cf. Matt. 21:38; 25:34; Mark 12:7; Luke 12:13; 20:14. See comment on Eph. 1:11; Luke 15:11-32 §173.

D. 1:13–2:23. Supremacy of Christ

1:13. God **delivered** (*errusato*) his people, which is not the same thing as saving them (*sōzō*). This expression is similar to the deliverance from an alien power, such as Egypt in the Old Testament (Exod. 14:30; Judges 6:9; cf.

Exod. 6:6; Judges 8:34), but also from danger, sickness, death, etc. (Pss. 33:18, 19; 79:9; 86:3). **Domain of darkness** is found in the Old Testament (Isa. 9:1; 60:2) referring to both sin and oppression. It is often, as here, contrasted with the deliverance provided by God. **Transferred** is a word used by Josephus to describe Tiglath-pileser's removal of the Transjordanian tribes to his own empire (*Ant.* 9.11.1 §235). Plato uses it with respect to the flight of a soul from darkness to light when a heavenly truth is revealed to it (*Republic* 7.518A; Schweizer, 51). The **kingdom of His beloved Son** hearkens back to God's promise to David that one of his descendants would sit on the throne forever (2 Sam. 7:16; Ps. 2:7; 4QFlor 1:11; Luke 1:33), though **son** can also refer to Israel (*Pss. Sol.* 17.1-46; *Jub.* 1.24; 4QFlor 1:7; cf. Ps. 2:2; 4QDib. Ham. 3:4-8, where God calls Israel "my firstborn son"; Schweizer, 52). The contrast between two realms—light and darkness—is common in Qumran literature where Belial and his "sons" (see comment on Eph. 2:2) are in darkness (1QS 2:5; 1QM 1:1, 5, 11; 4:2; 13:2) and opposed to God, his angels, and the "sons" of light (1QS 1:9; 2:16; 11:7, 8; 1QH 11:11, 12).

1:14. **Redemption** can mean deliverance in a general way (Exod. 21:8) or perhaps release of a prisoner when the appropriate price is paid (Zeph. 3:1; Dan. 4:34 LXX). The Exodus from Egypt is a primary example of God's "redemption" of Israel from servitude to become his people (Exod. 8:23; Deut. 7:8; 9:26; 13:5; 15:15; 24:18; 1 Chron. 17:21; cf. Ps. 49:7; Job 33:24; Isa. 43:3). This is accomplished by his might (Deut. 7:8; 9:26; Ps. 74:2; 77:15). Israel was to likewise redeem people and property that could not otherwise be freed (Lev. 25:25-26; 47-49). Provisions were made for people to go free from imprisonment by redemption (Exod. 21:29-30). Redemption is seen in Cyrus' decree for the exiles to be restored (Ezra 1:1-11), where redemption is attributed to God (Isa. 45:1-25; 52:3) in an Exodus-like manner (cf. Isa. 43:1-4, 14). It can generally refer to a deliverance from imprisonment to Beliar or bondage to evil (*T. Zeb.* 9.8; *T. Jos.* 18.2; cf. Dan. 4:34). The Qumran sectarians saw themselves as ones redeemed by God (1QM 1:12; 9:9; 14:5, 10; 15:1; 17:6). **Forgiveness of sins.** See comment on Eph. 1:7; Mark 2:1-13 §65.

1:15-20. Most scholars today consider 1:15-20 a hymn dating from before the penning of Colossians. It bears some resemblance to Jewish wisdom literature and suggests that Jesus is the incarnate Wisdom of God. Its origin and use are difficult to discern, though it seems clear (Col. 3:16) that the church at Colossae regularly worshiped with hymns, and the lines in vv. 15 and 18b seem to form new "stanzas." **Image of the invisible God.** **Image** (*eikōn*) hearkens to creation where man is said to be

---

"I learned both what is secret and what is manifest, for wisdom, the fashioner of all things, taught me. For in her there is a spirit that is intelligent, holy, unique, manifold, subtle, mobile, clear, unpolluted, distinct, invulnerable, loving the good, keen, irresistible, beneficent, humane, steadfast, sure, free from anxiety, all-powerful, overseeing all, and penetrating through all spirits that are intelligent and pure and most subtle. For wisdom is more mobile than any motion; because of her pureness she pervades and penetrates all things. For she is a breath of the power of God, and a pure emanation of the glory of the Almighty; therefore nothing defiled gains entrance into her. For she is a reflection of eternal light, a spotless mirror of the working of God, and an image of his goodness."

Wisdom 7.21-26

made in God's image (Gen. 1:26, 27) and for his glory (Isa. 43:7; cf. 1 Cor. 11:7). The term **image** may also come from Jewish wisdom literature. In Proverbs 8:22, Wisdom was with the Lord at creation (cf. *1 Enoch* 42.1; *Sir.* 1.4; 24.5, 9; Eusebius, *Preparation for the Gospel* 7.14.1; Philo, *Flight and Finding* 109), and some Jews thought Wisdom was an agent in God's creative activity (*Tg. Neof.* 1.1 [on Gen. 1:1]; 1QH 1:7:14-19). In *Wisdom* 7.25, God's personified wisdom is described as the **image** (*eikōn*) of God's goodness, that is, the revealer of God's goodness (O'Brien, 43). Plato and later Greeks thought of the cosmos as the visible image of God (*Timaeus* 92c; cf. *Corp. Herm.* 8.5; 11.15; 12.15; Pseud. Apul, *Asclepius* 10). **Firstborn of all creation:** In the Old Testament, Israel is described as God's "beloved son" (Exod. 4:22), while **firstborn** is used of God's Davidic king in Psalm 89:27. See comment on 1:13. In some Jewish texts Wisdom received personified status as an eternal entity sharing the throne of God (*Wisd.* 9.4, 9; Philo, *Conf. Tongues* 146; *Agriculture* 51; *Dreams* 1.215; *Flight and Finding* 109). Philo also says that the Logos is the **firstborn**, that is, the Messiah promised in Zech. 6:12 (*Conf. Tongues* 62; 146; *Agriculture* 51; *Dreams* 1.215; Schweizer, 68), and that wisdom is the perfect way which leads to God (*Unchanging* 142; *Migr. Abr.* 175). Here Paul uses language and imagery that was clearly attributed to wisdom and applies it to Christ. Rabbis understood the **firstborn** (Ps. 89:28) as the "King Messiah" (*Exod. Rabb.* 19.7 [on Exod. 13:1]). **For by Him all things were created** (1:16): Some Greeks thought all creation went back to nature for its origin (Marcus Aurelius, *Meditations* 4.23.2; cf. Ps-Aristotle, *Mund.* 6.397b; *Corp. Herm.* 5.10; *Paris Magical Papyrus* 4.2838; Lohse 49), while God and nature were viewed together as one (Philo, *Cherubim* 125). **In the heavens and on earth:** See comment on Eph. 1:20-23.

All things have been created by Him and for Him: Rabbis differed on why the world

"Rab said: The world was created only on David's account (that he might sing hymns and psalms to God); Samuel said: On Moses' account (That he might receive the Torah); R. Joh?anan said: For the sake of the Messiah."

b. Sanh. 98b.

was created (cf. *b. Sanh.* 98b). **In Him all things hold together.** Being **held together** (1:17) was used to denote the unity of the entire world in Platonic and Stoic philosophy (Plato, *Republic* 530a; Ps. Aristotle, *Mund.* 6; Philo, *Who is the Heir?* 281, 311), but the concept is closer to that used by Hellenistic Judaism, where the Spirit "of the Lord, indeed, fills the whole world, and that which holds all things together (*sunechon*) knows every word that is said" (*Wisd.* 1.7; O'Brien, 48; cf. Philo, *Flight and Finding* 112; Jos., *Ag. Ap.* 2.22 §190; *Sirach* 43.26).

He is also head of the body, the church (1:18). See comment on Eph. 1:20-23; 4:15-16; 5:23. Paul describes Christ as **firstborn from the dead . . . having first place in everything** (1:18). Philo considered both Wisdom and Logos as the beginning (Philo, *Allegorical Interpretation* 1.43; cf. Prov. 8:23). In the Old Testament, **firstborn** (*prōtokos*) and having **first place** are used together to describe the founding of a people (LXX Deut. 21:17; cf. Rom. 8:29; O'Brien, 50). **From the dead** (*nekrōn*) is in the plural suggesting Paul is not here referring to an abstract "death" but to Jesus as the first of many who arise from "the dead ones."

The Father's good pleasure (1:19) was normally associated with election (Pss. 44:3; 147:11; 149:4; cf. Isa. 8:18; 49:20; O'Brien, 52; 3 *Macc.* 2.16). In the Old Testament, God's **fullness** (1:19) is said to fill heaven and earth (LXX Jer. 23:23, 24; Isa. 6:3; Ezek. 43:5; 44:4; Ps. 72:19; cf. *Wisd.* 1.7) and is an expression of God's power, perhaps in allusion to the Holy Spirit.

Here it can refer to the totality of the divine powers and attributes or, perhaps, even the fullness of saving grace and power which belongs to one constituted as savior.

1:20. Having made peace (*eirēnopoiein*) is a rare word in the Bible. In the LXX of Isaiah 27:5, it refers to those who make peace with God and thus enjoy eschatological blessings (cf. Prov. 10:10; see comment on Matt. 5:9 § 29). *B. Ber.* 16b reads, "R. Saphra (ca. 300) used to pray, 'May it be your will, Yahweh our God, that you grant peace to the upper family (world of angels) and to the lower family (Israel) and to the students who busy themselves with your Torah'" (Lohse, 60). **Peace** is not something to come only at the end of time, but is currently present through the redemption of Christ (Phil. 2:10). Christ has restored creation and reconciled it with God (cf. Philo, *Special Laws* 2.192). **The blood of His cross:** Blood (*haima*) refers to a life given up in a violent death and, here, denotes a life offered up sacrificially and voluntarily in death. See comment on Eph. 2:13.

1:21. You were formerly alienated. Jews at Qumran recognized that God alone is able to end alienation between people and himself (1QS 11:13; 1QH 14:13; 16:12; Lohse, 63). Some Stoics thought of the **mind** (*dianoia*) as material to be formed as a carpenter works with timber or a shoemaker with hides (Epictetus, *Dissertation* 3.22.20). In Jewish thought, the **mind** (*dianoia*) was often interchangeable with the heart (Hebrew *lbb*; Gen. 8:21; 17:17; 24:45; 27:41; 34:3; Exod. 9:21; Deut. 6:5; *T. Reub.* 5.3). **Evil deeds.** Godlessness inevitably results in sinful practices (*T. Ash.* 6.5; *T. Zeb.* 9.7; *T. Gad* 3.1; cf. *Jos. Asen.* 12.5).

1:22. Reconciled (*apokatōllaxen*) is a term used of fixing public works fallen into disrepair (*OGIS* 483.8), restoration of property in legal disputes (*POxy* 1.67.9), or "balancing accounts" (*POxy* 1.70). For a discussion of the **cross** and crucifix-

ion, see comment on Mark 15:20, 21 §209 and Mark 15:24 §210. In the Old Testament, such mediation was a duty of priests (Deut. 10:8; 18:5, 7; 21:5; cf. Rom. 12:1; Schweizer, 93). **His fleshly body** refers to the frailty of the present life (*1 Enoch* 102.5) or the sinful nature (*Sir.* 23.17; cf. 1QpHab. 9:2) and may be meant to indicate Christ's taking on of our sinful nature (2 Cor. 5:21). It more likely, however, is used to distinguish his physical body, which was crucified, from his spiritual body, the church. The purpose of Christ's reconciliation is to **present you before Him** (see comment on Eph. 1:4) **holy and blameless and beyond reproach. Blameless** can also mean "unblemished" and is used in the OT of the proper sacrificial animal with no defects (Exod. 29:1; Lev. 1:3, 10; 3:1, 6; 4:3, 23, 28, 32; etc.; See comment on Philippians 2:15). **Beyond reproach** (*anegklētous*): In a papyrus from A.D. 20-50, a woman who was abandoned by her husband claims that she has "conducted (her)self blamelessly (*anegklēton*) in all respects" (*POxy* 2.281.12).

1:23. Firmly established (*themelioun*) is used in the Old Testament to designate the establishing of God's activity (LXX Pss. 8:4; 23:2; 101:26; Isa. 48:13; 51:13, 16) and the founding of God's eschatological city on Mount Zion (LXX Ps. 47:9; Isa. 14:32; 44:28; Hag. 2:18; Zech. 4:9; 8:9; Lohse, 66). The image of the community as God's building was used frequently at Qumran (1QS 5:6; 7:17; 8:7; 1:5; 1QH 6:25-27; 7:8). **Hope** in the coming of the Messiah was commonly expressed in crisis situations in Israel (2 *Bar.* 30.1; *Tg. Jer.* 31:6; *Tg. 2 Sam.* 23:4; Cf. Luke 2:25, 38).

1:24. Sufferings ... afflictions. Suffering was commonly expected in apocalyptic Judaism before the establishment of God's new creation (Dan. 12:1; *1 Enoch* 37.4; *1 Bar.* 14.1; *Jub.* 23.22; *4 Ezra* 4.51-5.13, 6.28; *Sib. Or.* 2.153f; *b. Sanh.* 96b; 97a; etc.), after which the anointed Messiah was to come (*b. Shab.* 118a; *b. Pes.* 118a).

1:26. Mystery (*mystērion*) in the OT is a Greek translation of the Aramaic *rz* found in Daniel 2:18, 19, 27-30, 47, with reference to something once hidden and then disclosed. Such "unknown" things were frequently being revealed in Jewish-Christian traditions, such as the meaning of a dream or vision (Dan. 2:19), a description of the end times (Dan. 2:27-29; *2 Bar.* 85.8; 1QpHab 7:1-5; *4 Ezra* 14.5; *1 Enoch* 9.6; 103.2), the divine structure of the universe (*1 Enoch* 71.4; *2 Bar.* 48.2), or an explanation of God's ways in human activity (*1 Enoch* 63.3; 1QM 14:14; 1QH 5:22-25; 9:23; Best [1998], 134). The early church understood **mystery** to refer to the sacraments (Ignatius, *Trallians* 2.3) or the gospel itself (*Letter to Diognetus* 4.6; 7.1; 8.10; 11.2; cf. *Didache* 11.11). See comment on Eph. 1:9.

1:28. Proclaim (*katangelein*) refers to a public announcement and is used in Christian writings for missionary preaching (Lohse, 77). **Admonishing** (*nouthetountes*) is a common expression in Greek literature for moral and intellectual correction (Plato, *Protagoras* 323D; *Republic* 399B; *Laws* 845B; Dio Chrysostom, *Orations* 32.27; Plutarch, *Adol. poet. aud.* 46B [15]; *Virt. mor.* 452C [12]; Lohse, 77). It is used in the New Testament only in Paul's exhortatory texts (1 Cor. 4:14; 1 Thess. 5:12, 14; Rom. 15:14; 2 Thess. 3:14). **Complete in Christ** (*teleion en Christō*): Walking in perfection was an expectation in the Old Testament (Deut. 18:13; 1 Kings 8:61; 11:4; 15:3, 14; 1 Chron. 28:9), in later Judaism (*Wisd.* 9.6; *Sirach* 44.17), and at Qumran (1QS 3:9; cf. 1QS 1:8; 2:2; 3:3; 4:22; 8:1; CD 1:21; 2:15; 7:5). Such perfection for Paul is accomplished **in Christ**, and this will be completely achieved at Christ's return (O'Brien, 89).

2:1. I want you to know how great a struggle I have on your behalf. **Struggle** (*agōn*) pictures an athletic contest which is both strenuous and demanding. **Laodicea** was a city located in the Lycus valley about 10 miles downstream from Colossae (see comment on 1:1). Founded by Antiochus II, it was named for his wife, Laodice, between 261 and 253 B.C. It was a center of financial and banking operations (Cicero, *Letter to Atticum* 5.15; *Epistulae ad familiars* 3.5; cf. Strabo, *Geography* 12.8.16) and gladiatorial contests (Cicero, *Letter to Atticum* 6.3.9). It suffered from frequent earthquakes and was desolated by them in A.D. 60, though rebuilt without the aid of Roman finances (Tacitus, *Annals* 14.27.1). See comment on 4:13, 16. **Those who have not personally seen my face.** Paul had not met the Colossians. See Introduction.

2:2. That their hearts may be encouraged. See comment on Eph. 3:17. **Knit together in love** (*sumbibasthentes en agapē*) may also translate, "being instructed in love," in an authoritative sense (Exod. 4:2, 15; 18:16; Lev. 10:11; Deut. 4:9; Judges 13:8; Isa. 40:13) but probably means "unite." Greeks used this expression to connote reconciliation of warring parties (Herodotus, *Histories* 1.74.17; Thucydides, *Peloponnesian War* 2.29.6; Plato, *Protagoras* 337E). Similar expressions are used by Aristotle to describe the connection between parts of the body (*Metaphysics* 4.4; 10.3; *Phys. Ausc.* 4.6; cf. Col. 2:19).

2:3. In whom are hidden . . . In *1 Enoch* 46.3 the heavenly "Son of Man" is the one who reveals all the treasures of that which is hidden. **Treasures** refers to material wealth (Josh. 6:19, 24; Prov. 10:2) but more importantly to spiritual attributes such as wisdom and the fear of God

"This is the Son of Man, to whom belongs righteousness, and with whom righteousness dwells. And he will open all the hidden storerooms; for the Lord of the Spirits has chosen him, and he is destined to be victorious before the Lord of the Spirits in eternal uprightness."

1 Enoch 46.3 OTP

(Isa. 33:6). **Wisdom and knowledge** are almost inseparable in Jewish thought (*Sir.* 1.16-18; 2.26; 7.13; 9.10; cf. 1QS 4:3, 22; 1QH 1:18, 19; CD 2:3; O'Brien 95; cf. *3 Enoch* 8.1).

2:4. Delude (*paralogizesthai*) refers to deception to oneself (Jas. 1:22) or, as here, deliberate deception of others (Gen. 29:25; Josh. 9:22; Judges 16:10, 13; Dio Chrysostom, *Orations* 11.108; Epictetus, *Dissertation* 2.20.7; *PAmh.* 2.35.12; *PMagd.* 29.5). It was used in ancient papyri of a keeper of a state library who had shown a willingness to make wrong use of certain documents (*POxy* 1.34; cf. *OGIS* 665.16; *PMagd* 29.5; *PAmh* 2.33.15). **Persuasive argument** (*pithanologia*) is a term used in Greek thought to designate high-sounding words of deceivers in the art of persuading. The connotation is clearly negative, as the deceivers are working under false pretenses (Plato, *Theaetetus* 162E; Aristotle, *Nic. Ethics* 1.3 [1094B]; *PLips* 1.40.3.7; Lohse, 83).

2:5. Discipline (*taxis*) can also mean "order" and is used to designate the careful arrangement of soldiers (Xenophon, *Anabasis* 1.2.18; Plutarch, *Pyrrhus* 16). **Stability** (*stereōma*) also has military uses and can describe the fortitude of an opponent's ranks (*1 Macc.* 9.14). The words do not necessarily have a military connotation here, rather they illustrate how the Colossians' lives are characterized by good order and firmness (cf. 1 Cor. 14:40). In the Old Testament, such

> "Moses received the Law from Sinai and committed it to Joshua, and Joshua to the elders, and the elders to the Prophets; and the prophets committed it to the men of the Great Synagogue. They said three things: Be deliberate in judgment, raise up many disciples, and make a fence around the Law"
>
> *m. 'Abot.* 1.1

language is used to describe the strength and steadfastness of God (Pss. 18:2; 71:3).

2:6-7. Received Christ Jesus the Lord... firmly rooted . . . built up . . . established in your faith . . . instructed . . . overflowing with gratitude: This passage is pivotal to the book of Colossians, as here Paul reminds his readers of what they had been taught as a basis for refuting the heresy that he will now address (2:8-23). Early Christians adopted the Jewish idea of transmitting and safeguarding a tradition. Botanical language seems to also be employed here. Some Jews saw their communities as growing plants (1QH 6:15; *Pss. Sol.* 14.3; Schweizer, 124; cf. *Odes Sol.* 38.16-18).

2:8. See to it (*blepete*) also translates "beware!" (cf. Gal. 5:15; 1 Cor. 8:9; 10:12, 18). **Takes you captive** (*sulag?gein*) occurs only here in the New Testament and is used in Greek writings to refer to literal kidnapping (Heliodorus, *Aethiopica* 10.35 [307]; cf. Aristaenetus, *Epistle* 2.22). **Through philosophy** (*philosophias*) refers to a learned way of thinking, including Judaism (*4 Macc.* 5.11; Philo, *Embassy to Gaius* 156; *Change of Names* 223; Jos., *J.W.* 2.8.2 §119; *Ant.* 18.1.2 §11), but is further described by three elements. First, it is **empty deception** (*ken? apat?*). Here the expression refers to those who claim there will be no judgment on sin. Empty words are those without meaning (Exod. 5:9) and insignificant vis-à-vis the Torah (Deut. 32:47). Empty words were said to spoil good deeds and deceive one's own soul (*T. Naph.* 3.1; cf. Col. 2:4, 8; Josephus, *Ag. Ap.* 2.31 §225). It is similar to Paul's description of "empty words." See comment on Eph. 5:6. Second, it is **according to the tradition of men** (*t?n paradosin t?n anthr?p?n*). In Greek mystery cults, initiation rites communicated to the devotee a sacred tradition (*paradosis*) which was thought to convey divine revelation (Athenaeus, *The Deipnosophists* 2.40d; Plutarch, *De Iside et Osiride* 2; Plutarch, *De Demetrio* 26.1; Ditt. *Syll* 704 E 12;

Apuleius, *Metamortph.* 11.21; Lohse, 95-96). The teachings of Greek philosophers, from Plato onwards, were passed on from teacher to pupil (Plato, *Theaet.* 36, 198b; O'Brien, 110). Third, the philosophy is **according to the elementary principles of the world.** Such principles were considered low (Xenophon, *Memor.* 2.1.1; Heb. 5:12) and of a very base nature (Diogenes Laertius 7.136) or material (*4 Macc.* 12.13; *Sir.* 7.17; 19.18; Philo, *Cherubim* 127; Jos., *Ant.* 3.3.7 §183), and they may have involved speculation on the coherence of the universe (*1 Enoch* 43.1; 60.11; 69.20-25; *2 Enoch* 19.1-4; Lohse, 98; cf. *T. Sol.* 8.3; 18.2). The Colossian heresy follows the latter principles **rather than** those **according to Christ** (*kata Christon*).

2:9. Philo compared the Logos to God in a similar manner (*Dreams* 1.75). Later Jews did so with Wisdom (*b. Sota* 48b). **Fulness** (*plērōma*) was a common element in Gnostic teachings. Adherents sought "discovery of the *plērōma*, for those who await the salvation which is coming from on high" (*Gospel of Truth* 1).

2:10. He is the head over... See comment on Eph. 1:20-23. **All rule and authority.** These powers are prevalent in the Old Testament and later Jewish literature, particularly in *2 Enoch 20-22* where classes of angels are ranked in the seventh heaven (cf. *1 Enoch* 61.10; *2 Macc.* 3.24). Ancient Judaism believed God had delegated some authority over nations to angelic beings, and that this is reflected in what happens on earth (cf. Dan. 10:13, 20; Deut. 32:17) and influences various aspects of life (*Jub.* 2.2; *1 Enoch* 60.11, 12). Early Christians interpreted these "powers" primarily as angelic (*T. Adam* 4.1; cf. *2 Enoch* 20.1). Satan himself was thought to be such a "power," who inhabits the air (Eph. 2:2; *1 Enoch* 61.10). Cf. comment on 1:16; 2:10, 15; Eph. 1:20-23.

2:11. Circumcised ... without hands. Without hands is a Greek expression for something that occurs naturally without human interference

(Herodotus, *History* 2.149; Xenophon, *Anabasis* 3.5; Jos., *Ant.* 15.9.4 §324; Schweizer, 140). In the Old Testament, idols were fashioned with human hands (Lev. 26:1; Isa. 46:1; cf. Philo, *Moses* 1.303; 2.165, 168; Josephus, *Ag. Ap.* 2.22 §188-92). The notion of such inward action is common both in Stoic philosophy (Euripides, *Madness of Hercules* 1345; Apuleius, *The Golden Ass* 5.1; Cicero, *Nat. d.* 1.8.20; Seneca, *Epistle* 41.3) and Judaism (Lev. 26:41; Deut. 10:16; Jer. 4:4; esp. 1 Sam. 16:7). In Jer. 9:25, the Lord warns that in the last days he will punish those who are circumcised *only* in the flesh, indicating something internal is required as well. Later Judaism understood circumcision of the heart as an eschatological act of God and as a gift of the Holy Spirit (*Jub.* 1.23; *Odes Sol.* 11.1-3; cf. Rom. 2.29; Schweizer, 141). See comment on Eph. 2:11.

2:12. Buried with Him in baptism...raised up with Him through faith. See comment on Rom. 6:4.

2:13-15. He made you alive together with Him. This phrase is described by a series of five modifying participles in the Greek describing the means by which the Colossians are

"Rabbi Akiba...used to say: all is given against a pledge, and the net is cast over all living; the shop stands open and the shopkeeper gives credit and the account-book lies open and the hand writes and every one that wishes to borrow let him come and borrow; but the collectors go their round continually every day and exact payment of men with their consent or without their consent, for they have that on which they can rely; and the judgment is a judgment of truth..."

m. Abot. 3.17

made alive with Christ: First, **having forgiven** (*carisamenos*) is used in Eph. 4:32 of God's forgiving men, while in Col. 3:13 it is used for men forgiving one another. Second, **having canceled out** (*exaleipsas*; v. 14) **the certificate of debt** (*cheirographon*): In the ancient world, a debtor issued a certificate of indebtedness in his own hand as an acknowledgment of his outstanding debt (Polybius, 30.8.4; *Ditt. Syl.* 2.742.50; *Tobit* 5.3; 9.5; Lohse, 108). **Decrees** (*dogmata*) in Hellenistic Judaism were a way of referring to the commandments of God (3 *Macc.* 1.3; *4 Macc.* 10.2; Josephus, *Ag. Ap.* 1.7 §42; *Ant.* 15.5.3 §136; Philo, *Giants* 52; *Allegorical Interpretation* 1.54). **He has taken it out of the way** is taken from Isa. 43:25 (LXX) where God wipes away the sins of the faithful (cf. LXX Ps. 50:1; Jer. 18:23). Rabbi Akiba described God as a shopkeeper who would lend money and goods freely, but the angels will demand repayment (*m. Abot.* 3.17). In the Old Testament, God promises, "I, even I, am the one who wipes out your transgressions for My own sake; And I will not remember your sins" (Isa. 43:25). What is taken away is no longer valid (1 Cor. 5:2; 1QS 2:16; cf. 2 Thess. 2:7; Matt. 13:47). This became an early Christian confession of the forgiveness accomplished by Christ (John 1:29, 36; 1 John 3:5; 1 Peter 2:24; Ignatius, *Ephesians* 9.1; *Trallians* 11.2; *Barn.* 9.8; 12.1; Lohse, 111).

Third, **having nailed it to the cross.** The expression is found only here in the New Testament, though it is used by Josephus, and means "to nail fast to the cross." The Jewish historian reports that the Roman procurator Florus took men in Jerusalem from the rank of soldiers, who were of Jewish heritage but were dressed according to Roman rank, had them scourged before his judgment seat, and then "nailed to the cross" (*J.W.* 2.14.9 §308). It refers to the manner of execution on the cross upon which the believers' debts are essentially crucified (cf. 2 Cor. 5:21; Gal. 2:20). This may also be a play on words for the practice of attaching a crucified man's indictment on his cross to indicate to onlookers what his crime was (cf. Mark 15:26; Dunn, 166).

Fourth, **When He had disarmed** (*apekdusamenos*; v. 15). In Christian hymnic writings, God is praised for his victory over **rulers and authorities** (Phil. 2:9-11; 1 Tim. 3:16; Heb. 1:9-14; *Odes Sol.* 22.3-5; Lohse, 112). Making **public display** (*deigmatizō*) is precisely what Joseph avoided of Mary (Matt. 1:19) for the shame it would bring.

Fifth, **having triumphed** (*thiambeusas*) **over them through Him.** When a Roman general defeated an enemy, he would lead a triumphal procession (*thriambeuō*) through the "triumphal gate" (Latin *Porta Triumphalis*) and then the streets of Rome, where he would flaunt the prisoners and spoils of war before the Roman citizens (Plutarch, *Aemilius Paulus* 32-34). The idea that the Resurrected One should lead the prisoners with him was already present in Ps. 68:19. See comment on Eph. 4:8.

2:16. In the Old Testament **food** laws, there were very few restrictions on **drink** (Lev. 10:9; 11:34, 36; Num. 6:3), so Paul may not be speaking of these laws. Later Judaism, and apparently the Colossian heretics, observed more strict dietary laws as important aspects of religious dedication (Philo, *Contemplative Life* 73; *T. Reub.* 1.10; *Let. Aris.* 142; cf. Luke 1:15; 7:33). **Festival or a new moon or a Sabbath day.** Paul enumerates three terms that often occur in the Old Testament in this combination and describe special days dedicated to God (Hos. 2:13; Ezek. 45:17; 1 Chron. 23:31; 2 Chron. 2:3; 31:3; cf. *Jub.* 1.14; *t. Ber.* 3.11; Justin, *Dial.* 8.4; Lohse, 115). The goddess Selene, along with Artemis and Hekate, was worshiped at Colossae. Her name in Greek is the word for moon.

2:17. Mere shadow (*skia*) **of what is to come.** Greek philosophy as far back as Plato saw a contrast between outer appearance and real

The Worship of Angels

In Col. 2:18 Paul speaks of the "worship of angels." Commentators sometimes think the apostle is criticizing those who worship or venerate angels. This is possible, but it seems strange that the apostle does not condemn such a heresy more vigorously, if that is what was in view. It may be that Paul was speaking of worshiping God in the way that the angels worship God. Thus, "worship of angels" does not mean worshiping the angels (as object), but worshiping (God) the way the angels do (as subject).

This interpretation may well be correct, for it helps make better sense of the actual language of Col. 2:18, which literally reads:

"Do not let anyone defraud you, having a desire for humility and worship of angels, which he has seen while entering (heaven), vainly puffed up by the mind of his flesh."

In other words, the apostle is complaining of those who are legalistic and self-right-eous, who believe that they experience heavenly visions, perhaps have even entered heaven (cf. 2 Cor. 12:2-4), where they have witnessed angels worshiping God. Having had this exalted experience, they judge other believers, robbing them of their joy in the Lord, insisting that they observe certain holidays, food laws, and aspects of humility.

---

substance (*Republic* 514b-518b; O'Brien, 139). For Philo the **shadow** (*skia*) had the same relation to the body as the name to the object, the copy to the original (*Decal.* 92; *Migr. Abr.* 12; *Conf. Tongues* 190; *Who is the Heir?* 72; *Moses* 2.74; Schweizer, 156; cf. Ps. 39:13; 1 Chron. 29:15; *Gen. Rab.* 96.2 [on Gen. 47:29]). According to Josephus, Archelaus was acting as king before he was given official authority to do so, which Josephus calls a shadow (*skian*) of a reign (*J.W.* 2.2.5 §28).

2:18 Self-abasement . . . taking his stand on visions he has seen. Humility was required in the Hellenistic world to receive visions (Hermas, *Vision* 3, 10, 6; *Similitudes* 5, 3, 7; Philo, *Dreams* 1.33-37; *Moses* 2.67-70; *QE* 2.39), and it seems that the Colossian heretics were **delighting** in ascetic practices as a prelude to the reception of heavenly visions (O'Brien, 142). Such **visions** were central to the mystery religions of Asia Minor. Pausanias (first century A.D.) claims that deities near the Meander River (see Introduction) offered visions to all who wanted to enter their inner sanctuaries in ritual initiation (*Descr.* 32.13). Such a vision is illustrated in the "Mithras Liturgy." Notice the extensive **vision** language. **The worship of the angels:** It is difficult to discern in the Greek whether **of angels** refers to angels *doing wor-*

The "Mithras Liturgy"

"You will see yourself being lifted up and ascending to the height, so that you seem to be in midair . . . you will see all immortal things. For in that day and hour you will see the divine order of the skies: the presiding gods rising into heaven, and others setting. Now the course of the visible gods will appear through the disk of god. . . . And you will see the gods staring intently at you and rushing at you . . . but rather going about in their own order of affairs."

ship or angels *being worshiped,* though it seems likely that the angels are being worshiped (v. 23; cf. *Asc. Isa.* 7.21).

2:19. Head ... body. Paul is borrowing language from ancient physiology found in several papyri (*POxy* 2.282.6-8; *POxy* 6.905.6; *PRainer* 1.27.12; *PLeid* 2.27; Lohse, 122). See comment on Eph. 1:20-23; 4:15-16; 5:23.

2:21. "Do not handle, do not taste, do not touch!" Here Paul seems to be quoting some of the ascetic prohibitions exhorted by the

Colossian heretics. They may have to do with restrictions regarding contact with objects that had been declared unclean or with forbidden foods (Lohse, 123). The expression may be borrowed from Judaism conveying the severity of the command (cf. Exod. 19:12 *m. Tam.* 1.4).

2:22. Teachings of men: This phrase is borrowed almost exactly from LXX Isa. 29:13 where the Lord chastises his people, "Because this people draw near with their words And honor Me with their lip service, But they remove their hearts far from Me, And their rev-

"Now so great was the prudence and wisdom which God granted Solomon that he surpassed the ancients, and even the Egyptians, who are said to excel all men in understanding, were not only, when compared with him, a little inferior but proved to fall far short of the king of sagacity. ... He also composed a thousand and five books of odes and songs, and three thousand books of parables and similitudes, for he spoke a parable about every kind of tree from the hyssop to the cedar and in like manner about birds and all kinds of terrestrial creatures and those that swim and those that fly. There was no form of nature with which he was not acquainted or which he passed over without examining, but he studied them all philosophically and revealed the most complete knowledge of their several properties. And God granted him knowledge of the art used against demons for the benefit and healing of men. He also composed incantations by which illnesses are relieved, and left behind forms of exorcisms with which those possessed by demons drive them out, never to return. And this kind of cure is of very great power among us to this day, for I have seen a certain Eleazar, a countryman of mine, in the presence of Vespasian, his sons, tribunes and a number of other soldiers, free men possessed by demons, and this was the manner of the cure: he put to the nose of the possessed man a ring which had under its seal one of the roots prescribed by Solomon, and then, as the man smelled it, drew out the demon through his nostrils, and, when the man at once fell down, adjured the demon never to come back into him, speaking Solomon's name and reciting the incantations which he had composed. Then, wishing to convince the bystanders and prove to them that he had this power, Eleazar placed a cup or foot-basin full of water a little way off and commanded the demon, as it went out of the man, to overturn it and make known to the spectators that he had left the man. And when this was done, the understanding and wisdom of Solomon where clearly revealed, on account of which we have been induced to speak of these things, in order that all men may know the greatness of his nature and how God favored him, and that no one under the sun may be ignorant of the king's surpassing virtue of every kind."

Josephus, *Ant.* 8.2.5 §§ 41-49 LCL

erence for Me consists of tradition learned by rote" (NASB; NIV follows the Greek and Hebrew more clearly: "taught by men").

2:23. Fleshly indulgence: The Colossian proponents' legalistic way of life leads only to satisfaction of the flesh. **Indulgence** (*pl?son?*) can be used for both good senses of fulfillment (Exod. 16:3, 8; Lev. 25:19; 26:5; Ps. 77:25; Hag. 1:6), and, as here, to denote the excesses that lead to sin and apostasy from the Lord (Ezek. 39:19; Hos. 13:6; O'Brien, 155; cf. Philo, *Contemplative Life* 35.37). Josephus refers to a tradition that wisdom, dating from Solomon, contained abilities to restrain evil spirits (*Ant.* 8.2.5 §§ 41-49).

II. 3:1–4:18. ETHICAL IMPLICATIONS OF CHRIST'S SUPREMACY

A. 3:1-4. Theological Basis for the Christian Life

3:1. If then you have been raised up with Christ, keep seeking the things above. The notion of heaven as an "upper world" was common in apocalyptic and Hellenistic Judaism (*1 Enoch* 17.2; 71.1; *Jub.* 2.2, 11, 30; *Sirach* 51.9; Philo, *Special Laws* 1.207; cf. Gen. 11:5; Exod. 19:20; Ps. 14:2; Schweizer, 173). Rabbis discussed good deeds as gathering treasures "for above" (*b. Hag.* 2.1). **Where Christ is, seated at the right hand of God.** Paul looks to Ps. 110:1 (cf. Eph. 1:20), which was likely an enthronement psalm for a king, and uses a well-attested Ancient Near Eastern expression of placing someone at the **right hand**. This was seen as bestowing the person with power, honor, and the right to act on behalf of the king. God's right hand is portrayed as a place of power (Exod. 15:6; Ps. 89:13; Isa. 48:13), victory (Pss. 20:6; 44:3; 48:10; Isa. 41:10), and favor (Ps. 80:18; Jer. 22:14). Here Jesus is said to be **seated**, an expression denoting the completion of an assigned task (cf. Heb.

1:3; 8:1; 10:12; 12:2; Rev. 3:21; 4:3; 5:1, 7; *T. Job* 36.3; *2 Bar.* 83.4).

3:2. Set your mind on the things above, not on the things that are on earth. Paul presumes the believer himself remains on earth. Gnostics believed that the true self of man ascends into the heavenly world, lays aside evil in its ascent through the spheres, and thus attains its own proper destination (Lohse, 133).

3:4. Christ, who is our life. Describing Christ as being life is an early Christian tradition seemingly developed by Paul (Phil. 1:21; cf. 1 John 5:12) and adopted particularly by Ignatius, who describes Christ as "our true life" (*Ephesians* 7.2; *Smyrneans* 4.1), our "everlasting life" (*Magnesians* 1.2), and "our inseparable life (*Ephesians* 3.2). . . . **Is revealed, then you also will be revealed with Him in glory:** Paul is here referring to the return of Christ.

B. 3:5-17. The Old and New Life

3:5. Consider the members of your earthly body as dead to immorality. This statement is similar to a Jewish proselyte catechism taken over by the church which lists ethical qualifications to be members of a community (cf. 1QS 5:3, 4; 1QS 2:24; 4:3, 4; 5:25) and which finds roots in the Old Testament (Deut. 30:15, 19; cf. Jer. 21:8; Ezek. 18:5-9, 15-17). **Immorality** (*porneia*) often denotes fornication but can generally refer to any sexual immorality (Gen. 34:31; 38:15; Lev. 19:29; Deut. 22:21; *m.'Abot.* 2.8; *T. Rub.* 1.6; *T. Judah* 13.6; *T. Benj.* 9.1). **Impurity** (*akatharsia*), though it can refer to ceremonial uncleanness (Num. 19:13; cf. Matt. 23:27), likewise denotes sexually immoral conduct. **Passion** (*pathos*) was used by the Stoics to describe the person who allowed himself to be dominated by his emotions and, therefore, could not attain tranquility (O'Brien, 182). **Desire** (*epithumia*) simply refers to a longing which can be positive (1 Thess. 2:17; Phil. 1:23) but which Paul here describes as **evil** (*kakōn*).

Greed (*pleonexia*) literally means, "a desire to have more," and is normally associated with an insatiable desire to have material things, giving birth to dishonesty and violence (Jer. 22:17; Ezek. 22:27; Hab. 2:9). Naturally, such greed was soundly condemned in Judaism (Philo, *Special Laws* 1.23-27; 1QpHab 6:1; 8:11, 12; 1QS 10:19; 11:12). **Which amounts to idolatry.** Jewish traditions say that Judah, on his deathbed, said, "My children, love of money leads to idolatry, because once they are led astray by money, they designate as gods those who are not gods. It makes anyone who has it go out of his mind" (*T. Jud.* 19.1 OTP). Polycarp similarly said, "If a man does not avoid love of money, he will be polluted by idolatry, and will be judged as one of the Gentiles, who are ignorant of the Lord's judgment" (*Phil.* 2.17). See comment on Matt. 6:24 §42.

3:6. For it is on account of these things that the wrath of God will come. Jews commonly expected a day of **wrath**, commonly called "the day of the Lord" (Zeph. 1:14-15).

3:8-11. But now you also, put them all aside. This language is similar to that used for taking off a garment (Job 29:14; Pss. 35:26; 109:29; 132:9; *2 Macc.* 8.35; Jos. *Ant.* 8.11.1 §266). Virtues and vices were often described in this way (Josephus, *Ant.* 13.1.4 §20; Plato, *Republic* 5.6 [457A]). **Anger, wrath, malice, slander:** Slander (*blasphēmia*) is the origin of the English "blasphemy." It usually referred to speaking in opposition to God by speaking against his representative (2 Kings 6:22; 19:4; Isa. 52:5; Ezek. 35:12, 13; *2 Macc.* 8.4; 9.28; 10.4, 34; O'Brien 187). **There is no distinction between Greek and Jew, circumcised and uncircumcised, barbarian** (v. 11)**:** For the Greeks or Romans, a barbarian was anyone not part of their own culture (Josephus, *Ag. Ap.* 2.38 §269). **Scythians** were northern people from along the northern coast of the Black Sea, in the modern Ukraine. They were regarded by Greeks as violent, une-

ducated, and uncivilized. Josephus says they, "delight in murdering people and are little better than wild beasts" (*Ag. Ap.* 2.38 §269 LCL).

3:12. Chosen of God. In the Old Testament, Israel saw itself as God's chosen people (Deut. 4:37; 7:7; Ps. 33:12), as did the sectarians at Qumran (1QpHab 10:13; 1QH 14:15; 4QpPs37 2:5; Lohse, 146). Christians likewise saw themselves as "a chosen race, a royal priesthood, a holy nation, a people for God's own possession" (1 Peter 2:9). **Compassion** (*splagxhna*) literally means "inward parts," as ancients often saw these as the seat of emotions. **Compassion** is an attribute most commonly associated with God in his dealings with his people (Pss. 24:6; 50:1; 102:4; 144; 9; cf. Exod. 34:6; 2 Chron. 30:9; cf. *T. Levi* 4.4; *T. Zeb* 8.2; *T. Naph.* 4.5; *T. Zeb* 8.1; O'Brien, 198-99). **Kindness** again is an attribute of God that he demonstrates in his acts in history (Pss. 25:7; 31:19; 65:11; etc.) and is used by the prophets to illustrate God's kindness in the face of his people's sin (Jer. 33:11; O'Brien, 199). At Qumran, members of the community were expected to show such kindness to one another as God had shown them (1QH 7:30; 10:16; 11:6, 9, 31; 12:21; 13:16; 1QS 4:3; cf. Col. 3:13). **Humility** occurs in a similar form in the Old Testament with respect to God bringing down the proud and lifting up the humble (cf. Amos 2:6, 7; Isa. 2:9; Job 5:11; Prov. 3:34; Pss. 10:17, 18; 25:18, etc.). **Gentleness** was a term of humility, particularly of the oppressed poor whom God will vindicate (cf. Isa. 32:7; Ps. 37:14; Job 24:4) and who find help from Yahweh alone (Ps. 40:7; Zeph. 2:3; 3:12; Isa. 41:17). It is seemingly used as a title of honor for the Messiah (Zech. 9:9) and is an identifying characteristic of Jesus' behavior toward others (Matt. 11:29; 21:5; O'Brien 201). **Patience** (*makrothumia*) means "long-suffering."

3:14. And beyond all these things put on love, which is the perfect bond of unity. Plutarch calls on a certain Numa to "be a bond of goodwill and friendship" (*Numa* 63e; Lohse, 149).

3:15. And let the peace of Christ rule in your hearts. Rule (*brabeuein*) can mean "to rule" or "to hold sway." It can be used as a judicial term where the bearer has an authoritative say in a decision (Philo, *Who is the Heir?* 95, *Moses* 1.163; *Wisd.* 10.12; *PMasp* 2.67151.21-23; Lohse, 149-50). **Heart** in the Old Testament was not a personal sphere of emotions but the center of one's personality and source of the will, emotion, thought, and affections (O'Brien, 204). **Thankful** (*eucharistoi*) is the root of our English word for Eucharist, the sacrament of the Lord's Supper.

3:16. Let the word of Christ richly dwell within you. As Wisdom found a dwelling place in Israel (*Sir.* 24.8) and the Spirit of God dwells in believers (1 Cor. 3:16; Rom. 8:9, 11), so the **word of Christ** should **dwell within** the Colossians (Lohse, 150). **Word of Christ** (*ho logos tou theou*) best refers to words concerning Christ rather than the words which Christ himself spoke. **With all wisdom teaching and admonishing.** See comment on 1:28. **Psalms**

(*psalmos*) normally refers to the Psalms of the Old Testament (Luke 20:42; 22:44; Acts 1:20; 13:33), which were surely part of Christian liturgy from an early date. **Hymns** (*hymnos*)—a unique term—are likewise worshipful songs (Cf. Matt. 26:30; Mark 14:26; Acts 16:25; Heb. 2:12). It is a term for an ode in praise of a deity (Plato, *Laws* 700b; Aristotle, *Poetics* $1448^{b}27$; Hesiod, *Works and Days* 657). **Spiritual songs** (*ōdais pneumatikais*) were perhaps songs employed in heavenly worship (Rev. 5:9; 14:3; 15:3). Most likely Paul sees these terms as synonymous, with little or no distinction between them (Jos., *Ant.* 12.7.8 §323 cf. *Ant.* 7.12.3 §305). Nothing is said of musical style, but, rather, that the object and content of the worship be **with your heart to the Lord.** *Sibylline Oracles* (8.496-500) says, "But rejoicing with holy minds and glad spirit, abundant love and hands that bring good gifts with gracious psalms and songs appropriate to God, we are bidden to sing your praises as imperishable and pure from all deceit, God, wise begetter of all" (OTP). See comment on Eph. 5:21.

"Parents have not only been given the right of exercising authority over their children, but the power of a master ... For parents pay out a sum many times the value of a slave on their children. They also invest nurses, tutors and teachers, in addition to the cost of their clothes, food and care in sickness and health from their earliest years until they are full grown.

Given all these considerations, children who honor their parents do nothing deserving of praise since even one of the items mentioned is in itself quite a sufficient call to show deep respect. And on the contrary, they deserve blame, a sharp reprimand, and extreme punishment who do not respect them as seniors nor listen to them as instructors nor feel the duty of repaying them as benefactors nor obey them as rulers nor fear them as masters.

Therefore, honor your father and mother next to God, he [Moses] says [Exod. 20:12]. ... For parents have little thought for their own personal interests and find their fulfillment and happiness in the high excellence of their children, and to gain this the children will be willing to listen to their instructions and to obey them in everything that is just and profitable; for the true father will give no instruction to his son that is foreign to virtue."

Philo, *Special Laws* 2.233-36 LCL

C. 3:18–4:1. Christian Home Life

3:18–4:1. Paul's teaching on the Christian household is marked by mutual selflessness and Christlikeness for all involved. All relationships here, **wives, husbands, children, parents, fathers, slaves, masters,** are most clearly illustrated as they reflect Christ and his Church. Philo illustrated the high regard one should hold for parents (*Special Laws* 2.233-36). Though apparently somewhat unique among his contemporaries, Seneca advocated the just treatment of slaves: "Associate with your slave on kindly, even on affable terms; let him talk with you, plan with you, live with you ... (and) value them according to their character" (*Epistle* 47.13, 15 LCL; cf. 47.1-21). Paul more fully explains these relationships in Ephesians. See comment on Eph. 5:22–6:9.

D. 4:2-6. Christian Lifestyle

4:2. Devote yourselves to prayer. See comment on Eph. 3:14.

4:3. Imprisoned (*dedemai*) can also mean "in chains." Such chains were an integral part of how Paul understood his ministry (cf. Phil. 1:7, 13-14, 17; Col. 4:18; 2 Tim. 1:16; Phile. 10, 13). See introduction to the Prison Epistles.

4:5. Making the most of the opportunity. See comment on Eph. 5:16.

4:6. Seasoned ... with salt. Salt is known for its preserving qualities. "Torah is like salt" is a common comparison found among the rabbis (O'Brien, 243). See comment on Matt. 5:13 §30.

E. 4:7-18. Conclusion

4:7. Tychicus is expected to set out for Colossae, and is mentioned in Acts 20:4 as one of the Asians who accompanied Paul on his journey to Jerusalem with the collection for that church. He is elsewhere named as a messenger of Paul (2 Tim. 4:2; Titus 3:12) and described as Paul's

beloved brother (*agapētos adelphos*), as were other members of the community (1:2). He was also a **faithful servant** (*pistos diakonos*), and, though **servant** comes from *diakonos*, it is not here meant as a particular office in the church but is used of anyone who discharges a specific ministry (Lohse, 171). **Fellow bond-servant in the Lord.** See comment on 1:8. **Will bring you information:** Those who carried letters also provided other information on the welfare of the sender (*PLond* 42).

4:9. Onesimus was apparently a common slave name (Galen, *De optima deoctrina liber* 1; Lohse, 171). This **Onesimus** is Philemon's fugitive slave (see Phile. 10) who met Paul, became a Christian, and ministered to Paul during his imprisonment. Colossae was Onesimus's hometown. The early church knew of a bishop named Onesimus (Ignatius, *Ephesians* 1.3; 2.1; 6.2), though it is uncertain whether Paul refers to the same man.

4:10. Aristarchus appears in Acts as a native of Thessalonica and traveling companion of Paul (Acts 19:29; 20:40). His conversion is the result of Paul's ministry in his native city (Acts 17:1-9), and he was with the apostle during the dangerous riot at Ephesus (Acts 19:29). He served as one of the two delegates from Thessalonica (Acts 20:4), who accompanied Paul and Luke from Caesarea perhaps all the way to Rome (Acts 27:2). **My fellow prisoner** suggests that Aristarchus was imprisoned with Paul, possibly during his Ephesian ministry. However, the phrase **my fellow prisoner** (*ho sunaichmalōtos mou*) literally means "my fellow-prisoner of war," in which case Paul could be referring to Aristarchus as a fellow prisoner of Christ in the sense that he sees the Christian life as spiritual warfare (see comments on Eph. 6:10-20). **Barnabas's cousin Mark** refers to John Mark, who was from Jerusalem (Acts 12:12, 25) and who traveled with Paul and Barnabas to Cyprus on the first missionary journey

(O'Brien, 250). Mark abandoned the effort at Perga and returned to Jerusalem (Acts 13:13), which was the source of sharp disagreement between Barnabas and Paul. On the next journey, Barnabas took his cousin back to Cyprus while Paul went with Silas (Acts 15:36-41). Under the careful guidance of Barnabas, Mark redeemed his reputation so that here he and the apostle to the Gentiles are again on friendly terms, for Mark is with Paul in his imprisonment (cf. Phile. 24; 2 Tim. 4:11; O'Brien, 250). Mark also appears as a companion of Peter (1 Peter 5:13), a tradition which has very strong support in early church history (Eusebius, *Ecclesiastical History* 3.39).

4:11. Jesus who is called Justus. Little is known about this man except that he may be a Jewish Christian who was with Paul (cf. Phile. 23). **Jesus** is the Greek form of Joshua. See comment on Matt. 1:21 §8. **Jesus** was a common name among Jews through the second century A.D., and **Justus** was common among Jews and proselytes (O'Brien, 251), and, as with many Jews in Greco-Roman culture, he took a second Hellenistic Roman name.

4:13. Laodicea and Hierapolis. It seems that Epaphras was the evangelist of all three congregations. Hierapolis lay about twelve miles northwest of Colossae and six miles north of Laodicea, along the road from Laodicea to Philadelphia. The ancient church figure Papias was bishop of that city, and tradition suggests that Philip and his daughters settled there prior to A.D. 70 (Dunn, 282). Laodicea was founded by Antiochus II in the middle of the third century B.C. and is the locus of one of the churches to which one of the seven letters of Revelation was written (Rev. 3:14-22; O'Brien, 255). It was a financial, medical, and administrative center and, though it suffered severe earthquakes in A.D. 17 and 60, was wealthy enough to reestablish itself without the benefit of government funding (Dunn, 282).

4:14. Only here is **Luke** called **the beloved physician** (*ho iatros ho agapētos*), which has led to the speculation that Luke was Paul's doctor during his imprisonment (O'Brien, 256). Little is known of **Demas**. He is mentioned only here, Phile. 24, and 2 Tim. 4:10, where Paul describes him as "in love with this present world" and as having deserted him. This suggests that some other interest took Demas to Thessalonica at a time when the apostle would have valued his continued presence (O'Brien, 256).

4:15. Nympha and the church that is in her house. House churches were common in Early Christianity. On occasion, a whole congregation was small enough to meet in a single member's home. Churches did not begin to own property perhaps until well into the third century (O'Brien, 256). In addition to the church that met in Nympha's home, we know that Philemon also housed a church in Colossae (Phile. 2).

4:16. Read my letter that is coming from Laodicea. See "Introduction" to Ephesians. Marcion confused this letter of Paul to the Laodiceans with that to the Ephesians (see Introduction to Ephesians). The content and fate of this letter is much debated, though all arguments are necessarily from silence, as there is no extant evidence of it (cf. 2 Bar. 86.1).

4:17. Archippus, called Paul's "fellow soldier" (Phile. 2), is a member of Philemon's household, and perhaps the latter's son (cf. Phil. 2:26).

4:18. I, Paul, write this greeting with my own hand. Remember my imprisonment. It seems that the letter itself was dictated by Paul but written by someone else, probably Timothy. Timothy would then serve as Paul's *amanuensis*, or secretary (see Introduction to the Prison Epistles). Writing in his own hand may have been a distinguishing mark to oppose forgery (2 Thess. 2:2), provide personal certification (Phile. 19), or to add emphasis (Gal. 6:11).

Introduction to 1 and 2 Thessalonians

Daniel M. Gurtner

Though having the distinction of being two of the earliest New Testament writings and providing some of the most explicit teachings on eschatology, the two epistles to the Thessalonians are often neglected in favor of the more developed theological treatises of Romans or Galatians.

Authorship. Both letters claim to have been written by Paul, and very few have challenged his authorship. Their vocabulary, style, and content are typical of Paul. Suggestions that 1 Thessalonians was written under Paul's name at a later date are confronted by its very early date (see below). Some scholars argue that while Luke claims that Paul spoke in the synagogue for three Sabbaths (Acts 17:2), his portrayal of Paul working at his trade in the city (1 Thess. 2:7-9) requires a longer period of time. Yet neither Acts nor Paul's letters give any precise account of the duration of the apostle's stay in Thessalonica.

More questions are raised, however, regarding the authorship of 2 Thessalonians. It has been suggested that the teachings of the end times (eschatology, from the Greek *eschatos* "last") in 2 Thessalonians are incompatible both with those of 1 Thessalonians and the other Pauline letters. In the latter, Christ's return is thought to take place suddenly, whereas in the former it is to be preceded by signs, including the appearance of the "man of lawlessness." The notion that such apocalypses require consistency, however, is a modern one not found in the first century, where Christians and Jews often combine the thoughts of the imminence of the end and of preparatory signs (CMM 345).

Similarly, readers of these epistles should not be surprised by the stark contrast in tone between them. The first is often seen as warm, colorful, and cordial whereas the second has elements that come across as cold and harsh. One must remember that the purpose and occasion of a letter largely determines its content and tone (see discussion below). Moreover, some scholars have seen the occasional precise repetition of phrases between the first and second epistles as evidence that Paul, who would have been too astute to repeat himself, was being deliberately copied. The similarities, however, are more easily attributable to a single author who, though using identical words and phrases, clearly uses them in differing contexts and for differing purposes. Thus, it seems best to accept both letters, as the majority of scholars do, as genuinely Pauline.

Church at Thessalonica. As a key city in the province of Macedonia and located along the Egnatian Way, Thessalonica was the home of a strategically important church for the ministry of Paul. That the city was the locus of a colony of Jews is evident from the existence of the synagogue that Paul visited, as was his custom on his trips to various cities (Acts 17:1). Having just left prison in Philippi, the apostle set out in the company of Silas and Timothy on his second missionary journey. Along with a number of Jews (Acts 17:4), the new church at Thessalonica was apparently comprised mostly of idol-worshipers won from heathenism (1 Thess. 1:9). Though the Old Testament is never specifically cited in either letter, it is often conjectured that there is some influence from a prevalent Jewish apocalyptic movement in the Thessalonian church, which may be in view in 1 Thessalonians 2:14-16. That this church was steeped in an erroneous eschatological orientation has been already noted and is clear throughout both epistles (1 Thess. 4:13-5:11; 2 Thess. 2:1-12). Such enthusiasm may have led to charges of political subversion (Acts 17:6-7). The church seems to have been comprised of both wealthy people, such as Jason and the "leading women" (Acts 17:4-5), and commoners from the working class (2 Thess. 3:11).

Provenance. Both letters appear to have been written from Greece, perhaps Athens or Corinth. Paul founded the church in Thessalonica and fled during a riot (Acts 17:1-9), then similarly left Berea for Athens (Acts 17:10-15). In Athens, his ministry bore little fruit (Acts 17:10-15), so he went to Corinth (Acts 18:1). While there, Silas and Timothy came to him (Acts 18:5) with good news regarding the church in Thessalonica. This seems to fit Paul's statement in 1 Thessalonians (3:6) that Timothy had just then arrived from them. It is possible that this meeting occurred in Athens, for Paul had also sent for them while there (Acts 17:15). If this is the case, then Paul must have sent them back because when the apostle was in Corinth they came to him from Macedonia (Acts 18:5; CMM 347). It seems more likely, however, that the Corinthian situation was the setting, as its later occasion allows for the development of the Thessalonians' situation (see below) as well as for their faith to become known "everywhere" (1 Thess. 1:8). The close relationship between the first and second epistles suggests they both were written from the same place.

Date. If the above scenario for a Corinthian origin is adopted, it is an integral factor for dating the epistles. Moreover, the lack of titles for church officials such as deacons, presbyters, etc., in favor of more general expressions (cf. 1 Thess. 5:12 "those . . . who are over you in the Lord"), suggests they had not yet developed, thus lending to the antiquity of the Thessalonian letters. Also, 1 Thess. 4:13-18 seems to address the errant expectation that the return of Christ would occur within Paul's lifetime. As he probably died ca. A.D. 63, the letter must date prior to that event.

An inscription found in Corinth states that the proconsul Gallio, before whom Paul was brought in Corinth (Acts 18:12), arrived in that city in the early summer of A.D. 51. Since the apostle ministered in Corinth before Gallio's arrival, his first letter probably dates from early in A.D. 50. The second was written some months after that. This makes the Thessalonian epistles the earliest extant Christian documents, with the possible exception of Galatians (see Introduction to Galatians).

Relation Between 1 and 2 Thessalonians. As outlined above, these two letters seem to be very early and portray a similar situation in the church to which they were written. So why was there a need for two letters, rather than one? Generally, both letters are quite similar, with the characteristic Pauline thanksgivings for his readers' faith. The primary unique feature is the eschatological section in 2 Thess. 2:1-12, after which appears a reminder of the missionaries' example and warning against idleness, found also in 1 Thess. 2:9-12. This accounts for the common conjecture that the two were written within a brief interval, one after the other (Bruce, xl). Some scholars have suggested that 2 Thessalonians is a replacement for the first, arguing that the new section (2 Thess. 2:1-12) adds that the coming of Christ would be preceded by the coming of the "man of lawlessness." Others have suggested that Paul has changed his opinion regarding the end times and writes 2 Thessalonians to offer a mediating view between his previous position and that of the church to which he writes. Still others suggest the letters were sent to two distinct groups within the church at Thessalonica, one Jewish and the other Gentile.

Some have suggested that 2 Thessalonians was written first, which seems possible since the traditional placement of the Pauline letters in the New Testament is based on length, not date (Bruce, xli). However, while 2 Thessalonians (2:15) seems to make reference to a previous letter (presumably 1 Thessalonians), 1 Thessalonians has no such allusion. Moreover, the distinctive eschatological teachings are best understood if the epistles are viewed in the traditional order. The first says that Christ will come when least expected (1 Thess. 5:2), which some may have taken to conclude that it was so imminent that there was no point going on with daily routines of work. 2 Thessalonians (2:1-12) seems to provide a corrective to the apparent over-realized eschatology of the Thessalonian church perhaps partially due to a misunderstanding of the first letter. Yes, Christ's return is imminent, but there is a significant enough delay and degree of uncertainty of its time that warrants continued, day-to-day living and work (2 Thess. 3:10).

Occasion and Purpose. As noted above, Timothy had just come from Thessalonica with good news about the church. Paul's use of "now about" (1 Thess. 4:9, 13; 5:1) may suggest he is replying to a letter which the Thessalonians wrote to him, as he does elsewhere (1 Cor. 7:1, 25; 8:1). Apparently, Jewish opponents were slandering Paul, accusing him of fabricating the gospel as a means of financial gain. The apostle thus spends a large portion of the first three chapters rebutting these and other charges. Practically, Paul charges the Thessalonians to avoid pagan sexual standards

(4:3-8). Some seem to have believed that Christ would return in their lifetimes and thus no longer saw the need to work (4:11-12). Moreover, when members of the church died, the survivors were afraid the deceased would miss the end times. Paul wrote to correct these misconceptions (4:13-18) and to teach them further regarding the end times (5:1-11). The authority of leaders may have been questioned (5:12-13) and some teaching on spiritual gifts required clarification (5:19-20; CMM 352).

2 Thessalonians, naturally, addresses very much the same situation. Paul here reinforces what he wrote in 1 Thessalonians, and the relative lack of self-defense in the letter may suggest his opponents were quieted. Idleness was still a problem (2 Thess. 3:6-13), and, as explained above, clarity on the return of Christ was needed (2 Thess. 2:1-12).

Contribution of 1 and 2 Thessalonians. Though providing numerous insights into the faith at its early stages, the most important contributions made by these letters relate to eschatology. We learn that when Christ returns believers will be the first to rise from the dead, then the living will be caught up with him in the air (1 Thess. 4:16-17). Toward the end of every chapter in 1 Thessalonians there is a reference to some aspect of the second coming (CMM 355). Despite providing the most explicit discussion of the so-called rapture in the New Testament, Paul discourages speculation about its date. Instead, he indicates that it will come unexpectedly (1 Thess. 5:1-2), emphasizing "that whether we are awake or asleep, we may live together with Him" (1 Thess. 5:10). As noted above, 2 Thessalonians repeats and develops themes from 1 Thessalonians. Believers should not be alarmed by speculations regarding the coming of Christ (2 Thess. 2:2), but rather, they should be assured that certain events, particularly the appearance of the "man of lawlessness" must come first (2 Thess. 2:3). Second Thessalonians, in particular, is steeped in Old Testament allusions and teachings about the coming Day of Judgment.

OUTLINE OF
1 THESSALONIANS

I. Greeting (1:1)
II. Prayer of Thanksgiving (1:2-4)
III. The Gospel and the Thessalonians
   (1:5–2:16)
IV. Paul and the Thessalonians (2:17–3:13)
V. Exhortations to Christian Living
(4:1-12)
VI. Problems Related to the Return of Christ
   (4:13–5:11)
VII. General Exhortations and Farewell
   (5:12-28)

OUTLINE OF
2 THESSALONIANS

I. Greeting (1:1-2)
II. Thanksgiving and Prayer (1:3-12)
III. The Day of the Lord (2:1-12)
IV. Thanksgiving and Prayer (3:1-5)
V. Godly Discipline (3:6-15)
VI. Conclusion (3:16-18)

RESOURCES

Best, Ernest, *The First and Second Epistles to the Thessalonians*. BNTC. London: Adam & Charles Black, 1972.

Bruce, F. F., *1 & 2 Thessalonians*. WBC 45. Waco, Tex.: Word Books, 1982.

Carson, D. A., Douglas J. Moo, and Leon Morris. *An Introduction to the New Testament*. Grand Rapids: Zondervan, 1992. (=CMM)

Jewett, Robert, *The Thessalonian Correspondence*. Philadelphia: Fortress Press, 1986.

Morris, Leon, *The First and Second Epistles to the Thessalonians*. NICNT. Grand Rapids: Eerdmans, 1959.

Wanamaker, Charles A., *The Epistles to the Thessalonians*. NIGTC. Grand Rapids: Eerdmans, 1990.

1 Thessalonians

Daniel M. Gurtner

I. 1:1. GREETING

1:1. Silvanus is mentioned in 2 Cor. 1:19 where he is said to have shared in the evangelistic activity of Paul and Timothy at Corinth. Though unclear whether he is the Silvanus of 1 Peter 5:12, Silvanus, also called Silas, this man was with his two colleagues in the evangelization of Thessalonica (Acts 17:1-9) and Corinth (Acts 18:5). He, along with Judas Barsabbas, was a member of the Jerusalem church charged with conveying the letter containing the apostolic decree (Acts 15:22, 27, 32). He accompanied Paul on his missionary journey through Asia Minor to Macedonia, where he was involved with evangelizing the cities of Philippi, Thessalonica, and Berea. It seems that Silvanus was, like Paul, a Roman citizen (Acts 16:37).

Timothy was a trusted colleague of Paul's who was instrumental in the churches in Thessalonica (3:2, 6), Corinth (1 Cor. 4:17; 16:10), and Philippi (Phil. 2:19). He was a native of a South Galatian city, perhaps Lystra. His mother was a Jew and his father a Greek. He was converted during Paul and Barnabas' first trip to that region, was circumcised, and taken along with Paul as a junior colleague. Timothy accompanied Paul and Silas to Macedonia (Acts 16:1-10; 17:14, 15) and later rejoined Paul in Corinth (Acts 18:5; Bruce, 6). See comment on Phil. 1:1.

Church (*ekklēsia*) **of the Thessalonians:** This is an unusual form, since typically the apostle writes "to the saints at" a particular city. The city **of the Thessalonians,** Thessalonica, was founded ca. 315 B.C. by Cassander, a former general of Alexander the Great. It was located at the head of the Thermaic Gulf (now the Gulf of Salonika), which contributed to its important role as a military and commercial port. It was made capital of one of the four administrative districts into which Macedonia was divided in 168 B.C. and became capital of the entire province when Macedonia was unified in 146 B.C. Thessalonica became a free city in 42 B.C., in return for its support of Antony and Octavian, for which it was given a degree of local autonomy, including the right to mint coins. It was also given freedom from military occupation and granted certain tax concessions. This favor also meant it would not be made a Roman colony, thus not subject to the Roman *ius Italicum* (see comment on Phil. 1:1) and would not be required to house demobilized Roman soldiers as Philippi had done. Though Thessalonica, as other Macedonian cities, suffered greatly from the Roman civil wars of 44 to 31 B.C., it subsequently enjoyed a period of unparalleled peace and generally improving economic circumstances as commercial activity underwent considerable development (Wannamaker, 4). Thessalonica remained the most important and populous city in Macedonia into the third, and perhaps fourth centuries A.D. A Greek inscription from the Vardar Gate, which stood over the nearby Egnatian Way on which Paul traveled from Philippi to Thessalonica (Acts 17:1), was discovered which uses the Greek word *politarch?s* ("civic official"), a term otherwise found only in Paul's account of his visit to that city (Acts 17:6).

Acts 17 contains the only substantive evidence of the existence of a Jewish community, and there is no reason to challenge this. Archaeological and inscriptional evidence, however, reveals that, in addition to Judaism, Thessalonica was the home of many mystery cults, such as those of Dionysus, Sarapis, and Cabirus. That of Cabirus in particular would have flourished in the first century, as civic officials intended to exploit it to unify the city and thus celebrated cultic feasts and festivals in its honor. In addition, the city widely recognized the imperial cult, as inscriptional evidence found in the city indicates.

Grace to you and peace. Peace (*eirēnē*) is the Greek equivalent of the Hebrew *shalom*, a very common OT expression found most prominently in the "Aaronic blessing" (Num. 6:22-27; cf. 10:19). It was associated with divine restoration (Jer. 29:11; 33:6) and was a characteristic of the Messianic age (Isa. 66:12; Ezek. 34:25; 37:26; Mic. 5:4-5; Hag. 2:9). Usually one found "mercy" (*eleos*) alongside **peace** (*eirēnē*) in Jewish letters, but not **grace** (Dan. 3:98 [4:1]; *2 Bar.* 78.2). See comment on Eph. 1:2; Col. 1:2; Phil. 1:2.

II. 1:2-4. PRAYER OF THANKSGIVING

1:2. We give thanks to God always for all of you, making mention of you in our prayers. Some ancient letters began with a thanksgiving to the gods. A third-century B.C. letter reads: "Toubias to Apollonios, greeting. If you are well and if all your affairs and everything else

is proceeding according to your will, many thanks to the gods" (*PCarZen* I 59076). Paul's introductions exclusively focus on the **Lord Jesus Christ** and **our God and Father** (v. 3). In 1 Thessalonians, this introduction serves to affirm his pastoral relationship, provides paraenetic exhortation (the church is often challenged to live up to the praises of the apostle), and anticipates the thanksgivings developed later in the epistle.

1:3. Constantly bearing in mind your work of faith and labor of love and steadfastness of hope in our Lord Jesus Christ in the presence of our God and Father. For God as **Father** see comment on Matt. 5:16 §30. **Constantly** is something that is done repeatedly and without interruption, such as the payment of taxes, service in an official position, a bad cough, repeated military attacks (Jos. *J.W.* 1.13.2 §252), continuous failure of a military campaign (Jos. *J.W.* 3.7.23 §241), or the constant pounding of a battering ram against a city wall (Jos. *J.W.* 5.7.2 §§298-302). **Faith ... love ... hope**, though appearing in varying order, is a surprisingly frequent combination in early Christian literature (esp. 1 Cor. 13:13; cf. Rom. 5:1-5; 1 Thess. 5:8; Eph. 4:2-5; Heb. 6:10-12; 1 Peter 1:3-8; *Barn.* 1.4; Polycarp, *Phil.* 3.2). **Labor** (*kopos*) in its noun and verb form often refers to Paul's missionary work (1 Cor. 15:10; Gal. 4:11; 1 Thess. 3:5) as well as that of others (1 Cor. 15:58; 16:16; 2 Cor. 10:15). He also uses it for the manual labor in which he is employed to support himself in his work (1 Cor. 4:12; 2 Thess. 3:8).

1:4. Brethren (*adelphoi*): Jews frequently regarded fellow Jews as brothers (Deut. 15:3; Jer. 22:18; 1QS 6:10, 22; CD 6:20; Philo, *Spec. Laws* 2.79; Josephus, *J.W.* 2.8.2 §122; *Ant.* 10.10.3 §201). **His choice of you.** In the Old Testament God had chosen Abraham (Neh. 9:7) and Israel (Deut. 4:37; 1 Kings 3:8; Isa. 41:8; 44:1; 49:7) to make himself known to the nations.

Roman Persecution of the Early Christians

Nero (64) blamed Christians for the fire of Rome.

Domitian (95) persecuted Christians for refusing to worship him as a god.

Marcus Aurelius (177) sanctioned severe persecution at Lyons.

Decius (250) required anyone who refused to sacrifice to the state gods to be executed.

Valerian (257) forbade Christian assembly, arrested and executed clergy and high-ranking laity.

Diocletian (303) ordered all churches destroyed and Scriptures burned.

III. 1:5–2:16. THE GOSPEL AND THE THESSALONIANS

1:5. Gospel (*euangelion*). Also translates "glad tidings," the verbal form of which is used in the Old Testament (Isa. 40:9; 52:7; 60:6; 61:1) to announce Zion's restoration after the Babylonian exile. The entire context of Isa. 40–66 in which these references are located is interpreted in the New Testament with reference to the Christian salvation (Isa. 52:7 in Rom. 10:15; Isa. 61:1 in Luke 4:18; etc.; Bruce, 14).

1:6. You also became imitators of us and of the Lord. Imitation of an ideal person was common in the ancient world (Isocrates, *Demai* 4.11; Seneca, *Ep. Mor.* 6.5-6; 7.6-9; Quintilian, *Inst. Orat.* 2.28; Philostratus, *Vit. Ap.* 1.19; 2 Macc. 6.2-28; 4 Macc. 9.23) and was particularly a model of Jewish education (see comment on Phil. 3:17). **Much tribulation** perhaps refers to social harassment (1 Thess. 2:2, 14-15; 3:1-5; 2 Thess. 1:4-7; cf. Acts 17:5-7) rather than full persecution, which was not established as official Roman policy until the reign of Domitian (81-

96). At this early stage of Christianity (see Introduction), the new faith was often seen as a sect of Judaism, which was legally protected from persecution at this point in Roman history.

1:7. You became an example to all the believers in Macedonia and in Achaia. An example (*tupos*) originally meant a mark left by a blow, but came to mean a pattern or example (cf. *PTebt.* 2.342.25; *PLond.* 1122b.3). Macedonia was the province in which Thessalonica was located (see comment on 1:1). **Achaia**, however, was made a separate province under Augustus in 27 B.C. Perhaps Paul had in mind the Philippian church in Macedonia (Phil. 4:15) and the Corinthian church in Achaia (1 Cor. 16:15; 2 Cor. 1:1).

1:8. For the word of the Lord has sounded forth from you. Sounded forth (*exēcheomai*) can also mean to thunder, and suggests an echoing like thunder or a sounding out as a trumpet. It indicates a sound that is made from a point and spreads out (Best, 80-81).

1:9. You turned to God from idols. An idol in the Old Testament was both the false god and the image made of it. In Thessalonica, the emperor cult, which promoted the worship of Caesar, was common, as were the cults of other gods such as Dionysus, Serapis, Isis, Zeus, Aphrodite, Demeter, and Cabirus. This is in opposition to the **living and true God**. Describing God in this way was common in the Old Testament (Num. 14:21; Deut. 32:40; Pss. 41:2; 83:3) as well as the New (Matt. 16:16; Acts 14:15; Heb. 3:12; 2 Cor. 3:3). Idols were considered dead gods who could do nothing (Pss. 96:5; 115:4). For the gods worshiped in Thessalonica, see Introduction. *Joseph and Aseneth* records a soliloquy saying, "I have heard many saying that the God of the Hebrews is a true God, and a living God, and a merciful God, and compassionate and long-suffering and pitiful and gentle, and does not count the sin of a humble person, nor expose

---

the lawless deeds of an afflicted person at the time of his affliction" (11.10 OTP).

1:10. Wait for His Son from heaven, whom He raised from the dead. Wait (*anamenein*) connotes that something is expected, and one is to hold out hope and confidence that it will arrive. Mystery religions in the Greek world were frequently concerned with life after death. The principal god of Thessalonica, Cabirus, was thought to have been killed by his two brothers but was expected to return to the city and help the poor. **Jesus, who delivers us from the wrath to come. Wrath** was something that God would pour out (Ezek. 20:33; Lam. 4:11), rise up (2 Chron. 36:16), send out (Job 20:23; Ps. 78:49), and perform (1 Sam. 28:18; Hos. 11:9; cf. *Sib. Or.* 8.1; *Asc. Isa.* 4.13).

2:1. Paul feels a need to defend himself at this point, and raises this as the first main issue of the letter. See "Occasion and Purpose" in the Introduction.

2:2. We had already suffered and been mistreated in Philippi. Paul is referring to the shameful treatment he received from officials at Philippi. See Acts 16:19-40. As he does in Philippians (1:27; 2:16; 3:14; 4:1), Paul uses athletic imagery to portray the suffering and struggling for faith in Hellenistic Judaism (*4 Macc.* 11.20; 16.16; 17.11-16). Suffering was commonly expected in apocalyptic Judaism before the establishment of God's new creation (Dan. 12:1; *1 Enoch* 37.4; *1 Bar.* 14.1; *Jub.* 23.22; *4 Ezra* 4.51-5.13, 6.28; *Sib. Or.* 2.153f; *b. Sanh.* 96b; 97a; etc.), after which the anointed Messiah was to come (*b. Shab.* 118a; *b. Pes.* 118a). **We had the boldness in our God to speak to you the gospel of God amid much opposition: Boldness** (*eparrēsiasametha*) is the verbal form of boldness (*parrēsion*) used in Ephesians 3:12, which is what believers have gained, along with access to the Father. The term was sometimes an expression used by Jews to describe pious prayer (LXX Job 22:26;

27:9, 10; Philo, *Special Laws* 1.203; Jos., *Ant.* 2.4.4 §52; cf. *Ant.* 5.1.3 §18). **Boldness** here really means frankness, or freedom of speech. *Letter of Aristeas* 125 speaks of a man receiving "frank (*parr?sion*) advice given him by his friends for his benefit" (OTP; cf. *T. Reub.* 4.2; Rom. 5:2; Heb. 3:6; 4:16; 10:35; 1 John 2:28; 3:21; 4:17; 5:14). The source of such assertiveness is **our God**, which was required **to speak to** them **the gospel ... amid much opposition. Opposition** refers to the difficulties Paul encountered while preaching to the Thessalonians. The word generally refers to the struggle put forth in competition (Aeschylus, *Agamemnon* 845) where the prize may be a crown (Herodotus, *Histories* 5.8, 102; cf. Aristophanes, *Plutus* 583). It can also be used as an action of legal maneuvering in a courtroom (Plato, *Apology* 24c; *Republic* 494e; Xenophon, *Lac* 8.4; *PTebt* 2.423.13; *POxy* 4.744.4).

2:3. For our exhortation does not come from error or impurity or by way of deceit: Exhortation (*paraklēsis*) suggests an appeal relating to the benefit of those being addressed. The term was used to encourage soldiers about to go into battle (*PGrenf* 1.32.10; *PTebt.* 2.392.26; *PFlor.* 3.323.6). **Impurity** (*akatharsia*) in the Old Testament refers to ritual impurity, though it often connoted ethical impurity as well (Prov. 3:32). **Deceit** (*dolos*) originally referred to the deceit used to catch a fish (Homer, *Odyssea* 12.253) and later developed into its present meaning of "deceit, cunning, treachery" (cf. *PLeid* 10.3.10).

2:4. God as one **who examines our hearts** was a common expression among Jews in the Old Testament for both the omniscience of God and the purity of man's motives (Pss. 7:9; 139:23; Prov. 17:3; Jer. 11:20; 12:3; 17:10; 1 Chron. 28:9).

2:5. For we never came with flattering speech, as you know, nor with a pretext for greed. Paul, like the Cynic philosopher Dio Chrysostom (*Oration* 32.5; cf. Aristotle, *Nic. Eth.* 4.6.9;

Theophrasuts, *Characters* 2), refused to employ flattery because it would compromise the integrity of his message and call into question his motivation in preaching the gospel (cf. 2 Cor. 2:17; 4:2; Wanamaker, 97). Dio Chrysostom further says, "flattery seems neither reputable nor honorable even when practiced to gain distinction, or from some other worthy motive. Nay, of all vices, I may say, flattery will be found to be the meanest" (*Third Discourse* 17). **God is witness** is employed often by Paul to affirm the truth of what he says (Rom. 1:9; Phil. 1:8; 1 Thess. 2:10), the practice of which comes from the Old Testament (Job 16:19; Ps. 89:37; cf. *Wisd.* 1.6). The authenticity and motivation of his message can be verified by God alone (Wanamaker, 98).

2:6. Nor did we seek glory from men, either from you or from others, even though as apostles of Christ we might have asserted our authority: The ancient world was full of wandering philosophers, prophets of new religions, magicians, and "divine men," about whom even secular writers warn as to their sincerity (Lucian, *De Morte Peregrini* 13; *Diologi Mortuorum* 10.8; Best, 99). Dio Chrysostom says that genuine philosophers would not seek such **glory** (*doxa*) **from men** (*Orations* 32.7-12).

2:7. Gentle (*ēpioi*) is a very uncertain reading, with the other option being "infants" (*nēpioi*), though the former is preferred by most translations (NIV, RSV, NAS, KJV). Though "infants" has the stronger manuscript evidence, **gentle** may make better sense in the context, as claiming to be both the infant and **nursing mother** confuses the metaphor. Cynics of Paul's day stressed the need for gentleness towards one's audience if one were to speak with boldness as well (Dio Chrysostom, *Orations* 77-78; Plutarch, *Moralia* [How to Tell a Flatterer from a Friend] 73C-74E; Wannamaker, 101). **Nursing mother** (*trophos*) is commonly called a "wet nurse," one who suckles children. These were widely used in the ancient world and were

important and loved figures in the household. Numerous papyri have been discovered which served as contracts between the nurse and the family. One such contract, dating from the first century B.C., shows that the nurse was taken into the home, provided food, clothing, and payment. The contract lasted two years (ND 1.1; cf. *BGU* 4.1058, 1106, 1109; *PGrenf.* 2.75). Here the image is metaphorical, as it is at Qumran where the Teacher of Righteousness is described as a nursing *father* to the community under his jurisdiction (1QH 7:20-22; 9:29-32).

2:8. Having thus a fond affection for you: Fond affection (*homeiromenoi*) is a term used in the Old Testament for an intense longing (Job 3:21). It is also used on a fourth century A.D. tombstone for parents "greatly desiring their [deceased] son" (*CIG* 3.4000.7).

2:9. For you recall, brethren, our labor and hardship, how working night and day so as not to be a burden to any of you, we proclaimed to you the gospel of God: Acts 18:3 describes Paul as a "tentmaker," which probably referred to a leather worker, though not a tanner as that would have been unclean for Jews. Rabbis in Paul's day often had a trade to support themselves in addition to study of the Law (cf. *m. Abot.* 2.2; 4.5). See comment on Acts 18:3.

2:10. Devoutly describes one's duty toward God. **Uprightly** describes one's duty toward others, though in view of a righteous life before God.

2:11. We were exhorting and encouraging and imploring each one of you as a father would **his own children:** Sons were to be imitators of their fathers (Isocrates, *To Demonicus* 4.11; 1 *Macc.* 2.51; Philo, *On the Birth of Abel and the Sacrifices Offered by Him and by His Brother Cain* 64), who were primarily responsible for their education. In Judaism, education was conducted most centrally in the home (Deut. 6:7; Prov. 13:24; *Sir.* 30.1-13; Philo, *Hypothetica: Apology for the Jews*

7.14; Josephus, *Ag. Ap.* 1.12 §60), where the Torah was primarily taught (Deut. 4:9; 6:7; 11:19; 32:46) and godly wisdom and discipline were espoused (Prov. 19:18; 22:6; 23:13, 14; 29:15; *Sirach* 7.23; cf. Philo, *On the Embassy to Gaius* 31; *Special Laws* 2.228; *Hypothetica: Apology for the Jews* 7.14). Josephus says of the Jews of his day, "Our ground is good, and we work it to our utmost, but our chief ambition is for the education of our children .... We take most pains of all with the instruction of children, and esteem the observation of the laws, and the piety corresponding with them, the most important affair of our whole life" (*Ag. Ap.* 1.12 §60; cf. 2.18 §178; 2.25 §204).

2:12. Walk in a manner worthy of the God who calls you into His own kingdom and glory. Walk (*parapateō*) is a metaphorical expression for moral and ethical behavior. In the Old Testament, King Hezekiah prayed, "Remember now, O LORD, I beseech Thee, how I have walked before Thee in truth and with a whole heart, and have done what is good in Thy sight" (2 Kings 20:3). Later Jewish laws and traditions, called *Halakah* (based on the Hebrew word *hlk*, meaning "to walk"), governed daily life. At Qumran, obedience to the Law was seen as "walking in the way of His (God's) delight" (1QS 5:10). See comment on 1 John 1:6-7 (cf. 1 John 2:6; 2 John 6; 3 John 3). **Worthy** (*axiōs*) literally means the balancing of scales, making things equivalent. Cf. Col. 1:10.

2:13. The word of God's message may hearken back to Isaiah 53:1: "Who has believed what he has heard from us?" which is used elsewhere in the New Testament as a testimony formula for the gospel message (John 12:38; Rom. 10:16). His **word** was seen as a powerful presence in creation (Gen. 1:3; Ps. 33:6) and in the redemption of Israel (Jer. 23:29).

2:14 For you, brethren, became imitators of the churches of God in Christ Jesus that are in

Judea. Judea includes not just Roman Judea but also Galilee and Samaria, which is normally called Palestine (cf. Luke 1:5; 23:5; Acts 10:37; Josephus, *Ant.* 1.7.2 §160; Tacitus, *History* 5.9). **For you also endured the same sufferings at the hands of your own countrymen. Your own countrymen** refers to the citizens of Thessalonica, who were primarily Gentiles, though it may include Jews who frequently incited opposition to Paul's mission (Acts 17:1).

2:15. Who both killed the Lord Jesus and the prophets, and drove us out. They are not pleasing to God, but hostile to all men. The accusation that the Jewish people were responsible for the death of prophets is not new to the New Testament (Matt. 23:29-37; Acts 7:52) nor contemporary Judaism (*Mart. Isa.* 5.1-14) but finds its origin in the Old Testament (1 Kings 19.10-14; cf. 2 Chron. 36:15; Wanamaker, 114; cf. Rom. 11:3; Jer. 2:30). **They are ... hostile to all men:** Other writers from antiquity expressed similar displeasure with Jews (Tacitus, *History* 5.5; Philostratus, *Life of Apollonius* 5.33).

2:16. They always fill up the measure of their sins. Here Paul draws from Gen. 15:16 (cf. Dan. 8:23; *2 Macc.* 6.14) which refers to the sins of the Amorites against Abraham, which Paul now turns against the Jews themselves (Best, 118).

The Wrath of God as Vindication of His People

"They persecuted Abraham when he was a nomad, and they harassed his flocks when they were pregnant, and they grossly mistreated Eblan, who had been born in this house. This is how they treated the nomadic people, seizing their wives and murdering them. But the wrath of God ultimately came upon them."

T. Levi 6.11 OTP

But wrath has come upon them to the utmost: Some think this refers to the Roman massacre of Jews in the temple courts on the Passover in A.D. 49 (Josephus, *J.W.* 2.12.1 §224-227; *Ant.* 20.5.3 §105-112) or the famine in A.D. 46 (Acts 11:28). However, there need not be a specific historical antecedent to this phrase and the warning may point to an impending, future judgment rather than a past one. **To the utmost** can mean "finally, in the end" or "forever" (Pss. 76:8; 78:5; 102:9 LXX), though it seems more likely to refer to "until the end," that is, when Christ returns (cf. Rom. 11:25-32; 1 Cor. 9:20). A legend attributed to Levi describes Shechem's and Hamor's mistreatment of Jews (Gen. 34:25-31) and the wrath of God coming upon them in their ultimately being murdered (*T. Levi* 6.11; cf. *Jub.* 30.1-26).

IV. 2:17–3:13. PAUL AND THE THESSALONIANS

2:17. But we, brethren, having been bereft of you for a short while—in person, not in spirit—were all the more eager with great desire to see your face: Bereft (*aporphanisthentes*) means to make one an orphan by separation.

2:18. For we wanted to come to you—I, Paul, more than once—and yet Satan thwarted us. I (*egō*) occurs five times in this letter (2:18; 3:5; 5:27), affirming the apostle's authorship and authority in it. **Thwarted** can mean "to cut into" and can be used to describe cutting down trees (*PFay* 113.10; *POxy* 6.892.10). It is also used for cutting up a road so as to make it impassable for a pursuing army (P.Alex. 4.3; Diogenes Laertes, 4.50; Polybius, 23.1.12; Vettius Valens, 6.9).

2:19. For who is our hope or joy or crown of exultation? Is it not even you, in the presence of our Lord Jesus at His coming? Crown of exultation. Though this expression is found in the Old Testament (Ezek. 16:12; 23:42; Prov. 16:31), here it probably refers to the victory wreath placed on the heads of victorious military commanders or the winners of athletic contests to signify their achievement (Wanamaker, 124; cf. 1QS 4:7). See comment on Phil. 4:1. **Coming** (*parousia*) can have two meanings, either or both of which may have influenced Paul's use of the term. One referred to the manifestation of a deity by a demonstration of his power, used by Josephus to describe the arrival of Yahweh at various key times in Israel's history (*Ant.* 3.5.2 §80, 3.8.5 §203; 9.2.3 §55). The other was used with reference to the arrival of an important person into a region which signified the dawn of a new era in that region's history. Such was used of Hadrian's arrival in Athens (A.D. 124). An inscription from A.D. 192/3 found at Tegea is dated, "in the year 69 of the first *parousia* of the god Hadrian in Greece." Such arrivals were traditionally accompanied by festive pomp and circumstance (Bruce, 57).

The Suffering of the Righteous

"And in those days if a man will live a jubilee and a half, they will say about him, 'He prolonged his life, but the majority of his days were suffering and anxiety and affliction. And there was no peace, because plague (came) upon plague, and wound upon wound, and affliction upon affliction, and evil report upon evil report, and sickness upon sickness, and every evil judgment of this sort one with another: sickness, and downfall, and sleet, and hail, and frost, and fever, and chills, and stupor, and famine, and death, and sword, and captivity, and all plagues, and suffering'."

Jubilees 23.12-13 OTP

3:1. Therefore when we could endure it no longer: Endure (*stegontes*) can be used with respect to holding back a leak in a boat (*PPetr.* 3.46.1.4) or the shielding from weather by a roof (cf. *Syll* 318; *PCairo Zen.* 2.59251.7; *POxy* 12.1450.9).

3:3. So that no man may be disturbed by these afflictions; for you yourselves know that we have been destined for this. In Jewish apocalyptic thought, the righteous were expected to undergo affliction or tribulation before the emergence of the new age (Dan. 12:1; *Jub.* 23.13; *2 Bar.* 70.2-10; *2 Esdras* 5.1-12; 13.30; Wanamaker, 130).

3:13. So that He may establish your hearts unblamable in holiness before our God and Father at the coming of our Lord Jesus with all His saints. Saints (*hagioi*) literally, "holy ones" (see comment on Col. 1:2) can also refer to angels or heavenly beings. The Old Testament describes Yahweh among his holy ones (Zech. 14:5). He appeared at Sinai to give the law among them (Deut. 33:2), and their presence with him is depicted in victory scenes (Ps. 68:1-35). They are among him on the Day of Judgment (Dan. 7:10), and early Christians associated their presence with the return of Christ (*Did.* 16.17cf. Pss. 50:3; 80:1; 107:20; Isa. 26:19; 63:9; Hab. 2:3; Zeph. 1:15; Mal. 4:1; Bruce, 73; cf. *1 Enoch* 1.9; *Tobit* 11.14; 12.15; *Asc. Isa.* 4.14, 16).

V. EXHORTATIONS TO CHRISTIAN LIVING (4:1-12)

4:3. For this is the will of God, your sanctification; that is, that you abstain from sexual immorality. Sanctification (*ho hagiasmos*) in the Old Testament referred to anything that was made holy by virtue of its association with God, particularly people (Lev. 11:44; 19:2; 20:7; 1 Peter 1:16). **Abstain from sexual immorality. Sexual immorality** (*porneia*) was strongly condemned

among Jews (Exod. 20:14; Lev. 20:10-23; *Jub.* 20.3-6; 39.6; *Sirach* 23.16-27; Philo, *Spec. Laws* 3.51) and was frequently considered the direct result of idolatry (*Wisd.* 14.12-31; Philo, *Allegorical Interpretation* 3.8; cf. *Jub.* 25.1; Wanamaker, 151). See comment on Eph. 5:3. Sexual integrity was by no means the norm either in Greek or Roman cultures. Though not necessarily representative of either, two examples serve to illustrate at least part of the ethical climate which the apostle confronted. Demosthenes (384-322 B.C.) says, "Mistresses we keep for the sake of pleasure, concubines for the daily care of our persons, but wives to bear us legitimate children and to be faithful guardians of our households" (Demosthenes, *Orations* 59.122). Horace describes the Stoic philosopher Cato (95-46 B.C.) who praised those men who would look to prostitutes to satisfy their sexual desires rather than another man's wife (*Satire* 1.2.31-35).

4:4. That each of you know how to possess his own vessel in sanctification and honor: Vessel (*skeuos*) can also mean wife (RSV), and scholars differ on whether Paul is exhorting each to "gain mastery over his body" (NEB) or "take a wife for himself" (RSV). Raba (d. ca. 352) says that the women of Vashti (Esther 2:1) were called his "vessels" (*b. Meg.* 12b). As the use here most clearly fits that of 1 Sam. 21:5, where it refers to controlling one's body, the former understanding is preferred. Rabbi Judah ben Pazzi (ca. 320) said that laws about relationships were present in the Old Testament to contribute to one's sanctity (*Lev. Rab.* 24.6 [on Lev. 19:8]).

4:5. Not in lustful passion, like the Gentiles who do not know God. In the Old Testament, particularly wisdom texts, those who did **not know God** were foolish people who likewise deny him by their behavior (Deut. 32:6 LXX; Jer. 4:22; Prov. 1:22; 4:10-14; 6:12; 9:1-18; cf. 1QS 3:13; 4:24; 9:12-21; 1QH 13:3; CD 12:21; 15:15). It was used to designate unbelievers (Jer. 10:25; Ps. 79:6; Gal. 4:8; 2 Thess. 1:8).

4:6. That no man transgress and defraud his brother in the matter because the Lord is the avenger in all these things, just as we also told you before and solemnly warned you: The Lord is the avenger: In the Old Testament, Yahweh was thought to be the **avenger** of evil deeds (Deut. 32:35; Pss. 94:1-7; 99:8; Micah 5:15; Nah. 1:2; cf. *2 Enoch* 60.1).

4:8. Consequently, he who rejects this is not rejecting man but the God who gives His Holy Spirit to you. In the Old Testament, God was said to give **His Holy Spirit**, here echoing the words of Ezek. 36:27; 37:14. The giving of the Spirit was often associated with the end times (Isa. 44:3; Ezek. 39:29; Joel 2:28-29; Acts 2:17-18).

4:9. Now as to the love of the brethren, you have no need for anyone to write to you, for you yourselves are taught by God to love one another: Brethren (*philadelphias*) was used by some Jews to refer almost exclusively to those of blood relation (*2 Macc.* 15.14; *4 Macc.* 13.23; 14.1; cf. Sophocles, *Antigone* 527; Xenophon, *Memorabilia* 2.3.17) but was adopted by Christians to have a metaphorical meaning (Rom. 12:10; Heb. 13:1; 1 Peter 1:22; 2 Peter 1:7). **Taught by God:** Some rabbis believed that Abraham was not taught the Law but learned it on his own, perhaps almost from birth (*Gen. Rab.* 95.3). The allusion here seems to be to Isa. 54:13, where the prophet looks to an eschatological day when instruction concerning God will no longer be necessary because God will already be known (cf. *Pss. Sol.* 17.32). See John 6:45; Jer. 31:33-34. **Love one another.** See comment on Matt. 5:43 §36.

4:10. Macedonia enjoyed a long, influential, but tumultuous history (cf. Herodotus, *Histories* 5.17-18, 173; 9.45; Polybius, *History* 7.9; 18.22-28; 31.29), including some encounters with Israel during the Babylonian captivity and afterward (Dan. 2:39; 7:6; 8:5-8; *1 Macc.* 1.1-7; 6.2). In Paul's day, it was a Roman province across which was built a great military road, the Egnatian Way, from the Adriatic Sea to the Aegean. It was made into an imperial province in A.D. 15 (Tacitus, *Annals* 1.76.4; 1.80.1), though divided again into a senatorial province by Claudius in 44 (Dio Cass. 60.24). Within its precincts were located the churches of the Thessalonians and Philippians.

4:11-12. And to make it your ambition to lead a quiet life and attend to your own business and work with your hands, just as we commanded you; so that you may behave properly toward outsiders and not be in any need. The Thessalonian Christians were so convinced of the imminence of Christ's return that they no longer saw a need to conduct their daily affairs and work. See Introduction to 1 and 2 Thessalonians.

VI. PROBLEMS RELATED TO THE RETURN OF CHRIST (4:13–5:11)

4:13. But we do not want you to be uninformed, brethren, about those who are asleep,

---

The God of Vengeance

"O Lord, God of vengeance; God of vengeance, shine forth! Rise up, O Judge of the earth; Render recompense to the proud. How long shall the wicked, O Lord, How long shall the wicked exult? They pour forth words, they speak arrogantly; All who do wickedness vaunt themselves. They crush Thy people, O Lord, And afflict Thy heritage. They slay the widow and the stranger, And murder the orphans. And they have said, 'The Lord does not see, Nor does the God of Jacob pay heed.'"

Psalm 94:1-7

that you may not grieve, as do the rest who have no hope. Concern about the time of the arrival of the Messiah and the implications of it were not unique to the Thessalonian Christians. Jewish apocalyptic texts suggest many believed that the Messianic age was accompanied by great suffering, and that it may have been better for them to have lived earlier to avoid it (4 Ezra 13.16-24; 2 Bar. 48.41; 10.6). There were, however, great blessings and benefits to be reaped upon the arrival of the Messiah (Pss. Sol. 18.7; 17.44), and some regarded the generation alive at the end with particular esteem (Dan. 12:12; 4 Ezra 13:24; Ps. Sol 17.50). **Sleep** was a common euphemism for death (cf. Job 14:12; Isa. 43:17; Pss. Sol. 16.1-4; Homer, Iliad 11.241; Sophocles, Electra 509; see Eph. 5:14). **Grieve ... as do the rest who have no hope:** While some philosophers held out hope for an afterlife, others suggested hope was only for the living. The dead have no hope (Theocritus, Idyll 4.42). A tomb inscription unearthed in Thessalonica reveals that beyond companionship with one's spouse in the grave, the dead had no hope (CIG 1973). Similarly, a letter of condolence from the second century A.D. reads, "I sorrowed and wept over your dear departed one as I wept over Didymas, ... but really, there is nothing one can do in the face of such things. So, please comfort each other" (POxy 115; Bruce, 96).

The Dead Have no Hope

"... for this woman had this surname, while she was still among the living. Because of her special disposition and good sense, her devoted husband created this tomb for her and also for himself, in order that later he would have a place to rest together with his dear wife, when he looks upon the end of life that has been spun out for him by the indissoluble threads of the Fates."

CIG 1973

4:14. We believe that Jesus died and rose again may be a creed dating before Paul. The Ascension of Isaiah says that when Christ returns, "the saints will come with the Lord with their robes which are stored up on the seventh heaven above; with the Lord will come those whose spirits are clothed, they will descend and be present in the world, and the Lord will strengthen those who are found in the body, together with the saints in the robes of the saints, and will serve those who have kept watch in this world" (4.16 OTP).

4:15. For this we say to you by the word of the Lord, that we who are alive, and remain until the coming of the Lord, shall not precede those who have fallen asleep. Whether this tradition stems from the teachings of the earthly Jesus not recorded in the gospels, a paraphrase of his teachings in Mark 13 and Matthew 24, or something particularly revealed to Paul on the Road to Damascus is unclear. Old Testament prophets believed that they gave the word of the Lord to God's people (Ezek. 34:1; 35:1; Hos. 1:1; Amos 5:1; Joel 1:1; cf. 1 Kings 13:2; 2 Chron. 30:12; Sir. 48:3; Best, 192; T. Abr. 13.4).

4:16. For the Lord Himself will descend from heaven with a shout, with the voice of the archangel, and with the trumpet of God; and the dead in Christ shall rise first. The Lord Himself employs deliverance language from Isa. 63:9. **Archangel** is a rare term, found only here and in Jude 9 in the New Testament. It recalls the Old Testament where the angel Michael, who is said to be "obedient in his benevolence over the people and the nations" (1 Enoch 20.5), is described with similar terminology (Dan. 10:13; cf. Dan. 12:1; 2 Esdr. 4.36). One should not think of a single figure, however, as Jewish tradition knew of seven (Tobit 12.15; 1 Enoch 20.1-7; cf. 4 Ezra 4.36; Rev. 8:2). The **trumpet of God** is an image frequently occurring in the Old Testament in the context of a manifestation of Yahweh (theophany) or of eschatological judgment (Exod. 19:16; Isa. 27:13; Joel 2:1; Zeph. 1:14-16; cf. also *Pss. Sol.* 11.1; *2 Esdras* 6.17-24; *Apoc. Mos.* 22, 37-38; Matt. 24:31; Rev. 8:2, 6, 13; 9:14; Wanamaker, 173). It was used in Isa. 27:13 of the summoning of the Jewish exiles home from Assyria and Egypt (cf. Joel 2:1, 15; Zech. 9:14; Bruce, 100-101).

Sibylline Oracles 8.239 claims the trumpet blast will be "mournful sounds" (OTP; cf. Cf. *4 Ezra* 6.23; *Jos. Asen.* 4.1; *LAE Apoc* 22.3; *Apoc. Elijah* 5.36; *Gk. Apoc. Ezra* 4.36). Some traditions claim that the angel Gabriel, who was thought to "oversee the garden of Eden, and the serpents, and the cherubim" (*1 Enoch* 20.7), will sound the trumpet (*Ques. Ezra* Rec B 13).

4:17-18. Then we who are alive and remain shall be caught up together with them in the clouds to meet the Lord in the air, and thus we shall always be with the Lord. Therefore comfort one another with these words. Clouds are typically mentioned in apocalyptic contexts as well as in relation to manifestations of Yahweh in the Old Testament (Exod. 19:16-25; Ps. 97:2). They are a vehicle for God (Ps. 104:3; Isa. 19:1; Ezek. 1:4-28) and the returning Christ (Matt. 26:64; Dan. 7:13). **Caught up** (*harpazein*) is used in Gen. 5:24 (LXX) for the taking up of Enoch to heaven, as well as in 2 Cor. 12:2, 4 in reference to Paul's ascent into the "third heaven." **Meet** (*eis apantēsin*) was a technical term in the Hellenistic world referring to the visits of dignitaries to cities (Jos. *Ant.* 11.8.4 §327; Best, 199). When a dignitary paid an official visit (*parousia*) to a city in the Hellenistic age, the action of the leading citizens in going out to meet him and escort him back to the final stage of his journey was signified with this term (*apant?sis*; Cicero, *Epistula ad Atticum* 8.16.2; 16.11.2; Bruce, 102). Some Jews likewise believed at the resurrection the faithful would meet with the Messiah (*1 Enoch* 62.13; 71.16).

5:1. Now as to the times and the epochs, brethren, you have no need of anything to be

---

Anticipating the End

"R. Samuel b. Nahmani said in the name of R. Jonathan: Blasted be the bones of those who calculate the end. For they would say, since the predetermined time has arrived, and yet has not come, he will never come. But [even so], wait for him, as it is written, *Though he tarry, wait for him.* . . . "

b. Sanhedrin 97b

---

written to you: Times (*kairōn*) **and the epochs** (*chronōn*) should probably be seen as synonymous terms, signifying that time which was seen by many Jews as the period, often the end time, when God would intervene and judge the world (Jer. 6:15; 18:23; Dan. 8:17; 11:35; 12:1; *3 Bar* 14:1; 1QS 9:13-15; 1QpHab 2:9-10; cf. Matt. 8:9; Mark 13:33; Acts 3:19-21; Rev. 1:3). Jews were also concerned about the time of the coming of the Messiah (*2 Bar.* 24.4; *4 Ezra* 6.59; cf. Jer. 25:22; Dan. 9:24).

5:2. The day of the Lord will come just like a thief in the night. Day of the Lord (*hemera kuriou*) comes from Jewish history in relation to God's decisive and final intervention. Most prevalent from the time of Amos onward, the expression is used to refer to the time of God's judgment on the wicked (Amos 5:18-10; Joel 1:15; Isa. 13:6) as well as deliverance for the faithful (Joel 2:32; 3:18; Obad. 15-17; Zech. 14:1-21; Best 206). **Thief in the night:** While there is no known pre-Christian Jewish apocalyptic evidence for this expression, Jews of the Old Testament clearly expected the Day of the Lord to be sudden (Mal. 3:1; Job 24:14; Joel 2:9; Obad. 5; cf. Euripides, *Iph. in Taur.* 1025-26; see comment on Matt. 24:43 §189). One tradition says, "Then when you hear that there is security in Jerusalem, tear your garments, O priests of the land, because the son of perdition will come soon" (*Apoc. Elijah* 2.40). Some rabbis spoke against anticipating the day and time of the end (*b. Sanh.* 97b).

5:3. While they are saying, "Peace and safety!" then destruction will come upon them suddenly: Peace and safety (*eirēnē kai asphaleia*) may allude to Old Testament condemnations of false prophets who proclaim such **peace and safety** when in reality destruction is imminent (Jer. 6:14; Ezek. 13:10). Yet some argue that the phrase more immediately derives from the contemporary Roman political environment in which **peace and safety** (Latin, *pax et securitas*) was an important component of Roman propaganda. This slogan has been found on coins, monuments, and official proclamations. Such language is found in Josephus' account of a Roman decree to the city of Pergamum (Jos. *Ant.* 14.10.22 §§247-55).

Birth pangs upon a woman with child is a metaphor found in the Old Testament commonly associated with the hardships accompanying the age of the coming Messiah (Isa. 13:8; 26:17; 66:7; Jer. 6:24; cf. *1 Enoch* 62.1-5; *T. Job* 18.4; Rom. 8:22; Gal. 4:19).

5:4-5. Darkness ... light. Darkness to **light** is a common expression for conversion (*Jos. Asen.*

Peace and Safety

"In the presidency of Cratippus, on the first month Daisios, a decree of the magistrates. As the Romans in pursuance of the practices of their ancestors have accepted dangerous risks for the common safety (*asphaleia*) of all humankind and strive emulously to place their allies and friends in a state of happiness and lasting peace (*eirēnē*), the Jewish nation and their high priest Hyrcanus have sent as an envoy to them. ..."

Josephus, *Ant.* 14.10.22 §§247-55 LCL

8.10; 15.13; Philo, *On the Virtues* 179; Acts 26:18; Col. 1:12, 13; 1 Peter 2:9; *Odes Sol.* 14.18, 19; cf. Heb. 6:4; 10:32). In the OT, light can refer to salvation and life from God (Ps. 27:1; Isa. 9:2; 10:17; 42:6, 16; 41:4; 60:1). At Qumran, the "War Scroll" (1QM) depicts a "War of the Sons of Light against the Sons of Darkness" (1QM 1:1-16; 3:6; 14:17; cf. 1QS 1:9, 10; 3:13, 19-21, 24, 25; *T. Levi* 14.4; *T. Benj.* 5.3). **Darkness** was clearly a metaphor depicting alienation from and opposition to God (Job 22:9-11; Pss. 74:20; 82:5; Isa. 2:5; cf. Amos 5:18-20; Joel 2:2; 3:31; 1QS 3:13-4:26; *T. Naph.* 2.7-10; *T. Benj.* 5.3).

5:5. Sons of light ... of day ... of night ... of darkness. "Sons of ... " expressions are Semitisms, similar to "son of stripes" (Deut. 25:2), describing one who deserves a flogging, or "son of death" (1 Sam. 26:16; 2 Sam. 12:5; Ps. 102:20), used of someone doomed to die. For killing his brother Abel (Gen. 4:8), Cain is called a "son of wrath" (*Ap. Moses* 3; cf. Gen. 4:11). See Eph. 2:3.

5:6. Let us not sleep as others do, but let us be alert and sober. Sleep was a common metaphor for death (see comment on 4:13). Here, though, it seems to be used to refer to attentiveness to the reality of the imminent return of Christ (cf. Matt. 24:43; Luke 12:39; Mark 13:35, 36).

5:8. But since we are of the day, let us be sober, having put on the breastplate of faith and love, and as a helmet, the hope of salvation. The **breastplate** is part of Yahweh's armor in Isa. 59:17 and *Wisd.* 5.18, with faith now being a quality put on by believers. A **breastplate** (*thōrax*) was a metal piece of armor protecting the chest, heart, and lungs (cf. 2 Cor. 6:7; cf. *T. Levi* 8.2). See comment on Eph. 6:14. **Helmet, the hope of salvation:** In the Old Testament, God is salvation and deliverance for the oppressed (Pss. 18:2, 46-48; 65:6; Isa. 33:2, 6; 45:17; 51:5; Jer. 31:33; Lincoln, 450).

Moreover, in Isaiah 59:17, God is a victorious warrior who wears the helmet of salvation, now here, Paul has it given to believers for protection. It is also seen as a defensive weapon used by the righteous in their eschatological battle against "the shameless one" (*Apoc. Elijah* 4.31 OTP).

5:11. Therefore encourage one another, and build up one another, just as you also are doing. Build up (*oikodomein*) is used in the Old Testament where God promises to **build up** Israel (Jer. 24:6; 31:4; 42:10). The verb was used in ancient papyri for the construction of a house (*PRyl* 2.133.13; *PGiss* 1.20.19; *PMagd* 27.4).

VII. GENERAL EXHORTATIONS AND FAREWELL (5:12-28)

5:12. But we request of you, brethren, that you appreciate those who diligently labor among you, and have charge over you in the Lord and give you instruction. Those who **have charge over** (*proistamenous*) the Thessalonians are unspecified. The term, however, refers to patrons or benefactors who supported various clients or associations as a guardian (Plato, *Republic* 565C; 599A; Xenophon, *Anabasis* 6.2.9; Herodotus, *Histories* 4.79). Some have suggested that this refers to a wealthy member of a congregation, such as Jason (Acts 17:5-9) who

may have had the time, resources, and education to facilitate the fledgling church.

5:14. And we urge you (*parakaleō*): Such exhortations were commonly found in ancient letters in which **entreat** was a common word for making an appeal to someone (Aeschylus, *Persae* 380; Euripides, *Phoenissae* 1254; Xenophon, *Anabasis* 3.1.24; Plato, *Republic* 523b). A papyrus fragment dating late in the second century contains a letter from a woman entreating a prefect of Egypt to decide a civil dispute (*ND* 6.144; cf. *P. Berol. Inv.* 16546). **Admonish the unruly. Unruly** (*ataktous*) is used in military contexts to describe soldiers who do not keep in step or obey orders (Xenophon, *Cyr* 7.2.6; Josephus, *Ant.* 17.10.10 §296). However, it can be used, as here, for anyone who is disorderly, undisciplined, or unruly (Aristotle, *Politics* 1319b.15; Plato, *Laws* 660b, 840e). The charge seems to be leveled against those who refuse to work because of the apparent imminence of Christ's return. See Introduction.

Encourage the fainthearted. Fainthearted (*oligopsychoi*) can also translate "timid" (NIV), and literally refers to one of "little soul." The term is used in the Old Testament of religious discouragement in the face of hardship (Exod. 6:9; Isa. 35:4; *Sirach* 7.10). It may refer to those anxious about Christ's return (4:13–5:11) or dis-

---

Vengeance Belongs to God

"He that takes vengeance will suffer vengeance from the Lord, and he will firmly establish his sins. Forgive your neighbor the wrong he has done, and then your sins will be pardoned when you pray. Does a man harbor anger against another, and yet seek for healing from the Lord? Does he have no mercy toward a man like himself, and yet pray for his own sins? If he himself, being flesh, maintains wrath, who will make expiation for his sins? Remember the end of your life, and cease from enmity, remember destruction and death, and be true to the commandments. Remember the commandments, and do not be angry with your neighbor; remember the covenant of the Most High, and overlook ignorance."

Sirach 28.1-7

heartened by persecution (1 Thess. 2:14; 3:1-5).

Help the weak. Weak probably does not refer to physical weakness but likely refers, as it does elsewhere in Paul's writings, to those who are hesitant about matters on which others, including Paul, have clear minds (1 Cor. 8:1-13; 10:1-33). Again, concerns may center around the return of Christ (1 Thess. 5:1-11) or one's behavior in the meantime (1 Thess. 4:3-8).

Be patient with all men. Patient (*makrothumia*) means "long-suffering," and is an ideal quality of God to be imitated by his people (Exod. 34:6; Ps. 103:8; cf. *T. Jos.* 2.7).

5:15. See that no one repays another with evil for evil, but always seek after that which is good for one another and for all men. Jews often left retribution in the hands of God: "Do not say, "I will repay evil"; Wait for the LORD, and He will save you" (Prov. 20:22; cf. 25:21; 1QS 10:17; *Tobit* 4.15; *Apoc. Sedr.* 7.9; *Jos. Asen.* 23.9; 28.4, 14; 29.3; *Sirach* 28.1-7).

5:19-20. Do not quench the Spirit. The language is similar to that of other New Testament passages where **quench** (*sbennute*) is used in reference to fire (Matt. 3:11; Luke 3:16; 12:49; Acts 2:3; Rom. 12:11) with respect to the work of the Holy Spirit. Here Paul has **prophetic utterances** in view (v. 20). The Spirit is quenched when the prophet refuses to utter the message he has been given or when others try to prevent him from uttering it. Jeremiah tried to withhold God's message in this way, which became "a burning fire shut up in [his] bones" (Jer. 20:9). The people in Amos' day tried to prevent prophecies from being said (Amos 2:23; cf. Mic. 2:6; *Tg. Neof.* Num. 11:28; Bruce, 125).

5:21. But examine everything carefully; hold fast to that which is good. Examine (*dokimazete*) is used in Christian writings as a means of determining the authenticity of a teaching, here designated **that which is good** (1 Cor. 12:3; 1 John 4:1-3; *Did.* 11.12). In Greek papyri,

examine (*dokimaz?*) is used, in judicial situations (*PRyl* 2.114.35; *POxy* 1.128.9; *PFlor* 2.119.4), of inspecting animals to see if they are fit for sacrifice (*PGen.* 1.32.8) or qualifying for public office (cf. inscription *OGIS* 90.3). **Hold fast** (*katechete*) is similar to a legal term used for retaining something that rightfully belongs to someone (*PTebt.* 1.5.47; *POxy* 2.237.8.22; *POxy* 4.713.15; *PAmh* 2.30.26).

5:22. Abstain from every form of evil. Verses 21 and 22 would sound familiar to those who had read Isa. 1:16-17, which says, "Wash yourselves; make yourselves clean; remove the evil of your doings from before my eyes; cease to do evil, learn to do good; seek justice, correct oppression; defend the fatherless, plead for the widow."

5:23. Sanctify you entirely. Entirely (*hooteleis*) is a very rare term, occurring only here in the New Testament. It is found on an inscription from A.D. 67 announcing "complete exemption from taxation" to all Greeks at the Isthmian Games (*SIG*³ 814.45; *IG* 7.2713.45; cf. Aristotle, *Plant.* 1.2.20.817b; *T. Dan* 5.2).

5:26 Greet all the brethren with a holy kiss: Holy kiss. Kisses in the ancient world were used within and outside the family. They communicated love, respect, and reconciliation. Though kissing among the **brethren** suggests kissing across sexes, kissing of the opposite sex was discouraged in earliest Christianity (*Apostolic Constitutions* 2.57.17). That the **kiss** is called **holy** suggests its religious connotation. Justin Martyr (c. A.D. 150) spoke of the exchange of kisses during the Eucharistic part of a service (Wanamaker, 208). Pagan religions employed cultic kisses of images to gain supernatural strength (Cicero, *Verr.* 2.4.94; Apul. *Met.* 11.17.3; Dio C. 41.9.2; Ovid. *Metam.* 7.631f).

2 Thessalonians

Daniel M. Gurtner

I. 1:1-2. GREETING

1:1. Paul and Silvanus and Timothy to the church of the Thessalonians in God our Father and the Lord Jesus Christ: The inclusion of all three names, along with the frequent use of "we" in this epistle (17 times) suggests that all should be considered as authors. The word "I" only occurs three times in 2 Thessalonians, perhaps affirming the personal greeting and authority of the apostle to the young church. It was customary in letter writing to begin with the name of the sender, the recipient, and a greeting; e.g., "Andron to his brother Milon greeting" (*Select Papyri; Letters*, 96.1 [LCL]). See comment on 1 Thess. 1:1.

1:2. Grace to you and peace from God the Father and the Lord Jesus Christ: The particular combination of **grace** and **peace** is unusual, but found in some Jewish literature (esp. *2 Bar.* 78.2; cf. *Jub.* 12.29; *1 Enoch* 1.8; 1QS 2:1-4). Here, however, Paul replaced the standard Hellenistic greeting of "greetings" (*chairein*) with a theological **grace** (*charis*). **Peace** (*eirēnē*) is the Greek equivalent of the Hebrew *shalom*. See comment on Col. 1:2.

II. THANKSGIVING AND PRAYER (1:3-12)

1:3. We ought always to give thanks to God for you brethren, as is only fitting. Ancient letters frequently began with a statement of thanks to various deities for the well-being of the recipients. See comment on 1 Thessalonians 1:2. **Ought . . . as is only fitting** implies a special obligation felt on the part of the apostle, which is similarly found in other Christian writings (*1 Clem.* 38.4; *Barn.* 5.3; 7.1). Jews also were reminded to thank God for their own redemption (*m. Pesah* 10.5).

1:4. Among the churches of God: Paul reveals in 1 Thessalonians 1:8 that the churches which are familiar with the faith of the Thessalonians are particularly those in Achaia and Macedonia. See comment on 1 Thess. 1:8. **Perseverance** (*hupomonēs*) is used by Paul to connote the endurance of a believer's faith through trials. It was used of Jews who displayed steadfastness in the face of martyrdom (*4 Macc.* 1.11; *Pss. Sol.* 2.40) or temptation to sin (*T. Jos.* 10.1). The term was also used of the power of a sword to sustain a blow (Polybius, *Frg.* 15.15.8) or the stamina of a plant to endure (Theophratus, *Causis Plantarum* 5.16.3). **Persecution and afflictions.** The Thessalonian Christians suffered from the moment of their conversion (1 Thess. 1:6; 2:2; cf. Acts 17:5-7). See comment on 1 Thess. 1:6.

1:5. This is a plain indication of God's righteous judgment: Plain indication (*endeigma*) can also mean "evidence" (Pl *Criti* 110b), and its verbal form may be used as a legal term for proof (*PMadg* 3.10; cf. *POxy* 3.494.9). **You may be considered worthy of the kingdom of God: Worthy** (*axiōs*) literally means the balancing of scales, making things equivalent (1 Thess. 2:12). That the verb **considered** is in the passive voice suggests it is God who will make the decision. The **kingdom of God** was probably seen as the presence and reign of God. See comment on Mark 1:15 §25. **Suffering** was understood to be the temporary lot of the faithful (*Pss. Sol* 13.9-10; *2 Macc.* 6.12-16; *2 Bar.* 13.3-10; 78.5). A Jewish theological understanding of suffering included the following; the recognition of God's retributive justice (cf. v. 6), the belief that such suffering was God's chastisement to prepare them to be worthy of future glory; the understanding that the peace then enjoyed by the wicked will one day be theirs while the lot of the wicked is destruction, and the recognition that the present suffering was evidence of God's election and justice (Wanamaker, 222). The Jews at Qumran expected a time of intense distress for believers prior to the arrival of the Messiah (1QH 3:2-18).

1:6. For after all it is only just for God to repay with affliction those who afflict you. The principle of divine retribution, *lex talionis* ("an

eye for an eye, a tooth for a tooth"), is often visible in the Old Testament with respect to the Day of the Lord. This verse is particularly dependent on Isaiah 66:6, which says, "A voice of uproar from the city, a voice from the temple, The voice of the LORD who is rendering recompense to His enemies" (cf. Ps. 137:8). While such retribution is forbidden to individuals (Matt. 5:38-48; Rom. 12:17), God may employ it because he has "righteous judgment" (1:5) and is himself **just** (cf. Rom. 2:6-8; 12:19; 2 Cor. 5:10; Col. 3:25).

1:7-8. The Lord Jesus shall be revealed from heaven with His mighty angels in flaming fire: Fire is often the medium through which an Old Testament theophany (manifestation of God, from the Greek *theos* ["God"] and *phanos* ["appearance, manifestation"]) took place (Exod. 3:2; 19:18; Deut. 5:4; Dan. 7:9; Isa. 66:15). Calling it a **flaming fire** emphasizes the glory of the appearance of the Lord, an appearance like that of a theophany in the Old Testament (Best, 259). Rather than **fire** here being thought of in terms of purification (Exod. 3:2), it should be understood in relation to **retribution** (v. 8; Isa. 66:15). **Retribution** (*ekdik?sis*) is not vindictive but a repayment (v. 6) of the wicked (Ezek. 25:14, 17; 2 Sam. 4:8; 22:48; Ps. 17:48). **Angels** were commonly thought to be present in Old Testament manifestations of Yahweh (Ps. 68:18; Zech. 14:5; cf. *1 Enoch* 1.9). Early Christians offered fanciful speculations on the return of Christ (*Ap. Elijah* 3.3; cf. *2 Bar* 29.3; *3 Bar* 1.8; *Asc. Isa.* 4.14, 15).

1:8. Dealing out retribution to those who do not know God and to those who do not obey the gospel of our Lord Jesus. Know God: Knowing (*gnōseēs*) is used in the Old Testament sense where God "knows" his people "in election and grace" (Exod. 33:12; Amos 3:2), and particularly, God's people knowing him "in love and obedience" to his self-revelation (Jer. 31:34; Hos. 6:3; cf. Wisd. 15.3; *Sib. Or.* 3.693; 1QS

Christ and the Angels

"When the Christ comes, he will come in the manner of a covey of doves with the crown of doves surrounding him. He will walk upon the heaven's vaults with the sign of the cross leading him. The whole world will behold him like the sun which shines from the eastern horizon to the western. This is how he will come with all his angels surrounding him."

Apocalypse of Elijah 3.2-4 OTP

> "For behold, the LORD will come in fire And His chariots like the whirlwind, To render His anger with fury, And His rebuke with flames of fire. For the LORD will execute judgment by fire And by His sword on all flesh, And those slain by the LORD will be many."
>
> Isaiah 66:15-16

1:12; 4:22; 11:16-20; Phil. 3:8). Those who do not **know God** are thought by some to refer to Gentiles (Jer. 10:25; Ps. 79:6; 1 Thess. 4:5), though Jews also, by both actions and lack of faith (in Christ), can likewise be said to not know God (Jer. 9:6; John 8:55). God's anger will be poured out on the nations who do not know him (Ps. 79:6). Paul seems to be borrowing the judgment language of Isa. 66:15-16.

1:9. And these will pay the penalty of eternal destruction, away from the presence of the Lord and from the glory of His power. These (hoitines) literally means "such people" and refers to those who persecute the Thessalonians (v. 6) and will undergo judgment. **Destruction** (olothron) is an Old Testament word used frequently for God's eschatological judgment (Jer. 28:55; 31:3; 32:17; Ezek. 6:14; 14:16). That it is **eternal** denotes the severity of the punishment awaiting the enemies of God (4 Macc. 10.15; Wanamaker, 229; cf. 1QS 2:15; 5:13; Pss. Sol. 2.35; 15.12). **Away from the presence of the Lord and from the glory of His power.** Unlike later Christian apocalypses, contemporary Jewish apocalypses and even parts of the New Testament, Paul views judgment in terms of the separation the judged will ultimately have from the Lord (Isa. 2:10, 19, 21; Best, 263).

1:11. We pray for you always: Ancient letters frequently included references to prayers for the health and well-being of the recipients. A letter

from a woman to her husband, written in 168 B.C., reads, "Isias to Hephaistion: Greeting. If you are well and your other affairs turn out in like fashion, it would be as I have been continually praying to the gods" (PLond 1.42; cf. PMich 8.499). Thessalonica contained numerous deities, though the apostle offers prayer to **our God. Worthy.** See comment on 1 Thess. 2:12.

III. 2:1-12. THE DAY OF THE LORD

2:1. With regard to the coming of our Lord Jesus Christ, and our gathering together to Him: Coming of our Lord Jesus Christ. Coming (parousia) see comment on 1 Thess. 2:19. **Our gathering together to Him** reflects Old Testament language from the exilic prophets reassembling Israel after its exile in Babylon (Isa. 43:4-7; 52:12; 56:8; Jer. 31:8; Ezek. 28:9; cf. Ps. 106:47; Joel 3:2; 2 Macc. 2.7).

2:2. That you may not be quickly shaken from your composure or be disturbed either by a spirit or a message or a letter as if from us, to the effect that the day of the Lord has come. Though uncertain of the medium, Paul clearly understands that someone has told them, claiming to be of his association, that the **day of the Lord has come.** Thus he provides a series of evidences listed to prove that the **day of the Lord** had not yet come. Paul here (vv. 2-12) lays out the first proof that Christ has not yet returned. The second is in 2:13-15.

2:3. Let no one in any way deceive you. Deceive connotes a deliberate misleading (Xenophon, Anabasis 7.1.25; Hesiodus, Theogonia 205) or enacting fraud in a business transaction (Syll 510.37; 533.47; POxy 3.471.42). **It will not come unless the apostasy comes first: Apostasy** is used in Josephus to denote a political rebellion, such as that of the Jews against the Romans (Life 43 §212-15). It is also used of religious defection, such as abandoning the Law of

---

Pompey as the "Lawless One"

"The lawless one laid waste our land, so that no one inhabited it; they massacred young and old and children at the same time. In his blameless wrath he expelled them to the west, and he did not spare even the officials of the country from ridicule. As the enemy (was) a stranger and his heart alien to our God, he acted arrogantly. So he did in Jerusalem all the things that gentiles do for their gods in their cities. And the children of the covenant (living) among the gentile rabble adopted these (practices). No one among them in Jerusalem acted (with) mercy or truth. Those who loved the assemblies of the devout fled from them as sparrows fled from their nest. (They became) refugees in the wilderness to save their lives from evil. The life of even one who was saved from them was precious in the eyes of the exiles. They were scattered over the whole earth by (these) lawless ones . . . See, Lord, and raise up for them their king, the son of David, to rule over your servant Israel in the time known to you, O God."

Psalms of Solomon 17.11-21 OTP

Moses (Acts 21:21) or his ordained leadership (Josh. 22:22; 2 Chron. 29:19; 33:19; Jer. 2:19; *1 Macc.* 2.15). A revolt against the law of God was foretold by some Jews (*Jub.* 23.24-23; *2 Esdr* 5.1-13; *1 Enoch* 91.3-10; 93.8-10; 1QpHab 2:1; cf. *b. Sanh.* 97). **And the man of lawlessness is revealed, the son of destruction:** The leader of this revolt is called **the man of lawlessness**. He is typically identified with one who elsewhere is called the Antichrist (1 John 2:18, 22; 4:3; 2 John 7; cf. Matt. 24:5, 23-24; Mark 13:21-22; Luke 21:8; Rev. 13:1-18). Some have argued that this phrase comes from the Old Testament "man of Belial" (2 Sam. 22:5; Ps. 18:4; 1 Kings 21:13). It connotes the origin, character, and destiny of the person so described (Bruce, 168). Belial comes from the Hebrew *b?liyya'al*, meaning "wickedness" and is used in various forms (Beliar, etc.) in later Judaism as a name for Satan (cf. *Jub.* 1.20; 15.33; *T. Reub.* 4.7; *T. Dan* 5.1; *Sib. Or.* 3.63-74; *Asc. Isa.* 1.8-9; 1QM 13:11; CD 16:5). *Psalms of Solomon* 17.11-22 describes Roman general Pompey's military campaign and entrance into the Holy of Holies in the Jerusalem temple in 63 B.C. in terms similar to Paul's depiction of the **man of lawlessness** (cf. Jos. *Ant.* 14.4.4; Jub 10.3; *Gk. Apoc. Ezra* 4.21; *Sib. Or.* 3.570; *Apoc. Elijah* 1.2, 10; 2.40; *Apoc. Dan.* 9.9). Similar language was also used of the emperor Caligula, who in A.D. 40 tried to set up a statue of himself in the temple and assert his claim to divinity (*Pss.Sol.* 2.1-37; Philo, *Embassy* 203-346; Jos. *Ant.* 18.8.2-9 §§261-309). **Son of destruction** (*ho huios t?s ap?leias*), KJV "son of perdition," is a Semitism, similar to "son of stripes" (Deut. 25:2), describing one who deserves a flogging, or "son of death" (1 Sam. 26:16; 2 Sam. 12:5; Ps. 102:20), used of someone doomed to die. For killing his brother Abel (Gen. 4:8), Cain is called a "son of wrath" (*Ap. Moses* 3.1-14; cf. Gen. 4:11; Eph. 2:3; 1QS 9:16; CD 6:15; 13:14).

2:4. Paul's language may be drawn from Dan. 11:36, which describes a certain king, probably Antiochus Epiphanes, who "will exalt and magnify himself above every god, and will speak monstrous things against the God of gods" (cf. *Apoc. Elijah* 3.5; *Asc. Isa.* 4.7). **Opposes:** In the Old Testament Satan is called "the opposer" (Zech. 3:1). **Object of worship** refers to objects used in worship (*Wisd.* 14.20; 15.17; Jos. *Ant.* 18.344). **The Temple of God:** Here what is recalled is the innermost part of the temple in Jerusalem. For someone to take a position in this location would require him to claim messianic status (*Tg. Zech.* 6:12; cf. Mal. 3:1; Best, 286). In the Old Testament, Yahweh himself was enthroned here on the cherubim and worshiped (Pss. 80:1; 99:1). **Displaying himself as being God.** Some believed a pagan could make such a claim (Philo, *Gaius* 162; cf. *Syb. Or.* 5.33) or an eschatological opponent of God (*Asc. Isa.* 4.6). Yet as has been said above, the language here most clearly reflects that of the Old Testament (Dan. 11:31, 36; Ezek. 28:2, 6, 9; Isa. 14:13), where the ideas of profanation of the temple, sitting on a throne, and claiming to be God are introduced (Best, 288). The king of Tyre was proclaiming "I am God, I sit in the seat of Gods" (Ezek. 28:2), while Herod Agrippa I also received honors of a deity (Acts 12:21-23; Jos. *Ant.* 19.8.2 §343-47).

2:5. I was telling you. The Greek verb, *elegon*, is in the imperfect tense, suggesting that Paul customarily or repeatedly told them **these things**.

2:6-7. These two verses have been seen by some scholars as the most difficult in all of Paul's writings. The phrase **you know what restrains him now** presupposes a shared knowledge between the author and Thessalonians of which readers are not aware. While modern scholars greatly vary in their understanding of the background of these verses, we must be content in concluding that they are speculative and that the apostle's readers had the necessary knowledge to interpret the passage. If not, Timothy, the bearer of the letter, could probably have easily explained it to them. Naturally, the issue largely revolves around how to understand **what restrains** (*to katechon*). The belief that in the end times Satan will be bound is commonly found in Jewish and Christian writings (*Tobit* 8.3; *1 Enoch* 10.4-11; 18.12-19.2; 21.1-6; 54.4; *T. Levi* 19.12; *Jub.* 48.15; Rev. 20:2; cf. *Acts of Pilate* 22.2). The identity of the restrainer is less clear. This figure is referred to in both neutral (a neuter participle **what restrains**, v. 6) and personal (a masculine participle **who . . . restrains**, v. 7) terms. Some have then suggested that it refers to the Roman Empire (neutral) and the Emperor (personal; Tertullian, ca. A.D. 200). Others suggest the principles of Law and Order along with the Roman political leaders are in view. Still others argue that the neutral is the gospel (*to euangelion* neuter noun) and the personal is Paul (*ho Paulos* masculine noun). Other suggestions include the power of God and God himself, the presence of the church and the Holy Spirit, and even the Jewish state and James of Jerusalem. It is widely agreed, however, that whatever the

---

"And forces from him will arise, desecrate the sanctuary fortress, and do away with the regular sacrifice. And they will set up the abomination of desolation. And by smooth words he will turn to godlessness those who act wickedly toward the covenant, but the people who know their God will display strength and take action. And those who have insight among the people will give understanding to the many; yet they will fall by sword and by flame, by captivity and by plunder, for many days. Now when they fall they will be granted a little help, and many will join with them in hypocrisy. And some of those who have insight will fall, in order to refine, purge, and make them pure, until the end time; because it is still to come at the appointed time. Then the king will do as he pleases, and he will exalt and magnify himself above every god, and will speak monstrous things against the God of gods; and he will prosper until the indignation is finished, for that which is decreed will be done. And he will show no regard for the gods of his fathers or for the desire of women, nor will he show regard for any other god; for he will magnify himself above them all."

Daniel 11:31-37

identity and nature of this restrainer, it is depicted as a positive thing for the Thessalonian church (cf. *Gk. Apoc. Ezra* 4.25; *LAB* 51.5). We do well to follow the model of Augustine, who said, "I admit that I am completely at a loss as to his meaning" (*City of God* 20.19 LCL).

2:7. For the mystery of lawlessness is already at work: Mystery (*mustērion*): See Introduction to Ephesians, comment on Eph. 1:9; Col. 1:26. The term commonly refers to the hitherto concealed but now disclosed purpose of God, with special reference to the fulfillment of his purpose (Bruce, 170). **Mystery of lawlessness** is a curious phrase without parallel in the New Testament. Its closest parallels are found in Qumran texts (1QH 5:36; 1Q 27:1:2, 7; 1QM 14:9), where it refers to "mysteries of sin," which are impeding God's divine purpose. Here it may refer to a lawlessness that is at work in secret (Best, 293).

2:8. And then that lawless one will be revealed whom the Lord will slay with the breath of His mouth and bring to an end by the appearance of His coming. Slay with the breath of His mouth borrows language from Isa. 11:4, where the princely descendent of David will, "strike the earth with the rod of His mouth, And with the breath of His lips He will slay the wicked" (cf. Pss. 32:6; 134:17; *1 Enoch* 14.2; 84.1; Job 4:9; Isa. 30:27-28; Rev. 19:15; *1 Enoch* 62.2; *4 Ezra* 13.10-11; *Pss. Sol.* 17.24, 35; *Apoc. Elijah* 2.41; *Asc. Isa.* 4.18). This is an image of warfare (Rev. 19:15), where the breath is a fierce weapon (Isa. 30:27; Rev. 2:16; 1QSb 5:24; Best, 303). The picture of the Messiah and Yahweh himself as warriors has Old Testament precedent (cf. Mal. 4:1; Isa. 42:13; 63:1-6). See comment on Eph. 6:11. **The appearance of His coming** connotes a more hostile and confrontational sense than merely **coming** (*2 Macc.* 2.21; 3.24; 12.22; 14.15; *3 Macc.* 5.8; cf. Joel 2:11; Mal. 3:22; Best, 304).

2:9. The one whose coming is in accord with the activity of Satan, with all power and signs and false wonders. In Rev. 13:2, the beast receives his power, throne, and authority from the red dragon (cf. *Apoc. Elijah* 3.6; *Asc. Isa.* 4.9).

2:10. With all the deception of wickedness for those who perish, because they did not receive the love of the truth so as to be saved. Deception of wickedness: In Revelation 13:13, the false prophet persuades people to worship the beast; here unbelievers are misled precisely because of their unbelief (cf. 1QS 4:23). **Love the truth. Truth** for Paul is used almost synonymously with the "gospel" (2 Cor. 4:2; 13:8; Gal. 5:8), and with **love;** (*agapē*) refers to love that has as its object the Christian gospel (Wanamaker, 261).

2:11. God will send upon them a deluding influence so that they might believe what is false: That God is the sender of such **deluding influence** is found elsewhere in the New Testament (Rom. 1:24, 26, 28) and the Old (Ps. 81:11; Ezek. 14:9; 1 Kings 22:23) as an act of judgment. **Deluding influence** (*energeian plan?s*) is also translated "strong delusion" (KJV, RSV), with the noun "delusion" (*plan?*) used of the strategy employed by a hunter stalking his game (*PKaibel* 351.3). **What is false** is to be contrasted with the gospel (v. 10), with such falsehoods clearly being in opposition to God (1QpHab 2:1, 2; 5:11).

2:13. But we should always give thanks to God for you. See comment on 1:3. Here Paul outlines his second proof that Christ has not yet returned. The first is in 2:2-12. **God has chosen you from the beginning for salvation through sanctification by the Spirit and faith in the truth:** In the Old Testament, Israel saw itself as God's chosen people (Deut. 4:37; 7:7; Ps. 33:12), as did the sectarians at Qumran (1QpHab 10:13; 1QH 14:15; 4QpPs37 2:5; Lohse, 146). Christians likewise saw themselves as "a chosen race, a royal priesthood, a holy nation, a people for God's own possession" (1 Peter 2:9; cf. Col. 3:12).

2:14. And it was for this He called you through our gospel, that you may gain the glory of our Lord Jesus Christ. Jews at Qumran believed that Adam lost his luster when he sinned, and that eschatological salvation would therefore include the return of the divine glory, that is, God's outward appearance of brilliance, to save humanity (1QS 4:23; CD 3:20; 1QH 17:15; Wanamaker, 268).

2:15. So then, brethren, stand firm. Stand firm (*stēkete*): Such steadfastness was an attribute of the ideal soldier who did not flinch regardless of potential threats (cf. Phil. 1:27; *PMag.Par.* 1.923; *PLips.* 40.2.4). **Stand firm** and **hold to** are both present imperatives in Greek, suggesting both actions are to be carried out on a continuous basis. **Traditions which you were taught** refers to their instructions in the faith from the apostles and his associates (cf. 1 Thess. 4:1).

IV. 3:1-5. THANKSGIVING AND PRAYER

3:1. Pray for us that the word of the Lord may spread rapidly. Spread rapidly (*trechein*) may be derived from the image of races held in Hellenistic stadiums. It seems more likely, though, that Ps. 147:15 was in view, in which such imagery is employed to display the majesty of God and the consequential necessity of extolling him (cf. Isa. 55:11; *Wisd.* 7.24).

3:2. That we may be delivered from perverse and evil men; for not all have faith. Deliverance from **evil men** is a common request to Yahweh from his people in the Old Testament (Ps. 139:1; Isa. 25:4), as well as for Paul (Rom. 15:31; 2 Cor. 1:10).

3:4. And we have confidence. This expression was sometimes used in ancient letters as a means of asserting pressure on the readers indirectly by compelling them to live up to the writer's expectations (*PMich* 485; *SB* 7656).

3:5. And may the Lord direct your hearts into the love of God and into the steadfastness of Christ. The word **direct** (*kateuthunai*) is used in a similar metaphorical sense in the Old Testament, where King David prayed, "Yahweh, God of Abraham, Isaac and Israel our ancestors, watch over this for ever, shape the purpose of your people's heart and direct their hearts to you, and give an undivided heart to Solomon my son to keep your commandments, your decrees and your statutes, to put them all into effect and to build the palace for which I have made provision" (1 Chron. 29:18-19; cf. 2 Chron. 12:14; 19:3; 20:33; Prov. 21:2; cf. *Sir.* 49.3). Here the Lord directs the will of an individual toward faithfulness to himself.

V. 3:6-15. GODLY DISCIPLINE

3:6. Keep aloof from every brother who leads an unruly life and not according to the tradition which you received from us. Keep aloof (*stellesthai*) can also refer to leaving behind or abandoning (cf. *3 Macc.* 1.19; *PKaibel* 691.4), or to restrictions as in a diet (Hippocrates, *Ancient Medicine* 5).

3:7. Follow our example. In Greco-Roman education, imitation of the teacher's example was an important aspect of learning. In Jewish education, disciples were expected to learn the master's teaching as well as to emulate his behavior (Philo, *Virtues* 66; *Congr.* 70; cf. Phil. 3:17). **Undisciplined manner** is used of an undisciplined or abandoning soldier (Xenophon, *Cyr.* 7.2.6; Demosthenes, *Third Olynth.* 11; Thucydides, *Peloponnesian War* 3.108; Bruce, 205).

3:8. With labor and hardship we kept work-

ing night and day so that we might not be a burden to any of you. Acts 17:7 suggests Paul and his companions stayed with Jason while in Thessalonica. See comment on 1 Thess. 2:9.

3:10. If anyone will not work, neither let him eat. Some scholars see this as a proverbial statement based on Gen. 3:19: "By the sweat of your face You shall eat bread, Till you return to the ground." Rabbi Abbahu reflected this belief: "If I do not work, I do not eat" (*Gen. Rab.* 2.2 [on Gen. 1:2]; cf. Prov. 10:4; *Ps-Phoc.* 153), as did some traditions in the early church (cf. *Did.* 12.1-5). Rabbis in Paul's day often had a trade to support themselves in addition to study of the Law (cf. *m. Abot.* 2.2; 4.5; *Midr. Qoh.* 2:17). See comment on Acts 18:3.

3:11. Doing no work at all . . . busybodies. The NIV best captures the Greek here by translating it "they are not busy; they are busybodies." Paul is using a play on words: **busy** (*ergazomenous*) with their work sounds like the word for **busybodies** (*periergazomenous*), which was commonly used for meddling in the affairs of another (*T. Reub.* 3.10; Plato, *Apology* 19B; *PLond.* 1912.90; *PGiss.* 1.57.5; cf. 1 Thess. 4:11; 1 Tim. 5:13).

3:14. Do not associate with him, so that he may be put to shame. The Qumran sectarians had similar regulations for discipline and restoring a wayward member. The disobedient were excluded from communal fellowship meals (1QS 6:24-7:25), and, though intended to be temporary, such shunning could also be permanent (cf. 1QS 9:1; CD 9:23; 20:3). The objective for Christians is repentance and restoration.

3:15. And yet do not regard him as an enemy, but admonish him as a brother. Marcus Aurelius comments that if someone is behaving roughly or rudely in the gymnasia, one is to simply "avoid him, yet not as an enemy" (*Meditations* 6.20; Bruce, 210).

3:16. Now may the Lord of peace Himself continually grant you peace in every circumstance. The Lord be with you all! Paul's letters typically ended with a benediction of peace (3:16), a personal greeting (3:17), and a benediction of grace (3:18).

3:17. I, Paul, write this greeting with my own hand, and this is a distinguishing mark in every letter; this is the way I write. Whether because of his chains or another reason, the apostle used a secretary, or *amanuensis*, who wrote what Paul dictated. See Introduction to the Prison Epistles. Such was a common practice in Paul's day, as was the inclusion of a personal greeting from the sender, perhaps functioning both to offer sentiments from his own hand and authenticate what was written by dictation (cf. *PGren* 89; Cicero, *Epistle to Atticum* 8.1; 13.28).

Earning One's Keep

"Everyone 'who comes in the name of the Lord' is to be welcomed. But then examine him, and you will find out – you will have insight – what is true and what is false. If the one who comes is merely passing through, assist him as much as you can. But he must not stay with you for more than two or, if necessary, three days. However, if he wishes to settle among you and is a craftsman, let him work for his living. But if he is not a craftsman, decide according to your judgment how he shall live among you as a Christian, yet without being idle. But if he does not wish to cooperate in this way, then he is trading on Christ. Beware of such people."

Didache 12.1-5

Introduction to the Pastoral Epistles

Robert W. Wall

Authorship. Without question, the most controversial issue in the modern study of the Pastoral Epistles (PE, 1-2 Timothy, Titus) is whether the historical Paul actually wrote them as attributed. During the nineteenth century a number of scholars began to question Pauline authorship of the PE. The decision one makes in this regard determines the historical setting one constructs for a precise interpretation of these letters. Virtually every detail of the social world of a composition is predicated on who wrote it, when, to whom, and for what reason. If Paul is not the real author of the PE, if Timothy and Titus are fictional recipients, if the date of composition is long after Paul's death for a church that did not know him in person, if the opponents mentioned are merely used as a rhetorical convention to respond to second-century controversies—as many scholars now contend—then the historical background of these letters would necessarily be cast in very different ways than if Paul actually wrote them sometime around 60 A.D.for young pastors of fledging congregations in Roman Asia.

To be sure, an historical investigation into the identity of the real "author" of an ancient letter is difficult to execute for lack of hard evidence. In addition, we know from his letters that Paul often dictated his advice and instructions to a scribe, such as Silvanus (1 Thess. 1:1), who would actually write them down in his own words. Moreover, Paul would deliver his letters through messengers, such as Timothy, who would presumably read the letter aloud and interpret its message for its auditors—again in his own words. The literary form of a Pauline letter and its initial transmission, then, was a collaborative effort, and the probable use of different secretaries and messengers, often due to Paul's personal circumstances (e.g., imprisonment, a mission in another city) and to the limits of the "print technology" of his day, may well explain differences in vocabulary, literary form, and even in the theological emphasis one finds when comparing any of the thirteen Pauline letters of the NT.

Modern biblical scholars typically classify the PE (and other Pauline letters) as "pseudonymous"—that is, letters attributed to Paul in their address but which were probably written by someone else following his death or in his absence. The unknown authors of these pseudonymous letters were likely associated with a "Pauline school" or were close associates of Paul's missionary organization. Although contested among scholars, most agree that a pseudonymous work, set within this deeply religious setting, would have hardly been the work of someone bent on defrauding the Christian public. In fact, the literary and ethical principles that guided the work of these pseudepigraphers were widely accepted and employed within Paul's Hellenistic world. Even the OT, which is a collection of anonymous books, attributes collections or individual books to famous figures of Israel's religious past (e.g., Moses, Samuel, Solomon). Moreover, the continuing authority of any biblical writing—whether authentic, pseudepigraphy, or anonymous—is measured by its theological accuracy and practical value in forming faith. That is, in final analysis it remains the content of a writing and not its authorship that commends a book's inspiration and authority.

In any case, this modern consensus regarding the Pauline authorship of the PE is often asserted as a matter of scholarly dogma without convincing support. The purported evidence is wellknown: 1) PE's use of a different and distinctive vocabulary; 2) images of a more developed (= post-Pauline) church structure (e.g., 1 Tim. 3:1-16; Titus 1:3-7); 3) routine appeal to traditions about Paul as an exemplary person worthy to be imitated (e.g., 1 Tim. 1:12-17; 2 Tim. 3:11-14) or to formulae of his teaching as the congregation's theological norm (e.g., 1 Tim. 2:3-7; Titus 2:11-14; 3:3-7; cf. the "faithful sayings" of 1 Tim. 1:15; 2 Tim. 1:9; 2:11-13), which many contend are motivated to preserve the blessed memory of a now-deceased Paul; 4) the imprecise description of Paul's opponents suggest they are fictionalized and used for rhetorical ends; 5) inconsistent teaching (e.g., PE use of "the faith" [of Paul] rather than "faith in" [Jesus]); and 6) finally many insist that the PE are shaped by a "sociology of domesticity" that points to a later time period when the ancient church's "countercultural" practices were replaced by a concern for long-term stability and political respectability (e.g., 1 Tim. 2:8-15; 6:1-2).

Such evidence, however, fails to convince other scholars on three counts. First, the diversity found in the PE when compared to the "authentic" Pauline letters (e.g., Romans, 1 Corinthians, Galatians, 1 Thessalonians) is roughly at the same level of diversity found when comparing any subgroup of Pauline letters. That is, the very character of the per se corpus of Pauline letters is variegated linguistically,

theologically, and sociologically according to variations of original audience, occasion, and Paul's own developing theological understanding. This is true even within the PE, where the scrupulous student will note real differences between 1 Timothy, 2 Timothy, and Titus in language, purpose, and theological emphasis. Indeed, the formation of the Pauline collection within the ancient church is grounded on a principle that is typically ignored by modern scholarship: that any biblical collection gathers together *diverse* (rather than similar) writings to envisage a more robust witness to the whole truth than mere uniformity would allow. For this reason, for instance, the church collected four different narratives of Jesus' life to render the single gospel story.

Second, the diversity inherent within the entire Pauline collection is a reflection of the complexity of Paul's missionary vocation. The speeches of the Paul of Acts reflect the skills of a missionary who adapts his message to his ever-changing audiences. The biblical reader should not be surprised when proceeding to the Pauline letters, then, to find Paul adapting a specific letter's advice to the particular demands of a different audience—to write in an idiom or to underwrite a theological theme that is most pertinent to the special circumstances and cultural settings of a letter's recipients. In fact, Scripture itself suggests that Paul's understanding and articulation of his core theological beliefs developed over time as a result of necessarily adapting them to ever-different situations.

Finally, the speculations of historical research about Pauline authorship will always be frustrated by lack of hard evidence, and historians always require more of it than actually exists! Biblical writings and the historical record behind them are a severely gapped. And yet if the student were to assume at face value the portrait of Paul and his mission supplied by the Book of Acts, along with the biographical materials found within the Pauline letters including the rather complicated network of personal references and contacts found in the PE, then one could easily date the PE from the early 60s—and 2 Timothy from a Roman prison. This early date will be accepted for the purposes of this Background Commentary, and also Paul as the real author of the PE and his younger associates as their first recipients. Moreover, even though these three letters are routinely treated as a discrete group of Pauline letters, it remains best to consider the occasion of each letter separately for the purpose of reconstructing their distinctive historical background.

Literary form. Letters took many forms in the ancient world. Most were written communication to bridge the distance between two parties. Oratory was an important social convention of Paul's world, and letters were the literary expression of both public and private speeches. Among the various kinds of letters preserved from the ancient world, perhaps the most common is private correspondence, which is similar in function and literary form to the PE. We now possess literally thousands of ancient papyrus letters, stored in museums across the world, which reflect a variety of interpersonal transactions that follow a standard literary pattern divided into three separate parts, each with a specific role to perform: an opening greeting, the main body, and a concluding benediction. Most of Paul's letters observe this same literary convention.

Of the various functions performed by private letters, the PE are letters of "instruction and order"—although the instructions contained in 1 Timothy and Titus are to order Christian congregations, mostly constituted of new converts, while those given in 2 Timothy are more personal and seek to reshape Timothy's life after Paul, his mentor and role model. While there are few exact parallels from this vast literary depository, the PE do bear a family resemblance to those we do possess; and this fact enables the scholar to make the following general observations about their literary form.

Letters of antiquity began with formal greetings so that the recipient would know the sender's identity immediately upon unrolling the scroll. For this reason, Paul's letters generally follow a well-known script: "Paul to recipient, greetings." In personal letters such as the PE, this formula was amplified to highlight the nature of the relationship between sender and recipient to justify a positive response of the letter's instructions. In the case of the PE, Paul's address does more than underwrite his personal relations with Timothy and Titus; his relationship to Jesus and the God of Israel are specified as well in order to stipulate his spiritual authority. Especially when the biblical reader approaches the PE with the Paul of Acts in mind, Paul's self-reference an "apostle of Christ Jesus" posits the religious importance of his mission and message for the future of the church, which Timothy and Titus are now delegated to organize in Ephesus and Crete.

The main body of a personal letter takes up the business at hand. (In this sense, it functions much like a sermon or homily does in today's worship service.) Differences of emphasis and vocabulary that the careful reader notes between different Pauline letters reflect the range of controversies and crises that Paul considers and seeks to resolve in the main body of his various letters. Advice is given, instruction rendered, commands made, doctrine corrected, false teachers rebuked according to his interpretation of Scripture (cf. 2 Tim. 3:16b) and religious experience (cf. 1 Tim. 1:12-16).

The subject matter of both 1 Timothy and Titus is similar, and is primarily concerned with conveying instructions that would order congregational life in pagan places—not unlike the early second-century *Didache* as well as other Christian writings written across the next several centuries for a developing, expanding missionary church. The main body of 2 Timothy is quite different, with a heightened sense of Paul's passing and the importance of Timothy's role to carry on his legacy to the next generation—a kind of literary "last will and testament" of the revered apostle.

The concluding words of a Pauline letter, including the PE, include many elements. While a benedictory blessing of some kind always ends a personal letter, miscellaneous greetings, exhortations, itinerary, summaries of concern, and other personal reminders are included in an epistolary benediction as well. What this suggests about the PE in particular is that they were not written to keep "private," but Paul intended them for a wider readership beyond their initial recipients.

Social world of Paul's urban missions. Francis Young famously said that "theology is always earthed in a context." The worlds that shape the ideals and idiom of Paul's instructions to both Timothy and Titus are Greco-Roman—the morality of its philosophers and social politics of its households—and Jewish—the theology of its Scriptures and structure of its synagogues. Yet, even more concretely, the congregations founded by Paul's mission were real life communities of believers. Converts to Jesus came from various social and religious backgrounds found in any large urban center in the Roman world in which Paul enjoyed his greatest successes as a missionary. Indeed, no shift in the composition of earliest Christianity is more remarkable than from the Palestinian/rural setting of the "Jesus movement" to the Roman/urban setting of Paul's missionary church; and the ethos of the PE reflects this new cultural horizon. To underwrite this observation, the biblical reader should note that the narrative world of Acts is constructed almost exclusively of cityscapes from Jerusalem to Rome, which surely reflects the urban background of earliest Christianity and much of the NT.

The cities of Paul's mission, including Ephesus (mentioned in 1-2 Timothy) and Nicopolis in Greece (mentioned in Titus), were typically important commercial centers of the Roman Empire, cosmopolitan in social makeup, and conveniently located for travel by land and sea. Most Roman cities were divided into ethnic neighborhoods, each with its own public places. Especially important was the large Jewish population in the Diaspora, which normally settled into enclaves within the city identified by its own synagogue (or "voluntary organization"). Otherwise, most ancient cities tolerated a diversity of religious cults devoted to the worship of local deities, deities of the Greek pantheon, "mystery" (or "new age") religions, and under pressure from Rome its Caesar.

The images of the "household" of an extended family are found throughout the PE; the household evidently was the setting for much of Paul's missionary activities and early Christian worship. Roman households were mostly larger "compounds" which combined shops, living accommodations, gathering places with yards for children to play. As Roman society's essential "building block," the household was ordered hierarchically, with its male head obligated to supervise and provide for its various members, whether familial or servants. Social convention and political legislation regulated relationships within the household, with each member held responsible for certain tasks to insure its good reputation and security.

As a Pharisee, Paul was bi-vocational by training, working as an artisan by day to support his mission and teaching interested people by night (cf. Acts 18:1-4). His missionary strategy and congregational gatherings alluded to throughout the PE and in the book of Acts were easily adapted to this household structure. Further, households were often large and always inclusive communities; each member held certain responsibilities and their relationships to others were predicated on these roles. The patterns of this political structure were also easily adapted to the congregational life. The "Christianization" of the Roman household curtailed any potential for internal conflict, even between household congregations within the same city, while also commending the gospel to outsiders who might measure its truth on the basis of Christian conduct. In part, this recognition explains Paul's abiding concern for virtuous character in his description of those who lead the Christian household/congregation.

At the same time, the household was a social "institution" shaped by a particular social hierarchy. The head of the house was typically the father or another older male; and indications of gender, social class, and rank are everywhere noted in the PE. For example, even though aspiring to the same virtuous persona, the poor widow occupies a different place within the Christian household (cf. 1 Tim. 5:1-16) than does the married woman of financial means (cf. 1 Tim. 2:9-15); and the instructions Paul gives to each reflect their very different social status. From the book of Acts, one is able to discern a broad range of social groups were represented within a Pauline congregation, reflecting the diversity within the city, including a substantial middle class. Paul's great "Magna Carta" of Gal. 3:28 (cf. Col. 3:11) is really a descriptive statement about the mixed membership of a congregation, perhaps asserted with the more revolutionary subtext that "in Christ" a diverse congregation of believers cuts across social, gender, ethnic, and geographical lines to achieve an uncommon solidarity because of him.

Diaspora Jews had settled particular neighborhoods of most Roman cities in which the synagogue (or "assembly place") was a central gathering point for their religious and social life. Because Christianity began as a messianic movement within Second Temple Judaism, its core theological beliefs, ethical behavior, religious and exegetical practices, worship liturgy, and social patterns were essentially Jewish. Perhaps in part because of the growing influence of Paul's mission to the nations, however, the church had begun to gradually separate itself from its Jewish legacy, primarily over controversies related to the conditions for initiating repentant pagans (i.e., non-Jews who had not first converted to Judaism) into Christian fellowship. Opponents to the Pauline mission appear on the scene to press for more Jewish forms of religious and theological expression, perhaps even challenging the manner by which Paul folded new converts into the community of believers. But these are "intramural" conflicts within the church, probably having as much to do with the social identity or political structures of a congregation belonging to the God of Israel than with its religious practices or theological beliefs.

Finally, it seems clear not only from Paul's autobiographical statements in his letters but also from his story told by Luke in Acts that his missionary organization included several colleagues, to whom he had delegated important responsibilities of his missionary enterprise (cf. Phil. 4:2-3). Clearly, Paul preferred to complete his work in person (cf. Rom. 1:10-11), no doubt believing that the very presence of his apostolic gifts mediated God's grace in more powerful and distinctive ways (cf. Rom. 1:5). Nonetheless, particular missionary associates, such as Timothy and Titus, were competent substitutes for the hard work of establishing Christian congregations in pagan places (cf. 1 Cor. 4:16-17; 16:10-11; 1 Thess. 3:2). In this sense, then, the instructions Paul gives to Timothy and Titus in the PE intend to establish a congregational expression of the Christian faith and reflect species of religious curriculum that he himself would have followed had he been able to plant these same congregations in downtown Ephesus (1-2 Timothy) or on the island of Crete (Titus).

Even the more personal tones and themes of 2 Timothy are suggestive of a "professional" relationship between a respected mentor and his young apprentice who needs equal measure of encouragement and of reminder to accomplish the difficult work at hand. This final observation is important for understanding the particular literary genre of the PE as "personal" letters (see above). In fact, Luke Johnson now classifies the literary genre of 1-2 Timothy as *mandata principis*—an "official" letter that mixes instruction (probably read publicly to the whole congregation) with personal exhortation (probably kept in private by its pastor) from a political superior to administrative associates for their use at a specific location.

The Pastoral Epistles within the Pauline Collection. One of the principal interests of biblical interpretation today is the canonical process that produced over time the final literary product of the Christian Bible. Whatever interest the individual scholar vests in this historical moment, the methodological presumption in every case is that this phenomenon reflects a process of selection by which certain writings of early Christian leaders were preserved and circulated for worship and religious education of various congregations in different locations. Individuals were eventually formed into collections by their faithful readers, and ultimately arranged together during the fourth and fifth centuries to form a New Testament as the written rule in forging a truly Christian theological definition of life and faith.

As one subplot of this canonical process, the PE circulated together during the second century but evidently separate from a nine- or ten-letter Pauline collection already known and used by Christian teachers by the end of the first century. Sometime during the second century, the PE were added to this collection already in circulation in order to complete it. In fact, the church did not fully recognize the authority of this Pauline canon for future generations of believers until only after the PE were added to it. The PE sub-collection was a necessary element in forming a final (or "canonical") edition of Paul's letters.

But why is this so, especially given the priority of other Pauline letters within the church, and given the general neglect of the PE in the church's teaching and scholarship? The PE were added to the Pauline collection during a period when the growing pains experienced by the second-century church required greater clarity regarding internal patterns of "ecclesiastical discipline" (as the Muratorian Canon phrased it around A.D. 200). Paul's more "charismatic"

conception of the Christian congregation, articulated in his letters to Corinthian believers, is largely defined by his own missionary vocation and experiences and by his convictions about the importance of the Holy Spirit's work within the congregation of believers. While his Corinthian correspondence, along with his so-called "prison" letters, supply his readers with general beliefs and practices concerning the church, more practical advice was required. In particular, the second-century urban church needed to understand more clearly how it should relate to the social institutions and morés of pagan culture. Moreover, the increasing diversity of its membership and complexity of its organization required more specific instructions to its leadership. For this reason, Paul's instructions to Timothy and Titus about practical matters related to a congregation's organization, its teaching and social ministries, its relationship with a pagan society, and so forth contribute to and complete Paul's overarching (and sometimes more "theoretical") understanding of the church—what it means to be the church and to do as the church ought.

RESOURCES

The following recently published commentaries on the PE are especially helpful in providing students with detailed information about the historical background and literary features of these Pauline letters. I acknowledge my debt to them, and to still other unnamed sources.

Collins, Raymond F. *I & II Timothy and Titus: A Commentary*. NTL. Louisville: Westminster John Knox Press, 2002.

Johnson, Luke Timothy. *The First and Second Letters to Timothy*. AB. New York: Doubleday, 2001.

Marshall, I. Howard. *The Pastoral Epistles*. ICC. Edinburgh: T&T Clark, 1999.

Quinn, Jerome D. and William C. Wacker. *The First and Second Letters to Timothy*. CEC Grad Rapids: Eerdmans, 1995.

Introduction to 1 Timothy

Robert W. Wall

First read the "Introduction to the Pastoral Epistles."

The purpose of 1 Timothy according to 1 Timothy is set out in the opening words of its main body: Paul commands Timothy to stay in Ephesus to correct the instruction (1:3) and manner (1:6-7) of false teachers to bring them into agreement with "the administration of God, which is by faith" (1:4) and whose goal (*telos*) is "love from a pure heart and a good conscience and a sincere faith" (1:5). Implied by this statement of purpose are four different elements that frame the background of his letter: 1) The relationship between Paul and Timothy, 2) the relationship between Ephesus, its church, and Paul's mission, 3) the problem of the false teachers in Ephesus, and 4) the theological meaning of "the administration of God."

The relationship between Paul and Timothy. Timothy is introduced to us in Acts 16:1-5. He is the product of a mixed marriage. Because his father is Greek and fathers typically determined the religious identification of their children, Timothy had inherited little of his mother's Jewish faith. According to Acts, Paul circumcises Timothy to restore his Jewish identity at least in part to aid Timothy in gaining entry into Jewish congregations while assuaging the worry of James who thought that the introduction of repentant but uncircumcised pagans into the church might lead to the attenuation of the Jewish legacy of the Christian

faith and its resurrection practices (cf. Acts 15:13-29). The conflict between Jewish and pagan religious backgrounds, which Timothy personifies, may well have prompted his disputations with those so-called "teachers of the Law" (see 1:7) whom Paul vigorously chastises.

In any case, according to Acts, Timothy accompanied Paul on his European mission and presumably was with him when he made his first stop in Ephesus (18:19) while on a personal pilgrimage to Jerusalem. He once again is mentioned as a member of Paul's entourage when leaving Ephesus some months later for Macedonia (20:4). Although Luke is not interested in telling Timothy's story and provides us with few details, it is plausible to suggest that he was a member of the missionary team that evangelized Ephesus over several months if not years, was familiar with its cultural currents and people, and therefore was a logical choice for Paul to appoint for the Ephesian work in his stead.

The relationship between Ephesus, its church, and Paul's mission. Ephesus was a great cosmopolitan city, a cultural and religious center of the ancient world, and the capital of Roman Asia—among the Empire's most prosperous regions. In time, Ephesus would also become the headquarters of the Pauline missionary organization. Paul's reference to himself as a teacher of the Gentiles (2:7) suggests that the congregations spread across the metropolis were largely non-Jewish and Hellenistic in their customs and sensibilities. The internal structure of the household seems more Jewish, however, not only in the tasks given its primary leaders (overseer, elder, deacon) but also in the makeup of its second tier of leadership in which respected widows and elderly men served the congregation in a variety of ways (5:1-25).

The problem of the false teachers in Ephesus. The identity of the false teachers whom Paul admonishes throughout this letter is difficult to determine. While names are given to them (1:20) and we are told they teach "different doctrines" (1:3), Paul reports little of what these doctrines consisted. Because he calls them "teachers of the law" (1:7) and later accuses them of teaching against marriage and certain foods (4:2-3) and articulating a false expression of "knowledge" (*gnosis*, 6:20), the impression is that they are conservative Jewish ascetics (not unlike those found at Qumran), formerly Christians (cf. 1:19-20; 4:1) with continuing influence within the church, but who advance a pattern of salvation that requires Gentiles to maintain certain Jewish practices as a condition of their membership and even of their life with God.

The theological meaning of "the administration of God." The central criticism Paul makes against their theology, however, is that they teach against "the administration of God" (1:4). Even though critical to our understanding of the instructions found in 1 Timothy, this expression is extremely difficult to translate and interpret. The word "administration" translates the Greek word, *oikonomia*, which builds upon its basic root word, *oikos*, or "household." In Hellenistic thought following Aristotle, the efficiently administrated household, whether political, religious, or social, followed patterns built into and fixed by the very nature of things. There was little upward mobility in Greco-Roman society; in fact, one's work within or responsibility to the community was in this sense predetermined by birth and the social status of one's extended family. This same concept extended even to the competent individual, whose "self-control" subdued internal passions for the good of society. From his Jewish perspective, Paul conceives of God's providential care of creation in a similar way. God's way of ordering reality, whether personal or societal, is apprehended by faith and aims at love (1:4b-5a). When the rule of faith is subverted, as is the case with the false teachers, then loving (or "orderly") relations within the congregation or between believers and outsiders are subverted. The instructions we find in 1 Timothy reflect Paul's understanding of God's way of ordering reality—that is, God's administration of a distinctively Christian life and household. The importance of such a theological belief would have been immediately understood by his first readers.

1 Timothy

Robert W. Wall

1:1-2. Paul Greets Timothy

Paul's reference to God as **our Savior**, a confession of trust that is repeated throughout the PE (1 Tim. 1:1; 2:3; 4:10; Titus 1:3; 2:10; 3:4), expresses a central Jewish belief in a way readily understood by the Greco-Roman world in which deities and important human leaders (e.g., rulers, military generals) were called "saviors." Not only were they saviors because they were thought to have rescued people from calamity but because they were the source of some benefaction that enhanced their lives.

In usual Pauline fashion, the letter's salutation (1:2) combines the traditional greetings of the pagan world, "grace," with that of Paul's Jewish world, "peace." Such a mixture, while also a judgment of the universal scope of God's salvation, would have especially resonated with Timothy who personified it (see above). In this way, the addition of "mercy" to this greeting probably reflects a theological interest of Paul's correspondence with Timothy rather than a response to a particular theological crisis facing the Ephesian church.

1:3-11. Paul Commissions Timothy

The use of the opening exhortation, **I urged you**, is frequently found in Hellenistic letters from a superior to underscore the seriousness of his instructions: this is serious business to which the apostle commissions his associate. The context for doing so—Paul's **departure for**

Macedonia (1:3a)—is provided by Acts 19–20, which gives a summary of Paul's third mission centered in Ephesus. Because of a summary's lack of details, the precise timing of this charge is unclear. What is evident from Acts, however, is that Paul frequently made forays from Ephesus into Macedonia and that Timothy was somehow involved in his missionary strategy (cf. Acts 19:21-22; 20:1-6).

Paul's specific instruction to Timothy is to correct those who **teach strange doctrines** (1:3b), which presumes the existence of an established "rule of faith" that measures the content of teaching within congregations founded by Paul (Ignatius, *Poly.* 3.1). That is, this teaching is considered "strange" and different because it disagrees with what Paul taught about the **administration of God** (1:4b, see above). Specifically, he is concerned about their interest in **myths and endless genealogies** (1:4a). Two contemporaries of Paul, Plutarch and Philo, described "myths" as "useless fabrications" (Plutarch, *Obs. Or.* 46) or "mistakes" made from inconclusive arguments (Philo, *Cong.* 53). The added adjective, "endless," underscores the uselessness of any commentary that retrieves theological or moral claims from biblical genealogies (see Titus 1:14; 3:9) or Jewish stories (see 4:7; 2 Tim. 4:4; Titus 1:14) to authorize either doctrine or practices that conflict with the church's Pauline rule of faith.

The distinctively Jewish flavor of Paul's

opponents is made even clearer in his subsequent polemic against those who want to be **teachers of the Law** (1:7a). Although "Law" has different connotations, the term is used elsewhere in the NT of Jewish interpreters of the biblical Torah (cf. Acts 5:34), especially the Pharisees (cf. Luke 5:17). Perhaps Paul has in mind the range of biblical commentary (or *midrash*) that includes *haggadah* (on Torah's "myths" or stories and genealogies) and *hallakah* (on Torah's law code), which speculate on a way of life and faith that disagrees with Paul's own christological *midrash* on his Scriptures (cf. Acts 17:2-3). He is not condemning the per se Jewish practices of biblical interpretation that he himself employed (e.g., 1 Tim. 2:13-15a); rather, he is criticizing the practical inutility of those *midrashim* that fail to inform **sound teaching, according to the glorious gospel of the blessed God** (1:10b-11a). Paul's teaching has established the norm for a right reading of God's gospel (e.g., 1 Tim. 2:3-7).

By contrast, not only is the content of their interpretation flawed, but also the manner of their presentation—**fruitless discussion** (1:6) and speaking confidently about matters of which they are ignorant (1:7)—characterizes them as spiritually immature. Philo writes, "There is no need, then to give injunctions or prohibitions to the perfect man formed after the (divine) image, for none of these does the perfect man require" ("Allegorical Interpretation" 1.94). This interplay between what is taught and the manner of life then influenced by sound doctrine is profoundly Jewish in its theological sensibility. Hence, Paul's keen emphasis on the character and content of the church's rabbinate.

The **soundness** (lit., "good health") of one's teaching was already a standard by which truth was measured. Homer (*Iliad* 8.524), Plato (*Repu.* 9.584e), Philo (*Abraham* 223), and especially Epictetus (*Discourses* 1.11.28; 2.15.2; 3.9.2-5) considered persuasive and edifying words "sound." In keeping with this general senti-ment, Paul writes that his gospel exemplifies **sound teaching** because it accords with God's very own gospel (1 Tim. 1:10-11). Moreover, Paul links the **soundness** of teaching inextricably with the godliness of one's lifestyle (see Titus 1:1; cf. 1 Tim. 6:3). Paul is a practical theologian, always interested in how truth performs in real life. For this reason, a healthy lifestyle is predicated on healthy doctrine.

In contrast to the "myths" and "fruitless discussions" of the false teachers, the goal of "sound teaching" is loving relations (1:5a). In Pauline thought, **love** (*agapē*) or loving relations, is the moral criterion of sound **instruction** (cf. Gal. 5:6). If a congregation's life with God is cultivated by teaching that agrees with God's mind, the moral precipitate will be friendship with God and one another. In this case, Paul's triad of inward qualities that forge loving relations within the congregation (1:5b) is unique in the NT, and reflects the social matrix of his mission to the nations (and perhaps in Ephesus). The first quality is a **pure heart** and is central to his Jewish morality (see 2 Tim. 2:22). According to Jewish psychology, heart is the epicenter of selfhood—one's emotions, affections, motives. According to the OT prophets, the human heart is what drives the outward expressions of one's personality—one follows the inclinations of one's heart, which follows the exhortation of the *Shema'* to love God with "your whole heart" (Deut. 6:4-5). Moreover, the Jewish purity laws, which Paul continued to observe following his conversion to Christ (cf. Acts 21:21-26), maintained covenant fellowship with God by whom one's inward motives and affections were constantly cleansed of deceit and self-centeredness. 1 Clem 41.1 connects a "pure heart" with the practices of Christian worship—prayers, sharing goods, fellowship, Scripture reading.

The quality of a believer's **good conscience** reflects agreement with the central element of Greco-Roman morality from Cicero through Seneca (e.g., *Happy Life*, 20.3-5). Secular morality influenced Jewish morality in the Diaspora, so that even though not mentioned in the OT, Philo can list the "good conscience" among his *Special Laws* (1:203) as the internal capacity to discern God's will with the intention of obeying it. Of course, if the *telos* of God's way of ordering reality (= "the administration of God") is loving relations, then both purity of heart and integrity of one's conscience direct a person's responses to befriend and care for others.

The final quality of a **sincere faith** adds a distinctively Christian dimension to Paul's triad. Different connotations have been made of Paul's use of "faith" in the PE; however, here it seems to infer a single-minded devotion to the things of God. Whether this is expressed in the decisions one makes or in the beliefs one adheres to, the force of this quality is to vigorously and rigorously embrace what is of God. Augustine writes that "if our faith involves no lie, then we do not love that which is not to be loved, and living justly, we hope for that which will in no way deceive our hope" (*On Christian Doctrine* 1:40-44).

In the PE, what conforms to **the glorious gospel of the blessed God** (1:11) in life and doctrine is considered "sound"—a Greek medical term that means "healthy" (1:10). The conviction that the practical engagement of Christian teaching fosters a healthy life is a familiar one in the ancient world. Maximus of Tyre wrote a century after Paul that "truth and healthy understanding and morality and knowledge of the law and right cannot be acquired in any other way than by actually doing them, just as one can never learn the craft of shoemaking unless one actually works at it" (*Discourses* 16.3). In this light, Paul's reflection on the Torah in 1:8-11, while revealed by God on Mt. Sinai and therefore inherently **good** (1:8; cf. Rom. 7:12), is evaluated by its practical use in the formation of Christian existence. That is, Paul lists paired vices, which generally follows the Decalogue's prohibitions, to diagnose what is unhealthy for human life. In effect, he per-

forms the role of a mature rabbi (teacher of the Law) to clarify the Torah's proper role in the Christian life. In doing so, he measures the results of the false teachers' attempt to perform the same role and finds it seriously deficient: their *hallakah* serve no useless purpose in forming a healthy Christian life.

Such catalogues of vices (and virtues) were a standard literary convention of the moral handbooks recovered from the ancient world, and are found throughout the NT. Some lists contain only the deadliest of vices or a short list of cardinal virtues, while other lists—especially in the Jewish world—were more exhaustive. (Philo's famous list in the *Sacrifices of Abel and Cain* contains 146 vices to avoid in a right relationship with God!) The rhetorical use of such lists, whether long or short, was to create mental impressions or even caricatures of the reprobate (vice) or productive (virtue) life. Usually, the author created his moral catalogues with a particular situation or audience in mind, ranking the most important first. In this case, the first pair of vices, **lawless and rebellious** (1:9), describes the social deviant, and may be an important subtext in the various instructions Paul gives Timothy beginning with chapt. 2. Theologically, this pairing may refer back to "the administration of God" (1:4), that seeks to bring order to the social chaos caused by sin. Unruly worship practices or reproachable leaders or disruptive internal relations, various expressions of an unruly congregation, not only subvert the prospect of a healthy spirituality but also the redemptive purposes of God (see 2:3-6).

1:12-17. Paul Thanks God

The "Pauline thanksgiving" is a standard (although not uniform) ingredient of his letters. According to the literary conventions of the ancient world, the writer expresses gratitude to the deity for the recipient of his letter. This is sometimes referred to as a *captatio benevolentiae*—a rhetorical device used when introducing a public speech that not only aims at cultivating the goodwill of one's auditors but also to establish the purpose or main themes of the speech that follows. In the case of 1 Timothy, Paul need not praise Timothy since their relationship is already close (see 1:2); rather, he gives praise of his conversion as the personification of God's loving way of reordering reality. By rehearsing the transforming effect of divine grace, Paul is able to provide Timothy with a personal standard by which the false teachers are condemned and the essential theological subtext of the various instructions that follow. The use of illustrative portraits is an important feature of ancient rhetoric (Aristotle, *Rhetoric* 1366a34-b11, 1398a33-b20). Paul is presented both as a role model whose conversion experience ought to be imitated by sinners (cf. 1:15); and as one whose life creates a pattern of orthodoxy—the normative way to conceive of God—for believers (cf. 1:17).

The problem of Paul's ignorance of God's redemptive purpose is a standard way by which sin was understood in Hellenistic Judaism, which distinguished between willful and unconscious rebellion against the Creator's kind intentions (Josephus, *Ant.* 3.231-32). Rabbi Yischmael (A.D. 135) taught that "it is better that an Israelite sin unknowingly than to sin with intent" (SB II, 264), presumably because God's mercy is more readily available for the ignorant than for those who know the truth but reject it (1:13; cf. Lev. 16:21; 22:14; Num. 15:29-30; Acts 3:17; 17:30).

The phrase, **it is a trustworthy statement** (1:15), appears five times in the PE (1 Tim. 1:15; 3:1; 4:9; 2 Tim. 2:11; Titus 3:8) and nowhere else in the NT. In each case, the phrase either introduces or concludes a compressed formulation of Paul's core beliefs about God's salvation. For example, the "trustworthy statement" included in this portrait of Paul's conversion is that **Christ came into the world to save sinners.** This saying aptly summarizes the

Christian message; it is what one contemporary scholar has called a "creedal cameo" (Raymond Collins, 43). How these catchphrases originated is difficult to determine. Most likely, however, they were created by Paul as a missionary's "sound bites"—memorable yet dense phrases that helped people conceptualize the experience of conversion.

The concluding doxology (1:17) would have had a familiar ring in both Hellenistic and Jewish worlds. Jewish prayers, picking up the idiom of the Psalter, spoke of Israel's God, the only God, as king of all (e.g., LXX Pss. 5:2; 23:7-10; 43:5; 46:3; 94:3). The divine attributes of immortality and invisibility come from Greek speculation, although that God is unseen is also a central claim of Jewish theology (see Exod. 33:20–34:8; cf. John 1:18). In his *Lives of Eminent Philosophers*, Diogenes Laertius (300 B.C.) writes, "First believe that God is a living being immortal and blessed, according to the notion of a god indicated by the common sense of humankind; and so believing, you shall not affirm of God aught that is foreign to his immortality or that does not agree with blessedness, but shall believe about God whatever may uphold both his blessedness and immortality" ("Epicurus" 10.123). This doxology, which complements one found at the end of this letter (see 6:15), was widely commented upon by the Church Fathers. Gregory of Nyssa commented that by it "we know that of all these names by which Deity is indicated some are expressive of the Divine majesty, employed and understood absolutely, and some are assigned with reference to the operations over us and all creation" (*Against Eunomius* 2.11).

1:18-20. Paul Repeats his Charge of Timothy

Paul repeats his earlier command to Timothy (see 1:3) and now adds that it accords with **the prophecies previously made concerning you.** While the source of these "prophecies" is not specified, it probably refers to the spiritual gift of prophecy used in worship and in continuity with the OT prophetic tradition to disclose the guiding word of the Lord to the people of God. Paul's other reference to this gift in 1 Timothy 4:14 implies that it is an element of a formal liturgy that officially transfers religious authority and mission from one leader to another—in this case, from Paul to Timothy in Ephesus. By the act of laying on hands, the congregation's elders confirm God's will as it was disclosed to them in the prophetic utterances of gifted believers (cf. Acts 13:1-4; Exod. 29:10; Lev. 4:15).

Paul's evocative exhortation that Timothy **fight the good fight** draws upon the images of warfare, which he frequently employs in other correspondence (cf. 2 Cor. 10:2-6; Eph. 6:10-20) and widely used by philosophers and literati of antiquity. For example, Epictetus asks rhetorically, "Do you not know that the business of life is a military campaign?" (*Diss.* 3.23.31). The War Scroll at Qumran (1QM 1.1-5) tells of the coming salvation of God by using the apocalyptic symbols of a cosmic battle between the forces of good and evil: "The first attack by the sons of light will be launched against the lot of the sons of darkness, against the army of Belial ... And after the war ... (there) will follow a time of salvation for the people of God and a period of rule for all the men of his lot, and of everlasting destruction for all the lot of Belial."

Paul's reference to **Hymenaeus and Alexander** (see 2 Tim. 2:17; 4:14) and to his practice of **delivering them over to Satan** (cf. LXX Job 2:6), which is probably a metaphor of excommunication (cf. 1 Cor. 5:5) rather than spiritual testing, envisages the importance of church discipline within new congregations set in pagan places. Not much is known about these two shadowy figures, although letter writers of antiquity frequently dropped known names into their letters without comment to pepper their points. However, a second-century pseudepigraphal work about Paul, *Acts of Paul and Thecla*, tells the story of an "Alexander"—

perhaps alluding to this Alexander—who plots to win the affections of Thecla, a protégée of Paul's, by bribes and finally by force, only then to be repelled by miracle and political intrigue to prove the spiritual resolve of Thecla (*Acts of Paul*, 3.26-36). Latter Christian stories often embellished the careers of people mentioned in passing by biblical writers such as Paul to form a kind of Christian *Midrash*—that is, a collection of interpretive narratives that fill in biblical gaps to clarify the text's meaning and to edify its readers.

2:1-15. Paul Instructs Timothy about Christian Worship

This entire chapter, among the most scrutinized in the PE, concerns the motive and manner of Christian worship. Paul begins his instructions, as any religious Jew would, with the topic of prayer as the quintessential mark of a congregation's worship: how people prays, for whom and to whom they pray, and why they pray, give public expression of their covenant relationship with the God of Israel, the only God.

At first glance, Paul's instruction to pray **for kings and all who are in authority** (2:2a) may seem disingenuous given the sometimes conflicted relations between secular authority and earliest Christianity. Yet such prayers were commonplace among all religious people of the day. For example, the pagan writer, Aelius Aristides (A.D. 150), observed that "it remains for each of us to go to our respective duties after a prayer to Poseidon, Amphitrite, Leucothea, Palaemon, the Nereids, and to all the gods and goddesses of the sea, to grant safety and preservation on land and sea to the great Emperor, to his whole family, and to the Greek race, and to us to thrive in oratory and in others respects as well" (*Discourses* 46, "The Isthmian Oration Regarding Poseidon" 42). In Paul's Diaspora Judaism, the practice of praying for one's pagan rulers was probably adapted from Darius's decree about the Jerusalem temple according to

Ezra 6, specifically that his instructions for the rebuilding of the temple were motivated in part so that Israel would offer acceptable sacrifices to God for "the life of the king and his sons" (6:10; cf. Bar. 1:11-12).

More importantly, Paul extends the scope of the congregation's prayers to include **all people** (2:1b). The motive for doing so is not political—that is, to cultivate a peaceful working environment in which believers could flourish—but rather theological—that is, to pray according to God's redemptive purpose: **God our Savior desires** *all people* **to be saved and to come to the knowledge of the truth** (2:4). Prayers for the Emperor, which routinely offered petitions for his personal safety and political wisdom, finally were offered to God in prospect of his salvation. While sometimes accused of praying only for Israel, Rabbi d. Chinena the Elder taught that the community's prayers should not fall short of the Lord's own interests (SB, 643); and if it is the Lord's desire that all people, including the Emperor, are saved, then the community's prayers should not fall short of God's desire (cf. 1 Sam. 12:23). Moreover, as Rabbi Hanina taught, the congregation is to "pray for the peace of the ruling power, since but for fear of it men would have swallowed up each other alive" (*m.'Abot* 3.2).

Paul's grand formulation of the theological foundation of his gospel in 2:3-6 is underwritten by traditional Jewish beliefs. For example, the singularity of God—that God is one God, the only God—is an affirmation of the Jewish Shema (Deut. 6:4) and of special importance in the Diaspora where the God of Israel had competition from many deities, local and national. For this reason, Chrysostom reminds us that the motive of Paul's confession, "there is one God," is to "distinguish the one God from idols, not from the Son" (*Homilies on 1 Timothy* 7). Given the influence and importance of the Emperor cult in the Roman world, Paul's insistence that there is one mediator, who is the human Jesus, should probably be understood

politically as a rejection of both the divinization of the Roman Caesar and his role as the sole medium of the gods. One God, one Messiah, one salvation all inform a particular conception of the truth. In Paul's understanding, then, conversion to Christianity requires one to **come of the knowledge of (this) truth.** It should also be noted that within a Jewish world Paul stresses that the character of the Lord's mediatorial role is messianic rather than priestly; that is, Jesus' role is to offer a ransom for all people (2:6) whereas the congregation's role is to pray for all people (2:1).

Paul's mention of the Lord's payment of a **ransom**—one human for all humanity—would have had special currency in a Roman world with a huge slave population, where it would have evoked images of a ransom price paid to set a slave free. Further, the prefix of the distinctive word Paul uses for ransom, "anti-," indicates that Jesus substitutes his own life on behalf of others. The very idea of a person substituting his life for a community or nation is the noblest definition of covenant loyalty in Jewish literature of Paul's day (see 4 *Macc.* 6:29; 17:21-22; 2 *Macc.* 7:37-38; cf. Deut. 32:36; Mark 10:45).

One of the most controversial passages in 1 Timothy concerns the social manners of Christian men (2:8) and women (2:9-15) when praying publicly with their congregation. Much of the confusion related to this passage eases with the recognition that the principal motive of Paul's instructions regarding worship practices is theological and set forth in 2:3-7: the matter and manner of a congregation's prayers is shaped by God's desire to save all people. There is no evidence that Paul is here responding to a problem with unruly men or immodest women who somehow have subverted the practice of worship in Ephesus. The background of this text is rather the cultural expectations of middle-class men and women who may well have influenced popular opinion regarding the respectability of the gospel. Worshiping men and women, then, are profiled by Paul in terms of widely held moral norms in both his Jewish and Hellenistic worlds. This sense of public decorum extended beyond personal relations to all public meetings, including Christian worship. According to an ancient inscription from Attica (A.D. 178), "no one may either sing or create a disturbance or applaud at the gatherings, but each shall say and act his allotted part with all good order and quietness under the direction of the priest."

For example, the posture of Christian men while praying is to **lift up holy hands.** Such is the normal posture of a Jewish man in prayer. Rabbi Joshua ben Levi says that "a priest should not raise his hands in holiness to God (so Ps. 134:2) unless to give a blessing" (*b. Sotah* 39a). Perhaps for this reason, then, Paul adds that the purity of the worshiper's hands (which might imply the ritual bathing of men prior to worship) extends to his heart: he should enter into worship only if he can do so **without wrath and dissension**. Rabbi Chiya ben Aschi taught that "he should not pray whose dispositions are not calm" (*Er.* 65a). Holy hands are symbolic not only of openness to God's desires but also of a solidarity with other members of the community.

The hallmark of Christian women is their **modest** or discrete behavior in public—a cardinal virtue thought to be the defining characteristic of the ideal women of Paul's day. Significantly, Philo envisions the virtuous wife as the personification of modesty, and in fact catalogues a long list of virtues as characteristic of a woman's modesty (*Abel and Cain* 26-27). Likewise, the Stoic moral philosopher Plutarch would write, "a virtuous woman puts on modesty, and the husband and wife bring modesty into their common relations as a token of supreme love" (*Mor.* 139c). The word that "modesty" translates refers to a person's moral capacity to control selfish desires for the common good. Aristotle understands it more generally to be characteristic of right moral thinking (*Rhet.* 1.9.9). In the PE, Paul turns it into a distinctive mark of one whose moral character has been transformed by divine grace.

Paul's instructions to women frame modesty in different arenas, not restricted but nevertheless relevant to worship—for the same reason that the prayers of a Christian man are predicated on his relations to God and neighbor (so 2:8). How a believer conducts her life away from worship insinuates itself upon the practice of worship. In this regard, then, simplicity of life and generosity of public service disclose a woman's modesty. Epictetus asks, "Can it be that the human is the only creature without a special virtue but must resort to his hair, clothes and ancestors?" Ancient (and contemporary!) religions often codified a communicant's attire and hairstyle so to prevent needless distractions in worship and disrespect in "polite society" (cf. 1 Cor. 11:2-16). For this reason, an overly scrupulous regard for clothing was criticized in Paul's Jewish world (cf. *T. Reub.* 5:1-5).

Another important element of a woman's modesty concerned her social manners toward men, especially those who were not her husband. The impression made by 2:9-10 is that Paul's instructions are intended for influential women—middle-class Roman women of religious conviction (2:10) who could afford to dress elaborately and braid their hair with gold (2:9), or, better, to give money to the needy (2:10). These were "public women," then, whose conduct in the town square would have been more carefully monitored by outsiders. For this reason, the reputation of the entire congregation depended to some extent on a Christian woman's honorable conduct, especially toward the important men in her life other than her husband.

In Paul's Hellenistic world no other male would have exercised more influence within a household than its teacher. While Jewish women were largely uneducated, Roman women of leisure had both money and access to a first-rate education, and for this reason Paul defines her modesty as a student. In the arena of learning, then, modesty is evinced by one's demeanor as a good student, as a woman who quietly receives and submits to the instruction of a male teacher. (Only men would have been employed as tutors in Paul's world.) Not to have done so as a student would have been regarded as shameful behavior and may have in turn subverted the congregation's capacity to convey to the general public God's desire to save all people. While the education of women was viewed as an important element of their domestic responsibilities (rather than the means to a successful career), Paul's purpose here is more religious: he is concerned to prevent the appearance of shameful conduct that might compromise the congregation's missionary vocation.

In support of these instructions, Paul appeals to the story of Eve in LXX Genesis (cf. 2:13-15a). His biblical commentary is characteristic of Jewish *midrash*, by which the plotline of a biblical narrative is re-read selectively to clarify and endorse God's redemptive purpose (cf. 2:3-6) in support of his prior definition of the "modest woman" (cf. 2:9-12). His typological use of Eve's story, which plots the story of every woman, is also thoroughly Jewish in exegetical sensibility. In this regard, Eve's story in Genesis is retold: from her creation (2:13; cf. Gen. 2:21-23), to her deception and transgression (2:14; cf. Gen. 3:1-13), and finally to the bearing of her first children when she exclaims her reunion and even partnership (i.e., reconciliation) with God (2:15a; cf. Gen. 4:1-2; 1:28). His concluding comment on Eve's prospective **preservation** (or salvation) **through the bearing of children** concentrates the reader's attention finally on that which is uniquely female—the act of childbearing—in order to underscore the woman's salvation as a woman. In this way, Paul is able to apply his grand theological norm—that God desires the salvation of everyone (2:4)—to the women of Ephesus.

Significantly, Paul departs from other Jewish *midrashim* on the creation story which blamed Eve for Adam's spiritual failure to justify the woman's more marginal status within the household (e.g., *Sir.* 25:24). This pervasive sense of the woman's moral inferiority within Judaism is reflected in the writings of Philo who interprets Eve's failure by her privileging of sensual perceptions over the rational mind by which God's heavenly purposes are discerned (*Op. Mund.* 165). Since rational judgment is characteristic of the male rather than the female, it is he who should lead the woman and not the reverse. Against this argument, Paul does not pull rank over women by steadfastly claiming she has equal access to God's saving grace because of Christ (cf. Gal. 3:28).

3:1-13. Paul Describes the Qualities of a Congregation's Leadership

Paul begins his instruction about those placed in leadership positions within the household of God in a provocative way: he *commends* those who **aspire** to be an **overseer** and **desire** to lead a congregation. The moral philosophers of his day routinely condemned those who "aspire" to political office because such ambitions were typically motivated by greed and power grabs; likewise, they also condemned those who "desire" a work because they were often prompted by a lust for power or sexual conquest. Paul challenges this more negative reading of human nature, suggesting that divine grace can transform the motives behind the actions.

The idea that a congregation should have only *one* **overseer**—and the Greek text strongly suggests this, and for this reason 3:2 is better translated "the overseer" rather than "a overseer"—probably derives from the sociology of the ancient household, which was led by one *paterfamilias* of singular authority. For this reason, the catalogue of sixteen qualities for the ideal overseer, especially since the overseer is by definition **the husband of one wife** (see Titus 1:6), regard men only (see 5:9). Although it is difficult to know what marital arrangement Paul has in mind by this cryptic phrase, clearly marital fidelity is the moral norm envisaged.

Scholars continue to debate whether this particular listing of virtues has a particular place in mind. On the one hand, they are similar to lists found in the writings of the Stoics. The great Epictetus, for example, defines the ideal citizen in conduct related to "marriage, raising children, reverence to God, care for parents" (*Discourses* 3.26). In a similar vein, Onasander describes the competent military officer as "temperate, self-restraining, vigilant, frugal, hard working, alert, not too young or too old, a father if possible, a good orator, with a good reputation" (*General*, 1.1). Isocrates (cf. 250 B.C.) writes, "Whenever you purpose to consult with any one about your affairs, first observe how he has managed his own. For he who has shown poor judgment in conducting his own business will never give wise counsel about the business of others" (*To Demonicus* 35). That is, Paul's list of a competent administrator's qualities agrees with the criterion in the ancient world by which any household's supervisor would have been assessed. On the other hand, even a cursory comparison between this list and the one found in Titus 1:6-9 reflects differences probably related to spiritual maturity (i.e., **not a new convert**) or the greater sophistication of Ephesian culture (see Titus 1:6-9). Further, Paul's insistence that leaders in Crete be "sensible" (Titus 1:8; 2:2, 4, 5, 6) may well reflect the general assessment that Cretan culture inclines one toward insensibility (see Titus 1:12)!

The term translated **deacon** has the original sense of "waiting on tables"—a hands-on server of others (cf. Acts 6:1-6). Generally, this list reflects more practical dispositions apropriate to this particular office. Significantly, however, Paul says that the deacon must **hold to the mystery of the faith with a clear conscience** (3:9)—a clearly theological requirement that infers the deacon must exemplify in his lifestyle the **mystery of godliness** defined in 3:16 (cf. Eph. 1:9; 3:4). According to

Hellenistic mores, religious beliefs when linked to a "mystery" implied the use of magical formulae or esoteric teachings, or to a initiation ritual known only to the membership of a so-called "mystery religion." But in Paul, the "mystery of faith" is publicly confessed and applicable to all. More importantly, Paul refers to **women** deacons (3:11) whose qualifications are the same as for male deacons with added concerns for propriety of speech and sobriety in bearing, probably reflecting a general cultural bias against old wives' tales and women gossips (see 5:13).

Modern scholars often compare this passage with other Christian writings from the second century in arguing that the congregation's governance reflects a later and more complex organizational structure (i.e., hierarchal episcopacy)—one closer to the third-century Catholic church than the first-century household assemblies reflected in other Pauline letters (e.g., 1 Cor. 11-12) or the informal Pauline congregations described in the book of Acts (e.g. Acts 20:7-12). This is doubtful. In fact, the simple structure more closely resembles the voluntary organizations of the Roman world or the synagogues of the Diaspora. Moreover, Paul's concerns are with a prospective leader's character, not her or his job description. The similarity noted between Paul's definition of competent character and the similar lists of a supervisor's attributes found in the secular writings of Greco-Roman philosophers suggest that the 1 Timothy understanding of leadership is perfectly at home in a first-century Roman world.

3:14-16. Paul's Confession of the Faith

Arguably, this is one of the most important passages in 1 Timothy and its ancient background is an important consideration of its interpretation. First of all, Paul states here the purpose of his letter to Timothy: to prepare him for a pastoral house-call. This is a natural reason to correspond with another, especially a friend whom one is about to visit. In Paul's case, however, his visits are "apostolic" and laden with official importance, typically with the exercise of his apostolic office whether to fortify a congregation's spiritual resolve (cf. Rom. 1:10-11; 15:20-22; 2 Cor. 13:1-2) or to check on their spiritual progress (cf. 1 Cor. 16:3-7; 1 Thess. 2:17–3:5; Phile. 22). In this sense, a personal visit embodies Paul's personal authority. For this reason, letters are sometimes written as a substitute for his personal presence, especially when a delay in his arrival is expected. First Timothy is the textual medium by which Paul gives instructions to Timothy that otherwise he would give in person. (This may explain why certain instructions are more expansive. For instance, Paul may have imagined the difficulty of Timothy's relations with certain women, whether because of their social status [2:9-15] or age [5:1-16], and for this reason provides more expansive directions.)

Paul writes to Timothy in order that he might organize the Christian congregation as the **household** (lit., house) **of God, which is the church of the living God** (3:15). Some have argued that the architecture of this passage—house, pillar, support—reflects a pagan temple, and Paul is positioning the "church" of God's people over and against those pagan congregations meeting in Ephesus' various temples or "houses" dedicated to false deities. It is probably the case, however, that **pillar and support of the truth** refers to Timothy's role within the congregation rather than to the church within the broader culture. More likely, he has the OT idea of Israel as comprising God's "whole household," with Timothy (as Paul's appointed delegate) performing the prophetic role of Moses (cf. Num. 12:6-8; Deut. 23:2-4; 31:30).

Of course, the sociology of the Roman household is a crucial subtext of the PE. God's plan for managing God's household bears a striking family resemblance to the traditional social patterns for organizing middle-class households in the cities of Paul's world (see

1:4-5; 5:1–6:2; 2 Tim. 2:20-21; Titus 1:5; 2:1-10). Each member of the household from the *paterfamilias* to its servants held a certain status within an extended family with various responsibilities to perform and social relations to observe. The stability of the city-state if not of the empire depended on maintaining this order. But Paul's concern for propriety and efficiency as God's household is motivated differently than others within Roman society: the primary vocation of God's household is religious, not political. The well-ordered Christian household is "the church of the living God" that serves God's chief desire, which is to save all people (see 2:4). For this reason, the church is ordered not by household codes or other instruments of social domestication, as some contend, but by the teaching of "sound doctrine" (see 1:10-11).

The lyrics of the hymn inserted by Paul in 3:16 comprise one of the NT's most important summaries of the Lord's messianic career, and stand at the epicenter of God's **glorious gospel** (see 1:10-11). Following the pattern of the OT Psalter, which contains many hymns, prayers, sermon fragments, and confessions that augment the story of Israel's faith, Paul frequently adorns his letters with similar literary conventions (e.g., Rom. 1:3-4; 16:25-27; 1 Cor. 15:3-7; Phil. 2:6-11; Col. 1:15-20). In most cases, the lyrics of hymns or creedal statements of a confession are formed before the letter is written and are therefore wellknown to his readers. In this case, Paul incorporates a hymn into his charge to Timothy to define a faith that is **by common confession** and not as one merely composed for this particular letter; its importance for the church is timeless rather than momentary. In addition, its literary form and christological content are wonderfully symmetrical, suggesting the shaping of a well-used text, perhaps already known by memory. In using this verse against the Arian heretic, Eunomius, Gregory of Nyssa wrote that these lyrics contain "all the declarations which the heralds of the faith are prone to make. By these is increased the marvelous character of him who manifested the super-abundance of his power by means external to his own nature" (*Against Eunomius* 5.3).

4:1-7a. Paul Warns Timothy about False Teachers

Only here in 1 Timothy does Paul turn to the teachings of the false teachers. Earlier he is satisfied only to describe the manner and motive of their teaching (see 1:3-7, 19-20)—the poor results of their instruction for Christian formation. In this passage, he condemns what they teach as an element of the deception of the **later times**. This is similar to Jesus' prediction of false prophets who will subvert Israel's preparation for its messiah (cf. Matt. 24; Mark 13; Luke 21); both Paul and Jesus are indebted to apocalyptic Judaism for their description of the end times. In particular, **deceitful spirits** in contrast with the "righteous spirit"—the Spirit who discloses God's truth (see 3:15-16) through the prophet to Israel—is characteristic of the Dead Sea Scrolls. For example, *The Rule of the Community* predicts that "due to the Angel of Darkness all the children of righteousness will stray, and all their sin, their iniquities, their failings and their deceitful works will be under his rule in compliance with the mysteries of God" (1QS 3:21b-23a). Other Jewish literature of the day, framed by the images of an imminent apocalypse, speak of "deceitful spirits" set loose on God's people to turn their minds away from God (*T. Reub.* 2:1-2; *T. Judah* 14:8; 20). Especially Matthew's gospel characterizes those who lead the Jewish opposition against Jesus as "hypocritical" (cf. Matt. 6:2, 16; 7:5; 22:18; 23:13-29; 24:51). Paul's polemic against the false teachers reflects the connection of personal character with one's capacity to receive and transmit truth, which is axiomatic of the moral literature of his day.

The **doctrines of demons** produce a world-denying asceticism. It has been difficult to place this false teaching, which includes both dietary restrictions and celibacy (4:3a), in Paul's world. Many scholars have argued that such a lifestyle reflects Gnosticism of the kind Irenaeus refuted during the second half of the second century. In *Against Heresies*, for example, he wrote, "(Gnostics) assert that marriage ... is from Satan" (1.24.2) and "some among them have introduced abstinence from animal food, thus proving they are ungrateful to God who created all things" (1.28.1). Not only are his reactions from a later period than the likely date of 1 Timothy, Jesus himself allows for a celibate life as an element of one's kingdom vocation (cf. Matt. 19:12), and he considered all foods kosher (Mark 7:19). Paul himself was celibate, not because he thought marriage is inherently evil but because its practical requirements could easily distract one from the church's mission (cf. 1 Cor. 7). Nevertheless his constant rumination on food and human sexuality in his letters (e.g., Rom. 14; 1 Cor. 5-7; 1 Thess. 4:3-6) suggest a keen interest in these same topics by his opponents. For the record, Paul supports a conventional marriage (e.g., 1 Cor. 7:1-7) and diet (e.g., 1 Cor. 8-11), and opposes behavior pertaining to either that divides the congregation, which seems to be Paul's motive here.

According to Acts, the leaders of the church gathered in Jerusalem to discuss issues of table fellowship. James in particular was deeply concerned that the initiation of repentant Gentiles into the Diaspora church, most of whom converted from paganism (rather than as proselyte Jews), might threaten the Jewish legacy of the faith. His solution, repeated three times in Acts for rhetorical effect (15:20, 29; 21:25), concerns food and sex. Indeed, religious practices related to these things defined the sometimes difficult relations between repentant Jews and Gentiles. Perhaps Paul's harsh words about the **hypocrisy of liars** and his appeal to God's good creation (4:4) and to the alternate religious practices of **the word of God and prayer** (4:5) have a similar setting in mind: certain Jewish Christian teachers are mandating a form of asceticism (no marriage, no foods) for nonproselyte Gentiles as a condition of their congregational membership.

Paul contrasts Timothy's pastoral duties as a **good servant of Christ Jesus** and adherence to the doctrinal standards of his Pauline legacy (4:6) with **worldly fables fit only for old women** (4:7a). While this sexist phrase may be merely rhetorical, since similar language is found frequently in philosophical polemic—Lucian, for example, criticizes his competition by calling their arguments "stories consisting of old wives' fables" (*Philopseudes* 9)—Paul may have a more historical referent in mind. Later in 1 Tim. 5:13 he criticizes certain widows for spending their days **talking about improper things** rather than nurturing the congregation in **the words of the faith.**

4:7b-16. Paul Charges Timothy to Serve Christ

Paul turns his attention back to the personal formation of his young delegate, Timothy, with a common image of the well-trained athlete: **discipline yourself for the purpose of godliness** (4:7b). Pseudo-Isocrates calls his students to "discipline by imposing toilsome tasks upon yourself that you may be able to deal with those that others impose upon you" (*Ad Demonicum* 21). In Paul's charge, the moral endgame is a practical godliness, which was the highest spiritual virtue of his Hellenistic world. Epictetus wrote "In piety towards the gods I would have you know the chief element is this: to have right opinions about them—that they exist and administrate the universe well and fairly—and to have set yourself to obey them and to submit to everything that happens, and to follow it freely in the belief that it is being fulfilled by the highest powers" (*Encheiridion* 31). Or, again, consider these words found in an inscription attributed to Antiochus 1 (ca.100 B.C.): "Piety is a sacred obligation to the gods and to our ancestors. I have made myself a model of such piety for my children and grandchildren by

many things, in the faith that they will have a good model to imitate."

Such a combination of piety and moral conduct is prudent since it profits a person in this life and in the next. But such is the result of **labor and striving** (4:10). Again, Epictetus compares the human struggle in becoming morally excellent with an athletic contest—with a long race or hard-fought wrestling match (*Discourse* 3.25.3) in which it is necessary for the athlete to fix his attention on its victorious completion. The goal of the hard work of spiritual discipline is the salvation promised by the **living God.**

The portrait of a youthful Timothy, introduced by a cautionary note to **let no one look down on your youthfulness** (4:12a), reflects a bias against youthful teachers especially common in the Roman world (as in our own) where an apprenticeship and field experience were viewed as requirements of mature instruction. While these are not unimportant to Paul, he rather appeals to personal credentials that transcend age: the exemplary life (4:12b), religious practices (4:13), the Spirit's gift and prophecy (4:14a), and Timothy's ecclesiastical ordination (4:14b). Significantly, this portrait of a minister's life is viewed holistically by Paul. For example, in a Jewish congregation the rabbi's public reading (or midrash) of Scripture is funded by his exemplary life; and the congregation's recognition of his spiritual authority is predicated on the inspired and inspiring exercise of his spiritual gift or *charism*, which in Timothy's case, is the **reading of Scripture, exhortation and teaching** of the congregation (see 5:22; 2 Tim. 1:6-7).

In a Jewish congregation, it is the responsibility of its most revered (and typically most senior) group of leading men both to recognize and confirm those charged with administrating the congregation's affairs—reminiscent of Moses laying hands upon Joshua, which is symbolic of transferring authority to his successor (cf. Num. 27:18-23; Deut. 34:9; Acts 6:6;

13:3). The presbytery (or "council of elders" [*presbyteroi*]) corresponds to the *gerousia* of the synagogue's elders who made appointments within the congregation.

Finally, the idea of a person's evident moral **progress** (4:15) is a hallmark of Stoic philosophy, following Aristotle for whom virtue is a habit which is developed only over time and with considerable practice (e. g., Plutarch, *Mor.* 75b-86a). In this same essay, "On Progress in Virtue," Plutarch extols the virtue of the person who stands up under his own scrutiny rather than disdainful of himself as an incompetent "witness" (81a), which may help one appreciate Paul's concluding charge for Timothy to **pay close attention to yourself and to your teaching** (4:16a).

5:1-16. Paul Instructs Timothy Concerning the Care of Widows

As explained earlier, the household was generally understood to be the essential unit of Roman society. Various household codes were written, depending upon the kind of household in view, to govern the conduct of their members. Well-run households were the necessary precondition of a civil and competent society. In Paul's mind, then, an orderly congregation of believers—"the household of God" (see 3:15)—is not only encouraged to care for its members but then on this basis to dispatch its missionary vocation according to God's chief desire to save all people (see 2:3-6). This mixture of responsible care for insiders and conscientious ministry to outsiders is characteristic of Paul's household code, which reflects extraordinary sensitivity to people of all ages.

Philo divided his Jewish congregation into six groups according to their ages: "old men, young men, boys, old women, grown women, maidens" (*Gaius* 227). Paul's initial prohibition against **sharply rebuking an older man** (5:1) reflects a sensibility of his Jewish upbringing that honored elderly men. Ben Sira taught that "kindness to one's father will not be forgotten

(by God)" (*Sir.* 3:14), and treatment of the elders was widely viewed in the ancient world as a litmus test of the community's moral maturity.

The primary group of Paul's concern is widows (5:3-16). He distinguishes between three groups of widows: those who are **widows indeed**—that is, those widows whose age precludes remarriage, who lack the financial support of an extended family, and whose piety is exemplary (5:3, 5-7, 9-10); widows who should expect the financial support of their children (5:4, 8, 16); and young widows who should expect to remarry (5:11-15). In part, Paul's instructions reflect his scrupulous attention to the Jewish Torah, which demands the faithful community take special care of its widows and orphans—those most vulnerable to the vicissitudes of life (cf. Exod. 22:22; Deut. 14:29; Zech. 7:9-10). In addition, his concern perhaps also reflects his understanding of Roman law, which required that if a dowry was paid upon marriage the widow would be provided for by the new head of her deceased husband's household—usually her son. If there was no son or the household was dissolved, then the proceeds of its sale would repay the dowry and the widow would be returned to her parents. Of course, if there was no dowry paid, nor a family to which a widow could return, as evidently is the case for the "widows indeed," then a subsistent *providentia* was provided to the widow by the city-state (in this case, Ephesus). Essentially, Paul's code is an attempt to reorder the congregation's welfare system according to Jewish practice (and the Torah) so that the congregation rather than the state takes financial responsibility for its poor as a matter of sacred (rather than civic) duty (cf. Acts 6:1-6; 9:39; Jas. 1:26-27; also Luke 7:11-17).

The practice of putting widows **on a list** (5:9) is well-known from Hellenistic literature: mercenary soldiers signed on to wage Rome's wars by adding their names to a general's list (Herodotus, *Persian War* 1:59; 7:1) or new initiates were added to the rolls of a religious group (Oxyrhynchus Papyrus 416) or newly elected members to the Senate's roster (Plutarch, *Life of Pompey* 13:7). This registry of widows in need of the congregation's material support has less to do with keeping a public record of those who are "widows indeed" as it is an encouragement to follow the protocol of discernment that Paul stipulates.

In this regard, among a widow's qualifications are her age and marital fidelity: **not less than sixty years old** and **the wife of one man** (5:9). Paul may be appealing to current "actuarial tables" for defining retirement age beyond which women could not be expected either to remarry or do hard work—sixty years old. Moreover, in Roman society the ideal of one marriage was honored (Livy, *Roman History*, 10.23.9), as well as in Judaism by which not remarrying would provide additional evidence of marital fidelity to her now deceased husband and of devotion to the Lord (cf. Jdth 8:4; 16:22; Luke 2:36-8). Paul is concerned that the congregation, whose vocation is to engage the wider culture with the gospel, is not at odds with social convention. At the same time, his concern is that widows who are supported by the congregation are known for their Christian piety (5:5) and for **good works** (5:10). Indeed, as Ambrose wrote, "the virtues of the widow have become the duties of old age" (*Concerning Widows* 2.9).

Even though the social convention of Paul's day—very nearly into the modern period—is that "younger widows" did not seek after remarriage, the verbal mood he uses in 5:11 is active: **I want younger widows to get married** (5:14). That is, his exhortation is for widows of marriageable age to actively pursue finding a Christian husband. In part, if this becomes her focus in life, Paul supposes she will more likely avoid the unseemly behaviors described in 5:11-13, which would only **give the enemy occasion for reproach**—the "enemy" in this case is probably Satan, God's principal antagonist borrowed from Paul's Jewish apocalyptic background. Rather than a reflection of his world's misogyny, his instruction is set against idlers (5:13; see Titus 1:11-2) who are easily perceived by outsiders as morally lax (cf. Aristotle, *Nicomachean Ethics* 1097b). With respect to the idle younger widows, who are evidently not called in Christian ministry (cf. 1 Cor. 7:25-35), this almost certainly would have carried a sexual innuendo in Paul's world (5:11; cf. Dio Cassius *Roman History* 47:15.4; 53:2.4) and so subverted the work of the gospel.

5:17-25. Paul Instructs Timothy Concerning the Care of Elderly Men

Leadership within an ancient middle-class household was determined by gender (male) and age (elderly); evidently Paul extends this social norm to the congregation—even though he is probably less concerned about chronological age than spiritual maturity (see 3:6; 4:12). Thus Philo could write of Moses that he "applied the name of 'elder' not to one who is bowed with old age but to one who is worthy of honor" (*Sobriety* 16). Yet, while **double honor** may well express the meaning of the Greek noun *timē*, it is probably better translated "double payment" in this context where Paul is concerned with the congregation's monetary compensation of its older members. This connotation is born out by the citation of LXX Deut. 25:4 (5:18a), followed by Paul's illustrative midrash (5:18b) probably based on LXX Num. 18:31, which underwrites the importance of those that work on behalf of the household. In this case, his midrash implies use of *qal-wa-homer*—an exegetical principle by which a lesser claim (in this case about farm animals) proves the ultimate importance of a greater good (in this case, wages paid to a laborer of the gospel).

In the case of older men (see 5:1), who while physically unable to labor in the marketplace are able to **work hard at preaching and teaching** (5:17), Paul does not mention a "list" as before (see 5:9) but does warn Timothy not to **receive an accusation against an elder** (5:19) or lay hands upon (an elder) (5:22) to exonerate him in a careless fashion. These instructions are cast with judicial images that imply certain procedures must be followed by a congregation when consideration is given to which of its elders are worthy of drawing a salary. As we should expect from Paul in 1 Timothy, the legal standards of an elder's value to the congregation are framed by concerns for his personal character—so that those who continue in sin (are) rebuked in the presence of all (5:20; cf. Matt. 18:15-17; 1 Cor. 5:6—6:8)—and especially for the character of his ministry—those who work hard at preaching and teaching (5:17). The word translated "preaching" is literarily "word" or "speech"—that is, a ministry of persuasive "speech" or "word-smithing" that Hellenistic culture would have considered a sine qua non of effective leadership.

Since it would be Timothy's responsibility—as the apostle's delegate in Ephesus—to monitor this legal protocol should it ever become necessary, Paul concludes his instructions with an intimate charge for Timothy to maintain these (instructions) without bias (5:21). Paul's command is not motivated by the need for Timothy to convene a legal review of certain elders currently under the care of the congregation, since the text supplies no evidence of such a problem; rather, he is motivated by an awareness of how Timothy's youth may be perceived by others (see 4:12) during the sometimes tricky nature of legal proceedings when sin is not always evident (cf. 5:24-25). His relative inexperience in such matters, coupled with the natural awkwardness of a young man's relationship with older men (cf. 5:1), may have added pressure to Timothy's already fragile psyche (see 2 Tim. 1:6-7). For this reason, we should read this text in light of Timothy's nerve for which the use of a little wine would have been viewed as medicinal. Greco-Roman physicians prescribed wine for a nervous stomach and the Talmud stipulates wine as the "first among medicines" (b.Ben Bat., 58b; cf. b. Ber. 35b)—

even though the Mishnah encourages abstinence from wine to maintain one's *spiritual* health (*m. 'Abot* 6:4). Chrysostom makes this distinction later when he writes on this verse: "Paul does not allow Timothy to indulge freely in wine, but as much as was for health and not for luxury" (*Homilies on 1 Timothy* 16).

6:1-2. Paul Instructs Timothy Concerning the Conduct of Slaves

The concluding entry in Paul's household code concerns the conduct of faithful slaves. Because servants were members of most middle-class households in the Greco-Roman world, conduct codes included a section of their duties. Doubtless the congregation at Ephesus comprised many slaves since slavery was integral to the economy of Roman urban society. Often Roman slaves were well-educated and exercised enormous influence in shaping the daily routines of the household. In this case, Paul's instruction is shaped by the fact that Christian slaves often belonged to households led by a nonbelieving *paterfamilias*. What is unusual in this passage is Paul's exhortation that Christian slaves should treat a Christian head of the household differently than were he a nonbeliever. The codes found in philosophical writings of the ancient world, Jewish and pagan, typically did not discriminate along ideological grounds. Paul seems alert to the egalitarian affect the gospel might have on the normal relations between household slaves and their believing master, which might in turn undermine the congregation's influence on the wider culture.

6:3-10. Paul Warns Timothy about the False Teachers

Paul's reflection on acquiring wealth should be considered conventional wisdom when viewed against the backdrop of Jewish and philosophical teaching on this important topic. Consider, for example, the words of Bion the Sophist who said, "The love of money is the mother city of all evils" (from Stobaeus, *Anthologium* 3.417, ca. 250 B.C.). Aristotle taught that "the life of money-making is limiting, and wealth is surely not the good we seek after, for it is at best only the means to something else" (*Nicomachean Ethics* 1.5.8). And Rabbi Jose b. Quisma (ca. A.D. 110) is reported to have said, "My son, even if you give me all the silver and gold of this world, I want to live in light of Torah nonetheless; because in the hour when one is separated from human life and he has no more silver nor gold nor jewels nor beads, only Torah and good works will accompany him" (*Aboth* 6.9). Against the background of this ancient and pervasive criticism related to making money as an end in itself, Paul's severe chastisement of the motive of false teachers who view **godliness as a means of (financial) gain** (6:5b) is more easily understood. Such a materialistic motive of ministry is contrary to the godliness that conforms to the **sound (or healthy) words of our Lord Jesus Christ** (6:3). As mentioned before (see 1:10), the ancient world did not judge the "soundness" of speech merely on the basis of what was said but also upon its salutary affect on people's lives (Homer, *Iliad* 8.524). Thus, the subtext of all Paul's instructions to both Timothy and Titus is a theological formula that equates sound doctrine with godly living—or in the case of false teachers, the advocacy of **different doctrine** (6:3; see 1:3) with the catalogue of moral vices found in 6:4-5.

Paul's reference to the "healthy words" of Jesus implies that the congregation already was following a collection of the Lord's sayings—i.e., words spoken by Jesus committed to memory and transmitted orally from congregation to congregation. This same word translated "words of" (*logois*) also can refer to "teachings about" his life, perhaps referring to stories of Jesus being circulated by professional storytellers (cf. Luke 1:1-2). In any case, Paul likely has in mind the Lord's teaching about wealth, one of the most important *topoi* of his

messianic instruction that he instantiated in his ministry among the poor and powerless of his Galilean world.

The ideal of self-sufficiency, which is envisaged by the sharp contrast found in 6:6-10, is well-known from Hellenistic moral philosophy. The Stoics lionized Socrates precisely because he refused to compromise his moral and religious ideals in exchange for wealth. In his *Lysis*, Plato proffers this famous exchange: "Will not the good man be measured by his self-sufficiency? Yes. Because the sufficient man has no need of anything other than the virtue of his sufficiency" (215a). Likewise, Diogenes the Cynic characterized the guiding norm of his teaching by describing the simplicity of his followers' clothing and diet. Of course, Paul's theological conception compels him to reinterpret the value placed on a simple lifestyle as the response of a "man of God" (= Timothy; 6:11) to the sufficiency of divine grace. By the same theological conception, his reference to the false teachers' **ruin and destruction** (6:9) expresses a belief in God's final judgment of the faithless and impious. For a vivid example, consider the DSS *Rule of the Community* in which the day of God's judgment is described as a "glut of punishments . . . for the scorching wrath of the God of revenge, for permanent error and shame without end with the humiliation of destruction by the fire of the dark regions" (1QS 4:11-13)! Paul's theological impulse, then, which contends the destiny of theological falsehood is eschatological ruin, would have been readily recognized by Timothy and the members of his congregation.

6:11-21. Paul's Benedictory Exhortation to Timothy

First Timothy concludes according to the standard pattern of a Hellenistic letter, with a final farewell ("grace be with you") and before that with a series of exhortations and instructions. Included is one of the most common literary forms used by ancient letter writers including

Paul—a list of moral virtues that characterize the **man of God** (6:11-12). This list defines the kind of person that would generate the respect of outsiders, but also is aimed at the problem of false teachers Paul has just castigated as money mongers without moral or spiritual scruples (see 6:3-10; cf. *Rule of the Community*, 1QS 3.13–4.26). In this sense, Timothy's virtuous character must stand in stark contrast to those who would subvert the congregation's life with God.

Paul recalls **the good confession** the Lord made (or "testified") before his Roman judge, Pontius Pilate, who was the Roman prefect of Judea at the time. This judicial allusion to Jesus' Roman trial, the only one found in the NT letters, underwrites the importance of the public confession made by Timothy **in the presence of many witnesses** (6:12; see 4:14; cf. 2 Tim. 1:6). That is, the board of elders who had earlier commissioned Timothy to his ministry now form a jury of "witnesses" with the quasi-legal authority to measure his compliance to his sacred calling.

Paul's startling reference to the Roman judge who supervised the execution of Jesus prepares us for his subsequent theological claim that God is **the blessed and only Sovereign, the King of kings and Lord of lords** (6:15). In addition to the traditional Jewish claim that the Creator God **gives life to all things** (6:13; cf. 1 Sam. 19:6) and on this basis is "King of kings and Lord of lords" (cf. Dan. 2:37; Deut. 10:17; Ps. 136:3; see Rev. 4:8-11!), Paul affirms there is but one **Sovereign**. One probable subtext of his doxology is the deified rulers of the Roman world, especially its Caesar who was routinely confessed as "Lord of lords." Another is Zeus who was considered "the most powerful, the mightiest of the gods, the far-seeing master who fulfills everything" (Homer, *Ode to Zeus* 1-2). Paul's implied claim is that such acclamations of divine sovereignty belong only to the Creator God and Lord Jesus Christ.

The important PE motif of Christ's epiphany (or "appearing") as "Lord of lords" may also continue Paul's polemical subtext against Roman worship of its rulers (see 2 Tim. 1:10; 4:1, 8; Titus 2:11, 13; 3:4; cf. 1 Thess. 3:13; 5:23; 2 Thess. 2:8). In explaining the Greek legend of Dionysus (= Bacchus), Diodorus writes (first cent. B.C.) that "all the plants perished in the flood at the time of Deucalion, and that when they sprang up again after the Deluge it was as if there had been a second epiphany of the god among men, and so the myth was created that Dionysus had been born again from the thigh of Zeus" (*Library of History* 3.62.10). Paul's theological claim is that Jesus' vindication as Lord will come at his "second epiphany"—his *Parousia*. In any case, these theological claims justify more completely why the congregation must pray that this **blessed and only Sovereign** save **the kings and all who are in authority** (2:2).

Paul returns to the topic of material riches, this time to sound a more constructive note related to wealthy members of the congregation who are encouraged to use their resources **in good works** (6:17-19). His exhortation is not unrelated to his prior affirmation of the sovereign Creator God **who gives life to all things** (6:13). The generosity of the rich is their logical response of devotion to a generous God; in fact, the **uncertainty of riches** (6:17) is contrasted with the certainly of a God **who richly supplies us with all things to enjoy** (see 4:1-5). Such a theme is deeply rooted in Paul's Jewish faith and reflects the teaching of Jesus who encourages his disciples to store up treasure in heaven rather than on earth (cf. Matt. 9:19-20; Luke 12:21-34).

This exhortation also reflects the diversity of social class within the urban congregations Paul founded. While clearly there are poor people who belong to Timothy's congregation (e.g., those who are "widows indeed" or household servants), there are also wealthy members from the middle class who have both time and money to engage in philanthropic works (see 2:9-10; 6:18). The measure of their religious commitment is how they use their time and money, whether on themselves or to improve society (see 2:9-10). For this reason, Augustine wrote in *The City of God* that "Those who have given liberally of their riches have had great gains to compensate them for light losses. Their joy at what they assured for themselves more securely by readiness to give outweighed their sadness at the surrender of possessions they more easily lost because they clung to them fearfully" (1.10.2).

Paul's final words to Timothy are consistent with the letter's function: he is to be the custodian of Paul's gospel and exemplar of godly living in Ephesus (see 1:10-11)—**to guard that which has been entrusted to you** (6:20a). And he is to do so in the face of opposition from those teachers who chatter on about **what is falsely called 'knowledge'** (6:20b; see 1:3-4, 6-7, 9). In this sense, the instructions Paul has given to Timothy by which to organize a Christian congregation purposes to protect believers from **going astray from the faith** (6:21; see 1:18-20).

Introduction to 2 Timothy

Robert W. Wall

Note the "Introduction to the Pastoral Epistles" and the Introduction to 1 Timothy.

Any reconstruction of the historical background behind 2 Timothy proceeds from the observation that its subject matter differs from the other two PE. While all three letters share a common literary form and purpose, the other two Pastoral letters are full of general instructions concerning "church orders" for the purpose of organizing Christian congregations in pagan places. The material found in 2 Timothy is mostly personal and concerns whether the congregation's leader, Timothy, is personally competent and spiritually mature enough to succeed Paul as a teacher of "sound doctrine."

For this reason, the subject matter of this letter is fashioned into an interplay between personal exhortation (*paraenesis*) and dramatic illustrations of good and bad individuals whom Paul recollects for Timothy's instruction. While the cast of characters mentioned by Paul is difficult to identify and locate on his missionary map, many are subsequently mentioned in the well-known second-century apocryphal writing (and Christian *midrash*), *Acts of Paul and Thecla*, even though under different circumstances than used in 2 Timothy. Whatever features their historical personae might have entailed, their collective role in 2 Timothy serves Paul's rhetorical purpose: they personify those traits that Timothy must emulate or avoid if he is to be a "man of God"

and spiritual leader of his congregation.

The sheer weight of personal information found in 2 Timothy about the elderly Paul and youthful Timothy, and also about their intimate relationship as master and apprentice, suggests slightly different historical circumstances than those that occasioned the writing of 1 Timothy and Titus. Not only is this letter written from an unnamed prison in Rome (1:8; 2:9; 4:16; cf. Acts 28:30-31), presumably because Paul and his gospel ministry had been discredited by others (1:16-17; 4:14-16), the tone of 2 Timothy suggests his imminent death (4:6) thereby occasioning the need for his succession (2:1-2). For this reason, many scholars contend that the literary genre of 2 Timothy is similar to a succession speech in which a departing (often dying) hero rehearses his legacy and gives instructions for his succession (similar to a last will and testament).

Well-known samples of this literary genre exist from the Greco-Roman world, where leaders or teachers would set forth the terms of an orderly succession by recollecting important moments from their lives as normative for and to be continued by those tradents left behind. First-century Jewish testamental literature (e.g., *Jubilees, Testaments of the Twelve Patriarchs*), builds upon Joseph's farewell speech found in Gen. 49 and had wide currency within earliest Christianity. Perhaps the most famous example of a succession speech in

Christian circles is from Paul made to the Ephesian elders at Miletus as reported by Luke in Acts 20:17-35. The salient elements of this speech are found in 2 Timothy, including 1) selective biography, 2) sense of imminent death, and 3) exhortation to successors to maintain the sacred traditions into the next generations.

Read from this perspective, the theological crisis that occasions 2 Timothy is the real threat facing a community dealing with loss—loss of its charismatic leader, loss of its distinctive identity, loss of hope for a better future, and so on. For a church that Paul had founded and whose charisma still guided even if from prison, coming to grips with his death must have been a traumatic experience, especially for this young protégé on whom the great Apostle had set his hands. Whereas the instructions found in 1 Timothy and Titus order the life and ministry of the congregation, then, 2 Timothy concerns new leadership who will continue to personify Paul's legacy in his absence. In this way, Paul seeks to maintain church order in the present while fostering hope in God's future.

The prospect of surviving as God's people into the future under Timothy's leadership is threatened in two different ways. First, is the intramural conflict between teachers within the very congregation Timothy is now leading. Among those Paul names in this letter are his opponents (2:17-18; 4:14) whose ministry of misinformation and false intentions has effectively eroded the spiritual fabric of the congregation's life together (3:1-8). Paul laments those believers who have turned away from the faith to their destruction (1:15; 4:10, 16). Second, Paul does not seem confident that Timothy is up to doing the tasks necessary in succeeding him to maintain the faith traditions into the next generation. Clearly, Paul's clarification that God gives the Spirit of power rather than one of "timidity" (1:7) and his disquiet over the embarrassment caused by his imprisonment (1:8) are linked to his prior reminder of Timothy's call (1:6). Especially since Paul repeatedly encourages Timothy to visit him in prison (4:9, 21), the letter's opening note is one of concern for Timothy's fortitude in staying the course of his divine calling as his successor.

Finally, there is perhaps a more benign impression left by Paul's various exhortations to Timothy as his "beloved son" (1:2) that this letter's advice is similar to the instruction used by ancient guilds in passing on inside knowledge of a particular craft to an apprentice who was typically the son of the artisan father or uncle. In this way, for example, medical practices often stayed within the same family for many generations. Against this background, then, 2 Timothy could be read as a letter written to strengthen the resolve and form the character of a young apprentice to continue the spiritual mastery of Paul. Only by doing so would a new Christian leader be properly formed to transmit the sacred tradition on to his generation of God's people.

2 Timothy

Robert W. Wall

1:1-2. Paul Greets Timothy

Paul begins his second letter to Timothy in typical fashion: by naming himself as sender and by greeting Timothy as recipient (see 1 Tim. 1:1-2; Titus 1:1-4). Paul's address differs somewhat from the other Pastoral Epistles (PE) in that he mentions **God's will** as the source of his apostolic authority (cf. 1 Cor. 1:1; 2 Cor. 1:1) and **the promise of life in Christ Jesus** as its purpose (see 1 Tim. 4:8). Both these elements of his greeting intend to shape Timothy's motive in responding to what Paul writes: he is to obey Paul because of his spiritual authority and because of the life-generating result of his instruction.

Once again Paul calls Timothy his **child** (see 1 Tim. 1:2), perhaps in the case of 2 Timothy to underwrite Timothy's job description as Paul's authorized successor (so 2 Tim. 2:1-2). Paul's traditional salutation, which combines the Hellenistic "grace" with the Jewish "peace," is complemented here by the familiar biblical motif "mercy" (see 1 Tim. 1:2) to ground all Christian relations—in this case between Paul and Timothy—in the confidence of God's merciful presence. Even as God's grace and peace extend to all people— to the Jew first and also to the Greek—so are all relationships within the community of believers imbued by this quality of divine mercy.

1:3-7. Paul Thanks God for Timothy

Giving thanks to the deity, noting one's petitions in doing so, is a typical convention of Hellenistic letter writing (see 1 Tim. 1:12), and it typically follows the greeting as is the case in most Pauline letters. In Paul's correspondence, however, the purpose of reporting the content of his petitions is to introduce the most important themes of a letter in an attitude of thankful worship. The thanksgiving of 2 Timothy is made extraordinary because of its intimacy. Paul's inner life is given expression here, not only by linking the fidelity of his ministry with **the way of my (biblical) forefathers**, but also for the emotional cast of his memories of Timothy—perhaps now intensified because of his personal suffering whilst in prison (see 4:9, 21). The idiom of Paul's thanksgiving, then, is rooted in his Jewish faith, not only expressed by the continuity he draws with his Jewish ancestors and by the piety evinced by his continual prayers for Timothy, but also by noting that Timothy's own faith is a spiritual property (**faith within you**) inherited from his Jewish mother and grandmother (cf. Acts 16:1).

The act of remembering others as important role models is consistent with the moral teaching of the Greco-Roman world. More importantly, however, the reader of this passage cannot help but take note of Paul's epistolary introduction as a challenge to those who would seek to rid the Christian faith of its

Jewish legacy. For as Origen wrote about verse 3, "We grant that there are some among us who may deny that the God of the Jews is truly God. Yet that is no reason to criticize those who prove from the same Scriptures that there is one and the same God for Jews and Gentiles. So also Paul came to Christianity from the Jews" (*Against Celsus* 5.61).

Paul recalls Timothy's **tears** as the occasion for a future visit and in prospect of personal joy. But to what does Paul's mention of Timothy's tears refer? In his letter to the Philippians, which is similar in many ways to 2 Timothy, Paul uses this same vocabulary (Phil. 2:1-2) as a metaphor of spiritual testing. "Tears" may refer to Timothy's spiritual struggle and testing which when resolved will occasion Paul's joy. For this reason, the recollection of Timothy's tears is logically linked by Paul to his recollection of Timothy's sacred calling (1:6), given from God and confirmed by Paul through the **laying on of my hands** (see 1 Tim. 4:14)—a Jewish practice denoting succession (cf. Num. 8:10). Hardly in view, however, is a succession of ecclesial office; this is a succession of common spiritual gift and ministry. That is, Timothy is Paul's successor in ministry. The two remembrances—of Timothy's tears and of his calling—are inextricably enjoined by Paul in the thanksgiving of his letter, which is then written to enable Timothy's exercise of his spiritual gift.

Timothy's gift is from the Holy Spirit whose properties are **power and love and self-discipline** (1:7; see 1:14) but which can be subverted by a human spirit of paralyzing **timidity** that is perhaps one's natural response to hardship, suffering, betrayal, loss of friends and supporters, trenchant opposition, and all the other various threats Paul himself encountered during his missionary career. This, then, is the central theme of 2 Timothy: those like Timothy, who by calling and spiritual gift succeed Paul in ministry, must finally own a future that is led by the empowering Spirit

rather than give in and give up to the "tears" which are sometimes occasioned by the hardships of a faithful ministry.

1:8-14. Paul Advises Timothy not to be Ashamed of Him

The first of Paul's several exhortations to his young protégé is in many ways his most decisive. His prayers for Timothy (1:3-7) disclose a spiritual threat: Timothy's "timidity," occasioned by personal hardship and opposition, may well be subverting his sacred calling for ministry and the enabling work of the Holy Spirit toward this end. For this reason, Paul advises Timothy to share in the suffering of the Lord and of Paul himself.

One of the most important elements of Hellenistic moral teaching is the use of personal example, which then the student is to emulate as a moral norm. As he often does in his letters, Paul provides autobiographical vignettes as illustrative of a manner of moral life worthy of imitation, even as his life follows the pattern established by **the testimony of our Lord** (1:8). Chrysostom's homily on this text makes the important point that often heresies—he notes those of Marcion, Manes, and Valentinus—arise because false teachers are "ashamed of the divine economy." He adds that when the cross of Christ is "viewed aright, it will appear full of dignity and a matter for boasting. For it was that death on the cross that saved the world when it was perishing" (*Homilies on 2 Timothy*).

The interpreter should note that Paul's exhortation to Timothy is bracketed by the idiom of shame: **do not be ashamed** (1:8) . . . **for I am not ashamed** (1:12). This literary inclusio reflects the psychological reality of Paul's Greco-Roman culture that measured personal value in terms of what brought honor or embarrassment to one's household or family. What brings honor to a person's extended family is a reflection of what society as a whole finds honorable; at the same time, what brings shame and embarrassment to an individual reflects what society deems ignoble. For Paul, of course, such a reality is shaped by the gospel, and what is deemed foolish by the world's standards—namely, the cross of Christ—is wisdom in God's mind (cf. 1 Cor. 1:18-25). For this reason, he writes that he is "not ashamed of the gospel" (Rom. 1:16) to underwrite his core conviction as a missionary that the proclamation of the gospel is the via medium by which the transforming grace of God is made available to sinners (see 1 Tim. 1:12-16). And, in fact, the costs one expends in preaching the gospel are a barometer of commitment to its claims. In Paul's case his missionary activities have landed him in jail as the Lord's **prisoner.**

An important literary element of the PE is Paul's use of hymns and creeds already in use among early Christian congregations. The inclusion of this traditional material in his letters always serves two functions. First, it clarifies Paul's theology—his principal ideas about God—which then warrants his exhortation or instruction. Second, his use of material sung or confessed by his readers reminds *them* of what *they* claim to believe as Christians. In this epistolary setting, Paul is concerned that Timothy will faithfully embrace his sacred calling, even if at considerable cost—a costly service that came to characterize the ministry of himself and also of Jesus.

To the exhortation of v. 8 he attaches a supporting statement about God in vv. 9-10—as though adding a supporting footnote to his earlier exhortation; this added comment consists of pre-formed lyrics from an early hymn about God's activity in calling people to saving tasks. In addition to the distinctive vocabulary found in vv. 9-10, this passage evinces the balanced structure typical of a hymn's lyrics, which is often noted by indentation in modern translations of vv. 9-10. In this case, the use of common verbal tenses and phraseology moves the reader seamlessly from lyric to theological lyric: (1) God saves, then calls. (9a) (2) God's sacred

calling is not related to personal achievement **but now** to God's eternal purpose disclosed in **our Savior Christ Jesus** (9b-10a) (3) through whom death has ended and eternal life has commenced (10b). (4) These claims stand at the epicenter of the gospel for which I (= Paul) was appointed to preach (10c-11).

The purpose of Paul's use of this theological hymn is self-evident in light of 1:6-7: Timothy, who is Paul's appointed successor, is to imitate Paul, who was appointed by God as a **preacher, apostle, teacher** (1:11). His reluctance to do so is a spiritual crisis precisely because one's **holy calling** concerns certain core convictions about the Holy Trinity—a God who saves, a Son who reveals, a Spirit who gifts.

The kerygmatic claim that Christ Jesus is **our Savior** should be understood as a political statement in a world that valorized the Roman Emperor as the world's "savior." Especially when paired with the image of the Lord's grand **appearance** to defeat the world's fiercest enemy (see 1 Tim. 3:16; Titus 2:11-14), which is death, the hymn's celebration of the powerful epiphany of a triumphant Savior must be read as an extraordinarily provocative claim in Paul's day. It is certainly decisive for an interpretation of the PE because it is the hallmark of its contribution to NT theology: reality changed with the "appearance"—the epiphany—of Christ Jesus to save sinners from death. Greeks loved and told tales of the grand appearances of legendary heroes (e.g., Alexander). Implied here, however, is the gospel's great reversal: Christ's triumph over humanity's greatest threat is utterly unexpected because it is through his suffering that death is abolished; and now Paul's own suffering and imprisonment follows in the Lord's way. Timothy's timidity reflects the world's value that the heroic savior avoids suffering by conventional means of power (military, statesmanship, economic, educational). The normative pattern in God's economy is the professed Word about Christ's cross; and it will often result in suffering because it rubs raw against the grain of a fallen and fractured world.

The combination of **sound** (= healthy) **words**—the doctrinal standard taught by Paul—and a virtuous life characterized by **the faith and love which are in Christ Jesus** (1:13) personified by Paul is thematic of the PE and central to its various instructions and personal exhortations. In 2 Timothy the use of Pauline traditions is weighed by the imminence of Paul's death (4:6) and the urgency of Timothy's succession of him (2:1-2). In this sense, the definition of "man of God" as one who subscribes to the "sound words" of Paul and who seeks to imitate his exemplary life is also the definition of one who can succeed him to ministry by providing gifted leadership to the church he has founded. Toward this end, then, Paul encourages Timothy to depend upon the Holy Spirit to protect this **treasure** (= Paul's gospel and the example of his life) given him.

Given that Paul's notion of what Timothy should "treasure" is autobiographical, it is apropos that he should extend his first exhortation to Timothy with an autobiographical note. Scholars have noticed that 1:15-18 is shaped as a literary *chiasm* (a-b-c-b'-c') to center this personal note on the image of Paul's imprisonment (cf: vv. 16b-17) since evidently this is a sign of disrespect for the gospel and a source of shame for Timothy in the Roman world. In this sense, then, both his reflections on the disaffection within the Asian church (a: 15, a': 18b) and the hospitality of Onesiphorus (b: 16a, b' 17b-18a) personify different responses and ultimate results to the embarrassment of Paul's imprisonment for Timothy to weigh. Obviously, he should not follow the lead of those in Asia **who turned away from me** but rather Onesiphorus's positive example, for **the Lord will grant him mercy on that day** (18a). The phrase, "on that day," draws upon the prophetic idiom of the OT when referring to the "day of the Lord" reserved for judgment and salvation (see 1 Tim. 4:8; cf. Matt. 25:36).

Not only is sharing in Paul's suffering a convention of his sacred calling, but Timothy should be motivated by this eschatological claim of divine mercy.

Nothing is known of Phygelus, Hermogenes, and Onesiphorus, who also are mentioned in the second-century apocryphal book *Acts of Paul and Thecla*. Some scholars suppose that the author of the *Acts of Paul* subsequently added details to their unrecorded story—in the fashion of Jewish midrashists in the ancient world—to clarify Paul's unstated motives when writing 2 Timothy. For example, in *Acts of Paul*, both Phygelus and Hermogenes (along with Demas, see 4:10) are portrayed as adversaries of Paul's mission who grow jealous by his success (*AP* 4) and subsequently come to disagree with his teaching about the resurrection of believers (see 2:18; *AP* 14). They claim against Pauline teaching that the resurrection from the dead has already been realized by believers both spiritually and inwardly rather than bodily and in the future at the Lord's return to earth (*AP* 11-14; cf. 1 Cor. 15). This latter Christian writing, then, when considered as a midrash of 2 Tim. 1:15-18, interprets the disaffection of Asian believers as prompted by their moral failure (= jealousy) and bad theology (= denial of a bodily resurrection "on that day"). In this way, the Christian midrashist who wrote the *Acts of Paul* wrote in part to clarify the motive of Paul's exhortation to Timothy to **retain the standard of sound words . . . in the faith and love which are in Christ Jesus** (1:13): maintenance of a moral life and orthodox theology are necessary attributes in maintaining a vigorous Christian ministry.

2:1-13. Paul Charges Timothy to Engage in the Tasks of His Calling

In this second exhortation Paul expands on the character of the spiritual gift Timothy has been given by God through the Holy Spirit (see 1:6-7, 14). In fact, his failure of nerve may have resulted in a paralysis of action to the determent of his congregation's Christian nurture: spiritual gifts are given by God to empower effective ministry among God's people. As we should expect, the tasks enabled by Timothy's spiritual gift are precisely those exemplified by his mentor, Paul. For this reason, Paul uses succession language in 2:2 to commission Timothy to teach and transmit to still other **faithful** believers (as opposed to disaffected ex-believers such as Phygelus and Hermogenes) those sacred traditions received from him.

This chain of sacred tradition—comprised of memories of Jesus (see 2:8; 1 Tim. 6:3) and Paul (see 1:13; 3:14; 1 Tim. 1:10-11; Titus 1:9) as well as Scripture (see 3:15-16)—moves fluidly from Paul to Timothy to still others and envisages the public protocol of Jewish catechesis. In this regard, tradition should not be viewed as static dogma but a living deposit of truth that is passed down, vested with new meaning, from generation to generation (see 1:3) to give direction and substance to a people's ongoing worship of God. It could be that Paul's reference to **things that you have heard me say in the presence of many witnesses** refers to Paul's commissioning of Timothy (see 1:6, "the laying on of my hands") before a congregation of elders (= "witnesses," see 1 Tim. 4:14); however, more likely the text refers to Paul's instruction of Timothy in preparation of his future ministry. In fact, the principal task of Timothy's vocation, for which the Spirit has gifted him and Paul has mentored him, is teaching others about the gospel of God.

The prospect of suffering, which is at the nub of Timothy's spiritual crisis (see 1:8), is examined by use of stock *typoi* Paul borrows from Hellenistic moral discourse: the Roman solider, the Greek athlete, and the Jewish farmer. Each is mentioned in passing knowing that his reader would be familiar with their use as metaphors of the disciplined worker who is able to overcome great obstacles in accomplishing conscripted tasks. The **good soldier** is one who does only what his recruiter commands of him and nothing else (cf. Epictetus, *Disc.* 3.22.69). The **competitive athlete** expends great effort to be crowned with the garland wreath given of a victor at athletic contests in the Greco-Roman world (cf. Herodotus, *PerWar* 8.59). The **hard-working farmer** receives payment from the fruit of the harvest in proportion to his effort in the fields (cf. Jospheus, *Ant.* 2.321). The cumulative effect of these familiar examples underwrites Paul's conception of Christian vocation: Timothy's future reward (if not also his very salvation—see 1 Tim. 4:16) is predicated on his present obedience to God's call, even though his obedience will require him to **suffer hardship with (Paul)** (cf. Phil. 2:5-8).

Chrysostom wonders why Paul would encourage Timothy to **remember Jesus Christ** (2:8), and answers his implied question by asserting that "it is directed chiefly against the heretics, at the same time to encourage Timothy by underscoring the divine blessings accompanying sufferings, since Christ, our Master, himself overcame death by suffering" (*Homilies on 2 Timothy* 4). Once again, Paul's exhortation to remember introduces an important element of his articulation of the Christian gospel (2:9), in this case Jesus' **resurrection from the dead** in vindication of his messianic status as a **descendant of David** (cf. Rom. 1:3-4). Although Chrysostom may be right that here Paul anticipates his later correction of heretical teaching (see 2:18), his immediate concern is Timothy's reluctance to share in his and the Lord's suffering. In this light, then, remembering Christ's resurrection recalls the deep logic of Paul's gospel by which Jesus triumphs over sin and death by "becoming obedience to the point of death, even death on a cross" (Phil. 2:8). It is further logical that this same obedience-suffering-triumph pattern is reflected by his own missionary experience (2:10).

Especially in the writings of Hellenistic Judaism (Philo, Josephus), the language of "glory" develops a connotation of human reputation (cf. Josephus, *Ant.* 15.376) that differs from OT (LXX) use of "glory" where it typically refers to the "weightiness" or ultimate importance of God's ongoing presence among God's people. Of course, in his doxologies Paul often recalls this biblical idea to celebrate God's **eternal glory** (see 1 Tim. 1:11; 3:16; 6:15-16; Titus 2:13). Here Paul splits the difference and speaks of faithful believers—those whose reputation is to endure suffering with their faith intact—as those who will ultimately participate in the eternal glory of God.

The extended **trustworthy saying** (2:11-13; see 1 Tim. 1:15, et. al.) that concludes Paul's exhortation is another part of his sacred tradition passed on to Timothy to teach still other faithful believers (see 2:2), presumably so that his entire congregation may share in the eternal glory of God (so 2:10). The compressed nature of these important sayings found throughout the PE, which all concern the nature and scope of God's saving grace, makes for a complex literary structure that is sometimes difficult to follow. This hard saying appears to be a midrash on Rom. 6:1-23 from a letter probably already in circulation and which Timothy probably knew.

It consists of a logical sequence of four conditional statements expressed in two contrasting pairs. The first pair (2:11-12a) sets forth the positive case of the faithful believer: If by faith we have died with Christ, then we now live with him (2:11; cf. Rom. 6:4-8); and if we endure our present suffering with our faith intact, then we will reign with him forever (2:12a; cf. Rom. 6:9-14). On the other hand, the second pair (2:12b-13) sets forth the negative case of the apostate who denies the gospel claims about Jesus: If the believer (= Paul's opponents) denies Paul's teaching about Christ, then Christ will deny his salvation (2:12b). The formulation of this statement envisages a kind of law code by which God's judgment of fidelity is based upon observance

of God's law—a point that Jesus frequently made (Matt. 7:21-26; 26:70). Paul gives a more positive formulation of 2 Tim. 2:12b in Rom. 6:17-19 when he thanks God that believers have been transformed to "become obedient from the heart to that form of teaching to which you were committed . . . so now present your members to righteousness, resulting in sanctification." This conditional is then paired with a final and climactic conditional, which is axiomatic of God's unchanging fidelity to covenantal promises made. That is, human faithlessness cannot subvert divine faithfulness **for God cannot deny himself** (2:13; cf. Rom. 6:23).

The faithfulness of God to promises made is a central theme of Scripture as is God's contrasting judgment of disobedience to God's law (cf. Jas. 2:8-13). What seems to be an innovation of the PE, however, is Paul's application of this theological principle to the congregation's leader and the execution of his appointed tasks. In doing them, the leader's salvation is insured (so 1 Tim. 4:16b; cf. 2 Tim. 4:8), even as those who are unfaithful to their calling face the prospect of God's eschatological judgment—or **denial** (so 2:12b). It is this theological claim that underwrites Paul's anxiety about Timothy and his persistent exhortation for him to faithfully discharge that which he has been set apart and gifted to do in this economy of God's salvation.

2:14–3:9. Paul Urges Timothy to Correct False Teachers

In the ancient church this extended passage from 2 Timothy was often cited in the church's debates with heretical teachers. Basil the Great appealed to 2:17 to argue that "in order that the sin slowly creeping farther may not spread like cancer, a disciple with evangelical precepts begs of God that the further outpouring of sin may cease and have definite bounds" (*Homilies* 11.6). In fact, Paul's admonitions profile his opponents in order to place boundaries around how the leader of a congregation should live and what doctrine he should teach.

Reconstructing an historical profile of Paul's opponents has been one of the most important yet difficult projects of modern biblical scholarship. Some scholars, perhaps out of frustration, have even suggested that Paul's polemics against false teachers is mere rhetoric; they are imaginary or fictional rivals drawn by Paul to allow him to build his own case by contrast more clearly. It was common in the ancient world—as in our own (think about any recent political contest!)—where an opponent's evils are exaggerated or even created in order to undercut his or her credibility. Thus, for example, philosophers would call their rival a "quack," a "hypocrite," a teacher of "falsehoods," or an "idle babbler" (Acts 17:18) in order to win the upper hand in a public debate. With Paul, teachers of the Greco-Roman world would provide commentary not only on the substantive criticisms of what their opponents taught, but also on how they taught—their oratory or pedagogy—as ineffective. In Paul's world, the manner of public speaking was as important as its content. For this reason, Paul typically criticizes his opponents for making claims that contradicted his teaching (e.g., 2:18) but also for the manner of their teaching (e.g., 2:14, 16). While this interpretation of Pauline polemic is certainly plausible, since it is a rhetorical strategy often employed by both Jewish rabbis and Hellenistic rhetors, it is entirely possible to separate out the purely rhetorical from those elements of Paul's description which have a basis in fact.

For instance, Timothy is likely doing battle with rival teachers for leadership of the Ephesian congregation. The familiar metaphor of a household (see Introduction to 1 Timothy) that contains both useful and unusable earthenware would seem to infer that some teachers edify believers while others do not—that is, some of this anti-Pauline teaching has contributed to a shameful lifestyle that is publicly evident. In this regard, note that Paul casts this intramural conflict in terms of the **honor-dishonor** culture of his day (2:20): false teachers whose teaching legitimates bad behavior bring dishonor to the household of God, while good teachers who **call on the Lord from a pure heart** cultivate a moral lifestyle and bring honor to the household. In this social setting to which Paul speaks of a culture of the **last days** (3:1), the Lord, who **knows those who are His** (2:19), will distribute honor and shame according to **every good work** (2:21).

In Paul's day, philosophers described the ideal teacher as one who adapted big ideas to real life in clear-headed ways (e.g., Plutarch's "Obsolescence of Oracles"). "Truth" that is truly true, in this sense, is never viewed as abstract or obtuse but as clearly communicated wisdom that works concretely to improve human lives and relations. Paul's comment that **talk will spread like gangrene** (2:17) is a reflection of this widespread conviction, and is the basis for his criticism that false teachers chatter away in profane and useless directions (2:16) while they engage in **foolish and ignorant speculations that produce quarrels** (2:23). Teaching style (pedagogy) is as important as the subject matter taught in Paul's world.

It is imperative for the interpreter of the PE to distinguish between the different groups of false teachers to whom Paul responds in these three different letters: the heretics of 1 Timothy are not those admonished in 2 Timothy or in Titus. Careful discrimination between these different groups, then, and especially the more precise criticisms that Paul makes of each, provide the basis for their historical profile. Two particular elements found in this passage are important in this regard. First, according to Paul's criticism found in 2:18 the false teachers of 2 Timothy evidently taught a wrong view of the resurrection of the dead, similar to the doctrine he had corrected earlier in Corinth (cf. 1 Cor. 15). Paul's own understanding of the resurrection has two sources: on the one hand, as a Pharisaic Jew with apocalyptic leanings, he hoped that God would one day enliven Israel's "dry bones" and bring back to eternal life a remnant of faithful Jews as the initial act of creation's restoration. On the other hand, Paul's Damascus Road experience with the risen Jesus transformed his Jewish belief in Nation Israel's end-time restoration into a conviction about the Lord's resurrection as proof for the prospect of God's coming triumph: when the risen Jesus returns, he will mediate the restoration of a "true" Israel (= church) to eternal life set within the bounds of a new creation. Belief in these two resurrections—of Christ in the past and church in the future—is inseparable in Paul's mind and may well be the theological subtext of this passage.

Evidently the particular point of apostasy concerns the resurrection of "dead" believers. If the claim of these apostates is that **the resurrection has already taken place** (2:18), then their teaching surely deviates from the reality of a future, bodily resurrection for eternal life in a new creation, which is central to the Pauline tradition Timothy has inherited. Evidently, these teachers have spiritualized and moralized Paul's doctrine of bodily resurrection. Being "resurrected from death unto life" with Jesus has become for some teachers a metaphor of an inward spiritual, mystical transformation by which the newly baptized convert achieves greater insight into a heavenly knowledge (= gnosis) or attains a morally virtuous life. Paul would not disagree with this use of Easter faith as a metaphor of personal transformation (cf. Rom. 6:4-8); however, the false teachers appear to restrict their definition of resurrection only to this more spiritual or moralistic experience, already realized, and deny at the same time a future, cosmic resurrection when God will triumph over all that is dead—spiritual and material, individual and creational, human and non-human, animate and inanimate. God who has created all things will repair all things when the risen Jesus

returns to earth to complete his messianic mission. It is against this background of a much fuller doctrine of the resurrection that Paul's criticism must be understood.

There is yet another specific element of Paul's criticism that concerns the questionable conduct of these false teachers. This should not come as a surprise since Paul often relates eschatology and ethics: what one thinks about the future shapes how one acts in the present. For this reason, contrasting catalogues of purity and profanity are central to this passage: the Christian leader is one who **flees from youthful lusts . . . and calls upon the Lord from a pure heart** (2:22). The conviction of a realized resurrection by which the new convert has already been initiated into a new existence, perhaps at Christian baptism, may well have formed the impression that one need no longer worry about the effects of "youthful lusts" or **worldly and empty chatter** (2:16) on relations with others or with God. Such a teaching subverts the believer's sense of needing to repent and grow in Christ, preventing thereby their escape **from the snare of the devil** (2:25-26).

Although the profile of Paul's opponents in 2 Timothy is an important historical construction, the most important element of this passage is the profile of Timothy as a congregational leader. Again, drafting both the persona and tasks of a competent successor, in whose hands the community can entrust its future, is central to this kind of testamental literature. The moral purpose of one's life—to **pursue righteousness** (2:22)—is a decisive ingredient of Timothy's future success as the congregation's teacher.

According to the Dead Sea Scrolls (CD 1.11; 20.32; 1QHab 2.2), the individual who had the most important role in shaping the life of the community was called "the Teacher of Righteousness" (*moreh hatsedeq*), a sobriquet that reflects his spiritual authority to interpret Torah and to exemplify the manner of holy life that might "direct (Israel) in the path of God's heart" (CD 1.11) and so the terms of eternal life (cf. 1QpHab 7.1-5). Significantly, the Scrolls also speak of the Teacher's opponent within Israel— a so-called "Wicked Priest" (cf. 1QpHab xi.4-8; 4Q171 4.8-10) who is sometimes called the "Liar" because he teaches falsehoods (cf. 1QpHab x.9)—as one who might lead Israel into Belial's traps (so CD 4.15; cf. 2:26). While the idiom used in the Scrolls to describe their unfriendly competition over Israel's future with God reflects the ascetic values of the Qumran community, it does emphasize the importance of purity in a way that rings true to Paul's expression throughout chapter two both to castigate his opposition (2:16-18) and to encourage Timothy to live a holy life (2:20-21).

Paul's description of moral decay, which is characteristic of "the last days," continues to draw out the conflict between Timothy and Paul's opponents in graphic, apocalyptic terms (3:1-9). Central to this text is the lengthy catalogue of vices that characterize the opponents whom Timothy is to avoid (3:2-5; see Titus 3:10). Each of these various vices can easily be found in the polemical writings of Greco-Roman philosophers such as Aristotle and Thucydides; and most are found in other Pauline letters although some appear only here in the NT. The purpose of these lists is to create an impression of people rather than to describe them literally. For example, some words Paul uses begin with the Greek letter alpha and others with the prefix "pro-," thereby creating literary alliteration that evokes an emotive response from its auditors when read aloud—as all his letters surely were (cf. Eph. 3:2).

Paul's symbolic world is primarily Jewish and biblical. His unqualified description of moral and societal chaos is a feature of apocalyptic writings such as 2 Esdras and Daniel, which had significant influence on Jesus' understanding of salvation's future (cf. Mark 13:5-27). And his reference to Jannes and Jambres for comparison (3:9) roots his entire "last days" polemic in the story of the Exodus.

Although their names are not found in the OT, these two shadowy figures were reputed to be members of the Pharaoh's court according to the Pseudo-Jonathan Targum on Exod. 1:15 and Midrash *Tanhuma* on Exod. 32:1. The Dead Sea Scroll, CD 5.17-19, says "For in ancient times God visited their deeds and His anger was kindled against their works; for it is a people of no discernment, it is a nation void of counsel inasmuch as there is not discernment in them. For in ancient times, Moses and Aaron arose by the hand of the Prince of Lights and Satan in his cunning raised up Jannes and his brother when Israel was first delivered." In fact, their story was so familiar to Paul's Judaism that he does not need to recall anything but their names to make his point; and set within the Exodus story implies the outcome of this contest: even as God delivered Israel from the Pharaoh, despite the opposition of Jannes and Jambres, so also will God expose the folly of those who reject the faith.

Finally, the reference to the opposition's tactic of influencing **weak women . . . led on by various impulses** (3:6) is based on a common caricature of immature, middle-class women found in the ancient world. (Working class women, employed perhaps as household servants, would not have the luxury to sit down and listen to the teaching of these men! It would not have been polite to do so in Paul's world, even if it had been permitted.) Epictetus denounced middle-class women as "silly," because they often used their freedom and leisure on material passions rather than on educating their minds (*Discourses* 15; see 1 Tim. 2:9-12). Paul's reference to **weak women weighed down with sins** is not a blanket statement about all women, any more than his exhortation to **avoid such men as these** constitutes a blanket statement about the proclivities of all men! Certainly, the reference to "household," Paul's most important metaphor for the church in the PE, indicates these are middle-class *Christian* women that worry Paul. But elsewhere in the PE he speaks of women who are mentors (see 1:5; cf. 1 Tim. 5:5) and also his missionary colleagues who are women (see 4:19-21). These "weak women," then, are probably new believers from influential families whose faith has not yet been brought to maturity by "sound doctrine" and as a result they are easily seduced by false teaching.

3:10-17. Paul Exhorts Timothy to Follow His Example

One of the most important properties of testamental literature such as 2 Timothy is the remembrance of personal examples to establish moral norms. By imitating Paul's life, Timothy is assured of doing every good work that is pleasing to God. Toward this end, then, Paul provides a robust summary of his life, which in contrast to those teachers Timothy must avoid/flee/shun exemplifies to what sort of leader he should aspire. The stipulation of Paul as Timothy's role model includes appropriate behavior (moral), missionary tasks (vocational), teaching (theological), suffering (experiential), and his anticipated destiny (eschatological); these are all conventional elements of *mimesis* in the ancient world.

Most of Paul's autobiography reprises themes mentioned earlier with his imprisonment and anticipated death (4:6) as their background; and reading Paul's recollection in context of the Book of Acts provides stories that help elucidate his **persecutions and sufferings . . . at Antioch, Iconium and at Lystra** (3:11; cf. Acts 13-14) as well as his work of **preaching the word . . . in season and out of season** (4:2). In many ways, his recollection here in 2 Timothy is anticipated by his great Miletus speech in Acts 20:18-35 in both purpose and content. In both texts, Paul distills his experiences into a simple formula: **all who desire to live godly in Christ Jesus will be persecuted** (3:12). Moreover, while Paul characterizes this godly life by catalogues of personal virtue (cf. 3:10; see 2:22), his principle

emphasis is on obedience to the tasks of his (= Timothy's) calling (see 1:6-7; 2:23-26).

Among the salient features of Paul's missionary calling is his interpretation of Scripture. We should expect this of a Pharisaic Jew for whom Scripture sets the norms of purity by which the way of a community's covenant relationship with God and its separation from a corrupt and evil world is made known. The portrait of Paul in Acts is fashioned by this emphasis, so that his primary missionary practice is teaching Scripture to give evidence that "Christ had to suffer and rise again from the dead" (Acts 17:2-3). Therefore, his statement about Scripture in 3:16 is contextualized both by his Jewish beliefs and by the practices of his evangelistic work.

It goes without saying that the endless controversies (especially within Protestantism!) generated by disagreements about the meaning of 2 Tim. 3:15-17 commends careful scrutiny of its historical background. When Paul refers to **sacred writings** that Timothy **knew from childhood** (see 1:5), he could not have been writing about a Christian Bible which did not exist in the first century and did not reach its final canonical shape until early in the fifth century. In fact, "sacred writings" is a set term used always by Hellenistic Jews like Paul in reference to their Hebrew Scriptures in Greek translation (from around 250 B.C. and called "the Septuagint")—which should be noted is not identical with a later edition of Hebrew Scriptures—the so-called "Masoretic" or rabbinical text—which the synagogue probably recognized as canonical sometime during the second century and in any case long after 2 Timothy was published. Because this same term, "sacred writings," also had currency in the secular world in reference to official documents, Paul may well also be referring to sacred traditions from Jesus (stories of his life and accounts of his teaching; see 1 Tim. 6:3) and also to formal summaries of his own gospel message—or what he calls "sound (or healthy) doctrine" (see 1 Tim. 1:10-11). In this sense, "sacred writings" takes on an expanded connotation of a body of living traditions—biblical, Christological, Pauline—that are formative of a believer's Christian faith.

The adjective "all" defines the scope of Scripture's importance to include its every part. This definition coheres to the ancient rabbis who taught that every part of Scripture held a word from God. In fact, Rabbi Akiva regulated readings of Scripture by his "*ribbui* (inclusion)-*mi'ut* (exclusion) rule," which stipulated that even the most familiar and least significant grammatical particles (e.g., "and," "or," "the," "a") could hold important meanings since by these particles God often discloses those included or excluded from covenant blessings. Moreover, the noun, "Scripture," is singular, which in keeping with his Pharisaic convictions infers that his Jewish Scripture (not "Scriptures") forms a "simultaneity:" every part of "all Scripture," even though expressed in differing idioms or with differing theological accent, bears common witness to the truth about one God, the only God.

The crux in understanding the meaning of Paul's beliefs about his Scripture is concentrated by a single Greek predicate, *theopneustos*, which NASB translates, "(is) inspired by God." The word is used only here in the NT and appears infrequently in other Greek writings. Hellenistic religious literature sometimes describes the speeches of religious men as "inspired," but usually in reference to their "mantic" experiences or even to the reception of their speeches by others who are "inspired" by their powerful rhetoric. For example, 4 Ezra (written about the same time as 2 Timothy) narrates the inspiration of the prophet Ezra this way: "And on the next day a voice called me, saying, 'Ezra, open your mouth and drink what I give you to bring.' So I opened my mouth, and a full cup was offered to me; it was full of something like water, but its color was like fire. I took it and drank; and when I had drunk it, my heart poured forth under-standing and my wisdom increased, for my spirit retained its memory and my mouth was opened and no longer closed" (4 *Es* 14:37-38).

Probably a better context for understanding Paul's meaning of *theopneustos* is Gen. 2:7, where "God breathed" life into Adam. The impression Paul creates by his allusion to the biblical story of man's creation, then, concerns less the "production" of the biblical text—since nowhere does Paul mention the inspiration of Scripture's authors—but rather to its ongoing "performance" when the community's authorized Scriptures are used profitably within the congregation for **teaching, reproof, correction, training in righteousness** (3:16b). For this reason, when this text is picked up and used by the church's Fathers (cited more than one hundred times through the first four centuries alone!), it is the performance of Scripture—its utility for Christian nurture—more than its production that is mentioned. In this sense, then, God "breathes newness of life" into those who actually use Scripture to learn God.

The catalogue of Scripture's uses, which includes both priestly (teaching, training) and prophetic (reproof, correction) roles, is also patterned on what rabbis understood to be the various roles of Torah. Not only is Torah the curriculum used by "rabbis-like-Moses" when teaching the congregation the truths about God (cf. Deut.), Torah is also used by "prophets-like-Moses" when calling the congregation to repentance (cf. Jeremiah, Isaiah). Paul's point in exhorting Timothy, then, is to underwrite both roles, with Scripture in hand: he is to reproof and correct the false teachers as a prophet, while teaching and training the congregation in living rightly before God. Such are the aspirations and **good work** of the **man of God** (3:17).

4:1-8. Paul Commands Timothy to Preach the Word in his Place

A final exhortation forms the poignant conclusion of Paul's instructions to Timothy. This passage effectively summarizes the letter's occasion: Paul anticipates his death (4:6) and thus the end of a successful ministry (4:7-8); and so in this light writes Timothy, his young successor, to command (= "charge") him to **endure hardship, do the work of an evangelist, fulfill your ministry** (4:5) with Paul as his example. The subtext of the entire letter is Timothy's own spiritual crisis, whether he is sufficiently mature and courageous to continue Paul's work (see 1:6-7).

This portion of 2 Timothy is especially characteristic of ancient testamental literature (see "Introduction" above): whose occasion is the impending death or departure of a charismatic leader, whose persona and work is remembered as exemplary, who writes to commission the appointed successor to perpetuate his example for the good of those left behind. In fact, the "last days" of Paul personify the "last days" of the present age, when Christ Jesus will appear **to judge the living and the dead** (4:1). In this light, Paul anticipates a future **crown of righteousness, which the Lord . . . will award me on that day** (4:8a) because he has **fought the good fight** to the finish (4:7). And this personal testimony becomes in turn the standard by which others, especially Timothy, may share in the eschatological awards (cf. 4:8b)—that is, if they too finish "the good fight."

Paul's careful connection of future blessing with vocation supplies motive to his charge for Timothy to **preach the word . . . in season and out of season** (4:2)—that is, in every circumstance and at every opportune moment. This "word" is Paul's gospel about Christ (see 2:8-9), the subject matter of **sound** (= healthy) **doctrine** (4:3) that now is challenged by false teachers within the congregation Timothy pastors. With characteristic vividness, Paul's polemic sounds a cautionary note that these false teachers will **tickle ears . . . and turn ears from the truth . . . to myths** (4:3-4).

Paul's contemporaries were well aware of the contrasting merits of mythology and truth telling. The most important philosophers of his day considered "myths" as opposing truth and common sense. Philo, for example, contrasted mythology and lasting truth (*Abel and Cain* 13) and Epictetus questioned Homer's enduring importance as author of "his myths" (*Discourses* 3.24.18). Similarly, the Eastern Father, Gregory of Nazianzus, commenting on this text for his day, wrote "there are certain persons who have not only their ears and their tongues but even, as I now perceive, their hands too, itching for words. They delight in profane babblings and the oppositions of science, falsely so-called, and strive over words which tend to no profit. Paul is the preacher and establisher of the 'word cut short' . . . who calls into question all that is excessive or superfluous in discourse" (*Orations* 27.1).

In 2 Timothy Paul expresses concern for Timothy's character, and in this concluding charge includes two virtue pairs, **patience and instruction** (4:2) and **sobriety and endurance** (4:5), that are widely recommended by the moralists of his day. Each asserts a practical response to typical problems faced by every leader. Thus, the effective leader must respond to his opponents with patient instruction, which includes **reproof, rebuke, exhortation** (4:2) based upon biblical teaching (see 3:16); and the effective leader must endure his hardship with sobriety, which refers to carefully thought out responses to real problems and which Plato taught is the most important quality of those in public life (*Laws* 11).

Finally, the use of athletic metaphors in Paul's summary of his life (4:5-8) for Timothy's sake is a common literary convention of the moral philosophers of his day: his race to the tape has engaged him in a disciplined struggle that required him to "endure hardship" and "keep the faith." As with any athlete, Paul's competence is motivated by the expectation of "the crown," which refers to the wreath awarded to the one who finishes first in athletic competition. "Righteousness" is not epexegetical of what the "wreath" is made of but is explanatory of what the athlete is made of; that is, Paul triumphs at day's end because he has lived a virtuous life, enduring his hardship with sobriety and responding to his many critics with patient instruction. And now Timothy must do likewise as his successor.

4:9-22. Paul Concludes His Letter with Personal Notes and Benediction

The conclusions of Hellenistic letters are noteworthy by their miscellany: they typically include epistolary summaries, travel itineraries, greetings and goodbyes to friends and colleagues, general exhortations, finally concluding with a benedictory prayer. Although often regarded as incidental to the main body of the letter, benedictions like this one often provide a window into the personal lives of their senders. And perhaps no other letter adds more to Scripture's biography of Paul than does 2 Timothy; again, the role of his portrait in a testamental letter such as this one is to provide the details of a life worth imitating. The keen impression of Paul's situation evoked by his concluding words is one of loneliness (4:10-11, 16-17), another expression of his suffering for the sake of the gospel (see 1:8-12; 2:3, 9; 3:11-12; 4:6).

Many of the names Paul drops into his concluding words to Timothy are unknown to us: we can account for nine of seventeen from other NT books. (There are forty names associated with Paul's missionary organization when counting all the names mentioned in the Pauline letters and Acts!) No matter; the impression shaped is that of a leader who is vested in his movement—today we call this "networking" or "taking care of business." The references to various places in Italy, Greece, and Roman Asia deepen the impression of the geographical extent of Paul's influence—an important theme in the narrative of Paul's mission in Acts.

The reference to Paul's library—his **books, especially the parchments** (4:13b)—is consistent with the tools of a rabbi's trade. In Judaism, "the books" often referred to the five books of Torah (cf. *1 Macc.* 1:56; 12:9) and "parchments" to scrolls of biblical commentary—yet another image of Scripture's importance in Paul's life (see 3:16). In light of Paul's earlier expression of his imminent death (see 4:6), Chrysostom comments, "What had Paul to do with books, who was about to depart and go to God? He needed them much, that he might deposit them in the hands of the faithful, who would retain them in place of his own teaching" (*Homilies on 2 Timothy* 10).

Even Paul's request for his **cloak** may allude to Elijah's mantel, the symbol of prophetic office (cf. 1 Kings 19:21-21; 2 Kings 4:18), even though more likely it is a personal request for warm clothing in preparation for a cold winter in prison (cf. 4:21). The evident urgency of Paul's request is probably not due to his immediate need for companionship but his awareness as an experienced traveler that travel arrangements become much more difficult when winter arrives in the Mediterranean world.

Paul's testimony that he was **delivered out of the lion's mouth** (4:17c) need not be a reference to a real event but more likely is an allusion to the biblical story of God's rescue of Daniel from the "mouth of lions" (Dan. 6:20-22; cf. Ps. 22:21; 1 Macc. 2:60; 4 Macc. 18:13). From this story Paul derives two theological assurances: that **the Lord stood with me . . . so that the gospel proclamation might be fully accomplished** (4:17ab) and that **the Lord will deliver me from every evil deed** (4:18a).

The grammar of Paul's benedictory blessing (4:22), which is stated in the singular **your spirit . . . you**," indicates the personal cast of this letter. However, the liturgical cast of this blessing may well indicate Paul's awareness that even personal correspondence would be read aloud for the spiritual edification of the worshiping congregation.

Introduction to Titus

Robert W. Wall

First read the "Introduction to the Pastoral Epistles," above.

The relationship between Paul and Titus. Passing mention of Titus is made in Galatians 2:1-3: he is a non-Jewish believer who stood at the center of religious controversy initiated by Jewish believers who believed that every convert to Christ should be "purified" and initiated into Christian fellowship through a protocol similar to that followed by Judaism, including Gentile circumcision. Paul refused, arguing that new life with Christ is initiated by trust and not by compliance to Jewish tradition. This earlier reference to Titus is an important subtext for understanding the opposition to his mission in Crete, which is led by "those of the circumcision" (1:10). He is mentioned in 2 Cor. 2:13 as Paul's "dear brother," a phrase that underwrites his importance to the Apostle and again as his "partner and fellow worker" (8:23), suggesting Titus's importance to Paul as a trusted missionary colleague; in fact, earlier Paul had recounted his happy meeting with Titus as a key element of an extensive missionary itinerary (7:5-16).

The relationship between Crete, its church and Paul's mission. We should assume Titus's close and trusted association with Paul when we pick up this letter for study. Perhaps that he is non-Jewish in his religious background before coming to knowledge of Christ is another bit of the background that makes more sense of this letter's occasion—Cretan believers are largely Gentile and his opposition there is largely Jewish. In any case, Titus is assigned by Paul to establish Christian congregations on the island of Crete while the apostle travels to Nicopolis on the Adriatic coast of western Greece (3:12). Although there is no record of a Pauline mission on the island, his intimate knowledge of Crete's coastline disclosed during his fateful voyage to Rome as narrated in Acts 27 may well indicate an earlier visit. In any case, Paul instructs Titus to correct false teaching and to appoint elders to lead each congregation in every city (1:5).

This seems especially important since comparisons between Titus and 1 Timothy, even though similar literary letters, suggests that the gospel's truth had only recently penetrated the island's population. Whereas in 1 Timothy, Paul can instruct his associate to avoid selecting new converts to lead the congregation to maturity (1 Tim. 3:6), in this letter Titus is expected to choose from recent converts (3:8) who nonetheless have a firm grasp of "sound doctrine" (1:9).

Every composition has a literary genre that shapes and conveys its teaching to others. Although passing mention is made of opponents in Titus (1:10-16; 3:9-11), no details are provided about what they teach. In fact, this is not a polemical letter but one full of exhortations, instructions, and theological summaries.

As with 1 Timothy, the genre of Titus is that of an official mandate—from Paul to a younger associate to whom he has delegated authority to grow new congregations in places removed from Paul's direct influence.

This sort of administrative composition in the Hellenistic world often contained the very literary conventions found in Titus (and 1 Timothy): lists of instructions, contrasting catalogues of vices and virtues, and personal examples. The purpose of these rhetorical devices was practical: to provide an easy-to-follow manual to a subordinate to insure his success in the field. Moreover, because administrative success depended upon theological orthodoxy, the structure of Titus (and 1 Timothy) is forged by closely related sections of congregational or personal instruction (2:1-10; 2:15—3:2) grounded on theological summary (2:11-14; 3:3-7).

The practical problems that occasion Paul's writing of this letter are similar to those that occasioned the writing of 1 Timothy, and are related to forming Christian congregations in pagan places. For example, Paul is concerned—as we are today—with identifying believers with the character and competence to lead these congregations (1:5-9). Compounding the lack of mature believers, the Cretan culture evidently has retarded the formation of good character making the prospect of finding and developing leaders more difficult (1:10-13a). This same concern shapes his instructions governing household etiquette and responsibilities (2:1-10).

The problem of the false teachers in Crete. The secondary crisis facing Titus concerns his theological opponents, whom Paul routinely castigates (1:10-16; 3:9-11). In part, the issue is political and related to their subversive effect on Titus's religious authority within the congregation; however, they also disrupt the spiritual formation of new believers (1:11). Vague references to their teaching would seem to indicate a Jewish influence: they are "of the circumcision" (1:10) who pay "attention to Jewish myths and commandments" (1:14) as well as "disputes about the Law" (3:9). But they are somehow affiliated with the church because Paul tells Titus that they "profess to know God" even though "worthless for any good deed" (1:16). He appears less concerned about the content of their teaching than about its divisive result within the congregation. Christian unity is a critical element of the gospel's advance in Crete.

Titus

Robert W. Wall

1:1-4. Paul Greets Titus

Paul typically opens his letters after the fashion of other letter-writers in the Greco-Roman world: "writer to recipient, greetings." This ancient literary formula is not incidental to the purpose of the letter, but often commends the proper posture of the letter's recipient to its writer and his message. In this case, Paul's religious authority is elaborated to underwrite the importance of his instructions to Titus. In particular, Paul refers to himself as **bond-servant of God . . . apostle of Jesus Christ**. These titles, appended to Paul's name much like today's business cards or signature block, define both his vocation and the perspective from which he writes to Titus. The first is unusual for Paul but familiar to Jewish readers of David's story in the OT where he considers his relationship to God as a "servant" (1 Sam. 23:10-11; 2 Sam. 7:27; cf. 1 Kings 8:28; Ezra 5:11; Isa. 42:19; 49:3). In describing his relationship in this way, Paul indicates his complete loyalty to God, a necessary attribute for an agent of God's salvation (see v. 3). This powerful sense of loyalty is deepened in a world in which the majority of members in Paul's urban congregations—perhaps even the one that Titus now pastors—had a résumé that included slavery (see 1 Tim. 6:1-2). Unlike the experience of most slaves in antebellum America, Roman slaves understood well the importance of obeying their masters who routinely entrusted important business and familial matters into their hands.

The second title, "apostle of Jesus Christ," is more typical of Paul and expresses his missionary calling (cf. Acts 9:15-16) as herald and teacher of God's gospel (see 1 Tim. 2:7). St. Jerome says that Paul "had designated himself with the title of apostle of Jesus Christ that he might strike awe into his readers by the authority of the name" (*Commentary on Titus*). More than inferring his missionary tasks, Christ's appointment of Paul to his apostolic order grants to him the requisite religious authority to define the terms of **the faith of those chosen of God and the knowledge of the truth**. The phrase "those chosen by God" recalls its use in Isaiah's prophecy for restored Israel (Isa. 42:1; 43:20; 45:4; 65:9, 15, 23); their social identity in the world is their affirmation of "the faith" that Paul is entrusted to preach (see 1 Tim. 1:10b-11).

The important combination of "knowledge of the truth" (see 1 Tim. 2:4) with "godliness" (see 1 Tim. 2:2), understood within the Pastoral Epistles (PE), defines the limits of Paul's pastoral purview in the most comprehensive way possible, combining both the truth of "sound doctrine" and the practical piety of "godliness." The reference to "truth" anticipates Paul's harsh characterization of both his religious opponents (1:10) and Cretan culture (1:12) as "liars." At Qumran, "knowledge of the truth" identified the community as God's covenant people—perhaps in contrast with other Jewish groups with different beliefs (1QS 6:15; 9:17-18; 1QH 10:20-29). In the Greco-Roman world, "godliness" was a cardinal virtue. Epictetus, an important Stoic philosopher, understood it as the very foundation of a moral life. Hellenistic Jews, such as Paul, recognized that obedience to God generated love for one another—piety begets morality. Thus, in the Pastoral Epistles, a life of "godliness" is often described in terms of religious practices/beliefs (e.g., 1 Tim. 6:3) that animates a particular lifestyle (e.g., 1 Tim. 6:5-6; cf. 2 Tim. 3:5).

A second combination, **in the hope of eternal life** with **promised long ages ago,** ascribes a temporal perspective to the content of faith. Drawn from Paul's Jewish background, God's truth extends *within* space and time from a distant past into an indeterminate future. The expression "hope of eternal life" encloses Paul's instructions to Titus (see 3:7), which then suggests the theological motive or objective for Titus' compliance to all these instructions: eternal life for God's people. In contemporary Jewish use, life with God is the objective of God's promise to Abraham and Sarah (cf. *2 Bar* 57:2). Insofar as God's promise is already envisaged at creation (cf. Gen. 1:27-28), it is a promise made "long ages ago" that will be realized in the eternal life of God's covenant people.

The climax of salvation's history is God's revelation in Christ. Paul's phrase **manifested, *even* His word**, however, reworks this same revelatory pattern to emphasize the authority of his message that leads people into God's salvation. That is, the theological content of Paul's **proclamation** agrees with the Word of God that is disclosed in Christ, so that by knowing this truth faithful people will enter into eternal life (cf. John 1:1-18; Jas. 1:18). The perspicuity of God's Word is stated by the striking claim that God "cannot lie," a phrase used by Jewish writers (*Wis* 7:7; Philo, *Ebr.* 139) and secular philosophers (cf. Plato, *Resp.* 2:382) of divine character: since deities do not lie, neither can

their "word" lead people astray. Thus, Clement of Rome says "nothing is impossible for God except to lie . . . and so let our souls be bound to him who is faithful to his promises" (*First Letter of Clement* 27).

The title, **God our Savior**, which is a central element of this letter's important theological statements (see 2:10, 13; 3:4, 6), is better translated "our Savior, God." God is the final note sounded in Paul's opening statement. In Greco-Roman culture, "our Savior," understood as a generous benefactor, had wide currency. City officials who distributed needed benefits to the rank-and-file were hailed as the people's "savior." Julius Caesar was celebrated as the "savior" of common folk, and was even worshiped as god personified (*SIG* 347, 760.6). Ancient deities such as Zeus were petitioned as savior by those in need of healing or rescue from harm's way. This definition of savior is the primary theological meaning of "savior" in the OT: God delivers Israel from the enemy and for a better life (Deut. 32:15; Pss. 24:5; 25:5; 278:8; 42:6; Isa. 12:2; 60:16).

This same idea is then extended to **Christ Jesus our Savior** (1:4), not so much to describe his importance—which would have been assumed by Titus—but to extend the work of salvation as a partnership between God and Jesus (see 2:11-14).

Titus is addressed as a **true child** perhaps in the manner of one who is authorized to interpret his mentor, which is then underwritten by Paul's recognition that they share a **common faith**—that is, they share the same **knowledge of the truth** (1:2). The background of the salutation itself is Diaspora Judaism—and perhaps the ethnically mixed audience of Paul's urban mission—in which both the Greek "grace" and Hebrew "peace" were traditional forms of greeting that stand for divine blessing.

1:5-9. Paul's Stipulations and Qualifications for the Congregation's Leaders

Unlike most Pauline letters in which expressions of thanksgiving and prayer follow the salutation, this letter moves directly to stipulate the reason Paul writes it: to instruct Titus in matters related to the organization of a Christian congregation on Crete, a large island in the Aegean Sea. This move directly from a salutation to the letter's occasion is relatively commonplace among Hellenistic letters. From Acts 14:23 we learn that Paul's missionary pattern called for the appointment of elders to supervise the practical matters of congregational life as an initial step in bringing stability to the fledgling church (see 1 Tim. 3:1-7; 5:17-22). The meaning of the verb, **to set in order**, does not infer a doctrinal dispute that requires correction but rather a protocol that church order needs to be established in the Cretan church.

The principal tasks given to the elders and overseer of a congregation are reflected by this catalogue of virtues that profiles them as competent leaders. Such lists were commonplace in Paul's world, with specific personal qualities stipulated for specific tasks. Isocrates, in *To Demonicus* 35 (250 B.C.), writes "Whenever you purpose to consult with any one about your affairs, first observe how he has managed his own; for he who has shown poor judgment in conducting his own business will never give wise counsel about the business of others." Paul extends this general moral rule to both private (home) and public affairs: Christian leaders must be **above reproach**, and their conduct is the criterion by which their competence is evaluated (see 1 Tim. 3:1-13).

This close connection between character and job performance is especially true of Jewish professional ethics. Since Crete maintained a large Jewish population—a source both of Christian converts and of opposition to the gospel (see 1:10)—it is natural for Paul to draft his profile of leadership as a practical matter of fidelity to the church's Jewish legacy. In particular, the elder must be **husband of one wife**. There is no mention of this phrase out-side of the PE (see 1 Tim. 3:2; cf. 5:9, 14), which allows many to suppose it is a metaphor of faithfulness in marriage. In fact, Josephus mentions polygamy (along with levirate marriage) as a practice still current among certain priestly families (*Ant.* 17.1, 2, 14), consistent with Israel's patriarchs who had multiple wives and the Torah's instruction which at points assumes polygamy (cf. Ex 21:8-11; Deut. 21:15; 25:5-10). Yet, polygamy was banned at Qumran as a feature of its community's moral rigor (CD IV.20-21) and monogamy was the norm throughout the Greco-Roman world. Paul may be responding to opponents who condemned marriage (cf. 1 Tim. 4:3) or, more likely, condemning the widespread practice of concubinage in the Roman world among the affluent who likely would have been pressed into service as leaders of their Christian congregation. Thus, Ambrose understood Paul to encourage "chastity in marriage to protect the grace of (a believer's) baptism" (*Letters* 63.62-63). A second, and more common measurement is that an elder's **children who believe**. In Paul's patriarchal world, fathers would have exercised final authority over their children's religious choices (cf. Acts 16:1-3). For this reason, whether or not one's children became believers would indicate something of the quality of the father's witness to the faith.

The "overseer" is distinguished from the congregation's elders, although the reason for this is not made clear. Evidently, the congregation has only one overseer who functions as **God's steward** and for this reason has qualities commensurate with good supervision. In his *Nicomachean Ethics*, Aristotle mentions the cardinal virtues Paul lists here as apropos qualities of the good citizen—in particular, being "sensible, just." (The four cardinal virtues in Greek philosophy are sensibility, justice, moderation, and courage, which are all marks of the Christian leader according to the PE.) Epictetus characterizes the good philosopher as the "manager of a well-ordered house" (*Dis.*

3.22.3-4; see 1 Tim. 1:4), and lists positive and negative qualities similar to those given Titus as pertinent to this task (*Dis.* 3.22).

The distinctively Christian characteristic listed is that this leader give oversight to **sound doctrine and to refute those who contradict.** Epictetus taught that the philosopher had the twofold responsibility of clarifying the truth and then defending it. Likewise, the overseer gives oversight to what is taught within the congregation and to protect what is taught from outside influence. The word translated "sound" is an ancient medical term for "healthy"—"sound doctrine" is teaching that promotes a congregation's spiritual health. Reference to **the faithful word which is in accordance with the teaching** stipulates the congregation's "rule of faith"—delineated by the core theological beliefs of Paul's gospel (cf. Rom. 1:16)—that measures the truthfulness of instruction within the congregation. The overseer is the principal custodian of this congregation's Pauline "rule."

1:10-16. Paul Argues Against False Teachers in Crete

The colorful characterization of false teachers follows in spirit those profiles used by ancient teachers to castigate their opponents. This catalogue of vices, which includes several words found only here in the NT, is the reverse of the virtues just listed by Paul for Christian leaders. They subvert the truth and any who search after it. The precise identity of Paul's opponents on Crete is more difficult to ascertain. Evidently certain members of the congregation have come under the influence of Jewish teachers, since Paul identifies them as **of the circumcision** and as **paying attention to Jewish myths and commandments.** We know nothing of their particular beliefs, although Josephus suggests that some Jews of Crete were susceptible to superstition (*Ant.*17.327). In a similar way, the plural "myths" is generally used negatively in the ancient world, not only because "myths" are

fictions that false teachers substitute for the truth but because they then would appeal to these fictions to justify unhealthy lifestyles (Plato, *Leg.* 1.636; *Rep.* 2.376E-383C). "Jewish myths" may refer to outrageous speculations about OT characters that were used to authorize beliefs and practices that opposed and even subverted Paul's witness. Likewise, the addition of "commandments" probably then refers to various codes of conduct, based upon these speculations, that stipulated what was clean or unclean. If Jewish in cast, then probably certain Gentile foods and perhaps even practices related to proper table fellowship between Jews and pagan converts are implied.

Epimenides the Crete (ca. 650 B.C.) is the unnamed author of the quotation Paul cites in v. 12. To castigate Cretans as liars and cheats agrees with public opinion; in the ancient world, the verb, "to Cretonize," was often used in reference to duplicitous acts! It may seem curious to Jewish readers (including his opponents) that Paul would refer to Epimenides as a "prophet"; however, according to the *Seder OlamR* 21, the non-Jewish world has its own "prophets" who speak accurately "of their own" and should be heeded by them. In this sense, Aristotle says of Epimenides the Cretan that he is not a prophet because he forecasts the future but because he brings the hidden to light (*Rhet.* 3.17.10). But in fact the low regard for Cretan integrity in religious matters was widely shared, in part because some pagan islanders claimed to possess the tomb of Zeus who cannot die (Callimachus, *Hymn to Zeus*, 8-9)! While Cretan Jews certainly would not have shared this fiction with their pagan neighbors, Paul may be coloring them with the same brush for rhetorical effect.

The language of health and disease was widely used by moral philosophers to describe the human condition (see 1 Tim. 6:4-5; 2 Tim. 2:17). The opponents have diseased (or "defiled") minds and consciences, so that Paul charges Titus to reprove them to restore them to spiritual health (or "sound" faith). When Paul speaks of the foundational importance of "sound doctrine" he does so by conjuring up the impression of teaching that is preventive medicine and makes for healthy, hardy faith.

2:1-10. Paul Describes the Church as the Household of God

The instructions found in 1 Timothy (see 3:1-13 and 5:1–6:2) and now here in Titus assume the social world of Roman households. One's status and role within the household depended on many things—gender (male/female), age (young/old), social rank (slave/master, rich/poor), marital status (single/widowed/married), and domestic role (wage earner, dependent, servant). To a large degree, one's public reputation was measured by the quality of domestic conduct toward members of the extended family: was the father/husband attentive to the financial needs of his family; did children obey his caring and careful direction; did their mother/wife devote herself to the efficient management of the household; and were household servants helpful in making the various endeavors of the family a success? True to the spirit of his age, Paul draws their familial obligations in terms of personal virtue rather than job description. What seems clear from this letter is that there is an inextricable connection between personal moral conduct and professional competence, so that the one implies the other. Chrysostom captures this ancient logic nicely when saying, "when observers see a slave who has been taught the philosophy of Christ display more self-command than those taught by their own philosophers, they will in every way admire the power of the gospel" (*Homilies on Titus* 3).

Among the household virtues listed by Paul, several are common to important Hellenistic moral philosophers such as Aristotle, Epictetus, Seneca, and the Jewish teacher Philo. In part, Paul's appropriation of secular moral norms is a piece of his mission-ary strategy, not wanting God's household to live on the margins of society where they would have no influence on others. At the same time, we must be alert to the decisively Christian ground into which these common norms are rooted: **sound (or healthy) doctrine** (2:1) and a belief in **God our Savior** (2:10). For this reason, the interpreter must not detach this ethical teaching about human relationships within the congregation from the densely theological passage that follows in 2:11-14, which articulates Paul's account of "sound doctrine."

The repetition of **sensible** (*sōphrosynē*) in 2:1-8 marks out its importance within the household of faith, and to such an extent that it is used again in the following passage as evidence of Christian conversion (see 2:12). In Greek literature (there is no precise Hebrew/OT equivalent) it is one of four "cardinal virtues" that personifies those who are able to control their frivolous desires—mind over emotion. Because the desires of men and women differed, so did the public expression of their moderate, sensible lifestyle (e.g., Aristotle, *Pol.* 1.5.8). Since a sensible lifestyle appears more difficult for youth, it frequently is listed by moral philosophers as the most important quality of virtuous youth (see, then, v. 6). Paul's point, then, is that the mature believer's choices reflect or bear witness to one's conversion to Christ; it personifies the earnest believer's commitment to "sound doctrine" rather than to self-centered appetites. Virtue is for him the calling card of Christian faith.

Older men are those around fifty years old according to the medical formula used by Hippocrates in a world where life-expectancy for males was probably mid- to late forties. Their moral profile is arranged by a pair of triads, a symbol of wholeness and a literary convention common to this kind of ancient moral literature (called *paraenesis*). The first triad consists of social virtues headed by a **temperate** or sober manner, while the second, qualified by Paul's catchword, **sound** (or "healthy"), defines the spirituality of the mature man. This second triad recalls the famous "Pauline triad" used in 1 Cor. 13:13 (cf. 1 Thess. 1:3) as the very ideal of a Christian life. More critically, given Paul's missionary sensibilities, the virtues of **faith, love, perseverance** would have wide currency in the religious world of his day. The subtext of Paul's list, of course, is that this sort of religious person is formed only by "sound doctrine" rather than by the false teaching of his opponents.

Older women are also in their fifties. They are to be **reverent in their behavior**, a phrase used by Hellenistic Jewish writers such as Philo to describe the religious practices of exemplary believers (*Abr.* 101; *Abel and Cain* 45; cf. *4 Macc.* 9:25). Paul's emphasis on the practical importance of edifying speech—**not malicious gossips . . . teaching what is good, that they may encourage the young women**—reflects a social world in which speech and virtue were intimately linked for the public good. The control of one's speech is especially critical of teachers (cf. Jas. 3), so that temperance in both drink and language was often sounded as a cautionary note for congregational leaders. Moreover, idle talk and drunkenness were elements of the caricatures of older (esp. middle-class) women in popular Hellenistic literature and also in the Talmud.

The primary aim of their teaching ministry is to cultivate female modesty in younger women—those "twenty-something's" who were beginning their careers as homemakers and wives. Although women had other careers in the ancient world, typically made necessary by financial need or social class, the ideal role women performed in the polite society of Paul's world was domestic. The list here in Titus is the standard job description of an ideal Roman wife baptized by Paul into a Christian motive, **that the word of God may not be dishonored**. His coda again reminds Titus that while there remains little difference in the character or duties of Christian and non-Christian households, Paul's commitment to social propriety is deeply rooted in a theology that believes God uses ordinary lives to persuade pagans of the truth of God's Word (see 1 Tim. 2:3-7).

Perhaps as many as half of those who lived in the Roman cities of Paul's world were **bondslaves**; they were typically important members of middle-class households and were responsible for a wide variety of chores—inside and outside the home—assigned by heads (or **masters**) of those households. Standard household codes in the ancient world prescribed duties to these domestic servants, encouraging them to work hard to insure their master's success and good reputation while guarding against illegal practices (e.g., **pilfering**). The word **adorn** refers to an orderly life that brings honor to a household—an important vestige in an ancient world where public honor and shame were judged ultimate social ends to achieve or avoid at all costs. In fact, this seems to be the motive of both the wife's (v. 5) and servant's (v. 9) submission to the household's master. In Paul's instructions, however, the honor that accrues to a Christian household by maintaining these domestic conventions extends to **the doctrine of God our Savior**. Ironically, in the ancient world the formal "liturgy" of freeing slaves often included an announcement that they were now in service of some deity. Perhaps this is the subtext of Paul's concluding phrase if only in a metaphorical sense: Christian slaves were to live as though now slaves to God rather than to their earthly masters (cf. 2:14).

From the perspective of moral philosophers, by teaching their "doctrine" people were made more "sensible" and were thereby "saved" from foolish choices—hence, the importance attached to good teaching (cf. Dio Chrys, *Or* 32.15-16; PsPlut., *Ed.* 7D-F). From Paul's perspective, however, the Christian motive for complying to this otherwise secular household code is to underwrite the truth of his claim that God is our Savior.

2:11-14 Paul's Doctrine of God Our Savior.

This important theological passage provides the ground on which Paul's prior instructions find firm footing. In fact, without this passage the prior household code would be virtually indistinguishable from those ideals taught by secular and Jewish moral philosophers of the day.

The confession of faith in **God our Savior** (v. 10; cf. 3:4) is commonplace among both Jews and pagans. In fact, in the Hellenistic world, deities were thought of as benefactors who granted favors (or "grace") to their subjects, especially when making holy "housecalls." The appearance of God, when grace is dispensed, serves an educative purpose—**instructing us** to live in a socially acceptable manner. This striking image is in keeping with the role of moral philosophers whose "doctrine" delivered people from making shameful choices. While Paul expresses God's grace differently here than in other letters, where grace saves sinners from death and for their benefit, the visitation of God's grace turns people from **ungodliness and worldly desires**, two of the cardinal faults in Stoicism, and toward moral character befitting those who belong to a Christian household (2:1-10). In this case, Paul is the mediator of divine grace because through his instruction people receive "healthy" doctrine about God that forges their moral character.

Paul defines this exemplary character by yet another triad of highly prized Greek virtues, **sensibly, righteously and godly**. Each virtue represents a moral ideal of Paul's world as one dimension of a robust response to divine favor: that is, the marks of a grace-filled life are to live "sensibly" (toward self), "righteously" (toward one's neighbors), and "godly" (toward God).

Also true to the spirit of Greco-Roman morality that helps shape Paul's instructions to Titus (and Timothy) is the dynamic sense of moral progress. From the first to the second **appearance** of Christ Jesus—what Paul refers to as **the present age**—the moral instruction of God's grace **redeems** and **purifies** a people who are **zealous for good deeds**. This formulation of the Christian life sounds loud echoes of another epiphany of God's grace, the Sinaitic revelation of Israel's Torah (cf. Exod. 19:5-6), especially if to **purify** for **good deeds** during **the present age** is preparatory for the **appearing of the glory of our great God and Savior, Christ Jesus**, since Israel purified itself (cf. Exod. 19:10-15) in preparation for its divine visitation (Exod. 19:16-20).

2:15–3:2. Paul Instructs Titus Regarding Leadership of a Congregation

The community's relations within wider society continue from 2:1-10 and fill in the last bit of Paul's "household code." The reminder **to be subject to rulers . . . authorities** agrees with the political imperative of Rome's imperial culture and is moral instruction frequently found in the ancient world (cf. Rom. 13:1-7). By Paul's day the Roman Empire was more than three centuries old and its social and political structures informed all of life. Perhaps this exhortation, then, reflects the sober realism of a Roman citizen and Diaspora Jew who recognized the importance of cooperating with civil powers as a means of survival. The irony of such behavior for those who confess that God alone is our Benefactor, not the Caesar, was nicely captured years later by John of Damascus who wrote, "If men honor emperors . . . how much more ought we to worship the King of kings" (*Ora.Imag.*, 3.41).

3:3-8a. Paul Defines the Theological Foundations of a Transformed Life

The "once-but when" contrast that gives rhetorical definition to this important passage reflects the distinctively Christian experience of conversion. Behind the Pauline letters are these two historical realities—the **appearance** of the Son of God Messiah on earth to redeem sinners (2:11-14) and the believer's ongoing experience of him through the **regeneration and renewing by the Holy Spirit**. Paul's own Jewish scruples share with Hellenistic moral philosophers of his day (esp. the Stoics) this core conviction that truly religious people must live their lives without sensual or illicit passions. For this reason, the manner of life from which the sinner is converted is characterized by those self-destructive passions listed—**lusts and pleasures . . . malice and envy, hateful, hating one another.**

Personal transformation is the work of God. This theological belief is central to Paul. But the idea is not novel to Christian faith. For example, unearthed near Rome is the following inscription dedicated to the Roman god Mithras, although dating from the second century A.D., inscribes an idea that probably extends back to the ancient church: " . . . the one well-pleasing to god who is reborn and re-created through sweet things." This ancient parallel speaks of conversion as a new creation, and "sweetness" may well refer to the purifying role that honey performed as an ancient salve. In fact, the complement belief that the believer's initiation (or baptism) into a new religion must be marked by personal changes—in a spiritual rebirth or renewal—is not unheard of in Paul's Judaism: Philo speaks of the soul's "regeneration" (*Herm. Trac.* 13.3) and Josephus uses this same image to express the more traditional hope of Israel's "regeneration" (*Ant.* 11.3.9. 66). The careful reader rightly notes similarities to Jesus' comments to Nicodemus according to John 3:1-15 that one must be born again by the Spirit in order to enjoy the delights of God's kingdom.

Some scholars argue this passage is based upon lyrics of an early Christian hymn sung during the baptism of new converts—perhaps even in Crete! In addition to the baptismal vocabulary resounding in the phrase, **by the washing of regeneration and renewing by the**

Holy Spirit, the cadence of the Greek text when spoken aloud is rhythmic and suggestive of the lyrics of a well-sung hymn. Moreover, Paul's concluding familiar phrase (see also 1 Tim. 1:15; 3:1; 4:9; 2 Tim. 2:11), **These things are good and profitable for men**, commends this prior passage—a single sentence in Greek—as theologically foundational for the instructions he has given Titus.

In fact, it is an apt formulation of Pauline theology—among the most important in the NT—the cornerstone of which is the repeated claim that God is "our Savior" (see 1:3; 2:10). The complement of attributes linked to this claim, including God's **kindness . . . love for mankind . . . mercy**, are all qualities of a benevolent ruler to whom cities would gladly open their gates in surrender. For example, the Rosetta Stone speaks of Ptolemy V's "kindness" toward his conquered in order to insure that his new subjects would show him their love and gratitude in return (cf. Plutarch, *Cicero* 21.4). How much greater love, then, would the appearance of the King of kings disclose to those "conquered" by God's mercy (cf. Philo, *Cher.* 99). For this same reason, some scholars recognize that Paul's hymn of praise to God reflects a familiar Greco-Roman myth of a deity's processional on earth to show clemency to humans as a dimension of his benevolent persona. Moreover, "mercy" was the chief attribute of the benevolent judge in the ancient world (cf. Plato, *Apology* 34-35). However familiar these claims about God were to his readers, the fundamental difference in Paul's understanding of God's salvation is that these divine characteristics are deeply rooted in an historical event—**Jesus Christ our Savior**—and a real experience—**washing of regeneration and renewing by the Holy Spirit.**

The word for "washing" means to take a bath. From ancient to modern times, the ritual of bathing in water has symbolized one's purification from the old and rebirth or initiation into the new. Paul's innovation, then, is not the idea of a baptism by which the new convert is initiated into a particular religion; such a ritual was practiced even by pagan religions. Rather his innovation is the connection of this sacramental "bath" with the work of "the Holy Spirit" (cf. Rom. 8:2-17). According to the Book of Acts, which introduces readers to the Pauline letters within the NT, the baptism of the Pentecostal Spirit empowers a new manner of corporate life in the world that bears real-time witness to the triumph of God over sin (cf. Acts 1:4-8; 2:37-47). Thus, the baptism indicated that the work of the Spirit was being initiated by a benevolent God within the congregation by which their lives would be transformed—"regenerated and renewed"—from those vices listed in v. 3 into a manner apropos for heirs of eternal life.

3:8b-15. Paul Concludes His Letter to Titus

The benedictions of Hellenistic letters are typically depositories of final exhortations, miscellaneous instructions, personal itineraries, and farewells. Paul urges Titus to avoid **foolish controversies and genealogies and strife and disputes about the Law,** which recalls his earlier definition of a "sound" (or healthy) faith that resists "Jewish myths" (1:14). This language reflects a situation that is influenced by a particular kind of Jewish spirituality that is shaped by scrupulous attention of a code of conduct that legislates, or so it is claimed, a lifestyle pleasing to God. Family myths and related genealogies of family trees were important literary conventions in ancient Jewish writings, especially commentaries on Genesis (*Jub, Ps.Philo,* 1QapGen, 4Q559, et.al.), and even in the biblical gospels (cf. Matt. 1:1-17; Luke 3:23-38). Locating one's family within Jewish history was a basis for an individual's religious authority. Paul's concern is that debating the meaning and motive of the Torah—but not the Torah itself—is finally **unprofitable and worthless** for Christian formation (cf. Rom. 7:12-13).

In this light, Paul's subsequent reference to **Zenas the lawyer,** who is otherwise unknown, may be especially pertinent. The profession of a lawyer in Paul's Jewish world concerns expertise in adapting the Torah's legal code to the ever-changing questions of faithful living. In the wider Greco-Roman world, however, the skills of a jurist depended upon his detailed knowledge of the Roman constitution. Since Zenas is a pagan name and probably reflects his work as a lawyer attached to the Roman courts, it may well be the case that Paul has recruited him to present the secular perspective to dismantle the debates over Jewish law now dividing the church of Crete. His traveling companion, **Apollos,** may well be the Alexandrian Jew introduced in Acts 18 and mentioned in 1 Cor. 1–4 as a leader of the church in this region and Paul's missionary colleague; however, this is a common Greek name and such a connection while apropos to this context should not be assumed.

Paul plans to winter in Nicopolis, which means "a city that overcomes." Nicopolis is a port city on the west coast of Crete just across the Bay of Actium from Italy. Paul asks Titus to join him there after he is relieved of his missionary duties by either **Artemas or Tychicus**—the latter mentioned in Acts 20:4. Some scholars hypothesize that the historical referent of Luke's prior reference to Paul's three-month rest in Acts 20:3a is to his winter stay mentioned here in Titus. No doubt it had become his custom to take winters off to rest and plan for his next missionary campaign—perhaps in this case to Spain. In any case, this personal detail, which expresses uncertainty about who will replace Titus on Crete, concern for his missionary colleagues, and authority over the details of the church's work, is a window to Paul's life that adds color and texture to his biblical portrait (see 2 Tim. 4:9-22).

Introduction to Philemon

Isobel A. H. Combes

Paul's letter to Philemon is the shortest of his writings. It contains no theological exposition or significant news and has no particular beauty of its own. However, despite that, it more than justifies its place in the canon as an unequalled insight into Paul's faith put into action and his relationships with his fellow Christians. Its authenticity is seldom challenged—it has been included among the letters of Paul since the earliest times and Marcion, Origen (*Homily on Jeremiah* 29), Tertullian (*Against Marcion* 5.42), and Eusebius (*Ecclesiastical History* 3.25) all accepted its Pauline authorship. The text has remained largely consistent over the centuries with only a few unimportant variations. The identification of the Onesimus of this letter with the Onesimus, bishop of Ephesus mentioned by Ignatius (Ignatius, *Letter to the Ephesians* 1:3) has even raised the possibility that Onesimus was the first editor of Paul's letters and so chose to include this certificate of his freedom in the collection.

The letter's odd amalgam of the private and public, the theological and practical, is one which becomes more significant and perhaps more bewildering as each passing age takes us further and further away from the social realities of the first-century world. It deals with a slave who has run into serious trouble with his master and is now with Paul. Paul, instead of aiding in the slave's escape, is sending him back to his master with a letter of recommenda-

tion which expresses the hope that the slave will be forgiven. It is no wonder that this text should be so disturbing to many modern readers and probably more than any other part of the New Testament it reminds us of the immense gulf that lies between our own society and that in which the Christian Church first took root. If anything will save us from the common tendency to view Paul as a middle-class character of our own time, this will. Slavery was an inescapable reality in the days of the early Church as it had been for many thousands of years before and would continue to be for nearly two thousand years after. It was as much taken for granted as any other domestic relationship and although the Christian teachers would have much to say on how this relationship should be conducted, it would be many years before any conceived of the idea that it could be dispensed with altogether.

When we look at Paul and the problem of slavery, we must take into account two separate traditions, the Jewish and the Greco-Roman. Both traditions involved slavery although there were many significant distinctions. Slavery in the Mesopotamian/Jewish world was largely associated with debt, and hence time limits were often set on its duration. The Jewish tradition distinguished between Jewish slaves and foreign slaves and established a separate code for each. Jewish slaves could not be held for more than seven years and had to be released at the Jubilee, though since any wife or child they acquired in that time would remain enslaved, they might choose to remain slaves themselves. However, there is evidence that these restrictions were sometimes ignored. Domestic slavery was relatively rare, except in the households of the wealthy, and the agricultural economy relied largely on the labour of free men. Jewish law set restrictions on the treatment of slaves by their masters and legislated for their humane treatment (Lev. 25:43 and Exod. 21:26-27, for example), although a degree of suspicion and resentment often remained on both sides.

In contrast to the Jewish world, that of the Greeks and Romans can be very much said to have been based on slavery. Plato regarded slaves as an essential part of a well-ordered society both for the sake of society and for their own, as slaves constituted that class of humans who were incapable of thinking for themselves and needed the control and guidance of their wiser masters. Slavery was necessary for society because it allowed the good and wise to be liberated from the drudgery of life so that they would be able to devote themselves to higher things. The Stoic tradition denied that there was any basis in nature for slavery, emphasizing the inner freedom of slaves and their spiritual equality with their masters. However they did not go so far as to call for the abolition of slavery. Roman law recognized that slavery was a law of the people *ius gentium* which was opposed to the law of nature *ius naturale* and the result of war (Florentius, *Digest* 1.5.4.1), but again, did not question the need for its existence. On the contrary, Rome made enormous use of slaves and these were distributed through all ranks of society. At the most miserable end of the scale were the chain gangs that worked the mines and the immense country estates of the Roman aristocracy. These were subjected to the most appallingly inhumane conditions and were virtually invisible in the minds of those who lived at the time. They are never mentioned in the New Testament. Above

these would be the higher class of agricultural labourers and overseers who would run the estates. The estate manager would almost invariably be a slave. Although these country slaves would have formed the vast bulk of the slave population, there would also be slaves in almost every household. Such slaves would not be restricted to menial jobs—teachers and secretaries would be slaves and probably far more educated and cultured than their masters. Some would work in the family business or even run businesses of their own almost entirely independently of their masters. It is fairly safe to say that the average domestic slave in a Roman city would have had a higher standard of living than many of the poorer free inhabitants. At the top of the ladder would be the slaves and freedmen of the emperor who constituted virtually the entire civil service. The emperor would have been surrounded by an inner circle of slaves who directed the affairs of the empire and came to have considerable power and influence, incurring much resentment from the freeborn population.

By the time of the later Empire, the emancipation of slaves after a certain period of satisfactory work had become so widespread as to be almost routine. It was common for slaves to be allowed a certain income of their own (*peculium*) and they would generally expect to save up enough of this to buy their own freedom and that of their spouse and children. Others might be freed as a reward for good work or through the self interest of the master who would continue to benefit from the legally enforced loyalty of the freedman without having to continue to be responsible for his or her upkeep. Slaves might also be freed by a childless master so as to be adopted, and female slaves might be freed so that the master could marry them.

It is this class of slave that appears in Paul's letters. Domestic slaves, as noted above, could be as educated as their masters and so able to participate fully in the Christian message. The way they are addressed by Paul shows that he expected them to be present during the reading of his letters. At no point does Paul forbid their participation or imply that they might not be able to understand things fully themselves (unlike women who are expected to ask their husbands if they do not understand something in church!). However, neither does he say anything that implies that they should cease to be slaves, and this is something that makes hard reading in this day and age.

The position of Paul in his instructions on domestic arrangements is clear on the point that slaves should respect their masters and obey them. Masters, in turn, should be kind and merciful to their slaves (Col. 3:22-4:1). There is the much disputed passage in 1 Cor. 7:20-24, which reads "but if you are able also to become free, rather do that (*mallon chresthai*)." The Greek here can either be read to mean "take advantage of the chance for freedom" or "even if you have a chance of freedom, make use rather of your slavery." Although there are those who argue that Paul is suggesting that slaves should accept emancipation, it is equally possible that he is saying quite the opposite— that slaves should use the opportunity of their slavery to glorify God and should remain in that position, even if the opportunity of freedom should come their way. After Paul, writers continue in much the same vein, generally discouraging slaves from seeking earthly freedom and urging them rather to concentrate on the spiritual freedom given them in Christ.

Modern sensibilities do not allow one to pass over all of this in silence. One cannot avoid questioning how something now regarded as one of the most fundamental injustices of society could have been affirmed by Christianity for so many years, with only the smallest amelioration in its cruelties. However, it has to be remembered that when an institution is so ingrained into the fabric of society it takes a mind-bending shift in perspective to envisage any other way of ordering human relations. It has taken this long to change society's view of slaves, women and children—it is always useful to ask oneself which of our own unalterable views will be remembered with horror by our descendants two thousand years hence. Furthermore, there is always a gap between any rules we give and our actual application of such rules to real people. This is what lies behind the great value of the Letter to Philemon. Now Paul, having laid down the rules of slavery for general application in the church is confronted with a real slave, and this is the story of what he does next.

RESOURCES

Bartchy, S. S., *Mallon Chresai: First Century Slavery and 1 Corinthians 7:21*, SBLDS, 11; Missoula, MT: SBL, 1973.

Bradley, K. R., *Slavery and Society at Rome*, Cambridge: Cambridge University Press, 1994.

Buckland, W. W., *The Roman Law of Slavery: The Condition of the Slave in Private Law from Augustus to Justinian*, Cambridge: Cambridge University Press, 1970.

Caird, G. B., *Paul's Letters from Prison*, Oxford: Oxford University Press, 1984.

Combes, I. A. H., *The Metaphor of Slavery in the Writings of the Early Church from the New Testament to the beginning of the Fifth Century*, JSNTSup 156, Sheffield: Sheffield Academic Press, 1998.

Finley, M. I., *Classical Slavery*, London,: Cass, 1987.

Fitzmyer, J. A., *The Letter to Philemon*, New York: Doubleday, 2000.

Gamsey, P., *Ideas of Slavery from Aristotle to Augustine*, Cambridge: Cambridge University Press, 1996.

Knox, J., *Philemon among the Letters of Paul: A New View of Its Place and Importance*, rev. ed., Nashville and New York: Abingdon; London: Collins, 1959.

Moule, C. F. D., *An Idiom Book of New Testament Greek,* Cambridge: Cambridge University Press, 1986.

Cambridge Greek Testament Commentary, Cambridge: Cambridge University Press, 1957.

Philemon

Isobel A. H. Combes

1. Paul, a prisoner of Christ. In all his letters, Paul defines himself in his introduction according to his relationship with Christ. In other letters he is an apostle of Christ or a slave, but here he uses "prisoner"(*desmios*). It may be he felt that "apostle of Jesus Christ" would be an unnecessarily blunt demonstration of the personal authority that he so carefully plays down in the rest of the letter. On the other hand, his other favourite title, "slave of Christ" (*doulos Cristou*), would have been somewhat tactless given the purpose of the letter. The use of *desmios*, is of course literal, unlike his use of *doulos* in other letters. Paul, writing from prison, is not a prisoner of Christ, of course, but imprisoned on account of his witness to Christ. There are some variations on this—New Testament Greek MS D substitutes *apostolos* here, while MS 629 has both *apostolos* and *desmios* and some MSS use even *doulos* ("slave") instead. These represent later attempts to bring this text into line with the other Pauline epistles. A number of locations have been suggested for the imprisonment referred to here, the two most likely being Rome and Ephesus. Rome has tended to be the preferred option, but locating Paul in Ephesus makes better sense of Paul's plans to visit Philemon, mentioned at the end of the letter.

To Philemon our beloved brother and coworker. Notice how even in these few words Paul sets up the atmosphere of the coming argument. He emphases the idea of brotherhood—

Timothy is "our brother" and Philemon is **our beloved brother**—and has already mentioned that he is a "prisoner," one deprived of his freedom. All these themes will reappear in the subsequent text.

It is generally agreed that Philemon came from Colossae, and as he is described as a **fellow worker** he was probably the leader of the church there—the *Apostolic Constitutions*, a later Christian text, identifies him as bishop of Colossae (*Apostolic Constitutions* 7.46), though there is no other evidence for this. Philemon is a well-attested Phyrgian name, deriving from the Greek word for love (*philein*) and Fitzmyer points out that Paul may be playing on that meaning when he describes Philemon as **beloved** (*agapetos*).

2. and to Apphia our sister. Apphia has traditionally been regarded as the wife of Philemon. Again the name is Phrygian as is Philemon and some versions read "beloved sister" giving her the same greeting as her husband.

Archippus our fellow soldier. Archippus is mentioned again in Col. 4:17. Here he appears as a follower of Epaphras and some ancient authorities hold that he succeeded Epaphras as bishop—he is mentioned in the *Apostolic Constitutions* 7.46 as the bishop of Laodicea. The designation **fellow soldier** is unusual for Paul and only used by him in one other place (cf. Phil. 2:25). There is no reason to

Was Archippus Onesimus's real master?

In Colossians, Archippus is intriguingly told to "fulfill the ministry that you have received in the Lord." There are some commentators such as John Knox who have argued that the real master of Onesimus was Archippus and that Col. 4:17 refers to Paul's request concerning Philemon. However, it seems highly unlikely that Archippus' name would have been placed after Philemon's if the letter had actually been intended for him. Furthermore it would be very strange if Paul should undo the tact and diplomacy with which he has composed Philemon with such a blunt and authoritative command in Colossians.

take this literally, and it was probably only another way of saying "fellow worker."

and to the church in your house. It would appear from this that the letter, in spite of its very personal content, is intended to be read before the congregation. It may be that Paul is thereby seeking witnesses to the content of the letter, to make it more difficult for Philemon quietly to disobey.

4. I thank my God always, making mention of you in my prayers. Paul frequently tells the recipients of his letters that he prays for them "always" or "without ceasing" (cf. Rom. 1:9; Eph. 1:16; Phil. 1:3; 1 Thess. 1:2; 2 Tim. 1:3).

5. because I hear of your love, and of the faith which you have toward the Lord Jesus, and toward all the saints. In his other letters the apostle rejoices to hear of the faith and love of Christian believers (e.g., Eph. 1:15; Phil. 1:27; Col. 1:4).

6-7. and I pray that the fellowship of your faith may become effective through the knowledge of every good thing which is in you for Christ's sake. For I have come to have much joy and comfort in your love, because the hearts of the saints have been refreshed through you, brother. Paul now begins to set up his case with a series of graceful compliments to Philemon, in which he again plants the themes he will use in his argument later. Hence love, fellowship, comfort, and brotherhood are again emphasised (cf. Gal. 5:6: "faith [pistis] working through love [agape]"). It is as if Paul is hoping for a self-fulfilling prophecy—if all these virtues are brought to bear, then Paul will get his way. If not, Philemon will be exposed as lacking them. **Fellowship** (koinonia) is a significant idea here and Paul will appeal to it again. It means both participation in and partnership with. Philemon's participation in the faith and his partnership with Paul (and the wider Christian community) must now be demonstrated in the realisation of the good things which God has in mind for him.

8-9. Therefore, though I have enough confidence in Christ to order you to do what is proper, yet for love's sake I rather appeal to you—since I am such a person as Paul, the aged and now also a prisoner for Christ. Paul now leads into the point of the letter with an elegant chiastic structure, contrasting what he has just said with his own "humble" position and sandwiching the contrast between love and authority in the middle. He opens with the word dio, which is a strong form of "therefore," linking back to what has just been said. We might read the lines thus — the first and last lines contrast with each other as do the third and fourth:

Therefore, although (on account of the fact that you are a good and admirable Christian)

I have the authority in Christ to command you to do the right thing

I would rather appeal out of love instead

The Lord Jesus Christ

This phrase occurs throughout the New Testament and early Christian witness, but it is worth considering it for a moment here. Although Jesus is frequently addressed as "lord" (*kyrie*), the title "Lord" (*kyrios*), appears to be virtually unknown in the gospels with the exception of John 13:13 and possibly John 20:28. While *kyrie* amounts to little more than a polite formula of respect, the title *kyrios* is heavy with connotations of kingship, authority, and mastery and it is widely used as a title for Christ throughout the rest of the New Testament. The conflict between the Christian and the State in the centuries after the New Testament would frequently centre on this idea of *kyrios*. Was the emperor *kyrios* or was Christ *kyrios*? This question became central with the imposition of the imperial cult and Domitian's claim to be *Dominus et Deus* ("Lord and God"), and on this conflict hung the lives of so many Christian martyrs. In the context of this particular letter, there is also the relationship of the *kyrios* (as "master") and the *doulos* ("slave"). Paul is writing to Onesimus's *kyrios* but also reminding him that he too has a *kyrios* who is Jesus Christ, as in Col. 4:1: "You masters (*kyrioi*), be just and fair to your slaves, knowing that you too have a master (*kyrios*) in heaven . . ."

(on account of the fact that I am just) Paul, an old man and a prisoner.

Already Philemon is put in a position where he can hardly refuse Paul's request without appearing to be an unfeeling brute!

Translators differ over the word *presbutes* (**aged**) used here. Some, the New English Bible, for example, prefer to take its meaning as ambassador (Greek: *presbeutes*). However, there is no evidence for this variation in the Greek MSS, although it was common for the two words to be confused, and it is so clear that Paul is placing himself in a position of humility here in contrast to Philemon that it would seem counterproductive to assert his status while he is still pointing out his metaphorical chains.

10. I appeal to you for my child, whom I have begotten in my imprisonment, Onesimus: Paul has here put "old man" and "child" (i.e., *presbeutes* and *teknon*) in apposition, both followed by prisoner and imprisonment. Hence

. . . Paul a *presbutes* and now also a prisoner (*desmios*) . . .

. . . my *teknon* whom I have begotten in imprisonment (*desmois*).

Paul makes frequent use of the metaphor of parenthood to describe his converts. See also 1 Cor. 4:14 "In Christ Jesus you are my offspring" and 1 Cor. 4:17 "I have sent Timothy who is my beloved and faithful child in the Lord" (as well as 1 Tim. 1:2; 2 Tim. 1:2; Titus 1:4; Gal. 4:19). He leaves the identification of Onesimus to the end, giving priority to the relationship he now has with Paul.

11. who formerly was useless to you , but is now useful both to you and me. It was common for slaves to be given names that reflected the behaviour expected of them "faithful," "profitable," and so on. The name "Onesimus" means "useful" and is a well-attested slave name of the time. Paul immediately plays on this by saying that Onesimus was *achreston* ("useless") to Philemon but is now *euchreston* ("very useful") to both him and Paul.

12. And I have sent him back to you in person. Here is the crunch for modern readers. Why is Onesimus with Paul and why has Paul sent him back? In the first place, is Onesimus a runaway slave? Philemon will be urged to accept him back as "more than a slave, a beloved brother," and the name Onesimus certainly appears to be a slave name so we can be reasonably certain that the traditional view of Onesimus as a runaway slave is the true one. There are commentators, indeed, who have disputed this. Onesimus has been variously identified as a messenger sent by Philemon's church to minister to Paul and as Philemon's brother who has quarrelled with him. Neither of these interpretations is convincing. However, if Onesimus had been sent deliberately by the church at Colossae then there is no reason for Paul to call him useless, or to make mention of Onesimus having "wronged you." The idea that Onesimus might have been Philemon's brother is even less convincing.

If Onesimus can be understood as a runaway slave, then the next question is, how has he come to know Paul? It would certainly not be the case, as it would at first appear, that Onesimus is Paul's fellow prisoner, having been captured in his flight. Paul would have been kept, not in a formal prison as his letter implies, but more probably under some form of house arrest or, at the very least, under some sort of very liberal regime. He would certainly not have encountered runaway slaves as his fellow prisoners.

So if Onesimus was not a fellow prisoner, another traditional view is that he came to Paul for the very sanctuary demanded by Jewish law (Deut. 23:16-17, "You shall not give up to his master a slave who escapes from his master to you; he shall dwell with you, in your midst . . .") and forbidden by Rome. (*Digest* 11.4.1.1-6). However, since Onesimus is clearly a Gentile from a Gentile context, it is unlikely that he would have felt himself able to appeal to the former law. It is even more unlikely that Paul could have offered such sanctuary. Being under arrest himself, he would hardly compound his situation by the criminal act of sheltering a slave, not to mention that Onesimus would have been arrested by Paul's guards.

How could a runaway slave, then, have come to be in Paul's circle and to have been

---

To Sabinianus,

That freedman of yours with whom you said you were angry has been to me, flung himself at my feet, and clung to me as if I were you. He begged my help with many tears, though he left a good deal unsaid; in short, he convinced me of his genuine penitence. I believe he has reformed, because he realised he did wrong. You are angry, I know, and I know too that your anger was deserved, but mercy wins most praise when there was just cause for anger. You loved the man once, and I hope you will love him again, but it is sufficient for the moment if you allow yourself to be appeased. You can always be angry again if he deserves it, and will have more excuse if you were once placated. Make some concession to his youth, his tears, and your own kind heart, and do not torment him or yourself any longer—anger can only be a torment to your gentle self.

I'm afraid you will think I am using pressure, not persuasion, if I add my prayers to his—but this is what I shall do, and all the more freely and fully because I have given the man a very severe scolding and warned him firmly that I will never make such request again. This was because he deserved a fright, and is not intended for your ears; for maybe I shall make another request and obtain it, as long as it is nothing unsuitable for me to ask and you to grant.

Pliny, *Letters* 9.21
(tr. B. Radice)

there long enough, unmolested, to have converted to Christianity? The first-century Roman jurist Proculus, is recorded as saying that a slave who, having angered his master, takes refuge with a friend of the master, for the purpose of asking that friend to intercede for him, is not legally a runaway (*Digest* 21.1.17.4). Onesimus could, therefore, have come legally to Paul, so long as he was doing so in order to ask Paul to act as an *amicus domini* ("friend of the master") and to reconcile him with Philemon. It would seem that he is being sent back with exactly what he asked for, a letter asking Philemon to take him back and waive any punishment. In the writings of Pliny the Younger (ca. 61-113 A.D.), we have an example of just such a letter, where Pliny intercedes in quite similar terms, for a freedman who has fallen foul of his master. If Paul is here acting as the *amicus domini*, then his actions are understandable. Onesimus is returning of his own free will but carrying with him the letter that will ensure that he is at least spared punishment, and as Paul will go on to imply, perhaps bring about an even better end.

that is, sending you my own heart. Paul throws himself fully into this plea, saying that he is sending Philemon his very *splagchna*. *Splagchna* means literally the inward parts, bowels or entrails which, like the heart today, were identified as the source of human emotion. Paul is sending Philemon his "very inward self." This refers also back to the *splagchna* of the faithful which have been refreshed through Philemon's goodness and looks forward to Paul's expectation later that Philemon will also refresh Paul's *splagchna* through his cooperation.

13. whom I wished to keep with me, that in your behalf he might minister to me in my imprisonment for the gospel. It was not unusual for slaves to act on behalf of their masters. Under certain circumstances they could stand in for their masters for the sake of legal contracts. This concept was certainly abused.

Pliny the Younger also mentions the scandal of slaves who have been sent to take their masters' place in the army (Pliny, *Letters* 10.29), and some later Christians did attempt to protect their own souls by sending their slaves to perform ritual pagan sacrifices in their stead (a practice condemned in the *Canons* of Peter of Alexandria, *Canons* 6 and 7, in A.D. 311).

14. but without your consent, I did not want to do anything, that your goodness should not be as it were by compulsion, but of your own free will. Once again Paul sets up the apposition between his own right to force compliance on Philemon and his actual surrender of his right. He has reminded Philemon of the gospel which has put him in prison and the right he would have to expect his friends to minister to him, but immediately puts that aside, assuring Philemon that he would rather the good came from his own free will. A similar concern is expressed in Pliny's letter: "I'm afraid you will think I am using pressure, not persuasion." However, the implication is once again that Paul has every right to compel him but is surrendering that right out of love. See also 2 Cor. 8:9 ("I am not speaking this as a command, but as proving through the earnestness of others the sincerity of your love also") and 2 Cor. 9:7. Earlier he has prayed that Philemon's fellowship may be made effective in goodness. Now the nature of that goodness is unambiguously laid out. In the following verse, Paul calls for backup.

15. For perhaps he was for this reason parted from you for a while, that you should have him back forever. This grammatical form in the New Testament is known as a *theological passive* and is a common way of expressing the action of God in human life. Paul in Rom. 1:1 is "called to be an apostle" and "separated for the gospel." Here, Paul is not just being euphemistic, tactfully stepping aside from Onesimus' misdeed, but he is actually attributing the action of Onesimus to the will of God and suggesting that

Philemon's wholehearted forgiveness of Onesimus is therefore part of God's own plan.

16. no longer as a slave, but more than a slave, a beloved brother, especially to me, but how much more to you, both in the flesh and the Lord. Paul has said that Philemon will have Onesimus back "into eternity" but the nature of the "having" is immediately turned on its head as Philemon is to have Onesimus back, not as a slave but as a "beloved brother." This we saw seeded right at the beginning of the letter. Philemon was greeted by Paul and Timothy as a beloved brother, now he is called upon to bestow this very title on Onesimus. Paul is clear that Onesimus is beloved "especially to me" and Philemon clearly cannot continue his own relationship with Paul unless he too accepts Onesimus as a "beloved brother." There is no incompatibility in the New Testament between that and Onesimus remaining a slave. People might be masters and slaves in the flesh but brothers in the Lord. No one in the early church appears to have had any problem with that idea at all. However, Paul does not leave it there— Onesimus is to be accepted as **a beloved brother . . . both in the flesh and in the Lord**. This cannot mean, as some commentators have it, that Onesimus is actually Philemon's brother but has had a disagreement with him. However, it might be read in another and more startling way. Throughout the discussions of slavery in the New Testament and early church and indeed in some philosophies of the time, a constant dichotomy is brought up between the master and slave relationship "in the flesh" and "in the spirit." Those who are master and slave "in the flesh" or in the earthly sense can at the same time be brothers and sisters in the spiritual sense, and although the church never called for the wholesale emancipation of slaves it was always clear that all were equal in the sight of God and in their spiritual relationships. However, here Paul is saying that Onesimus should be accepted as a brother **both in the flesh and in the Lord**. Whereas he could have simply asked that Onesimus be accepted as a brother **in the Lord** and by implication as a slave **in the flesh**, he has clearly applied the status of "brother" both to Onesimus's status "in the flesh" (*en sarki*) and "in the Lord." We can compare this to Col. 3:19 "slaves should obey in all things those who are their masters according to the flesh [*kata sarka*]." Paul is surely saying that Onesimus' status is to be changed as much in the earthly as the spiritual sphere.

17. If then you regard me as a partner, accept him as you would me. Aware of what a serious request he has made of Philemon, Paul proceeds to back it up with what amounts to a thinly veiled threat. If Philemon does not accept Onesimus on Paul's terms, then the implication is that he cannot view himself as a partner (*koinon*) in Paul's ministry. This looks back to the beginning of the letter where is he has prayed that the *koinonia* ("fellowship") of Philemon's faith may be made effective.

18. But if he has wronged you in any way, or owes you anything, charge that to my account. Turning now to practical matters, Paul brings up the subject of the wrong Onesimus "might" have done or what he "might" owe to Philemon. For a letter from an *amicus domini* seeking forgiveness for a slave, the nature of Onesimus's crimes is left surprisingly vague. Pliny's letter to Sabinius, our other evidence of such a letter, is very explicit about the repentance of the errant freedman and his determination not to sin again. Paul, on the other hand, makes no mention whatsoever of any definite misdeed on Onesimus's part, nor of any repentance nor, indeed, of any need for repentance.

19. I, Paul am writing this with my own hand, I will repay it (lest I should mention to you that you owe me even your own self as well). The implication is that Paul hardly believes Onesimus to be at fault at all, but if there should be any outstanding debt he undertakes, with his own signature, to repay it. However, he has no sooner signed his IOU note than he turns it on its head by reminding Philemon that he himself owes Paul his "own self." This figure of speech is known as a *paraleipsis*, where the speaker pretends to pass over something, while mentioning it all the same. One is reminded, although not deliberately on Paul's part, of the parable of the slave who though his debts are forgiven by his own master will not forgive the debts of a fellow slave (Matt. 18:23-35). This is not the only example of Paul adding his own handwriting to a letter (see Gal. 6:11-12).

20. Yes, brother, let me benefit from you in the Lord; refresh my heart in Christ. In "let me benefit" (*oniamen*) we have the only case in the whole New Testament of the use of the first person optative (the third person optative, e.g., "let it not be so," is the more common form) and here it takes a strongly imperative tone. Ignatius of Antioch, in his letter to the Ephesians, later picked up on this same wordplay with "May I always have 'profit' from you if I am worthy" (Ignatius, *Epistle to the Ephesians* 2:2). Philemon is also requested to refresh Paul's *splagchna* (i.e., "inward being"), just as he has already refreshed the *splagchna* of the saints in v. 7. Again there is a repetition of vocabulary—Paul calls him brother as he has done in a similar context in v. 7 and as he has asked him to regard Onesimus, driving home yet again the brotherhood that should exist between all Christians and guide their behavior.

21. Having confidence in your obedience, I write to you, since I know that you will do even more than I say. Having confidence (*pepoithos*) is sometimes translated as "being persuaded" and is the same word used at the beginning of Paul's famous declaration of faith in Rom. 8:38, "For I am persuaded that neither death nor life . . . is able to separate us from the love of God in Christ Jesus our Lord."

(However, the specific grammatical form of *pepoitha* with the dative of the thing being trusted is found nowhere else in the New Testament.) The word expresses a deep sense of conviction and Paul's complete confidence in Philemon's obedience—despite his earlier assurances that he was not using his authority to exact such obedience. Earlier on, Paul has hinted in a delicate manner that he expects Onesimus to be set free to be a Christian brother "in the flesh" as well as "in the Lord" and here he seems to be alluding to this request again. Or else it may be that he is asking Philemon to go even further than this and to fulfil Paul's own desire to have Onesimus back with him.

22. At the same time also prepare for me a lodging; for I hope that through your prayers I shall be given to you. This is, literally, "prepare hospitality for me" and is not just a request for accommodation but another subtle threat. If Paul is to visit he will be able to see for himself whether Philemon has acted in accordance with his wishes. This verse has bearings on the question of the location of Paul's imprisonment during the composition of this letter and would seem to favor Ephesus. It would be strange for Paul to mention his visit in this casual way were it to entail the long and arduous journey by land and sea from Rome. There is no evidence, however, that the visit was ever made.

What was the result of the letter? Did Paul get his way and was Onesimus emancipated and allowed to join him? The very fact that this letter survives suggests a happy ending, as it is unlikely that Philemon would have held on to such a thing if he had not cooperated with Paul's instructions. It has even been suggested that it was Onesimus himself, as bishop of Ephesus, who eventually collected together the canon of Pauline epistles as we have them today, including among them the story of his own conversion and release. The letter to the Colossians mentions "Onesimus, our trustworthy and dear brother, who is one of yourselves" (4:9), and

> "Do not behave arrogantly towards slaves, male or female. But let them not be puffed up. Rather let them be enslaved all the more to the glory of God, so that they may come to a greater freedom from God. Let them not desire to be manumitted out of the common chest, so that they may not be found slaves of lust."
>
> Ignatius, *Epistle to Polycarp* 4:3

there is no reason not to believe that this is the same Onesimus. More doubtfully, Ignatius of Antioch identifies him with Onesimus who was bishop of Ephesus around A.D. 115 There were certainly cases of ex-slaves who went on to hold office in the church, such as the freedman Callistus who became bishop of Rome in A.D. 217. It is hard to know what Paul himself thought of the emancipation of slaves. There is no doubt that he makes some firm statements about the duties of slaves, as in 1 Tim. 6:1 "If the masters are believers, the slaves must not respect them any less for being their Christian brethren." There is, of course, the ambiguous "but if you are able also to become free, rather do that" (*mallon chresthai*, lit. "rather, take advantage of it"). Whether this means that slaves should take advantage of their state of slavery or of the chance to be liberated has never been satisfactorily settled. If Philemon is to be taken as a request for emancipation, it may indicate that Paul supported slaves seeking freedom where the opportunity arose. Ignatius of Antioch, in the early second century, warns slaves against the practice of seeking to have their emancipation paid for by the Church's common chest, which suggests that there was such a practice at some point and the liberation of one's slaves soon came to be seen as a Christian virtue, though more for ascetic than humanitarian reasons.

The early church never seriously challenged the institution of slavery. That would take nearly two thousand years and a radically different economic and social structure. What it did, however, was to stand firm on the slave's right to be seen as an equal in the sight of God, and in so far as was practical, in the sight of the church. There were a few, very few, tentative protests against the idea of slavery. John Chrysostom in the fourth century A.D., claimed that early Christians had set their slaves free and that one should ideally do without them at all. Gregory of Nyssa, his contemporary, went further and condemned the whole idea of slavery, but did not go so far as to extend this to the practical sphere. Christian writers in general simply urged masters to treat their slaves well, and ensure their spiritual well-being. What they could not imagine at the time was a world where such an injustice could be dispensed with altogether.

Gregory of Nyssa's condemnation of slavery

"Who can buy a man, who can sell him, when he is made in the likeness of God, when he is ruler over the whole earth, when he has been given as his inheritance by God authority over all that is in the earth? Such power belongs to God alone, or rather it does not even belong to God himself. For as Scripture says, 'The gifts of God are irrevocable.' Of his own free will God called us into freedom when we were slaves to sin. In that case he would hardly reduce human beings to slavery. But if God does not enslave what is free, who dares to put his own authority higher than God's?"

Gregory of Nyssa, *In Ecclesiastem* 4
(tr. T. J. Dennis, 1982)